The
Mackintosh
Treasury

The Mackintosh Treasury

Miscellaneous Writings
by C.H. Mackintosh

❀

⬛GBV⬛

GUTE BOTSCHAFT Verlag
P. O. Box 80
D-35673 Dillenburg
Germany

The Mackintosh Treasury
by C. H. Mackintosh

Copyright © 1976 by LOIZEAUX BROTHERS, Inc.

A Nonprofit Organization, Devoted to the Lord's Work
and to the Spread of His Truth

Originally published in 1896 in six volumes under the title:
Miscellaneous Writings

First Edition in One Volume - 1976
Third Loizeaux Brothers, Inc. Reprint - 1987

1999 Believers Bookshelf Reprint Edition
ISBN 0-88172-229-4
Reprinted by Permission

BELIEVERS BOOKSHELF INC.
5205 Regional Rd. #81, Unit #3
Beamsville, Ontario, Canada L0R 1B3

BELIEVERS BOOKSHELF INC.
P.O Box 261
Sunbury, Pennsylvania 17801, USA
www.bbusa.org

Distributed in the United Kingdom by:

CHAPTER TWO
13 Plum Lane
LONDON
SE18 3AF, ENGLAND

PRINTED IN THE CZECH REPUBLIC

CONTENTS

(The number in parentheses following each title indicates
the volume number in the original set)

THE AUTHORITY OF SCRIPTURE

THE PERSON OF CHRIST

LESSONS FROM THE OLD TESTAMENT

THE CHRISTIAN LIFE

DOCTRINE

DOCTRINE
(continued)

THE CHURCH – THE BODY OF CHRIST

THE LORD'S COMING

Of all the groups of Christian believers that developed in the English-speaking world in the nineteenth century, the one which produced the greatest number of gifted writers was the Brethren. Of their founder himself, John Nelson Darby, over forty substantial volumes were published. But of all this notable group of writers, the one whose works have been most frequently printed is Charles Henry Mackintosh, generally known as C.H.M., which is all that appeared on the title pages of his major writings.

Charles H. Mackintosh was born in October 1820, at Glenmalure Barricks, County Wicklow, Ireland, the son of the captain of a Highland regiment. Mackintosh was converted at the age of eighteen through the letters of a devout sister, and the prayerful reading of J.N. Darby's *Operations of the Spirit.* When he was twenty-four years of age, he opened a private school at Westport, but it was not long before he concluded he must give himself entirely to the ministry of the Word of God, in writing and in public speaking. Soon thereafter he felt led to establish a periodical, which he continued to edit for twenty- one years, *Things New and Old.*

The opening pages of the first issue of *Things New and Old* outline its purpose:

In presenting to the reader the first number of our periodical, we feel called upon to state our reasons for entering upon such a service, and also the objects which we hope, by the grace of God, to effect.

We do not deem any apology necessary for adding another to the numerous publications already extant, having for their object the circulation of pure truth. We want them all, and thousands more, if we could get them. We cannot have too many agencies for the furtherance of that which is good, and the suppression of that which is evil.

For, first of all, it is a lamentable fact that the enemy of souls has wrought, far more diligently, at the printing press, than the servants of the living God. Numerous as are the books, the pamphlets, the tracts, and the periodicals in which the words of eternal truth shine, for the instruction and comfort of souls, yet are they outnumbered, to an appalling amount, by publications of an infidel, immoral, and irreligious tendency.

2. We believe that the art of printing was designed, by a gracious Providence, as a powerful engine for the diffusion of scriptural knowledge; but we cannot shut our eyes to the startling fact that the enemy is making diligent use of that very art, for the purpose of corrupting, in all directions, the springs of thought and feeling. He is publishing, in the cheapest and most attractive form, gross evil, soul-destroying error, and perverted truth. And, we may safely say, if positive error has slain its thousands, perverted truth has slain its tens of thousands.

3. Now, we are fully assured that, notwithstanding all the enemy's efforts, the Lord is gathering out His own—that He is accomplishing His purposes, and hastening His everlasting kingdom. But should this be a reason for slackness, coldness, and indifference, on the part of the servants of Christ? The very reverse; yea, the assurance thereof is the basis of "stedfast" and "unmovable" service. It is because we know, on divine authority, that "our labour shall not be in vain in the Lord," that therefore we work. Thank God for such a solid foundation! It would be sad, indeed, if what our God has graciously given as a soul-stirring encouragement to *work* should be used as a plea for *inactivity* if the assurance of reaching God's end were to be a reason for neglecting God's means. This would be a grievous use to make of the goodness and faithfulness of God.

4. But, further, we undertake this service because we feel bound to serve and testify, while the time for service and testimony lasts. The day is rapidly approaching, in the which we shall not be called upon to render such fruits. When we get into the Master's presence, we shall admire and worship; but, now, in "the little while," in the night of His absence, it is our holy and happy privilege to be "always abounding in the work of the Lord" (1 Cor. 15:58). We are responsible to let the light shine forth, in every possible way—to circulate

11

the truth of God, by all means, by word of mouth, by "paper and ink," in public and private, "in the morning and in the evening," "in season and out of season"; we should "sow beside all waters." In a word, whether we consider the importance of divine truth, the value of immortal souls, or the fearful progress of error and evil, we are imperatively called upon to be up and doing, in the name of the Lord, under the guidance of His word, and by the grace of His Spirit.

Mr. Mackintosh took a great interest in, and actively participated in, the great revival of 1859 and 1860. He died on November 2, 1896, and was buried in Cheltenham Cemetery, where, in what is known as the Plymouth Brethren plot, "the graves of Exclusive and Open Brethren lie side by side awaiting the resurrection morn."

Now that more than seventy years have passed since his death, it is difficult to come upon much factual detail concerning his own personal life. He was a man of a much milder spirit than Darby, and breathed an atmosphere of deep devotion, and a love not only for Christian believers but for lost souls. He had a gracious spirit, avoiding conflict as far as possible.

Mr. Mackintosh's fame rests primarily upon the work which is herewith being republished in a single volume, *Notes on the Pentateuch,* beginning with a volume of 334 pages on Genesis, and concluding with a two-volume work on Deuteronomy extending to over 800 pages.

Another series by Mr. Mackintosh also was frequently reprinted, under the general heading of *Miscellaneous Writings,* six volumes, totaling over 2500 pages, and most of it still definitely worth reading.

Let me especially call attention to Mr. Mackintosh's excellent comments on Evangelization, which seem to be remarkably up-to-date in this time when we are witnessing so much world-wide evangelization. In volume IV is a very thorough, illuminating, and sensible discussion of ninety pages on the Great Commission of Luke 24:44-49. His statements at the very beginning are refreshing to read:

> Our divine Master called upon sinners to repent and believe the gospel. Some would have us to believe that it is a mistake to call upon persons dead in trespasses and sins to do anything. "How," it is argued, "can those who are dead repent? They are incapable of any spiritual movement. They must first get the power ere they can either repent or believe."
>
> What is our reply to all this? A very simple one indeed—our Lord knows better than all the theologians in the world what ought to be preached. He knows all about man's condition—his guilt, his misery, his spiritual death, his utter helplessness, his total inability to think a single right thought, to utter a single right word, to do a single right act; and yet He called upon men to repent. This is quite enough for us. It is no part of our business to seek to reconcile seeming differences. It may seem to us difficult to reconcile man's utter powerlessness with his responsibility; but "God is His own interpreter, and He will make it plain." It is our happy privilege, and our bounden duty, to believe what He says, and do what He tells us. This is true wisdom, and it yields solid peace.
>
> Our Lord preached repentance, and He commanded His apostles to preach it; and they did so constantly.

Because many are teaching otherwise, one rejoices to see the author's emphasis on the need for genuine repentance.

In volume III there is a section of eighty-six pages with the general heading, "Papers on Evangelism," in the midst of which is a long and excellent commentary of Acts 16:8-31. I cannot help but quote a few lines from these rich pages:

> We increasingly feel the immense importance of an earnest, fervent gospel testimony everywhere; and we dread exceedingly any falling off therein. We are imperatively called to "do the work of an evangelist," and not to be moved from that work by any arguments or considerations whatsoever .... We observe, with deep concern, some who were once known amongst us as

earnest and eminently successful evangelists, now almost wholly abandoning their work and becoming teachers and lecturers.

This is most deplorable. *We really want evangelists.* A true evangelist is almost as great a rarity as a true pastor. Alas! alas! how rare are both! The two are closely connected . . . . We are perfectly aware of the fact that there is in some quarters a strong tendency to throw cold water upon the work of evangelization. There is a sad lack of sympathy with the preacher of the gospel; and, as a necessary consequence, of active co-operation with him in his work . . . . We have invariably found that those who think and speak slightingly of the work of the evangelist are persons of very little spirituality; and on the other hand, the most devoted, the most truehearted, the best taught saints of God, are always sure to take a profound interest in that work . . . . But I find in the Gospels, and in the Acts of the Apostles, that a quantity of most blessed evangelistic work was done by persons who were not specially gifted at all, but who had an earnest love for souls, and a deep sense of the preciousness of Christ and His salvation.

In the midst of these papers, our author discusses what I think is very rare in his writing, his own participation in the great revival in 1859 in Ulster.

Personally, I thought it would be appropriate, in the light of the famous Loizeaux Brothers firm publishing from time to time these twelve volumes of Mr. Mackintosh and so many other worthwhile books, that we might read again what our gifted author said nearly one hundred years ago about reaching the souls of men through Christian bookstores, what he calls tract depots:

And how can we best reach the people, for whom the tracts and books are prepared? I believe by having the books and tracts exposed for sale in a shop window, where that is possible, so that people may see them as they pass, and step in and purchase what they want. Many a soul has been laid hold of in this way. Many, I doubt not, have been saved and blessed by means of tracts, seen for the first time in a shop window or arranged on a counter. . . . It seems to me that a grand point would be gained if the tract depot were placed on its proper footing, and viewed as an integral part of the evangelistic work, to be taken up in responsibility to the Lord, and carried on in the energy of faith in the living God. Every branch of gospel work—the depot, the preaching, the Sunday-school—must be carried on in this way.

WILBUR M. SMITH

(The above is taken from the article specially written by Dr. Smith for the one-volume GENESIS TO DEUTERONOMY: NOTES ON THE PENTATEUCH.)

The Authority
of Scripture

THE BIBLE

ITS SUFFICIENCY AND SUPREMACY

SOME, we are aware, would fain persuade us that things are so totally changed since the Bible was penned, that we need other guidance than that which its precious pages supply. They tell us that society is not what it was; that the human race has made progress; that there has been such a development of the powers of nature, the resources of science, and the appliances of philosophy, that to maintain the sufficiency and supremacy of the Bible, at such a point in the world's history as the nineteenth century of the Christian era, can only be regarded as childishness, ignorance, or imbecility.

Now, the men that tell us these things may be very clever and very learned; but we have no hesitation whatever in telling them that, in this matter, "they do greatly err, not knowing the Scriptures, nor the power of God." We certainly do desire to render all due respect to learning, genius, and talent, whenever we find them in their right place, and at their proper work; but when we find them lifting their proud heads above the Word of God; when we find them sitting in judgment, and casting a slur upon that peerless revelation, we feel that we owe them no respect whatever; yea, we treat them as so many agents of the devil, in his efforts to shake those eternal pillars on which the faith of God's people has ever rested. We cannot listen for a moment to men, however profound in their reading and thinking, who dare to treat God's book as though it were man's book, and speak of those pages that were penned by the Allwise, Almighty, and Eternal God, as though they were the production of a shallow and short-sighted mortal.

It is important that the reader should see clearly that men must either deny that the Bible is the Word of God, or admit its sufficiency and supremacy in all ages, and in all countries—in all stages and conditions of the human race. Grant us but this, that God has written a book for man's guidance, and we argue that that book *must* be amply sufficient for man, no matter when, where, or how we find him. "All scripture is given by inspiration of God . . . that the man of God may be *perfect* ($\alpha\rho\tau\iota o\varsigma$), *throughly furnished* unto *all* good works" (2 Tim. 3:16-17). This, surely, is enough. To be perfect and thoroughly furnished, must needs render a man independent of all the boasted powers of science and philosophy, falsely so called.

We are quite aware that, in writing thus, we expose ourselves to the sneer of the learned rationalist, and the polished and cultivated philosopher. But we are not very careful about this. We greatly admire the answer of a pious, but, no doubt, very ignorant woman to some very learned man who was endeavoring to show her that the inspired writer had made a mistake in asserting that Jonah was in the whale's belly. He assured her that such a thing could not possibly be, inasmuch that the natural history of the whale proved it could not swallow anything so large.

"Well," said the poor woman, "I do not know much about natural history; but this I know, that if the Bible were to tell me that Jonah swallowed the whale I would believe it."

Now, it is quite possible many would pronounce this poor woman to have been under the influence of ignorance and blind credulity; but, for our part, we should rather be the ignorant woman, confiding in God's Word, than the learned rationalist trying to pick holes in it. We have no doubt as to who was in the safer position.

But, let it not be supposed that we prefer ignorance to learning. Let none imagine that

17

we despise the discoveries of science, or treat with contempt the achievements of sound philosophy. Far from it. We honor them highly in their proper sphere. We could not say how much we prize the labors of those learned men who have consecrated their energies to the work of clearing the sacred text of the various errors and corruptions which, from age to age, had crept into it, through the carelessness or infirmity of copyists, taken advantage of by a crafty and malignant foe. Every effort put forth to preserve, to unfold, to illustrate, and to enforce the precious truth of Scripture, we most highly esteem; but, on the other hand, when we find men making use of their learning, their science, and their philosophy, for the purpose of undermining the sacred edifice of divine revelation, we deem it our duty, to raise our voice, in the clearest and strongest way, against them, and to warn the reader, most solemnly, against their baneful influence.

We believe that the Bible, as written in the original Hebrew and Greek languages, is the very word of the only wise and the only true God, with whom one day is as a thousand years, and a thousand years as one day, who saw the end from the beginning, and not only the end, but every stage of the way. We therefore hold it to be nothing short of positive blasphemy to assert that we have arrived at a stage of our career in which the Bible is not sufficient, or that we are compelled to travel outside its covers to find ample guidance and instruction for the present moment, and for every moment of our earthly pilgrimage. The Bible is a perfect chart, in which every exigency of the Christian mariner has been anticipated. Every rock, every sand-bank, every shoal, every strand, every island, has been carefully noted down. All the need of the Church of God, its members, and its ministers, has been most fully provided for. How could it be otherwise, if we admit the Bible to be the Word of God? Could the mind of God have devised, or His finger sketched an imperfect chart? Impossible. We must either deny the divinity or admit the sufficiency of *The Book*. We are absolutely shut up to this alternative. There is not so much as a single point between these

two positions. If the book is incomplete, it cannot be of God; if it be of God it must be perfect. But if we are compelled to betake ourselves to other sources for guidance and instruction, as to the path of the Church of God, its members or its ministers, then is the Bible incomplete, and being such, it cannot be of God at all.

What then are we to do? Whither can we betake ourselves? If the Bible be not a divine and therefore all-sufficient guide-book, what remains? Some will tell us to have recourse to tradition. Alas! what a miserable guide. No sooner have we launched out into the wide field of tradition than our ears are assailed by ten thousand strange and conflicting sounds. We meet, it may be, with a tradition which seems very authentic, very venerable, well worthy of respect and confidence, and we commit ourselves to its guidance; but, directly we have done so, another tradition crosses our path, putting forth quite as strong claims on our confidence, and leading us in quite an opposite direction. Thus it is with tradition. The mind is bewildered, and one is reminded of the assembly at Ephesus, concerning which we read that, "Some cried one thing, and some another; for the assembly was confused." The fact is, we want a perfect standard, and this can only be found in a divine revelation, which, as we believe, is to be found within the covers of our most precious Bible. What a treasure! How we should bless God for it! How we should praise His name for His mercy in that He hath not left His Church dependent upon the *ignis fatuus* of human tradition, but upon the steady light of divine revelation! We do not want tradition to assist revelation, but we use revelation as the test of tradition. We should just as soon think of bringing out a rush-light to assist the sun's meridian beams, as of calling in human tradition to aid divine revelation.

But there is another very ensnaring and dangerous resource presented by the enemy of the Bible, and alas! accepted by too many of the people of God, and that is expediency, or the very attractive plea of doing all the good we can, without due attention to the way in which that good is done. The tree of expediency is a wide-spreading one, and yields most tempting clusters. But remember, its clusters will prove bitter as wormwood in the end. It is, no doubt, well to do all the good we can; but let us look well to the way in which we do it. Let us not deceive ourselves by the vain imagination that God will ever accept of services based upon positive disobedience to His Word. "It is a gift," said the elders, as they boldly walked over the plain commandment of God, as if He would be pleased with a gift presented on such a principle. There is an intimate connection between the ancient "corban" and the modern "expediency," for "there is nothing new under the sun." The solemn responsibility of obeying the Word of God was got rid of under the plausible pretext of "corban," or "it is a gift" (Mark 7:7-13).

Thus it was of old. The "corban" of the ancients justified, or sought to justify, many a bold transgression of the law of God; and the "expediency" of our times allures many to outstep the boundary line laid down by divine revelation.

Now, we quite admit that expediency holds out most attractive inducements. It does seem so very delightful to be doing a great deal of good, to be gaining the ends of a large-hearted benevolence, to be reaching tangible results. It would not be an easy matter duly to estimate the ensnaring influences of such objects, or the immense difficulty of throwing them overboard. Have we never been tempted as we stood upon the narrow path of obedience, and looked forth upon the golden fields of expediency lying on either side, to exclaim, "Alas! I am sacrificing my usefulness for an idea"? Doubtless; but then what if it should turn out that we have the very same foundation for that "idea" as for the fundamental doctrines of salvation? The question is, What is the idea? Is it founded upon "Thus saith the Lord"? If so, let us tenaciously hold by it, though ten thousand advocates of expediency were hurling at us the grievous charge of narrow-mindedness.

There is immense power in Samuel's brief but pointed reply to Saul, "Hath the Lord as great delight in burnt offerings and sacrifices, as in obeying the voice of the Lord! Behold, to obey is better than sacrifice, and to hearken than the fat of rams" (1 Sam. 15:22). Saul's word was *"Sacrifice."* Samuel's word was *"Obedience."* No doubt the bleating of the sheep and the lowing of the oxen were most exciting. They would be looked upon as substantial proofs that something was being done; while on the other hand, the path of obedience seemed narrow, silent, lonely, and fruitless. But oh! those pungent words of Samuel! *"to obey is better than sacrifice."* What a triumphant answer to the most eloquent advocates of expediency! They are most conclusive—most commanding words. They teach us that it is better, if it must be so, to stand, like a marble statue, on the pathway of obedience, than to reach the most desirable ends by transgressing a plain precept of the Word of God.

But let none suppose that one must be like a statue on the path of obedience. Far from it. There are rare and precious services to be rendered by the obedient one—services which can only be rendered by such, and which owe all their preciousness to their being the fruit of simple obedience.* True, they may not find a place in the public record of man's bustling activity; but they are recorded on high, and they will be published at the right time. As a dear friend has often said to us, "Heaven will be the safest and happiest place to hear all about our work down here." May we remember this, and pursue our way, in all simplicity, looking to Christ for guidance, power, and blessing. May His smile be enough for us. May we not be found looking askance to catch the approving look of a poor mortal whose breath is in his nostrils, nor sigh to find our names amid the glittering record of the great men of the age. The servant of Christ should look far beyond all such things. The grand business of the servant is to obey. His object should not be to do a great deal, but simply to do what he is told. This makes all plain; and, moreover, it will make the Bible precious as the depository of

---

* What a pattern of this we have in our blessed Lord! who for thirty years lived here in retirement, known by men only as "the carpenter" (Mark 6:3), but known by, and the delight of, the Father, as the Holy One of God, the perfect meat-offering of Lev. 6:19-33—wholly burnt upon the altar. [ED.]

the Master's will, to which he must continually betake himself to know what he is to do, and how he is to do it. Neither tradition nor expediency will do for the servant of Christ. The all-important inquiry is, "What saith the Scriptures."

This settles everything. From the decision of the Word of God there must be no appeal. When God speaks man must bow. It is not by any means a question of obstinate adherence to a man's own notions. Quite the opposite. It is a reverent adherence to the Word of God. Let the reader distinctly mark this. It often happens that, when one is determined, through grace, to abide by Scripture, he will be pronounced dogmatic, intolerant and imperious; and, no doubt, one has to watch over his temper, spirit, and style, even when seeking to abide by the Word of God. But, be it well remembered, obedience to Christ's commandments is the very opposite of imperiousness, dogmatism, and intolerance. It is not a little strange that when a man tamely consents to place his conscience in the keeping of his fellow, and to bow down his understanding to the opinions of men, he is considered meek, modest, and liberal; but let him reverently bow to the authority of the holy Scripture, and he will be looked upon as self-confident, dogmatic, and narrow-minded. Be it so. The time is rapidly approaching when obedience shall be called by its right name, and meet its recognition and reward. For that moment the faithful must be content to wait, and while waiting for it, be satisfied to let men call them whatever they please. "The Lord knoweth the thoughts of man, that they are vanity."

But we must draw to a close, and would merely add, in conclusion, that there is a third hostile influence against which the lover of the Bible will have to watch, and that is *rationalism*—or the supremacy of man's reason. The faithful disciple of the Word of God will have to withstand this audacious intruder, with the most unflinching decision. It presumes to sit in judgment upon the Word of God—to decide upon what is and what is not worthy of God—to prescribe boundaries to inspiration. Instead of humbly bowing to the authority of Scripture, which

continually soars into a region where poor blind reason can never follow, it proudly seeks to drag Scripture down to its own level. If the Bible puts forth aught which, in the smallest degree, clashes with the conclusions of rationalism, then there must be some flaw. God is shut out of His own book if He says anything which poor blind, perverted reason cannot reconcile with her own conclusions—which conclusions, be it observed, are not unfrequently the grossest absurdities.

Nor is this all. Rationalism deprives us of the only perfect standard of truth, and conducts us into a region of the most dreary uncertainty. It seeks to undermine the authority of a Book in which we can believe everything, and carries us into a field of speculation in which we can be sure of nothing. Under the dominion of rationalism the soul is like a vessel broken from its safe moorings in the haven of divine revelation, to be tossed like a cork upon the wild watery waste of universal skepticism.

Now we do not expect to convince a thorough rationalist, even if such a one should condescend to scan our unpretending pages, which is most unlikely. Neither could we expect to gain over to our way of thinking the decided advocate of expediency, or the ardent admirer of tradition. We have neither the competency, the leisure, nor the space, to enter upon such a line of argument as would be required were we seeking to gain such ends as these. But we are most anxious that the Christian reader should rise up from the perusal of this volume with a deepened sense of the preciousness of his Bible. We earnestly desire that the words, *"The Bible: its sufficiency and supremacy,"* should be engraved, in deep and broad characters, upon the tablet of the reader's heart.

We feel that we have a solemn duty to perform, at a moment like the present, in the which superstition, expediency, and rationalism are all at work, as so many agents of the devil, in his efforts to sap the foundations of our holy faith. We owe it to that blessed volume of inspiration, from which we have drunk the streams of life and peace, to bear our feeble testimony to the divinity of its every page—to give expression, in this permanent form, to our profound reverence for its authority, and our conviction of its divine sufficiency for every need, whether of the believer individually, or the church collectively.

We press upon our readers earnestly to set a higher value than ever upon the Holy Scriptures, and to warn them, in most urgent terms, against every influence, whether of tradition, expediency, or rationalism, which might tend to shake their confidence in those heavenly oracles. There is a spirit abroad, and there are principles at work, which make it imperative upon us to keep close to Scripture—to treasure it in our hearts—and to submit to its holy authority.

May God the Spirit, the Author of the Bible, produce, in the writer and reader of these lines, a more ardent love for that Bible! May He enlarge our experimental acquaintance with its contents, and lead us into more complete subjection to its teachings in all things, that God may be more glorified in us through Jesus Christ our Lord. Amen.

DIVINE TITLES

IT IS AT ONCE INTERESTING, instructive, and edifying to mark the various titles under which God appears in the Holy Scriptures. These titles are expressive of certain characters and relationships in which God has been pleased to reveal Himself to man; and we are persuaded that the Christian reader will find solid profit and real spiritual refreshment and blessing in the study of this subject. We can do little more in this brief paper than offer a suggestion or two, leaving the reader to search the Scriptures for himself, in order to obtain a full understanding of the true meaning and proper application of the various titles.

In the first chapter of Genesis we have the first great title—"God" (Elohim): "In the beginning God created the heaven and the earth." This presents God in unapproachable, incomprehensible Deity. "No man hath seen God at any time." We hear His voice and see His work in creation; but Himself no man hath seen or can see. He dwelleth in the light which no man can approach unto.

But in Gen. 2, we have another title added to God, namely, "Lord" (Jehovah). Why is this? Because man is now on the scene, and "Lord" is expressive of the divine relation with man. Precious truth! It is impossible to read these two chapters and not be struck with the difference of the titles "God" and "the Lord God"—"Elohim" and "Jehovah Elohim"; and the difference is at once beautiful and instructive.*

Gen. 7:16 presents an interesting example. "And they that went in, went in male and female of all flesh, as *God* had commanded him: and the *Lord* shut him in." God, in His government, was about to destroy the human race, and every living thing. But Jehovah, in infinite grace, shut Noah in. Mark the distinction. If a mere man were writing the history, he might transpose the titles, not seeing what was involved. Not so the Holy Spirit.

---

* We shall here give the various divine titles given in Scripture; and the reader can, if so led, examine for himself the passages in which they occur, and see the way in which they are applied.

"Elohim"—God. "Jehovah"—Lord. "Adonai," also rendered Lord, see Ps. 16:2. Adonai, or Adon, has been taken to mean *Ruler*, or *Sovereign*, from the root "Dan," to judge. In some English Bibles, Jehovah is rendered in capital letters, LORD; Adonai, Lord. Thus the distinction is easily seen. "O my soul, thou hast said, Jehovah, Thou art my Adonai" (Ps. 16:2). This is very striking and most beautiful.

Then, in Gen. 14:22, we have "Elion"—the Most High God. This is His millennial title. And in chapter 17:1 we have "Shaddai"—the Almighty. "I am the Almighty God: walk before Me, and be thou perfect." In Psalm 91:1-2, we have a very beautiful application: "He that dwelleth in the secret places of Elion shall abide under the shadow of Shaddai. I will say of Jehovah, He is my refuge and my fortress; my Elohim; in Him will I trust." All this is full of precious instruction; and we trust the reader may be led to pursue the study for himself. It is hardly needful to add that, for the ineffable title and relationship of "Father" we must turn to the New Testament.

He brings out the lovely point of Jehovah's relationship with Noah. Elohim was going to judge the world; but as Jehovah He had His eye upon His beloved servant Noah, and graciously sheltered him in the vessel of mercy. How perfect is Scripture! How edifying and refreshing to trace the moral glories of the divine volume!

Let us turn to a passage in 1 Sam. 17, where we have the record of David's encounter with Goliath. He boldly tells the giant what he is about to do, both to him and to the host of the Philistines, in order "that all *the earth* may know that there is a *God* (Elohim) in Israel. And all this assembly shall know that the *Lord* (Jehovah) saveth not with sword and spear: for the battle is Jehovah's, and He will give you into our hands" (vers. 46-47).

"All the earth" was to know and own the presence of God in the midst of His people. They could know nothing of the precious relationship involved in the title "Jehovah." This latter was for the assembly of Israel alone. They were to know not only His presence in their midst, but His blessed mode of acting. To the world He was Elohim, to His beloved people He was Jehovah.

Well may these exquisite touches command our hearts' admiration. Oh, the living depths, the moral glories, of that peerless Revelation which our Father has graciously penned for our comfort and edification! We must confess it gives us unspeakable delight to dwell on these things and point them out to the reader, in this infidel day when the divine inspiration of Holy Scripture is boldly called in question, in quarters where we should least expect it. But we have something better to do just now than replying to the contemptible assaults of infidelity. We are thoroughly persuaded that the most effective safeguard against all such assaults is to have the Word of Christ dwelling in us richly, in all its living, formative power. To the heart thus filled and fortified, the most plausible and powerful arguments of all infidel writers are but as the pattering of rain on the window.

We shall give the reader only one more illustration of our subject from the Old Testament. It occurs in the interesting history of Jehoshaphat (2 Chron. 18:31). "And it came to pass, when the captains of the chariots saw Jehoshaphat, that they said, It is the king of Israel. Therefore they compassed about him to fight: but Jehoshaphat cried out, and *the Lord* (Jehovah) helped *him;* and *God* (Elohim) moved *them* to depart from him."

This is deeply affecting. Jehoshaphat had put himself into an utterly false position. He had linked himself with the most ungodly of Israel's kings. He had even gone so far as to say to the wicked Ahab, "I am as thou art, and my people as thy people; and we will be with thee in the war." No marvel, therefore, if the Syrian captains mistook him for Ahab. It was only taking him at his word. But when brought down to the very lowest point—into the very shadow of death—"he cried out"; and that cry went up to the gracious and ever-attentive ear of Jehovah, who had said, "Call upon Me in the day of trouble; I will deliver thee." Precious grace!

But mark the lovely accuracy in the use and application of the divine titles—for this is our thesis. "He cried out, and Jehovah helped him;" and—what then? A mere human author would doubtless have put it thus: "Jehovah helped him, and moved them." But no; Jehovah had, as such, nothing to do with uncircumcised Syrians. His eye was upon his dear, though erring, servant; His heart was toward him, and His everlasting arms around him. There was no link between Jehovah and the Syrians; but Elohim, whom they knew not, moved them away.

Who can fail to see the beauty and perfection of all this? Is it not plain that the stamp of a divine hand is visible upon the three passages which we have culled for consideration? Yes, and so it is upon every clause, from cover to cover, of the divine volume. Let no one suppose for a moment that we want to occupy our readers with curious points, nice distinctions, or learned criticisms. Nothing is further from our thoughts. We would not pen a line for any or all of these objects. As God is our witness, our one great object in writing this paper is to deepen in the hearts of our readers the sense of the preciousness, beauty and excellency of the Holy Scriptures, given of God for the guidance, help and blessing of His people in this dark world. If this object be gained, we have our full reward.

But we cannot close without referring, for a moment, to the precious pages of the New Testament. We shall ask the reader to turn to Rom. 15, in which we have God presented to us under three distinct titles, each one of which is in perfect and beautiful keeping with the immediate subject in hand. Thus, in the opening verses of the chapter, which properly belong to chapter 14, the inspired apostle is urging upon us the necessity of patience, forbearance, and kindly consideration one of another.

And to whom does he direct us for power to respond to those holy and much-needed exhortations? "To the God of patience and consolation." He presents God in the very character in which we need Him. Our small stock of patience would soon be exhausted in seeking to meet the varied characters which cross our path, even in intercourse with our brethren. There are constant claims upon our patience and forbearance; and most surely others have need of patience and forbearance with us. Where are we all to get the means of meeting all these claims? At the exhaustless treasury of "the God of patience and consolation." Our tiny springs would soon dry up if not kept in unbroken connection with that ever-flowing Fountain. The weight of a feather would be an overmatch for *our* patience; how much more the ten thousand things that come before us even in the Church of God!

Hence the need of the beautiful prayer of the apostle, "Now the God of patience and consolation grant you to be likeminded one toward another, according to Christ Jesus; that ye may with one mind and one mouth glorify God, even the Father of our Lord Jesus Christ. Wherefore receive ye one another, as Christ also received us to the glory of God."

Here lies the grand secret, the divine power of receiving one another, and going on together in holy love, heavenly patience, and tender consideration. We cannot get on otherwise. It is only by habitual communion with the God of patience and consolation that we shall be able to rise above the numberless hindrances to confidence and fellowship that continually present themselves, and walk in fervent love to all who love our Lord Jesus Christ in sincerity.

But we must draw this paper to a close, and shall merely glance at the other divine titles presented in our chapter. When the apostle speaks of the future glory, his heart at once turns to God in the very character suited to the subject before him. "Now *the God of hope* fill you with all joy and peace in believing, that ye may abound in hope, through the power of the Holy Ghost." If we would have the hope of glory heightened in our souls—and truly we need it—we must turn our eyes to "the God of hope."

How marked and striking is the application of the divine titles, wherever we turn! Whatever may be the character of our need, God presents Himself to our hearts in the very way adapted to meet it. Thus, at the close of the chapter, when the apostle turns his eyes towards Judea, and the difficulties and the dangers awaiting him, his heart springs up to *the God of peace.*" Precious resource in all our varied exercises, anxieties, sorrows, and cares!

In a word, whatever we want, we have just to turn in simple faith to God, and find it all in Him. God—blessed forever be His name—is the one grand and all-sufficient answer to our every need, from the starting-point to the goal of our Christian career. Oh for artless faith to use Him!

LIFE AND TIMES OF JOSIAH

2 Chronicles 34—35

TWO THOUSAND FOUR HUNDRED years have rolled away since king Josiah lived and reigned; but his history is pregnant with instruction, which can never lose its freshness or its power. The moment at which he ascended the throne of his fathers was one of peculiar gloom and heaviness. The tide of corruption, swollen by many a tributary stream, had risen to the highest point; and the sword of judgment, long held back in divine patience and longsuffering, was about to fall in terrible severity upon the city of David. The brilliant reign of Hezekiah had been followed by a long and dreary period of fifty-five years under the sway of his son Manasseh; and albeit the rod of correction had proved effectual in leading this great sinner to repentance and amendment, yet no sooner had the sceptre fallen from his hand than it was seized by his godless and impenitent son Amon, who "did that which was evil in the sight of the Lord, as did Manasseh his father: for Amon sacrificed unto all the carved images which Manasseh his father had made, and served them; and humbled not himself before the Lord, as Manasseh his father had humbled himself: but Amon trespassed more and more. And his servants conspired against him, and slew him in his own house. . . . And the people of the land made Josiah his son king in his stead" (2 Chron. 33:22-25).

Thus, then, Josiah, a child of eight years, found himself on the throne of David, surrounded by the accumulated evils and errors of his father and his grandfather—yea, by forms of corruption which had been introduced by no less a personage than Solomon himself. If the reader will just turn for a moment to 2 Kings 23, he will find a marvelous picture of the condition of things at the opening of Josiah's history. There were "idolatrous priests, whom the kings of Judah had ordained to burn incense in the high places, in the cities of Judah, and in the places round about Jerusalem; those also that burned incense unto Baal, to the sun, and to the moon, and to the planets, and to all the host of heaven."

Ponder this! Only think of kings of Judah, successors of David, ordaining priests to burn incense to Baal! Bear in mind too that each of these kings of Judah was responsible to "write him a copy of the book of the law," which he was to keep by him, and in which he was to "read *all the days of his life*, that he may learn to fear the Lord his God, to keep *all the words of this law*, and those statutes to do them" (See Deut. 17:18-19). Alas! how sadly had they departed from "all the words of the law," when they could actually set about ordaining priests to burn incense to false gods!

But further, there were "horses that the kings of Judah had given *to the sun*," and that, moreover, "at the entering in of the house of the Lord," and "chariots of the sun," and "high places which *Solomon* the king of Israel had builded for Ashtoreth the abomination of the Zidonians, and for Chemosh the abomination of the Moabites, and for Milcom the abomination of the children of Ammon."

All this is most solemn, and worthy of the serious consideration of the Christian reader. We certainly ought not to pass it over as a mere fragment of ancient history. It is not as though we were reading the historic records of Babylon, of Persia, of Greece, or of Rome. We should not marvel at the kings of those nations burning incense to Baal, ordaining idolatrous priests, and worshiping the host of heaven; but when we see kings of Judah, the sons and successors of David, children of Abraham, men who had access to the book of the law of God, and who were responsible to make that book the subject of their profound and constant study—when we see such men falling under the power of dark and debasing superstition, it sounds in our ears a warning voice, to which we cannot with impunity refuse to give heed. We should bear in mind that all these things have been written for our learning; and although it may be said that we are not in danger of being led to burn incense to Baal, or to worship the host of heaven, yet we may be assured we have need to attend to the admonitions and warnings with which the Holy Ghost has furnished us in the history of God's ancient people. "Now all these things happened unto them for ensamples; and they are written for our admonition, on whom the ends of the ages have come" (1 Cor. 10:11). These words of the inspired apostle, though directly referring to the actings of Israel in the wilderness, may nevertheless apply to the entire history of that people—a history fraught with the deepest instruction from first to last.

But how are we to account for all those gross and terrible evils into which Solomon and his successors were drawn? What was their origin? *Neglect of the Word of God.* This was the source of all the mischief and all the sorrow. Let professing Christians remember this; let the whole Church of God remember it. The neglect of the Holy Scriptures was the fruitful source of all those errors and corruptions which blot the page of Israel's history, and which brought down upon them many heavy strokes of Jehovah's governmental rod. "Concerning the works of men, by the word of Thy lips, I have kept me from the paths of the destroyer" (Psa. 17:4). *"From a child* thou hast known the Holy Scriptures, which are able to make thee wise unto salvation through faith which is in Christ Jesus. All Scripture is given by inspiration of God, and is profitable for doctrine, for reproof, for correction, for instruction in righteousness, that the man of God may be perfect ($\alpha\rho\tau\iota o\varsigma$), throughly furnished unto all good works" (2 Tim. 3:15-17).

In these two precious quotations we have the Word of God presented in its twofold virtue; it not only perfectly preserves us

from evil, but perfectly furnishes us unto all good, it keeps us from the paths of the destroyer, and guides us in the ways of God.

How important, then, is the study—the diligent, earnest, prayerful study of Holy Scripture! How needful to cultivate a spirit of reverential submission, in all things, to the authority of the Word of God! Mark how continually and how earnestly this was impressed upon the ancient people of God. How often were such accents as the following sounded in their ears!—"Now therefore harken, O Israel, unto the statutes and unto the judgments which I teach you, for to do them, that ye may live, and go in and possess the land which the Lord God of your fathers giveth you. Ye shall not add unto the word which I command you, neither shall ye diminish aught from it, that ye may keep the commandments of the Lord your God which I command you. . . . Behold, I have taught you statutes and judgments, even as the Lord my God commanded me, that ye should do so in the land whither ye go to possess it. Keep, therefore, and do them; *for this is your wisdom and your understanding in the sight of the nations*, which shall hear all the statutes, and say, Surely, this great nation is a wise and understanding people. For what nation is there so great, who hath God so nigh unto them, as the Lord our God is in all things that we call upon Him for? And what nation is there so great, that hath statutes and judgments so righteous as all this law, which I set before you this day? *Only take heed to thyself*, and *keep thy soul diligently*, lest thou forget the things which thine eyes have seen, and lest they depart from thy heart all the days of thy life; but teach them thy sons, and thy sons' sons" (Deut. 4:1-9).

Let it be carefully noticed here, that "wisdom and understanding" consist simply in having the commandments of God treasured in the heart. This, moreover, was to be the basis of Israel's moral greatness, in view of the nations around them. It was not the learning of the schools of Egypt, or of the Chaldeans. No; it was the knowledge of the Word of God, and attention thereto—the spirit of implicit obedience in all things to the holy statutes and judgments of the Lord their

God. This was Israel's wisdom; this their true and real greatness; this their impregnable bulwark against every foe—their moral safeguard against every evil.

And does not the self-same thing hold good with respect to God's people at the present moment? Is not obedience to the Word of God our wisdom, our safeguard, and the foundation of all true moral greatness? Assuredly. Our wisdom is to obey. The obedient soul is wise, safe, happy, and fruitful. As it was, so it is. If we study the history of David and his successors, we shall find (without so much as a single exception) that those who yielded obedience to the commandments of God were safe, happy, prosperous, and influential. And so it will ever be. Obedience will always yield its own precious and fragrant fruits—not that its fruits should be our *motive* for rendering obedience; we are called to be obedient, irrespective of everything.

Now it is obvious that in order to be obedient to the Word of God, we must be acquainted with it, and in order to be acquainted with it, we must carefully study it. And how should we study it? With an earnest desire to understand its contents, with profound reverence for its authority, and with an honest purpose to obey its dictates, cost what it may. If we have grace to study Scripture in some small degree after this fashion, we may expect to grow in knowledge and wisdom.

But alas! there is a fearful amount of ignorance of Scripture in the professing church. We are deeply impressed with a sense of this; and we may as well, at this point, just tell the reader that our main object in calling his attention to the subject of "Josiah and his times" is to wake up in his soul an intense desire after a closer acquaintance with God's holy Word, and a more entire bowing down of his whole moral being— heart, conscience, and understanding—to that perfect standard.

We feel the commanding importance of this subject, and we must discharge what we believe to be a sacred duty to the souls of our readers and to the truth of God. The powers of darkness are abroad. The enemy is succeeding to an appalling extent in drawing hearts after various forms of error and evil, in casting dust in the eyes of God's people, and in blinding the minds of men. True we have not got Ashtoreth, Chemosh, and Milcom; but we have ritualism, infidelity, spiritualism, etc. We have not to cry against burning incense to Baal, and worshiping the host of heaven, but we have something far more ensnaring and dangerous. We have the ritualist, with his sensuous and attractive rites and ceremonies; we have the rationalist, with his learned and plausible reasonings; we have the spiritualist, with his boasted converse with the spirits of the departed—and what multitude of other delusions and insidious attacks upon the truth!

We doubt if the minds of Christians generally are alive to the real character and extent of these formidable influences. There are at this moment millions of souls throughout the length and breadth of the professing Church who are building their hopes for eternity upon the sandy foundation of ordinances, rites, and ceremonies. There is a very marked return to the traditions of the fathers, as they are called; an intense longing after those things which gratify the senses— music, painting, architecture, vestments, lights, incense—all the appliances, in short, of a gorgeous and senuous religion. The theology, the worship, and the discipline of the various churches of the Reformation are found insufficient to meet the religious cravings of the people. They are too severely simple to satisfy hearts that long for something tangible on which to lean for support and comfort—something to feed the senses, and fan the flame of devotion.

Hence the strong tendency of the religious mind in the direction of what is called ritualism. If the soul has not got hold of *the truth*, if there is not the living link with Christ, if the supreme authority of Holy Scripture be not set up in the heart, there is no safeguard against the powerful and fascinating influences of ceremonial religiousness. The most potent efforts of mere intellectualism, eloquence, logic, all the varied charms of literature, are found to be utterly insufficient to hold that class of minds to which we are now referring. They *must* have the forms and offices of religion; to these they will flock; around these they will gather; on these they will build.

It is painfully interesting to mark the efforts put forth in various quarters to act upon the masses and keep the people together. It is very evident to the thoughtful Christian that those who put forth such efforts must be sadly deficient in that profound faith in the power of the Word of God and of the cross of Christ which swayed the heart of the apostle Paul. They cannot be fully aware of the solemn fact that Satan's grand object is to keep souls in ignorance of divine revelation, to hide from them the glory of the cross and of the person of Christ. For this end he is using ritualism, rationalism, and spiritualism now, just as he used Ashtoreth, Chemosh, and Milcom in the days of Josiah. "There is nothing new under the sun." The devil has ever hated the truth of God, and he will leave no stone unturned to keep it from acting on the heart of man. Hence it is that he has rites and ceremonies for one man, the powers of reason for another; and when men tire of both, and begin to sigh for something satisfying, he leads them into converse and communion with the spirits of the departed. By all alike are souls led away from the Holy Scriptures, and from the blessed Saviour which those Scriptures reveal.

It is solemn and affecting beyond expression to think of all this, and not less so to contemplate the lethargy and indifference of those who profess to have the truth. We do not stop to inquire what it is that ministers to this lethargic state of many professors. That is not our object. We desire, by the grace of God, to see them thoroughly roused out of it, and to this end it is that we call their attention to the influences that are abroad, and to the only divine safeguard against them. We cannot but feel deeply for our children, growing up in such an atmosphere as that which at present surrounds us, and which will become yet darker and darker. We long to see more earnestness on the part of Christians in seeking to store the minds of the young with the precious and soul-saving knowledge of the Word of God. The child Josiah, and the child Timothy, should incite us to greater diligence in the instruction of the young, whether in the bosom of the family, in the Sunday school, or in any way we can reach them. It will not do for us to fold our arms, and say, "When God's time comes, our children will be converted; and till then, our efforts are useless." This is a fatal mistake. "God is a rewarder of them that diligently seek Him" (Heb. 11). He blesses our prayerful efforts in the instruction of our children. And further, who can estimate the blessing of being early led in the right way—of having the character formed amid holy influences, and the mind stored with what is true and pure and lovely? On the other hand, who will undertake to set forth the evil consequences of allowing our children to grow up in ignorance of divine things? Who can portray the evils of a polluted imagination—of a mind stored with vanity, folly, and falsehood—of a heart familiarized from infancy with scenes of moral degradation? We do not hesitate to say that Christians incur very heavy and awful responsibility in allowing the enemy to preoccupy the minds of their children at the very period when they are most plastic and susceptible.

True, there must be the quickening power of the Holy Ghost. It is as true of the children of Christians as of any other that they "must be born again." We all understand this. But does this fact touch the question of our responsibility in reference to our children? Is it to cripple our energies or hinder our earnest efforts? Assuredly not. We are called upon by every argument, divine and human, to shield our precious little ones from every evil influence, and to train them in that which is holy and good. And not only should we so act in respect to our own children, but also in respect to the thousands around us, who are like sheep having no shepherd, and who may each say, alas, with too much truth, "No man careth for my soul."

May the foregoing pages be used by God's Spirit to act powerfully on the hearts of all who may read them, that so there may be a real awakening to a sense of our high and holy responsibilities to the souls around, and a shaking off of that terrible deadness and coldness over which we all have to mourn.

Part 2

In studying the history of Josiah and his times, we learn one special and priceless lesson, namely, *the value and authority of the Word of God*. It would be utterly impossible for human language to set forth the vast importance of such a lesson—a lesson for every age, for every clime, for every condition—for the individual believer and for the whole Church of God. The supreme authority of Holy Scripture should be deeply impressed on every heart. It is the only safeguard against the many forms of error and evil which abound on every hand. Human writings, no doubt, have their value; they may interest the mind as a reference, but they are perfectly worthless as authority.

We need to remember this. There is a strong tendency in the human mind to lean upon human authority. Hence it has come to pass that millions throughout the professing Church have virtually been deprived altogether of the Word of God, from the fact that they have lived and died under the delusion that they could not know it to be the Word of God apart from human authority. Now this is, in reality, throwing the Word of God overboard. If that Word is of no avail without man's authority, then, we maintain, it is not God's Word at all. It does not matter, in the smallest degree, what the authority is, the effect is the same. God's Word is declared to be insufficient without something of man to give the certainty that it is God that is speaking.

This is a most dangerous error, and its root lies far deeper in the heart than many of us are aware. It has often been said to us, when quoting passages of Scripture, "How do you know that that is the Word of God?" What is the point of such a question? Plainly to overthrow the authority of the Word. The heart that could suggest such an inquiry does not want to be governed by Holy Scripture at all. The *will* is concerned. Here lies the deep secret. There is the consciousness that the Word condemns something that the heart wants to hold and cherish, and hence the effort to set the Word aside altogether.

But how are we to know that the book which we call the Bible is the Word of God? We reply, It carries its own credentials with it. It bears its own evidence upon every page, in every paragraph, in every line. True, it is only by the teaching of the Holy Spirit, the divine Author of the book, that the evidence can be weighed and the credentials appreciated. But we do not want man's voice to accredit God's book; or, if we do, we are most assuredly on infidel ground as regards divine revelation. If God cannot speak directly to the heart—if He cannot give the assurance that it is He Himself who speaks, then where are we? whither shall we turn? If God cannot make Himself heard and understood, can man do it better?—can he improve upon God? Can man's voice give us more certainty? Can the authority of the Church, the decrees of general councils, the judgment of the fathers, the opinion of the doctors, give us more certainty than God Himself? If so, we are just as completely at sea—just as thoroughly in the dark as though God had not spoken at all. Of course, if God has not spoken, we are completely in the dark; but if He has spoken, and yet we cannot know His voice without man's authority to accredit it, where lies the difference? Is it not plain that if God in His great mercy has given us a revelation, it must be sufficient of itself; and on the other hand, that any revelation which is not sufficient of itself cannot possibly be divine? And further, is it not equally plain that if we cannot believe what God says because He says it, we have no safer ground to go upon when man presumes to affix his accrediting seal?

Let us not be misunderstood. What we insist upon is this: the all-sufficiency of a divine revelation apart from and above all human writings—ancient, mediæval, or modern. We value human writings; we value sound criticism; we value profound and accurate scholarship; we value the light of *true* science and philosophy; we value the testimony of pious travelers who have sought to throw light upon the sacred text; we value all those books that open up to us the intensely interesting subject of biblical antiquities; in short, we value everything that tends to aid us in the study of the Holy Scriptures: but after all, we return with deeper emphasis to our assertion as to the all-sufficiency and supremacy of the Word of God. That Word must be received on its own divine authority, without any human recommendation, or else it is not the Word of God to us. We believe that God can give us the certainty in our own souls that the Holy Scriptures are, in very deed, His own Word. If He does not give it, no man can; and if He does, no man need. Thus the inspired apostle says to his son Timothy, "Continue thou in the things which thou hast learned, and *hast been assured of* knowing *of whom* thou hast learned; and that from a child thou hast known the Holy Scriptures, which are able to make thee wise unto salvation through faith which is in Christ Jesus" (2 Tim. 3:14-15).

How did Timothy know that the Holy Scriptures were the Word of God? He knew it by divine teaching. He knew of *whom* he had learned. Here lay the secret. There was a living link between his soul and God, and he recognized in Scripture the very voice of God. Thus it must ever be. It will not do merely to be convinced in the intellect, by human arguments, human evidences, and human apologies, that the Bible is the Word of God; we must know its power in the heart and on the conscience by divine teaching; and when this is the case, we shall no more need human proofs of the divinity of the book than we need a rushlight at noonday to prove that the sun is shining. We shall then believe what God says because He says it, and not because man accredits it, nor because we feel it. "Abraham *believed God*, and it was counted unto him for righteousness." He did not want to go to the Chaldeans, or to the Egyptians, in order to find out from them if what he had heard was in reality the Word of God. No; he knew *whom* he had believed, and this gave him holy stability. He could say, beyond all question, "God has established a link between my soul and Himself, by means of His Word, which no power of earth or hell can ever snap." This is the true ground for every believer—man, woman, or child, in all ages and under all circumstances. This was the ground for Abraham and Josiah, for Luke and Theophilus, for Paul and Timothy; and it must be the ground for the writer and the reader of these words, else we shall never be able to stand against the rising tide of infidelity, which is sweeping away the very foundations on which thousands of professors are reposing.

However, we may well inquire, can a merely national profession, a hereditary faith, an educational creed, sustain the soul in the presence of an audacious skepticism that reasons about everything and believes nothing? Impossible! We must be able to stand before the skeptic, the rationalist, and the infidel, and say, in all the calmness and dignity of a divinely wrought faith, *"I know whom I have believed."* Then we shall be little moved by such books as, "The Phases of Faith," "Essays and Reviews," "Broken Lights," "Ecce Homo," or "Colenso." They will be no more to us than gnats in the sunshine. They cannot hide from our souls the heavenly beams of our Father's revelation. God has spoken, and His voice reaches the heart. It makes itself heard above the din and confusion of this world, and all the strife and controversy of professing Christians. It gives rest and peace, strength and fixedness, to the believing heart and mind. The opinions of men may perplex and confound. We may not be able to thread our way through the labyrinths of human systems of theology; but God's voice speaks in Holy Scripture—speaks to the heart—speaks to *me*. This is life and peace. It is all I want. Human writings may now go for what they are worth, seeing I have all I want in the ever-flowing fountain of inspiration—the peerless, precious volume of my God.

But let us now turn to Josiah, and see how all that we have been dwelling upon finds its illustration in his life and times.

"Josiah was eight years old when he began to reign" (2 Chron. 34:1). This tells a tale as to the condition and ways of God's people. Josiah's father had been murdered by his own servants, after a brief and evil reign of two years, in the twenty-fourth year of his age. Such things ought not to have been. They were the sad fruit of sin and folly—the humiliating proofs of Judah's departure from Jehovah. But God was above all; and although we should not have expected ever to find a child of eight years of age on the throne of David, yet that child could find his sure resource in the God of his fathers: so that in this case, as in all others, "where sin abounded, grace did much more abound." The very fact of Josiah's youth and inexperience only afforded an occasion for the display of divine grace, and the setting forth of the value and the power of the Word of God.

This pious child was placed in a position of peculiar difficulty and temptation. He was surrounded by errors in various forms and of long standing; but "he did that which was right in the sight of the Lord, and walked in the ways of David his father, and declined neither to the right hand nor to the left. For in the eighth year of his reign, while he was yet young, he began to seek after the God of David his father: and in the twelfth year began to purge Judah and Jerusalem from the high places, and the groves, and the carved images, and the molten images."

This was a good beginning. It is a great matter, while the heart is yet tender, to have it impressed with the fear of the Lord. It preserves it from a host of evils and errors. "The fear of the Lord is the beginning of wisdom," and it taught this pious youth to know what was "right," and to adhere to it with unswerving fixedness of purpose. There is great force and value in the expression, "He did that which was right *in the sight of the Lord.*" It was not that which was right in his own eyes, nor yet in the eyes of the people, nor in the eyes of those that had gone before him; but simply what was right in the sight of the Lord. This is the solid foundation of all right action. Until the fear of the Lord gets its true place in the heart, there can be nothing right, nothing wise, nothing holy. How can there be, if indeed that fear is the *beginning* of wisdom? We may do many things through the fear of man, many things through force of habit, through surrounding influences; but never can we do what is really right in the sight of the Lord until our hearts are brought to understand the fear of His holy name. This is the grand regulating principle. It imparts seriousness, earnestness, and reality—rare and admirable qualities! It is an effectual safeguard against levity and vanity. A man, or a child, who habitually walks in the fear of God is always earnest and sincere, always free from trifling and affectation, from assumption and bombast, life has a purpose, the heart has an object, and this gives intensity to the whole course and character.

But further, we read of Josiah that "he walked in the ways of David his father, and *declined neither to the right hand nor to the left.*" What a testimony for the Holy Ghost to bear concerning a young man! How we do long for this plain decision! It is invaluable at all times, but especially in a day of laxity and latitudinarianism—of false liberality and spurious charity like the present. It imparts great peace of mind. A vacillating man is never peaceful; he is always tossed to and fro. "A double-minded man is unstable in all his ways." He tries to please everybody, and in the end pleases nobody. The decided man, on the contrary, is he who feels he has "to please but *One.*" This gives unity and fixedness to the life and character. It is an immense relief to be thoroughly done with men-pleasing and eye-service—to be able to fix the eye upon the Master alone, and go on with Him through evil report and through good report. True, we may be misunderstood and misrepresented; but that is a very small matter indeed; our great business is to walk in the divinely appointed path, "declining neither to the right hand nor to the left."

We are convinced that plain decision is the only thing for the servant of Christ at the present moment; for so surely as the devil finds us wavering, he will bring every engine into play in order to drive us completely off the plain and narrow path. May God's Spirit work more mightily in our souls, and give us increased ability to say, "My heart is fixed, O God; my heart is fixed: I will sing and give praise."

We shall now proceed to consider the great work which Josiah was raised up to accomplish; but ere doing so, we must ask the reader to notice particularly the words already referred to, namely, "In the eighth year of his reign, while he was yet young, *he began to seek after the God of David his father.*" Here, we may rest assured, lay the true basis of all

Josiah's valuable service. He began by seeking after God. Let young Christians ponder this deeply. Hundreds, we fear, have made shipwreck by rushing prematurely into work. They have become occupied and engrossed with their service before the heart was rightly established in the fear and love of God. This is a very serious error indeed, and we have met numbers, within the last few years, who have fallen into it. We should ever remember that those whom God uses much in public He trains in secret; and further, that all His most honored servants have been more occupied with their Master than with their work. It is not that we undervalue work; by no means; but we do find that all those who have been signally owned of God, and who have pursued a long and steady course of service and Christian testimony, have begun with much deep and earnest heart-work, in the secret of the divine presence. And on the other hand, we have noticed that when men have rushed prematurely into public work—when they began to teach before they had begun to learn, they have speedily broken down and gone back.

It is well to remember this. God's plants are deeply rooted, and often slow of growth. Josiah "began to seek God" four years before he began his public work. There was in his case a firm ground-work of genuine personal piety, on which to erect the superstructure of active service. This was most needful. He had a great work to do. "High places and groves, carved images and molten images," abounded on all hands, and called for no ordinary faithfulness and decision. Where were these to be had? In the divine treasury, and there alone. Josiah was but a child, and many of those who had introduced the false worship were men of years and experience. But he set himself to seek the Lord. He found his resource in the God of his father David. He betook himself to the fountain-head of all wisdom and power, and there gathered up strength wherewith to gird himself for what lay before him.

This, we repeat, was most needful; it was absolutely indispensable. The accumulated rubbish of ages and generations lay before him. One after another of his predecessors

had added to the pile; and notwithstanding the reformation effected in the days of Hezekiah, it would seem as though all had to be done over again. Harken to the following appalling catalog of evils and errors: "In the twelfth year, Josiah began to purge Judah and Jerusalem from the high places, and the groves, and the carved images, and the molten images. And they break down the altars of Baalim in his presence; and the images that were on high above them he cut down; and the groves, and the carved images, and the molten images, he brake in pieces, and *made dust* of them, and strewed it upon the graves of them that had sacrificed unto them. And he burnt the bones of the priests upon their altars, and cleansed Judah and Jerusalem. And so did he in the cities of Manasseh and Ephraim and Simeon, even unto Naphtali, with their mattocks round about. And when he had broken down the altars and the groves, and had beaten the graven images into *powder*, and cut down all the idols throughout *all the land of Israel*, he returned to Jerusalem."

See also the narrative given in 2 Kings 23, where we have a much more detailed list of the abominations with which this devoted servant of God had to grapple. We do not quote any further. Enough has been given to show the fearful lengths to which even the people of God may go when once they turn aside, in the smallest measure, from the authority of Holy Scripture. We feel that this is one special lesson to be learned from the deeply interesting history of this best of Judah's kings, and we fondly trust it may be learned effectually. It is indeed a grand and all-important lesson. The moment a man departs, the breadth of a hair, from Scripture, there is no accounting for the monstrous extravagance into which he may rush. We may feel disposed to marvel how such a man as Solomon could ever be led to "build high places for Ashtoreth the abomination of the Zidonians, and for Chemosh the abomination of the Moabites, and for Milcom the abomination of the children of Ammon." But then we can easily see how that having in the first place disobeyed the Word of his Lord in going to those nations for wives, he easily enough fell into the deeper error of adopting their worship.

But let us remember that all the mischief, all the corruption and confusion, all the shame and dishonor, all the reproach and blasphemy, had its origin in the neglect of the Word of God. We cannot possibly ponder this fact too deeply. It is solemn, impressive, and admonitory beyond expression. It has ever been a special design of Satan to lead God's people away from Scripture. He will use anything and everything for this end—tradition, the church so-called, expediency, human reason, popular opinion, reputation and influence, character, position, and usefulness—all those he will use in order to get the heart and conscience away from that one golden sentence—that divine, eternal motto, *"It is written."* All that enormous pile of error which our devoted young monarch was enabled to "grind into *dust*, and beat into *powder*"—all, all had its origin in the gross neglect of this most precious sentence. It mattered little to Josiah that all these things could boast of antiquity, and the authority of the fathers of the Jewish nation. Neither was he moved by the thought that these altars and high places, these groves and images, might be regarded as proofs of largeness of heart, breadth of mind, and a liberality of spirit that spurned all narrowness, bigotry, and intolerance—that *would* not be confined within the narrow bounds of Jewish prejudice, but could travel forth through the wide, wide world, and embrace all in a circle of charity and brotherhood. None of these things, we are persuaded, moved him. If they were not based upon "Thus saith the Lord," he had but one thing to do with them, and that was to *"beat them into powder."*

Part 3

The various periods in the life of Josiah are very strongly marked. "In the *eighth* year of his reign, he began to seek after the God of David his father"; "in the *twelfth* year he began to purge Judah and Jerusalem"; and "in the *eighteenth* year of his reign, when he had purged the land and the house, he sent Shaphan the son of Azaliah, and Maaseiah the governor of the city, and Joah the son of Joahaz the recorder, to repair the house of the Lord his God."

Now in all this we can mark that progress which ever results from a real purpose of heart to serve the Lord. "The path of the just is as a shining light, which shineth more and more unto the perfect day." Such was the path of Josiah; and such, too, may be the path of the reader, if only he is influenced by the same earnest purpose. It does not matter what the circumstances may be. We may be surrounded by the most hostile influences, as Josiah was in his day; but a devoted heart, an earnest spirit, a fixed purpose, will, through grace, lift us above all, and enable us to press forward from stage to stage of the path of true discipleship.

If we study the first twelve chapters of the book of Jeremiah, we shall be able to form some idea of the condition of things in the days of Josiah. There we meet with such passages as the following: "I will utter My judgments against them touching *all their wickedness*, who have forsaken Me, and have *burned incense unto other gods*, and *worshiped the works of their own hands*. Thou therefore gird up thy loins, and arise, and speak unto them all that I command thee: *be not dismayed at their faces*, lest I confound thee before them." "Wherefore I will yet plead with you, saith the Lord, and with your children's children will I plead. For pass over the isles of Chittim, and see; and send unto Kedar, and consider diligently, and see if there be such a thing. Hath a nation changed their gods, which are yet no gods? but My people have changed their glory for that which doth not profit." So also in the opening of chap. 3, we find the most terrible imagery used to set forth the base conduct of "backsliding Israel and treacherous Judah."

Harken to the following glowing language in chap. 4: "Thy way and thy doings have procured these things unto thee; this is thy wickedness, because it is bitter, because it reacheth unto thy heart. My bowels! my bowels! I am pained at my very heart; my heart maketh a noise in me; I cannot hold my peace, because thou hast heard, O my soul, the sound of the trumpet, the alarm of war. Destruction upon destruction is cried; for the whole land is spoiled: suddenly are my tents spoiled, and my curtains in a moment. How long shall I see the standard, and hear the sound of the trumpet? For My people are foolish, they have not known Me; they are sottish children, and they have none understanding: they are wise to do evil, but to do good they have no knowledge. I beheld the earth, and lo, it was without form and void; and the heavens, and they had no light. I beheld the mountains, and, lo, they trembled, and all the hills moved lightly. I beheld, and, lo, there was no man, and all the birds of the heavens were fled. I beheld, and, lo, the fruitful place was a wilderness, and all the cities thereof were broken down at the presence of the Lord, and by His fierce anger."

What vivid language! The whole scene seems, in the vision of the prophet, reduced to primæval chaos and darkness. In short, nothing could be more gloomy than the aspect here presented. The whole of these opening chapters should be carefully studied, if we would form a correct judgment of the times in which Josiah's lot was cast. They were evidently times characterized by deep-seated and wide-spread corruptions, in every shape and form. High and low, rich and poor, learned and ignorant, prophets, priests, and people—all presented an appalling picture of hollowness, deceit, and heartless wickedness, which could only be faithfully portrayed by an inspired pen.

But why dwell upon this? Why multiply quotations in proof of the low moral condition of Israel and Judah in the days of king Josiah? Mainly to show that, no matter what may be our surroundings, we can individually serve the Lord, if only there be the purpose of heart to do so. Indeed, it is in the very darkest times that the light of true devotedness shines forth most brightly. It is thrown into relief by the surrounding gloom. The very circumstances which indolence and unfaithfulness would use as a plea for yielding to the current will only furnish a devoted spirit with a plea for making head against it. If Josiah had looked around him, what would

he have seen? Treachery, deceit, corruption, and violence. Such was the state of public morals. And what of religion? Errors and evils in every imaginable shape. Some of these were hoary with age. They had been instituted by *Solomon* and left standing by *Hezekiah*. Their foundations had been laid amid the splendors of the reign of Israel's wisest and wealthiest monarch, and the most pious and devoted of Josiah's predecessors had left them as they found them.

Who, then, was Josiah, that he should presume to overturn such venerable institutions? What right had he, a mere youth, raw and inexperienced, to set himself in opposition to men so far beyond him in wisdom, intelligence, and mature judgment? Why not leave things as he found them? Why not allow the current to flow peacefully on through those channels which had conducted it for ages and generations? Disruptions are hazardous. There is always great risk in disturbing old prejudices.

These and a thousand kindred questions might doubtless have exercised the heart of Josiah; but the answer was simple, direct, clear and conclusive. It was not the judgment of Josiah against the judgment of his predecessors, but it was the judgment of God against all. This is a most weighty principle for every child of God and every servant of Christ. Without it, we can never make head against the tide of evil which is flowing around us. It was this principle which sustained Luther in the terrible conflict which he had to wage with the whole of christendom. He too, like Josiah, had to lay the axe to the root of old prejudices, and shake the very foundation of opinions and doctrines which had held almost universal sway in the Church for over a thousand years. How was this to be done? Was it by setting up the judgment of Martin Luther against the judgment of popes and cardinals, councils and colleges, bishops and doctors? Assuredly not. This would never have brought about the Reformation. It was not Luther *versus* Christendom, but Holy Scripture *versus* Error.

Ponder this! We feel it is a grand and all-important lesson for this moment, as it surely was for the days of Luther and for the days of

Josiah. We long to see the supremacy of Holy Scripture—the paramount authority of the Word of God—the absolute sovereignty of divine revelation reverently owned throughout the length and breadth of the Church of God. We are convinced that the enemy is diligently seeking, in all quarters and by all means, to undermine the authority of the Word, and to weaken its hold upon the human conscience. And it is because we feel this that we seek to raise, again and again, a note of solemn warning, as also to set forth, according to our ability, the vital importance of submitting, in all things, to the inspired testimony—the voice of God in Scripture. It is not sufficient to render a merely formal assent to that popular statement, "The Bible, and the Bible alone, is the religion of Protestants." We want more than this. We want to be, in all things, absolutely governed by the authority of Scripture—not by our fellow-mortal's interpretation of Scripture, but by Scripture itself. We want to have the conscience in a condition to yield, at all times, a true response to the teachings of the divine Word.

This is what we have so vividly illustrated in the life and times of Josiah, and particularly in the transactions of the eighteenth year of his reign, to which we shall now call the reader's attention. This year was one of the most memorable, not only in the history of Josiah, but in the annals of Israel. It was signalized by two great facts, namely, *the discovery of the book of the law and the celebration of the feast of the Passover.* Stupendous facts!—facts which have left their impress upon this most interesting period, and rendered it pre-eminently fruitful in instruction to the people of God in all ages.

It is worthy of note that the discovery of the book of the law was made during the progress of Josiah's reformatory measures. It affords one of the ten thousand proofs of that great practical principle that "to him that hath shall more be given"; and again, "If any man *will do* His will, he *shall know* of the doctrine."

"Now in the eighteenth year of his reign, when he had purged the land and the house, he sent Shaphan the son of Azaliah, and Maaseiah the governor of the city, and Joah the son of Joahaz the recorder, to repair the house of the Lord his God. And when they came to Hilkiah the priest, they delivered the money that was brought into the house of God. ... And when they brought out the money that was brought into the house of the Lord, Hilkiah the priest found a book of the law of the Lord given by Moses. And Hilkiah the priest answered and said to Shaphan the scribe, I have found the book of the law in the house of the Lord. And Hilkiah delivered the book to Shaphan. And Shaphan carried the book to the king. ... And Shaphan read it before the king. And it came to pass, when the king had heard the words of the law, that he rent his clothes" (2 Chron. 34:8-19).

Here we have a tender conscience bowing under the action of the Word of God. This was one special charm in the character of Josiah. He was, in truth, a man of a humble and contrite spirit, who trembled at the Word of God. Would that we all knew more of this! It is a most valuable feature of the Christian character. We certainly do need to feel much more deeply the weight, authority, and seriousness of Scripture. Josiah had no question whatever in his mind as to the genuineness and authenticity of the words which Shaphan had read in his hearing. We do not read of his asking, "How am I to know that this is the Word of God?" No; he trembled at it; he bowed before it; he was smitten down under it; he rent his garments. He did not presume to sit in judgment upon the Word of God, but, as was meet and right, he allowed the Word to judge him.

Thus it should ever be. If man is to judge Scripture, then Scripture is not the Word of God at all; but if Scripture is in very truth the Word of God, then it must judge man. And so it is and so it does. Scripture *is* the Word of God, and it judges man thoroughly. It lays bare the very roots of his nature—it opens up the foundations of his moral being. It holds up before him the only faithful mirror in which he can see himself perfectly reflected. This is the reason why man does not like Scripture—cannot bear it—seeks to set it aside—delights to pick holes in it—dares to sit in judgment upon it. It is not so in reference to other books. Men do not trouble themselves so much to discover and point out flaws and discrepancies in Homer or Herodotus, Aristotle or Shakespeare. No; but Scripture judges them—judges their ways, their lusts. Hence the enmity of the natural mind to that most precious and marvelous Book, which, as we have already remarked, carries its own credentials with it to every divinely prepared heart.

There is a power in Scripture which must bear down all before it. All must bow down under it, sooner or later. "The word of God is quick and powerful, and sharper than any two-edged sword, piercing even to the dividing asunder of soul and spirit, and of the joints and marrow, and is a discerner of the thoughts and intents of the heart. Neither is there any creature that is not manifest in His sight; but all things are naked and opened unto the eyes of Him with whom we have to do" (Heb. 4:12-13).

Josiah found it to be even so. The Word of God pierced him through and through. "And it came to pass, when the king had heard the words of the law, that he rent his clothes. And the king commanded Hilkiah, and Ahikam the son of Shaphan, and Abdon the son of Micah, and Shaphan the scribe, and Asaiah a servant of the king's, saying, Go inquire of the Lord for me, and for them that are left in Israel and in Judah, concerning the words of the book that is found; for great is the wrath of the Lord that is poured out upon us, because our fathers have not kept the word of the Lord, to do after all that is written in this book." What a striking contrast between Josiah, with contrite heart, exercised conscience, and rent garments, bowing down under the mighty action of the Word of God, and our modern skeptics and infidels, who, with appalling audacity, dare to sit in judgment upon that very same Word. Oh that men would be wise in time, and bow their hearts and consciences in reverent submission to the Word of the living God before that great and terrible day of the Lord in the which they shall be compelled to bow, amid "weeping and wailing and gnashing of teeth."

God's Word shall stand forever, and it is utterly vain for man to set himself up in opposition to it, or seek by his reasonings and skeptical speculations to find out errors and contradictions in it. "Forever, O Lord, Thy word is settled in heaven." "Heaven and earth shall pass away, but My words shall not pass away." "The word of the Lord endureth forever." Of what possible use is it, therefore, for man to resist the Word of God? He can gain nothing; but oh! what may he lose? If man could prove the Bible false, what should he gain? but if it be true after all, what does he lose? A serious inquiry! May it have its weight with any reader whose mind is at all under the influence of rationalistic or infidel notions.

We shall now proceed with our history.

"And Hilkiah and they that the king had appointed went to Huldah the prophetess, the wife of Shallum the son of Tikvath, the son of Hasrah, keeper of the wardrobe; (now she dwelt in Jerusalem, in the college;) and they spake to her to that effect." At the opening of this paper we referred to the fact of a child of eight years old being on the throne of David as indicative of the condition of things amongst the people of God. Here, too, we are arrested by the fact that the prophetic office was filled by a woman. It surely tells a tale. Things were low; but the grace of God was unfailing and abundant, and Josiah was so thoroughly broken down that he was prepared to receive the communication of the mind of God through whatever channel it might reach him. This was morally lovely. It might, to nature's view, seem very humiliating for a king of Judah to have recourse to a woman for counsel; but then that woman was the depository of the mind of God, and this was quite enough for a humble and a contrite spirit like Josiah's. He had thus far proved that his one grand desire was to know and do the will of God, and hence it mattered not by what vehicle the voice of God was conveyed to his ear, he was prepared to hear and obey.

Let us consider this. We may rest assured that herein lies the true secret of divine guidance. "The meek will He guide in judgment, and the meek will He teach His way" (Ps. 25:9). Were there more of this blessed spirit of meekness among us, there would be less confusion, less controversy, less striving about words to no profit. If we were all meek, we should all be divinely guided and divinely taught, and thus we should see eye to eye; we should be of one mind, and speak the same thing, and avoid much sad and humbling division and heart-burning.

See what a full answer the meek and contrite Josiah received from Huldah the prophetess—an answer both as to his people and as to himself. "And she answered them, Thus saith the Lord God of Israel, Tell ye the man that sent you to me, Thus saith the Lord, Behold, I will bring evil upon this place, and upon the inhabitants thereof, even all the curses that are written in the book which they have read before the king of Judah. Because *they have forsaken Me*, and have burned incense unto other gods, that they might provoke Me to anger with all the works of their hands; therefore My wrath shall be poured out upon this place, and shall not be quenched."

All this was but the solemn reiteration and establishment of what had already fallen upon the open and attentive ear of the king of Judah; but then it came with fresh force, emphasis, and interest, as a direct personal communication to himself. It came enforced and enhanced by that earnest sentence, "Tell ye *the man* that sent you to me."

But there was more than this. There was a gracious message directly concerning Josiah himself. "And as for the king of Judah, who sent you to inquire of the Lord, so shall ye say unto him, Thus saith the Lord God of Israel concerning the words which thou hast heard: *Because thy heart was tender*, and thou didst *humble thyself before God* when thou heardest His words against this place, and against the inhabitants thereof, and *humbledst thyself before Me*, and didst rend thy clothes and *weep before Me;* I have even heard thee also, saith the Lord. Behold, I will gather thee to thy fathers, and thou shalt be gathered to thy grave in peace, neither shall thine eyes see all the evil that I will bring upon this place and upon the inhabitants of the same. So they brought the king word again" (2 Chron. 34:23-28).

All this is full of instruction and encouragement for us in this dark and evil day. It teaches us the immense value, in the divine estimation, of deep personal exercise of soul and contrition of heart. Josiah might have deemed the case hopeless—that nothing could avert the mighty tide of wrath and judgment which was about to roll over the city of Jerusalem and the land of Israel—that any movement of his must prove utterly unavailing—that the divine purpose was settled—the decree gone forth, and that, in short, he had only to stand by and let things take their course. But Josiah did not reason thus. No; he bowed before the divine testimony. He humbled himself, rent his clothes, and wept. God took knowledge of this. Josiah's penitential tears were precious to Jehovah, and though the appalling judgment had to take its course, yet the penitent escaped. And not only did he himself escape, but he became the honored instrument in the Lord's hand of delivering others also. He did not abandon himself to the influence of a pernicious fatalism, but in brokenness of spirit and earnestness of heart he cast himself upon God, confessing his own sins and the sins of his people. And then, when assured of his own personal deliverance, he set himself to seek the deliverance of his brethren also. This is a fine moral lesson for the heart. May we learn it thoroughly.

Part 4

It is deeply interesting and instructive to mark the actings of Josiah when his heart and conscience had been brought under the powerful influence of the Word of God. He not only bowed down under that Word himself, but he sought to lead others to bow likewise. This must ever be the case where the work is real. It is impossible for a man to feel the weight and solemnity of truth and not seek to bring others under its action. No doubt a quantity of truth may be held in the intellect—held superficially—held in a merely speculative, notional way; but this will have no practical effect; it does not tell upon the heart and conscience after a divine, living fashion; it does not affect the life and character. And inasmuch as it does not affect our own souls, neither will our mode of presenting it be very likely to act with much power upon others. True, God is sovereign, and He may use His own Word even when spoken by one who has never really felt its influence; but we are speaking now of what may properly and naturally be looked for; and we may rest assured that the best way in which to make others feel deeply is to feel deeply ourselves.

Take any truth you please. Take, for example, the glorious truth of the Lord's coming. How is a man most likely to affect his hearers by the presentation of this truth? Unquestionably by being deeply affected himself. If the heart be under the power of that solemn word, "the Lord is at hand"—if this fact be realized in all its solemnity as to the world, and in its sweet attractiveness as to the believer individually and the Church collectively, then it will assuredly be presented in a way calculated to move the hearts of the hearers. It is easy to see when a man *feels* what he is saying. There may be a very clear and clever exposition of the doctrine of the second advent, and of all the collateral truths; but if it be cold and heartless, it will fall powerless on the ears of the audience. In order to speak to *hearts*, on any subject, the heart of the speaker must feel it. What was it that gave such power to Whitefield's discourses? It was not the depth or the range of truth contained in them, as is manifest to any intelligent reader. No. The secret of their mighty efficacy lay in the fact that the speaker *felt* what he was saying. Whitefield wept over the people, and no marvel if the people wept under Whitefield. He must be a hardened wretch indeed who can sit unmoved under a preacher who is shedding tears for his soul's salvation.

Let us not be misunderstood. We do not mean to say that anything in a preacher's manner can of itself convert a soul. Tears cannot quicken: earnestness cannot regenerate. It is "not by might, nor by power, but by My Spirit, saith the Lord." It is only by the powerful action of the Word and Spirit of God that any soul can be born again. All this we fully believe, and would ever bear in mind; but at the same time, we as fully believe and would also bear in mind that God blesses earnest preaching, and souls are moved by it. We have far too much mechanical preaching—too much routine work—too much of what may justly be called *going through a* service. We want more earnestness, more depth of feeling, more intensity, more power to weep over the souls of men, a more influential and abiding sense of the awful doom of impenitent sinners, the value of an immortal soul, and the solemn realities of the eternal world. We are told that the famous Garrick was once asked by a bishop how it was that he produced far more powerful results by his fiction than the bishop could by preaching truth. The reply of the actor is full of force. "My lord," said he, "the reason is obvious: I speak fiction as though it were truth, whereas you speak truth as though it were fiction."

Alas! it is much to be feared that too many of us speak truth in the same way, and hence the little result. We are persuaded that earnest, faithful preaching is one of the special wants of this our day. There are a few here and there, thank God, who seem to *feel* what they are at—who stand before their audience as those who consider themselves as channels of communication between God and their fellows—men who are really bent on their work—bent, not merely on preaching and teaching, but on saving and blessing souls. The grand business of the evangelist is to *bring* the soul and Christ together; the business of the teacher and pastor is to *keep* them together. True it is, most blessedly true, that God is glorified and Jesus Christ magnified by the unfolding of truth, whether men will hear or whether they will forbear; but is this fact to be allowed to interfere, in the smallest degree, with the ardent desire for *results* in reference to souls? We do not for a moment believe it. The preacher should look for results, and should not be satisfied without them. He should no more think of being satisfied to go on without results than the husbandman thinks of going on from year to year without a crop. Some preachers there are who only succeed in preaching their hearers away, and then they content themselves by saying, "We are a sweet savor to God." Now, we believe this is a great mistake, and a fatal delusion.

What we want is to live before God for the results of our work—to wait upon Him—to agonize in prayer for souls—to throw all our energies into the work—to preach as though the whole thing depended upon us, although knowing full well that we can do just nothing, and that our words must prove as the morning cloud if not fastened as a nail in a sure place by the Master of assemblies. We are convinced that, in the divine order of things, the earnest workman must have the fruit of his labor; and that according to his faith, so shall it be. There may be exceptions, but as a general rule, we may rest assured that a faithful preacher, will, sooner or later, reap fruit.

We have been drawn into the foregoing line of thought while contemplating the interesting scene in the life of Josiah presented to us at the close of 2 Chronicles 34. It will be profitable for us to dwell upon it. Josiah was a man thoroughly in earnest. He felt the power of truth in his own soul, and he could not rest satisfied until he gathered the people around him, in order that the light which had shone upon him might shine upon them likewise. He did not, he could not, rest in the fact that he was to be gathered to his grave in peace—that his eyes were not to see the evil that was coming upon Jerusalem—that he was to escape the appalling tide of judgment which was about to roll over the land. No; he thought of others, he felt for the people around him; and inasmuch as his own personal escape stood connected with and based upon his true penitence and humiliation under the mighty hand of God, so he would seek, by the action of that Word which had wrought so powerfully in his own heart, to lead others to like penitence and humiliation.

"Then the king sent and gathered together all the elders of Judah and Jerusalem. And the king went up into the house of the Lord, and all the men of Judah, and the inhabitants of Jerusalem, and the priests, and the Levites, and all the people, great and small; and he read in their ears all the words of the book of the covenant that was found in the house of the Lord. And the king stood in his place, and made a covenant before the Lord, to walk after the Lord, and to keep His commandments and His testimonies and his statutes *with all his heart* and *with all his soul,* to perform the words of the covenant which are written in this book. And he caused all that were present in Jerusalem and Benjamin to stand to it. And the inhabitants of Jerusalem did according to the covenant of God, the God of their fathers. And Josiah took away all the abominations out of all the countries that pertained to the children of Israel, and made all that were present in Israel to serve, even to serve the Lord their God. And all his days they departed not from following the Lord, the God of their fathers."

There is a fine moral lesson in all this for us—yea, many lessons to which we, with all our light, knowledge, and privilege, may well sit down. What first of all strikes us at this moment is the fact that Josiah felt his responsibility to those around him. He did not put his light under a bushel, but rather allowed it to shine for the full benefit and blessing of others. This is all the more striking, inasmuch as that great practical truth of the unity of all believers in one body was not known to Josiah, because not revealed by God. The doctrine contained in that one brief sentence, "There is one body and one Spirit," was not made known until long after the times of Josiah, even when Christ the risen Head had taken His seat at the right hand of the Majesty in the heavens.

But although this truth was "hid in God," nevertheless there was the unity of the nation of Israel. There was a national unity, though there was not the unity of a body; and this unity was always recognized by the faithful, whatever might be the outward condition of the people. The twelve loaves on the table of show-bread in the sanctuary were the divine type of the perfect unity and yet the perfect distinctness of the twelve tribes. The reader can see this in Leviticus 24. It is full of interest, and should be deeply pondered by every student of Scripture and every earnest lover of the ways of God. During the dark and silent watches of the night, the seven lamps of the golden candlestick threw their light upon the twelve loaves ranged by the hand of the high-priest according to the commandment of God upon the pure table. Significant figure!

It was on this grand truth that Elijah the Tishbite took his stand, when on Mount Carmel he built an altar "with twelve stones, according to the number of the tribes of the sons of Jacob, unto whom the word of the Lord came, saying, 'Israel shall be thy name' " (1 Kings 18). To this same truth Hezekiah had regard when he commanded "that the burnt-offering and the sin-offering should be made for *all Israel*" (2 Chron. 29:24). Paul, in his day referred to this precious truth, when in the presence of king Agrippa he spoke of "our twelve tribes, instantly serving God day and night" (Acts 26:7).

Now, if any one of those men of faith had been asked, "Where are the twelve tribes?" could he have given an answer? could he have pointed them out? Assuredly he could; but not to sight—not to man's view, for the nation was divided—its unity was broken. In the days of Elijah and Hezekiah there were the ten tribes and the two; and in the days of Paul, the ten tribes were scattered abroad, and only a remnant of the two in the land of Palestine, under the dominion of Daniel's fourth beast. What then? Was the truth of God made of none effect by Israel's outward condition? Far be the thought! "Our twelve tribes" must never be given up. The unity of the nation is a grand reality to faith. It is as true at this moment as when Joshua pitched the twelve stones at Gilgal. The Word of our God shall stand forever. Not one jot or tittle of aught that He has spoken shall ever pass away.

Change and decay may mark the history of human affairs, death and desolation may sweep like a withering blast over earth's fairest scenes, but Jehovah will make good His every word, and Israel's twelve tribes shall yet enjoy the promised land, in all its length, breadth, and fulness. No power of earth or hell shall be able to hinder this blessed consummation. And why? What makes us so sure? How can we speak with such absolute certainty? Simply because the mouth of the Lord hath spoken it. We may be more sure that Israel's tribes shall yet enjoy their fair inheritance in Palestine than that the house of Tudor once held sway in England. The

former we believe on the testimony of God, who cannot lie; the latter on the testimony of man only.

It is of the utmost importance that the reader should be clear as to this, not only because of its special bearing upon Israel and the land of Canaan, but also because it affects the integrity of Scripture as a whole. There is a loose mode of handling the Word of God, which is at once dishonoring to Him and injurious to us. Passages which apply distinctly and exclusively to Jerusalem and to Israel are made to apply to the spread of the gospel and the extension of the Christian Church. This, to say the least of it, is taking a very unwarrantable liberty with divine revelation. Our God can surely say what He means, and as surely He means what He says; hence, when He speaks of Israel and Jerusalem, He does not mean the Church; and when He speaks of the Church, He does not mean Israel or Jerusalem.

Expositors and students of Scripture should ponder this. Let no one suppose that it is merely a question of prophetic interpretation. It is far more than this. It is a question of the integrity, value, and power of the Word of God. If we allow ourselves to be loose and careless in reference to one class of Scriptures, we are likely to be loose and careless as to another, and then our sense of the weight and authority of all Scripture will be sadly enfeebled.

But we must return to Josiah, and see how he recognized, according to his measure, the great principle on which we have been dwelling. He certainly proved no exception to the general rule, namely, that all the pious kings of Judah had regard to the unity of the nation of Israel, and never suffered their thoughts, their sympathies, or their operations to be confined within any narrower range than "our twelve tribes." The twelve loaves on the pure table were ever before the eye of God and ever before the eye of faith. Nor was this a mere speculation—a non-practical dogma— a dead letter. No; it was in every case a great practical, influential truth. "Josiah took away *all* the abominations out of *all the countries that pertained to the children of Israel.*" This was acting in the fullest harmony with his pious predecessor, Hezekiah, who "commanded that the burnt-offering and the sin-offering should be made for *all Israel.*

And now, mark the application of all this to your own souls at this present moment. Do you heartily believe, upon divine authority, in the doctrine of the unity of the body of Christ? Do you believe that there is such a body on this earth now, united to its divine and living Head in Heaven by the Holy Ghost? Do you hold this great truth from God Himself, upon the authority of Holy Scripture? Do you, in one word, hold as a cardinal and fundamental truth of the New Testament the indissoluble unity of the Church of God? Do not turn round and ask, "Where is this to be *seen?*" This is the question which unbelief must ever put, as the eye rests upon Christendom's numberless sects and parties, and to which faith replies, as the eye rests upon that imperishable sentence, "There is one body and one Spirit." Mark the words!— "There *is.* " It does not say there *was* at one time and there shall be again "one body." Neither does it say that such a thing exists in Heaven. No; but it says, "There *is* one body and one Spirit" now on this earth. Can this truth be touched by the condition of things in the professing Church? Has God's Word ceased to be true because man has ceased to be faithful? Will any one undertake to say that the unity of the body was only a truth for apostolic times, and that it has no application now, seeing that there is no exhibition of it?

We solemnly warn you to beware how you admit into your heart a sentiment so entirely infidel as this. Rest assured it is the fruit of positive unbelief in God's Word. No doubt, appearances argue against this truth; but what truth is it against which appearances do not argue? And say, is it on appearances that faith ever builds? Did Elijah build on appearances when he erected his altar of twelve stones, according to the number of the tribes of the sons of Jacob? Did king Hezekiah build on appearances when he issued that fine commandment that the burnt-offering and the sin-offering should be made for *all Israel?* Did Josiah build on appearances when he carried his reformatory operations into all the countries that pertained to the children of Israel?

Surely not. They built upon the faithful Word of the God of Israel. That Word was true whether Israel's tribes were scattered or united. If God's truth is to be affected by outward appearances, or by the actings of men, then where are we? or what are we to believe? The fact is, there is hardly a truth in the entire compass of divine revelation to which we could with calm confidence commit our souls if we suffer ourselves to be affected by outward appearances.

No; the only ground on which we can believe anything is this one eternal clause, *"It is written"!* Do you not admit this? Does not your whole soul bow down to it? Do you not hold it to be a principle entirely vital? We believe you do, as a Christian, hold, admit, and reverently believe this. Well, then, *it is written,* "There is one body and one Spirit" (Eph. 4). This is as clearly revealed in Scripture as that "we are justified by faith," or any other truth. Do outward appearances affect the saving, fundamental doctrine of justification by faith? Are we to call in question this precious truth because there is so little exhibition of its purifying power in the lives of believers? Who could admit such a fatal principle as this? What a complete upturning of all the foundations of our faith is necessarily involved in the admission of this most mischievous line of reasoning! We believe because it is written in the Word, not because it is exhibited in the world. Doubtless it ought to be exhibited, and it is our sin and shame that it is not. To this we shall afterward refer more fully; but we must insist upon the proper ground of belief, namely, divine revelation; and when this is clearly seen and fully admitted, it applies as distinctly to the doctrine of the unity of the body as it does to the doctrine of justification by faith.

Part 5

We feel it to be of real moment to insist upon this principle, namely, that the *only* ground on which we can believe any doctrine is its being revealed in the divine Word. It is thus we believe all the great truths of Christianity. We know nothing and can believe nothing of what is spiritual, heavenly, or divine, save as we find it revealed in the Word of God. How do I know I am a sinner? Because Scripture hath declared that "all have sinned." No doubt I feel that I am a sinner; but I do not believe because I feel, but I feel because I believe, and I believe because God has spoken. Faith rests upon divine revelation, not on human feelings or human reasonings. "It is written" is quite sufficient for faith. It can do with nothing less, but it asks nothing more. God speaks: faith believes. Yes, it believes simply because God speaks. It does not judge God's Word by outward appearances, but it judges outward appearances by the Word of God.

Thus it is in reference to all the cardinal truths of the Christian religion, such as the Trinity, the deity of our Lord Jesus Christ, His atonement, His priesthood, His advent, the doctrine of original sin, of justification, judgment to come, eternal punishment. We believe these grand and solemn truths, not on the ground of feeling, of reason, or of outward appearances, but simply on the ground of divine revelation.

Hence, then, if it be asked, On what ground do we believe in the doctrine of the unity of the body? we reply, Upon the self-same ground that we believe the doctrine of the Trinity, the deity of Christ, and the atonement. We believe it because it is revealed in sundry places in the New Testament. Thus, for example, in 1 Cor. 12 we read, "For as *the body is one*, and hath many members, and all the members of that *one body*, being many, are *one body;* so also *is Christ*. For by one Spirit are we all baptized into *one body*, whether we be Jews or Gentiles, whether we be bond or free; and have been all made to drink into one Spirit." Again, "God hath tempered the body together, having given more abundant honor to that part which lacked, that there should be no schism in the body. . . . Now, *ye are the body of Christ*, and members in particular."

Here we have distinctly laid down the perfect and indissoluble unity of the Church of God, the body of Christ, on precisely the same authority as any other truth commonly received amongst us; so that there is just as much ground for calling in question the deity of Christ as there is for calling in question the unity of the body. The one is as true as the other; and both are divinely revealed. We believe that Jesus Christ is God over all, blessed forever, because Scripture tells us so; we believe that there is one body because Scripture tells us so. We do not reason in the one case, but believe and bow; nor should we reason in the other case, but believe and bow. "There is one body and one Spirit."

Now, we must bear in mind that this truth of the unity of the body is not a mere abstraction—a barren speculation—a powerless dogma. It is a practical, formative, influential truth, in the light of which we are called to walk, to judge ourselves and all around us. It was so with the faithful in Israel of old. The unity of the nation was a real thing to them, and not a mere theory to be taken up or laid down at pleasure. It was a great formative, powerful truth. The nation was one in God's thoughts; and if it was not manifestly so, the faithful had only to take the place of self-judgment, brokenness of spirit, and contrition of heart. Witness the case of Hezekiah, Josiah, Daniel, Nehemiah, and Ezra. It never once occurred to these faithful men that they were to give up the truth of Israel's unity because Israel had failed to maintain it. They did not measure the truth of God by the actings of men; but they judged the actings of men, and themselves likewise, by the truth of God. This was the only true way to act. If the manifested unity of Israel was marred through man's sin and folly, the truehearted members of the congregation owned and mourned over the sin, confessed it as their own, and looked to God. Nor was this all. They felt their responsibility to act on the truth of God whatever might be the outward condition of things.

This, we repeat, was the meaning of Elijah's altar of twelve stones, erected in the face of Jezebel's eight hundred false prophets, and despite the division of the nation in man's view (1 Kings 18). This, too, was the meaning of Hezekiah's letters sent to *"all Israel"* to invite them to "come to the house of the Lord at Jerusalem, to keep the passover unto the Lord God of Israel." Nothing can be more touching than the spirit and style of these letters. *"Ye children of Israel, turn again unto the Lord God of Abraham, Isaac, and Israel, and He will return to the remnant of you that are escaped out of the hand of the kings of Assyria.* And be not ye like your fathers and like your brethren, which trespassed against the Lord God of their fathers, who therefore gave them up to desolation, as ye see. Now, *be ye not stiff-necked,* as your fathers were, but *yield your-selves unto the Lord,* and enter into His sanc-tuary, which He *hath sanctified forever;* and serve the Lord your God, that the fierceness of His wrath may turn away from you. *For if ye turn again unto the Lord, your brethren and your children shall find compassion* be-fore them that lead them captive, so that they shall come again into this land; for the Lord your God is gracious and merciful, and will not turn away His face from you" (2 Chron. 30:6-9).

What was all this but simple faith acting on the grand, eternal, immutable truth of the unity of the nation of Israel? The nation was *one* in the purpose of God, and Hezekiah looked at it from the divine standpoint, as faith ever does, and he acted accordingly. "So the posts passed from city to city, through *the country of Ephraim and Manasseh,* even unto Zebulun; but *they laughed them to scorn, and mocked them."* This was very sad, but it is only what we must expect. The act-ings of faith are sure to call forth the scorn and contempt of those who are not up to the standard of God's thoughts.

Doubtless these men of Ephraim and Manasseh regarded Hezekiah's message as a piece of presumption or wild extravagance. Perhaps the great truth that was acting with such power on his soul, forming his character and ruling his conduct, was in their judgment a myth, or at best a valueless theory—a thing of the past—an institution of bygone ages, having no present application. But faith is never moved by the thoughts of men, and therefore Hezekiah went on with his work, and God owned and blessed him. He could afford to be laughed at and turned into ridi-cule, while he beheld divers of Asher and Manasseh and Zebulun humbling themselves

and coming to Jerusalem. Hezekiah and all who thus humbled themselves under the mighty hand of God reaped a rich harvest of blessing, while the mockers and scorners were left in the barrenness and deadness with which their own unbelief had surrounded them.

Mark the force of those words of Hezekiah, "If *ye* turn again unto the Lord, *your breth-ren and your children shall find compassion* before them that lead them captive." Does not this approach very near to that precious truth of the New Testament times, that we are members one of another, and that the conduct of one member affects all the rest? Unbelief might raise the question as to how this could possibly be—as to how the actings of one could possibly affect others far away; yet so it was in Israel, and so it is now in the Church of God.

Witness the case of Achan, in Joshua 7. There, one man sinned; and, so far as the nar-rative informs us, the whole congregation was ignorant of the fact; and yet we read that *"the children of Israel committed a trespass* in the accursed thing." And again, *"Israel* hath sinned." How could this be? Simply be-cause the nation was one, and God dwelt among them. This, plainly, was the ground of a double responsibility, namely, a responsibil-ity to God, and a responsibility to the whole assembly and to each member in particular. It was utterly impossible for any one member of the congregation to shake off this high and holy responsibility. A person living at Dan might feel disposed to question how his con-duct could affect a man living at Beersheba; yet such was the fact, and the ground of this fact lay in the eternal truth of Israel's indis-soluble unity and Jehovah's dwelling in the midst of His redeemed assembly. (See Exo-dus 15:2, and the many passages which speak of God's dwelling in the midst of Israel.)

We do not attempt even to quote the num-erous Scriptures which speak of God's presence in the congregation of Israel—His dwelling in their midst. But we would call the attention of the reader to the all-important fact that those Scriptures *begin* with Exodus 15. It was when Israel stood, as a fully re-deemed people, on Canaan's side of the Red

Sea that they were able to say, "The Lord is my strength and my song, and He is become my salvation: He is *my God*, and I will prepare Him *a habitation.*" Redemption formed the ground of God's dwelling among His people, and His presence in their midst secured their perfect unity. Hence no one member of the congregation could view himself as an isolated independent atom. Each one was called to view himself as part of a whole, and to view his conduct in reference to all those who, like himself, formed part of that whole.

Now, reason could never grasp a truth like this. It lay entirely beyond the ken of the most powerful human intellect. Faith alone could receive it and act upon it, and it is of the deepest interest to see that the faithful in Israel ever recognized it and acted upon it. Why did Hezekiah send letters to "all Israel"? Why did he expose himself to scorn and ridicule in so doing? Why did he command that "the burnt-offering and the sin-offering should be made for all Israel"? Why did Josiah carry his reformatory operations into all "the countries that pertained to the children of Israel"? Because those men of God recognized the divine truth of Israel's unity, and they did not think of throwing this grand reality overboard because so few saw it or sought to carry it out. "The people shall dwell alone;" and "I, the Lord, will dwell among the children of Israel." These imperishable truths shine, like most precious gems of heavenly lustre, all along the page of Old Testament Scripture; and we invariably find that, just in proportion as any one was living near to God—near to the living and ever-gushing fountain of life and light and love—just in proportion as he entered into the thoughts, purposes, sympathies, and counsels of the God of Israel, did he apprehend and seek to carry out that which God had declared to be true of His people, though His people had proved so untrue to Him.

And now, we would ask you a very plain and pointed question, which is this: Do you not recognize in the unity of the Jewish nation the foreshadowing of a higher unity now existing in that one body of which Christ is the Head? We trust you do. We fondly hope

that your whole moral being bows down, with reverent submission, to the mighty truth, "There *is* one body." But then we can well imagine that you feel yourself not a little perplexed and confounded when you cast your eye around you through the length and breadth of the professing Church, in search of any positive expression of this unity. You see Christians scattered and divided—you see innumerable sects and parties; and what perhaps puzzles you most of all, you see those who profess to believe and act upon the truth of the unity of the body divided amongst themselves, and presenting anything but a spectacle of unity and harmony.

All this, we confess, is very perplexing to one who looks at it from a merely human standpoint. We are not the least surprised at people being stumbled and hindered by these things. Still the foundation of God standeth sure. His truth is perfectly indestructible; and if we gaze with admiration upon the faithful worthies of a bygone age who believed and confessed the unity of Israel when there was not a trace of that unity visible to mortal eyes, why should we not heartily believe and diligently carry out the higher unity of the one body? "There is one body and one Spirit," and herein lies the basis of our responsibility to one another and to God.

Are we to surrender this all-important truth because Christians are scattered and divided? God forbid. It is as real and as precious as ever, and it ought to be as formative and as influential. We are bound to act upon the truth of God, irrespective of consequences, and utterly regardless of outward appearances. It is not for us to say, as so many do, "The case is hopeless: everything has gone to pieces. It is impossible to carry out the truth of God amid the heaps of rubbish which lie around us. The unity of the body was a thing of the *past;* it may be a thing of the *future,* but it cannot be a thing of the *present.* The idea of unity must be abandoned as thoroughly utopian, it cannot be maintained in the face of Christendom's numberless sects and parties. Nothing remains now but for each one to look to the Lord for himself, and to do the best he can, in his own *individual* sphere, and according to the dictates of his own conscience and judgment."

Such is, in substance, the language of hundreds of the true people of God; and as is their language, so is their practical career. But we must speak plainly, and we have no hesitation in saying that this language savors of sheer unbelief in that great cardinal verity of the unity of the body; and, moreover, that we have just as much warrant for rejecting the precious doctrine of Christ's deity, of His perfect humanity, or of His vicarious sacrifice, as we have for rejecting the truth of the perfect unity of His body, inasmuch as this latter rests upon precisely the same foundation as the former, namely, the eternal truth of God—the absolute statement of Holy Scripture. What right have we to set aside any one truth of divine revelation? What authority have we to single out any special truth from the Word of God and say that it no longer applies?

We are bound to receive *all truth*, and to submit our souls to its authority. It is a dangerous thing to admit for a moment the idea that any one truth of God is to be set aside, on the plea that it cannot be carried out. It is sufficient for us that it is revealed in the Holy Scriptures: we have only to *believe* and to *obey*. Does Scripture declare that there is "one body"? Assuredly it does. This is enough. We are responsible to maintain this truth, cost what it may; we can accept nothing else—nothing less—nothing different. We are bound, by the allegiance which we owe to Christ the Head, to testify, practically, against everything that militates against the truth of the indissoluble unity of the Church of God, and to seek earnestly and constantly a faithful expression of that unity.

True, we shall have to contend with false unity on the one hand and false individuality on the other; but we have only to hold fast and confess the truth of God, looking to Him, in humility of mind and earnest purpose of heart, and He will sustain us in the path, let the difficulties be what they may. No doubt there are difficulties in the way—grave difficulties, such as we in our own strength cannot cope with. The very fact that we are told to "*endeavor* to keep the unity of the Spirit in the bond of peace" is sufficient to prove that there are difficulties in the way; but the grace of our Lord Jesus Christ is amply sufficient for all the demands that may be made upon us in seeking to act upon this most precious truth.

In contemplating the present condition of the professing Church we may discern two very distinct classes. In the first place, there are those who are seeking unity on false grounds; and secondly, those who are seeking it on the ground laid down in the New Testament. This latter is distinctly a spiritual, living, divine unity, and stands out in vivid contrast with all the forms of unity which man has attempted, whether it be national, ecclesiastical, ceremonial, or doctrinal. The Church of God is not a nation, not an ecclesiastical or political system. It is a body united to its divine Head in Heaven, by the presence of the Holy Ghost. This is what it was, and this is what it is. "There is one body and one Spirit." This remains unalterably true. It holds good now just as much as when the inspired apostle penned Ephesians 4. Hence anything that tends to interfere with or mar this truth must be wrong, and we are bound to stand apart from it and testify against it. To seek to unite Christians on any other ground than the unity of the body is manifestly opposed to the revealed mind of God. It may seem very attractive, very desirable, very reasonable, right, and expedient; but it is contrary to God, and this should be enough for us. God's Word speaks *only* of the unity of the body and the unity of the Spirit. It recognizes no other unity: neither should we.

The Church of God is one, though consisting of many members. It is not local, or geographical; it is corporate. All the members have a double responsibility; they are responsible to the Head, and they are responsible to one another. It is utterly impossible to ignore this responsibility. Men may seek to shirk it; they may deny it; they may assert their individual rights, and act according to their own reason, judgment, or will; but they cannot get rid of the responsibility founded upon the fact of the one compact body. They have to do with the Head in Heaven and with the members on earth. They stand in this double relationship—they were incorporated thereinto by the Holy Ghost, and to deny it is to deny their very spiritual existence. It is founded in life, formed by the Spirit, and taught and maintained in the Holy Scriptures.

There is no such thing as independency. Christians cannot view themselves as mere individuals—as isolated atoms. "We are members one of another." This is as true as that we are "justified by faith." No doubt there is a sense in which we are individual: we are individual in our repentance; individual in our faith; individual in our justification; individual in our walk with God and in our service to Christ; individual in our rewards for service, for each one shall get a white stone and a new name engraved thereon known only to himself. All this is quite true, but it in no wise touches the other grand practical truth of our union with the Head above and with each and all of the members below.

And we would here call attention to two very distinct lines of truth flowing out of two distinct titles of our blessed Lord, namely, Headship and Lordship. He is Head of His body the Church, and He is Lord of all, Lord of each. Now, when we think of Christ as Lord, we are reminded of our individual responsibility to Him, in the wide range of service to which He, in His sovereignty, has graciously called us. Our reference must be to Him in all things. All our actings, all our movements, all our arrangements, must be placed under the commanding influence of that weighty sentence (often, alas! lightly spoken and penned), "If *the Lord* will." And, moreover, no one has any right to thrust himself between the conscience of a servant and the commandment of his Lord. All this is divinely true, and of the very highest importance. The Lordship of Christ is a truth the value of which cannot possibly be overestimated.

But we must bear in mind that Christ is *Head* as well as *Lord;* He is Head of a body, as well as Lord of individuals. These things must not be confounded. We are not to hold the truth of Christ's Lordship in such a way as to interfere with the truth of His Headship. If we merely think of Christ as Lord, and ourselves as individuals responsible to Him, then we shall ignore His Headship, and

lose sight of our responsibility to every member of that body of which He is Head. We must jealously watch against this. We cannot look at ourselves as isolated, independent atoms; if we think of Christ as Head, then we must think of all His members, and this opens up a wide range of practical truth. We have holy duties to discharge to our fellow-members, as well as to our Lord and Master; and we may rest assured that no one walking in communion with Christ can ever lose sight of the grand fact of his relationship to every member of His body. Such an one will ever remember that his walk and ways exert an influence upon Christians living at the other side of the globe. This is a wondrous mystery, but it is divinely true. "If one member suffer, *all* the members suffer with it" (1 Cor. 12:26). You cannot reduce the body of Christ to a matter of locality: the body is one, and we are called to maintain this practically in every possible way, and to bear a decided testimony against everything which tends to hinder the expression of the perfect unity of the body, whether it be false unity or false individuality. The enemy is seeking to associate Christians on a false ground, and gather them around a false centre; or, if he cannot do this, he will send them adrift upon the wide and tumultuous ocean of a desultory individualism. *We are thoroughly persuaded, before God, that the only safeguard against both these false and dangerous extremes is divinely wrought faith in the grand foundation-truth of the unity of the body of Christ.*

Part 6

It may here be proper to inquire what is the suited attitude of the Christian in view of the grand foundation-truth of the unity of the body. That it is a truth distinctly laid down in the New Testament cannot possibly be questioned. If any reader of these pages be not fully established in the knowledge and hearty belief of this truth, let him prayerfully study 1 Corinthians 12 and 14, Ephesians 2 and 4, Colossians 2 and 3. He will find the doctrine referred to in a practical way in the opening of Romans 12; though it is not the design of the Holy Ghost, in that magnificent Epistle, to give us a full unfolding of the truth respecting the Church. What we have to look for there is rather the soul's relationship with God through the death and resurrection of Christ. We might pass through the first eleven chapters of Romans and not know that there is such a thing as the Church of God, the body of Christ; and when we reach chap. 12, the doctrine of the one body is assumed, but not dwelt upon.

There is, then, "one body" actually existing on this earth, formed by the "one Spirit," and united to the living Head in Heaven. This truth cannot be gainsaid. Some may not see it; some may find it very hard to receive it, in view of the present condition of things; but nevertheless it remains a divinely established truth that "there is one body," and the question is, how are we individually affected by this truth? It is as impossible to shake off the responsibility involved therein as it is to set aside the truth itself. If there is a body of which we are members, then do we, in every truth, stand in a holy relationship to every member of that body on earth, as well as to the Head in Heaven; and this relationship, like every other, has its characteristic affections, privileges, and responsibilities.

And be it remembered, we are not speaking now of the question of association with any special company of Christians, but of the whole body of Christ upon earth. No doubt each company of Christians, wherever assembled, should be but the local expression of the whole body. It should be so gathered and so ordered, on the authority of the Word, and by the power of the Holy Ghost, as that all Christ's members who are walking in truth and holiness might happily find their place there. If an assembly be not thus gathered and thus ordered, it is not on the ground of the unity of the body at all. If there be anything, no matter what, in order, discipline, doctrine, or practice, which would prove a barrier to the presence of any of Christ's members whose faith and practice are according to the Word of God, then is the unity of the body practically denied. We are solemnly responsible to own the truth of the unity of the body. We should so meet that all

the members of Christ's body might, simply as such, sit down with us and exercise whatever gift the Head of the Church has bestowed upon them. The body is one. Its members are scattered over the whole earth. Distance is nothing: locality nothing. It may be New Zealand, London, Paris, or Edinburgh: it matters not. A member of the body in one place is a member of the body everywhere, for there is but "one body and one Spirit." It is the Spirit who forms the body, and links the members with the Head and with one another. Hence, a Christian coming from New Zealand to London ought to expect to find an assembly so gathered as to be a faithful expression of the unity of the body, to which he might attach himself; and furthermore, any such Christian ought to find his place in the bosom of that assembly, provided always there be nothing in doctrine or walk to forbid his hearty reception.

Such is the divine order, as laid down in 1 Cor. 12 and 14; Eph. 2 and 4, and assumed in Rom. 12. Indeed, we cannot study the New Testament and not see this blessed truth. We find in various cities and towns saints gathered by the Holy Ghost in the name of our Lord Jesus Christ; as, for example, at Rome, Corinth, Ephesus, Philippi, Colosse, and Thessalonica. These were not independent, isolated, fragmentary assemblies, but parts of the one body, so that a member of the Church in one place was a member of the Church everywhere. Doubtless, each assembly, as guided by the one Spirit, and under the one Lord, acted in all local matters, such as receiving to communion, or putting away any wicked person from their midst; meeting the wants of their poor, and such like; but we may be quite assured that the act of the assembly at Corinth would be recognized by all other assemblies, so that if any one was separated from communion there, he would, if known, be refused in all other places; otherwise it would be a plain denial of the unity of the body. We have no reason to suppose that the assembly at Corinth communicated or conferred with any other assembly previous to the putting away of "the wicked person" in chapter 5, but we are bound to believe that that act would be duly recognized and sanctioned by every assembly upon the earth, and that any assembly knowingly receiving the excommunicated man would have cast a slur upon the assembly at Corinth, and practically denied the unity of the body.

This we believe to be the plain teaching of the New Testament Scriptures—this, the doctrine which any simple, true-hearted student of these Scriptures would gather up. That the Church has failed to carry out this precious truth is, alas! painfully true; and that we are all participators in this failure is equally true. The thought of this should humble us deeply before God. Not one can throw a stone at another, for we are all verily guilty in this matter. Let not the reader suppose for a single moment that our object in these pages is to set up anything like high ecclesiastical pretensions, or to afford countenance to hollow assumption, in the face of manifest sin and failure. God forbid! we say with our very heart of hearts. We believe that there is a most urgent call upon all God's people to humble themselves in the dust on account of our sad departure from the truth so plainly laid down in the Word of God.

Thus it was with the pious and devoted king Josiah, whose life and times have suggested this entire line of thought. He found the book of the law, and discovered in its sacred pages an order of things wholly different from what he saw around him. How did he act? Did he content himself by saying, "The case is hopeless: the nation is too far gone: ruin has set in, and it is utterly vain to think of aiming at the divine standard; we must only let things stand, and do the best we can"? Nay, such was not Josiah's language or mode of action; but he humbled himself before God, and called upon others to do the same. And not only so, but he sought to carry out the truth of God. He aimed at the very loftiest standard, and the consequence was, that "from the days of Samuel the prophet, there was no passover like to Josiah's kept in Israel; neither did all the kings of Israel keep such a passover."

Such was the result of faithful reference and adherence to the Word of God, and thus it will ever be, for "God is a rewarder of them that diligently seek Him." Look at the actings of the remnant that returned from Babylon in the days of Ezra and Nehemiah. What did they do? They set up the altar of God; they built the temple, and repaired the walls of Jerusalem. In other words, they occupied themselves with the true worship of the God of Israel, and with the grand centre or gathering-point of His people. This was right. It is what faith always does, regardless of circumstances.

If the remnant had looked at circumstances, they could not have acted. They were a poor contemptible handful of people, under the dominion of the uncircumcised Gentiles. They were surrounded by active enemies on all sides, who, instigated by the enemy of God, of His city, of His people, left nothing undone to hinder them in their blessed work. These enemies ridiculed them, and said, "What do these feeble Jews? Will they fortify themselves? will they sacrifice? will they make an end in a day? will they revive the stones out of the heaps of the rubbish which are burned?" Nor was this all; not only had they to contend with powerful foes without, there was also internal weakness, for "Judah said, The strength of the bearers of burdens is decayed, and there is much rubbish, so that we are not able to build the wall" (Neh. 4). All this was very depressing. It was very different from the brilliant and palmy days of Solomon. His burden-bearers were many and strong, and there was no rubbish covering the great stones and costly with which he built the house of God, nor any contemptuous foe to sneer at his work.

And yet, for all that, there were features attaching to the work of Ezra and Nehemiah which are not to be found in the days of Solomon. Their very feebleness, the piles of rubbish which lay before them, the proud and insulting enemies who surrounded them—all these things conspired to add a peculiar halo of glory to their work. They built and prospered, and God was glorified, and He declared in their ears these cheering words: "The glory of this latter house shall be greater than of the former, saith the Lord of Hosts: and in this place will I give peace, saith the Lord of Hosts" (Hag. 2:9).

It is of importance, in connection with the

subject that has been engaging our attention, that the reader should carefully study the books of Ezra and Nehemiah, Haggai and Zechariah. They are full of most blessed instruction, comfort, and encouragement in a day like the present. Many, nowadays, it may be, are disposed to smile at the bare mention of such a subject as the unity of the body; but let them ask themselves, Is it the smile of calm confidence, or the sneer or unbelief? One thing is certain, the devil as cordially hates the doctrine of the unity of the body as he hates any other doctrine of divine revelation, and he will as assuredly seek to hinder any attempt to carry it out as he sought to hinder the rebuilding of Jerusalem in the days of Nehemiah. But let us not be discouraged. It is enough for us that we find in God's Word the precious truth of the one body. Let us bring the light of this to bear upon the present condition of the professing Church, and see what it will reveal to our eyes. It will most assuredly put us on our faces in the dust before our God because of our ways; but at the same time, it will lift our hearts up to the contemplation of the divine standard. It will so enlighten and elevate our souls as to render us thoroughly dissatisfied with everything that does not present some expression, however feeble, of the unity of the body of Christ. It is wholly impossible that any one can drink into his soul the truth of the one body and rest satisfied with any thing short of the practical recognition thereof. True, he must make up his mind to bear the brunt of the enemy's opposition. He will meet a Sanballat here, and a Rehum there, but faith can say,

> Is God for *me*? I fear not, though
> all against me rise;
> When I call on Christ my Saviour,
> the host of evil flies.

There is ample encouragement for our souls in the Word of God. If we look at Josiah, just *before the captivity*, what do we see? A man simply taking the Word as his guide— judging himself and all around by its light—rejecting all that was contrary to it, and seeking, with earnest purpose of heart, to carry out what he found written there. And what was the result? The most blessed passover that had been celebrated since the days of Samuel.

Again, if we look at Daniel, *during the captivity*, what do we see? A man acting simply on the truth of God and praying toward Jerusalem, though death stared him in the face as the consequence of his act. What was the result? A glorious testimony to the God of Israel, and the destruction of Daniel's enemies.

Finally, if we look at the remnant, *after the captivity*, what do we see? Men, in the face of appalling difficulties, rebuilding that city which was, and shall be, God's earthly centre. And what was the result? The joyous celebration of the feast of tabernacles, which had not been known since the days of Joshua the son of Nun.

Now, if we take any of the above interesting cases, and inquire as to the effect of their looking at surrounding circumstances, what answer shall we get? Take Daniel, for instance. Why did he open his window toward Jerusalem? Why look toward a city of ruins? Why call attention to a spot which only bore testimony to Israel's sin and shame? Would it not be better to let the name of Jerusalem sink into oblivion? Ah? we can guess at Daniel's reply to all such inquiries. Men might smile at him too, and deem him a visionary enthusiast; but he knew what he was doing. His heart was occupied with God's centre, the city of David, the grand gathering-point for Israel's twelve tribes. Was he to give up God's truth because of outward circumstances? Surely not. He could not consent to lower the standard even the breadth of a hair. He would weep, and pray, and fast, and chasten his soul before God, but never lower the standard. Was he going to give up God's thoughts about Zion because Israel had proved unfaithful? Not he. Daniel knew better than this. His eye was fixed on God's eternal truth, and hence, though he was in the dust because of his own sins and his people's, yet the divine banner floated above his head, in its unfading glory.

Just so now we are called to fix the gaze of faith upon the imperishable truth of the one body; and not only to gaze upon it, but seek to carry it out in our feeble measure. This should be our one definite and constant aim.

We should ever and only seek the expression of the unity of the body. We are not to ask, "How can this be?" Faith never says, "How?" in the presence of divine revelation; it believes and acts. We are not to surrender the truth of God on the plea that we cannot carry it out. The truth is revealed, and we are called to bow to it. We are not called to form the unity of the body. Very many seem to think that this unity is a something which they themselves are to set up or form in some way or another. This is a mistake. The unity exists. It is the result of the presence of the Holy Ghost in the body, and we have to recognize it, and walk in the light of it. This will give great definiteness to our course. It is always immensely important to have a distinct object before the heart, and to work with direct reference thereto. Look at Paul, that most devoted of workmen. What was his aim?—for what did he work? Hear the answer in his own words: "I now rejoice in my sufferings for you, and fill up that which is behind of the afflictions of Christ in my flesh for His body's sake, which is the *Church:* whereof I am made a minister, according to the dispensation of God which is given to me for you, to fulfil the word of God; even the mystery which hath been hid from ages and from generations, but now is made manifest to His saints: to whom God would make known what is the riches of the glory of this mystery among the Gentiles; which is Christ in you, the hope of glory: whom we preach, warning every man, and teaching every man in all wisdom; that we may present every man perfect in Christ Jesus; whereunto I also labor, striving according to His working, which worketh in me mightily" (Col. 1:24-29).

Now, this was a great deal more than the mere conversion of souls, precious as that is, most surely. Paul preached the gospel with a direct view to the body of Christ; and this is the pattern for all evangelists. We should not rest in the mere fact that souls are quickened; we should keep before our minds their incorporation, by the one Spirit, into the one body. This would effectually preserve us from sect-making—from preaching to swell the ranks of a party—from seeking to get persons to *join* this, that, or the other denomination. We should know nothing whatever but the one body, because we find nothing else in the New Testament. If this be lost sight of, the evangelist will not know what to do with souls when they are converted. A man may be used in the conversion of hundreds—a most precious work indeed—precious beyond all expression; and if he does not see the unity of the body, he must be at sea as to their further course. This is very serious, both as to himself and them, and also as to the testimony for Christ.

May God's Spirit lead all Christians to see this great truth in all its bearings. We have but glanced at it, in connection with our theme; but it demands much serious attention at the present moment. It may be that some of our readers are disposed to find fault with what they may deem a long digression from the subject of "Life and Times of Josiah"; but in truth it should not be looked on as a digression, but as a line of truth flowing naturally out of that subject—a line, too, which cannot possibly be overestimated.

Part 7

In closing our remarks on "The Life and Times of Josiah," we shall in few words advert, first, to the fact of his celebration of the passover; and secondly, to the solemn close of his history. Our sketch of this truly interesting period would unquestionably be incomplete were these things omitted.

And first, then, as to the fact—so full of interest and encouragement—that at the very close of Israel's history there should be one of the brightest moments that Israel had ever known. What does this teach us? It very manifestly teaches us that in darkest times it is the privilege of the faithful soul to act on divine principles and to enjoy divine privileges. We look upon this as a most weighty fact for all ages, but specially weighty at the present moment. If we did nothing more by writing our papers on Josiah than to impress this great fact on the mind of the Christian reader, we should consider that we had not written in vain. If Josiah had been influenced by the spirit and principle which, alas! seem to actuate so many in this our day, he never could have attempted to celebrate the passover at all. He would have folded his arms and said, "It is useless to think of maintaining any longer our great national institutions. It can only be regarded as a piece of presumption to attempt the celebration of that ordinance which was designed to set forth Israel's deliverance from judgment by the blood of the lamb, when Israel's unity is broken, and its national glory faded and gone."

But Josiah did not reason like this; he simply acted upon the truth of God. He studied the Scriptures, and rejected what was wrong and did what was right. "Moreover, Josiah kept a passover unto the Lord in Jerusalem; and they killed the passover on the fourteenth day of *the first month*" (2 Chron. 35:1). This was taking higher ground than Hezekiah had taken, inasmuch as he kept his passover "on the fourteenth day of *the second month*" (chap. 30:15). In so doing, Hezekiah was, as we know, availing himself of the provision which grace had made for cases of defilement (see Num. 9:9-11). The divine order, however, had fixed "the first month" as the proper period, and to this order Josiah was enabled to conform. In short, he took the very highest ground, according to the truth of God, while lying low under the deep sense of personal and national failure. This is ever the way of faith.

"And he set the priests in their charges, and encouraged them to the service of the house of the Lord, and said unto the Levites that taught *all Israel*, which were holy unto the Lord, Put the holy ark in the house which *Solomon*, the *son of David, king of Israel*, did build: it shall not be a burden on your shoulders; serve now the Lord your God, and *His people Israel*. And prepare yourselves by the houses of your fathers, after your courses, *according to the writing of David king of Israel*, and according to the writing of Solomon his son, and stand in the holy place, according to the divisions of the families of the fathers of your brethren the people, and after the division of the families of the Levites. So kill the passover, and sanctify yourselves, and prepare your brethren, *that they may do according to the word of the Lord by the hand of Moses.*"

Here we have Josiah taking the loftiest ground and acting on the highest authority. The most cursory reader cannot fail to be arrested, as he scans the lines just quoted from the inspired record, by the names of "Solomon," "David," "Moses," "all Israel," and above all, by the expression—so full of dignity, weight, and power—"That they may do according to the word of the Lord." Most memorable words! May they sink down into our ears and into our hearts. Josiah felt it to be his high and holy privilege to conform to the divine standard, notwithstanding all the errors and evils which had crept in from age to age. God's truth must stand forever. Faith owns and acts on this precious fact, and reaps accordingly. Nothing can be more lovely than the scene enacted on the occasion to which we are now referring.

Josiah's strict adherence to the Word of the Lord is not more to be admired than his large-hearted devotedness and liberality. "He gave to the people of the flock, lambs and kids, all for the passover-offerings, for all that were present, to the number of thirty thousand, and three thousand bullocks: these were of the king's substance. And his princes gave willingly unto the people, to the priests, and to the Levites. . . . So the service was prepared, and the priests stood in their place, and the Levites in their courses, according to the king's commandment. . . . And the singers, the sons of Asaph, were in their place, according to the commandment of David, and Asaph, and Heman, and Jeduthun the king's seer; and the porters waited at every gate; they might not depart from their service; for their brethren the Levites prepared for them. So all the service of the Lord was prepared the same day, to keep the passover, and to offer burnt-offerings upon the altar of the Lord, according to the commandment of king Josiah. And *the children of Israel* that were present kept the passover at that time, and the feast of unleavened bread seven days. And there was no passover like to that kept in Israel from the days of Samuel the prophet; neither did all the kings of Israel keep such a passover as Josiah kept, and the priests, and the Levites, and all Judah and Israel that were present, and the inhabitants of Jerusalem. In the eighteenth year of the reign of Josiah was this passover kept."

What a picture! King, princes, priests, Levites, singers, porters, all Israel, Judah, and the inhabitants of Jerusalem—all gathered together—all in their true place and at their appointed work, "according to the word of the Lord"—and all this "in the eighteenth year of the reign of Josiah," when the entire Jewish polity was on the very eve of dissolution. Surely this must speak to the heart of the thoughtful reader. It tells its own impressive tale, and teaches its own peculiar lesson. It tells us that no age, no circumstances, no influence, can ever change the truth of God or dim the vision of faith. "The word of the Lord endureth forever," and faith grasps that Word and holds it fast in the face of everything. It is the privilege of the believing soul to have to do with God and His eternal truth; and, moreover, it is the duty of such an one to aim at the very loftiest standard of action, and to be satisfied with nothing lower. Unbelief will draw a plea from the condition of things around to lower the standard, to relax the grasp, to slacken the pace, to lower the tone. Faith says "No!"— emphatically and decidedly, "No!" Let us bow our heads in shame and sorrow on account of our sin and failure, but keep the standard up. The failure is ours: the standard is God's.

Josiah wept and rent his clothes, but he did not surrender the truth of God. He felt and owned that he and his brethren and his fathers had sinned, but that was no reason why he should not celebrate the passover according to the divine order. It was as imperative upon him to do right as it was upon Solomon, David, or Moses. It is our business to obey the Word of the Lord, and we shall assuredly be blessed in our deed. This is one grand lesson to be drawn from the life and times of Josiah, and it is undoubtedly a seasonable lesson for our own times. May we learn it thoroughly. May we learn to adhere with holy decision to the ground on which the truth of God has set us, and to occupy that ground with a larger measure of true devotedness to Christ and His cause.

Most gladly would we linger over the brilliant and soul-stirring scene presented in the opening verses of 2 Chronicles 35, but we must bring this paper to an end, and we shall merely glance very rapidly at the solemn and admonitory close of Josiah's history. It stands in sad and painful contrast with all the rest of his most interesting career, and sounds in our ears a note of warning to which we are bound to give our most serious attention. We shall do little more than quote the passage, and then leave the reader to reflect upon it, prayerfully and humbly, in the presence of God.

"*After all this*, when Josiah had prepared the temple, Necho king of Egypt came up to fight against Charchemish by Euphrates; and Josiah went out against him. But he sent ambassadors to him, saying, What have I to do with thee, thou king of Judah? I come not against thee this day, but against the house wherewith I have war; for God commanded me to make haste: forbear thee from meddling with God, who is with me, that He destroy thee not. Nevertheless, Josiah would not turn his face from him, but *disguised himself*, that he might fight with him, and harkened not to the words of Necho *from the mouth of God* and came to fight in the valley of Megiddo. And the archers shot at king Josiah; and the king said to his servants, Have me away, for I am sore wounded. His servants therefore took him out of that chariot and put him in the second chariot that he had; and they brought him to Jerusalem: and he died, and was buried in one of the sepulchres of his fathers. And all Judah and Jerusalem mourned for Josiah" (2 Chron. 35:20-24).

All this is very sad and humbling. We do not wish to dwell upon it further than is absolutely needful for the purpose of instruction and admonition. The Holy Spirit does not expatiate, but He has recorded it for our learning. It is ever His way to give us men as they were—to write the history of their "deeds, *first and last*"—good and bad—one as well as another. He tells us of Josiah's piety at the "first," and of his wilfulness at the "last." He shows us that so long as Josiah walked in the light of divine revelation, his path was illuminated by the bright beams of the divine countenance; but the moment he attempted to act for himself—to walk by the light of his own eyes—to travel off the straight and narrow way of simple obedience, that moment dark and heavy clouds gathered around him, and the course that had opened in sunshine ended in gloom. Josiah went against Necho without any command from God—yea, he went in direct opposition to words spoken "from the mouth of God." He meddled with strife that belonged not to him, and he reaped the consequences.

"He disguised himself." Why do this, if he was conscious of acting for God? Why wear a mask, if treading the divinely appointed pathway? Alas! Josiah failed in this, and in his failure he teaches us a salutary lesson. May we profit by it. May we learn more than ever to seek a divine warrant for all we do, and to do nothing without it. We can count on God to the fullest extent if we are walking in His way, but we have no security whatever if we attempt to travel off the divinely appointed line. Josiah had no command to fight at Megiddo, and hence he could not count on divine protection. "He disguised himself," but that did not shield him from the enemy's arrow. "The archers shot him"—they gave him his death wound, and he fell, amid the tears and lamentations of a people to whom he had endeared himself by a life of genuine piety and earnest devotedness.

May we have grace to imitate him in his piety and devotedness, and to guard against his wilfulness. It is a serious thing for a child of God to persist in doing his own will. Josiah went to Megiddo when he ought to have tarried at Jerusalem, and the archers shot him, and he died; Jonah went to Tarshish when he ought to have gone to Nineveh, and he was flung into the deep: Paul persisted in going to Jerusalem though the Spirit told him not, and he fell into the hands of the Romans. Now, all these were true, earnest, devoted servants of God; but they failed in these things; and though God overruled their failure for blessing, yet they had to reap the fruit of their failure, for *our* God is a consuming fire" (Heb. 12:29).

DECISION FOR CHRIST

MORDECAI THE JEW AND DANIEL THE PROPHET

IN APPROACHING THE SUBJECT of "Decision for Christ," there are two or three obstacles which lie in our way—two or three difficulties which hang around the question, which we would fain remove, if possible, in order that the reader may be able to view the matter on its own proper ground, and in its own proper bearings.

In the first place, we encounter a serious difficulty in the fact that very few of us, comparatively, are in a condition of soul to appreciate the subject, or to suffer a word of exhortation thereon. We are, for the most part, so occupied with the question of our soul's salvation—so taken up with matters affecting ourselves, our peace, our liberty, our comfort, our deliverance from the wrath to come, our interest in Christ—that we have but little heart for aught that purely concerns Christ Himself—His name, His person, His cause, His glory.

There are, we may say, two things which lie at the foundation of all true decision for Christ, namely, a conscience purged by the blood of Jesus, and a heart that bows with reverent submission to the authority of His Word in all things. Now we do not mean to dwell upon these things in this paper; first, because we are anxious to get at once to our immediate theme; and secondly, because we have so often dwelt on the subject of establishing the conscience in the peace of the gospel, and on setting before the heart the paramount claims of the Word of God. We merely refer to them here for the purpose of reminding the reader that they are absolutely essential materials in forming the basis of decision for Christ. If my conscience is ill at ease, if I am in doubt as to my salvation, if I am filled with "anxious thought" as to whether I am a child of God or not, decision for Christ is out of the question. I must know that Christ died for me before I can intelligently and happily live for Him.

So, also, if there be any reserve in the heart as to my entire subjection to the authority of Christ as my Lord and Master; if I am keeping some chamber of my heart, be it ever so remote, ever so small, closed against the light of His Word, it must of necessity hinder my whole-hearted decision for Him in this world. In a word, I must know that *Christ is mine* and *I am His* ere my course down here can be one of unswerving, uncompromising decision for Him. If the reader hesitates as to this, if he is still in doubt and darkness, let him pause and turn directly to the cross of the Son of God and hearken to what the Holy Spirit declares as to all those who simply put their trust therein. Let him drink into his inmost soul these words: "Be it known unto you, therefore, that through this Man is preached unto you the forgiveness of sins; and by Him *all* that *believe are* justified from *all* things from which ye could not be justified by the law of Moses." Yes, these are the glad tidings for you. "*All*, from *all*," by faith in a crucified and risen Lord.

But we see another difficuly in the way of our subject. We greatly fear that while we speak of decision for Christ, some of our readers may suppose that we are contending for some notion or set of notions of our own; that we are pressing some peculiar views or principles to which we vainly and foolishly venture to apply the imposing title of "Decision for Christ." All this we do most solemnly disclaim. The words which stand at the head of this paper are the simple expression of our thesis. We do not contend

for attachment to sect, party, or denomination; for adherence to the doctrines or commandments of men. We write in the immediate presence of Him who searcheth the hearts and trieth the reins of the children of men; and we distinctly avow that our one object is to urge upon the Christian reader the necessity of decision for Christ. We would not, if we know ourselves, pen a single line to swell the ranks of a party, or draw over adherents to any particular doctrinal creed or any special form of church polity.

We are impressed with the conviction that where Christ has His right place in the heart, all will be right; and that where He has not, there will be nothing right. And further, we believe that nothing but plain decision for Christ can effectually preserve the soul from the fatal influences that are at work around us in the professing Church. Mere orthodoxy cannot preserve us. Attachment to religious forms will not avail in the present fearful struggle. It is, we feel persuaded, a simple question of Christ as our *life*, and Christ as our *object*. May the Spirit of God now enable us to ponder aright the subject of "Decision for Christ"!

It is well to bear in mind that there are certain great truths—certain immutable principles—which underlie all the dispensations of God from age to age and which remain untouched by all the failure, the folly and the sin of man. It is on these great moral truths, these foundation principles, that faith lays hold, and in them finds its strength and sustenance. Dispensations change and pass away, men prove unfaithful in their varied positions of stewardship and responsibility, but the Word of the Lord endureth forever. It never fails. "Forever, O Lord, Thy word is settled in heaven." And again, "Thou hast magnified Thy word above all Thy name."*

Nothing can touch the eternal truth of God, and therefore what we want at all times is to give that truth its proper place in our hearts; to let it act on our conscience, form our character, and shape our way. "Thy word have I hid in my heart, that I might not sin against Thee." "Man shall not live by bread

---

* "Thou hast magnified Thy word [or saying] according to all Thy Name," seems more exactly to give the meaning of the passage. [ED.]

alone, but by every word that proceedeth out of the mouth of the Lord." This is true security. Here lies the real secret of decision for Christ. What God has spoken must govern us in the most absolute manner ere our path can be said to be one of plain decision. There may be tenacious adherence to our own notions, obstinate attachment to the prejudices of the age, a blind devotion to certain doctrines and practices resting on a traditionary foundation, certain opinions which we have received to hold without ever inquiring as to whether or not there be any authority whatever for such opinions in Holy Scripture. There may be all this and much more, and yet not one atom of genuine decision for Christ.

Now we feel we cannot do better than furnish our readers with an example or two drawn from the page of inspired history, which will do more to illustrate and enforce our theme than aught that we could possibly advance. And first, then, let us turn to the book of Esther, and there contemplate for a few moments the instructive history of *Mordecai the Jew.*

This very remarkable man lived at a time in which the Jewish economy had failed through the unfaithfulness and disobedience of the Jewish people. The Gentile was in power. The relationship between Jehovah and Israel could no longer be publicly acknowledged. The faithful Jew had but to hang his harp on the willows and sign over the faded light of other days. The chosen seed was in exile; the city and temple where their fathers worshiped were in ruins, and the vessels of the Lord's house were in a strange land. Such was the outward condition of things in the day in which Mordecai's lot was cast. But in addition to this there was a man very near the throne occupying only the second place in the empire, sitting beside the very fountain-head of authority, possessing princely wealth, and wielding almost boundless influence. To this great man, strange to say, the poor exiled Jew sternly refuses to bow. Nothing will induce him to yield a single mark of respect to the second man in the kingdom. He will save the life of Ahasuerus, but he will not bow to Haman.

Why was this? Was this blind obstinacy, or bold decision—which? In order to determine this we must inquire as to the real root or principle of Mordecai's acting. If, indeed, there was no authority for his conduct in the law of God, then must we at once pronounce it to have been blind obstinacy, foolish pride, or, it may have been, envy of a man in power. But if, on the other hand, there be within the covers of the five inspired books of Moses a plain authority for Mordecai's deportment in this matter, then must we, without hesitation, pronounce his conduct to have been the rare and exquisite fruit of attachment to the law of his God, and uncompromising decision for Him and His holy authority.

This makes all the difference. If it be merely a matter of private opinion—a question concerning which each one may lawfully adopt his own view—then, verily, might such a line of conduct be justly termed the most narrow-minded bigotry. We hear a great deal nowadays about narrow-mindedness on the other hand, and large-heartedness on the other. But as a Roman orator, over two thousand years ago, exclaimed in the senate-house of Rome, "Conscript fathers: long since, indeed, we have lost the true names of things," so may we, in the bosom of the professing Church, at the close of the nineteenth century, repeat, with far greater force, "Long since we have lost the true names of things." For what do men now call bigotry and narrow-mindedness? A faithful clinging to and carrying out of "Thus saith the Lord." And what do they designate large-heartedness? A readiness to sacrifice truth on the altar of politeness and civility.

Reader, be thou fully assured that thus it is at this solemn moment. We do not want to be sour or cynical, morose or gloomy: but we must speak the truth if we are to speak at all. We desire that the tongue may be hushed in silence, and the pen may drop from the hand, if we could basely cushion the plain, bold, unvarnished truth through fear of scattering our readers, or to avoid the sneer of the infidel. We cannot shut our eyes to the solemn fact that God's truth is being trampled in the dust—that the name of Jesus is despised and rejected. We have only to pass from city to city, and from town to town, of highly-favored England, and read upon the walls the melancholy proofs of the truth of our assertions. Truth is flung aside, in cold contempt. The name of Jesus is little set by. On the other hand, man is exalted, his reason deified, his will indulged. Where must all this end? "In the blackness of darkness forever."

How refreshing, in the face of all this, to ponder the history of Mordecai the Jew! It is very plain that he knew little and cared less about the thoughts of men on the question of narrow-mindedness. He obeyed the Word of the Lord; and this we must be allowed to call real breadth of mind, true largeness of heart. For what, after all, is a narrow mind? A narrow mind we hold to be a mind which refuses to open itself to admit the truth of God. And what, on the contrary, is a large and liberal heart? A heart expanded by the truth and grace of God. Let us not be scared away from decision in the path of obedience by the scornful epithets which men have bestowed upon that path. It is a path of peace and purity, a path where the light of an approving conscience is enjoyed, and upon which the beams of divine favor ever pour themselves in undimmed lustre.

But why did Mordecai refuse to bow to Haman? Was there any great principle at stake? Was it merely a whim of his own? Had he a "Thus saith the Lord" for his warrant in refusing a single nod of the head to the proud Amalekite? Yes. Let us turn to the seventeenth chapter of the book of Exodus, and there we read, "And the Lord said unto Moses, Write this for a memorial in a book, and rehearse it in the ears of Joshua: for I will utterly put out the remembrance of Amalek from under heaven. And Moses built an altar, and called the name of it Jehovah-nissi; for he said, Because the Lord hath sworn that the Lord will have war with Amalek from generation to generation."*

Here, then, was Mordecai's authority for not bowing to Haman the Agagite. A faithful Jew could not do reverence to one with whom Jehovah was at war. The heart might plead a thousand excuses and urge a thousand reasons. It might seek an easy path for itself on the plea that the Jewish system was in ruins and the Amalekite in power, and that therefore it was worse than useless, yea, it was positively absurd, to maintain such lofty ground when the glory of Israel was gone and the Amalekite was in the place of authority.

"Of what use," it might be argued, "can it be to uphold the standard when all is gone to pieces? You are only making your degradation more remarkable by the pertinacious refusal to bow your head. Would it not be better to give just one nod? That will settle the matter. Haman will be satisfied, and you and your people will be safe. Do not be obstinate. Show a tendency to be courteous. Do not stand up in that dogged way for a thing so manifestly non-essential. Besides, you should remember that the command in Exodus 17 was only to be rehearsed in the ears of Joshua, and only had its true application in his bright and palmy days. It was never meant for the ears of an exile, never intended to apply in the days of Israel's desolation."

All this, and much beside, might have been urged on Mordecai; but ah, the answer was simple: "God hath spoken. This is enough for me. True, we are a scattered people; but the word of the Lord is not scattered. He has not reversed His word about Amalek, nor entered into a treaty of peace with him. Jehovah and Amalek are still at war, and Amalek stands before me in the person of this haughty Agagite. How can I bow to one with whom Jehovah is at war? How can I do homage to a man whom the faithful Samuel would hew in pieces before the Lord?"

"Well, then," it might be further urged upon this devoted Jew, "you will all be destroyed. You must either bow or perish." The answer is still most simple: "I have nothing to do with consequences. They are in the hand of God. Obedience is my path, the results are with Him. It is better to die with a good conscience than live with a bad one. It is better to go to Heaven with an uncondemning heart than remain upon earth

* It is deeply interesting to note that neither the Jews' best Friend nor their worst enemy is once formally named in the book of Esther; but faith could recognize both the one and the other.

with a heart that would make me a coward. God has spoken. I can do no otherwise. May the Lord help me! Amen."

Oh, how well we can understand the mode in which this faithful Jew would be assulted by the enemy. Nothing but the grace of God can ever enable any one to maintain a deportment of unflinching decision at a moment in which everything within and around is against us. True it is, we know that it is better to suffer anything than deny our Lord or fly in the face of His commandments; but yet how little are some of us prepared to endure a single sneer, a single scornful look, a single contemptuous expression, for Christ's sake. And perhaps there are few things harder, for some of us at least, to bear than to be reproached on the ground of narrow-mindedness and bigotry. We naturally like to be thought large-hearted and liberal. We like to be accounted men of enlightened mind, sound judgment, and comprehensive grasp. But we must remember that we have no right to be liberal at our Master's expense. We have simply to obey.

Thus it was with Mordecai. He stood like a rock, and allowed the whole tide of difficulty and opposition to roll over him. He would not bow to the Amalekite, let the consequence be what it might. Obedience was his path. The results were with God. And look at the result! In one moment the tide was turned. The proud Amalekite fell from his lofty eminence, and the exiled Jew was lifted from his sackcloth and ashes and placed next the throne. Haman exchanged his wealth and dignities for gallows; Mordecai exchanged his sackcloth for a royal robe.

Now it may not always happen that the reward of simple obedience will be as speedy and as signal as in Mordecai's case. And moreover, we may say that we are not Mordecais, nor are we placed in his position. But the principle holds good, whoever and wherever we are. There is not one of us, however obscure or insignificant, that has not a sphere within which our influence is felt for good or for evil. And besides, independent altogether of our circumstances and the apparent results of our conduct, we are called upon to obey implicitly the Word of the

Lord—to have His Word hidden in our hearts—to refuse with unswerving decision, to do or say aught that the Word of the living God condemns. "How can I do this great wickedness, and sin against God?" This should be the language, whether it be the question of a child tempted to steal a lump of sugar, or the most momentous step in evil that one can be tempted to take.

The strength and moral security of Mordecai's position lay in this fact, that he had the Word of God for his authority. Had it not been so, his conduct would have been senseless in the extreme. To have refused the usual expression of respect to one in high authority, without some weighty reason, could only be regarded as the most unmeaning obstinacy. But the moment you introduce a "Thus saith the Lord," the matter is entirely changed. The Word of the Lord endureth forever. The divine testimonies do not fade away or change with the times and seasons. Heaven and earth shall pass away, but one jot or tittle of what our God hath spoken shall never pass away. Hence, what had been rehearsed in the ears of Joshua, as he rested in triumph under the banner of Jehovah, was designed to govern the conduct of Mordecai, though clothed in sackcloth as an exile, in the city of Shushan. Ages and generations had passed away; the days of the judges and the days of the kings had run thier course; but the commandment of the Lord with respect to Amalek had lost—could lose—none of its force. "The Lord *hath sworn* that the Lord will have war with Amalek," not merely in the days of Joshua, nor in the days of the judges, nor in the days of the kings, but "from generation to generation." Such was the record—the imperishable and immutable record of God; and such was the plain, solid and unquestionable foundation of Mordecai's conduct.

And here let us say a few words as to the immense importance of entire submission to the Word of God. We live in a day which is plainly marked by strong self-will. Man's reason, man's will and man's interest are working together, with appalling success, to ignore the authority of Holy Scripture. So long as the statements of the Word of God chime in with man's reason, so long as they do not run counter to his will, and are not subversive of his interests, so long will he tolerate them; or, it may be, he will quote them with a measure of respect, or at least with self-complacency; but the moment it becomes a question of Scripture *versus* reason, will, or interest, the former is either silently ignored or contemptuously rejected. This is a very marked and solemn feature of the days that are now passing over our heads. It behooves Christians to be aware of it, and to be on their watchtower.

We fear that very few, comparatively, are truly alive to the real state of the moral atmosphere which enwraps the religious world. We do not refer here so much to the bold attacks of infidel writers. To these we have alluded elsewhere. What we have now before us is rather the cool indifference on the part of professing Christians as to Scripture; the little power which pure truth wields over the conscience; the way in which the edge of Scripture is blunted or turned aside. You quote passage after passage from the inspired volume, but it seems like the pattering of rain upon the window: the *reason* is at work, the *will* is dominant, *interest* is at stake, human opinions bear sway, God's truth is practically, if not in so many words, set aside.

All this is deeply solemn. We know of few things more dangerous than intellectual familiarity with the letter of Scripture where the spirit of it does not govern the conscience, form the character, and shape the way. We want to tremble at the Word of God, to bow down in reverential submission to its holy authority in all things. A single line of Scripture ought to be sufficient for our souls on any point, even though, in carrying it out, we should have to move athwart the opinions of the highest and best of men. May the Lord raise up many faithful and true-hearted witnesses in these last days—men like the faithful Mordecai—who would rather ascend a gallows than bow to an Amalekite!

For the further illustration of our theme, we shall ask the reader to turn to the sixth chapter of the book of Daniel. There is a special charm and interest in the history of these living examples presented to us in the Holy Scriptures. They tell us how the truth of God was acted upon, in other days, by men of like passions with ourselves; they prove to us that in every age there have been men who so prized the truth, so reverenced the Word of the living God, that they would rather face death, in it most appalling forms, than to depart one hair's breadth from the narrow line laid down by the authoritative voice of their Lord and Master.

It is healthful to be brought into contact with such men—healthful at times, but peculiarly so in days like the present, when there is so much laxity and easy-going profession—so much of mere theory—when every one is allowed to go his own way, and hold his own opinion, provided always that he does not interfere with the opinions of his neighbor—when the commandments of God seem to have so little weight, so little power over the heart and conscience. Tradition will get a hearing; public opinion will be respected; anything and everything, in short, but the plain and positive statements of the Word of God, will get a place in the thoughts and opinions of men. At such a time, it is, we repeat, at once healthful and edifying to muse over the history of men like Mordecai the Jew, and Daniel the prophet, and scores of others, in whose estimation a single line of Holy Scripture rose far above all the thoughts of men, the decrees of governors, and the statutes of kings, and who declared plainly that they had nothing whatever to do with consequences where the Word of the Lord was concerned. Absolute submission to the divine command is that which alone becomes the creature.

It is not, be it observed and well remembered, that any man or any number of men have any right to demand subjection to their decisions or decrees. No man has any right to enforce his opinions upon his fellow. This is plain enough, and we have to bless God for the inestimable privilege of civil and religious liberty, as enjoyed under this government. But what we urge upon our readers, just now, is plain decision for Christ, and implicit subjection to His authority, irrespective of everything, and regardless of consequences. This is what we do most earnestly desire for ourselves and for all the people of God in these last days. We long for that condition of soul, that attitude of heart, that quality of conscience, which shall lead us to bow down in implicit subjection to the commandments of our Lord and Saviour Jesus Christ.

No doubt there are difficulties, stumbling blocks, and hostile influences to be encountered. It may be said, for instance, that "It is very difficult for one, now-a-days, to know what is really true and right. There are so many opinions and so many ways, and good men differ so in judgment about the simplest and plainest matters, and yet they all profess to own the Bible as the only standard of appeal; and, moreover, they all declare that their one desire is to do what is right, and to serve the Lord, in their day and generation. How, then, is one to know what is true or what is false, seeing that you will find the very best of men ranged on opposite sides of the same question?"

The answer to all this is very simple. "If thine eye be single thy whole body shall be full of light." But, most assuredly, my eye is not single if I am looking at men, and reasoning on what I see in them. A single eye rests simply on the Lord and His Word. Men differ, no doubt—they have differed, and they ever will differ, but I am to harken to the voice of my Lord and do His will. His Word is to be my light and my authority, the girdle of my loins in action, the strength of my heart in service, my only warrant for moving hither and thither, the stable foundation of all my ways. If I were to attempt to shape my way according to the thoughts of men, where should I be? How uncertain and unsatisfactory would my course be! If I really want to be guided aright, my God will surely guide me; but if I am looking to men, if I am governed by mixed motives, if I am seeking my own ends and interests, if I am seeking to please my fellows, then, undoubtedly, my body shall be full of darkness, heavy clouds shall settle down upon my pathway, and uncertainty mark all my goings.

Christian reader, think of these things.

Think deeply of them. Depend upon it they have a just claim upon your attention. Do you earnestly desire to follow your Lord? Do you really aim at something beyond mere empty profession, cold orthodoxy, or mechanical religiousness? Do you sigh for reality, depth, energy, fervor, and whole-heartedness? Then make Christ your one object, His Word your rule, His glory your aim. May the blessed Spirit be pleased to use for the furtherance of these ends our meditation on the interesting narrative of *Daniel the prophet.*

"It pleased Darius to set over the kingdom a hundred and twenty princes, which should be over the whole kingdom; and over these, three presidents, of whom Daniel was first; that the princes might give accounts unto them, and the king should have no damage. Then this Daniel was preferred above the presidents and princes, because an excellent spirit was in him; and the king thought to set him over the whole realm. Then the presidents and princes sought to find occasion against Daniel concerning the kingdom; but they could find none occasion or fault; forasmuch as he was faithful, neither was there any error or fault found in him" (Dan. 6:1-4).

What a testimony! How truly refreshing to the heart! "No error or fault!" Even his most bitter enemies could not put their finger upon a single blemish in his character, or a flaw in his practical career. Truly this was a rare and admirable character—a bright witness for the God of Israel, even in the dark days of the Babylonish captivity—an unanswerable proof of the fact that no matter where we are situated, or how we are circumstanced, no matter how unfavorable our position, or how dark the day in which our lot is cast, it is our happy privilege so to carry ourselves, in all the details of daily life, as to give no occasion to the enemy to speak reproachfully.

How sad when it is otherwise! How humiliating when those who make a high profession are found constantly breaking down in the most commonplace affairs of domestic and commercial life! There are few things which more tend to discourage the heart than that.

No doubt worldly people are only too ready

to find occasion against those who prefess the name of Jesus; and, further, we have to remember that there are two sides to every question, and that, very frequently, a broad margin must be left for exaggeration, high coloring, and false impressions. But still, it is the Christian's plain duty so to walk in every position and relationship of life, as that "no error or fault" may be found in him. We should not make any excuses for ourselves. The duties of our situation, whatever it may happen to be, should be scrupulously performed. A careless manner, a slovenly habit, an unprincipled mode of acting, on the part of the Christian, is a serious damage to the cause of Christ, and a dishonor to His holy name.

And, on the other hand, diligence, earnestness, punctuality, and fidelity, bring glory to that name. And this should ever be the Christian's object. He should not aim at his own interest, his own reputation, or his own advancement, in seeking to carry himself aright in his family and in his calling in life. True, it will promote his interest, establish his reputation, and further his progress, to be upright and diligent in all his ways; but none of these things should ever be his motive. He is to be ever and only governed by the one thing, namely, to please and honor his Lord and Master.

The standard which the Holy Ghost has set before us, as to all these things, is furnished in the words of the apostle to the Philippians, "That ye may be blameless and harmless, the sons of God without rebuke in the midst of a crooked and perverse nation, among whom ye shine as lights in the world." We should not be satisfied with anything less than this. "They could find none occasion nor fault, forasmuch as he was faithful, neither was there any error or fault found in him." Noble testimony! Would that it were more called forth, in this our day, by the deportment, the habits, the temper, and ways of all those who call themselves Christians.

But there was one point in which Daniel's enemies felt they could lay hold of him. "Then said these men, We shall not find any occasion against this Daniel, except we find it against him concerning *the law of his God.*" Here was a something in the which occasion might be found to ruin this beloved and honored servant of God. It appears that Daniel had been in the habit of praying three times a day, with his windows open toward Jerusalem. This fact was well known, and was speedily laid hold of, and turned to account. "Then these presidents and princes assembled together to the king, and said thus unto him, King Darius, live for ever. All the presidents of the kingdom, the governors, and the princes, the counsellors, and the captains, have consulted together to establish a royal statute, and to make a firm decree, that whosoever shall ask a petition of any god or man for thirty days, save of thee, O king, he shall be cast into the den of lions. Now, O king, establish the decree, and sign the writing, that it be not changed, according to the law of the Medes and Persians, which altereth not. Wherefore king Darius signed the writing and the decree."

Here, then, was a deep plot, a subtle snare, laid for the blameless and harmless Daniel. How would he act in the face of all this? Would he not feel it right to lower the standard? Well, if the standard was something of his own, he might surely lower it, and perhaps he ought. But if it were something divine—if his conduct was based upon the truth of God, then clearly it was his place to hold it up as high as ever, regardless of statutes, decrees, and writings established, signed, and countersigned. The whole question hinged upon this.

Just as in the case of Mordecai the Jew, the question hinged upon the one point of whether he had any divine warrant for refusing to bow to Haman; so, in the case of Daniel the prophet, the question was, had he any divine authority for praying toward Jerusalem. It certainly seemed strange and odd. Many might have felt disposed to say to him, "Why persist in this practice? What need is there for opening your windows and praying toward Jerusalem, in such a public manner? Can you not wait until night has drawn her sable curtain around you, and your closet door has shut you in, and then pour out your heart to your God? This would be prudent, judicious, and expedient. And, surely, your God does not exact this of you. He does not regard time, place, or attitude. All times and places are alike to Him. Are you wise—are you right, in persisting in such a line of action under such circumstances? It was all well enough before this decree was signed, when you could pray when and as you thought right; but now it does seem like the most culpable fatuity and blind obstinacy to persevere; it is as though you really courted martyrdom."

All this, and much more, we may easily conceive, might be suggested to the mind of the faithful Jew; but still the grand question remained, "What saith the Scripture?" Was there any divine reason for Daniel's praying toward Jerusalem? Assuredly there was! In the first place, Jehovah had said to Solomon, in reference to the temple at Jerusalem, "Mine eyes and My heart shall be there perpetually." Jerusalem was God's earthly centre. It was, it is, and ever shall be. True, it was in ruins—the temple was in ruins; but God's Word was not in ruins; and here is faith's simple but solid warrant.

King Solomon had said, at the dedication of the temple, hundreds of years before Daniel's time, "If Thy people sin against Thee, (for there is no man that sinneth not,) and Thou be angry with them, and deliver them over before their enemies, and they carry them away captive unto a land far off or near. Yet if they bethink themselves in the land whither they are carried captive, and turn and pray unto Thee, in the land of their captivity, saying, We have sinned, we have done amiss, and have dealt wickedly; if they return to Thee with all their heart and with all their soul in the land of their captivity, whither they have carried them captive, and pray toward their land, which Thou gavest unto their fathers, and toward the city which Thou hast chosen, and toward the house which I have built for Thy name: then hear Thou from the heavens, even from Thy dwelling-place, their prayer and their supplications, and maintain their cause, and forgive Thy people which have sinned against Thee" (2 Chron. 6:36-39).

Now this was precisely what Daniel was doing—this was the ground he took. He was a captive exile, but his heart was at Jerusalem, and his eyes followed his heart. If he could not sing the songs of Zion, he could at least breathe his prayers toward Zion's hill. If his harp was on the willows at Babylon, his fond affections turned toward the city of God, now a heap of ruins, but ere long to be an eternal excellency, "the joy of the whole earth." It mattered not to him that a decree had been signed by earth's greatest monarch, forbidding him to pray toward the city of his fathers and to his father's God. It mattered not to him that the lion's den was yawning to receive him, and the lion's jaws ready to devour him. Like his brother Mordecai, he had nothing to do with consequences. Mordecai would rather mount the gallows than bow to Haman, and Daniel would rather descend to the lion's den than cease to pray to Jehovah. These, surely, were the worthies. They were men whose hearts and consciences were governed absolutely by the Word of God. The world may dub them bigots and fools; but, oh! how the heart does long for such bigots and fools, in these days of false liberality and wisdom!

It might have been said to Mordecai and Daniel that they were contending for mere trifles—for things wholly indifferent and non-essential. This is an argument often used; but, oh! it has no weight with an honest and devoted heart. Indeed, there is nothing more contemptible, in the judgment of every true lover of Jesus, than the principle that regulates the standard as to essentials and non-essentials. For, what is it? Simply this, "All that concerns my salvation is essential; all that merely affects the glory of Christ is non-essential." How terrible is this! Dost thou not utterly abhor it? What! shall we accept salvation as the fruit of our Lord's death, and deem aught that concerns Him non-essential? God forbid. Yea; rather let us entirely reverse the matter, and regard all that concerns the honor and glory of the name of Jesus, the truth of His Word, and the integrity of His cause, as vital, essential, and fundamental; and all that merely concerns ourselves as non-essential and indifferent. May God grant us this mind! May nothing be deemed trivial by us which has for its foundation the Word of the living God!

Thus it was with those devoted men whose history we have been glancing at. Mordecai would not bow his head, and Daniel would not close his window. Blessed men! The Lord be praised for such, and for the inspired record of their actings. Mordecai would rather surrender life than diverge from the truth of God, and Daniel would rather do the same than turn away from God's centre. Jehovah had said that He would have war with Amalek from generation to generation, and therefore Mordecai would not bow. Jehovah had said of Jerusalem, "Mine eyes and My heart shall be there perpetually"; therefore Daniel would not cease to pray toward that blessed centre. The Word of the Lord endureth forever, and faith takes its stand on that imperishable foundation. There is an eternal freshness about every word that has come forth from the Lord. His truth holds good throughout all generations; its bloom can never be brushed away, its light can never fade, its edge can never be blunted. All praise be to His holy name.

But let us look for a moment at the result of Daniel's faithfulness. The king was plunged into the deepest grief when he discovered his mistake. "He was sore displeased with himself." So well he might. He had fallen into a snare; but Daniel was in good keeping. It was all right with him. "The name of the Lord is a strong tower, the righteous runneth into it, and is safe." It matters not whether it be a lion's den at Babylon or a prison at Philippi; faith and a good conscience can make a man happy in either. We question if Daniel ever spent a happier night on this earth, than the night he spent in the lion's den. He was there for God, and God was there with him. He was there with an approving conscience and an uncondemning heart. He could look up from the very bottom of that den straight into Heaven: yea, that den was Heaven upon earth to his happy spirit. Who would not rather be Daniel in the den than Darius in the palace? The one happy in God; the other "sore displeased with himself." Darius would have every one pray to him; Daniel would pray to none but God. Darius was bound by his own rash decree; Daniel was bound only by the Word of the living God. What a contrast!

And then see in the end what signal honor was put upon Daniel. He stood publicly identified with the one living and true God. "O Daniel," cried the king, "servant of the living God." Truly he had earned this title for himself. He was, unquestionably, a faithful servant of God. He had seen his three brethren cast into a furnace because they would worship *only* the true God, and he had been cast into the lion's den because he would pray *only* to Him; but the Lord had appeared for them and him, and given them a glorious triumph. He had allowed them to realize that precious promise made of old to their fathers, that they should be the head and their enemies the tail; that they should be above and their enemies below. Nothing could be more marked—nothing could more forcibly illustrate the value which God puts upon plain decision and true-hearted devotedness, no matter where, when, or by whom exhibited.

Oh! for an earnest heart in this day of lukewarmness! O Lord, revive Thy work!

THE LIVING GOD AND A LIVING FAITH

THERE IS ONE GREAT SUBSTANTIAL fact standing prominently forth on every page of the volume of God, and illustrated in every stage of the history of God's people—a fact of immense weight and moral power at all times, but specially in seasons of darkness, difficulty, and discouragement, occasioned by the low condition of things among those who profess to be on the Lord's side. The fact is this, *That faith can always count on God, and God will always answer faith.*

Such is our fact, such our thesis; and if the reader will turn with us, for a few moments, to 2 Chronicles 20, he will find a very beautiful and very striking illustration.

This chapter shows us the good king Jehoshaphat under very heavy pressure indeed—it records a dark moment in his history. "It came to pass after this also, that the children of Moab, and the children of Ammon, and with them other besides the Ammonites, came against Jehoshaphat to battle. Then" (for people are ever quick to run with evil tidings) "there came some that told Jehoshaphat, saying, There cometh a great multitude against thee from beyond the sea, on this side Syria."

Here was a difficulty of no ordinary nature. This invading host was made up of the descendants of Lot and of Esau; and this fact might give rise to a thousand conflicting thoughts and distracting questions in the mind of Jehoshaphat. They were not Egyptians or Assyrians, concerning whom there could be no question whatever; but both Esau and Lot stood in certain relations to Israel, and a question might suggest itself as to how far such relations were to be recognized.

Not this only. The practical state of the entire nation of Israel—the actual condition of God's people, was such as to give rise to the most serious misgivings. Israel no longer presented an unbroken front to the invading

foe. Their visible unity was gone. A grievous breach had been made in their battlements. The ten tribes and the two were rent asunder, the one from the other. The condition of the former was terrible, and that of the latter, shaky enough.

Thus the circumstances of king Jehoshaphat were dark and discouraging in the extreme; and, even as regards himself and his practical course, he was but just emerging from the consequences of a very humiliating fall, so that his reminiscences would be quite as cheerless as his surroundings.

But it is just here that our grand substantial fact presents itself to the vision of faith, and flings a mantle of light over the whole scene. Things looked gloomy, no doubt; but God was to be counted upon by faith, and faith could count upon Him. God is a never failing resource—a great reality, at all times, and under all circumstances. "God is our refuge and stength, a very present help in trouble. Therefore will not we fear, though the earth be removed, and though the mountains be carried into the midst of the sea. Though the waters thereof roar and be troubled, though the mountains shake with the swelling thereof. There is a river, the stream whereof shall make glad the city of God, the holy place of the tabernacles of the Most High. God is in the midst of her, she shall not be moved: God shall help her, and that right early. The heathen raged, the kingdoms were moved: He uttered His voice, the earth melted. The Lord of hosts is with us; the God of Jacob is our refuge" (Psa. 46:1-7).

Here, then, was Jehoshaphat's resource in the day of his trouble; and to it he at once betook himself, in that earnest faith which never fails to draw down power and blessing from the living and true God, to meet every exigency of the way. "And Jehoshaphat feared, and set himself to seek the Lord, and proclaimed a fast throughout all Judah. And Judah gathered themselves together, to ask help of the Lord; even out of all the cities of Judah they came to seek the Lord. And Jehoshaphat stood in the congregation of Judah and Jerusalem, in the house of the Lord, before the new court, and said, O Lord God of our fathers, art not Thou God in heaven? and rulest not Thou over all the kingdoms of the heathen? and in Thy hand is there not power and might, so that none is able to withstand Thee? Art not Thou our God, who didst drive out the inhabitants of this land before Thy people Israel, and gavest it to *the seed of Abraham Thy friend for ever?*"

These are the breathings of faith—faith that enables the soul to take the very highest possible ground. It mattered not what unsettled questions there might be between Esau and Jacob; there were none between Abraham and the Almighty God. Now, God had given the land to Abraham, His friend. For how long? *For ever.* This was enough. "The gifts and calling of God are without repentance." God will never cancel His call, or take back a gift. This is a fixed foundation principle; and on this faith always takes its stand with firm decision.

The enemy might throw in a thousand suggestions; and the poor heart might throw up a thousand reasonings. It might seem like presumption and empty conceit, on the part of Jehoshaphat, to plant his foot on such lofty ground. It was all well enough in the days of David, or of Solomon, or of Joshua, when the unity of the nation was unbroken, and the banner of Jehovah floated in triumph over the twelve tribes of Israel. But things were sadly changed; and it ill became one in Jehoshaphat's circumstances to use such lofty language or assume to occupy such a high position.

What is faith's reply to all this? A very simple, but a very powerful one—God never changes. He is the same yesterday, to-day, and forever. Had He not made Abraham a present of the land of Canaan? Had He not bestowed it upon his seed forever? Had He not ratified the gift by His word and His

oath—these two immutable things in which it was impossible for Him to lie? Unquestionably.

But then what of the law? Did not that make some difference? None whatever, as regards God's gift and promise. Four centuries previous to the giving of the law, was the great transaction settled and stablished between the Almighty God and Abraham His friend—and settled and stablished forever. Hence nothing can possibly touch this. There were no legal conditions proposed to Abraham. All was pure and absolute grace. God gave the land to Abraham by promise, and not by law, in any shape or form.

Now, it was on this original ground that Jehoshaphat took his stand; and he was right. It was the only thing for him to do. He had not one hair's breadth of solid standing ground, short of these golden words, "Thou gavest it to the seed of Abraham Thy friend forever." It was either this or nothing. *A living faith always lays hold on the living God.* It cannot stop short of Him. It looks not at men or their circumstances. It takes no account of the changes and chances of this mortal life. It lives and moves and has its being in the presence of the living God; it rejoices in the cloudless sunlight of His blessed countenance. It carries on all its artless reasonings in the sanctuary, and draws all its happy conclusions from the facts discovered there. It does not lower the standard according to the condition of things around, but boldly and decidedly takes up its position on the very highest ground.

Now, these actings of faith are always most grateful to the heart of God. The living God delights in a living faith. We may be quite sure that the bolder the grasp of faith, the more welcome it is to God. We need never suppose that the blessed One is either gratified or glorified by the workings of a legal mind. No; He delights to be trusted without a shadow of reserve or misgiving. He delights to be fully counted upon and largely used; and the deeper the need, and the darker the surrounding gloom, the more is He glorified by the faith that draws upon Him.

Hence, we may assert with perfect confidence, that the attitude and the utterances of Jehoshaphat, in the scene before us, were in full accordance with the mind of God. There is something perfectly beautiful to see him, as it were, opening the original lease, and laying his finger on that clause in virtue of which Israel held as tenants forever under God. Nothing could cancel that clause or break that lease. No flaw there. All was ordered and sure. "Thou *gavest* it to the seed of Abraham Thy friend *forever.*"

This was solid ground—the ground of God—the ground of faith, which no power of the enemy can ever shake. True, the enemy might remind Jehoshaphat of sin and folly, failure and unfaithfulness. Nay, he might suggest to him that the very fact of the threatened invasion proved that Israel had fallen, for had they not done so, there would be neither enemy nor evil.

But for this, too, grace had provided an answer—an answer which faith knew well how to appropriate. Jehoshaphat reminds Jehovah of the house which Solomon had built to His name. "They have built Thee a sanctuary therein for Thy name, saying, If, when evil cometh upon us, as a sword, judgment, or pestilence, or famine, we stand before this house, and in Thy presence (for Thy name is in this house), and cry unto Thee in our affliction, then Thou wilt hear and help. and now, behold, the children of Ammon, and Moab, and mount Seir, whom Thou wouldest not let Israel invade, when they came out of the land of Egypt, but they turned from them, and destroyed them not. Behold, I say, how they reward us, to come to cast us out of *Thy possession, which Thou hast given us to inherit.* O our God, wilt Thou not judge them? for we have no might against this great company that cometh against us; neither know we what to do, but *our eyes are upon Thee"* (vers. 8-12).

Here, truly, is a living faith dealing with the living God. It is no mere empty profession—no lifeless creed—no cold uninfluential theory. It is not a man "saying he has faith." Such things will never stand in the day of battle. They may do well enough when all

is calm, smooth, and bright; but when difficulties have to be grappled with—when the enemy has to be met face to face, all merely nominal faith, all mere lip profession, will prove like autumn leaves before the blast. Nothing will stand the test of actual conflict but a living personal faith in a living personal Saviour-God. This is what is needed. It is this which alone can sustain the heart, come what may. Faith brings God into the scene, and all is strength, victory, and perfect peace.

Thus it was with the king of Judah, in the days of 2 Chron. 20. "We have no might; neither know we what to do; but our eyes are upon Thee." This is the way to occupy God's ground, even with the eyes fixed on God Himself. This is the true secret of stability and peace. The devil will leave no stone unturned to drive us off the true ground which, as Christians, we ought to occupy in these last days; and we, in ourselves, have no might whatever against him. Our only resource is in the living God. If our eyes are upon Him, nothing can harm us. "Thou wilt keep him in perfect peace, whose mind is stayed on Thee, because he trusteth in Thee."

Art thou on God's ground? Canst thou give a "Thus saith the Lord" for the position which thou occupiest, at this moment? Art thou consciously standing on the solid ground of holy Scripture? Is there anything questionable in thy surroundings and associations? We beseech thee to weigh these questions solemnly as in the divine presence. Be assured they are of moment just now. We are passing through critical moments. Men are taking sides; principles are working and coming to a head. Never was it more needful to be thoroughly and unmistakably on the Lord's side.

Jehoshaphat never could have met the Ammonites, Moabites, and Edomites, had he not been persuaded that his feet were on the very ground which God had given to Abraham. If the enemy could have shaken his confidence as to this, he would have had an easy victory. But Jehoshaphat knew where he was; he knew his ground. He understood his bearings; and therefore he could fix his eyes with confidence upon the living God. He had no misgivings as to his position. He did not say, as many do, now-a-days, "I am not quite sure. I hope I am; but sometimes clouds come over my soul, and make me hesitate as to whether I am really on divine ground."

Ah! no, the king of Judah would not have understood such language at all. All was clear to him. His eye rested on the original grant. He felt sure he was on the true ground of the Israel of God; and albeit all Israel were not there with him, yet God was with him, and that was enough. His was a living faith in the living God—the only thing that will stand in the day of trial.

There is something in the attitude and utterance of the king of Judah, on that memorable occasion, well worthy of the reader's profound attention. His feet were firmly fixed on God's ground, and his eyes as firmly fixed on God Himself; and in addition to this, there was the deep sense of his own thorough nothingness. He had not so much as a shadow of a doubt as to the fact of his being in possession of the very inheritance which God had given him. He knew that he was in his right place. He did not *hope* it; still less did he doubt it; no, he knew it. He could say, "I believe and am sure."

This is all-important. It is impossible to stand against the enemy, if there is anything equivocal in our position. If there be any secret misgiving as to our being in our right place—if we cannot give a "Thus saith the Lord" for the position which we occupy, the path we tread, the associations in which we stand, the work in which we are engaged, there will, most assuredly, be weakness in the hour of conflict. Satan is sure to avail himself of the smallest misgiving in the soul. All must be settled as to our positive standing, if we would make any headway against the enemy. There must be an unclouded confidence as to our real position before God, else the foe will have an easy victory.

Now, it is precisely here that there is so much weakness apparent among the children of God. Very few, comparatively, are clear, sound, and settled as to their foundation—very few are able, without any reserve, to take the blessed ground of being washed in the blood of Jesus, and sealed with the Holy Spirit. At times they hope it. When things go well with them; when they have had a good time in the closet; when they have enjoyed nearness to God in prayer, or over the Word; while they are sitting under a clear, fervent, forcible ministry—at such moments, perhaps, they can venture to speak hopefully about themselves.

But, very soon, dark clouds gather; they feel the workings of indwelling sin; they are afflicted with wandering thoughts; or it may be, they have been betrayed into some levity of spirit, or irritability of temper; then they begin to *reason* about themselves, and to question whether they are, in reality, the children of God. And from reasonings and questionings, they very speedily slip into positive unbelief, and then plunge into the thick gloom of a despondency bordering on despair.

All this is most sad. It is, at once, dishonoring to God, and destructive to the soul's peace; and as to progress, in such a condition, it is wholly out of the question. How can any one run a race, if he has not cleared the starting post? How can he erect a building, if he has not laid the foundation? And, on the same principle, how can a soul grow in the divine life, if he is always liable to doubt whether he has that life or not?

But it may be that some of our readers are disposed to put such a question as the following, "How can I be sure that I am on God's ground?—that I am washed in the blood of Jesus and sealed with the Holy Spirit?" We reply, How do you know that you are a lost sinner? Is it because you feel it? Is mere feeling the ground of your faith? If so, it is not a divine faith at all. True faith rests *only* on the testimony of holy Scripture.

No doubt, it is by the gracious energy of the Holy Ghost that any one can exercise this living faith; but we are speaking now of the true ground of faith—the authority—the basis on which it rests, and that is simply the holy Scriptures which, as the inspired apostle tells us, are able to make us wise unto salvation, and which even a child could know, without the church, the clergy, the fathers, the doctors, the councils, the colleges, or any other human intervention whatsoever.

"Abraham believed God." Here was divine faith. It was not a question of feeling. Indeed, if Abraham had been influenced by his feelings, he would have been a doubter instead of a believer. For what had he to build upon in himself? "His own body now dead." A poor ground surely on which to build his faith in the promise of an innumerable seed. But, we are told, "He considered not his own body now dead" (Rom. 4). What, then, did he consider? He considered the word of the living God, and on that he rested. Now this is faith. And mark what the apostle says: "He staggered not at the promise of God through unbelief" (for unbelief is always a staggerer), "but was strong in faith, giving glory to God: and being fully persuaded that what He had promised, He was able also to perform. And *therefore* it was imputed to him for righteousness."

"Ah! but," the anxious reader may say, "what has all this to say to my case? I am not an Abraham—I cannot expect a special revelation from God. How am I to know that God has spoken to me? How can I possess this precious faith?" Well, dear friend, mark the apostle's further statement. "Now," he adds, "it was not written for his [Abraham's] sake alone, that it was imputed to him; but for us also, to whom it shall be imputed, if"—if what?—if we feel, realize, or experience aught in ourselves? Nay, but "if we believe on Him that raised up Jesus our Lord from the dead; who was delivered for our offences, and was raised again for our justification."

All this is full of solid comfort and richest consolation. It assures the anxious inquirer that he has the selfsame ground and authority to rest upon that Abraham had, with an immensely higher measure of light thrown on that ground, inasmuch as Abraham was called to believe in a promise, whereas we are privileged to believe in an accomplished fact. He was called to look forward to something which was to be done; we look back at something that is done, even an accomplished redemption, attested by the fact of a risen and glorified Saviour, at the right hand of the Majesty in the Heavens.

But as to the ground or authority on which we are called to rest our souls, it is the same in our case as in Abraham's and all true believers' in all ages—it is the Word of God—the holy Scriptures. There is no other foundation of faith but this; and the faith that rests on any other is not true faith at all. A faith resting on human tradition—on the authority of the Church—on the authority of so-called general councils—on the clergy—or on learned men, is not divine faith, but mere superstition; it is a faith which "stands in the wisdom of men," and "not in the power of God" (1 Cor. 2:5).

Now, it is utterly impossible for any human pen or mortal tongue to overstate the value or importance of this grand principle—this principle of a living faith. Its value at the present moment is postively unspeakable. We believe it to be the divine antidote against most, if not all, the leading errors, evils, and hostile influences of the day in which our lot is cast. There is a tremendous shaking going on around us. Minds are agitated. Disturbing forces are abroad. There is a loosening of the foundations. Old institutions, to which the human mind clings, as the ivy to the oak, are tottering on every side; and many are actually fallen: and thousands of souls that have been finding shelter in them are dislodged and scared, and know not whither to turn. Some are saying, "The bricks are thrown down, but we will build with hewn stone." Many are at their wit's end, and most are ill at ease.

Nor is this all; there is a numerous class, for the most part, of those who are not so much concerned about the condition and destiny of religious institutions and ecclesiastical systems, as about the condition and destiny of their own precious souls—of those who are not so much agitated by questions about "broad church," "high church," "low church," "state church," or "free church," as about this one great question, "What must I do to be saved?" What have we to say to these latter? What is the real want of their souls? Simply this, "A living faith in the living God." This is what is needed for all who are disturbed by what they *see* without, or feel within. Our unfailing resource is in the living God and in His Son Jesus Christ, as revealed by the Holy Spirit in the holy Scriptures.

Here is the true resting-place of faith, and to this we do, most earnestly, most urgently and solemnly, invite the anxious reader. In one word, we entreat him to stay his whole soul on the Word of God—the holy Scriptures. Here we have authority for all that we need to know, to believe, or to do.

Is it a question of anxiety about my eternal salvation? Hear the following words, "Therefore, thus saith the Lord God, Behold, I lay in Zion *for a foundation*, a stone, a tried stone, a precious corner stone, *a sure foundation:* he that believeth shall not make haste" (Isa. 28:16). These precious words, so pregnant with tranquilizing power, are quoted by the inspired apostle in the New Testament Scriptures: "Wherefore also it is contained in the scripture, Behold, I lay in Sion a chief corner stone, elect, precious: and *he that believeth on Him shall not be confounded"* (1 Peter 2:6).

What solid comfort—what deep and settled repose for the anxious soul is here! God has laid the foundation, and that foundation is nothing less than His own eternal and co-equal Son, the Son who had dwelt from all eternity in His bosom. This foundation is, in every respect, adequate to sustain the whole weight of the counsels and purposes of the eternal *Three in One*—to meet all the claims of the nature, the character, and the throne of God.

Being all this, it must needs be fully adequate to meet all the need of the anxious soul, of what kind soever that need may be. If Christ is enough for God He must of necessity be enough for man—for any man—for the reader; and that He is enough is proved by the very passage just quoted. He is God's own foundation, laid by His own hand, the foundation and centre of that glorious system of royal and victorious grace set forth in the word "Zion." (See Heb. 12:22-24.) He is God's own precious, tried, chief corner stone—that blessed One who went down into death's dark waters—bore the heavy judgment and wrath of God against sin—robbed death of its sting, and the grave of its victory—destroyed him

that had the power of death—wrested from the enemy's grasp that terrible weapon with which sin had armed him, and made it the very instrument of his eternal defeat and confusion. Having done all this, He was received up into glory, and seated at the right hand of the Majesty in the heavens.

Such is God's foundation, to which He graciously calls the attention of every one who really feels the need of something divinely solid on which to build, in view of the hollow and shadowy scenes of this world, and in prospect of the stern realities of eternity. You are now invited to build upon this foundation. Be assured it is for you as positively and distinctly as though you heard a voice from Heaven speaking to your own very self. The word of the living God is addressed "to every creature under heaven"—"whosoever will" is invited to come.

The inspired volume has been placed in your hand and laid open before your eyes; and for what think you? Is it to mock or to tantalize you by presenting before you what was never intended for you? Ah! no; such is not God's way. Does He send His sunlight and showers to mock and to tantalize, or to gladden and refresh? Do you ever think of calling in question your own very personal welcome to study the book of Creation? Never; and yet there might be some show of foundation of such a question, inasmuch as, since that wondrous volume was thrown open, sin has entered and thrown its dark blots over the pages thereof.

But, spite of sin and all its forms and all its consequences, spite of Satan's power and malice, God has spoken. He has caused His voice to be heard in this dark and sinful world. And what has He said? "Behold, I lay in Zion a foundation." This is something entirely new. It is as though our blessed, loving, and ever gracious God had said to us, "Here, I have begun on the new. I have laid a foundation, on the ground of redemption, which nothing can ever touch, neither sin, or Satan, or aught else. I *lay* the foundation, and pledge My word that whosoever believes—whosoever commits himself, in childlike, unquestioning confidence, to My foundation—whosoever rests in My Christ—whosoever is satisfied with My precious, tried, chief corner stone, shall never—no, never—no, never be confounded—never be put to shame—never be disappointed—shall never perish, world without end."

Beloved reader, dost thou still hesitate? We solemnly avow we cannot see even the shadow of a foundation of a reason why thou shouldest. If there were any question raised, or any condition proposed, or any barrier erected, reason would that thou mightest hesitate. If there were so much as a single preliminary to be settled by thee—if it were made a question of feeling or of experience, or of aught else that thou couldst do, or feel, or be, then verily thou mightest justly pause. But there is absolutely nothing of the sort. There is the Christ of God and the Word of God, and—what then? "He that believeth shall not be confounded."

In short, it is simply "A living faith in the living God." It is taking God at His word. It is believing what He says because He says it. It is committing your soul to the word of Him who cannot lie. It is doing what Abraham did when he believed God and was counted righteous. It is doing what Jehoshaphat did when he planted his foot firmly on those immortal words, "Thou gavest it to the seed of Abraham Thy friend, forever." It is doing what the patriarchs, the prophets, the apostles, the saints in all ages have done, when they rested their souls for time and eternity upon that Word which "is settled forever in heaven," and thus lived in peace and died in hope of a glorious resurrection. It is resting calmly and sweetly on the immovable rock of holy Scripture, and thus proving the divine and sustaining virtue of that which has never failed any who trusted it, and never will, and never can.

Oh! the unspeakable blessedness of having such a foundation in a world like this where death, decay, and change are stamped upon all; where friendship's fondest links are snapped in the twinkling of an eye by death's rude hand; where all that seems, to nature's view, most stable, is liable to be swept away in a moment by the rushing tide of popular revolution; where there is absolutely nothing on which the heart can lean, and say, "I have now found permanent repose." What a mercy, in such a scene, to have "A living faith in the living God."

"They shall not be ashamed that wait for Me." Such is the veritable record of the living God—a record made good in the experience of all those who have been enabled, through grace, to exercise a living faith. But then we must remember how much is involved in those three words, *"wait for Me."* The waiting must be a real thing. It will not do to *say* we are waiting on God, when, in reality, our eye is askance upon some human prop or creature confidence. We must be absolutely "shut up" to God. We must be brought to the end of self, and to the bottom of circumstances, in order fully to prove what the life of faith is, and what God's resources are. God and the creature can never occupy the same platform. It must be God alone. "My soul, wait thou *only* upon God; for my expectation is from Him. He *only* is my rock and my salvation" (Psa. 62:5-6).

Thus it was with Jehoshaphat, in that scene recorded in 2 Chron. 20. He was wholly cast upon God. It was either God or nothing. "We have no might." But what then? "Our eyes are upon Thee." This was enough. It was well for Jehoshaphat not to have so much as a single atom of might—a single ray of knowledge. He was in the very best possible attitude and condition to prove what God was. It would have been an incalculable loss to him to have been possessed of the very smallest particle of creature strength or creature wisdom, inasmuch as it could only have proved a hindrance to him in leaning exclusively upon the arm and the counsel of the Almighty God. If the eye of faith rests upon the living God—if He fills the entire range of the soul's vision, then what do we want with might or knowledge of our own? Who would think of resting in that which is human when he can have that which is divine? Who would lean on an arm of flesh, when he can lean on the arm of the living God?

Art thou, at this moment in any pressure, in any trial, need, or difficulty? If so, let us entreat thee to look simply and solely to the living God. Turn away thine eyes completely from the creature: "Cease from man, whose breath is in his nostrils." Let thy faith take hold now on the strength of God Himself. Put thy whole case into His omnipotent hand. Cast thy burden, whatever it is, upon Him. Let there be no reserve. He is as willing as He is able, and as able as He is willing, to bear all. Only trust Him fully. He loves to be trusted—loves to be used. It is His joy, blessed be His name, to yield a ready and a full response to the appeal of faith. It is worth having a burden, to know the blessedness of rolling it over upon Him. So the king of Judah found it in the day of his trial, and so shall the reader find it now. God never fails a trusting heart. "They shall not be ashamed that wait for Me." Precious words! Let us mark how they are illustrated in the narrative before us.

No sooner had Jehoshaphat cast himself completely upon the Lord, than the divine response fell, with clearness and power, upon his ear. "Harken ye, all Judah, and ye inhabitants of Jerusalem, and thou king Jehoshaphat; thus saith the Lord unto you, Be not afraid or dismayed by reason of this great multitude; for the battle is not yours, but God's...ye shall not need to fight in this battle. Set yourselves, stand ye still, and see the salvation of the Lord with you, O Judah and Jerusalem: fear not, nor be dismayed; to-morrow go out against them; for the Lord will be with you."

What an answer! "The battle is not yours, but God's." Only think of God's having a battle with people! Assuredly there could be little question as to the issue of such a battle. Jehoshaphat had put the whole matter into God's hands, and God took it up and made it entirely His own. It is always thus. Faith puts the difficulty, the trial, and the burden into God's hands, and leaves Him to act. This is enough. God never refuses to respond to the appeal of faith; nay, it is His delight to answer it. Jehoshaphat had made it a question between God and the enemy. He had said, "They have come to cast us out of *Thy* possession, which Thou hast given us to inherit."

Nothing could be simpler. God had given Israel the land, and He could keep them in it, spite of ten thousand foes. Thus faith would reason. The self-same Hand that had placed them in the land could keep them there. It was simply a question of divine power. "O our God, wilt Thou not judge them? for we have no might against this great company that cometh against us; neither know we what to do; but our eyes are upon Thee."

It is a wonderful point in the history of any soul, to be brought to say, "I have no might." It is the sure precursor of divine deliverance. The moment a man is brought to the discovery of his utter powerlessness, the divine word is, "Stand still, and see the salvation of God." One does not want "might" to "stand still." It needs no effort to "see the salvation of God." This holds good in reference to the sinner in coming to Christ, at the first; and it holds equally good in reference to the Christian in his whole career from first to last. The great difficulty is to get to the end of our own strength. Once there, the whole thing is settled.

There may be a vast amount of struggle and exercise ere we are brought to say "without strength!" But, the moment we take that ground, the word is, "Stand still, and see the salvation of God." Human effort, in every shape and form, can but raise a barrier between our souls and God's salvation. If God has undertaken for us, we may well be still. And has He not? Yes, blessed be His holy name, He has charged Himself with all that concerns us, for time and eternity; and hence we have only to let Him act for us, in all things. It is our happy privilege to let Him go before us, while we follow on "in wonder, love, and praise."

Thus it was in that interesting and instructive scene on which we have been dwelling. "Jehoshaphat bowed his head, with his face to the ground: and all Judah and the inhabitants of Jerusalem fell before the Lord, worshiping the Lord. And the Levites, of the children of the Kohathites, and of the children of the Korhites, stood up to praise the Lord God of Israel with a loud voice on high."

Here we have the true attitude and the proper occupation of the believer. Jehosha-phat withdrew his eyes from "that great company that had come against him," and fixed them upon the living God. Jehovah had come right in and placed Himself between His people and the enemy, just as He had done in the day of the exodus, at the Red Sea, so that instead of looking at the difficulties, they might look at Him.

This is the secret of victory at all times, and under all circumstances. This it is which fills the heart with praise and thanksgiving, and bows the head in wondering worship. There is something perfectly beautiful in the entire bearing of Jehoshaphat and the congregation, on the occasion before us. They were evidently impressed with the thought that they had nothing to do but to praise God. And they were right. Had He not said to them, "Ye shall not need to fight"? What then had they to do? What remained for them? Nothing but praise. Jehovah was going out before them to fight; and they had but to follow after Him in adoring worship.

"And they rose early in the morning, and went forth in the wilderness of Tekoa: and as they went forth, Jehoshaphat stood and said, Hear me, O Judah, and ye inhabitants of Jerusalem; believe in the Lord your God, so shall ye be established; believe His prophets, so shall ye prosper" (2 Chron. 20:20).

It is of the very last importance that God's Word should ever have its own supreme place in the heart of the Christian. God has spoken. He has given us His Word; and it is for us to lean unshaken thereon. We want nothing more. The divine Word is amply sufficient to give confidence, peace, and stability to the soul. We do not need evidences from man to prove the truth of God's Word. That Word carries its own powerful evidences with it. To suppose that we require human testimony to prove that God's Word is true, is to imply that man's word is more valid, more trustworthy, more authoritative, than the Word of God. If we need a human voice to interpret, to ratify, to make God's revelation available, then we are virtually deprived of that revelation altogether.

We call the special attention of the reader to this point. It concerns the integrity of Holy Scripture. The grand question is this, Is God's Word sufficient or not? Do we really want man's authority to make us sure that God has spoken? Far be the thought! This would be placing man's word above God's Word, and thus depriving us of the *only* solid ground on which our souls can lean.

This is precisely what the devil has been aiming at from the very beginning, and it is what he is aiming at now. He wants to remove from beneath our feet the solid rock of divine revelation, and to give us instead the sandy foundation of human authority. Hence it is that we do so earnestly press upon our readers the urgent need of keeping close to God's Word, in simple unquestioning faith. It is really the true secret of stability and peace. If God's Word be not enough for us, without man's interference, we are positively left without any sure basis of our soul's confidence; yea, we are cast adrift on the wild watery waste of skepticism, we are plunged in doubt and dark uncertainty: we are most miserable.

But, thanks and praise be to God, it is not so. "*Believe in the Lord your God, so shall ye be established: believe His prophets, so shall ye prosper.*" Here is the resting-place of faith in all ages. God's eternal Word, which is settled for ever in Heaven, which He has magnified according to all His name, and which stands forth in its own divine dignity and sufficiency before the eye of faith. We must utterly reject the idea that aught in the way of human authority, human evidences, or human feelings, is needful to make the testimony of God full weight in the balances of the soul.

Grant us but this, that God has spoken, and we argue with bold decision that nothing more is needed as a foundation for genuine faith. In a word, if we want to be established and to prosper, we have simply to "Believe in the Lord our God." It was this that enabled Jehoshaphat to bow his head in holy worship. It was this that enabled him to praise God for victory ere a single blow was struck. It was this that conducted him into "the valley of Berachah" (*blessing*) and surrounded him with spoil more than he could carry away.

And now we have the soul-stirring record: "And when he had consulted with the people, he appointed *singers unto the Lord*, and that should praise the beauty of holiness, as they went out before the army, and to say, Praise the Lord: for His mercy endureth forever." What a strange advance guard for an army! A company of singers! Such is faith's way of ordering the battle.

"And when they began to sing and to praise, the Lord set ambushments against the children of Ammon, Moab, and Mount Seir, which were come against Judah, and they were smitten." Only think of the Lord setting ambushments! Think of His engaging in the business of military tactics! How wonderful! God will do any thing that His people need, if only His people will confide in Him, and leave themselves and their affairs absolutely in His hand.

"And when Judah came toward the watch-tower in the wilderness, they looked unto the multitude, and, behold, they were dead bodies fallen to the earth, and none escaped." Such was the end of "that great company"—that formidable host—that terrible foe. All vanished away before the presence of the God of Israel. Yes, and had they been a million times more numerous, and more formidable, the issue would have been the same, for circumstances are nothing to the living God, and nothing to a living faith. When God fills the vision of the soul,

difficulties fade away, and songs of praise break forth from joyful lips.

"And when Jehoshaphat and his people came to take away the spoil of them" (for that was all they had to do) "they found among them in abundance both riches with the dead bodies, and precious jewels, which they stripped off for themselves, more than they could carry away; and they were three days in gathering of the spoil, it was so much. And on the fourth day, they assembled themselves in the valley of Berachah; for there they blessed the Lord."

Such must ever be the result of a living faith in the living God. More than two thousand five hundred years have rolled away since the occurrence of the event on which we have been dwelling; but the record is as fresh as ever. No change has come over the living God, or over the living faith which ever takes hold of His strength, and counts on His faithfulness. It is as true to-day as it was in the day of Jehoshaphat, that those who believe in the Lord our God shall be established, and shall prosper. They shall be endowed with strength, crowned with victory, clothed with spoils, and filled with songs of praise. May we, then, through the gracious energy of the Holy Spirit, ever be enabled to exercise "*a living faith in the living God!*"

A RISEN SAVIOUR'S CHALLENGE

Luke 24

THE PERIOD during which our blessed Lord lay in the tomb must needs have proved a dark and bewildering moment to many of those who looked for redemption in Israel. It would demand a calm, clear and vigorous faith to raise the heart above the heavy clouds which gathered just then upon the horizon of God's people, and it does not appear that many possessed such a faith at that trying moment.

We may doubtless look upon the two disciples who travelled together to Emmaus as illustrating the condition of many, if not all, the beloved saints of God during the three days and three nights that our beloved Lord lay in the heart of the earth. They were thoroughly bewildered and at their wits' end. "They talked together of all these things which had happened. And it came to pass that, while they communed together and reasoned, Jesus Himself drew near, and went with them. But their eyes were holden that they should not know Him."

Their minds were full of surrounding circumstances. All hope seemed gone. Their fondly cherished expectations were blasted, apparently. The whole scene was overcast by the dark shadow of death, and their poor hearts were sad.

But mark how the risen Saviour's challenge falls upon their drooping spirits! "And He said unto them, What manner of communications are these that ye have one to another, as ye walk, and are sad?"

Surely this was a reasonable and weighty question for those dear disciples—a question eminently calculated to recall them, as we say, to their senses. It was precisely what they wanted at the moment, occupied as they were with circumstances instead of resting in the eternal and immutable truth of God. Scripture was clear and plain enough had they only hearkened to its voice. But instead of listening only to the distinct testimony of the eternal Spirit in the Word they had allowed their minds to get thoroughly down under the action and influences of outward circumstances. Instead of standing with firm foot on the everlasting rock of divine revelation, they were struggling amid the billows of life's stormy ocean. In a word, they had for a moment fallen under the power of death so far as their minds were concerned, and no marvel if their hearts were sad and their communications gloomy.

And does it not sometimes happen that you and I in like manner get down under the power of things seen and temporal, instead of living by faith in the light of things unseen and eternal? Yes, even we who profess to know and believe in a risen Saviour—who believe that we are dead and risen with Him—who have the Holy Ghost dwelling in us, do not we at times sink and cower? And do we not at such moments stand in need of a risen Saviour's challenge? Has not that precious, loving Saviour oftimes occasion to put the question to our hearts, "What manner of communications are these that ye have one to another?"

Does it not often happen that when we come together or when we walk by the way our "communications" are anything but what they ought to be? It may be gloomily moping together over the depressing circumstances which surround us—the weather—the prospects of the country—the state of trade—our poor health—the difficulty of making both ends meet—anything and everything, in short, but the right thing.

Yes, and so occupied do we become with such things that our spiritual eyes are holden, and we do not take knowledge of the blessed One who in His tender faithful love is at our side, and He has to challenge our vagrant hearts with His pointed and powerful question, "What manner of communications are these that ye have?"

Let us think of this. It really demands our consideration. We are all far too apt to allow our minds to fall under the power and pressure of circumstances, instead of living in the power of faith. We get occupied with our surroundings instead of dwelling upon "things above"—those bright and blessed realities which are ours in Christ.

And what is the result? Do we better our circumstances, or brighten our prospects by gloomily moping over them? Not in the smallest degree. What then? We simply make ourselves miserable and our communications depressing; and, worst of all, we bring dishonor on the cause of Christ.

Christians forget how much is involved in their temper, manner, look, and deportment in daily life. We forget that the Lord's glory is intimately bound up with our daily deportments. We all know that, in social life, we judge of the character of the head of a household by what we see of his children and servants. If we observed the children looking miserable and downcast, we should be disposed to pronounce their father morose, severe and arbitrary. If we see the servants crushed and overwrought, we consider the master hard-hearted and grinding. In short, as a rule, you can form a tolerably fair estimate of the head of a house by the tone, spirit, style and manner of the members of his household.

How earnestly, then, should we seek, as members of the household of *God*, to give a right impression of what He is by our temper, spirit, style, and manner! If men of the world—those with whom we come in contact from day to day in the practical details of life—if they see us looking sour, morose, downcast—if they hear us giving utterance to doleful complaints about this, that and the other—if they see us occupied about our own things—grasping, griping, and driving as hard bargains as others—if they see us grinding our servants with heavy work, low wages, and poor fare—what estimate can they form of Him whom we call our Father and our Master in Heaven?

Let us not despise and turn away from such homely words. Depend upon it there is need of such in this day of much profession. There is a vast amount of intellectual traffic in truth which leaves the conscience unreached, the heart untouched, the life unaffected. We know we are dead and risen; but when anything occurs to touch *us*, either in our persons, in our relations, or in our interests, we speedily shew how little power that precious truth has upon us.

May the Lord give us grace to apply our hearts very seriously and earnestly to these things, so that there may be, in our daily course, a more faithful exhibition of a genuine Christianity—such an exhibition as shall glorify our own most gracious God and Father, and our Lord and Saviour Jesus Christ—and such, too, as shall afford to those who come in contact with us a fair specimen of what pure religion really is in its action upon the entire course and character.

May we all realize more a risen Saviour's presence, and find therein a triumphant answer to all the dark suggestions of the enemy, the depressing reasonings of our own hearts, and the deadening influence of surrounding circumstances. God, in His infinite mercy, grant it, for Jesus' sake.

It is impossible to read this charming section of inspiration (Luke 24) and not be struck with what we may venture to call the rallying power of a risen Saviour's voice and presence. We see the dear disciples scattered hither and thither in doubt and perplexity, fear and despondency—some running to the sepulchre; some coming from it; some going to Emmaus, and some crowded together at Jerusalem, in various states and conditions.

But the voice and realized presence of Jesus rallied, reassured, and encouraged them all, and brought all together around His own blessed Person in worship, love, and praise. There was an indescribable power in His presence to meet every condition of heart and mind. Thus it was; thus it is; thus it ever must be, blessed and praised be His precious name! There is power in the presence of a risen Saviour to solve our difficulties, remove our perplexities, calm our fears, ease our burdens, dry our tears, meet our every need, tranquilize our minds and satisfy every craving of our hearts.

> Jesus! Thou art enough,
>   The mind and heart to fill;
> They life—to calm the anxious soul,
>   Thy love—its fear dispel.

The two disciples going to Emmaus proved something of this, if we are to judge from their own glowing words to one another. "Did not our heart burn within us, while He talked with us by the way, and while He opened to us the Scriptures?" Yes, here lay the deep and precious secret: *"He* talked with us"—and *"He* opened to us the Scriptures"! What seraphic moments! what high communion! what loving ministry! A risen Saviour rallying their hearts by His marvelous words and mighty exposition of the Scriptures.

What was the effect—what the necessary result? The two travellers instantly returned to Jerusalem to seek their brethren. It could not be otherwise. If we lose sight of a risen Saviour we are sure to get away from our brethren, sure to get occupied with our own things; to pursue our own way—to get into coldness, deadness, darkness, and selfishness. But, on the other hand, the moment we get really into the presence of Christ, when we hear His voice and feel the sweetness and power of His love, when our hearts are brought under the mighty moral influence of His most precious loving ministry, then we are led out in true affection and interest after all our brethren and in earnest desire to find our place in their midst in order that we may communicate to them the deep joy that is filling our own souls.

We may lay it down as a fixed principle—a spiritual axiom—that it is utterly impossible to breathe the atmosphere of a risen Saviour's presence and remain in an isolated, independent, or fragmentary condition. The necessary effect of His dear presence is to melt the heart and cause it to flow out in streams of tender affection toward all that belong to Him.

But let us pursue our chapter.

"And they rose up the same hour" of the night—thus proving they had but little

business at Emmaus, or how paramount was the blessed object now before them, "and returned to Jerusalem, and found the eleven gathered together, and them that were with them, saying, The Lord is risen indeed, and hath appeared to Simon. And they told what things were done in the way, and how He was known of them in breaking of bread. And as they thus spake, Jesus Himself stood in the midst of them, and saith unto them, Peace be unto you. But they were terrified and affrighted, and supposed that they had seen a spirit."

They, too, needed a risen Saviour's challenge to bring them to their senses—to calm their fears and raise their drooping spirits. They needed to realize the power of His presence as the risen One. They had just declared to their two brethren from Emmaus that "The Lord is risen indeed"; but yet when their risen Lord appeared to them they did not know Him, and He had to challenge their hearts with His stirring words, "Why are ye troubled? and why do thoughts arise in your hearts? Behold My hands and My feet, that it is I Myself: handle Me, and see; for a spirit hath not flesh and bones, as ye see Me have. And when He had thus spoken, He shewed them His hands and His feet. And while they yet believed not for joy, and wondered, He said unto them, Have ye here any meat? And they gave Him a piece of a broiled fish, and of an honeycomb. And He took it, and did eat before them."

What tender love! What gracious condescension to their weakness and need! What compassionate entrance into all their feelings, spite of their folly and unbelief! Gracious Saviour! Who would not love Thee? Who would not trust Thee? May the whole heart be absorbed with Thee! May the whole life be cordially devoted to Thy blessed service! May Thy cause command all our energies! May all we have and all we love be laid on Thine altar as a reasonable service! May the eternal Spirit work in us for the accomplishment of these grand and longed for objects!

But ere closing this brief article there is one point of special interest and value to which we must call attention, and that is, the way in which the risen Saviour puts honor upon the written Word. He rebuked the two travellers for their slowness of heart to believe the Scriptures. "And beginning at Moses and all the prophets, He expounded unto them in all the Scriptures the things concerning Himself."

So also in His interview with the eleven and the rest at Jerusalem. No sooner had He satisfied them as to His identity than He sought to conduct their souls to the same divine authority—the Holy Scriptures. "And He said unto them, These are the words which I spake unto you, while I was yet with you, that all things must be fulfilled, *which were written* in the law of Moses, and in the Prophets, and in the Psalms, concerning Me. Then opened He their understanding, that they might understand *the Scriptures*, and said unto them, *Thus it is written*, and thus it behoved Christ to suffer, and to rise from the dead the third day: and that repentance and remission of sins should be preached in His name among all nations, beginning at Jerusalem."

All this is of the deepest possible importance at the present moment. We feel persuaded that professing Christians everywhere need to have their hearts stirred up in reference to the paramount claims of the Word of God, its absolute authority over the conscience, its formative power, its complete sway over the entire course, character and conduct.

It is to be feared, greatly feared, that Holy Scripture is fast losing its divine place in the hearts of those who profess to take it as the divine rule of faith and morals. We have often heard that watchword sounded in our ears, "The Bible, and the Bible alone, is the religion of Protestants." Alas! if this motto were ever really true we fear that its truth at this moment is more than questionable.

Very few, comparatively, even of those who occupy the very highest platform of profession seem to admit, and still fewer actually acknowledge practically, that *in all things*—whether of faith or morals—in all the practical details of life, in the Church, in the family, in the business, and in our private walk from day to day—we are to be governed absolutely by that commanding, that mighty, that morally glorious sentence, "It is written"—a sentence enhanced exceedingly in value and heightened in its moral glory by the telling fact that it was used thrice by our adorable Lord at the opening of His public career, in His conflict with the adversary, and sounded in the ears of His loved ones just as He was about to ascend into the heavens.

Yes, "It is written" was a favorite sentence with our divine Master and Lord. He ever obeyed the Word. He yielded a hearty and unqualifed submission to its holy authority in all things. He lived on it and by it from first to last. He walked according to it and never acted without it. He did not reason or question, imply or infer, He did not add or diminish, or qualify in any one way—*He obeyed*. Yes; He, the eternal Son of the Father—Himself God over all blessed for ever—having become a man, lived on the Holy Scriptures and walked by their rule continually. He made them the food of His soul, the material and the basis of His marvelous ministry—the divine authority of His perfect path.

In all this He was our great Exemplar. Oh, may we follow His blessed footsteps! May we bring ourselves, our ways, our habits, our associations, our surroundings, to the test of Holy Scripture, and reject with wholehearted decision everything, no matter what or by whom propounded, that will not bear that searching light.

We are most thoroughly persuaded that in hundreds of thousands of cases the first grand point to be gained is to recall the heart to that delightful attitude in which the Word of God is *fully* owned and submitted to as an absolute authority. It is positively labor lost to be arguing and disputing with a man who does not give Scripture the self-same place that our Lord Jesus Christ gave it. And when a man does this there is no need of argument. What is really needed is to make the Word of God the basis of our individual peace and authority of our individual path. May we all do so!

The Person of
Christ

THE ALL-SUFFICIENCY OF CHRIST

Part 1

WHEN ONCE THE SOUL has been brought to feel the reality of its condition before God—the depth of its ruin, guilt, and misery—its utter and hopeless backruptcy, there can be no rest until the Holy Spirit reveals a full and an all-sufficient Christ to the heart. The only possible answer to our total ruin is God's perfect remedy.

This is a very simple, but a most important truth; and we may say, with all possible assurance, the more deeply and thoroughly the reader learns it for himself the better. The true secret of peace is, to get to the very end of a guilty, ruined, helpless, worthless self, and there find an all-sufficient Christ as God's provision for our very deepest need. This truly is rest—a rest which can never be disturbed. There may be sorrow, pressure, conflict, exercise of soul, heaviness through manifold temptations, ups and downs, all sorts of trials and difficulties; but we feel persuaded that when a soul is really brought by God's Spirit to see the end of self, and to rest in a full Christ, it finds a peace which can never be interrupted.

The unsettled state of so many of God's dear people is the result of not having received into their hearts a full Christ, as God's own very provision for them. No doubt this sad and painful result may be brought about by various contributing causes, such as a legal mind, a morbid conscience, a self-occupied heart, bad teaching, a secret hankering after this present world, some little reserve in the heart as to the claims of God, of Christ, and of eternity. But whatever may be the producing cause, we believe it will be found, in almost every case, that the lack of settled peace, so common amongst the Lord's people, is the result of not seeing, not believing, what God has made His Christ to be to them and for them, and that forever.

Now, what we propose in this paper, is to show the anxious reader, from the precious pages of the Word of God, that there is treasured up for him in Christ all he can possibly need, whether it be to meet the claims of his conscience, the cravings of his heart, or the exigencies of his path. We shall seek, by the grace of God, to prove that the *work* of Christ is the only true resting-place for the *conscience;* His *Person*, the only true object for the *heart;* His *Word*, the only true guide for the *path*.

And first, then, let us dwell for a little upon *the work of Christ as the only resting-place for the conscience.*

In considering this great subject, two things claim our attention: first, what Christ has done for us; secondly, what He is doing for us. In the former, we have atonement; in the latter, advocacy. He died for us on the cross: He lives for us on the throne. By His precious atoning death He has met our entire condition as sinners. He has borne our sins, and put them away forever. He stood charged with all our sins—the sins of all who believe in His name. "Jehovah laid on Him the iniquity of us all" (Isa. 53). And again, "For Christ also hath once suffered for sins, the just for the unjust, that He might bring us to God" (1 Pet. 3:18).

This is a grand and all-important truth for the anxious soul—a truth which lies at the very foundation of the whole Christian position. It is impossible that any truly awakened soul, any spiritually enlightened conscience, can enjoy divinely settled peace until this most precious truth is laid hold of in simple faith. I must know, upon divine authority, that all my sins are put away forever out of God's sight; that He Himself has disposed of them in such a manner as to satisfy all the claims of His throne and all the attributes of His nature; that He has glorified Himself in the putting away of my sins, in a far higher and more wonderful manner than if He had sent me to an everlasting hell on account of them.

Yes, He Himself has done it. This is the very gist and marrow—the heart's core of the whole matter. God has laid our sins on Jesus, and He tells us so in His holy Word, so that we may know it upon divine authority—an authority that cannot lie. God planned it; God did it; God says it. It is all of God, from first to last, and we have simply to rest in it like a child. How do I know that Jesus bore my sins in His own body on the tree? By the very same authority which tells me I had sins to be borne. God, in His marvelous and matchless love, assures me, a poor guilty, hell-deserving sinner, that He has Himself undertaken the whole matter of my sins, and disposed of it in such a manner as to bring a rich harvest of glory to His own eternal name, throughout the wide universe, in presence of all created intelligence.

The living faith of this must tranquilize the conscience. If God has satified Himself about my sins, I may well be satisfied also. I know I am a sinner—it may be, the chief of sinners. I know my sins are more in number than the hairs of my head; that they are black as midnight—black as hell itself. I know that any one of these sins, the very least, deserves the eternal flames of hell. I know—because God's Word tells me—that a single speck of sin can never enter His holy presence; and hence, so far as I am concerned, there was no possible issue save eternal separation from God. All this I know, upon the clear and unquestionable authority of that Word which is settled forever in Heaven.

But, oh, the profound mystery of the cross!—the glorious mystery of redeeming love! I see God Himself taking all my sins—the black and terrible category—all my sins, as He knew and estimated them. I see Him laying them all upon the head of my blessed Substitute, and dealing with Him about them. I see all the billows and waves of God's righteous wrath—His wrath against my sins—His wrath which should have consumed me, soul and body, in hell, throughout a dreary eternity; I see them rolling over the Man who stood in my stead, who represented me before God, who bore all that was due to me, with whom a holy God dealt as He should have dealt with me. I see inflexible justice, holiness, truth, and righteousness dealing with my sins, and making a clear and eternal riddance of them. No one of them is suffered to pass! There is no connivance, no palliation, no slurring over, no indifference. This could not possibly be, once God Himself took the matter in hand. His glory was at stake; His unsullied holiness, His eternal majesty, the lofty claims of His government.

All these had to be provided for in such wise as to glorify Himself in view of angels, men, and devils. He might have sent me to hell—righteously, justly, sent me to hell—because of my sins. I deserved nothing else. My whole moral being, from its profoundest depths, owns this—must own it. I have not a word to say in excuse for a single sinful thought, to say nothing of a sin-stained life from first to last—yes, a life of deliberate, rebellious, high-handed sin.

Others may reason as they please as to the injustice of an eternity of punishment for a life of sin—the utter want of proportion between a few years of wrong-doing and endless ages of torment in the lake of fire. They may reason, but I thoroughly believe, and unreservedly confess, that for a single sin against such a Being as the God whom I see at the cross, I richly deserved everlasting punishment in the deep, dark, and dismal pit of hell.

I am not writing as a theologian; if I were, it would be a very easy task indeed to bring an unanswerable array of Scripture evidence in proof of the solemn truth of eternal punishment. But no; I am writing as one who has been divinely taught the true desert of sin, and that desert, I calmly, deliberately, and solemnly declare, is, and can be, nothing less than eternal exclusion from the presence of God and the Lamb—eternal torment in the lake that burneth with fire and brimstone.

But—eternal halleluiahs to the God of all grace!—instead of sending us to hell because of our sins, He sent His Son to be the propitiation for those sins. And in the unfolding of the marvelous plan of redemption, we see a holy God dealing with the question of our sins, and executing judgment upon them in the Person of His well-beloved, eternal, and coequal Son, in order that the full flood-tide of His love might flow down into our hearts. "Herein is love, not that we loved God, but that He loved us, and sent His Son to be the propitiation for our sins" (1 John 4:10).

Now, this must give peace to the conscience, if only it be received in the simplicity of faith. How is it possible for a person to believe that God has satisfied Himself as to his sins and not have peace? If God says to us, "Your sins and iniquities I will remember no more," what could we desire further as a basis of peace for our conscience? If God assures me that all my sins are blotted out as a thick cloud—that they are cast behind His back—forever gone from His sight, should I not have peace? If He shows me the Man who bore my sins on the cross, now crowned at the right hand of the Majesty in the heavens, ought not my soul to enter into perfect rest as to the question of my sins? Most assuredly.

For how, let me ask, did Christ reach the place which He now fills on the throne of God? Was it as God over all, blessed forever? No; for He was always that. Was it as the eternal Son of the Father? No; He was ever that—ever in the bosom of the Father—the object of the Father's eternal and ineffable delight. Was it as a spotless, holy, perfect Man—One whose nature was absolutely pure, perfectly free from sin? No; for in that character, and on that ground, He could at any moment, between the manger and the cross, have claimed a place at the right hand of God. How was it, then? Eternal praise to the God of all grace! it was as the One who had by His death accomplished the glorious work of redemption—the One who had stood charged with the full weight of our sins—the One who had perfectly satisfied all the righteous claims of that throne on which He now sits.

This is a grand, cardinal point for the anxious reader to seize. It cannot fail to emancipate the heart and tranquilize the conscience. We cannot possibly behold, by faith, the Man who was nailed to the tree, now crowned on the throne, and not have peace with God. The Lord Jesus Christ having taken upon Himself our sins, and the judgment due to them, He could not be where He now is if a single one of those sins remained unatoned for. To see the Sin-bearer crowned with glory is to see our sins gone forever from the divine presence. Where are our sins? They are all obliterated. How do we know this? The One who took them all upon Himself has passed through the heavens to the very highest pinnacle of glory. Eternal justice has wreathed His blessed brow with a diadem of glory, as the Accomplisher of our redemption—the Bearer of our sins; thus proving, beyond all question, or possibility of a question, that our sins are all put away out of God's sight forever. A crowned Christ and a clear conscience are, in the blessed economy of grace, inseparably linked together. Wondrous fact! Well may we chant, with all our ransomed powers, the praises of redeeming love.

But let us see how this most consolatory truth is set forth in holy Scripture. In Romans 3, we read, "But now the righteousness of God with law [χωρὶς νόμου] is manifested, being witnessed by the law and the prophets; even the righteousness of God by faith of Jesus Christ unto all and upon all them that believe; for there is no difference: for all have sinned, and come short of the glory of God; being justified freely by His grace through the redemption that is in Christ Jesus: *whom God hath set forth a* propitiation through faith in His blood, to declare His righteousness for the remission [or passing over] of sins that are past [in time gone by], through the forbearance of God; to declare at this time His righteousness; that He might be just and the justifier of him which believeth in Jesus."

Again, in chapter 4, speaking of Abraham's faith being counted to him for righteousness, the apostle adds, "Now it was not written for his sake alone, that it was imputed to him; but for us also, to whom it shall be imputed, if we *believe on Him that raised up Jesus our Lord from the dead; who was delivered for our offenses, and raised again for our justification."* Here we have God introduced to our souls as the One who raised from the dead the Bearer of our sins. Why did He do so? Because the One who had been delivered for our offenses had perfectly glorified Him respecting those offenses, and put them away forever. God not only sent His only begotten Son into the world, but He bruised Him for our iniquities, and raised Him from the dead, in order that we might know and believe that our iniquities are all disposed of in such a manner as to glorify Him infinitely and everlastingly. Eternal and universal homage to His name!

But we have further testimony on this grand fundamental truth. In Hebrews 1 we read such soul-stirring words as these: "God, who at sundry times and in divers manners [or in divers measures and modes] spake in time past unto the fathers by the prophets, hath in these last days spoken unto us by [His] Son, whom He hath appointed heir of all things, by whom also He made the worlds; who being the brightness of His glory, and the express image of His Person, and upholding all things by the word of His power, *when He had by Himself purged our sins*, sat down on the right hand of the Majesty on high." Our Lord Christ, blessed be His name! would not take His seat on the throne of God until He had, by the offering of Himself on the cross, purged our sins. Hence, a risen Christ at God's right hand is the glorious and unanswerable proof that our sins are all gone, for He could not be where He now is if a single one of those sins remained. God raised from the dead the self-same Man on whom He Himself had laid the full weight of our sins. Thus all is settled—divinely, eternally settled. It is as impossible that a single sin can be found on the very weakest believer in Jesus as on Jesus Himself. This is a wonderful thing to be able to say, but it is the solid truth of God, established in manifold places in holy Scripture, and the soul that believes it must possess a peace which the world can neither give nor take away.

Part 2

Thus far, we have been occupied with that aspect of the work of Christ which bears upon the question of the forgiveness of sins, and we earnestly trust that the reader is thoroughly clear and settled on this grand point. It is assuredly his happy privilege so to be, if only he will take God at His word. "Christ hath once suffered for sins, the just for the unjust, that He might bring us to God."

If, then, Christ hath suffered for our sins, should we not know the deep blessedness of being eternally delivered from the burden of those sins? Can it be according to the mind and heart of God that one for whom Christ suffered should remain in perpetual bondage, tied and bound with the chain of his sins, and crying out, from week to week, month to month, and year to year, that the burden of his sins is intolerable?

If such utterances are true and proper for the Christian, then what has Christ done for us? Can it be true that Christ has put away our sins and yet that we are tied and bound with the chain of them? Is it true that He bore the heavy burden of our sins and yet that we are still crushed beneath the intolerable weight thereof?

Some would fain persuade us that it is not possible to know that our sins are forgiven—that we must go on to the end of our life in a state of complete uncertainty on this most vital and important question. If this be so, what has become of the precious gospel of the grace of God—the glad tidings of salvation? In the view of such miserable teaching as this, what mean those glowing words of the blessed apostle Paul in the synagogue of Antioch?—"Be it known unto you therefore, men and brethren, that through this Man [Jesus Christ, dead and risen] is preached [not promised as a future thing, but proclaimed now] the forgiveness of sins; and by Him all who believe *are* [not shall be, or hope to be] justified from *all things*, from which ye could not be justified by the law of Moses" (Acts 13:38-39).

If we were resting on the law of Moses, on our keeping the commandments, on our doing our duty, on our feeling as we ought, on our valuing Christ and loving God as we ought, reason would that we should be in doubt and dark uncertainty, seeing we could have no possible ground of assurance. If we had so much as the movement of an eyelash to do in the matter, then, verily, it would be the very height of presumption on our part to think of being certain.

But on the other hand, when we hear the voice of the living God, who cannot lie, proclaiming in our ears the glad tidings that through His own beloved Son, who died on the cross, was buried in the grave, raised from the dead, and seated in the glory—that through Him alone—through Him, without any thing whatever of ours—through His one offering of Himself once and forever, full and everlasting remission of sins is preached, as a present reality, to be enjoyed now by every soul who simply believes the precious record of God, how is it possible for any one to continue in doubt and uncertainty? Is Christ's work finished? He said it was. What did He do? He put away our sins. Are they, then, put away, or are they still on us?—which?

Reader, say which? where are thy sins? Are they blotted out as a thick cloud? or are they still lying as a heavy load of guilt, in condemning power, on thy conscience? If they were not put away by the atoning death of Christ, they will never be put away; if He did not bear them on the cross, you will have to bear them in the tormenting flames of hell forever and ever and ever. Yes; be assured of it, there is no other way of disposing of this most weighty and momentous question. If Christ did not settle the matter on the cross, you must settle it in hell. It must be so, if God's Word be true.

But glory be to God, His own testimony assures us that Christ hath once suffered for sins, the just for the unjust, that He might bring us to God; not merely bring us to Heaven when we die, but bring us to God *now*. How does He bring us to God? Tied and bound with the chain of our sins? with an intolerable burden of guilt on our souls? Nay, verily; He brings us to God without spot or stain or charge. He brings us to God in all His own acceptableness. Is there any guilt on

Him? No. There was, blessed be His name, when He stood in our stead, but it is gone—gone forever—cast as lead into the unfathomable waters of divine forgetfulness. He was charged with our sins on the cross. God laid on Him all our iniquities, and dealt with Him about them. The whole question of our sins, according to God's estimate thereof, was fully gone into and definitively, because divinely, settled between God and Christ, amid the awful shadows of Calvary. Yes, it was all done, once and forever, there. How do we know it? By the authority of the only true God. His Word assures us that *we have* redemption through the blood of Christ, the remission of sins, according to the riches of His grace. He declares to us, in accents of sweetest, richest, deepest mercy, that our sins and our iniquities He will remember no more. Is not this enough? Shall we still continue to cry out that we are tied and bound with the chain of our sins? Shall we thus cast a slur upon the perfect work of Christ? Shall we thus tarnish the lustre of divine grace, and give the lie to the testimony of the Holy Ghost in the Scripture of truth? Far be the thought! It must not be so. Let us rather hail with thanksgiving the blessed boon so freely conferred upon us by love divine, through the precious blood of Christ. It is the joy of the heart of God to forgive us our sins. Yes, God delights in pardoning iniquity and transgression. It gratifies and glorifies Him to pour into the broken and contrite heart the precious balm of His own pardoning love and mercy. He spared not His own Son, but delivered Him up, and bruised Him on the cursed tree, in order that He might be able, in perfect righteousness, to let the rich streams of grace flow forth from His large, loving heart, to the poor, guilty, self-destroyed, conscience-smitten sinner.

But should it be that the reader still feels disposed to inquire how he may have the assurance that this blessed remission of sins—this fruit of Christ's atoning work—applies to him, let him harken to those magnificent words which flowed from the lips of the risen Saviour as He commissioned the earliest heralds of His grace.—"And He said unto them, 'Thus it is written, and thus *it was necessary* for Christ to suffer, and to rise from the dead the third day; and that repentance and remission of sins should be preached in His name among all nations, beginning at Jerusalem' " (Luke 24:46-47).

Here we have the great and glorious commission—its basis, its authority, its sphere. Christ has suffered. This is the meritorious ground of remission of sins. Without shedding of blood there is no remission of sins; but by the shedding of blood, *and by it alone*, there is remission of sins—a remission as full and complete as the precious blood of Christ is fitted to effect.

But where is the authority? *"It is written."* Blessed, indisputable authority! Nothing can ever shake it. I know, on the solid authority of the Word of God, that my sins are all forgiven, all blotted out, all gone forever, all cast behind God's back, so that they can never, by any possibility, rise against me.

Finally, as to the sphere. It is, "all nations." This includes me, beyond all question. There is no sort of exception, condition, or qualification. The blessed tidings were to be wafted, on the wings of love, to all nations—to all the world—to every creature under heaven. How could I exclude myself from this world-wide commission? Do I question, for a moment, that the beams of God's sun are intended for me? Surely not. And why should I question the precious fact that remission of sins is for me? Not for a single instant. It is for me as surely as though I were the only sinner beneath the canopy of God's heaven. The universality of its aspect precludes all question as to its being designed for me.

And surely, if any further encouragement were needed, it is found in the fact that the blessed ambassadors were to "begin at Jerusalem"—the very guiltiest spot on the face of the earth. They were to make the earliest offer of pardon to the very murderers of the Son of God. This the apostle Peter does in those words of marvelous and transcendent grace, "Unto you first God, having raised up His Son, sent Him to bless you, by turning away every one of you from your iniquities" (Acts 3:26).

It is not possible to conceive any thing richer or fuller or more magnificent than this. The grace that could reach the murderers of the Son of God can reach any one: the blood that could cleanse the guilt of such a crime can cleanse the vilest sinner outside the precincts of hell.

Do you, can you, still hesitate as to the forgiveness of your sins? Christ has suffered for sins. God preaches remission of sins. He pledges His own Word on the point. "To Him give all the prophets witness, that through His name whosoever believeth in Him shall receive remission of sins." What more would you have? How can you any longer doubt or delay? What are you waiting for? You have Christ's finished work and God's faithful word. Surely these ought to satisfy your heart and tranquilize your mind. Do, then, let us entreat you to accept the full and everlasting remission of all your sins. Receive into your heart the sweet tidings of divine love and mercy, and go on your way rejoicing. Hear the voice of a risen Saviour, speaking from the throne of the Majesty in the heavens, and assuring you that your sins are all forgiven. Let those soothing accents, from the very mouth of God Himself, fall, in their enfranchising power, upon your troubled spirit:"Your sins and iniquities will I remember no more." If God thus speaks to me, if He assures me that He will no more remember my sins, should I not be fully and forever satisfied? Why should I go on doubting and reasoning when God has spoken? What can give certainty but the Word of God, that liveth and abideth forever? It is the only ground of certainty; and no power of earth or hell—human or diabolical—can ever shake it. The finished work of Christ and the faithful Word of God are the basis and the authority of full forgiveness of sins.

But, blessed forever be the God of all grace, it is not only remission of *sins* which is announced to us through the atoning death of Christ. This in itself would be a boon and a blessing of the very highest order; and, as we have seen, we enjoy it according to the largeness of the heart of God, and according to the value and efficacy of the death of

Christ, as God estimates it. But besides the full and perfect remission of sins, we have also *entire deliverance from the present power of sin.*

This is a grand point for every true lover of holiness. According to the glorious economy of grace, the same work which secures the complete remission of *sins* has broken forever the power of *sin.* It is not only that the *sins of the life* are blotted out, but the *sin of the nature* is condemned. The believer is privileged to regard himself as dead to sin. He can sing, with a glad heart,

> For me, Lord Jesus, Thou hast died,
>   And I have died in Thee;
> Thou'rt risen, my bands are all united,
>   And now Thou livest in me.
> The Father's face of radiant grace
>   Shines now in light on me.

This is the proper breathing of a Christian. "I am crucified with Christ, nevertheless I live; yet not I, but Christ liveth in me." This is Christianity. The old "I" crucified, and Christ living in me. The Christian is a new creation. Old things are passed away. The death of Christ has closed forever the history of the old "I"; and hence, though sin dwells in the believer, its power is broken and gone forever. Not only is its guilt canceled, but its terrible dominion completely overthrown.

This is the glorious doctrine of Romans 6—8. The thoughtful student of this most magnificent Epistle will observe that from chapter 3:21 to chapter 5:11 we have the work of Christ applied to the question of *sins;* and from chapter 5:12 to the end of chapter 8 we have another aspect of that work, namely, its application to the question of *sin*—"our old man"—"the body of *sin*"—"*sin* in the flesh." There is no such thing in Scripture as the forgiveness of sin. God has condemned sin, not forgiven it—an immensely important distinction. God has set forth His eternal abhorrence of sin in the cross of Christ. He has expressed and executed His judgment upon it, and now the believer can see himself as linked and identified with the One who died on the cross and is raised from the dead. He has passed out of the sphere of sin's

dominion into that new and blessed sphere where grace reigns through righteousness. "God be thanked," says the apostle, "that ye *were* [once, but now no longer are to be] the servants of sin, but ye have obeyed from the heart that type of doctrine to which ye were delivered (margin). Being then made *free from sin* [not merely sins forgiven], ye became the servants of righteousness. I speak after the manner of men, because of the infirmity of your flesh; for as ye have yielded your members servants to uncleanness and to iniquity unto iniquity, even so now yield your members servants to righteousness unto holiness. For when ye *were* the servants of sin, ye were free from righteousness. What fruit had ye then in those things whereof ye are now ashamed? for the end of those things is death. But now being made *free from sin*, and become servants to God, ye have your fruit unto holiness, and the end everlasting life" (Rom. 6:17-22).

Here lies the precious secret of holy living. We are dead to sin; alive to God. The reign of sin is over. What has sin to do with a dead man? Nothing. Well, then, the believer has died with Christ; he was buried with Christ; he is risen with Christ, to walk in newness of life. He lives under the precious reign of grace, and he has his fruit unto holiness. The man who draws a plea from the abundance of divine grace to live in sin, denies the very foundation of Christianity. "How shall we that have died to sin, live any longer therein?" Impossible. It would be a denial of the whole Christian standing. To imagine the Christian as one who is to go on, from day to day, week to week, month to month, and year to year, sinning and repenting, sinning and repenting, is to degrade Christianity and falsify the whole Christian position. To say that a Christian *must* go on sinning because he has the flesh in him is to ignore the death of Christ in one of its grand aspects, and to give the lie to the whole of the apostle's teaching in Romans 6—8.

Thank God, there is no necessity whatever why the believer should commit sin. "My little children, these things write I unto you that ye sin not." We should not justify ourselves in a single sinful thought. It is our sweet privilege to walk in the light, as God is in the light; and most surely, when we are walking in the light, we are not committing sin. Alas! we get out of the light and commit sin; but the normal, the true, the divine idea of a Christian is, walking in the light, and not committing sin. A sinful thought is foreign to the true genius of Christianity. We have sin in us, and shall have it so long as we are in the body; but if we walk in the Spirit, the sin in our nature will not show itself in the life. To say that *we need not sin* is to state a Christian privilege; to say that *we cannot sin* is a deceit and a delusion.

Part 3

From what has already passed before us, we learn that the grand result of the work of Christ in the past is to give us a divinely perfect standing before God. "He has perfected forever them that are sanctified." He has introduced us into the Divine Presence, in all His own perfect acceptability, in the full credit and virtue of His name, of His Person, and of His work; so that, as the Apostle John declares, "as He is, so are we in this world" (1 John 4:17).

Such is the settled standing of the very feeblest lamb in all the blood-bought flock of Christ. Nor could it possibly be otherwise. It must be either this or eternal perdition. There is not the breadth of a hair between this standing of absolute perfectness before God and a condition of guilt and ruin. We are either in our sins or in a risen Christ. There is no middle ground. We are either covered with guilt or complete in Christ. But the believer is declared, by the authoritative voice of the Holy Ghost in Scripture, to be "complete in Christ"—"perfect, as pertaining to his conscience"—"perfected in perpetuity" —"clean every whit"—"accepted in the Beloved"—"made [or become] the righteousness of God in Christ."

And all this through the sacrifice of the cross. That precious atoning death of Christ forms the solid and irrefragable foundation of the Christian's standing. "This Man, after He had offered one sacrifice for sins, forever sat down on the right hand of God." A seated Christ is the glorious proof and the perfect definition of the believer's place in the presence of God. Our Lord Christ, having glorified God about our sins, and borne His judgment on our entire condition as sinners, had offered one sacrifice for sins, forever sat Himself, into a place, not only of forgiveness, acceptance, and peace, but of complete deliverance from the dominion of sin—a place of assured victory over every thing that could possibly be against us, whether indwelling sin, the fear of Satan, the law, or this present evil world.

Such, we repeat, is the absolutely settled standing of the believer, if we are to be taught by holy Scripture. And we earnestly entreat the Christian reader not to be satisifed with any thing less than this. Let him not any longer accept the muddled teachings of christendom's creeds, and its liturgical services, which only drive the soul back into the darkness, distance, and bondage of Judaism—that system which God found fault with, and which He has forever abolished, because it did not meet His holy mind, or satisfy His loving heart, in giving the worshiper perfect peace, perfect liberty, perfect nearness to Himself, and that forever.

We solemnly call upon all the Lord's people, throughout the various sections of the professing Church, to consider where they are, and to see how far they understand and enjoy the true Christian position, as set forth in the various passages of Scripture which we have quoted, and which might easily be multiplied a hundredfold. Let them diligently and faithfully compare the teachings of christendom with the Word of God, and see how far they agree. In this way they will find how completely the professing Christianity of the present day stands in contrast with the living teachings of the New Testament; and as a consequence, souls are robbed of the precious privileges which belong to them as Christians, and they are kept in the moral distance which characterized the Mosaic economy.

All this is most deplorable. It grieves the

Holy Spirit, wounds the heart of Christ, dishonors the grace of God, and contradicts the plainest statements of holy Scripture. We are most thoroughly persuaded that the condition of thousands of precious souls at this moment is enough to make the heart bleed; and all this, to a large extent, is traceable to christendom's teachings, its creeds, and its formularies. Where will you find, amid the ordinary ranks of Christian profession, a person in the enjoyment of a perfectly purged conscience, of peace with God, of the Spirit of adoption? Is it not true that people are publicly and systematically taught that it is the height of presumption for any one to say that his sins *are* all forgiven—that he *has* eternal life—that he *is* justified from all things—that he *is* accepted in the Beloved—that he *is* sealed with the Holy Ghost—that he cannot be lost, because he is actually united to Christ by the indwelling Spirit? Are not all these Christian privileges practically denied and ignored in christendom? Are not people taught that it is dangerous to be too confident—that it is morally safer to live in doubt and fear—that the very utmost we can look for is the hope of getting to Heaven when we die? Where are souls taught the glorious truths connected with the new creation? Where are they rooted and grounded in the knowledge of their standing in a risen and glorified Head in the heavens? Where are they led into the enjoyment of those things which are freely given of God to His beloved people?

Alas! we grieve to think of the only true answer which can be given to such inquiries. The flock of Christ is scattered upon the dark mountains and desolate moors. The souls of God's people are left in the dim distance which characterized the Jewish system. They know not the meaning of the rent vail, of nearness to God, of conscious acceptance in the Beloved. The very table of the Lord is shrouded with the dark and chilling mists of superstition, and surrounded by the repulsive barriers of a dark and depressing legality. Accomplished redemption, full remission of sins, perfect justification before God, acceptance in a risen Christ, the Spirit of adoption, the bright and blessed hope of the coming of the Bridegroom—all these grand glorious realities—these chartered privileges of the Church of God are practically set aside by christendom's teachings and religious machinery.

Some, perhaps, may think we have drawn too gloomy a picture. We can only say—and we say it with all sincerity—would to God it were so! We fear the picture is far too true—yea, the reality is far more appalling than the picture. We are deeply and painfully impressed with the fact that the condition, not merely of the professing Church, but of thousands of the true sheep of the flock of Christ, is such, that if we only realized it as God sees it, it would break our hearts.

However, we must pursue our subject, and by so doing, furnish the very best remedy that can possibly be suggested for the deplorable condition of so many of the Lord's people.

We have dwelt upon that precious work which our Lord Jesus Christ has accomplished for us, in the putting away of our *sins*, and in the condemnation of *sin*, securing for us perfect remission of the former, and entire deliverance from the latter, as a ruling power. The Christian is one who is not only forgiven, but delivered. Christ has died for him, and he has died in Christ. Hence he is free, as one who is raised from the dead and alive unto God, through Jesus Christ our Lord. He is a new creation. He has passed from death unto life. Death and judgment are behind him, and nothing but glory before him. He possesses an unblotted title and an unclouded prospect.

Now, if all this be indeed true of every child of God—and Scripture says it is—what more do we want? Nothing, as to title; nothing, as to standing; nothing, as to hope. As to all these, we have absolute, divine perfection; but then our *state* is not perfect, our *walk* is not perfect. We are still in the body, compassed about with manifold infirmities, exposed to manifold temptations, liable to stumble, to fall, and to wander. We are unable of ourselves to think a right thought, or to keep ourselves for one moment in the blessed position into which grace has introduced us. True it is, we have everlasting life, and we are linked to the living Head in Heaven, by the Holy Ghost sent down to earth, so that we are eternally secure. Nothing can ever touch our life, inasmuch as it is "hid with Christ in God."

But while nothing can touch our life, or interfere with our standing, yet, seeing that our state is imperfect and our walk imperfect, our communion is liable to be interrupted, and hence it is that we need *the present work of Christ for us.*

Jesus lives at the right hand of God for us. His active intervention on our behalf never ceases for a single moment. He has passed through the heavens, in virtue of accomplished atonement, and there He ever carries on His perfect advocacy for us before our God. He is there as our subsisting righteousness, to maintain us ever in the divine integrity of the position and relationship into which His atoning death has introduced us. Thus we read, in Romans 5:10, "If, while we were enemies, we were reconciled to God by the death of His Son, much more, being reconciled, we shall be saved by His life." So also in Hebrews 4 we read, "Seeing then that we have a great High-Priest that has passed through the heavens, Jesus the Son of God, let us hold fast the confession. For we have not a High-Priest which cannot be touched with the feeling of our infirmities; but was in all points tempted, in like manner, without sin. Let us therefore come boldly unto the throne of grace, that we may obtain mercy, and find grace to help in time of need." Again, in chapter 7—"But this Man, because He continueth forever, hath an unchangeable priesthood. Wherefore He is able also to save them to the uttermost that come unto God by Him, seeing He ever liveth to make intercession for them." And in chapter 9—"For Christ is not entered into the holy places made with hands, which are the figures of the true; but into heaven itself, now to appear in the presence of God for us."

Then, in the first Epistle of John, we have the same subject presented under a somewhat different aspect: "My little children, these things write I unto you, that ye sin not. And if any one sin, we have an Advocate with the Father, Jesus Christ the righteous: and He is the propitiation for our sins; and not our sins only, but also for the whole world."

How precious is all this to the true-hearted Christian, who is ever conscious—deeply and painfully conscious—of his weakness, need, infirmity, and failure! How, we may lawfully inquire, is it possible for any one, with his eye resting on such passages as we have just quoted, to say nothing of his own self-consciousness—the sense of his own imperfect state and walk, to call in question the Christian's need of the unceasing ministry of Christ on his behalf? Is it not marvelous that any reader of the Epistle to the Hebrews, any observer of the state and walk of the most advanced believer, should be found denying the application of Christ's priesthood and advocacy to Christians now?

For whom, let us ask, is Christ now living and acting at the right hand of God? Is it for the world? Clearly not; for He says, in John 17, "I pray not for the world, but for them which Thou hast given Me; for they are Thine." And who are these? are they the Jewish remnant? Nay; that remnant is yet to appear on the scene. Who are they, then? Believers—children of God—Christians, who are now passing through this sinful world, liable to fail and to contract defilement every step of the way. These are the subjects of Christ's priestly ministry. He died to make them clean: He lives to keep them clean. By His death He expiated our guilt, and by His life He cleanses us, through the action of the Word by the power of the Holy Ghost. "This is He that came by water and blood; not by water only, but by water and blood." We have expiation and cleansing through a crucified Saviour. The double stream emanated from the pierced side of Christ, dead for us. All praise to His name!

We have all, in virtue of the precious death of Christ. Is it a question of our guilt? It is canceled by the blood of atonement. Is it a question of our daily short-comings? We have an Advocate with the Father—a great High-Priest with God. "If any man sin." He does not say, If any man repent. No doubt there is, and must be, repentance and self-judgment; but how are they produced? whence do they proceed? Here it is: "We have an Advocate with the Father." It is His all-prevailing intercession that procures for the sinning one the grace of repentance, self-judgment, and confession.

It is of the very utmost importance for the Christian reader to be thoroughly clear as to this great cardinal truth of the advocacy or priesthood of Christ. We sometimes erroneously think that when we fail in our work, something has to be done on our part to set matters straight between our souls and God. We forget that ere we are even conscious of the failure—before our conscience becomes really cognizant of the fact, our blessed Advocate has been to the Father about it; and it is to His intercession we are indebted for the grace of repentance, confession, and restoration. "If any man sin, we have"—what? The blood to return to? No; mark carefully what the Holy Ghost declares. "We have an Advocate with the Father, Jesus Christ the righteous." Why does He say, "the righteous"? why not the gracious, the merciful, the sympathizing? Is He not all this? Most surely; but not any one of these attributes would be in place here, inasmuch as the blessed apostle is putting before us the consolatory truth that in all our errors, our sins, and our failures, we have "a righteous" representative ever before the righteous God, the holy Father, so that our affairs can never fall through. "He *ever* liveth to make intercession for us;" and because He ever liveth, "He is able to save *to the uttermost*"—right through to the very end—"them that come unto God by Him."

What solid comfort is here for the people of God! and how needful for our souls to be established in the knowledge and sense of it! Some there are who have an imperfect sense of the true *standing* of a Christian, because they do not see what Christ has done for them in the past; others, on the contrary, have such an entirely one-sided view of the *state* of the Christian that they do not see our need of what Christ is doing for us now. Both must be corrected. The former are ignorant of the extent and value of the atonement; the latter are ignorant of the place and application of the advocacy. Such is the perfection of our *standing*, that the apostle can say, "As He is, so are we in this world." If this were all, we should certainly have no need of priesthood or advocacy; but then, such is our *state*, that the apostle has to say, "If any man sin." This proves our continual need of the Advocate. And, blessed be God, we have Him continually; we have him *ever living for us*. He lives and serves on high. He is our subsisting righteousness before our God. He lives to keep us always right in Heaven, and to set us right when we go wrong upon earth. He is the divine and indissoluble link between our souls and God.

Part 4

Having, in the three preceding papers of this series, sought to unfold the grand foundation-truths connected with the work of Christ for us—His work in the past and His work in the present—His atonement and His advocacy, we shall now seek, by the gracious aid of the Spirit of God, to present to the reader something of what the Scriptures teach us as to the second branch of our subject, namely, *Christ as an object for the heart.*

It is a wonderfully blessed thing to be able to say, "I have found an object which perfectly satisfies my heart—I have found Christ." It is this which gives true elevation above the world. It renders us thoroughly independent of the resources to which the unconverted heart ever betakes itself. It gives *settled rest*. It imparts a calmness and quietness to the spirit which the world cannot comprehend. The poor votary of the world may think the life of the true Christian a very slow, dull, stupid affair indeed. He may marvel how such an one can manage to get on without what he calls amusement, recreation, and pleasure; no theaters, no balls or parties, no concerts, no cards or billiards, no hunts or races, no club or news-room, no cricket or croquet parties.

To deprive the unconverted man of such things would almost drive him to despair or lunacy; but the Christian does not want such things—would not have them. They would be a perfect weariness to him. We speak, of course, of the true Christian, of one who is not merely a Christian in name, but in reality. Alas! many profess to be Christians, and take very high ground in their profession, who are, nevertheless, to be found mixed up in all the vain and frivolous pursuits of the men of this world. They may be seen at the communion-table on the Lord's day, and at the theater or a concert on Monday: they may be found assaying to take part in some one or other of the many branches of Christian work on Sunday, and during the week you may see them in the ball-room, at the race-course, or some such scene of folly and vanity.

It is very evident that such persons know nothing of Christ as an object for the heart. Indeed, it is very questionable how any one with a single spark of divine life in the soul can find pleasure in the wretched pursuits of a godless world. The true and earnest Christian turns away from such things— turns away instinctively; and this, not merely because of the positive wrong and evil of them—though most surely he feels them to be wrong and evil—but because he has no taste for them, and because he has found something infinitely superior, something which perfectly satisfied all the desires of the new nature. Could we imagine an angel from Heaven taking pleasure at a ball, a theater, or a race-course? The bare thought is supremely ridiculous. All such scenes are perfectly foreign to a heavenly being.

And what is a Christian? He is a heavenly man; he is a partaker of the divine nature. He is dead to the world—dead to sin—alive to God. He has not a single link with the world: he belongs to Heaven. He is no more of the world than Christ his Lord. Could Christ take part in the amusements, gayeties, and follies of the world? The very idea were blasphemy. Well, then, what of the Christian? Is he to be found where his Lord could not be? Can he consistently take part in things which he knows in his heart are contrary to Christ? Can he go into places and scenes and circumstances in which, he must admit, his Saviour and Lord can take no part? Can he go and have fellowship with a world which hates the One to whom he professes to owe every thing?

It may perhaps seem to some of our readers that we are taking too high ground. We would ask such, what ground are we to take? Surely, Christian ground, if we are Christians. Well, then, if we are to take Christian ground, how are we to know what that ground really is? Assuredly, from the New Testament. And what does it teach? Does it afford any warrant for the Christian to mix himself, in any shape or form, with the amusements and vain pursuits of this present evil world? Let us hearken to the weighty words of our blessed Lord in John 17. Let us hear from His lips the truth as to our portion, our position, and our path in this world. He says, addressing the Father, "I have given them Thy Word; and the world hath hated them, because *they are not of the world, even as I am not of the world.* I pray not that Thou shouldest take them out of the world, but that Thou shouldest keep them from the evil. *They are not of the world, even as I am not of the world.* Sanctify them through Thy truth; Thy Word is truth. As Thou hast sent Me into the world, even so have I also sent them into the world" (ver. 14-18).

Is it possible to conceive a closer measure of identification than that set before us in these words? Twice over, in this brief passage, our Lord declares that we are not of the world, even as He is not. What has our blessed Lord to do with the world? Nothing. The world has utterly rejected Him and cast Him out. It nailed Him to a shameful cross, between two malefactors. The world lies as fully and freshly under the charge of all this as though the act of the crucifixion took place yesterday, at the very centre of its civilization, and with the unanimous consent of all. There is not so much as a single moral link between Christ and the world. Yea, the world is stained with His murder, and will have to answer to God for the crime.

How solemn is this! What a serious consideration for Christians! We are passing through a world that crucified our Lord and Master, and He declares that we are not of that world, even as He is not of it. Hence it follows that in so far as we have any fellowship with the world, we are false to Christ. What should we think of a wife who could sit and laugh and joke with a set of men who had murdered her husband? and yet this is precisely what professing Christians do when they mix themselves up with this present evil world, and make themselves part and parcel of it.

It will perhaps be said, What are we to do? are we to go out of the world? By no means. Our Lord expressly says, "I pray not that Thou shouldest take them out of the world, but that Thou shouldest keep them from the evil." In it, but not of it, is the true principle for the Christian. To use a figure, the Christian in the world is like a diver. He is in the midst of an element which would destroy him, were he not protected from its action, and sustained by unbroken communication with the scene above.

And what is the Christian to do in the world? what is his mission? Here it is: "As Thou hast sent Me into the world, even so have I sent them into the world." And again, in John 20:21—"As My Father hath sent Me, even so send I you."

Such is the Christian's mission. He is not to shut himself within the walls of a monastery or convent. Christianity does not consist in joining a brotherhood or a sisterhood. Nothing of the kind. We are called to move up and down in the varied relations of life, and to act in our divinely appointed spheres, to the glory of God. It is not a question of what we are doing, but of how we do it. All depends upon the object which governs our hearts. If Christ be the commanding and absorbing object of the heart, all will be right; if He be not, nothing is right. Two persons may sit down at the same table to eat; the one eats to gratify his appetite, the other eats to the glory of God—eats simply to keep his body in proper working order as God's vessel, the temple of the Holy Ghost, the instrument for Christ's service.

So in every thing. It is our sweet privilege to set the Lord always before us. He is our model. As he was sent into the world, so are we. What did He come to do? To glorify God.

How did He live? By the Father. "As the living Father hath sent Me, and I live by the Father, so he that eateth Me, even he shall live by Me" (John 6:57).

This makes it all so simple. Christ is the standard and touchstone for every thing. It is no longer a question of mere right and wrong according to human rules; it is simply a question of what is worthy of Christ. Would He do this or that? would He go here or there? "He left us an example, that we should follow *His* steps;" and most assuredly, we should not go where we cannot trace His blessed footsteps. If we go hither and thither to please ourselves, we are not treading in His steps, and we cannot expect to enjoy His blessed presence.

Here lies the real secret of the whole matter. The grand question is just this: Is Christ my one object? what am I living for? Can I say, "The life that I live in the flesh, I live by the faith of the Son of God, who loved me, and gave Himself for me"? Nothing less than this is worthy of a Christian. It is a poor miserable thing to be content with being saved, and then to go on with the world, and live for self-pleasing and self-interest—to accept salvation as the fruit of Christ's toil and passion, and then live at a distance from Himself. What should we think of a child who only cared about the good things provided by his father's hand, and never sought his father's company—yea, preferred the company of strangers? We should justly despise him; but how much more despicable is the Christian who owes his present and his eternal all to the work of Christ and yet is content to live at a cold distance from His blessed Person, caring not for the furtherance of His cause—the promotion of His glory!

Part 5

If the reader has been enabled, through grace, to make his own of what has passed before our minds in this series of papers, he will have a perfect remedy for all uneasiness of conscience and all restlessness of heart. The work of Christ, if only it be laid hold of by an artless faith, must, of blessed necessity, meet the former; and the Person of Christ, if only He be contemplated with a single eye, must perfectly meet the latter. If, therefore, we are not in the enjoyment of peace of conscience, it can only be because we are not resting on the finished work of Christ; and if the heart is not at ease, it proves that we are not satisfied with Christ Himself.

And yet, how few, even of the Lord's beloved people, know either the one or the other. How rare it is to find a person in the enjoyment of true peace of conscience and rest of heart! In general, Christians are not a whit in advance of the condition of Old Testament saints. They do not know the blessedness of an accomplished redemption; they are not in the enjoyment of a purged conscience; they cannot draw nigh with a true heart, in full assurance of faith, having the heart sprinkled from an evil conscience, and the body washed with pure water; they do not apprehend the grand truth of the indwelling of the Holy Ghost, enabling them to cry, "Abba, Father"; they are, as to their experience, under law; they have never really entered into the deep blessedness of being under the reign of grace. They have life. It is impossible to doubt this. They love divine things; their tastes, their habits, their aspirations—yea, their very exercises, their conflicts, their anxieties, doubts, and fears all go to prove the existence of divine life. They are, in a way, separated from the world, but their separation is rather negative than positive. It is more because they see the utter vanity of the world, and its inability to satisfy their hearts, than because they have found an object in Christ. They have lost their taste for the things of the world, but they have not found their place and their portion in the Son of God where He now is at the right hand of God. The things of the world cannot satisfy them, and they are not in the enjoyment of their proper heavenly standing, object, and hope; hence they are in an anomalous condition altogether; they have no certainty, no rest, no fixedness of purpose; they are not happy; they do not know their true bearings; they are neither one thing nor the other.

Is it thus with the reader? We fondly hope not. We trust he is one of those who, through infinite grace, "know the things that are freely given them of God"; who know that they have passed from death unto life—that they have eternal life; who enjoy the precious witness of the Spirit; who realize their association with a risen and glorified Head in the heavens, with whom they are linked by the Holy Ghost, who dwells in them; who have found their object in the Person of that blessed One whose finished work is the divine and eternal basis of their salvation and peace; and who are earnestly looking for the blessed moment when Jesus shall come to receive them to Himself, that where He is, they may be also, to go no more out forever.

This is Christianity. Nothing else deserves the name. It stands out in bold and striking contrast with the spurious religiousness of the day, which is neither pure Judaism on the one hand, nor pure Christianity on the other, but a wretched mixture, composed of some of the elements of each, which unconverted people can adopt and go on with, because it sanctions the lusts of the flesh, and allows them to enjoy the pleasures and vanities of the world to their heart's content. The archenemy of Christ and of souls has succeeded in producing an awful system of religion, half Jewish, half Christian, combining, in the most artful manner, the world and the flesh, with a certain amount of Scripture, so used as to destroy its moral force and hinder its just application. In the meshes of this system souls are hopelessly entangled. Unconverted people are deceived into the notion that they are very good Christians indeed, and going on all right to Heaven; and on the other hand, the Lord's dear people are robbed of their proper place and privileges, and dragged down by the dark and depressing influence of the religious atmosphere which surrounds and almost suffocates them.

It lies not, we believe, within the compass of human language to set forth the appalling consequences of this mingling of the people of God with the people of the world in one common system of religiousness and theological belief. Its effect upon the former is to blind their eyes to the true moral glories of Christianity as set forth in the pages of the New Testament; and this to such an extent, that if any one attempts to unfold these glories to their view, he is regarded as a visionary enthusiast, or dangerous heretic: its effect upon the latter is to deceive them altogether as to their true condition, character, and destiny. Both classes repeat the' same formularies, subscribe the same creed, say the same prayers, are members of the same community, partake of the same sacrament, are, in short, ecclesiastically, theologically, religiously one.

It will perhaps be said in reply to all this, that our Lord, in His wonderful discourse in Matthew 13, distinctly teaches that the wheat and the tares are to grow together. Yes; but where? in the *Church?* Nay; but "in the field"; and He tells us that *"the field is the world."* To confound these things is to falsify the whole Christian position, and to do away with all godly discipline in the assembly. It is to place the teaching of our Lord in Matthew 13 in opposition to the teaching of the Holy Ghost in 1 Corinthians 5.

However, we shall not pursue this subject further just now. It is far too important and too extensive to be disposed of in a. brief article like the present. We may perhaps discuss it more fully on some future occasion. That it demands the serious consideration of the Christian reader we are most thoroughly convinced; bearing, as it does, so manifestly on the glory of Christ, on the true interests of His people, on the progress of the gospel, on the integrity of Christian testimony and service, it would be quite impossible to overestimate its importance. But we must leave it for the present, and draw this paper to a close by a brief reference to the third and last branch of our subject, namely, *the Word of Christ as the all-sufficient guide for our path.*

If Christ's work suffices for the conscience, if His blessed Person suffices for the heart, then, most assuredly, His precious Word suffices for the path. We may assert, with all possible confidence, that we possess in the divine volume of holy Scripture all we can ever need, not only to meet all the exigencies of our individual path, but also the varied necessities of the Church of God, in the most minute details of her history in this world.

We are quite aware that in making this assertion we lay ourselves open to much scorn and opposition, in more quarters than one. We shall be met on the one hand by the advocates of tradition, and on the other by those who contend for the supremacy of man's reason and will; but this gives us very little concern indeed. We regard the traditions of men, whether fathers, brothers, or doctors, *if presented as an authority,* as the small dust of the balance; and as to human reason, it can only be compared to a bat in the sunshine, dazzled by the brightness, and blindly dashing itself against objects which it cannot see.

It is the deepest joy of the Christian's heart to retire from the conflicting traditions and doctrines of men into the calm light of holy Scripture; and when encountered by the impudent reasonings of the infidel, the rationalist, and the skeptic, to bow down his whole moral being to the authority and power of holy Scripture. He thankfully recognizes in the Word of God the only perfect standard for doctrine, for morals, for every thing. "All Scripture is given by inspiration of God, and is profitable for doctrine, for reproof, for correction, for instruction in righteousness; that the man of God may be *perfect* ($\alpha\rho\tau\iota o\varsigma$), *throughly furnished unto all good works."*

What more can we need? Nothing. If Scripture can make a child "wise unto salvation," and if it can make a man "perfect," and furnish him "throughly to all good works," what do we want of human tradition or human reasonings? If God has written a volume for us, if He has graciously condescended to give us a revelation of His mind, as to all we ought to know and think and feel and believe and do, shall we turn to a poor fellow-mortal—be he ritualist or rationalist—to help us? Far away be the thought! As well might we turn to our fellow-man to add something to the finished work of Christ, in order to render it sufficient for our conscience, or to supply some deficiency in the Person of Christ, in order to render Him a sufficient object for the heart, as to betake ourselves to human tradition or human reason to supply some deficiency in divine revelation.

All praise and thanks to our God, it is not so. He has given us in His own beloved Son all we want for the conscience, for the heart, for the path—for time, with all its changing scenes—for eternity, with its countless ages. We can say:

> Thou, O Christ, art all we want;
> More than all in Thee we find.

There is, there could be, no lack in the Christ of God. His atonement and advocacy must satisfy all the cravings of the most deeply exercised conscience. The moral glories—the powerful attractions of His divine Person must satisfy the most intense aspirations and longings of the heart. And His peerless revelation—that priceless volume—contains within its covers all we can possibly need, from the starting-post to the goal of our Christian career.

Christian reader, are not these things so? Dost thou not, from the very center of thy renewed moral being, own the truth of them? If so, art thou resting, in calm repose, on Christ's work? art thou delighting in His Person? art thou submitting, in all things, to the authority of His Word? God grant it may be so with thee, and with all who profess His name! May there be a fuller, clearer, and more decided testimony to "the all-sufficiency of Christ," till "that day."

THE MINISTRY OF CHRIST

PAST, PRESENT, AND FUTURE

Exodus 21:1-6; John 13:1-10; Luke 12:37

"FOR EVEN THE SON OF MAN came not to be ministered unto, but to minister, and to give His life a ransom for many" (Mark 10:45).

It is very necessary to retire from all thoughts about our service to the Lord, and our work for Him, and to have our hearts occupied with His service toward us. And when I say this, you will not suppose for a moment that it is my desire or thought to weaken in any heart in this assembly, in the smallest degree, the desire to work for Christ, whatever sphere He may open for you, or according to whatever gift He may have bestowed upon you. Quite the reverse; indeed, I would seek in every way to strengthen and intensify that desire. But then one knows, both from experience and observation, that we may be so occupied with *our* work and *our* services that our hearts may lose the sense of what Christ is toward us in His marvelous character as a servant.

Here let me say that my immediate thesis is the Lord Jesus as the servant of His people's necessities. That is the field into which we are introduced by these Scriptures. The Lord Jesus is the servant of the soul's necessities in every stage of its history, from first to last—from the depths of your ruin and degradation as sinners, in all your weakness and failure as saints from day to day, until He plants you in the joys of His own kingdom. And His services will not end there; for, as we read in Luke 12:37, He will gird Himself, and serve us in the glory. Thus His work as a servant overlaps the whole of the soul's history, past, present, and future. He has served us in the past, He is serving us now, and He will serve us forever.

And here allow me to say that the line of truth which I have to bring before you is of a directly individual character. We were speaking, previously, of the truth with respect to our corporate condition and character, and therefore I feel all the more free on this occasion to enter upon what is more directly personal—to speak of truth which bears directly on the soul's individual condition and wants. And I would ask you to place yourselves, so far as through grace you can, in all simplicity and reality, straight in view of this theme—Christ the servant of our necessities.

It is possible there may be souls who want to begin at the very beginning with this most precious theme. They want to know Christ as the One who came into this world to serve them in all their deep and varied need as lost, self-destroyed, guilty, hell-deserving sinners. If there be any such, I would ask them to ponder deeply that verse which I have read, "The Son of Man is come to serve and to give."

This is a divine reality. Jesus came into this world to meet our need, to serve us in all that in which we need His precious service, and to give His life a ransom for many; to serve us by bearing our sins in His own body on the tree, and working out a full and an eternal salvation. He did not come to get—He did not come to take—He did not come to be ministered to—He did not come to be gazed at—He came to be used; and therefore, while the soul that is exercised may be raising this harassing question, "What can I do for the Lord?" the answer is, "You must pause and see and believe what the Lord has done for you. You must stand still and see the salvation of God." Remember those words of divine and evangelistic sweetness. "To him that *worketh not*, but believeth on Him that justifieth the ungodly, his faith is counted for righteousness" (Rom. 4:5). You can never intelligently or properly serve Christ until you know and believe how He has served you. You must cease your restless doings, and rest in a divinely accomplished work. Then, but not until then, will you be able to start on a career of Christian service. It is most necessary for all anxious souls to understand that all true Christian service begins with the possession of eternal life, and

is rendered in the power of the Holy Ghost, the indwelling Spirit, in the light and on the authority of holy Scripture. This is the divine idea of Christian work and service.

Now, though the primary object is for those who are saints of God, who have set out on their course, still I do not think it would be according to the heart and sympathies of Christ to overlook the face that there may be some soul that wants, as I said, just to begin at the very beginning with this precious mystery—Christ the servant; that have never taken the attitude of simple repose in Christ's finished work. They have, it may be, begun to think of their soul's salvation, to think about eternity; but they are occupied with the thought that the Lord is claiming something from them: "I must do this, I must do that, and I must do the other." Now, if such there be, I repeat, with deepest earnestness, you must cease altogether from your own doings, cease from your own reasonings, cease from your own feelings; because, be assured of it, it is neither feeling nor thinking nor reasoning nor doing at all, but it is pausing and gazing. It is hearing and believing. It is looking off from yourselves and your service to Christ and His service. It is ceasing from your restless and worthless doings, and reposing in full, unquestioning confidence in the one offering of Jesus Christ, which has perfectly satisfied and perfectly glorified God as to the great question of your sin and guilt. Here lies the divine secret of peace—peace in Jesus—peace with God— eternal peace. Nothing will ever be right till you get on this ground. If you are occupied with your doings for Christ, you will never get peace; but if you will only take God at His word, and rest in His Christ, you shall possess a peace which no power of earth or hell can ever disturb.

Now, I ask you, before I proceed, this question, Is there a heart that has not yet rested here? Is there a heart that will say, I am not satisfied with Christ's service; I cannot rest in His work? What! The Son of God has stooped to serve you. The One who made you, the One who gave you life and breath and all things, the One to whom all are responsible, He has stooped to become your servant. It is not a question of asking you to do any thing, or asking you to give any thing, because—mark those words—they are words which sweep all through the history of the Son of Man—they are words which, in all their length and breadth and fullness, you can take up and use as if you were the only object of this service in the world—"The Son of Man is come to serve and to give." He is not come to get; He is not come to ask.

The legal mind leads you to think that God is an exactor—that He is making demands upon you—that He wants your services in one way or another. But oh, remember, that your first great business, your primary and all-important work, is to believe in Jesus—to rest sweetly in Him, and in what He has done for you on the cross, and in what He is doing for you on the throne. "This is the work of God, that ye believe on Him whom He hath sent." You remember the interesting question of the Psalmist—a question asked when his eye rested on the magnitude and multitude of Jehovah's benefits—"What shall I render unto the Lord for all His benefits?" What is the reply? "I will take the cup of salvation, and call upon the name of the Lord."

Is this the way to "render unto the Lord"? Yes, this is just the way that gratifies and glorifies Him. If you really want to *render*, you must *take*. Take what? "The cup of salvation"—a full and brimming cup, most surely; and as you drink of that cup, as the glories of God's salvation shine in the vision of your soul, then will streams of living praise flow from your grateful heart. And you know He says, "Whoso offereth praise, glorifieth Me."

In a word, then, you must, first of all, allow your soul to dwell upon the marvelous mystery of Christ's service toward you in all the depth of your need; and the more you dwell upon that, the more will you be in the true attitude to serve Him.

Take another striking illustration. When David, as you remember, in that remarkable passage in the second book of Samuel (chap. 7), sat in his house of cedar, and looked around at all that God had done for him, he said, "I must rise and build a house."

Immediately the prophet was despatched to David to correct him on this point: "You shall not build Me a house, but I will build you a house." You must reverse the matter. God wants you to sit down and gaze yet more fully and intently upon His actings on your behalf. He wants you to look, not only at the past and the present, but to look on into the bright future; to see your entire history overlapped by His own magnificent grace.

And what was the effect of all this upon the heart of David? We have the answer in that one pithy statement: "Then went King David in, and sat before the Lord, and said, 'Who am I?'" Mark the attitude, and ponder the question. They are full of deep meaning. *"He sat."* This is rest and sweet repose. He wanted to go to work too soon. No, says God, you must sit down and look at My work, and trace My actings on your behalf in the past, the present, and the future.

And then the question, *"Who am I?"* In this we see the blessed fact that self was for the moment lost sight of. It was flung into the shade by the lustre of divine revelation. Self and its poor little actings were set aside by the glory of God and the rich magnificence of His actings on behalf of His servant.

Now, some might have thought that David was an active, useful man when he was rising to take the trowel to build the house; and they might have thought him a good-for-nothing man to be sitting still when there was work to be done. But, let us remember that God's thoughts are not as our thoughts. He prizes our worship much more highly than our work. Indeed, it is only the true and intelligent worshiper that can be a true and intelligent workman. No doubt God most graciously accepts our poor services, even stamped as they so often are with mistakes of all sorts. But when it becomes a question of the comparative value of service and worship, the former must give place to the latter; and we know that when our brief span of working time shall have expired, our eternity of worship shall begin. Sweet thought!

And let me further remark, ere leaving this part of our subject, that no one need fear in the least that the practical effect of what I have been saying will be to cripple your service, or lead you to fold your arms in culpable idleness or cold indifference. The very reverse is the case, as you may see in the history of David himself. Study at your leisure 1 Chronicles 28—29. There you have a splendid presentation of service—a most triumphant answer to all who would place work before worship. There you see, as it were, King David rising from the attitude of a worshiper into that of a workman, and making ample provision for the building of that very house of which he was not allowed to set one stone upon another.

And not only does he make provision according to the claims of holiness, but, as he says, "Because I have set my affection to the house of my God, I have of mine own proper good, of gold and silver, which I have given to the house of my God, *over and above all* that I have prepared for the holy house, even three thousand talents of gold of the gold of Ophir, and seven thousand talents of refined silver, to overlay the walls of the house." In other words, as we should express it, out of his own private purse, he gave the princely sum of over sixteen millions as a free gift toward the house which was to be reared by the hand of another. This, as he informs us, was "over and above what he had prepared for the holy house," which latter greatly exceeded the amount of England's national debt.

Thus we see that it is the true worshiper that makes the effective servant. It is when we have sat and gazed on the actings of Christ for us that we are enabled in any small degree to act for Him. And then, too, we shall be able to say with David, as he surveyed the untold wealth prepared for the house of God, "It is all Thine, and of Thine own have we given Thee."

I. But we must now turn for a few moments to the opening paragraph of Exodus 21—"If thou buy a Hebrew servant, six years he shall serve; and in the seventh, he shall go out free for nothing. If he came in by himself, he shall go out by himself: if he were married, then his wife shall go out with him. If his master have given him a wife, and she have borne him sons or daughters; the wife and her children shall be her master's, and he shall go

out by himself. And if the servant shall plainly say, I love my master, my wife, and my children; I will not go out free: then his master shall bring him unto the judges; he shall also bring him to the door, or unto the door-post; and his master shall bore his ear through with an awl; and he shall serve him forever."

Here, then, we have one of the shadows of good things to come—a shadow or figure of the True Servant, the Lord Jesus Christ, that blessed One who loved the Church and gave Himself for it. The Hebrew servant, having served the legal time, was perfectly free to go out; but he loved his wife and his children, and that, too, with such a love as led him to surrender his own personal liberty for their sakes. He proved his love for them by sacrificing himself. He might have gone forth and enjoyed his freedom, but what of them? How could he leave them behind? Impossible. He loved them too well for that; and hence he deliberately walked to the door-post, and there, in the presence of the judges, had his ear bored in token of perpetual service.

This was love indeed. There was no mistake about it. The wife and each child, as they gazed ever after on that bored ear, could read the touching and powerful proof of the love of that servant's heart.

Here is something for the heart to dwell upon—yea, something over which the heart may well break itself. We see in this Old Testament type the everlasting Lover of our souls—Jesus, the true servant. You remember that remarkable occasion in our Lord's life when He was setting before His disciples the solemn fact of His approaching cross and passion. You will find it in the eighth chapter of the Gospel of Mark: "And He began to teach them that the Son of Man must suffer many things, and be rejected of the elders, and of the chief priests, and scribes, and be killed, and after three days rise again. And He spake that saying openly. And Peter took Him, and began to rebuke Him." Peter would fain, though he knew it not, have interrupted the True Servant in His movement to the door-post. He would have Him pity Himself, and maintain His own personal freedom. But oh, hearken to the withering rebuke administered to the very man who just before had made such a fine confession of Christ! "But when he had turned about and looked on His disciples, He rebuked Peter, saying, 'Get thee behind Me, Satan; for thou savorest not the things that be of God, but the things that be of men.'"

Mark the action. "He turned and looked on His disciples," as though He would say, If I harken to your counsel, Peter—if I pity Myself—if I retreat from that cross which lies before Me, then what is to become of these? It is the Hebrew servant saying, "I love my wife, I love my children, I will not go out free."

It is of the very last possible importance for us to see that there was no necessity whatever laid upon the Lord Jesus Christ to walk to the cross; there was no necessity whatever laid upon Him to leave the glory which He had with the Father from all eternity and come down here; and when He had come down into this world, and taken perfect humanity upon Him, there was no necessity laid upon Him that He should have gone to the cross; for at any moment during the whole of His blessed history, from the manger of Bethlehem to the cross of Calvary, He might have gone back to where He came from. Death had no claim upon Him. The prince of this world came and had nothing in Him. He could say, speaking of His life, "No man taketh it from Me, but I lay it down of Myself" (John 10:18). And on His way from the garden to the cross we hear Him saying, "Thinkest thou that I cannot now pray to My Father, and He shall presently give Me more than twelve legions of angels? But how then shall the Scriptures be fulfilled, that thus it must be?" And may we not say there was much more truth than the utterers were aware of in these accents of mockery which fell on the blessed Saviour's ear as He hung on the cross—"He saved others; Himself He cannot save"? But they might have said, Himself He will not save.

Ah, no! blessed forever be His name! He did not pity or spare Himself, but He pitied us. He beheld us in our hopeless ruin, guilt, misery, and danger. He saw that there was no eye to pity, no arm to save; and—all

praise to His matchless name!—He laid aside His glory, came down into this wretched world, became a man, that as a man He might, by the sacrifice of Himself, deliver us from the lake of fire, and associate us with Himself on the new and eternal ground of accomplished redemption, in the power of resurrection-life, according to the eternal counsels of God, and to the praise of His glory.

Now, we cannot possibly overestimate the importance of dwelling upon the fact that there was no necessity whatever laid upon our blessed Lord Jesus Christ to die on the cross, and to endure the wrath of God. Neither in His person, in His nature, nor in His relations was He obnoxious to death. He was God over all, blessed forever. He was the Eternal Son of God. And in His human nature He was pure, spotless, sinless, perfect. He knew no sin. He did always and only the things that please God. He glorified Him, and finished His work; and He has saved us in such a way as to glorify God in the most wonderful manner. He was, to use the language of our type, free to go out by Himself; but ah, had He done so, your place and mine must inevitably have been the lake of fire forever.

To all this the Holy Ghost delights to bear testimony, as one of our own poets has sweetly sung:

> And, Lord, Thy perfect fitness
> To do a Saviour's part,
> The Holy Ghost doth witness
> To each believer's heart.

Most true: and we might with equal truth say, "His fitness to do a servant's part," because it was the very height of His glory, the very dignity of His person; it was the glory whence He had descended, that enabled Him to stoop down to the very depths of their condition, that He has not not a necessity—no, not one—in the deepest range of His people's history, or in the lowest depths of their condition, that He has not reached in His marvelous character and His divine ministry as the servant of His people's necessities.

Brethren, let us never forget this. Nay, rather let us constantly cherish in our hearts the most grateful remembrance of it. The more we dwell upon the height of Christ's personal glory, the more fully we shall see the depths of His humiliation. The more profoundly we meditate upon the glory of what He *was*, the more we must be arrested by the grace of what He *became*. "Ye know the grace of our Lord Jesus Christ, that, though He was rich, yet for your sakes He became poor, that ye through His poverty might be rich."

Who can measure the heights and the depths of those two words, "rich" and "poor," in their application to our adorable Lord and Saviour? No created intelligence can fathom them; but most assuredly we should cultivate the habit of dwelling upon the love that shines all along the pathway of the divine Servant as He walked to the cross for us. It is as we dwell upon His love to us that our hearts shall be drawn out by the Holy Ghost in the power of responsive love to Him. "The love of Christ constraineth us; because we thus judge, that if One died for all, then were all dead; and that He died for all, that they which live should not henceforth live unto themselves, but unto Him which died for them, and rose again" (2 Cor. 5:14-15).

II. Having thus glanced at our Lord's service toward us in the past, let us look for a few moments at His present service—at what He is now doing for us continually in the presence of God. This we have most blessedly presented to us in John 13. The same precious grace shines in this as in all that on which we have been dwelling. If we look back at the past, we behold the Perfect Servant nailed to the cross for us; if we look up to the throne now, we behold Him girded for us, not only according to our present need, but according to the perfect love of His heart—His love to the Father, His love to the Church, His love to each individual believer from the beginning to the end of time.

"Now before the feast of the passover, when Jesus knew that His hour was come that He should depart out of this world unto the Father, having loved His own which were in the world, He loved them unto the end. And during supper [see Greek], the devil having now put into the heart of Judas Iscariot, Simon's son, to betray Him; Jesus knowing that the Father had given all things into His hands, and that He was come from God, and went to God; He riseth from supper, and laid aside His garments; and took a towel, and girded Himself. After that He poureth water into a basin, and began to wash the disciples' feet, and to wipe them with the towel wherewith He was girded."

Here, then, we have a most marvelous presentation of Christ's present service toward "His own which are in the world." There is something peculiarly precious in the expression, *"His own."* It brings us so very near to the heart of Christ. It is so sweet to think that He can look at such poor, feeble, failing creatures as we are, and say, They are Mine. It matters not what others may think about them; they belong to Me, and I must have them in a condition worthy of the place whence I came, and whither I am going.

This is ineffably precious and edifying for our souls. It was in the sense of His personal glory, in the consciousness that He had come from God and was going to God, that He could stoop down and wash His people's feet. There was nothing, could be nothing, higher than the place whence Jesus had come; there was nothing, could be nothing, lower than the defiled feet of His disciples: but, blessed and praised forever be His name! He fills up in His own divine person and marvelous service every point between those two extremes. He can lay one hand on the throne of God, and the other on our feet, and be Himself the divine and eternal link between.

Now, there are three things in this Scripture which I am anxious to put clearly before you. In the first place, we have the special action of our Lord toward His own in the world; secondly, the spring of that action; and thirdly, the measure of the action: the action, its spring, and its measure.

1. And first, the action itself. You will bear in mind that what we have presented here is not "the washing of regeneration."

That pertains to the first stage of our Lord's service on our behalf. "His own which are in the world"—all who belong to that highly privileged class (and that is simply all who believe in His name) have passed through that great washing, in virtue of which Christ can pronounce them "clean every whit."

There is not a spot or a stain upon the very feeblest of that blessed number whom He calls "His own." "He that is washed needeth not save to wash his feet, but *is clean every whit: and ye are clean*, but not all." If a single spot could be detected on one of Christ's own, it would be a dishonor cast upon Him, inasmuch as He has washed us from all our guilt according to the perfection of His work as the Servant of our need, and, far above all, the Servant of the eternal counsels, purposes, and glory of God. He found us clean never a whit, and He has made us "clean every whit."

This is the washing of regeneration, which is never repeated. We have a figure of this in the case of the priests of the Mosaic economy. On the great day of their inauguration they were washed in water. This action was never repeated. But after this, from day to day, in order to fit them for the daily discharge of their priestly functions, they had to wash their hands and their feet in the brazen laver in the tabernacle, or the brazen sea in the temple. This daily washing is the figure of the action in John 13. The two washings, being distinct, must never be confounded; and being intimately connected, must never be separated. The washing of regeneration is divinely and eternally complete: the washing of sanctification is being divinely and continually carried on. The former is never repeated; the latter is never interrupted. That gives us a part *in* Christ, of which nothing can rob us; and this gives us a part *with* Christ, of which any thing may deprive us. The one is the basis of our eternal life; the other is the ground of our daily communion.

See that you understand the meaning of having your feet washed, moment by moment, by the hands of that blessed One who is girded as the divine Servant of your present need. It is utterly impossible for any one to overestimate the importance of this

work; but we may at least gather something of its value from our Lord's words to Peter; for Peter, like ourselves, alas! was very far from seizing the full significance of what his Lord was doing. "Then cometh He to Simon Peter; and Peter saith unto Him, 'Lord, dost Thou wash my feet?' Jesus answered and said unto him, 'What I do thou knowest not now; but thou shalt know hereafter.' Peter saith unto Him, 'Thou shalt never wash my feet.' Jesus answered him, 'If I wash thee not, thou hast no part *with* Me.' "

Here is the grand point—"part with Me." The washing of regeneration gives us a part *in* Christ: the daily washing of sanctification gives us a part *with* Christ. In order to full, intelligent, happy communion, we must have a clean conscience, and clean feet. The blood of atonement secures the former; the water of purification maintains the other. But both the blood and the water flowed from a crucified Christ. The death of Christ is the necessary basis of every thing. He died to make us clean; He lives to keep us clean. We are made as clean as His death can make us; we are kept as clean as His life can keep us.

And, be it remembered, this marvelous ministry of Christ on our behalf never ceases. He ever liveth to act *for* us on high, and to act *on* us and *in* us by His Word and Spirit. He speaks to God for us, and He speaks to us for God. He came from God, and traveled down to the profoundest depths of our need. He has gone back to God, to bear us ever on His heart, to meet our daily need, and to maintain us in the integrity of the position and relationship into which He has introduced us.

This is replete with solid comfort for the soul. We are passing through a defiling world, where we are constantly liable to contract evils of one kind or another which, though they cannot touch our eternal life, can very seriously affect our communion. It is impossible for us to tread the sanctuary of the divine presence with soiled feet; and hence the deep and unspeakable blessedness of having One ever in the presence of God for us—One who, having been in this scene, knows its true character; and One who, having come from God, and gone back to Him, knows the full extent of His claims, and all that is needful to fit us for fellowship with Him. The provision is divinely perfect. Sin or uncleanness can never be found in the presence of God. If we can make light of either the one or the other, God cannot and will not. The holiness that shines in the demand for purity is as bright as the grace that provides it. Grace has made the provision, but holiness demands the application thereof. The goodness of God provided a laver for the priests of old, but the holiness of God demanded that the priests should use that laver. The great washing of inauguration introduced them to the office of the priesthood; the washing in the laver fitted them for the duties of that office. How could acceptable priestly service be discharged with unclean hands? Impossible. And we may say it is as impossible that we can walk in the pathway of holiness if our feet are not washed and wiped by that blessed One who has girded Himself to serve us in this matter perpetually.

All this is divinely simple. There are two links in Christianity; namely, the link of eternal life, which can never be snapped by any thing; and the link of personal communion, which can be snapped in a moment by the weight of a feather. Now, it is as our ways are cleansed by the holy action of the Word, through the Holy Ghost, that our communion is maintained in its unbroken integrity. But if I am afraid to face the Word of God, or if I am willfully refusing its action, how can I enjoy communion with God?

I am not speaking now of ignorance of the Word of God. The Lord bears with a wonderful amount of ignorance in us—far more than we could bear with in one another. I do not now refer to the question of ignorance. But suppose a case. A young person entered these walls a few weeks ago, and took her seat on one of these benches. She was dressed out in all the fashion of this world—her head adorned with feathers and flowers, and her fingers with jewels. Her heart full of vanity and folly. Here the grace of God met her in all its fullness and freeness. The arrow of divine conviction entered her soul. She was broken down under the mighty power of the Word, in the hands of the Holy

Ghost. She was brought to repentance toward God, and faith in the Lord Jesus Christ. She was saved, there and then, and left the place rejoicing in a full salvation. This joy continued for many days. She was engrossed with her newly found treasure. She never thought about her feathers, her flowers, or her jewels. True, she continued to wear them, simply because she as yet saw nothing wrong in so doing. She knew not as yet that there was so much as a single sentence in the Word of God bearing upon such things.

Brethren, let me just remind you that we should be prepared for such a case as this, and be prepared to meet it. Some of us, I fear, have but little wisdom or patience to deal with cases of this type. We are in undue haste to enter upon what I may call the stripping process. This is a mistake. We must allow time for the hidden virtues of the kingdom of God to develop themselves. We must not attempt to reduce the Christian assembly into a place in which a certain livery is adopted. This will never do. We really cannot reduce all to a dead level. We must allow the Word of God to act on the life which the Spirit of God has implanted. I do nothing but mischief to people if I get them to adopt a certain style of dress merely at my suggestion. The grand thing is to allow the kingdom of God to assert its holy sway over the entire character. This is to His glory and reduce all to a dead level. We must allow the

Let us pursue our case. Our young friend, in the course of her reading, is arrested by the following pointed passage: "In like manner also, that women adorn themselves in modest apparel, with shamefacedness and sobriety; not with broidered hair, or gold, or pearls, or costly array; but (which becometh women professing godliness) with good works" (1 Tim. 2:9-10). And again, "Whose adorning let it not be that outward adorning of plaiting the hair, and of wearing of gold, or of putting on of apparel; but let it be the hidden man of the heart, in that which is not corruptible, even the ornament of a meek and quiet spirit, which is in the sight of God of great price" (1 Pet. 3:3-4).

Now, here, we have illustrated for us the

present ministry of Christ—the action of the Word upon the soul—the application of the basin to the feet—the washing of water by the Word. It is Jesus stooping down to wash the feet of this young disciple. The question is, How will she receive the action? Will she resist it, or yield to it? Will she push away the basin? Will she refuse the gracious ministry? "If I wash thee not, thou hast no part *with* Me."

This is very solemn, and it demands our most serious attention. Next in moral importance to having the conscience purged by the blood of Christ stands this cleansing of our ways by the action of the Word, through the power of the Holy Ghost. The former gives us a part *in* Christ; the latter, a part *with* Christ. That is never repeated; this must never be interrupted. If we really desire fellowship with Christ, we must allow Him to wash our feet moment by moment. We cannot tread the pure precincts of the sanctuary of God with defiled feet any more than we can enter them with a defiled conscience.

Hence, therefore, let us look well to it that we have our ways continually submitted to the purifying action of the precious Word of God. Let us put away every thing which that Word condemns; let us abandon every position and every association and every practice which that Word condemns, that so our holy fellowship with Christ may be maintained in its freshness and integrity. Nothing is more dangerous than to trifle with evil in any shape or form. Ignorance God can and does most graciously bear with, but the willful resistance of His Word in any one point is sure to lead to disastrous results. The heart becomes hardened, the conscience seared, the moral sense blunted, and the whole moral being gets into a most deplorable condition. We get away from the Lord, and make shipwreck of faith and a good conscience. May the Lord keep us near to Himself, walking with Him in tenderness of conscience and uprightness of heart. May His Word ever tell in living formative power upon our souls, that so our way be cleansed according to the claims of the sanctuary of God.

2. But let us now inquire for a moment into the spring of this action on which we have been dwelling. This is presented with touching sweetness and power in the first verse of John 13—"Having loved His own which were in the world, He loved them unto the end."

Here, then, we have the mighty spring of Christ's present ministry. It is the changeless love of His heart—a love that was stronger than death, and which many waters could not quench. "Christ loved the Church, and gave Himself for it; that He might sanctify and cleanse it with the washing of water by the Word" (Eph. 5:25-26). This is the blessed basis and the motive-spring of that marvelous ministry which our Lord Jesus Christ is now carrying on for us and toward us. He knew what He was undertaking when He uttered those words in the fortieth Psalm, "Lo, I come to do Thy will, O God." He knew what it would cost Him when He took up our case. But His love was and is divinely equal to all. We need not be afraid of exhausting that love which triumphed over all the unutterable horrors of Calvary, and went down under the deep and dark waters of death and judgment. We may at times feel ashamed to have so often to bring our defiled feet to that blessed One to cleanse them; but His love is equal to all, and that love is the spring of His precious and indispensable ministry.

It is a common saying that love is blind, but I look upon it as a libel upon love. Most certainly it does not and could not apply to the love of Christ. He knew all that was in us, and He knows now all our ways and all our weakness and all our follies; but He loves us notwithstanding all, and in the power of that love He acts toward us in order to deliver us from all that He sees in us and about us which would hinder our holy fellowship with the Father and with His Son.

Of what use would a blind love be to you or to me? Surely, none whatever. How could we ever repose in a love which only acted toward us in ignorance of our blots and blemishes! Impossible. What we want is a love superior to all our imperfections, and a love that can deliver us from them. This love we have in

Christ, blessed be His name! It is a love that, however it may expose us to ourselves, will never expose us to another. It is a love that comes to us with the basin and towel, and stoops down in infinite tenderness and lowly, matchless grace to wash away every soil, and give us the comfortable sense of being "clean every whit." This is the love which you and I need, and this is the love which we have found in divine fullness and power in the heart of that perfect Servant who is girded for us ever before the throne.

"Having loved *His own* which were in the world, He loved them"—how long? As long as they behaved themselves, and walked with unsoiled feet? Ah, no! this would never do for such as we. "He loved them *unto the end.*" Precious, perfect, divine, everlasting love! a love that overlaps and underlies and outlives all our blots and blemishes, our failings and falterings, our wants and weaknesses, our wanderings and waywardness; a love that has come to us armed with all that our condition could possibly demand; a love that will never cease to act for us and toward us and in us, until it presents us in unblemished perfectness before the throne of God.

3. And now one word as to the measure of Christ's present action for us and toward us. This is a point of unspeakable value and importance. It is essential for us to know that, whether it be a question of Christ's service for us in the past or His present service, the measure of both the one and the other is and can be nothing less than the claims of the sanctuary, the throne, and the nature of God. We might suppose that the measure would be our necessities, but this would never do. If we think of Christ's atoning work, we know, and rejoice to know, that precious work has done very much more than meet the deepest measure of our necessities as sinners. Blessed be God! the work of the cross has divinely met all the claims of God. It could never give solid peace to our souls merely to know that the very highest claims of human conscience had been met by the atoning death of Christ. We must be assured on divine authority that the highest claims of the government, the character, the nature, and the glory of God

have all been perfectly met by the precious work of Christ.

Thus it is through infinite grace, and here every divinely exercised soul can find settled and eternal peace. Nor is it otherwise in respect to Christ's present work for us. It could never satisfy our souls to be told that that work is measured by our very deepest need. That need is met, no doubt; but it is because Christ's present ministry goes far beyond that need, and reaches to, and satisfies the claims of, the sanctuary of God.

Unspeakable mercy! Here we may rest in perfect tranquility. We have One on high undertaking for us, ever living in the presence of God for us; One who not only knows our necessities, but knows also the claims of God. He knows what this scene is through which we are passing, and He knows what that scene is into which He has entered; and, all praise to His name! He meets in His own perfect ministry both the one and the other. He must needs meet all our claims since He meets all God's claims, for the less must ever be included in the greater.

What solid comfort is here! What unruffled repose! We have One in the presence of God for us, in whose hands all our affairs are perfectly, because divinely, safe. They can never fall through, never go wrong. We may say that ere ever the very weakest of those whom Christ calls "His own in the world" can fail, Christ Himself must fail, and that can be *never.* His own are as safe as Himself.

What a grand reality! With what perfect confidence may we refer every objector, every accuser, every opposer, to this blessed manager! And what folly, on our part, to attempt to answer such ourselves! Oh, may we learn to lean more confidently on that blessed One who thus presents Himself before our souls as the girded servant of our deep and manifold necessities. May we prize His precious ministry more and more—His ministry for us, His ministry to us. May we repose more sweetly in the assurance that He is speaking to the Father for us, in all our failures, in all our shortcomings, in all our sins.

May we remember, for our exceeding comfort, that even before we slip, He has been pleading for us, as He pleaded for Peter. "I have prayed for thee," said the loving One, "that thy faith fail not." Oh, the matchless grace of these words! He did not pray that Peter might not fall, but that, having fallen, his confidence might not give way, his faith might not fail. Thus, too, He pleads for us, and thus we are sustained, and thus we are restored when we fall, else we should very speedily go from bad to worse, and make shipwreck altogether. "He ever liveth to make intercession for us." We are sustained by His precious and powerful ministry every moment. We could not stand for a single hour without Him.

Things are continually turning up which would prove destructive of our fellowship, if we had not that blessed One acting for us, whose intervention on our behalf never ceases. He knows not only our need, but He knows what the sanctuary demands; and not only does He know it, but He provides for it, according to His own infinite perfectness and acceptance before God, meeting His people's necessities.

Now, there are some people who have got such a one-sided notion of the standing of the believer, that they throw the Lord's priestly ministry overboard altogether. I say it is one-sided, and there is nothing more dangerous than one-sided truth—nothing. I would far rather see a man going through the length and breadth of London publishing palpable error, such as the simplest mind could detect. I would have far less apprehension of the mischievous result of his ministry than of the teaching of a man who takes up one side of a truth, and presses it in such a way as to interfere with some other truth.

Now, there is an adjusting power in the truth of God—an adjusting power in Scripture that constitutes one of its brightest moral glories; and hence we find that while the Word of God most fully and blessedly establishes the truth that the believer stands complete in Christ, justified from all things, accepted in the Beloved, "clean every whit," it, at the same time with equal clearness and fullness, sets forth the fact that the believer is, in himself, a poor feeble creature, exposed

to manifold snares, temptations, and hostile influences; liable at any moment to fall into error and evil; utterly unable to keep himself, or to grapple with the difficulties and dangers which surround him; liable at any moment to contract defilement, which would unfit him for the holy fellowship and worship of the sanctuary.

How, then, are all those things to be met? How is the Christian to be kept in the face of such things? Having an evil nature, a crafty foe, and a hostile world to cope with, how is he to get on? How is he to be kept? How is he to be restored if he wanders? How is he to be lifted up if he falls? The answer to all these questions is found in that ever-precious sentence of inspiration, "He ever liveth to make intercession for us"; and again, "He is able to save to the uttermost"; and again, "We shall be saved by His life"; and again, "Because I live, ye shall live also"; and again, "We have an advocate with the Father."

How the heart delights to give forth and to ponder over such utterances as these! They are marrow and fatness to the soul. How can any one, in the face of such passages—to say nothing of his own necessary experiences as to himself and his surroundings—think of calling in question the grand foundation-truth of the priesthood of Christ, in its application to believers now? I can only say, I know not. But alas! there is no accounting for the depths of error into which we may fall, if we allow our minds to work, and get away from the direct authority of holy Scripture. And we may truly say that a most palpable proof of our need of the intercession of Christ is to be found in the sad fact that any of His servants should be found to deny it.

I shall add no more on this point, save to warn all the Lord's dear people against the terrible error of denying our continual need of the priestly ministry, the precious intercession and all-prevailing advocacy of our Lord Jesus Christ—an error second only to the denial of His atoning work. For most surely our need of His priesthood is second only to our need of His atoning blood.

III. Having then briefly, and, alas! imperfectly, glanced at our Lord's ministry in the past and in the present, we cannot close without a reference to His ministry in the future. Some may feel disposed to say, I do not understand how our Lord can ever be found serving us in the future. I can understand His serving us now on the throne, but how He is to serve us in the kingdom is, I confess, beyond me.

No doubt it is most marvelous, and had we not His own veritable words for it, we might well hesitate in our statement of the fact that our Lord Christ shall serve His people in the very brightness of the glory. But let us hear what He Himself saith to us. Turn for a moment to Luke 12:35: "Let your loins be girded about, and your lights burning; and ye yourselves like unto men that wait for their lord, when he will return from the wedding; that when he cometh and knocketh, they may open unto him immediately. Blessed are those servants, whom the lord when he cometh shall find watching: verily I say unto you, that *he shall gird himself, and make them to sit down to meat, and will come forth and serve them."*

This is distinct and unmistakable. Most marvelous, no doubt, but as plain as it is marvelous. Christ will serve us in the kingdom. He will serve us forever. His ministry overlaps our entire history. It reaches down to the very deepest depths of our need as sinners, and up to the very loftiest heights of the glory. It goes back to the past, it covers the present, and it stretches away into the boundless future. Blessed be His name! He loves to serve us, and He gives us the assurance that the very moment, as it were, that He enters upon the glory of His own kingdom, He will gratify His loving heart by making us sit down amid the very brightness of that glory, and there serving us in the same love that has characterized His service from the very first. All praise and eternal homage to His peerless name!

But mark another thing in this twelfth chapter of Luke. At the forty-first verse Peter puts the question, " 'Lord, speakest Thou this parable unto us, or even to all?' And the Lord said, 'Who then is that faithful and wise steward whom his lord shall make ruler over his household, to give them their

portion of meat in due season? Blessed is that servant, whom his lord when he cometh shall find so doing. Of a truth I say unto you, that he will make him ruler over all that he hath.' "

Thus we have two things, namely, "*watching*" and "*doing*." Which does Christ value most? The former, unquestionably, as is proved by the higher reward attached to it. To have Christ serving us in the glory is something far beyond any position which He may in His goodness assign to us.

Let us, then, ever bear in mind, brethren, that our blessed Lord values, above all things, that loving attitude of the heart which expresses itself by *watching for* His return. No doubt it is blessed and important to be found "*doing*" also, whatever He gives us to do, whether it be sweeping a crossing or evangelizing a nation; He will not allow the very smallest act of service to go unrequited. It is not that He values service less, but He values watching more, and we can understand this; even nature itself will teach it to us. Suppose the head of a family is absent from home; the servants are told to have things in readiness for his return, and each will be found doing his or her appointed work. They will say, Master is coming home; we must see and have all square and right for him. This is as it should be; but is there not something far deeper and higher than this? Is there not something that answers to the heart of that absent one? Surely there is; there is the earnest longing of an affectionate wife, without which the best ordered house would be but a poor, cold, cheerless thing to come back to.

Thus it is, be assured of it, with our beloved absent Lord. He prizes, above all things, the affectionate, earnest longings of our hearts to see His face. Something of what shone in Mephibosheth, when he said to David, "Let him take all, seeing my lord the king is come in peace." Oh, let us cultivate more of this, dearly beloved in the Lord; let us see to it that we are of those who *love* the appearing of our adorable Lord and Saviour! May the cry of our hearts be continually, "Why tarry the wheels of His chariot?"

Will this make us deficient in service? The

very reverse. Nay, it is this which will give the true spring to all service, and impart a holy fragrance to the very smallest act which may be done. Whereas, if this deep personal affection be lacking, the most splendid and showy acts of service are as nothing to the heart of Jesus. The two mites of the widow were more precious to Christ than the most princely gifts of heartless offerers. Show me a heart that is watching for Christ, and I will show you a pair of hands occupied for Him in some way or another. It does not matter in the least what we are doing, provided it be the very thing which our Lord has given us to do, and there is nothing that will so quickly enable us to know what service to do as a loving heart. There is an instinct, a tact about true love, that leads it to find out at once what is grateful to its object.

This is what is wanting, brethren. There may be a vast amount of busy activity—of running hither and thither—of coming and going; but if the *heart* be not occupied with Christ, the hands and feet and head are little worth. He, blessed forever be His name! has given us a whole heart, and nothing can satisfy Him in return but a whole heart from us. His entire service—past, present, and future—is the fruit of His perfect love; and nothing can meet His desire, with respect to us, save a heart responsive in its affections to Him. And where there is this, it will express itself in an anxious, earnest longing for His coming. "Blessed are those servants, whom their lord when he cometh shall find watching."

May the eternal Spirit fill our hearts with genuine love to the Person of our own adorable Lord and Saviour; that so our one grand and undivided purpose may be to live for Him in this scene from which He has been cast out, and to wait for that moment when we shall see Him as He is, and be like Him and with Him forever.

THE THREE APPEARINGS

Hebrews 9:24-28

"FOR CHRIST is not entered into the holy places made with hands, which are the figures of the true; but into heaven itself, *now to appear* in the presence of God for us: nor yet that He should offer Himself often, as the high priest entereth into the holy place every year with blood of others; for then must He often have suffered since the foundation of the world: but now once in the end of the ages *hath He appeared* to put away sin by the sacrifice of Himself. And as it is appointed unto men once to die, but after this the judgment: so Christ was once offered to bear the sins of many; and unto them that look for Him *shall He appear* the second time apart from sin unto salvation."*

The foregoing passage sets before us three great facts in the life of our Lord Jesus Christ. It speaks of what we may venture to call three distinct appearings, namely, an appearing in the past; an appearing in the present; and an appearing in the future. He *hath* appeared in this world to do a certain work; He *doth* appear in Heaven to carry on a certain ministry; and He *shall* appear in glory. The first is Atonement; the second is Advocacy; the third is the Advent.

First, then, let us dwell for a few moments on *the Atonement*, which is here presented in its two grand aspects, first, Godward; and secondly, usward. The apostle declares that Christ hath appeared "to put away *sin*"; and also "to bear the sins of many." This is a distinction of the utmost importance, and one not sufficiently understood or attended to.

---

* The English reader should be informed that the three words which are rendered in the above passage, "appear," are not the same in the original Greek; but our object is to deal with the facts set forth, rather than with the words employed.

Christ has put away sin by the sacrifice of Himself. He has glorified God in reference to the question of sin in its very broadest aspect. This He has done altogether irrespective of the question of persons or the forgiveness of the *sins* of individuals. Even though every soul, from the days of Adam down to the very last generation, were to reject the proffered mercy of God, yet would it hold good that the atoning death of Christ had put away sin—had destroyed the power of Satan—had perfectly glorified God, and laid the deep and solid foundation on which all the divine counsels and purposes can rest for ever.

It is to this fact that the Baptist refers in these memorable words, "Behold the Lamb of God, which taketh away the *sin* of the world" (John 1:29). The Lamb of God has wrought a work in virtue of which every trace of sin shall be obliterated from the creation of God. He has perfectly vindicated God in the very midst of a scene in which He had been so grossly dishonored, in which His character had been traduced and His majesty insulted. He came to do this at all cost, even at the sacrifice of Himself. He sacrificed Himself in order to maintain, in view of Heaven, earth, and hell, the glory of God. He has wrought a work by the which God is infinitely more glorified than if sin had not entered at all. God shall reap a richer harvest by far in the fields of redemption than ever He could have reaped in the fields of an unfallen creation.

It is well that the reader should deeply ponder this glorious aspect of the atoning death of Christ. We are apt to think that the very highest view we can take of the cross is that which involves the question of our forgiveness and salvation. This is a grave mistake. That question is divinely settled, as we shall seek to show; for the less is always included in the greater. But let us remember that our side of the atonement is the less, God's side of it the greater.

It was infinitely more important that God should be glorified than that we should be saved. Both ends have been gained, blessed be God, and gained by one and the same work, the precious atonement of Christ; but

we must never forget that the glory of God is of far greater moment than the salvation of men; and further, that we never can have so clear a sense of the latter as when we see it flowing from the former. It is when we see that God has been perfectly and for ever glorified in the death of Christ, that we can really enter into the divine perfectness of our salvation. In point of fact, both are so intimately bound up together that they cannot be separated; but still God's part in the cross of Christ must ever get its own proper pre-eminence.

The glory of God was ever uppermost in the devoted heart of the Lord Jesus Christ. For this He lived, for this He died. He came into this world for the express purpose of glorifying God, and from this great and holy object He never swerved a moment from the manger to the cross. True it is—blessedly true—that in carrying out this object He has perfectly met our case; but the divine glory ruled Him in life and in death.

Now it is on the ground of atonement, looked at in this its higher aspect, that God has been dealing with the world in patient grace, mercy and forbearance for well nigh six thousand years. He sends His rain and His sunbeams upon the evil and upon the good, upon the just and the unjust. It is in virtue of the atonement of Christ—though despised and rejected—that the infidel and the atheist live, and enjoy God's daily mercies; yea, the very breath that they spend in opposing the revelation and denying the existence of God they owe to Him in whom they live, move, and have their being.

We speak not here, by any means, of the forgiveness of *sins*, or of the soul's salvation. This is another question altogether, and to it we shall refer presently. But, looking at man in reference to his life in this world, and looking at the world in which he lives, it is the Cross which forms the basis of God's merciful dealing with both the one and the other.

Furthermore, it is on the ground of the atonement of Christ, in the same aspect of it, that the evangelist can go forth "into *all the world*, and preach glad tidings to *every creature*." He can declare the blessed truth that God has been glorified as to sin—His claims satisfied—His majesty vindicated—His law magnified—His attributes harmonized. He can proclaim the precious message that God can now be just and yet the justifier of any poor ungodly sinner that believes in Jesus. There is no hindrance, no barrier of any kind whatsoever.

The preacher of the gospel is not to be cramped by any dogmas of theology. He has to do with the large, loving heart of God, which, in virtue of atonement, can flow forth to every creature beneath the canopy of Heaven. He can say to each and to all—and say it without reserve—"*Come!*" Nay, more, he is bound to "*beseech*" them to come. "We *pray* you in Christ's stead, be ye reconciled to God." Such is the proper language of the evangelist, the herald of the cross, the ambassador of Christ. He knows no less a range than the wide, wide world; and he is called to drop his message into the ear of every creature under heaven.

And why? Because "Christ hath put away sin by the sacrifice of Himself." He has, by His most precious death, changed completely the ground of God's dealings with man and with the world, so that, instead of having to deal with them on the ground of sin, He can deal on the ground of atonement.

Finally, it is in virtue of the atonement, in this broad and lofty aspect, that every vestige of sin, and every trace of the serpent shall be obliterated from the wide universe of God. Then shall be seen the full force of that passage above referred to, "The Lamb of God, which taketh away the sin of the world."

Thus much as to what we may call the primary aspect of the atoning death of Christ—an aspect which cannot be too thoughtfully studied. A clear understanding of this weighty point would tend to remove a great deal of difficulty and misunderstanding in reference to the full and free preaching of the gospel. Many of the Lord's honored servants find themselves hindered in the presentation of the glad tidings of salvation, simply because they do not see this wide aspect of the atonement. They confine the death of Christ merely to its bearing upon the sins of God's elect; and they therefore deem it wrong to preach the gospel to all, or to invite, yea to beseech and entreat, all to come.

Now, that Christ did die for the elect, Scripture distinctly teaches in manifold places. He died for the elect nation of Israel, and for the elect Church of God—the bride of Christ. But Scripture teaches more than this. It declares that "He died for *all*" (2 Cor. 5:14); that "He tasted death for *every man*" (Heb. 2:9). There is no need whatever for seeking to avoid the plain force and meaning of these and kindred statements of inspiration. And further, we believe it to be quite wrong to add our own words to God's words in order to reconcile them with any particular system of doctrine.

When Scripture affirms that Christ died for all, we have no right to add the words, "the elect." And when Scripture states that Christ "tasted death for every man," we have no right to say, "every elect man." It is our place to take God's Word as it stands, and reverently bow to its authoritative teaching in all things. We can no more systematize God's Word than we can systematize God Himself. His Word, His heart, and His nature, are quite too deep and comprehensive to be included within the limits of the very broadest and best constructed human system of theology that was ever framed.

We shall, ever and anon, be discovering passages of Scripture which will not fall in with our system. We must remember that God is love, and this love will tell itself out to all without limit. True, God has His counsels, His purposes, and His decrees; but it is not these He presents to the poor lost sinner. He will instruct and interest His saints about such things; but to the guilty, heavy-laden sinner, He presents His love, His grace, His mercy, His readiness to save, to pardon, and to bless.

And let it be well remembered that the sinner's responsibility flows out of what is *revealed*, and not out of what is *secret*. God's decrees are secret; His nature, His character, Himself is revealed. The sinner will not be judged for rejecting what he had no means of knowing. "This is the condemnation, that light is come into the world, and men loved darkness rather than light, because their deeds were evil" (John 3:19).

We are not writing a theological treatise; but we do feel it to be a matter of the gravest moment to press upon the reader that his responsibility, as a sinner, is based upon the fact that the aspect of the salvation of God, and of the atonement of Christ, is most distinctly and decidedly "unto all," and not merely to a certain number of the human family. The glorious message is sent forth into all the world. Every one who hears it is invited to come. This is grounded upon the fact that Christ has put away sin—that the blood of atonement has been carried into the presence of God— that the barrier which sin presented has been flung down and abolished, and now the mighty tide of divine love can flow freely forth to the very vilest of the sons of men.

Such is the message; and when any one through grace believes it he can be further told that not only has Christ put away *sin*, but that also He has borne his *sins*—the actual sins of all His people—of all who believe in His name. The evangelist can stand up in the midst of assembled thousands, and declare that Christ has put away sin—that God is satisfied—that the way is open for all; and he can whisper the same in the ear of each and every sinner under Heaven. Then, when any one has bowed down to this testimony—when the repentant, broken-hearted, self-judged sinner receives the blessed record—he can be further taught that his *sins* were all laid on Jesus, all borne and for ever put away by Him when He died on the cross.

This is the plain doctrine of Hebrews 9:26, 28; and we have a striking type of it in the two goats of Leviticus 16. If the reader will just turn to the passage he will find there, first, the *slain* goat; and secondly the *scape-goat*. The blood of the slain goat was brought into the sanctuary and sprinkled there. This was a type of Christ putting away *sin*. Then the high priest, on behalf of the congregation, confessed all their *sins* upon the head of the scape-goat, and they were borne away into a land not inhabited. This

was a type of Christ bearing the sins of His people. The two goats, taken together, give us a full view of the atonement of Christ, which, like the righteousness of God in Romans 3, is "unto all, and upon all them that believe."

All this is most simple. It removes many difficulties out of the way of the earnest seeker after peace. These difficulties arise in many cases from the conflicting dogmas of theological systems, and have no foundation whatever in Holy Scripture. There, all is as plain and as clear as God can make it. Each one who hears the message of God's free love is bound, not to say invited, to receive it; and judgment will, most assuredly, fall upon each and all who refuse or neglect the proffered mercy.

It is utterly impossible for any one who has ever heard the gospel, or ever had the New Testament in his hand, to get rid of the awful responsibility that rests upon him to accept God's salvation. Not a single soul will have to say, I could not believe, because I was not one of the elect, and did not get power to believe. No one will ever dare to say or even to think this. If any could take such ground, then where were the force or the meaning of the following burning words?—"The Lord Jesus shall be revealed from heaven with the angels of His power, in flaming fire taking vengeance on them that know not God, and that obey not the gospel of our Lord Jesus Christ" (2 Thess. 1:7-8). Will any one ever be punished for not obeying the gospel if he is not responsible to yield that obedience? Most assuredly not. "Shall not the Judge of all the earth do right?"

But does God send His gospel to people merely to place them under responsibility and increase their guilt? Far be the monstrous thought! He sends His gospel to the lost sinner in order that he may be *saved*, for God is not willing that any should perish, but that all should come to repentance. All, therefore, who perish shall have none but themselves to blame.

It is of the very last importance that the reader should be established in the knowledge and practical sense of what the atonement of Christ has accomplished for all who simply trust in Him. It is, we need hardly say, the only basis of peace. He has put away sin by the sacrifice of Himself; and He has borne our sins in His own body on the tree. It is, therefore, impossible that any question as to sin or guilt can ever arise. All has been "once and for ever" settled by the atoning death of the Lamb of God.

True it is—alas, how true!—we all have sin in us; and we have, daily and hourly, to judge ourselves and judge our ways. It will ever hold good of us, so long as we are in a body of sin and death, that "in me (that is, in my flesh) dwelleth no good thing." But then nothing can ever touch the question of our soul's perfect and eternal acceptance. The conscience of the believer is as completely purged from every soil and stain as will be the whole creation by-and-by. If it were not so, Christ could not be where He now is. He has entered into the presence of God, there to appear for us.

This leads us in the second place to consider *the Advocacy.* Very many souls are apt to confound two things which, though inseparably connected, are perfectly distinct, namely, advocacy and atonement. Not seeing the divine completeness of the atonement, they are in a certain way looking to the advocacy to do for them what the atonement has done. We must remember that though as to our standing we are not in the flesh but in the Spirit, yet as to the actual fact of our condition we are in the body. We are in spirit and by faith seated in heavenly places in Christ; but yet we are actually in the wilderness, subject to all sorts of infirmities, liable to fail and err in a thousand ways.

Now it is to meet our present actual state and wants that the advocacy, or priesthood, of Christ is designed. God be praised for the blessed provision! As those who are in the body passing through the wilderness, we need a great High Priest to maintain the link of communion, or to restore it when broken.

Such a One we have, ever living to make intercession for us; nor could we get on for a single moment without Him. The work of atonement is never repeated; the work of the Advocate is never interrupted. When once the blood of Christ is applied to the soul by the power of the Holy Ghost, the application is never repeated. To think of a repetition is to deny its efficacy and to reduce it to the level of the blood of bulls and goats.

No doubt people do not see this, and most assuredly they do not mean it; but such is the real tendency of the thought of a fresh application of the blood of sprinkling. It may be that persons who speak in this way really mean to put honor upon the blood of Christ, and to give expression to their own felt unworthiness; but, in truth, the best way to put honor upon the blood of Christ is to rejoice in what it has done for our souls; and the best way to set forth our own unworthiness is to feel and remember that we were so vile that nothing but the death of Christ could avail to meet our case. So vile were we that nothing but His blood could cleanse us. So precious is His blood that not a trace of our guilt remains. "The blood of Jesus Christ, God's Son, cleanseth us from all sin."

Thus it stands in reference to the very feeblest child of God whose eye scans these lines. "All sins forgiven." Not a trace of guilt remains. Jesus is in the presence of God for us. He is there as a High Priest before God—as an Advocate with the Father. He has by His atoning death rent the veil—put away sin—brought us nigh to God in all the credit and virtue of His sacrifice, and now He lives to maintain us by His advocacy in the enjoyment of the place and privileges into which His blood has introduced us.

Hence the apostle says, "If any man sin, we have"—what? The blood? Nay, but "an Advocate with the Father, Jesus Christ the righteous." The blood has done its work, and is ever before God according to its full value in His sight. Its efficacy is ever the same. But we have sinned; it may be only in thought; but even that thought is quite enough to interrupt our communion. Here is where advocacy comes in. If it were not that Jesus Christ is ever acting for us in the sanctuary above, our faith would most assuredly fail in moments in the which we have in any measure yielded to the voice of our sinful nature.

Thus it was with Peter in that terrible hour

of his temptation and fall: "Simon, Simon, behold, Satan hath desired to have you, that he may sift you as wheat: but I have prayed for thee, that thy faith fail not: and when thou art converted (or restored), strengthen thy brethren" (Luke 22:21, 32).

Let the reader note this. "I have prayed for thee, that"—What? Was it that he might not fail? Nay, but that, having failed, his faith might not give way. Had Christ not prayed for his poor, feeble servant, he would have gone from bad to worse, and from worse to worst. But the intercession of Christ procured for Peter the grace of true repentance, self-judgment and bitter sorrow for his sin, and finally complete restoration of his heart and conscience, so that the current of his communion—interrupted by sin, but restored by advocacy—might flow on as before.

Thus it is with us when, through lack of that holy vigilance which we should ever exercise, we commit sin: Jesus goes to the Father for us. He prays for us; and it is through the efficacy of His priestly intercession that we are convicted and brought to self-judgment, confession, and restoration. All is founded on the advocacy, and the advocacy is founded on the atonement.

And here it may be well to assert, in the clearest and strongest manner possible, that it is the sweet privilege of every believer not to commit sin. There is no necessity whatever why he should. "My little children," says the apostle, "these things write I unto you, that ye sin not." This is a most precious truth for every lover of holiness. *We need not sin.* Let us remember this. "Whosoever is born of God doth not commit [or, *practice*] sin; for His seed remaineth in him: and he cannot sin, because he is born of God" (1 John 3:9).

This is the divine idea of a Christian. Alas, we do not always realize it! but that does not, and cannot, touch the precious truth. The divine nature, the new man, the life of Christ in the believer cannot possibly sin, and it is the privilege of every believer so to walk as that nothing but the life of Christ may be seen. The Holy Ghost dwells in the believer on the ground of redemption, in order to give effect to the desires of the new nature, so that the flesh may be as though it did not exist, and nothing but Christ be seen in the believer's life.

It is of the utmost importance that this divine idea of Christian life should be seized and maintained. People sometimes ask the question, Is it possible for a Christian to live without committing sin? We reply in the language of the inspired apostle, "My little children, these things write I unto you, that ye sin not" (1 John 2:1). And again, quoting the language of another inspired apostle, "How shall we, that are dead to sin, *live* any longer therein?" (Rom. 6:2)

The Christian is viewed by God as "dead to sin"; and hence, if he yields to it he is practically denying his standing in a risen Christ. Alas, alas, we do sin, and hence the apostle adds, "If any man sin, we have an Advocate with the Father, Jesus Christ the righteous: and He is the propitiation for our sins: and not for ours only, but also for the whole world."

This gives wonderful completeness to the work on which our souls repose. Such is the perfect efficacy of the atonement of Christ that we have one Advocate with us in order that we may not sin, and another Advocate with the Father if we do sin. The word rendered "Comforter" in John 14:16 is rendered "advocate" in 1 John 3:1. We have one divine Person caring for us here, and we have another divine Person caring for us in Heaven, and all this on the ground of the atoning death of Christ.

Will it be said that in writing thus we furnish a license for committing sin? God forbid! We have already declared, and would insist upon, the blessed possibility of living in such unbroken communion with God—of walking so in the Spirit—of being so filled and occupied with Christ—as that the flesh, or the old nature, may not appear. This we know is not always the case. "In many things we all offend," as James tells us. But no rightminded person, no lover of holiness, no spiritual Chrisian, could have any sympathy with those who say we *must* commit sin. Thank God, it is not so. But what a mercy it is to know that when we do fail there is One at the right hand of God to restore the broken link of communion! This He does by producing in our souls, by His Spirit who dwells in us—that "other Advocate"—the sense of failure, and leading us into self-judgment and true confession of the wrong, whatever it be.

We say *"true* confession," for it must be this if it be the fruit of the Spirit's work in the heart. It is not lightly and flippantly saying we have sinned, and then as lightly and flippantly sinning again. This is most sorrowful and most dangerous. We know nothing more hardening and demoralizing than this sort of thing. It is sure to lead to the most disastrous consequences. We have known cases of persons living in sin and satisfying themselves by a mere lip confession of their sin, and then going and committing the sin again and again; and this has gone on for months and years, until God in His faithfulness caused the whole thing to come out openly before others.

All this is most dreadful. It is Satan's way of hardening and deceiving the heart. Oh that we may watch against it, and ever keep a tender conscience! We may rest assured that when a true-hearted child of God is betrayed into sin the Holy Ghost will produce in him such a sense of it—will lead him into such intense self-loathing, such an abhorrence of the evil, such thorough self-judgment in the presence of God—as that he cannot lightly go and commit the sin again. This we may learn from the words of the apostle when he says, "If we confess our sins, He is faithful and just to forgive us our sins, and"—mark this weighty clause—"to *cleanse us from all unrighteousness.*"

Here we have the precious fruit of the double advocacy. It is all presented in its fulness in this part of the First Epistle of John. If any man sin, the blessed Paraclete on high intercedes with the Father, pleads the full merits of His atoning work, prays for the erring one on the ground of His having borne the judgment of that very sin. Then the other Paraclete acts in the conscience, produces repentance and confession, and brings the soul back into the light in the sweet sense

that the sin is forgiven, the unrighteousness cleansed, and the communion perfectly restored. "He restoreth my soul: *He leadeth me in the paths of righteousness* for His name's sake" (Ps. 23:3).

We trust the reader will be enabled to understand this great fundamental truth. Many, we are aware, find it difficult to reconcile the idea of intercession with the truth of a perfect atonement. If, say they, the atonement is perfect, what need is there of intercession? If the believer is made as white as snow by the blood of Christ—so white that the Spirit of God can dwell in his heart—then what does he want of a priest? If by one offering Christ has perfected for ever all them that are sanctified, then what need have these perfected and sanctified ones of an advocate? Surely we must either admit the thought of an imperfect atonement or deny the need of advocacy?

Such is the reasoning of the human mind, but such is not the faith of Christians. Scripture does most surely teach us that the believer is washed as white as snow; that he is accepted in the Beloved—complete in Christ—perfectly forgiven and perfectly justified through the death and resurrection of Christ; that he can never come into judgment, but is passed from death unto life; that he is not in the flesh, but in the Spirit—not in the old creation, but in the new—not a member of the first Adam, but of the last; that he is dead to sin, dead to the world, dead to the law, because Christ has died, and the believer has died in Him. All this is largely unfolded and constantly insisted upon by the inspired writers. Scores of passages might easily be quoted in proof, were it needful.

But then there is another aspect of the Christian which must be taken into account. He is not in the flesh as to the ground of his standing, but he is in the body as to the fact of his condition. He is in Christ as to his standing, but he is also in the world as to the fact of his existence. He is surrounded by all sorts of temptations and difficulties, and he is in himself a poor feeble creature full of infirmities, not sufficient even to think anything as of himself.

Nor is this all. Each true Christian is ever ready to acknowledge that in him, that is, in his flesh, there dwelleth no good thing. He is saved, thank God, and all is eternally settled; but then he has, *as a saved one*, to get through the wilderness; he has to labor to enter into God's rest, and here it is that priesthood comes in. The object of priesthood is not to complete the work of atonement, inasmuch as that work is as perfect as the One who accomplished it.

But we have to be carried through the wilderness and brought into the rest that remains for the people of God, and for this end we have a great High Priest who is passed into the heavens, Jesus the Son of God. His sympathy and succor are ours, and we could not get on for one moment without them. He ever liveth to make intercession for us, and by His ministry in the heavenly sanctuary He sustains us day by day in the full credit and value of His atoning work. He lifts us up when we fall, restores us when we wander, repairs the link of communion when snapped by our carelessness. In a word, He appears in the presence of God for us, and there carries on an uninterrupted service on our behalf, in virtue of which we are maintained in the integrity of the relationship into which His atoning death has introduced us.

Thus much as to the atonement and advocacy. It only remains for us to treat of the advent. We wish specially to remind the reader that in treating of the death of Christ we have left wholly untouched one grand point therein, namely, our death in Him.* This we may, if God permit, go into on another occasion. It is immensely important as the power of deliverance from indwelling sin as well as from this present evil world and from the law. There are many who merely look to the death of Christ for pardon and justification, but they do not see the precious and emancipating truth of their having died in Him and their deliverance in consequence from the power of sin in them. This latter is the secret of victory over self and the world, and of deliverance from every form of legality and mere fleshly pietism.

Thus we have glanced at two of the weighty subjects presented to us in the closing verses of Heb. 9, namely, first, the precious atoning death of our Lord Jesus Christ in its two aspects; and secondly, His all-prevailing advocacy at God's right hand for us.

It only remains for us to consider in the third place *His Advent*, which is here presented to us in immediate connection with those great foundation truths which have already engaged our attention, and which, moreover, are held and prized by all true Christians. Is it true that Christ hath appeared in this world to put away *sin* by the sacrifice of Himself? and to bear the *sins* of the many who though grace put their trust in Him? Is it true that He has passed into the heavens and taken His seat on the throne of God, there to appear for us? Yes, blessed be God, these are grand, vital and fundamental verities of the Christian faith.

Well, then, it is equally true that He shall appear again, apart from the question of sin, unto salvation. "As it is appointed unto men once to die, but after this the judgment: so Christ was once offered to bear the sins of many; and unto them that look for Him shall He appear the second time apart from sin unto salvation."

Here, then, we have the matter most definitely stated. *As* truly as Christ hath appeared on this earth—as truly as He lay in the manger of Bethlehem—was baptized in the waters of Jordan—was anointed with the Holy Ghost—was tempted of the devil in the wilderness—went about doing good, and healing all that were oppressed of the devil—groaned, and wept, and prayed in Gethsemane—hung upon Calvary's accursed tree, and died, the Just for the unjust—was laid in the dark, silent tomb—rose victorious on the third day—ascended into the heavens, there to appear in the presence of God for His people—*so* truly shall He appear ere long in the clouds of Heaven to receive His people to Himself.

If we refuse one we must refuse all. If we question one we must question all. If we are unsettled as to one we must be unsettled as

* This has been touched upon in "Sin in the Flesh, and Sin on the Conscience" in this volume.

to all, inasmuch as all rest upon precisely the same basis, namely, the Holy Scriptures. How do I know that Jesus *hath* appeared? Because Scripture tells me so. How do I know that He *doth* appear? Because Scripture tells me so. How do I know that He *shall* appear? Because Scripture tells me so.

In a word, then, the doctrine of the Atonement, the doctrine of the Advocacy, and the doctrine of the Advent all rest on one and the same irrefragable foundation, namely, the simple declaration of the Word of God, so that if we receive one we must receive all.

How is it then that while the Church of God in all ages has held and prized the doctrines of atonement and advocacy, she has practically lost sight of the doctrine of the advent? How comes it to pass that while the first two are regarded as essential, the last is deemed non-essential? Nay, we may go further and say, how is it that while a man who does not hold the first two is regarded as a heretic, and justly so, yet the man who holds the last is by many regarded as hardly sound in the faith or bringing in strange doctrine?

What answer can we give to these questions? Alas! the Church has ceased to look for her Lord. Atonement and advocacy are held because they concern us; but the advent has been virtually let slip, although it so deeply concerns Him. It is due to the One who suffered and died on this earth that He should reign; to the One who wore a crown of thorns that He should wear a crown of glory; to the One who humbled Himself to the very dust of death that He should be exalted and that every knee should yet bow before Him.

Most surely this is so; and the God and Father of our Lord Jesus Christ will see to it and bring it to pass in His own appointed time. "Sit Thou at My right hand, until I make Thine enemies Thy footstool" (Ps. 110; Heb. 1). The moment is rapidly approaching when that blessed One who is now hidden from the eyes of men shall appear in glory. Every eye shall see Him. As surely as He hung upon the cross and is now seated on the throne, so surely shall He appear in glory.

Seeing these things are so, art thou among the number of "those that look for Him"? This is a solemn question. There are those who look for Him and there are those who do not. Now it is to the former that He shall appear unto salvation. He will come and receive His people unto Himself, that where He is, there they may be also (John 14). These are His own loving words, spoken at the moment of His departure for the solace and comfort of His sorrowing disciples. He counted on their being troubled at the thought of His leaving them, and He seeks to comfort them by the assurance of His coming back. He does not say, Let not your hearts be troubled, for you shall soon follow Me. No; but "I will come again."

This is the proper hope of the Christian. Christ is coming. Are we ready? Are we looking for Him? Do we miss Him? Do we mourn His absence? It is impossible that we can be in the true attitude of waiting for Him if we do not feel His absence. He is coming. He may be here to-night. Ere another sun arises the voice of the archangel and the blast of the trumpet may be heard in the air.

And what then? Why then the sleeping saints—all who have departed in the faith of Christ—all the redeemed of the Lord whose ashes repose in the graveyards and cemeteries around us or in the mighty depths of the ocean—all these shall rise. The living saints shall be changed in a moment, and all shall ascend up to meet the Lord in the air (1 Cor. 15:51-54; 1 Thess. 4:13—5:11).

But what of the unconverted—the unbelieving—the unrepentant—the unprepared? What of all such? Ah! this is a question of awful solemnity. It makes the heart sink to reflect upon the case of those who are still in their sins—of those who have turned a deaf ear to all the entreaties and all the warnings which God in His long-suffering mercy has sent to them from week to week and year to year—of those who have sat under the sound of the gospel from their earliest days, and who have become, as we say, gospel-hardened. How dreadful will be the condition of all such when the Lord comes to receive His own! They shall be left behind to fall under the deep and dark delusion which God will assuredly send upon all who have heard and rejected the gospel. And what then? What is to follow this deep and dark delusion? The deeper and darker damnation of the lake that burneth with fire and brimstone.

Oh! shall we not sound a note of alarm in the ears of our fellow-sinners? Shall we not more earnestly and solemnly warn them to flee from the wrath to come? Shall we not seek by word and deed—by the double testimony of the lips and the life—to set before them the weighty fact that "the Lord is at hand"? May we feel it more deeply, and then we shall exhibit it more faithfully. There is immense moral power in the truth of the Lord's coming if it be really held in the heart and not merely in the head. If Christians only lived in the habitual expectation of the advent it would tell amazingly upon the unconverted around them.

May the Holy Ghost revive in the hearts of all God's people the blessed hope of their Lord's return, that they may be as men that wait for their Lord, that when He cometh and knocketh they may open unto Him immediately!

BETHANY

John 11—12

Part 1

TURN WITH US to John 11—12; and if we mistake not, you will find therein a very rare spiritual treat. In chapter 11, we see what the Lord Jesus was to the family of Bethany; and in chapter 12 we see what the family of Bethany was to Him. The entire passage is full of the most precious instruction.

In chapter 11 we have three great subjects presented to us, namely, first, our Lord's own path with the Father; secondly, His profound sympathy with His people; and, thirdly, His grace in associating us with Himself in His work, in so far as that is possible.

"Now a certain man was sick, named Lazarus, of Bethany, the town of Mary and her sister Martha. (It was that Mary which anointed the Lord with ointment, and wiped His feet with her hair, whose brother Lazarus was sick.) Therefore his sisters sent unto Him, saying, Lord, behold he whom Thou lovest is sick. When Jesus heard that, He said, This sickness is not unto death, but for the glory of God that the Son of God might be glorified thereby."

The sisters, in their time of trouble, turned to the true Source—their divine Friend: Jesus was a sure resource for them, as He is for all His tried ones wherever, however, or whoever they are. "Call upon Me in the time of trouble; I will deliver thee, and thou shalt glorify Me." We make a most serious mistake when, in any time of need or pressure, we turn to the creature for help or sympathy. We are sure to be disappointed. Creature-streams are dry. Creature-props give way. Our God will make us prove the vanity and folly of all creature-confidences, human hopes, and earthly expectations. And on the other hand, He will prove to us, in the most touching and forcible manner, the truth and blessedness of His own Word, "They shall not be ashamed that wait for Me."

No, never! He, blessed be His name, never fails a trusting heart. He cannot deny Himself. He delights to take occasion from our wants, our woes and weaknesses, to express and illustrate His tender care and lovingkindness, in a thousand ways. But He will teach us the utter barrenness of all human resources. "Thus saith the Lord; Cursed be the man that trusteth in man, and maketh flesh his arm, and whose heart departeth from the Lord. For he shall be like the heath in the desert, and shall not see when good cometh; but shall inhabit the parched places in the wilderness, in a salt land and not inhabited."

Thus it must ever be. Disappointment,

barrenness and desolation are the sure and certain results of trusting in man. But, on the other hand—and mark the contrast, "Blessed is the man that trusteth in the Lord, and whose hope the Lord is: for he shall be as a tree planted by the waters, and that spreadeth out her roots by the river, and shall not see when heat cometh, but her leaf shall be green; and shall not be careful in the year of drought, neither shall cease from yielding fruit" (Jer. 17:5-8).

Such is the unvarying teaching of Scripture on both sides of this great practical question. It is a fatal mistake to look even to the very best of men, to betake ourselves, directly or indirectly, to poor human cisterns. But the true secret of blessing, strength and comfort is to look to Jesus—to betake ourselves at once, in simple faith, to the living God whose delight ever is to help the needy, to strengthen the feeble, and lift up those that are cast down.

Hence, the sisters of Bethany did the right thing, when in the hour of need and pressure they turned to Jesus. He was both able and willing to help them: yet that blessed One did not at once respond to their call. He did not see fit at once to fly to their relief, much as He loved them. He fully entered into their sorrow and anxiety. He took it all in and measured it perfectly. He was thoroughly with them in it. There was no lack of sympathy, as we shall see in the sequel.

Yet He paused; and the enemy might cast in all sorts of suggestions; and their own hearts might conceive all sorts of reasonings. It might seem as though "The Master" had forgotten them. Perhpas their loving Lord and Friend was changed toward them. Something may have occurred to bring a cloud between them. We all know how the poor heart reasons and tortures itself at such times. But there is a divine remedy for all the heart's reasonings, and a triumphant answer to all the enemy's dark and horrible suggestions. What is it? Unshaken confidence in the eternal stability of the love of Christ.

Here lies the true secret of the whole matter. Let nothing shake your confidence in the unalterable love of your Lord. Come what may—let the furnace be ever so hot; let the waters be ever so deep; let the shadows be ever so dark; let the path be ever so rough; let the pressure be ever so great—still hold fast your confidence in the perfect love and sympathy of the One who has proved His love by going down into the dust of death—down under the dark and heavy billows and waves of the wrath of God, in order to save your soul from everlasting burnings. Be not afraid to trust Him *fully*—to commit yourself, without a shadow of reserve or misgiving, to Him.

Do not measure His love by your circumstances. If you do, you must, of necessity, reach a false conclusion. Judge not according to the outward appearance. Never reason from your surroundings. Get to the heart of Christ, and reason out from that blessed centre. Never interpret His love by your circumstances; but always interpret your circumstances by His love. Let the beams of His everlasting favor shine upon your darkest surroundings, and then you will be able to answer every infidel thought, no matter whence it comes.

> Judge not the Lord by feeble sense,
> But trust Him for His grace:
> Behind a frowning providence
> He hides a smiling face.

It is a grand thing to be able, ever to vindicate God; even if we can do nothing more, to stand as a monument of His unfailing faithfulness to all who put their trust in Him. What though the horizon around be dark and depressing—though the heavy clouds gather and the storm rage, God is faithful, and will not suffer us to be tempted above that we are able; but will, with the temptation, make a way of escape, that we may be able to bear it.

Besides, we must not measure divine love by the mode of its manifestation. We are all prone to do so; but it is a great mistake. The love of God clothes itself in varied forms, and not unfrequently the form seems to us, in our shallowness and short-sightedness, mysterious and incomprehensible. But, if only we wait patiently and in artless confidence, divine light will shine upon the dispensation of divine providence, and our hearts shall be filled with wonder, love, and praise.

We leave it to Himself,
To choose and to command:
With wonder filled, we soon shall see
How wise, how strong, His hand.

We comprehend Him not;
Yet earth and heaven tell,
God sits as Sovereign on the throne
And ruleth all things well.

God's thoughts are not as our thoughts; nor His ways as our ways; nor His love as our love. If we hear of a friend in distress or difficulty of any kind, our first impulse is to fly to his help and relieve him of his trial, if possible. But this might be a great mistake. In place of rendering help, it might be doing serious mischief. We might actually be running athwart the purpose of God, and taking our friend out of a position in which divine government had placed him for his ultimate and permanent profit. The love of God is a wise and faithful love. It abounds toward us in all wisdom and prudence.

We, on the contrary, make the gravest mistakes, even when most sincerely desiring to do what is right and good. We are not competent to take in all the bearings of things, or scan the windings and workings of providence, or weigh the ultimate results of the divine dealings. Hence, the urgent need of waiting much on God; and, above all things, of holding fast our confidence in His unchanging, unfailing, unerring love. He will make all plain. He will bring light out of darkness, life out of death, victory out of seeming defeat. He will cause the deepest and darkest distress to yield the very richest harvest of blessing. He will make all things work together for good.

But He is never in a hurry. He has His own wise ends in view, and He will reach them in His own time and way; and, moreover, out of what may seem to us to be a dark, tangled, inexplicable maze of providence, light will spring forth and fill our souls with praise and adoration.

The foregoing line of thought may help us to understand and appreciate our Lord's bearing towards the sisters of Bethany on hearing of their trouble. He felt there was much more involved in the case than the mere matter of relieving those whom He,

nevertheless, deeply loved. The glory of God had to be considered. Hence, He says, "This sickness is not unto death, but for the glory of God, that the Son of God might be glorified thereby." He saw in this case an occasion for the display of the divine glory, and not merely for the exhibition of personal affection, however deep and real that might be—and with Him, surely, it was both deep and real, for we read, "Jesus loved Martha and her sister and Lazarus."

But, in the judgment of our blessed and adorable Lord, the glory of God took precedence of every other consideration. Neither personal affection nor personal fear had the smallest sway over His movements. He was ruled, in all things, by the glory of God. From the manger to the cross, in life and in death, in all His words, and all His works, and all His ways, His devoted heart was set, with firm and unalterable purpose, upon the glory of God. Hence, though it might be a good thing to relieve a friend in distress, it was far better and higher to glorify God; and we may be sure, that the beloved family of Bethany sustained no loss by a delay which only made room for the brighter out-shining of the divine glory.

Let us all remember this in seasons of trial and pressure. It is an all-important point, and when fully apprehended, will prove a very deep and blessed source of consolation. It will help us marvelously to bear up under sickness, pain, death, bereavement, sorrow, and poverty. How blessed to be able to stand beside the sick bed of a friend and say, "This sickness is not unto death, but for the glory of God!" And this is faith's privilege. Yea, not only in the sick chamber, but by the open grave, the true believer may see the beams of the divine glory shining forth over all.

No doubt the skeptic might cavil at the statement that "The sickness is not unto death." He might object and reason and argue on the ground of the apparent fact that Lazarus *did* die. But faith reasons not from appearances: it bring God in, and there finds a divine solution for *all* difficulties. Such is the moral elevation—the reality of a life of faith. It sees God above and beyond all circumstances. It reasons from God downward—not from circumstances upward. Sickness and death are nothing in the presence of divine power. All difficulties disappear from the pathway of faith. They are, as Joshua and Caleb assured their unbelieving brethren, simply bread for the true believer.

Nor is this all. Faith can wait God's time, knowing that His time is the best. It staggers not, even though He may seem to linger. It rests with calmness in the assurance of His unchanging love and unerring wisdom. It fills the heart with the sweetest confidence that if there be delay—if the relief be not sent all at once—it is all for the best, inasmuch as "all things work together for good to them that love God," and all must in the long run redound to the glory of God. Faith enables its happy possessor to vindicate God amid the greatest pressure, and to know and confess that divine love always does the very best for its object.

Part 2

It gives great rest to the heart to know that the One who has undertaken for us, in all our weakness, our need, and the exigencies of our path from first to last, has first of all secured, in every respect, the glory of God. That was His primary object in all things. In the work of redemption, and in all our history, the glory of God has the first place in the heart of that blessed One with whom we have to do. At all cost to Himself He vindicated and maintained the divine glory. To that end He gave up everything. He laid aside His own glory, humbled, emptied Himself. He surrendered Himself and yielded up His life, in order to lay the imperishable foundation of that glory which now fills all Heaven—and shall soon cover the earth, and shine through the wide universe for ever.

The knowledge and abiding sense of this must give profound repose to the spirit in reference to everything that concerns us,

whether it be the salvation of the soul, the forgiveness of sins, or the needs for the daily path. All that could possibly be a matter of exercise to us, for time or for eternity, has been provided for, all secured on the selfsame basis that sustains the divine glory. We are saved and provided for; but the salvation and provision—all praise to our glorious Saviour and Provider!—are inseparably bound up with the glory of God. In all that our Lord Jesus Christ has done for us, in all that He is doing, in all that He will do, the glory of God is fully maintained.*

And, further, we may add that in our trials, difficulties, sorrows, and exercises, if instant relief be not afforded, we have to remember there is some deep reason connected with the glory of God and our real good, why the desired relief is withheld. In seasons of pressure we are apt to think only of the one thing, namely, relief. But there is very much more than this to be considered. We should think of the glory of God. We should seek to know His object in putting us under the pressure. We should earnestly desire that His end might be gained, and His glory promoted. This would be for our fullest and deepest blessing, while the relief which we so eagerly desire might be the worst thing we could get. We must always remember that, through the marvelous grace of God, His glory and our true blessing are so inseparably bound up together, that when the former is maintained, the latter must be perfectly secured.

This is a most precious consideration, and one eminently calculated to sustain the heart in all seasons of affliction. All things must ultimately redound to the glory of God, and "all things work together for good to those that love God, to them who are the called according to His purpose." It may not, perhaps, be so easy to see this when the pressure is upon us. When anxiously watching by the sick-bed of a beloved friend; or when treading the chamber of sorrow; or when laid on a bed of pain and languishing

---

* Entering the Sanctuary, Israel's high priest had over his forehead the plate of pure gold on which was engraved "*Holiness to the Lord*"; and on the breastplate, securely fastened upon his breast over the ephod, were engraved on twelve jewels the names of each tribe in Israel. So, in perfect love, our blessed Lord bears every one of His people upon His heart, maintaining at the same time God's holy character with His people. [Ed.]

ourselves; or when overwhelmed by sudden tidings of the loss of our earthly all: under such circumstances it may not be so easy to see the glory of God maintained, and our blessing secured; but faith can see it for all that; and as for "blind unbelief," it is always "sure to err."

If those beloved sisters of Bethany had judged by the sight of their eyes, they would have been sorely tried during those weary days and nights spent at the bedside of their much loved brother. And not only so, but when the terrible moment arrived, and they were called to witness the closing scene, many dark reasonings might have sprung up in their crushed and desolate hearts.

But Jesus was looking on. His heart was with them. He was watching the whole process, and that, too, from the very highest standpoint—the glory of God. He took in the entire scene, in all its bearings, its influences and its issues. He felt *for* those afflicted sisters—felt *with* them—felt as only a perfect human heart could feel. Though absent in person, He was with them in spirit, as they traveled through the deep waters. His loving heart perfectly entered into all their sorrow, and He only waited for "God's due time" to come to their aid, and light up the darkness of death and the grave with the bright beams of resurrection glory.

"When He had heard that Lazarus was sick, He abode two days still in the same place where He was." Things were allowed to take their course as we say; death was allowed to enter the much loved dwelling; but all this was for the glory of God. The enemy might seem to have it all his own way, but it was only in appearance; in reality death itself was but preparing a platform on which the glory of God was to be displayed. "This sickness is not unto death, but for the glory of God, that the Son of God might be glorified thereby."

Such, then, was the path of our blessed Lord—His path with the Father. His every step, His every act, His every utterance, had direct reference to the claims of the Father's glory. Much as He loved the family of Bethany, His personal affection led Him not into the scene of their sorrow till the moment

was come for the display of the divine glory, and then no personal fear could keep Him away. "Then after that He saith to His disciples, Let us go into Judea again. His disciples say unto Him, Master, the Jews of late sought to stone Thee, and goest Thou thither again? Jesus answered, Are there not twelve hours in the day? If any man walk in the day, he stumbleth not, because he seeth the light of this world. But if a man walk in the night he stumbleth, because there is no light in him."

Thus that blessed One walked, in the full blaze of the glory of God. His springs of action were all divine—all heavenly. He was a perfect stranger to all the motives and objects of the men of this world, who are stumbling along in the thick moral darkness that enwraps them—whose motives are all selfish, whose objects are earthly and sensual. He never did a single thing to please Himself. His Father's will, His Father's glory, ruled Him in all things. The stirrings of deep personal affection took Him not to Bethany, and no personal fear could keep Him away. In all He did, and in all He did not do, He found His motive in the glory of God.

Precious Saviour! teach us to walk in Thy heavenly footsteps! Give us to drink more into Thy spirit! This, truly, is what we need. We are so sadly prone to self-seeking and self-pleasing, even when apparently doing right things and ostensibly engaging in the Lord's work. We run hither and thither, do this and that, travel and preach and write, and all the while we may be pleasing ourselves, and not really seeking to do the will of God and promote His glory. May we study more profoundly our divine Exemplar! May He be ever before our hearts as the One to whom we are predestinated to be conformed! Thank God for the sweet and soul-sustaining assurance that we shall be like Him, for we shall see Him as He is. It is but a little while and we shall be done forever with all that now hinders our progress and interrupts our communion. Till then may the blessed Spirit work in our hearts, and keep us so occupied with Christ, so feeding by faith on His preciousness, that our practical ways may be a more living expression of Himself, and that we may bring forth more abundantly the fruits of righteousness which are by Jesus Christ to the glory and praise of God.

Part 3

We may now meditate for a few moments on the deeply interesting theme of Christ's sympathy with His people, so touchingly illustrated in His dealings with the beloved family of Bethany. He allowed them to go through the exercise, to wade through the deep waters, to be thoroughly tested, in order that "the trial of their faith, being much more precious than of gold that perisheth, though it be tried with fire, might be found unto praise and honor and glory. Looked at from nature's standpoint, it might seem as though all hope was gone and every ray of light faded away from the horizon. Lazarus was dead and buried. All was over. And yet the Lord had said, "This sickness is not unto death." How was this? What could He mean?

Thus nature might reason; but we must not listen to the reasonings of nature, which are sure to carry us down into the regions of the shadow of death. We must listen to the voice of Jesus; we must harken to His living, cheering, strengthening, encouraging accents. In this way we shall be able to vindicate and glorify God, not only at the sick-bed, but in the chamber of death, and at the very grave itself. Death is not death if Christ be there. The grave itself is but the sphere in which the glory of God shines out in all its power. It is when all that belongs to the creature is gone from the scene—when the platform is thoroughly cleared of all that is merely of man, it is then that the beams of the divine glory can be seen in all their brightness. It is when all is gone, or seems to be, that Christ can come in and fill the scene.

This is a grand point for the soul to get hold of and understand. It is only faith that can really enter into it. We are all so terribly prone to lean on some creature-prop, to sit beside some creature-stream, to trust in an arm of flesh, to cling to what we can see, to rest in the palpable and tangible. "The things that are seen and temporal" have ofttimes more weight with us than "the things which are unseen and eternal." Hence it is our ever-faithful Lord sees it right and good to sweep away our creature-props, and dry up our creature-streams, in order that we may lean on Himself, the eternal Rock of our salvation, and find all our springs in Himself, the living and exhaustless Fountain of all blessing. He is jealous of our love and confidence, and He will clear the scene of everything that might divide our hearts with Himself. He knows it is for our souls' full blessing to be wholly cast upon Himself, and hence He seeks to purify our hearts from every hateful idol.

And should we not praise Him for all this? Yes, truly; and not only so, but we should welcome whatever means He is pleased to use for the accomplishment of His wise and gracious end, even though, to nature's view, it may seem harsh and severe. He may often have to say to us as He said to Peter, "What I do thou knowest not now, but thou shalt know hereafter."

Yes, by and by we shall know and appreciate all His dealings. We shall look back upon the whole course from the light of His own blessed presence, and see and own that "the very heaviest stroke of His hand was the very strongest expression of His love at the time." Martha and Mary might wonder why death had been allowed to enter their dwelling. Doubtless they looked day after day, hour after hour, moment after moment, for their beloved Friend to enter; but instead of that He kept away, and death entered, and all seemed gone.

Why was this? Let Himself reply. "These things said He: and after that He saith unto them, *Our friend* Lazarus sleepeth." What touching affection! What gracious intimacy! What a tender linking of Himself with the family of Bethany on the one hand, and His disciples on the other! "Our friend Lazarus sleepeth." It was but a gentle sleep. Death is not death in the presence of the Prince of life. The grave is but a sleeping place. "I go, that I may awake him out of sleep." Such words could not have been uttered had Lazarus been raised from a sick-bed. "Man's extremity is God's opportunity"; and we can see without difficulty that the grave afforded God a far better opportunity than a sick-bed.

This, then, was the reason why Jesus kept away from His beloved friends. He waited for the fitting moment, and that moment was when Lazarus had lain in the grave four days already; when every human hope had vanished; when all human agency was powerless and valueless. "I go"—not to raise him from a sick-bed, but "that I may awake him out of sleep." The platform was cleared of the creature in order that the glory of God might shine out in all its brightness.

And is it not well to have the scene thus cleared of the creature? is it not a mercy—not in disguise, as some people say, but a plain, positive, palpable mercy—to have every human prop gone? Faith says, "Yes"— unhesitatingly and emphatically. Nature says, "No!" The poor heart craves something of the creature to lean upon, something that the eye can see. But faith—that most precious, priceless, divinely-wrought principle—find its true sphere in being called to lean absolutely and abidingly upon the living God.

But it must be a real thing. It is of little use talking about faith if the heart be a stranger to its power. Mere profession is perfectly worthless. God deals in moral realities. "What doth it profit, my brethren, though a man *say* he have faith?" He does not say, "What doth it profit though a man *have* faith?" Blessed be God, those who through grace have it, know that it profits *much* every way. By faith the sinner is brought in living relationship with God, is justified, and lives unto Him.

Faith glorifies God as nothing else can. It lifts the soul above the depressing influences of things seen and temporal. It tranquilizes the spirit in a most blessed manner. It enlarges the heart, by leading us out of our own narrow circle of personal interests, sympathies, cares and burdens, and connecting us livingly with the eternal, exhaustless spring of goodness. It works by love, and draws us out in gracious activity toward every object of need, but especially toward those who are of the household of faith.

It is faith alone that can move along the path where Jesus leads. To mere nature that path is dreadful. It is rough, dark, and lonely. Even those who surrounded our blessed Lord on the occasion of the death of Lazarus seemed wholly unable to comprehend His thoughts or follow intelligently in His footsteps. When He said, "Let us go into Judea again," they could think only of the Jews stoning Him. When He said, "I go, that I may awake him out of sleep," they replied, "If he sleep, he shall do well." When He spoke of his death, they thought that He had spoken of taking rest in sleep. When "He said unto them plainly, "Lazarus is dead: and I am glad *for your sakes* that I was not there, *to the intent that ye may believe*," poor unbelieving nature, speaking through the lips of Thomas Didymus, said, "Let us also go, that we may die with Him."

In a word, we see total inability to take in the true bearing of the case, as viewed from a divine standpoint. Nature sees nothing but death and darkness, where faith basks in the sunlight of the divine presence. "Let us also go, that we may *die* with Him." Alas, was this all that even a disciple had to say? How absurd are the conclusions of unbelief! Let us go with the Prince of life, that—what? "we may die with Him"! What blindness even while attached to the Lord! Should not Thomas have said: "Let us go, that we may behold His glory; that we may see His marvelous doings in the very region of the shadow of death; that we may share in His triumphs; that we may shout, at the very gates of the grave, our hallelujahs to His deathless name?"

Part 4

We have already noticed the three prominent subjects presented to us in John 11, namely, our Lord's own path with the Father; secondly, His profound sympathy with us; thirdly, His grace in linking us with Himself, in so far as that is possible, in all His blessed work. He ever walked with God, in calm, unbroken communion. He walked in the most implicit obedience to the will of God, and was ruled in all things by His glory. He walked in the day, and stumbled not. The will of God was the light in which the perfect workman ever carried on His work. He found His *only* motive for action in the divine will—His *only* object in the divine glory. He came down from Heaven, not to do His own will, but the will of the Father, in which He ever found His meat and drink.

But His great, loving heart flowed out in perfect sympathy with human sorrow. This we see attested in the most touching manner as He moved, in company with the afflicted sisters, to the tomb of their brother. If any question had arisen in their hearts during the season of trial, in the absence of their Lord, it was abundantly answered, yea, we may add, completely demolished, by the manifestion of His deep and tender affection as He moved toward the spot where the beams of the divine glory were so soon to shine out over the dreary region of death.

We do not here dwell upon the interesting interview between the two sisters and their beloved Lord, so full of teaching, so illustrative of His perfect mode of dealing with His people in their varied measures of intelligence and communion. We pass at once to the inspired statement in verse 33 of our chapter. "When Jesus therefore saw her weeping, and the Jews also weeping which came with her, He groaned in the spirit, and was troubled, and said, Where have ye laid him? They said unto Him, Lord, come and see. Jesus wept."

How wonderful! The Son of God groaned and wept. Let us never forget it. He, though God over all, blessed forever; though the Resurrection and the Life; though the Quickener of the dead; though the Conqueror of the grave; though on His way to deliver the body of His friend from the grasp of the enemy—sample of what He will soon do for all who belong to Him—yet, so perfectly did He enter into human sorrow, and take in all the terrible consequences of sin, all the misery and desolation of this sin-stricken world, that He groaned and wept! And those tears and groans emanated from the depths of a perfect human heart that felt as only a perfect human heart could feel—felt

according to God—for every form of human sorrow and misery. Though perfectly exempt, in His own divine person, from sin and all its consequences—yea, because exempt—He could in perfect grace enter into it all and make it His own as only He could do.

"Jesus wept"! Wondrous, significant fact! He wept not for Himself, but for others. He wept with them. Mary wept. The Jews wept. All this is easily grasped and understood. But that Jesus should weep reveals a mystery which we cannot fathom. It was divine compassion weeping through human eyes over the desolation which sin had caused in this poor world, weeping in sympathy with those whose hearts had been crushed by the inexorable hand of death.

Let all who are in sorrow remember this. Jesus is the same yesterday, to-day, and forever. His circumstances are changed, but His heart is not. His position is different, but His sympathy is the same. "We have not a high priest that can not be *touched* with the feeling of our infirmities, but was in all points tempted like as we are, apart from sin." There is a perfect human heart on the throne of the Majesty of the heavens, and that heart sympathizes with us in all our sorrows, in all our trials, in all our infirmities, in all our pressure and exercise. He perfectly enters into it all. Yea, He gives Himself to each one of His beloved members here upon earth as though He had only that one to look after.

How sweet and soothing to think of this! It is worth having a sorrow to be allowed to taste the preciousness of Christ's sympathy. The sisters of Bethany might say, "Lord, if Thou hadst been here, my brother had not died." But if their brother had not died, they would not have seen Jesus weeping, or heard His deep groan of sympathy with them in their sorrow. And who would not say that it is better to have the sympathy of His heart with us in our sorrow than the power of His hand in keeping or taking us out of it? Was it not much better, much higher, much more blessed, for the three witnesses in Dan. 3 to have the Son of God walking with them in the furnace than to have escaped the furnace by the power of His hand? Unquestionably.

And thus it is in every case. We have ever

to remember that this is not the day for the display of Christ's power. By and by He will take to Himself His great power, and reign. Then all our sufferings, our trials, our tribulations, will be over forever. The night of weeping will give place to the morning of joy—the morning without clouds—the morning that shall never know an evening. But now it is the time of Christ's patience, the time of His precious sympathy; and the sense of this is most blessedly calculated to sustain the heart in passing through the deep waters of affliction.

And there *are* deep waters of affliction. There *are* trials, sorrows, tribulations, and difficulties. And not only so, but our God means that we should feel them. His hand is in them for our real good, and for His glory. And it is our privilege to be able to say, "We glory in tribulation also; knowing that tribulation worketh patience; and patience, experience; and experience, hope; and hope maketh not ashamed, because the love of God is shed abroad in our hearts by the Holy Ghost, which is given unto us."

The Lord be praised for all this! But it were folly to deny that there are trials, sorrows and tribulations of all sorts. Nor would our God have us insensible to them. Insensibility to them is folly; glorying in them is faith. The consciousness of Christ's sympathy, and the intelligence of God's object in all our afflictions, will enable us to rejoice in them; but to deny the afflictions, or that we ought to feel them, is simply absurd. God would not have us to be stoics; He leads us into deep waters to walk with us through them; and when His end is reached, He delivers us out of them, to our joy and His own everlasting praise.

"He said unto me, My grace is sufficient for thee; for My strength is made perfect in weakness. Most gladly *therefore* will I rather glory in my infirmities, that the power of Christ may rest upon me. Therefore I take pleasure in infirmities, in reproaches, in necessities, in persecutions, in distresses, for Christ's sake; for when I am weak then I am strong." At the first, Paul longed to be rid of the thorn in the flesh, whatever it was. He besought the Lord thrice that it might depart from him. But the thorn in the flesh was better than pride in the heart. It was better far to be afflicted than puffed up—better to have Christ's sympathy with him in his temptation than the power of His hand in delivering him out of it.

Part 5

It is deeply touching to mark the two groans of our Lord, as He moved toward the tomb of His friend. The first groan was called forth by the sight of the weeping mourners around Him. "When Jesus therefore saw her weeping, and the Jews also weeping which came with her, He groaned in the spirit, and was troubled." The margin reads, "He troubled Himself."

How precious is the thought of this to the crushed and sorrowing heart! The sight of human tears drew forth a groan from the loving, sympathizing heart of the Son of God. Let all mourners remember this. Jesus did not rebuke Mary for weeping. He did not rally her on account of her sorrow. He did not tell her she ought not to feel; that she ought to be above everything of that sort. Ah, no! this would not be like Him. Some heartless folk may talk in this style; but He knew better. He, though Son of God, was a real man; and hence, He felt as a man ought to feel, and He knew what man must feel, while passing through the dark vale of tears.

Some of us talk largely and loftily about being above nature, and not feeling the snapping of tender links, and much in that strain. But in this we are not wise. We are not in sympathy with the heart of the Man, Christ Jesus. It is one thing to put forth, in heartless flippancy, our transcendental theories, and it is quite another to pass through the deep waters of grief and desolation with a heart exercised according to God. It will generally be found that those of us who declaim the loudest against nature, prove ourselves to be just like other people, when called to meet bodily sickness, sorrow of heart, mental pressure, or pecuniary loss.

The great point is to be real, and to go through the stern realities of actual life with a heart truly subject to God. Fine-drawn theories will not stand the test of real sorrow, trial, and difficulty; and nothing can be more absurd than to talk to people, with human hearts, about not feeling things. God means us to feel; and—precious, soothing, consolatory thought!—Jesus feels with us.

Let all the sons and daughters of sorrow remember these things for the consolation of their sorrowing hearts. "God comforts those that are cast down." If we were never cast down, we should not know His precious ministry. A stoic does not need the comfort of God. It is worth having a broken heart to have it bound up by our most merciful High Priest.

"Jesus groaned"—"Jesus wept." What power, what divine sweetness in these words! What a blank there would be were these words erased from the page of inspiration! Surely we could not do without them, and therefore our own most gracious God has, by His Spirit, penned these unspeakably precious words for the comfort and consolation of all who are called to tread the chamber of sorrow, or to stand at the grave of a friend.

But there was another groan evoked from the heart of our blessed Lord. Some of the Jews, when they heard His groan, and saw His tears, could not help exclaiming, "Behold how He loved him!" But alas! others only found, in such affecting proofs of true and profound sympathy, occasion for the display of heartless skepticism—and skepticism is always heartless. "Some of them said, could not this man, that opened the eyes of the blind, have caused that even this man should not have died?"

Here the poor human heart lets itself out, in its ignorant reasonings. How little did these skeptics understand either the person or the path of the Son of God! How could they appreciate the motives that actuated Him either in what He did, or in what He did not do? He opened the eyes of the blind, in order that "the works of God might be made manifest in him." And He did not prevent the death of Lazarus, that God might be glorified thereby.

But what did they know about all this?

Absolutely nothing. The blessed One moved at far too high an elevation to be within the ken of worldly religionists and skeptical reasoners. "The world knew Him not." God understood and appreciated Him perfectly. This was enough. What were the thoughts of men to One who ever walked in calm communion with the Father? They were utterly incapable of forming a correct judgment either of Himself or of His ways. They carried on their reasonings in that thick moral darkness in which they dwelt.

Thus it is still. Human reasonings are begun, continued, and ended in darkness. Man reasons about God; reasons about Christ; reasons about Scripture; reasons about Heaven, about hell, about eternity; about all sorts of things. But all his reasonings are worse, far worse, than worthless. Men are no more capable of understanding or appreciating the written Word now, than they were of understanding or appreciating the living Word, when He was amongst them. Indeed, the two things must go together.

As the living Word and the written Word are one, so to know the one we must know the other; but the natural, the unrenewed, the unconverted man knows neither. He is totally blind, in utter darkness, dead; and when, without reality, he made a religious profession, he is "twice dead"—dead in nature and dead in his religion. What are his thoughts, his reasonings, his conclusions worth? They are baseless, false, ruinous.

Nor is there the slightest use in arguing with unconverted people. It only tends to deceive them by leading them to suppose that they can argue. It is always the best way to deal solemnly with them as to their own moral condition before God. We do not find our Lord taking any notice of the unbelieving reasonings of those around Him. He only again groans and goes on His way. "Jesus *therefore*, again groaning in Himself, cometh to the grave. It was a cave, and a stone lay upon it."

This second groan is deeply affecting. He groaned, at first, in sympathy with the mourners around Him. He groaned again over the hardness and dark unbelief of the human heart, and of the heart of Israel in particular. But, be it carefully noted, He does not attempt to explain His reasons for not having hindered the death of His friend, although He had opened the eyes of the blind.

Blessed, perfect Servant! It was no part of His business to explain or apologize. He had to work on in the current of the divine counsels, and for the promotion of the divine glory. He had to do the Father's will, not explain Himself to those who could not possibly understand the explanation.

This is a weighty point for us all. Some of us lose a quantity of time in argument, apology, and explanation, in cases where such things are not the least understood. We really do mischief. Better far pursue, in holy calmness of spirit, singleness of eye, and decision of purpose, the path of duty. That is what we have got to do, not to explain or defend ourselves, which is sorry work at best for any one.

But let us look a moment at the tomb of Lazarus, and there see with what lovely grace our adorable Lord and Master sought to associate His servants with Himself in His work, in so far as that was possible; though, even here, too, He is sadly intruded upon by the dark unbelief of the human heart. "Jesus said, Take ye away the stone." This they could do, and hence He graciously calls upon them to do it. It was all they could do, so far. But here unbelief breaks in and casts its dark shadows over the heart. "Martha, the sister of him that was dead, saith unto Him, Lord, by this time he stinketh; for he hath been dead four days."

And what of that? Could the humiliating process of decomposition, even if completed, stand for one moment in the way of Him who is the resurrection and the life? Impossible! Bring Him in, and all is clear and simple; leave Him out, and all is dark and impracticable. Let but the voice of the Son of God be heard, and death and corruption must vanish like the darkness of night before the beams of the rising sun.

"Behold, I shew you a mystery: We shall not all sleep, but we shall all be changed, in a moment, in the twinkling of an eye, at the last trump; for the trumpet shall sound, and the dead shall be raised incorruptible, and we shall be changed. So when this corruptible shall have put on incorruption, and this mortal shall have put on immortality, then shall be brought to pass the saying that is written, Death is swallowed up in victory. O death, where is thy sting? O grave, where is thy victory? The sting of death is sin; and the strength of sin is the law. But thanks be to God, which giveth us the victory through our Lord Jesus Christ."

How magnificent! What are death, the grave and decomposition in the presence of such power as this? Talk of being dead four days as a difficulty! Millions that have been mouldering in the dust for thousands of years, shall spring up in a moment into life, immortality, and eternal glory, at the voice of that blessed One to whom Martha ventured to offer her unbelieving and irrational suggestion.

Part 6

In our Lord's reply to Martha we have one of the most blessed utterances that ever fell on the human ear. "Said I not unto thee, that, *if thou wouldest believe, thou shouldest see the glory of God?*" What living depth, what divine power, what freshness and comfort in these words! They present to us the very gist and marrow, the essential principle of the divine life. It is only the eye of faith that can see the glory of God. Unbelief sees only difficulties, darkness, and death. Faith looks above and beyond all these, and ever basks in the blessed beams of the divine glory. Poor Martha saw nothing but a decomposed human body, simply because she was under a spirit of dark and depressing unbelief. Had she been swayed by an artless faith she would have walked to the tomb in company with Him who is the resurrection and the life, assured that, instead of death and decomposition, she should see the glory of God.

This is a grand principle for the soul to grasp. It is utterly impossible for human language to overstate its value and importance. Faith never looks at difficulties, except indeed it be to feed on them. It looks not at the things that are seen, but at the things that are unseen. It endures as seeing Him who is invisible. It takes hold of the living God. It leans on His arm; it makes use of His strength; it draws on His exhaustless treasury; it walks in the light of His blessed countenance, and sees His glory shining forth over the darkest scenes of human life.

The inspired volume abounds in striking illustrations of the contrast between faith and unbelief. Let us glance at one or two of them. Look, for example, at Caleb and Joshua, in contrast with their unbelieving brethren, in Num. 13. These latter saw only the difficulties which stood in their way. "Nevertheless the people be strong that dwell in the land"—not stronger than Jehovah, surely—"and the cities are walled, and very great"—"not greater than the living God:—"and moreover we saw the children of Anak there."

It is very clear that they did not see the glory of God; indeed, they saw anything and everything but that. They were wholly governed by a spirit of unbelief, and hence they could only "bring up an evil report of the land which they had searched unto the children of Israel, saying, The land, through which we have gone to search it, is a land that eateth up the inhabitants thereof; and *all* the people that *we saw* in it are men of *great stature*"—they did not *see* a single small man: they looked at everything through the magnifying-glass of unbelief. "There *we saw* the giants"—no doubt!—"the sons of Anak, which come of the giants." Anything more? Ah, God was shut out; they could not see Him at all through the glasses they used. They could only see the terrible giants and towering walls: "and we were in our own sight as grasshoppers, and so were we in their sight."

But what of Jehovah? Alas, He was left out! Unbelief invariably leaves God out of its calculations. It can take a very full account of the difficulties, the hindrances, the hostile influences; but as for the living God, it sees Him not. There is a melancholy consistency in the utterances of unbelief, whether we listen to them in the wilderness of Kadesh, or,

fourteen hundred years afterwards, at the tomb of Lazarus. Unbelief is always and everywhere the same; it begins, continues and ends with the absolute exclusion of the one living and true God. It can do naught save to cast dark shadows over the pathway of every one who will listen to its voice.

How different are the accents of faith! Harken to Joshua and Caleb, as they seek to stem the rising ride of unbelief. "And Joshua the son of Nun, and Caleb the son of Jephunneh, which were of them that searched the land, rent their clothes: and they spake unto all the company of the children of Israel, saying, The land, which we passed through to search it, is an exceeding good land. *If the Lord delight in us*"—here lies the secret—"then He will bring us into this land, and give it us; a land which floweth with milk and honey. Only rebel not ye against the Lord, neither fear ye the people of the land; for *they are bread for us*"—faith actually feeds on the difficulties which terrify unbelief:—"their defence is departed from them, and the Lord is with us: fear them not."

Glorious words! It does the heart good to transcribe them. "Said I not unto thee, that, if thou wouldest believe, thou shouldest see the glory of God?" Thus it is always. If there is a melancholy consistency in the utterances of unbelief, there is a glorious consistency in the accents of faith, wherever we harken to them. Caleb and Joshua saw the glory of God, and in the light of that glory what were giants and high walls? Simply nothing. If anything, they were *bread* for the nourishment of faith. Faith brings in God, and He dispels all difficulties. What walls or giants could stand before the Almighty God? "If God be for us, who can be against us?"

Such is ever the artless but powerful reasoning of faith. It conducts its arguments and reaches its conclusions in the blessed light of the divine presence. It sees the glory of God. It looks above and beyond the heavy clouds which at times gather upon the horizon, and finds in God its sure and never-failing resource. Precious faith!—the only thing in the world that really glorifies God, and makes the heart of the Christian truly bright and happy.

Take another illustration. Turn to 1 Kings 17, and contrast the widow of Sarepta with Elijah the Tishbite. What was the difference between them? Just the difference that ever exists between unbelief and faith. Listen again to the utterances of unbelief. "And she said, As the Lord thy God liveth, I have not a cake, but a handful of meal in a barrel, and a little oil in a cruse: and, behold, I am gathering two sticks, that I may go in and dress it for me and my son, that we may eat it, *and die.*"

Here, truly, is a gloomy picture. An empty barrel, an exhausted cruse, and death! Was that all? That was all for blind unbelief. It is the old story of the giants and lofty walls over again. God is shut out, though she could say, "As the Lord *thy* God liveth." In reality she was out of His presence, and had lost the sense of His all-sufficiency to meet her need and that of her house. Her circumstances excluded God from the vision of her soul. She looked at things that were seen, not at the things which were unseen. She saw not the invisible One; she saw nothing but famine and death. As the ten unbelieving spies saw nothing but the difficulties; as Martha saw nothing but the grave and its humiliating results; so the poor Sareptan saw nothing but starvation and death.

Not so the man of faith. He looked beyond the barrel and the cruse. He had no thought of dying of hunger. He rested on the word of the Lord. Here was his precious resource. God had said, "I have commanded a widow woman there to sustain thee." This was quite enough for him. He knew that God could multiply the meal and the oil to sustain him and her. Like Caleb and Joshua, he brought God into the scene, and found in Him the happy solution of every difficulty. They saw God above and beyond the walls and the giants. They rested on His eternal word. He had promised to bring His people into the land, and hence, though there were nothing but walls and giants from Dan to Beersheba, He would most surely fulfil His word.

And so with Elijah the Tishbite. He saw the living and almighty God above and beyond the barrel and the cruse. He rested upon that word which is settled forever in Heaven, and which never can fail a trusting heart. This tranquilized his spirit, and with this he sought to tranquilize the widow too. "And he said unto her, *Fear not*"—precious, soul-stirring utterance of faith!—"go, and do as thou hast said. . . . For *thus saith the Lord God of Israel*, The barrel of meal shall not waste, neither shall the cruse of oil fail, until the day that the Lord sendeth rain upon the earth."

Here was the solid ground on which the man of God rested when he ventured to offer a word of encouragement to the poor, desponding widow of Sarepta. It was not in the light-heartedness, or blind recklessness, of nature that he spoke to her. He did not deny that the barrel and cruse were almost empty, as the woman had said. This could have given her no comfort, inasmuch as she knew too well the facts of her case. But he brought the living God and His faithful Word before her aching heart; and hence he could say, "Fear not." He sought to lead her soul to the true resting-place where he himself had found repose, namely, *the Word of the living God*—blessed, unfailing, divine resting-place for every anxious soul!

Thus it was with Caleb and Joshua. They did not deny that there were giants and high walls: they brought God in, and sought to place Him between the hearts of their desponding brethren and the dreaded difficulties. This is what faith always does, and thus gives glory to God and keeps the soul in peace, let the difficulties be ever so great. It would be folly to deny there are obstacles and hostile influences in the way: and there is a certain style of speaking of such things which cannot possibly minister comfort or encouragement to a poor, troubled heart. Faith accurately weights the difficulties and trials, but, knowing that the power of God outweighs them all, it rests in holy calmness on His word, and in His perfect wisdom and everlasting love.

The reader's mind will no doubt recur to many other instances in which the Lord's people have been cast down by looking at circumstances, instead of looking at God. David, in a dark moment, could say, "I shall one day perish by the hand of Saul." What a sad mistake!—the mistake of unbelief. What should he have said? Denied that the unrelenting hand of Saul was against him? Surely not. What comfort would that have given him, inasmuch as he knew too well that it was really so. But he should have remembered that the hand of *God* was with him, and that hand was stronger than ten thousand Sauls.

So with Jacob in his day of darkness and depression. "All these things," said he, "are against me." What should he have added? "But God is for me." Faith has its *"buts"* and *"ifs"* as well as unbelief; but faith's buts and ifs are all bright because they express the passage of the soul—its rapid passage—from the difficulties to God Himself. *"But* God who is rich," etc. And again, *"If* God be for us, who can be against us?" Thus faith ever reasons. It begins with God, it places Him between the soul and all its surroundings, and thus imparts a peace which passeth all understanding, a peace which nothing can disturb.

But we must, ere closing this paper, return for a moment to the tomb of Lazarus. The rapid glance we have taken through the inspired volume will enable us to appreciate more fully those most precious words of our Lord to Martha, "Said I not unto thee, that, if thou wouldest believe, thou shouldest see the glory of God?" Men tell us that seeing is believing; but we can say that believing is seeing. Yes, reader, get hold of this grand truth. It will carry you through and bear you above the darkest and most trying scenes of this dark and trying world. *"Have faith in God."* This is the mainspring of the divine life. "The life that I live in the flesh, I live by the faith of the Son of God, who loved me, and gave Himself for me."

Faith knows, and is persuaded, that there is nothing too hard, nothing too great—yea, and nothing too small—for God. It can count on Him for everything. It basks in the very sunlight of His presence, and exults in the manifestations of His goodness, His faithfulness, and His power. It ever delights to see the platform cleared of the creature, that the glory of God may shine forth in all its lustre. It turns away from creature streams and creature props, and finds all its resources in the one living and true God.

Only see how the divine glory displays itself at the grave of Lazarus, even spite of the unbelieving suggestion of Martha's heart; for God, blessed be His name, delights at times to rebuke our fears as well as to answer our faith. "Then they took away the stone where the dead was laid. And Jesus lifted up His eyes, and said, Father I thank Thee that Thou hast heard Me. And I knew that Thou hearest Me always: but because of the people which stand by I said it, that they may believe that Thou hast sent Me. And when He thus had spoken, He cried with a loud voice, Lazarus, come forth! And he that was dead came forth, bound hand and foot with grave clothes; and his face was bound about with a napkin. Jesus saith unto them, Loose him, and let him go."

Glorious scene! displaying our Jesus as the Son of God with power, by resurrection of the dead. Gracious scene! in which the Son of God condescends to use man in rolling away the stone and removing the grave clothes. How good of Him to use us in any little way! May it be our joy to be ever ready—in a holy readiness to be used, that God in all things may be glorified!

Lessons from the
Old Testament

THE CALL OF GOD

ABRAHAM AND LOT

Genesis 12

IN A DAY of such widely extended profession as the present, it is specially important that Christians should be deeply impressed with the necessity of realizing *personally the call of God*, without which there can be no permanency or steadiness in the Christian course.

It is a comparatively easy thing to make a profession at a time when profession prevails; but it is never easy to walk by faith—it is never easy to give up present things, in the hope of "good things to come." Nothing but that mighty principle which the apostle denominates *"the substance* of things hoped for, the evidence of things not seen" (Heb. 11:1), can ever enable a man to persevere in a course which in a world where all is wrong—all out of order, must be thorny and difficult. We must feel *"persuaded"* of something yet to come—something worth waiting for—something that will reward all the toil of a pilgrim's protracted course, ere we rise up out of the circumstances of nature and the world, to "run with patience the race that is set before us" (Heb. 12:1).

All this is fully exemplified in Abraham, and the exemplification receives additional force from the contrast exhibited in the character of Lot and others who are introduced in the course of the narrative.

In the seventh of Acts, we have the following words which bear directly upon the subject before us. "The God of glory appeared unto our father Abraham, when he was in Mesopotamia, before he dwelt in Charran, and said unto him, Get thee out of thy country and from thy kindred, and come into the land that *I shall show thee"* (vers. 1-2). Here then we are presented with the first dawning of that light which attracted Abraham out of the darkness of "Ur, of the Chaldees," and which shining in upon his wearisome path, from time to time, gave fresh vigor to his soul, as he journeyed in quest of "that city which hath foundations, whose builder and maker is God." "The God of glory" caused Abraham to see, in the light of His character, the true condition of things in Ur, and further, to believe, as some one has observed, *a report concerning future glory and inheritance*, and he therefore hesitates not, but instantly girds himself up for the journey.

However, upon a close comparison of the opening of the seventh of Acts, with the first verse of this twelfth chapter of Genesis, we get an important principle. From the time that God appeared unto Abraham, until he finally gets up into the land of Canaan, an event occurs involving much deep instruction to us. I allude to the death of Abraham's father, as we read in Acts 7, "From thence, *when his father* was dead, He removed him into this land wherein ye now dwell" (ver. 4). This will enable us to understand the force of the expression in Gen. 12, "The Lord *had* said unto Abram" etc. (ver. 1). From both these passages, it would plainly appear the movement made by Terah and his family, recorded in Gen. 10:31, was the result of a revelation made by "the God of glory" to Abram, but it would not appear that *Terah* had received any such revelation from God. He is presented to us rather as a hindrance to Abram than any thing else, for until he died, Abram did not come into the land of Canaan—his divinely appointed destination.

Now, this circumstance, trivial as it may

seem to a cursory reader, confirms in the strongest manner the statement already advanced, namely, that unless the call of God—the revelation from "the God of glory" be *personally realized*, there can be no permanency or steadiness in the Christian course. Had Terah realized that call, he would neither have been a clog to Abram in his path of faith, nor yet would he have dropped off, like a mere child of nature, ere reaching the future land of promise. We get the same principle illustrated in Laban afterward in Gen. 24. Laban, as some one has well observed, was fully alive to the value of the gold and silver jewels which the servant of Abraham had brought with him, but he had not heart to value *the report* concerning future things, which dropped from his lips. In other words, he did not receive a revelation from "the God of glory," and as a consequence, he remained, as the same writer has observed, "*a thorough man of the world.*"

In the conversion of Saul of Tarsus, we are taught the same truth. There were other persons with him when he was struck to the ground by the lustre of the glory of the Lord Jesus; these persons "saw indeed the light"—they witnessed many of the external circumstances which had arrested the furious zealot; but as he himself states, "*they heard not the voice of Him that spake to me*" (Acts 22:9). Here is the grand point. The voice must speak "to me"—"the God of glory" must appear "to me," ere I can take the place of a pilgrim and stranger in the world, and perseveringly, "run the race that is set before me." It is not *national faith*, nor *family faith*, but *personal faith* that will constitute us real witnesses for God in the world.

But when Abram was released from the clog which he had experienced in the person of his father, he was enabled to enter with vigor and decision upon the path of faith—a path which "flesh and blood" can never tread—a thorny path beset with difficulties from first to last, in which God alone can sustain the soul. "And Abram passed through the land unto the place of Sichem, unto the plain of Moreh. *And the Canaanite was then in the land*. And the Lord appeared unto Abram, and said, "Unto thy seed will I give this land: *and there builded he an altar unto the Lord who appeared unto him*" (Gen. 12:6-7). Here Abram at once takes his stand as *a worshiper*, in the face of "the Canaanite." The altar marks him as one who, having been delivered from the idols of Ur of the Chaldees, had been taught to bow before the altar of the one true God, "who made heaven and earth." In the following verse, we get the second grand feature in the character of the man of faith, namely, "*the tent*," denoting strangership in the world. "By faith he sojourned in the land of promise, as in a *strange country, dwelling in tabernacles* with Isaac and Jacob, *the heirs* with him of the same *promise*" (Heb. 11:9).

We shall have occasion to notice more fully, as we proceed, these two important points in the life of Abraham, and shall therefore rest satisfied for the present with establishing the fact that the tent and the altar do most clearly present him to us as a *stranger* and a *worshiper*, and that as such, he was a man entirely separated from the course of this evil world.

Scarcely had Abram entered upon his course, when he had to encounter one of those difficulties which have a special tendency to test the genuineness of faith, both as to its quality and its object. "And there was a famine in the land." The difficulty meets him in the very place into which the Lord had called him. Now, it is no easy matter when we perceive trial and sorrow, privation and difficulty awaiting us, while walking in "the strait and narrow way," still to persevere—still to pursue the onward path, and especially if we observe within our reach, as Abram did, an entire exemption from the particular trial under which we may be smarting. The men of this world "are not in trouble as other men, neither are they plagued as other men." This feeling is still further increased by the entire absence of every thing, as far as sight is concerned, which could act as a confirmation of our hope. Abram had not so much as to set his foot upon—famine was raging around him on every side, *save in Egypt*. Could he only find himself *there*, he would be able to live in ease and abundance.

Here, however, the man of faith must pursue the path of simple obedience. God had said, "Get thee out of thy country . . . unto a land that I will show thee." Abram may, it is true, afterward discover that obedience to this command will involve his abiding in a land where nothing but starvation, apparently, awaits him. But even though it should be so, God had not in any way qualified the command. No, the word was simple and definite: "Into a land that *I* will show thee." This should have been as true and as binding upon Abram when famine reigned around him, as when peace and abundance prevailed. Famine should not, therefore, have induced him to leave the land, neither should abundance have induced him to remain. The influential words were, "I will show thee."

But Abram leaves this land—he succumbs, for the moment, to the heavy trial, and bends his footsteps down to Egypt, leaving behind him his tent and altar. There he obtained ease and luxury; he escaped, no doubt, the formidable trial under which he had suffered in the land of promise; but he lost, for the time being, his worship and strangership— things which should ever be dearest to the heart of a pilgrim.

There is nothing in Egypt for Abram to feed upon as a spiritual man; it might, and doubtless did, afford abundance for him as a natural man, but that was all. Egypt would give nothing to Abram unless he sacrificed his character both as a stranger and as a worshiper of God. It is needless to observe that it is exactly so at this very hour. There is plenty in the world upon which our old nature could feed most luxuriously. There are the rich delights "of the flesh and of the mind," and abundant means of gratifying the desires of the heart, but what of all these, if the enjoyment thereof leads, as it must necessarily do, right out of the path of faith—the path of simple obedience.

Here then is the question for the Christian: which shall I have, the gold and silver, the flocks and herds—the present ease and affluence of Egypt, or the tent and altar of "the land of promise"? Which shall I have: the carnal ease and delight of the world, or a peaceful holy walk with God *here*, and

eternal blessedness and glory hereafter? We cannot have both, for, "If *any man* love the world, the love of the Father is not in him."

But, we may ask, why was it that Abram had to experience famine and trial in the land of promise? Why did he not find a home and plenty there? Simply because "the Canaanite and Perizzite dwelt then in the land" (chap. 13:7). The land had not as yet been fitted up to be the residence of God's redeemed ones. Abram's faith might have enabled him to penetrate through the long and dreary period which should intervene ere the promise could be consummated; but that very principle of faith it was that made him "a pilgrim and a stranger." He could wait for God's time, and until then remain without "so much as to set his foot on" (Acts 7:5). So should it be now.

Genesis 13

This beautiful chapter shows us the man of faith recovering himself, through the faithfulness and loving-kindness of God, who never allows such to wander far, or tarry long away. The gold and silver, the flocks and herds of Egypt, could not long prove a satisfying portion for Abram, while deprived of his tent and his altar, and he therefore once more, in the renewed energy of faith rises, as it were, from the dust of Egypt, and retraces his steps to the land of promise. Happy recovery! Certain evidence of a fixed and honest purpose to serve the Lord. "The ship may be tossed by the waves and the winds, but *the magnet still points to the north.*"

But some expressions in the opening of this chapter confirm most fully a thought already expressed, namely, that Abram gained nothing, "as before God," by his visit to Egypt. Thus, for example, "Abram went on his journeys . . . unto the place where his tent had been *at the beginning*, unto the place of the altar which he had made there *at the first*" (vers. 3-4). The words "beginning," and "at the first," prove that Abram had made no progress while in Egypt, but that, while there, all his time was, as it were, lost. No doubt he learnt a wholesome lesson, and it is well when by our failures we learn to distrust our own hearts, and dread the pernicious influence of the world. Abram learnt that there could be no tent or altar in Egypt. It is only faith that can enable a man to raise an altar or erect a tent, but in Egypt all is sight and not faith, and hence, the moment Abram set his foot there he ceased to show forth the genuine fruits of faith—yea, the very principle which led him to leave the land of promise. Led him, at the same time, to relinquish his character as a stranger and a worshiper.

How forcibly are we here reminded of a proposal made long after this, by a king of Egypt, to Abraham's seed. "And Pharaoh called for Moses and Aaron, and said: Go ye, sacrifice to your God in the land" (Exod. 8:25). Thus, it would seem ever to have been the design of the enemy to get the people of God, the holy seed, to defile themselves by worshiping or sacrificing to God, *in the world;* i.e., to make their character, as worshipers of God, accord with that of men of the world—men holding a place in society where Christ is an outcast; thus, of course, declaring that there is no difference between the religion of the world and the religion of God—a truly fearful delusion, calculated to lead many souls out of the way of truth and holiness.

It is most sad to hear, at times, those who surely ought to know better, in order, as they say, to manifest a *liberal spirit*, speaking of the religion of the world in all its multiplied forms, as if it were all right; or, as if it were a matter of total indifference whether we remained in communion with error or not. Oh, let us not be deceived! God's principle of separation is as strong and as binding to-day as it was in the days of Abram or Moses. "Come out from among them, and be ye separate, and touch not the unclean thing," must hold good as long as the "unclean thing" exists; nor can any outward form alter the character—the true essential character of "the unclean thing" so as to make it "a clean thing."

Moses, then, was not liberal, in the above acceptation of the word, for he at once refused to countenance the religion of the world. "It is not meet so to do." Memorable words! Would that there were more amongst us who, when invited to countenance the religion of the world, would reply, "It is not meet so to do." Abram could not worship in Egypt, neither could his seed.

But Abram had more difficulties than one to encounter in his course. The path which every man of faith is called to tread lies between two dangerous extremes. One is the temptation to return to the world; the other, to strive with brethren by the way. Abram had just recovered himself from the effects of the former, and we have now to behold him buffeting the latter.

The moment Abram emerged from Egypt, he appeared in a special manner to move under a new responsibility, namely, responsibility to his brother to walk with him in harmony. While in Egypt, this responsibility stood quite in the shade. The institutions—laws—habits—luxury and ease of Egypt, would in an eminent degree tend to do away with every such feeling. All these things would have had the effect of erecting barriers around each individual tending to prevent him from recognizing the fact that he was his "brother's keeper." Nor is it otherwise now. So long as we continue in the world—the religious world, as it is termed—we shall find ourselves completely relieved from the difficult task of being our "brother's keeper." Those who advocate a continuance therein may deny this fact, but it is all in vain, for Scripture and experience alike demonstrate it. Abram and Lot *did not strive in Egypt*, and a religious establishment presents this attraction at least—and it is by no means a feeble one—it effectually prevents *brotherly collision;* and, of course, where there is no collision there can be no strife—no dispute; where collision takes place, there must be either grace to enable us to walk in unity of mind, or strife and contention. But Egypt saps the very springs of grace by leading us out of a place of simple dependence upon the Lord, (for dependence ever genders grace and forbearance) and because she does so, she, at the same time, teaches us, or attempts at least to teach us, that we do not need grace, by leading us into a sphere in which responsibility to brethren is never realized; thus the need is not felt; weakness is mistaken for strength, folly for wisdom.

When the Christian at first starts on his course, he fondly dreams of nothing but perfection in his fellow Christians; but in this he soon finds himself mistaken, for we have all our infirmities, and as the apostle states, "In many things we offend all." But why, we may ask, was there such a speedy development of infirmity upon their coming up out of Egypt? Because they were now called to walk in the power of a naked principle, without any of the props or barriers of Egypt. They were called to walk by faith, and "faith worketh by love."

Now "the Canaanite," etc., "was then in the land." This should have acted as a hindrance to any strife between "*brethren*," for the Canaanite cannot understand anything about the infirmities of believers, and he therefore puts all their failure down to some defect in the principle professed.

But in every strife between brethren, there must be fault somewhere. In the contention between Paul and Barnabas there was fault somewhere. Nor can we be at any loss to decide where it lay. Barnabas wished to take *his relative* with him, but this relative had before proved himself unfit, or at least unwilling, to "endure hardness," therefore it could not have been with a single eye to the Lord's work that Barnabas desired his company. The Lord Himself, too, at once takes Paul's side of the question by providing him with a dear son and fellow-laborer, in the person of Timothy, with whom he had "none like-minded."

So it is exactly in the case before us. We can have no hesitation in asserting that Lot was the man in error here. Lot does not appear to have fully got rid of the spirit of the world, and where there is this spirit predominating in any one he will ever find the path of faith too strait for him to walk in, and so it was, "They could not dwell together."

If, then, it be asked on what grounds one would pronounce Lot to have been in the wrong? The answer is, first, Lot's subsequent conduct; and, secondly, the Lord's dealings with Abram, "after that Lot was separated from him."

What then did Lot do? "*He lifted up his eyes.*" This is ever our mode of acting when not under the direct power of faith. Whenever we lift up our eyes without divine direction, we are sure to go wrong. I say, without divine direction, for we find the Lord afterwards directing Abram to lift up his eyes, but then that was totally different from Lot's act, which was simply the suggestion of mere human wisdom and foresight. Human wisdom and foresight, however, can never assist our progress as men of faith—no, quite the reverse; human wisdom will ever suggest things which, if acted upon, will lead us right athwart the path of a man of faith. Therefore Lot, in lifting up his eyes, could not penetrate beyond the "things that are seen and temporal." Such was the utmost bound of his range of vision. The things on which his eyes rested were those with which he had been conversant while in Egypt, as we read, "He beheld all the plain of Jordan that it was well watered everywhere . . . *like the land of Egypt*" (ver. 10). Here we observe that Lot had never been really detached in heart and affection from Egypt—he had never learnt the vanity and unsatisfactoriness of all her resources in the light of a better order of things—he had never contrasted her with that "*city which hath foundations*, whose builder and maker is God"—in a word, he "having put his hand to the plow," was now beginning "to look back," and thus to prove himself "unfit for the kingdom of heaven."

There is a striking notice of all this afforded in the opening verse of this chapter, "Abram went up out of Egypt and *Lot with him*." Here we get the secret of Lot's after instability. He appears to have gone up rather *with Abram* than *with God*, and the consequence was that, when he parted with Abram, he had nothing to lean upon. He had been hitherto moving under Abram's protection and guidance instead of being directly before the Lord, and therefore when he lost Abram he went astray.

Now then is the moment for Abram to "lift up his eyes," at the Lord's command, and oh, what a different range of vision was his! While Lot could not penetrate beyond the narrow limits of the present scene, Abram was enabled to survey the length and breadth of God's inheritance. He soars on the strong and rapid pinion of faith, and is, as it were, lost in the unbounded beneficence of God; while Lot, the man walking by sight, is well-nigh lost in the deep gulf of Sodom's corruption.

Let us then, ere we enter upon the next chapter, take a view of the different circumstances of these two men who had started together. "Lot lifted up his eyes," and the prospect on which they rested was, as might be expected, such as suited his natural desires, "well-watered plains," which, however fair in man's view, were nevertheless, in the sight of the Lord, filled with exceeding wickedness (comp. vers. 10 and 14). Abram, on the contrary, had allowed his eye to wander over the length and breadth of the *promised* inheritance—uninfluenced by all else, he viewed the portion which God was *reserving* for him and his seed, and took up his position accordingly.

Thus do we find Lot in the unhallowed region of Sodom; and Abram—the pilgrim and stranger, with his tent and altar—"in the plain of Mamre, which is in Hebron."

Genesis 14

Here we have a very minute account of a battle fought by "four kings with five," and we may ask, What connection had this strife between "the potsherds of the earth," with the history of the people of God? With Abram indeed none, in one sense, for *he* was outside it all. *His tent* marked him as a stranger to all these things—it marked him as one to whom the battle of "four kings with five" would be a matter of very trivial moment. And then his altar marked him as one whose pursuits were quite of another character, even a heavenly. His tent showed him to be a stranger on earth—his altar showed him to be at home in Heaven. Happy man! Happy pilgrim! who could thus from his high elevation, even the lofty watch-tower of faith,

look down, as a passer-by, upon the battle fields of an evil world. It mattered not to Abram whether the laurel of victory were about to wreath the brow of the king of Sodom, or of Chedorlaomer, king of Elam; his portion was not in danger through their strife, because he had it in that place "where thieves *do not* break through and steal."

But, though it was the happy lot of Abram to have his being and his portion in a place where wars could have no influence, yet such was not the case with his more worldly-minded brother. His position was such as to place him in the midst of the strife, and consequently the issue of this battle could not fail to be of the deepest moment to him. If the child of God will stoop so low as to mix himself up with the world, he must calculate upon being made a participator in its convulsions, and woe be to that man who shall have his portion in the world in that day (now fast approaching) when all things shall be shaken by the mighty hand of God in judgment.

I would here observe that what has ever made the history of nations and the movements of mighty kings and conquerors, matters of interest to the Holy Spirit, has been the connection of such things with the history of the people of God. Beyond this they possessed nothing of moment to Him. He could find no pleasure in dwelling upon the abstract history of man. The busy strife and tumult of nations—the fierce contests of ungodly tyrants grasping after power—the movements of armies, could not attract the notice of the Spirit of peace; nevertheless, when such things became, in the least degree, connected with the history of a "righteous soul," the Holy Ghost can be most minute in detailing the circumstances of a battle, as is observable in the case under consideration.

What then were the results of this contest to Lot? Ruin to him and his family. He was made prisoner and all his goods were taken (ver. 12). He had laid up treasure for himself upon earth, and the thieves had broken through; and thus, while Abram was above it all, in the power—the separating power of communion with God, *he* found himself a prisoner and a beggar. He had sown to the flesh, and of the flesh he must now "reap corruption."

But this was just the moment for Abram to show himself in the powerful activities of love. He had, as above observed, hitherto surveyed with calm indifference these movements of "kings and their armies," but the very same faith which had made him indifferent about the strifes of men, made him quick to take cognizance of *a brother* in distress. Faith not only purifies the heart from worldly and carnal desires, but it also "works by love," as is powerfully shown in Abram's case, for "when Abram saw that *his brother* was taken captive he armed his trained servants," etc. (ver. 14).

Now, it is to be observed that it is in the hour of distress and difficulty that the relationship *of brother* gets the prominent place. In days of unruffled peace, Lot might be known to Abram as "his brother's son," but now he was in sorrow, and therefore the claims of brotherhood act, and act powerfully and effectually.

We are now called to witness a deeply interesting scene. Abram himself is about to meet a temptation—a temptation at once repulsed indeed by the power of God in him, but nevertheless, a temptation. The king of Sodom was about to come forth to display his treasures before the eye of Abram, and he had by nature a heart to value those treasures.

That man knows not his own heart who could say that the world does not present many—very many attractions to the natural heart. There is a species of misanthropy which looks like elevation above the world, but which, after all, is not it. The cynic philosopher Diogenes, when he told Alexander to get out of his sunshine, was as proud and as worldly a man as Alexander himself. The only true and real way in which to be separated from, and elevated above, the world, is by the knowledge of heavenly things, and Abram was led, through the mercy of God, into that knowledge.

But the victory obtained by Abram, was not owing to any power in himself. He had, as I have observed, a heart to value the things which the enemy had to give him; and, therefore, if he triumphed, it was through the operation of a power outside himself. In all this transaction, the One who had watched over His dear servant during the dark season of his sojourn in Egypt, and who, moreover, had, by that very sojourn, taught him a lesson as to the true character of the world, was now closely observing his ways, and making preparations for his relief; He was cognizant of the movements and designs of the enemy, from first to last, and He therefore prepares to supply a heavenly antidote to nullify his poison.

It is particularly worthy of observation that between the time at which the king of Sodom went forth to meet Abram, and that wherein he made the proposal to him with reference to "the persons and the goods," there is a remarkable character introduced, namely, Melchizedek. This stranger, commissioned by God, was on his way to fortify Abram's heart at the very moment when the enemy was on his way to attack (comp. ver. 17, 18, and 21). Now, why did not "the priest of the Most High God" come to meet Abram before? Because this was the very moment in which Abram most needed the strength which he had to bring. The enemy was about to display his gilded bait before the eye of the man of God, and therefore is Melchizedek at hand to display in his view the divine realities of the kingdom. He was about to feed and strengthen his soul with the "bread," and cheer him with the "wine," of the kingdom, in order that, "in the strength of that meat" he might mount above the influence of all the allurements of the world. From all this we may learn that it is communion with the joys and glories of the kingdom that can alone cause the heart to reject the pollutions of the world.

Reader, upon what are *you* now feeding? What constitutes your habitual food? Is it "the bread and wine" which the Lord provides, or "the goods" of Sodom? Are your ears open to the pernicious suggestions of the *King of Sodom*, or to the heavenly communications of the *King of Salem?* The Lord grant that our hearts may ever choose that in which He delights.

But to proceed, Melchizedek leads Abram's soul into present communion with "*The Most High God, the possessor of heaven and earth*," and thus completes the wondrous contrast between "the King of Sodom" and "the Most High God, possessor of heaven and earth"—"the goods of Sodom" and the extensive possessions of Heaven and earth. Blessed contrast, which faith ever draws! It is needless to say that Abram at once rejects the offer of the King of Sodom. The bread and wine, and the benediction of "the priest of the Most High God," had raised Abram to such a height that he could, in one comprehensive glance, take in the vast possessions of Heaven and earth, and further, look down from thence upon the despicable proposal of the King of Sodom and reject it. Melchizedek had just said, "the Most High God, the possessor of heaven and earth," and Abram had laid hold on these words and made use of them in his reply to the adversary. "I have lifted up my hand," said he, "to the Lord, the Most High God, the possessor of heaven and earth, that I will not take from a thread even to a shoe-latchet and that I will not take anything that is thine, lest thou shouldest say, I have made Abram rich" (vers. 22-23).

Abram appears to breathe the very atmosphere of the presence of Him, "who hath measured the waters in the hollow of His hand, and meted out heaven with a span, and comprehended the dust of the earth in a measure, and weighed the mountains in scales, and the hills in a balance, in whose sight the nations are as a drop of a bucket, and are counted as the small dust of the balance. Behold! he taketh up the isles as a very little thing, and Lebanon is not sufficient to burn, nor the beasts thereof sufficient for a burnt-offering. All nations before Him are as nothing, and they are counted to Him as less than nothing and vanity" (Isa. 40:12, 15-18).

And surely, we may say, it was only thus that Abram could triumph; and let no one who moves not, in some measure, in the same sphere, affect to despise the world—nothing can be more truly vain. There must be the experimental acquaintance with *the* better thing—the fondly cherished hope of "*good*

things to come"—ere we can obtain full victory over present things, and our own worldly desires. "Ye took joyfully the spoiling of your goods, *knowing in yourselves* that ye have *in heaven a better and an enduring substance*" (Heb. 10:34). If we are really waiting for the manifestation of the glory, we shall be found standing apart from everything which will be judged in that day: and it is written, "Yet once more, I shake not the earth only but also heaven; and this word, yet once more, signifieth the removing of those things that are shaken, as of things that are made, that those things which cannot be shaken may remain" (Heb. 12:26-27).

We have, in the last verse of our truly interesting chapter, a happy feature in the character of the true man of faith. Abram would not force others to walk according to his elevated standard. Although *he* might be able to reject, in the most unreserved manner, the offers of the king of Sodom, yet *others* might not be able to do so, and therefore he says, with regard to "Aner, Eshcol, and Mamre, *let them* take *their portion*." Our walk should ever be "according as God hath dealt to every man the measure of faith" (Rom. 12:3). We have seen, in our own day, many persons led, at the outset, to give up a variety of worldly things, and afterwards plunge still deeper into those things; and why? Because they acted through mere excitement or human influence, and were not able to say with Abram, "*I have lift up my hand unto the Lord*."

Genesis 15

In the opening verse of this chapter, we have a principle fraught with comfort and encouragement to us—a principle eminently calculated to call out into full exercise a spirit of true devotedness to the Lord. We observe here, the Lord's grace in acknowledging and accepting the sacrifice laid upon His altar—the willing offering of the devoted heart of His servant. Our God is never slow in owning such things, nor in rewarding them a hundredfold. Abram had just been manifesting a spirit of self-denial in refusing the attractive offers of the King of Sodom. He had refused to be enriched from such a source, and had taken "the Most High God" for his portion and his reward, therefore the Lord comes forth to confirm the soul of his servant with these words, "Fear not, Abram, I *am* thy shield, and thy exceeding great reward." "God is not unrighteous to forget the work and labor of love" (Heb. 6:10). A similar principle is presented to us in chapter 13, where Abram is seen giving way to Lot, in the matter of choosing the land. Abram's whole anxiety in that matter was about the Lord's honor, as maintained in the harmonious walk of "*brethren*" before the "Canaanite and the Perizzite." "Let there be no strife," says he, "between me and thee . . . *for we be brethren.*" Nor did Abram desire to suppress the strife, by *exacting concessions* from Lot. No; he was willing to concede everything himself—to surrender every claim—to sacrifice every advantage, provided the strife were suppressed. "Is not the *whole land* before thee?" *Take* what you please—possess yourself of the fairest spot in all the region round about. Here, as some one has observed, is the liberality—the unselfishness of faith. What was land to Abram in comparison with the Lord's glory? Nothing. He could give up anything, or everything, for that. How then does the Lord meet this self-sacrifice on the part of His servant? Just as He does in this chapter 15, by coming in, in the plenitude of His goodness, to make it up to him a hundredfold. "Lift up *now* thine eyes . . . for *all the land which thou seest* to thee will I give it, and to thy seed after thee" (13:14-15). How truly gracious it is of the Lord to enable His servant to make a sacrifice for Him, and then reward that sacrifice by a vast increase of blessing. Such are His ways—His ever adorable ways.

We are now called to trace in Abram the development of a feature which, in a special manner, demonstrates the high order of his communion with God. After all God's revelations and promises to him, his soul still breathes after an object without which all besides was defective. True, he had surveyed, with the eye of faith, the promised inheritance—the magnificent gift of divine benevolence: yet, notwithstanding all this, was there a great desideratum—a mighty blank. He sighed for a *Son.* A son *alone* could render complete, in Abram's estimation, all his previous privileges. "And Abram said, Lord God, what wilt Thou give me, seeing I go childless, and *the steward of my house is this Eliezer of Damascus.* And Abram said, Behold to me thou hast given no seed: and lo, *one born in my house* is mine heir" (vers. 2-3). Now, we have, in tracing the path of this remarkable man, beheld him, at times, displaying some very noble features of character. His generosity—his high elevation of mind—his pilgrim-like habits—all these things denote a man of the very highest order; yet I hesitate not to say, that we find him, in the passage just quoted, exhibiting a temper of soul, more in harmony with the mind of Heaven than anything we have met hitherto. Abram desired to have his house enlivened by the cry of a child. He had been long enough conversant with the spirit of bondage breathed by "the steward of his house," but the titles of *lord* and *master*, though all very good in their place, could not satisfy the heart of Abram, for Abram had been taught of God, and God ever instructs His children in those things which He loves, and which He exhibits in His dealings with them. And I would just observe, in connection with this, that we see in the case of the prodigal in Luke 15, the development of a principle very much in connection with what we have been saying. He says, in the very midst of all his misery "I will arise and go unto my Father, and will say unto him, *Father.*" Here we have a fine feature in the character of this poor wanderer. He had such a sense of the grace of him against whom he had sinned, that he could yet say "*Father*," notwithstanding his long course of rebellion and folly.

But let us observe with what accuracy Abram lays hold of the great principle afterwards brought out by the Spirit in Romans 8. "*If children, then heirs.*" Abram felt that sonship and heirship were inseparably connected, so much so, that without the former the latter could not be.

This is the meaning of his question, "Lord God, what wilt thou give me, seeing I go childless, and the steward of my house is this Eliezer of Damascus?" Abram rightly judged that to have "*no seed*" was to have *no inheritance*, for the word is, not if *stewards or servants*, *then heirs*, but "if *children*, then heirs" (Rom. 8:17).

How very important it is that we should ever bear in mind, that all our present privileges and future prospects stand connected with our character as "*sons*." It may be all well and very valuable, in its right place, to realize our responsibility to act as "faithful and wise stewards," in the absence of our Master; still the most ample privileges—the highest enjoyments—the brightest glories, which belong to us through the grace and mercy of our God, stand intimately connected with our character and place as "*sons*" (comp. John 1:12; Rom. 8:14, 19; 1 John 3:1-2; Eph. 1:5; 5:1; Heb. 12:5).

In the vision presented to us in the close of our chapter, and which was granted to Abram as an answer to his question, "Lord God, whereby shall I know that I shall inherit it?" we have a further illustration of the teaching of Romans 8. Abram is taught by the vision, that the *inheritance* was only to be reached through *suffering*—that *the heirs* must pass through *the furnace*, previous to their entering upon the enjoyment of that which God was reserving for them; and I doubt not that, were we more deeply and experimentally taught in the divine life, we should more fully apprehend the moral fitness of such training. Suffering then, is not connected, in this chapter, with *sonship*, but with *heirship*; and so we are taught in Romans 8. "If children, then heirs, heirs of God, and joint heirs with Christ, if so be that *we suffer* with Him, that we may be also *glorified* together." Again, we must, "through much *tribulation*, enter into the kingdom of God" (Acts 14:22). The Lord Jesus Himself, likewise, stands as the great illustration of the principle upon which we are dwelling. He occupied the place and enjoyed the favor of a Son from before all worlds (Prov. 8), yet ere He could lay His hand upon the inheritance He must pass

through suffering. He had a baptism to be baptized with, and was straitened (συνεχομενος) until it was accomplished. So also when He remembered that "a corn of wheat must fall into the ground and die," or else abide *alone*, His soul was "*troubled*." Now, we are to "know Him in the fellowship of His sufferings," before we can know Him in the fellowship of His glory; hence it is that the palmed multitude mentioned in Revelation 7 had to pass through "great tribulation" (της μεγαλης θλιψεως) ere they reached their peaceful, heavenly home. Passages of Scripture might be multiplied in proof of this point, but I will merely refer to the following, viz.—Phil. 1:29; 1 Thess. 3:4; 2 Thess. 1:5; 1 Tim. 4:10; 2 Tim. 2:12; 1 Peter 5:10.

But, in this remarkable vision, there are two points which, as they appear prominently in the whole of Israel's after history, deserve to be particularly noticed. I allude to "the smoking furnace, and the burning lamp" (ver. 17). It has been well observed, by a recent writer, that Israel's history might be summed up in these two words, "the furnace and the lamp." Egypt was a trying furnace to the seed of Abraham. There the fire burned fiercely, but it was soon followed by "the burning lamp" of God's own deliverance. The cry of the suffering seed had come up into the ears of Jehovah. He had heard their groanings and seen their afflictions, and had come down to display above their heads "the lamp" of salvation. "I am come down to deliver them," said He to Moses. Satan might take delight in kindling the furnace, and in adding to its intensity, but the blessed God, on the other hand, ever delighted in letting the rays of His lamp fall upon the dark path of His suffering heirs. So, when Jehovah had, in the faithfulness of His love, brought them into the land of Canaan, they again and again, kindled a furnace by their sins and iniquities; He, as frequently, raised up deliverers in the persons of the judges which were as so many lamps of deliverance to them. Further, when by their aggravated rebellion, they were plunged into the furnace kindled at Babylon, even there we observe the glimmerings of "the burning lamp," and finally it shone out for their full deliverance, in the decree of Cyrus.

Now, the Lord was constantly reminding the children of Israel of the above truth. He says to them, "But the Lord hath taken you, and brought you forth out of the *iron furnace*" (Deut. 4:20; 1 Kings 8:51). Again, "Cursed be the man that obeyeth not the words of this covenant, which I commanded your fathers, in the day that I brought them forth out of the land of Egypt, from *the iron furnace*" (Jer. 11:3-4).

Finally, we may ask, are the seed of Abraham now suffering in the furnace, or are they enjoying the lamp of God?—for they must be experiencing either the one or the other—the furnace, assuredly. They are scattered over the face of the earth as a proverb and a byword, a reproach and a hissing among all the nations of the earth. Thus are they in the iron furnace. But, as it has ever been, "the burning lamp" will assuredly follow "the smoking furnace," for "all Israel shall be saved; as it is written, there shall come out of Sion *the Deliverer*, and shall turn away ungodliness from Jacob" (Isa. 59:20; Rom. 11:26).

Thus we see how that Israel's eventful history has all along stood connected with the smoking furnace and the burning lamp, here seen in vision by Abram. They are either presented to us in the furnace of affliction, through their own sin, or enjoying the fruits of God's salvation; and even at this moment, when, as has been already observed, they are manifestly in the furnace, we can witness the fulfillment of God's promise, so often repeated, "And unto his son will I give one tribe, that David My servant may have a *lamp* [margin] always before Me in Jerusalem, the city which I have chosen Me to put My name there" (1 Kings 11:36; 15:14; 2 Kings 8:19; Psalm 132:17). If it be asked where does this lamp shine now? Not on earth, for Jerusalem, the place of its earthly display, is "trodden down of the Gentiles," but the eye of faith can behold it shining with undimmed lustre "in the true tabernacle," where it will continue to shine "until the fulness of the Gentiles be come in"; and then, when the furnace, seen in this chapter by Israel's great

progenitor, shall have been heated to the very highest degree of intensity, when the blood of Israel's tribes shall flow like water round the walls of Jerusalem, even then, shall the blessed lamp come forth from the place where it now shines, and cast its cheering rays upon the dark path of the oppressed and sorrowing remnant, bringing to mind those oft-illustrated words, "*O Israel, thou hast destroyed thyself; but in Me is thy help.*"*

Genesis 16—17

These two chapters give us an account of Abram's effort to obtain the promised seed by harkening to the voice of his wife, also of God's mode of teaching him the unprofitableness of such an appeal to the mere energy of nature as that which his effort involved.

At the very opening of Abram's course we find his faith put to the test in the matter of the famine, but here we find him tried in quite another way, a way moreover, which involved a far higher exercise of faith and spiritual power. "His own body now dead and the deadness of Sarah's womb;" although, in the main, "he considered them not," must have acted upon his mind to a considerable extent.

Now, as is the case of the famine already alluded to, Egypt was at hand, holding out a refuge from anxiety as to present supply, so here, "*an Egyptian maid*"—one of those maid-servants, doubtless, which Abram had gotten during his sojourn in that evil place—was presented to him as a relief in the time of anxiety touching the promised seed. "*Abram hearkened to the voice of Sarai.*"

But why introduce the element of bondage into his house? Why did not Abram's mind shrink from the thought of "the bondwoman and her son" as much as it had shrunk from the thought of "the steward of his house"? Might not the question, "Lord, what wilt Thou give me," be asked in connection with one as well as the other? Surely it was as

* I would refer the reader to the following Scriptures in confirmation of what has been above advanced on the subject of "the lamp."—Exod. 27: 20; 2 Sam. 22: 29; Ps. 119: 105; Prov. 6: 23; 13: 9; Isa. 62: 1.

much opposed to the divine economy to grant the inheritance to the seed of *"a bond-woman,"* as to a *"servant."* In either case it would be an allowance of the claims of nature, which cannot be.

The principles involved in this act of Abram's are fully laid open to us in the inspired commentary given in the Epistle to the Galatians. There we read, "Abram had two sons, the one by a bondmaid, the other by a free woman. But he who was of the bondwoman was born after the flesh; but he of the free woman was by promise. Which things are an allegory: for these are the two covenants; the one from the Mount Sinai, which gendereth to bondage, which is Agar. For this Agar is Mount Sinai in Arabia, and answereth to Jerusalem which now is, and is in bondage with her children. But Jerusalem which is above is free, which is the mother of us all" (chap. 4:22-26).

The churches of Galatia had been led away from the simplicity and liberty of Christ and had returned to *"the flesh."* They were beginning to substitute religious ceremonies for the energies of the Spirit of Christ. Hence it is that the apostle, in the course of his reasoning with them on their unhappy movement, refers to the matter recorded in our chapters, and the way in which he expounds it to them renders it unnecessary to dwell longer upon it. This step of Abram's only "gendered to bondage;" it introduced an unhealthy and an unhappy element into his house which, as we shall see when we proceed further with our subject, he had to expel ere he could reach the highest point of elevation in his course.

In chapter 17 we have God's remedy presented to us, and most consolatory it is to observe how the Blessed One at once comes in in order to lead back His servant to the *simple* yet *difficult* position of faith in Himself—simple, because therein we have but *one object* with which to be occupied—difficult, because therein we have to contend against the workings of "an evil heart of unbelief," leading us to "depart from the living God."

"And when Abram was ninety years old and nine, the Lord appeared to Abram and said unto him, *I am the Almighty God; walk before Me, and be thou perfect."* Here was at once the effectual cure for all impatient anxiety. *"I am Almighty"*—I can quicken the dead—I can call those things that be not as though they were—I can, if needs be, raise up of stones, children unto you—no flesh shall glory in My presence. "I am Almighty, walk before Me and be thou perfect."

It is perhaps one of the finest principles with which the mind can be occupied, that our God desires that He may ever be learnt, in the variety of His perfections, by the need of His people. We have already met a striking illustration of this important principle, in the matter of Abram's conflict with the king of Sodom, in chapter 14. There, when Abram was tempted by the offers of the enemy, he found relief in the apprehension of God's character as "the Most High God, the possessor of heaven and earth." The character of the communion into which Melchizedek led the soul of Abram was suited to the circumstances in which he stood. So is it exactly in this 17th chapter. Communion with God as "the Almighty" was the sole remedy for impatient anxiety as to the fulfillment of any promise.

Now, when once the Lord exhibits Himself in His character of "Almighty," there can be no obstacle whatsoever to the outflow of His grace; for, when almighty power and almighty grace combine in behalf of the sinner, faith may count upon a rich and an abundant harvest.

The promises, therefore, with which this chapter abounds are just such as we might have expected. "I will make thee exceeding fruitful, and I will make nations of thee, and kings shall come out of thee. And I will establish my covenant between Me and thee and thy seed after thee in their generations for an everlasting covenant, to be a God unto thee and to thy seed after thee. And I will give unto thee, and to thy seed after thee, the land wherein thou art a stranger, all the land of Canaan, for an everlasting possession; and I will be their God" (17:6-8). Surely these are promises which *almighty grace* alone could utter, *almighty power* alone fulfill.

The above promises stand connected with

"the covenant of circumcision" which is specially important as looked at in connection with Abram's effort to obtain the seed otherwise than by the operations of God's own hand. It would be profitable to dwell for a little upon the doctrine of this covenant of circumcision but my design in taking up this history, is not by any means to handle it in a doctrinal way, but rather to draw from it some of those valuable principles of a decidedly practical tendency with which it so richly abounds; and therefore I pass rapidly over chapters 16—17, which contain a mine of precious doctrinal truth quite sufficient to occupy a separate treatise.*

Ere closing my observations on this section of our narrative, I would add that it is *faith* alone which can enable one to listen, as Abraham here does, to the promises of Almighty God, and when faith listens, God will surely continue to speak. Abram here gets his name changed to Abraham, and the Lord unfolds to him the future greatness and number of his seed, while Abraham hearkens in the unquestioning silence of faith. But when the "Almighty God" goes on to say with reference to Sarai, "As for Sarai thy wife, thou shalt not call her name Sarai, but Sarah shall her name be. And I will bless her, and give thee a son also of her; yea, I will bless her, and she shall be a mother of nations; kings of people shall be of her" (vers. 15-16), he is at once overwhelmed by the pledges of such marvelous power and grace to be exercised towards him. They exceeded anything he had as yet known, and "Abraham fell on his face." This is very instructive. Abraham with his face in the dust, overcome by the plenitude of almighty power and grace! Surely, we may say, while dwelling upon such a Scripture as this, it is only *faith* that can rightly entertain the "*Almighty God*," it *alone* can give Him His due and proper place and honor Him as He should be honored. When the Almighty displays Himself, *self* must be excluded, hence we find that *Abram* is set aside in all this—*Sarai* is lost sight of—"*the bondwoman and her son*"

are, for the moment, put far out of view, and nothing is seen but "the Almighty God" in the sovereignty and fulness of His grace and power, and the faith that could lie prostrate in the dust, in silent adoration of such a display of the divine glories.

How different is this from the preceding chapter! There we find Abram hearkening to the suggestion of Sarai his wife, with regard to the bondwoman—here we find him hearkening to the voice of Jehovah, as Almighty, who is about to quicken the dead womb of Sarah, and to call those things that be not as though they were, that no flesh might glory in His presence. There it is Abram and Sarai *without God*—here it is God *without Abram and Sarai*. In a word, there it is *flesh*—here it is spirit—there it is *sight*—here it is *faith*. Wondrous contrast! Exactly similar to that afterwards displayed by the apostle to the churches of Galatia, when he sought to restore them from the sad influence of "the beggarly elements" of the flesh and the world, to the full liberty wherewith Christ had made them free.

Genesis 18—19

I class these two chapters together because, like those we have just been considering, they furnish us with a contrast—a contrast most marked and striking between the position occupied by Abraham in chapter 18, and that occupied by Lot in chapter 19.

The Lord Jesus when asked by Judas, not Iscariot, "How is it that Thou wilt manifest Thyself unto us and not unto the world?" replied, "If a man love Me, he will keep My words: and My Father will love him, and We will come unto him and make Our abode with him" (John 14:23). Again, "Behold, I stand at the door and knock: if any man hear My voice, and open the door, I will come in to him, and will sup with him, and he with Me" (Rev. 3:20). Now, Abraham furnishes us with an exceedingly happy exemplification of the

---

* I would observe here that the doctrine of the Epistle to the Galatians stands intimately connected with chap. 16—17, and I might add, the important doctrine of Israel's future restoration. We also get the doctrine of justification by faith fully illustrated in chap. 15.

truth stated in the above passages. "The Lord appeared unto him in the plains of Mamre: and He sat in *the tent door* in the heat of the day" (chap. 18:1). Here we find Abraham again in the full exhibition of his stranger character. *Mamre* and *the tent* are associated in our minds with the day of his triumph over the king of Sodom. Abraham is still a stranger and a pilgrim "dwelling in tabernacles." The revelation made unto him by the Almighty God had not altered the tone of his character in this respect, but had rather imparted fresh vigor and energy thereto. A simple dependence upon the promise of the Almighty God was the most effectual means of maintaining him in his stranger condition.

Now, it is, in the very highest degree, instructive to see the honor here put upon the character and condition of the stranger. Throughout the wide range of the world there was just *one spot* in which the Lord could accept the rites of hospitality and make Himself at home, and that was *in the tent of "a pilgrim and stranger."* The Lord would not honor the sumptuous halls and princely palaces of Egypt with His presence. No. All His sympathies and all His affections hung around the stranger of Mamre, who was the only one who, in the midst of an evil world, could be induced to take God for his portion.

What a season of enjoyment it must have been to Abraham while those heavenly strangers sat with him and partook of the offerings of his generous heart. Mark how he calls forth into action all the energies of his house to do honor to his guests. He hastens from the tent to the field, and from the field to the tent again, and seems to lose sight of himself in his effort to make others happy.

Nor is it merely by partaking of Abraham's hospitality that the Lord gives expession to the high estimation in which He holds him; He renews His promise to him with regard to the son—He opens up His counsels to him with reference to Sodom. "Shall I," says He, "hide from Abraham that thing which I do; seeing that Abraham shall surely become a great and mighty nation, and all the nations of the earth shall be blessed in him? *For I know him,* that he will command his children

and his household after him, and they shall keep the way of the Lord, to do justice and judgment; that the Lord may bring upon Abraham that which He hath spoken of him" (vers. 17-19).

Here Abraham is seen as "*the friend of God.*" "The servant knoweth not what his lord doeth," but Abraham was made acquainted with what the Lord was about to do to Sodom, while Lot—the one who was so deeply interested in the solemn event—was left in profound ignorance about it.

How then does Abraham make use of his favored position? Does he use it to strengthen more fully, and place on a firmer basis, the future interests of his house? Surely the natural heart would at once have prompted him to make such a use of his present advantage in the matter of nearness to Jehovah. Does he use it thus? Nay. Abraham had learnt too much of the ways of God to act in a way savoring so much of the selfishness of a heartless world. But, even had he thought of such a thing, he had no need to utter a syllable on the subject, for "*the Almighty God*" had most amply satisfied his heart with regard to the everlasting interests of his house—He had fixed it upon such a foundation that an anxious thought would have evidenced a complete want of moral order in Abraham's soul. He therefore entertained not a thought about himself or his house, but like a genuine man of faith, *he takes advantage of his place in the presence of God to intercede for a brother, whose worldliness had plunged him into the very midst of that place which was about to be given over to everlasting destruction.* "And Abraham drew near, and said, Wilt thou also destroy the righteous with the wicked?" (ver. 23) "*The righteous!*" to whom can he allude? Can it be to the man who had so deliberately turned aside out of the path of faith to take up his abode at Sodom? Yes; he speaks of Lot—he calls him "*righteous*"—he speaks of him in the very same terms as the Spirit in the apostle afterward speaks of him when he calls him a "righteous soul." Abraham, therefore, was taught of God when he could recognize in the man surrounded by all the pollution of Sodom "a righteous soul."*

I doubt not it will be admitted by every one taught of God that the conduct of Abraham in this chapter, furnishes us with one of the most important results of a holy and separated walk. We observe in it a man pleading with God in a most urgent strain for one who had turned his back upon him, and selected Sodom as the place of his abode. How completely must Abraham's soul have been lifted above "the things that are seen" when he could thus forget "the strife" and the departure, worldliness and evil of Lot, and plead for him still as "a righteous soul." If Abraham appears as "the *friend* of God" under other circumstances and other scenes, surely he is here seen as the *child* of God exhibiting most sweetly those principles which he had learnt in communion with his heavenly Father.

We shall now leave Abraham, for a little, enjoying his happy place before the Lord, while we contemplate the last sad scene in the life of one who seems to have valued the things of this life more highly than was consistent with the character of "a stranger and pilgrim" or "a righteous soul."

From the time that the separation took place between Abraham and Lot, the former seems to have proceeded "from strength to strength;" while the latter, on the contrary, seems to have proceeded only downwards, from one stage of weakness to another, until we find him, at the close, making shipwreck of everything, and merely "escaping with his life." The loss of all his goods in the battle between the "four kings and five" does not seem to have had any effect upon the mind of Lot in the way of teaching him the evil of being mixed up with the world; yea, he seems to have become more deeply involved in worldliness after that event than he had been before; for, at the first, he merely "pitched his tent *towards* Sodom" (chap. 13:12); but now we find him sitting "in the gate" (chap. 19:1), which, as we know, was then the place of honor. When once a man has put his hand to the plow if he begin to look back, we have

been told by Him who cannot err, that "he is not *fit* for the kingdom of God." Nor is it possible to count upon the fearful lengths to which a man may go when once the world, in any one of its varied aspects, has taken possession of his heart, or when once he has begun to turn his back upon the people of God. The terrible declension spoken of in Hebrews 10, which stops not short of "trampling under foot the Son of God," has its beginning in the apparently simple act of "forsaking the assembling of ourselves together." How needful, therefore, it is that we should take heed to our ways, and watch the avenues of our hearts and minds, lest any evil thing should get dominion over us, which, however trivial in itself, might lead to the most appalling results.

Now, it strikes me, that we have in the circumstance presented to us in the opening of chapter 19 the full evidence of Lot's fallen condition. The Lord Himself does not appear at all. He remains at a distance from the unholy place, and merely sends *His angels* to execute His commission upon the devoted city of Sodom. The angels, too, exhibit all the symptoms of distance and strangership—they refuse to go into Lot's house when invited, saying, "*Nay, but we will abide in the street all night*." True, they subsequently enter into his house; but, if they do so, it is not so much to enjoy refreshment as to counteract the sad effects of Lot's wrong circumstances. How different was the scene at Lot's house from that which they had so lately witnessed at the tent of the stranger of Mamre! The tumult of the men of Sodom—to whom, notwithstanding all their ungodly deeds and ungodly speeches, Lot applies the title of "*brethren*"—the evident embarrassment of Lot at being discovered in such painful circumstances—the shocking proposal which he is constrained to make in order to screen his guests from the violence of the ungodly men of Sodom—the struggle at the door, and Lot's danger—all these things must have shocked the heavenly strangers, and stood in marked contrast with the holy peace and retirement of Abraham's tent, together

* Although I consider Lot the principal object in Abraham's mind, while interceding before the Lord, I do not forget that there is mention made of "fifty," etc.

with his own calm and dignified demeanor throughout the scene. Well might those angels have been astonished to find "a righteous soul" in such a place, when he could have enjoyed, in company with his separated brother, the peaceful and holy joys of his steady and consistent course.

But the time had now arrived for the pouring out of the cup of divine wrath upon Sodom. "The men said unto Lot, Hast thou here any besides? . . . bring them out of *this place*: for we will destroy this place, because the cry of them is waxen great before the face of the Lord; and the Lord hath sent us to destroy it" (vers. 12-13). The critical moment which the Lord Jesus, in the gospel, notes by the exceedingly solemn word "*until*," was now at hand for the careless inhabitants of Sodom, who dreamed not of any interruption to their "eating, and drinking, buying and selling, marrying and giving in marriage." A moment's respite is allowed, during which Lot bears a message to his son-in-law, a testimony as to the rapidly approaching judgment; but, ah! what power could the testimony of one who had voluntarily come in and settled amongst them, have upon those who had lived and moved from their earliest infancy in the midst of the ungodly scene? How could Lot expect that his *words* would have any weight when his *ways* had so sadly contradicted them? He might now, with terrified aspect and earnest entreaties, urge them to leave a place which he knew was doomed to everlasting destruction, but they could not forget the calm and deliberate way in which he had at first "pitched his tent toward Sodom," and finally taken his seat "in the gate;" hence, as might be expected, "he seemed as one that mocked unto his sons-in-law" (ver. 14). And how, so far as he was concerned, could it be otherwise? His sons-in-law might be, and doubtless were, responsible before God for the rejection of the testimony; but Lot could not, by any means, expect them to heed him much, indeed, we find that even he himself was tardy in departing from the place; for "*while he lingered*"—while his heart still went after some object or another that was dear to him—"the men *laid hold upon his hand*, and

upon the hand of his wife, and upon the hand of his two daughters; the Lord being merciful to him, and *they brought him forth* and set him without the city" (ver. 16). From this statement, it is manifest that, had not the men "laid hold of, and brought forth" Lot, he would, no doubt, have "lingered" on "*until*" the fire of God's judgment had fallen upon him, and prevented even his "escaping with his life." But they "pulled him out of the fire," because "the Lord had mercy upon him."

But this escape of Lot's only served to put fresh honor upon Abraham, for we read that "when God destroyed the cities of the plain, *he remembered Abraham and sent Lot out of the midst of the overthrow*" (ver. 29). Thus, as Abraham's sword had delivered Lot in the time of the conquest of Sodom, his prayer delivered him in the time of its final overthrow, "for the effectual fervent prayer of a righteous man availeth much." Nor does the contrast between those two men stop here. There is yet another scene in which they stand at a great distance from each other as to the moral condition of their souls. "Abraham gat him up early in the morning, to the place where he stood before the Lord" (ver. 27). Here the man of faith, the holy pilgrim, once more raises his head amid the mighty scene of desolation. All was over with Sodom and its guilty inhabitants, "the smoke of the country went up as the smoke of a furnace." Sad spectacle! The din and bustle of that once stirring city was hushed; silence reigned around—the buying and selling—the eating and drinking—the marrying and giving in marriage—all the intercourse of social life had been awfully broken in upon. The solemn "*until*" had come at last—the only one in all that wicked place who, notwithstanding his failure, could be regarded as "the salt," had been removed— the measure of Sodom's iniquity had been filled up—the day of divine longsuffering closed, and nothing now met the eye of Abraham but misery and desolation throughout all the plain. How melancholy! And yet it was but a type of the far more terrible desolation which shall sweep across this guilty world when the Son of man makes His appearance, "when every eye shall see

Him, and all the tribes of the earth shall mourn and wail because of Him."

Thus, "Abraham stood *before the Lord*" completely exempt from all the sad effects of the recent visitation, as far as he was personally concerned. His stranger condition which, in the days of Chedorlaomer, had enabled him to live outside of Sodom and all its circumstances, still kept him free, and was the means of his escape from Sodom's unutterable woe and misery. Had Abraham, when solicited by the King of Sodom, mixed himself up with the things of Sodom, he would have been involved, in some measure, as was his brother Lot, in its overthrow. He himself would have been saved, but his work would have been burnt up. But Abraham was looking for "a city that hath foundations," and he knew at once that Sodom was not that city, and hence he would have nothing whatever to do with it. He would "hate even the garment spotted by the flesh"—he would "touch not the unclean thing," and now he was permitted to realize the blessed results of his conduct, for, while Lot had to retreat in confusion and sorrow to a cave in the mountains, his wife and all his possessions being lost, Abraham takes his stand, in all that blessed calmness and dignity which ever characterized him, in the presence of Jehovah, and from thence surveys the heart-rending scene.

But what of Lot? How did he end his course? "Oh, tell it not in Gath! publish it not in the streets of Askelon!" Well may we desire to throw a veil over the closing scene of the life of one who does not seem to have ever realized, as he should, the power of *the call of God*. He had always displayed a secret desire for the things of Egypt or those of Sodom. His heart does not seem to have been thoroughly detached from the world, and therefore his course was always unsteady; from the time he separated himself from Abraham, he went from bad to worse—from one stage of evil to another, until at last the scene closes with the shocking transaction in the cave; the sad results of which were seen in the persons of Moab and Ammon, the enemies of the people of God.

Thus ended the course of Lot, whose

history ought to be a solemn warning to all Christians who feel a tendency to be carried away by the world. The history has not been left on record without a purpose. "Whatever things were written aforetime, were written for our learning," may we therefore learn from the above narrative, "not to lust after evil things," for, although "the Lord knows how to deliver the godly out of temptation," yet it is our place to keep as much out of the way of temptation as we can, and our prayer should ever be "lead us not into temptation." "The world passeth away, and the lust thereof; but he that doeth the will of God abideth forever" (1 John 2:17).

Genesis 20—21

Lot has now passed off the scene—his sun has gone down amid thick clouds and a gloomy atmosphere; it now remains for us to pursue, for a few moments longer, the narrative of Abraham's ways, and God's dealings with him.

There was one point involved in chapter 12 which I left untouched, knowing that it would come before us again in this place.

When Abraham went down into Egypt, he entered into a compact with Sarah his wife *to conceal part of the truth*, "Say, I pray thee," said he, "thou art my sister" (chap. 12:13). One evil ever leads to another. Abraham was moving in the wrong direction when he went down into Egypt for help, and therefore did not exhibit that refinement of conscience which would have told him of the moral unsoundness of this mental reservation. "Speak every man truth with his neighbor," being a divine principle, would always exercise an influence upon one walking in communion with God; but Abraham's desire to get out of present trial was an evidence of failure in communion, and hence "his moral sense," as a recent writer has termed it, was not as keen or as elevated as it should have been. However, although the Lord plagued Pharaoh's house because of his having taken Sarah into it, and further, although Pharaoh rebukes Abraham for his acting in the matter, yet the latter says nothing whatever about the deliberate compact into which he had entered with his wife, to keep back part of the truth; he silently takes the rebuke and goes on his way, but the root of the evil remained still in his heart, ready to show itself at any time if circumstances should arise to draw it out.

Now, it is marvelous to behold Abraham coming up out of Egypt—building an altar and pitching a tent—exhibiting the noble generosity of faith—vanquishing Chedorlaomer and repulsing the temptation of the King of Sodom—urging his request for a son and heir, receiving the most gracious answer—on his face before God in the sense of His almighty grace and power—entertaining the heavenly strangers and interceding for his brother Lot. In a word, I say, it is marvelous to behold Abraham passing through such brilliant scenes, comprising a series of years, and, all the while, this moral point, in which he had erred at the very threshold of his course, remains unsettled in his heart. True, it did not develop itself during the period to which I have just referred, but why did it not? Because Abraham was not in circumstances to call it out, but there it was notwithstanding. The evil was not *fully brought out*—not confessed, not got rid of—and the proof of this is, that the moment he again finds himself in circumstances which could act upon *his weak point*, it is at once made manifest that the weak point is there. The temptation through which he passed in the matter of the King of Sodom, was not by any means calculated to touch this peculiar point; nor was anything that occurred to him from the time he came up out of Egypt until he went down into Gerar, calculated to touch it, for had it been touched, it would no doubt have exhibited itself.

We never can know what is in our hearts until circumstances arise to draw it out. Peter did not imagine that he could deny his Lord, but when he got into circumstances which were calculated to act upon his peculiar weakness, he showed that the weakness was there.

It required the protracted period of forty years in the wilderness to teach the children of Israel "what was in their hearts" (Deut. 8:2); and it is one of the grand results of the course of discipline through which each child of God passes, to lead him into a more profound knowledge of his own weakness and nothingness. "We had the *sentence of death in ourselves*, that we should not trust in ourselves, but in God which raiseth the dead" (2 Cor. 1:9). The more we are growing in the sense of our infirmities, the more shall we see our need of clinging more closely to Christ—drawing more largely upon His grace, and entering more fully into the cleansing virtue and value of His atoning blood. The Christian, at the opening of his course, never knows his own heart; indeed, he could not bear the full knowledge of it; he would be overwhelmed thereby. "The Lord leads us not by the way of the Philistines lest we should see war," and so be plunged in despair. But He graciously leads us by a circuitous route, in order that our apprehension of His grace may keep pace with our growing self-knowledge.

In chapter 20, then, we find Abraham again, after the lapse of many years, falling into the old error, a suppression of truth, for which he has to suffer a rebuke from a mere man of the world. The man of the world, in this scene, seemed, for the moment, to possess a more refined moral sense than the man of God. "Said he not unto me," says he, " 'She is my sister'! and she, even she herself said, 'He is my brother': in the integrity of my heart and innocency of my hands have I done this." But mark how God enters the scene for the purpose of vindicating His servant. He says to Abimelech, "Behold, thou art but a dead man." Yes, with all "the integrity of his heart and innocency of his hands"—with all his fine moral sense of right and wrong, he was "but a dead man," when it came to be a question, for one moment, between him and even an erring child of God. God, in His grace, was looking at His dear servant from quite a different point of view from that adopted by Abimelech. All that the latter could see in Abraham was a man guilty of a manifest piece of deception, but God saw more than that, and therefore He says to Abimelech, "Now therefore restore the man his wife; *for he is a prophet, and he shall pray for thee, and thou shalt live.*" What dignity is here put upon Abraham! God himself vindicates him before the world! Not a syllable of reproof!—not a breath of disapprobation!—no, "he is a prophet and he shall pray for thee and thou shalt live." How truly consolatory it is for the poor, weak, and harassed believer to remember that His Father is ever viewing him through the medium of the Lord Jesus Christ. He sees nothing whatever upon His child but the excellency and perfectness of Jesus. Thus, while a man of the world may have to rebuke a child of God, as in the case before us, God declares that He values that character which the believer has received from Him more than all the amiability, integrity, and innocency that nature can boast of.

This reminds us of the way in which the Lord vindicates the Baptist before the multitude, although He had sent a message to himself which must have exercised him deeply: "I say unto you, among those that are born of women there is not a greater prophet then John the Baptist" (Luke 7:28). Thus, whatever unfavorable aspect the child of God may wear in the world's view, God will ever show Himself the vindicator of such. "He suffered no man to do them wrong; yea, he reproved kings for their sakes, saying, Touch not mine anointed and do my prophets no harm" (1 Chron. 16:21-22).

However, as was observed with regard to John the Baptist, the message sent from the Lord to His servant must have exercised his spirit deeply in secret, so is it in Abraham's case. Abraham must have felt deeply humbled in his soul at the thought of what had occurred, and the consciousness of the fact that God would not enter into judgment with him about it would have augmented that feeling. When Abraham fell into the same error in Egypt we do not find that Pharaoh's reproof produced any manifest effect. He was not humbled by it to such a degree as to make a full confession of the whole thing. He takes his departure out of Egypt, but *the root* of evil remains in his heart, ready to shoot forth its pernicious branches again. Not so in chapter 20; here we get at once at the root of the matter—Abraham opens up his whole

heart, he confesses that from the very first moment of his course he had retained this thing in his heart which had twice betrayed him into an act, which, to say the least of it, would not bear the light. And as there is the full confession of the evil on his part, so is there the complete renunciation of it—he gets rid of it fully, root and branch. The leaven is put forth out of every corner of his heart, he hearkens to Abimelech's reproof and profits by it; it was God's instrument by which He brought out the matter, and delivered the soul of his servant from the power of evil.

But, in addition to the point upon which we have been dwelling, there was yet another question to be settled ere Abraham could reach the most elevated point of his course as a man of faith. The bondwoman and her son were yet in the house. He must put forth these from *his house* as he had put forth the evil from *his heart*. The house and the heart must be cleared out. In chapter 21 we find matters brought to a crisis with regard to the bondwoman and her son, concerning whom we have heard comparatively nothing until now. The element of bondage had heretofore lain dormant in Abraham's house because not roused into action, by anything of an opposite nature and tendency. But in the birth of Isaac—the son of the free woman—the child of promise—we see a new element introduced. The spirit of liberty and the spirit of bondage are thus brought into contact, and the struggle must issue in the expulsion of either one or the other. They cannot move on in harmony, for "how can two walk together except they be agreed."

Now we are invited by the apostle, in his Epistle to the Galatians, to behold in these two children, "the two covenants," the one gendering to *bondage*, the other to *liberty;* and further, to behold in them samples of the fleshly and spiritual seed of Abraham, the former, "born after the flesh," the latter, "born after the Spirit." Nor can anything be more marked than the line of demarcation between, not only the two covenants, but the two seeds. They are totally distinct the one from the other, and can never, by any operation, be brought to coalesce. Abraham was made to feel, and that painfully, this fact. "Cast out this bondwoman and her son; for the son of this bondwoman shall not be heir with my son, even with Isaac" (chap. 21:10). Here the natural result shows itself. The two elements could not mingle. As well might the north and the south winds be expected to blow in all their strength without exciting a convulsion in the elements.

But it was most painful work to Abraham to be obliged thus to thrust forth his son. "The thing was very grievous in Abraham's sight because of his son;" but it mattered not, he must be put out, for the son of a bondwoman could never inherit the promises made only to the spiritual seed. If Ishmael were to have been retained, it would have been an open allowance of the claims of the flesh. Abraham would have found something "as pertaining to the flesh" and would thus have had "whereof to glory." But no—all God's promises are to be made good to those who, like Isaac, are the children of promise, born after the Spirit, "not of blood, nor of the will of the flesh, nor of the will of man, but of God" (John 1:13). Ishmael was manifestly born "of the will of the flesh, and of the will of man," and "flesh and blood cannot inherit the kingdom of God." The flesh must therefore be set aside and kept under, no matter how "grievous" it may be to our hearts. The Christian will often find it grievous enough to keep down the old principle which ever lusts against the new, but the Lord gives spiritual power for the struggle so that "we are more than conquerors through Him that loves us."

But it is not my present purpose to pursue the doctrinal matter involved in this instructive history; were I to do so it would carry me far beyond the limits I have prescribed for myself in this little paper, the design of which is, as before observed, simply to direct attention to a few leading principles put forward in the narrative. I will therefore pass on to the next chapter which is the last of the section laid out for consideration.

Genesis 22

The circumstances through which Abraham passed in chapters 20 and 21 were most important indeed. An evil which had long been harbored in his heart had been put away; the bondwoman and her son, who had so long retained quiet possession of his house, were cast out, and he now stands forth as "a vessel sanctified and meet for the master's use, prepared unto every good work."

"And it came to pass *after these things*, that God did tempt [or try] Abraham." Here Abraham is at once introduced into a place of real dignity and honor. When God tries an individual it is a certain evidence of His confidence in him. We never read that "God did tempt Lot"—no, the goods of Sodom furnished a sufficiently strong temptation for Lot. The enemy laid a snare for him in the well-watered plains of Sodom which he seemed but too prone to fall into. Not so with Abraham. He lived more in the presence of God, and was, therefore less susceptible of the influence of that which had ensnared his erring brother.

Now, the test to which God submits Abraham—the furnace in which He tries him, marks at once a pure and genuine metal. Had Abraham's faith not been of the purest and most genuine character, he would assuredly have winced under the fiery ordeal through which we behold him passing in this beautiful chapter. When God promised Abraham a son, he believed the promise "and it was counted unto him for righteousness." "He staggered not at the promise of God through unbelief, but was strong in faith, giving glory to God." But then, having received this son, having realized the truth of the promise, was there not a danger that he would rest in *the gift* instead of in *the Giver?* Was there not a danger that he would lean upon Isaac, in thinking upon the future seed and future inheritance, rather than upon God Himself who had promised him the seed? Surely there was; and God knew that, and therefore tries His servant in a way, more than anything, calculated to put him to the test as to the object on which his soul was resting. The grand inquiry put to Abraham's heart, in this wondrous transaction, was, "are you still walking before *the Almighty God, the quickener of the dead*?" God desired to know whether he could apprehend in Him the One who was as able to raise up children from the ashes of his sacrificed son as from the dead womb of Sarah. In other words, God desired to prove that Abraham's faith reached forth, as some one has observed, *to resurrection*, for if it stopped short of this, he never would have responded to the startling command, "Take now, thy son, thine only son Isaac whom thou lovest, and get thee into the land of Moriah; and offer him there for a burnt-offering upon one of the mountains which I will tell thee of" (chap. 22:2). But Abraham "staggered not." He at once responds to the call. God had asked for Isaac, and Isaac must be given, and that too without a breath of murmur. He could give up anything or everything so long as his eye rested upon "the Almighty God." And mark the point of view in which Abraham puts this journey of his to Mount Moriah, "I and the lad will go yonder *and worship*." Yes, it was an act of worship, for he was about to lay upon the altar of the Quickener of the dead the one in whom all God's promises centred. It was an act of worship—most elevated worship, for he was about to prove, in the sight of Heaven and hell, that no other object filled his soul but the Almighty God. Hence, what calmness! what self-possession! what pure devotion! what elevation of mind! what self-renunciation! He never falters throughout the scene. He saddles the ass, prepares the wood, and sets off to Mount Moriah, without giving expression to one anxious thought, although, as far as human eye could see, he was about to lose the object of his heart's most tender affection, yea, the one upon whom the future interests of his house, to all appearance, depended.

Abraham, however, showed most fully that his heart had found a nearer and dearer object than Isaac, dear as he was; he showed also that his faith was resting upon another object altogether, with reference to the future interests of his seed, *and that he was as simply resting upon the promise of Almighty God after the birth of Isaac as before it.*

Behold, then, this man of faith as he ascends the mount, taking with him his "well-beloved"! What a scene of breathless interest!* How must the angelic hosts have watched this illustrious father from stage to stage of his wondrous journey, until at last they beheld his hand stretched forth for the knife to slay his son—that son for which he had so long and ardently wished, and for which he had so steadily trusted God. Then again, what an opportunity for Satan to ply his fiery darts! What abundant room for such suggestions as the following, viz., "What will become of the promises of God with regard to the seed and the inheritance, if you thus sacrifice your only son? Beware that you are not led astray by some false revelation; or, *if it be true* that God has said so and so, doth not God know that, in the day you sacrifice your son, all your hopes will be blasted? Further, think of Sarah; what will she do if she lose Isaac, after having induced you to expel from your house Ishmael?" All these suggestions, and many beside, the enemy might bring to bear upon the heart of Abraham. Nor would Abraham himself have been beyond the region of those thoughts and reasonings which, at such a time, would not fail to arise within him. What then was his answer to all such dark suggestions? *Resurrection!* "By faith Abraham, when he was tried, offered up Isaac; and he that had received the promises offered up his only begotten son, of whom it was said, that in Isaac shall thy seed be called: *Accounting that God was able to raise him up, even from the dead; from whence also he received him in a figure*" (Heb. 11:17-19).

Resurrection is God's mighty remedy for all the mischief and ruin introduced by Satan; when once we arrive at this point, we have done with the power of Satan, the last exercise of which is seen in death. Satan cannot touch the life that has been received in resurrection, for the last exercise of his power is seen in the grave of Christ; beyond that he can do nothing. Hence the security of

---

* It strikes me that we get, in Abraham's journey to Mount Moriah, a remarkable type of the mysterious scene afterwards exhibited at Calvary, when God was really providing Himself a lamb. We can have no difficulty in losing sight of Herod and Pilate, the chief priests and scribes, the Pharisees and the multitude, and thus we have none remaining but *the Father and the Son*, who, in company, ascend the Mount and carry out the gracious work of redemption in the unbroken solitude of that place.

the Church's place; her "life is hidden with Christ in God." Blessed hiding place! May we rejoice in it more and more each day.

I will now draw this paper to a close. We have followed Abraham in his course, from Ur of the Chaldees up to the Mount Moriah—we have seen him resign, at the call of God, family and kindred, lands and possessions, worldly ease and prosperity; and lastly, we have seen him, in the power of faith, at the same call of God, ascend the solitary mount, for the purpose of laying "his only begotten" upon God's altar, and thus to declare that he could give up everything and every one but God Himself—and that, being acquainted with the meaning of *"the Almighty"* and *"Resurrection,"* he cared not though he were called to look to the stones for the raising up of seed unto him.

On the other hand, we have followed Lot from Ur of the Chaldees also; but alas! his path was a far different one from that of his brother. He does not seem to have realized the power of the call of God in his own soul; he moved rather under Abraham's influence than under that of Johovah; hence we find

that, while Abraham was, at every step of his journey, letting go the world, Lot was doing the very reverse; he was grasping at the world in every shape and form, and he obtained that at which he was grasping, but what then? What of the end? Ah, that is the point. What of Lot's end? Instead of being a noble spectacle unto angels, and a pattern to all future generations of the faithful—of what faith can enable a man "to do and to suffer" for God—he was just the reverse; he was led away by the enemy of his soul, who ensnared him by means of the things of the world; he spent his days amid the uncleanness of Sodom, and the scene closes with the sad circumstances in the cave. All he did for God or his people was to beget the Ammonite and the Moabite, the enemies of both.

How wondrous then is that grace, which, speaking of the history of such an one, could say, "And delivered just Lot, vexed with the filthy conversation of the wicked; for that righteous man dwelling among them, in seeing and hearing, vexed his righteous soul from day to day with their unlawful deeds" (2 Peter 2:7-8).

THE HISTORY OF THE TRIBE OF LEVI

THE TRIBE OF LEVI
ARRANGED ACCORDING
TO THEIR FAMILIES

Name	Meaning
First Class	
Gershon	*A stranger, or exile*
Lael	*Dedicated, or belonging to God*
Eliasaph	*God hath added*
Shimei	*Renowned*
Libni	*White*
Second Class	
Kohath	*Assembly*
Hebron	*Association, communion*
Amram	*Exalted people, of the exalted One*
Izhar	*Oil*
Uzziel	*The strength of God*

	Third Class
Merari	*Bitter*
Mahli	*Sick, sickly*
Mushi	*Yielding, forsaking*
Abihail	*Father of strength*
Zuriel	*My rock is God*

THERE ARE FEW EXERCISES more profitable for the Christian than that of reflecting upon the character of God as unfolded in the history of the saints and fathers of ancient times recorded in the Scriptures of the Old Testament: and indeed this might be expected from the very nature of the subject, which is such that, whatever be its extent, it unfolds principles to us which stand intimately connected with all that is important for us to know or be established in. Thus, whether we get the dealings of God on a limited scale, as with any one of the fathers *personally*, or more widely extended, as with the seed of Israel afterwards, it is nevertheless the same lesson we are called upon to learn, namely, *God and man*.

Now, this is what should enhance exceedingly the value of the Old Testament to the Christian; almost the great body of its teaching is of the above character: and not only so, but it also (as looked at in this point of view) guards effectually against the mere exercise of imagination; for when we consider the history of any man or people, it is not necessary that we should decide positively what is *shadowed out* therein;* it is enough for us to see that we have before us a more or less extensive development of the character and actings of God and man; and this, without ever descending beneath the surface of Scripture, cannot fail of being instructive and edifying to the soul.

But, of all the histories of the Old Testament embodying instruction of the above character, I believe there are few more copious, deep and varied than that which is about to engage our attention. If the narrative of a soul taken up by sovereign and eternal grace from the pit of corruption and deep depravity, carried through the various stages which grace and truth had enacted for sinful man, until at last he is set down in the very sanctuary of God and established in the enjoyment of the covenant of life and peace forever; if, I say, such a narrative would possess charms and present attractions to us, then does the history of Levi abound in this. It is only a matter of astonishment that a history fraught with such rich and varied instruction has not occupied more of the thoughts of those luminaries of the Church whose writings have been a source of comfort and instruction to all who have been taught to value the truth of God.

Yet, much as I see in the history of Levi, and much as I admire what I do see, I could

not think of directing the reader's thoughts to the subject without informing him that I purpose doing little more than to bring before his mind in a connected way the various Scriptures which treat of this most interesting question; however, these Scriptures are so plain and striking that no one who is at all familiar with Scripture truths can fail to enter into them. Now, as I purpose, with the Lord's blessing and grace, to follow the history of Levi through all the Scriptures in which it is brought before us, I will commence with *his birth*, as recorded in Genesis 29:34; "And she [Leah] conceived again, and bare a son: and said, Now this time will my husband be *joined* unto me, because I have borne him three sons: therefore was his name called Levi" (that is, "joined").

Here, then, we are presented with the birth and name of this most remarkable character—a name of wondrous significance as looked at in connection with his after history, whether in nature's wild and lawless extravagance, in which we find him "*joined*" with his brother in the perpetration of a deed of blood and murder (Gen. 34), or in the day when he was called to drink deeply and largely of the cup of God's electing grace, when "*joined*" with Aaron in "the work of the tabernacle" (Num. 8).

Genesis 34:25-26: "And it came to pass on *the third day*, when they were sore, that two of the sons of Jacob, Simeon and Levi, Dinah's brethren, took each man his sword, and came upon the city boldly, and slew all the males. And they slew Hamor and Shechem his son with the edge of the sword, and took Dinah out of Shechem's house and went out."

As the Spirit of God in Jacob has furnished us with a striking commentary on the above piece of cruelty, we will consider the Scripture in which the commentary is given, namely, Genesis 49:5-7: "Simeon and Levi *are brethren*; instruments of cruelty are in their habitations. O my soul, *come not thou into their secret; unto their assembly, mine honor, be not thou united:* for in their anger they slew a man, and in their self-will they

---

* In many of the Old Testament narratives, however, the instruction is so manifestly typical that even the most cautious reader, if at all familiar with Scripture, cannot refuse to look at it in that point of view.

digged down a wall. Cursed be their anger, for it was fierce; and their wrath, for it was cruel; *I will divide them in Jacob, and scatter them in Israel.*"

We have here a truly humbling view of human nature as looked at in the light of the holiness of God. It is as if the Lord would say to us, Look here! behold a man clothed in nature's blackest garb, and presenting nature's most forbidding aspect. Examine him closely, in order that you, seeing what *man is* when stripped of all that false clothing which ignorance or vain self-righteousness would put upon him, may know the rich aboundings of My grace, which can avail to lift even such a one into the loftiest heights of communion—heights which human conception would utterly fail to mount, but which My grace, through the blood of the cross, can make available to the very chief of sinners.

In reading such a description as that which the above passage presents to us, how needful it is for the sinner to bear in mind that it is not only in the light of *God's holiness* that he is called to look at himself, but also in the light of *His grace.* When this is learned he needs not be afraid to penetrate deeply into the dark recesses of his heart's corruption; for if God in grace *fill* the scene, the sinner (so far as his own righteousness is concerned) must necessarily be *out* of the scene; and then it is no longer a question of what *we* think about sin, but how *God* will deal with it in grace, and that is simply to put it away forever—yea, to bury it forever in the waters of His forgetfulness: thus it will be placing *our sin* side by side with *God's grace;* which is what the gospel invites us to do, and which, moreover, is the only way to arrive at a proper settlement of the question of sin.

On the other hand, where this saving principle is not known—not believed—the sinner will undoubtedly seek to make the load of his guilt as light as possible, in order that he may have as little to do as he may. This will ever lead to the most unutterable and intolerable bondage; or if not to this, to that which is much worse, even to detestable religious pride, which is of all things most truly abominable in the sight of God.

If you have not as yet got the question of

sin settled between your conscience and God, ponder, I do beseech you, what I have now stated; for to know this principle in spirit is life eternal. Christ has, *once for all*, borne sin's deepest curse in His own body on the tree, and now even *Levi* can lift up his head; for although he be by nature only conversant with "*instruments of cruelty,*" things which must have kept God forever at a distance from "his secret and his assembly;" although he be by nature *cruel, fierce, self-willed, scattered, and divided*, yet God can, in the exercise of His mercy, make him conversant with "the instruments of the tabernacle," bring him into the enjoyment of the covenant of *life* and *peace, in union* with the great head of the priestly family, and, in the power of this blessed union, cause him to have his "*lights and perfections with his Holy One*" (Deut. 33:8; Mal 2:4-5).

However, we must not anticipate the teaching of passages which are yet to come under our notice; I will therefore close my remarks on this part of our subject by requesting my reader to compare attentively the character of Levi, as above recorded, with that which the Apostle Paul, quoting from the Psalms, has given of man generally, whether Jew or Gentile: "There is *none* righteous, no, not one; there is *none* that understandeth, there is *none* that seeketh after God. They are *all* gone out of the way, they are *together* become unprofitable; there is none that doeth good, no, not one. Their throat is an open sepulchre; with their tongues they have used deceit; the poison of asps is under their lips, whose mouth is full of cursing and bitterness: *their feet are swift to shed blood: destruction and misery are in their ways; and the way of peace have they not known:* there is no fear of God before their eyes" (Rom. 3:10-18).

Exodus 32:25-29; "And when Moses saw that the people were naked; (for Aaron had made them naked unto their shame among their enemies:) then Moses stood in the gate of the camp, and said, Who is on the Lord's side? let him come unto me. And all the sons of Levi gathered themselves together unto him. And he said unto them, Thus saith the Lord God of Israel, Put every man his sword by his side and go in and out from gate to gate throughout the camp, and slay every man his brother, and every man his companion, and every man his neighbor. And the children of Levi did according to the word of Moses: and there fell of the people that day about three thousand men. For Moses had said, Consecrate yourselves to-day to the Lord, even every man upon his son, and upon his brother; that He may bestow upon you a blessing this day."

Here a new scene opens to us, and we are called to witness the dawning of a new day upon Levi; a day, moreover, which may justly lead us to anticipate great things. It is true we get him here likewise with his sword by his side, but, oh, for what a different purpose, and in what a different cause! It is not now in anger and self-will slaying a man, but in holy jealousy and care for the honor of the Lord God of Israel, and in simple obedience to His command; and although this may, and will, lead to the very cutting off of a brother, a son, or a friend, Levi cares not; for the word is, "Consecrate yourselves to the Lord, that He may bestow upon you a blessing."

This was enough for Levi; and although by nature he was vile and utterly unfit either for the fellowship or service of God, yet is he now the foremost in jealous vindication of His holy name and worship against those who would seek to "turn their glory into the similitude of an ox that eateth grass." Nor is Levi now seen *"joined"* with his brother Simeon—no, he might join in league with him in the days of his wickedness for the perpetration of deeds of blood; but here, as I before observed, we get the opening of a new scene, and therefore he is seen "joined" with the Lord and His servant Moses for the execution of righteous judgment upon idolatry.

And henceforth, in following the footsteps of Levi, we shall find that, instead of being "swift to shed blood," they are to be "swift" in following the movements of the cloud, and "swift" in performing the service of the tabernacle.

It would, of course, be quite foreign to our subject to dwell upon the sad and humbling scene that called out the above act of service

on the part of Levi. Suffice it to say that it was, as we know, on the part of Aaron and the camp, a ceasing to exercise faith in the fact that Moses was *alive* in the presence of God for them. The consequence of which was an entire forgetfulness of the mighty Hand and stretched out Arm that had brought them up out of the land of Egypt, and of their present position *in the wilderness;* hence, as might be expected, "the people *sat down to eat and drink* and rose up to play." May the Lord preserve us from like forgetfulness; and, seeing "those things were written for our admonition," may we be truly admonished thereby not to "lust after evil things."

We shall now pass on to the next Scripture, where we get the Lord's own thoughts upon the above act of service, namely, Deuteronomy 33:8-11: "And of Levi he [Moses] said, Let thy Thummim and thy Urim be with thy Holy One, whom thou didst prove at Massah, and with whom thou didst strive at the waters of Meribah; who said unto his father and to his mother, I have not seen him; neither did he acknowledge his brethren, nor knew his own children: for they have observed Thy word and kept Thy covenant. They shall teach Jacob Thy judgments, and Israel Thy law; they shall put incense before Thee, and whole burnt sacrifice upon Thine altar. Bless, Lord, his substance, and accept the work of his hands: smite through the loins of them that rise against him, and of them that hate him, that they rise not again."

In this passage we have real Levite service brought before us in the words, "who said unto his father and mother, I have not seen him," etc. The *true* and *decided* servant of God will ever have to experience something of this; indeed, the measure thereof will just be in proportion to the faithfulness and power of his walk: "flesh and blood cannot inherit the kingdom of God"; therefore every heir of that kingdom must show himself in readiness to deny all the claims which "flesh and blood" would make on him, whether in himself or in others. Most happily does the address to "the queen," in Ps. 45, connect itself with this point: "*Harken*, O daughter, and *consider*, and *incline thine ear; forget also thine own people* and thy father's house;

so shall the King greatly desire thy beauty: for He is thy Lord, and worship thou Him" (vers. 10-11).

We have all to watch against a tendency to be influenced by the claims of flesh and blood, in our testimony for Christ. He Himself has said on this subject that "no man having put his hand to the plow and *looking back*, is fit for the kingdom of God" (Luke 9:62). And, as some one has observed, it was upon this point that the prophet Elisha's character seemed a little defective, for when Elijah cast his mantle over him, or, in other words, when he had put upon him the high honor of making him a prophet of the Lord God, Elisha's heart seemed to yearn after home, and he said, "Let me, I pray thee, *kiss my father and my mother*, and *then* I will *follow thee*" (1 Kings 19:20).

Now this was most natural, and, as some would say, amiable and affectionate; but, oh, amiability and natural affection have often hindered people from entering as they should into the Lord's service; and although it is one of the marks of the latter-day apostasy to be "without natural affection," yet does Moses, in the above-cited passage, ask the Lord to bless Levi, because "he said unto his father and his mother, I have not seen him, neither did he acknowledge his brethren, nor knew his own children." How grossly inconsistent would it have been for Levi to have said, "Let me kiss my father and my mother," when called to enter upon the Lord's work; and not less so is it for us to allow the claims of "flesh and blood" to interfere with our true-hearted Levite service to our God, who has done so much for *us*.

But let us carefully observe the blessed consequences of this decision of character on the part of Levi. These are, first, "They shall *teach Jacob* Thy judgments, and Israel Thy law." Secondly, "They shall put incense before Thee, and whole burnt sacrifice upon *Thine altar*." Thirdly, "Bless his substance." Fourthly, "Accept the work of his hands." Fifthly, "Smite through the loins of them that rise against him, and of them that hate him, that they rise not again." All these fruits are distinct, and yet intimately connected, as springing from the same source, namely,

simple, devoted and uncompromising obedience to the Lord.

As to the first of these fruits, how true it is that it is only the man who himself endeavors to walk in power before God that can speak with effect to the hearts and consciences of others; nothing else will do—nothing else will tell, either upon the hearts or in the lives of Christians. There may be, and, alas, is much of mere systematic teaching and preaching of things which the mere intellect may have received, and which, by a natural fluency of language, we may be able to give out; but all such teaching is vain, and had much better be avoided in the sight of God. True, it might often give to our public assemblies an appearance of barrenness and poverty which our poor, proud hearts could ill brook; but would it not be far better to keep silence than to substitute mere carnal effort for the blessed energy of the Holy Spirit?

True ministry, however, the ministry of the Spirit, will always commend itself to the heart and conscience. We can always know the source from which a man is drawing who speaks in "the words which the Holy Ghost teacheth," and with the ability which God giveth; and while we should ever pray to be delivered from the mere effort of man's intellect to handle the truth of God amongst us, we should diligently cultivate that power to teach which stands connected, as in Levi's case, with the denial of the claims of flesh and blood, and with entire devotedness to the Lord's service.

In the second consequence above referred to we have a very elevated point: "They shall put incense before Thee, and whole burnt sacrifice upon Thine altar." This is worship. We put incense before God when we are enabled, in the power of communion, to present in His presence the sweet odor of Christ in His person and work. This is our proper occupation as members of the chosen and separated tribe.

But it is particularly instructive to look at both the above mentioned consequences in connection; i.e., the Levites in ministry to their brethren, and the Levites in worship before God: it was as acceptable in the sight of God, and as divine an exercise of his functions, for a Levite to instruct his brethren as it was for him to burn incense before God. This is very important. We should never separate these two things. If we do not see that it is the same Spirit who must qualify us to speak *for* God as to speak *to* Him, there is a manifest want of moral order in our souls. If we could keep this principle clearly before our minds, it would be a most effectual means of maintaining amongst us the true dignity and solemnity of ministry in the Word: having lost sight of it has been productive of very sad consequences.

If we imagine for a moment that we can teach Jacob by any other power or ability than that by which we put incense before God, or if we imagine that one is not as acceptable before God as the other, we are not soundly instructed upon one of the most important points of truth; for, as some one has observed, "Let us look at this point illustrated in the personal ministry of Christ, and we shall no longer say that teaching by the Holy Ghost is inferior to praise by the same, for surely the apostleship of Christ when He came *from God* was as sweet in its savor to God as His priesthood when *He went to God* to minister to Him in that office. The candlestick in the holy place which diffused the light of life—God's blessed name—was as valuable, at least in His view, as the altar in the same place, which presented the perfume of praise."

We now come to speak of the third point, namely, "Bless, Lord, his substance." This is just what we might have expected; an *increase* of blessing will ever be the result of real true-hearted devotedness to Christ. "Every branch in Me that beareth fruit He purgeth, that it may bring forth more fruit;" "The diligent soul shall be made fat;" and "To him that hath shall *more* be given." Levi had exhibited much diligence of soul in the Lord's service—he had shown himself in readiness to vindicate His name in strong and decided opposition to every mere human thought and affection; and now the Lord will show Levi that He is not unrighteous to forget his work and labor of love, "for He will bless his substance."

We find the Apostle Paul bringing forward the same principle to his son Timothy when he tells him to "meditate on these things; *give thyself wholly* to them, that *thy profiting may appear to all.*" Here he connects the "profiting" with the "giving himself wholly": this will ever be the case; and if we would experience more than we do the meaning and power of the words, "Bless, Lord, his substance," we must first endeavor to enter into the meaning of what goes before, namely, "who said to his father and to his mother, I have not known him," etc. "Every one that hath forsaken houses, or brethren, or sisters, or father, or mother, or wife, or children, or lands, for My name's sake, shall receive an hundredfold, and shall inherit everlasting life" (Matt. 19:29).

Not less striking is the connection between what has just been stated and our fourth point, namely, "Accept the work of his hands." This I conceive to be a point of the greatest importance to us, and one which involves a question upon which we frequently display much want of intelligence. We often find it difficult to reconcile the idea of salvation through free grace with that of an increase of blessing and power for walking in obedience; and yet we find the two things constantly maintained in Scripture; thus we read, "He that hath My commandments, and keepeth them, he it is that loveth Me; and he that loveth Me shall be loved of My Father, and I will love him, and *will manifest Myself* to him." And, again, "If a man love Me, he will keep My words; and My Father will love him, *and We will come unto him and make Our abode with him*" (John 14: 21, 23).

This is very clear and decided upon the subject: we see here that the manifestation of the Son is made to depend on our keeping the commandments of Christ. Grace takes up a sinner and leads him into the knowledge of the full forgiveness of his sins through faith in the blood of the Lord Jesus Christ: but all this is simply a means to an end: it is, in a word, to set him down in a position of responsibility to Christ, which position he by nature could never have sustained, because "the carnal mind is enmity against God; it is not subject to the law of God, neither indeed can be." If, then, a man be put into a place of responsibility, it is clear that the more faithfully and diligently he maintains that place, the more enlarged will be his communion.

A father may have two children, the one obedient, the other the very reverse; now, they are both his children; neither the obedience of the one nor the disobedience of the other can interfere in the least with the relationship existing between them; but can we have a question as to which of them would enjoy most of the father's presence and affection? Surely not; a father likes to be obeyed, and will love the obedient child. There may be extraordinary cases where, from a warped judgment or a blind and unmeaning partiality, the disobedient, lawless son may have more of the heart of the parent than the other; but this is not so with God: His judgment is clear and unerring: He can accurately distinguish between the one that honors Him and the one that despises Him: the former "He will honor," the latter He will "lightly esteem."

The Lord does not ask a sinner *dead* in trespasses and sins to serve Him, for all such a one could do would be polluted with sin—his very prayers are polluted—his meditations are polluted—his acts of benevolence are polluted; in a word, he is all polluted, from the crown of his head to the sole of his foot, and therefore can do nothing acceptable in the sight of God. But the Lord quickens those that are dead in trespasses and sins, and then teaches them to "walk worthy of Him as dear children," and to be fruitful in every good word and work, to the praise of His name: and when we do this He graciously condescends to "accept the work of our hands."

But not only does Scripture abound with precepts which confirm what has been above stated, it also affords numerous examples and illustrations of the same; thus, for instance, the case of Abraham and Lot, in the opening of the book of Genesis. These were both servants of God, but yet how differently they walked! one loved God; the other loved the well-watered plains of Sodom: and the consequence was, that while the Lord Himself could meet with Abraham, and sup

with him, and, moreover, unfold to him His counsels with reference to Sodom, He merely sends *angels* to Sodom, and we can plainly perceive in their manner toward Lot their marked disapproval of his circumstances, for when he invites them into his house, they reply, "*Nay, but we will abide in the street all night.*"

This is plain: the angels of the Lord would rather abide all night in the streets of guilty Sodom than go in to a child of His who was not walking in obedience; nor does the fact that they afterwards consented to go in at all interfere with the point which I am seeking to establish; no, their answer speaks volumes of the most solemn and practical instruction to us; they enter into *Lot's house*, it is true; but if they do, it is only to counteract the sad effects of *Lot's sin.* May we, then, seek, by prayer and communion with God, to keep ourselves in the path of obedience, so that we may prove in our soul's happy experience the meaning of the prayer in our text, "Accept the work of his hands."

We have now arrived at the fifth and last point in this branch of our subject, namely, "Smite through the loins of them that rise against him, and of them that hate him, that they rise not again." This is properly the last point, when there shall be neither "adversary nor evil occurrent," we shall rest from our labor and conflict, and enter into possession of that upon which hope now feeds; therefore, when it can be said of our enemies "that they rise not again," we shall be happy indeed.

However, there is much of practical value in this point in the connection in which it stands here, i.e., as *a consequence* of obedience; there is nothing that gives the soul such marvelous power over enemies as an obedient, holy walk. Every step we take in real obedience to Christ is, so far, a victory gained over the flesh, and the devil; and every fresh victory ministers fresh power for the conflict which follows; thus we grow. And on the other hand, every battle *lost* only serves to weaken us, while it gives power to our enemies to attack us again.

Thus we see that the man whose heart is truly devoted to the Lord will have power to teach—power to worship; he will increase in substance, for Christ causes those that love Him "to inherit *substance*" (Prov. 8). He will enjoy more of God's favor and of the light of His countenance, for "them that honor Me I will honor"; and, finally, he will have enlarged power over all enemies. All these are the fruits of that true Levite devotedness which will enable a man to say "to his father, and to his mother, I have not seen him"; or, in other words, those fruits can only be enjoyed by one who is ready to "leave all and follow Christ."

This being the case, then, we can have little difficulty in accounting for the poverty in gifts of ministry—the poverty in worship—the meagreness of growth—the many interruptions in the enjoyment of divine favor—the almost total lack of power over enemies of which we have all to complain. Many seek to satisfy themselves by saying that we cannot expect the same power in gifts and worship now as that which fell to the lot of the saints in the apostolic day, and this, of course, we are not going to deny; but then, the question is, Have we as much power and freshness in these things as we might have? I believe we have not—and why? Is not Levi's God our God? Yes, He is, blessed be His name, and the same everlasting and abundant fountain of blessing as ever He was, but we, alas, are *far behind* in the matter of Levi's true devotedness; and this is the root of it all, for it remains unalterably true that "to him that hath shall *more* be given," and "we cannot serve two masters." This is true—solemn—and practical.

We are now called to consider a Scripture which will unfold to us at once the wondrous secret of how a sinner so degraded as Levi could hold a place of such elevation and nearness to God as that which he afterwards occupied. There is nothing in a sinner by nature with which God could hold any intercourse; therefore, if ever He brings any one into a place of blessing and high communion, He does so in *pure grace*, and thus *excludes* "boasting" altogether, for "no flesh shall glory in His presence." Those who look upon it as presumption in a sinner to speak of holding a place of such nearness to

God, seem to lose sight of this completely.

It could never be *pride* that would lead any one into a place where *he* would be broken to pieces, and be shown that he was altogether corrupt and worthless; if God were to elevate *flesh*, and bring flesh into a place of nearness to Himself, then indeed there would be some force in the objection on the ground of presumption; but God does no such thing: the flesh is so far gone in ruin that it cannot be improved, and therefore God declares in the Cross His mind about the flesh, namely, that it is a condemned thing; but He, by the same Cross, gives the poor sinner *life*, and in the power of *that life*, and not in the power of life in the flesh, He brings the sinner into His presence and sets him down at His table; so that it is not the presumption of a poor prodigal that assigns the place which he is to occupy, but the *grace* and boundless lovingkindness of the father: thus, God says to Noah, "The end of all flesh is come before Me," and what then? "Make thee an ark of gopher wood"—and in that ark is Noah raised up beyond the region of judgment, and a judged world, into a place of undisturbed communion.

Now, we shall find the very same principles developed in God's dealings with Levi, in the Scripture which is about to engage our attention. I shall first consider their cleansing; and secondly, their position and service. First, their cleansing as recorded in Numbers 8:5-14: "And the Lord spake unto Moses, saying, Take the Levites from among the children of Israel, and cleanse them. And thus shalt thou do unto them, to cleanse them: Sprinkle water of purifying upon them, and let them shave all their flesh, and let them wash their clothes, and so make themselves clean. Then let them take a young bullock with his meat offering, even fine flour mingled with oil; and another young bullock shalt thou take for a sin offering. And thou shalt bring the Levites before the tabernacle of the congregation: and thou shalt gather the whole assembly of the children of Israel together: and thou shalt bring the Levites before the Lord: and the children of Israel shall put their hands upon the Levites: and Aaron shall offer the Levites before the Lord for an offering of the children of Israel, that they may execute the service of the Lord. And the Levites shall lay their hands upon the heads of the bullocks: and thou shalt offer the one for a sin offering, and the other for a burnt offering, unto the Lord, to make an atonement for the Levites. And thou shalt set the Levites before Aaron, and before his sons, and offer them for an offering unto the Lord. Thus shalt thou separate the Levites from among the children of Israel: and the Levites shall be Mine."

This passage furnishes us with a very rich and blessed branch of our interesting subject. We were enabled to see, in looking at Levi by nature, that such was his character that God would have no fellowship with him whatever, and that, so far as Levi was concerned, he should abide forever in *his own habitation*, in company with the "instruments of cruelty" which were therein. But God will not leave him there, and therefore God must Himself provide the remedy—God Himself must cleanse this self-willed, cruel and fierce man.

And here we are invited to recall a thought which occurred to the mind in the opening of this paper, viz., that man's sin must ever be brought into the presence of God's grace. Levi had nothing else to look to; his sin was such as to preclude every thought of human remedy; the law condemned Levi's nature; and God had pronounced him unfit for His presence. And what, then, had Levi to do? Could he set himself with heart and soul to keep the law? Impossible: the law had not only condemned his works, but pronounced the curse of God upon his very nature. The law said, "Thou shalt do no murder;" and having said this, it added, "*Cursed* is every one that continueth not in all things that are written in the book of the law, to do them." But Levi had murder in his nature, therefore Levi's nature was cursed.

What, then, could Levi do? Might he not cast himself over upon the mercy of God, with the hope that He would deal lightly with his sins? No; by no means: God had given forth His solemn and unalterable decree, "O my soul, come not thou into their secret";

God could not come into a habitation wherein were "instruments of cruelty."

Thus, then, Levi was completely shut up, without a single means of escape; the law nailed him down to this one point, "Answer my demands." And all that Levi had towards the discharge of these demands was, "anger, fierceness, murder, self-will, cruelty," etc.: poor resources, alas! Nor would the law of God enter into any composition with the sinner; it should have "the uttermost farthing," or else the word was, "*cursed art thou.*" Therefore Levi, *as a man alive in the flesh*, or, in other words, Levi, as seeking to get life through the law, was judged, condemned, and set aside, and it only remained for him to take thus the place of *one dead*, in order that God might *in grace* quicken him into new life, which God was ready and willing to do, and which, as we shall see, He graciously did, according to His own marvelous thoughts, and in His own way.*

Levi, then, had just to see himself as one that was, in God's account, *dead*, as we read, "for they [i.e., the Levites] are wholly given unto Me from among the children of Israel; *instead* of such as open every womb, even *instead* of the first-born of all the children of Israel, have I taken them unto Me: for all the first-born of the children of Israel are Mine, both man and beast: on the day that I smote every first-born in the land of Egypt, *I sanctified them for Myself; and I have taken the Levites for all the first-born of the children of Israel*" (chap. 8:16-18).

The Lord passed through the land of Egypt with the sword of justice unsheathed, to smite *all* the first-born, nor would Israel's first-born have escaped, had not the sword fallen upon the neck of the spotless victim and thus, as some one has beautifully observed, "There was death in every house, not only in the houses of the Egyptians, but also in those of the Israelites: in the former, it was the *death of Egypt's first-born*; in the latter, the death of God's Lamb."

The Levites, then, were taken *instead* of those upon whom the sword of the destroying

* The reader will, of course, bear in mind that what is stated about Levi in this paper is to be regarded as *typical* of that which the believer now knows in *reality* through the Holy Ghost.

angel should have fallen; or, in other words, *the Levites were, typically, a dead and risen people*, and thus were no longer looked at in the circumstances of nature, but of *new life* through grace, in which they were placed by God Himself. And here let me observe that this is the path which every sinner must travel if he would know experimentally anything of Levi's after history.

There is no other way in which to escape from the judgment of the law on the one hand, or from the horrid workings of indwelling corruption on the other, than simply to see ourselves "*dead*" to both, and "*alive* unto God through Jesus Christ." "How shall we," says the apostle, "that are *dead to sin* live any longer therein? Know ye not that so many of us as were baptized into Jesus Christ were baptized into His death? Therefore we are buried with Him by baptism into death; that, like as Christ was raised up from the dead by the glory of the Father, even so we also should walk in newness of life" (Rom. 6:2-4). And, again, "Wherefore, my brethren, ye also are become *dead* to the *law* by the body of Christ, that ye should be *married to another*, even to Him who is raised from the dead, that we should bring forth fruit unto God" (chap. 7:4).

But not only are death and resurrection the only possible means by which a sinner can escape the condemnation of the law and the tyrannical sway of sin, they are also the only means by which he can acceptably serve God. The flesh, or carnal mind, cannot serve God, for it is not subject to His law, neither indeed can be; therefore we infer that the sources of that life by which we can serve God are not to be found in the flesh, but only in union with the Lord Jesus in resurrection. "If a man abide not *in Me*, he is cast forth as a branch and is withered" (John 15:6).

Consequently, when God would bring Levi into a place of nearness and service to Himself, He shows him to us as passing through those circumstances which, in the clearest manner, illustrate *death and resurrection;* for they are taken instead of those that were as dead, but who escaped

through the death of the lamb: and then, having thus passed through the circumstances of death, they are told in chap. 8 to "*put off the old man and put on the new*"—for that is the meaning of the "washing of water," and "shaving of the flesh," etc.

This is in full keeping with what the apostle states to his son Titus: "For we ourselves also were sometime foolish, disobedient, deceived, serving divers lusts and pleasures, *living in malice and envy*, hateful, and hating one another. But after that the kindness and love of God our Saviour toward man appeared, not by works of righteousness which we have done, but according to His mercy He saved us, by the *washing of regeneration*, and renewing of the Holy Ghost, which He shed on us abundantly through Jesus Christ our Saviour" (Titus 3:3-6).

But in order that we may have a clearer and more comprehensive view of the ground upon which the Levites stood before God, I would refer, in as brief and concise a manner as I can, to the offerings connected with their consecration: these were the burnt offering, the meat offering, and the sin offering; all, as we shall see, showing out the Lord Jesus Christ in His varied aspects.* And first, the burnt offering: the principles unfolded in this offering are brought out in the first chapter of Leviticus, where we read, "If his offering be a burnt sacrifice of the herd, let him offer a male without blemish: he shall offer it of his own voluntary will at the door of the tabernacle of the congregation before the Lord" (ver. 3).

Here, then, is something real for the soul to feed on and rejoice in. We have in the burnt offering the Lord Jesus Christ, in all His fulness and perfections, as offering Himself "*without spot to God,*" and also as accepted before God *for us*. In this He was found to be "*a male without blemish*"; so much so, that the One in whose sight the very heavens are not clean, could say, "In whom I am well pleased": and again, "Mine elect, in whom My soul delighteth."

But further, this unblemished offering

---

* It may be well just to observe here that in considering the offerings above referred to I have merely looked at them with reference to the question of Levi's history.

presents Himself voluntarily at the door of the tabernacle. "No man," says the Lord Jesus, speaking of His life, "taketh it from Me, but I lay it down of Myself: I have power to lay it down, and I have power to take it again: this commandment have I received of My Father." And truly, in tracing the way of the blessed Jesus through this defiled world, we can recognize this feature of the burnt offering in a very striking manner. From first to last His course was marked with all the steadiness and divine uninterrupted calmness of true devotedness to God.

The billows of dark and fierce temptation might roll and toss themselves with a range and fury which would have crushed one less than God. The devil might stir up all his deadly malice against Him; man might display all his enmity—enmity which could only be outdone by the eternal friendship of this devoted One. His disciples, moreover, may refuse to "watch with Him one hour." Death may arm himself with all his ghastly terrors, and pour out a cup mixed with hell's bitterest ingredients; and further, display his deadly sting in all its infernal keenness and power to wound. The grave may conjure up all its unutterable horrors to make one grand struggle for "*victory,*" but *all* in vain. The answer of this unblemished voluntary offering to all these was, "My meat and My drink is to do the will of Him that sent Me, and to finish His work."

He had His eye upon one object, and that was "the joy that was set before Him." He looked forward to the moment when He would be able to draw forth from the inexhaustible treasuries of eternal love the rich and princely fruits of His hard-bought victory, and pour them forth in divine profusion upon the "travail of His soul"; even the Church, which He loved, and purchased with His own precious blood. He eagerly anticipated "the morning without clouds," when, surrounded by the myriads of His ransomed brethren, He will sound forth in everlasting strains the mighty answer to all the foul aspersions of the enemy as to the love of God toward the sinner. All these attractions, I say, He had before Him, and therefore He marched onward in the

greatness of His strength; "He *steadfastly* set His face to go to Jerusalem." Lord Jesus Christ, invigorate our poor cold hearts to sound forth the eternal honors of Thine adorable name; and may our lives be more and more the decided evidence of our hearts—love to Thee, for "Thou alone art worthy!"

All this is surely most blessed for us; but, blessed as it is, it is not all; there are other strokes from the pencil of the Divine Artist, calculated, in the highest degree, to captivate our spiritual tastes, yea, more, to feed our souls. "He shall put his hand upon the head of the burnt offering; and *it shall be accepted for him,* to make atonement for him" (ver. 4). Here, then, is grace! Levi, the self-willed, cruel, fierce, and blood-shedding Levi, is accepted in all the perfectness and acceptableness of this "unblemished male" before God: whatever of excellency, whatever of value, whatever of purity, God beheld in this offering, that did He likewise behold in Levi as "accepted *in* the offering."

Thus, look at Levi *apart from* the offering, and you will find him such that God could not come into *his* assembly: but look at him as *in the offering,* and you find him, through grace, as pure and as perfect as the offering itself. Nothing could surpass this most excellent grace. The grace that could take up a sinner from such a pit of corruption as that in which Levi lay groveling, and lead him into such high elevation, deserves the highest note of praise; and, blessed be God, it shall, ere long, have it from all who, like Levi, have felt its sacred power.

However, we must not enter too minutely into the detail of this burnt offering, and there are just two points further to which I will refer. The first is presented to us in ver. 6: "And he shall flay the burnt offering, and cut it into his pieces." Here we see at once to what a process of strict, jealous and uncompromising scrutiny the Lord Jesus exposed Himself in offering Himself before God. It was not enough that the animal should be *apparently* "without blemish," for the skin, or *outward surface,* might look very well, and at the same time the offering be not at all fit for God's altar; therefore the *outward surface* must be removed, in order that this offering may be examined in all its sinews, joints and veins, and thus be found, as to *the springs of action, the structure of his frame,* and the source and channels of the life that animated him, a perfectly unblemished offering.

But further, "*he shall cut it into his pieces,*" i.e., take the offering asunder, and examine its various parts, in order that it may not only form a perfect whole, but that each distinct joint may be found perfect. Thus, in whatever aspect we look at the Lord Jesus, we get divine perfection. He could say to God, "Thou hast tried Me, and shalt find nothing;" and God could answer, "I am well pleased." He could say of the devil, "The prince of this world cometh, and hath nothing *in Me*;" and the devil could reply, "I know Thee, who thou art, the *Holy One of God.*" He could say to men, "Which of you convinceth Me of sin?" and man could answer, "Truly this was a *righteous man.*"

Thus, I say, our divine burnt-offering, who voluntarily presented Himself at God's altar, and there poured forth His most precious blood, was found, in every feature and in every aspect, pure and perfect in the very highest sense of the word, and confessed so by heaven, earth, and hell.*

All, therefore, having been found pure, and fit for God's altar, it becomes the happy place of *Aaron's sons* to send up before God the sweet savor of this most acceptable offering, as we read: "And the *sons of Aaron* the priest shall put fire upon the altar, and lay the wood in order upon the altar, and lay the wood in order upon the fire. And *the priests*, Aaron's *sons*, shall lay the parts, the head and the fat, in order upon the wood that is on the fire which is upon the altar. But *his inwards and his legs* shall he wash in water: and the priest shall burn *all* on the altar, to be a burnt sacrifice, an offering made by fire, of a sweet savor unto the Lord" (vers. 7-9).

The fat of the offering was God's peculiar part; no one could with impunity touch that;

yea, the punishment for so doing was the same as for eating blood; i.e., it was as wrong and as daringly presumptuous for a man to intrude upon God's portion of the offering as it was for him to assume life in his own right, which latter was an open denial of the state of death and ruin in which he was by reason of sin. God, then, I say, claimed the fat. He alone could feed upon the inward excellency and peerless perfections of Jesus, just as in the case of the unmeasured ointment in Exodus 30, where we see, as well as in the above cited passage, that the infinite mind of God could alone appreciate the infinite value of Christ. But we find *the head* burnt in connection with the fat, showing us, I suppose, that both the hidden energies of the Lord Jesus and the seat of His understanding were equally suited to be a sweet savor unto God.

Lastly, the inwards and legs were washed and burned upon the altar, showing us that the secret thoughts, purposes and counsels of the Lord Jesus, as well as the outward development of these in His *walk,* were perfectly pure and fit for the altar: and, in connection with this last point, one cannot help dwelling with comfort upon the marvelous contrast between the Lord Jesus and His poor people.

How often may our *outward walk,* typified by "the legs," appear quite right in the eye of man, when, at the same time, perhaps, in the eye of God, our "*inwards*" may be full of gross impurity. But it is well for us that such was not the case with our great Head: in Him *all was alike,* for *all was pure.* May our hearts enter more and more fully, under the teaching of the Spirit, into the intrinsic excellency of the Lord Jesus; and may we be enabled daily, standing at the altar before God, to send up in His presence the savor of all this!

As to the meat offering, we need not enter minutely into it. It was composed, as we know, of that which sprang from *the earth,* and such as aptly shadowed out "the Man

* We may also observe, in the act of cutting the offering into his pieces, this important truth, that in whatever relationship of life we contemplate the Lord Jesus, we find the same unsullied perfection; whether we consider Him as a public or as a private character, in one position or another, all is alike. Now so with man—here there must be failure in one way or another. If a man is a good public character, he may be the very plague of the family circle, and *vice versa*. And, surely, in all this we learn the glorious truth which shall shortly be owned by all created intelligences, that "He *alone* is worthy."

Christ Jesus," the frankincense thereon marking the entire devotedness of all the actings of Christ's human nature to God His Father. Nothing was done by Him to meet man's eye, or man's approbation; nothing was done to produce mere effect; no, *all was directly before God*. Whether we trace the footsteps of the Lord Jesus, while, for thirty years, *He was subject* to His parents at home; or while, for three years, He was engaged in public ministry amongst the Jews—all was alike: all showed forth the pure frankincense that marked Him, in all things, as God's peculiar and devoted servant. We may observe further that this meat offering was *baked* with oil, and *anointed* with oil; thus showing forth, I suppose, the incarnate Son of God, who was first "*conceived* of the Holy Ghost" (Matt. 1:20), and then "*anointed* with the Holy Ghost" (Matt. 3:16; Acts 10:38).

We now come to speak of the sin offering, and may the Lord graciously refresh our spirits while dwelling for a little on the blessed principles unfolded therein. The sin offering is brought before us in Leviticus 4, from whence we may select one case for our present purpose. "If the priest that is anointed do sin according to the sin of the people, then *let him* bring for his sin which he hath sinned a young bullock without blemish unto the Lord for a sin offering. *And he shall bring* the bullock unto the door of the tabernacle of the congregation before the Lord, and shall lay his hand upon the bullock's head and kill the bullock before the Lord" (vers. 3-4).

The reader will, no doubt, observe a marked difference between the above passage and that in which the burnt offering was referred to; and the difference so far mainly consists in this, that in the last cited passage the words "*voluntary will*" are not found, and this was quite to be looked for. In the burnt offering we were enabled to recognize the Lord Jesus Christ *offering* Himself voluntarily before God, in which aspect of His blessed work He could say, "No man taketh it [My life] from Me, *I lay it down of Myself*." In other words, He offered Himself "of His own voluntary will at the door of the tabernacle of the congregation before the Lord."

But in the sin offering it is quite different: "*He shall be brought*" and "*He shall be killed*"; i.e., instead of *coming*, He shall be *brought*; and instead of laying down His life of *Himself*, His life *shall be taken from Him*. These, I say, are important distinctions, and such as arise from the very nature of the two offerings. In the burnt offering the Lord Jesus is seen offering Himself in all the unblemished perfectness which belonged to Him; and in this His soul had great delight, because He was presenting that before God which was so acceptable to Him. But in the sin offering the Lord Jesus is seen standing in connection with that which His pure and spotless soul must have deeply abhorred and keenly resented—abhorred and resented, indeed, in a way of which we cannot form the faintest idea. He is seen, in a word, as standing in connection with *sin*: yea, more, as "made sin" (2 Cor. 5:21).

Thus it was that the prophet, through the Spirit, viewed Him when he said, "He was wounded for our transgressions, He was bruised for our iniquities; the chastisement of our peace was upon Him; and with *His stripes* we are healed. All we like sheep have gone astray; we have turned every one to his own way; and the Lord hath laid on Him the iniquity of us all" (Isa. 53: 5-6).

Now I believe that by looking at the two offerings in connection we get a very deep and wondrous view of sin's dark and dreadful enormity in the sight of God: for sin in this point of view appears sinful just according to the measure of Christ's perfectness in God's account. If in the burnt offering we were enabled to see that such was the beauty and excellency of Christ that His *whole man* could go up before God as a sweet savor, and that God could "find nothing in Him" but perfection, as a necessary consequence then we must see in the sin offering the blackness and heinousness of sin, which could oblige God to hide His face from "His elect, in whom His soul delighted."

This brings us to the next point connected with the sin offering, viz., "He shall lay his hand upon the bullock's head" (ver. 4). Here we have at once the secret of the deep and profound mystery of the three hours' darkness.

It was before observed that God had to hide His face from the Lord Jesus on the cross, but how are we to account for such a mysterious circumstance? Simply by the words, "he (the sinner) shall lay his hand upon the bullock's head." If, in contemplating the burnt offering, we were struck by the fact that all the perfectness of the offering was communicated to the "fierce and cruel" Levi, so here we are called upon to adore the grace that devised the wondrous plan whereby that could be effected, which was by imputing to the offering all the sin and defilement of Levi, and dealing with the sin of Levi in the person of the sin offering, in order that Levi himself might be dealt with in the person of the burnt offering.

And all this, be it observed, is conveyed to us in the action of "the laying on of hands." This action was performed in both cases; i.e., Levi laid his hands on the head of the burnt-offering, and Levi laid his hands on the head of the sin offering. As to the *act*, it was the same in each case; but oh, how different the results! they were, in a word, as different as life and death, Heaven and hell, sin and holiness. In fact, we cannot conceive a wider contrast than that which is observable in the results of this action, to all appearance the same in each case.

We may, perhaps, be able to form some idea of it by considering that the act of imposition of hands was at once the imputation of *sin* to one "*who knew no sin,*" but was "holy, harmless, undefiled," and whose very nature abhorred *all sin.* And, on the other hand, it was the imputation of *perfect righteousness* to one who was by nature "a cruel, fierce, and self-willed murderer."* Furthermore, the act of

imposition of hands obliged the One who from before all worlds dwelt in the bosom of the Father to travel far away into the cold and barren regions of death and darkness, where the genial and life-giving rays of His Father's countenance, which He alone could truly appreciate, had never penetrated; and standing upon the confines of which, He cried out, "*If it be possible,* let this cup pass from Me!" and again, when these gloomy regions, with their ten thousand unutterable horrors, burst upon His spotless soul, "My God, My God, *why hast Thou* forsaken Me?"

And, on the other hand, it enabled the one who dwelt in "the habitations of cruelty," into whose "assembly" God could not come, to stand in the very blaze of the light of God's throne. These considerations, I say, may perhaps assist our conceptions in some measure upon this astounding truth. Now, the apostle states the same truth in the didactic language of the New Testament when he says, "He [God] hath *made Him* to be *sin for us,* that *we* might be *made the righteousness* of God *in Him*" (2 Cor. 5:21). That is, He hath made the One whose perfectness is seen in the burnt offering to be judged *as sin,* and treated as such in the sin offering, in order that *we,* who deserved the treatment of the sin offering, might be treated as accepted in the burnt offering.

I would also observe here that there is much force and value in the word "*made*": it shows out most fully that righteousness was just as foreign to the nature of man as sin was to the nature of Christ. Man had no righteousness of his own, or in other words, he knew no righteousness, and therefore he had to be "*made*" righteousness. Christ "*knew no sin,*" and therefore had to be "*made sin*" in order that we might be *made* righteousness, even "the righteousness of God *in Him.*" But further, we learn from the

---

* I would observe here that in speaking of "the imputation of righteousness," I by no means desire to be understood as giving any countenance to the prevailing theory of "the imputed righteousness of Christ." Of this expression, so much in use in the theology of the present day, it would be sufficient to say that it is nowhere to be found in the oracles of God. I read of "the righteousness of God" (Rom. 3 passim), and, moreover, of the imputation of righteousness (Rom. 4: 11), but never of "the righteousness of Christ." It is true, we read of the Lord Jesus being "*made of God* unto us righteousness" (Jer. 23: 6), but these passages do not support the above theory. I would further add that the moral effect of this idea will be found to be decidedly pernicious, because it of *necessity* supposes the believer as standing apart from the Lord Jesus, whereas the doctrine of Scripture is that the believer is "made the righteousness of God *in Him*" (2 Cor. 5:21). And again, "we are *in Him* that is true, even in *His Son Jesus Christ*" (1 John 5: 20).

passage to which we are referring that the Lord Jesus having been "made sin for us," is not more real, not more true, not more palpable, than that the believer is *"made righteousness* in Him."

If there be any truth or reality in the record concerning the cross and passion of the Lord Jesus, then, it is plain that the moment a soul acts in faith upon Christ in His death and resurrection, that moment he is accepted in all the acceptableness of Christ. His consciousness of this is, of course, quite another question: a truth and the realization of a truth are quite distinct.

The measure of our realization will be in proportion to the measure of our communion with God. If we are satisfied to move at a cold and heartless distance from God, our consciousness of the power and value of any truth will, as a consequence, be meagre and shallow: while, therefore, it is not to be forgotten that the root and source of all life and communion is the truth stated in the passage to which we are alluding, it is manifest that the more we walk in communion with Him who gives us the life, the more shall we enjoy both Himself and the life which He gives.

Let us pray that the cross and passion of the Lord Jesus may sink so deeply into our hearts that we may have on the one hand such a view of the loathsomeness of sin as shall lead us to abhor it with a holy abhorrence "all the days of our life," and on the other hand such a view of the amazing love of God as shall constrain us "to live not unto ourselves but unto Him who died for us and rose again."

Thus, then, we see that the laying on of hands shows forth nothing less than a *change of places* on the part of the sinner and the Saviour. The sinner was *out* of the favor of God: "O my soul, come not thou into their habitation." The Saviour was *in* the favor of God, *"daily His delight,"* dwelling in His bosom from before all worlds. But the amazing plan of redemption *shows us the Saviour out of the favor of God, and God forsaking Him, while at the same time a condemned malefactor is brought at once into the very presence of a loving and pardoning God.*

Amazing, deep, inconceivable, eternal love! unfathomable wisdom! love which soars far aloft above the most gigantic conception! wisdom which has written everlasting contempt upon all the power and base designs of the great enemy of God and man! For, ere Levi could be introduced into the enjoyment of the "covenant of *life* and *peace*" (Mal. 2:5), a spotless Victim must stand the shock of the king of terrors and all his thunders. But who is this Victim? We ask not, "Who is this King of glory?" but *Who* is this Victim? The answer to this question it is which gives to the plan of redemption its grandest and most divine characteristic. The Victim was none less than the Son of God Himself! Yes! here was love, here was wisdom. The Son of God had to stoop because man had exalted himself.

And surely we may say, If God had not entered upon the work, *all, all* were lost, and that forever. No mere mortal could have entered into that dark scene where sin was being atoned for; no one but the Son of God could have sustained the weight which, in the garden and on the cross, rested on the shoulders of the "One that was mighty."

And here we might refer to the Lord's language to His disciples when He was about to enter into conflict with the adversary: "Hereafter I will not talk much with you; for the prince of this world cometh, and hath nothing in Me" (John 14: 30). Why could He not "talk much with them"? Because He was just going to enter upon the work of atonement, in which they could do nothing, because the prince of this world, had he come, would have had *plenty in them;* but then, the moment He, as it were, in spirit passes through that sorrowful hour, He says, *"Arise,* let us go hence"; i.e., although we could not move a single step in the achievement of the victory, yet we could enjoy the fruits of it; and not only so, but *display* the fruits of it in a life of service and fruit-bearing to God, which forms the subject of teaching in the next chapter.

Here, then, is what gives peace to the awakened conscience of the sinner. God Himself has done the work. God has triumphed over all man's wickedness and rebellion, and now every soul who feels his need of pardon and peace can draw near in faith and holy confidence and reap the fruits of this wondrous triumph of grace and mercy.

And now, if *you* have not as yet made these wondrous fruits your own; if you have not as yet cast the whole burden of your sins on God's eternal love as seen in the cross, I ask you, Why do you stand aloof? Why do you doubt? Perhaps you feel the hardness of your heart, perhaps you are ready to say that you feel yourself even now unmoved by the contemplation of all the deep sorrow endured by the Son of God. Well, what of that? If it be a question of *your* guilt, you may go much farther than even this, for in that hour of which we have been speaking you stood unmoved, looked on with cold and heartless indifference, while all creation owned the wondrous fact.

Yea, more, you yourself crucified the incarnate God, you spat in His face, and plunged your spear into His side. Do you shrink back and say, "Oh, not so bad!" I say *it was the act of the human heart*; and if you have a human heart, it was your act. But the Scriptures at once decide this point, for it is written, "For of a truth against Thy holy child Jesus, whom Thou hast anointed, both Herod and Pontius Pilate, *with the Gentiles* and the people of Israel, were gathered together" (Acts 4:27). This passage, I say, proves that all the world were *representatively* around the cross. But why insist on this? Simply to show forth the riches of the grace of God, which can only be seen in all its effulgent lustre in the cross; and therein it is seen mounting far above all man's sin and malignant rebellion; for when man, in the fiendish pride of his heart, could plunge his spear into the side of incarnate Deity, God's cry was—*Blood!* and through *that blood* *"remission of sins, beginning at Jerusalem."* Thus, where *sin* abounded, *grace* did *much more abound*," and "grace *reigns* through righteousness by Jesus Christ our Lord."

Enough, I trust, has been said to show the grounds upon which the Levites stood before God. These grounds were free and *eternal grace*—grace exercised toward them through the blood, which is the only channel through which grace can flow. Man has been found to be *utterly ruined* before God, and therefore it must be a question either of salvation through *free grace*, or eternal damnation; for "by the deeds of the law there shall no flesh living be justified." But then, while man is by nature utterly unfit to render anything like an acceptable righteousness or service to God, yet, when God gives us *new life* through grace, He, of course, looks for the development of that life. In other words, grace brings the soul into circumstances of responsibility and service, and it is as we meet those circumstances that God is glorified in us and our souls grow in the knowledge of God. Thus it was in the case of the leper: up to a certain point in his history he had nothing to do, *the priest* was the sole actor. But when the priest had done his part; when, by virtue of *the blood* which had been shed, he had pronounced him "clean," the leper had *then* to begin to "*wash himself*" (Lev. 14:8). Now we shall find that the history of Levi develops all these principles most fully.

We have hitherto been engaged with Levi's condition and character by nature and also the wondrous remedy devised by grace to meet him in his lost estate, and not only to save him *from* that estate but also to raise him up to an elevation which could never have entered into the heart of man, even into the very tabernacle of God.

We shall now, with God's blessing and grace, proceed to examine that high elevation to which we have referred, and also the service which it involved, as put before us in Numbers 3: "And the Lord spake unto Moses, saying, *Bring the tribe of Levi near*, and present them before Aaron the priest, that they may minister unto him. And they shall keep his charge, and the charge of the whole congregation before the tabernacle of the congregation, to do the service of the tabernacle. And they shall keep *all the instruments of the tabernacle* of the congregation, and the charge of the children of Israel, to do the service of the tabernacle. And thou shalt give the Levites unto Aaron, and to his sons: they are wholly given unto him out of the children of Israel" (vers. 5-9).

Here, then, God's marvelous purposes of grace toward Levi fully open before us, and *truly* marvelous they are indeed. We see that the sacrifices were but a means to an end; but both the means and the end were in every way worthy of each other. The means were, in one word, "death and resurrection," and *all included therein*. The end was, *nearness* to God, and *all included therein*.

Looking at Levi by nature, there could not be any point farther removed from God than that at which he stood; but *grace* in exercise, through the blood, could *lift him up* out of that ruin in which he stood, and "bring him nigh," yea, bring him into association with the great head of the priestly family, there to serve in the tabernacle. Thus, we read, "You *hath He quickened who were dead* in trespasses and sins, wherein in time past ye walked according to the course of this world, according to the prince of the power of the air, the spirit that now worketh in the children of disobedience. . . . *But God*, who is *rich in mercy*, for His *great love* wherewith *He loved us*, even *when we were dead in sins*, hath quickened us *together with Christ* (by grace ye are saved), and hath raised us up together, and made us sit together in heavenly places in Christ Jesus" (Eph. 2:1-6). And again, "But *now, in Christ Jesus*, ye who sometime were *afar off*, are *made nigh* by the blood of Christ" (ver. 13).

When *nature* is left free to work, it will ever go as far away from *God* as it can. This is true since the day when man said, "I heard *Thy voice*, and I was *afraid* and I hid myself" (Gen. 3:10). But when *grace* is left free and sovereign to work, it will ever bring the soul "nigh." Thus it was with Levi. He was by nature *"black as the tents of Kedar"*; by grace, "comely as the curtains of Solomon": by *nature* he was *"joined"* in a convenant of murder; by *grace* "joined" in a convenant of "life and peace." The former, because he was *"fierce and cruel"*; the latter, because he feared and was afraid of the Lord's name. (Comp. Gen. 49:6-7; Mal. 2:5).

Furthermore, Levi was by *nature* conversant with the "instruments of cruelty"; by *grace*, with "*the instruments of God's tabernacle"*: by *nature* God could not come into *Levi's assembly*; by *grace*, Levi is brought into *God's assembly*: by nature "his feet were swift *to shed blood"*: by grace, *swift* to follow the movements of the cloud through the desert, in real, patient service to God. In a word, Levi had become a *"new creature*," and "old things had passed away," and therefore he was no longer to "live unto himself," but unto Him who had done such marvelous things for him in grace.

I would further observe, on the last cited passage, that the Levites are, in the first place, declared to be God's property, and then they are *"Wholly given unto Aaron."* Thus we read: *"Thine they were, and Thou gavest them Me, and they have kept Thy word"* (John 17:6). And again, "All that *the Father giveth Me* shall come to Me" (John 6:37).

I would now look a little into the detail of their service, in which, I doubt not, we shall find much to edify and refresh us.

We find that although the whole tribe of Levi were, *as to standing, "joined with Aaron*," yet, as to *service*, they were divided into classes. "All had not the same office;" and this is what we might have expected, for, although in the matter *of life* and *standing* they were all *on a level*, yet, in the development of that life, and in the manifestation of the power of that standing, they would, no doubt, display different measures; and not only so, but there would also be seen an assignment to each of distinct position and line of service, which would serve to distinguish him from his brethren in a very marked and decided manner.

And here I would observe that I know of nothing connected with the walk and service of the Christian which demands more attention than this point to which I am now alluding, viz., *unity* in the matter of life and standing, and at the same time the greatest variety in the manifestation of character and in the line of service. A due attention to this important point would save us from much of that "unwise" comparing of ourselves and our service with the persons and services of others, which is most unholy, and, as a consequence, most unhealthy.*

And not only would it lead thus to beneficial results in a negative point of view, it would also have a most happy effect in producing and cultivating originality and uniqueness of Christian character. But while there was this diversity in the line of service amongst the Levites, it is also to be remembered that there was *manifested unity*. The Levites were *one people*, and seen as such; they were "*joined*" with Aaron in the work of the tabernacle; moreover, *they had one standard*, round which they *all* rallied, and that was "the tabernacle of the congregation," the well known type of Christ in His character and offices. And, indeed, this was one of the ends which God had in view in calling out the Levites by His grace from amongst the people of Israel; it was that they should stand in marked association with Aaron and his sons, and in that association bear the tabernacle and all pertaining thereto on their shoulders, through the barren wilderness around.**

God did not call out the Levites *merely* that they might escape the sad effects of God's absence from their assembly; or, in other words, God had more than *their* blessing and security in view in His dealings with them. He designed that they should serve in the tabernacle, and thus be to His praise and glory. We shall, however, I trust, see this principle upon which I am dwelling in a clearer and stronger point of view as we proceed in our subject.

We find that Levi had three sons, viz., "Gershon, and Kohath, and Merari" (Num. 3: 17). These formed the heads of the three classes alluded to, and we shall find that the nature of the service of each was such as of necessity to impart that tone of character signified by their very name. Thus: "Of Gershon was the family of the Libnites and the family of the Shimites: these are the families of the Gershonites. And the chief of the house of the father of the Gershonites shall be Eliasaph, the son of Lael. And the charge of the sons of Gershon in the tabernacle of the congregation shall be the tabernacle and the tent, the covering thereof, and the hanging for the door of the tabernacle of the congregation, and the hangings of the court, and the curtain for the door of the court, which is by the tabernacle, and by the altar round about, and the cords of it for all the service thereof" (ver. 21-26).

Here was Gershon's work, to carry through the waste and howling wilderness the tabernacle and its coverings. This was indeed *true Levite service*, but it was most blessed service, and its antitype in the Church now is what we should much seek after, because it is that which alone puts the Christian into his right place in the world, i.e., the place of a *stranger*. There could be but little attractiveness in the rams' skins and badgers' skins; but, little as there was, it was, nevertheless, the high privilege of the Gershonite to take them all up and bear them cheerfully on his shoulders across the trackless sands. What, then, are we to understand by the covering of the tabernacle? I believe, in a word, it shadowed out the character of the Lord Jesus Christ. It was that which would meet the eye. There might be, and were, other services among the Levites of a very blessed nature, but surely it was most elevated service to carry through the desert that which so strikingly prefigured the character of Christ.

This is what makes the saint "a stranger" (as the name Gershon imports) in the world. If we are walking in *the manifestation of the character of the Lord Jesus*, and in so doing realize our place as *in the wilderness*, we may

---

* It is worthy the serious attention of the Christian reader who may desire the unity of the Church, that the tribe of Levi in the desert was a truly striking example of what may be termed "unity in diversity." Gershon was in one sense totally different from Merari, and Merari was totally different from Kohath; and yet Gershon, Merari and Kohath were *one*: they should not, therefore, contend about their service, because they were *one*; nor yet would it have been right to confound their services, because they were totally different. Thus, attention to *unity* would have saved them from contention, and attention to *diversity* would have saved them from confusion. In a word, all things could only be "done decently and in order" by a due attention to the fact of there being "unity in diversity."

* * I say "one of the ends," for we should ever remember that the grand object before the divine mind in redemption is to show in the ages to come His kindness towards us through Christ Jesus; and this object will be secured even though our poor puny services had never been heard of.

rest assured it will impart a very decided tone of strangership to our character in the world. And oh, would that we knew much more of this. The Church has laid down the rams' skins and badgers' skins, and with them the Gershonite character: in other words, the Church has ceased to walk in the footsteps of her rejected Lord and Master, and the consequence has been that instead of being the wearied and worn stranger, as she should be, treading the parched and sterile desert, with the burden on the shoulders, she has settled herself down in the green places of the world and made herself at home.

But there was another feature of the stranger character shadowed out in the curtain, viz., *anticipation*. This was most blessed—God dwelling in curtains showed plainly that neither God nor the ark of His strength had found a resting-place, but were *journeying on* towards "*a rest that remained*."

And how could there be *a rest* in the desert? There were no rivers and brooks *there*—no old corn *there*—no milk and honey *there*. True, the smitten rock sent forth its refreshing streams to meet their need, and Heaven sent down their *daily bread;* but all this was not Canaan. They were still in the desert, eating wilderness food and drinking wilderness water, and it was Gershon's holy privilege to carry upon his shoulders that which in the fullest manner expressed all this, viz., *the curtain*. "Thus saith the Lord, Shalt thou build Me an house for Me to dwell in? Whereas I have not *dwelt* in any house since the time that I brought up the children of Israel out of Egypt, even to this day, but have *walked* in a *tent* and in a *tabernacle*" (2 Sam. 7:5-6). Here, too, we have sadly failed. The Church grew weary of the curtain, and wished to build a house before the time; she grew weary of "*walking in a tent*," and earnestly desired to "*dwell in a house*."

And truly we have all to watch and pray against this disposition to grow weary of our Gershonite character. There is nothing so trying to nature as continual labor in a state of expectancy; our hearts love rest and fruition, and therefore nothing but the continual remembrance that "our sufficiency is of God" can at all sustain us in our Gershon or stranger condition.

Let us therefore remember that we bear on our shoulder the curtains, and have beneath our feet the sand of the desert, above our heads the pillar of cloud, and before us "the land of rest" clothed in never-withering green, and, both as a stimulus and a warning, let us remember that "He that endureth to the end *the same* shall be saved."*

We shall next consider the Merarite feature of character; for, although the family of Merari does not stand next in order in the chapter, yet there is a kindredness of spirit, as it were arising out of the very nature of their service, that would link them together in the mind. But, not only is there this intimate connection between the services of these two classes of Levites, which would lead us to link them together thus, the Lord Himself presents them to us in marked unity of service, for we read, "And the Kohathites set forward bearing the sanctuary; and *the other* (i.e., the Gershonites and the Merarites) *did set up the tabernacle against they came*" (Num. 10: 21).

Here, then, we see that it was the great business of these two families to pass onward through the desert in holy companionship, bearing with them, wherever they went, "*the tabernacle*," and, moreover, the tabernacle as looked at in its character of outward manifestation or testimony; which would, as a matter of course, put those who carried it thus into a place of *very laborious* discipleship. "And under the custody and charge of the sons of Merari shall be the boards of the tabernacle, and the bars thereof, and the pillars thereof, and the sockets thereof, and all the vessels thereof,

* It would surely be of all importance in this day, when so many are declining from the narrow path of obedience to the written Word, and entering upon the wide and bewildering field of human tradition, to bear in mind that the Levite, when carrying the tabernacle through the desert, found no support nor guide *from beneath*; no, *the grace* in which he stood was his *sole support*, and *the pillar above* his *sole guide*. It would have been miserable indeed had he been left to find a guide in the footmarks on the sand, which would change at every wind that blew. *But all the sand did for him was to add to his labor and toil while he endeavored to follow the heavenly guide above his head.*

and all that serveth thereto, and the pillars of the court round about, and their sockets, and their pins, and their cords" (chap. 3:36-37). Here, then, was what Merari had to do: he had to take his place here or there, according to the movement of the cloud, and *set up* the boards of the tabernacle in their sockets of silver—and all this, be it remembered, upon the sand of the desert.*

Could anything be more opposed to another than the nature of all that Merari had to set up was to the waste and howling wilderness around? What could be more unlike than silver and barren sand? But Merari might not shrink from all this; no, his language was, when he had arrived at a spot in the desert at which the cloud halted, "I am come to set up the patterns of things in heaven in the very midst of all the desolation and misery of the wilderness around." All this was most laborious, and would, no doubt, impart to the character of Merari a tone of sadness or sorrow which was at once expressed in his name, which means "*sorrow.*"

And surely the antitype of all this in the Church now will fully confirm what has been stated about the character of Merari. Let any one take his stand firmly and decidedly in the world *for Christ*—let him penetrate into those places where "the *world*" is really seen in its vigor—let him oppose himself, *firm as a rock*, to the deep and rapid tide of worldliness, and *there* let him begin to set up "*the sockets of silver*," and, rest assured of it, he will find such a course attended with very much sorrow and bitterness of soul; in a word, he will realize it to be a path in which the cross is to be taken up "*daily*," and not only taken up, but borne.

Now, if any further proof were needed of the above interpretation, we have a most striking one in the fact that there are but *very few* of the laborious Merarite character to be found; and why is this? Simply because the exhibition of such a character will ever be attended with very much labor and sorrow to nature, and nature loves ease, and therefore human nature never could be a Merarite; nothing will make us true Merarites but deep communion with Him who was "*the Man of sorrows.*"

There is something in the service of Gershon from which one does not shrink so much as from that of Merari. For what had Gershon to do? He had to place the curtains and badgers' skins over the boards *which had been already set up by his laborious and sorrowful brother*. And just so now: if a laborious servant of God has gone to a place where hitherto the world and Satan have reigned supreme, and there raised a testimony for Christ, it will be comparatively easy for another to go and walk on in the simple *manifestation* of Christian character, which would of itself put him into the place of "a stranger."

But, although nature may assume the character of a misanthropist, yet nothing but grace can make us Merarites, and *the true Merarite* is the *true philanthropist*, because he introduces that which alone *can bless*; and the very fact that a Merarite should have to take a place of sorrow is a most convincing proof that the world is an evil place. There was no need of a Merarite in Canaan, nor a Gershonite either: for the Merarite was *happy there*, and the Gershonite *at home*. But the world is not the Levite's home, and therefore if any will carry the curtains, he must be a stranger; and if any will carry the sockets and boards, he must be a man of sorrow; for when He who was a true Gershonite and a true Merarite came into the world He was emphatically *the Man of sorrows, who had not where to lay His head*.

However, if the Gershonite and the Merarite had to occupy a place in which they endured not a little of "the burden and heat of the day," yet the Lord graciously met them in that with a very rich reward, for "He is not unrighteous to forget your work and labor of

---

* It has been well observed that in the tabernacle God was seen bringing all His glory into immediate connection with *the sand of the desert*: and when the high priest went into the holy place, he found himself in the very presence of that glory, *with his feet upon the sand of the desert* likewise. In the temple, however, this was not the case, for the floor of the house was *overlaid with gold* (1 Kings 6:30).

So is it with the Christian now; he has not as yet his feet upon the "pure gold" of the heavenly city, but his deepest and most abiding knowledge of God is that which he obtains in connection with his sorrow, toil and conflict in the wilderness.

love," and therefore, if they had to labor and toil *amongst* their brethren, they were blessedly ministered to *by* their brethren.

Thus we read concerning the offerings of the princes: "And the Lord spake unto Moses, saying, Take it of them, that they may be to do the service of the tabernacle of the congregation; and thou shalt give them unto the Levites, to every man according to his service. And Moses took the wagons and the oxen and gave them unto the Levites. Two wagons and four oxen he gave unto the sons of Gershon, according to their service. And four wagons and eight oxen he gave unto the sons of Merari according unto their service, under the hand of Ithamar the son of Aaron the priest. *But unto the sons of Kohath he gave none*, because *the service of the sanctuary* belonging unto them was that they should bear upon their shoulders" (Num. 7: 4-9).

Here we see that the service of Gershon and Merari was that which met the rich and blessed ministrations of their brethren. Grace had filled the hearts and affections of the princes, and not only filled but overflowed them, and in its overflow it was designed to refresh the spirits of the homeless Gershonite and sorrowful Merarite: on the other hand, the Kohathites had no part in these ministrations; and why? Because *their service*, as we shall see presently, was in *itself* a rich reward indeed. We see the very same doctrine taught in the case of the Levites generally, as contrasted with the priests, in chap. 18, where we read: "And the Lord spake unto Aaron, Thou shalt have no inheritance in their land, neither *shalt thou have any part among them: I am thy part and thine inheritance among the children of Israel*" (ver. 20).

On the other hand, He says of the Levites, "Behold, I have given the children of Levi all the tenth in *Israel for an inheritance, for their service which they serve*, even the service of the tabernacle of the congregaton."

And again, "Ye shall eat it in every place, ye and your households, for *it is your reward* for your service in the tabernacle of the congregation" (ver. 21, 31).

Aaron occupied a position so truly elevated

that any inheritance in the way of earthly things would have been to him most degrading; whereas the Levites (looked at in one aspect) had not this high standing, but had much hard labor; and consequently, while Aaron's very place and service was "*his reward*," the Levites had to get *a tenth* for "*their reward*."

We come now to consider the third and last division of the Levites, viz., the Kohathites, of whom we read, "The families of the sons of Kohath shall pitch on the side of the tabernacle southward. And the chief of the house of the father of the families of the Kohathites shall be Elizaphan the son of Uzziel. And their charge shall be the ark, and the table, and the candlestick, and the altars, and the vessels of the sanctuary wherewith they minister, and the hanging, and all the service thereof" (chap. 3: 29-31). We can now have no difficulty in understanding why it was that Kohath had no share in the ministrations of the princes. Gershon and Merari might need wagons and oxen to carry the boards, etc., but not Kohath; his charge was too precious to be committed to any or aught but himself, and therefore it was his high and honored place to carry all upon his shoulders.

What a privilege, for example, to be allowed to carry *the ark, the table,* or *the golden candlestick!* And would it not have argued an entire absence of ability to appreciate his elevated calling if he had sought for the assistance of oxen in his holy service? What, then, we ask, would have been the effect produced upon the character of Kohath by this his service? Would it not have imparted a very elevated tone thereto? Surely it would.

What can be more elevated, at least as far as development of character in the world is concerned, than the display of that congregational spirit which is expressed in the name of Kohath? Should not Christians be found rebuking, by a *real* union *in everything*, man's oft-repeated attempt at forming associations for various purposes? And how can they effect that if it be not by gathering more closely around their common centre, Christ, in all the blessed fulness and variety of that Name? a fulness and variety typified by the varied furniture of the tabernacle, some of the most precious parts of which were designed to be borne on the shoulders of this favored division of the tribe of Levi.

And surely we may safely assert that what would lead the saints now into more of the congregational spirit is just communion with Him whom the ark and table shadowed forth. If we were more conversant with Christ as the ark, covering in this scene of death, and, moreover, with the table of showbread, whereon stood *the food of the priests*—if, I say, we knew more of Christ in these blessed aspects of His character—we should not be as we are, *a proverb* and a byword by reason of our gross disunion.

But, alas, as the Church grew weary of the curtains and the boards, and laid aside her Gershonite and Merarite character, so has she laid aside her Kohathite character, because she has ceased to carry the ark and the table upon her shoulder, and cast those precious pearls which were, through the grace of God, her peculiar property, to the swine, and thus has she lost her elevated character and position in the world.

Thus, let us review those three grand features of character shown forth in the tribe of Levi.

Strangership. "Therefore the world knoweth *us not*, because it knew Him not." "Here we have no abiding city." "Dearly beloved, I beseech you *as strangers and pilgrims*, abstain from fleshly lusts, which war against the soul."

Sorrow in the world. "*In the world* ye shall have tribulation." "If they have *persecuted Me*, they will also *persecute you*." "I *reckon* that *the sufferings of this present* time are not worthy to be compared with the glory which shall be revealed in us." "After that *ye have suffered awhile*, make you perfect"—"*ye have need* of patience"—"ye yourselves know that ye are appointed thereunto." "If we *suffer* with Him, we shall also reign with

Him." "These are they that came out of *great tribulation*, and have washed their robes and made them white in the blood of the Lamb."

Union. "That they *all may be one*." "He should gather together in *one* the children of God that are *scattered* abroad." "That He might reconcile *both* unto God in *one* body by the cross." And here, again, I would request of my reader to bear in mind that, while there was this beautiful diversity in the character and line of service of the Levites, yet they were *one people*, and that *manifestly*—they were *one* in *life*, *one* in standing, *one* in calling, *one* in inheritance; and so should it be with Christians *now*. We are not to expect uniformity of opinion on every point, nor yet are we to look for a perfect correspondence in the line of service and development of life; but then the saints should be seen as *one people—one* in worship,* *one* in labor, *one* in object, *one* in sympathy; in a word, *one* in everything that belongs to them in common as the people of God.

How sadly out of order it would have been for a Levite to call upon one of the uncircumcised of the nations around to assist him in carrying any part of the tabernacle! and yet we hear Christians now justifying and insisting upon the propriety of conduct not less disorderly, viz., calling upon the openly unconverted and profane to put their hands to the Lord's work. Thus we see that the Levites have become scattered, and have forsaken their posts. The Gershonite has refused to carry the curtains because he has become weary of the stranger condition; the Merarite has laid down the boards and sockets because he grew weary of bearing the cross, and the Kohathite has degraded his high and holy office by making it the common property of those who have not authority from God to put their hands thereunto.

Thus the name of God is blasphemed among the heathen by us, and we do not "sigh and cry for the abominations" thus practiced, but lift up our heads in proud indifference as if it all were right, and as if the camp of God

* I say, *one in worship*; and I would press this point, because at the present day it seems to be a thought in the minds of many that there may be unity in service and at the same time the greatest diversity in worship. I would appeal to the spiritual mind of the Christian reader, and I would ask him, Can this really be? What should we say to a family who would unite, or appear to do so, for the purpose of carrying on their father's work, but who could not, by reason of division, meet around their father's table? Could such unity satisfy a father who loved his children?

were moving onward in all heavenly order, under the guidance of the cloud, communicated by the silver trumpets. "My brethren, these things ought not so to be." May we walk more humbly before our God, and, while we mourn over the sad fact that "Overturn, overturn, overturn" has been written by the finger of God upon all human arrangements, let us remember that it is only "*until He come whose right it is*," and then *all* shall be set right forever, for God, in all things, shall be fully glorified through Jesus Christ.

Thus have we followed Levi in his course; and oh, what a marvelous course has it been! a course, every step of which displays the visible marks of sovereign grace abounding over man's sin—grace, which led God to stoop from His throne in the heavens to visit "the habitations of cruelty," in order to lift a poor perishing sinner from thence, and bring him, through the purging power of the blood, into a place of marvelous blessing indeed, even into the very tabernacle of God, there to be employed about the instruments of God's house. We have found Levi to have been indeed the one who "was *dead* and is *alive* again, who was *lost* and is found."

May we, then, adore the grace that could do such mighty acts! and if we have felt in our hearts the operations of the same grace in delivering us from the death and darkness of Egypt, may we remember that its effects should be to constrain us to live, not unto ourselves, but unto Him who died for us and rose again. We are now in the wilderness, where we are called to carry the tabernacle. May we cheerfully move onward, "*declaring plainly* that we seek a country," and anxiously look out the "*the rest that remains.*"

JEHOVAH'S DEMAND AND SATAN'S OBJECTIONS

"Let My people go, that they may hold a feast to Me in the wilderness" (Exodus 5:1).

WHAT A VOLUME OF TRUTH is contained in this sentence! It is one of those comprehensive and suggestive passages which lie scattered up and down the divine volume, and which seize, with peculiar power, upon the heart, and open up a vast field of most precious truth. It sets forth, in plain and forcible language, the blessed purpose of the Lord God of Israel to have His people completely delivered from Egypt and separated unto Himself, in order that they might feast with Him in the wilderness. Nothing could satisfy His heart, in reference to them, but their entire emancipation from the land of death and darkness. He would free them not only from Egypt's brick-kilns and task-masters, but from its temples and its altars, and from all its habits and all its associations, from its principles, its maxims, and its fashions. In a word, they must be a thoroughly separated people, ere they could hold a feast to Him in the wilderness.

Thus it was with Israel, and thus it is with us. We, too, must be a fully and consciously delivered people ere we can properly serve, worship, or walk with God. We must not only know the forgiveness of our sins, and our entire freedom from guilt, wrath, judgment, and condemnation; but also our complete deliverance from this present evil world and all its belongings, ere we can intelligently serve the Lord. The world is to the Christian what Egypt was to Israel; only, of course, our separation from the world is not local or physical, but moral and spiritual. Israel left Egypt in person; we leave the world in spirit and principle. Israel left Egypt in fact; we leave the world in faith. It was a real, out-and-out, thorough separation for them, and it is the same for us. "Let My people go, that they may hold a feast to Me in the wilderness."

1. To this rigid separation, as we very well

know, Satan had and still has many objections. His first objection was set forth in the following words, spoken by the lips of Pharaoh, "Go ye, *and sacrifice to your God in the land.*" These were subtle words—words well calculated to ensnare a heart that was not in communion with the mind of God. For it might with great plausibility and apparent force be argued, Is it not uncommonly liberal on the part of the king of Egypt to offer you toleration for your pecular mode of worship? Is it not a great stretch of liberality to offer your religion a place on the public platform? Surely you can carry on your religion as well as other people. There is room for all. Why this demand for separation? Why not take common ground with your neighbors? There is no need surely for such extreme narrowness.

All this might seem very reasonable. But then, mark Jehovah's high and holy standard! Hearken to the plain and positive declaration, "Let My people go!" There is no mistaking this. It is impossible, in the face of such a statement, to remain in Egypt. The most plausible reasonings that ever could be advanced vanish into thin air in the presence of the authoritative demand of the Lord God of Israel. If He says, "Let My people go," then go we must, spite of all the opposing power of earth and hell, men and devils. There is no use in reasoning, disputing, or discussing. We must obey. Egyptians may think for themselves; Jehovah must think for Israel; the sequel will prove who is right.

And here let us just offer a word, in passing, as to the subject of "narrowness," about which we hear so much now-a-days. The real question is, "Who is to fix the boundaries of the Christian's faith? Is it man or God—human opinion or divine revelation?" When this question is answered, the whole matter is easily settled. There are some minds terribly scared by the bugbear of "narrow-mindedness." But then we have to inquire what *is* narrowness, and what breadth of mind? Now, what we understand by a narrow mind is simply a mind which refuses to take in and be governed by the whole truth of God. A mind governed by human opinions, human reasonings, worldly

maxims, selfish interests, self-will—this we unhesitatingly pronounce to be a narrow mind.

On the other hand, a mind beautifully subject to the authority of Christ—a mind that bows with reverent submission to the voice of Holy Scripture—a mind that sternly refuses to go beyond the written Word—that absolutely rejects what is not based upon "Thus saith the Lord"—this is what we call a broad, elevated mind.

Is it not—must it not be so? Is not God's Word—His mind, infinitely more comprehensive, wide, and full than the mind and ways of man? Is there not infinitely greater breadth in the Holy Scriptures than in all the human writings under the sun? Does it not argue more largeness of heart, and devotion of soul to be governed by the thoughts of God than by our own thoughts or the thoughts of our fellows? It seems to us there can be but one reply to these questions; and hence the entire subject of narrowness resolves itself into this simple but very telling motto, "We must be as narrow as Christ, and as broad as Christ."

We must view everything from this blessed standpoint, and then our entire range of vision will be correct, and our conclusions thoroughly sound. But if Christ be not our standpoint, but self, or man, or the world, then our entire range of vision is false, and our conclusions thoroughly unsound.

All this is as clear as a sunbeam to a single eye and an honest and loyal heart. And, really, if the eye be not single, and the heart true to Christ, and the conscience subject to the Word, it is a complete loss of time to argue or discuss. Of what possible use can it be to argue with a man who, instead of obeying the Word of God, is only seeking to turn aside its edge? None whatever. It is a hopeless task to reason with one who has never taken in the mighty moral import of that most precious word—obey.

We must now return to our immediate theme. There is something uncommonly fine in Moses' reply to Satan's first objection, "It is not meet so to do: for we shall sacrifice the abomination of the Egyptians to the Lord our God: lo, shall we sacrifice the abomination of the Egyptians before their eyes, and will they not stone us? We will go three days' journey into the wilderness, and sacrifice to the Lord our God, as He shall command us" (Exod. 8:26).

There would have been a lack of moral fitness in presenting to Jehovah, in sacrifice, the object of Egyptian worship. But, more than this, Egypt was not the place in which to erect an altar to the true God. Abraham had no altar when he turned aside into Egypt. He abandoned his worship and his strangership when he went down thither; and if Abraham could not worship there, neither could his seed. An Egyptian might ask, Why? But it is one thing to ask a question, and another thing to understand the answer. How could the Egyptian mind enter into the reasons of a true Israelite's conduct? Impossible. What could such an one know of the meaning of a "three days' journey"? Absolutely nothing.

"Beloved, the world knoweth us not, because it knew Him not." The motives which actuate, and the objects which animate, the true believer lie far beyond the world's range of vision; and we may rest assured that in the exact proportion in which the world can enter into and appreciate a Christian's motives the Christian must be unfaithful to his Lord.

We speak, of course, of proper Christian *motives*. No doubt there is much in a Christian's life that the world can admire and value. Integrity, honesty, truthfulness, disinterested kindness, care for the poor, self-denial—all these things may be understood and appreciated; but, admitting all this, we return to the apostolic statement that "The world knoweth us not": and if we want to walk with God—if we would hold a feast unto Him—if it is our heart's true and earnest desire to run a consistent heavenly course, we must break with the world altogether, and break with *self* also, and take our stand outside the camp, with a world-rejected, Heaven-accepted Christ. May we do so, with fixed purpose of heart, to the glory of His own precious and peerless name!

2. Satan's second objection is very near akin to his first. If he cannot succeed in keeping Israel in Egypt, he will at least try to keep them as near to it as possible. "I will let you go, that ye may sacrifice to the Lord your

God in the wilderness; only *ye shall not go very far away*" (chap. 8: 28).

There is more damage done to the cause of Christ by an apparent, partial, half-hearted giving up of the world, than by remaining in it altogether. Wavering, undecided, half-and-half professors injure the testimony of the Lord more than out-and-out worldlings. And, further, we may say, there is a very wide difference indeed between giving up certain worldly things, and giving up the world itself. A person may lay aside certain forms of worldliness, and, all the while, retain the world deep down in the heart. We may give up the theatre, the ball-room, the race-course, the billiard-table, etc., yet cling to the world all the same. We may lop off some of the branches, and yet cling with tenacity to the old trunk.

This must be carefully seen to. We feel persuaded that what multitudes of professing Christians need is to make a clean break with the world—that very comprehensive word. It is utterly impossible to make a proper start, much less to make any progress, while the heart is playing fast and loose with the holy claims of Christ. We do not hesitate to express it as our settled conviction that, in thousands of cases, where souls complain of doubts and fears, ups and downs, darkness and heaviness, lack of assurance and comfort, of light, liberty, joy, peace, and vivid realization, it is owing to the simple fact that they have not really broken with the world. They either seek to hold a feast to the Lord in Egypt, or they remain so near as to be easily drawn back again; so near that they are neither one thing nor the other.

How can such people be happy? How can their peace flow as a river? How can they possibly walk in the light of a Father's countenance, or in the joy of a Saviour's presence? How can the blessed beams of that sun that shines in the new creation reach them through the murky atmosphere that envelops the land of death and darkness? Impossible! They must break with the world, and make a clear, decided, whole-hearted surrender of themselves to Christ. There must be a full Christ for the heart, and a full heart for Christ.

Here, we may rest assured, lies the grand secret of Christian progress. We must make a proper start before ever we can get on; and in order to make a proper start we must break our links with the world, or, rather, we must believe and practically carry out the fact that God has broken them for us in the death of our Lord Jesus Christ. The cross has separated us for ever from this present evil world. It has not merely delivered us from the eternal consequences of our sins, but from the present power of sin, and from the principles, maxims, and fashions of a world that lieth in the hands of the wicked one.

It is one of Satan's masterpieces to lead professing Christians to rest satisfied with looking to the Cross for salvation while remaining in the world, or occupying a border position—"not going very far away." This is a terrible snare, against which we most solemnly warn the Christian reader. What is the remedy? True heart-devotedness to and fellowship with a rejected and glorified Christ. To walk with Christ, to delight in Him, to feed upon Him, we must be apart from the godless, Christless, wicked world—apart from it in the spirit of our minds and in the affections of our hearts—apart from it, not merely in its gross forms of moral pravity, or the wild extravagance of its folly and gaiety, but apart from its religion, its politics, and its philanthropy—apart from the world in all that goes to make up that comprehensive phrase.

But here we may be asked, "Is Christianity merely a stripping, an emptying, a giving up? Does it only consist of prohibition and negation?" We answer, with hearty and blissful emphasis, *No!* A thousand times, *No!* Christianity is preeminently positive—intensely real—divinely satisfying. What does it give us in lieu of what it takes from us? It gives us "unsearchable riches" in place of "dung and dross." It gives us "an inheritance incorruptible, undefiled and unfading, reserved in heaven," instead of a poor passing bubble on the stream of time. It gives us Christ, the joy of the heart of God, the object of Heaven's worship, the theme of angels' song, the eternal sunlight of the new creation, in lieu of a few moments of sinful gratification and guilty pleasure. And, finally, it gives us an eternity of ineffable bliss and glory in the Father's house above, instead of an eternity in the awful flames of hell.

Reader, what sayest thou to these things? Is not this a good exchange? Can we not find here the most cogent reasons for giving up the world? It sometimes happens that men favor us with their reasons for resigning this, that, and the other branch of worldliness; but it strikes us that all such reasons might be summed up in one, and that one be thus enunciated: "The reason for resigning the world—*I have found Christ*." This is the real way to put the matter. Men do not find it very hard to give up cinders for diamonds, ashes for pearls, dross for gold. No; and in the same way, when one has tasted the preciousness of Christ, there is no difficulty in giving up the world.

If Christ fills the heart, the world is not only driven out, but kept out. We not only turn our back upon Egypt, but we go far enough away from it never to return. And for what? To do nothing? To have nothing? To be gloomy, morose, melancholy, sour, or cynical? No; but to "hold a *feast* to the Lord." True, it is "in the wilderness"; but then the wilderness is heaven begun, when we have Christ there with us. He is our Heaven, blessed be His name—the light of our eyes, the joy of our hearts, the food of our souls; for even Heaven would be no Heaven without Him, and the wilderness itself is turned into a heaven by His dear, bright, soul-satisfying presence.

Nor is this all. It is not merely that the *heart* is thoroughly satisfied with Christ; but the *mind* also is divinely tranquilized as to the difficulties of the path, and the questions that so constantly crop up to trouble and perplex those who do not know the deep blessedness of making Christ their object, and viewing all in direct reference to Him.

For instance, if I am called to act for Christ in any given case, and, instead of looking at the matter simply in its bearing upon Him and His glory, I look at how it will affect *me*, I shall most assuredly get into darkness and perplexity, and reach a wrong conclusion. But if I simply look at *Him*, and consider *Him*, and see how the matter bears upon *Him*, I shall see the thing as clear as a sunbeam, and move with holy elasticity and firm purpose along that blessed path which is ever illuminated by the bright beams of God's approving countenance. A single eye never looks at consequences, but looks straight to Christ, and then all is simple and plain; the body is full of light, and the path marked by plain decision.

This is what is so needed in this day of easy-going profession, worldly religiousness, self-seeking, and man-pleasing. We want to make Christ our *only* standpoint—to look at self, the world, and the so-called Church, from thence, regardless of consequences. Oh that it may be so with us, through the infinite mercy of our God! Then we shall understand something of the force, depth, beauty, and fulness of the opening sentence of this paper, "Let My people go, that they may hold a feast to Me in the wilderness."

Note the way in which Satan disputes every inch of the ground in the grand question of Israel's deliverance from the land of Egypt. He would allow them to worship *in* the land, or *near* the land; but their absolute and complete deliverance *from* the land is what he will, by every means in his power, obstinately resist.

But Jehovah, blessed be His eternal name, is above the great adversary, and He will have His people fully delivered, spite of all the powers of hell and earth combined. The divine standard can never be lowered—"Let My people go, that they may hold a feast to Me in the wilderness." This is Jehovah's demand, and it must be made good, though the enemy were to offer ten thousand objections. The divine glory is intimately involved in the entire separation of Israel from Egypt, and from all the people that are upon the face of the earth. "The people shall dwell alone, and shall not be reckoned among the nations." To this the enemy demurs; and to hinder it he puts forth all his malignant power, and all his crafty schemes. We have already considered two of his objections, and we shall now proceed to the third.

3. "And Moses and Aaron were brought again unto Pharaoh: and he said unto them, Go, serve the Lord your God: but who are they that shall go? And Moses said, We will go with our young and with our old, with our sons and with our daughters, with our flocks and with our herds we will go; for we must hold a feast unto the Lord. And he said unto them, Let the Lord be so with you, as I will let you go, and your little ones: look to it; for evil is before you. Not so: go now ye that are men, and serve the Lord; for that ye did desire. And they were driven out from Pharaoh's presence" (Exod. 10:8-11).

These words contain a very solemn lesson for the hearts of all Christian parents. They reveal a deep and crafty purpose of the arch-enemy. If he cannot keep the parents in Egypt, he will at least seek to keep the children, and in this way mar the testimony to the truth of God, tarnish His glory in His people, and hinder their blessing in Him. Parents in the wilderness, and their children in Egypt!—how opposed to the mind of God, and utterly subversive of His glory in the walk of His people.

We should ever remember—strange that we should ever forget!—that our children are part of ourselves. God's creative hand has made them such; and, surely, what the Creator has joined together, the Redeemer would not put asunder. Hence we invariably find that God links a man and his house together. "Thou and thy house" is a phrase of deep practical import. It involves the very highest consequences, and conveys the richest consolation to every Christian parent; and, we may truly add, the neglect of it has led to the most disastrous consequences in thousands of family circles.

Very many—alas, how many!—Christian parents, through an utterly false application of the doctrines of grace, have allowed their children to grow up around them in wilfulness and worldliness; and while so doing they have comforted themselves with the thought that they could do nothing, and that in God's time their children would, if included in the eternal purpose, be gathered in. They have virtually lost sight of the grand practical truth that the One who has decreed the end has fixed the means of reaching it, and that it is the height of folly to think of gaining the end while neglecting the means.

Do we, then, mean to assert that all the children of Christian parents are, of necessity, included in the number of God's elect; that they will all be infallibly saved?—and if not, that it is the parents' fault? We mean to assert nothing of the kind. "Known unto God are all His works from the beginning of the world." We know nothing of God's eternal decrees and purposes. No mortal eye has scanned the page of His secret counsels.

What, then, is involved in the weighty expression, "Thou and thy house"? There are two things involved in it. In the first place, there is a most precious privilege; and, in the second place, a deep responsibility. It is unquestionably the privilege of all Christian parents to count on God for their children; but it is also their bounden *duty*—do we dislike the homely word?—to train their children for God.

Here we have the sum and substance of the whole matter—the two sides of this great question. The Word of God, in every part of it, connects a man with his house. "This day is salvation come to *this house*." "Believe on the Lord Jesus Christ, and thou shalt be saved, and *thy house*" (Luke 19; Acts 16). Here lies the solid basis of the privilege and responsibility of parents. Acting on the weighty principle here laid down, we are at once to take God's ground for our children, and diligently bring them up for Him, counting on Him for the result. We are to begin at the very beginning, and go steadily on, from day to day, month to month, year to year, training our children for God.

Just as a wise and skillful gardener begins, while his fruit trees are young and tender, to train the branches along the wall where they may catch the genial rays of the sun, so should we, while our children are young and plastic, seek to mould them for God. It would be the height of folly, on the part of the

gardener, to wait till the branches become old and gnarled, and then seek to train them. He would find it a hopeless task. And, most surely, it is the very greatest folly, on our part, to suffer our children to remain for years and years under the moulding hand of Satan, and the world, and sin, ere we rouse ourselves to the holy business of moulding them for God.

Let us not be misunderstood. Let no one suppose that we mean to teach that grace is hereditary, or that we can, by any act or system of training, make Christians of our children. No! nothing of the kind. Grace is sovereign, and the children of Christian parents must, like all others, be born of water and of the Spirit, ere they can see or enter the kingdom of God. All this is as plain and as clear as Scripture can make it; but, on the other hand, Scripture is equally clear and plain as to the duty of Christian parents to "bring up their children in the nurture and admonition of the Lord."*

And what does this "bringing up" involve? What does it mean? In what does it consist? these, surely, are weighty questions for the heart and conscience of every Christian parent. It is to be feared, that very few of us indeed really understand what Christian training means, or how it is to be carried on. One thing is certain, namely, that Christian training means a great deal more than drilling religion into our children, making the Bible a task-book, teaching our children to repeat texts and hymns like a parrot, and turning the family circle into a school. No doubt it is very well to store the memory of a child with Scripture and sweet hymns. No one would think of calling this in question. But is it not too frequently the case that religion is made a weariness to the child, and the Bible a repulsive school-book?

This will never do. What is really needed is to surround our children with a thoroughly Christian atmosphere, from their earliest moments; to let them breathe the pure air of the new creation; to let them see in their

---

* In Abraham we see how paternal control and exercise of authority over his household is coupled with the Lord's promise and blessing: "And the Lord said, Shall I hide from Abraham that thing which I do? . . . For I know him, *that he will command his children and his household after him,* and they shall keep the way of the Lord . . . that the Lord may bring upon Abraham that which He hath spoken of him" (Gen. 18:17-19). [Ed.]

parents the genuine fruits of spiritual life—love, peace, purity, tenderness, holy disinterestedness, genuine kindness, unselfishness, loving thoughtfulness of others. These things have a mighty moral influence upon the plastic mind of the child, and the Spirit of God will assuredly use them in drawing the heart to Christ—the centre and the source of all these beauteous graces and heavenly influences.

But, on the other hand, who can attempt to define the pernicious effect produced upon our children by our inconsistencies, by our bad temper, our selfish ways, our worldliness, and covetousness? Can we be said to bring our children out of Egypt when Egypt's principles and habits are seen in our whole career? It may be we use and teach the phraseology of the wilderness or of Canaan; but our ways, our manners, our habits are those of Egypt, and our children are quicksighted enough to mark the gross inconsistency, and the effect upon them is deplorable beyond expression. We have but little idea of the way in which the unfaithfulness of Christian parents has contributed to swell the tide of infidelity which is rising around us with such appalling rapidity.

It may be said, and said with a measure of truth, that children are responsible spite of the inconsistency of their parents. But, most assuredly, whatever amount of truth there may be in this statement, it is not for parents to urge it. It ill becomes us to fall back upon the responsibility of our children in view of our failure in meeting our own. They are responsible, no doubt, but so are we; and if we fail to exhibit before the eyes of our children those living and unanswerable proofs that we ourselves have left Egypt, and left it for ever, need we marvel if they remain?

Of what possible use is it to talk about wilderness life, and our being in Canaan, while our manners, our habits, our ways, our deportment, our spirit, the bent of our whole life, bears and exhibits the impress of Egypt? None whatever. The language of the life gives the lie to the language of the lips, and we know full well that the former is far more telling than the latter. Our children will judge from our conduct, not from our talk, where we really are; and is this to be wondered at? Is not conduct the real index of conviction? If we have really left Egypt, it will be seen in our ways; and if it be not seen in our ways, the talk of the lips is worse than worthless; it only tends to create disgust in the minds of our children, and to lead them to the conclusion that Christianity is a mere sham.

All this is deeply solemn, and should lead Christian parents into the most profound exercise of soul in the presence of God. We may depend upon it there is a great deal more involved in this question of training than many of us are aware of. Nothing but the direct power of the Spirit of God can fit parents for the great and holy work of training their children, in these days in which we live, and in the midst of the scene through which we are passing. That word falls upon the heart with heavenly sweetness and power: "My grace is sufficient for thee." We can, with fullest confidence, reckon upon God to bless the very feeblest effort to lead our dear children forth out of Egypt. But the effort must be made, and made, too, with real, fixed, earnest purpose of heart. It will not do to fold our arms and say, "Grace is not hereditary. We cannot convert our children. If they are of the number of God's elect they must be saved; if not, they cannot."

All this is one-sided and utterly false. It will not stand; it cannot bear the light of the judgment-seat of Christ. Parents cannot get rid of the holy responsibility of training their children for God; that responsibility begins with, and is based upon, the relationship; and the right discharge of it demands continual exercise of soul before God, in reference to our children. We have to remember that the foundation of character is laid in the nursery. It is in the early days of infancy that Christian training begins, and it must be steadily pursued, from day to day, month to month, and year to year, in simple, hearty dependence upon God who will, most assuredly, in due time, hear and answer the earnest cry of a parent's heart, and crown with His rich blessing the faithful labors of a parent's hands.

And, while on this subject of training children, we would, in true brotherly love, offer a suggestion to all Christian parents as to the immense importance of inculcating a spirit of implicit obedience.

If we mistake not, there is very wide-spread failure in this respect, for which we have to judge ourselves before God. Whether through a false tenderness, or indolence, we suffer our children to walk according to their own will and pleasure, and the strides which they make along this road are alarmingly rapid. They pass from stage to stage with great speed, until, at length, they reach the terrible goal of despising their parents altogether, throwing their authority entirely overboard, and trampling beneath their feet the holy order of God, and turning the domestic circle into a scene of godless misrule and confusion.

How dreadful this is we need not say, or how utterly opposed to the mind of God, as revealed in His holy Word. But have we not ourselves to blame for it? God has put into the parents' hands the reins of government, and the rod of authority, but if parents, through indolence, suffer the reins to drop from their hands; and if through false tenderness or moral weakness, the rod of authority is not applied, need we marvel if the children grow up in utter lawlessness? How could it be otherwise? Children are, as a rule, very much what we make them. If they are made to be obedient, they will be so; and if they are allowed to have their own way, the result will be accordingly.

Are we then to be continually chucking the reins and brandishing the rod? By no means. This would be to break the spirit of the child, instead of subduing his will. Where parental authority is thoroughly established, the reins may lie gently on the neck, and the rod be allowed to stand in the corner. The child should be taught, from his earliest hour, that the parent only wills his good, but the parent's will must be supreme. Nothing is simpler. A look is enough for a properly trained child. There is no need whatever to be continually hawking our authority; indeed nothing is more contemptible whether in a husband, a father, or a master. There is a quiet dignity about one who really possesses authority; whereas the spasmodic efforts of weakness only draw out contempt.

We have found, through many years of experience and careful observation, that the real secret of successful training lies in the proper adjustment of firmness and tenderness. If the parent, from the very beginning, establishes his authority, he may exercise as much tenderness as the most loving heart can desire or display. When the child is really made to feel that the reins and rod are under the direct control of sound judgment and true affection, and not of a sour temper and an arbitrary will, there will be little difficulty in training him.

In a word, firmness and tenderness are the two essential ingredients in all sound education; a firmness which the child will not dare to question; a tenderness which takes account of the child's every real want and right desire. It is sad indeed if the idea which a child forms of parental authority be that of arbitrary interference with, or a cold indifference to, his little wishes and wants. It is not thus our heavenly Father deals with us; and He is to be our model in this as in all beside.

If it be written, and it is written, "Children, obey your parents in all things"; it is also, in beautiful adjusting power, written, "Fathers, provoke not your children, lest they be discouraged." Again, if it be said, "Children, obey your parents in the Lord; for this is right"; it is also said, "Ye fathers, provoke not your children to wrath; but bring them up in the nurture and admonition of the Lord." In short, the child must be taught to obey; but the obedient child must be allowed to breathe an atmosphere of tenderness, and to walk up and down in the sunshine of parental affection. This is the spirit of Christian education.

Most gladly would we dwell further on this great practical subject; but we trust sufficient has been said to rouse the hearts and consciences of all Christian parents to a sense of their high and holy responsibilities in reference to their beloved offspring; and also to shew that there is a great deal more involved in bringing our children out of

Egypt, and taking God's ground for them, than many of us are aware of. And if the reading of the foregoing lines be used of God to lead any parent into prayerful exercise in this most weighty matter, we shall not have penned them in vain.

4. We shall close this paper with the briefest possible reference to the enemy's fourth and last objection, which is embodied in the following words, "And Pharaoh called unto Moses, and said, Go ye, serve the Lord; only let your flocks and your herds be stayed: let your little ones also go with you." He would let them go, but without resources to serve the Lord. If he could not keep them in Egypt, he would send them away crippled and shorn. Such is the enemy's last demurrer.

But mark the noble reply of a devoted heart. It is morally grand. "And Moses said, Thou must give us also sacrifices and burnt-offerings, that we may sacrifice unto the Lord our God. Our cattle also shall go with us; there shall not a hoof be left behind: for thereof must we take to serve the Lord our God; and"—ponder these suggestive words—"*We know not with what we must serve the Lord until we come thither.*"

We must be fully and clearly on God's ground and at His stand-point, before ever we can form any true idea of the nature and extent of His claims. It is utterly impossible, while surrounded by a worldly atmosphere, and governed by a worldly spirit, worldly principles, and worldly objects, to have any just sense of what is due to God. We must stand on the lofty ground of accomplished redemption—in the full-orbed light of the new creation—apart from this present evil world, ere we can properly serve Christ.

It is only when, in the power of an indwelling Spirit, we see where we are brought by the death and resurrection of Christ—"three days' journey"—that we can at all understand what true Christian service is; and then we shall clearly see and fully own, that "all we are, and all we have, belong to Him." "We know not with what we must serve the Lord until we come thither." Precious words! May we better understand their force, meaning, and practical application! Moses, the man of God, meets all Satan's objections by a simple but decided adherence to Jehovah's demand, "Let My people go, that they hold a feast unto Me in the wilderness."

This is the true principle we are called to maintain spite of all objections. If that standard be lowered, ever so little, the enemy gains his point, and Christian service and testimony are undermined—if not made impossible.

"GILGAL"

Joshua 5

Part 1

"WHATSOEVER THINGS were written aforetime were written for our learning, that we through patience and comfort of the Scriptures might have hope" (Rom. 15:4). These few words furnish a title, distinct and unquestionable, for the Christian to range through the wide and magnificent field of Old Testament Scripture, and gather therein instruction and comfort, according to the measure of his capacity and the character or depth of his spiritual need. And were any further warrant needed, we have it with equal clearness in the words of another inspired Epistle: "Now all these things happened unto them [Israel] for ensamples; and they are written for our admonition, upon whom the ends of the world are come" (1 Cor. 10: 11).

No doubt, in reading the Old Testament, as in reading the New, there is constant need of watchfulness—need of self-emptiness, of dependence upon the direct teaching of the Holy Spirit, by whom all Scripture has been indited. The imagination must be checked, lest it lead us into crude notions and fanciful interpretations, which tend to no profit, but rather to the weakening of the power of Scripture over the soul, and hindering our growth in the divine life.

Still, we must never lose sight of the divine charter made out for us in Rom. 15:4—never forget for a single moment that "whatsoever things were written aforetime were written for our learning." It is in the strength of these words that we invite the reader to accompany us back to the opening of the book of Joshua, that we may together contemplate the striking and instructive scenes presented there, and seek to gather up some of the precious "learning" there unfolded. If we mistake not, we shall learn some fine lessons on the banks of the Jordan, and find the air of Gilgal most healthful and bracing for the spiritual constitution.

We have all been accustomed to look at Jordan as the figure of death—the death of the believer—his leaving this world and going to Heaven. Doubtless the believer was often read and heard these lines:

Could we but stand where Moses stood,
    And view the landscape o'er,
Not Jordan's stream nor death's cold flood
    Could fright us from the shore.

But all this line of thought, feeling and experience is very far below the mark of true Christianity. A moment's reflection in the true light which Scripture pours upon our souls would be sufficient to show how utterly deficient is the popular religious thought as to Jordan. For instance, when a believer dies and goes to Heaven, is he called to fight? Surely not. All is rest and peace up yonder—ineffable, eternal peace. Not a ripple on that ocean. No sound of alarm throughout that pure and holy region. No conflict there. No need of armor. We shall want no girdle, because our garments may flow loosely around us. We shall not need a breast-plate of righteousness, for divine righteousness has there its eternal abode. We shall have no need of sandals, for there will be no rough or thorny places in that fair and blissful region. No shield called for there, inasmuch as there will be no fiery darts flying. No helmet of salvation, for the divine and eternal results of God's salvation shall then be reached. No sword, inasmuch as there will be neither enemy nor evil occurrent throughout all that blissful, sunny region.

Hence, therefore, Jordan cannot mean the death of the believer and his going to Heaven, for the simplest of all reasons, that it was when Israel crossed the Jordan that their fighting, properly speaking, began. True they had fought with Amalek in the wilderness; but it was in Canaan that their real war commenced. The careful reader of the Scriptures will readily see this.

But does not Jordan represent death? Most surely it does. And must not the believer cross it? Yes; but he finds it dry, because the Prince of Life has gone down into its deepest depths, and opened up a pathway for His people, by the which they pass over into their heavenly inheritance.

Moses, from Pisgah's top, gazed upon the promised land. *Personally*, under the governmental dealings of God, he was prevented from going over Jordan. But looking at him *officially*, we know that the law could not possibly bring the people into Canaan; so Moses' course must end there, for he represents the law.

But Christ, the true Joshua, has crossed the Jordan, and not only crossed it, but turned it into a pathway by which the ransomed host can pass over dry-shod into the heavenly Canaan. The Christian is not called to stand shivering on the brink of the river of death, as one in doubt as to how it may go with him. That river is dried up for faith. Its power is gone. Our adorable Lord "has abolished death, and brought life and incorruptibility to light by the gospel." Faith can now, therefore, sing triumphantly, "O death, where is thy sting? O grave, where is thy victory? The sting of death is sin; and the strength of sin is the law; but thanks be to God, which giveth us the victory through our Lord Jesus Christ" (1 Cor. 15: 55-57).

Glorious, enfranchising fact! Let us praise Him for it. Let all our ransomed powers adore Him. Let our whole moral being be stirred up to chant the praises of Him who has taken the sting from death, and destroyed him who had the power of death, that is, the devil, and conducted us into a sphere which is pervaded throughout with life, light, incorruptibility, and glory. May our entire practical career be to His glory!

We shall now proceed to examine more particularly the teaching of Scripture on this great subject, and may the Holy Spirit Himself be our immediate instructor!

"And Joshua rose early in the morning; and they removed from Shittim, and came to Jordan, he and all the children of Israel, and lodged there before they passed over. And it came to pass after three days, that the officers went through the host; and they commanded the people, saying, When ye see the ark of the covenant of the Lord your God, and the priests, the Levites, bearing it, then ye shall remove from your place, and go after it. *Yet there shall be a space between you and it*, about two thousand cubits by measure: come not near unto it, *that ye may know the way by which ye must go: for ye have not passed this way before*" (Josh. 3: 1-4).

There are three deeply important points in Israel's history which the reader would do well to ponder. There is, first, the blood-stained lintel, in the land of Egypt; secondly, the Red Sea; thirdly, the river Jordan.

Now in each of these we have a type of the death of Christ, in some one or other of its grand aspects—for, as we know, that precious death has many and various aspects, and nothing can be more profitable for the Christian, and nothing, surely, ought to be more attractive, than the study of the profound mystery of the death of Christ. There are depths and heights in that mystery which eternity alone will unfold; and it should be our delight now, under the powerful ministry of the Holy Ghost, through the perfect light of Holy Scripture, to search into these things for the strength, comfort and refreshment of the inward man.

Looking, then, at the death of Christ, as typified by the blood of the paschal lamb, we see in it that which screens us from the judgment of God. "I will pass through the land of Egypt this night, and will smite all the firstborn in the land of Egypt, both man and beast; and against all the gods of Egypt I will execute judgment; I am the Lord. And the blood shall be to you for a token upon the houses where ye are; and when I see the blood, I will pass over you, and the plague shall not be upon you to destroy you, when I smite the land of Egypt" (Exod. 12).

Now, we need hardly say, it is of the deepest moment for the exercised, consciously guilty soul, to know that God has provided a shelter from wrath and judgment to come. No right-minded person would think for a moment of undervaluing this aspect of the death of Christ. "When *I* see the blood, I will pass over you." Israel's safety rested upon God's estimate of the blood. He does not say, "When *you* see the blood." The Judge saw the blood, knew its value, and passed over the house. Israel was screened by the blood of the lamb—by God's estimate of that blood, not by their own. Precious fact!

How prone we are to be occupied with our thoughts about the blood of Christ, instead of with God's thoughts! We feel we do not value that precious blood as we ought—who ever did, or ever could? and then we begin to question if we are safe, seeing we so sadly fail in our estimate of Christ's work and in our love to His person.

Now if our *safety* depends in the smallest degree upon our estimate of Christ's work, or our love to His person, we are in more imminent danger than if it depended upon our keeping the law. True it is—most true—who could think of denying it?—we ought to value Christ's work, and we ought to love Himself. But if all this be put upon the footing of a righteous claim, and if our safety rests upon our answering to that claim, then are we in greater danger and more justly condemned than if we stood on the ground of a broken law. For just in proportion as the claims of Christ are higher than the claims of Moses, and in proportion as Christianity is higher than the legal system, so are we worse off, in greater danger, farther from peace, if our safety depends upon our response to those higher claims.

Mark, it is not that we ought not to answer to such claims; we most certainly ought. But who among us does? and hence, so far as we are concerned, our ruin and guilt are only made more manifest, and our condemnation more righteous, if we stand upon the claims of Christ, because we have not answered to them. If we are to be saved by our estimate of Christ, by our response to His claims, by our appreciation of His love, we are worse off by far than if we were placed under the claims of the law of Moses.

But, blessed be God, it is not so. We are saved by grace—free, sovereign, divine and eternal grace—not by our sense of grace. We are sheltered by the blood, not by our estimate of the blood. Jehovah did not say, on that awful night, "When *you* see the blood, and estimate it as you ought, I will pass over you." Nothing of the kind. This is not the way of our God. He wanted to shelter His people, and to let them know that they were sheltered—perfectly, because divinely sheltered—and therefore He places the matter wholly upon a divine basis. He takes it entirely out of their hands, by assuring them that their safety rested simply and entirely upon the blood, and upon His estimate thereof. He gives them to understand that they had nothing whatever to do with providing the shelter. It was His to *provide*. It was theirs to *enjoy*.

Thus it stood between Jehovah and His Israel in that memorable night; and thus it stands between Him and the soul that simply trusts in Jesus now. We are not saved by *our* love, or *our* estimate, or *our* anything. We are saved by the blood behind which faith has fled for refuge, and by God's estimate of it, which faith apprehends. And just as Israel, within that blood-stained lintel screened from judgment—safe from the sword of the destroyer—could feed upon the roasted lamb, so may the believer, perfectly sheltered from the wrath to come—sweetly secure from all danger, screened from judgment—feed upon Christ in all the preciousness of what He is.

But more of this by and by.

We are specially anxious that the reader should weigh the point on which we have been dwelling, if he be one who has not yet found peace, even as to the question of safety from judgment to come, which, as we shall see (if God permit) ere we close this paper, is but a part, though an ineffably precious part, of what the death of Christ has procured for us.

We have very little idea indeed of how much of the leaven of self-righteousness cleaves to us, even after our conversion, and how immensely it interferes with our peace, our enjoyment of grace, and our consequent progress in the divine life. It may be we fancy we have done with self-righteousness when we have given up all thought of being saved by our works; but alas, it is not so, for the evil takes new forms; and of all these, none is more subtle than the feeling that we do not value the blood as we ought, and the doubting our safety on that ground. All this is the fruit of self-righteousness. We have not done with *self*. True, we are not, it may be, making a saviour of our *doings*, but we are of our *feelings*. We are seeking, unknown to ourselves perhaps, to find some sort of title in our love to God or our appreciation of Christ.

Now all this must be given up. We must rest simply on the blood of Christ, and upon God's testimony to that blood. He sees the blood. He values it as it deserves. He is satisfied. This ought to satisfy us. He did not say to Israel, When I see how you behave yourselves; when I see the unleavened bread, the bitter herbs, the girded loins, the shod feet, I will pass over you.

No doubt all these things had their proper place; but that proper place was not as the ground of safety, but as the secret of communion. They were called to behave themselves—called to keep the feast; but it was as *being*, not *in order to be*, a sheltered people. This made all the difference. It was because they were divinely screened from judgment that they could keep the feast. They had the authority of the Word of God to assure them that there was no judgment for them; and if they believed that Word, they could celebrate the feast in peace and safety. "Through faith he kept the passover, and the sprinkling of blood, lest He that destroyed the firstborn should touch them" (Heb. 11: 28).

Here lies the deep and precious secret of the whole matter. It was by faith he kept the passover. God had said, "When I see the blood, I will pass over you," and He could not deny Himself. It would have been a denial of His very nature and character, and an ignoring of His own blessed remedy, had a single hair of an Israelite's head been touched on that deeply solemn night. It was not, we repeat, in anywise a question of Israel's state or Israel's deservings. It was simply and entirely a question of the value of the blood *in God's sight*, and of the truth and authority of His own Word.

What stability is here!—what peace and rest! What a solid ground of confidence! The blood of Christ! the Word of God! True, divinely true—let it never be forgotten or lost sight of—it is only by the grace of the Holy Spirit that the Word of God can be received, or the blood of Christ relied upon. Still, it is the Word of God and the blood of Christ, and nothing else, which give peace to the heart as regards all question of coming judgment. There can be no judgment for the believer. And why? Because the blood is on the mercy-seat, as the perfect proof that judgment has been already executed.

He bore on the tree the sentence for me,
And now both the Surety and sinner are free.

Yet, all praise to His name, thus it stands as to every soul that simply takes God at His word, and rests in the precious blood of Christ. It is as impossible that such an one can come into judgment, as that Christ Himself can. All who are sheltered by the blood are as safe as the Word of God is sure—as safe as Christ Himself. It seems perfectly wonderful for any poor sinful mortal to be able to pen such words; but the blessed fact is, it is either this or nothing. If there is any question as to the believer's safety, then the blood of Christ is not on the mercy-seat, or it is of no account in the judgment of God. If it be a question of the believer's state, of his worthiness, of his feelings, of his experience, of his walk, of his love, of his devotedness, of his appreciation of Christ, then would there be no force, no value, no truth in that glorious sentence,

"When I see the blood, I will pass over"; for in that case the form of speech should be entirely changed, and a dark and chilling shade be cast over its heavenly lustre. It should then be, "When I see the blood, and——"

But no, it is not, and it never can be, thus. Nothing must ever be added—not the weight of a feather, to that precious blood which has perfectly satisfied God as a Judge, and which perfectly shelters every soul that has fled for safety behind it. If the righteous Judge has declared Himself satisfied, surely the guilty culprit may well be satisfied also. God is satisfied with the blood of Jesus; and when the soul is satisfied likewise, all is settled, and there is peace as regards the question of judgment. "There is no condemnation to them that are in Christ Jesus." How can there be, seeing He has borne the condemnation in their stead? To doubt the believer's exemption from judgment is to make God a liar, and to make the blood of Christ of none effect.

Thus far we have been occupied only with the question of deliverance from judgment—a most weighty question surely. But, as we shall see, there is far more secured for us by the death of Christ than freedom from judgment and wrath, blessed as that is. That peerless sacrifice does a great deal more for us than keep God out as a Judge.

Art thou sheltered by the blood of Jesus? Do not rest until you can answer with a clear and unhesitating "Yes." Remember, you are either sheltered by the blood, or exposed to the horrors of eternal judgment.

Part 2

Israel under the shelter of the blood is a grand reality, most surely: who could duly estimate it? What human language could suitably unfold the deep blessedness of being screened from the judgment of God by the blood of the Lamb—of being within that hallowed circle where wrath and judgment can never come? Who can speak aright of the privilege of feeding in perfect safety on the Lamb whose precious blood has forever averted from us the wrath of sin-hating God?

But blessed as all this is, there is much more than this. There is far more comprehended in the salvation of God than deliverance from judgment and wrath. We may have the fullest assurance that our sins are forgiven, that God will never enter into judgment with us on account of our sins, and yet be very far indeed from the enjoyment of the true Christian position. We may be filled with all manner of fears about ourselves— fears occasioned by the consciousness of indwelling sin, the power of Satan, the influence of the world. All these things may crop up before us, and fill us with the gravest apprehensions.

Thus, for example, when we turn to Exod. 14, we find Israel in the deepest distress, and almost overwhelmed with fear. It would seem as if they had for the moment lost sight of the fact that they had been under the cover of the blood.

Let us look at the passage.

"And the Lord spake unto Moses, saying, Speak unto the children of Israel, that they turn and encamp before Pi-hahiroth, between Migdol and the sea, over against Baal-zephon: before it shall ye encamp by the sea. For Pharaoh will say of the children of Israel, They are entangled in the land, the wilderness hath shut them in. And I will harden Pharaoh's heart, that he shall follow after them: and I will be honored upon Pharaoh, and upon all his host; that the Egyptians may know that I am the Lord. And they did so. And it was told the king of Egypt that the people fled: and the heart of Pharaoh and of his servants was turned against the people, and they said, Why have we done this, *that we have let Israel go from serving us?*"—mark these words: "And he made ready his chariot, and took his people with him. And he took six hundred chosen chariots, and all the chariots of Egypt, and captains over every one of them. And the Lord hardened the heart of Pharaoh king of Egypt, and he pursued after the children of Israel: and the children of Israel went out with a high hand. But the Egyptians pursued after them, all the horses and chariots of Pharaoh, and his horsemen, and his army, and overtook them, encamping by the sea,

beside Pi-hahiroth, before Baal-zephon. And when Pharaoh drew nigh, the children of Israel lifted up their eyes, and, behold, the Egyptians marched after them; and they were *sore afraid*: and the children of Israel *cried out* unto the Lord."

Now, are these the people whom we have seen so recently feeding, in perfect safety, under the cover of the blood? The very same. Whence, then, these fears, this intense alarm, this agonizing cry? Did they really think that Jehovah was going to judge and destroy them, after all? Not exactly. Of what then were they afraid? Of perishing in the wilderness after all. "And they said unto Moses, Because there were no graves in Egypt, hast thou taken us away to die in the wilderness? Wherefore hast thou dealt thus with us, to carry us forth out of Egypt? Is not this the word that we did tell thee in Egypt, saying, Let us alone, that we may serve the Egyptians! For it had been better for us to serve the Egyptians, than that we should die in the wilderness."

All this was most gloomy and depressing. Their poor hearts seem to fluctuate between "graves in Egypt" and death in the wilderness. There is no sense of deliverance; no adequate knowledge either of God's purposes or of God's salvation. All seems utter darkness, almost bordering upon hopeless despair. They are thoroughly hemmed in and "shut up." They seem in a worse plight than ever. They heartily wish themselves back again amid the brick-kilns and stubble fields of Egypt. Desert sands on either side of them; the sea in front; Pharaoh and all his terrific hosts behind!

The case seemed perfectly hopeless; and hopeless it was, so far as they were concerned. They were utterly powerless, and they were being made to realize it, and this is a very painful process to go through; but very wholesome and valuable, yea, most necessary for all. We must all, in one way or another, learn the force, meaning, and depth of that phrase, "without strength." It is exactly in proportion as we find out what it is to be without strength, that we are prepared to appreciate God's "due time."

But is there aught in the history of God's

people now answering to Israel's experience at the Red Sea? Doubtless there is; for we are told that the things which happened unto Israel are our ensamples, or types. And, most surely, the scene at the Red Sea is full of instruction for us. How often do we find the children of God plunged in the very depths of distress and darkness as to their state and prospects!

It is not that they question the love of God, or the efficacy of the blood of Jesus, nor yet that God will reckon their sins to them, or enter into judgment with them. But still, they have no sense of full deliverence. They do not see the application of the death of Christ to their *evil nature*. They do not realize the glorious truth that by that death they are completely delivered from this present evil world, from the dominion of sin, and from the power of Satan. They see that the blood of Jesus screens them from the judgment of God; but they do not see that *they* are "dead to sin"; that their "old man is crucified with Christ"; that not only have their sins been put upon Christ at the cross, but *they themselves*, as sinful children of Adam, have been, by the act of God, identified with Christ in His death; that God pronounces them *dead and risen with Christ*. (See Col. 3:1-4 and the sixth chapter of Romans.)

But if this precious truth, is not apprehended, by faith, there is no bright, happy, emancipating sense of full and everlasting salvation. They are, to speak according to our type, at Egypt's side of the Red Sea, and in danger of falling into the hands of the prince of this world. They do not see "*all* their enemies dead on the seashore." They cannot sing the song of redemption. No one can sing it, until he stands by faith on the wilderness side of the Red Sea, or, in other words, until he sees his complete deliverence from sin, the world, and Satan—the great foes of every child of God.

Thus, in contemplating the facts of Israel's history, as recorded in the first fifteen chapters of Exodus, we observe that they did not raise a single note of praise until they had passed through the Red Sea. We hear the cry of sore distress under the cruel lash of Pharaoh's task-masters, and amid the grievous toil of Egypt's brick-kilns. And we hear the cry of terror when they stood "between Migdol and the sea." All this we hear; but not one note of praise, not a single accent of triumph, until the waters of the Red Sea rolled between them and the land of bondage and of death, and they saw all the power of the enemy broken and gone. "Thus the Lord saved Israel that day out of the hand of the Egyptians; and Israel saw the Egyptians dead upon the sea-shore. And *Israel saw that great work which the Lord did* upon the Egyptians: and the people feared the Lord and His servant Moses. *Then sang* Moses and the children of Israel."

Now, what is the simple application of all this to us as Christians? What grand lesson are we to learn from the scenes on the shores of the Red Sea? In a word, of what is the Red Sea a type? And what is the difference between the blood-stained lintel and the divided sea?

The Red Sea is the type of the death of Christ, in its application to all our spiritual enemies, sin, the world, and Satan. By the death of Christ the believer is completely and forever delivered from the *power* of sin. He is, alas! conscious of the *presence* of sin; but its power is gone. He has died to sin, in the death of Christ; and what power has sin over a dead man? It is the privilege of the Christian to reckon himself as much delivered from the dominion of sin as a man lying dead on the floor. What power has sin over such an one? None whatever. No more has it over the Christian. Sin *dwells* in the believer, and will do so to the end of the chapter; but its *rule* is gone. Christ has wrested the sceptre from the grasp of our old master, and shivered it to atoms. It is not merely that His blood has purged our *sins;* but His death has broken the power of *sin*.

It is one thing to know that our sins are forgiven, and another thing altogether to know that "the body of sin is destroyed"—its rule ended—its dominion gone. Many will tell you that they do not question the forgiveness of their past sins, but they do not know what to say as to indwelling sin. They fear lest, after all, that may come against them, and bring them into judgment. Such persons are, to use the figure, "between Migdol and the sea." They have not learnt the doctrine of Rom. 6. They have not as yet, in their spiritual intelligence and apprehension, reached the resurrection side of the Red Sea. They do not know what it is to be dead unto sin, and alive unto God through Jesus Christ our Lord.

And let the reader particularly note the force of the apostle's word, *"reckon."* How very different it is, in every way, from our word, *"realize"!* This latter word may do very well where natural or human things are concerned. We can realize physical or material facts; but where a spiritual truth is involved, it is not a question of realizing, but of reckoning. How can I realize that I am dead to sin? All my own experience, my own feelings, my inward self-consciousness seems to offer a flat contradiction to the truth. I cannot realize that I am dead; but God tells me I am. He assures me that He counts me to have died to sin when Christ died. I believe it; not because I feel it, but because God says it. I reckon myself to be what God tells me I am. If I were sinless, if I had no sin in me, I should never be told to reckon myself dead to sin; neither should I ever be called to listen to such words as, "Let not sin, therefore, *reign* in your mortal body." But it is just because I have sin dwelling in me, and in order to give me full practical deliverance from its reigning power, that I am taught the grand enfranchising truth, that the dominion of sin is broken by the death of Christ in which I also died.

How do I know this? Is it because I feel it? Certainly not. How could I feel it? How could I realize it? How could I ever have the self-consciousness of it, while in the body? Impossible. But God tells me I have died in the death of Christ. I believe it. I do not reason about it. I do not stagger at it because I cannot find any evidence of its truth in myself. I take God at His word. I reckon myself to be what He tells me I am. I do not endeavor to struggle, and strive, and work myself into a sinless state which is impossible. Neither do I imagine myself to be in it, which were a deceit and a delusion; but

by a simple, childlike faith, I take the blessed ground which faith assigns me, in association with a dead Christ. I look at Christ there, and see in Him, according to God's Word, the true expression of where I am, in the Divine Presence. I do not reason from myself upwards, but I reason from God downwards.

This makes all the difference. It is just the difference between unbelief and faith—between law and grace—between human religion and divine Christianity. If I reason from self, how can I have any right thought of what is in the heart of God?—all my conclusions must be utterly false. But if, on the other hand, I listen to God and believe His Word, my conclusions are divinely sound. Abraham did not look at himself and the improbability, nay, the impossibility of having a son in his old age; but he believed God and gave glory to Him. And it was counted to Him for righteousness.

It is an unspeakable mercy to get done with self, in all its phases and in all its workings, and to be brought to rest, in all simplicity, on the written Word, and on the Christ which that written Word presents to our souls. Self-occupation is a death-blow to fellowship, and a great barrier to the soul's rest and progress. It is impossible for any one to enjoy settled peace so long as he is occupied with himself. He must cease from self, and harken to God's Word, and rest, without a single question, on its pure, precious, and everlasting record. God's Word never changes. I change; my frames, my feelings, my experience, my circumstances, change continually; but God's Word is the same yesterday, and to-day, and forever.

Furthermore, it is a grand and essential point for the soul to apprehend that Christ is the only definition of the believer's place before God. This gives immense power, liberty, and blessing. "As He is, so are we, in this world" (1 John 4:17). This is something perfectly wonderful! Let us ponder it: let us think of a poor, wretched, guilty slave of sin, a bondslave of Satan, a votary of the world, exposed to an eternal hell—such an one taken up by sovereign grace, delivered completely from the grasp of Satan, the dominion of sin, the power of this present evil world—

pardoned, washed, justified, brought nigh to God, accepted in Christ, and perfectly and forever identified with Him, so that the Holy Ghost can say, as Christ is, so is he in this world!

All this seems too good to be true; and, most assuredly, it is too good for us to get; but, blessed be the God of all grace, and blessed be the Christ of God, it is not too good for Him to give. God gives like Himself. He will be God, spite of our unworthiness and Satan's opposition. He will act in a way worthy of Himself, and worthy of the Son of His love. Were it a question of our deservings, we could only think of the deepest and darkest pit of hell. But seeing it is a question of what is worthy of God to give, and that He gives according to His estimate of the worthiness of Christ, then, verily, we can think of the very highest place in Heaven. The glory of God, and the worthiness of His Son, are involved in His dealings with us; and hence everything that could possibly stand in the way of our eternal blessedness, has been disposed of in such a manner as to secure the divine glory, and furnish a triumphant answer to every plea of the enemy.

Is it a question of trespass? "He has forgiven us all trespasses." Is it a question of sin? He has condemned sin at the cross, and thus put it away. Is it a question of guilt? It is canceled by the blood of the cross. Is it a question of death? He has taken away its sting, and actually made it part of our property. Is it a question of Satan? He has destroyed him, by annulling all his power. Is it a question of the world? He has delivered us from it, and snapped every link which connected us with it.

Thus, it stands with us if we are to be taught by Scripture, if we are to take God at His Word, if we are to believe what He says. And we may add, if it be not thus, we are in our sins; under the power of sin; in the grasp of Satan; obnoxious to death; part and parcel of an evil, Christless, Godless world, and exposed to the unmitigated wrath of God—the vengeance of eternal fire.

Oh that the blessed Spirit may open the eyes of God's people, and give them to see their proper place, their full and eternal deliverance in association with Christ who died for them, and *in whom they have died*, and *thus* passed out of the power of all their enemies!

Part 3

Having glanced at two of the leading points in our subject, namely, Israel freed from guilt under the shelter of the blood, and Israel freed from all their enemies in the passage of the Red Sea, we have now to contemplate for a few moments Israel crossing the Jordan, and celebrating the paschal feast of Gilgal, in which they represent the risen position of Christians now.

The Christian is one who is not only sheltered from judgment by the blood of the Lamb, not only delivered from the power of all his enemies by the death of Christ, but is also associated with Him where He now is, at the right hand of God; he is, with Christ, passed out of death, in resurrection, and is blessed with all spiritual blessings, in the heavenlies, in Christ. He is thus a heavenly man, and, as such, is called to walk in this world in all the varied relationships and responsibilities in which the good hand of God has placed him. He is not a monk, or an ascetic, or a man living in the clouds, fit neither for earth or heaven. He is not one who lives in a dreamy, misty, unpractical region; but, on the contrary, one whose happy privilege it is, from day to day, to reflect, amid the scenes and circumstances of earth, the graces and virtues of Christ, with whom, through infinite grace, and on the solid ground of accomplished redemption, he is linked in the power of the Holy Ghost.

Such is the Christian, according to the teaching of the New Testament. Let the reader see that he understands it. It is very real, very definite, very positive, very practical. A child may know it, and realize it, and exhibit it. A Christian is one whose sins are forgiven, who possesses eternal life, and knows it; in whom the Holy Ghost dwells; he is accepted in and associated with a risen and glorified Christ; he has broken with the world, is dead to sin and the law, and finds his object and his delight, and his spiritual sustenance, in the Christ who loved him and gave Himself for him, and for whose coming he waits every day of his life.

This, we repeat, is the New Testament description of a Christian. How immensely it differs from the ordinary type of Christian profession around us we need not say. But let the reader measure himself by the divine standard, and see wherein he comes short; for of this he may rest assured, that there is no reason whatsoever, so far as the love of God, or the work of Christ, or the testimony of the Holy Ghost, is concerned, why he should not be in the full enjoyment of all the rich and rare spiritual blessings which appertain to the true Christian position. Dark unbelief, fed by legality, bad teaching, and spurious religiousness, rob many of God's dear children of their proper place and portion. And not only so, but, from want of a thorough break with the world, many are sadly hindered from the clear perception and full realization of their position and privileges as heavenly men.

But we are rather anticipating the instruction unfolded to us in the typical history of Israel, in Josh. 3—5, to which we shall now turn. "And Joshua rose early in the morning; and they removed from Shittim, and came to Jordan, he and all the children of Israel, and lodged there before they passed over. And it came to pass, after three days, that the officers went through the host. And they commanded the people, saying, When ye see the ark of the covenant of the Lord your God, and the priests the Levites bearing it, then ye shall remove from your place, and go after it. *Yet there shall be a space between you and it*, about two thousand cubits by measure: *come not near unto it, that ye may know the way by which ye must go; for ye have not passed this way heretofore*" (Josh. 3:1-4).

It is most desirable that the reader should, with all simplicity and clearness, seize the true spiritual import of the river Jordan. It typifies the death of Christ in one of its grand aspects, just as the Red Sea typifies it in another. When the children of Israel stood on the wilderness side of the Red Sea, they sang the song of redemption. They were a delivered people—delivered from Egypt and the power of Pharaoh. They saw all their enemies dead on the seashore. They could even anticipate, in glowing accents, their triumphal entrance into the promised land. "Thou in Thy mercy hast led forth the people which Thou hast redeemed; Thou hast guided them in Thy strength unto Thy holy habitation. The people shall hear, and be afraid: sorrow shall take hold on the inhabitants of Palestina. Then the dukes of Edom shall be amazed; the mighty men of Moab, trembling shall take hold upon them: all the inhabitants of Canaan shall melt away. Fear and dread shall fall upon them; by the greatness of Thine arm they shall be still as a stone; till Thy people pass over, O Lord, till the people pass over which Thou hast purchased. Thou shalt bring them in, and plant them in the mountain of Thine inheritance, in the place, O Lord, which Thou hast made for Thee to dwell in; in the sanctuary, O Lord, which Thy hands have established. The Lord shall reign for ever and ever" (Exod. 15:13-18).

All this was perfectly magnificent, and divinely true. But they were not yet in Canaan. Jordan—of which, most surely, there is no mention in their glorious song of victory—lay between them and the promised land. True, in the purpose of God and in the judgment of faith, the land was theirs; but they had to traverse the wilderness, cross the Jordan, and take possession.

How constantly we see all this exemplified in the history of souls! When first converted, there is nothing but joy and victory and praise. They know their sins forgiven; they are filled with wonder, love, and praise. Being justified by faith, they have peace with God, and they can rejoice in hope of His glory, yea, and joy in Himself through Jesus Christ our Lord. They are in Rom. 5:1-11; and, in one sense, there can be nothing higher. Even in Heaven itself we shall have nothing higher or better than "joy in God." Persons sometimes speak of Rom. 8 being higher than Rom. 5: but what can be higher than "joy in God"? If we are brought to God, we have reached the most exalted point to which any soul can come. To know Him as our portion, our rest, our stay, our object, our all; to have all our springs in Him, and know Him as a perfect covering for our eyes, at all times, and in all places, and under all circumstances—this is heaven itself to the believer.

But there is this difference between Rom. 5 and 8, that 6 and 7 lie between; and when the soul has traveled practically through these latter, and learns how to apply their profound and precious teaching to the great questions of indwelling sin and the law, then it is in a better state, though, most assuredly, not in a higher standing.

We repeat, and with emphasis, the words "*traveled practically.*" For it must be even so, if we would really enter into these holy mysteries according to God. It is easy to talk about being "dead to sin" and "dead to the law"—easy to see these things written in Rom. 6 and 7—easy to grasp, in the intellect, the mere theory of these things. But the question is, have we made them our own—have they been applied practically to our souls by the power of the Holy Ghost? Are they livingly exhibited in our ways to the glory of Him who, at such a cost to Himself, has brought us into such a marvelous place of blessing and privilege?

It is much to be feared that there is a vast amount of merely intellectual traffic in these deep and precious mysteries of our most holy faith, which, if only laid hold of in spiritual power, would produce wonderful results in practice.

But we must return to our theme; and in doing so, we would ask the reader if he really understands the true spiritual import of the river Jordan? What does it really mean? We have said that it typifies the death of Christ. But in what aspect? for that precious death, as we are now considering, has many and various aspects. We believe the Jordan sets forth the death of our Lord Jesus Christ as that by which we are introduced into the inheritance He has obtained for us. The Red Sea *delivered Israel from* Egypt and the power of Pharaoh. Jordan *brought them into* the land of Canaan.

We find both in the death of Christ. He, blessed be His name, has, by His death on the cross—His death for us—delivered us from our sins, from their guilt and condemnation, from Satan's power, and from this present evil world.

But more than this: He has, by the same infinitely precious work, brought us *now* into an entirely new position, in resurrection and in living union and association with Himself, where He is at God's right hand. Such is the distinct teaching of Eph. 2. "But God, who is rich in mercy, for His great love wherewith He loved us, even when we were dead in sins, *hath quickened us together with Christ,* (by grace ye are saved;) and *hath raised us up together,* and made us *sit together in the heavenlies* in Christ Jesus" (vers. 4-6).

Note the little word "*hath.*" He is not speaking of what God *will* do, but of what He *hath* done—done for us, and with us, in Christ Jesus. The believer has not to wait till he passes out of this life to enjoy his inheritance in Heaven. In the person of his living and glorified Head, through faith, by the Spirit, he belongs there now, and is free to all that God has given to all His own.*

Is all this real and true? Yes! As real and true as that Christ hung on the cross and lay

---

* There are three very distinct aspects of the death of Christ which, to apprehend clearly, is of unspeakable value to the soul.

1. That which is typified in the blood of the paschal lamb on Israel's doors in Egypt. This is the judgment of God against the sinner in the person of the Substitute provided for him. Rom. 3: 23-27 applies to this.

It brings peace to the soul who believes, for his judgment is passed. Christ has borne it in our stead.

2. As revealed at the passage of the Red Sea. There it is fully manifested that God is *for* His people; He has completely overcome their enemy and freed them from his power forever. The prince and his hosts, who ruled over them unto death, are drowned in the sea. God's people have passed out of his dominions, and can now go on with God in perfect freedom. No condemnation remains. Henceforth, in faith, Satan is a vanquished foe. God's people are delivered; they can now, in settled peace, worship, praise, and serve their God. Blessed, holy deliverance and service! Rom. 6—7 gives the full teaching of this aspect of the death of Christ.

3. As seen in the passage of Jordan. There is no judgment to escape there; no foe pressing behind. It is a question of entering the good land which is just across. It is the death of Christ here as *the ending of His people's history as children of Adam*; that, by resurrection, He may now introduce them, as having died and risen with Him, into the place of glory where He has gone. By this it can be said, "As He is, so are we in this world" (1 John 4:17).

Col. 2:10—3:4, is the New Testament doctrine of this precious truth. [Ed.]

in the grave; as real and true as that we were dead in trespasses and sins; as real and true as the truth of God can make it; as real and true as the indwelling of the Holy Spirit in the body of every true believer.

Mark, we are not now speaking of the practical working-out of all this glorious truth in the life of Christians from day to day. This is another thing altogether. Alas, if our only idea of true Christian position were to be drawn from the practical career of professing Christians, we might give up Christianity as a myth or a sham.

But, thank God, it is not so. We must learn what true Christianity is from the pages of the New Testament, and, having learnt it there, judge ourselves, our ways, our surroundings, by its heavenly light. In this way, while we shall ever have to confess and mourn our shortcomings, our hearts shall ever, more and more, be filled with praise to Him whose infinite grace has brought us into such a glorious position, in union and fellowship with His own Son—a position, blessed be God, in nowise dependent upon our personal state, but which, if really apprehended, must exert a powerful influence upon our entire course, conduct, and character.

Part 4

The more deeply we ponder the typical instruction presented in the river Jordan, the more clearly we must see that the whole Christian position is involved in the standpoint from which we view it. Jordan means death, but, for the believer, a death that is *past*—the death we have gone through as identified with Christ, and which, through resurrection, has brought us on the other side—the Canaan side—where He is now. He, typified by the ark, has passed over before us into Jordan, to stem its torrent for us, and make it a dry path for our feet, so that we might pass clean over into our heavenly inheritance. The Prince of Life has destroyed, on our behalf, him that had the power of death. He has taken the sting from death; yea, He has made death itself the very means by which we reach, even now, in spirit and by faith, the true heavenly Canaan.

Let us see how all this is unfolded in our type. Mark particularly the commandment given by the officers of the host. "When ye see the ark of the covenant of the Lord your God, and the priests the Levites bearing it, then ye shall remove from your place, and go after it." The ark must go first. They dared not to move one inch along that mysterious way, until the symbol of the divine Presence had gone before.

"Yet there shall be a space between you and it, about two thousand cubits by measure: *come not near unto it that ye may know the way by which ye must go;* for ye have *not passed this way heretofore.*" It was an awful flood ahead of them. No mortal could tread it with impunity. Death and destruction are linked together. "It is appointed unto men once to die; but after this the judgment" (Heb. 9). Who can stand before the king of terrors? Who can face that grim and terrible foe? Who can encounter the swellings of Jordan? Who, except the Ark go first, can face death and judgment? Poor Peter thought he could; but he was sadly mistaken. He said unto Jesus, "Lord, whither goest thou? Jesus answered him, Whither I go, *thou canst not follow Me now;* but thou shalt follow Me afterwards."

How fully these words explain the import of that mystic "space" between Israel and the ark. Peter did not understand that space. He had not studied aright Josh. 3:4. He knew nothing of that terrible pathway which his blessed Master was about to enter upon. "Peter said unto Him, Lord, why cannot I follow Thee now? I will lay down my life for Thy sake."

Poor dear Peter! How little he knew of himself, or of that which he was—sincerely, no doubt, though ignorantly—undertaking to do! How little did he imagine that the very sound of death's dark river, heard even in the distance, would be sufficient so to terrify him, as to make him curse and swear that he did not know his Master! "Jesus answered him, Wilt thou lay down thy life for My sake? Verily, verily, I say unto thee, the cock shall not crow till thou hast denied Me thrice."

"Yet there shall be a space between you and it." How needful! How absolutely essential! Truly there was a space between Peter and his Lord. Jesus had to go before. He had to meet death in its most terrific form. He had to tread that rough path in profound solitude—for who could accompany Him? "There shall be a space between you and it: come not near to it, that ye may know the way by which ye must go; for ye have not passed this way heretofore."

"Thou canst not follow Me *now:* but thou shalt follow Me *afterwards."* Blessed Master! He would not suffer His poor feeble servant to enter upon that terrible path, until He Himself had gone before, and so entirely changed its character, that the pathway of death should be lighted up with the beams of life and the light of God's face. Our Jesus has "abolished death, and brought life and incorruptibility to light by the gospel."

Thus death is no longer death to the believer. It was death to Jesus, in all its intensity, in all its horrors, in all its reality. He met it as the power which Satan wields over the soul of man. He met it as the penalty due to sin. He met it as the just judgment of God against sin—against us. There was not a single feature, not a single ingredient, not a single circumstance, which could possibly render death formidable which did not enter into the death of Christ. He met all; and, blessed be God, *we are accounted as having gone through all in and by Him.* We died in Him, so that death has no further claim upon us, or power over us. Its claims are disposed of, its power broken and gone for all believers. The whole scene is cleared completely of death, and filled with life and incorruptibility.

And hence, in Peter's case, we find our Lord, in the last chapter of John, most graciously meeting the desire of His servant's heart—a desire in which he was perfectly sincere—the desire to follow his beloved Lord. "Verily, verily, I say unto thee, When thou wast young, thou girdest thyself, and walkedst whither thou wouldest; but when thou shalt be old, thou shalt stretch forth thy hands, and another shall gird thee, and carry thee whither thou wouldest not.

This spake He signifying by what death he should glorify God." Thus death, instead of being the judgment of God to overwhelm Peter, was turned into a means by which Peter could glorify God.

What a glorious change! What a stupendous mystery! How it magnifies the cross, or rather the One who hung thereon! What a might revolution, when a poor sinful man can, by death, glorify God! So completely has death been robbed of its sting, so thoroughly has its character been changed that, instead of shrinking from it with terror, we can meet it, if it does come, and go through it with song of victory; and instead of its being to us the wages of sin, it is a means by which we can glorify God. All praise to Him who has so wrought for us! to Him who has gone down into Jordan's deepest depths for us, and made there a highway by which His ransomed people can pass over into their heavenly inheritance! May our hearts adore Him! May all our powers be stirred up to magnify His holy name! May our whole life be devoted to His praise! May we appreciate the grace and lay hold of the inheritance.

But we must proceed with our type.

"And Joshua spake unto the priests, saying, Take up the ark of the covenant, and pass over before the people. And they took up the ark of the convenant, and went before the people. And the Lord said unto Joshua, This day will I begin to magnify thee in the sight of all Israel, that they may know that as I was with Moses, so I will be with thee." Joshua stands before us as a type of the risen Christ, leading His people, in the power of the Holy Ghost, into their heavenly inheritance. The priests bearing the ark into the midst of Jordan typify Christ going down into death for us, and destroying completely its power. "He passed through death's dark raging flood, to make our rest secure"; and not only to make it secure, but to lead us into it, in association with Himself, now, in spirit and by faith; by-and-by, in actual fact.

"And Joshua said unto the children of Israel, Come hither, and hear the words of the Lord your God. And Joshua said, Hereby ye shall know that the *living* God is among you, and that He will without fail drive out from before you the Canaanites. . . . Behold, the ark of the covenant of the Lord of all the earth passeth over before you into Jordan."

The passage of the ark into Jordan proved two things, namely, the presence of the living God in the midst of His people; and that He would most surely drive out all their enemies from before them. The death of Christ is the basis and the guarantee of everything to faith. Grant us but this, that Christ has gone down into death for us, and we argue, with all possible confidence, that, in this one great fact, all is secured. God is with us, and God is for us. "He that spared not His own Son, but delivered Him up for us all, how shall He not with Him also freely give us all things?" The difficulty of unbelief is, "How shall He?" The difficulty of faith is, "How shall He *not?*"

Israel might wonder how all the hosts of Canaan could ever be expelled from before them: let them gaze on the ark in the midst of Jordan, and cease to wonder, cease to doubt. The less is included in the greater. And hence we can say, What may we not expect, seeing that Christ has died for us? There is nothing too good, nothing too great, nothing too glorious, for God to do for us, and in us, and with us, seeing He has not spared His only-begotten Son, but delivered Him up for us all. Everything is secured for us by the precious death of Christ. It has opened up the everlasting floodgates of the love of God, so that the rich streams thereof might flow down into the very depths of our souls. It fills us with the sweetest assurance that the One who could bruise His only-begotten Son, on the cursed tree, for us, will meet our every need, carry us through all our difficulties, and lead us into the full possession and enjoyment of all that His eternal purpose of grace has in store for us. Having given us such a proof of His love, even when we were yet sinners, what may we not expect at His hands now that He views us in association with that blessed One who glorified Him in death—the death that He died for us? When Israel saw the ark in the midst of Jordan, they were entitled to consider that all was secured. As our Lord also said to His disciples before leaving them, "Be of good cheer, I have

overcome the world"; and, in view of His cross, He would say, "Now is the prince of this world cast out." True, Israel had, as we know, to take possession: they had to plant their feet upon the inheritance; but the power that could stem death's dark waters, could also drive out every foe from before them, and put them in peaceful possession of all that God had promised.

Part 5

In closing these meditations on Gilgal, we must turn our thoughts to the practical application of that which has been engaging our attention. If it be true—and it is true—that Jesus died for us, it is equally true that we have died in Him; as one of our own poets has sweetly put it:

> For me, Lord Jesus, Thou hast died
>   And I have died in Thee:
> Thou'rt risen—my bands are all untied,
>   And now Thou livest in me.
> The Father's face of radiant grace
>   Shines now in light on me.

Now this is a great practical truth—none more so. It lies at the very foundation of all true Christianity. If Christ has died for us, then, in very deed, He has taken us completely out of our old condition, with all that appertained to it, and placed us upon an entirely new footing. We can look back from resurrection-ground on which we now stand, into the dark river of death, and see there, in its deepest depths, the memorial of the victory gained for us by the Prince of Life. We do not look forward to death; we look back at it. We can truly say, "The bitterness of death is past."

Jesus met death for us in its most terrible form. Just as the river of Jordan was divided when it presented its most formidable appearance—"for Jordan overfloweth all its banks all the time of harvest"—so our Jesus encountered our last great enemy, vanquished him in the most fearful form, and left behind, in the very centre of death's dark domain, the imperishable record of His glorious victory. All praise, homage, and adoration to His peerless name! It is our privilege, by faith and in spirit, to stand on Canaan's side of Jordan, and erect our memorial of what the Saviour, the true Joshua, has done for us.

"And it came to pass, when all the people were clean passed over Jordan, that the Lord spake unto Joshua, saying, Take you twelve men out of the people, *out of every tribe a man*. And command ye them, saying, Take you hence out of the midst of Jordan, *out of the place where the priests' feet stood firm*, twelve stones; and ye shall carry them over with you, and leave them in the lodging-place where ye shall lodge this night. Then Joshua called the twelve men whom he had prepared of the children of Israel, *out of every tribe a man*. And Joshua said unto them, Pass over before the ark of the Lord your God, into the midst of Jordan, and take you up *every man of you* a stone upon his shoulder, according unto the number of the tribes of the children of Israel: that this may be a sign among you, that when your children ask their fathers in time to come, saying, What mean ye by these stones? then ye shall answer them, That the waters of Jordan were cut off before the ark of the covenant of the Lord; when it passed over Jordan, the waters of Jordan were cut off: and these stones shall be *for a memorial* unto the children of Israel for ever" (Josh. 4:1-7).

The great fact was to be seized, and practically carried out by the whole assembly, "of every tribe a man"—"every man of you a stone upon his shoulder," a stone taken from the very spot where the priests' feet stood firm. All were to be brought into living personal contact with the great mysterious fact that the waters of Jordan were cut off. All were to engage in erecting such a memorial of this fact as should elicit inquiry from their children as to what it meant. It was never to be forgotton.

What a lesson is here for us! Are we erecting our memorial? Are we giving evidence—such evidence as may strike even the mind of a child—of the fact that our Jesus has vanquished the power of death for us? Are we affording any practical proof in daily life that Christ has died for us, and that we have died in Him? Is there aught in our actual history, from day to day, answering to the figure set forth in the passage just quoted—"every man of you a stone upon his shoulder"? Are we declaring plainly that we have passed clean over Jordon—that we belong to Heaven—that we are not in the flesh, but in the Spirit? Do our children see aught in our habits and ways, in our spirit and deportment, in our whole character and manner of life, leading them to inquire, "What mean ye by these things?" Are we living as those who are dead with Christ—dead to sin—dead to the world? Are we practically freed from the world—letting go our hold of present things, in the power of communion with a risen Christ?

These are searching questions for the soul. Let us seek to meet them honestly, as in the Divine Presence. We profess these things, we hold them in theory. We say we believe that Jesus died for us, and that we died in Him. Where is the proof—where the abiding memorial—where the stone on the shoulder? Let us judge ourselves honestly before God. Let us no longer rest satisfied with anything short of the thorough, practical, habitual carrying out of the great truth that "we are dead, and our life is hid with Christ in God." Mere profession is worthless. We want the living power—the true result—the proper fruit.

"And the people came up out of Jordan on the tenth day of the first month, and encamped in Gilgal, in the east border of Jericho. And *those twelve stones which they took out of Jordan*"—stones of peculiar import—no other stones could tell such a tale, teach such a lesson, or symbolize such a stupendous fact—no other stones like them—"those twelve stones did Joshua pitch in Gilgal. And he spake unto the children of Israel, saying, When your children shall ask their fathers in time to come, saying, What mean these stones? then ye shall let your children know, saying, *Israel came over this Jordan on dry land*. For the Lord your God dried up the waters of Jordan from before you, until ye were passed over, as the Lord your God did to the Red Sea, which He dried up from before us, until we were gone over: that all the people of the earth might know the hand of the Lord, that it is mighty: that ye might fear the Lord your God forever."

Here, then, we see Israel at Gilgal. "Everything was finished that the Lord commanded Joshua to speak unto the people, according to all that Moses commanded Joshua." Every member of the host had passed clean over Jordan—not one had been suffered to feel the slightest touch of the river of death. Grace had brought them all safely over into the inheritance promised to their fathers. They were not only separated from Egypt by the Red Sea, but actually brought into Canaan across the dry bed of the Jordan, and encamped in Gilgal, in the plains of Jericho.

Now mark what follows. "And it came to pass, when all the kings of the Amorites which were on the side of Jordan westward, and all the kings of the Canaanites which were by the sea, heard that the Lord had dried up the waters of Jordan from before the children of Israel, until we were passed over, that their heart melted, neither was there spirit in them any more, because of the children of Israel. *At that time*"—note the words!—when all the nations were paralyzed with terror at the very thought of this people— "at that time the Lord said unto Joshua, Make thee *sharp knives*, and circumcise again the children of Israel the second time."

How deeply significant is this! How suggestive are these "sharp knives"! How needful! If Israel are about to bring the sword upon the Canaanites, Israel must have the sharp knife applied to themselves. They had never been circumcised in the wilderness. The reproach of Egypt had never been rolled away from them. And ere they could celebrate the passover, and eat of the old corn of the land of Canaan, they must have the sentence of death written upon them. No doubt this was aught but agreeable to nature; but it must be done. How could they take possession of Canaan with the reproach of Egypt resting upon them? How could uncircumcised people dispossess the Canaanites? Impossible! The sharp knives had to do their work throughout the camp of Israel ere they could eat of Canaan's food or prosecute the warfare which of necessity belongs to it.

"And Joshua made him sharp knives, and circumcised the children of Israel at the hill of the foreskins. And this is the cause why Joshua did circumcise. All the people that came out of Egypt that were males, even all the men of war, died in the wilderness by the way, after they came out of Egypt. . . . And their children, whom he raised up in their stead, them Joshua circumcised: for they were uncircumcised, because they had not circumcised them by the way. . . . And the Lord said unto Joshua, This day have I rolled away the reproach of Egypt from off you. Wherefore the name of the place is called Gilgal ["rolling"] unto this day. And the children of Israel encamped in Gilgal, and kept the passover on the fourteenth day of the month, at even, in the plains of Jericho. And they did eat of the old corn of the land on the morrow after the passover, unleavened cakes and parched corn, in the selfsame day. And the manna ceased on the morrow after they had eaten of the old corn of the land; neither had the children of Israel manna any more; but they did eat of the fruit of the land of Canaan that year."

Here, then, we have a type of the full Christian position. The Christian is a heavenly man, dead to the world, crucified with Christ, associated with Him where He now is, and, while waiting for His appearing, occupied in heart with Him, feeding by faith upon Him as the proper nourishment of the new man.

Such is the Christian's position—such his portion. But in order to enter fully into the enjoyment thereof, there must be the application of the "sharp knife" to all that belongs to mere nature. There must be the sentence of death written upon that which Scripture designates as "the old man."

All this must be really and practically entered into if we would maintain our position or enjoy our proper portion as heavenly men. If we are indulging nature; if we are living in a low, worldly atmosphere; if we are going in for this world's pursuits, its pleasures, its politics, its riches, its honors, its fashions, and its distinctions—then, verily, it is impossible that we can be enjoying fellowship with our risen Head and Lord.* Christ is in Heaven, and to enjoy Him we must be living, in spirit and by faith, where He is. He is not of this world; and if we are of it, we cannot be enjoying fellowship with Him. "If we say that we have fellowship with Him, and walk in darkness, we lie, and do not the truth" (1 John 1: 6).

This is most solemn. If I am living in and of the world, I am walking in darkness, and I can have no fellowship with a heavenly Christ. "Wherefore," says the blessed apostle, "if ye be dead with Christ from the rudiments of the world, why, *as though living in the world*, are ye subject to ordinances?" Do we really understand these words? Have we weighed the full force of the expression, "living in the world"? Is the Christian not to be as one living in the world? Clearly not. He is to live, in spirit, where Christ is. As to fact, he is obviously on this earth, moving up and down, and in and out, in the varied relations of life, and in the varied spheres of action in which the hand of God has set him. But his home is in Heaven. His life is there. His object, his rest, his proper *all*, is in Heaven. He does not belong to earth. His citizenship is in Heaven; and in order to make this good in practice from day to day, there must be the denial of self, the mortification of our members.

All this comes vividly out in Col. 3. Indeed, it would be impossible to give a more striking exposition of the entire subject of "Gilgal" than that presented in the following lines: "If ye then be risen with Christ, seek those things which are above, where Christ sitteth on the right hand of God. Set your affections on things above, not on things on the earth. For ye have died, and your life is hid with Christ in God. When Christ our life shall appear, then shall ye also appear with Him in glory." And now comes the true spiritual import and application of "Gilgal" and its "sharp knives"—"Mortify, therefore, your members which are upon the earth."

May the Holy Spirit lead us into a deeper and fuller understanding of our place, portion and practice as Christians. Would to God that we better knew what it is to feed upon the old corn of the land, at the true spiritual Gilgal, that thus we might be better fitted for the conflict and service to which we are called!

---

* The reader may here remark that "the old corn of the land of Canaan" is a type of Christ risen and glorified. The manna is a type of Christ in His humiliation. The remembrance of Him in the latter is ineffably precious to the soul. It is sweet to look back and trace His way as the lowly, humble, self emptied man. This is to feed upon the hidden manna—"Christ, once humbled here." Nevertheless, a risen, ascended and glorified Christ is the true object for the heart of the Christian; but to enjoy Him there, the reproach of this present evil world—all conformity to it—must be rolled away from us by the spiritual application of the circumcision of Christ. He was not conformed to this world, and we must be prepared to identify ourselves with Him in this.

GIDEON AND HIS COMPANIONS

Judges 6—8

Part 1

IN STUDYING THE HISTORY of the nation of Israel, we notice two distinct eras, namely, the era of *unity*, and the era of *individuality*—the period in which the twelve tribes acted as one man, and the period in the which one man was called to act for the twelve tribes. We may take the book of Joshua as illustrating the former; and the book of Judges as a sample of the latter. The most cursory reader cannot fail to discern the difference between these two books. The one is characterized by external power and glory; the other, by weakness and failure. Power is stamped on the former, ruin on the latter. In that, Jehovah gives the land to Israel; in this, Israel fails to take the land from Jehovah.

Now, all this is expressed in the two words which may be regarded as the motto of the two books, namely, "Gilgal" and "Bochim." In the book of Joshua we find the congregation always starting from Gilgal to prosecute the war, and returning thither to celebrate their victory. Gilgal was their centre, because there they were circumcised; and there the reproach of Egypt was rolled away (see Josh. 5: 9-10).

But no sooner have we opened the book of Judges than the eye rests upon the sad record, "The angel of the Lord came up *from Gilgal to Bochim*, and said, I made you to go up out of Egypt, and have brought you unto the land which I sware unto your fathers; and I said, I will never break my covenant with you. And ye shall make no league with the inhabitants of this land; ye shall throw down their altars, but ye have not obeyed my voice; why have ye done this? Wherefore I also said, I will not drive them out from before you; but they shall be as thorns in your sides, and their gods shall be a snare unto you. And it came to pass, when the angel of the Lord spake these words unto all the children of Israel, that the people lifted up their voice, and wept. And they called the name of that place Bochim, that is, weepers; and they sacrificed there unto the Lord" (Judges 2: 1-5).

Here, then, we have, very remarkably, the contrast between the two books of Joshua and Judges—the book of unity and the book of individuality—the book of external power and glory, and the book of internal weakness, failure, and ruin. Alas! the glory speedily departed. Israel's national greatness soon faded away. "The people served the Lord all the days of Joshua, and all the days of the elders that outlived Joshua, who had seen all the great works of the Lord, that He did for Israel. And Joshua the son of Nun, the servant of the Lord, died, being an hundred and ten years old . . . . And also all that generation were gathered unto their fathers: and there arose another generation after them, which knew not the Lord, nor yet the works which He had done for Israel. And the children of Israel did evil in the sight of the Lord, and served Baalim . . . . And they

forsook the Lord, and served Baal and Ashtaroth. And the anger of the Lord was hot against Israel, and He delivered them into the hands of spoilers that spoiled them, and He sold them into the hands of their enemies round about, so that they could not any longer stand before their enemies. Whithersoever they went out, the hand of the Lord was against them for evil, as the Lord had said, and as the Lord had sworn unto them; and they were greatly distressed."

This, truly, is a gloomy and humiliating record. Joshua's sword was sheathed. Those bright days in the which he had led Israel's compact host to splendid victories over the kings of Canaan, were passed and gone. The moral influence of Joshua and of the elders that survived him had passed away, and the whole nation had rushed, with terrible avidity, into the gross moral evils and abominable idolatries of those nations whom they ought to have driven out from before them. In a word, the ruin was complete, so far as Israel was concerned. Like Adam, in the garden; and Noah, in the restored earth; so Israel, in the land of Canaan, utterly failed. Adam ate the forbidden fruit; Noah got drunk; and Israel bowed before the altars of Baal.

Thus much as to man. But, thank God, there is another side of the picture. There is what we may call a bright and beauteous "*Nevertheless*"; for God will be God, no matter what man may prove himself to be. This is an unspeakable relief and consolation to the heart. God abideth faithful. Here is faith's stronghold, come what may. God is always to be counted upon, spite of all man's failure and shortcoming. His goodness and faithfulness form the resource and the refuge of the soul amid the darkest scenes of human history.

This soul-sustaining truth shines out with remarkable lustre in the very passage from which we have just given such a depressing quotation. "Nevertheless, the Lord raised up judges, which delivered them out of the hand of those that spoiled them." But mark the following words, so illustrative of the individuality of the book of Judges: "And when the Lord raised them up judges, then *the Lord was with the judge*, and delivered them out of the hand of their enemies *all the days of the judge:* for it repented the Lord because of their groanings by reason of them that oppressed them and vexed them" (Judges 2:16-18).

In these last quoted words, we have the great root principle of the book of Judges—the divine secret of the ministry of the Baraks, the Gideons, the Jephthahs, and the Samsons, the record of whose ministry occupies so large a portion of this most interesting section of inspiration. Israel had failed—sadly, shamefully, inexcusably failed. They had forfeited all claims to the protection of Jehovah's shield. They were justly given over into the ruthless hands of the kings of Canaan. As to all this there could be no possible question. "Nevertheless" Jehovah's heart could feel for His poor, oppressed, and groaning Israel. True, they had proved themselves naughty and unworthy, yet His ear was ever ready to catch their very earliest groan; yea, we are even told, in chapter 10, that "His soul was grieved for the misery of Israel."

What touching words! What tenderness! What deep compassion! How such a statement lets us into the profound depths of the heart of God! The misery of His people moved the loving heart of Jehovah. The very faintest and earliest symptoms of brokenness and contrition, on the part of Israel, met with a ready and gracious response, on the part of Israel's God. It mattered not how far they had wandered, how deeply they had sunk, or how grievously they had sinned; God was ever ready to welcome the feeblest breathings of a broken heart. The springs of divine mercy and compassion are absolutely inexhaustible. The ocean of His love is boundless and unfathomable; and hence, the very moment His people take the place of confession, He enters the place of forgiveness. He delights to pardon, according to the largeness of His heart, and according to the glory of His own Name. He finds His peculiar joy in blotting out transgressions, in healing, restoring, and blessing, in a manner worthy of Himself.

This glorious truth shines in the history of Israel; it shines in the history of the Church; and it shines in the history of every individual believer.

But we turn to our immediate subject, namely, "Gideon and his companions," as presented in Judges 6—8. May the eternal Spirit unfold and apply its precious contents to our souls!

Chapter 6 opens with a very sad and depressing record—a record only too characteristic of Israel's entire history: "And the children of Israel did evil in the sight of the Lord; and the Lord delivered them into the hand of Midian seven years. And the hand of Midian prevailed against Israel; and because of the Midianites the children of Israel made them the dens which are in the mountains, and caves, and strongholds." What a humiliating picture! What a contrast to the conquering host that had crossed the Jordan and walked across the ruins of Jericho! How sad, how humbling, to think of Israel crouching and hiding in the dens and caves of the mountains, through the terror of the uncircumcised Midianites!

It is well for us to consider this picture, and receive its salutary lesson. Israel's power and glory consisted simply in having the presence of God with them. Without that, they were as water spilt upon the ground, or the autumn leaf before the blast. But the divine presence could not be enjoyed in connection with allowed evil; and therefore, when Israel forgot their Lord, and wandered away from Him into the forbidden paths of idolatry, He had to recall them to their senses by stretching out His governmental rod, and causing them to feel the crushing power of one or another of the nations around.

Now all this has a voice and a lesson for us. So long as God's people walk with Him in holy obedience, they have nothing to fear. They are perfectly safe from the snares and assaults of all their spiritual foes. Nought can, by any means, harm them while they abide in the shelter of God's own presence. But, clearly, that presence demands and secures holiness. Unjudged evil cannot dwell there. To live in sin and talk of security—to attempt to connect the presence of God with sanctioned evil—is wickedness of the deepest dye. No, it must not be! "God is greatly to be feared in the assembly of the saints; and to be had in reverence of all them that are round about Him." "Thy testimonies are very sure; holiness becometh Thy house, O Lord, forever."

If God's people forget these wholesome truths, He knows how to recall them to their remembrance by the rod of discipline; and, blessed forever be His name, He loves them too well to spare that rod, however reluctant He may be to use it. "Whom the Lord loveth He chasteneth, and scourgeth every son whom He receiveth. If ye endure chastening, God dealeth with you as with sons: for what son is he whom the father chasteneth not? But if ye be without chastisement, whereof all are partakers, then are ye bastards, and not sons. Furthermore, we have had fathers of our flesh, which corrected us, and we gave them reverence: shall we not much rather be in subjection unto the Father of spirits, and live? For they verily for a few days chastened us after their own pleasure; but He for our profit, that we might be partakers of His holiness. Now no chastening for the present seemeth to be joyous, but grievous; nevertheless afterward it yieldeth the peaceable fruit of righteousness unto them which are exercised thereby. *Wherefore lift up the hands which hang down, and the feeble knees"* (Hebrews 12: 6-12).

These are encouraging words for the people of God, at all times. The discipline may be—no doubt is—painful; but when we know a Father's hand is in it, and when we realize what His object is, we can pass through the trial with exercised hearts, and thus reap the peaceable fruits of righteousness. On the other hand, if we meet the discipline with an impatient spirit, a rebellious will, an unsubdued mind, we only render it necessary for the pressure to be continued and augmented, for our loving Father will never let us alone. He will have us in holy subjection to Himself, cost what it may. He graciously takes our part against ourselves, subdues the proud risings of our will, and crushes all that in us which hinders our growth in holiness, grace, and divine knowledge.

Oh! what infinite grace shines in the fact that our God occupies Himself with our very failure and follies, our waywardness and wilfulness, our sins and shortcomings, in order to deliver us from them! He knows all about us. He understands and takes into account all our surroundings and all our inward tendencies, and He deals with us in infinite wisdom and perfect patience, keeping ever before Him that one gracious object, to make us partakers of His holiness, and—wondrous thought!—to bring out in us the expression of His own nature and character. Surely, then, in the presence of such abounding grace and mercy, we may well "lift up the hands that hang down, and the feeble knees."

Part 2

There is one truth which shines out with uncommon lustre in the book of Judges, and that is, that God is ever to be counted upon, even amid the darkest scenes of human history; and, moreover, faith can always count upon God; God never fails a trusting heart—no, never. He never has failed, never will, never can fail the individual soul that confides in Him, that takes hold of His precious word, in the artless simplicity of a faith that trusts Him in the face of man's deepest failure and shortcoming.

This is most consolatory and encouraging, at all times, and under all circumstances. True it is—alas! how true! man fails in everything. Trace him where you will; mark him in whatever sphere of action or responsibility he occupies, and it is the same sad tale, over and over again, of unfaithfulness, failure, and ruin. Let man be set up in business, as often as he may, with the largest capital and the fairest prospects, and he is sure to become a bankrupt. It has ever been so, from the days of Eden down to the present moment. We may assert, without fear of contradiction, that there has not been one solitary exception to the dismal rule, in the history of Adam's fallen race. We must never forget this. True faith never forgets it. It would be the blindest folly to attempt to ignore the fact that *ruin* is stamped, in characters deep and broad, upon the entire of man's story, from first to last.

But, in the face of all this, God abideth faithful. He cannot deny Himself. Here is the resource and the resting-place of faith. It recognizes and owns the ruin; but it counts on God. Faith is not blind to human failure; but it fixes its gaze on divine faithfulness. It confesses the ruin of man; but it counts on the resources of God.

Now, all this comes strikingly out in the interesting and instructive story of Gideon. He, truly, was made to realize, in his own person and experience, the fact of Israel's fallen condition. The contrast between Joshua and Gideon is as striking as can be, so far as regards the question of their condition and circumstances. Joshua could place his foot on the necks of the kings of Canaan. Gideon had to thrash his wheat in a corner to hide it from the Midianites. The day of Joshua was marked by splendid victories; the day of Gideon was a day of small things. But the day of small things for man is the day of great things for God. So Gideon found it. True, it was not permitted him to witness the sun and moon arrested in their course, or the cities of the uncircumcised levelled with the ground. His was a day of barley cakes and broken pitchers, not of astounding miracles and brilliant achievements. But God was with him; and this was enough. "There came an angel of the Lord, and sat under an oak which was in Ophrah, that pertained unto Joash the Abiezrite; and his son Gideon threshed wheat by the winepress, to hide it from the Midianites. And the angel of the Lord appeared unto him, and said unto him, The Lord is with thee, *thou mighty man of valor*" (Judges 6:11-12).

What words were these to fall upon the ear of Gideon, cowering in the winepress, through fear of the enemy! They were words from Heaven to lift his soul above the trials, and sorrows, and humiliations of earth—words of divine power and virtue to infuse vigor into his depressed and sorrowing heart. "Thou mighty man of valor!" How hard was it for Gideon to take such wondrous accents in! How difficult to apply them to himself!

Where was the might or where was the valor? Most surely not in himself or in his surroundings. Where then? In the living God; precisely where Joshua found his might and his valor. Indeed there is a striking similarity in the terms in which both these eminent servants of God were addressed. The similarity of the terms is quite as marked as is the contrast in their circumstances. Here are the terms to Joshua: "Have not I commanded thee? Be strong and of a good courage: be not thou afraid, neither be thou dismayed: for the Lord thy God is with thee whithersoever thou goest." And the terms to Gideon are: "The Lord is with thee, thou mighty man of valor."

Precious words! Soul-stirring, heart-strengthening accents! And yet Gideon was slow to make them his own—slow to grasp them, in the lovely appropriating power of faith, which so delights the heart of God, and glorifies His name. How often is it thus with us! How constantly we fail to rise to the height of God's gracious thoughts and purposes towards us! We are prone to *reason* about ourselves and our suroundings, instead of believing God, and resting, in sweet tranquility, in His perfect love and faithfulness.

Thus it was with that dear man of God on whose history we are dwelling. The divine statement was clear, full, absolute, and unconditional: "The Lord *is* with thee." There was no ground, in these words, for any question or doubt, whatsoever; and yet mark Gideon's reply: "And Gideon said unto Him, O my Lord, *if* the Lord be with us, why then is all this befallen us? And where be all His miracles which our fathers told us of, saying, Did not the Lord bring us up from Egypt? but now the Lord hath forsaken us, and delivered us into the hands of the Midianites" (verse 13).

Here, as is evident, Gideon reasons from his surroundings. Hence the "*if*"—that little monosyllable of unbelief. It is a familiar remark amongst us, "If you want to be miserable, look within; if you want to be distracted, look around; if you want to be peaceful and happy, look up—'look off unto Jesus.' " This is most true. So surely as we become occupied with self, or with men and things, the circumstances which surround us, we must be unhinged and unhappy. Our only strength, our only comfort, our only light, is to keep the eye of faith fixed on Jesus, and the heart firmly centred in Him. Most certainly Gideon's surroundings were of the gloomiest character. His "sensible horizon" was overhung with dark and heavy clouds. But there was one bright and blessed ray which shone in upon his depressed spirit—a ray emanating from the very heart of God, and conveyed in that one brief but comprehensive sentence, "The Lord is with thee." There was no "if" in this—no doubt, no reserve, no condition. It was distinct and unqualified, and needed only one thing to make it a spring of joy, strength, and victory in Gideon's soul, and that was to mix it with faith. But then "if" is not faith. True faith never answers God with ifs, for the simplest of all reasons, that it looks only at God, and there are no ifs with Him. Faith reasons from God downwards; not from man upwards. Faith has only one difficulty, and that difficulty is embodied in the question, "How shall He *not?*" It never says, "How shall He?" This is the language of sheer unbelief.

But, it may be asked by some, was there not some foundation for Gideon's "if" and "why?" Certainly not in God or in His word, whatever there had been in Israel and their actings. No doubt, if Gideon had only cast his eye back over the pages of his national history, he might have discovered ample reason for the sad and humiliating condition in which he found himself. Those blotted pages would have furnished an abundant answer to his question, "Why then is all this befallen us?" But had Israel's actings dimmed the lustre of Jehovah's mighty "miracles"? Not in the vision of faith, most surely. God had done great and glorious things for His people; and the record of those doings lay ever under the eye of faith, in all its soul-sustaining virtue. No doubt Israel had failed—shamefully failed; and the record of that failure lay also under the eye of faith, and furnished a solemn answer to Gideon's inquiry, "Why is all this befallen us?" Faith recognizes God's government as well as His

grace, and moreover it bows, in solemn awe, before each stroke of His governmental rod.

It is well to keep all this in mind. We are apt to forget it. God has, at times, to stretch forth his hand and lift the rod of authority. He cannot own what is contrary to His Name and His nature. Now, Gideon needed to remember this. Israel had sinned, and this was the reason why they were under the rod, of which the power of the Midianites was the expression in Gideon's day.

Gideon, we repeat, was called to enter practically into the meaning of all this; and not only so, but to taste the reality of identification with his people in all their pressure and affliction. This latter, as we know, was the portion and experience of every true servant of God in Israel. All had to pass through those deep exercises of soul consequent upon their association with the people of God. It mattered not whether it were a judge, a prophet, a priest, or a king; all had to participate in the sorrows and trials of the nation of Israel; nor could any true heart—any genuine lover of God or His people—desire exemption from such deep and holy exercises. This was pre-eminently true of the only perfect Servant that ever stood upon this earth. He, though personally exempt from all the consequences of Israel's sin and failure—though pure and spotless, divinely holy in nature and in life—did nevertheless, in perfect grace, voluntarily identify Himself with the people in all their sorrow and humiliation. "In all their affliction He was afflicted." Thus it was with our blessed Lord Jesus Christ; and all who, in any degree, partook of His Spirit, had, according to their measure, to taste of the same cup, though none could ever come up to Him in this or in aught else.

But when we come to compare closely the angel's words to Gideon, with his reply, we notice a point of deep interest, and one which illustrates the individual character of the book of Judges. The angel says, "The Lord is with *thee.*" Gideon replies, "If the Lord be with *us.*" This is very interesting and instructive; moreover it is in full keeping with a passage already referred to, in chap. 3: "And when the Lord raised them up judges, then the Lord was *with the judge.*" It does not say, "with the people," but adds, with touching grace, "and *delivered them* out of the hand of their enemies all the days of the judge; for it repented the Lord because of their groanings by reason of them that oppressed them and vexed them" (ver. 18).

There is peculiar sweetness and beauty in this. If Jehovah had to hide His face from His people, and give them over, for the time, into the hand of the uncircumcised, yet His loving heart was ever turned towards them, and ever ready to mark and recognize the faintest traces of a repentant spirit. "Who is a God like unto Thee, that pardoneth iniquity, and passeth by the transgression of the remnant of His heritage? He retaineth not His anger forever, because He delighteth in mercy. He will turn again, He will have compassion upon us; He will subdue our iniquities; and Thou wilt cast all their sins into the depths of the sea. Thou wilt perform the truth to Jacob, and the mercy to Abraham, which Thou hast sworn unto our fathers from the days of old" (Micah 7:18-20).

Part 3

Nothing can be more encouraging to the heart than the mode in which the Lord deals with the soul of Gideon—the way in which He prepares him for the course of action to which He was calling him. Gideon, like ourselves, was full of "ifs" and "whys,"—those little words so big with unbelief. The poor human heart is ever slow to take in the magnificence of divine grace; our feeble vision is dazzled by the brilliancy of divine revelation. It is only artless faith which can cause the soul to feel perfectly at home in the presence of the richest unfoldings of the goodness and loving-kindness of God. Faith never says "if" or "why?" It believes what God says, because He says it. It rests, in sweet tranquility, upon ever word that proceedeth out of the mouth of God. Unbelief looks at circumstances and reasons from them: faith looks at God, and reasons from Him. Hence the vast difference in their conclusions. Gideon, judging from his surroundings, concluded that Jehovah had

forsaken His people. A simple faith would have led him to the very opposite conclusion; it would have enabled him to see and know and remember that Jehovah would ever be true to His promise to Abraham, Isaac, and Jacob, however He might, in His governmental dealings, have to hide His face from their rebellious and sinful offspring. Faith always counts on God; and God, blessed be His name, ever honors faith. He first produces it in us, and then owns it.

But not only does God graciously honor faith; He rebukes our fears. He rises above our unbelief, and hushes all our silly reasonings. Thus, in His dealings with His chosen servant Gideon, it would seem as though He heard not the "if" or the "why?" He goes on to unfold His own thoughts, to display His own resources, and to fill the soul of His servant with a confidence and a courage which were to lift him above all the depressing influences with which he was surrounded.

"And the Lord looked upon him, and said, Go in this thy might, and thou shalt save Israel out of the hand of the Midianites: have not I sent thee?" Here we have the true secret of strength: "The Lord looked upon him." There was divine power in this look, if Gideon could only have taken it in. But, alas! he was still full of questions. "And he said unto Him, O my Lord, wherewith shall I save Israel? Behold, my family is poor in Manasseh, and I am the least in my father's house."

Thus, unbelief turns the eye in upon self, or out upon our surroundings. It leads us to compare our visible resources with the work to which God is calling us. Jehovah had said, "Go in this thy might." What was the "might?" In what did it consist? Was it great wealth, lofty position, or great physical power? Nothing of the kind. "Jehovah looked upon him, and said, Go in this thy might, and thou shalt save Israel." This was absolute and unqualified. It left no room for Gideon's "wherewith?" It made it very plain that the might with which he was to deliver Israel was not in himself or in his father's house, but in the God of Israel. It mattered little whether his family was rich or poor; whether he was little or great. It was God who was about to use him. What was wealth or greatness to Him? He could use a barley cake or a broken pitcher. Indeed we may observe this special feature in the varied instruments taken up in the book of Judges, namely, that "no flesh shall glory in God's presence." How does human glory fade away before the humiliating fact that Israel's hosts were called forth to battle under the leadership of a woman! What a stain on human pride in the fact of deliverance coming through the agency of a "left-handed man"!

But, on the other hand, we find that just in proportion as man's glory fades away, the divine glory shines out. The humbler the instrument, the more we see the power of God. What difference does it make to the Almighty God whether His instrument be left-handed or right-handed—a man or a woman—a dwarf or a giant? The instrument is nothing: God is all in all. True, He deigns to use instruments; but all the power is His, and His shall be the eternal and universal praise. Gideon had to learn this; and so had Moses; and so have we all. It is an invaluable lesson. We are all so prone to think of *our* competency for any work or service which may lie before us, when we ought to remember that of all His works that are done upon the earth, God is the doer of them. Our sufficiency is of Him. We can do nothing; and if we could do aught, it would be badly done. The human finger can only leave a soil behind. The works of men perish like their thoughts. The work of God abideth forever. Let us remember these things, that we may walk humbly and lean ever and only on the mighty arm of the living God. Thus the soul is kept in a well-balanced condition, free from self-confidence and fleshly excitement, on the one hand; and from gloom and depression, on the other. If we can do nothing, self-confidence is the height of presumption. If God can do every thing, despondency is the height of folly.

But in the case of Gideon, as in that of all God's servants, we observe two things worthy of our deepest attention. In the first place, we have the divine commission, as embodied in those weighty words, "*Have not I sent thee?*" And in the second place, we have the assurance of the divine presence, as set forth in these encouraging words, "*Surely I will be with thee.*"

These are the two grand points for all who will serve God in their day and generation. They must know that the path they tread has been marked out distinctly by the hand of God; and, furthermore, they must have the sense of His presence with them along the path. These things are absolutely essential. Without them we shall waver and vacillate. We shall be running from one line of work to another. We shall take up certain work, go on with it for a while, and then abandon it for something else. We shall work by fits and starts; our course will be faltering, our light flickering: "Unstable as water, we shall not excel." We shall never succeed at anything. There will be no certainty, no stability, no progress.

These are weighty matters for all of us. It is of immense importance for every servant of Christ, every child of God, to know that he is at his divinely appointed post, and at his divinely given work. This will give fixedness of purpose, moral elevation, and holy independence. It will preserve us from being tossed about by human thoughts and opinions—being influenced by the judgment of one or another. It is our happy privilege to be so sure that we are doing the very work which the Master has given us to do, that the thoughts of our fellows respecting us shall have no more weight with us than the pattering of rain on the window.

Not—be it carefully observed—that we should, for a moment countenance, much less cultivate, a spirit of haughty independence. Far away be the thought! We as Christians, can never, in one sense, be independent one of another. How can we, seeing we are members one of another? We are united to one another and to our risen Head in glory, by the one Spirit who is with us and in us. The most intense individuality—and our individuality should be as intense as our unity is indissoluble—can never touch the precious truth of the one body and one Spirit.

All this is divinely true, and most fully and thankfully owned. But, at the same time, we must insist upon the truth of our individuality, and of our personal responsibility. This must be maintained with all possible energy and decision. Each servant has to do with his Lord, in that particular sphere of work to which he has been called. And, moreover, each should know his work, and give himself to it diligently and constantly. He should possess the holy certainty and authority imparted to the soul by that divine and powerful sentence, "Have not I sent thee?"

It will perhaps be said, "We are not all Gideons or Joshuas. We are not all called to occupy such a prominent place or tread such a brilliant path as those illustrious servants." True; but we are called to serve; and it is essential to every servant to know his commission, to understand his work, and to be fully assured in his own soul that he is doing the very work which the Lord has given him to do, and treading the very path which the hand of God has marked out for him. If there be any uncertainty as to this, we do not see how there can be any progress.

But there is more than this. It is not enough to know that we are treading the divinely appointed path. We want to realize the divine presence. We want to have the precious words made good in our experience, "Surely I will be with thee." This completes the servant's equipment. The divine commission and the divine presence are all we want; but we must have these in order to get on. With these priceless realities it matters not who we are. The Lord can use a feeble woman, a left-handed man, a cake of barley meal, or a broken pitcher. The instrument is nothing. God is the workman. Unbelief may cry out, "O my Lord, wherewith shall I save Israel? Behold my family is *poor* in Manasseh, and I am the *least* in my father's house." Faith can cry out in reply, "What of all this if God be for us? Does He want the rich or the noble? What are riches or greatness to Him? Nothing." "Ye see your calling, brethren, how that not many wise men after the flesh, not many mighty, not many noble, are called; but God hath chosen the foolish things of the world to confound the wise; and God hath chosen the weak things of the world to confound the things which are mighty; and base things of the world, and things which are despised, hath God chosen, yea, and things which are not to bring to nought things that are: that no flesh should glory in His presence" (1 Cor. 1: 26-29).

These are wholesome words for all of us. It is an unspeakable mercy for every dear servant of Christ to be kept in the abiding sense of his own utter nothingness—to be taught to realize, in some measure, the depth, fulness, and power of that one brief but most comprehensive statement, "Apart from Me ye can do nothing." There is not a single branch in all the vine, however imposing or widespreading it may seem to be, which, if separated from the parent stem by the thickness of a gold leaf, can produce the very smallest atom of fruit. There must be the abiding realization of our vital union with Christ—the practical, living, abiding in Him, by faith, day by day, in order to bring forth any fruit that God can accept. It is as we abide in Christ that the living sap circulates freely through us, and gives forth the healthy bud, the green leaf, and the seasonable fruit.

Here lies the grand secret of power. It is abiding in the living Vine. "Blessed is the man that trusteth in the Lord, and whose hope the Lord is; for he shall be as a tree planted by the waters, and that spreadeth out her roots by the river; and shall not see when heat cometh, but her leaf shall be green; and shall not be careful in the year of drought, neither shall cease from yielding fruit" (Jer. 17:7-8).

All this is intensely personal. We must each, for himself and herself, cling by faith to Christ. It is of the very first importance for Christians to bear in mind that Christianity is a thoroughly individual thing. We are individual in our repentance, in our faith, in our salvation, in our communion, in our service, and in our reward. Look at the addresses to the seven churches in Rev. 2—3. Hearken to those pointed words, "*He* that hath an ear"—"To *him* that overcometh." What do they mean? Do they not set forth, in the most distinct and forcible manner, that blessed individuality of which we speak?

Unquestionably. But do they touch unity? Not in the smallest degree. They leave its sacred domain wholly untouched. "There is one body and one Spirit." This must ever hold good, spite of all the ruin and failure of the professing Church.

Nevertheless, the writings of John are pre-eminently individual.* From the opening lines of his Gospel to the closing sentence of his Apocalypse, we trace this feature. He shows us the Philips, the Simons, the Andrews, and the Nathanaels coming, in their individuality, to Jesus. He tells us of a Jewish ruler here, and a Samaritan sinner there, who were drawn by the Father to Jesus. He tells us of the good Shepherd who calleth His sheep by name. He tells us of the branches clinging to the living Vine. Thus it is in John's Gospel; and when we turn to his Epistles, we find the same principle running through them all. He writes to an elect lady, and to his beloved Gaius; and if he once speaks of "the Church," it is but to weep over its departed glory, and to raise amid its ruins that warning note for individual ears, "*Look to yourselves.*" And as to the Revelation, it ends as it begins, with a solemn appeal "*to him that heareth.*"

Part 4

The more closely we study the narrative of the Lord's dealings with Gideon, the more we must be struck with the marvelous way in which He prepares him for his after course. Like all God's servants, in all ages, Gideon had to undergo a course of secret training and discipline, ere he was fit to appear in public. The space of time occupied in this training may vary, as may also the character of the discipline; but of this we may rest assured that all who will be used of God in public must be taught of God in private. It is a fatal mistake for any one to rush into prominence without proper equipment, and that equipment can only be attained in the secret of the divine presence. It is in profound and hallowed retirement with God.

that vessels are filled, and instruments fitted for His work.

Let us never forget this. Moses had to spend forty years at "the back side of the desert" ere he was fit to enter upon his public career. David had to feed his father's flock, ere he was called to rule the nation of Israel. He slew a lion and a bear in secret, ere he was called to slay Goliath in public. The great apostle of the Gentiles spent three years in Arabia, notwithstanding his very remarkable conversion and call. The apostles spent three years and a half in companionship with their Master, and then had to tarry until they were endued with power from on high. Thus it has been with all those who have ever been called to occupy a prominent place in the Lord's work; and even the blessed Master Himself—though surely needing no training or discipline, inasmuch as He was ever perfect—to set us an example, spent thirty years in retirement ere He came forth in public.

All this is full of most wholesome instruction for our souls. Let us seek to take it in and profit by it. No one can ever get on in public work without this private teaching in the school of Christ. It is this which gives depth, solidity, and mellowness to the character. It imparts a tone of reality and a fixedness of purpose most desirable in all who engage in any department of the Lord's work. It will invariably be found that where anyone goes to work without this divine preparation, there is shallowness and instability. There may perhaps for a time be more flash and show in those superficial characters than in those who have been educated in the school of Christ; but it never lasts. It may create a momentary sensation, but it soon passes away like the morning cloud or the early dew. Nothing will stand but that which is the direct result of private communion with God—secret training in His presence—the excellent discipline of the school of God.

Let us see how all this is exemplified in Gideon's case. It is very evident that this

---

* Eternal life and its manifestations—first in our Lord, and then in the children of God—being the general line of truth in John's Gospel and Epistles, is individual and personal. In Paul's Epistles the unity of the saints as baptized by one Spirit into one body, with what flows from it, is brought out. [Ed.]

honored servant was called to pass through deep exercises of soul before ever he took a single step in public action, yea, before he ever unfurled the standard of testimony in his father's house. He had to begin with himself, with his own personal condition, with his own heart. Those who will be used for others must begin with themselves. So Gideon found it. Let us pursue his history.

"And the Lord said unto Gideon, Surely I will be with thee, and thou shalt smite the Midianites as one man. And he said unto Him, If now I have found grace in Thy sight, then show me a sign that Thou talkest with me. Depart not hence, I pray thee, until I come unto Thee, and bring forth my present, and set it before Thee. And He said, I will tarry till thou come again. And Gideon went in and made ready a kid, and unleavened cakes of an ephah of flour; the flesh he put in a basket, and he put the broth in a pot, and brought it out unto Him under the oak, and presented it. And the angel of God said unto him, Take the flesh and the unleavened cakes; and lay them upon this rock, and pour out the broth. And he did so. Then the angel of the Lord put forth the end of the staff that was in His hand, and touched the flesh and the unleavened cakes; and there rose up fire out of the rock and consumed the flesh and the unleavened cakes. Then the angel of the Lord departed out of his sight. And when Gideon perceived that He was an angel of the Lord, Gideon said, Alas, O Lord God! for because I have seen an angel of the Lord face to face. And the Lord said unto him, Peace be unto thee; fear not: thou shalt not die" (Judges 6:16-23).

Here we reach a profoundly interesting stage of Gideon's preparatory course. He is called to enter practically and experimentally into the great and universal law for the servants of God, namely, "When I am weak, then I am strong." This is a most precious law, and one which forms an indispensable element in the education of all Christ's servants. Let no one imagine that he can ever be used in the Lord's work, or ever make progress in the divine life, without some measure of real entrance into this invaluable principle. We hold it to be absolutely

essential in forming the character of the true servant of Christ. Where it is not known, where it has not been felt, where it has not been to some extent realized, there is sure to be unsubduedness, unbrokenness, self-occupation, in some form or another. There will be more or less of self-confidence, and various points and angles turning up here and there, and acting as a sad hindrance to all that is good, useful, and holy.

On the other hand, when one has learnt that great family motto quoted above—when one has learnt, in the divine presence to say, "When I am weak, then I am strong"—when nature has been weighed in the balance of the sanctuary, there you will always find a measure of brokenness, softness, and tenderness of spirit; and not only so, but also largeness of heart, and readiness for every good work, and that lovely elasticity of mind which enables one to rise above all those petty, selfish considerations, which so sadly hinder the work of God. In short, the heart must first be broken, then made whole; and, being made whole, be undividedly given to Christ and to His blessed service.

It is impossible to run the eye along the brilliant array of Christ's workmen, and not see the truth of this. Moses, Joshua, David, Isaiah, Jeremiah, Ezekiel, and Daniel, in Old Testament times; and Peter, Paul, and John, in those of the New, all stand before us as vivid illustrations of the value of broken material. All those beloved and honored servants had to be broken in order to be made whole—to be emptied in order to be filled—to learn that, of themselves, they could do nothing, in order to be ready, in Christ's strength, for anything and everything.

Such is the law of the household—the law of the vineyard—the law of the kingdom. So Gideon found it in his day. His "alas!" was followed by Jehovah's "Peace; fear not," and then he was ready to begin. He had been brought face to face with the angel of God, and there he learnt not only that his family was poor in Manasseh, and he the least in his father's house, but that in himself he was perfectly powerless, and that all his springs must be found in the living God. Priceless lesson this, for the son of Joash, and for us all!—a lesson not to be learnt in the schools and colleges of this world, but only in the deep and holy retirement of the sanctuary of God.

And now let us see what was Gideon's first act after his fears were hushed, and his soul filled with divine peace. His very first act was to build an altar. "Then Gideon built an altar there unto the Lord, and called it Jehovah-shalom: unto this day it is yet in Ophrah of the Abi-ezrites." He takes the happy place of a worshiper, and his worship is characterized by the revelation of the divine character. He calls his altar by that precious title, "The Lord send peace." He had gone through many and deep exercises of soul—exercises which none can know save those who are called out into a prominent place amongst God's people. He felt the ruin and the weakness of all around him. He felt the fallen and humiliating condition of his beloved people. He felt his own littleness, yea, his own emptiness, and nothingness. How could he come forward? How could he smite the Midianites? How could he save Israel? Who was sufficient for these things? It is all very well for those persons who live an easy, irresponsible kind of life; who know not the toils, the cares, and anxieties connected with the public service of Christ and the testimony for His name in an evil day. These know nothing of Gideon's painful exercises of soul; nothing of the pressure upon his spirit as he looked forth from beneath the shade of his father's oak-tree, and contemplated the dangers and responsi-bilities of the battle-field. They can enter but feebly into the meaning of those words of one high up in the school of Christ, "We had the sentence of death in ourselves that we should not trust in ourselves, but in God who raiseth the dead."

These are weighty words for all Christ's servants; but we must be His servants in reality, in order to enter into their deep significance. If we are content to live a life of indolence and ease, a life of self-seeking and self-pleasing, it is impossible for us to understand such words, or indeed to enter into any of those intense exercises of soul

through which Christ's true-hearted servants and faithful witnesses, in all ages, have been called to pass. We invariably find that all those who have been most used of God in public have gone through deep waters in secret. It is as the sentence of death is written practically upon *self*, that the power of resurrection-life in Christ shines out. Thus Paul could say to the Corinthians, "Death worketh in us; but life in you." Marvelous words! Words which let us into the profound depths of the apostle's ministry. What a ministry must that have been which was carried on upon such a principle as this! What power! what energy! Death working in the poor earthen vessel, but streams of life, heavenly grace, and spiritual power flowing into those to whom he ministered.

This, we may depend upon it, is the true secret of all effective ministry. It is an easy matter to talk about ministry; to set up to be ministers of Christ; but oh, how has the professing Church departed from the divine reality of ministry! Alas! the heart sinks at the bare thought of it. Where are the Pauls, the Gideons, and the Joshuas? Where are the deep heart-searchings and profound soul exercises which have characterized Christ's servants in other days? We are flippant and wordy, shallow and empty, self-sufficient and self-indulgent. Need we wonder at the small results? How can we expect to see life working in others when we know so little about death working in us?

May the eternal Spirit stir us all up, and work in us a more powerful sense of what it is to be the true-hearted, single-eyed, devoted servants of Jesus Christ!

Part 5

We are now to contemplate Gideon called forth into action. He has received his commission from Jehovah. His questions have been answered, his fears hushed, his heart tranquilized, and he is enabled to build an altar. All this had reference to his own personal condition, to the state of his own soul, to the attitude of his own heart as in the sight of God.

Thus it must ever be. We must all begin in

this way, if we are ever to be used of God to act on others. We must have to do with God in the secret of our own souls, else we shall prove to be but sorry workmen in the sequel. All who go forth in public work without this secret training, are sure to prove flimsy and shallow. Self must be measured in the divine presence. We must learn that nature is of no account in the Lord's work. "Not by might, nor by power, but by My Spirit, saith the Lord of hosts" (Zech. 4: 6).

It was not until Gideon had gone through somewhat of this holy discipline in secret that he was led out into service. And let us carefully note where he had to commence. "It came to pass the same night, that the Lord said unto him, Take thy father's young bullock, even the second bullock, of seven years old"—for Jehovah knew how many bullocks Joash had and the age of each—"and throw down the altar of Baal that thy father hath, and cut down the grove that is by it. And build an altar unto the Lord thy God upon the top of this rock, in the ordered place, and take the second bullock, and offer a burnt sacrifice with the wood of the grove which thou shalt cut down."

Here we see that Gideon had to begin *at home*. He was called to unfurl the standard of testimony in the very bosom of his family—in the very centre of his father's house. This is intensely interesting, and deeply practical. It teaches a lesson to which we should all bend our ears and apply our hearts. Testimony must begin at home. It will never do to rush forth into public work while our private and domestic ways are anything but what they ought to be. It is useless to set about throwing down the altar of Baal in public, while the selfsame altar remains standing at home.

This is of the very first importance. We are all of us imperatively called upon to show piety at home. Nothing is more sorrowful than to meet with persons who, abroad amongst their fellow men or their fellow Christians, are marked by a high tone of spirituality—a style of speaking which would lead one to suppose them far beyond the ordinary level of Christians, and yet when you come to close quarters with them—when

you become acquainted with their private life and ways, their actual history from day to day, you find them very far indeed from bearing testimony for Christ to those with whom they come in contact. This is most deplorable. It dishonors the Lord Jesus, grieves the Spirit, stumbles and repulses young believers, gives occasion to the enemy to speak reproachfully, and to our brethren to speak doubtfully of us.

Surely these things ought not to be. There ought to be a testimony yielded at home. Those who see most of us should see most of Christ in us. Those who know us best ought best to know that we are Christ's. But alas! how often is it otherwise! How often the home circle is just the place where the lovely traits of Christian character are least exhibited! The wife or the husband, the parent or the child, the brother or the sister, the master or the servant, the fellow-servant or some other companion in daily life, is just the one in whose sight we least display the beauteous fruits of divine life. It is in private life that all our weak points come out—our oddities and peculiarities, our silly tendencies and sinful tempers: instead of which it ought to be in that very sphere that the grace of Jesus is most faithfully manifested.

Let us not turn away from the word of reproof, of admonition, or exhortation. It may not be pleasant; but, we may rest assured, it is salutary. It may not be agreeable to the flesh; but it is wholesome to the soul. We are called, like Gideon, to begin at home, if we would prove helpful to our brethren, or act effectively against the common foe.

No doubt there are difficulties involved in this home testimony. It is often very hard, for example, for a child to bear witness against the worldliness of a parent, or of the whole family; but where there is humility of mind and simple dependence upon God, He maintains and carries us through marvelously. One thing is certain, there is nothing like decision. "The first blow is half the battle," yea, the whole battle is often gained by a single blow, when that blow is dealt in full communion with the mind of Christ.

On the other hand, where there is weakness and vacillation—playing fast and loose with the truth of God, trifling with divine principles and one's own conscience, a looking at consequences and a weighing of probable results—there the enemy is sure to have the upper hand, and the testimony altogether fails. God acts with those who act for Him. This is the grand secret of their success; but where the eye is not single, there is no real progress, no divine result.

Here is where so many of us signally fail. We are not whole hearted, not decided, not thoroughly out-and-out for Christ. Hence there is no result for God, no action on others. We have no idea of what may be accomplished by a single devoted heart, one earnest and energetic soul. Such an one may be used to raise up a standard round which thousands will flock who might never have had the courage or energy to unfurl the standard themselves.

Look at Gideon. See how he wrought for God and how God wrought with him. "Then Gideon took ten men of his servants, and did as the Lord had said unto him; and so it was, because he feared his father's household, and the men of the city, that he could not do it by day, that he did it by night. And when the men of the city rose early in the morning, behold, the altar of Baal was cast down, and the grove was cut down that was by it, and the second bullock was offered upon the altar that was built. And they said one to another, Who hath done this thing? And when they inquired and asked, they said, Gideon the son of Joash hath done this thing. Then the men of the city said unto Joash, Bring out thy son that he may die; because he hath cast down the altar of Baal, and because he hath cut down the grove that was by it."

This is what we may call striking at the very root of the matter. The worship of Baal is completely overturned. This was no trifle. We have little idea of what it cost the son of Joash to do this thing; but by the grace of God he did it. True, it may have been with fear and trembling, still he did it. He dealt one vigorous blow at the entire system of Baal, and it crumbled into dust beneath his feet. No half measures would have availed. It would have been of no possible use to pick a stone here and there out of the idol's altar;

the whole fabric had to be overturned from its very foundation, and the idol itself degraded in the very presence of its deluded worshipers. A bold decisive stroke was needed, and that stroke was given by the hand of Gideon the son of Joash, God's "mighty man of valor."

There is nothing, we repeat, like plain decision—bold, uncompromising faithfulness for Christ, cost what it may. Had Gideon been less decided, had his line of action been less thorough, his father Joash would not have been so perfectly won over. It needed just such a method of dealing with Baal to convince a rational person that the worship of such a god was a sham and a falsehood. "And Joash said unto all that stood against him, Will ye plead for Baal? *will ye save him?* he that will plead for him, let him be put to death whilst it is yet morning: if he be a god, let him plead for himself, because one hath cast down his altar. Therefore on that day he called him Jerubbaal, saying, Let Baal plead against him, because he hath thrown down his altar."

This was very simple reasoning, "If he be a god, let him plead for himself." Gideon's decided course had brought matters to a point. Baal was either a reality or a most complete delusion. If the former, let him plead for himself. If the latter, who would think of pleading for him? Nothing could be simpler. Gideon's action was a complete success. The worship of Baal was overturned; and the worship of Jehovah Elohim set up instead.

Thus we see that the divine work in the soul of Gideon is making very rapid but very real progress. He is conducted from strength to strength. How little idea had he, when first the divine voice fell on his ear, that, in so short a time, he would take so bold a step. If any one had said to him then, "In a few hours you will overturn the worship of Baal in the very midst of your father's house," he would not have believed it. But the Lord led him along, step by step, gently yet firmly; and as the heavenly light broke in upon his soul, his confidence and courage grew.

Thus it is the Lord ever deals with His servants. He does not expect them to run before they have learnt to walk; but where the heart is true, and the purpose honest and firm, He graciously supplies the needed strength, moment by moment. He causes mountains of difficulty to remove, rolls away many a dark and heavy cloud, fortifies the heart, and girds up the loins of the mind, so that the very feeblest are armed with giant strength, and the coward heart filled with wonder, love, and praise at the triumph of divine grace.

Having broken down Baal's altar, Gideon is now led to encounter Midian's hosts. "Then all the Midianites and the Amalekites and the children of the east were gathered together, and went over, and pitched in the valley of Jezreel. But the Spirit of the Lord came upon Gideon, and he blew a trumpet, and Abi-ezer was gathered after him. And he sent messengers throughout all Manasseh, who also was gathered after him; and he sent messengers unto Asher, and unto Zebulun, and unto Naphtali; and they came up to meet them."

In short there was a thorough awakening. The tide of spiritual energy rose majestically, and bore hundreds and thousands upon its bosom. The work which had begun in Gideon's heart was extending itself far and wide, throughout the length and breadth of the land. The Spirit of the Lord was displaying His mighty energy, and multitudes were stirred up to gather round the standard which the hand of faith had unfurled.

But just at this point, it would seem that Gideon's faith needed fresh confirmation. It may be his spirit was overawed when he saw the mighty host of the uncircumcised mustering before him; and then, for a moment, his courage failed, and his heart craved a fresh sign from the Lord. "And Gideon said unto God, If Thou wilt save Israel by my hand, *as Thou hast said*"—alas! the poor heart can place its unbelieving "if" right in front of the word of God who cannot lie—"behold, I will put a fleece of wool in the floor; and if the dew be on the fleece only, and if it be dry upon all the earth beside, *then shall I know* that Thou wilt save Israel by mine hand, *as Thou hast said*."

How marvelous! And yet we need not marvel if we know aught of our own hearts. Anything for the poor human heart but the naked word of the living God. A sign, a token, something that the eye can see. The word of God is not enough for unbelieving nature.

But oh! the matchless grace of God! His unupbraiding love! His tender considerateness! He graciously meets the weakness of His poor servant, for "It was so: for he rose up early on the morrow, and thrust the fleece together, and wringed the dew out of the fleece, *a bowl full of water*." What condescending grace! Instead of severely rebuking Gideon's unbelieving "if," He graciously confirms his wavering faith by superabounding evidence.

And yet all this sufficed not. Gideon seeks still further confirmation. "And he said unto God, Let not thine anger be hot against me, and I will speak but this once. Let me prove, I pray Thee, but this once with the fleece; let it now be dry only upon the fleece, and upon all the ground let there be dew. And God did so that night: for it was dry upon the fleece only, and there was dew upon all the ground." Such is the abounding grace and patience of the God with whom we have to do. Forever adored be His holy Name! Who would not trust Him, and love Him, and serve Him?

Part 6

We shall now ask the reader to open his Bible at the seventh chapter of the book of Judges. Here Gideon's companions are brought before us; and their history, as well as that of their leader, is full of interest and profit for us. They had to be trained and tested as well as he. Let us ponder the narrative.

"Then Jerubbaal, who is Gideon, and all the people that were with him, rose up early and pitched beside the well of Harod: so that the host of the Midianites were on the north side of them, by the hill of Moreh, in the valley. And the Lord said unto Gideon, The people that are with thee are too many for Me to give the Midianites into their hands, lest Israel vaunt themselves against Me, saying, Mine own hand hath saved me."

The clear and soul-stirring blast of Gideon's trumpet had drawn around him a very large and imposing company; but this company had to be tested. It is one thing to be moved by the zeal and energy of some earnest servant of Christ, and it is quite another thing to possess those moral qualities which alone can fit a man to be an earnest servant himself. There is a vast difference between following in the wake of some devoted man of God, and walking with God ourselves—being propped up and led on by the faith and energy of another, and leaning upon God in the power of individual faith for ourselves.

This is a serious consideration for all of us. There is always great danger of our being mere imitators of other people's faith; of copying their example without their spiritual power; of adopting their peculiar line of things without their personal communion. All this must be carefully guarded against. We specially warn the young Christian reader against it. Let us be simple, and humble, and real. We may be very *small*, our sphere very narrow, our path very retired; but it does not matter in the least, provided we are precisely what grace has made us, and occupying the sphere in which our blessed Master has set us, and treading the path which He has opened before us. It is by no means absolutely necessary that we should be great, or prominent, or showy, or noisy in the world; but it is absolutely necessary that we should be real and humble, obedient and dependent.

Thus our God can use us, without fear of our vaunting ourselves; and then, too, we are safe, peaceful, and happy. There is nothing more delightful to the true Christian, the genuine servant of Christ, than to find himself in that quiet, humble, shady path where *self* is lost sight of, and the precious light of God's countenance enjoyed—where the thoughts of men are of small account, and the sweet approval of Christ is everything to the soul.

Flesh cannot be trusted. It will turn the very service of Christ into an occasion of self-exaltation. It will use the very name of Him who made Himself nothing in order to make itself something. It will build up its own reputation by seeming to further the cause of Him who made Himself of none. Such is flesh! Such are we in ourselves! Silly, self-exalting creatures, ever ready to vaunt ourselves, while professing to be nothing in ourselves, and to deserve nothing but the flames of an everlasting hell.

Need we marvel at the testing and proving of Gideon's companions? All must be tested and proved. The service of Christ is a very solemn and a very holy thing; and all who take part therein must be self-judged, self-distrusting, and self-emptied; and not only so, but they must lean, with unshaken confidence, upon the living God. These are the grand qualities that go to make up the character of the true servant of Christ, and they are strikingly illustrated on the page of inspiration which now lies open before us.

Let us proceed with the narrative.

"The people that are with thee are too many for Me to give the Midianites into their hands. . . . Now, therefore, go to, proclaim in the ears of the people, saying, Whosoever is fearful and afraid, let him return and depart early from mount Gilead. And there returned of the people twenty and two thousand; and there remained ten thousand."

Here the first grand test is applied to Gideon's host—a test designed to bring out the measure of the heart's simple confidence in Jehovah. A coward heart will not do for the day of battle; a doubting spirit will not stand in conflict. The same principle is set forth in Deuteronomy 20:8 "And the officers shall speak further unto the people, and they shall say, What man is there that is fearful and fainthearted? let him go and return unto his house, lest his brethren's heart faint as well as his heart."

Faintheartedness is terribly contagious. It spreads rapidly. It withers the arm that should bear the shield, and paralyses the hand that should wield the sword. The only cure for this malady is simple confidence in God, a firm grasp of His faithfulness, a child-like trust in His Word, true personal acquaintance with Himself. We must know God for ourselves, in such a way that His Word is everything to us, and that we can walk alone with Him, and stand alone with Him in the darkest hour.

Reader, is it thus with thee? Hast thou this blessed confidence in God—this solid hold of His Word? Hast thou, deep down in thy heart, such an experimental knowledge of God and His Christ as shall sustain thee even though thou hadst not the support or sympathy of another believer under the sun? Art thou prepared to walk alone in the world?

These are weighty questions, and we feel the need of pressing them upon the Church of God at the present moment. There is a wide diffusion of the precious truth of God, and numbers are getting hold of it. Like the blast of Gideon's trumpet, so the clear testimony which has widely gone forth of late years has attracted many; and while we quite feel that there is real ground for thankfulness in this, we also feel that there is ground for very serious reflection indeed. Truth is a most precious thing, if it be truthfully found and truthfully held; but let us remember that in exact proportion to the preciousness of the truth of God so is the moral danger of trafficking therein without a self-judged heart and an exercised conscience.

What we really need is faith—unfeigned, earnest, simple faith, which connects the soul, in living power, with God, and enables us to overcome all the difficulties and discouragements of the way. Of this faith there can be no imitation. We must either possess it in reality or not at all. A sham faith will speedily come to the ground. The man who attempts to walk by faith, if he have it not, must speedily totter and fall. We cannot face the hosts of Midian unless we have full confidence in the living God. "Whosoever is fearful and afraid, let him return." Thus it must ever be. None can go to battle save those who are braced up by a faith that grasps the unseen realities of eternity, and endures as seeing Him who is invisible. May this faith be ours, in larger measure.

It is full of instruction for the heart to notice the effect of the first test upon the host of Gideon. It thinned his ranks amazingly. "There returned of the people twenty and two thousand, and there remained ten

thousand." This was a serious reduction. But it is far better to have ten thousand that can trust God than ten thousand times ten thousand who cannot. Of what use are numbers, if they be not energized by a living faith? None whatever. It is comparatively easy to flock around a standard raised by a vigorous hand; but it is a totally different thing to stand, in personal energy, in the actual battle. Nought but genuine faith can do this; and hence when the searching question is put, "Who can trust God?" the showy ranks of profession are speedily thinned.

But there was yet another test for Gideon's companions. "And the Lord said unto Gideon, The people are yet too many; bring them down unto the water, and I will try them for thee there: and it shall be, that of whom I say unto thee, This shall go with thee, the same shall go with thee; and of whomsoever I say unto thee, This shall not go with thee, the same shall not go. So he brought down the people unto the water: and the Lord said unto Gideon, Every one that lappeth of the water with his tongue, as a dog lappeth, him shalt thou set by himself; likewise every one that boweth down upon his knees to drink. And the number of them that lapped, putting their hand to their mouth, were three hundred men: but all the rest of the people bowed down upon their knees to drink water. And the Lord said unto Gideon, By the three hundred men that lapped will I save you, and deliver the Midianites into thine hand: and let all the other people go every man unto his place" (7:4-7).

Here then we have another great moral quality which must characterize those who will act for God and His people, in an evil day. They must not only have confidence in God, but they must also be prepared to surrender self. This is a universal law in the service of Christ. If we want to swim in God's current, we must sink self; and we can only sink self in proportion as we trust Christ. It is not, need we say, a question of salvation; it is a question of service. It is not a question of being a child of God, but of being a proper servant of Christ. The thirty-one thousand seven hundred that were dismissed from

Gideon's army, were just as much Israelites as the three hundred that remained; but they were not fitted for the moment of conflict; they were not the right men for the crisis. And why? Was it that they were not circumcised? Nay. What then? They could not trust God and surrender self. They were full of fear when they ought to have been full of faith. They made refreshment and comfort their object instead of conflict.

Here lay the true secret of their moral unfitness. God cannot trust those who do not trust Him and sink self. This is pre-eminently solemn and practical. We live in a day of easy profession and self-indulgence. Knowledge can, now-a-days, be picked up at very small cost. Scraps of truth can be gathered, second hand, in all directions. Truth which cost some of God's dear servants years of deep soul-ploughing and heart-searching exercise, is now in free circulation and can be intellectually seized and flippantly professed, by many who know not what soul-ploughing or heart-exercise means.

But let us never forget—yea, let us constantly remember—that the life of faith is a reality; service is a reality; testimony for Christ, a reality. And further let us bear in mind that if we want to stand for Christ in an evil day—if we would be men for the crisis, genuine servants, true witnesses—then verily we must learn the true meaning of those two qualities, namely, confidence in God, and self-surrender.

Part 7

There is something peculiarly striking in the fact that out of the many thousands of Israel, in the days of Gideon, there were only three hundred men who were really fit for conflict with the Midianites; only this small band fit for the occasion. This truly is a suggestive and admonitory fact. There were hundreds of thousands of true Israelites— truly circumcised sons of Abraham—members of the congregation of the Lord, who were by no means up to the mark, when it was a question of war to the knife with Midian—a question of genuine confidence in

God and self-surrender. We are safe in saying that the men who were morally fitted for the grand crisis in the day of battle were not one in a thousand. How solemn! Not one in a thousand who could trust God and deny self.

Is not this something worthy of deep and serious thought? Does it not, very naturally, suggest the inquiry as to whether it is otherwise at this moment? Is it not painfully evident that we live in a day in which little is known of the blessed secret of confidence in God, and still less of the exercise of self-surrender? In point of fact, these things can never be rightly separated. If we attempt to divorce self-surrender from confidence in God, it will land us in the deep and dark delusions of monasticism, asceticism, or ritualism. It will issue in nature trying to subdue nature. This, we need hardly say, is the direct opposite of Christianity. This latter starts with the glorious fact that the *old self* has been condemned and set aside by the cross of Christ, and therefore it can be practically surrendered, every day, by the power of the Holy Ghost. This is the meaning of those fine words in Colossians 3, "Ye *are* dead, and your life is hid with Christ in God." He does not say, "Ye *ought to be* dead." No; but "ye *are* dead." What then? "Mortify your members which are on the earth." So also in the profound and precious teaching in Romans 6, "How shall we that *are* dead to sin, live any longer therein? Know ye not, that so many of us as were baptized unto Jesus Christ were baptized unto His death?" What then? "Likewise reckon ye also yourselves to be dead indeed unto sin, but alive unto God through Jesus Christ our Lord."

Here then lies the secret of all true self-surrender. If this be not understood and practically entered into, it will simply be *self* in one form trying to subdue *self* in another. This is a fatal delusion. It is a snare of the devil into which earnest souls are in imminent danger of falling, who sigh after holiness of life, but do not know the power of accomplished redemption, and the indwelling of the Holy Ghost—are not built upon the solid foundation of Christianity.

We specially warn against this insidious error. It distinctly savors of monasticism or asceticism. It clothes itself in the garb of pietism and sanctimoniousness, and is peculiarly attractive to a certain class of ardent spirits who long for victory over the lusts, passions, and tendencies of nature; but, not knowing how to attain it, are turning their back upon Christ and His cross, and betaking themselves to the resources of a spurious religion.

It is against this most mischievous and delusive system that the apostle warns us, in Colossians 2, "Let no man," he says, "beguile you of your reward in a voluntary humility and worshiping of angels, intruding into those things which he hath not seen, vainly puffed up by his fleshly mind, and not holding the head, from which all the body by joints and bands having nourishment ministered, and knit together, increaseth with the increase of God. Wherefore if ye be dead with Christ from the rudiments of the world, why, as though living in the world, are ye subject to ordinances"—such as, "touch not; taste not; handle not; which all are to perish with the using—after the commandments and doctrines of men? Which things have indeed a show of wisdom in will worship, and humility, and neglecting of the body; not in any honor to the satisfying of the flesh" (Colossians 2: 18-23).

We deem it needful to say thus much lest any of our readers should at all mistake us on the subject of self-surrender. We desire it to be distinctly understood that the only possible ground of self-surrender is the knowledge of accomplished redemption, and our union with Christ through the power of the Holy Ghost. This is the essential basis of all Christian conduct. In short, a known salvation is the basis; the Holy Ghost indwelling, the power; and the Word of God, the directory of all true self-surrender.

But what did Gideon and his companions know of these things? Nothing, as Christians now know them. But they had confidence in God, and further, they did not make their own refreshment or comfort their object, but simply took it up by the way as a means to an end. Herein they teach a fine lesson even to those whose privilege it is to walk in the full light of New Testament Christianity. If they,

in the dim twilight in which they lived, could trust God, and surrender self for the moment, even in measure, then what shall we say for ourselves who, with all our light and privileges, are so ready to doubt God and seek our own things?

Is it not painfully evident that, in this our day of light and privilege, there is but little moral preparedness for the path of service and conflict which we are called to tread? Alas! we cannot deny it. There is a deplorable lack of genuine trust in the living God, and of the true spirit of self-surrender. Here, we may rest assured, is the deep secret of the whole matter. God is not practically known and habitually trusted; self is exalted and indulged. Hence our unfitness for the warfare, our failure in the day of battle. It is one thing to be saved, and quite another thing to be a soldier; and we cannot shake off the painful conviction that, in this day of widely extended profession, the proportion of workmen and warriors would not be found a whit greater than it was in the days of Gideon and his companions. The fact is, we want men of faith, men whose hearts are fixed and their eyes single; men so absorbed with Christ and His cause that they have no time for aught beside. We greatly fear that, if the double test which was applied to Israel in the days of Gideon, were to be applied now to those who stand on the very highest platform of profession, the practical result would not differ very materially.

We shall only touch on two more leading points, and then leave our readers to meditate closely upon the whole subject for themselves.

The close of Judges 7 shews us Gideon and his companions completely victorious. "The cake of barley bread" and "the broken pitchers" proved a match for all the power of the Midianites, although they "lay along in the valley like grasshoppers for multitude, and their camels were without number, as the sand by the sea-side for multitude." God was with those represented by the cake of barley bread and broken pitchers, as He will ever be with those who are prepared to take the low place; prepared to be nothing, but to make Him their all in all; prepared to trust

Him and to sink self. This, let it never be forgotten, is the great root principle in all service and in all conflict. Without it, we can never succeed; with it, we can never fail. It matters not what the difficulties, or what the numbers and power of our enemies, all must give way before the presence of the living God; and that presence will ever accompany those who trust Him and sink self.

Nor is this all. Not only is firm trust in God and self-surrender the secret of victory over external enemies; it is also the secret of overcoming, disarming, and melting down proud and jealous brethren, though these latter are often far more difficult to deal with than open enemies. Thus no sooner had Gideon reached the point of victory over the uncircumcised, than he was called to encounter the petty and contemptible jealousy of his brethren. "And the men of Ephraim said unto him, Why hast thou served us thus, that thou calledst us not when thou wentest to fight the Midianites? And they did chide with him sharply" (chapter 8:1).

All this was most uncalled for and unworthy. Had they not heard the sound of the trumpet calling Israel to the battle field? Had they not heard that the standard was unfurled? Why had they not rushed to the battle at the first? It was an easy matter to come in at the close and reap the spoil, and then find fault with the one who had been God's real instrument on the occasion.

However, we shall not dwell upon the unlovely conduct of the men of Ephraim; but turn, for a moment, to the exquisite way in which Gideon was enabled to meet them. "And he said unto them, What have I done now in comparison of you. . . . God hath delivered into your hands the princes of Midian, Oreb, and Zeeb; and what was I able to do in comparison of you? Then their anger was abated toward him when he had said that."

Here is the true way to vanquish jealous and envious brethren. The cake of barley bread and the broken pitcher can vanquish jealous Ephraimites as well as hostile Midianites. A self-hiding spirit is the grand secret of victory over envy and jealousy, in all their odious forms. It is difficult, if not impossible, to quarrel with a man who is down in the dust, in true self-abasement. "What have I done now in comparison of you?" This is the language of one who had learnt something of the real meaning of self-surrender; and we may safely assert that such language must ever disarm the envy and jealousy of the self-occupied and self-sufficient. May we know more of the truth of this!

We must now look at the closing scene of Gideon's remarkable history—a scene full of admonition for every servant of Christ. From it we learn that it is easier to gain a victory than to make a good use of it; easier to reach a position than to occupy it aright. We shall quote the passage. "Then the men of Israel said unto Gideon, Rule thou over us, both thou, and thy son, and thy son's son also: for thou hast delivered us from the hand of Midian. And Gideon said unto them, I will not rule over you, neither shall my son rule over you: the Lord shall rule over you."

So far, this was very fine. It was in full keeping with the self-surrender of Gideon's previous course. Every true servant of Christ will ever seek to connect souls with his Master, and not with himself. Gideon would not indeed displace Jehovah as the ruler of Israel. But, alas! his great victory fills his mind, and he will make a perpetual glory of it by an ephod (a priestly garment) of gold; and this, simply because his self-surrender was not complete. There has been but One whose self-surrender was, and that One must, in all things, have the preeminence. "And Gideon said unto them, I would desire a request of you, that ye would give me every man the earrings of his prey. (For they had golden earrings, because they were Ishmaelites.) And they answered, We will willingly give them. And they spread a garment, and did cast therein every man the earrings of his prey . . . . And Gideon made an ephod thereof, and put it in his city, even in Ophrah: and all Israel went thither a whoring after it: which thing became a snare unto Gideon, and to his house" (8: 22-27).

Such is man, even the best of men, when left to himself. Here we see the very man who had led his brethren on to victory over Midian, now leading them into dark and abominable idolatry. The earrings of the Ishmaelites did what their swords could not do; and the love-tokens of the men of Israel proved far more dangerous than the sharp chidings of the men of Ephraim. The latter drew out a lovely spirit of self-emptiness: the former proved a snare to Gideon and to the whole house of Israel.

Let us remember all this. If Gideon had refused the earrings as well as the throne, it would have been well for him and for his brethren; but the devil laid a snare for him into which he fell and carried all his brethren with him. May we all take warning from Gideon's fall, and draw encouragement from Gideon's victories. May we remember that it is one thing to gain a victory, and another to make good use of it; it is easier to reach a position than to occupy it aright. May God grant to the reader and writer of these lines, more simple confidence in Himself, and more of the true spirit of self-surrender! May such be the result of our meditations upon Gideon and his companions.

THE LIFE AND TIMES OF DAVID

THE LIFE OF FAITH

INTRODUCTION

THE STEPS which led to the setting up of a king in Israel are easily traced, and easily accounted for, by all who have studied with any attention the humbling history of the human heart, either as presented in themselves or in others.

In the opening chapters of First Samuel we are furnished with a most instructive and solemn picture of Israel's condition. The house of Elkanah is taken up by the sacred penman as a striking illustration of Israel after the flesh, and Israel after the Spirit. "He had two wives; the name of the one was Hannah, and the name of the other Peninnah; and Peninnah had children, but Hannah had no children."

Thus we have in the domestic circle of this Ephrathite the early scenes of Sarah and Hagar enacted over again. Hannah was the barren woman—and she was made to feel it deeply, for "her adversary also provoked her sore, for to make her fret, because the Lord had shut up her womb."

The barren woman is in Scripture the type of nature's ruined and helpless condition. There is no ability to do anything for God—no power to bring forth any fruit to Him; all is death and barrenness. Such is the real condition of every child of Adam. He can neither do anything for God nor for himself, as regards his eternal destiny. He is emphatically "without strength"; he is "a dry tree," "a heath in the desert." Such is the lesson taught us by the barren woman.

However, the Lord caused His grace to abound over all Hannah's weakness and need, and put a song of praise into her mouth. He enabled her to say, "My horn is exalted in the Lord; my mouth is enlarged over mine enemies; because I rejoice in Thy salvation." It is the Lord's special province to make the barren woman rejoice. He alone can say, "Sing, O barren, thou that didst not bear; break forth into singing, and cry aloud, thou that didst not travail with child; for more are the children of the desolate than the children of the married wife, saith the Lord" (Isa. 54:1).

Hannah realized this, and widowed Israel will ere long realize it also, "for her Maker is her husband; the Lord of Hosts is His name; and her Redeemer the Holy One of Israel." The beautiful song of Hannah is the soul's thankful acknowledgment of God's actings in reference to Israel. "The Lord killeth, and maketh alive: He bringeth down to the grave, and bringeth up. The Lord maketh poor, and maketh rich: He bringeth low, and lifteth up. He raiseth up the poor out of the dust, and lifteth up the beggar from the dunghill, to set them among princes, and to make them inherit the throne of glory." All this will be most fully exemplified in Israel in the latter day; and it is now exemplified in the person of every one who through grace is raised from his ruined condition in nature to blessedness and peace in Christ.

The birth of Samuel filled up a great blank, not only in the heart of Hannah, but doubtless in the heart of every faithful Israelite who sighed for the true interests of the Lord's house and the purity of the Lord's offering, both of which were alike disregarded and trampled upon by the unholy sons of Eli. In Hannah's desire for *"a man child,"* we perceive not merely the development of the heart of a *mother*, but that of an *Israelite*. She had, no doubt, beheld and mourned over the ruin of everything connected with the temple of the Lord. The dimmed eye of Eli— the vile actings of Hophni and Phinehas—the fading lamp—the desecrated temple—the despised sacrifice—all conspired to tell Hannah that there was a real want, which want could alone be supplied by the precious gift of a man-child from the Lord. Hence she says to her husband, "I will not go up until the child be weaned, and then I will bring him, *that he may appear before the Lord, and there abide forever."*

"Abide forever!" Nothing short of this could satisfy the longing soul of Hannah. It was not the mere matter of wiping away her own reproach that rendered Samuel so precious in her eyes. No! she longed to see "a faithful priest" standing before the Lord; and by faith her eye rested on one who was to

abide there forever. Precious, elevating faith—that holy principle which lifts the soul above the depressing influence of things seen and temporal, into the light of things unseen and eternal!

In chapter 3 we have the prediction of the terrible downfall of Eli's house. "And it came to pass at that time, when Eli was laid down in his place, *and his eyes began to wax dim, that he could not see;* and ere the lamp of God went out in the temple of the Lord, where the ark of God was, and Samuel was laid down to sleep; *that the Lord called Samuel."* This was very expressive—solemnly expressive. Eli's eyes "dim," and the Lord's call to Samuel: in other words, Eli's house is passing away, and the faithful priest is about to enter upon the scene. Samuel runs to Eli, but, alas, all the latter could say was, *"Lie down again."* He had no message for the child. Hoary and dim, he could spend his time in sleep and darkness, while the Lord's voice was sounding so very near him. Solemn, most solemn warning!

Eli was a priest of the Lord, but he failed to walk watchfully, failed to order his house according to the testimonies of God, failed to restrain his sons; hence we see the sad end to which he came. "And the Lord said to Samuel, Behold, I will do a thing in Israel at which both the ears of every one that heareth it shall tingle. In that day I will perform against Eli all things which I have spoken concerning his house: when I begin, I will also make an end. For I have told him that I will judge his house forever for the iniquity which he knoweth; because his sons made themselves vile, and he restrained them not" (1 Sam. 3:11-13).

"Whatsoever a man soweth," says the apostle, "that shall he also reap." How true is this in the history of every child of Adam!— how peculiarly true in the history of every child of God! According to our sowing shall be our reaping. So Eli was made to feel; and so shall the writer and the reader of this. There is much more of solemn, practical reality in this divine statement than many are apt to imagine. If we indulge in a wrong current of thought, if we adopt a wrong habit of conversation, if we pursue a wrong line of acting, we must inevitably reap the fruits of it sooner or later.* May this reflection lead us to more holy watchfulness in our ways; may we be more careful to "sow to the Spirit," that so, of the Spirit, we may "reap life everlasting"!

In chapter 4 a humiliating picture of Israel's condition in connection with the declining house of Eli is presented. "Now Israel went out against the Philistines to battle, and pitched beside Ebenezer: and the Philistines pitched in Aphek. And the Philistines put themselves in array against Israel: and when they joined battle, Israel was smitten before the Philistines: and they slew of the army in the field about four thousand men." Here Israel was being made to realize the curse of a broken law. See Deut. 28:25. They could not stand before their enemies, being weak and powerless by reason of their disobedience.

And observe the nature and ground of their confidence, in this their time of need and pressure: "And when the people were come into the camp, the elders of Israel said, Wherefore hath the Lord smitten us to-day before the Philistines? Let us fetch the ark of the covenant of the Lord out of Shiloh unto us, that, when it cometh among us, it may save us out of the hand of our enemies." Alas, what a miserable ground of confidence! Not a word about *the Lord Himself*. They thought not of *Him* as the source of their strength; they made not *Him* their shield and buckler. No! they trusted in the ark; they vainly imagined that it could save them. How vain! How could *it* avail them aught when unaccompanied by the presence of the Lord of hosts, the God of the armies of Israel? Impossible! But He was no longer there; He had been grieved away by their unconfessed and unjudged sin; nor could any symbol or ordinance ever supply His place.

However, Israel vainly imagined that the ark would do all for them; and great was their joy, though not well founded, when it made its appearance among them, accompanied, not by Jehovah, but by the wicked priests Hophni and Phinehas. "And when the ark of the covenant of the Lord came into the camp, all Israel shouted with a great shout, so that the earth rang again." All this was very imposing; but, ah, it was hollow; their triumph was as baseless as it was unbecoming; they ought to have known themselves much better than to make such an empty display. Their shout of triumph harmonized badly with their low moral condition in the sight of God; and yet it will ever be found that those who know least of themselves set up the highest pretensions, and assume the highest position.

The Pharisee in the Gospel looked down with an air of proud indifference on the self-abased publican; he imagined himself very high up and the publican very low down in the scale; yet how different were God's thoughts about the two! Thus it is the broken and contrite heart will ever be the dwelling-place of God, who, blessed be His name, knows how to lift up and comfort every such heart as none else can do. Such is His peculiar work—the work in which He delights.

But the men of this world will always attach importance to high pretensions. They like them, and, generally speaking, give a high place in their thoughts to those who assume to be somewhat; while, on the other hand, they will seek to put the really self-abased man still lower. Thus, in the instructive scene before us in this chapter, the Philistines attached no small importance to the shout of the men of Israel. It was like

---

* The statement in the text, I need hardly say, does not by any means interfere with the eternal stability of divine grace and the perfect acceptance of the believer in all the acceptableness of Christ before God. This is a great foundation truth. Christ is the believer's life, and Christ is his righteousness—the ground of his peace with God. He may lose the enjoyment of it, but the thing itself God has established upon an indestructible basis, and before ever it can be touched the fact of Christ's resurrection must be called in question, for clearly He could not be where He is if the believer's peace were not perfectly settled. In order to have perfect peace, I must know my perfect justification: and in order to know my perfect justification, I must know, by faith in God's Word, that Christ has made a perfect atonement. This is the divine order—perfect atonement as the ground of my perfect justification; and perfect justification as the ground of my perfect peace. God has joined those three together, and let not man's unbelieving heart put them asunder.

Hence, therefore, the statement in the text will not, I trust, be misunderstood or misapplied. The principle contained therein may be thus illustrated: If my child does wrong, he may injure himself and grieve and displease me; but he is my child all the while. The apostolic statement is as broad as possible—"Whatsoever a man soweth, that shall he also reap." He does not say whether it is a converted or an unconverted man, and therefore the passage should have its full application. It could not possibly touch the question of pure and absolute grace.

themselves, and therefore they could apprehend and appreciate it.

"And when the Philistines heard the noise of the shout, they said, What meaneth the noise of this great shout in the camp of the Hebrews? And they understood that the ark of the Lord was come into the camp. And the Philistines were afraid; for they said, God is come into the camp," etc. They naturally supposed that the shout of triumph was based on a reality: they saw not what was beneath the surface; they understood not the meaning of a defiled priesthood, a despised sacrifice, a desecrated temple. They beheld the outward symbol, and imagined that power accompanied it; hence their fear. How little did they know that their fear and Israel's triumph were alike groundless. "Be strong," said they, "and quit yourselves like men, O ye Philistines, that ye be not servants to the Hebrews, as they have been to you: quit yourselves like men, and fight."

Here was the resource of the Philistines—"quit yourselves *like men.*" Israel could not do this. If prevented by sin from bringing the resources of God to bear upon their circumstances, they were weaker than other men; Israel's only hope was in God; and if God were not there, if it were a mere conflict between man and man, an Israelite was no match for a Philistine. The truth of this was most fully established on the occasion to which we are referring. "The Philistines fought, and Israel was smitten." How else could it be? Israel could but be smitten and fly when their shield and buckler, even God Himself, was not in their midst. They were smitten; the glory departed from them; the ark was taken: they were shorn of their strength; their shout of triumph was exchanged for the piercing cry of sorrow; their portion was defeat and shame; and the aged Eli, whom we may regard as the representative of the existing system of things, fell with that system, and was buried in its ruins.

Chapters 5 and 6 embrace the period during which "Ichabod" was written upon the nation of Israel. During this time God ceased to act publicly for Israel, and the ark of His presence was carried about from city to city of the uncircumcised Philistines. This period

is full of instruction. The ark of God among strangers, and Israel for the time being set aside, are circumstances which cannot fail to interest the mind and fix the attention of the intelligent and thoughtful student of Scripture.

"And the Philistines took the ark of God, and brought it from Eben-ezer to Ashdod. When the Philistines took the ark of God, they brought it into the house of Dagon, and set it by Dagon." Here we are presented with the sad and humiliating result of Israel's unfaithfulness. With what a careless hand and faithless heart had they kept the ark of God when it could ever be brought to find a lodging-place in the temple of Dragon! How deeply Israel had failed! They had let go everything; they had given up that which was most sacred, to be profaned and blasphemed by the uncircumcised.

And now the ark of Jehovah, which belonged to the holiest of all, is placed by the Philistines in the house of their god. The shadow of Dagon was to be substituted for the wings of the cherubim and the beams of the divine glory. Such were the thoughts of the lords of the Philistines; but not so God's thoughts. Israel, on the one hand, had failed in defending the ark; they had failed to recognize the great truth that it should ever have been connected with the presence of God among them.

On the other hand, the lords of the Philistines might presume to insult the sacred symbol of the divine presence by impiously associating it with Dagon their god. In a word, the Israelites might prove faithless, and the Philistines profane, but the God of Israel must ever be true to Himself, ever true to His own holiness, and Dagon must fall prostrate before the ark of His presence. "And when they of Ashdod arose early on the morrow, behold, Dagon was fallen upon his face to the earth before the ark of the Lord. And they took Dagon, and set him in his place again. And when they arose early on the morrow morning, behold, Dagon was fallen upon his face to the ground before the ark of the Lord; and the head of Dagon and both the palms of his hands were cut off upon the threshold: only the stump of Dagon was left to him" (chap. 5:3-4).

We can hardly conceive a more humiliating condition of things at this crisis in Israel's history. They beheld the ark snatched from their midst; they had proved themselves unfit and unable to occupy the place of God's witnesses in the view of the nations around them; and as to the grounds of triumph by the enemies of the truth, it was enough to say, "The ark is in the house of Dagon." This was truly terrible, when looked at from one point of view; but oh, how ineffably glorious when looked at from another! Israel had failed, and had let go everything that was sacred and precious; they had allowed the enemy to lay their honor in the dust, and trample on their glory; yet God was above all, beyond all; He remained sovereign over all.

Here was the deep source of consolation to every faithful heart. If Israel would not act in defence of God's truth, He must act Himself; and so He did. The lords of the Philistines had vanquished Israel; but the gods of the Philistines must fall prostrate before that ark which of old had driven back the waters of Jordan. Here was divine triumph. In the darkness and solitude of the house of Dagon —where there was no eye to see, no ear to hear—the God of Israel was acting in defence of those great principles of truth which His Israel had so failed to maintain. Dagon fell, and in his fall proclaimed the honor of the God of Israel. The darkness of the moment only afforded an opportunity for the divine glory to shine out with brilliancy. The scene was so thoroughly emptied of the creature that the Creator could show Himself in His own proper character. "Man's extremity was God's opportunity." His failure made room for the divine faithfulness. The Philistines had proved stronger than Israel; but Jehovah was stronger than Dagon.

Now all this is replete with instruction and encouragement at a time like the present, when the people of God are so sadly declining from that deep tone of devotedness and separation which ought to characterize them. We should bless the Lord for the full assurance of His faithfulness—"He cannot deny Himself"; "The foundation of God standeth sure, having this seal, the Lord

knoweth them that are His, and let every one that nameth the name of Christ depart from iniquity." Hence, in darkest times He will maintain His truth and raise up a witness for Himself, even though it should be in the house of Dagon. Christians may depart from God's principles, but the principles remain the same: their purity, their power, their heavenly virtue, are in no wise affected by the fickleness and inconsistency of faithless professors, and in the end truth will triumph.

However, the effort of the Philistines to keep the ark of God among them proved a complete failure. They could not make Dagon and Jehovah dwell together—how blasphemous the attempt! "What concord hath Christ with Belial?" None! The standard of God can never be lowered so as to accommodate itself to the principles which govern the men of this world; and the attempt to hold Christ with one hand and the world with the other must issue in shame and confusion of face. Yet how many are making that effort! How many are there who seem to make it the great question, how much of the world they can retain without sacrificing the name and privileges of Christians! This is a deadly evil, a fearful snare of Satan, and it may with strict propriety be denominated the most refined selfishness. It is bad enough for men to walk in the lawlessness and corruption of their own hearts; but to connect evil with the holy name of Christ is the climax of guilt.

"Thus saith the Lord of hosts, the God of Israel . . . . Behold, ye trust in lying words, that cannot profit. Will ye steal, murder, and commit adultery, and swear falsely, and burn incense unto Baal, and walk after other gods whom ye know not, and come and stand before Me in this house, which is called by My name, and say, We are delivered to do all these abominations?" (Jer. 7:3, 8-10) Again, we read, as one of the special characteristics of the last days, that men shall have "a form of godliness, but deny the power thereof."

The *form* suits the worldly heart, because it serves to keep the conscience at ease, while the heart enjoys the world in all its attractiveness. What a delusion! How needful the apostolic admonition, *"From such turn away"!* Satan's masterpiece is the amalgamation of things apparently Christian with things decidedly unholy. He deceives more effectually by this scheme than any other, and we need more spiritual perception to detect it in consequence. The Lord grant us this, for He knows how much we need it.

Chapter 7. Passing over much that is valuable in chapters 5 and 6 we must dwell a little upon Israel's happy restoration, in connection with the ministry of "the faithful priest."

Israel had been allowed to mourn for many a day the absence of the ark; their spirits drooped under the withering influence of idolatry; and at length their affections began to go out after the Lord. But in this revival we learn how deeply they had been sunk in death. This is always the case.

When Jacob of old was called upon to go up to Bethel from amid the defilement of Shechem, he had but little idea of how he and his family had become entangled in the meshes of idolatry. But the call to *"go up to Bethel"* roused his dormant energies, quickened his conscience, and sharpened his moral perception. Hence he says to his household, "Put away the strange gods that are among you, and be clean, and change your garments." The very idea of Bethel, where God had appeared to him, exerted a reviving influence on the soul of Jacob; and he being revived himself was enabled to lead others also in fresh power.

Thus it is with Jacob's seed in this chapter. "And Samuel spake unto all the house of Israel, saying, If ye do return unto the Lord with all your hearts, then put away the strange gods and Ashtaroth from among you, and *prepare your hearts unto the Lord,* and serve Him *only;* and He will deliver you out of the hand of the Philistines." We observe here what a downward course Israel had been pursuing in connection with the house of Eli. The first step in evil is to place confidence in a form apart from God; apart too from those principles which make the form valuable. The next step is to set up an idol. Hence we find Israel saying of the ark, "That *it* may save us." But now the word of the prophet is, "Put away the strange gods and Ashtaroth from among you."

Is there not a solemn admonition in all this

for the professing Church? Truly there is. The present is pre-eminently a day of form without power. The spirit of cold and uninfluential formalism is moving upon the face of christendom's troubled waters, and soon all will settle down in the deathlike calm of false profession, which will be broken in upon only by "the shout of the archangel and the trump of God."

However, the attitude assumed by Israel in chapter 7 forms a perfect contrast to the scene in chapter 4: "And Samuel said, Gather all Israel to Mizpeh, and I will pray for you unto the Lord. And they gathered together to Mizpeh, and drew water, and poured it out before the Lord" (an expression of their weak, helpless condition) "and fasted on that day, and said there, We have sinned against the Lord." This was real work, and we can say, *God is here now.* There is no confidence in a mere symbol or lifeless form; there is no empty pretension or vain assumption, no shout or baseless vaunting; all is deep and solemn reality. The earnest cry, the water poured out, the fast, the confession—all tell out the mighty change which had taken place in Israel's moral condition.

They now betake themselves to the faithful priest, and through him to the Lord Himself. They speak not now of fetching the ark. No; their word is, "Cease not to cry unto the Lord our God for us, that *He* will save us out of the hand of the Philistines. And Samuel took a sucking-lamb, and offered it for a burnt-offering wholly unto the Lord; and Samuel cried unto the Lord for Israel; and the Lord heard him." Here was the source of Israel's power. The sucking-lamb—God's gracious providing in tender remembrance of their need—gave a new aspect to their circumstances; it was the turning-point in their history on this occasion.

And observe, the Philistines seem to have been in total ignorance of all that was going on between Jehovah and Israel. They doubtless imagined that, inasmuch as they heard no shout of triumph, the Israelites were, if possible, in a more impoverished condition than before. They do not make the earth to ring again, as in chap. 4; but ah, there was a silent work going on which a Philistine's eye could not see, nor a Philistine's heart appreciate! What could a Philistine know about the penitential cry, the water poured out, or the sucking-lamb offered up? Nothing.

The men of this world can only take cognizance of that which lies on the surface. The outward show, the pomp and glare, the assumption of strength and greatness in the flesh, are well understood by the world; but they know nothing of the reality of a soul exercised before God. And yet this latter is what the Christian should most earnestly seek after. An exercised soul is most precious in the sight of God; He can dwell with such at all times. Let us not assume to be anything, but simply take our proper place in the sight of God, and He will surely be our spring of power and energy, according to the measure of our need.

"And as Samuel was offering up the burnt-offering, the Philistines drew near to battle against Israel: but the Lord thundered with a great thunder on that day upon the Philistines, and discomfited them, and they were smitten before Israel." Such were the happy results of simple dependence upon the God of the armies of Israel: it was somewhat like the glorious display of Jehovah's power on the shores of the Red Sea.

"The Lord is a man of war" when His people need Him, and their faith can count on Him as their present help in time of need. Whenever Israel truly turned to Jehovah, He was ever ready to appear in their behalf; but the glory must be *all* His own. Israel's shout of empty triumph must be hushed, in order that the voice of Jehovah may be distinctly heard. And how blessed to be silent, and let Jehovah speak! What power in His voice to bring peace to His people, and to strike terror into the hearts of His enemies! "Who shall not fear Thee, O Lord, and glorify Thy name?"

Chapter 8. In this chapter we have a very marked step towards the setting up of a king in Israel. "And it came to pass, when Samuel was old, that he made his sons judges over Israel. ... And his sons walked not in his ways, but turned aside after lucre, and took bribes, and perverted judgment." Sad picture! How like man in every age! Man

corrupts himself and all committed to him at the first opportunity. Moses and Joshua foresaw Israel's turning away after their departure (Deut. 31:29; Josh. 23:15-16); and Paul could say to the Ephesian elders: "I know that after my departure shall grievous wolves enter in among you, not sparing the flock." So here; Israel no sooner recovers from the effects of the immorality of Eli's sons than they are made to feel the direful effects of the avarice of Samuel's sons, and thus are they hurried along the path which ended in the rejection of Jehovah and the setting up of Saul.

"When Samuel was old, *he made* his sons judges." But this was a very different thing indeed from God's appointment. The faithfulness of Samuel was no guarantee for his sons; just as we find in the boasted theory of apostolic succession. What kind of successors have we seen? How far have they resembled their predecessors? Paul could say, "I have coveted no man's silver or gold": can the so-called successors say so? Samuel could say, "Behold, here I am: witness against me before the Lord, and before His anointed: whose ox have I taken? or whose ass have I taken? or whom have I defrauded? whom have I oppressed? or of whose hand have I received any bribe to blind mine eyes therewith?" But alas, Samuel's sons and successors could not say this! To them "filthy lucre" was the leading spring of action.

Now we find in this chapter that Israel makes this evil of Samuel's sons the ostensible reason for asking a king. "Behold, thou art old, and thy sons walk not in thy ways: now make us a king to judge us *like all the nations.*" Fearful declension! Israel satisfied to come down to the level of the nations around! and all because Samuel was old and his sons covetous. The Lord is shut out. Had they looked up to Him, they would have had no reason for seeking to put themselves under the guardianship of a poor mortal like themselves.

But ah, the Lord's ability to guide and keep them was little thought of in all this scene! They cannot see beyond Samuel and his sons: if no help can be found from them, they must at once step down from their high elevation of having Jehovah as their King and make to themselves a human head like the nations around them. The attitude of faith and dependence on God cannot be maintained by the natural man. *Outwardly* God had been owned as their King; but now it is not so: a king must now be their recognized head. We shall soon see the sad result of all this.

Chapters 9—13. These chapters furnish us with the character of Saul, together with his anointing and the opening of his rule. I shall not dwell upon it in this introduction, being merely desirous to call the reader's attention to the steps which led to the setting up of a king in Israel.

Saul was emphatically the man after Israel's heart: he had all that the flesh could desire—"a choice young man, and a goodly; and there was not among the children of Israel a goodlier person than he: from his shoulders and upward he was higher than any of the people." This was all very imposing to those who could only look upon the outward appearance; but what lay beneath this attractive exterior! Saul's whole course is marked with selfishness and pride, under the cloak of humility. True, the Spirit came upon him as one set apart to be an office-bearer among the people of God;* but he was throughout a self-seeker, and he only used the name of God for his own ends, and the things of God as a pedestal on which to set forth his own glory.

The scene at Gilgal is truly characteristic, and develops much of Saul's principle of action. Impatient to wait for God's time, he "forces himself," and offers a burnt-offering, and has to hear from the lips of Samuel these solemn words: "Thou hast done foolishly; thou hast not kept the commandment of the Lord thy God which He commanded thee: for now would the Lord have established thy kingdom upon Israel for ever. But now thy kingdom shall not continue: the Lord hath

sought Him a man after His own heart, and the Lord hath commanded him to be captain over His people, because thou hast not kept that which the Lord commanded thee."

This is just the sum of the matter, so far as Saul is concerned. "Thou hast done foolishly; thou hast not kept the commandment of the Lord; thy kingdom shall not continue." Solemn verities! Saul, the man after man's heart, is set aside, to make room for the man after God's heart. The children of Israel had abundant opportunity of testing the character of the man whom they had chosen to lead them forth, and fight their battles.** The reed on which they had so earnestly desired to lean had broken, and was about to pierce their hand.

Man's king, alas, what was he? Set him in an emergency, and how does he carry himself? Bustling self-importance marks all his actings. No dignity, no holy confidence in God, no acting on the broad principles of truth. Self, self, and that, too, in the most solemn scenes, and while apparently acting for God and His people. Such was man's king.

Chapter 14. This beautiful chapter furnishes a striking contrast between the efficacy of Israel's expedient, and that of the *old principle* of simple faith in God. Saul sits beneath a pomegranate tree, in display of empty pomp without any real power; while Jonathan, acting in the spirit of faith, is made the happy instrument of working salvation for Israel. Israel, in unbelief, had asked for a king to fight their battles, and doubtless they imagined that, when blessed with a king, no enemy could stand before them: but was it so? One word in chap. 13 gives the reply: "All the people followed him *trembling*." What a change! How different from the mighty host who, of old, had followed Joshua into the strongholds of Canaan! And yet they now had their longed-for king before them; but, God was not there, and hence their trembling.

---

* My reader should accurately distinguish between the Holy Ghost coming *upon* people and the Holy Ghost dwelling and acting *in* them. The statement in 1 Sam. 10: 6 may present a difficulty to some minds. "The Spirit of the Lord will come *upon* thee, and thou shalt prophesy with them, and shalt be turned into another man." This is not the Spirit producing the new birth, but merely fitting Saul to be an office-bearer. Were it regeneration, it would not merely be the Spirit coming *upon*, but acting *in*, a man. Saul the *office-bearer* and Saul the *man* are quite distinct, and this distinction must be maintained in reference to many of the characters both in the Old and New Testament Scriptures.

** It is to be noted that Saul, though appointed by God's order to Samuel, is nevertheless the *people's* choice and acclaimed by them as such (1 Sam. 10:24)—God thus selecting for them the man after *their* heart. [Ed.]

Let man have the fairest, the most impos-ing ordinance, without the sense of God's presence, and he is weakness itself. Let him have the presence of God in power, and nothing can resist him. Moses had, of old, done wonders with a simple rod in his hand; but now, Israel, with the man after their own heart full in their view, could do nought but tremble before their enemies. "All the people followed him trembling." How truly humiliating! "Nay; but we will have a king over us . . . that our king may judge us, and *go out before us and fight our battles.*" Truly "it is better to trust in the Lord, than to put confidence in princes." Jonathan proved this, most blessedly. He goes up against the Phil-istines in the power of that word, "There is no restraint with the Lord to save by many or by few." It was "the Lord" who filled his soul, and having Him, "many or few" made no dif-ference. Faith does not reckon on circum-stances, but on God.

And mark the change upon Israel the moment that faith begins to act amongst them. The trembling was transferred from Israel to the Philistines; "and there was a trembling in the host, in the field, and among all the people; the garrison and the spoilers, they also trembled; and the earth quaked; so it was a very great trembling." Israel's star was now decidedly in the ascendant, simply because Israel was acting upon the principle of faith. Jonathan looked not to his father Saul for deliverance, but to Jehovah; he knew that He was a man of war, and on Him he leaned for the deliverance of Israel in the day of trouble. Blessed dependence! None like it.

Human ordinances perish—human re-sources vanish away; but "they that trust in the Lord shall be as Mount Zion, which cannot be removed, but abideth for ever." "It was a very great trembling," for God was putting His terror into their hearts, and fill-ing Israel with joy and triumph. Jonathan's faith was owned of God in the establishment of those who had previously fled from the field of conflict into the mountains. Thus it is ever; one can never walk in the power of faith without giving an impetus to others; and, on the other hand, one coward heart is sufficient

to deter a great many. Moreover, unbelief always drives one from the field of service or conflict, while faith, as surely, leads one into it.

But what of Saul in all this? How did he co-operate with the man of faith? He was perfectly incapable of any such acting. He sat under the pomegranate tree, unable to in-spire courage into the hearts of those who had chosen him to be their captain; and when he did venture to move, or rather to bustle forth, he could do nought but hinder the precious results of faith by his rashness and folly. But we must hasten on to the close of these introductory remarks.

Chapter 15 presents us with the final test-ing and setting aside of man's king. *"Go, smite Amalek."* This is the test which really made manifest the moral condition of Saul's heart. Had he been right before God, he would have executed God's judgment upon Amalek. But the issue proved that Saul had too much in common with Amalek to carry out the divine will in his destruction. What had Amalek done? "Thus saith the Lord of hosts, I remember that which Amalek did to Israel, how he laid wait for him in the way, when he came up from Egypt." In a word, Amalek stands before the spiritual mind as the first great obstacle to the progress of the redeemed from Egypt to Canaan; and we know what it is which fills a similar place in reference to those who now set out to follow the Lord Jesus.

Now, Saul had been just showing himself as a most decided obstacle in the way of the man of faith; indeed, his entire course was one of hostility to the principles of God. How, then, could he destroy Amalek? Impossible. "He spared Agag." Just so. Saul and Agag suited each other but too well, nor had he power to execute the judgment of God on this great en-emy of His people. And mark the ignorance and self-complacency of this unhappy man. "And Samuel came to Saul; and Saul said unto him, Blessed be thou of the Lord: *I have per-formed the commandment of the Lord.*" Per-formed the commandment of the Lord, while Agag, king of the Amalekites, was yet alive! Oh, to what lengths of vain delusion will one go when not walking uprightly before God!

"What meaneth then this bleating of the sheep in my ears?" Solemn, heart-searching inquiry! In vain is recourse had to the plausible matter of *"sacrifice unto the Lord."* Miserable resource for disobedient hearts! As if the Lord would accept a sacrifice from one walking in positive rebellion against His commandment. How many since Saul's day have sought to cover a disobedient spirit with the plausible mantle of "sacrifice unto the Lord." Samuel's answer to Saul is of universal application, viz.: "Hath the Lord as great delight in burnt offerings and sacrifices as in obeying the voice of the Lord? Behold, to obey is better than sacrifice, and to hearken than the fat of rams. For rebellion is as the sin of witchcraft, and stubbornness is as iniquity and idolatry." The Lord seeks not offerings, but obedience: the subject heart and acquiescent spirit will glorify Him more than the cattle upon a thousand hills.

How important to have this great principle pressed home upon the conscience, when so many are cloaking all sorts of disobedience with the word, sacrifice, sacrifice! *"To obey is better than sacrifice."* It is far better to have the will in subjection to God than to load His altar with the costliest sacrifices. When the will is in subjection, everything else will take its due place; but for one whose will is in rebellion against God to talk of sacrificing to Him is nothing but deadly delusion. God looks not at the amount of the sacrifice, but at the spirit from which it springs. Moreover, it will be found that all who, in Saul's spirit, speak of sacrificing unto the Lord, have concealed beneath some selfish object—some Agag or other—the best of the sheep—or something attractive to the flesh, which is more influential than the service or worship of the blessed God.

May all who read these pages seek to know the real blessedness of a will entirely subject to God, for in it will be found that blessed rest which the meek and lowly Jesus promised to all who were heavy laden—the rest which He Himself found in being able to say, "I thank Thee, O Father . . . *for so it seemed good in Thy sight."* God had desired Saul to destroy Amalek, but his heart desired to spare something which to *him*, at least, seemed good and desirable; he was ready to carry out the will of God in reference to all that was *"vile and refuse,"* but he thought he might make some exceptions, as if the line of distinction between that which was "refuse" and that which was "good" was to be drawn by his judgment, and not by the unerring judgment of Him who looked at Amalek from a true point of view, and saw in Agag one who, with all his delicacy, would resist Israel as strongly as ever, and this was His ground of controversy with Amalek, which Saul was unable to understand or appreciate.

The close of this chapter shows us, but too plainly, the current in which Saul's thoughts and desires were flowing. He had just heard the solemn appeal of Samuel, and the denunciations of God against him, concluded with these solemn words, "The Lord hath rent the kingdom of Israel from thee this day, and hath given it to a neighbor of thine, that is better than thou." These stunning words had just fallen upon his ear; yet so full was he of self, that he could say, *"Honor me* now, I pray thee, before the elders of my people, and before Israel."

This was Saul. *"The people,"* said he, "spared what should have been destroyed"— it was their fault, but *"honor me."* Alas, what vanity! A heart steeped in iniquity seeking honor from his fellow-worms. Rejected of God as an office-bearer, he clings to the thought of human honor. It seems that, provided he could maintain his place in the estimation of his people, he cared but little what God thought of him. But he was rejected of God, and the kingdom torn from him; nor did it avail him much that Samuel turned again, and stood by, while Saul went through the form of worshiping the Lord, in order that he might not forfeit his place and influence amongst his people.

"Then said Samuel, Bring hither to me Agag, the king of the Amalekites; and Agag came unto him delicately. And Agag said, Surely the bitterness of death is past. And Samuel said, As thy sword hath made women childless, so shall thy mother be childless, among women. *And Samuel hewed Agag in pieces before the Lord in Gilgal."* Agag's delicacy could not deceive one who was taught of God. How remarkable to find him hewing Agag in pieces *at Gilgal!* Gilgal was the place where the reproach of Egypt was rolled away from Israel;* and, in tracing their history, we find it associated with much power over evil. Here it was, then, that this Amalekite came to his end by the hand of righteous Samuel.

This is most instructive. When the soul is blessed with the realization of its full deliverance from Egypt, by the power of death and resurrection, it is in the best position for obtaining victory over evil. Had Saul known anything of the spirit and principle of Gilgal, he would not have spared Agag. He was ready enough to go thither to "renew the kingdom," but by no means so to crush and set aside all that savored of the flesh. But Samuel, acting in the energy of the Spirit of God, dealt with Agag according to the principles of truth; for it is written, "The Lord hath sworn that the Lord will have war with Amalek from generation to generation." *The king of Israel ought to have known this.*

Part 1

DAVID ANOINTED

We now come to our theme—our rich and varied theme—the life and times of David, king of Israel.

In looking through Scripture, we observe how wonderfully the blessed God has ever brought good out of evil. It was Israel's sin to reject their King, Jehovah, and seek to set up a man over them; and in that man, who first wielded the sceptre over them, they had learnt how vain was the help of man. The Lord was now about to bring blessing to His people out of all their evil and folly.

Saul had been set aside, in the government of God; he had been weighed in the balance, and found wanting; his kingdom was to pass away from under his hand, and a man after God's own heart was about to be set upon the throne, to the glory of God, and the blessing of His people. "And the Lord said unto Samuel, How long wilt thou mourn for Saul, seeing I have rejected him from reigning over Israel?"

These words let us into the secret of Samuel's sorrow in reference to Saul, during the long period of his separation from him. In the last verse of chap. 15 we read, "And Samuel came no more to see Saul until the day of his death; nevertheless Samuel mourned for Saul." This was natural. There was much that was affecting—deeply affecting to the heart in the melancholy fall of this unhappy man. He had once elicited from Israel the shout of "God save the king." Many an eye, full of enthusiasm, had doubtless rested upon "the choice young man and the goodly," and now all this was gone; Saul was rejected, and Samuel felt constrained to take a position of entire separation from him as one whom God had set aside.

This was the second office-bearer whom it had been Samuel's lot to see stripped of his robes of office; he had been the bearer of heavy tidings to Eli, at the opening of his career; and now, at the close of it, he was called upon to deliver, in the ear of Saul, the announcement of the judgment of Heaven against his course.

However, Samuel was called to enter into the thoughts of God in reference to Saul. "How long wilt *thou* mourn for Saul, seeing *I* have rejected him?" Communion with God will ever lead us to acquiesce in His ways. Sentimentalism may weep over fallen greatness, but faith grasps the great truth that God's unerring counsel shall stand, and He will do all His pleasure. Faith could not shed a tear over Agag, when hewed in pieces before the Lord, neither would it continue over a rejected Saul, because it ever flows in harmony with God, in His ways. But there is a wide difference between nature and faith; while the former sits down to weep, the latter arises and fills the horn with oil.

It is well to ponder this contrast. We are all too apt to be carried away by mere sentiment, which is often truly dangerous. Indeed, inasmuch as it is of nature, it must flow in a

---

* It was at Gilgal, upon their crossing Jordan, that Israel was circumcised after the forty years' uncircumcision in the wilderness; and to this place Joshua oft led them back after their victories. The meaning of this for us Christians is given in Phil. 3: 3—no self-confidence. [Ed.]

current different from the thoughts of the Spirit of God. Now, the most effectual remedy against the working of mere sentiment is a strong, deep, thorough, abiding conviction of the reality of the purpose of God. In the view of this, sentimentality withers and dies, while, on the other hand, faith lives and flourishes in the atmosphere of the purpose of God. This is impressively taught in the first verse of chap. 16: "How long wilt thou mourn? . . . Fill thy horn with oil, and go: I will send thee to Jesse the Bethlehemite: for I have provided Me a king among his sons."

Yes; human sorrow must flow on until the heart finds repose in the rich resources of the blessed God. The varied blanks which human events leave in the heart can only be filled up by the power of faith in the precious word, *"I have provided."* This really settles everything. This dries the tear, alleviates the sorrow, fills the blank. The moment the spirit rests in the provision of God's love, there is a period put to all repinings. May we all know the power and varied application of this truth; may we know what it is to have our tears dried up, and our horn filled by the conviction of our Father's wise and merciful provision.

This is a rare blessing; it is difficult to get completely above the region of human thought and feeling. Even a Samuel is found replying to the divine command, and manifesting a slowness to run in the way of simple obedience. The Lord said, *"Go;"* but Samuel said, *"How can I go?"* Strange inquiry! yet how fully it develops the moral condition of the human heart. Samuel had been mourning for Saul, and now, when told to go and anoint one to fill his place, his reply is, "How can I?" Now we may be quite sure that faith never says this. There is no such word as "how" in the vocabulary of faith. No; the divine command no sooner marks out the path, than faith takes it up in willing obedience, not counting the difficulties.

However, the Lord, in tender mercy, meets His servant in his difficulty. "And the Lord said, Take a heifer with thee, and say, I am come to sacrifice to the Lord." Thus with a full horn and a sacrifice he sets off to the city of David, where an obscure and unthought-of youth tended a few sheep in the wilderness.

Amongst the sons of Jesse, there would seem to have been some very fair specimens of nature—some whom Samuel, if left to the exercise of his own judgment, would have fixed upon to succeed to the crown of Israel. "And it came to pass when they were come, that he looked upon Eliab, and said, Surely the Lord's anointed is before Him." But it was not so. Natural attraction had nothing to do with the Lord's election. He looks beneath the gilded surface of men and things, and judges according to His own unerring principles. We learn something of Eliab's haughty and self-sufficient spirit in chap. 17. But the Lord puts no confidence in the legs of a man, and thus Eliab was not His chosen vessel.

It is very remarkable to find Samuel so much and so often astray in this chapter. His mourning for Saul, his hesitation to go and anoint David, his mistake about Eliab, all shows how much astray he was as to the ways of God. How solemn is the Lord's word, "Look not on his countenance, or on the height of his stature; because I have refused him: for the Lord seeth not as man seeth; for man looketh on the outward appearance, but the Lord looketh on the heart." This is the great difference; *the outward appearance,"* and *"the heart."* Even Samuel was well-nigh snared by the former, had not the Lord graciously interfered to teach him the value of the latter. "Look not on his countenance." Memorable words!

"Then Jesse called Abinadab, and made him pass before Samuel. And he said, Neither hath the Lord chosen this. Then Jesse made Shammah to pass by. And he said, Neither hath the Lord chosen this. Again, Jesse made *seven of his sons* to pass before Samuel. And Samuel said unto Jesse, The Lord hath not chosen these." Thus the perfection, as it were, of nature passed before the prophet, but all in vain; nature could produce nought for God or His people.

And, what is still more remarkable, Jesse thought not of David in all this! The ruddy youth was in the solitude of the wilderness, with the sheep, and came not into mind in this review of nature's offspring. But, ah, the eye of Jehovah was resting upon this despised youth, and beholding in him the one who was to stand in the line through which, according to the flesh, Christ should come, to occupy the throne of David, and rule over the house of Israel for ever. Truly "God seeth not as man seeth," for He "hath chosen the foolish things of the world, to confound the wise; and God hath chosen the weak things of the world, to confound things which are mighty; and base things of the world, and things which are despised, hath God chosen— yea, and things which are not, to bring to nought things that are; that no flesh should glory in His presence" (1 Cor. 1:27-29).

If Eliab, or Shammah, or Abinadab, or any one of the "seven sons" of Jesse had had the anointing oil poured upon his head, flesh might have gloried in the presence of God; but the moment David—the forgotten David —appears on the scene, we recognize in him one who would give all the glory to Him who was about to put the sceptre into his hand. In a word, David stands before us as the marked type of the Lord Jesus, who, when He appeared amongst men, was despised, over- looked, and forgotten. And I may just add here, that we shall find, in ranging through David's instructive history, how strikingly he shadowed forth the true beloved of God.

"And Samuel said unto Jesse, Are here all thy children? And he said, There remaineth yet the youngest, and, behold, he keepeth the sheep. And Samuel said unto Jesse, Send and fetch him: for we will not sit down till he come hither. And he sent, and brought him in. Now he was ruddy, and withal of a beauti- ful countenance, and goodly to look at. And the Lord said, Arise, anoint him: *for this is he.*" "There remaineth yet the youngest." Surely he could not be the elect one, thought Jesse. Man cannot understand the ways of God. The very instrument which God is about to make use of is overlooked or despised by man. "Arise, anoint him: for this is he," is God's perfect reply to the thoughts of Jesse and Samuel.

And how happy it is to note David's occupation. "Behold, he keepeth the sheep." This was afterwards referred to by the Lord,

when He said to David, "I took thee from the sheep-cote, from following the sheep, to be ruler over My people, over Israel." Nothing can more sweetly illustrate God's thoughts of the kingly office than the work of a shepherd. Indeed, when it is not executed in the spirit of a shepherd, it fails of its end. King David fully entered into this, as may be seen in those touching words, *"These sheep*, what have they done?"

The people were the Lord's sheep, and he, as the Lord's shepherd, kept them on the mountains of Israel, just as he had kept his father's sheep in the retirement of Bethle- hem. He did not alter his character when he came from the sheep-cote to the throne, and exchanged the crook for the sceptre. No; he was the shepherd still, and he felt himself re- sponsible to protect the Lord's flock from the lions and bears which ever prowled around the fold.

The prophetic allusion to the true David is touching and beautiful. "Therefore will I save My flock, and they shall no more be a prey; and I will judge between cattle and cattle. And I will set up one shepherd over them, and He shall feed them, even My servant David; He shall feed them, and He shall be their shepherd. And I the Lord will be their God, and My servant David a prince among them; I the Lord have spoken it" (Ezek. 34:22-24). Our Lord in John 10 presents Himself as the faithful and good Shepherd who loves and cares for His sheep; and, doubtless, in John 6, He had more or less reference to His shepherd character.

"And this is the Father's will which hath sent Me, that of all which He hath given Me, I should lose nothing, but should raise it up again at the last day." This is a great principle of truth. Independent of His own personal love for the sheep—so wonderfully attested in life and in death—the Lord Jesus, in the above memorable passage, presents Himself as one responsible—voluntarily so, no doubt—to the Father, to keep every member of the loved and valued flock through all the vicissitudes of this life, and present them in resurrection-glory, at the last day.

Such is the Shepherd to whom a Father's

hand has committed us; and, oh, how has He provided for us for time and eternity, by placing us in such hands—the hands of an ever-living, ever-loving, all-powerful Shepherd, whose love many waters cannot quench; whose power no enemy can countervail; who holds in His hand the keys of death and hell, and who has established His claim to the guardianship of the flock, by laying down His life for it. Truly we may say, "The Lord is my Shepherd, I shall not want." How can we want while Jesus feeds us? Impossible. Our foolish hearts may often desire to feed on noxious pasture, and our Shepherd may have to prove His gracious care by denying us the use of such, but one thing is certain, that those whom Jesus feeds shall not want any *good* thing.

There is something in the shepherd character which would seem to be much in harmony with the divine mind, inasmuch as we find the Father, the Son, and the Spirit, all acting in that character. The twenty-third psalm may be primarily viewed as the experience of Christ delighting in the assurance of His Father's shepherd-care. Then, in John 10, we find the Son presented as the good Shepherd. Lastly, in Acts 20 and 1 Pet. 5, we find the Holy Ghost acting in that blessed capacity, by raising up and gifting for the work the subordinate shepherds. It is edifying to mark this. It is like our God to present Himself in the most endearing relationship, and that most calculated to win our confidence and draw out our affections. Blessed be His name forever! His ways are all perfect; there is none like Him.

I would just direct the reader's attention to the contrast between the circumstances in which Samuel found David, and those in which he found Saul. Remember that Saul was in pursuit of his father's asses, when he came in contact with Samuel. I do not interpret this fact, I merely refer to it. I believe it is expressive, in the way of evil, just as David's occupation, in the sheep-cote, was expressive of his future career, as the shepherd of Israel.* When we see David tending his father's sheep in the wilderness, overlooked, or thought little of in the circle of his brethren, we are led to look for something corresponding in his after-course; nor are we disappointed. Just so, when we see Saul in search of his father's asses, we are led to look for something corresponding in his character and habits afterwards.

Trifling circumstances often teach a great deal. David's affectionate and tender solicitude for the Lord's flock and forgetfulness of self, may all be traced in the circumstances in which he is introduced to our notice; and, on the other hand, Saul's ambitious, self-seeking spirit may be traced in the object of his pursuit when he came in contact with Samuel. However, I simply leave the suggestion with the reader to use as the Lord may lead him, only reminding him that nothing can be insignificant which the Spirit has recorded concerning men who appear throughout in such marked contrast, and who each, in his way, occupied such an important place in the history of the people of God.

One can only say, Blessed be the grace which took up one to be ruler over His people, who manifested those traits of character which were most blessedly adapted to his work. "Then Samuel took the horn of oil, and anointed him in the midst of his brethren: and the Spirit of the Lord came upon David from that day forward." Thus, then, David is fully before us as the Lord's anointed, and we have now to trace him in all his wanderings and vicissitudes, while rejected of man, and waiting for the kingdom.

Part 2

THE VALLEY OF ELAH

No sooner had the anointing oil of the Lord been poured upon David, than he was called forth from his retirement to stand before king Saul, now forsaken of God, and troubled with an evil spirit. This unhappy man needed the soothing notes of David's harp to dispel

---

* "Yea, man is born as a wild ass's colt" says Job 11: 12, describing man's natural condition—wilful, unmanageable, unclean. Compare Exod. 13:13, and Hosea 8:9. Saul and Israel were only too manifestly pictured in this unsuccessful search after his father's asses. David was the keeper of his father's sheep. [Ed.]

the horrid influence of that spirit which now haunted him from day to day. Wretched man! sad monument of the results of a self-seeking course!

David, however, did not hesitate to take his place as *a servant*, even in the house of one who was afterwards to prove his most bitter enemy. It was quite the same to him where he served or what he did; he would protect his father's flocks from lions and bears, or dispel an evil spirit from Saul. In fact, from the moment David's history opens, he is seen as a servant, ready for every kind of work, and the valley of Elah furnishes a most striking manifestation of his servant character.

Saul would seem to have had little idea of who it was that stood before him, and whose music refreshed his troubled spirit; he knew not that he had in his presence the future king of Israel. "He loved him greatly; and he became his armor-bearer." The selfish Saul would gladly use the services of David in his need, though ready to shed his blood when he understood who and what he was.

But let us turn our thoughts to the deeply interesting scenes in the valley of Elah.

"Now the Philistines gathered together their armies to battle." Here now we come to something calculated to bring out the true character and worth of Saul and David, the man of form and the man of power. It is trial that brings out the reality of a man's resources. Saul had already been proved, for "all the people had followed him trembling," nor was he likely to prove a more soul-stirring leader on this occasion. A man forsaken of God, and plagued by an evil spirit, was but little adapted to lead on an army to battle, and still less to meet, single-handed, the powerful giant of Gath.

The struggle in the valley of Elah was rendered exceedingly peculiar by the challenge, on the part of Goliath, to decide the matter by single combat; it was the very method in which an *individual* might be signalized. It was not, as in ordinary cases, army against army, but it was a question of who, throughout all the host of Israel, would venture to stand before the terrific uncircumcised foe. In fact, it is plain that the

blessed God was about to make manifest again to Israel that, as a people, they were utterly powerless, and that their only deliverance, as of old, was the arm of Jehovah, who was still ready to act in His wondrous character of "a man of war," whenever faith addressed Him as such.

For forty successive days did the Philistine draw near and present himself in the view of the unhappy Saul and his awe-struck army. And observe his bitter taunt—"Am not I a Philistine, and *ye servants to Saul?*" Alas! it was but too true; they had come down from their high elevation as servants to Jehovah to become mere servants to Saul. Samuel had forewarned them of all this—he had told them that they would become footmen, bakers, cooks, and confectioners to their self-chosen master; and all this, as their choice, instead of having the Lord God of Israel as their sole master and King. Nothing will teach man, however, save bitter experience; and the cutting taunts of Goliath would, no doubt, teach Israel afresh the real nature of their condition under the crushing rule of the Philistines. "Choose you *a man* for you, and let him come down to me," said the giant. How little did he know who was about to be his antagonist. He, in all his boasted fleshly strength, vainly imagined that no Israelite could stand before him.

And here we may inquire, what of Jonathan in all this scene? He who had acted in such simple faith and energy in chap. 14, why was he not now ready to go forth against this champion? I doubt not if we look particularly at his actings, we shall find that his faith was not of that simple, independent character which would carry a man through all kinds of difficulties. The defect in his faith appears in the words, "*If* they say thus," etc.

Faith never says "if"; it has to do only with God. When Jonathan said "There is no restraint to the Lord," he uttered a fine principle of truth, and one which should have carried him on without an "if." Had Jonathan's soul been reposing simply in the ability of *God*, he would not have sought for a sign. True, the Lord graciously gave him the sign, just as He had given one to Gideon before, for He ever meets His servants in all their needs.

However, Jonathan does not make his appearance in the valley of Elah; he had, it seems, done his work, and acted according to his measure; but, in the scene now before us, there was a demand for something far deeper than anything Jonathan had known.

But the Lord was secretly preparing an instrument for this new and more difficult work. And may we not say it is ever thus that the blessed God acts? He trains in secret those whom He is about to use in public. He makes His servants acquainted with Himself in the secret solemnity of His sanctuary, and causes His greatness to pass in review before them, that thus they may be able to look with a steady gaze at the difficulties of their path.

Thus it was with David. He had been alone with God while keeping the sheep in the wilderness; his soul had become filled with the thought of God's power; and now he makes his appearance in the valley of Elah, in all the simplicity and self-renouncing dignity of a man of faith. The emptiness of man had been fully proved by the forty days of Goliath's haughty boasting. Saul could avail nothing; Jesse's three eldest sons could avail nothing; yea, even Jonathan could avail nothing; all was lost, or seemed to be, when the stripling David entered the scene, clothed in the strength of Him who was about to lay in the dust the pomp and glory of the proud Philistine.

The words of Goliath were reported to David, and in them he at once recognized a blasphemous defiance of the living God. "Who," said he, "is this uncircumcised Philistine, that he should defy the armies of *the living God?*" David's faith recognized in the trembling host before him the army of the living God, and he at once made it a question between Jehovah and the Philistine.

This is most instructive: for no change of circumstances can ever rob the people of God of their dignity in the eye of faith. They may be brought low in the view of man, as in Israel's case on the present occasion, but faith ever recognizes what God has imparted; and hence David, as he beheld his poor brethren fainting in the view of their terrible enemy, was enabled to acknowledge those with whom the living God had identified Himself, and who ought not, therefore, to be defied by an uncircumcised Philistine.

When faith is in exercise, it brings the soul into direct connection with the grace and faithfulness of God and His purposes toward His people. True, Israel had brought all this sorrow and humiliation upon themselves by their unfaithfulness; it was not of the Lord that they should quail in the presence of an enemy; it was the fruit of their own doing, and faith would ever apprehend and acknowledge this. Still, the question is, "Who is this uncircumcised Philistine?"

This is the inquiry of faith. It was not the army of *Saul* that the man of faith beheld. No; it was the army of the *living God*—an army under the command of the same Captain that had led His hosts through the Red Sea, through the terrible wilderness, and through Jordan. Nothing less, nothing lower than this, was in the eye of faith.

But then, how little are the judgment and the actings of faith understood or valued when things get low amongst the people of God! This is very apparent on every page of Israel's history, and, we may say, on every page of the Church's history also. The path of simple, childlike faith is far removed from human sight; and if the Lord's people sink into a low, carnal state, they can never understand the principle of power in the soul of one really acting by faith. He will be misunderstood in various ways, and have wrong motives attributed to him; he will be accused of setting himself up, or acting wilfully, independently. All these things must be expected by one who stands in the breach, at a time when things are low. Through lack of faith in the majority, a man is left alone, and then, when he is led to act for God, he will be misinterpreted.

Thus it was in David's case. Not only was he left alone in the time of difficulty, but he had to endure the taunt of the flesh, administered by Eliab, his eldest brother. "And Eliab his eldest brother heard when he spake unto the men; and Eliab's anger was kindled against David, and he said, Why camest thou down hither? and with whom hast thou left those few sheep in the wilderness? *I know thy pride, and the naughtiness of thy heart;*

for thou art come down that thou mightest see the battle" (chap. 17:28). This was the judgment of Eliab, in reference to the actings of David. "And David said, What have I now done? Is there not a cause?"

David was borne onward by an energy quite unknown to Eliab, nor was he careful to enter upon a defence of his course to his haughty brother. Why had not Eliab acted himself for the defence of his brethren? Why had not Abinadab or Shammah acted? Because they were faithless; simply this. Not only had those three men remained powerless, but the whole congregation had remained terror-stricken in the presence of the enemy, and now, when one appeared in their midst whom God was about to use marvelously, not one could understand him.

"And David said to Saul, Let no man's heart fail because of him; thy servant will go and fight with this Philistine." Precious faith! no difficulty deters it—nothing stands in its way. What was the Philistine to David? Nothing. His tremendous height, his formidable armor, were mere circumstances; *and faith never looks at circumstances, but looks straight to God.* Had not David's soul been buoyed up by faith, he could not have uttered the words, "Thy servant will go"; for, harken to the words of him who ought to have been the first to face Israel's dreadful enemy: "And Saul said to David, Thou art not able to go against this Philistine." What language for the king of Israel! What a contrast between the man of office and the man of power!

Surely Saul ought to have gone forth in the defence of the flock which had been intrusted to his care; but, ah! Saul cared not for Israel, unless so far as Israel was connected with himself, and hence his exposing his person on their behalf never, we may safely say, entered his selfish heart; and not only was he unable and unwilling to act himself, but would fain clog the energies of one who, even now, was putting forth the precious fruits of that divine principle implanted within him, and which was about to prove him so fit for the high office which the purpose of God had assigned to him, and to which His anointing oil had dedicated him.

"*Thou* art not able." True, but Jehovah was; and David was leaning simply upon the strength of His arm. His faith laid hold of the ability of Him who had appeared to Joshua beneath the walls of Jericho, with a sword drawn in His hand, as "Captain of the host of the Lord." David felt that Israel had not ceased to be the Lord's host, though so far sunk from what they were in Joshua's day. No; they were still the army of the Lord, and the battle was just as much the Lord's battle as when the sun and the moon were arrested in their course in order that Joshua might execute the judgment of God upon the Canaanites. Simple faith in God sustained the spirit of David, though Eliab might accuse him of pride, and Saul might talk of his want of ability.

There is nothing that can possibly give such energy and persevering power as the consciousness of acting *for God*, and that God is acting *with us*. This removes every obstacle; it lifts the soul above all human influence, and brings it into the very region of power omnipotent. Let us only be fully assured that we *are* on the Lord's side, and that His hand is acting with us, and nothing can drive us from the path of service and testimony—conduct us whither it may. "I can do all things," said the apostle, "through Christ which strengtheneth me." And again, "Most gladly therefore will I rather glory in my infirmities, that the power of Christ may rest upon me." The very weakest saint can do all things through Christ. But if man's eye rests on this weak saint, it seems like presumption to talk of "doing all things."

Thus, when Saul looked upon David, and compared him with Goliath, he judged rightly when he said, "Thou art not able to go against this Philistine to fight with him: for thou art but a youth, and he a man of war from his youth." It was a comparison of flesh with flesh, and, as such, it was quite correct. To compare a stripling with a giant would leave little room for hesitation as to the issue of the conflict; but he ought to have compared the strength of Goliath with that of the God of the armies of Israel. This was what David did.

"And David said unto Saul, Thy servant

kept his father's sheep, and there came a lion and a bear, and took a lamb out of the flock: and I went out after him, and smote him, and delivered it out of his mouth: and when he arose against me, I caught him by his beard, and smote him, and slew him. Thy servant slew both the lion and the bear: and this uncircumcised Philistine shall be as one of them, seeing he hath defied the armies of the living God." This was the argument of faith. The hand that had delivered from one difficulty would deliver from another. There is no "if" in all this. David did not wait for a sign; he simply said, "*Thy servant will go.*" David had felt the power of God's presence with him in secret before he came forth to present himself in public as the servant of God and of Israel.

As another has remarked, David had not boasted of his triumph over the lion and the bear; no one seemed to have heard of it before; nor would he probably have spoken of it, had it not been for the purpose of showing what a solid ground of confidence he had in reference to the great work on which he was about to enter. He would fain show that it was not in his own strength he was going forth. So was it in the matter of Paul's rapture to the third Heaven: for fourteen years had that circumstance remained buried as a secret with the apostle, nor would he have divulged it, had not the carnal reasonings of the Corinthians compelled him to do so.

Now, both these cases are full of practical instruction for us. With the majority of us, alas, there is too great a readiness to talk of our doings, or, at least, to think much of them. The flesh is prone to glory in anything that might exalt *self;* and if the Lord, despite of the evil in us, has accomplished any little service by our instrumentality, how speedily is it communicated in a spirit of pride and self-complacency. It is all right to speak of the Lord's grace, and to have our hearts filled with thankful adoration because of it; but this is very different from boasting of things connected with self.

David, however, kept the secret of his triumph over the lion and the bear concealed in his own bosom, and did not bring it forth

until the fitting occasion; nor does he, even then, speak of himself as having achieved aught, but he simply says, "*The Lord that delivered me* out of the paw of the lion, and out of the paw of the bear, He will deliver me out of the hand of this Philistine." Precious, self-renouncing faith!—faith that counts on God for everything, and trusts the flesh in nothing—faith which brings God into every difficulty, and leads us, with deepest thankfulness, to hide self, and give Him all the glory.

But it frequently needs much spirituality to detect the vast difference between the language of faith and the language of mere commonplace and formal religiousness. Saul assumed the garb and phraseology of religiousness; we have already seen much of this in his history, and we see it in his interview with David. Mere *religiousness* and *faith* here are seen in marked contrast. When David had made the clear and unequivocal statement of faith in the presence and power of Jehovah, Saul added, "*Go, and the Lord be with thee.*" But, ah, how little did he know what was involved in having the Lord with him. He *seemed* to trust the Lord, but *in reality* he trusted his armor. Had he understood what he said, why think of putting on armor? "The Lord be with thee" was in Saul's mouth a mere commonplace: it really meant nothing, for he had no idea of David's going *simply* with the Lord.

It is well to dwell upon, and distinctly point out, the evil of this—the evil of using words which, so far as we are concerned, mean nothing, but which involve a trifling with the Lord's name and truth. How often do we speak of trusting the Lord, when, in reality, we are leaning on some circumstance, or set of circumstances. How often do we speak of living by the day, in simple dependence upon God, when, if we judged the positive condition of our souls before God, we should find that we were looking to some human or earthly source of supply. This is a sad evil, and should be most carefully watched against.

It was just what Saul exhibited, when, having made use of the apparently devout expression, "The Lord be with thee," he proceeded to "arm David with his armor, and he put a helmet of brass upon his head; also he armed him with a coat of mail." He had no other idea but that David was to fight in the usual way. No doubt, it was *professedly* in the name of the Lord; but he thought David *ought to use means*. But it happens that we frequently speak of using means and really shut out God; we profess to use means in dependence upon God, and, in reality, use the mere name of God in dependence upon the means. This is virtually, and according to the judgment of faith, to make a God of our means. Whether had Saul more confidence, in the Lord or in the armor? In the armor, no doubt; and so with all who do not truly walk by faith; it is the *means* they lean upon, and not upon God.

Perceive how strikingly all this bears upon the title of this little book, viz.; "The Life of Faith." We can hardly dwell upon any point in our subject more important than that suggested by the interesting scene on which we are immediately dwelling. The man of means, and the man of faith, are really before us; and we can at once perceive how far the latter proceeds in the use of means. Means are to be used, no doubt, but only such means as are perfectly consistent with the full and blessed action of faith, and also with the untarnished glory of the God of all power and grace. Now David felt that Saul's armor and coat of mail were not such means, and he, therefore, refused them. Had he gone with them, the victory would not have been so manifestly the Lord's. But David had professed his faith in the Lord's deliverance, and not in human armor. True, means will be used; but let us take care that our means do not shut out God.*

"And David girded his sword upon his armor, and he assayed to go; for he had not proved it. And David said unto Saul, I cannot go with these; for I have not proved them. And David put them off him." Happy deliverance from the trammels of human policy! It has been observed, and most truly so, that

David's trial was not when he met the giant, in actual conflict, but when he was tempted to use Saul's armor. Had the enemy succeeded in inducing him to go with that, all was gone; but, through grace, he rejected it, and thus left himself entirely in the Lord's hands, and we know what security he found there. This is faith. It leaves itself in God's hand.**

And may we not apply this with much profit to the case of a poor helpless sinner in reference to the forgiveness of his sins? I believe we may. Satan will tempt such an one to seek some addition to the finished work of Christ—something that will detract from the glory of the Son of God as the *only* Saviour of sinners. Now to such I would say, It matters not *what* you add to the work of Christ—you make it of no avail. If it might be permitted to add anything, surely circumcision would have been admitted, as being an ordinance of divine institution; yet the apostle says, "Behold, I Paul say unto you, that if ye be circumcised, Christ shall profit you nothing. For I testify again to every man that is circumcised, that he is a debtor to do the whole law. Christ is become of no effect unto you, whosoever of you are justified by the law; ye are fallen from grace" (Gal. 5:2-4).

In a word, then, we must have Christ *alone;* we want no more, we can do with no less. If our works are to be put in with Christ's, then He is not sufficient. We dishonor the sufficiency of His atonement if we seek to connect aught of our own with it, just as David would have dishonored the Lord by going forth to meet the Philistine champion in Saul's armor. Doubtless many a so-called prudent man would have condemned what seemed to him to be the rashness and foolhardiness of the stripling; indeed, the more practised a man was in human warfare, the more likely would he have been to condemn the course adopted by the man of faith. But what of that? David knew in whom he had believed; he knew it was not rashness that

---

* Faith, waiting on God, allows Him to use what means soever He pleases. It does not ask Him to bless *our* means, but lets Him use His own.

** How often it happens that the child of God or the servant of Christ, harnessed with human devices for his work, finds himself burdened and hampered with these trammels to obedience and faith. Let them be but shaken off, through grace, and the soul cast upon God finds at once the joy and liberty for the service and energy of faith. [Ed.]

was leading him on, but simple faith in God's willingness and ability to meet him in his need.

Few, perhaps, in Saul's army knew the weakness of David as realized by himself in that trying moment. Though all eyes were fastened upon him as one having much self-confidence, yet we know what it was that buoyed up his heart, and gave firmness to his step as he went forth to meet the terrible foe. We know that the power of God was there just as manifestly as when the waters of the sea were divided to make a way for the ransomed to pass over; and when faith brings the power of God into action, nothing can stand in the way.

Verse 40 shows us David's armor. "And he took his staff in his hand, and chose him five smooth stones out of the brook, and put them in a shepherd's bag which he had, even in a scrip; and his sling was in his hand: and he drew near to the Philistine." So, we see, David did use means; but what means! What contempt does David cast upon the ponderous armor of his enemy! How his sling must have contrasted with Goliath's spear like a weaver's beam! In fact, David could not have inflicted a deeper wound upon the Philistine's pride than by coming against him with such weapons. Goliath felt this. "Am I a dog?" said he. It mattered not, in the judgment of faith, what he was, dog or giant; he was an enemy of the people of God, and David was meeting him with the weapons of faith.

"Then said David to the Philistine, Thou comest to me with a sword, and with a spear, and with a shield: but I come to thee in the name of the Lord of hosts, the God of the armies of Israel, whom thou hast defied. This day will the Lord deliver thee into my hand . . . that all the earth may know that there is a God in Israel. And all this assembly shall know that *the Lord saveth not with sword and spear:* for the battle is the Lord's, and He will give you into our hands."*

Here we have the true object of the man of faith, viz., that Israel and all the earth might have a glorious testimony to the power and presence of God in the midst of His people. If David had used Saul's armor it would not have been known that the Lord saved not by sword and spear—his warfare would just seem like any other; but the sling and the stone while giving little prominence to him that used it, gave the glory to Him from whom the victory came.**

Faith ever honors God, and God ever honors faith. David, as has been already remarked, put himself into the hands of God, and the happy result of so doing was victory —full, glorious victory. "David prevailed over the Philistine with a sling and with a stone, and smote the Philistine, and slew him; *but there was no sword in the hand of David."* Magnificent triumph! Precious fruit of simple faith in God! How should it encourage the heart to cast away from it every carnal confidence, and to cling to the only true source of power.

David was made the happy instrument of delivering his brethren from the galling and terrifying threats of the uncircumcised Philistine; he had come into their midst, from the retirement of a shepherd's life, unknown and despised, though the anointed king of Israel; he had gone forth single-handed to meet the enemy of the congregation; he had laid him prostrate, and made a show of him openly; and all this, be it remembered, as *the servant* of God, and the servant of Israel, and in the energy of a faith which circumstances could not shake. It was a wondrous deliverance, gained by a single blow—no manoeuvring of armies—no skill of generals—no prowess of soldiers. No; a stone from the brook, slung by a shepherd's hand, settled the whole matter. It was the victory of faith.

"And when the Philistines saw that their champion was dead, they fled." How vain are those hopes which are based on the perishable resources of flesh, in its greatest apparent strength and energy! Who that saw the giant and the stripling about to engage in

---

* For the important distinction between the expressions, "Lord" and "God"—Jehovah and Elohim—see *Notes on the Book of Genesis*, chap. 2.

** It is interesting to observe David's address to Goliath. He does not say, "I come to thee *with a sling and a stone.*" No; but, "in the name of the Lord of hosts." With him, it is not the means, but "the Lord of Hosts" on which he fixes his eyes.

conflict, but would have trembled for the latter? Who would have thought that all the massy armor would come to nothing before a sling and a stone? Yet see the end. The champion of the Philistines fell, and with him all their fondly-cherished hopes. "And the men of Israel and of Judah arose, and shouted, and pursued the Philistines." Yes: they might well shout, for God was manifestly gone out before them, to deliver them from the power of their enemies. He had been working powerfully by the hand of one whom they knew not, nor recognized, as their anointed king, but whose moral grace might well attract every heart.

But amidst the many thousands who beheld the victory, we read of one whose whole soul was drawn forth in ardent affection for the victor. The most thoughtless must have been struck with admiration of the victory; and, no doubt, it affected individuals differently. At such times, in a certain sense, "the thoughts of many hearts are revealed." Some would envy, some would admire; some would rest in the victory; some in the instrument; some would have their hearts drawn up to "the God of the armies of Israel" who had again come amongst them with a drawn sword in His hand. But there was one devoted heart who was powerfully attracted to *the person* of the conqueror, and this was Jonathan.

"And it came to pass, when he had made an end of speaking unto Saul, that *the soul of Jonathan was knit with the soul of David*, and Jonathan loved him as his own soul" (chap. 18:1.) No doubt Jonathan participated more fully in the joy of all in the triumph of David; but there was more than this in it; it was not merely the triumph, but the person of the triumphant one that drew out the deep and ardent affections of Jonathan's soul. Saul might selfishly seek to retain the valiant David about his person, not because of love for his person, but simply to magnify himself. Not so Jonathan; he *loved* David. David had removed a load from his spirit, and filled up a great blank in his heart.

The challenge of the giant had, as it was each day repeated, developed the poverty of Israel. The eye might have ranged up and down the ranks in search of one able to meet the urgent need, but in vain. As the giant's vaunting words fell on their ears, *"all* the men of Israel, when they saw the man, fled from him, and were sore afraid." "All," yes; all fled, when they heard his words, and saw his size. Terrible was the blank, therefore, left in the heart on this solemn occasion; and when a beloved one appeared to fill up that blank, what wonder that Jonathan's whole soul was drawn out in genuine affection for that one. And be it remembered, that it was David himself, and not his work only, that touched Jonathan's heart. He admired his victory surely, but his person more. It is well to note this, and trace its striking application to the true David.

That we are warranted in making such application will, surely, not be questioned. The whole scene, from first to last, is too remarkable to admit of a question. In Goliath we behold the power of the enemy by which he held the soul in grievous bondage. From this power there was no means of deliverance within human reach. The challenge might be repeated from day to day—but all in vain. From age to age might the solemn verdict be heard throughout the myriads of Adam's fallen posterity, "It is appointed unto men once to die, but after this the judgment"; and the only response which man could yield was, like Israel's response in the valley of Elah, dismay—deep, deep dismay. "Through fear of death, all our lifetime subject to bondage." This was man's response. The need was felt— the void unfilled. The human heart yearned for something, and yearned in vain. The claims of justice could not be met—death and judgment frowned in the distance, and man could only tremble at the prospect.

But blessed be the God of all grace, a deliverer has appeared—One mighty to save, the Son of God, the true David, the Anointed King of Israel and of all the earth. He has met the need, filled up the blank, satisfied the yearnings of the heart. But how? where? when? By His death on Calvary, in that terrible hour when all creation was made to feel the solemn reality of what was being transacted. Yes, the cross was the field where the battle was fought, and the victory won. There it was that the strong man had all his armor taken from him, and his house spoiled. There, justice had its utmost claims fully satisfied; there, the handwriting of ordinances, which was against us, was nailed to the tree. There, too, the curse of a broken law was forever obliterated by the blood of the Lamb, and the needs of a guilty conscience satisfied by the same.

"The precious blood of Christ, as of a lamb without blemish and without spot," settled everything for the believing soul. The poor trembling sinner may stand by and behold the conflict, and the glorious issue thereof, and behold all the power of the enemy laid low by one stroke of his glorious Deliverer, and feel the heavy burden rolled away from his struggling spirit. The tide of divine peace and joy may flow into his soul, and he may walk abroad in the full power of the emancipation purchased for him by the blood, and proclaimed to him in the gospel.

And shall not one thus delivered love *the Person* of the deliverer?—not merely the work, but the Person? Ah! how can it be otherwise? Who that has felt the real depth of his need, and groaned beneath the burden of his sins, can fail to love and adore that gracious One who has satisfied the one and removed the other? The work of Jesus is infinitely precious; it meets the sinner's need, and introduces the soul into a position in which it can contemplate the Person of Christ. In a word, then, the *work* of the Saviour is for the *sinner;* the *Person* of the Saviour is for the saint: what He has *done*, is for the former; what He *is*, is for the latter.

But there may be a mere formal following of Christ while the heart is cold and remains unacquainted with His person. In the sixth chapter of John, we find a multitude of persons following the Lord Jesus merely on selfish grounds, and He is constrained to tell them so: "Verily, verily, I say unto you, Ye seek Me, not because ye saw the miracles, but because ye did eat of the loaves, and were filled." It was not for what He *was* they were seeking Him, but for mere carnal advantage; and hence, when He applies to their hearts the searching statement, "Except ye eat the flesh of the Son of man, and drink His blood,

there is no life in you," we read, "Many of His disciples went back, and walked no more with Him." Now, eating His flesh, and drinking His blood, is, in other words, the soul finding its food, its satisfaction, in the offering of Himself in sacrifice for us.

The whole Gospel of John is a development of the personal glory of the Incarnate Word who is presented to us as "the Lamb of God which taketh away the sin of the world." Yet the natural heart could not receive Him thus, and therefore, "many went back, and walked no more with Him." The majority could not bear to have this truth pressed upon them. But harken to the testimony of one taught of God: "Peter answered and said, Lord, to whom shall we go? Thou hast the words of eternal life; and we believe and are sure that Thou art the Christ, the Son of the living God." Here we have the two things, viz.: what He *had* for them, what He *was* to them. He had eternal life to give, and He was the Son of the living God; by the former, the sinner is drawn to Him; by the latter, the saint is bound to Him. He not only meets all our necessities as sinners by His work, but also satisfies our affections and desires as saints by His Person.

This train of thought has been suggested by the deeply interesting and touching interview between David and Jonathan, when the conflict was over. The many thousands of Israel had raised the shout of triumph, and pursued the Philistines to reap the fruits of victory, while Jonathan was delighting himself in the person of the victor. "And Jonathan stripped himself of the robe that was upon him, and gave it to David, and his garments, even to his sword, and to his bow, and to his girdle." This was love, pure, simple, unaffected love—undivided occupation with an attractive object. Love strips itself for the sake of its object. David had forgotten himself and put his life in jeopardy for God and the congregation, and now Jonathan would forget himself for David.

Reader, let us remember that love to Jesus is the spring of true Christianity. Love to Jesus makes us strip ourselves; and, we may say, that to strip self to honor Jesus is the fairest fruit of the work of God in the soul.

Talk they of morals? O Thou bleeding Lamb,
   The great morality is love to Thee.

Very different were the feelings with which Saul regarded the person and work of David. He had not learnt to forget himself and rejoice to see the work done by another. It is the work of grace to be able to do this. We all naturally like to be or to do something—to be looked at and thought of. Thus it was with Saul; he was a self-important man, and was, therefore, little able to bear the songs of the maids of Israel: "Saul hath slain his thousands, and David his ten thousands." Saul could not brook the idea of being second. He forgot how he had trembled at the voice of Goliath; though cowardly he would fain be counted brave and valiant. "And Saul eyed David from that day and forward." Terrible eye!—the eye of envy and bitter jealousy.*

We shall have the occasion to trace the development both of Jonathan's love and Saul's hatred, as we proceed in this work, and must now trace the man of faith through other scenes.

Part 3

THE CAVE OF ADULLAM

From amid the brilliant lustre of the valley of Elah, David passed into very different scenes in the household of Saul, where envious looks and heartless attempts upon his life were the only returns for the soothing notes of his harp, and the valiant exploits of his sling and his sword. Saul owed his continuance on the throne, under God, to David, yet the javelin was Saul's return. But the Lord in His mercy kept His dear servant, amid all the intricacies of his extremely difficult position. "David behaved himself wisely in all his ways; and the Lord was with him. Wherefore, when Saul saw that he behaved himself very wisely, he was afraid of him. But all Israel and Judah loved David, because he went out and came in before them."

Thus was David, while anointed king of Israel, called upon to endure the hatred and reproach of the ruling power, though loved by all who were enabled to trace his moral worth. It was impossible that Saul and David could continue to dwell together; being of totally opposite principles, a separation must necessarily take place. David knew that he was anointed king, but Saul occupied the throne, and he was quite content to wait on God, and in meekness abide His time. Till then, the Spirit of Christ led him in the path of an exile. His way to the throne lay through multiplied sorrows and difficulties. He, like his blessed Master and antitype, was called to suffering first, and glory afterwards.

David would have served Saul to the end—he honored him as "the Lord's anointed." If the moving of his finger would have set him on the throne, he would not have taken advantage of it. Of this we have the fullest evidence in his having twice saved Saul's life, when, to all appearance, the Lord had put him in his power. David waited simply upon God. Here was his strength, his elevation—his entire dependence. He could say, "My soul wait thou *only* upon God, for my expectation is from Him."

Hence we see that David was carried happily through all the snares and dangers of his path as a servant in the household and army of Saul. The Lord delivered him from every evil work, and preserved him unto that kingdom which He had prepared for him, and to which it was His purpose to raise him "after that he had suffered a while." David had, as it were, but just issued from the place of secret discipline and training, to appear in the battle-field, and, having accomplished his work there, he was called to take his place again on the form, to learn some deeper lessons in the school of Christ.

The Lord's lessons are often painful and difficult, because of the waywardness or indolence of our hearts; but every fresh lesson learned, every fresh principle imbibed, only fits us the more for all that is yet before

---

* It requires a very simple heart and single eye to be able to rejoice as unfeignedly in the fruit of another's labors as in that of our own hands. Had the glory of God and the good of His people filled Saul's heart, he would not have spent a thought upon the question as to the numbers attributed to him or to David. Alas, he sought his own glory. This was the secret of his envy and jealousy. Oh, what sacred rest, what true elevation, what perfect quietness of spirit flows from self-renunciation, such self-renunciation as results from having the heart wholly occupied with Christ! When we are honestly seeking the promotion of Christ's glory we shall not be careful as to the instrument.

us. Yet it is blessed to be the disciples of Christ, and to yield ourselves to His gracious discipline and training. The end will unfold to us the blessedness of such a place. Nor need we wait for the end; even now, the soul finds it most happy to be subject, in all things, to the Master. "Come unto Me, all ye that labor and are heavy laden, and I will give you rest. *Take My yoke upon you,* and learn of Me; for I am meek and lowly in heart: and *ye shall find rest unto your souls*. For My yoke is easy, and My burden is light" (Matt. 11:28-30). There are, we may say, three rests spoken of in Scripture. *First*, is the rest which, as sinners, we find in the accomplished work of Christ. *Secondly*, the present rest, which, as saints, we find in being entirely subject to the will of God; this is opposed to *restlessness*. *Thirdly*, the rest that remains for the people of God.

Now, David knew much of the blessedness of the second of these rests, inasmuch as he was entirely subject to the counsel and will of God, in reference to the kingdom. He was prepared to wait for God's time, being assured that it was the best and wisest time. He could say,

> My times are in Thy hand;
> Father, I wish them there.

How desirable this subjection! It saves us from much anxiety of heart and restlessness. When we walk in the habitual conviction that God is making "all things to work together for our good," the spirit is most wonderfully tranquilized. We shall never set about planning for ourselves if we believe that God is planning for us; we shall be satisfied to leave *all* to Him. But alas, how often is it otherwise with us. How often do we vainly imagine that we can manage matters better than the blessed God. We may not say so in so many words; yet we virtually feel and act as if it were so. The Lord grant unto us a more subdued and confiding spirit. The supremacy of the will of God over that of the creature will characterize the millennial age; but the saint is called *now* to let the will of God rule him in all things.

It was this subjection of spirit that led David to give way in the matter of the kingdom, and to take his place in the lonely cave of Adullam. He left Saul, and the kingdom, and his own destinies in the hands of God, assured that all would yet be well. And, oh, how happy was it for him to find himself outside the unhealthy atmosphere of Saul's house, and from under the jealous glance of Saul's eye! He could breathe more freely in the cave, however it might seem in man's view, than in the household of Saul. So will it ever be; the place of separation is the freest and the happiest. The Spirit of the Lord was departed from Saul, and this was faith's warrant for separation from his person, while, at the same time, there was the fullest subjection to his power as the king of Israel. The intelligent mind will have no difficulty in distinguishing between these two things. The separation and the subjection should both be complete.*

But we must view Saul not only in a secular but also in a religious point of view; and it was in reference to the religious element in his personal character and official capacity, that there was the greatest need for distinct and decided separation. Saul had manifested throughout a desire to rule the conscience in religious matters; witness the scene in chap. 14, where, as we have seen, spiritual energy was cramped and hindered by Saul's religious rule. Now, when such rule is set up, there is no alternative but separation. When form without power prevails, the solemn word of the Holy Ghost is, "From such turn away." Faith never stops to inquire, Whither shall I "turn"? We are told what to turn away *from*, and we may be sure that, when we have yielded obedience to this, we shall be left at no loss as to the rest.

However, we shall see this principle in a much clearer light when we regard David in a typical point of view. In reality, David was forced into the place of separation, and thus, as one rejected of man, and anointed of God, we see him a type of Christ in His present rejection. David was, in principle, God's king,

---

* The New Testament teaches the Christian to be subject to the powers that be, but it *never* contemplates the idea of his being in the place of power. Hence, there are no directions for a Christian as a king or a magistrate, though there is ample guidance for a Christian as a husband, a father, a master, or a servant. This speaks volumes.

and as such experienced man's hostility, being driven into exile to avoid death. The cave of Adullam became the great gathering point for all who loved David and were wearied of the unrighteous rule of Saul. So long as David remained in the king's house, there was no call upon any one to separate; but the moment the rejected David took his place outside, no one could remain neutral; wherefore we read, "Every one that was in distress, and every one that was in debt, and every one that was discontented, gathered themselves unto him; and he became a captain over them: and there were with him about four hundred men."

Here was, then, the line of distinction clearly marked. It was now David, or Saul. All who loved form, loved an empty name, a powerless office, continued to adhere to Saul; but all who were dissatisfied with these things, and loved the person of God's anointed king, flocked around him in the hold. The prophet, priest, and king were there—the thoughts and sympathies of God were there, and though the company assembled there must have presented a strange appearance to the carnal and the worldly, yet it was a company gathered round the person of David, and linked with his destinies. It was composed of men whose very condition seems to have driven them to David, but who were now deriving character and distinction from their nearness and devotedness to the person of the beloved. Away from Saul, away from all that marked the day of his power, they could enjoy the sweetness of unhindered fellowship with the person of him who, though now rejected, was ere long to ascend the throne and wield the sceptre, to the glory of God and the joy of His people.

You may clearly perceive in David and his despised company a precious sample of the true David, and those who prefer companionship with Him to all the joys, the honors, and emoluments of earth. Those who had cast in their lot with David—what had they to do with the interests of Saul? They had found a new object, a new centre, and communion with God's annointed.

Nor was their place about the person of

David dependent on, or connected with, what they had been. No; it mattered not what they had been; they were now the servants of David, and he was their captain. This gave them their character. They had cast in their lot with God's exile; their interest and his were identical. Happy company! Happy to escape from the rule and influence of Saul—still more happy to find themselves in companionship with God's anointed king. Their discontent, their distress, their debt, were all forgotten in their new circumstances. The grace of David was their present portion; the glory of David their future prospect.

Just so should it be with Christians now. Through grace, and the gentle leadings of the Father, we have found our way to Jesus—the anointed and rejected Jesus—now hidden with God. No doubt, we all had our respective features of character in the days of our guilt and folly—some discontented, some in distress, all in heavy debt to God—miserable, ruined, guilty, void of everything which could recommend us to Christ: yet God has led us to the feet of His dear Son, where we have found pardon and peace through His precious blood: Jesus has removed our discontent, alleviated our distress, cancelled our debt, brought us near His beloved person.

What return are we making for all this grace? Are we gathering, in ardent affection, round the Captain of our salvation? Are we weaned from the state of things under Saul? Are we living as those who are waiting for the day when our David shall mount the throne? Are our affections set upon things above? "If ye then be risen with Christ," says the apostle, "seek those things which are above, where Christ sitteth on the right hand of God. Set your affection on things above, not on things on the earth. For ye have died, and your life is hid with Christ in God. When Christ, who is our life, shall appear, then shall ye also appear with Him in glory" (Col. 3:1-4).

It is greatly to be feared that few really enter into the true nature and practical consequences of their position as associated with the crucified and risen Jesus—few really enter into the depth and meaning of our Lord's words, "They are not of the world, even as I am not of the world"; or of the Spirit's word, "The Sanctifier and the sanctified are all of one." The measure of the saint's separation from the world is nothing less than Christ's; i.e., the principle of it. Looked at practically, alas, it is quite another thing; but in principle there is no difference. It is of vast importance to enforce this principle. The actual standing, calling and hopes of the Church as so feebly apprehended.

Yet the feeblest believer in Christ is, in God's view, as separate from all belonging to earth as Jesus. It is not a matter of attainment, but of our standing, through grace: not an object after which we must strive, but a point from which we must start. Many have been led astray by the idea that we must work up to a heavenly position by shaking off the things of earth. This is to begin at the wrong end. It is the same error, only in reference to another department of truth, as to assert that we must work up to a condition of justification, by mortifying the sins of the flesh. Now, we do not mortify self *in order to be* justified, but *because we are* justified; yea, dead and risen with Christ.

In like manner, we do not put away things of earth in order to become heavenly, but because we are so. Abram's calling was to leave kindred and go to Canaan; *our* calling is a heavenly one (of which Canaan was a type), and in proportion as we enter into it we will be separate from earth. But to make our standing the result of conduct, instead of conduct the result of standing, is a grievous error.

Ask a saint, really intelligent as to the heavenly calling, to give a reason for his standing apart from the present world: what will he reply? Will he tell you that he does so in order to become heavenly? Nay. Will he tell you that it is because the present world is under judgment? Nay. No doubt *it is* under judgment, but this is not the true ground of separation. What then? "We have died, and our life is hid with Christ in God."—"They are not of the world, even as I am not of the world." "Holy brethren, partakers of the heavenly calling," etc. Here we have the grand reason for the saint's present separation from the world. It does not matter what the world is, be it good or bad; he is not *of* it, though *in* it, as the place of his daily toil, conflict, and discipline.

Christian! ponder well your heavenly calling—it is the only thing that will give full deliverance from the power and influence of worldliness. Men may seek *abstraction* from the world in various ways, but there is only one in which to attain *separation* from it. Again, men may seek to render themselves *unearthly* in various ways; there is only one way in which we can become really *heavenly.* Abstraction is not separation; nor is unearthliness to be mistaken for heavenliness. The monastic system illustrates very fully the distinction between these things. A sincere monk is unearthly, in a certain sense, but by no means heavenly; he is unnatural, but by no means spiritual; he is abstracted from the world, but by no means separated from it.

The Christian's heavenly calling is in virtue of *what* Christ is, and *where* He is. The heart instructed by the Holy Ghost as to the meaning of Heb. 2:11, finds the reason and power of his deliverance from the principles, habits, pursuits, feelings, and tendencies of this present age. The Lord Jesus has taken His place on high as Head of the body, the Church; and the Holy Ghost has come down to lead all the foreknown and predestinated members of Christ into living fellowship with the living Head, now rejected from earth, and hidden with God. Hence in the gospel, as preached by Paul, the remission of sins is inseparably connected with the heavenly calling, inasmuch as he preached the unity of the one body on earth with its Head in Heaven. He preached justification, not merely as an abstract thing, but as the result of what the Church is, as one with Christ, who is now at the right hand of God, Head over all things to His Church, angels and principalities being made subject to Him. Paul preached remission of sins, no doubt, but he preached it all with the fulness, depth, power, and energy which the doctrine of the Church imparts to it.

The Epistle to the Ephesians teaches us not only that God can forgive sinners, but far more than this: it unfolds to us the wondrous truth that believers are members of the body of Christ; "for we," says the apostle, "are members of His body, of His flesh, and of His bones." Again, "But God, who is rich in mercy, for His great love wherewith He loved us, even when we were dead in sins, hath quickened us together with Christ (by grace ye are saved); and hath raised us up together, and made us sit together in heavenly places in Christ Jesus." Again, "Christ also loved the Church, and gave Himself for it; that He might sanctify and cleanse it with the washing of water by the Word. That He might present it to Himself a glorious Church, not having spot, or wrinkle, or any such thing; but that it should be holy and without blemish." These passages present far more than mere remission of sins. To be the bride of the Lamb is a very much higher, very much more glorious thing than only to have our sins forgiven.

> Yet 'tis not that we know the joy
>   Of cancell'd sin alone,
> But, happier far, Thy saints are call'd
>   To share Thy glorious throne.

The blessed God has gone beyond all man's thoughts in His mode of dealing with the Church. He has called us, not only to walk here below in the full sense of His pardoning love, but also to know the love of Christ to His body, the Church, and the high and holy dignity of that Church, as seated in the heavenlies.

My reader may perhaps inquire what has the cave of Adullam to do with the Church's place in the heavens? It has to do with it only so far as it illustrates the present place of rejection into which Christ has entered, and which all must know who enjoy fellowship with Him. Of course, neither David nor his men knew anything about the heavenly calling as the Church now knows it. We may frequently discover in Old Testament

Scriptures, foreshadowings of the heavenly calling, in the character, walk, and circumstances of certain prominent persons which are introduced to our notice.

But the heavenly calling, properly speaking, was not known until the Lord Jesus took His seat on high, and the Holy Ghost came down to baptize believers, Jew and Gentile, into one body; then the heavenly calling was developed in all its power and fulness. This truth was peculiarly committed to Paul; it was an essential part of the mystery committed to him, and was embodied in these words, "Why persecutest thou *ME?*" Saul was persecuting the saints, and the Lord Jesus appeared to him in heavenly glory, and told him that these saints were part of Himself—His members on earth. Henceforce this became Paul's great thesis; in it was involved the oneness of the Church with Christ, and therefore the heavenly calling of the Church.

Observe that all this was not merely an admission of the Gentile into the Jewish fold.* No, it was taking both Jew and Gentile out of their circumstances in nature, and setting them down in new circumstances— new to both. The work of the Cross was needful to break down the middle wall of partition, and to make of twain one new man, i.e., to make of Jew and Gentile a new heavenly man, separated from earth and its aims. The present place of Christ in the heavens is connected with His rejection by Israel, during what is called the Church period, and serves to bring out still more distinctly the heavenly character of the Church of God. She belongs to Heaven, and is called to manifest on earth the living energy of the Holy Ghost who dwells in her.

Thus, as David's men were withdrawn from all connection with Saul's system by virtue of their association with him, so all those who are led by the Spirit to know their

---

* I would say a word here, on the opening verses of John 10.

The Lord Jesus presented Himself at the door of the Jewish fold, and having obtained entrance, called out His sheep that were therein, and then He says, "Other sheep I have which are not of this fold; them also I must bring, and they shall hear My voice; and there shall be one *flock*, and one Shepherd." It is strange that the translators should have rendered this "one fold," when the word fold (αυλης) actually occurs in the same verse. Nor is the distinction unimportant. A fold is an enclosure for the separation and safety of the sheep; hence the word is properly applied to the Jewish economy. Now, however, it is no longer a fold—an earthly arrangement—a penning up of sheep here below. But the heavenly Shepherd has called forth His Jewish sheep from the earthly fold, and His Gentile sheep from the dark mountains of this wide world, and made them one flock, giving them freedom, and committed them into the Father's hand. Thus we see the difference between the words "fold" and "flock."

oneness with the rejected Jesus, must feel themselves dissociated from present things, by reason of that blessed oneness with Him.

Hence, if you ask a heavenly man why he does not mix himself up with the plans and pursuits of this age, his reply will be, Because Christ is at the right hand of God, and I am identified with Him. He has been cast out by this world and I take my place with Him, apart therefore from its objects and pursuits. All who understand the true nature of the heavenly calling will walk in separation from the world; but those who do not, will just take their portion here, and live as others.

Many, alas, are satisfied with the mere knowledge of the forgiveness of sins, and never think of going further. They have passed through the Red Sea, it may be, but manifest no desire to cross the Jordan, and eat the old corn of the land of promise. Just as it was in the day of David's rejection; many, though Israelites, did not cast in their lot in rejection with him. It was one thing to be an Israelite; it was another thing to be with David in the hold. Even Jonathan was not there; he still adhered to the old system of things. Though loving David as his own soul, he lived and died in companionship with Saul. True, he ventured to speak *for* David, and sought his company when he could. He had stripped himself to clothe David; yet he did not cast in his lot *with* him. And, consequently, when the names and the deeds of David's worthies are heralded by the Holy Ghost, we look in vain for the name of the affectionate Jonathan; when the devoted companions of David's exile were mustering round his throne in the sunshine of his royal countenance, poor Jonathan was mingled with the dust, having ingloriously fallen, on mount Gilboa, by the hands of the uncircumcised Philistines!

Oh that all who profess to love the Lord Jesus Christ may seek a more decided identification with Him in this the time of His rejection! The citizens have sent a message after Him, saying, "We will not have this man to reign over us"; and shall we go and associate ourselves with those citizens to forward their Christ-rejecting plans? God forbid. May our hearts be with Him where He

is. May we know the hallowed fellowship of the cave of Adullam, where the Prophet, Priest, and King are to be found, embodied in the beloved Person of Him who loved us, and washed us from our sins in His own blood.

We cannot walk with Saul and David at the same time. We cannot hold Christ and the world—we must take our choice. The Lord grant us grace to reject the evil and choose the good, remembering the solemn words of the apostle: "This is a faithful saying; for if we be *dead with Him*, we shall also *live with Him*; if we *suffer*, we shall also *reign* with Him; if we deny Him, He also will deny us." This is the time of suffering, the time for enduring afflictions and hardness; we must wait for the time of rest and glory.

David's men were called, by reason of their association with him, to undergo much toil and fatigue, but love made all light and easy to them; and their names and exploits were recorded and faithfully remembered when David was at rest in his kingdom. None were forgotten. The twenty-third chapter of Second Samuel will furnish the reader with the precious catalogue, and will, no doubt, lead his mind onward to the time when the Lord Christ shall reward *His* faithful servants—those who from love to His person, and by the energy of His Spirit, have performed acts of service for Him in the time of His rejection. These acts may not be seen, known, or thought of by men; but Jesus knows them, and will publicly declare them from the throne of His glory. Who would ever have known the acts of David's worthies if the Holy Ghost had not recorded them? Who would have known of the three who drew water from the well of Bethlehem? Who would have known of the slaying of a lion in a pit, in the time of snow?

Just so now: many a heart throbs with love to the Person of the Saviour, unknown to all; and many a hand may be stretched forth in service to Him, unobserved by human eye. It is sweet to think it is so, specially in an age of cold formality like the present—sweet to think of those who love the Lord Jesus Christ in sincerity. Some there are, alas, who are not only indifferent to His beloved Person, but who even go as far as to traduce Him—to rob Him of His dignity, and make Him little better than Elias, or one of the prophets. But we shall not dwell upon these; we have, thank God, a happier theme, and we shall, with His help, pursue it.

We shall think of those valued men who jeoparded their lives for the sake of their captain, and who, the instant he uttered his desire, were ready, at all cost, to gratify it. Love never pauses to calculate. It was quite sufficient for those worthies to know that David longed for a drink from the well of Bethlehem, and they procured it at any cost to themselves: "And these three mighty men brake through the host of the Philistines, and drew water out of the well of Bethlehem, that was by the gate, and took it and brought it to David: nevertheless he would not drink thereof, but poured it out unto the Lord."* Lovely scene! Sweet sample of what the Church ought to be! Loving not her life unto the death for Christ's sake.

Oh that the Holy Ghost may kindle within us a flame of ardent love to the person of Jesus—may He unfold to our souls more of the divine excellencies of His person, that we may know Him to be the fairest amongst ten thousand, and altogether lovely, and be able to say with a true worthy, "Yea, doubtless, and I count all things but loss for the excellency of the knowledge of Christ Jesus my Lord; for whom I have suffered the loss of all things, and do count them but dung, that I may win Christ" (Phil. 3:8).

* There is something peculiarly touching and beautiful in the above scene, whether we contemplate the act of the three mighty men in procuring the water for David, or David's act in pouring it out to the Lord. It is evident that David discerned, in an act of such uncommon devotedness, a sacrifice which none but the Lord Himself was worthy to receive. The odor of such a sacrifice was far too fragrant for him to interrupt it in its ascent to the throne of the God of Israel. Wherefore he, very properly and gracefully, allows it to pass him by, in order that it might go up to the One who alone was worthy to receive it, or able to appreciate it. All this reminds us, forcibly, of that beautiful compendium of Christian devotedness set forth in Phil. 2: 17-18: "Yea, and if I be poured out upon the sacrifice and service of your faith, I joy and rejoice with you all; for this cause do ye also joy and rejoice with me." In this passage, the apostle represents the Philippian saints in their character as priests, presenting a "sacrifice" and performing a priestly ministration to God; and such was the intensity of his self-forgetting devotedness, that he could rejoice in his being poured out as a drink offering upon their sacrifice, so that all might ascend, in fragrant odor, to God. The Philippians laid a sacrifice on God's altar, and the apostle was poured out upon it, and all went up to God as an odor of sweet smell. It mattered not who put the sacrifice on the altar, or who was poured out thereupon, providing that God received what was acceptable to Him. This, truly, is a divine model for Christian devotedness. Would that we had grace to form our ways according to it. There would, then, be far less of "*my* sayings," and "*my* doings," and "*my* goings."

Part 4

NABAL AND ABIGAIL

1 Samuel 25

It is interesting to observe, as we pass from stage to stage of David's history, how different individuals were affected toward his person, and the consequent position assumed in reference to him. It required energy of faith to discern, in the despised outcast, the future king of Israel. In this chapter we are presented with two striking examples of persons thus variously affected in reference to David's person and career.

"There was a man in Maon, whose possessions were in Carmel; and the man was very great, and he had three thousand sheep, and a thousand goats; and he was shearing his sheep in Carmel. Now the name of the man was Nabal." This Nabal was an Israelite, and he appears in marked contrast with David, who, though anointed king of Israel, had not where to lay his head, but was a wanderer from mountain to mountain, and from cave to cave. Nabal was a selfish man, with no sympathy for David. If he had blessings, he had them for himself; if he was "great," he had no idea of sharing his greatness with any one else, and least of all with David and his companions.

"And David heard *in the wilderness* that Nabal did shear his sheep. And David sent out ten young men, and David said to the young men, Get you up to Carmel, and go to Nabal, and greet him in my name," etc. David was in the wilderness; this was his place. Nabal was surrounded by all the comforts of life. The former owed all his sorrows and privations to what he was; the latter owed all his possessions and enjoyments to what he was.

Now, we generally find that where advantages are derived from religious distinction and profession, much selfishness exists. The profession of truth, if not connected with self-denial, will be connected with positive self-indulgence; and hence we may observe at the present day a determined spirit of worldliness connected with the very highest profession of truth. This is a grievous evil. The apostle was made to feel the anguish of it, even in his time. "Many," says he, "walk, of whom I have told you often, and now tell you even weeping, that they are the enemies of *the cross of Christ:* whose end is destruction, whose God is their belly, and whose glory is in their shame, *who mind earthly things*" (Phil. 3:18-19). Observe, they are the enemies of the *Cross* of Christ. They do not throw off any semblance of Christianity; far from it. "Many *walk*." This expression shows a measure of profession.

The persons here pictured would, doubtless, be much offended were any to refuse them the appellation of Christians; but then they do not want to take up the *Cross;* they desire not practical identification with a crucified Christ; whatever amount of professed Christianity can be had apart from all self-denial is welcome to them, but not one jot beyond this. "Their God is their belly, and they mind earthly things." Ah, how many must plead guilty to the charge of minding earthly things! It is easy to make a profession of the religion of Christ, while Christ Himself is unknown, and the cross of Christ is hated. It is easy to take up the name of Jesus into the lips, and walk in self-indulgence and love of the world, which the human heart knows so well how to estimate. All this finds its full illustration in the person of the churlish Nabal, who having shut himself up in the midst of his luxuries and wealth, cared not for God's anointed, nor felt for him in the season of his painful exile and sojourn in the wilderness.

What was his reply to David's touching appeal? "Who is David? and who is the son of Jesse? there be many servants now-a-days that break away every man from his master.

Shall I then take my bread, and my water, and my flesh that I have killed for my shearers, and give it unto men whom I know not whence they be?" Here was the secret of this worldly man's estrangement of heart; *he did not know him;* had he known him, it would have been a very different matter: but he neither knew who he was nor whence he was; he did not know that he was railing on the Lord's anointed, and casting from him, in his selfish folly, the privilege of ministering to the need of the future king of Israel.

The moral of all this is deeply instructive. It demands the clear vision of faith to enable any one to discern the true glory of Christ, and cleave to Him in the time of His rejection. It is one thing to be a Christian, as people say, and another thing to confess Christ before men. Indeed, one can hardly find anything more sefish than that condition of heart which would lead us to take all that Jesus has to give, and yield Him nothing in return. "Provided *I* am saved, all the rest is unessential." This is the secret thought of many a heart, and if thrown into a more honest form would be this, "If I am sure of salvation, it matters little about the glory of Christ."

This was just Nabal's mode of acting; he reaped all the advantage he could from David; but the moment David put in his claim for sympathy and aid, his worldly spirit developed itself. "One of the young men told Abigail, Nabal's wife, saying, Behold, David sent messengers out of the wilderness, to salute our master; and he railed on them. But the men were very good unto us, and we were not hurt, neither missed we anything, as long as we were conversant with them when we were in the fields. They were a wall unto us both by night and by day, all the while we were with them keeping the sheep." This was all very well. Nabal could well understand the value of David's *protection,* though he cared not for David's *person.* So long as David's men were a wall to his possessions, he would tolerate them; but when they would become a burden, they were rejected and railed upon.

Now, as might be expected, Nabal's acting was directly contrary to Scripture, as his spirit was decidedly contrary to the spirit of its divine Author. It is written in the fifteenth chapter of Deuteronomy, "If there be among you a poor man of one of thy brethren, within any of thy gates, in the land which the Lord thy God giveth thee, thou shalt not harden thy heart, nor shut thy hand from thy poor brother; but thou shalt open thy hand wide unto him, and shalt surely lend him sufficient for his need, in that which he wanteth. Beware that there be not a thought in thy wicked heart, saying, The seventh year, the year of release is at hand; and thine eye be evil against thy poor brother, and thou givest him nought; and he cry unto the Lord against thee, and it be sin unto thee." Precious grace! How like God. How unlike Nabal! Grace would keep the heart wide open to every object of need; whereas selfishness would close it against every applicant. Nabal ought to have obeyed the word, independently of his knowledge of David; but his selfishness was too deep a character to allow of his obedience to the Lord's word, or his love to the Lord's anointed.

However, Nabal's selfishness led to very important results; it led, in David's case, to the exhibition of much that was calculated to humble him in the presence of God. He is here seen to come down from the high elevation which usually characterized him, through the grace of God. No doubt, it was deeply trying to meet with such base ingratitude from one to whom he had been a wall of defence; it was galling, too, to be reproached on the very ground of those circumstances in which faithfulness had called him; to be accused of breaking away from his master at the very time that he was being hunted as a partridge through the mountains. All this was hard to bear, and, in the first ebullition of feeling, David gives expression to words which would not bear the examination of the sanctuary. *"Gird ye on every man his sword,"* was not just the language which we should have expected from one who had hitherto walked in such a meek and gentle spirit. The Scripture just quoted presents the resource of the poor brother, viz.: to "cry unto the Lord," not to draw his sword for revenge.

Nabal's selfishness could never have been remedied by the sword of David, nor would faith ever have adopted such a course. We do not find David acting thus in reference to Saul; he left him entirely to God, and even when induced to cut off the skirt of his robe, his heart smote him. Why did he not act thus toward Nabal? Because he was not in communion; he was off his guard, and the enemy took advantage of him. Nature will ever lead us to vindicate ourselves, and resent every injury. The heart will secretly murmur, "He had no right to treat me thus; I really cannot bear it, nor do I think I ought to do so." This may be so, but the man of faith at once rises above all such things; he sees God in everything; the jealousy of Saul, the folly of Nabal, all is looked at as coming from the hand of God, and met in the secret of His holy presence. The instrument is nothing to faith; God is in all. This gives real power to move on through all sorts of circumstances. If we do not trace God in everything, we shall be constantly ensnared.

We shall have occasion, as we proceed with our subject, to trace this principle more fully, and shall now turn to another character introduced to our notice in this instructive chapter. This is Abigail, the wife of Nabal, "a woman of good understanding, and of a beautiful countenance." A noble testimony, surely, and one which shows that grace can manifest itself in the most untoward circumstances. The house of the churlish Nabal must have been a withering scene to one like Abigail; but she waited on God, and, as we shall see, was not disappointed.

The case of this remarkable woman is full of encouragement and instruction to all who may find themselves cramped and hindered by unavoidable connections and associations. To all such the history of Abigail simply says, Be patient, wait on God, do not suppose yourself void of all opportunity for testimony. The Lord may be much glorified by meek subjection, and will, assuredly, give relief and victory in the end. True, some may have to reproach themselves for having formed such connections, or entered into such associations; but even so, if the folly and evil are really felt, confessed, and judged before

God, and the soul brought into an attitude of thorough subduedness, the end will be blessing and peace.

In Abigail we see one who was actually used to correct no less a personage than David himself. It may be that her course, up to the time at which the sacred historian introduces her to our notice, had been marked by much that was painful and trying; indeed, it could hardly have been otherwise, associated with such an one as Nabal. Time, however, brought to light the grace that was in her. She had suffered in obscurity, and was now about to be raised to an unusually high elevation. Few had seen her patient service and testimony; but many beheld her exaltation. The burden which she had borne in secret was about to drop off before many witnesses. The preciousness of Abigail's service did not consist in her having saved Nabal from the sword of David, but in keeping David from drawing the sword at all.

"Now David had said, Surely in vain have I kept all that this fellow hath in the wilderness, so that nothing was missed of all that pertained unto him; and he hath requited me evil for good." This was terrible! And David was rashly taking himself out of the place of dependence—the only happy, the only holy place. Nor was it on behalf of the congregation of the Lord. No, it was to avenge himself on one who had treated him badly. Sad mistake! Happy was it for him, that there was an Abigail in the house of Nabal who was about to be used of God to keep him from answering a fool according to his folly. This was just what the enemy desired. Nabal's selfishness was used by Satan to ensnare David, and Abigail was the Lord's instrument to deliver him.

It is well when the man of God can detect Satan's working; to be able so to do, he must be much in the presence of God, for there alone can he find light and spiritual power to enable him to cope with such a foe. When out of communion, the soul becomes distracted by looking at secondary causes, and subordinate agents, just as David was distracted by looking at Nabal. Had he paused to view the matter calmly before God, we should not have had such words as, "In vain have I kept all that this fellow hath in the wilderness"; he would have passed on, and left "this fellow" to himself. Faith imparts real dignity to the character, and superiority over the petty circumstances of this transient scene. Those who know themselves as pilgrims and strangers, will remember that the sorrows as well as the joys of this life are evanescent, and they will not be inordinately affected by either the one or the other. "Passing away," is written on everything; the man of faith must, therefore, look upwards and onward.

Now Abigail, by the grace of God, delivered David from the unhappy influence of the *present*, by leading his soul onward into the *future:* we learn this from her exquisite address to him. "And when Abigail saw David, she hasted, and lighted off the ass, and fell before David on her face, and bowed herself to the ground, and fell at his feet, and said, Upon me, my lord, upon me let this iniquity be; and let thine handmaid, I pray thee, speak in thine audience, and hear the words of thine handmaid. Let not my lord, I pray thee, regard this man of Belial, even Nabal; for as his name is, so is he; Nabal is his name, and folly is with him: but I thine handmaid saw not the young men of my lord, whom thou didst send. Now, therefore, my lord, as the Lord liveth, and as thy soul liveth, seeing the Lord hath withholden thee from coming to shed blood, and from avenging thyself *with thine own hand*, now let thine enemies and they that seek evil to my lord, be as Nabal . . . for *the Lord will certainly make my lord a sure house; because my lord fighteth the battles of the Lord*, and evil hath not been found in thee all thy days.

"Yet a man is risen to pursue thee, and to seek thy soul; *but the soul of my lord shall be bound in the bundle of life with the Lord thy God; and the souls of thine enemies, them shall He sling out, as out of the middle of a sling. And it shall come to pass, *when the Lord shall have done to my lord according to all the good that He hath spoken concerning thee, and shall have appointed thee ruler over Israel*, that this shall be not grief unto thee, nor offence of heart unto my lord, either that thou hast shed blood causeless, or that my lord hath avenged himself; but when the Lord shall have dealt well with my lord, then remember thine handmaid."

We can hardly conceive anything more touching than this address; every point in it was calculated to touch the heart. She presents to him the evil of seeking to avenge himself; the weakness and folly of the object of his revenge,—she reminds him of his proper occupation, viz., "fighting *the Lord's battles*. This must have brought home to his heart the humiliating circumstances in which Abigail met him, even rushing on to fight *his own* battle.

However, perceive that the leading point in this address is the special reference to the future. "The Lord *will* certainly make my lord a sure house." "The soul of my lord *shall* be bound in the bundle of life with the Lord thy God." "When the Lord *shall* have done to my lord," etc.; "and *shall* have appointed thee ruler over Israel." All these allusions to David's future blessing and glory were eminently calculated to withdraw his heart from his present grievance. The sure house, the bundle of life, and the kingdom, were far better than Nabal's flocks and herds; and in the view of these glories, David could well afford to leave him to his portion, and his portion to him.

To the heir of a kingdom, a few sheep could have but little attraction; and one who knew that he had the anointing oil of the Lord upon his head might easily bear to be called a runaway servant. All these things Abigail knew—knew as matters of faith. She knew David, and knew his high destinies. By faith she recognized in the despised outcast the future king of Israel. Nabal knew not David. He was a man of the world, swallowed up with present things. With him there was nothing more important, nothing more influential, than "*my* bread, *my* flesh, *my* shearers"; it was all self; there was no room for David or his claims. This might be expected from such an one; but surely it was not for David to go down from his elevation to grapple with a poor worldling about his perishable possessions. Ah, no; the kingdom should have filled his eye, and engaged his thoughts, and lifted his spirit above all lower influences.

Look at the Master Himself, as He stood at the bar of a poor worm—the creation of His own hand—how did He conduct Himself? Did He call upon His little band of followers to gird on every man his sword? Did He say of the man who dared to sit as His judge, "In vain have I imparted unto this fellow all he is, and all he has?" No; He looked above and beyond Pilate, Herod, the chief priests, and scribes. He could say, "The cup which *My Father* hath given Me, shall I not drink it?" This kept His spirit tranquil, while, at the same time, He could look forward into the future, and say, "*Hereafter* shall ye see the Son of Man sitting on the right hand of power, and coming in the clouds of heaven." Here was real power over present things. The millennial kingdom, with all its untold joys, with all its heights and depths of glory, glistened in the distance with everlasting light and brilliancy, and the eye of the Man of Sorrows rested upon it, in that dark hour when the scoffs and sneers, the taunts and reproaches of guilty sinners were falling upon His blessed person.

This is our model; thus ought we to meet the trials and difficulties, the reproach, obloquy, and desertion of this present time. We should view *all* in the light of "*hereafter."* "Our light affliction," says an eminent sufferer, "which is but for a moment, worketh for us a far more exceeding and eternal weight of glory." Again, "But the God of all grace, who hath called us to His eternal glory by Christ Jesus, after that ye have suffered a while, make you perfect, stablish, strengthen, settle you." "O fools, and slow of heart to believe all that the prophets have spoken! Ought not Christ to have *suffered* these things, and to enter into His *glory?*" Yes; suffering must come first and glory afterwards; and any one who, by his own hand, would seek to take off the edge of present suffering and reproach, proves that the kingdom is not filling the vision of his soul—that *now* is more influential with him than "*hereafter."*

How we ought to bless our God for having opened to us such a vista of glory in the ages to come! How it enables us to tread, with a buoyant step, our rugged path through the wilderness! How it lifts us above the things which engross the children of this world!

We're not of the world, which fadeth away,
We're not of the night, but children of day;
The chains that once bound us by Jesus are riven,
We're strangers on earth, and our home is in Heaven.

May we prove the sacred reality of this more, as we pass along through "this vale of tears." Truly the heart would sink and the spirit faint, were we not sustained by hope—even the hope of glory, which, thank God, maketh not ashamed, for the Spirit is the earnest of it in our hearts.

In pursuing the narrative of David and Abigail a little further, we have a still more striking example of the vast difference between the child of nature and the child of faith. Abigail returned from her interview with David, and found Nabal "very drunken; wherefore she told him nothing, less or more, until the morning light. But it came to pass in the morning, when the wine was gone out of Nabal, and his wife had told him these things, that his heart died within him, and he became as a stone. And it came to pass, about ten days after, that the Lord smote Nabal, that he died." What a sad picture of a man of the world! Sunk in intoxication during the night, and when the morning dawned, struck with terror, pierced by the arrow of death.

How solemnly like the multitudes whom the enemy has succeeded, in every age, in alluring and intoxicating with the perishing joys of a world which lies under the curse of God, and awaits the fire of His judgment. "They that sleep, sleep in the night, and they that be drunken are drunken in the night;" but, ah! the morning is at hand, when the wine (apt symbol of this world's joy) shall have altogether evaporated—the feverish excitement in which Satan now involves the spirits of the men of this world shall have calmed down, and then comes the stern reality of an eternity of misery—unspeakable misery, in company with Satan and his angels.

Nabal did not even meet David face to face; yet the very thought of his avenging sword filled his soul with deadly fear. How much more terrible will it be to meet the gaze of a despised and rejected Jesus! Then the Abigails and the Nabals will find their respective places; those who had known and loved the true David, and those who had not. God, in His mercy, grant that my reader may be amongst the happy number of the former.

I would only observe, further, that the interesting narrative of this chapter gives us a striking picture of the Church and the world, as a whole; the one united to the king, and associated with Him in His glory; the other plunged in irretrievable ruin. "Seeing then that all these things shall be dissolved, what manner of persons ought ye to be in all holy conversation and godliness; looking for and hasting unto the coming of the day of God, wherein the heavens being on fire shall be dissolved, and the elements shall melt with fervent heat? Nevertheless we, according to His promise, look for new heavens and a new earth, wherein dwelleth righteousness. Wherefore, beloved, seeing that ye look for such things, be diligent, that ye may be found of Him in peace, without spot, and blameless" (2 Pet. 3:11-14).

Such are the soul-stirring, momentous facts presented to us throughout the Book of God, in order to detach our hearts from present things, and bind them in genuine affection to those objects and prospects which stand connected with the person of the Son of God. Nor will aught else, save the deep and positive conviction of the reality of these things, produce such effects.

We know the intoxicating power of this world's schemes and operations; we know how the human heart is borne away, as upon the surface of a rapid current, when such things are presented: schemes of improvement, commercial operations, political movements—aye, and popular religious movements too—all these things produce upon the human mind an effect similar to that produced by Nabal's wine, so that it is almost useless to announce the stern facts presented in the above solemn quotation. Still, they must be announced, must be reiterated, "and so much the more, as we see the day approaching." "The day of the Lord will come as a thief in the night." "All these things shall be dissolved." "The heavens being on fire shall be dissolved, and the elements shall melt with fervent heat; the earth also, and the works that are therein, shall be burned up." Such is the prospect presented to all who, like Nabal, surcharged with "surfeiting, and drunkenness, and cares of this life," have rejected the claims and appeals of Jesus.

The world is being prepared, with inconceivable rapidity, for the introduction of that one who, by the energy of Satan, will head up all its institutions, embody all its principles, concentrate all its energies. Let but the last elect one be gathered out, the last member be incorporated into the body of Christ by the quickening energy of the Holy Ghost, the last stone be set in its appointed places in the temple of God, and then shall the salt be removed, which now preserves the world from corruption; the barrier presented by the presence of the Holy Ghost in the Church shall be taken out of the way, and then comes forth "the lawless one" on the stage of this world, "whom the Lord shall consume with the spirit of His mouth, and destroy with the brightness of His coming. Even him whose coming is after the working of Satan, with all power, and signs, and lying wonders, and with all deceivableness of unrighteousness in them that perish; because they received not the love of the truth, that they might be saved."

Surely these things ought to check the career of the men of this world, and lead them, with solemnized minds, to "consider *their latter end.*" "The long-suffering of our Lord is salvation." Precious word! Most precious! But let it not be abused; let it not be mistaken for *"slackness."* The Lord waits to be gracious to *sinners,* not to connive at *sin.*

However, as has been already observed, it is almost useless to speak to men about the *future* who are wholly engrossed with the *present.*

Blessed be God, there are some who have ears to hear the testimony about the kindness and grace of Jesus, as well as about His coming judgment. Thus it was with Abigail; she believed the truth about David, and acted accordingly; and all who believe the truth about Jesus will be found separating themselves diligently from this present world.

Part 5

ZIKLAG

In dwelling upon a history such as that now before us, which manifestly presents much failure and infirmity, it is well for us to keep in memory what we ourselves are, lest we be found pointing out the lapses of others in a spirit of self-complacency. The divine penman has set before us, with unflinching fidelity, all the imperfections of those whose history He records. His object is to present God to the soul in all the fulness and variety of His resources, and in all His competency to meet the helpless sinner in his very deepest need. He has not written the history of angels, but of men—men "of like passions with us"; and this is what makes Old Testament narratives so exceedingly instructive to us; we are presented with facts which speak to the heart; we are conducted through scenes and circumstances which unfold to us, with touching simplicity, the hidden springs of our nature, and also the hidden springs of grace.

We learn that man is the same in every age: in Eden, in Canaan, in the Church, in millennial glory, he is proved to be made of the same humbling materials; but we learn also, for our joy and encouragement, that God is the same—"the same yesterday, to-day, and for ever"—"Patient, gracious, powerful, holy"—patient, to bear with our grievous and manifold provocations; gracious, to blot out our oft-repeated sins, and restore our wandering souls; powerful, to deliver us out of Satan's entangling snares, and from the energy of nature and the world; holy, to execute judgment in His house, and to chasten His sons, that they may be partakers of His holiness. Such is the God with whom we have to do; and we see the wondrous unfoldings of His character in the deeply-interesting sketches with which the Old Testament history abounds, and in none, perhaps, more than in that now before us.

Few characters exhibit more variety of

experience than David. He truly knew the depths and heights which mark the course of the man of faith. At one moment, we find him giving forth from his harp the most sublime strains; at another, pouring forth the sorrows of a defiled conscience and a wounded spirit. This variety of experience rendered David a fit subject for illustrating the varied grace of God. It is ever thus. The poor prodigal would never have known such high communion, had he not known the humiliating depths of the far country. The grace which decked him in the best robe would not have shone so brightly, had he not been clad in filthy rags.

God's grace is magnified by man's ruin; and the more keenly the ruin is felt, the more highly the grace is valued. The elder brother never got a kid that he might make merry with his friends; and why? Because he imagined he had earned it. "Lo," says he, "these many years do I serve thee, neither transgressed I at any time thy commandment." Vain man! How could he expect the ring, the robe, or the fatted calf? Had he obtained them, they would have been but the trappings of self-righteousness, and not the ornaments with which grace decks the believing sinner.

Thus was it with Saul and David. Saul never knew his need as David knew it, nor have we any record of such flagrant sins in his case; at least, what man would pronounce flagrant. Saul was the outwardly moral and religious man, but, withal, a self-righteous man; hence we have such expressions as these, "I have performed the commandment of the Lord"—"Yea, I have obeyed the voice of the Lord, and have gone the way which the Lord sent me." How could this man value grace? Impossible. A heart unbroken, a conscience unconvinced, can never enter into the meaning of the term Grace. How different was it with David! He felt his sins, groaned under them, confessed them, judged them, in the presence of God whose grace had blotted them all out for ever. There is a great difference between a man ignorant of his sins and walking in self-complacency, and one deeply conscious of his sins, yet happy in the full forgiveness of them.

The above train of thought introduces us to the circumstances connected with David in Ziklag of the Philistines—circumstances which fully manifest human infirmity and divine grace and mercy.

"And David said *in his heart*, I shall now perish one day by the hand of Saul; there is nothing better for me than that I should speedily escape into the land of the Philistines." This was David's second visit to the land of the Philistines. In chapter 21 we read, "And David arose and fled that day for fear of Saul, and went to Achish the king of Gath." Here we find David really taking himself out of the hands of God, and putting himself into the hands of Achish. He leaves the place of dependence, and goes into the very midst of the enemies of God and of Israel. And, be it remarked, he has in his hand the very sword of the Philistine champion. Nor is it to act in his true character as the servant of God; this would have been happy indeed; but no; he goes to act the madman, in the presence of those before whom he had so recently acted as the champion of Israel.

"The servants of Achish said unto him, Is not this David, the king of the land? Did they not sing one to another of him in dances, saying, Saul hath slain his thousands, and David his ten thousands?" The Philistines recognized David's true character as "king of the land"—the slayer of ten thousands; they imagined that he could not possibly act otherwise than as their enemy. Little were they able to enter into the moral condition of his soul at that extraordinary stage of his history; little did they think that the slayer of Goliath had fled to them for protection from the hand of Saul. The world cannot understand the vicissitudes of the life of faith. Who that had seen David in the valley of Elah could ever suppose that he would so soon fear to avow with boldness the results of that faith with which God had endowed him? Who could have thought that with Goliath's sword in his hand he could tremble to avow himself the victor of Goliath? Yet so it was. "David laid up these words in his heart, and was sore afraid of Achish, the king of Gath. And he changed his behavior before them, and feigned himself mad in their hands, and scrabbled on the doors of the gate, and let his spittle fall down upon his beard."

Thus must it ever be when a saint deserts the path of simple dependence upon God and strangership in the world. The "behavior" must be "changed," the real character abandoned, and instead thereof a course is adopted which is marked by positive deceit before God and folly before the world. This is most sorrowful. A saint should always maintain his dignity—the dignity which flows from the consciousness of the presence of God. But the moment faith gives way, the power of testimony is gone, and the man of faith is despised as a "madman."

When David "said in his heart, I shall now perish one day by the hand of Saul," he forsook the only path of real power. Had he continued as a homeless wanderer through the mountains, he would never have presented such a melancholy picture in the view of the servants of Achish—he would never have been pronounced a madman. Achish would not have dared to call David by such a name in the valley of Elah! No, nor in the cave of Adullam; but, alas, David had put himself into the power of this stranger, and therefore he should either suffer for his past faithfulness, or give all up, and pretend to be a fool in their eyes. They rightly judged him to be the king of the land, but he, afraid of the consequences of maintaining such a high dignity, denied his kingship, and became a fool. How frequently may we trace the working of this same evil in the walk of Christians!

How frequently may we see a man who, by his past actings in the energy of the Spirit of God, has attained a very high position in the thoughts, not only of his brethren, but even of the children of this world, and yet, when such an one gets out of communion, he is really afraid to maintain his position; and, at the very moment when those without are looking only for an unbending and unqualified testimony against their ways, he changes his behavior, and instead of being esteemed and reverenced, he is actually despised. We should most carefully guard against this; it can only be effectually avoided by walking in the full and blessed consciousness of God's sufficiency. So long as we feel that God is sufficient for *all* our need, we are entirely independent of the world; if it be not thus with us, we shall just compromise the truth of God, and deny our real character as heavenly men.

How completely must David have lost the sense of God's sufficiency when he could say, "There is *nothing better* for me than that I should speedily escape into the land of the Philistines." Nothing better for a man of faith than to go back to the world for refuge! Strange confession! The confession of one who had allowed circumstances to come between his soul and God. When we slip off the narrow path of faith, we are liable to run into the wildest extremes; and nothing can more forcibly exhibit the contrast between one looking at God and one looking at circumstances, than David in the valley of Elah and David scrabbling on the doors of the Philistine king. The contrast is full of solemn instruction and warning. It is well calculated to teach us what we are, and how little the best of us can be depended upon.

Ah! what are we? Poor, failing, stumbling creatures; prone, at every turn in our path, to wander into error and evil—prone to forsake the Rock of Ages, and lean upon the broken reeds of the world—prone to forsake the fountain of living waters, and hew out for ourselves broken cisterns that can hold no water. Truly we have need, deep need, to walk humbly, watchfully, and prayerfully, before our God—deep need to utter David's own prayer, continually, "Uphold me according unto Thy word, that I may live; and let me not be ashamed of my hope. Hold Thou me up, and I shall be safe; and I will have respect unto Thy statutes continually." We need to have our feet made as hinds' feet, so that we may walk on the high and slippery places through which our path lies. Nothing short of grace divine can enable us to pursue a course of steady devotedness: for, if left to ourselves, there is no extreme of evil into which we may not run. They alone are safe whom God keeps in the hollow of His hand.

Truly happy is it for us to have to do with one who is able to bear with us in all our waywardness, and able also to restore and revive our souls when faint and withering under the influence of the atmosphere of evil around us. God forbid that we should make any other use of what we may term the Ziklag portion of David's history, save to apply it to our own hearts before God, and use it as a matter of solemn and soul-searching warning; for though it may be said that there is a wide difference between the standing and privileges of David and those of the Church of God now, yet, in every age and dispensation, nature is the same; and we seriously wrong our own souls if we fail to learn a wholesome lesson from the falls of one so high up in the school of Christ as David. Dispensations differ, no doubt, in their great leading features; but there is a wonderful analogy in God's principles of discipline at all times, let the standing of His people differ as it may.

In following David, in his further sojourn in the land of the Philistines, we only find fresh cause of humiliation. He obtains the grant of Ziklag, where he sojourns for sixteen months, during which period, though free from all fear with respect to Saul, he was at a distance from God and from Israel. It is, in one sense, a very easy matter to get out of a place of trial; but then we get out of a place of blessing also. It would have been much happier for David to have remained in a position which left him exposed to Saul, while, at the same time, he enjoyed the protection of the God of Israel, than to seek safety from the arm of the king of Gath. However, when the pressure of trial is upon us, the thought of relief is sweet, and we are in danger of seeking relief in our own way.

The enemy always has a by-road open to the man of faith. He had an Egypt for Abraham, and a Ziklag for David; and now he has the world, in all its varied forms, for us. "And truly, if they had been mindful of that country from whence they came out, they might have had opportunity to have returned." It is the opportunity to return that proves the genuine fixedness of purpose to go forward. The Lord leaves His people

free, in order that they may "declare *plainly* that they seek a country." This is what glorifies God. It would avail nothing if we were to be compelled, as with bit and bridle, to go from earth to Heaven; but when, through grace, we voluntarily abandon the things of earth to seek those things which are above, this is to the glory of God, because it demonstrates that what He has to give is far more attractive than this present world.*

David, however, accepted Ziklag, and instead of remaining as a homeless stranger in the cave of Adullam, he becomes a citizen in the land of the Philistines. Nor does he now act the madman, as before: no; he now acts the part of a positive deceiver. He wages war on the Geshurites and Gezrites, and tells a lie about it, lest he should again lose his self-chosen place of protection. Yea, so far does he proceed in his unhappy course, that when Achish proposes to him to act as ally to the Philistines, his answer is, "Surely thou shalt know what thy servant can do . . . . And Achish said to David, Therefore will I make thee keeper of my head for ever . . . . Now the Philistines gathered together all their armies to Aphek; and the Israelites pitched by a fountain which is in Jezreel. And the lords of the Philistines passed on by hundreds and by thousands; *but David and his men passed on in the rearward with Achish.*"

Here, then, we have a strange anomaly—a king of Israel about to be made keeper of the head of a Philistine, and about to draw the sword against the armies of the living God. Was ever anything like this? The slayer of Goliath, servant to a Philistine! Who could have looked for such a thing? Truly difficult is it for us to determine where all this would have ended, had David been left to the full results of his false position. But this could not be. God was graciously watching His poor wanderer, and had rich and manifold mercies in store for him, as well as some humbling lessons and painful exercises of soul.

The very lords of the Philistines were the instruments made use of by the Lord to deliver David from his strange position. They, judging from his past ways, could not

---

* "*He led them forth* by the right way, that *they might go* to a city of habitation" (Ps. 107:7). Grace not only leads forth from Egypt, but imparts the capacity and the desire to go to Canaan.

be induced to trust him as an ally. "Is not this David, and how can we confide in him?" A Philistine could never rely upon a Hebrew for co-operation against Hebrews. In a word, the men of this world can never place full confidence in one who has once been decided for the truth of God. A saint who has got out of communion and gone back to the world, though he may go to a great length, will never be regarded or confided in as one of themselves; he will be suspected, just as David was by the Philistines. "Make this fellow return, that he may go again to his place which thou hast appointed him, and let him not go down with us to battle, lest in the battle he be an adversary to us."

They could give him a certain place amongst them, but when it became a question of war between them and Israel, they would not acknowledge him. And they were wise; for let David *assume* what character he might, be could be *really* nought else save an enemy to the Philistines. He might *feign* himself to be mad; he might *pretend* to make war upon the south of Judah; but when matters came to a positive issue, David could only act consistently with his true character, as the slayer of ten thousands of Philistines. The fact is, from first to last David was misunderstood; the Philistines did not know what it was that had sent him into their midst. There was far more in the apparent madman than they could fathom. They thought that he desired to be reconciled to his master, Saul, little imagining that they had before them one who was so soon to lay his hand upon the sceptre of Israel, and to make them feel the weight of his power.

However, the Lord would not allow David to appear in the field against Israel. He sent him back, or rather He led him aside, in order that He might deal with him in secret about his course. "So David and his men rose up early to depart in the morning, to return into the land of the Philistines . . . . And it came to pass, when David and his men were come to Ziklag, on the third day, that the Amalekites had invaded the south, and Ziklag, and smitten Ziklag, and burned it with fire; and had taken the women captives that were

therein; they slew not any, either great or small, but carried them away, and went on their way."

David is here made to feel the bitter result of his having sought to Achish for help in the day of his need. He had taken up his position amongst the uncircumcised, and must, therefore, be made a partaker of their wretchedness. Had he remained amongst the mountains of Judah, he would have escaped all this sorrow; his God would have been a wall of fire round about him. But he had fled to Ziklag to escape Saul; and then, as it were, at the very moment when Saul was falling on Mount Gilboa, David was weeping over the ruins of Ziklag. Surely it was not thus we should have expected to find David. "Then David and the people that were with him lifted up their voice and wept, until they had no more power to weep . . . . And David was greatly distressed, for the people spake of stoning him."

In all this God was dealing with His dear child, not to crush him, but to bring him to a right sense of the course he had been pursuing amongst the Philistines. Surely when David beheld the smouldering ashes of Ziklag, and felt himself deprived of his wives, children, and all, he had a practical lesson as to the evil and sorrow of taking anything from the world. We can hardly picture to ourselves a condition more painful than that in which David found himself on his return to Ziklag. He had been, for a year and four months, pursuing a course which might have left him with an uneasy conscience toward God; he was cast off by those on whose protection he had thrown himself; his place of refuge was burned; his wives and property were gone; and lastly, his companions, those who had followed him in all his wanderings, were threatening to stone him.

Thus was David sunk to the very lowest ebb, in every point of view; all creature-streams were dried up; and not only so, but the enemy might effectually ply his fiery darts at such a moment—conscience might work, and memory call up the scenes of the past: his abandoning the place of dependence; his flight to Achish; his change of behavior; his acting the madman; his telling a lie; his volunteering to fight against Israel, as the servant of the Philistines: all these things must have augmented, in no small degree, his anguish of soul.

But David was a man of faith after all, and, notwithstanding all, *he knew the Lord,* and His "boundless stores of grace." This was his joy and comfort in this exceedingly dark moment of his career. Had he not been able to roll his heavy burden over upon infinite grace, he must have given up in utter despair. He had never before been so tested. He had met the lion and the bear in the wilderness; he had met the giant of Gath in the valley of Elah; but he had never met such an overwhelming array of circumstances before. Yet God was sufficient, and David knew this. Hence we read, *"David encouraged himself in the Lord his God."* Happy, well-founded encouragment! Happy the soul that knows it! Happy he who could rise from the very deepest depths of human misery, up to God, and His neverfailing resources! Faith knows God to be fully equal to all human need, human weakness, human failure, human sin. God is above all, beyond all, beneath all; and the heart that apprehends Him is lifted above all the trials and difficulties of the way.

There is no condition in which the Christian can find himself in which he may not count upon God. Is he crushed beneath the pressure of trial from external circumstances? Let him bring God's omnipotent power to bear upon these things. Is the heart oppressed by the burden of personal infirmity?—truly a heavy burden! Let him draw upon the exhaustless springs of Divine compassion and mercy. Is the soul filled with horror, by the sense of sin and guilt? Let him have recourse to the boundless grace of God, and the infinitely-precious blood of Christ. In a word, whatever be the burden, the trial, the sorrow, or the need, God is more than equal to all, and it is the province of faith to use Him. "David encouraged himself in the Lord his God" when everything around was dark and depressing.

May we know the true blessedness of this. To have to do with God is rest to the soul, and happiness and power. To disentangle our hearts from self and the things which surround us, and rise upward into the holy calmness of the Divine presence, imparts comfort and consolation beyond what one can utter. Satan's object is ever to hinder this. He would fain lead us to make present things the boundary of our soul's horizon; he would seek to surround us with a thick, dark, impenetrable cloud, so that we might not recognize our Father's countenance, and our Father's hand in our circumstances.

But faith pierces the cloud, and gets upward to God; it looks not at the things which are seen, but at the things which are unseen: it endures, as seeing Him who is invisible; it can say to God,

In darkest shades, if Thou appear,
    My dawning is begun;
Thou art my soul's bright morning star,
    And Thou my rising sun.

Truly David's return to Ziklag was a dark hour—one of his darkest; yet God appeared, and his dawning began. God appeared for his relief and restoration; He graciously removed the weight from his spirit; He burst the fetters, and let the prisoner go free. Such is the manner of God. He permits His children to taste the bitter fruit of their own ways, in order that they may return to Him, and realize they can only be truly happy in His gracious and holy presence. Ziklag may shelter for a time, but it will perish; and even while it lasts, must be purchased by the sacrifice of a good conscience toward God, and toward His people. A heavy price, surely, for a temporary relief from pressure! How much better to endure the pressure for a time!

But, blessed be our God, "all things work together for good to them that love Him." The death of the Philistine champion, and the sixteen months' sojourn in Ziklag; the cave of Adullam, and the house of Achish—all worked for David's good. The Lord makes the very failure of His children to yield them blessing, inasmuch as it leads them to seek more prayerful vigilance of spirit, and a closer walk with Him. If our stumbles teach us to lean more implicitly upon God, we shall still thank Him, however much we may have to be humbled at the remembrance of them. Humbling as David's Ziklag experience must have been to him, we may be sure he would not have been without it. It taught him more of the deep reality of God's grace and faithfulness; it enabled him to see, that when brought down to the very bottom of human things, he could find God there in all the fulness of His grace. This was a valuable lesson, and it will be our place to learn from it also.

Are we able to lean on the Lord amid the ruin around us? Is He beyond every one and everything to our souls? Can we encourage ourselves in Him when all without and within seems directly against us? Is His name dear to us in this day of faithlessness and cold formality? Are we prepared to pursue the rest of our course through the desert in solitariness and desertion, if such should be needful? It may be, we have learnt to cease looking, in any way, to the children of this world; but are we prepared to lose the approval and confidence of our brethren? David's companions spake of stoning him; but the Lord was more to him than all; the Lord was *"his refuge"*; do we know the power and comfort of this? The Lord grant that we may know it more.

Before closing of this chapter, I would call attention to the instructive scene between David and the young man who was servant to the Amalekite. I do not say that we are to regard it as a positive type; but we are certainly warranted in looking at it as a very striking illustration. An illustration of what? Let us see.

In order to appreciate the teaching of the Spirit in this Scripture (chap. 30: 11-16) we must bear in mind the difference between Egypt and Amalek; the former is associated with Israel in the blessing of the latter day, "In that day shall Israel be the third with Egypt and with Assyria, even a blessing in the midst of the land; whom the Lord of hosts shall bless, saying, Blessed be Egypt My people, and Assyria the work of My hands, and Israel Mine inheritance." Amalek, on the contrary, is thus spoken of, "The Lord hath sworn that the Lord will have war with Amalek from generation to generation." An Egyptian, therefore, and an Amalekite stood in a very different relationship to Israel.

Now this young man was an Egyptian, servant to an Amalekite, and his master left him because he had fallen sick. This was the treatment he had received from his Amalekite master; he had abandoned him in the hour of his need, because he was no longer able to be of service to him. But his very ruin and wretchedness threw him upon the sympathies of David, who refreshed him and revived his spirit. He found him faint and weak from the effects of his former service, and having restored his spirit he inquired, "Canst thou bring me down to this company?" He here puts in his claim upon the service and devotedness of one who owed him everything under God; but the young man, though fully restored, was unable to act with David until possessed of the full assurance of *life* and *liberty*. "Swear unto me by God," said he, "that thou wilt neither kill me, nor deliver me into the hands of my master, and I will bring you down to this company." He could not serve David until fully assured of deliverance from the power of his old master.

All this is very striking as an illustration of the apostle's teaching in Romans 6. The believer needs to know his entire emancipation from the dominion of his old master, the flesh, before ever he can, with confidence, apply himself to the service of Christ. We have felt the bitterness of serving the flesh; as the apostle says, "What fruit had ye then in those things whereof ye are now ashamed? For the end of those things is death." It is impossible to walk in peace and liberty of heart until we know where death and resurrection have placed us. Until we know and believe that sin has no dominion over us, we must, of necessity, be occupied about ourselves, for we shall be constantly discovering the working of indwelling corruption, and thus be filled with apprehension of being delivered over into the hands of our former oppressor. We may be very clear as to the theory of justification by faith; we may understand what it is to rest in the accomplished work of Christ in reference to sins that are past, and yet be so troubled about indwelling sin as to be quite hindered in our service to Christ and His Church.

The gospel of the grace of God, when entered into in its divine fulness, sets the soul at rest, not only as to the past, but also the present and the future. The Lord forgives *all* our sins, not *some* of them; and not only does He forgive sins, but also delivers from the power of sin, as we read in Roman 6—"Sin shall not have dominion over you: for ye are not under the law, but under grace." This is a truly precious truth for those who are daily harassed with the seeds of evil within. Though sin *dwells*, it shall not *reign*. And how is this deliverance accomplished! By death and resurrection. "He that has died is justified from sin" (RV). What claim has sin upon a dead man? None! Well, then, God looks upon the believer as dead—dead with Christ, and risen again; and his power to deny the working of sin consists in his reckoning himself to be what God tells him he is.

Thus, as David's oath set the young man's mind at rest, and enabled him to act with him against the Amalekites, so the word of Christ banishes fear and hesitation from the heart of the believer, and enables him, through the Spirit, to act against his former master—the flesh. Grace assures us that all our interests, for time and eternity, have been most fully provided for in the death and resurrection of Christ, and gives us to see that our only business now is to live to the praise of Him who died for us, and rose again.

"Shall we continue in sin?" Could the young man in this Scripture have gone back again to his Amalekite master? Impossible. What fruit had he from his former service? Ruin and desertion. And what fruit had we? Death. The wages of sin is death. The world, the flesh, and the devil, can only lead us down to hell. Serve them how we may, death and destruction must be the end. Men may not see this; they may not wish to see it; yet it is not the less true. "It is appointed unto men once to die, but after this the judgment." This is the appointment.

But Christ has borne all for the believer; death and judgment have passed away, and nothing remains but for the believer to accompany, in liberty and joy of heart, the true David against his enemies. Christ has done all for us, that we might act for Him in this the time of His rejection. He has suffered for us without the gate, and now calls upon us to go forth to Him, bearing His reproach. The believer does not act in order to get life, but because he has it. He starts on his Christian career with the full assurance of pardon and acceptance in the Beloved. Perfect justification is his starting-post, and glory the goal. "Whom He justified, them He also glorified."

It is well to be exceedingly simple in our apprehension of this great truth. Some imagine that we can never know that our sins are forgiven while here. Now, if we cannot know that our sins are forgiven, we cannot know that God's Word is true, and Christ's work perfect. Will any one maintain this? If not, both rest on the same basis. The forgiveness of sins and the truth of God's Word are linked together in the precious gospel of Christ. Doubt the forgiveness of sins, and you call in question the truth of Christ's words, *"It is finished"*—words uttered under the most solemn circumstances.

Yet we know how hard it is for the heart to repose with unquestioning simplicity on the truth of God, in reference to the perfect remission of sins through the blood of Christ. Our thoughts are too shallow and contracted to take in all the effulgence of divine grace. We are too full of legalism, too full of self. We vainly think that we must add something to what Christ has done, whether that something be in the shape of works, feelings, or experiences. All this must be set aside. Christ *alone* is the great foundation, the eternal rock, the tower of salvation. To add even circumcision would be to make Christ of none effect, to fall from grace, and to make ourselves debtors to keep the whole law, and thus to expose ourselves to curse and wrath. "As many as are of the works of the law are under the curse."

May we cling to Christ, with a deeper sense of our own vileness and His perfectness. May we wrap ourselves up, as it were, in Him, while passing on through this cold and faithless world

Part 6

THE RETURN OF THE ARK

2 Samuel 6 and 1 Chronicles 13

We are now called to follow David from the scenes of his exile to those of his government. Saul has passed off the stage of history, having met death by the hand of the Amalekite—one of that very nation which he had disobediently spared. Solemn warning! Jonathan, too, had fallen in company with his father, Saul, on Mount Gilboa, and David had given utterance to his sublime lament over both. David had ever carried himself towards Saul with the fullest sense of his being the Lord's anointed; nor did he manifest anything bordering upon a spirit of exultation when informed of his death; on the contrary, he wept over him, and called on others to do the same.

Neither do we find anything like unbecoming haste to ascend the throne left vacant for him; he waited upon the Lord about it. "David inquired of the Lord, saying, Shall I go up into any of the cities of Judah? And the Lord said unto him, Go up. and David said, Whither shall I go up? And He said, Unto Hebron."* This was real dependence. Nature would have been eager to rush into the place of honor; but David waited on the Lord, and only moved as directed of Him. It was this confidence in and dependence upon God—delighting himself in Jehovah—that forms the peculiar loveliness of David's character, "the man after God's own heart." Happy would it have been for him had he continued thus to move on in child-like dependence.

But, alas; we have to trace far more of nature in David during the period of his elevation than during the period of His rejection. A time of peace and prosperity tends to develop and bring to maturity many seeds of evil which might be nipped and blighted by the keen blast of adversity. David found the kingdom more thorny and dangerous than the wilderness.

After his accession to the throne over all Israel, David's lovely desire, to have the ark of the Lord near himself in the city of Jerusalem, is followed by a great error. His desire was most commendable; the only question was, how was it to be done? The Word of God was exceedingly plain and distinct in reference to this important matter; it pointed out a very simple and definite way of carrying the ark of the Lord of Hosts, even upon the shoulders of living men, who had been taken up and set aside for that purpose (See Num. 3 and 8.)

When the Philistines sent the ark of Jehovah back to its own land and people, they knew nothing of this, and therefore devised a way of their own, which, as might be expected, was directly opposed to God's way, for "the natural man receiveth not the things of the Spirit of God, neither can he know them, because they are spiritually discerned." Therefore, though the plan adopted by the Philistines was very decent and orderly, as men would say, yet it was not of God. The ministers of the house of Dagon were poorly qualified to arrange the order of the divine service. They thought a wooden cart would do as well as anything else; it might have answered for the service of Dagon, and they knew no difference. They had once trembled at the sight of the ark, but, through the unfaithfulness of Israel, it had lost its solemnity in their eyes; and though it had been most solemnly and impressively vindicated in their view by the destruction of their god, they understood not its deep significancy, they knew not its wondrous contents; it was quite beyond them, and therefore they could devise nothing better than a mere lifeless ordinance for conveying it to its place.

But David ought to have known God's thoughts, and have acted upon them at the first; he should not have followed the thoughts and traditions of men in the service of God; he should have drawn his directions from the lucid lines of the book of the law. It is a terrible thing when the children of the kingdom form themselves after the model of the men of the world, and tread in their

---

* Hebron means *Communion;* it is in communion with Himself the Lord ever calls His servants in entering the field of service to which He calls and for which He prepares. [Ed.]

footsteps. They never can do so without serious damage to their own souls, and at the sacrifice of God's truth and testimony.

The Philistines might construct a cart to carry the ark, and nothing whatever occur to show them the error of so doing; but God would not allow David so to act. And so now; the men of this world may put forth their canons, enact their laws, and decree their ceremonies in religion; but shall the children of God come down from their high position and privileges, as those who are guided by the Holy Ghost and the blessed Word of God, and suffer themselves to be guided and influenced by such things? They may do so, but they shall assuredly suffer loss.

David was made to learn his mistake by bitter experience, for "when they came unto the threshing-floor of Chidon, Uzza put forth his hand to hold the ark; for the oxen stumbled." The weakness and inconsistency of the whole thing was here manifested. The Levites, the ministers of God, had borne the ark from Horeb to Jordan, and yet we have no record of any stumble. The shoulders of His servants was God's way; but the cart and oxen were man's way. And who would have thought that an Israelite would have deposited the ark of the God of Israel upon a wooden cart, to be drawn by oxen? Yet such is ever the sad effect of departing from the written Word to follow human traditions. "The oxen stumbled." The arrangement was "weak and beggarly," in the judgment of the Holy Ghost; and the Lord was only making this fully manifest. The ark should never have been in such a dishonoring position; oxen should never have been the bearers of such a burden.

"And the anger of the Lord was kindled against Uzza, and He smote him, because he put his hand to the ark; and there he died before God." Truly, "judgment must begin at the house of God." The Lord judged David for doing what the Philistines had done without notice. The nearer a man is to God, the more solemnly and speedily will he be judged for any evil. This need not afford any encouragement to the worldling, for, as the apostle says, "If judgment first begin at us, what shall the end be of those that obey not

the gospel of God? And if the righteous scarcely be saved, where shall the ungodly and the sinner appear?" If God judges His people, what shall become of the poor worldling! Though the Philistines escaped the judgment of God in the matter of the cart, they had to meet it in another way. God deals with all according to His own holy principles, and the breach upon Uzza was designed to restore David to a right apprehension of the mind of God in reference to the ark of His presence.

Yet it did not seem, at first, to produce the proper effect. "David was displeased because the Lord had made a breach upon Uzza: wherefore the name of the place is called Perez Uzza to this day. And David was afraid of God that day, saying, How shall I bring the ark of God home to me?" There is much deep instruction in this. David was doing a right thing in a wrong way, and when God executed judgment upon his way of acting, he despaired of doing the thing at all. This is a very common error.

We enter upon some right course of acting in a wrong way, or in a wrong spirit, which God cannot own; and then our spirit, or method of acting, is confounded with the service in which we were engaged. But we must ever distinguish between *what* men do, and *how* they do it. It was right for David to bring up the ark; it was wrong to put it on an ox-cart. The Lord approved the former, but disapproved and judged the latter.

God will never suffer His children to persist in carrying on His work upon wrong principles. They may go on for a time with much apparent success, as "David and all Israel played before God with all their might, and with singing, and with harps, and with psalteries, and with timbrels, and with cymbals, and with trumpets." This was very imposing. It would have been a difficult matter for any one to raise an objection to the course of David in this proceeding. The king and all his captains were engaged in it; and the burst of music would have drowned any objection. But, ah, how soon was all this exultation checked! "The oxen stumbled"— "Uzza put forth his hand," vainly imagining that God would suffer the ark of His presence to fall to the ground. He who had maintained the dignity of that ark, even in the dark solitude of the house of Dagon, would surely preserve it from dishonor amid the mistakes and confusion of His people. It was a solemn thing to come near the ark of God—a solemn thing to approach that which was the special symbol of the Divine presence in the midst of His congregation.

It is a solemn thing to be the bearer of the name of Jesus, and the depositaries of the truth connected with His holy person. We should all feel this solemnity more deeply than we do. We are too apt to regard it as a light thing to put our hand to the ark; but it is not; and those who attempt it will suffer for their error.

But, it may be asked, has anything been entrusted to the care and keeping of the Church answering to the ark? Yes; the Person of the Son of God answers to the ark of old. His divine and human nature answers to the gold and shittim wood of the ark. The *materials* of the ark typified His *Person* as the God-man; while the *purposes* of the ark and mercy-seat typified His *work*, whether in life or in death. The ark enclosed the tables of testimony; and the Son of God could say, in connection with the body prepared of God for Him, "Thy law is within My heart." (See Psalm 40.) Again, the mercy-seat spoke of peace and pardon, of mercy rejoicing against judgment, where the poor sinner meets God in peace; as the apostle says, "He [Christ] is a mercy-seat for our sins." And again, "Whom God hath set forth to be a mercy-seat." (The word used in Rom. 3 is precisely the same as that used in Exodus 25, viz., *hilasteerion*— propitiatory).

Thus we perceive what a marked type the ark of the covenant was of Him who magnified the law and made it honorable— even Jesus the Son of God, whose glorious person should be the special object of the saints' reverent and affectionate guardianship. And, just as Israel's moral power was ever connected with the right acknowledgment and preservation of the ark amongst them, so the Church's power will be found connected with her due maintenance of the doctrine, the great and all-important

doctrine, of the Son. It is in vain that we exult in the work of our hands, and boast ourselves in our knowledge, our testimony, our assemblies, our gifts, our ministry, our anything: if we are not maintaining the honor of the Son, we are really worthless—we are merely walking in the sparks of our own kindling—sparks which shall be speedily extinguished, when the Lord is obliged, in very faithfulness, to come in and make a breach upon us. "David was displeased" at the breach. It was a grievous check to all the joy and gladness of the occasion; but it was needful. A faithful eye detected the wrong moral condition of soul which was betrayed by the wooden cart; and the breach upon Uzza was designed as a corrective; and it proved an effectual one.

"David brought not the ark of God home to himself to the city of David, but carried it aside into the house of Obed-edom, the Gittite." This was David's loss; he forfeited much blessing and privilege by thus stopping short, for the ark of God could do nought but bless all who were rightly connected with it, though it was judgment to be connected with it otherwise, as in the men of Bethshemesh, and Uzza. It was a happy time for Obed-edom while the ark was in his house, for "the Lord blessed his house and all that he had." All the time that David was *"afraid"* and without the ark, Obed-edom was *"blessed"* with the ark. True, things might not just look so cheering; the blessing, instead of being diffused through the whole nation, as it would have been had all been right, was confined to the immediate circle of him who had the ark in his house. Still the blessing, though contracted, was as real and positive, as pure and truthful, as if the whole nation had been enjoying it. It could not be otherwise, inasmuch as it was the result of the presence of the ark.

God will ever be true to His own principles, and will ever make those happy who walk in obedience; and as He blessed Obed-edom during the three months that the ark was in his house, though even king David was "afraid," so will He now bless those who seek to meet in truth and simplicity, in the name of Jesus. "Where two or three are gathered together in My name, there am I." This is the great charter of our meeting. Where the presence of Christ is, there must be blessing. Weakness there may be, no doubt, and paucity, but still blessing and comfort because Jesus is there; and the more we feel our own weakness, emptiness, and nothingness, the more will His presence be prized and loved.

Christians should seek to know more of the presence of Christ in their meetings. We do not want sermons, power of eloquence, human intellect, or anything that merely comes from man; we want the presence of Jesus, without which all is cold, barren, and lifeless. But, oh the sweetness of realizing the presence of the Master! Who can give expression to the preciousness known by those on whom the dew of the divine blessing falls? Blessed be God that any know it! Blessed be God that in this day, when the sad effects of human tradition are but too apparent in the Church, there is such a thing as the house of Obed-edom the Gittite, where the presence of the ark, and the consequent blessing of God, can be known and enjoyed! Let us prize this more and more, while shadowy and unsatisfying forms and ceremonies prevail around us.

We shall now dwell, for a little, upon God's gracious method of restoring the soul of His servant David. The life of faith* is little more than a series of falls and restorations, errors, and correction; displaying, on the one hand, the sad weakness of man, and on the other, the grace and power of God. This is abundantly exemplified in David.

There is a considerable difference in the way in which the return of the ark is recorded in Samuel and in Chronicles; in the one we have the simple statement of the facts; in the other, we have the moral training through which the soul of David passed during the time that he was afraid of God, or, in other words, during the time that he was laboring under the effects of his own

mistake. In Samuel we read, "And it was told king David, saying, The Lord hath blessed the house of Obed-edom, and all that pertaineth unto him, because of the ark of God. So David went and brought up the ark of God from the house of Obed-edom, into the city of David with gladness." David learned that so far from standing aloof from the ark through fear, it was really his privilege and blessing to be near it.

In 1 Chronicles 14, we find David in conflict with the Philistines, and obtaining victory over them. "David inquired of God, saying, Shall I go up against the Philistines? and wilt Thou deliver them into my hand? And the Lord said unto him, Go up; for I will deliver them into thy hand. So they came up to Baal-perazim; and David smote them there. Then David said, God hath broken in upon mine enemies by my hand, like the breaking forth of waters: therefore they called the name of that place Baal-perazim (i.e., a place of breaches)." There is a very great difference between "a breach" and "a place of breaches."

God had made a breach upon Israel because of their error in reference to the ark; but as to the Philistines, it was not merely a breach made upon them, they were altogether in a place of breaches; and David might have learnt what a poor example he had followed when he, like them, made the cart to carry the ark. And he did learn his mistake, for in chapter 15 we read, "And David made him houses in the city of David, and prepared a place for the ark of God, and pitched for it a tent. Then David said, None ought to carry the ark of God but the Levites; for them hath the Lord chosen to carry the ark of God, and to minister unto Him for ever." And again, addressing the chief of the fathers of the Levites, he says, "Sanctify yourselves, both ye and your brethren, that ye may bring up the ark of the Lord God of Israel unto the place that I have prepared for it. For *because ye did it not at the first*, the

---

* Not exactly the "life of *faith*," but the life of saints. The conflicts and trials so general in the people of God, while they testify to faith within, result from the flesh which, not having been kept under judgment, reasserts itself against the Spirit in the child of God. It is of this Gal. 5: 16-25 speaks. Were the "walk in the Spirit" a constant thing with us, the lust and warrings of the flesh would be kept under—kept in the place of death, where God has assigned the flesh. The apostle could say as to himself, "Always bearing about in the body the dying of the Lord Jesus, that the life also of Jesus might be made manifest in our mortal flesh" (2 Cor. 4: 10). [Ed.]

Lord our God made a breach upon us, for that we sought Him not *after the due order."*

Thus had David learned by the "breach" upon Uzza. He was brought to see that to follow in the current of man's thoughts was contrary to "the due order." None can teach like God. When David was wrong, God made a breach upon him by His own hand. He would not allow the Philistines to do this: on the contrary, He allows David to see them in a place of breaches, and enables him to smite them—to break in upon them, like the breaking forth of waters. Thus God taught, and thus David learned, what was "the due order"—thus he learned, as it were, to remove the ark from the new cart, and place it upon the shoulders of the Levites, whom the Lord had chosen to minister unto Him for ever—thus he was taught to cast aside human traditions, and follow, in simplicity, the written Word of God, in which there was not a word about a cart and oxen to carry the ark. *"None* ought to carry the ark of God but the Levites." This was very distinct. The entire mistake had risen from forgetfulness of the Word, and following the example of the uncircumcised, who had no capacity to understand the mind of God on any question, much less the solemn and important one of carrying the ark.

But in what a wonderfully gracious way did the Lord teach His servant! He taught him by victory over His enemies! Thus it is the Lord frequently leads His children into the apprehension of His mind, when they vainly seek to follow in the track of the men of this world. He shows them that they should not adopt such models. *The breach* taught David his mistake; *the place of breaches* taught him God's due order: by the former he learnt the folly of the cart and oxen; by the latter he learnt the value of the Levites, and the place which they held in the service of God. He would not allow His people to depart from His prescribed order with impunity. And the ark might have remained to the end in the house of Obed-edom, had David not learned to lay aside his own way of bringing it up, and take up God's way.

"So the priests and the Levites sanctified themselves to bring up the ark of the Lord God of Israel. And the children of the Levites bare the ark *upon their shoulders*, with the staves thereon, *as Moses commanded, according to the word of the Lord."* The Lord was glorified in all this, and He could therefore give real joy and gladness, strength and energy. There was no more stumbling of oxen—no more human effort to keep the ark from falling; the truth of God was dominant, and the power of God could act.

There can be no real power where truth is sacrificed. There may be the appearance of it, the assumption of it, but no reality. How can there be? God is the source of power, but He cannot associate Himself with what is at variance with His truth. Hence, although "David and all Israel played before God with all their might," there was no divine power. God's order was shut out by the human arrangement, and all ended in confusion and sorrow. How different is it in chap. 15. There is real joy—real power. "It came to pass, when *God helped the Levites* that bare the ark of the covenant of the Lord, that they offered seven bullocks and seven rams. And David was clothed with a robe of fine linen, and all the Levites that bare the ark, and the singers, and Chenaniah the master of the song, with the singers."

In a word, this was a scene with which God could consistently connect Himself. He did not help the oxen; He did not help Uzza; the oxen had not borne the ark, of old, through the waters of Jordan; neither had they borne it round the walls of Jericho. No; it was on the shoulders of the Levites that God had put it, and His order is the only happy one. It may not always commend itself to human judgment; yet it will ever have the stamp of Divine approval, and this is abundantly sufficient for every faithful heart. David was enabled to bear the sneer of contempt from Michal, the daughter of Saul, because *he was acting before the Lord.* Hear his fine reply to her reproach: "It was before the Lord, which chose me before thy father, and before all his house to appoint me ruler over the people of the Lord, over Israel; *therefore will I play before the Lord. And I will yet be more vile than thus, and will be base in mine own sight.*" Precious determination! May it be ours, through grace. Base in our own eyes—happy in God. Humbled to the very dust in the sense of our own vileness—lifted up on high, in the sense of the grace and loving-kindness of our God.

The reader will remark that 1 Chronicles 16 is just the development of the spirit breathed in the above quotation. It is the hiding of self and the setting forth the character and ways of God. In short, it is a song of praise, which one has only to read to be refreshed thereby. I would only direct attention to the last verse, in which we will find the four great characteristics of the people of God fully set forth. "Save us, O God of our salvation, and gather us together, and deliver us from the heathen, that we may give thanks to Thy holy name, and glory in Thy praise." The Church of God is a *saved* company. Salvation is the basis of everything. We cannot answer to any of the other characteristics in this copious verse, until we know ourselves as saved by the grace of God, through the death and resurrection of Christ.

In the power of this salvation the Church is gathered by the energy of the Holy Ghost sent down from Heaven. The true effect of the Spirit's operation will be to lead into fellowship all who submit to His leading. His order is not isolation, but blessed association and unity in the truth. But if there be ignorance as to salvation, our gathering together will not be to the glory of God, but rather for the promotion of our own spiritual interests, as it is termed. Men frequently associate on religious grounds without the assurance of being perfectly saved by the precious blood of Christ. This is not the Spirit's mode of gathering, for He gathers to Christ on the glorious ground of what He has accomplished. Confessing Christ, as the Son of the living God, is the rock on which the Church is built. It is not agreement in religious views that constitutes church-fellowship, but the possession of a common life, in union with the Head in Heaven.

Now, the more this divine unity is realized, the more will we enter into the next characteristic presented to us, viz., *separation:* "and deliver us from the heathen."

The Church is called out of the world, though called to witness for Christ in it. All within the Church is to be under the government of the Holy Ghost; all outside alas, is morally under the lordship of Satan, the prince of this world.

Finally, we have the Spirit of a worshiping people: "That we may give thanks to Thy holy name." This follows from all that we have been looking at. Salvation, association, separation, and worship are all connected together. The Church, breathing the atmosphere of God's salvation, is led by the Spirit into holy and happy fellowship, and thus being separated unto the Lord Jesus, without the camp, presents the fruit of her lips to God, giving thanks to His name.

Part 7

DAVID'S HOUSE AND THE HOUSE OF GOD

2 Samuel 7 and 1 Chronicles 29

There is nothing in which the narrowness of the human heart is so manifested as in its apprehensions of divine grace. Legalism is that to which we are most prone, because it gives self a place, and makes it something. Now this is the very thing which God will not allow. "No flesh shall glory in His presence," is a decree which can never be reversed. God must be all, fill all, and give all.

When the psalmist inquired, "What shall I render to the Lord for all His benefits?" the answer is *"I will take* the cup of salvation." The way to "render" to God is to "take" yet more largely from His bounteous hand. To be a thankful, unquestioning recipient of grace glorifies God far more than all we could render unto Him.

The gospel of God's grace comes to man as a ruined, guilty, helpless being. Hence God must be a great Actor in redemption. By His counsel alone it was planned; through His mercy alone it was accomplished in "the one offering of Jesus Christ once for all"; and by the Spirit's power alone is the sinner quickened into life and believes the glorious and peace-giving tidings of salvation.

Now, this stops man's mouth altogether as to his own righteousness. It excludes boasting, for we cannot boast of what we are but the unworthy recipients. How happy should all this make us! How happy it is to be the subjects of such grace—grace which blots out all our sins, sets the conscience at rest, and sanctifies all the affections of the heart! Blessed forever be the Fountain from which this saving grace flows to guilty sinners!

The seventh chapter of 2 Samuel is full of instruction as to the great principle of grace. The Lord had done much for His servant David; He had raised him from the depth of obscurity to an exceedingly high elevation, and David felt this, and was disposed to look around him and survey the precious mercies which, in rich profusion, strewed his path.

"And it came to pass, when the king sat in his house, and the Lord had given him rest round about from all his enemies, that the king said unto Nathan the prophet, See now, I dwell in a house of cedar, but the ark of God dwelleth within curtains." Observe, "David *sat in his house.*" He was surrounded by his own circumstances, and thought it needful to do something for God; but, again, he was in error as to his thoughts of building a house for Jehovah. The ark was within curtains, truly, because the time had not yet come for it to find a resting-place.

God had ever moved in the fullest sympathy with his people. When they were plunged in the furnace of Egyptian bondage, He was in the burning bush; when they were treading their long and dreary journey across the burning desert, His chariot traveled in company with them all the way. When they stood beneath the frowning walls of Jericho, He was there as a man of war, with a drawn sword in His hand, to act for, and in sympathy with, them. Thus, at all times, God and His Israel were together. While they toiled, He toiled, and until they could rest, He would not rest. But David desired to build a house, and find a resting-place for God, while there were both "enemies and evil occurrent."

This could not be. It was contrary to the thoughts and counsels of the God of Israel. "It came to pass *that night*, that the word of the Lord came unto Nathan, saying, Go and tell My servant David, Thus saith the Lord, Shalt thou build Me a house for Me to dwell in?—whereas I have not dwelt in any house since the time that I brought up the children of Israel out of Egypt, even to this day, but have walked in a tent and in a tabernacle." The Lord would not allow another sun to rise without correcting the error of His servant. He sets before him His own past actings toward Israel and toward himself; He reminds David that He had never sought a house or a rest for Himself, but had wandered up and down with His people in all their wanderings, and been afflicted in all their afflictions. "In all the places wherein *I have walked* with all the children of Israel, spake I a word with any of the tribes of Israel whom I commanded to feed My people Israel, saying, Why build ye not Me a house of cedar?"

What lovely, what soul-stirring grace breathes in these words! The blessed God came down to be a traveler with His traveling people. He would set His foot on the sand of the desert, because Israel was there; He caused His glory to dwell beneath a covering of badgers' skins, because His redeemed ones were in militant circumstances. Jehovah sought not a house of cedar; it was not for that He had come down to visit His people in the hour of their affliction in Egypt; He had come down to *give*, not to *take*; to dispense and minister to His people, not to exact from then. True, when the people had put themselves under a convenant of works, at Mount Horeb, God had to test them by a ministration which was characterized by the words *"do"* and *"give;"* but had they only walked in the power of God's original covenant with Abraham, they would never have heard such words uttered in connection with the terrific thunders of Mount Sinai.

When God came down to redeem them out of the hand of Pharaoh, and out of the house of bondage; when He bore them on eagles' wings, and brought them unto Himself; when He made a way through the sea for His ransomed to pass over, and overwhelmed the hosts of Egypt in the depths; when He showered down manna from Heaven, and caused the refreshing stream to gush from the rock; when He took His place in the pillar of fire by night, and the pillar of cloud by day, to guide them through the trackless desert; when He did all these things for them, and many more, surely it was not on the ground of anything they could *give* or *do;* but simply on the ground of His own everlasting love, and the covenant of grace made with Abraham. Yes, this was the ground of His acting toward them. What *they* did was to reject His grace; trample on His laws; despise His warnings; refuse His mercies; stone His prophets; crucify His Son; resist His Spirit! Such were their actings, from the beginning, the bitter fruits of which they are now reaping, and shall reap, until they are brought, humbly and thankfully, to bow to His covenant of grace.

By bringing all these past ways of God in review before David, the Lord taught David his mistake in seeking to build Him a house. "Shalt thou build Me a house? whereas . . . . Now, therefore, so shalt thou say to My servant David, Thus saith the Lord of hosts, I took thee from the sheepcote, from following the sheep, to be ruler over My people, over Israel: and I was with thee whithersoever thou wentest, and have cut off thine enemies out of thy sight, and have made thee a great name, like unto the name of the great that are in the earth. Moreover, I will appoint a place for My people Israel, and will plant them, that they may dwell in a place of their own, and move no more; neither shall the children of wickedness afflict them any more, as beforetime, and as since the time that I commanded judges to be over My people Israel, and have caused thee to rest from all thine enemies. Also the Lord telleth thee that He will make thee a house."

David is here taught that his own history, like that of his people, was to be a history of grace from first to last. He is conducted, in thought, from the sheep-cote to the throne, and from the throne into the ages of the future, and sees the whole course marked by the actings of sovereign grace. Grace had taken him up; grace had set him on the throne; grace had subdued his enemies;

grace was to bear him onward; grace was to build up his throne and his house to all generations. It was all grace.

David might justly feel that the Lord had done much for him: the house of cedar was a great thing for the shepherd of Bethlehem; but what was it when compared with the future? What was all that God had done, compared with what He would do? "When thy days be fulfilled, and thou shalt sleep with thy fathers, I will set up thy seed after thee, which shall proceed out of thy bowels, and I will establish his kingdom. He shall build a house for My name, and I will establish the throne of his kingdom forever." Thus we see, that it was not merely his own short span of forty years that was to be characterized by such actings of grace; his house too was spoken of "for a great while to come," even forever.

To whom, think you, are we directed in all these promises made to David? Are we to regard them as fully actualized in the reign of Solomon? Surely not. Glorious as was the reign of that monarch, it by no means corresponded to the bright picture presented to David. It was, in one sense, but a passing moment, during which a bright gleam of sunshine flashed across Israel's horizon; for hardly are we conducted to the lofty pinnacle on which Solomon was elevated, when the chilling words fall on the ear, "*But Solomon loved many strange women,*" etc. Hardly has the cup of exquisite delight been raised to the lips than it is dashed to the ground, and the disappointed heart cries out, "Vanity of vanities, all is vanity and vexation of spirit."

The book of Ecclesiastes will tell us how far short the reign of Solomon came of actualizing the magnificent promises made to David in this seventh chapter of 2 Samuel. In that book we trace the yearnings of a heart that felt an aching void, and was ranging through creation's wide domain in search of a satisfying object, but ranged in vain. We must, therefore, look beyond the reign of Solomon to a greater than he, even to Him of whom the Spirit in Zacharias speaks, in that fine prophecy in Luke 1, "Blessed be the Lord God of Israel; for He hath visited and redeemed His people, and hath raised up a horn of salvation for us in the house of His servant David; as He spake by the mouth of His holy prophets, which have been since the world began; that we should be saved from our enemies, and from the hand of all that hate us; to perform the mercy promised to our fathers, and to remember His holy covenant, the oath which He sware to our father Abraham."

Again, in the angel's address to Mary, "Behold, thou shalt conceive in thy womb, and bring forth a son, and shalt call His name Jesus. He shall be great, and shall be called the Son of the Highest; and the Lord God shall give unto Him the throne of His father David; and He shall reign over the house of Jacob forever; and of His kingdom there shall be no end." Here the heart can repose without a single check. There is no doubt, no hesitation, no interruption, no exception. We feel that we have beneath our feet a solid rock, the Rock of Ages, and that we are not, like the writer of Ecclesiastes, constrained to lament the absence of an object capable of filling our hearts, and satisfying our desires; but rather, as some one has observed, like the bride in Canticles, to confess our entire lack of capacity to enjoy the glorious object presented to us, who is the "fairest among ten thousand, and altogether lovely."

"Of His kingdom there shall be no end." The foundations of His throne are laid in the deep recesses of eternity; the stamp of immortality is upon His sceptre, and of incorruptibility upon His crown. There shall be no Jeroboam then, to seize upon ten parts of the kingdom; it shall be one undivided whole forever, beneath the peaceful sway of Him who is "meek and lowly in heart."

Such are God's promises to the house of His servant David. Well might the astonished recipient of such mercies, when speaking of all that had been done for him, exclaim, "And this was yet a small thing in Thy sight, O Lord God." What was the past when compared with the future! *Grace* shone in the past, but *glory* glistened in the future. "The Lord will give grace and glory." Grace lays the foundation; glory garnishes the superstructure. This is true of all; it is true, in an eminent degree, of the Church, as we learn from the Epistle to the Ephesians.

"Blessed be the God and Father of our Lord Jesus Christ, who hath blessed us with all spiritual blessings in the heavenlies in Christ; according as He hath chosen us in Him before the foundation of the world, that we should be holy and without blame before Him in love . . . to the praise of the glory of His *grace*, wherein He hath made us accepted in the beloved . . . that in the dispensation of the fulness of times . . . we should be to the praise of His glory." And again, "But God, who is rich in mercy, for His great love wherewith He loved us, even when we were dead in sins, hath quickened us together with Christ (by grace ye are saved), and hath raised us up together, and made us sit together in the heavenlies in Christ Jesus: that in the ages to come, He might show the exceeding riches of His grace in His kindness toward us through Christ Jesus."

Here we have grace and glory set forth most blessedly: grace securing, on immutable principles, the full forgiveness of sins through the precious blood of Christ, and full acceptance in His beloved Person; glory in the distance, gilding with its immortal beams the ages to come. Thus it is that the Word of God addresses itself to two great principles in the soul of the believer, viz., faith and hope. Faith reposes upon the past; hope anticipates the future; faith leans upon God's work already accomplished; hope looks forward with earnest desire to His actings yet to be developed. This puts the Christian into a deeply interesting position; it shuts him up to God in everything. As to the past, he leans on the Cross; as to the present, he is sustained and comforted by Christ's priesthood and promises; and as to the future, he "rejoices in hope of the glory of God."

But let us inquire what was the effect produced upon David by all this burst of grace and glory on his spirit? One thing is certain, it effectually corrected his mistake in seeking, as another has said, to exchange the *sword* for the *trowel*. It made him really feel his own thorough littleness, and the greatness of God in His counsels and actings. "Then went king David in, and *sat* before the Lord, and he said, *Who am I*, O Lord God?"

It is impossible to convey, in human language, the deep experience of David's soul, as expressed in his attitude and inquiry on this occasion. First, as to his attitude, "*he sat.*" This gives us the idea of the most complete repose in God, without a single intervening cloud. There is no doubt, no suspicion, no hesitancy. God, as the almighty and gracious Actor, filled his soul's vision, and hence, to have entertained a doubt would be calling in question either God's willingness or ability to do all that He had said. How could he doubt? Impossible! The record of the past furnished too many substantial arguments in proof of both the will and ability of God to admit of a doubt on the subject.

And truly blessed it is thus to realize our place before the Lord—to allow the heart to dwell upon His wondrous ways of grace—to sit in His presence in the full, unclouded sense of His pardoning love. True, it is hard to understand why it should be so—why He should set His love on creatures such as we. Yet so it is; and we have only to believe and rejoice.

But observe his inquiry, "*Who am I?*" Here we have the hiding of self. David felt that God was all, and self nothing, when he sat before the Lord. He no longer speaks of his actings, his house of cedar, his plan of building a house, etc. No; he expatiates on the actings of God, and his own little doings sink into their proper nothingness in his estimation. The Lord had said, "Shalt thou build Me a house?" And again, "The Lord telleth thee that He will make thee a house." In other words, the Lord taught David that He should be superior in everything, and that He could not, therefore, be anticipated in building a house. This might seem an easy lesson; but all who know anything of their own proud, self-righteous hearts, know that it was far otherwise. Abraham, David, Job, Paul, and Peter experienced the difficulty of hiding self and exalting God. This is, in fact, the most difficult lesson for a man to learn; for our whole being since the fall is set upon the very opposite, viz., the exaltation of self, and the setting aside of God.

It is needless to adduce any proofs of this; Scripture and experience alike demonstrate the fact that man seeks to be somewhat; and this cannot be attempted without setting aside the claims of God. Grace, however, reverses the matter, and makes man nothing, and God everything. "Is this the manner of man?" No, indeed, it is not the manner or law of man, but it is the manner of God. Man's manner is to set himself up, to rejoice in the works of his own hands, to walk in the sparks of his own kindling; God's manner, on the contrary, is to turn man away from himself, to teach him to look upon his own righteousness as filthy rags, to loathe and abhor himself, and repent in dust and ashes, and cling to Christ, as the shipwrecked mariner clings to the rock.

Thus was it with David when he sat before the Lord, and, losing sight of himself, allowed his soul to go out in holy adoration of God and His ways. This is true worship, and is the very reverse of human religiousness. The former is the acknowledgment of God by the energy of faith; the latter is the setting up of man in the spirit of legalism. No doubt, David would have appeared, to many, a more devoted man when seeking to build a house for the Lord than when sitting in His presence. In the one case, he was trying to do something; in the other, he was apparently doing nothing. Like the two sisters at Bethany, of whom one would seem, in the judgment of nature, to have been doing all the work, and the other to have been sitting idle. How different are God's thoughts! David sitting before the Lord was in a right position, rather than seeking to build.

It must, however, be observed, that while grace leads us away from our own actings, it does not hinder real acting for God. Far otherwise. It only hinders self-importance. It does not abolish service; it only puts it in its right place. Hence, when David learnt that he was not the man, nor his the time to lay aside the sword and take up the trowel, how readily did he acquiesce! How readily did he draw forth his sword from its scabbard, and take his place once more on the field of battle! How ready was he to be the militant servant to the end, and allow the curtain to drop upon him as builder! How ready was he to retire, and allow another to do the work!

In chapter 8 we find David smiting, slaying, taking, and thus earning for himself a still more extensive fame as a man of war, and proving how effectually he had learnt the Lord's lesson. Thus will it ever be with all who have learned in the school of God. It matters little what the character of service may be, whether building the house, or subduing the foes of the Lord. The true servant is ready for anything. David came forth from amid the holy repose of the Lord's house to fight the Lord's battles, in order that he might clear the ground for another to lay the foundation of that house, which his heart had so fondly desired to build. Thus David was the servant throughout. In the sheepfold, in the valley of Elah, in the house of Saul, on the throne of Israel, he maintained the character of a servant.

But we must pass to other scenes, in order to learn other and deeper principles in reference to David's connection with the house of God. He had to learn, in a remarkable manner, where the foundation of the Lord's house was to be laid. Let the reader turn to 1 Chronicles 21 and read it. It is parallel with 2 Samuel 24, and furnishes the account of David's fall in numbering the people. He became proud of his hosts, or rather the Lord's hosts, which he would fain regard as his. He desired to count his resources, and, alas! he had to learn the emptiness thereof: the sword of the destroying angel mowed down seventy thousand of his boasted numbers, and brought home to his conscience, in terrible solemnity, his grievous sin in attempting to number the Lord's people.

However, it had the effect of eliciting much of the sweet, self-renouncing grace that was in David. Hear his touching words, as he exposes his own bosom to the stroke of judgment: "And David said unto God, Is it not I that commanded the people to be numbered? even *I* it is that have sinned and done evil indeed; but as for these sheep, what have they done? Let Thy hand, I pray thee, O Lord my God, be on me, and on my father's house; but not on *Thy* people, that they should be plagued." This was precious grace. He learned to say, "Thy people," and was ready to stand between them and the foe.

But there was mercy in the midst of wrath. By the threshing-floor of Ornan the Jebusite, the angel of judgment sheathed his sword. "Then the angel of the Lord commanded Gad to say to David, that David should go up, and set up an altar unto the Lord in the threshing-floor of Ornan the Jebusite." Here, then, was the place where mercy triumphed, and caused her voice to be heard above the roar of judgment. Here the blood of the victim flowed, and here the foundation of the Lord's house was laid.

At that time, when David saw that the Lord had answered him in the threshing-floor of Ornan the Jebusite, then he sacrificed there. For the tabernacle of the Lord, which Moses made in the wilderness, and the altar of the burnt-offering, were at that season in the high place at Gibeon: but David could not go before it to inquire of God: for he was afraid, because of the sword of the angel of the Lord. Then David said, This is the house of the Lord God, and this is the altar of the burnt-offering for Israel. And David commanded to gather together the strangers that were in the land of Israel: and he set masons to hew wrought stones to build the house of God."

Blessed discovery! Thus impressively and solemnly, and effectually, was David taught the place where the Lord's house should be built, and its deep significance! The Lord knows how to lead His people, and to instruct them in the deep secrets of His mind. He taught His servant David by the instrumentality of judgment first, and mercy afterwards, and thus led him to the place and its meaning where He would have His temple built. It was by his necessities he learnt about the temple to God, and he went forth to make preparation for it as one who had learnt God's character by his own deep failure.

"This is the house of the Lord God"—the place where mercy rejoiced against judgment —the place where the blood of the victim flowed—the place where David had his sin blotted out. This was very different from going to build on the ground of his dwelling in a house of cedar, as in 2 Samuel 7. Instead of saying, "Lo, I dwell in a house of cedar," he might say, "Lo, I am a poor, pardoned sinner." It is one thing to act on the ground of what *we* are; and quite another thing to act on the ground of what *God* is. The house of God must ever be the witness of His mercy, and this holds good whether we look at the temple of old or the Church now. Both show forth the triumph of mercy over judgment.

At the cross we behold the stroke of justice falling upon the spotless Victim, and then the Holy Ghost came down to gather men around the person of Him who was raised from the dead. Just as David began to gather the hewed stones, and the materials for the joinings of the house, the moment the place of the foundation was settled. The Church is the temple of the living God, of which Christ is the chief corner stone. The materials for this building were all provided, and the place of its foundation purchased, in the season of Christ's trouble; for David represents Christ in His sufferings, as Solomon represents Him in His glory. David was the man of war; Solomon, the man of rest. David had to grapple with enemies; Solomon was able to say, "There is neither enemy nor evil occurrent." Thus do these two kings shadow forth Him who, by His cross and passion, made ample provision for the building of the temple which shall be manifested in divine order and perfectness in the day of His coming glory.

David proved, in the end, that though his *thoughts* as to the time of building the house needed to be corrected, his *affection* for the house itself was not the less fervent. He says, at the close, "Now I have prepared with all my might for the house of my God, the gold for things to be made of gold, and the silver for things of silver, and the brass for things of brass, the iron for things of iron, and wood for things of wood: onyx-stones, and stones to be set, glistening stones and of divers colors, and all manner of precious stones, and marble stones in abundance" (1 Chron. 29:2).*

Thus does grace put service into its proper place, and not only so, but imparts an energy to it which ill-timed service can never exhibit. David had learnt lessons when he sat in the Lord's presence, and when he stood on the threshing-floor of Ornan the Jebusite, which wonderfully fitted him for making the needed preparations for the temple. He could now say, "I have prepared with *all my might.*" And again, "Because I have set *my affection* to the house of my God, I have of my own proper good, of gold and silver, which I have given to the house of my God, *over and above* all that I have prepared for the holy house, even three thousand talents of gold," etc. His strength and affection were both devoted to a work which was to be brought to maturity by another.

Grace enables a man to hide himself and make God his object. When David's eye rested on the glittering pile which his devoted heart had raised, he was able to say, "Of *Thine own* have we given Thee." "Blessed be Thou, Lord God of Israel our father, for ever and ever. Thine, O Lord, is the greatness, and the power, and the glory, and the victory, and the majesty: for all that is in the heaven and in the earth is Thine; Thine is the kingdom, O Lord, and Thou art exalted as head above all. Both riches and honor come of Thee, and Thou reignest over all; and in Thy hand is power and might, and in Thy hand it is to make great, and to give strength unto all. Now, therefore, our God, we thank Thee, and praise Thy glorious name. But *who am I*, and what is my people, that we should be able to offer so willingly after this sort? for *all things come of Thee*, and of Thine own have we given Thee. For we are strangers before Thee, and sojourners, as were all our Fathers; our days on the earth are as a shadow, and there is none abiding. O Lord our God, all this store that we have prepared to build Thee a house for Thy holy name, cometh of Thy hand, and is all Thine own."

"Who am I?" What a question! David was nothing, and God was all and in all. If ever he had entertained the thought that he could offer anything to God, he entertained it no longer. It was all the Lord's, and He, in His grace, had allowed them to offer it all. Man

---

* In 2 Samuel 24: 24, we read, "So David bought the *threshing-floor* and the *oxen* for fifty shekels of silver." And in 1 Chron. 21: 25, we read, "So David gave to Ornan *for the place six hundred* shekels of gold by weight." In Samuel, only the "threshing-floor and the oxen" for sacrifice at the time of the plague are mentioned; while in Chronicles "the place"—the whole temple hill—seems to be comprehended.

can never make God his debtor, though he is ever seeking to do so. The fiftieth psalm, the first of Isaiah, and the seventeenth of Acts, all prove that the unceasing effort of man, whether Jew or Gentile, is to give something to God; but it is a vain effort. The reply to man, thus endeavoring to make God his debtor, is, "If I were hungry, I would not tell thee." God must be the giver, man the receiver. "Who," says the apostle, "hath *first* given to Him?"

The Lord will graciously take from those who are taught to say, "Of Thine own have we given Thee," but eternity will declare God to be *the great first Giver*. Blessed that it should be so! Blessed for the poor, guilty, broken-hearted sinner, to recognize in God the giver of all—of life, pardon, peace, holiness, everlasting glory! Happy was it for David, as he drew near the end of his checkered career, to hide both himself and his offerings behind the rich abundance of divine grace! Happy for him to know, as he handed the plan of the temple to Solomon, his son, that it should ever be the monument of God's triumphant mercy! The house was, in due time, to rise in magnificence and splendor from its foundation; the effulgence of divine glory was yet to fill it from end to end; yet would it never be forgotten that it stood on that sacred spot where the devastating progress of judgment had been stayed by the hand of sovereign mercy, acting in connection with the blood of a spotless victim.

And in passing from the temple of Solomon to that which in the latter day shall arise in the midst of God's beloved people, how fully may we trace the development of the same heavenly principles! Still more, when we pass from the earthly to the heavenly temple, may we behold the glorious triumph of mercy over every barrier; yea, rather, the glorious harmony effected between mercy and truth, righteousness and peace. From amid the brightness of millennial glory, shall Israel below, and the Church above, look backward to the cross as the place where justice sheathed its sword, and the Hand of mercy began to erect that superstructure which shall shine, with everlasting light and glory,

to the praise and honor of God, the blessed Giver of all.

Part 8

THE CONSPIRACY

We are again called to follow David into the valley of humiliation—a deep valley indeed where grievous sin and its bitter fruits are fully seen. It is really wonderful to trace the checkered path of this remarkable man. No sooner has the hand of love restored his soul, and set his feet again upon the rock, than he is plunged into the depths of corruption. We have just seen his error in reference to the house of God graciously corrected, and we are now to behold him led captive in the chains of natural desire. Such, alas, is man—a poor, halting, stumbling creature, needing at every moment the fullest exercise of divine grace and forbearance.

The history of the most obscure believer will be found to exhibit, though on a smaller scale, all the roughnesses, inequalities, and inconsistencies observable in David's course. Indeed, it is this that renders the narrative of his life and times so peculiarly, so touchingly interesting to us.

Where is the heart that has not been assailed by the power of unbelief, like David when he fled for refuge to the king of Gath? or by mistaken notions in reference to the Lord's service, like David when he sought to build a house for God, before the time? or by emotions of self-complacency and pride, like David when he sought to number the people? or by the vile lustings of nature, like David in the matter of Uriah the Hittite? If there be such a heart, it will find but little interest in tracing the ways of David. But I trust my reader has not such a heart, for wherever there is a human heart there is also the susceptibility of all that I have been enumerating, and, therefore, the grace that could meet David must be precious to every heart that knows its own plague.

The section of our history on which we are now entering is an extensive one, embracing many important principles of Christian experience and divine dealing. The facts of the case are, doubtless, familiar, but it will be profitable to look closely at them. David's sin led to Absalom's conspiracy. "And it came to pass, after the year was expired, at the time when kings go forth to battle, that David sent Joab, and his servants with him, and all Israel; and they destroyed the children of Ammon, and besieged Rabbah. *But David tarried still at Jerusalem*" (2 Sam. 11:1). David, instead of being out at the head of his army, exercising himself in the hardships and fatigues of war, was quietly reposing at home. This was giving the enemy a manifest advantage over him. The moment a man absents himself from his post of duty, or retires from the place of conflict, he renders himself weak. He has taken off the harness, and will, undoubtedly, be pierced by the arrow of the enemy.

While at work for the Lord, be the work what it may, nature is kept under pressure; but when at ease, nature begins to work, and feel the action and influence of external things. We should seriously ponder this. Satan will ever find mischief for idle hearts, as well as idle hands. David was made to feel this. Had he been at Rabbah with his army, his eye would not have rested upon an object calculated to act upon the corrupt principle within; but the very act of tarrying at home afforded an opening for the enemy to come in upon him.

It is well to be ever on the watch, for we have a watchful enemy. "Be sober, be vigilant," says the apostle, "because your adversary, the devil, as a roaring lion, walketh about, seeking whom he may devour." Satan watches his opportunity, and when he finds a soul unoccupied with his proper service, he will surely seek to involve him in evil. It is, therefore, safe and healthful to be diligently engaged in service—service flowing out of communion with God, for we are thus in an attitude of positive hostility to the enemy; but if we are not acting in hostility, he will use us as instruments for his own ends. When David failed in energy as the captain of the hosts of Israel, he became the slave of lust. Sad picture! Solemn, most solemn warning for our souls!

The believer is the subject either of the energy of the Spirit, or the energy of the flesh; if he fails in the former, the latter will most assuredly predominate, and then he becomes an easy prey to the enemy. Thus it was with David. "At the time when kings go forth to battle" he was at rest in his house, and Satan presented a bait which proved too much for his poor heart. He fell—grievously, shamefully fell! Nor was his fall now a mere mistake. No; he fell into a deep pit of moral evil, of vile corruption, and his fall utters the solemn admonition, *"Keep under the body."* Nature must be judged, or we shall make shipwreck.

And mark the fearful lengths to which David was carried in the commission of evil. Having sacrificed his character to indulge nature, he endeavors to make Uriah a cloak to screen him from the public eye. His reputation must be maintained at all cost. He tries kindness, but in vain; he makes the wronged and dishonored Uriah drunk, but to no purpose; at last, he murders him by the sword of the children of Ammon. How dreadful!

Did David really think that all was over when Uriah was out of the way.? Did he forget that the eyes of the Lord were resting upon him in his evil course? It would seem that his conscience was hardened on this occasion, and not susceptible of conviction as we should expect. Had it been so, he would assuredly have faltered and hesitated ere he added the sin of murder to that of adultery, he would have mourned under the sharp reproof of Uriah—only the sharper because perfectly unintentional—when he said, "The ark, and Israel, and Judah, abide in tents; and my lord Joab and the servants of my lord are encamped in the open fields: shall I then go into my house?" What a rebuke to David! The Lord and His people were in the open fields, conflicting with the uncircumcised foes of Israel, but David was at home enjoying the ease and indulging the desires of nature.

Surely we may say, there was a time when David would not have been found reclining on his couch when the hosts of the Lord were warring with the enemy; there was a time when he would not have exposed a faithful servant to the assault of the enemy in order to save his own reputation. Such, however, is man—the best of men. When pride swells the heart, or lust dims the eye, who shall attempt to draw a limit to human depravity? Who shall define the fearful lengths to which even a David can go, when out of communion? Blessed for ever be the God of all grace, who has ever proved Himself equal to all the demands of His wayward children! Who but God could deal with even one saint for a single stage of his history? When we remember His perfect estimate of the odiousness of sin, His perfect grace toward the sinner must fill the soul with adoring gratitude!

The Lord must maintain His holiness, however He may deal with the sinner; and hence, in David's case, we find Him denouncing the most solemn judgment upon his house because of his sin. Nathan is sent to him in order to lead his conscience into the immediate presence of the holiness of God. This is the proper place for conscience to find itself. When not there, it will find various expedients, subterfuges, and various cloaks. David said, when told of the success of his diabolical scheme in reference to Uriah, "Thus shalt thou say to Joab, Let not this thing displease thee, for the sword devoureth one as well as another." Thus did he think to hush up the whole matter. He vainly imagined that, when Uriah was out of the way, all would be well.

But, ah, there was an Eye that could penetrate through all this covering which David's insensibility has cast over his heart and conscience. "The sword devoureth one as well as another," no doubt, and war has its vicissitudes; but this would not satisfy the holiness of God. No; the whole matter must be exposed—the dreadful meshes of evil in which Satan had entangled the feet of his victim must all be disentangled, the holiness of God's house must be maintained at all cost, His name and truth fully vindicated, and His servant scourged in the view of the whole congregation—yea, "in the sight of the sun." It might seem, in man's judgment, to be wiser to hide from public view the chastisement of one who stood so high, but such is not God's mode; He will prove to every spectator that He has no fellowship with evil, by the judgment which He executes in the midst of

His people. Nothing could avail to wipe off the stain which had been cast upon the truth of God but the public judgment of the transgressor. The men of the world may go on for the present, and sin with a high hand; but those who stand in association with the name of the Lord, must keep themselves pure or else be judged.

However, David would seem to have been most wonderfully insensible in this whole transaction. Even when Nathan's touching parable had set before him the blackness of his conduct, he, though roused to indignation at the selfish conduct of the rich man, never took it to himself. "And David's anger was greatly kindled against the man; and he said to Nathan, As the Lord liveth, the man that hath done this thing shall surely die." Thus did he pronounce judgment upon himself unconsciously; he felt not his own sin as yet; perhaps he would have proceeded to find out and punish the offender, had not the prophet's word proved to be the very arrow of the Almighty to pierce his obtuse conscience. *"Thou art the man."*

Tremendous discovery! The sin was traced to its source, and David stood as a conscience-smitten, broken-hearted sinner in the presence of God. There is no more effort to screen himself, or maintain his reputation. *"I have sinned against the Lord,"* is the acknowledgment which flows forth from his wounded spirit. His soul was subdued by the power of the truth, and the 51st psalm was his penitential utterance, as he lay prostrate in the dust, in the deep sense of his own personal vileness before the Lord. "Have mercy upon me, O God, according to Thy loving-kindness; according to the multitude of Thy tender mercies blot out my transgressions." Here was David's well-known, oft-tried resource. He brings his heavy burden and lays it down beside the loving-kindness and tender mercy of God—the only place in which his harassed spirit could find repose. He felt his sin to be so heinous that nothing but the mercy of God could avail to blot it out. There, however, he found a "vast abyss" which could "swallow up" all his evil, and give him profound peace in the view of his own wretchedness.

Nor was it merely to be forgiven his sins that David desired; this he needed, no doubt, but he needed more; he needed to be inwardly cleansed from the defiling power of sin itself. *"Wash me thoroughly* from mine iniquity, and cleanse me from my sin." The apostle says, "If we confess our sins, He is faithful and just to forgive us our sins, *and to cleanse us from all unrighteousness."* To be cleansed from unrighteousness is more than to be forgiven our sins; and David desired the latter, as well as the former. Both are made to depend on the confession of our sins.

It is a much more difficult thing to confess our sin, than to ask for forgiveness. Really to confess before God the sin which we have committed, is a much more humbling thing than to ask for pardon in a general way. It is an easy thing to ask the Lord for pardon; but it is in vain unless we confess our sins; and then, observe, it is a matter of simple faith to know that sins are forgiven us. The word is, "If *we confess"*; David confessed his sin.

"I acknowledge my transgressions; and my sin is ever before me. Against Thee, Thee only, have I sinned, and done this evil in Thy sight; that Thou mightest be justified when Thou speakest, and be clear when Thou judgest." This was true conviction. There was no attempt at palliation; no laying blame on circumstances; no looking at individuals. It is simply *"I"* and *"Thee"*; I a sinner, and Thou the God of truth. "Let God be true, and every man a liar." The secret of true restoration consists in taking our real place, as sinners, in the light of the truth of God. This is the apostle's teaching in the third of Romans. The truth of God is there set up as the great standard by which man's condition is to be tested.

The effect of this is to bring the sinner down to the very bottom, as it were, of his moral and practical condition in the sight of God; it strips him of everything, and lays his inmost soul bare before a holiness which will not tolerate the least speck of sin in its presence. But when thus brought down into the dust of self-abasement and genuine confession, what do we find? We find God, in the solitariness and sovereignty of His grace, working out a perfect righteousness for the guilty and self-condemned sinner.

Here we find truth and grace presented to us in this most important section of inspiration. Truth breaks the heart, grace binds it up; that stops the mouth, this opens it; stops it, that it may no longer boast of human merit; opens it, that it may show forth the praise and honor of the God of all grace.

David traveled in spirit through the truth afterwards set forth in Rom. 3. He, too, was led down into the profound depths of his nature. "Behold," he says, "I was shapen in iniquity, and in sin did my mother conceive me." Here he looks down to the very lowest point of depression. Man's original—*shapen in sin!* What good could ever flow from such a thing? Nothing! It is irrecoverable.

And then observe the contrast: "Behold, Thou desirest truth in the inward parts." God demands truth. What could David do therefore but confess what he does? for that was the truth concerning himself. What could now meet the need of such a man? Nothing but the precious blood of Christ. "Purge me with hyssop, and I shall be clean: wash me, and I shall be whiter than snow." In other words, David throws himself as a helpless sinner into the arms of redeeming love. Happy resting-place! God alone can purge a sinner, and make him fit for His own presence. "Make me to hear joy and gladness; that the bones which Thou hast broken may rejoice."

God must do all—purge his conscience, open his ear again to the notes of joy and gladness, open his mouth to tell transgressors of His ways of love and mercy, create a clean heart within him, restore to him the joy of His salvation, uphold him by His free Spirit, deliver him from blood-guiltiness. In short, when Nathan's words fell with divine power upon David's heart, he cast the crushing weight of his burden upon infinite grace, (exercised through the precious blood of atonement) and thus was brought humbly to rejoice in a perfect settlement of the question which his sin had raised between his conscience and God. Grace gained a glorious triumph; and David retired from the field, scarred indeed, and sorely wounded, yet with a deepened experience of what God was, and what grace had done for his soul.

Still, David's sin produced its own bitter fruits in due time. This must ever be so. Grace does not set aside that solemn word of the apostle, "Whatsoever a man soweth, that shall he also reap." Grace may pardon the individual, but the results of sin will assuredly appear, even though the sinner may enjoy the deepest and sweetest experiences of divine love and restoring grace, while actually under the rod. We shall see this abundantly exemplified in David. He was, as we know, fully, blessedly, divinely pardoned, washed, and restored; nevertheless he had to harken to the solemn denunciation, "Now, therefore, the sword shall never depart from thy house; because thou hast despised Me, and hast taken the wife of Uriah the Hittite to be thy wife."

Observe, "Thou hast despised *Me.*" David had sought to hide his sin from public view by putting Uriah out of the way, forgetting the all-seeing eye of Jehovah, and forgetting, too, the honor of His holy name. Had he remembered the Lord at the moment when nature was causing her voice to be heard within, he would not have fallen into the snare. The sense of God's presence is the great preservative from evil; but how often are we more influenced by the presence of our fellow-man than we are by the presence of God. "I have set the Lord always before me; because He is on my right hand, I shall not be moved." If we fail to realize God's presence as a preservative *against* evil, we shall be made to feel it as a judgment *because* of it.

"The sword shall never depart from thy house." Contrast this with the glorious promises made to David in chap. 7, and yet it is the same voice that falls on the ear in the denuciation and in the promise, though in a tone so awfully different: in the latter, grace; in the former, holiness is heard. "Because by this deed thou hast given great occasion to the enemies of the Lord to blaspheme, the child that is born unto thee shall surely die." The death of the child, however, was but the first sound of the tornado of judgment about to burst upon David's house. He might fast, pray, humble himself, and lie prostrate in the dust, but the child must die; judgment must take its course, the consuming fire burn up every particle of the material submitted to its action.

The sword of man "devours one as well as another"; but the sword of God falls on the head of the *offender*. Things must be made manifest; the stream may flow for a time under ground, but sooner or later it will break out. We may go on for years in a course of secret evil, in the cultivation of some unholy principle, in the indulgence of some unholy lust, in the gratification of some unholy temper or feeling, but the smoldering flame must ultimately break forth, and show us the real character of our actings. This is a truly solemnizing reflection. We cannot hide things from God, nor cause *Him* to think that our wrong ways are all right. We may try to reason ourselves into such a thought; we may persuade our hearts by plausible arguments that such and such things are right, good, or lawful; but "God is not mocked: whatsoever a man soweth, that shall he also reap."

Yet what grace shines out in this, as in every scene of David's remarkable career. Bathsheba becomes the mother of Solomon, who occupied the throne of Israel in its most glorious period, and who also stands in that privileged line through which, according to the flesh, Christ came! This is truly divine! It is altogether worthy of God. The darkest scene in David's life becomes, under the hand of God, the means of richest blessings—divine grace is reflected on a dark background. Thus did the eater yield meat, and the strong, sweetness. We know how this principle characterizes all the ways of God with His people. He judges their evil, surely, but pardons their sin, and makes their very failures the channel through which, after humiliation and self-judgment, grace flows to them. Blessed forever be the God of all grace, who pardons our sins, restores our souls, bears with our many infirmities, and finally causes us to triumph through Him that loves us!

How must David have felt ever after, as his eye rested upon his Solomon, *"the man of rest"*—his Jedidiah, *"the beloved of the Lord"*! He would remember his own humiliating fall; he would remember God's adorable grace. And, is it not just thus with ourselves? What is our history day by day, but a history of falls and restorations, of ups and downs? Nothing more; and thank God for the assurance that "Grace all the work shall crown, through everlasting days."

At the close of this twelfth chapter, we find David again in conflict with the enemy—his proper place. "And David gathered all the people together, and went to Rabbah, and fought against it and took it. ... And he brought forth the people that were therein, and put them under saws, and under harrows of iron, and under axes of iron, and made them pass through the brick-kiln; and thus did he to all the cities of the children of Ammon. So David and all the people returned to Jerusalem."

And now begins the heavy tale of David's woes, the fulfilment of the prophet's denunciation, that the sword should never depart from his house. Chapter 13 records two of the most diabolical acts that ever stained a family circle. Amnon, the son of David, offers dishonor to the sister of Absalom, and Absalom murders Amnon, and then flees to Geshur, where he remains three years. David allows him to return, contrary to the positive command of the law. Even had he been but a manslayer, he should have remained in a city of refuge; but he was a murderer, and, with his murder upon him, he is received back again upon natural grounds—no confession, no judgment, no atonement.

"The king kissed Absalom." Yes, the king kissed the murderer, instead of allowing the law of the God of Israel to take its course. What then? "It came to pass after this, that Absalom prepared chariots and horses, and fifty men to run before him." This was the next step. David's inordinate tenderness only paved the way for Absalom's open rebellion. Terrible warning! Deal tenderly with evil, and it will assuredly rise to a head, and crush you in the end. On the other hand, meet evil in the name of the Lord, and your victory is sure. Sport not with the serpent, but at once crush it beneath your foot. Plain, unflinching decision is, after all, the safest and happiest path. It may be trying at first, but the end is peaceful.

But observe how Absalom works. He begins by creating a want in the hearts of the men of Israel. "And Absalom rose up early, and stood beside the way of the gate: and it was so, that when any man that had a controversy came to the king for judgment, then Absalom called unto him, and said, Of what city art thou? ... See thy matters are good and right; but *there is no man deputed of the king to hear thee.* Absalom said, moreover, Oh, that I were made judge in the land, that every man which hath any suit or cause might come unto me, and I would do him justice. And it was so that when any man came nigh to him to do him obeisance, he put forth his hand and kissed him. ... So Absalom stole the hearts of the men of Israel." The enemy's way is first to create a want, to produce a blank, and then proceed to fill it up with something, or some one, of his own providing. Those whose hearts were fully satisfied with David had no room for Absalom.

This is a fine principle when applied to our hearts in reference to Christ. If we are filled with Him we have no room for aught beside. It is only when Satan succeeds in creating a want in our hearts that he introduces something of his own. When we are able in truth to say, "The Lord is my portion," we are safe from the influence of Satan's attractive baits. The Lord keep us in the happy and holy enjoyment of Himself, that so we may be able to say with one of old, "I try to lay up all my good things in Christ, and then a little of the creature goes a great way."

However, Absalom stole the hearts of the men of Israel. He came in by flatteries, and usurped David's place in their thoughts and affections. He was a comely person, well adapted to captivate the multitude. "In all Israel there was none to be so much praised as Absalom for his beauty: from the sole of his foot even to the crown of his head there was no blemish in him." But his beauty and his flattery had no effect upon *those who were near the person of David.* When the messenger came, saying, "The hearts of the men of Israel are after Absalom," it became manifest who were for David.

"And David said unto all his servants that were with him at Jerusalem, Arise, and let us flee. . . . And the king's servants said unto the king, Behold, thy servants are ready to do whatsoever my lord the king shall appoint . . . .And the king went forth, and all the people after him, and tarried in a place that was far off. And all his servants passed on *beside him*, and all the Cherethites, and all the Pelethites, and all the Gittites, six hundred men which came after him from Gath, passed on before the king. . . . And all the country wept with a loud voice, and all the people passed over; the king also himself passed over the brook Kidron, and all the people passed over, toward the way of the wilderness."

Thus were there many hearts who loved David too well to be drawn away by the ensnaring influence of Absalom. Those who had been with David in the days of his exile were near his beloved person in this day of his deep sorrow. "And David went up by the ascent of Mount Olivet, and wept as he went up, and had his head covered; and he went barefoot; and all the people that were with him covered every man his head, and they went up, weeping as they went up."

This is a deeply touching scene. David's grace shines out more during this conspiracy than at any period of his life. And not only does David's grace appear in a striking point of view, but the genuine devotedness of his dear people also. When we behold a loving band of followers thronging round the weeping, the barefooted David, our hearts are far more deeply touched than when we see them thronging round his throne. We are more thoroughly convinced that his *person*, and not his office, was the centre of attraction. David had nothing to offer his followers now save fellowship in his rejection; yet was there a charm about him, to those who knew his person, that bound them to him at all times. They could weep with him, as well as conquer with him. Hear the language of a genuine lover of David: "And Ittai answered the king, and said, As the Lord liveth, and as my lord the king liveth, surely in what place my lord the king shall be, whether in death or life, even there also will thy servant be." Life or death; he would be in companionship with David.

In looking through these chapters, there is nothing that so strikes us as David's beautiful subjection of spirit. When Zadok would bring the ark in his weeping train, he says, "Carry back the ark of God into the city; if I shall find favor in the eyes of the Lord, He will bring me again, and show me both it, and His habitation; but if He thus say, I have no delight in thee, behold, here am I, let Him do to me as seemeth good unto Him."

When the insulting Benjamite, Shimei, came forth to curse and cast stones at him, and Abishai desired permission to take off his head, his answer is, "What have I to do with you, ye sons of Zeruiah? So let him curse, because the Lord hath said unto him, Curse David. Who shall then say, Wherefore hast thou done so?" In short, he meekly bows his head to the dispensation of God. He felt, no doubt, that he was only reaping the fruit of his sin, and he accepted it. He saw God in every circumstance, and owned Him with a subdued and reverent spirit. To him it was not Shimei, but the Lord. Abishai saw only the man, and desired to deal with him accordingly; like Peter afterwards, when he sought to defend his beloved Master from the band of murderers sent to arrest Him. Both Peter and Abishai were living upon the surface, and looking at secondary causes. The Lord Jesus was living in the most profound subjection to the Father. "The cup which My Father hath given Me, shall I not drink it?" This gave Him power over anything. He looked beyond the instrument to God—beyond the cup to the hand which had filled it. It mattered not whether it were Judas, Herod, Caiaphas, or Pilate; He could say in all, "the cup which *My Father* hath given Me to drink."

Thus, too, was David, in his measure, lifted above subordinate agents. He looked right up to God, and with unshod feet, and covered head, he bowed before Him. "The Lord hath said unto him, Curse David." This was enough.

Now, there are, perhaps, few things in which we so much fail as in apprehending the presence of God, and His dealing with our souls in every circumstance of daily life. We are constantly ensnared by looking at secondary causes; we do not realize *God in every-thing*. Hence Satan gets the victory over us. Were we more alive to the fact that there is not an event which happens to us, from morning to night, in which the voice of God may not be heard, the hand of God seen, with what a holy atmosphere would it surround us! Men and things would then be received as so many agents and instruments in our Father's hand; so many ingredients in our Father's cup.

Thus would our minds be solemnized, our spirits calmed, our hearts subdued. Then we shall not say with Abishai, "Why should this dead dog curse my lord the king? let me go over, I pray thee, and take off his head." Nor shall we, with Peter, draw the sword of natural excitement. How far below their respective masters were both these affectionate though mistaken men! How must the sound of Peter's sword have grated on his Master's ear, and offended His spirit! And how must Abishai's words have grieved the meek and submitting David! Could David defend himself while God was dealing with his soul in a manner so solemn and impressive? Surely not. He dare not take himself out of the hands of the Lord. He was His, for life or death—as a king or an exile. Blessed subjection!

But, as has been already remarked, the record of this conspiracy not only exhibits David's subjection to God, but also the devotedness of David's friends to his person, whether mistaken or otherwise. His mighty men are seen thronging round him on his right hand and his left, and sharing with him the insults and execrations of Shimei. They had been with him in the hold, with him on the throne, with him in the field, and they are now with him in his humiliation.

Now Shobi and Barzillai come forth to minister to him and his men with princely liberality. In short, the thoughts of many hearts were revealed in the season of David's sorrow. It was manifest who loved David for his own sake; and, no doubt, he returned to his house and his throne with a fuller and deeper confidence in the genuine affection of those around him.

There is, however, one character introduced to our notice, upon which we must dwell for a little. I allude to Mephibosheth, the son of Jonathan.

Hardly had David taken his seat on the throne, when he gave utterance to those memorably gracious words, "Is there yet any that is left of *the house of Saul*, that I may show *the kindness of God* unto him?" "The house of Saul!" "The kindness of God!" What words! Saul had been his most implacable enemy; yet, being now on the throne, the brilliancy of his position, and the fulness of divine grace, enabled him to sink in oblivion the acts of the past, and to manifest, not merely the kindness of David, but the kindness of God.

Now, the kindness of God is marked by this special characteristic, exercised toward His enemies. "If, while we were enemies, we were reconciled to God by the death of His Son," etc. Such was the kindness which David desired to show to a member of the house of Saul. "Now, when Mephibosheth the son of Jonathan, the son of Saul, was come unto David, he fell on his face, and did reverence. ... And David said unto him, Fear not, for I will surely show thee kindness ... and thou shalt eat bread at my table continually. And he bowed himself, and said, What is thy servant, that thou shouldest look on such a dead dog as I am?" Here, then, is a lovely specimen of the kindness of God, and here, too, we are presented with the ground of Mephibosheth's devotedness to David. Though having no more claim upon him than an enemy, or a dead dog, yet is he taken up in grace, and set down at the king's table.

But Mephibosheth had a faithless servant, who, to promote his own ends, misrepresented him to the king. The opening verses of chapter 16 will furnish the reader with an account of Ziba's actings. He pretends kindness to David, and blackens the character of Mephibosheth, in order to get possession of his lands. He takes advantage of his master's weakness of body to deceive and malign him. What a picture!

The truth, however, came to light, and the wronged one was fully vindicated. On David's return, when all the trouble was over, and Absalom perished from the scene, "Mephibosheth, the son of Saul, came down to meet the king, and had neither dressed his feet, nor trimmed his beard, nor washed his clothes, from the day the king departed until he came again in peace."

Such is the Spirit's testimony to this faithful man. While David was away, Mephibosheth was a mourner: true picture of what the saint ought to be now, during the period of his Master's absence. Fellowship with an absent Lord imparts a tone of thorough separation to the Christian character. The question is not at all what a Christian may, or may not do. No; an affectionate heart will suggest the true course to be adopted by all those who are looking for the king's return. What a truly divine spring of action does the absence of Jesus furnish! "If ye then be risen with Christ, seek those things which are above." Ask the spiritual man, why does he abstain from things which he might enjoy? His answer is, *Jesus is absent.* This is the highest motive.

We do not want the rules of a cold and barren formalism to regulate our ways; but we want a more fervent affection for the person of Christ, and a more lively desire for His speedy return. We, like Mephibosheth, have experienced the kindness of God— precious kindness! We have been taken up from the depths of our ruin, and set among the princes of God's people. Should we not, therefore, love our Master? should we not desire to see His face? should we not regulate our present conduct by constant reference to Him? Would that we were more like Mephibosheth. But we are all too well disposed to minister to our odious nature—too ready to walk in the unchecked enjoyment of the things of this life—its riches, its honors, its comforts, its refinements, its elegancies, and the more so because we imagine we can do all these things without forfeiting our title to the name and privileges of Christians. Vain, detestable selfishness! Selfishness, which shall be put to the blush in the day of Christ's appearing.

Had Ziba's account of Mephibosheth been true, how could the latter have replied to David when he said, "Wherefore wentest thou not with me, Mephibosheth?" But he was able to answer, "My lord, O king, my servant deceived me; for thy servant said, I will saddle me an ass, that I may ride thereon, and go to the king; because thy servant is lame. And he hath slandered thy servant unto my lord the king; but my lord the king is an angel of God; do, therefore, what is good in thine eyes. For all of my father's house were but dead men before my lord the king; yet didst thou set thy servant among them that did eat at thine own table. What right, therefore, have I yet to cry any more unto the king?" Here was simple integrity of heart. Unaffected devotedness must develop itself.

The contrast between Ziba and Mephibosheth is truly striking. The former was seeking for the inheritance; the later only desired to be near the king. Hence, when David said, "Why speakest thou any more of thy matters? I have said, Thou and Ziba divide the land," Mephibosheth at once proved the direction in which his thoughts and desires were flowing; "Yea," said he, *'let him take all,* forasmuch as my lord the king is come again in peace unto his own house." His heart was engaged about David, not about the "matters." How could he stand on a footing with Ziba? How could he divide the land with such an one? Impossible! The king had returned; this was enough for him. To be near to him was better far than all the inheritance of the house of Saul. "Let him take *all.*" Nearness to the person of the king so filled, so satisfied the heart of Mephibosheth, that he could, without any difficulty, give up all that for which Ziba had so diligently acted the deceiver and the slanderer.

Just so will it be with those who love the name and person of the Son of God. The prospect of His loved appearing will deaden their affections for the things of this world. With them it will not be a question of lawfulness or unlawfulness: such terms are far too cold for an affectionate heart. The very fact of their looking out for the morning, will, of necessity, turn their hearts away from all beside; just as gazing intently at any special object necessarily turns one away from everything else.

If Christians realized more the power of our blessed hope, how they would walk above and apart from the world. The enemy is well aware of this, and hence he has labored hard to reduce this hope to the level of speculative doctrine—a peculiar tenet, possessing little or no practical power to attract the heart. That section of inspiration, too, which specially unfolds the events connected with the coming of Christ, he has succeeded in involving in almost total neglect. The book of Revelation has, until very recently, been regarded as a book of such profound and inextricable mystery, that few, if any, could approach it. And even since the attention of Christians has been more particularly directed to its study, he has introduced and built up such conflicting systems—has set forward such jarring interpretations, that simple minds are well-nigh scared away from a subject which seems, in their judgment, to be inseparably connected with mysticism and confusion.

Now there is just one grand remedy for all this evil, viz., *a genuine love of the appearing of Jesus*. Those who are waiting for that will not dispute much about the mode of it. Indeed, we may set it down as a fixed principle, that in proportion as affection becomes dead, will the spirit of controversy prevail.

All this is very simply and very strikingly illustrated in the narrative of Mephibosheth. He felt that he owed everything to David; that he had been saved from ruin, and raised to dignity. Hence, when David's place was occupied by a usurper, Mephibosheth's whole appearance and manner proved that he had no sympathy with the existing state of things; he was estranged from it all, and only sighed for the return of him whose kindness had made him all he was. His interests, his destinies, his hopes, were all bound up with David, and nothing but his return could make him happy.

Oh, that it were thus with us! Would that we really entered more into our true character, as strangers and pilgrims, in the midst of a scene where Satan rules. The time is coming when our beloved King shall be brought back, amid the affectionate acclamations of His people, when the usurper shall be hurled from his throne, and every enemy crushed beneath the footstool of our glorious

Immanuel. The Absaloms, the Ahithophels, the Shimeis, shall find their proper place; and, on the other hand, all who, like Mephibosheth, have mourned the absent David, shall have all the desires of their longing hearts abundantly satisfied. "How long, O Lord?" May this be our cry, as we eagerly look for the earliest sound of His chariot wheels. The way is long, rough, and painful; the night dark and depressing; but the word is, "Be patient, brethren." "He that shall come will come, and will not tarry. Now the just shall live by faith; but if any man draw back, My soul shall have no pleasure in him."

Into the further details of Absalom's conspiracy I do not now mean to enter. He met the end his deeds merited, though a father's heart might grieve and a father's tears flow for him. Moreover, his history may justly be viewed as a type of that great prophetic character, who, as Daniel informs us, "shall obtain the kingdom by flatteries." This, however, and many other points full of interest, I shall leave the reader to deduce from the sacred text for himself, praying the Lord to make the study of His own Word refreshing and edifying, in this day of darkness and confusion. Never was there a time when Christians needed more to give themselves to the prayerful study of Scripture. Conflicting opinions and judgments, strange notions and baseless theories are abroad, and the simple mind knows not whither to turn. Blessed be God, His Word is before us in all its lucid simplicity, and in it we have the eternal fountain of truth, the immutable standard by which everything must be judged; all, therefore, that we need is a mind fully subject to its teaching. "If thine eye be single, thy whole body shall be full of light."

Part 9

THE SONG AND LAST WORDS

The twenty-second chapter of 2 Samuel contains David's magnificent song, and is parallel with the 18th psalm. It is the utterance of the Spirit of Christ in David, connected with His triumph over death, through the mighty energy of the power of God (Ephes. 1:19). In it, as the inspired heading teaches us, David presents his praise to God for deliverance from the hand of all his enemies, and the hand of Saul particularly. He thankfully recounts the glorious actings of God on his behalf, yet in such language as at once leads us from David and all his conflicts, to that terrible conflict which raged around the grave of Jesus, when all the powers of darkness were ranged, in fierce array, against God. Tremendous was the scene! Never before, and never since, was such a battle fought, or such a victory gained, whether we look at the contending powers, or the consequences resulting. Heaven on the one side, and hell on the other. Such were the contending powers.

And as to the consequences resulting, who shall recount them? The glory of God and of His Christ, in the first place; the salvation of the Church; the restoration and blessing of Israel's tribes; and the full deliverance of creation's wide domain from the lordship of Satan, the curse of God, and the thraldom of corruption. Such were some of the results. Fierce, therefore, was the struggle of the great enemy of God and man at the cross and at the grave of Christ; violent were the efforts of the strong man to prevent his armor from being taken, and his house from being spoiled, but all in vain; Jesus triumphed. "When the waves of death compassed me, the floods of ungodly men made me afraid; the sorrows of hell compassed me about; the snares of death prevented me; in my distress I called upon the Lord, and cried to my God: and He did hear my voice out of His temple, and my cry did enter into His ears."

Here was apparent weakness, but real power. The apparently vanquished one became the victor. "Jesus was crucified in weakness, but He liveth by the power of God." Having shed His blood as the victim for sin, He left Himself in the hands of the Father, who, by the eternal Spirit, brought Him again from the dead. He resisted not, but suffered Himself to be trampled upon, and thus crushed the power of the enemy. Satan, by man's agency, nailed Him to the cross, laid Him in the grave, and set a seal upon Him, that He might not rise; but He came up out of the horrible pit, and out of the miry clay, "having spoiled principalities and powers." He went down into the very heart of the enemy's dominion, only that He might make a show of him openly.

From ver. 8-20, we have the interference of Jehovah on the part of His righteous servant, set forth in language sublime and powerful beyond expression. The imagery used by the inspired Psalmist is of the most solemn and impressive character, "The earth shook and trembled; the fountains of heaven moved and shook, because He was wroth. . . . He bowed the heavens also, and came down; and darkness was under His feet. And He rode upon a cherub and did fly; and He was seen upon the wings of the wind. And He made darkness pavilions round about Him, dark waters and thick clouds of the skies . . . . The Lord thundered from heaven, and the Most High uttered His voice. And He sent out arrows, and scattered them; lightning, and discomfited them. And the channels of the sea appeared, the foundations of the world were discovered, at the rebuking of the Lord, at the blast of the breath of His nostrils. He sent from above, He took me; He drew me out of many waters."

What language is here! Where shall we find anything to equal it? The wrath of the Omnipotent, the thunder of His power, the convulsion of creation's entire framework, the artillery of Heaven—all these ideas, so glowingly set forward here, outstrip all human imagination. The grave of Christ was the centre round which the battle raged in all its fierceness, for there lay the Prince of life. Satan did his utmost; he brought all the power of hell to bear, all "the power of darkness," but he could not hold his captive, because all the claims of justice had been met. The Lord Jesus triumphed over Satan, death, and hell, in strict conformity with the claims of righteousness. This is the sinner's joy, the sinner's peace. It would avail nothing to be told that God over all, blessed for ever, had vanquished Satan, a creature of His own creation. But to be told that He, as man's representative, as the sinner's substitute, as the Church's surety, gained the victory, this, when believed, gives the soul ineffable peace; and this is just what the gospel tells us—this is the message which it conveys to the sinner's ear. The apostle tells us that "He [Christ] was delivered for our offences, and raised again for our justification." Having taken upon Himself our sins, and gone down into the grave under the weight of them, resurrection was necessary as the divine proof of His accomplished work. The Holy Ghost, in the gospel, presents Him as risen, ascended, and seated at God's right hand in the heavens, and thus dispels from the believer's heart every doubt, every fear, every hesitation. "The Lord is risen indeed"; and His precious blood is new and living wine.

The great argument of the apostle in 1 Cor. 15 is based upon this subject. The forgiveness of sins is proved by the resurrection of Christ. "If Christ be not raised, ye are yet in your sins." And, as a consequence, if Christ be raised, ye are *not* in your sins. Hence resurrection and forgiveness stand or fall together. Recognize Christ risen, and you recognize sin forgiven. "But now," says the triumphant reasoner, "is Christ risen from the dead, and become the first-fruits of them that slept." This settles all. The moment you take your eye off a risen Christ, you lose the full, deep, divine, peace-giving sense of the forgiveness of sins. The richest fund of experience—the widest range of intelligence will not do as a ground of confidence. Nothing, in short, but *Jesus risen.*

From ver. 21-25, we have the ground of Jehovah's interference on behalf of His servant. These verses prove that in this entire song we have a greater than David. David could not say, "The Lord rewarded me according to my righteousness; according to the cleanness of my hands hath He recompensed me. For I have kept the ways of the Lord, and have not wickedly departed from my God. For all His judgments were before me; and as for His statutes, I did not depart from them. I was also upright before Him, and have kept myself from mine iniquity. Therefore the Lord hath recompensed me according to my righteousness; according to my cleanness in His eyesight." How different is this language from that of Psalm 51, on which we have already dwelt. There it is, "Have mercy upon me, according to Thy loving kindness; according to the multitude of Thy tender mercies." This was suitable language for a fallen sinner, as David felt himself to be. He dare not speak of his righteousness, which was as filthy rags; and as to his recompense, he felt that the lake of fire was all that he could, in justice, claim, on the ground of what he was.

Hence, therefore, the language of our chapter is the language of Christ, who alone could use it.* He, blessed be His name, could speak of His righteousness, His uprightness, and the cleanness of His hands. And here we see the wondrous grace that shines in redemption. The righteous One took the place of the guilty. "He hath made Him to be sin for us who knew no sin, that we might be made the righteousness of God in Him." Here is the sinner's resting-place. Here he beholds the spotless victim nailed to the accursed tree, *for him*; here he beholds a full redemption flowing from the perfect work of the Lamb of God; here, too, he may behold Jehovah interfering on behalf of his glorious and gracious representative, and, as a consequence, on his behalf; and that, moreover, on strictly righteous grounds. What deep peace this gives to the sin-burdened heart! Deep, ineffable, divine peace!

David's song closes with a fine allusion to the glories of the latter day, which imparts to it a character of completeness and enlarged compass particularly edifying. "Strangers shall submit themselves unto me." "I will give thanks unto Thee among the heathen," etc. Thus are we conducted along a wondrous path, commencing at the cross, and ending in the kingdom. The One who lay in the grave is

---

* In a subordinate or partial way, we may say it also applies to David. Save that terrible fall, in the matter of Uriah, his life was an exemplary one—walking in the love and fear of God all his days. Though grossly and persistently wronged by Saul, never would David touch his life because he was the anointed of Jehovah. 1 Kings 15: 4-5 and 2 Sam. 23: 1 give us a divine estimate of his life. [Ed.]

to sit on the throne; the hand that was pierced with the nail shall wield the sceptre; and the brow that was dishonored with a crown of thorns shall be wreathed with a diadem of glory. And never will the top-stone be laid on the superstructure which redeeming love has begun to erect, until the crucified Jesus of Nazareth shall ascend the throne of David, and rule over the house of Jacob. Then shall the glories of redemption be truly celebrated in Heaven and on earth, because the Redeemer shall be exalted and the redeemed rendered perfectly and eternally happy.

In David's last words, as in the history of other servants of God, we see how they all found in God their unfailing portion, and a sure refuge. Thus was it with him whose history we have been dwelling upon. Through his whole career, David had learned that divine grace *alone* could meet his need; and, at the close, he gives full expression to this. Whether we look at his "song," or his "last words," the great prominent subject is one and the same, viz., the sufficiency of divine grace.

However, David's last words derive point and energy from the knowledge of God's requirements, in reference to the character of a ruler. "He that ruleth over men must be just, ruling in the fear of God." This is God's standard. Nothing less will do; and where amongst the ranks of human rulers shall we find any to come up to it? We may travel down the entire catalogue of those who have occupied the thrones of this world, and not find so much as one who could answer to the great characteristics set forth in the above comprehensive verse. He "must be just," and "rule in the fear of God."

Psalm 82 furnishes us with the divine challenge of all those who have been set in places of authority. "God standeth in the congregation of the mighty; He judgeth among the gods." What does He find? Justice and the fear of His name? Ah! no; far from it. "How long will ye judge unjustly, and accept the persons of the wicked?" Such is man. "They know not, neither *will* they understand; they walk on in darkness; all the foundations of the earth are out of course."

What, then, is the resource in view of such a humiliating state of things? "Arise, O God, judge the earth; for Thou shalt inherit all nations." The Lord Jesus is here presented as the one alone competent to fill the throne according to the thoughts of God, and Psalm 72 gives us a lovely sketch of what His government will be.

"He shall judge Thy people with righteousness, and Thy poor with judgment." "He shall judge the poor of the people, He shall save the children of the needy, and shall break in pieces the oppressor." "He shall come down like rain upon the mown grass; as showers that water the earth." In short, the entire psalm must be read as a sample of the millennial kingdom of the Son of Man, and the reader will perceive how entirely David's last words harmonize with the spirit of it. "And He shall be as the light of the morning, when the sun riseth, even a morning without clouds; as the tender grass springeth out of the earth by clear shining after rain."

Truly refreshing and soul-reviving is this! And how does the heart rejoice to turn away from the dark and dreary scene through which we are passing, to contemplate a morning without clouds. The "morning without a cloud" is not now. How could it be? How could a fallen race, a groaning world, enjoy a cloudless sky? Impossible, until the atoning efficacy of the Cross shall have been applied to all, and the whole creation shall have entered into its full repose beneath the shadow of Immanuel's wings. Bright and happy prospect!

But it has been remarked, that no human office-bearer ever came up to the divine standard, as set forth in David's last words. David himself felt this. "My house is not so with God." Such was his humble, soul-subduing sense of what he was. We have already seen how fully, how deeply, how unaffectedly, he entered into the vast distance between what he was *personally* and the divine requirement, when he exclaimed, *I* was born in sin"; "*Thou* desirest truth in the inward parts." His experience was the same when he looked at himself *officially*. "My house is not so with God." Neither as a *man* nor as a *king* was he what he ought to be.

And hence it was that grace was so precious to his heart. He looked into the mirror of God's perfect law, and saw therein his own deformity; he then turned round and looked at God's "convenant, ordered in *all* things and *sure*," and here he rested with unquestioning simplicity.

Though David's house was not ordered in all things, yet God's covenant was, and David could therefore say, "This is all my salvation, and all my desire." He had learnt to look away from himself and his house straight to God, and His everlasting covenant of grace. And, we may say, that just as his apprehension of his own personal and official nothingness was deep and real, would his sense of what grace had done for him be deep and real also. The view of what God was had humbled him; the view of what God was had lifted him up. It was his joy, as he traveled to the end of all human things, to find his resting-place in the blessed covenant of his God, in which he found embodied, and eternally secured, all his salvation and all his desire.

How blessed it is to find thus our *all* in God! not merely to use Him as one who makes up our deficiency, but our all; to use Him as one who supersedes every one and everything in our estimation. This is what we want. God must be set above all, not merely in reference to the forgiveness of sins but also in reference to our every necessity. Many who trust God for salvation, nevertheless, fail much in the minute details of life; and yet God is glorified in being made the depositary of all our cares, and the bearer of all our burdens. There is nothing too small as not to be brought to Him, and nothing so small as not to be more than a match for our capacity, did we but enter into the sense of our nothingness.

But we find another element in this chapter 23, an element, too, which might seem introduced rather abruptly: I allude to the record of David's mighty men. This has been already alluded to; but it is interesting to notice it in connection with God's covenant.

There were two things to cheer and comfort David's heart, viz., the faithfulness of God, and the devotedness of his servants.* And, in looking at the close of Paul's course, we find that he had the same springs of comfort and encouragement. In the Second Epistle to Timothy, he glances at the condition of things around him; he sees the "great house," which assuredly was "not so with God" as He required it; he sees all that were in Asia turned away from him; he sees Hymeneus and Philetus teaching false doctrine, and overturning the faith of some; he sees Alexander the coppersmith doing much mischief; he sees many with itching ears, heaping to themselves teachers, and turning away from the truth to fables; he sees the perilous times setting in with fearful rapidity: in a word, he sees the whole fabric, humanly speaking, going to pieces.

But he, like David, rested in the assurance that "the foundation of God standeth sure," and he was also cheered by the individual devotedness of some who, like mighty men, through the grace of God were standing faithful amid the wreck. He remembered the faith of a Timothy, the love of an Onesiphorus; and, moreover, he was cheered by the fact that in darkest times there would be a company of faithful ones who would call on the Lord out of a pure heart. These latter he exhorts Timothy to follow, having purged himself from the dishonorable vessels of the great house.

Thus was it with David. He could count his worthies, and record their deeds. Though his own house was not what it ought to be, and though "the sons of Belial" were around him, yet he could speak of an Adino, a Dodo, and a Shammah, men who had hazarded their lives for him, and had signalized their names by deeds of prowess against the uncircumcised.

Thank God, He will never leave Himself without a witness; He will always have a people devoted to His cause in the world. Did we not know and believe this, at a time like the present our hearts might indeed sink within us. A few years have wrought a

---

* May not this review of David's worthies and companions in tribulation set forth, or at least remind us, of that time when our Lord shall review with us our path with Him down here? A similar thought seems to be brought before us in Romans 16, in the apostle's salutations. [Ed.]

mighty change in the sphere of action of many Christians. Things are not as they once were amongst us, and we may with truth say, "Our house is not so with God." Many of us have, it may be, been disappointed; we looked for much, and, alas, it has come to little—oh, how little! We have found that we were just like others, or, if we differed in aught, it was in our making a higher profession, and, as a consequence, incurring higher responsibilities, and exhibiting greater inconsistencies. We thought we were somewhat, but we grievously erred, and are now learning our error. The Lord grant that we may learn it rightly, learn it thoroughly—in the dust, in His presence, that we may lift our heads proudly no more, but walk in the abiding sense of our own emptiness. The Lord's address to Laodicea must be remembered, and we may ponder it with profit.

If our past experience leads us to cling more simply to Jesus, we shall have reason to bless the Lord for it all; and, as it is, we cannot but feel it to be a special mercy to be delivered from every false ground of confidence. If we were seeking to build up a system, it is well to be delivered from its influence and to be brought to adhere simply to the Word and Spirit of God, which are the appointed companions of the Church's path through the wilderness.

Nor are we, either, void of the sweet encouragement to be derived from the devotedness of one or another here and there. There are many who are proving their affection for the person of Christ, and the high estimation in which they hold the doctrine of the Church. This is a great mercy. The enemy, though he has done much mischief, has it not all his own way. There are those who are ready to spend their strength and energy in the defence of the gospel. May the Lord add to their number—may He also add to the vigor of their testimony; and, finally, may He make us increasingly thankful for His grace in having set before us, in His Word, the true position and path of His servants, and those principles which can alone sustain us in the midst of strife and confusion.

David had thought to do much in his day, and was sincere in the thought; but he had to learn that the will of God concerning him was that he should "serve his generation." We, too, must learn this—we must learn that a humble mind, a devoted heart, a tender conscience, an honest purpose, are far more precious in the sight of God than mere outward services, however showy and attractive. "To obey is better than sacrifice; and to harken than the fat of rams." Salutary words, these, for a day of religiousness, like the present, wherein divine principle is so loosely held.

The Lord keep us faithful to the end, so that whether like those who have gone before us, we fall asleep in Jesus, or be caught up to meet Him in the air, we "may be found of Him in peace, without spot, and blameless." Meanwhile, let us rejoice in the apostle's word to his son Timothy—"The foundation of God standeth sure, having this seal, The Lord knoweth them that are His;" and, "Let every one that nameth the name of Christ depart from iniquity."

THE LIFE AND TIMES OF ELIJAH

INTRODUCTION

THE EXERCISE OF PROPHETIC ministry in Israel, of old, was always a proof of the nation's decline. So long as the great national institutions were maintained in their vigor, and the machinery of the Mosaic economy carried out according to its original design, there was no need of anything extraneous, and therefore the voice of a prophet was not heard; but when failure had set in—when those laws and institutions which had been enacted, and set on foot by God Himself, ceased to be carried out in their pristine spirit and power, then there was a demand for something additional, and that something was supplied by the energy of the Spirit in the prophets.

There were no materials in the whole range of Levitical rites and ceremonies for the formation or maintenance of such a ministry as that of Elijah the Tishbite; there was too much of the carnal element in them for that. The message of a prophet could only be delivered in the power of the Holy Ghost, and therefore, so long as the Levitical institutions fulfilled their end, the Spirit had no need to put forth any fresh energy.

There was no need of such a minister as Elijah in the days of Solomon's glory and greatness; all was in order then—the whole machinery was in a sound condition—every wheel and every screw worked effectually in its own place—the king on the throne wielded the sceptre for the maintenance of Israel's civil interest—the priest in the temple discharged in due order his religious functions—the Levites and the singers were all at their respective posts: in a word, all moved on in such a measure of order as to render the voice of a prophet unnecessary.

However, the scene soon changed; the mighty tide of evil soon set in, and swept away the very foundations of Israel's civil and religious system: ungodly men, in process of time, ascended the throne of David, and sacrificed the interests of the people of God at the shrine of their own vile lusts; and to such a height did wickedness rise, that at last the wicked Ahab, with his consort Jezebel, occupied that throne from which Solomon had administered the judgment of God.

Jehovah could no longer forbear; He could not allow the tide of evil to rise any higher, and He therefore sent forth from His quiver a polished shaft to pierce the conscience of Israel, if haply He might bring them back to their place of happy allegiance to Himself. This shaft was none other than Elijah the Tishbite—the bold and uncompromising witness for God who stood in the breach at a moment when every one seemed to have fled from the field of conflict, unable to stem the overwhelming torrent.

But, before we proceed to the consideration of the life and ministry of this remarkable man, it may be well just to make one observation upon the two-fold character of prophetic ministry. We shall find, in considering the ministry of the prophets, that, not only had each prophet a distinct ministry committed to him, but that, also, in one and the same prophet, there was a double purpose carried out: the Lord dealt with the conscience about present evil, while He pointed the eye of the faithful one to the future glory. The prophet, by the Holy Ghost, brought the light and truth of God to bear upon the heart and conscience—he laid open fully and faithfully the hidden chambers of evil within—he spoke plainly of the people's sad declension and departure from God, and removed the foundations of that false religious system which they were erecting around them.

But the prophet did not stop here; it would have been sad indeed had he been confined to the humiliating story of Israel's failure, and the departure of their ancient glory; he was able, through grace, to add to the solemn announcement, "O Israel, *thou* hast destroyed thyself," the consolatory assurance, "but *in Me* is thy help"; and herein we have developed to us the two elements which composed the ministry of the prophets, namely, Israel's total failure, and God's triumphant grace—the departure of the glory as connected with, and based upon, the obedience of Israel, and its final return and establishment as connected with, and based upon, the obedience and death of the Son of God.

Truly, we may say, this was ministry of a very elevated and holy character; it was a glorious commission to be told to stand amid the fragments of a crushed and ruined system, and there to point to the time—the happy time—when God would display Himself in the immortal results of His own redeeming grace, to the joy of His ransomed ones in Heaven and on earth.

Part 1

THE PROPHET'S FIRST MESSAGE

The reign of Ahab, the son of Omri, was a dark and dreary time for the house of Israel; iniquity had risen to a fearful height; the sins of Jeroboam were little when compared with the black catalogue of Ahab's transgressions; the wicked Jezebel, the daughter of the uncircumcised king of the Zidonians, was chosen to be the partner of his heart and his throne, and this circumstance alone was enough to secure the oppression of Israel, and the entire subversion of their ancient worship. In a word, the Spirit sums up the whole matter with these words, "Ahab did more to provoke the Lord God of Israel to anger than all the kings of Israel that were before him" (1 Kings 16:33). This was saying enough for him. The whole line of kings from Jeroboam down, had done evil in the sight of the Lord; but to do more than all of them, marked a character of no ordinary degree of guilt. Yet such was Ahab—such was the man that occupied the throne of God's ancient people, when Elijah the Tishbite entered upon his course of prophetic testimony.

There is something particularly sorrowful to the spirit in contemplating a scene like that which the reign of Ahab presents. Every light had been extinguished, every voice of testimony hushed; the firmament in which many a brilliant luminary had shone from time to time, had become overcast with dark clouds; death seemed to spread itself over the whole scene, and the devil to carry every thing with a high hand, when, at length, God in His mercy to His poor oppressed and misguided people, raised up a bright and powerful witness for Himself in the person of our prophet. But then it is just at such a time that a real witness for God is likely to produce the most powerful effect, and exert the most extensive influence. It is after a long drought that a shower is likely to be felt in all its refreshing virtue. The state of things at this time in Israel called for some mighty man of valor to come forth and act in divine energy against the tide of evil.

However, it is instructive to observe that Elijah is presented to us, in common with all his fellowservants, in circumstances of secret training and exercise ere he appears in public. This is a feature in the history of all the servants of God, not excepting Him who was emphatically *the Servant;* all have been trained in secret with God previous to their acting in public with man; and, moreover, those who have entered most deeply into the meaning and value of the secret training will be found the most effective and permanent in their public service and testimony. That man has much cause to tremble for his destiny who has arrived at a position in public which exceeds the measure of his secret exercise of soul before God; he will assuredly come short.

If the superstructure exceed the measure of the foundation below, the building will totter or fall. If a tree shoot forth its branches into the air to a degree exceeding the depth of its roots, it will be unequal to the violence of the storm, and will come to the ground: so is it with the man who enters a place of public service; he must be *alone with God*; his spirit must be exercised in private; he must pass through the deep waters in his own experience, otherwise he will be but a theorist, and not a witness; his ear must be opened to hear, ere his tongue can be fitted to speak as the learned.

What has become of all those apparently brilliant lights which have suddenly flashed across the path of the Church of God from time to time, and as suddenly disappeared behind the cloud? Whence came they, and whither have they gone, and why have they been so evanescent? They were but sparks of human kindling; there was no depth, no power of endurance, no reality in them; hence they shone for a time, and speedily vanished away, producing no result save to increase the darkness around, or at least the sad consciousness thereof.

Every true minister of God should be able, in measure, to say with the apostle, "Blessed be God, even the Father of our Lord Jesus Christ, the Father of mercies, and the God of all comfort, who comforteth us in all our tribulation, that we may be able to comfort them which are in any trouble, by the comfort wherewith we ourselves are comforted of God" (2 Cor. 1: 3-4).

1 Kings 17, gives us Elijah's first appearance in public; but the Spirit, in James, has graciously furnished us with the account of a yet earlier stage in his history, and one full of instruction to us, be our sphere of service what it may. The sacred historian introduces our prophet in a way which might seem abrupt. He presents him to us as at once boldly entering upon his sphere of labor, with this grand and solemn announcement, "Thus saith the Lord."

But he does not tell us, in this place, anything of the prophet's previous exercise; he speaks not of how it was he came to learn how the Lord would have him to speak: of all this, though most important for us to know, the Spirit in the historian says nothing; He simply introduces him to our notice in the holy exercise of a power which he had obtained in secret with God: He shows us Elijah acting in public, and nothing more. But the apostle lets us into the secret of Elijah's

prayer *to God*, before ever he came out in active service before *man*. "Elias was a man subject to like passions as we are, and he prayed earnestly that it might not rain; and it rained not on the earth by the space of three years and six months" (James 5: 17).

Now, if the Holy Ghost had not informed us about this important fact, by the pen of James, we should have lacked a very powerful incentive to prayer; but Scripture is perfect—divinely perfect, lacking nothing that it ought to have, and having nothing that it ought to lack; hence it is that James tells us of Elijah's secret moments of prayer and wrestling, and shows him to us in the retirement of the mountains of Gilead, where he had, no doubt, mourned over the lamentable state of things in Israel, and also fortified his spirit for the part he was about to act.

This circumstance in the life of our prophet teaches us a truly profitable lesson. We live in a time of more than usual barrenness and spiritual dearth. The state of the Church may well remind us of Ezekiel's valley of dry bones. We have not merely to cope with evils which have characterized by-gone ages, but also with the matured corruption of a time wherein the varied evils of the Gentile world have become connected with, and covered by, the cloak of the Christian profession.

And when we turn to the state of those whose knowledge of truth and high profession might naturally encourage the expectation of more healthy and vigorous Christian action, we find alas! in many that the knowledge is but cold and uninfluential theory, and the profession but superficial, having no power over the feelings and affections of the inward man. Amongst persons of this class it will also be found that the truth of God possesses little or no interest, or attractive power; they know so much in the intellect that nothing can be presented to them with which they are not already acquainted: hence the lifelessness with which they harken to every statement of truth.

In such a condition of things, what is the resource of the faithful one? To what should he betake himself? Prayer; patient, persevering prayer; secret communion with God; deep and real exercise of soul in His presence, where alone we can arrive at a true estimate of ourselves, and things around us: and not only so, but also obtain spiritual power to act for God amongst our brethren, or toward the world without.

"Elias was a man of like passions with us;" and he found himself in the midst of dark apostasy, and wide-spread alienation of heart from God. He beheld the faithful failing from amongst the children of men; he saw the tide of evil rising around him, and the light of truth fast fading away: the altar of Baal had displaced the altar of Jehovah, and the cries of the priests of Baal had drowned the sacred songs of the Levites; in a word, the whole thing was one vast mass of ruin before his view. He felt it; he wept over it; he did more—*"he prayed earnestly."*

Here was the resource—the sure unfailing resource of the grieved prophet; he retreated into the presence of God; he poured out his spirit there, and wept over the ruin and sorrow of his beloved people; he was really engaged about the sad condition of things around him, and therefore prayed about it—prayed as he ought, not coldly, formally, or occasionally, but "earnestly," and perseveringly.

This is a blessed example for us. Never was there a time when fervent prayer was so much needed in the Church of God as at this moment. The devil seems to be exerting all his malignant power to crush the spirits and hinder the activities of the people of God; with some, he makes use of their public engagements; with others, their domestic trials; and with others, personal sorrow and conflict; in a word, "There are many adversaries," and nothing but the mighty power of God can enable us to cope with them and come off victorious.

But Elijah was not merely called to pass unscathed, as an individual, through the evil; he was called to exert an influence upon others: he was called to act for God in a degenerate age; he had to make an effort to bring his nation back to the God of their fathers; how much more, therefore, did he need to seek the Lord in private; to gather up

spiritual strength in the presence of God, whereby alone he could not only escape himself, but be made an instrument of blessing to others also. Elijah felt all this, and therefore "he prayed earnestly that it might not rain."

Thus it was he brought God into the scene, nor did he fail of his object. "It rained not." God will never refuse to act when faith addresses Him on the ground of His own glory, and we know it was simply upon this ground that the prophet addressed Him. It could afford him no pleasure to see the land turned into a parched and sterile wilderness, or his brethren wasted by famine and all its attendant horrors. No; it was simply to turn the hearts of the children to the fathers—to bring the nation back to its early faith—to eradicate those principles of error which had taken fast hold of the minds of the people: for such ends as these did our prophet pray earnestly that it might not rain, and God harkened and heard, because the prayer was the offspring of His Spirit in the soul of His dear servant.

Truly we may say, *it is good to wait upon God:* it not only leads to happy results as seen in God's answer to it, but there is also much sweetness and comfort in the exercise itself. How truly happy it is for the tried and tempted believer to find himself along with God! how blessed to allow his spirit to flow out, and his affections to ascend to Him who alone is able to lift him above the depressing power of present things into the calmness and light of His own most blessed presence! May we all be found, then, waiting more upon God—making the very difficulties of our day an occasion for drawing near to the mercy-seat, and then we shall not only exert a salutary influence in our respective spheres, but our own heart will be comforted and encouraged by private waiting upon our Father, for the promise has never yet failed, "They that wait on the Lord shall renew their strength!" Precious promise! May we make full proof of it!

Thus, Elijah the Tishbite entered upon his path of service; he came forth armed from the sanctuary of God with divine power to deal with, and act upon, his fellow-men.

There is much power in the words, "as the Lord God of Israel liveth *before whom I stand*"; they bring before us in a very special way the basis on which the soul of this eminent servant of God was resting, as also the principle which sustained him in his course of service. He stood before "*the Lord God of Israel*," and so standing, he could speak with a measure of power and authority.

But how very little did Ahab know of the secret exercises of Elijah's soul, ere he had thus come forth to speak to his conscience! He knew not that Elijah had been on his knees in secret before he presented himself in public. He knew nothing of all this, but Elijah did, and hence he could boldly confront the very head of the evil; he could speak to king Ahab himself, and announce to him the judgments of an offended God. In this, our prophet may be viewed as a fine model for all who are called upon to speak in the name of the Lord.

All who are so called should feel themselves, in virtue of their divine commission, entirely lifted above the influence of human opinion. How often does it happen that men who can speak with a measure of power and liberty in the presence of some, are before others cramped, and, it may be, altogether hindered! This we know would not be the case did they but realize with distinctness, not only that they had received their commission from on high, but also that they executed it in the presence of *the living God*. The messenger of the Lord should never be affected by those to whom he delivers his message; he should be above them, while at the same time he takes the humble place of a servant. His language should be, "But with me it is a very small matter that I should be judged of you, or of man's judgment" (ἀνθρωπίνης ἡμέρας).

This was pre-eminently the case with our blessed Master. How little was He affected by the thoughts or judgments of those to whom He spoke! They might thwart, oppose, and reject, but that never led Him for a moment to lose sight of the fact that He was sent of God. He carried with Him, throughout His entire course, the holy, soul-sustaining assurance expressed in the synagogue of Nazareth, "The Spirit of the Lord is upon Me, because He hath anointed Me to preach the gospel to the poor," etc. (Luke 4:18). Here was the basis of His ministry as Son of man. It was "in the power of the Spirit," and hence He ever felt Himself to be the minister of God, and as such raised quite above the influence of those with whom He had to do. "My doctrine is not Mine," said He, "but His that sent Me." He could truly say, "The Lord God of Israel, *before whom I stand:*" He was ever "the Lord's messenger," speaking "in the Lord's message unto the people" (Hag. 1: 13).

And should not all who fill the place of servants or messengers of the Lord, seek to know more of this holy elevation of mind above men and circumstances? Should they not aim at being less under the power of human thoughts and feelings? What have we to do with the thoughts of men about us? Nothing. Whether they will hear, or whether they will forbear; whether they will accept, or whether they will reject; whether we shall be highly esteemed for our work's sake, or made of no reputation—still let it be our aim, our constant aim, to "approve ourselves as the ministers of God."

But observe further, the power and authority with which our prophet speaks, "There shall not be dew nor rain these years but according to my word." He felt such perfect assurance in the fact that he was standing in the Lord's presence, and speaking the Lord's words, yea, that he was thoroughly identified with Him, that he could say, "according to my word."

Such was the privilege of the Lord's messenger, when delivering the Lord's message. Such are the wondrous results of secret prayer. "Elias was a man of like passions as we are, and he prayed earnestly that it might not rain; and it rained not on the earth by the space of three years and six months." May it prove a powerful incentive to all those who desire to act for God in this day of weakness! We want to be more in the presence of God, in the real sense of our need; if we felt our need more, we should have more of *the spirit of prayer*. And it is the spirit of prayer we want—that spirit which puts God in His own proper place of *giver*, and us into our proper place of *receivers*.

But how often are we deceived by the mere form of prayer—with the formal utterance of words which have no reality in them! There are many who make a kind of god of prayer—many who let their very prayers get between their souls and the God of prayer. This is a great snare. We should always take care that our prayers are the natural outflow of the Spirit within us, and not of the mere superstitious performance of what we think ought to be done.*

Part 2

THE PROPHET IN RETIREMENT

Hardly had our prophet delivered his testimony when he was again called away from public observation into retirement and solitude. "And the word of the Lord came unto him, saying, Get thee hence, and turn thee eastward, and *hide thyself* by the brook Cherith, that is before Jordan."

These words are full of deep instruction. Elijah had taken a very prominent place in the presence of Israel, and though his having done so was the result of previous retirement and exercise of soul in the presence of God, yet did the faithful One for whom he was acting see it needful to have him away again into privacy, that so he might not only occupy a high place in the presence of his brethren, but also a low place in the presence of God. All this is full of teaching for us. We must be kept low. Flesh must be crushed. Our time of *training in secret*, must far exceed our time of *acting in public*. Elijah stood, as it were, for a brief moment, in public testimony, and

that too, after having been alone with God, and he must at once be led away into seclusion for three years and a half.

Oh! how little can man be trusted; how badly can we bear to be set in a place of honor! How soon we forget ourselves and God! We shall see presently, how much our honored prophet needed to be thus kept in retirement. The Lord knew his temperament and tendencies, and dealt with him accordingly. It is truly humiliating to think how little we can be trusted in the way of public testimony for Christ; we are so full of self; we vainly imagine that *we* are something, and that God will do much by *us;* hence it is that we need, like our prophet, to be told to "hide ourselves," to get away from public view, that we may learn, in the holy calmness of our Father's presence, our own proper nothingness.

And the spiritual mind can at once see the importance of all this. It would never do to be always before the eye of man; no creature could stand it: the Son of God Himself constantly sought the solitary place, apart from the din and bustle of the city, where He might enjoy a quiet retreat for prayer, and of secret communion with God. "Jesus went unto the Mount of Olives." "Rising up a great while before day, He departed into a solitary place and there prayed."

But it was not because He needed to hide Himself, for His entire path on earth was, blessed be His name, a hiding of self. The spirit of His ministry is brought out in these words, "My doctrine is not Mine, but His that sent Me." Would that all the Lord's servants knew more of this! We all want to hide self more—much more than we do.

The devil acts so on our poor silly hearts; our thoughts so revolve round ourselves; yea, we so often make our very service, and

---

* I would offer a few words here on the subject of united prayer among Christians, an exercise which seems so sadly neglected by us at a time when it is so specially needed. It will be generally found that collective life and energy, service and testimony, will be in proportion to the measure of collective waiting upon God. Where there are not public prayer-meetings, there is sure to be a lack of service and testimony; the interests of the Church of God are not realized, and, as a consequence, the things of earth occupy a place of undue prominence in the minds of Christians. If we *felt* our collective weakness, there would be a collective utterance of that weakness, and, moreover, a renewal of our collective strength. Now I think it will be found that all important movements among the people of God have been the result of united heartfelt prayer. And surely we may say it is natural that it should be so. We are not to expect that God will pour forth His reviving grace on those who rest satisfied with their deadness and coldness. The word is, "Open thy mouth wide, and I will fill it." If we will not open our mouths, how can they be filled? If we are satisfied with what we have, how can we expect to get more? Let it be, therefore, the aim of the Christian reader to stir up his fellow-Christians around him to seek the Lord in united prayer, and, he may be assured of it, the happy results will speedily be seen.

the truth of God, a pedestal on which to show forth our own glory. No marvel, therefore, that we are not much used: how could the Lord make use of agents who will not give Him the glory? How can the Lord use Israel, when Israel is ever prone to vaunt himself? Let us then pray to be made more truly humble, more self-abased, more willing to be looked upon as "a dead dog, or a flea," or "the off-scouring of all things," or nothing at all, for the name of our gracious Master.

In His lonely retreat by the brook Cherith, Elijah was called to sojourn many days; not, however, without a precious promise from the Lord God of Israel in reference to his needed provision, for he went accompanied by the gracious assurance, "*I have commanded* the ravens to feed thee there." The Lord would take care of His dear servant while hidden from public view, and minister to his necessities, even though it should be by the instrumentality of ravens. What a strange provision! What a continual exercise of faith was there involved in being called to look out for the daily visits of birds that would naturally desire to devour the prophet's meal! But was it upon the ravens that Elijah lived? Surely not. His soul reposed in the precious words, "*I have commanded.*" It was God, and not the ravens, for him. He had the God of Israel with him in his hiding place—he lived by faith. And how truly blessed for the spirit thus to cling, in unaffected simplicity, to the promise of God!

How happy to be lifted above the power of circumstances, in the apprehension of God's presence and care! Elijah was hiding himself from man, while God was showing Himself to Elijah. This will ever be so. Let us only set self aside, and we may be assured that God will reveal Himself in power to our souls. If Elijah had persisted in occupying a prominent and a public place, he would have been left unprovided for. *He must be hidden;* for the streams of divine provision and refreshment only flowed for him in the place of retirement and self-abasement. "I have commanded the ravens to feed thee *there.*" If the prophet were anywhere else but "*there*" he would have gotten nothing at all from God.

What teaching for us in all this! Why are our souls so lean and barren? Why do we so little drink of the streams of divinely provided refreshment? Because we are not hiding self sufficiently. We cannot expect that God will strengthen and refresh us for the purpose of earthly display. He will strengthen us for Himself. If we could but realize more that we are "not our own," we should enjoy more spiritual power.

But there is also much meaning in the little word "*there.*" Elijah should be "*there*" and nowhere else, in order to enjoy God's supplies; and just so is it with the believer now; he must know where God would have him to be, and there abide. We have no right to choose our place, for the Lord "orders the bounds of our habitation," and happy for us is it to know this, and submit to His wise and gracious ordering. It was at the brook Cherith, and there alone, that the ravens were commanded to convey bread and flesh to the prophet; he might wish to sojourn elsewhere, but, if he had done so he should have provided for himself: how much happier to allow God to provide for him! So Elijah felt, and therefore he went to Cherith, for the Lord had "commanded the ravens to feed him *there.*" The divinely appointed provision is alone to be had in the divinely appointed place.

Thus was Elijah conveyed from solitude to solitude. He had come from the mountains of Gilead, with a message from the Lord God of Israel to Israel's king, and having delivered that message, he was again conducted, by the hand of God, into unbroken solitude, there to have his spirit exercised, and his strength renewed in the presence of God.

And who would be without those sweet and holy lessons learnt in secret? Who would lack the training of a Father's hand? Who would not long to be led away from beneath the eye of man, and above the influence of things earthly and natural, into the pure light of the Divine Presence, where self and all around are viewed and estimated according to the judgment of the sanctuary? In a word, who would not desire to be alone with God?—alone, not as a merely sentimental expression, but really, practically, and experimentally alone; alone like Moses at the mount of God; alone, like Aaron in the holiest of all; alone, like our prophet at the brook Cherith; alone, like John in the island of Patmos; and above all, alone, like Jesus on the mount.

And here, let us inquire what it is to be alone with God. It is to have self and the world set aside; to have the spirit impressed with thoughts of God and His perfections and excellencies; to allow all His goodness to pass before us; to see Him as the great Actor *for* us, and *in* us; to get above flesh and its reasonings, earth and its ways, Satan and his accusations; and, above all, to feel that we have been introduced into this holy solitude, simply and exclusively through the precious blood of our Lord Jesus Christ.

These are some of the results of our being alone with God. But, in truth, it is a term which one can hardly explain to another, for each spiritually-minded saint will have his own feelings on the subject, and will best understand what it means in his own case. This, at least, we may well crave, to be truly found in the secret of our Father's presence; to be done with the weariness and wretchedness of endeavoring to maintain *our character*, and to know the joy, the liberty, the peace, and unaffected simplicity of the sanctuary, where God in all His varied attributes and perfections rises before our souls and fills us with bliss ineffable.

> To find my place within the veil,
>   To know that God is mine,
> Are springs of joy that will not fail,
>   Unspeakable, divine.

But, though Elijah was thus happily alone by the brook Cherith, he was not exempt from the deep exercise of soul consequent upon a life of faith. The ravens, it is true, in obedience to the divine command, paid him their daily visits, and Cherith flowed on in its tranquil and uninterrupted course, so that the prophet's bread was given him, and his water was sure, and thus, as far as he was personally concerned, he might forget that the rod of judgment was stretched out over the land.

But faith must be put to the test. The man of faith cannot be allowed to settle on his lees; he must be emptied from vessel to vessel; the child of God must pass from form to form in the school of Christ, and having mastered, through grace, the difficulties of one, he must be called to grapple with those of another. It was, therefore, needful that the soul of the prophet should be tried in order that it might be seen whether he was depending upon Cherith, or upon the Lord God of Israel; hence, "it came to pass, after awhile, that *the brook dried up*."

We are ever in danger, through the infirmity of our flesh, of having our faith propped up by circumstances, and when these are favorable, we think our faith is strong, and *vice versa*. But faith never looks at circumstances; it looks straight to God; it has to do exclusively with Him and His promises. Thus it was with Elijah; it mattered little to him whether Cherith continued to flow or not; he could say:

> In vain the creature streams are dry,
>   I have a fountain still.

God was his fountain, his unfailing exhaustless fountain. The brook might yield to the influence of the prevailing drought, but no drought could affect God, and the prophet knew this; he knew that the Word of the Lord was as certain a portion, and as sure a basis in the drying up of Cherith, as it had been during the time of his sojourn upon its banks; and so it was, for "the word of the Lord came to him, saying, Arise, get thee to Zarephath, which belongeth to Zidon, and dwell there; behold *I have commanded* a widow woman there to sustain thee."

Elijah's faith must still rest upon the same immutable basis. "I have commanded." How truly blessed is this! Circumstances change; human things fail; creature streams are dried up, but God and His Word are the same yesterday, to-day, and forever. Nor does the prophet seem to have been the least disturbed by this fresh order from on high. No; for, like Israel of old, he had learned to pitch and strike his tent according to the movement of Jehovah's cloud. The camp, of old, was called to watch attentively the wheels of that heavenly chariot which rolled onward toward the land of rest, and here and there halted in the wilderness to find them out a resting-place; and just so was it with Elijah; he would take up his solitary post by the banks of Cherith, or tread his weary way to Zarephath of Zidon in undeviating obedience to "the word of the Lord."

Israel of old were not allowed to have any plans of their own; Jehovah planned and arranged everything for them. He told them when and where they were to move and halt; at various intervals He signified His sovereign pleasure to them by the movement of the cloud above their heads. "Whether it were two days, or a month, or a year, that the cloud tarried upon the tabernacle, remaining thereon, the children of Israel abode in their tents, and journeyed not; but when it was taken up they journeyed. At the commandment of the Lord they rested in their tents, and at the commandment of the Lord they journeyed" (Num. 9: 22-23).

Such was the happy condition of the Lord's redeemed, while passing from Egypt to Canaan. They never could have *their own way*, as regards their movements. If an Israelite had refused to move when the cloud moved, or to halt when it halted, *he would have been left to starve in the wilderness.* The rock and the manna followed them while they followed Jehovah; in other words, food and refreshment were alone to be found in the path of simple obedience. Just so was it with Elijah; he was not permitted to have a will of his own; he could not fix the time of his sojourn at Cherith, nor the time for his removal to Zarephath; "the word of the Lord" settled all for him, and when he obeyed it he found sustenance.

What a lesson for the Christian in all this! The path of obedience is alone the path of happiness. If we were more successful in doing violence to self, our spiritual condition would be far more vigorous and healthy than it is. Nothing so ministers to health and vigor of soul as undeviating obedience; there is strength gained by the very effort to obey. This is true in the case of all, but specially so as regards those who stand in the capacity of ministers of the Lord. Such must walk in obedience if they would be used in ministry.

How could Elijah have said, as he afterwards did, upon mount Carmel, "If the Lord be God, *follow Him,*" if his own private path had exhibited a wilful and rebellious spirit? Impossible. The path of a servant must be the path of obedience, otherwise he ceases to be a servant. The word *servant* is as inseparably linked with *obedience*, as is *work* with *workman*. "A servant," as another has observed, "must move when the bell rings."

Would that we were all more alive to the sound of our Master's bell, and more ready to run in the direction in which it summons us. *"Speak, Lord, for Thy servant heareth."* Here is our proper language. Whether the Word of the Lord summons us from our retirement into the midst of our brethren, or from thence into retirement again, may our language ever be, "Speak, Lord for Thy servant heareth." The Word of the Lord, and the attentive ear of a servant, are all we need to carry us safely and happily onward.

Now, this path of obedience is by no means an easy one; it involves the constant abandonment of self, and can only be pursued as the eye is steadily kept on God, and the conscience kept under the action of His truth. True, there is a rich reward in every act of obedience, yet flesh and blood must be set aside, and this is no easy work. Witness the path of our prophet. He was first called to take his place by the brook Cherith, to be fed by ravens! How could flesh and blood understand this?

Then again, when the brook failed, he is called away to a distant city of Zidon, there to be nourished by a destitute widow who seemed to be at the very point of dying of starvation! Here was the command: "Arise, get thee to Zarephath, which belongeth to Zidon, and dwell there: behold, I have commanded a widow woman there to sustain thee."

And what confirmation did Elijah derive from appearances, upon his arrival at this place? None whatever; but everything to fill him with doubts and fears had he been looking at circumstances in the matter. "So he arose, and went to Zarephath. And when he came to the gate of the city, behold, the widow woman was there gathering of sticks;

and he called to her, and said, Fetch me, I pray thee, a little water in a vessel, that I may drink. And as she was going to fetch it, he called to her, and said, Bring me, I pray thee, a morsel of bread in thine hand. And she said, As the Lord thy God liveth, I have not a cake, but a handful of meal in a barrel, and a little oil in a cruse: and behold, I am gathering two sticks, that I may go in and dress it for me and my son, that we may eat it, and die."

This was the scene that presented itself to the eye of the prophet when he had arrived at his divinely appointed destination. Truly a gloomy and depressing one to flesh and blood. But Elijah conferred not with flesh and blood; his spirit was sustained by the immutable Word of Jehovah; his confidence was based upon the faithfulness of God, and he needed no aid from things around him. The horizon might look dark and heavy to mortal vision, but the eye of faith could pierce the clouds, and see beyond them all "the firm foundation which is laid for faith in Jehovah's excellent word."

How precious, then, is the Word of God! Well might the psalmist say, "Thy testimonies have I taken as an heritage forever." Precious heritage! Pure, incorruptible, immortal truth! How should we bless our God for having made it our inalienable portion—a portion which, when all sublunary things shall have vanished from view, when the world shall have passed away and the lust thereof, when all flesh shall have been consumed as withered grass, shall prove to the faithful a real, an eternal, an enduring substance. "Thanks be to God for His unspeakable gift."

But what were the circumstances which met the prophet's eye upon his approach to Zarephath? A widow and her son starving, two sticks, and a handful of meal! And yet the word was, "I have commanded a widow woman there to sustain thee." How trying, how deeply mysterious, was all this!

Elijah, however, staggered not at the promise of God through unbelief, but was strong in faith, giving glory to God. He knew that it was the Most High and Almighty God, the possessor of Heaven and earth, that was

to meet his necessities; hence, though there had been neither oil nor meal, it would have made no matter to him, for he looked beyond circumstances to the God of circumstances. He saw not the widow, but God. He looked not at the handful of meal, but at the divine command; therefore his spirit was perfectly calm and unruffled in the midst of circumstances which would have crushed the spirit of one walking by sight, and he was able, without a shadow of doubt, to say, "Thus saith the Lord God of Israel, The barrel of meal shall not waste, neither shall the cruse of oil fail, until the day that the Lord sendeth rain upon the earth."

Here we have the reply of faith to the language of unbelief. "Thus saith the Lord" settles everything. The moment the spirit apprehends God's promise, there is an end to the reasonings of unbelief. Unbelief puts circumstances between the soul and God; faith puts God between the soul and circumstances. This is a very important difference. May we walk in the power and energy of faith, to the praise of Him whom faith ever honors!

But there is another point in this lovely scene to be particularly noticed: it is the way in which death ever hovers around the spirit of one not walking by faith. "That we may eat it and die" is the language of the widow. Death and unbelief are inseparably linked together. The spirit can only be conducted along the path of life by the energy of faith: hence if faith be not in energy, there is no life, no power, no elevation.

Thus was it with this poor widow: her hope of life was based upon the barrel of meal and the cruse of oil: beyond these she saw no springs of life, no hope of continuance. Her soul knew not as yet the real blessedness of communion with the living God to whom alone belong the issues from death. She was not yet able against hope to believe in hope. Alas, what a poor, frail, tottering thing is that hope which rests only on a cruse of oil and a barrel of meal! How scanty must be those expectations which only rest on the creature!

And are we not all but too prone to lean upon something quite as mean and paltry in

God's view as a handful of meal? Truly we are; and it must be so where God is not apprehended by the soul. To faith it is either God or nothing. A handful of meal will afford, in the hand of God and to the view of faith, as efficient materials as the cattle upon a thousand hills. "We have here but five loaves and two small fishes; but *what are these amongst so many?*" This is the language of the human heart; but faith never says what are *these* amongst so many? but what is *God* among so many? Unbelief says *we* are not able; faith says, but *God* is well able.

And would it not be well, ere we turn from this interesting point in our subject, to apply these principles to the poor, conscience-smitten sinner? How often is such an one found clinging to some vain resource for the pardon of his sins, rather than to the accomplished work of Christ upon the cross, which has forever satisfied the claims of divine justice, and ought therefore, surely, to satisfy the cravings of his guilty conscience.

"I have no man, when the water is troubled, to put me into the pool; but while I am coming, another steppeth down before me." Such is the language of one who had not as yet learned to look beyond all human aid, straight to Jesus. "*I have no man,*" says the poor, guilty, unbelieving sinner: but I have *Jesus*, says the believer; and he may add, Thus saith the Lord, The cleansing efficacy of the blood shall not fail, nor its preciousness diminish, until the time that the Lord shall have safely housed His ransomed forever in His own heavenly mansions.

Hence, if these pages should meet the eye of any poor, halting, trembling, fearful sinner, I would invite him to take comfort from the precious truth that God has, in His infinite grace, set the cross of Jesus between him and his sins, if only he will believe the divine testimony. The great difference between a believer and an unbeliever is this: the former has Christ between him and his sins; the latter has his sins between him and Christ.

Now, with the former, Christ is the all-engrossing object: he looks not at the enormity of his sin, but at the value of the blood and the preciousness of the person of Christ: he knows that God is not now on the judgment-seat, but on the mercy-seat: if He were on the former, His thoughts would be simply occupied about the question of sin, but being on the latter, His thoughts are, blessed be His name, as purely occupied about the blood. Oh for more simple and abiding communion with the mind of Heaven, and more complete abstraction from the things and thoughts of earth! The Lord grant more of both to all His saints!

It has been already observed that the man of faith must be emptied from vessel to vessel; each successive scene and stage of the believer's life is but his entrance upon a new form in the school of Christ, where he has to learn some fresh and, of course, more difficult lesson.

But, it may be asked, what more trying circumstances had Elijah to grapple with at Zarephath than at Cherith? Was it not better to be cast upon human sympathies than to have ravens as his channel of supply? And further, was it not more pleasing to the spirit to be domesticated with human beings than to dwell in the loneliness and solitude of the brook Cherith? All this might have been so, no doubt; yet solitude has its sweets, and association its trials. There are selfish interests which work amongst men, and hinder that refined and exquisite enjoyment which human society ought to yield, and which it will yield, when humanity stands forth in its divinely-imparted perfections.

Our prophet heard no such words as "*me and my son*" when he took up his abode by the brook. There was there no selfish interest acting as a barrier to his sustenance and enjoyment. No, but the moment he passed from his retirement into human society, then he was called to feel that the human heart does not like to have its own objects in the least interfered with; he was called to enter into the deep meaning of the words "*me and my son,*" which unfold the hidden springs of selfishness, which actuate humanity in its fallen condition.

But it will doubtless be observed that it was natural for the widow's heart to entertain thoughts of herself and her son in preference to any one else, and surely it was *natural*; it is what nature ever does. Harken to the following words of a genuine child of nature: "Shall I then take my bread, and my water, and my flesh that I have killed for my shearers, and give it unto men whom I know not whence they be?" (1 Sam. 25: 11)

Nature will ever seek its own first; nor does it come within the compass of this perishing world so to fill the human soul as to make it overflow for the benefit of others. It is the province of God alone to do this. It is utterly in vain to try to expand the heart of man by any instrumentality save the abundant grace of God. This it is which will cause him to open wide the door of his affections to every needy applicant. Human benevolence may do much where abundant resources prevent the possibility of personal privation, but grace alone will enable a man to trample personal interests under foot to meet the claims of another. "Men will praise thee when thou doest well to thyself." This is the world's principle, and nothing can make us unlearn it but the knowledge of the fact that God has done well for us, and, moreover, that it is our best interest to let Him continue to do so unto the end.

Now it was the knowledge of this divine principle that enabled our prophet to say, "Make *me* thereof a little cake *first*, and bring it unto *me*, and *after* make for thee and thy son." Elijah was, in his address, simply putting in the divine claim upon the widow's resources; and, as we know, the result of a true and ready response to that claim will be a rich harvest of blessing to the soul. There was, however, a demand upon the widow's faith in all this. she was called to act a trying and difficult part, in the energy of faith in a divine promise, "Thus saith the Lord God of Israel, The barrel of meal shall not waste, neither shall the cruse of oil fail, until the day that the Lord sendeth rain upon the earth."

And is it not thus with every believer? Undoubtedly it is; we must act in faith. The promise of God must ever constitute the great moving principle in the soul of the Christian. There would have been no room for the exercise of faith on the part of the widow had the barrel been full; but when it was exhausted, when she was reduced to her

last handful, to be told to give of that handful to a stranger *first*, was surely a large demand, to which nothing but faith could have enabled her to respond.

But the Lord often deals with His people as He dealt with His disciples in the matter of feeding the multitude. "This He said to prove them, for He Himself knew what He would do." He frequently tells us to take a step involving considerable trial, and in the very act of taking it we not only see the reason of it, but also get strength to proceed. In fact, all the divine claims upon us for action are based upon the principle involved in the command to the children of Israel of old, "Speak to the children of Israel that they go forward."

Whither were they to go? Through the sea. Strange path! Yet behind this trying command we see grace providing the ability to execute it in the word to Moses, "But lift thou up thy rod, and stretch out thy hand over the sea, and divide it; and the children of Israel shall go on dry ground through the midst of the sea" (Exod. 14:16). Faith enables a man, being called, to go out not knowing whither he goes.

But there is more than the mere principle of obedience to be learned from this truly interesting scene between Elijah and the widow of Zarephath: we learn, also, that nothing but the superior power of divine grace can lift the human mind above the freezing atmosphere of selfishness in which fallen man lives, and moves, and has his being. The effulgence of God's benevolence shining in upon the soul disperses those mists in which the world is enveloped, and enables a man to think and act upon higher and nobler principles than those which actuate the moving mass around him. This poor widow had left her house influenced by no higher motive than self-interest and self-preservation, and having no more brilliant object before her mind than death.

And is it in any wise different with multitudes around us? Yea, is it a whit better in the case of any unregenerate man on earth? Not a whit. The most illustrious, the most intellectual, the most learned—in a word, every man upon whose spirit the light of divine grace has never shone, will be found, in God's estimation, like this poor widow, influenced by motives of self-interest and self-preservation, and having no brighter prospect before him than death.

The truth of God, however, speedily alters the aspect of things. In the case of the widow it acted most powerfully: it sent her back to her house occupied about and interested for another, and with her soul filled with cheering thoughts of life. And so will it ever be. Let but the soul get into communion with the truth and grace of God, and it is at once delivered from this present evil world, it is turned aside out of the current which is rapidly hurrying millions away upon its surface. It becomes actuated by heavenly motives, and animated by heavenly objects.

Grace teaches a man to live and act for others. The more our souls taste the sweetness of redeeming love, the more earnest will be our desire to serve others. Oh that we all felt more deeply and abidingly the constraining power of the love of Christ, in this day of lamentable coldness and indifference! Would to God we could all live and act in the remembrance that we are not our own, but bought with a price!

The widow of Zarephath was taught this truth. The Lord not only put His claim to the handful of meal and the cruse of oil, but also laid His hand upon her son—the cherished object of her affections. Death visits the house in which the Lord's prophet, in company with the widow and her son, were feeding together on the precious fruits of divine benevolence. "It came to pass, after these things, that the son of the woman, the mistress of the house, fell sick; and his sickness was so sore that there was no breath left in him."

Now this son, as we know, had, in common with herself, stood in her way in the matter of her ready response to the divine claim as put forward by Elijah; hence there is solemn instruction for the saint in the death of this child. So surely as we allow *any object*, whether it be parent or child, husband or wife, brother or sister, to obstruct us in our path of simple obedience and devotedness to Christ, we may rest assured that object will

be removed. This widow had given her son a higher place in her thoughts than the Lord's prophet, and the son was taken from her that she might learn that it was not merely, "the handful of meal" that should be held in subjection to the Lord and in readiness for Him, but also her dearest earthly object.

It needs no small measure of the spirit of Christ to hold everything in mere stewardship for God. We are so prone to look upon things as ours, instead of remembering that all we have, and all we are, belongs to the Lord, and should ever be given up at His call. Nor is this a mere matter of rightful obedience; it is for our lasting benefit and happiness.

The widow responded to God's claim on her handful of meal; and what follows? She and her house are sustained for years! Again the Lord lays His hand upon her son; and what follows? Her son is raised from the dead by the mighty power of God, thus teaching her that the Lord could not only sustain life, but impart it. Resurrection-power is brought to bear upon her circumstances, and she receives her son now, as she had received her supplies before, directly from the hand of the Lord God of Israel.

How happy to be a dependent upon such bounty! How happy to go to our barrel of meal, or our cruse of oil, and find it daily replenished by our Father's generous hand! How happy to hold the dearest object of our affections in the power of resurrection ties! Such are the privileges of the weakest believer in Jesus.

Before, however, I turn from this branch of our subject, I would observe that the effect which the divine visitation produced upon this widow was to awaken a solemn inquiry in her conscience as to her sin. "Art thou come to call my sin to remembrance?" When the Lord comes near to us, there will always be observed a divine quickness and sensitiveness of conscience which are most earnestly to be sought after.

One may often pass on from day to day in the ordinary routine of life, in the enjoyment, too, of a replenished barrel and cruse, without much deep exercise of conscience before God. The latter will only be found where there is really close walking with God, or some special visitation of His hand. Had the Lord merely met the poor widow's need from day to day, there might never have been a question of "sin" raised in her mind; but when death entered, conscience began to work, for death is the wages of sin.

There is a twofold action in all the divine dealings with us, namely, an action of *truth*, and an action of *grace*. The former discovers the evil, the latter puts it away; that unfolds what man is, this what God is; that brings out into the light the hidden workings of evil in the heart of man, this brings out, in contrast, the rich and exhaustless springs of grace in the heart of God. Now, both are needful: *truth*, for the maintenance of God's glory; *grace*, for the establishment of our blessing; that, for the vindication of the divine character and attributes, this for the perfect repose of the sinner's heart and conscience.

How blessed to know that both "grace and truth came by Jesus Christ." The divine dealings with the widow of Zarephath would not have been complete had they not elicited from her the confession contained in the last verse of our chapter, "By *this* I know thou art a man of God, and that the word of the Lord in thy mouth is *truth*." She had learnt *grace* in the marvelous supply of her need; she learnt *truth* in the death of her son.

And if we were only more spiritually sensitive and quick-sighted, we should at all times perceive these two features in our Father's mode of dealing with us. We are the constant recipients of His grace, and again and again we get examples of His truth in the dealings of His hand which are more particularly designed to bring out the evil from the hidden chambers of the heart, in order that we may judge and put it away. While we see our barrel and cruse replenished, conscience is apt to slumber, but when Jehovah knocks at the door of our hearts by some chastening dispensation, forthwith it wakes up and enters with vigor upon the seasonable work of self-judgment.

Now, while we cannot too strongly deprecate that form of self-examination which frequently genders doubt as to the fact of the soul's acceptance, yet we must remember that *self must be judged* or we shall break down altogether. The believer is not told to examine himself with any such idea as that the examination may issue in the discovery that he is not in the faith. This idea is often based upon an unsound interpretation of 2 Cor. 13:5, "Examine yourselves, whether ye be in the faith," etc.

Now, the idea in the mind of the apostle was the very reverse of what is sought to be deduced from his words, as may at once be seen by a little attention to the context. It would seem that the assembly at Corinth had given a place amongst them to certain false apostles who presumed to call in question the ministry of the Apostle Paul, thus rendering it necessary for the latter to enter upon a defense of his apostleship, which he does, first, by a reference to his general course of service and testimony; and secondly, by a touching appeal to the Corinthian saints. "Since," says he, "ye seek a proof of Christ speaking in me . . . examine yourselves."

The most powerful and, to them at least, affecting proof of the divine authority of his apostleship was to be deduced from the fact that they were in the faith. It cannot therefore for a moment be supposed that he would have told them to examine themselves in order to prove his heavenly mission if that examination were to issue in the discovery that they were not in the faith at all: on the contrary, it was because he had a well-grounded assurance that they were "sanctified in Christ Jesus," that he could confidently appeal to them as an evidence that his mission was from above.

There is, however, considerable difference between what is called "self-examination" and self-judgment; not so much in the abstract things themselves as in the ideas which we attach to them. It is a most blessed exercise to judge nature—honestly, solemnly and rigidly to judge that evil nature which we carry about with us, and which ever clogs and hinders us in running the race set before us. The Lord grant us all more spiritual power to exercise this judgment continually. But then we must take great care that our examination of self does not savor of mistrusting God. It is upon the ground of

God's grace and faithfulness that I judge myself. *If God be not God, there is an end of everything.*

But there was also a voice in this visitation for Elijah. He had presented himself to the widow in the character of a man of God, and he therefore needed to establish his claims to that character. This Jehovah graciously did for him by the resurrection of the child. "By *this* I know," said she, "that thou art a man of God." It was resurrection that vindicated his claim upon her confidence.

There must be the exhibition of a measure of resurrection power in the life of the man of God ere his claim to that character can be fully established. This power will show itself in the form of victory over self in all its odious workings. The believer is risen with Christ—he is made a partaker of the divine nature, but he is still in the world, and bears about with him a body of humiliation; and if he does not deny himself, he will soon find his character as a man of God called in question.

It would, however, be but a miserable object merely to seek *self-vindication.* The prophet had a higher and nobler aim, namely, to establish the truth of the Word of the Lord in his mouth. This is the proper object of the man of God. His own character and reputation should be matters of small moment with him, save as they stand connected with the Word of the Lord in his mouth. It was simply for the purpose of maintaining the divine origin of the gospel which he preached that the Apostle Paul entered upon the defense of his apostleship in his Epistles to the Galatians and Corinthians. It mattered little to him what they thought of Paul, but it mattered much what they thought of Paul's gospel. Hence, for their sakes, he was anxious to prove that the Word of the Lord in his mouth was truth.

How important, then, was it for the prophet to have such a testimony to the divine origin of his ministry before entering upon the scenes in which he is seen moving in chap. 18! He gained thus much at least by his retirement at Zarephath; and surely it was not a little. His spirit was blessedly confirmed; he received a divine seal to his ministry; he approved himself to the conscience of one with whom he had sojourned for a long period, and was enabled to start afresh upon his public career with the happy assurance that he was a man of God, and that the Word of the Lord in his mouth was truth.*

We have now arrived at the close of a very important stage of Elijah's history, embracing a period of three years and a half, during which he was hidden from the view of Israel. We have been occupied simply with the consideration of those principles of truth which lie on the surface of Elijah's personal history. But may we not draw instruction from his course viewed in a mystic sense? I believe we may. The reference of Christ Himself to the prophet's mission to the Gentile widow may justly lead us to see therein the blessed foreshadowing of the gathering of the Gentiles into the Church of God.

"But I tell you of a truth, many widows were in Israel in the days of Elias, when the heaven was shut up for three years and six months, when great famine was throughout all the land; but unto none of them was Elias sent, save unto Sarepta, a city of Zidon, unto a woman that was a widow" (Luke 4:25-26). The Lord Jesus had presented Himself to Israel as the prophet of God, but found no response; the daughter of Zion refused to hear the voice of her Lord. "The gracious words which proceeded out of His mouth"

---

* I may just add a word here on the subject of self-vindication. It is truly sorrowful when the servant of God is obliged to vindicate himself; it shows there must be something wrong either in himself or in those who have rendered it needful for him thus to act. When, however, such a course becomes necessary, there is one grand object to be kept clearly before the mind, namely, the glory of Christ, and the purity of the truth committed to his trust. It too frequently happens that when any charge is brought either against our ministry or our personal character, the pride of our hearts is drawn out, and we are quick to stand up in self-defense. Now, we should remember that, apart from our connection with Christ and His saints, we are but vile atoms of the dust, utterly unworthy of a thought or word; it should therefore be far from our thoughts to seek the establishment of our own reputation. We have been constituted the depositaries, to a certain extent, of the reputation of Christ; and provided we preserve that unsullied, we need not be careful about self.

The Lord grant us all grace to walk in the abiding consciousness of our high dignities and holy responsibilities as the "epistle of Christ, known and read of all men"!

were answered by the carnal inquiry, "Is not this Joseph's son?" He therefore finds relief for His spirit, in the view of Israel's scorn and rejection, in the happy reflection that there were objects beyond Jewish bounds to whom the divine grace of which He was the channel could flow out in all its richness and purity.

The grace of God is such that if it be stopped by the pride, unbelief, or hardness of heart of some, it will only flow more copiously to others, and so, "Though Israel be not gathered, yet shall I be glorious in the eyes of the Lord, and My God shall be My strength. And He said, It is a light thing that Thou shouldst be My servant to raise up the tribes of Jacob, and to restore the preserved of Israel: I will also give Thee for *a light to the Gentiles*, that Thou mayest be My salvation unto the end of the earth" (Isa. 49: 5-6).

The precious truth of the call of the Gentiles is largely taught in Scripture, both by type and precept, and it might be serviceable at another time to enter fully upon the consideration of it in its various ramifications; but my object, in this paper, is rather to consider the life and ministry of our prophet in a simple and practical way, with the hope that the Lord would be graciously pleased to acknowledge such simple reflections for the comfort and edification of His people of every name and denomination.

Part 3

THE HOUSE OF AHAB

We must now leave our prophet, for a season, and turn our attention to the sad condition of things in Israel during the time that he was hidden with God. Terrible indeed must be the condition of things on earth when "the heaven is shut up." Sterile and dreary must be the aspect of this lower world when Heaven withholds its refreshing showers, and specially of that land which was to "drink water of the rain of heaven." Egypt might not have regarded much the shutting up of Heaven, seeing she had never been wont to look thither for her supplies. She had her resources in herself. "My river is mine own," was her independent language.

But such was not the case with the Lord's land—"the land of hills and valleys." If Heaven yielded not its supplies, all was parched and sterile. Israel could not say, "My river is mine own." No; they were ever taught to look up; their eyes were always to be upon the Lord, as the Lord's eyes were ever upon them. Hence, when anything arose to hinder the intercourse between Heaven and earth, the land of Canaan was made to feel it with painful intensity.

Thus it was "in the days of Elias, when the heaven was shut up three years and six months, when great famine was throughout all the land." Israel was made to feel the dreadful consequences of departure from their only source of real blessing. "There was sore famine in Samaria, and Ahab said unto Obadiah, Go into the land, unto all fountains of water, and unto all brooks; peradventure we may find grass to save the horses and mules alive, that we lose not all the beasts. So they divided the land between them, to pass throughout it; Ahab went one way by himself, and Obadiah went another way by himself."

Israel had sinned, and Israel must feel the rod of Jehovah's righteous anger. What a humbling picture of God's ancient people, to see their king going forth to look for grass! What a contrast between all this and the rich abundance and glory of Solomon's day! But God had been grossly dishonored, and His truth rejected. Jezebel had sent forth the pestilential influence of her principles by the instrumentality of her wicked prophets— Baal's altar had superseded the altar of God; hence the Heaven above was iron, and the earth beneath brass; the physical aspect of things was but the expression of Israel's hardness of heart and low moral condition.

Now there is not so much as a word about God in Ahab's directions to his servants—not a syllable about the sin that had called down the heavy displeasure and judgment of God upon the land. No; the word is, "Go unto all fountains and brooks." Such was Ahab's thought, his poor groveling thought; his heart turned not, in true humility, to

Jehovah; he cried not to Him in the hour of his need; hence his word is, "peradventure *we may find grass.*" God is shut out, and self is the all-engrossing object. Provided he could find *grass*, he cared not about finding *God.*

He could have enjoyed himself in the midst of Jezebel's idolatrous prophets, had not the horrors of famine driven him forth: and then, instead of searching out the cause of the famine, in true self-judgment and humility, and seeking for pardon and restoration at the hand of God, he goes forth, in impenitent selfishness, to look for grass. Alas! he had sold himself to work wickedness; he had become the slave of Jezebel; his palace had become a cage of every unclean bird; Baal's prophets, like so many vultures, hovered around his throne, and from thence spread the leaven of idolatry over the whole land.

Oh, it is a truly awful thing to allow the heart to depart from the Lord. One cannot tell where it may end. Ahab was an Israelite, but he had allowed himself to be ensnared by a false religious system, at the head of which was Jezebel his wife; he had made shipwreck of faith and a good conscience, and was driven headlong into the most abandoned wickedness. There is no one so bad as the man who turns aside from the ways of God. Such an one is sure to plunge into more profound depths of wickedness than even the ordinary victims of sin and Satan. The devil seems to take special delight in making such an one an instrument in carrying out his malignant designs against the truth of God.

If you have ever been taught to value the ways of truth and holiness, if you have ever taken delight in God and His ways, be watchful; "keep thy heart with all diligence;" beware of false religious influence; you are moving through a scene in which the very atmosphere you breathe is noxious, and destructive of spiritual life. The enemy has with hellish sagacity—a sagacity sharpened by well-nigh six thousand years' acquaintance with the constitution of the human mind—laid his snares on all sides of you, and nothing but permanent communion with your heavenly Father will avail to preserve your soul. Remember Ahab, and pray continually to be kept from temptation.

The following passage of Scripture may well be used, in connection with Ahab, as a solemn and seasonable warning: "Cursed be the man that trusteth in man, and maketh flesh his arm, and whose heart departeth from the Lord. For he shall be like the heath in the desert, and shall not see when good cometh; but shall inhabit the parched places in the wilderness, in a salt land and not inhabited" (Jer. 17: 5-6).

Such was the wretched Ahab—wretched though favored with a diadem and a sceptre. He cared neither for God nor his people. In his sayings and doings, on the melancholy occasion to which we are referring, we find as little about Israel as about God. There is not one word about the people that had been committed to his care, and who ought, after God, to have been his great object. His earthly mind seems to have been unable to reach beyond "the horses and mules." Such were the objects of Ahab's anxious solicitude in the day of Israel's direful calamity.

Alas, what a contrast between all this low and groveling selfishness and the noble spirit of the man after God's own heart, who, when the land was trembling beneath the heavy stroke of Jehovah's chastening rod, could say, "Is it not I that have commanded the people to be numbered: *even I it is that have sinned and done evil indeed;* but as for *these sheep*, what have they done? let Thy hand, I pray Thee, O Lord my God, be on me, and on my father's house; but not on Thy people, that they should be plagued" (1 Chron. 21: 17).

Here was the true spirit of a king. David, in the spirit of his blessed Master, would expose his own bosom to the stroke, in order that the sheep might escape; he would "stand between them and the foe"; he would turn the sceptre into a shepherd's crook; he thought not of his "horses and mules"; yea, he thought not of himself or his father's house, but of the people of God's pasture, and the sheep of His hand. Happy, ineffably happy, will it be for Israel's scattered tribes to find themselves again under the tender care of the true David.

It might be profitable to follow out a little more fully the history of Ahab; to dwell upon his unprincipled treatment of the righteous Naboth; of the alluring influence exerted by him over the mind of the good king Jehoshaphat, and of many other circumstances in his unhappy reign; but all this would lead us too far from our subject. We shall therefore advert for a few moments to the character of an important member of Ahab's household, and then return to Elijah.

Obadiah, the governor of Ahab's house, was one who, in the secret of his own spirit, feared the Lord, but who was planted in a most unhallowed atmosphere. The house of the wicked Ahab, and his still more wicked consort, must have been a painful school for the righteous soul of Obadiah; and so he found it. He was hindered in service and testimony. What he did for the Lord was done by stealth. He was afraid to act openly and decidedly; yet he did quite enough to show what he would have done had he been planted in a more congenial soil, and cherished by a more healthful atmosphere. "He took a hundred prophets, and hid them by fifty in a cave, and fed them with bread and water." This was a most precious token of devotedness of heart to the Lord—a blessed triumph of divine principle over the most untoward circumstances.

Thus it was with Jonathan in the house of Saul. He, too, was sadly hindered in his service to God and to Israel. He should have stood forth in more entire separation from the evil in which his father lived, and moved; his place at Saul's table should have been vacant as well as David's: the cave of Adullam would have been his proper place, where, in holy companionship with the rejected David and his despised band of followers, he might have found a wider and more suited range in which to manifest his affectionate devotedness to God and His anointed.

Human expediency, however, might, and doubtless would, have recommended Jonathan to remain in Saul's house, and Obadiah to remain in Ahab's house, as being "the sphere in which Providence had placed them"; but expediency is not faith, nor will it aid a man in his path of service, whatever it may be. Faith will ever lead a man to break through the freezing rules of human expedi-

ency, in order that it may express itself in a way not to be mistaken.

Jonathan felt constrained at times to leave the table of Saul in order that he might embrace David: but he should have abandoned it altogether; he should have cast in his lot entirely with David; he ought not to have rested satisfied with speaking *for* his brother, he should have identified himself *with* him. But he did not do so, and therefore he fell on Mount Gilboa, by the hand of the uncircumcised. Thus, in his life he was harassed and hindered by the unrighteous principle of rule which Saul had set up to entangle and bind the consciences of the faithful, and in his death he was ingloriously mingled with the uncircumcised.

Just so it was with Obadiah. It was his lot to stand in connection with the man who occupied the lowest step of that ladder of apostasy whereby the kings of Israel had descended from original principles. Hence he was obliged to act stealthily for God and His servants; he was afraid of Ahab and Jezebel; he lacked boldness and energy to stand out in decided testimony against all abominations; he had no room for the development of his renewed energies or affections; his soul was withered by the noxious vapors around him, and he could therefore exert but little influence on his day and generation.

Hence, while Elijah was boldly confronting Ahab, and openly serving the Lord, Obadiah was openly serving Ahab, and stealthily serving the Lord. While Elijah was breathing the holy atmosphere of Jehovah's presence, Obadiah was breathing the polluted atmosphere of Ahab's wicked court. While Elijah was receiving his daily supplies from the hand of the God of Israel, Obadiah was ranging the country in search of grass for Ahab's horses.

Truly a most striking contrast! And is there not at this moment many an Obadiah similarly occupied? Is there not many a God-fearing man sharing, in common with the children of this world, its death and misery, and laboring in co-operation with them to avert its impending ruin? Doubtless there is. And is this fit work for such? Should "the mules and horses" of an ungodly world engross the thoughts and energies of the Christian instead of the interests of the Church of God? Ah no! it should not be so. The Christian should have a nobler end in view—a higher and more heavenly sphere in which to use his energies. God, and not Ahab, demands and deserves our devotion.

This is a very wide question, and there are few amongst us that may not learn a lesson from it. Let us ask ourselves honestly, as before the Searcher of hearts, what are we doing? What object are we carrying out? What end have we in view? Are we sowing to the flesh? Are we working for merely earthly objects? Have we no higher end in view than self or this present world?

Oh these are searching questions, when rightly put! The tendency of the human heart and affections is ever downward—ever toward earth and the things of earth. The palace of Ahab holds out far more powerful attractions to our fallen nature than the lonely banks of Cherith or the house of the starving widow of Zarephath. But ah, *let us think of the end!* The end alone is the true criterion by which to judge in such matters. "Until I went into *the sanctuary of God;* then understood I *their end"* (Psa. 73:17).

Elijah knew, by being in the sanctuary, that Ahab stood in a slippery place; that his house would speedily crumble in the dust; that all his pomp and glory was about to end in the lonely tomb, and his immortal spirit to be summoned to render its final account. These things the holy man of God thoroughly understood, and he was therefore well content to stand apart from it all. His leathern girdle, his homely fare, his lonely path, were far better, he felt, than all the pleasures of Ahab's court. Such was his judgment, and we shall see, ere we close this paper, that his judgment was sound.

"The world passeth away, and the lust thereof, but he that doeth the will of God abideth forever." Would that all who love the name of Jesus were more uncompromising and energetic in their testimony for Him! The time is rapidly approaching when we would give worlds that we had been more *true and real* in our ways here below. We are too lukewarm, too much inclined to make terms with the world and the flesh, too ready to exchange the leathern girdle for the robe in which Ahab and Jezebel are most willing to array us.

May the Lord give all His people grace to testify against this world that the deeds thereof are evil, and to stand apart from its ways, it maxims and principles; in a word, from everything which properly belongs to it. "The night is far spent, and the day is at hand." Let us then cast off the works of darkness and stand clothed in the armor of light; let us, as those that are risen with Christ, set our affection on things above, and not on things on the earth; having "our citizenship in heaven," let us, with unceasing eagerness, "look for the Saviour from thence, who shall change the body of our humiliation, that it may be fashioned like unto the body of His glory, according to the working whereby He is able even to subdue all things to Himself."

Part 4

THE PROPHET ON MOUNT CARMEL

In the opening verse of chapter 18 a new order is issued to our prophet. "And it came to pass, after many days, that the word of the Lord came to Elijah in the third year, saying, Go show thyself unto Ahab, and I will send rain on the earth."

Here Elijah is summoned away from his retirement at Zarephath, to make his appearance in public and stand again before king Ahab. To one occupying the position, and exhibiting the spirit, of a true servant, it matters not what summons he receives. Whether it be "Go *hide* thyself," or "Go *show* thyself," he is ready, through grace, to obey. The Lord had been training His servant for three years and a half in secret. At Cherith and Zarephath He had taught him many important lessons; and when the time was come for his showing unto Israel, he was called to leave the desert and appear again as the public witness of Jehovah.

Nor did he hesitate. No, not for a moment, however much he might have preferred retirement to the stormy scenes and harassing vicissitudes of public life. Elijah was *a servant*, and that was enough. He was as ready to confront the angry Ahab, and all the prophets of Baal, as he had been to seclude himself for three years and a half. Truly we may well covet the spirit of a servant—a humble, obedient servant. Such a spirit will carry us through many difficulties; will save us from much contention; will send us along the path of service while others are disputing about it. If only we be willing to obey, and to serve, we shall never lack opportunity, nor be at a loss as to the path we should pursue.*

We have already had occasion to notice the prophet's unhesitating obedience to the Word of the Lord. Such obedience will ever involve the abandonment of self. To be told, for example, to leave one's sweet retreat in order to appear before an angry tyrant who, with his wicked queen, led on to the contest a host of idolatrous prophets, called for no small measure of self-renunciation. But Elijah, through grace, was ready. He felt he was not his own. *He was a servant*, and as such ever stood with girded loins and open ears to attend his Master's summons, whatever it might be. Blessed attitude! May there be many found therein!

Elijah, therefore, goes to meet king Ahab, and we are called to follow him now into one of the most important scenes of his life.

Before, however, he comes in contact with Ahab, he crosses the path of Obadiah, and his meeting with him is perfectly characteristic. Obadiah certainly does not meet the prophet with that affectionate cordiality which ought to appear in the bearing of one brother towards another, but rather in the cold formality of one who had been moving much in the world's society. "Art thou that *my lord* Elijah?"

Now, though all this might have been occasioned by the overawing solemnity of Elijah's appearance and manner, still the thought forces itself upon one that there ought to have been more holy familiarity between two servants of the Lord. Elijah, too, seems to maintain this distance. "I am," said he; "go tell thy lord, Behold, Elijah is here." Elijah felt himself to be the depositary of the secret of the Lord, of which secret his brother knew nothing.

And how could he? Ahab's house was not the place to obtain an entrance into the divine counsels. Obadiah was out on a mission perfectly in keeping with the place from whence he had come, and with the person who had sent him; and so was Elijah. The former had as his immediate object grass—if peradventure he might find it; and as his ultimate object, the preservation of Ahab's horses and mules; the latter had as his immediate object the announcement of Jehovah's indubitable purpose concerning rain; and as his ultimate object, the bringing back of the nation to its early faith and devotedness.

True they were both men of God; and, moreover, it may be said by some that Obadiah was as much in his place as Elijah, seeing he was serving his master. No doubt he was serving his master; but should Ahab have been his master? I believe not. I believe his service to Ahab was not the result of communion with God. True it did not rob him of his name and character as one that feared the Lord greatly, for the Holy Ghost has graciously recorded this concerning him; but truly it was a miserable thing for one that feared the Lord greatly to own as his master the worst of Israel's apostate kings. Elijah would not have done so. We cannot think of him as going forth on such a mission as that which was commanding the energies of his more worldly brother. Elijah would not own Ahab as his *master*, though he was bound to own him as his *king*.

There is a great difference between being *a*

---

* In every age the servant character is marked by the Holy Ghost as one of special value. It is, in fact, the only thing that will stand in times of general declension. Of this we have numerous examples in Scripture. When the house of Eli was about to fall before the divine judgment, Samuel occupied the position of a servant whose ear was opened to hear. His word was, "Speak, Lord, for *Thy servant* heareth." When all Israel had fled from the face of the Philistine champion, the servant character again stood prominently forth. "*Thy servant* will go and fight," etc. The Lord Jesus Himself had the title of Servant applied to Him by Jehovah, in the words of the prophet, "Behold My *Servant*," etc. Furthermore, when the Church had failed, and had become "the great house," "the *servant* of the Lord" was told how he ought to carry himself. And lastly, it is mentioned as one of the special features of the heavenly Jerusalem, that "His *servants* shall *serve* Him." The Lord grant us more of this spirit!

subject and one in a position under a monarch. People argue thus: "The powers that be are ordained of God," therefore it is right to hold office under them. But those who argue thus seem to lose sight of the manifest distinction between *subject to* and *co-operating with* the powers that be: the former is a sound and scriptural service—an act of positive obedience to God; the latter is an unsound and unscriptural assumption of worldly authority, for the wielding of which we have no direction, and which, moreover, will be found a sad obstruction in the path of the servant of God.

We would not enter into judgment upon those who feel they can enlist their energies in the government of this world; but this much we would say—they will find themselves in an extremely awkward position in reference to the service of their heavenly Master. The principles of this world are diametrically opposed to those of God, and it is therefore hard to conceive how a man can be carrying out both at the same time.

Obadiah is a remarkable example of this. Had he been more openly on the Lord's side, he would have had no need to say, "Was it not told my lord what I did?" His hiding the prophets seems, in his estimation, to have been such a remarkable thing that he wondered if all had not heard it. Elijah had no need to ask such a question; it was well known "what he did." His acts of service to God were no phenomena in his history. And why? Because he was not trammeled by the arrangements of Ahab's house. *He was free,* and could therefore act for God without reference to the thoughts of Ahab or Jezebel.

In acting thus, however, he had to lie under the charge of troubling Israel. "Art thou he that troubleth Israel?" The more faithful one is to God and His truth, the more exposed he is to this charge. If all be allowed to sleep "in dead supineness," the god of this world will be well pleased, and his domain untroubled; but only let some faithful one make his appearance, and he is sure to be regarded as a troubler, and an intruder upon peace and good order.

But it is well to have that peace and order broken up which stand connected with the open denial of the Lord's truth and name. The hearts of the earthly-minded may only be occupied with the question, "Is it peace?" utterly regardless as to whether that peace is procured at the expense of truth and holiness. Nature loves ease, and may often be found, even amongst Christians, pleading for peace and quietness, where faithfulness to Christ and His principles would call for plain dealing with unsound doctrine or evil practice.

The tendency of the age is to hold all religious questions in abeyance. The things pertaining to the world and the flesh are of far too much importance, in the estimate of this generation, to have them interfered with for a moment by questions of eternal importance. Elijah, however, thought not so. He seems to have felt that the peaceful slumber of sin must be interrupted at all cost. He beheld the nation wrapped in the deep sleep of idolatry, and he thought it well to be the instrument of raising a storm around them.

So it was, and so it is. The storm of controversy is always preferable to the calm of sin and worldliness. Truly happy is it when there is no need of raising such a storm; but when it is needed—when the enemy would stretch forth over the people of God "the leaden sceptre" of unholy repose—it is a matter of thankfulness to find that there is life enough even to break in upon such repose. Had there been no Elijah in Israel in the days of Ahab and Jezebel, had all been like Obadiah or the seven thousand, Baal and his prophets might have held undisputed sway over the minds of the people.

But God raised up a man who cared not about his own ease; no, nor about the nation's ease, if that ease were to be purchased at the expense of God's honor and Israel's early principles. He feared not, in the strength of the Lord, to face a terrific array of eight hundred and fifty prophets, whose living depended upon the nation's delusion, headed, as they were, by a furious woman who could turn her weak-minded lord whithersoever she would.

All this, surely, called for no small amount of spiritual vigor and energy. It needed deep and powerful convictions of the reality of divine truth, and a very clear insight into Israel's low and degraded condition, to enable a man to leave his quiet retreat at Zarephath and burst into the midst of Baal's votaries, thus to bring upon himself a fierce storm of opposition from every quarter. Elijah might, to speak after the manner of men, have remained in quiet retirement, in undisturbed repose, had he been satisfied to let Baal alone, and to allow the strongholds of idolatry to remain untouched. But this he could not do, and therefore he comes forth and meets the angry Ahab with these solemn and heart-searching words, "I have not troubled Israel; but thou and thy father's house, in that ye have forsaken the commandments of the Lord, and thou hast served Baalim."

This was tracing the evil up to its right source. It was departure from God and His holy commandments that had brought all this trouble upon them. Men are ever prone to forget the sin that has occasioned trouble, and think only of the trouble; but true wisdom will ever lead us to look from the trouble to the procuring cause.

Thus, too, when unsound doctrine has insidiously crept in, and gained power over many minds—if some faithful one should feel called to make a firm and decided stand against it, he must count upon being regarded as a troubler, and as being the cause of all the commotion consequent upon such acting; whereas the intelligent and reflecting mind will at once trace the matter, not to the faithful one who has made a stand for truth against error, but to him who may have introduced the error, and to those who have received and entertained it.

True, the defender of truth will need to watch his spirit and temper, lest, while he attacks error in doctrine, he fall into evil in practice. Many who have set out in real sincerity of heart to vindicate some neglected or disputed truth have failed in this particular, and have thus, in a great degree, nullified their valuable testimony; for their sagacious enemy is always ready to act upon the narrowmindedness and unreasonableness of men by leading them to fasten upon the petty infirmities of temper, and lose sight of the important principle advocated.

But our prophet entered the arena well equipped; he had come from "the secret place of the Most High"; he had been learning, in solitude, those lessons of self-judgment and self-subjugation which could alone qualify him for the momentous scenes on which he was about to enter. Elijah was no angry or stormy controversialist; he had been too much in the secret of the divine presence for that; he had been blessedly solemnized in his spirit ere he was called to confront Baal's host of prophets. Hence he stands before them in all the calm elevation and holy dignity which ever marked his bearing. We see no haste about him, no perturbation, no hesitancy. He was before God, and therefore he was self-possessed and tranquil.

Now it is in such circumstances that a man's spirit is really tested. Nothing but the mighty power of God could have maintained Elijah in his extraordinary position on mount Carmel. "He was a man of like passions with us;" and being the only one of his day who possessed sufficient moral courage and spiritual power to make a public stand for God against the power of idolatry, the enemy might readily suggest to his poor heart, "What a great man you are to stand forth thus as the solitary champion of Israel's ancient faith!" But God held up His dear servant so far. He carried him through this very trying scene, because he was His witness, and His servant.

And so it will ever be. The Lord will ever stand by those that stand by Him. Had Obadiah only made a stand against Ahab and Jezebel, the Lord would have owned him and carried him through, so that instead of being the servant of Ahab, he might have been the yokefellow of Elijah in his great reformation. But this was not the case, and therefore, like Lot of old, "his righteous soul was vexed" by the errors and evils of an idolatrous house.

O let us aim at something beyond this! Let us not be chained down to earth by deliberate connection with this world's systems or plans. Heaven is our home; there, too, our hope is; we are not of the world; Jesus has purchased us, and delivered us from it, in order that we might shine as lights and walk as heavenly men while passing onward to our heavenly rest.

However, it was not merely in his deportment and manner that Elijah acquitted himself as a servant of God; he also showed himself to be one taught of God in reference to those principles on which the needed reformation should be based. Personal deportment and manner would avail but little if soundness in the faith were lacking. It would be an easy thing to put on a leathern girdle, and assume a solemn and dignified manner; but nothing save a spiritual apprehension of divine principles will enable any one to exert a reforming influence on the men of his age.

But Elijah possessed all those needed qualifications. Both his appearance and his faith were such as, in an eminent degree, suited a thorough reformer. Conscious, therefore, that he was in possession of a secret which would deliver the spirits of his brethren from the unhallowed thraldom of Baal, he says to Ahab, "Now, therefore, send and gather to me all Israel unto mount Carmel, and the prophets of Baal four hundred and fifty, and the prophets of the groves four hundred, which eat at Jezebel's table."

He is determined to bring Baal and the God of Israel face to face, in the view of the nation. He felt that matters should be brought to a test. His brethren must no longer be left to "halt between two opinions." What strength there is in the prophet's words as he stands before the assembled thousands of Israel! "How long halt ye between two opinions? If the Lord be God, follow Him; but if Baal, then follow him."

This was very simple. The prophets of Baal could not gainsay nor resist it. The prophet only asked for decision of character. There could be nothing gained on either side by vacillating ways. "I would ye were either cold or hot." We know from the Lord's own words to Elijah, in the next chapter, that there were seven thousand in Israel who had not bowed the knee to Baal, and who, we may suppose, were only waiting for some vigorous hand to

plant the standard of truth in order that they might rally round it. No one amongst them would seem to have had power for such a bold step, but they would no doubt rejoice in Elijah's boldness and ability to do so.

This has often been the case in the history of the people of God. In times of greatest darkness there have always been those whose spirits mourned in secret over the widespread evil and apostasy, who longed for the bursting in of spiritual light, and were ready with joy to welcome its earliest beams. God has never left Himself without a witness; and although it is only here and there we can perceive a star of sufficient magnitude and brilliancy to pierce through the clouds of night and enlighten the benighted Church in the wilderness, yet we know, blessed be God, that let the clouds be ever so dark and gloomy, the stars have been there in every age, though their twinkling has been but little seen.

Thus it was in the days of Elias; there were seven thousand such stars whose light was obscured by the thick clouds of idolatry—who would not yield to the darkness themselves, though they lacked power to enlighten others; yet was there but one star of sufficient power and brightness to dispel the mists and create a sphere in which others might shine. This was Elijah the Tishbite, whom we now behold, in heavenly power and light, breaking into the very stronghold of Baal, upsetting Jezebel's table,* writing folly upon the whole system of Baal's worship, and in fact, by God's grace, effecting a mighty moral change in the nation—bringing the many thousands of Israel down into the dust in real self-abasement, and mingling the blood of Baal's prophets with the waters of Kishon.

How gracious of the Lord to raise up such a deliverer for His deluded people! And what a death-blow to the prophets of Baal! We may safely assert they never offered a more unwilling sacrifice to their idol than that which our prophet suggested. It was the sure precursor of his downfall, and of theirs also. What a sad aspect they present, "crying and

---

* False religion has always sought the sunshine of this world's favor, whereas true religion has always been more pure and genuine when the world has frowned upon it. *"The prophets of the groves eat at Jezebel's table."* If Jezebel had had no table, she would have had not prophets either; it was *her table*, and not *her souls*, they sought.

cutting themselves with knives and lancets till the blood gushed out," and crying out, with unavailing earnestness, "O Baal, hear us!" Alas, Baal could not hear nor answer them!

The true prophet, conscious in his inmost soul of the sinful folly of the whole scene, mocks them: they cry more earnestly, and leap with frantic zeal upon the altar; but all in vain. They were now to be unmasked in the view of the nation. Their craft was in imminent danger. Those hands which, through their influence, had so often been lifted up in the diabolical worship of a sinful absurdity, were speedily about to seize them and drag them to their merited fate. Well, therefore, might they cry, "O Baal, hear us!"

How solemn, how immutably true, are those words of Jeremiah, "Cursed is the man whose heart departeth from the Lord"! It matters not on whom, or on what, we place our confidence: whether it be a religious system or a religious ordinance, or anything else, it is a departure of the heart from God; a curse follows it, and when the final struggle comes the Baal will be invoked in vain; "there will be neither voice, nor any to answer, nor any to regard."

How awful is the thought of departure from the living God! How dreadful to find, at the end of our history, that we have been leaning upon a broken reed! O, if you have not found solid and abiding peace for your guilty conscience in the atoning blood of Jesus, if you have a single emotion of fear in your heart at the thought of meeting God, let me put the prophet's question to you, "How long halt ye between two opinions?" Why do you stand aloof when Jesus calls you to come unto Him and take His yoke upon you? Believe me, the hour is coming when, if you have not fled for refuge to Jesus, a greater than Elijah will mock at your calamity.

Harken to these solemn words: "Because I have called, and ye refused; I have stretched out My hand, and no man regarded; but ye have set at naught all My counsel, and would none of My reproof; I also will laugh at your calamity; I will mock when your fear cometh; when your fear cometh as desolation, and your destruction cometh as a whirlwind;

when distress and anguish cometh upon you" (Prov. 1:24-27).

Awful words! inconceivably awful! How much more awful the reality! Flee to Jesus. Betake yourself to the open fountain, and there find peace and refuge ere the storm of divine wrath and judgment bursts upon your head. "When once the master of the house has risen up and shut to the door," you are lost, and lost forever. Oh think of this, I implore of you, and let not Satan drag your precious soul into everlasting perdition!

We now turn to another side of the picture. The prophets of Baal were signally defeated. They had leaped, cut themselves, and cried to no purpose. Their whole system had been proved a gross fallacy; the superstructure of error had been trampled to the ground, and it only now remained to rear the magnificent superstructure of truth in the view of those who had been so long enslaved by vanity and lies. "And Elijah said unto all the people, Come near unto me. And all the people came near unto him. *And he repaired the altar of the Lord that was broken down.* And Elijah took twelve stones, according to the number of the tribes of the sons of Jacob, unto whom the word of the Lord came, saying, Israel shall be thy name: and with the stones he built an altar in the name of the Lord."

It is always well to wait patiently, and allow evil and error to find their own level. Time will surely bring the truth to light; and let error array itself ever so carefully in the venerable robes of antiquity, yet will time strip it of these robes, and display it in all its naked deformity. Elijah felt this, and therefore he could stand quietly by and allow all the sands of Baal's glass to run out ere he began to exhibit the pattern of a more excellent way. Now it needs a very real apprehension of divine principles to enable one to adopt this patient course. Had our prophet been shallow-minded, or badly taught, he would have been in much greater haste to display his system and raise a storm of opposition against his antagonists.

But a spirit gifted with true elevation is never in haste, never perturbed; he has found a centre round which to move, and in revolving round that he finds himself carried out of the region of every other influence. Such an one was Elijah, a really elevated, independent, holy man—one who in every scene of his extraordinary career maintained a heavenly dignity which is earnestly to be sought after by all the Lord's servants. When he stood on mount Carmel, beholding the fruitless bodily exercise of Baal's prophets, he presented the appearance of one who was fully conscious of his heavenly mission; and not only in his manner, but also in his principles of acting, he acquitted himself as a prophet of the Lord.

What, then, were those principles on which Elijah acted? They were, in a word, those on which the unity of the nation was based. The first thing he does is to "repair the altar of the Lord that was broken down." This was Israel's centre, and to this every true reformer directed his attention. Those who seek to carry out a one-sided reformation may rest satisfied with merely throwing down that which is false, without proceeding further to establish a sound basis on which to erect a new superstructure: but such reformation will never stand; it will carry with it too much of the old leaven to admit of its being a testimony. The altar of Baal must not only be thrown down, but the altar of the Lord must be set up.

Some there are who would sacrifice to the Lord on the altar of Baal; in other words, they would retain an evil system, and rest satisfied with giving it a right name. But no; the only centre of unity which God can recognize is the name of Jesus—simply and exclusively that. The people of God must not be looked at as members of a system, but as members of Christ. God sees them as such, and it should be their business to reckon themselves to be what God tells them they are, and manifestly to take that blessed place.

And we may further remark that Elijah in his actings on mount Carmel does not stop short of the recognition of Israel's unbroken unity. He takes *twelve stones*, according to *the number of the sons of Jacob*, unto whom the Word of the Lord came, saying *"Israel shall be thy name."* This was taking high ground—yea, the very highest. Solomon

could have taken no higher. To recognize the twelve tribes of Israel at a time when they were divided, and weakened, and degraded, evidenced true communion with the mind of God in reference to His people.

Yet this is what the Spirit will ever suggest. "Our twelve tribes" must never be given up. True they may, through their own weakness and folly, become scattered and divided; yet the God of Israel can only think of them in that unbroken unity which they once exhibited, and which, moreover, they will exhibit again when, having been united by the true David, they shall in holy fellowship tread the courts of the Lord forever.

Now the Prophet Elijah, through the Spirit, saw all this. With the eye of faith, he penetrated the long, dreary time of Israel's humiliating bondage, and beheld them in their visible unity, no longer Judah and Israel, but *Israel,* for the word is, *"Israel shall be thy name."* His mind was occupied, not with what Israel was, but with what God had said. This was faith. Unbelief might say, "You are taking too high a stand; it is presumption to talk about twelve tribes when there are but ten; it is folly to speak of unbroken unity when there is nothing but division." Such will ever be the language of unbelief, which can never grasp the thoughts of God, nor see things as He sees them.

But it is the happy privilege of the man of faith to rest his spirit on the immutable testimony of God, which is not to be nullified by man's sinful folly. *"Israel shall be thy name."* Precious promise! Most precious! Most permanent! Nothing could for a moment interfere with it—neither Rehoboam's childishness nor Jeroboam's cunning policy; no, nor yet Ahab's vileness could hinder Elijah from taking the loftiest position that an Israelite could take, even the position of a worshiper at an altar built of twelve stones, according to the names of the twelve tribes of Israel.

Now in Elijah the Tishbite we have an example of the power of faith in the promise of God at a time when everything around him seemed to stand opposed. It enabled him to rise above all the evil and sorrow around him, and to build an altar of twelve stones with as much holy confidence and unclouded assurance as did Joshua when, amid the triumphant hosts of Israel, he erected his trophy on the banks of Jordan.

But I must bring this section to a close, having already extended it further than I had intended. We have seen the principle upon which our prophet desired to carry out the reformation. It was a sound one, and God honored it. The fire from Heaven at once confounded the prophets of Baal, confirmed the prophet's faith, and delivered the people from their sad condition of halting between two opinions. Elijah's faith had given God room to act; he had made a trench and filled it with water; in other words, he had made the difficulty as great as possible in order that the divine triumph might be complete: and truly it was so.

God will always respond to the appeal of simple faith. "Hear me," said the prophet, "O Lord, hear me; that this people may know that Thou art the Lord God, and that Thou hast turned their heart back again."

This is intelligent prayer. The prophet is engaged solely about God and His people. He does not say, "Hear me, that this people may know that I am a true prophet." No; his only object was to bring the people back to the God of their fathers, and to have the claims of God established in their consciences, in opposition to the claims of Baal. And God harkened and heard; for no sooner had he concluded his prayer than "the fire of the Lord fell, and consumed the burnt sacrifice, and the wood, and the stones, and the dust, and licked up the water that was in the trench. And when all the people saw it they fell on their faces: and they said, The Lord, He is the God; the Lord, He is the God."

Truth triumphs! The prophets are confounded! The prophet, in holy indignation, mingles their blood with the waters of the Kishon, and thus, evil being judged, there remains no further hindrance to the communication of the divine blessing, which Elijah announces to Ahab in these words, "Get thee up, eat and drink, for there is a sound of abundance of rain." How do these words convey to us Ahab's true character! *"Eat and drink."* This was all he knew, or

cared to know. He had come forth to look for grass, and nothing more; and the prophet conveyed to him that intelligence which he knew he desired. He could not ask him to come and join him in thanksgiving to God for this glorious triumph over evil, for he knew well he would meet with no response.

And yet they were both Israelites: but one was in communion with God, and the other was the slave of sin; hence, while Ahab found his enjoyment in getting up to "eat and drink," Elijah sought his in retirement with God. Blessed, holy, heavenly enjoyment!

But mark the difference between Elijah's bearing in the presence of man and in the presence of God. He had met Obadiah, a saint in wrong circumstances, with an air of dignity and elevation; he had met Ahab in righteous sternness; he had stood amid the thousands of his deluded and erring brethren with the firmness and grace of a true reformer; and lastly, he had met the wicked prophets of Baal with mocking, and then with the sword of vengeance. Thus had he carried himself in the presence of man.

But how did he meet God? "He cast himself down upon the earth, and put his face between his knees." Thus he carried himself before God. All this is lovely. Our prophet knew his place both before God and man. In the presence of man he acted in the wisdom of the Spirit, as the case demanded; in the presence of God he prostrated himself in unfeigned and reverent humility. Thus may all the Lord's servants know how to walk in all their complicated relations here below.

We must now accompany our prophet to widely different scenes.

Part 5

THE PROPHET ON MOUNT HOREB

There are few who have taken a prominent place in the history of the Church of God whose course has not been marked, in a special manner, by vicissitude: of such, as of "those that go down to the sea in ships, that do business in great waters," it may be said, "They mount up to the heaven, they go down again to the depths; their soul is melted because of trouble." They are sometimes seen on the mount, sometimes in the valley; at one time basking in the sunshine, at another beaten by the storm.

Nor is this the case merely with prominent characters; almost every Christian, be his path ever so retired and noiseless, knows something of this vicissitude. Indeed, it would seem as if no one could run the race which is marked out for the man of faith without finding inequalities in his way. The path through the desert must be rough, and it is well that is so; for there is no right-minded person who would not rather be set in a rough than in a "slippery" way. The Lord sees our need of being exercised by roughness and hardness, not only that we may find the rest at the end sweeter, but also that we may be the more effectually trained and fitted for the place we are yet to occupy.

True we shall have no need for trials in the kingdom, but we shall have need of those graces and habits of soul which were formed amid the trials and sorrows of the wilderness. We shall yet be constrained to acknowledge that our path here below was not a whit too rough, but that on the contrary we could not have done without a single exercise of all those that had fallen to our lot. We now see things indistinctly, and are often unable to see the needs-be for many of our trials and sorrows: moreover our impatient nature may often feel disposed to murmur and rebel; but only let us be patient and we shall be able without hesitation, and with the full assent of every thought and feeling, to say, "He led us forth by *a right way*, that He might bring us to *a city of habitation.*"

The above train of thought is suggested by the circumstances of our prophet in chapter 19. He seems to have had little anticipation of the terrific storm which was about to burst upon him: he had come from the top of mount Carmel, and in the energy of the Spirit outstripped Ahab in his chariot to the entrance of Jezreel; but there he was destined to receive a check, and that, too, from one who had hitherto kept herself in the background. This was the wicked Jezebel. I say, she had kept herself in the background;

but she had not been idle there. She had no doubt influenced her weak-minded lord, and used his power for her wicked ends. She had opened her house and spread a table for the prophets of Baal. These things she had done in furtherance of her master's interests.

Jezebel is not to be looked at merely as an individual: she stands before the spiritual mind as the representative of a class—yea, more, as the impersonation of a principle which has from age to age been working in hostility to the truth of God, and which appears in its full maturity in the person of the great whore spoken of in the Apocalypse. The spirit of Jezebel is a persecuting spirit—a spirit that will carry its own point in opposition to everything—an active, energetic, persevering spirit, in which satanic vigor appears very manifestly.

Very different is the Ahab spirit. In Ahab we see one who, provided he could attain the gratification of his carnal and worldly desires, cared but little about religion. He troubled himself but little to decide between the claims of Jehovah and those of Baal. To him they were all alike. Now it was such an one that Jezebel could wield according to her mind. She took care to have his desires gratified while she actively and sagaciously used his power in opposition to the truth of God. The Ahabs are always found to be fit instruments for the Jezebels; hence, in the Apocalypse, where all those principles which have been, are now, or are yet to be, at work, are seen in their full maturity, we find the woman riding the beast: that is, corrupt religion wielding the secular power, or the full-grown Jezebel-spirit making use of the full-grown Ahab-spirit.

All this has a solemn voice for the present generation; and those that have ears to hear, let them hear. Men are becoming increasingly heedless as to the interests and destinies of the truth of God in the earth. Christ and Belial are all alike, provided the wheels of the vast machine of utilitarianism be not clogged in their movement. You may hold what principles you please provided you hold them in the background; and thus men of the most conflicting principles can unite and hold those principles in abeyance while with ardor and energy they pursue the phantom of worldliness.

Such is the spirit and tendency of the age, and all that is needed is that a Jezebel-spirit should arise and lead men on along the path upon which they have manifestly entered—a path which will most assuredly end in the blackness of darkness forever. Solemn, most solemn thought! Again I say, "He that hath ears to hear, let him hear."

But we have said it was from Jezebel that the prophet Elijah received the check which seems so to have overwhelmed his spirit. "And Ahab told Jezebel all that Elijah had done, and withal how he had slain all the prophets with the sword." Observe, "Ahab told Jezebel"; he had neither sufficient interest in the matter to lead him to take an active part himself, nor, even if he had the interest, did he possess sufficient energy. To him, perhaps, the abundance of rain seemed to stand connected with the death of the prophets, and therefore he could quietly stand by and see them put to death.

What was Baal to him, or Jehovah either? Nothing. Let Ahab and all of that school get enough to "eat and drink," and all questions of truth and religion will be but lightly regarded. Gross and unmeaning abomination! Miserable, infatuated sensualism! Ye children of this world, whose sentiments are expressed in the words "let us eat and drink, for to-morrow we die," think of Ahab; remember his terrible end—the end of his eating and drinking. What was it? "The dogs licked his blood." And as to his soul—ah, eternity will unfold its destinies!

But in Jezebel we see one who lacked neither interest nor energy. To her the controversy was one of the deepest moment, and she was determined to act with decision. "Then Jezebel sent a messenger unto Elijah, saying, So let the gods do to me, and more also, if I make not thy life as the life of one of them by to-morrow about this time."

Here then the prophet was called to endure the storm of persecution. He had been on mount Carmel, where he had stood against all the prophets of Baal; his course had hitherto been a triumphant one, the result of communion with God; but now his sun seemed, in his view, to be about to go down, and his horizon to become dark and gloomy.

"And when he saw that, he arose *and went for his life*, and came to Beersheba, which belongeth to Judah, and left his servant there. But he himself went a day's journey into the wilderness, and came and sat down under a juniper tree: and he requested for himself that he might die; and said, It is enough; now, O Lord, take away my life; for I am not better than my fathers."

Elijah's spirit sinks altogether; he looks at everything through the dark cloud in which he was enveloped; all his labor seems, in his view, to have been for nought and in vain, and he has only to lie down and die. His spirit, harassed by what he deemed fruitless efforts to bring the nation back to its faith, longed to enter into rest.

Now, in all this we perceive the workings of impatience and unbelief. Elijah said nothing about longing to depart when he stood on mount Carmel. No; there all was triumph; there he seemed to be achieving something—he seemed to be of some use, and therefore he thought not of his departure. But the Lord would show His servant not only what he "must do," but also what he "must suffer." The former we like well enough, the latter we are not so well prepared for. And yet the Lord is as much glorified in a patient sufferer as in an active servant. The graces that are developed by one who is enabled to endure protracted suffering are as fragrant in their perfume as all the fruits of active service. This our prophet should have borne in mind. But ah, the heart can well understand and sympathize with him in his gloom and despondency.

There are few of the Lord's servants who have not, at some time or other, eagerly desired to put off their harness and cease from the toils of conflict, particularly at times when all their labor and testimony would seem to be in vain, and when they are disposed to look upon themselves as mere cumberers of the ground. Yet we must wait God's time, and until then seek to pursue our way in patient, uncomplaining service. There is a vast difference between longing to get away from trial and sorrow, and longing to be at home in our Father's house.

No doubt the thought of rest is sweet, ineffably sweet, to the laboring man. It is sweet to think of the time when our own gracious God shall wipe away all tears from our eyes, sweet to think of those green pastures and living fountains to which the Lamb will lead His flock throughout the coming ages of glory. In a word, the whole prospect presented to the view of faith is sweet and cheering; yet we have no right to say, "O Lord, take away my life." Nothing but an impatient spirit could ever dictate such language.

How different is the spirit breathed in the following words of the apostle Paul! "For I am in a strait betwixt two, having a desire to depart, and to be with Christ, which is *far better*. Nevertheless, to abide in the flesh is *more needful for you*. And having this confidence, I know that *I shall abide and continue with you all, for your furtherance and joy of faith*" (Phil. 1:23-25).

These words exhibit a truly Christian spirit. The servant of the Church should seek the Church's good, and not his own advantage. If Paul had considered himself, he would not have tarried a moment on earth; but when he considered the Church, he desired to abide and continue for the purpose of furthering its joy and faith. This should have been Elijah's desire too: he should have desired to remain for the benefit of the nation. But here he failed. He had fled into the wilderness under the influence of unbelief, and for the purpose of saving his life, and then desired that his life might be taken away simply to escape from the trials which his position involved.

In all this we may learn a most profitable lesson. Unbelief is sure to drive us from the place of testimony and service. So long as Elijah walked by faith, so long he occupied the place of a servant and a witness; but the moment his faith gave way, he abandoned both and fled into the wilderness. Unbelief ever unfits us for the place of service, and renders us useless. We never can act for God save in the energy of faith. We should remember this at a time like the present,

when so many are giving up and turning aside. I suppose we may lay it down as a fixed principle of truth, that whenever a man abandons any distinctive position of testimony, it is from positive unbelief in the truth which led him into it.

Thus, for example, at the present day we see many who at one time took up a very distinct and prominent position from having learnt (as they stated) that great truth, the presence of the Holy Ghost in the Church. Now, when this truth is really learnt, and held in power, it delivers from man's authority in matters of faith, and leads Christians out of those systems where such authority is acknowledged and defended.

If the Holy Ghost rules in the Church, then man has no right to interfere, no right to decree and institute ceremonies; for in doing so he is most presumptuously interfering with the divine prerogative. If therefore a man sincerely believe this important truth, his belief will certainly influence his conduct so far that he will feel himself called upon to bear testimony against every system in which this truth is practically denied, by separating from it.

It is not a question of what or whom he will attach himself to. No; this is another, and an after, consideration. A man's first business is to "cease to do evil," and after that to "learn to do well."

However, many who once professed to see this truth, and to act upon it, have since lost confidence in it, and as a consequence have retired from their distinct position, and gone back to those systems from which they had emerged. Like Elijah, they have not realized all their expectations; the results which they looked for have not appeared, therefore they have fled from the scene, and doubtless many have felt disposed to say, *"It is enough."*

Yes, many a heart which once cherished high and fond expectations respecting the Church is now bowed down with sorrow and disappointment. Those who professed to see and act upon the truth of the presence of the Holy Ghost in the Church, and other collateral truths, have, to say the least, failed to carry them into practice, and not only failed, but in many instances have made a most humiliating exhibition of themselves; and the enemy has not been backward in making his own use of all this. He has used it especially to discourage the hearts of those who, no doubt, desired to stand in testimony for Christ, but who, seeing the failure of everything like corporate testimony on the earth, have given up in despair.

However, let Christians observe this: it was unbelief that made Elijah fly into the wilderness, and it is unbelief which causes any one to give up that position of testimony into which the truth of the Holy Ghost's presence in the Church would necessarily lead him.

Those who thus retreat prove that it was not with God and His eternal truth, but with man and his circumstances, that they had to do. If God's truth be the basis of our acting, we shall not be affected by man's mutability and failure. Man may, and assuredly will, fail in his very best and purest efforts to carry out the truth of God; but shall man's failure make the truth of God of none effect? "God forbid; yea, let God be true and every man a liar."

If those who profess to hold the blessed doctrine of the unity of the Church should split into parties; if those who hold the doctrine of the Spirit's presence in the Church for the purpose of rule and ministry should nevertheless practically lean upon man's authority; if those who profess to be looking for the personal appearance and reign of the Son of man should be found grasping with eagerness after the things of this present world, shall these things nullify those heavenly principles? Certainly not. Thank God, truth will be truth to the end. God will be God, though man should prove himself a thousandfold more imperfect than he is. Wherefore, instead of giving up in despair because men have failed to make a right use of God's truth, we should rather hold fast that truth as the only stay of our souls amid universal ruin and shipwreck.

Had Elijah held fast the truth which filled his soul when he stood on mount Carmel, he would never have been found beneath the juniper tree, nor would he have given utterance to such words as "Take away my life, for I am not better than my fathers."

Yet the Lord can graciously meet his poor servant even asleep under a juniper tree. "He knoweth our frame, He remembers that we are dust," and therefore, instead of granting the petulant request of His harassed and disappointed servant, He rather seeks to feed and strengthen him for further exertion. This is not "the manner of man," but it is, blessed forever be His name, the manner of God, whose ways and thoughts are not as ours. Man would often deal roughly and harshly with his fellow, making no allowance for him, but acting towards him in haste and severity. Not so God. He ever deals in the deepest pity and tenderness. He understood Elijah, and He remembered the stand he had recently made for His name and truth, and therefore He would minister to him in the season of his depression.

"And as he lay and slept under a juniper tree, behold, then an angel touched him, and said unto him, Arise and eat. And he looked, and behold, there was a cake baken on the coals, and a cruse of water at his head. And he did eat and drink, and laid him down again. And the angel of the Lord came again the second time, and touched him, and said, Arise and eat; because the journey is too great for thee. And he arose, and did eat and drink, and went in the strength of that meat forty days and forty nights unto Horeb the mount of God" (chap. 19:5,8).

The Lord knows better than we do the demands that may be made on us, and He graciously strengthens us according to His estimate of those demands. The prophet wished to sleep for sorrow, but the Lord wished to strengthen and nerve him for future service. Like the disciples in the garden, who, overwhelmed with deep sorrow at the apparent failure of all their fondly cherished hopes, allowed themselves to sink into profound slumber while their blessed Master would have had them girding up their loins and nerving their arms for the trying scenes on which they were about to enter.

But Elijah did eat and drink; and being thus strengthened, he proceeded to mount Horeb. Here again we have to trace the sorrowful actings of an impatient spirit.

Elijah seems determined to retire from his place of service and testimony altogether. If he cannot sleep under the juniper tree, he will hide himself in a cave. "He came thither unto a cave, and lodged there."

When once a man allows himself to slip aside from the position in which faith would keep him, there is no accounting for the extremes into which he may run. Nothing but abiding faith in the Word of God can maintain any one in the path of service, because *faith makes a man satisfied to wait for the end,* whereas unbelief, looking only at surrounding circumstances, sinks into complete despondency.

The Christian must make up his mind to meet with nothing but trial and disappointment here. We may often dream of rest and satisfaction in some condition or other here; but it is only a dream. Elijah had no doubt hoped to see a mighty moral change brought about by his instrumentality; and instead of that, his life was threatened. But he ought to have been prepared for this.

The man who had fearlessly faced Ahab and all the prophets of Baal ought surely to have been able to bear a message from a woman. Yet no; his faith had given way. When a man's faith gives way, his own shadow will deter him. In contemplating the prophet's position on mount Horeb, one is disposed to ask, Can it be the same man whom we saw so recently standing on mount Carmel, at an altar of twelve stones, and there so blessedly vindicating the God of Israel in the presence of his brethren?

Alas! what a powerless creature man is when not sustained by simple faith in the testimony of God! David could, at one time, meet Goliath in the power of faith, and afterwards say, "I shall one day perish by the hand of Saul." Faith gets above circumstances and looks at God; unbelief loses sight of God, and looks only at circumstances. Unbelief says, "We were in our own sight as grasshoppers, and so were we in their sight;" faith says, "We are well able to overcome them."

However, the Lord does not leave His servant in the cave; He still follows him, and seeks to bring him again and again back to that post which he had abandoned in his impatience and unbelief. "And behold, the word of the Lord came to him, and He said unto him, What doest thou here, Elijah?" What a reproof! Why did Elijah thus bury himself in a cave? Why had he retreated from the honorable post of testimony? Because of Jezebel's message, and because his ministry had not been as fully owned as he expected. He thought to have reaped a more cheering harvest from all his labor than a threatening message and apparent desertion, and therefore he had sought the retirement of a mountain cave, as a place suited to indulge his feelings.

Now, it must be admitted that there was much—very much to wound the prophet's spirit; he had come from his quiet retreat at Zarephath to face the whole nation, headed by Jezebel and a host of wicked priests and prophets. He had confounded the latter, through God's grace; God had sent down fire from Heaven in answer to his prayer; all Israel had seemed to acknowledge the truth as proclaimed by him. All these things must have raised his expectations to no ordinary height; yet, after all, his life is threatened, he sees no one to stand by him, he is enveloped in a thick cloud, he abandons the field of conflict, and hides himself in a cave.

It is much easier to censure another than to act aright, and we must be exceedingly slow in pronouncing judgment upon the actions of so honored a servant as Elijah the Tishbite. But though we should not deal much in censure, we may, at least, draw instruction and warning from this section of our prophet's history. We may learn a lesson of which we stand very much in need. "What doest thou here?" is a question which might justly be put to many of us from time to time, when, in impatience or unbelief, we leave our proper place of service amongst our brethren, to sleep under a juniper tree, or hide ourselves in a cave.

Are there not many at this moment who, aforetime, were powerful advocates of the principles connected with the unity and worship of the people of God, to be found either asleep or hidden in caves? that is, they are doing nothing for the furtherance of those truths which they once advocated. This is a truly sorrowful reflection. To such the question, "What doest thou here?" should come with special force. Yes, what are such doing? or rather, what are they not doing in the way of positive mischief to the sheep of Christ? A man who thus retires is not merely harmless, he is noxious; he is really injuring his brethren.

It would be far better never to have appeared as the advocates of important truth, than having done so to retire; to call special attention to some leading principles of divine truth, and then to abandon them, is most culpable. "If many man be ignorant, let him be ignorant." We can pity ignorance, or endeavor to instruct it; but the man, who, having professed to see truth, afterwards abandons it, can neither be looked upon as an object of pity, nor a subject for instruction.

But it is not merely unbelief and disappointment in reference to certain truths that drive men into unhappy isolation; apparent failure in ministry has the same effect. The latter was, perhaps, what more especially affected Elijah. The triumph on mount Carmel had, doubtless, led to much elation of spirit in reference to the results of his ministry, and he was not prepared for the sad reverse.

Now, the sovereign remedy for both these maladies, that is, for unbelief in important truth and disappointment as regards our ministry, is to keep the eye simply and steadily fixed on Jesus.

If, for example, we see men professing those two grand and all-important truths— the unity of the Church, and the abiding presence of the Holy Ghost in the Church—professing, I say, to see these things, and yet failing most sadly in carrying them out, shall we turn aside, and say there is no unity, and no abiding presence of the Holy Ghost? God forbid. This would be to make God's truth dependent upon man's faithfulness, which cannot be endured for a moment by the spiritual mind. No, let us rather look into the precious Word of God, and see the Church as the body of Christ, each member thereof written in God's book from everlasting to everlasting.

And, in like manner when we see Jesus at God's right hand in the Heavens, we see the unfailing ground of the Spirit's presence in the Church. Thank God for the blessed stability of all this. "The gifts and calling of God are without repentance."

Finally, if any be tried in the matter of their ministry, if the enemy would endeavor to make them give up in chagrin or disappointment, let them try to keep their eyes more simply on Jesus, remembering that, however depressing the aspect of things here may be, the time is speedily approaching when all who have served the Lord simply, from love to Him, shall reap a full reward. We must take care, however, that we allow not our ministry, or the fruits thereof, to get between our souls and Christ. There is great danger of this. A man may set out in unaffected devotedness to his Master, and yet, through the craft of the enemy, and the weakness of his own heart, he may, ere long, give his work a more prominent place in his thoughts than Christ Himself. Had Elijah kept the God of Israel more before him, he would not have given up in despair.

But we learn the real state of the prophet's soul from his reply to the divine challenge: "I have been very jealous," said he, "for the Lord God of hosts; for the children of Israel have forsaken Thy covenant, thrown down Thine altars, and slain Thy prophets with the sword: and I, even I only, am left; and they seek my life to take it away." How different is this language from that which dropped from his lips on mount Carmel! There he vindicated God,—here he vindicates himself; there he endeavored to convert his brethren by presenting before them the truth of God,—here he accuses his brethren, and recounts their sins before God.*

"I have been very jealous;" but "they have forsaken," etc. This was the strain in which

* It is instructive to observe the order in which Elijah recounts the sins of Israel: 1—"they have forsaken Thy covenant;" 2—"they have thrown down Thine altars;" 3—"they have slain Thy prophets with the sword." The ground of all this evil was their having forsaken the covenant of God, the natural consequence of which was the throwing down of God's altars, and the abandonment of His worship, which latter was followed out by killing the prophets. We can understand this order.

the disappointed prophet spoke from his cave on mount Horeb. He seems to have looked upon himself as the only one that had done, or was doing, anything for God. "I only am left, and they seek my life to take it away." Now all this was the natural consequence of his position.

The moment a man retires from his place of testimony and service among his brethren, he must begin to extol himself, and accuse them; yea, his very act expresses at once the assumption of his faithfulness, and their failure. But to all who thus separate from, and accuse their brethren, the searching question is, "What doest thou here?" "He that hath ears to hear, let him hear."

Our prophet, however, is called forth from his isolated place. "Go forth," said Jehovah, "and stand upon the mount before the Lord. And, behold, the Lord passed by, and a great and strong wind rent the mountains, and brake in pieces the rocks before the Lord; but the Lord was not in the wind: and after the wind an earthquake; but the Lord was not in the earthquake: and after the earthquake a fire; but the Lord was not in the fire: and after the fire *a still small voice.*"

The Lord, by these solemn and varied exhibitions of Himself and His wondrous actings, would teach His servant most impressively that He was not to be confined to one agent in carrying out His designs. The wind was an agent, and a powerful one, yet it did not accomplish the end; and the same might be said of the earthquake and the fire. They, by their very terribleness, served but to pave the way for the last, and apparently the weakest agent, namely, the still small voice.

Thus the prophet was taught that he must be satisfied to be an agent, and one of many. He might have thought that all the work was to have been done by him. Coming, as he did, with all the terrible vehemence of the mighty wind, he supposed he should have carried off every obstacle, and brought the nation back to its place of happy allegiance to God. But ah! how little does even the most elevated instrument apprehend his own insignificance! The most devoted, the most gifted and the most elevated are but stones in the superstructure, screws in the vast machine; and whoever supposes he is *the* instrument, will find himself much mistaken.

"Paul may plant, and Apollos water, but God giveth the increase." And so Elijah had to learn that the Lord was not confined to him. He had other shafts in His quiver, which He would discharge in due time. The wind, the earthquake, and the fire must all do their work, and then the still small voice could be heard distinctly and effectually. It is the sole province of God to make Himself heard, even though He speak in "a still small voice." Elijah remained in the cave until this voice reached his ear, and then "he wrapped his face in his mantle, and went out, and stood in the entering in of the cave."

It is only "before the Lord" that we get into our right position. We may conceive high thoughts of ourselves and our ministry, until we are brought into the divine presence, and then we learn to wrap our face in a mantle; in other words, we learn, in reality, to hide ourselves. When Moses found himself in the divine presence "he trembled, and durst not behold." When Job found himself there, "he abhorred himself, and repented in dust and ashes"; and so has it been with every one who has ever gotten a view of himself in the light of God's presence; he has learned his own thorough nothingness, he has been led to see that God could do without him.

The Lord is ever ready to acknowledge the smallest act of service done to Him, but the moment a man makes a centre of his service, the Lord will teach him that He wants him no longer. Thus it was with Elijah. He had retired from the field of labor and conflict, and earnestly desired to be gone: he thought himself a solitary witness, a forsaken and disappointed servant, and Jehovah makes him stand forth before Him, and there, as it were, give up his commission, and hear the names of his successors in the field of labor.

"The Lord said unto him, Go, return, on thy way to the wilderness of Damascus; and when thou comest, anoint Hazael to be king over Syria: and Jehu the son of Nimshi shalt thou anoint to be king over Israel: and Elisha the son of Shaphat, of Abel-meholah, shalt thou anoint to be prophet in thy room. And it shall come to pass, that him that escapeth the sword of Hazael shall Jehu slay; and him that escapeth the sword of Jehu shall Elisha slay. Yet I have left Me seven thousand in Israel, all the knees which have not bowed unto Baal, and every mouth which hath not kissed him."

This statement must have thrown much light on the prophet's mind. Seven thousand! although he had thought himself left alone. Jehovah will never be at a loss for instruments. If the wind will not do, He has the earthquake; and if the earthquake will not do, He has the fire; and last of all, He has "the still small voice."

And so Elijah was taught that Israel had to be acted upon by other ministry besides his: Hazael, Jehu, and Elisha had yet to appear on the scene, and as the still small voice had proved effectual in drawing him forth from his mountain cave, so would the gracious ministry of Elisha prove effectual in drawing forth from their lurking-places the thousands of faithful ones whom he had altogether overlooked. Elijah was not to do all. He was but one agent. "The eye cannot say to the hand I have no need of thee: nor again the head to the feet, I have no need of you."

Such, I believe, was the important lesson taught to our prophet by the impressive scenes on mount Horeb. He had gone up thither full of thoughts of himself alone; he stood there filled with the idea that he was *the* witness, the *only* witness; he went down from thence with the humbling yet wholesome consciousness that *he was but one of seven thousand.* A very different view of the case indeed. None can teach like God. When He desires to teach a lesson He can teach it effectually, blessed be His name. He had so taught Elijah his own insignificance that he was satisifed to retrace his steps, to come forth from his cave and down from the mount, to lay aside all his complaints and accusations, and humbly, silently, obediently, and willingly cast his prophetic mantle over the shoulders of another.

All this is most instructive. The silence of Elijah, after he hears of the seven thousand, is most remarkable. He had learnt a lesson which mount Carmel could not teach him—a lesson which neither Zarephath nor Cherith had taught him. In these places he had learnt much about God and His truth, but on Horeb he had learnt his own littleness, and as the result of that learning he comes down from the mount and gives up his office to another; and not merely this, but in so doing he says, "What have *I* done?"

In a word, we see in this dear servant the most complete renunciation of self from the moment he learnt that he was but one of many. He delivers a message to Ahab in the vineyard of Naboth; a message to Ahaziah in his sick chamber; then he takes his departure from earth, leaving the work which he had begun to be finished by other hands. Like John the Baptist, who, as we know, came in the spirit and power of Elias, he was satisfied to usher in another and then retire.

Oh that we all knew more of this humble, self-renouncing spirit—the spirit which leads a man to do the work and think nothing of it; or if it should be so, to see the work done by others and rejoice therein. The Baptist had to learn this as well as the Tishbite; he had to learn to be content to end his brilliant career in the gloom of a prison while another was doing the work. John too thought it strange that it should be thus with him, and sent a message to Christ to inquire, "Art Thou He that should come, or look we for another?" As if he had said, Can it be possible that He to whom I have borne witness is indeed the Christ and yet I am left to perish, neglected, in Herod's dungeon?

Thus it was, and John had to learn to be content. He had said at the commencement of his ministerial course, "He must increase, but I must decrease"; but it may be he had not just counted upon such a mode of decreasing: yet such was the divine counsel concerning this honored servant. How different are God's thoughts from those of man! John, after having fulfilled a most important mission, even the mission of ushering in the Son of God, was destined to have his head cut off at the will of a wicked woman, and lest an ungodly tyrant should break his oath.

Just so was it with Elijah the Tishbite. His course, no doubt, had been a most brilliant one; he had passed before the eyes of Israel in all the dignity and majesty of a heavenly man—a heavenly messenger. Divine truth had fallen from his lips, and God had abundantly honored him in his work; yet the moment he began to think of himself as anything; the moment he began to say, "*I* have been very jealous, and *I* only am left." the Lord taught him his mistake, and told him to appoint his successor.

May we learn from all this to be very humble and self-renouncing in our service, whatever it be. Let us not presume to survey ourselves as if we were anything, or our service as if we had achieved some great thing. And even though our ministry should be unproductive, and we ourselves despised and rejected, may we be able *to look forward to the end*, when everything shall be made manifest. This was what our blessed Master did. He kept His eye fixed on "the joy that was set before Him," and regarded not the thoughts of men as He passed along. Nor did He complain of or accuse those who rejected, despised, and crucified Him. No; His dying words were, "Father, forgive them." Blessed Master, impart unto us more of Thy meek, loving, gracious and forgiving spirit! May we be like Thee, and tread in Thy steps across this dreary world!

Part 6

THE PROPHET'S RAPTURE

From the moment that Elijah had cast his mantle upon the shoulders of Elisha we may consider his prophetic career as almost ended. He delivered a message or two, as has already been noticed; but as regards his ministerial connection with Israel, it may be looked upon as closed from the moment that Elisha the son of Shaphat, of Abel-meholah, was anointed to be prophet in his room.

Indeed, he abandoned the work himself. "He arose, and fled for his life;" so that it was, to speak after the manner of men, high time to think of appointing a successor.

But we must not confine our thoughts to Elijah's ministerial character when reflecting upon his life and times. We must not only look at him as a *prophet*, but also as a *man;* not only as a *servant*, but also a *child;* not only *officially*, but also *personally*. As a prophet, the steady continuance and successful termination of his course would depend, in a great measure, on his own faithfulness. Hence, when he allowed himself to be carried away by a spirit inconsistent with the character of a genuine servant, he had to resign his office into the hands of another.*

There were, however, better things in store for Elijah. He might be hasty; he might hide himself in a cave, and from thence make intercession against Israel; he might impatiently long to depart from the trying scene in which he had been called to move; he might do all this, and in consequence thereof be called to resign his place: still the blessed God had thoughts of grace about him which never could have entered into his heart.

How truly blessed to allow God to adopt His own manner in dealing with us! We are sure to sustain loss when we interfere with the divine method of proceeding; and yet it has ever been man's tendency thus to interfere. Man will not allow God to adopt His own method of justifying him, but will ever be intruding into the wondrous plan of redemption: and even when he has submitted himself, through the operation of the Holy Ghost, to God's righteousness, he will again and again, notwithstanding repeated experience of God's superior wisdom, seek to interfere with the divine method of training and leading him; as if he could make better arrngements for himself than God! Presumptuous folly!—the fruits of which, to some, will be eternal perdition; to others,

---

* It may be needful just to notice an objection which may be made to the view I have taken of the prophet's actings. It may be said that he was raised up at a special era of Israel's history, and for a special purpose, and that when that purpose had been effected another kind of instrument was needed. All this is most true. Yet we can have no difficulty in perceiving the haste and impatience of Elijah in desiring to resign his post because things had not turned out as he had expected. God's counsels and man's acting are very distinct. The ministry of Elijah had filled its proper place in the nation's history, no doubt; and moreover, another kind of instrument might be needed; yet this leaves quite untouched the question of his spirit and actings in the matter. Joshua might be needed to succeed Moses; and yet it was for hastiness of spirit that Moses was refused permission to go over Jordan.

present forfeiture of blessing in the way of enlarged knowledge and experience of God's character and ways.

Had Elijah received his request, how much he would have lost! How much better to be carried up to Heaven in a chariot of fire, than to be taken away in a fit of impatience! Elijah asked for the latter, but God gave him the former. "And it came to pass, when the Lord would take up Elijah into heaven by a whirlwind, that Elijah went with Elisha from Gilgal" (2 Kings 2:1).

It would be foreign to my present design to dwell upon the circumstances of Elisha's introduction into the prophetic office, his slowness at first in accompanying Elijah, and his unwillingness afterward to leave him. We find him in this chapter accompanying Elijah from Gilgal to Bethel, and from Bethel to Jericho, and from Jericho to Jordan. All these places were famous in Israel's history. Bethel, or the house of God, was the spot where Jacob of old had seen the mystic ladder stretching from earth to Heaven, the apt expression of God's future purposes concerning the heavenly and earthly families. To this same place did Jacob return, by the express command of God, after he had cleansed himself from the defilement of Shechem (Gen. 35:1).

Bethel, therefore, was a spot of deep interest to the heart of an Israelite. But alas, it had become polluted! Jeroboam's calf had effectually obliterated the sacred principles of truth taught by Jacob's ladder. The latter conducted the spirit from earth to Heaven—it led upward and onward; upward to God's eternal purpose of *grace;* onward to the display of that purpose in *glory.* The former, on the contrary, bound the heart down to a degrading system of political religion—a system in which the *names* of things heavenly were used to secure for self the things earthly.

Jeroboam made use of *the house of God* to secure for himself *the kingdom of Israel.* He was well content to remain at the bottom of the ladder, and cared not to look upward. His earthly heart desired not to scale those sublime heights to which Jacob's ladder led; earth and its glory were all he wanted; and

provided he obtained these, he cared not whether he worshiped before Baal's calf at Bethel, or Jehovah's altar at Jerusalem. What was it to him? Jerusalem, Bethel, or Dan, was but a name in the estimate of this politico-religious man—yea, and in the estimate of every other such man.

Religion is but an instrument in the hands of the children of this world—an instrument by which they dig into the bowels of the earth; not a ladder by which they mount from earth to Heaven. Man pollutes everything sacred. Place in his hands the purest, the most heavenly truth, and ere long he will defile it: commit to his guardianship the most precious, the most impressive ordinance, and he will ere long convert it into a lifeless form, and lose therein the principles sought to be conveyed. So was it with Bethel. So was it with everything sacred that man had anything to do with.

Then as to Gilgal, the place from whence the two prophets started: it too was a place of interest. It was there the Lord rolled away the reproach of Egypt from His people; there Israel kept their first passover in the land of Canaan, and were refreshed by the old corn of the land. Gilgal was the rallying point for Joshua and his men of war; from thence they went forth in the strength of the Lord to obtain glorious triumphs over the uncircumcised, and thither they returned to enjoy the spoils.

Thus was Gilgal a place round which the affections of a Jew might well entwine themselves—a place of many hallowed recollections. Yet it too had lost all its reality. The reproach of Egypt had rolled back upon Israel. the principles which once stood connected with Gilgal had lost their sway over the hearts of God's professing people. Bochim (the place of weepers) had long since taken the place of Gilgal in reference to Israel, and Gilgal had become an empty form—ancient, no doubt, but powerless, for Israel had ceased to walk in the power of the truth taught at Gilgal.

Again, as to Jericho, There it was that the hosts of the Lord, under their mighty Captain, gained their first victory in the land of promise, and exhibited the power of faith.

And lastly, at Jordan it was that Israel had had such an impressive manifestation of Jehovah's power in connection with the ark of His presence. Jordan was the place where death had been, in type, overcome by the power of life; and in its midst, and on its banks, it presented the trophies of victory over the foe.

Thus were these varied places—namely, Bethel, Gilgal, Jericho, and Jordan—deeply interesting to the heart of a true child of Abraham; but their power and meaning were lost: Bethel had ceased to be the house of God save in name; Gilgal was no longer valued as the place where the reproach of Egypt had been rolled away. The walls of Jericho which had been destroyed by faith were built again. Jordan was no longer viewed as the scene of Jehovah's power.

In a word, all these things had become mere form without power, and the Lord might, even in Elijah's time, have to speak to the house of Israel concerning them in the following impressive words: "Thus saith the Lord unto the house of Israel, *Seek ye Me*, and ye shall live: but seek not Bethel, nor enter into Gilgal, and pass not to Beersheba: for Gilgal shall surely go into captivity, and Bethel shall come to naught. Seek the Lord, and ye shall live" (Amos 5:4-6). Here is an important truth for all those whose hearts are prone to cling to ancient forms.

We are taught by this striking passage that nothing but the divine reality of personal communion with God will stand. Men may plead, in defense of forms, their great antiquity, but where can we find greater antiquity than that which Bethel and Gilgal could boast? Yet they failed and came to naught, and the faithful were admonished to abandon them all and look up in simple faith to the living God.

Through all the above places, then, our prophet passed in the energy and elevation of a heavenly man. His destination lay beyond and above them all. He would seek to leave Elisha behind him while he pressed onward along his heavenward path; but the latter clings to him, and accompanies him as it were to the very portals of Heaven, and checks the busy intrusion of his less intelligent brethren by the words, "Hold ye your peace."

But Elijah moves on in the power of his heavenly mission. "The Lord hath sent me," says he; and in obedience to the divine command he passes through Gilgal, Bethel, Jericho, and on to Jordan; leaving far behind him all those ancient forms and sacred localities which might engage the affections of any who were not, like Elijah the Tishbite, carried forward by a heavenly hope.

The sons of the prophets might tarry amid those things, and perhaps, too, have many a hallowed recollection awakened by them; but to one whose spirit was filled with the thought of his rapture to Heaven, things of earth be they ever so sacred, ever so venerable, could present no attraction. Heaven was his object, not Bethel or Gilgal. He was about to take his departure from earth and all its harassing scenes; he was about to leave Ahab and Jezebel behind to meet their terrible doom; to pass beyond the region of broken covenants, ruined altars, and slain prophets—in a word, to pass beyond the gloom and sorrow, trial and disappointment of this stormy world; and that not by the agency of death, but by a heavenly chariot.

Death was to possess no power against this heavenly man. No doubt his body was changed in the twinkling of an eye, for "flesh and blood cannot inherit the kingdom of God, neither doth corruption inherit incorruption"; but death can have no power over him; he rather stepped like a conqueror into his triumphal chariot, and thus passed away into his rest.

Happy man! his conflict was over, his race run, his victory secure. He had been a stranger here—unlike the men of this world; yea, unlike many of the children of the kingdom. He had come forth from the mountains of Gilead as the girded witness, and the stern intruder upon the course of a professing world. He had no home or resting-place here below, but as a stranger and pilgrim pressed onward toward his heavenly rest.

Elijah's path from first to last was a unique one. Like John the Baptist, he was a voice "crying in the wilderness," away from the haunts of men; and whenever he did make his appearance, he was like some heavenly meteor, the origin and destiny of which were alike beyond the reach of human conception. The man with the leathern girdle was only known as the witness against evil—the bearer of the truth of God. He had no fellowship with man as such, but in all his ways maintained an elevation which at once repulsed all intrusion and secured reverence and respect. There was so much of the sacred solemnity of the sanctuary about him that vanity or folly could not live in his presence. He was not, like his successor Elisha, a social man; his path was solitary.

"He came neither eating nor drinking." In a word, he was peculiar in everything; peculiar in his entrance upon his prophetic career, peculiar in his passage out of it. He was an exception, and a marked one. The very fact of his not being called to pass through the gates of the grave would be quite sufficient to draw special attention to him.

But let us observe the path pursued by our prophet as he journeyed toward the scene of his rapture. He retraced the path of the camp of old. Israel had journeyed from Jordan to Jericho, but Elijah journeyed from Jericho to Jordan. In other words, as Jordan was that which separated the wilderness from the land, the prophet crossed it, thus leaving Canaan behind him. His chariot met him, not *in the land, but in the wilderness.* The land was polluted, and was speedily to be cleansed of those who had introduced the pollution; the glory was soon to take its departure from even the most favored spot. Ichabod might be written upon it all; wherefore the prophet leaves it and passes into the wilderness, thus pointing out to the spiritual mind that nothing remained for heavenly men but the wilderness and the rest above.

Earth was no longer to be the resting-place, or portion, of the man of God; it was polluted. The Jordan had been divided to allow Israel to pass from the wilderness to Canaan; it was now to be divided to allow a heavenly man to pass from Canaan to the wilderness where his chariot awaited him, ready to convey him from earth to Heaven.

Earthly things and earthly hopes had passed away from the mind of Elijah, he had learnt the thorough vanity of everything here below, and nothing now remained for him but to look beyond it all. He had toiled amid Israel's broken altars; he had labored and testified for years among a disobedient and gainsaying people; he had longed to depart and be at rest; and now he was about to do so in a way worthy of God—Jehovah Himself was about to place His everlasting arms around and underneath His servant to shield him from the power of death. In his case death was to have no sting and the grave no victory.

Elijah was privileged, as he stood upon the sand of the wilderness, to look right upward and, unimpeded by the humiliating circumstances of sickness and death, see Heaven open to receive him. Not one of the circumstances of fallen humanity fell to the lot of our prophet in the matter of his exit from earth. He exchanged his prophet's mantle for a chariot of fire. He could cheerfully let his mantle drop to earth while he ascended to Heaven. To him earth was but a perishable and polluted speck in God's creation, and most happy was he to lay aside everything which marked his connection with it.

What a position! And yet it is only the position which every heavenly man should occupy. Nature and earth have no longer any claims on the man who believes in Jesus. The Cross has broken all the chains which once bound him to earth. As Jordan separated Elijah from Canaan, and brought him into the wilderness to meet Jehovah's chariot, so the Cross has introduced the believer into new ground; it has brought him into purely wilderness circumstances; it has placed him, too, at the other side of death, with no other object before him than his rapture to meet the Lord in the air.

Such is the real, unquestionable portion of every saint, be he ever so weak, ever so ignorant. The happy experience thereof is, of course, a very different thing. To attain to this we need to be much alone with God, and much in the exercise of a spirit of self-judgment. Flesh and blood can never be brought to understand the rapture of a heavenly man.

Indeed, we find that the sons of the prophets did not understand it either, for they say to Elisha, "Behold now, there be with thy servants fifty strong men: let them go, we pray thee, and seek thy master, lest, peradventure, the Spirit of the Lord hath taken him up, and cast him upon some mountain, or into some valley." Here was their highest thought about the prophet's rapture—"The Spirit of the Lord hath cast him upon some mountain, or into some valley." They could not conceive such a thing as his being carried up to Heaven in a chariot of fire.*

They still tarried amid the things of earth, and had not their spiritual senses sufficiently exercised to perceive and appreciate a truth so glorious. Elisha yielded to their importunity, but they learnt the folly of their thoughts by the fruitless toil of their messengers. Fifty strong men could nowhere find the raptured prophet. He was gone; and it required other strength than that of nature to travel the same road. "The natural man receiveth not the things of the Spirit of God, neither can he know them, because they are spiritually discerned." Those who walk in the Spirit will best understand the prophet's privilege in being delivered from the claims of mortality, and being introduced in a manner so glorious into his heavenly rest.

Such, then, was the end of our prophet's course. A glorious end! Who would not say, "Let my last end be like this"? Blessed be the love that so arranged it that *a man* should be thus honored! Blessed be the grace that led the Son of God—the Prince of life—to stoop from His glory in the heavens and submit to a shameful death upon the cross, by virtue of which, even though yet only in prospect, the prophet Elijah was exempted from the penalty of sin, permitted to pass into the regions of light and immortality without the smell of death having passed upon him!

How we should adore this love, dear Christian reader! Yes; while we trace the footsteps of the remarkable man whose history we have been dwelling upon; while

we follow him from Gilead to Cherith, from Cherith to Zarephath, from Zarephath to Carmel, from Carmel to Horeb, and from Horeb *to Heaven*, we must feel constrained to cry out, "Oh, the matchless love of God!" Who could conceive that mortal man could tread such a course? Who but God could bring about such things?

The path of Elijah the Tishbite magnifies exceedingly the grace of God, and confounds the wisdom of the enemy. The rapture of a saint to Heaven is one of the richest fruits and most magnificent results of redemption. To save a soul from hell is in itself a glorious achievement, a splendid triumph; to raise up the body of a sleeping saint is even a more marked display of divine grace and power; but to take a living man, in the freshness and energy of his natural existence, and carry him from earth to Heaven, is a finer display of the power of God and the value of redemption than anything we can conceive.

Thus it was with Elijah. It was not merely the salvation of his soul, nor the resurrection of his body; but it was the rapture of his person—"body, soul, and spirit." He was taken away from the midst of all the turmoil and confusion around him. The tide of evil might yet have to flow onward; men and principles might continue to work and show themselves. The measure of Israel's iniquities might still have to be filled up and the proud Assyrian enter the scene as the rod of Jehovah's anger to chastise them; but what was all this to the raptured prophet? Nothing. Heaven had opened upon him as he stood a homeless wanderer in the wilderness. He was now to be done with the land of Canaan, with its defilement and degradation, and to take his place above, there to await those momentous scenes in which he was, and is yet, to take a part.

Having thus seen our prophet go into Heaven, our reflections on his life and times might naturally close. Yet there is one scene in particular in which he appears in the New Testament; and did we not dwell for a little upon it, our sketch of him would be

---

* It has been observed by another that the little children who came out of Bethel, and said to Elisha, "Go up, thou bald head," were mocking the idea of rapture. If this be so, they afford a sample of the world in their thoughts about the rapture of the Church.

incomplete. I allude to the mount of transfiguration, where Moses and Elias appeared in glory, and spoke with the Lord Jesus Christ of His decease which He should accomplish at Jerusalem.

The Lord Jesus had taken with Him Peter, James, and John, and brought them up into a high mountain, apart, in order to exhibit in their view a sample of His future glory, that thus their spirits might be fortified against the trying scenes through which both He and they had yet to pass.

What a company! The Son of God, in white and glistering raiment: Moses, type of those who sleep in Jesus; Elias, type of the raptured saints; and Peter, James, and John, who have been styled the pillars of the New Testament Church! Now it is evident that our Lord designed to prepare His apostles for the scene of His sufferings by showing them a specimen of the glory that should follow. He saw the cross, with all its accompanying horrors, in the distance before Him.

Shortly before His transfiguration He said to them, "The Son of man must suffer many things, and be rejected of the elders, and chief priests, and scribes, and be slain, and be raised the third day": but previous to His entering into all this, He would show them something of His glory. The cross is in reality the basis of everything. The future glory of Christ and His saints, the joy of restored Israel in the land of Canaan, and the deliverance of creation from the bondage of corruption, all hang upon the cross of the Lord Jesus Christ. His sorrows and sufferings have secured the Church's glory, Israel's restoration, and the blessing of the whole creation.

No marvel, therefore, that the cross should form the subject of discourse between Christ and His glorious visitors. "They spoke of His decease which He should accomplish at Jerusalem." Everything hung upon this. The past, the present and the future all rested on

the cross as upon an immortal basis. Moses could see and acknowledge in the cross that which superseded the law, with all its shadowy rites and ceremonies; Elijah could see and acknowledge in it that which could give efficacy to all prophetic testimony. The law and the prophets pointed to the cross as the foundation of the glory which lay beyond it.

How profoundly interesting, therefore, was the subject of converse upon the mount of transfiguration, in the midst of the excellent glory! It was interesting to earth, interesting to Heaven, interesting to the wide creation of God. It forms the centre of all the divine purposes and counsels; it harmonizes all the divine attributes; it secures upon immutable principles the glory of God and the sinner's peace; on it may be inscribed in indelible characters "Glory to God in the highest, and on earth peace, good will toward men."

No marvel, therefore, again I say, that Moses and Elias could appear in glory and talk of such a momentous subject. They were about to return to their rest, while their blessed Master had to descend again into the arena of conflict to meet the cross in all its tremendous reality; but they knew full well that He and they would yet meet in the midst of a glory which shall never be overshadowed by a cloud—a glory of which He, the Lamb, was to be the source and the centre forever—a glory which shall shine with everlasting brilliancy when all human and earthly glories shall be overcast by the shadows of an eternal night.

But what of the disciples during all this wondrous converse? How were they employed? They were asleep! Asleep while Moses and Elias conversed with the Son of God concerning His cross and passion! Marvelous insensibility! Nature can sleep in the very presence of the excellent glory.*

"And when they were awake they saw His

* It is not a little remarkable that we find these same disciples asleep during the season of our Lord's agony in the garden. They slept in the view of the glory, and also in the view of the cross. Nature can as little enter into the one as the other. And yet the blessed Master does not rebuke them in either case, save to say to the most prominent and self-confident among them, "Couldst *thou* not watch with Me one hour?" He knew whom He had to do with; He knew that "the spirit is willing, but the flesh is weak." Gracious Master, Thou wast ever ready to make allowance for Thy poor people, and didst say, "Ye are they who have continued with Me in My temptation," to those who had slept on the mount, slept in the garden, and who were about to deny and desert Thee in the hour of Thy deepest need!

glory, and the two men that stood with Him. And it came to pass, as they departed from Him, Peter said unto Jesus, Master, it is good for us to be here; and let us make three tabernacles—one for Thee, one for Moses, and one for Elias—not knowing what he said."

No doubt it was good to be there—far better than to go down from their elevation and glory to meet all the contradiction and trying obloquy of man. When Peter saw the glory, and Moses and Elias, it instantly occurred to his Jewish mind that there was no hindrance to the celebration of the feast of tabernacles. He had been asleep while they spoke of "the decease"; he had been indulging nature whilst his Master's sufferings had formed the subject of discourse; and when he awoke, he would fain pitch his tent in the midst of that scene of peace and glory, beneath the open heavens. But ah, he knew not what he said. It was but a passing moment.

The heavenly strangers were soon to depart; the Lord Jesus was to be delivered into the hands of men. He was to pass from the mount of glory to the place of suffering; Peter himself, too, had yet to be sifted by Satan—to be deeply humbled and broken under a sense of his shameful fall—to be girded by another, and carried whither he would not; a long and a dreary season, a dark night of sorrow and tribulation, was in store for the Church; the armies of Rome were yet to trample the holy city in the dust, and lay waste her bulwarks; the thunders of war and political revolution were yet to roll, with terrible vehemence, over the whole civilized world;—all these things, and many more, were to come to pass, ere the fond thought of poor Peter's heart could be realized on earth. The prophet Elijah must visit the earth again "before the coming of the great and dreadful day of the Lord" (Mal. 4:5). "Elias must first come and restore all things."

How long, O Lord? May this be the continual inquiry of our hearts as we pass along to that rest and glory which lie before us. "Time is short," and eternity, with all its divine and glorious realities, is at hand. May we live in the light of it! May we ever be able, by the eye of faith, to see the bright beams of

the millennial morning—the morning without clouds—irradiating the distance hills!

Everything points to this; every event that happens, every voice that reaches the ear, tells of the speedy approach of the kingdom: the sea and the waves may be heard roaring—nations are convulsed, thrones overturned;—all these things have a voice for the circumcised ear, and the voice is, "Look up!"

Those who have received the Holy Ghost have received the earnest of the future inheritance; and the earnest, as we know, is part of the thing to be received. They have been on the mount; and although the cloud may overshadow them too—although they too may have to come down from the mount to meet the trial and sorrow below—yet they have a foretaste of the joy and blessedness which shall be theirs forever; and they can unfeignedly thank God, as they journey on from day to day, that their hopes are not bounded by this world's gloomy horizon, but that they have a home beyond it all.

> Oh wondrous grace, oh love divine,
>   To give us such a home!
> Let us the present things resign,
>   And seek this rest to come.
> And gazing on our Saviour's cross,
>   Esteem all else but dung and dross;
> Press forward till the race be run,
>   Fight till the crown of life be won.

CONCLUSION

Although, in the character of his ministry, Elijah the Tishbite much resembled John the Baptist, as has been already observed, yet looking at him personally, and considering his unearthly and pilgrim path, and specially his rapture to Heaven, he stands before us as a remarkable illustration of the Church, or heavenly family. Taking this view of him, I think a few observations on the important doctrine of the Church will not be considered out of place as a conclusion to the foregoing sketch of his life and times.

It is of the utmost importance that the Christian reader should understand the doctrine of the Church's heavenly character. It will be found to be the only preservative against the varied forms of evil and unsound doctrine which prevail around us. To be soundly instructed in the heavenly origin, heavenly position, and heavenly destiny of the Church, is the most effectual safeguard against worldliness in the Christian's present path, and also against false teaching in reference to his future hopes.

Every system of doctrine or discipline which would connect the Church with the world, either in her present condition or her future prospects, must be wrong, and must exert an unhallowed influence. The Church is not of the world. Her life, her position, her hopes, are all heavenly in the very highest sense of that word. The calling and existence of the Church are, humanly speaking, consequent upon the present rejection of Israel and the world.

The garden of Eden and the land of Canaan were successively the scenes of divine operation; but sin, as we have often heard, marred them both, and now all who believe the gospel of the grace of God, preached to them in the name of a crucified, risen and ascended Saviour, are constituted living members of the body of Christ, and are called upon to abandon every earthly hope. Being quickened by the voice of Him who has passed into the heavens, and not only so, but being united to Him by the Holy Ghost, they are called to occupy the place of strangers and pilgrims on earth.

The position of Elijah the Tishbite as he stood on the wilderness side of Jordan, waiting for his rapture to Heaven, aptly represents the condition of the Church collectively or the believer individually.* The Church, properly so called, finds (as another has said) "the termini of her existence to be the cross and the coming of the Lord"; and surely, we may say, earth has no place between these sacred bounds. To think of the Church as a worldly corporation, be it ever so sound and scriptural, is to sink far below the divine thought about it.

The doctrine of the Church's heavenly character was developed in all its power and

beauty by the Holy Ghost in the apostle Paul. Up to his time, and even during the early stages of his ministry, the divine purpose was to deal with Israel. There had been all along a chain of witnesses, the object of whose mission was exclusively the house of Israel.

The prophets, as has been already observed in the opening of this paper, bore witness to Israel, not only concerning their complete failure, but also the future establishment of *the kingdom* agreeably to the covenant made with Abraham, Isaac, Jacob, and David. They spoke not of the Church as the body of Christ. How could they, when the thing was a profound mystery, "not revealed to the sons of men"?

The thought of a Church composed of Jew and Gentile, "seated *together* in the heavenlies," lay far beyond the range of prophetic testimony. Isaiah, no doubt, speaks in very elevated strains of Jerusalem's glory in the latter day; he speaks of Gentiles coming to her light, and kings to the brightness of her rising; but he never rises higher than the kingdom, and as a consequence never brings out anything beyond the covenant made with Abraham, which secures everlasting blessedness to his seed, and through them to the Gentiles. We may range through the inspired pages of the law and the prophets, from one end to the other, and find nothing concerning "*the great mystery*" of the Church.

Then, again, in the ministry of John the Baptist we observe the same thing. We have the sum and substance of his testimony in these words: "Repent, for *the kingdom* is at hand." He came as the great precursor of the Messiah, and sought to produce moral order amongst all ranks. He told the people what they were to do in that transition state into which his ministry was designed to conduct them, and pointed to Him that was to come. Have we anything of the *Church* in all this? Not a syllable. The *kingdom* is still the very highest thought. John led his disciples to the waters of Jordan—the place of confession in view of the kingdom; but it was not yet that

* When I say the wilderness side of Jordan, I only speak of Jordan in reference to the prophet's path. If we look at it in reference to the path of Israel from Egypt to Canaan, we learn a different truth. The spiritual reader will understand both.

character of repentance produced in them who are made members of the body of Christ.

The Lord Jesus Himself then took up the chain of testimony. The prophets had been stoned; John had been beheaded; and now "the Faithful Witness" entered the scene, and not only declared that the kingdom was at hand, but presented Himself to the daughter of Zion as her King. He too was rejected, and, like every previous witness, sealed His testimony with His blood. Israel would not have God's King, and God would not give Israel the kingdom.

Next came the twelve apostles, and took up the chain of testimony. Immediately after the resurrection they inquired of the Lord, "Wilt Thou at this time restore again *the kingdom* to Israel?" Their minds were filled with the thought of the kingdom. "We trusted," said the two disciples going to Emmaus, "that it had been He which should have redeemed Israel." And so it was. The question was, *when?* The Lord does not rebuke the disciples for entertaining the thought of the kingdom; He simply tells them, "It is not for you to know *the times or the seasons*, which the Father hath put in His own power. But ye shall receive power, after that the Holy Ghost is come upon you: and ye shall be *witnesses* unto Me both in Jerusalem, and in all Judea, and in Samaria, and unto the uttermost part of the earth" (Acts 1: 7-8).

Agreeably to this, the Apostle Peter, in his address to Israel, offers them *the kingdom*. "Repent ye therefore, and be converted, that your sins may be blotted out, and the times of refreshing shall come from the presence ($\alpha\pi o$ $\pi\rho o\delta\omega\pi o\nu$) of the Lord; and He shall send Jesus Christ which before was preached unto you; whom the heaven must receive until the times of restitution of all things, which God hath spoken by the mouth of all His holy prophets since the world began."

Have we here the development of the Church? No. The time had not yet arrived for this. The revelation of the Church was yet to be, as it were, forced out as something quite extraordinary—something quite out of the regular course of things. The Church as seen in the opening of the Acts exhibits but a sample of lovely grace and order, exquisite indeed in its way, but not anything beyond what man could take cognizance of and value. In a word, it was still the kingdom, and not the great mystery of the Church. Those who think that the opening chapters of Acts present the Church in its essential aspect have by no means reached the divine thought on the subject.

Peter's vision in Acts 10 is decidedly a step in advance of his preaching in chapter 3. Still, however, the grand truth of the heavenly mystery was not yet unfolded. In the council held at Jerusalem for the purpose of considering the question that had arisen in reference to the Gentiles, we find the apostles all agreeing with James in the following conclusion: "Simeon hath declared how God at the first did visit the Gentiles, to take out of them a people for His name. And to this agree the words of the prophets; as it is written, After this I will return, and will build again the tabernacle of David, which is fallen down; and I will build again the ruins thereof, and I will set it up; that the residue of men might seek after the Lord, and all the Gentiles, upon whom My name is called, saith the Lord, who doeth all these things" (Acts 15:14-17).

Here we are taught that the Gentiles, as such, are to have a place with the Jews in the kingdom.

But did the council at Jerusalem apprehend the truth of the Church, of Jews and Gentiles so truly formed in "one body" that they are no more Jew nor Gentile? I believe not. A few members might have heard it from Paul (see Gal. 2:12), but as a whole they do not seem to have understood it as yet.

We infer, therefore, that the preaching of the gospel to the Gentiles by the mouth of Peter was not the development of *the great mystery* of the Church, but simply the opening of *the kingdom*, agreeably to the words of the prophets, and also to Peter's commission in Matt. 16: "And I say unto thee that thou art Peter, and upon this rock I will build My Church; and the gates of hell shall not prevail against it. And I will give unto thee the keys *of the kingdom* of heaven: and whatsoever thou shalt bind *on earth* shall be bound in heaven; and whatsoever thou shalt loose *on earth* shall be loosed in heaven."

Mark, it is "the kingdom," and not the Church. Peter received the keys of the kingdom, and he used those keys, first to open the kingdom to the Jew, and then to the Gentile. But Peter never received a commission to unfold the mystery of the Church. Even in his Epistles we find nothing of it. He views believers on earth; as strangers, no doubt, but yet on earth; having their hope in Heaven and being on their way thither, but never as the body of Christ seated there in Him.

It was reserved for the great apostle of the Gentiles to bring out, in the energy and power of the Holy Ghost, the mystery of which we speak. He was raised up, however, as he himself tells us, before the time. "Last of all, He was seen of me also, as of one born out of due time." Things were not sufficiently matured for the development of the new revelation of which he was made the peculiar minister, and hence he styles himself one born *before* the time; for such is the real force of the original word. And how was he before the time? Because Israel had not as yet been finally set aside. The Lord was still lingering over His beloved city, unwilling to enter into judgment; for, as another has said, "Whenever the Lord leaves a place of mercy, or enters a place of judgment, He moves with a slow and measured pace."

This is most true; and hence, although the apostle of the Gentiles had been raised up and constituted the depositary of a truth which was designed to carry all who should receive it far away beyond the bounds of Jewish things, yet did he make the house of Israel his primary object; and in so doing he worked in company with the twelve, although not a debtor to them in any one way. "It was necessary," says he to the Jews, "that the word of God should *first* have been spoken to you; but seeing ye put it from you,

and judge yourselves unworthy of everlasting life, lo, we turn to the Gentiles" (Acts 13:46).

Why was it necessary? Because of God's long-suffering and grace. Paul was not only the depositary of the divine counsels, but also of divine affections. As the former, he should act upon his peculiar commission; as the latter, he would linger over "his brethren, his kinsmen according to the flesh": as the former, he was called upon to lead the Church into the knowledge of "a mystery which in other ages was not made known to the sons of men"; as the latter, he would, like his Master, with "a slow and measured step," turn his back upon the devoted city and the infatuated nation.

In a word, as the gospel with which he was entrusted could only be proclaimed upon the ground of the total abandonment of earth, the earthly city, and the earthly nation, and as Paul's heart yearned over that nation and city, therefore it was that he was so slow to make known publicly the gospel which he preached. He delayed for fourteen years, as he himself informs us. "Then fourteen years after I went up again to Jerusalem with Barnabas, and took Titus with me also. And I went up by revelation, and communicated unto them that gospel which I preach among the Gentiles, but privately to them which were of reputation, lest by any means I should run, or had run, in vain" (Gal. 2: 1-2).

This is a very important passage on the question now before us. Paul had been raised up quite out of the regular course of things; his ministry was totally divested of the earthly, human and Jewish element; so much so indeed as to give rise to numerous questions as to its divine origin.*

To him was committed what he emphatically styles *his* gospel. But, as has been remarked, it was a question whether things were ripe as regards the divine counsels respecting Israel, for the public development of this gospel. The apostle felt

* There have not been wanting modern teachers who have labored to deprive Paul's ministry of its peculiarly heavenly character by placing him among the regular college of apostles, whose aspect and bearing were manifestly Jewish. This they do by calling in question the election of Matthias. But to all those who need more than the exercise of spiritual judgment to guide them in this matter it may be sufficient to say that the Holy Ghost raised no question as to the validity of Mattias's election, for He fell upon him in common with his fellow-apostles. However, we can well understand why those who feel themselves called upon to uphold human systems should labor so diligently to reduce our apostle's ministry to a human, or earthly level.

this to be a momentous question: hence his caution in communicating it *severally* to a few. He could not, even in the midst of the Church at Jerusalem, speak openly on this grand question, because he feared that the full time had not come, and that, should he develop it prematurely, few had sufficient spiritual intelligence or largeness of mind to understand or enter into it. His fears, as we know, were well grounded. There were few at Jerusalem who were at all prepared for Paul's gospel.

Even some years later we find James, who seems to have taken a very prominent place in the Church of Jerusalem, inducing Paul to purify himself and shave his head. And what was this for? Just to prevent a break-up of the earthly thing.

"Thou seest, brother," said James, "how many thousands of Jews there are which believe; and they are all zealous of the law. And they are informed of thee that thou teachest all the Jews which are among the Gentiles to forsake Moses, saying that they ought not to circumcise their children, neither to walk after the customs. What is it therefore? The multitude must needs come together; for they will hear that thou art come. Do therefore this that we say to thee: we have four men which have a vow on them; them take, and purify thyself with them, and be at charges with them, that they may shave their heads; and all may know that those things whereof they were informed concerning thee are nothing, but that thou thyself also walkest orderly, and keepest the law" (Acts 21:20-24). Here, then, we have abundant proof of the fact that the great mystery was not understood and would not be received by the Church at Jerusalem.*

Now, one can well understand how the spirit of James would have shrunk from the terrible break-up which must have resulted from the public declaration of Paul's gospel amongst those whose hearts still clung to the earthly thing. True, it was the privilege of believing Jews to breathe a purer atmosphere than that of an earthly

sanctuary, yet they were not prepared for the strong meat of Paul's gospel, and moreover the heart would cling with peculiar fondness to the thought that Jerusalem was to be a great focus of Christian light and testimony from whence the rays of gospel truth should emanate to enlighten all around. But if the mystery which Paul had communicated to them privately were to be made known to the multitude, "the many thousands of Jews" would not receive it, and thus the great centre of light would have become the centre of division.

Moreover, the very same motive which had actuated Paul on the occasion of his former visit to Jerusalem, when he communicated his gospel only to a few, lest he should run in vain if things were not ripe for the revelation—the same motive, we say, might have led him at a later period to hold his gospel in abeyance, and accommodate himself to the thoughts and feelings of those who had not as yet got beyond the earthly order of things.

Every affection of Paul's heart as a man and a Jew would have led him to linger at Jerusalem, and also to hesitate in the development of a doctrine which would cast Jerusalem and all earthly things into the shade, and raise the thoughts and affections into a far higher and purer region than had yet been realized. Paul knew full well the vanity and emptiness of vows and purifications. He saw nothing in the temple and its splendid ceremonies save a vast system of shadows of which the substance was in Heaven.

Yet his affectionate heart yearned over his brethren who were still captivated by it all, and therefore he hesitated to let the full blaze of the light which had been communicated to him shine upon them, lest it should dazzle them, habituated as they were to the shadows of bygone days.

If this be a sound view of the conduct of our apostle in the matter of the vow, etc., it places him before us in a most truly interesting point of view, and also brings out

* The circumstance to which allusion is made in the above quotation occurred some years later than the visit to which Paul refers in Gal. 2. The latter would seem to have been occasioned by the controversy respecting the Gentiles. This fact gives additional force to the expression "Severally to them which were of reputation." Paul could not communicate his gospel to them *en masse*.

very distinctly the two features of his character, namely, as the participator in the divine affections towards Israel, and also as the depositary of the divine counsels respecting the Church. Both these are lovely in their way. His fervent affection for Israel and his faithfulness to his own peculiar commission are both exquisite. Some may think he allowed the former to interfere at times with the latter, as in the matter of the vow; but it was an interference which we can well understand and account for.

His heart, however, led him to tarry in Jerusalem; yea, to tarry until the Lord had to compel him to leave it. His commission was to the Gentiles; and yet, again and again he betakes himself to Jerusalem, and in his unwillingness to depart from it reminds us of the "slow and measured steps" with which the glory as seen by Ezekiel had departed from the temple.

But the Lord would insist upon His servant's leaving Jerusalem. "*Make haste*," said He, "and *get thee quickly* out of Jerusalem; for they will not receive *thy* testimony concerning Me." Paul's Jewish heart still lingers. He replies, "They know that I imprisoned and beat in every synagogue them that believed on Thee; and when the blood of Thy martyr Stephen was shed, I was also standing by and consenting unto his death, and kept the raiment of them that slew him."

What pleading is here! "Their unbelief is all my fault; my vileness acts as the great barrier to their reception of the testimony—only let me remain." Impossible! "Depart: for I will send thee *far hence, to the Gentiles*." Yes; the truth must be brought out; the divine counsels must be fulfilled; the time was come, and it was in vain for James to seek to stem the mighty current of events, or for Paul to linger or hesitate any longer: the crisis had arrived, and if Paul will after all this return to Jerusalem again, he must be carried away from it in bonds! He does return again.

The passage we have just quoted is Paul's own account of what the Lord had said to him on a former occasion, to which we have no allusion till now. Thus, although he had been expressly told to depart from Jerusalem because they would not receive his testimony, he goes thither again; and we know the result of this visit. It was his last.

The very thing that James dreaded and sought to avoid came upon them: an uproar was raised, and Paul was delivered over into the hands of the Gentiles. The Lord was determined to send him to the Gentiles. If he would not go as a free man, he must go as "an ambassador in bonds." He could say, however, that it was for "the hope of Israel that he was bound with this chain." If his heart had not longed so after Israel, he might have escaped the bonds. He left Israel without excuse, but he himself became a prisoner and a martyr.

Thus then, at length, Paul took leave of Jerusalem. He had visited it again and again, and would have tarried there; but it was not his place. Jerusalem had been for ages the object of divine regard and the centre of divine operation, but it was speedily about to be trodden down of the Gentiles; its temple was about to be laid in ruins, and the flock of Christ that had been gathered there was about to be scattered abroad; a few short years, and that spot which had stood so long connected with all God's thoughts about earth would be laid low, even with the dust, beneath the rude foot of the Roman.

Now Paul's departure may be looked upon as the immediate precursor of all this. The peculiar truth of which he was the depositary could only be brought out in all its fulness and power in connection with the abandonment of earth as the *manifested* scene of divine operation. Hence Paul's journey from Jerusalem to Rome must be viewed with deepest interest by the intelligent and reflecting Christian.*

* It is a thought full of interest, in connection with the subject before us, that Paul's voyage to Rome gives us the history of the Church as regards its earthly destinies. The vessel sets out in due order, as a compact and well regulated thing, framed to endure the violence of the stormy ocean over which it had to pass. After a time the apostle offers a certain suggestion, which, being rejected, the ship is dashed to pieces by the waves. There was, however, an important distinction between the vessel and the individuals on board: the former was lost, the latter were all saved. Let us apply all this to the history of the Church in its earthly path. The testimony, as we know, emanated from Jerusalem, whence Paul started on his way to Rome. Apostolic testimony was designed to guide the Church in its earthly course, and preserve it from shipwreck; but this being rejected, failure and ruin were the consequences. But, in the progress of the failure, we perceive the distinction between the preservation of the Church's

But we may ask, did our apostle, when he turned his back upon Jerusalem, take leave also of Israel? No; he did not yet despair. True they had not received his testimony at Jerusalem, but perhaps they might receive it at Rome: they had not given him a place in the East, perhaps they would in the West. At all events he would try. He would not abandon Israel, though Israel had rejected him.

Hence we read that "after three days [from the time of his arrival at Rome] Paul called *the chief of the Jews* together; and when they were come together, he said unto them, Men and brethren, though I have committed nothing against the people or customs of our fathers, yet was I delivered prisoner from Jerusalem into the hands of the Romans. . . . For this cause therefore have I called for you, to see you, and to speak with you; because that for the hope of Israel I am bound with this chain. . . . And when they had appointed him a day, there came many to him into his lodging; to whom he expounded and testified the kingdom of God, persuading them concerning Jesus, both out of the law of Moses and out of the prophets, from morning till evening" (Acts 28: 17, 20, 23).

Here, then, we have this blessed "ambassador in bonds" still seeking out "the lost sheep of the house of Israel," and offering them, in the first place, "the salvation of God." But "they agreed not among themselves," and at last Paul is constrained to say, "Well spake the Holy Ghost by Esaias the prophet unto our fathers, saying, Go unto this people and say, Hearing ye shall hear, and not understand; and seeing ye shall see, and not perceive; for the heart of this people is waxed gross, and their ears are dull of hearing, and their eyes have they closed, lest they should see with their eyes, and hear with their ears, and understand with their heart, and should be converted and I should heal them. *Be it known therefore unto you, that the salvation of God is sent unto the Gentiles, and that they will hear it."*

There was now no more hope. Every effort that love could make had been made, but to no purpose; and our apostle, with a reluctant heart, shuts them up under the power of that judicial blindness which was the natural result of their rejection of the salvation of God. Thus every obstacle to the clear and full development of Paul's gospel was removed. He found himself in the midst of the wide Gentile world—a prisoner at Rome and rejected of Israel. He had done his utmost to tarry among them; his affectionate heart led him to delay as long as possible ere he would reiterate the prophet's verdict; but now all was over—every expectation was blasted—all human institutions and associations present to his view nothing but ruin and disappointment; he must therefore set himself to bring out that holy and heavenly mystery which had been hid in God from ages and generations—the mystery of the Church as the body of Christ united to its living Head by the Holy Ghost.

Thus closes the Acts of the Apostles, which, like the Gospels, is more or less connected with the testimony to Israel. So long as Israel could be regarded as the object of testimony, so long the testimony continued; but when they were shut up to judicial blindness, they ceased to come within the range of testimony, wherefore the testimony ceased.

And now let us see what this "mystery," this "gospel," this "salvation," really was, and wherein its peculiarity consisted. To understand this is of the utmost importance. What, therefore, was Paul's gospel? Was it a different method of justifying a sinner from that preached by the other apostles? No; by no means. Paul preached both to the Jews and also to the Gentiles "repentance toward God, and faith toward our Lord Jesus Christ." This was the substance of his preaching.

The peculiarity of the gospel preached by Paul had not so much reference to God's way of dealing with *the sinner* as with *the saint;* it was not so much how God justified a sinner as

corporate testimony and individual faithfulness and salvation. "He that hath ears to hear" will always find a word of instruction and guidance for him in times of thickest darkness. The waves may dash in pieces the corporate thing—everything connected with earth may vanish away, "but he that doeth the will of God abideth forever." The above picture might be traced far more minutely by those who feel they have intelligence and warrant to do so.

what He did with him when justified. Yes; it was the place into which Paul's gospel conducted the *saint* that marked its peculiarity. As regards the justification of a sinner, there could be but one way, namely, through faith in the one offering of the Lord Jesus Christ.

But there could be numerous degrees of elevation as regards the standing of the saint. For example, a saint in the opening of Acts had higher privileges than a saint under the law. Moses, the prophets, John, our Lord in His personal ministry, and the twelve, all brought out varied aspects of the believer's position before God. But Paul's gospel went far beyond them all. It was not the kingdom offered to Israel on the ground of repentance, as by John the Baptist and our Lord; nor was it the kingdom opened to Jew and Gentile by Peter in Acts 3 and 10; but it was *the heavenly calling of the Church of God composed of Jew and Gentile, in one body, united to a glorified Christ by the presence of the Holy Ghost.*

The Epistle to the Ephesians fully develops the mystery of the will of God concerning this. There we find ample instruction as to our heavenly standing, heavenly hopes, and heavenly conflict. The apostle does not contemplate the Church as a pilgrim *on earth*, (which, we need not say, is most true,) but as sitting *in Heaven:* not as toiling *here*, but resting *there*. "He hath raised us up together, and made us *sit* together in heavenly places in Christ Jesus." It is not that He *will* do this, but "He hath" done it. When Christ was raised from the dead, all the members of His body were raised also; when He ascended into Heaven, they ascended also; when He sat down, they sat down also; that is, in the counsel of God, and to be actualized in process of time by the Holy Ghost sent down from Heaven.

Such was the thought and purpose of the divine mind concerning them. Believers did not know this at the first; it was not unfolded by the ministry of the twelve, as seen in the Acts of the Apostles, because the testimony to Israel was still going on; and so long as earth was the manifested scene of divine operation, and so long as there was any ground of hope in connection with Israel, the heavenly mystery was held back; but when earth had been abandoned and Israel set aside, the apostle of the Gentiles, from his prison at Rome, writes to the Church, and opens out all the glorious privileges connected with its place in the Heavens with Christ.

When Paul arrived at Rome as a prisoner, he had, as it were, arrived at the end of all human things. He no longer thought of the Church as exhibiting anything like a perfect testimony on earth. He knew how things would turn out as regards the Church's earthly path; he knew that it would fare with it even as it had fared with the vessel in which he had sailed from Jerusalem to Rome; but his spirit was buoyed up by the happy assurance that nothing could touch the unity of the body of Christ, because it was a unity infallibly maintained by God Himself.*

This was the spring of Paul's joy as he lay a despised and neglected prisoner in the dungeon of Nero. He was not ashamed, for he knew that the Church, though broken in pieces here, was nevertheless held in the everlasting grasp of the Son of God, and that He was able to keep it until the happy moment of its rapture to meet Him in the air.**

But it may be asked: How can believers be said to be seated in heavenly places when they are yet in the world, struggling with its difficulties, its sorrows and temptations? The same question may be asked in reference to

* I believe it is of the deepest moment that the believer should avoid all looseness of thought, or indifference, in reference to the presence of the Holy Ghost in the Church and the unity of the body of Christ. The man who holds the former will assuredly seek the latter.

** A letter has been put into my hand, from a dear and valued servant of Christ, from which I extract the following statements, which are well worthy of attention: "The Holy Ghost came down from heaven to form one body on the earth; 'for by one Spirit are we all baptized into one body.' This is the unity we are responsible to maintain—the unity of the Spirit; the other, final one, God secures infallibly. If God set in the Church 'healings,' it certainly is not in heaven. One has only to read 1 Cor. 10:11 to learn that the unity of the Church on earth is a fundamental, essential, divine institution—the cardinal truth which will distinguish, I believe, those who have faith to walk devotedly in these last days, and without which the expectation of Christ will be only personal deliverance, and not 'The Spirit and the Bride say, Come.' "

the important doctrine of Rom. 6: How can believers be represented as dead to sin when they find sin working in them continually? The answer to both is one and the same.

God sees the believer as dead with Christ, and He also sees the Church as raised with and seated in Christ; but it is the province of faith to lead the soul into the reality of both. "Reckon yourselves to be" what God tells you you are. The believer's power to subdue indwelling corruption consists in his reckoning himself to be dead to it; and his power of separation from the world consists in his reckoning himself to be raised with Christ and seated in Him. The Church, according to God's estimation, has as little to do with sin and the world as Christ has; but God's thoughts and our apprehensions are very different things.

We must never forget that every tendency of the human mind not only falls short of but stands actually opposed to all this divine truth about the Church. We have seen how long it was ere man could take hold of it—how it was forced out, as it were, and pressed upon him; and we have only to glance at the history of the Church for the last eighteen centuries to see how feebly it was held and how speedily it was let go. The heart naturally clings to earth, and the thought of an earthly corporation is attractive to it.

Hence we may expect that the truth of the Church's heavenly character will only be apprehended and carried out by a very small and feeble minority.

It is not to be supposed that the Protestant reformers exercised their thoughts on this momentous subject. They were made instrumental in bringing out the precious doctrine of justification by faith from amid the rubbish of Romish superstition, and also in letting in upon the human conscience the light of inspiration in opposition to the false and ensnaring dogmas of human tradition.

This was doing not a little: yet it must be admitted the position and hopes of the Church engaged not their attention. It would have been a bold step from the church of Rome to the Church of God; and yet it will be found in the end that there is not distinct neutral ground between the two; for every church, or, to speak more accurately, every religious corporation, reared up and carried on by the wisdom and resources of man, be its principle ever so pure and ever so hostile to Catholicism, will be found, when judged by the Spirit, and in the light of Heaven, to partake more or less of the element of the Romish system.

The heart clings to earth, and will with difficulty be led to believe that the only time wherein God ceases to be manifestly occupied about earth—that the only unnoticed interval in the history of time—is just the period wherein He, by the Holy Ghost, is gathering out the Church to form the body of Christ; and moreover, that when God was dealing publicly with earth, the Church, properly so called, was not contemplated; and that when He shall resume His public dealings with the earth and with Israel, the Church will be out of the scene.

To understand all this requires a larger measure of spirituality than is to be found with many Christians.* The question naturally arises in the mind of the inquirer after truth, "What is the most scriptural form of Church government?" To what body of Christians should I attach myself?" The answer to such questions is, "Attach yourself to those who are 'endeavoring to keep the unity of the Spirit in the bond of peace.'"

Sects are not the Church, nor religious parties the body of Christ. Hence, to be attached to the sects is to find ourselves in some of those numerous tributary streams which are rapidly flowing onward into the terrible vortex of which we read in Rev. 17

---

* The reader will, I trust, understand the distinction between God's *public* actings and His secret operations by His providence. The former ceased when Israel was set aside, and will be resumed when Israel comes again into notice; the latter are going on now. God controls the wheels of government and the counsels of kings to bring about His own great designs.

Deep in unfathomable mines
Of never-failing skill,
He treasures up His bright designs,
And works His sovereign will.

and 18. Let us not be deceived—principles will work, and systems will find their proper level. Prejudice will operate, and hinder the carrying out of those heavenly principles of which we speak.

Those who will maintain Paul's gospel will find themselves, like him, deserted and despised amid the splendid pomp and glitter of the world. The clashing of ecclesiastical systems, the jarring of sects, and the din of religious controversy, will surely drown the feeble voices of those who would speak of the heavenly calling and rapture of the Church.

But let the spiritual man who finds himself in the midst of all this sad and heart-sickening confusion remember the following simple principle: *Every system of ecclesiastical discipline, and every system of prophetic interpretation, which would connect the Church, in any one way, with the world, or things of the world, must be contrary to the spirit and principles of the great mystery developed by the Holy Ghost in the apostle of the Gentiles.*

The Church stands in no need of the world's aid in the matter of order or discipline. The Holy Ghost dwells in the Church, broken and scattered though it be, notwithstanding all man's unbelief about it; and if there be any introduction of the earthly or human element, it can only have the sad effect of grieving Him whose presence is the very light of believers and the spring and power of ministry and discipline.

And then, as to the Church's hope, "we look for the Saviour," and not for the accomplishment of any earthly event. Thank God, believers are not taught to wait for the revelation of Antichrist, but for the appearing of the blessed Son of God, who loved them and gave Himself for them. Christians should understand that they have nothing to look for save their rapture into the air to meet the Lord. The world may ridicule the idea, and false teachers may build up systems hostile to it, for the purpose of shaking the faith of the simple-minded; but through grace we will continue to "comfort one another" with the assurance that "the days are at hand, and the effect of every vision."

I must now close this paper. I am deeply conscious of how feebly and incoherently I have developed what I have in my mind concerning the doctrine of the Church; but I have no doubt of its real importance, and feel assured that as the time draws near much light will be communicated to believers about it. At present, it is to be feared, few really enter into it.

If it were understood, there would be far less effort to attain a name and a place on earth. Paul, the great witness of the Church's heavenly calling, must have exhibited a poor spectacle in the view of the children of this world, and so will all who maintain his principles and walk in his steps; but he comforted his spirit with the thought that "the foundation of God standeth sure, having this seal, the Lord knoweth them that are His"; and he also knew that in the very darkest time there would be a few who would "call on the Lord out of a pure heart." May our lot be cast among such, in the midst of this sorrowful scene, until we shall see Jesus as He is, and be made like Him forever!

JEHOSHAPHAT

WORLDLINESS

IN TRACING THE INSPIRED RECORD of the houses of Israel and Judah, from the period of their separation, under Rehoboam, we can without difficulty recognize the marked distinction between them. The line of kings from Jeroboam to Hosea presents only a dark and sorrowful catalogue of evil-doers in the sight of the Lord: we look in vain for an exception. Even Jehu, who manifested so much zeal and energy in the abolition of idolatry, proved, in the sequel, that his heart was far from being right with God. In fact, a dark cloud of idolatry seems to have settled upon the whole house of Israel, until they were carried away beyond Babylon, and scattered amongst the Gentiles.

Not so, however, with Judah. Here we find some happy exceptions—some pleasant rays from that lamp which the Lord so graciously granted in Jerusalem for David His servant's sake. The soul is refreshed by the history of such men as Josiah, Asa, Joash, and Hezekiah—men whose hearts were devoted to the service of the sanctuary, and who therefore exerted a holy influence on their times.

It is on the narrative of one of these blessed exceptions that I desire to dwell for a little, trusting the Lord to give instruction and profit in so doing.

Jehoshaphat, king of Judah, is introduced to our notice in 2 Chronicles 17. In this chapter, we find God, in His grace, establishing His servant in the kingdom, and the people of God acknowledging him therein. Jehoshaphat's first act was to "strengthen himself against Israel." This is worthy of notice. Israel and Israel's king were ever a snare to the heart of Jehoshaphat. But in the opening of his course, in the season of his early freshness, he was able to fortify his kingdom against the

power of Israel. Now, one frequently observes this in the history of Christians; the evils which in after life prove their greatest snares are those against which there is the greatest watchfulness at first.

Most happy is it when the spirit of watchfulness increases with our increasing knowledge of the tendencies and capabilities of our hearts. But this, alas! is not always the way: on the contrary, how frequently do we find Christians of some years' standing indulging in things which at first their consciences would have shrunk from. This may seem to be but a growing out of a legal spirit; but should it not rather be viewed as a growing out of a tender and sensitive conscience? It would be sad if the result of more enlarged views were to be a careless spirit or a seared conscience; or if high principles of truth did but tend to render those who were once self-denying and separated, self-indulgent, careless, and worldly. But it is not so. To grow in the knowledge of truth is to grow in the knowledge of God, and to grow in the knowledge of God is to grow in practical holiness. The conscience that can let pass without reproof things from which it would formerly have shrunk is, it is much to be feared, instead of being under the action of the truth of God, under the hardening influence of the deceitfulness of sin.

The whole scene presented to us (chap. 17) is full of interest. Jehoshaphat not only retains the conquests of Asa, his father, but goes on to extend, by his personal exertions, the interests of his kingdom. All is well ordered. "The Lord was with Jehoshaphat, because he walked in *the first ways* of his father David, and sought not unto Baalim; but sought to the Lord God of his father, and walked in His commandments, and not after

337

the doings of Israel. Therefore the Lord established the kingdom in his hand; and all Judah brought to Jehoshaphat presents; and he had riches and honor in abundance. And his heart was lifted up in the ways of the Lord: moreover, he took away the high places and groves out of Israel." Here was the true secret of his prosperity: "His heart was lifted up in the ways of the Lord." When the heart is *thus* lifted up, every thing goes well.

In chap. 18, however, we have a very different state of things. Jehoshaphat's prosperity is used by the devil as a snare for him. "Jehoshaphat had riches and honors in abundance, and *joined affinity with Ahab.*" We have already observed Jehoshaphat fortifying his *kingdom;* but the enemy comes upon him in a way for which Jehoshaphat does not seem to have prepared himself; he does not attack his *kingdom*, he attacks his *heart*. He comes not as the lion, but as the serpent. Ahab's "sheep and oxen" are found more suitable and effectual than Ahab's men of war. Had Ahab declared war against Jehoshaphat, it would only have cast him upon the Lord; but he does not. Jehoshaphat's kingdom is fortified against Ahab's hostilities, but his heart lies open to Ahab's allurements. This is truly solemn! We often make a great effort against evil in one shape, while we are allowing it to get in upon us in another.

Jehoshaphat had at first strengthened himself against Israel, but now he joins affinity with Israel's king. And why? Had any change for the better taken place? Had Ahab's heart become more tender toward the Lord? By no means. *He* was still the same, but Jehoshaphat's conscience had lost much of its early tenderness and sensitiveness: he had come near to the evil, and tampered with it; he had touched the pitch, and was defiled by it. "He joined affinity with Ahab." Here was the evil—an evil which, however slow in its operation, would certainly produce its own fruit sooner or later. "He that soweth to his flesh shall of the flesh reap corruption" (Gal. 6:8). The truth of this must inevitably be realized. Grace may triumph in the forgiveness of sin, but the legitimate fruit

will spring forth in due time. The Lord put away David's sin in the matter of Uriah, but the child died, and Absalom arose in rebellion. So it will ever be. If we sow to the flesh, we must reap corruption; the flesh can produce naught else.

In Jehoshaphat's case, it was not until *after years* that the results of his false steps began to show themselves: "And after certain years, he went down to Ahab to Samaria; and Ahab killed sheep and oxen for him in abundance, and for the people he had with him, and persuaded him to go up with him to Ramoth-gilead." Satan knows his ground; he knows where the seed of evil has taken root; he knows the heart that is prepared to respond to his temptation; he knew that the "affinity" into which the king of Judah had entered with the king of Israel had prepared him for further steps in a downward course. When a Christian enters into connection with the world, he lays himself open to be *"persuaded"* by the world, to enter upon an *un*christian course of action. David took Ziklag from Achish (1 Sam. 27:6), and the next step was, to join Achish against Israel (1 Sam. 28:1).

The world will never give any thing to a child of God without making large demands in return. When the king of Judah had allowed Ahab to kill sheep and oxen for him, he would have found it difficult not to meet Ahab's desire in reference to Ramoth-gilead. The safest way therefore is, to be no debtor to the world. Jehoshaphat should have had nothing whatever to do with Ahab; he should have kept himself pure. The Lord was not with Ahab, and though it might seem a desirable thing to recover one of the cities of refuge out of the hand of the enemy, yet Jehoshaphat should have known that he was not to do evil that good might come. If we join with the world in its schemes, we must expect to be identified with it in its convulsions.

Ramoth-gilead had been of old assigned as a city of refuge for the slayer (Deut. 4:43), and to recover this city from the king of Syria was the object of Ahab's expedition. But behind this we can detect the snare of the enemy, who cared little about the city, provided he could thereby betray a child of God from the path of purity and separation. The devil has always found religious and benevolent objects most effectual in their influence upon the people of God. He does not come at first with something openly ungodly; he does not tempt a believer to join the world for some wicked design, because he knows that the sensitive conscience would shrink from such a thing; his way is rather to present in the distance some desirable object—to cover his schemes with the cloak of religion or benevolence, and thus insnare.

There is, however, one truth which would, if realized, effectually deliver the Christian from all connection with the men of this world. The apostle, by the Holy Ghost, teaches us that unbelievers are "unto *every* good work reprobate" (Tit. 1:16). This is enough for an obedient soul. We must not join with those who are so represented. It matters not what they propose—be it a work of benevolence or a work of religion,—Scripture tells us they are reprobate, yes, "reprobate," though they profess that they know God. This should be sufficient. God cannot accept or acknowledge the works or offerings of those whose hearts are far from Him; nor should the Church mingle with such, even though it be for the accomplishment of desirable ends. "Keep thyself pure" is a valuable admonition for us all. "To obey is better than sacrifice, and to hearken than the fat of rams." It would have been infinitely better and more acceptable for Jehoshaphat to have kept himself pure from all contact with Ahab's defilement than to have recovered Ramoth from the Syrians, even had he succeeded in doing so.

However, he had to learn this by painful experience. And thus it is that most of us learn our lessons. We may *speak* much of certain points of truth, while we know but little of having learnt them experimentally. When Jehoshaphat at the commencement of his career strengthened himself against Israel, he had little idea of the way in which he would afterward be insnared by the very worst of Israelites. The only effectual safeguard against evil is, to be in communion with God about it. When we look at evil in the light of the holiness of God, we not only look at the *act,* but at the *principle;* and if the principle be unsound, no matter what the result may be, we should have nothing to do with it. But to deal thus with evil requires much exercise of soul before God—much spirituality, much self-judgment, much prayer and watchfulness. The Lord grant us these, and also more tenderness and godly sensitiveness of conscience.

We have no idea of the sad consequences of a mistake on the part of a child of God. It is not always that the full results appear to us; but the enemy takes care to make his own use of the matter, not in injury done to the one who makes the mistake merely, but to others who witness and are influenced by it. Jehoshaphat did not only fall into the snare himself, but he led others in also. "I am as thou art," said he; and further, "My people as thy people." What miserably low ground for a man of God to take! and what a place to put the people of God into—"*I am as thou art*"! Thus spake Jehoshaphat, and well was it for him that his words were not verified throughout. God did not judge of *him* as He judged of *Ahab;* here was his real security, even in the midst of the terrible consequences of his unguarded conduct. He was not as Ahab in the close of his career, though he had joined affinity with him for the purpose of carrying out his plans; he was not as Ahab when Ahab was pierced by an arrow; he was not as Ahab when the dogs licked Ahab's blood. The Lord had made him to differ.

But we should remember that when the Christian joins with the world for any purpose whatsoever, whether of religion or of benevolence, he is just saying (as Jehoshaphat said to Ahab), "I am as thou art." Let the Christian reader ask his own heart, Is this right? Is he prepared to say this? It will not do to say, "We are not to judge others." Jehoshaphat ought to have judged, as is manifested from the language of Jehu the prophet, when he met him on his return from Ramoth, "Shouldst thou help the ungodly, and love them that hate the Lord?" How was he to know who was ungodly, or who hated the Lord, if he did not exercise judgment? We have certainly no right to judge those that are without, but we are bound to exercise judgment as to those with whom we enter into fellowship. Nor does this in the least involve of necessity the idea of one's own personal superiority in any one particular. No; it is not, "Stand by thyself: *I* am holier than *thou;*" but, "I must stand apart, because *God is holy.*" This is the true principle. It is upon the ground of what God is (not of what we are) that we separate from known evil. "Be *ye* holy, for *I* am holy."

Jehoshaphat, however, failed to maintain this separation; and, as has been already remarked, in failing himself, led others into failure. In this we may learn a most solemn lesson. Jehoshaphat had, we may suppose, gained very considerable influence over the hearts of the people by his previous devotedness; he had established himself in their confidence and affections; and, to a certain extent, rightly so. It is right that those who walk devotedly should be loved and confided in; but then we must watch most jealously against the dangerous tendency of mere personal influence. No one save a man of extensive influence could have said, "My people are as thy people." He might have said, "I am as thou art," but no more. His extensive influence, when used out of communion, only made him a more efficient instrument of evil. Satan knew this; he knew his mark; he did not fasten on an ordinary man of Judah, but on the most prominent and influential man he could find, well knowing that if he could only succeed in drawing him aside, others would follow in his train.

Nor was he mistaken. Many would no doubt say, "What harm can there be in joining Ahab's expedition? Surely, if there were any thing wrong in it, such a good man as king Jehoshaphat would not engage in it. So long as we see *him* there, *we* may make our minds easy about the matter." But if this were not the language of some in Jehoshaphat's day, it certainly is of many in our own. How often do we hear Christians say, "How can such-and-such things be wrong, when we see such good men in connection with them, or engaging in them?" Now all that can be said of such reasoning is

that it is utterly false; it is beginning quite at the wrong end. We are responsible to God to act upon principle, let others do as they may. We should be able, through grace, humbly, yet decidedly, to render a sound and intelligent reason for whatever course of action we may adopt, without any reference to the conduct of others. Moreover, we know full well that good men go astray, and do wrong things. They are not, therefore, nor can they be, our guides. "To his own master he standeth or falleth." A spiritual mind, a conscience enlightened by the Word of God, a real sense of personal responsibility, together with honesty of purpose, are what we specially need. If we lack these, our path will be defective.

But it may be said, there are few, if any, who occupy a position in which their conduct could exert such an extensive influence as that of king Jehoshaphat. To meet this, it may be needful to dwell a little upon a truth sadly neglected in the present day, namely, that of *the unity of the body of Christ, and the consequent effect which the conduct of each member, however obscure, must produce upon the whole body.*

The great doctrine of the unity of the Church upon earth is, it is to be feared, feebly apprehended and feebly carried out, even by the most spiritually minded and intelligent of the Lord's people. The reason of this is very apparent. The doctrine is viewed rather in the light of the Church's present condition, than of her condition as presented in the New Testament; and this being so, the unity never can be understood. If we simply take Scripture for our guide, we shall have no difficulty about it. There we read, "If *one* member suffer, *all* the members suffer with it." This principle did not hold good in the days of king Jehoshaphat, because the body of Christ, properly so called, had no actual existence. All the members of it were written in God's book; but "as yet there was none of them"—they existed in the purpose of God, but that purpose had not been actualized. Hence, though so many were led astray by the influence of Jehoshaphat, it was not by any means on the principle stated in the above passage; it was not all suffering from the act of one because they were one body, but many being led astray by one because they followed his example. The distinction is very important. There is no member of the Church, how obscure soever, whose path and conduct do not affect, in some measure, all the members. "By one Spirit are we all baptized into one body, whether we be Jews or Gentiles, whether we be bond or free; and have been all made to drink into one Spirit." Hence, if a Christian be walking loosely or carelessly,—if he be out of communion—if he fail in prayer, in watchfulness, or in self-judgment, he is really injuring the whole body; and, on the contrary, when he is walking in spiritual health and vigor, he is promoting the blessing and interest of all.

It was not without a struggle that Jehoshaphat yielded to the solicitations of Ahab. The working of conscience is observable in the words, "Inquire, I pray thee, at the word of the Lord today." But ah! how futile was prayer for guidance, when he had already said, "I am as thou art, and my people as thy people; and we will be with thee in the war"! It is but solemn mockery to ask for guidance when we have made up our minds; and yet how frequently we do so! How frequently do we decide on a course of action, and then go and ask the Lord about it! All this is wretched; it is only honoring God with the lips, while the heart is in positive rebellion against Him. Instead of getting that guidance for which we profess to ask, may we not rather expect a lying spirit to be sent forth to us? (verse 21) Ahab was at no loss for counselors. He speedily "gathered together four hundred prophets," who were ready to counsel him according to his heart's desire: "Go up, for God will deliver it into the king's hand." This was what he wanted. Nor need we marvel at Ahab's being quite satisfied with prophets like these. They suited him well.

But surely Jehoshaphat should not have even appeared to acknowledge them to be prophets of the Lord, as he evidently did, by saying, "Is there not here a prophet of the Lord *besides?*" (or, as the margin reads, "yet one more?") Had he been faithful to the Lord, he would at once have denied the right of these false prophets to give counsel. But, alas! he was giving full countenance to the religion of the world, and to these its ministers. He could not bring himself to hurt Ahab's feelings by dealing faithfully with his prophets. They were all, it would seem, proper men.

How dreadful a thing it is to allow ourselves to get into a condition of soul in which we are unable to bear distinct and faithful testimony against the ministers of Satan! "We must," it is said, "be liberal;" "we must not hurt people's feelings;" "there are good men every where." But truth is truth, and we are not to put error for truth, nor truth for error. Nothing but a secret desire to stand well with the world will ever lead to this careless method of dealing with evil. Now, if we want to stand well with the world, let us do it at our own charges, and not at the expense of God's truth. It is often urged, "We must present truth in such an aspect as will attract," when what is really meant is this, that truth is to be made a kind of variable, elastic thing, which can be turned into any shape, or stretched to any length, to suit the taste and habits of those who would fain put it out of the world altogether.

Truth, however, cannot be thus treated; it can never be made to reduce itself to the level of this world. Those who profess to hold it may seek to use it thus, but it will ever be found the same pure, holy, faithful witness against the world and all its ways. It will speak distinctly, if its voice be not stifled by connection with the practice of its faithless professors. When Jehoshaphat had stooped so low as to acknowledge the false prophets for the purpose of gratifying Ahab, who could observe any distinct testimony for God? All seemed to sink down to the one common level, and the enemy to have it all his own way. The voice of truth was hushed: the prophets prophesied falsely: God was forgotten. Thus must it ever be.

The attempt to accommodate truth to those who are of the world can only end in complete failure. There can be no accommodation. Let it stand upon its own heavenly height; let saints stand fully and firmly with it; let them invite sinners up to them; but let them not descend to the low and groveling pursuits and habits of the world, and thus rob truth, so far as in them lies, of all its edge and power. It is far better to allow the contrast between God's truth and our ways to be fully seen, than to attempt to identify them in appearance, when they really do not agree. We may think to commend truth to the minds of the worldly people by an effort to conform to their ways; but, so far from commending it, we in reality expose it to secret contempt and scorn. Jehoshaphat certainly did not further the cause of truth by conforming to Ahab's ways, or by acknowledging the claims of his false prophets. The man who conforms to the world will be the enemy of Christ, and the enemy of Christ's people. It cannot be otherwise. "The friendship of the world is enmity with God; whosoever, therefore, will be a friend of the world is the enemy of God."

How fully was this proved in the case of king Jehoshaphat! He became the friend and companion of Ahab, who hated Micaiah, the servant of God; and as a consequence, although he did not himself positively persecute the righteous witness, yet he did what was bad; for he sat beside Ahab, and beheld the Lord's prophet first struck, and then committed to prison, simply because he would not tell a lie to please a wicked king, and harmonize with four hundred wicked prophets. What must have been the feelings of Jehoshaphat when he beheld his brother smitten and imprisoned for his faithfulness in testifying against an expedition in which he himself was engaged! Yet such was the position into which his connection with Ahab had forced him that he could not avoid being a witness of these wicked proceedings; yea, and moreover, a partaker of them also. When a man associates himself with the world, he must do so thoroughly. The enemy will not be satisfied with half measures; on the contrary,

he will use every effort to force a saint out of communion into the most terrible extremes of evil.

The beginning of evil is like the letting out of water. Small beginnings lead to fearful results. There is first a slight tampering with evil at a distance; then, by degrees, a nearer approach to it; after this, a taking hold of it more firmly; and finally, a deliberate plunge into it, whence nothing but the most marked interposition of God can rescue. Jehoshaphat "joined affinity with Ahab"; then accepted of his hospitality; after that, was "persuaded" into open association with him; and finally, took *his* place at the battle of Ramoth-gilead. He had said to Ahab, "I am as thou art," and Ahab takes him at his word; for he says to him, "I will disguise myself, and will go to the battle; but put thou on thy robes."

Thus, so completely did Jehoshaphat surrender his personal identity, in the view of the men of the world, that "it came to pass, when the captains of the chariots saw Jehoshaphat, that they said, '*It is the king of Israel.*' " Terrible position for Jehoshaphat! To find him personating, and thus mistaken for, the worst of Israel's kings is a sad proof of the danger of associating with the men of the world. Happy was it for Jehoshaphat that the Lord did not take him at his word when he said to Ahab, "I am as thou art." The Lord knew that Jehoshaphat was not Ahab, though he might personate and be mistaken for him. Grace had made him to differ, and conduct should have *proved* him to be what grace had made him. But, blessed be God, "He knows how to deliver the godly out of temptation," and He graciously delivered His poor servant out of the evil into which he had plunged himself, and in which he would have perished, had not the hand of God been stretched out to rescue him. "Jehoshaphat cried out, and the Lord helped him; and God moved them to depart from him."*

* The reader will doubtless observe how the inspired writer presents God under two different titles in the above verse. "*The Lord*" brings out His connection with His distressed servant—His connection in grace; while the expression "*God*" shows out the powerful control which He exercised over the Syrian captains. It is needless to say that this distinction is divinely perfect. As Lord, He deals with His own redeemed people,—meeting all their weakness, and supplying all their need; but as God, He holds in His omnipotent hand the hearts of all men, to turn them whithersoever He will. Now we generally find unconverted persons using the expression "God," and not "Lord." They think of Him as One exercising an influence from a distance, rather than as One standing in near relationship. Jehoshaphat knew who it was that "*helped him*," but the Syrian captains did not know who it was that "*moved them.*"

Here we have the turning-point in this stage of Jehoshaphat's life. His eyes were opened to see the position into which he had brought himself; at least, he saw his danger, if he did not apprehend the moral evil of his course. Encompassed by the captains of Syria, he could feel something of what it was to have taken Ahab's place. Happily for him, however, he could look up to the Lord from the depth of his distress,—he could cry out to Him in the time of his extremity; had it not been thus, the enemy's arrow, lodged deep in his heart, might have told out the sorrowful result of his ungodly association.

"Jehoshaphat cried out," and his cry came up before the Lord, whose ear is ever open to hear the cry of such as feel their need. "Peter went out and wept bitterly." The prodigal said, "I will arise, and go to my father;" and the father ran to meet him, and fell on his neck, and kissed him. Thus is it that the blessed God ever meets those who, feeling that they have hewn out for themselves broken cisterns, which can hold no water, return to Him, the fountain of living waters. Would that all who feel that they have in any measure departed from Christ and slipped into the current of this present world might find their way back, in true humility and contrition of spirit, to Him who says, "Behold, I stand at the door, and knock; if any man hear My voice, and open the door, I will come in to him, and will sup with him, and he with Me."

How different Ahab's case! He, though carrying in His bosom a mortal wound, propped himself up in his chariot until the evening, fondly desiring to hide his weakness, and accomplish the object of his heart. We find no cry of humility, no tear of penitence, no looking upward. Ah, no; we find not any thing but what is in full keeping with his entire course. He died as he had lived—doing evil in the sight of the Lord. How fruitless were his efforts to prop himself up! Death had seized upon him; and though he struggled for a time to keep up an appearance, yet "about the time of the sun going down he died." Terrible end!— the end of one who had "sold himself to work wickedness." Who would be the votary of the world? Who that valued a life of simplicity and purity would mix himself up with its pursuits and habits? Who that valued a peaceful and happy termination of his career would link himself with its destinies?

Christian reader, let us, with the Lord's help, endeavor to shake off the world's influence, and purge ourselves from its ways. We have no idea how insidiously it creeps in upon us. The enemy at first weans from really simple and Christian habits, and by degrees we drop into the current of the world's thoughts. Oh that we may, with more holy jealousy and tenderness of conscience, watch against the approach of evil, lest the solemn statement of the prophet should apply to us, "Her Nazarites *were* purer than snow, they *were* whiter than milk, they *were* more ruddy in body than rubies, their polishing *was* of sapphire: [but such is the sorrowful change, that] their visage *is* blacker than a coal, *they are not known in the streets*, their skin cleaveth to their bones; it is withered, it is become like a stick"!

We shall now look a little at chapter 19. Here we see some blessed results from all that Jehoshaphat had passed through. "He returned to his house in peace to Jerusalem." Happy escape! The Lord's hand had interposed for him, and delivered him from the snare of the fowler, and, we may say, he would no doubt have his heart full of gratitude to Him who had so made him to differ from Ahab, though he had said, "I am as thou art." Ahab had gone down to his grave in shame and degradation, while Jehoshaphat returned to his house in peace. But what a lesson he had learned! How solemn to think of his having been so near the brink of the precipice! Yet the Lord had a controversy with him about what he had done. Though He allowed him to return in peace to Jerusalem, and did not suffer the enemy to hurt him, He would speak to his conscience about his sin; He would bring him aside from the field of battle, to deal with him in private. "And Jehu, the son of Hanani the seer, went out to meet him, and said to king Jehoshaphat, 'Shouldst thou help the ungodly, and love them that hate the Lord? therefore is wrath upon thee from before the Lord.'" This was a solemn appeal, and it produced its own effect. Jehoshaphat "went out again through the people, from Beersheba to mount Ephraim, and brought them back unto the Lord God of their fathers." "When thou art converted, strengthen thy brethren."

Thus did Peter; thus too did king Jehoshaphat; and blessed is it when lapses and failings lead, through the Lord's tender mercy, to such a result. Nothing but divine grace can ever produce this. When, after beholding Jehoshaphat surrounded by the Syrian captains (chap. 18), we find him here going out through the length and breadth of the land to instruct his brethren in the fear of the Lord, we can only exclaim, "What hath God wrought!" But he was just the man for such a work. It is one who has felt in his own person the terrible fruits of a careless spirit that can most effectually say, *"Take heed what ye do."* A restored Peter, who had himself denied the Holy One, was the chosen vessel to go and charge others with having done the same, and to offer them that precious blood which had cleansed his conscience from the guilt of it. So likewise the restored Jehoshaphat came from the battle of Ramoth-gilead to sound in the ears of his brethren with solemn emphasis, "Take heed what ye do." He that had just escaped from the snare could best tell what it was, and tell how to avoid it.

And mark the special feature in the Lord's character which engaged Jehoshaphat's attention: "There is no iniquity with the Lord our God, *nor respect of persons, nor taking of gifts.*" Now his snare seems to have been the gift of Ahab: "Ahab slew sheep and oxen for him in abundance, and for the people he had with him, and persuaded him to go up with him to Ramoth-gilead." He allowed his heart to be warmed by Ahab's gift, and was thereby the more easily swayed by Ahab's arguments. Just as Peter accepted the compliment of being let into the high-priest's fire, and, being warmed thereby, denied his Lord. We can never canvass, with spiritual coolness, the world's arguments and suggestions, while we are breathing its atmosphere, or accepting its compliments. We must keep outside and independent of it, and thus we shall find ourselves in a better position to reject its proposals, and triumph over its allurements.

But it is instructive to mark how Jehoshaphat, after his restoration, dwells upon that feature in the divine character from the lack of which he had so grievously failed. Communion with God is the great safeguard against all temptation; for there is no sin to which we are tempted, of which we cannot find the opposite in God; and we can only avoid evil by communion with good. This is a very simple but deeply practical truth. Had Jehoshaphat been in fellowship with God, he could not have sought fellowship with Ahab.

May we not say this is the only divine way in which to look at the question of worldly association. Let us ask ourselves, Can our association with the world go hand in hand with our fellowship with God? This is really the question. It is a miserable thing to ask, May I not partake of all the benefits of the name of Christ, and yet dishonor that name by mixing myself up with the people of the world, and taking common ground with them? How easily the matter is settled when we bring it into the divine presence, and under the searching power of the truth of God: "Shouldst thou help the ungodly, and love them that hate the Lord?" Truth strips off all the false covering which a heart out of communion is wont to throw around things. It is only when *it* casts its unerring beams on our path that we see things in their true character.

Mark the way in which divine truth exposed the actings of Ahab and Jezebel. Jezebel would fain put a fair cloak on her shocking wickedness: "Arise," said she, "and take possession of the vineyard of Naboth the Jezreelite, which he refused to give thee for money; for Naboth is not alive but dead." Such was her way of putting the matter. But how did the Lord view it? "Thus saith the Lord, 'Hast thou killed, and also taken possession' " (in other words, Hast thou committed murder and robbery?) God deals with realities. In His estimation, men and things get their proper place and value; there is no gilding, no affectation, no assumption—

all is real. Just so was it with Jehoshaphat; his scheme which might in human estimation be regarded as a religious one, was in the divine judgment pronounced to be simply a helping of the ungodly, and loving them that hated the Lord. While men might applaud him, "there was wrath upon him from before the Lord."

However, Jehoshaphat had to be thankful for the salutary lesson which his fall had taught him; it had taught him to walk more in the fear of the Lord, and caused him to impress that more upon others also. This was doing not a little. True, it was a sad and painful way to learn; but it is well when we learn even by our falls; it is well when we can tell even by painful experience the terrible evil of being mixed up with the world. Would to God we all felt it more! Would that we more walked in the solemn apprehension of the defiling nature of all worldly association, and of our own tendency to be defiled thereby! we should then be more efficient teachers of others! we should be able to say, with somewhat more weight, "Take heed what ye do;" and again, "Deal courageously, and the Lord shall be with the good."

In chapter 20 we find Jehoshaphat in far more healthful circumstances than in chap. 18. He is here seen under trial from the hand of the enemy: "It came to pass after this also, that the children of Moab, and the children of Ammon, and with them others beside the Ammonites, came against Jehoshaphat to battle." We are in far less apprehension for Jehoshaphat when we behold him the object of the enemy's hostilities than when we beheld him the subject of Ahab's kindness and hospitality. And very justly so; for in the one case he is about to be cast simply on the God of Israel, whereas in the other he was about to fall into the snare of Satan. The proper place for the man of God is to be in positive opposition to the enemies of the Lord, and not in conjunction with them.

We never can count upon divine sympathy or guidance when we join with the enemies of the Lord. Hence we observe what an empty thing it was of Jehoshaphat to ask counsel of the Lord in a matter which he knew to be wrong. Not so, however, in the scene before us. He is really in earnest when "he sets himself to seek the Lord, and proclaims a fast throughout all Judah." This is real work. There is nothing like trial from the hand of the world for driving the saint into a place of separation from it. When the world smiles, we are in danger of being attracted; but when it frowns, we are driven away from it into our stronghold; and this is both happy and healthful. Jehoshaphat did not say to a Moabite or an Ammonite, "I am as thou art." No; he knew well this was not so, for they would not let him think so. And how much better it is to know our true position in reference to the world!

There are three special points in Jehoshaphat's address to the Lord (verses 6-12).

1. The greatness of God.

2. The oath to Abraham about the land.

3. The attempt of the enemy to drive the seed of Abraham out of that land.

The prayer is most precious and instructive—full of divine intelligence. He makes it altogether a question between the God of Abraham and the children of Ammon, Moab, and mount Seir. This is what faith ever does, and the issue will ever be the same. "They come," says he, "to cast us out of *Thy possession, which Thou hast given us to inherit.*" How simple! *They* would take what *Thou* hast given! This was putting it, as it were, upon God to maintain His own convenant. "O our God, *wilt Thou not judge them? for we have no might* against this great company that cometh against us; neither know we what to do; but our eyes are upon Thee." Surely, we may say, victory was already secured to one who could thus deal with God. And so Jehoshaphat felt. For "when he had consulted with the people, *he appointed singers unto the Lord*, and that should praise the beauty of holiness, as they went out before the army, and to say, Praise the Lord: for His mercy endureth forever." Nothing but faith could raise a song of praise before even the battle had begun. "Faith counts the promise sure." And as it had enabled Abraham to believe that God would put his seed into the possession of Canaan, so it enabled Jehoshaphat to believe that He would keep them therein, and he therefore did not need to wait for victory in order to praise; he already stood in the full results of victory. Faith could say, "Thou *hast guided* them in Thy strength unto Thy holy habitation," though they had but just entered upon the wilderness.

But what a strange sight it must have been for the enemies of Jehoshaphat, to see a band of men with musical instruments instead of weapons in their hands. It was something of the same principle of warfare as that adopted by Hezekiah afterward, when he clothed himself in sackcloth instead of armor (Isa. 37:1).* Yes, it was the same, for both had been trained in the same school, and both fought under the same banner. Would that our warfare with the present age—with its habits, manners, and maxims—were more conducted on the same principle. "Above all, taking the shield of faith, wherewith ye shall be able to quench all the fiery darts of the wicked one."

What a contrast between Jehoshaphat personating Ahab at Ramoth-gilead, and standing with the Lord against his enemies the Moabites! Yes, what a contrast, in every particular! His mode of seeking help and guidance of the Lord was different, his mode of proceeding to battle was different; and oh, how different too the end! Instead of being well-nigh overwhelmed by the enemy, and crying out in the depth of his distress and danger, we find him joining in a loud chorus of praise to the God of his fathers, who had given him a victory without his striking a blow, who had made his enemies destroy one another, and who had graciously conducted him from the dark valley of Achor into the valley of Berachah. Blessed contrast! May it lead us to seek a more decided path of separation, and of abiding dependence on the Lord's grace and faithfulness. The valley of Berachah, or praise, is ever the place into which the Spirit of God would conduct; but He cannot lead us thither when we join ourselves with the "Ahabs" of this world, for the purpose of carrying out their schemes. The word is, "Come out from among them, and be ye separate, saith the Lord, and touch not the

* "The proud king of Assyria was at the gates of Jerusalem with a mighty conquering host, and one would naturally expect to find Hezekiah in the midst of his men of war, buckling on his armor, girding on his sword, mounting his chariot; but no; Hezekiah was different from most kings and captains—he had found out a place of strength which was quite unknown to Sennacherib—he had discovered a field of battle in which he could conquer without striking a blow. And mark the armor with which he girds himself: 'And it came to pass, when Hezekiah heard it, that he rent his clothes, and *covered himself with sackcloth*, and went into the house of the Lord.' Here was the armor in which the king of Judah was about to cope with the king of Assyria. Strange armor!—the armor of the sanctuary. What would Sennacherib have said had he seen this? He had never met such an antagonist before—he had never come in contact with a man who, instead of covering himself with a coat of mail, would cover himself with sackcloth; and instead of rushing forth into the field of battle in his chariot, would fall upon his knees in the temple. This would have appeared a novel mode of warfare in the eyes of the king of Assyria. He had met the kings of Hamath and Arphad, etc.; but if he had, it was upon his own principle, and in his own way; but he had never encountered such an antagonist as Hezekiah. In fact, what gave the latter such uncommon power in this contest was the feeling that *he* was nothing—that an 'arm of flesh' was of no avail;—in a word, that it was just Jehovah or nothing. This is specially seen in the act of spreading the letter before the Lord. Hezekiah was enabled by faith to retire out of the scene, and make it altogether a question between Jehovah and the king of Assyria. It was not Sennacherib and Hezekiah, but Sennacherib and Jehovah. This tells us the meaning of the sackcloth. Hezekiah felt himself to be utterly helpless, and he took the place of helplessness. He tells the Lord that the king of Assyria had reproached *Him;* he calls upon Him to vindicate His own glorious name, feeling assured that in so doing He would deliver His people. Mark, then, this wondrous scene. Repair to the sanctuary, and there behold one poor, weak, solitary man on his knees, pouring out his soul to Him who dwelt between the cherubim. No military preparations, no reviewing of troops: the elders of the priests, covered with sackcloth, pass to and fro from Hezekiah to the prophet Isaiah: all is apparent weakness. On the other hand, see a mighty conqueror leading on a numerous army flushed with victory, eager for spoil. Surely, one might say, speaking after the manner of men, all is over with Hezekiah and Jerusalem! Surely Sennacherib and his proud host will swallow up in a moment such a feeble band! And observe, further, the ground which Sennacherib takes in all this (Isa. 36:4-7). Here we observe that Sennacherib makes the very reformation which Hezekiah had effected a ground of reproach; thus leaving him, as he vainly thought, no resting-place or foundation for his confidence. Again, he says, 'Am I come up without the Lord against this land to destroy it? *The Lord said unto me, Go up against this land, and destroy it.*' (v. 10) This was indeed putting Hezekiah's faith to the test: faith must pass through the furnace. It will not do to *say* that we trust in the Lord; we must *prove* that we do, and that too when every thing apparently is against us. How, then, does Hezekiah meet all those lofty words? In the silent dignity of faith. 'The King's commandment was, saying, Answer him not' (v. 21). Such was the king's bearing in the eyes of the people; yea, rather, such is ever the bearing of faith: calm, self-possessed, dignified, in the presence of man; while, at the same time, ready to sink into the very dust in self-abasement in the presence of God. The man of faith can say to his fellow, 'Stand still, and see the salvation of God!' and, at the same moment, send up to God the cry of conscious weakness. (See Exod. 14:13-15.) So it was with the king of Judah at this solemn and trying crisis. Harken to him while, in the retirement of the sanctuary, shut in with God, he pours out the anxieties of his soul in the ear of One who was willing to hear and ready to help (chap. 37:15-20)."—*Practical Reflections on the Life and Times of Hezekiah.*

unclean thing; and I will receive you, and will be a Father unto you, and ye shall be My sons and daughters, saith the Lord Almighty" (2 Cor. 6:17-18).

It is wonderful how worldliness hinders, yea, rather destroys, a spirit of praise; it is positively hostile to such a spirit, and, if indulged in, it will either lead to deep anguish of soul, or to the most thorough and open abandonment of all semblance of godliness. In Jehoshaphat's case, it was happily the former. He was humbled, restored, and led into larger blessedness.

But it would be sad indeed were any one to plunge into worldliness with the hope that it might lead to an issue similar to that of Jehoshaphat. Vain, presumptuous hope! Sinful expectation! Who that valued a pure, calm, and peaceful walk could for a moment entertain it? "The Lord knoweth how to deliver the godly out of temptation," but shall we, on that account, go and deliberately plunge ourselves into it? God forbid!

Yet, ah! who can sound the depths of the human heart—its profound, malignant depths? Who can disentangle its complicated mazes? Could any one imagine that Jehoshaphat would again, after such solemn lessons, join himself with the ungodly, to further their ambitious, or rather their avaricious, schemes? No one could imagine it, save one who had learned something of his own heart. Yet so he did. "He joined himself with Ahaziah, king of Israel, who did very wickedly. And he joined himself with him, to make ships to go to Tarshish; and they made the ships in Ezion-gaber. Then Eliezer, the son of Dodavah of Mareshah, prophesied against Jehoshaphat, saying, 'Because thou hast joined thyself with Ahaziah, the Lord hath broken thy works.' And the ships were broken, and they were not able to go to Tarshish" (verses 35-37). What is man! A poor, stumbling, failing, halting creature; ever rushing into some new folly or evil. Jehoshaphat had, as it were, but just recovered from the effects of his association with Ahab, and he forthwith joins himself with Ahaziah. He had with difficulty, or rather through the special and most gracious interference of the Lord, escaped from the arrows of the Syrians, and again we find him in league with the kings of Israel and Edom, to fight against the Moabites.

Such was Jehoshaphat—such his extra-ordinary course. There were some "good things found in him"; but his snare was, worldly association; and the lesson which we learn from the consideration of his history is, to beware of that evil. Yes; we would need to have sounded in our ears, with ceaseless solemnity, the words, "*Come out, and be separate.*" We cannot, by any possibility, mix ourselves up with the world, and allow ourselves to be governed and led by its maxims and principles, without suffering in our own souls, and marring our testimony.

I would only remark, in conclusion, that it seems like a relief to the spirit to read the words, "Jehoshaphat slept with his fathers" (chap. 21:1), as we feel assured, that he has at last got beyond the reach of the enemy's snares and devices; and further, that he comes under the Spirit's benediction, "Blessed are the dead which die in the Lord; for they rest from their labors"—yes, a rest from their conflicts, snares, and temptations also.

JOB AND HIS FRIENDS

THE BOOK OF JOB occupies a very peculiar place in the volume of God. It possesses a character entirely its own, and teaches lessons which are not to be learnt in any other section of inspiration. It is not by any means our purpose to enter upon a line of argument to prove the genuineness, or establish the fact of the divine inspiration, of this precious book. We take these things for granted; being fully persuaded of them as established facts, we leave the proofs to abler hands. We receive the book of Job as part of the Holy Scriptures given of God for the profit and blessing of His people. We need no proofs of this for ourselves, nor do we attempt to offer any to our reader.

And we may further add that we have no thought of entering upon the field of inquiry as to the authorship of this book. This, howsoever interesting it may be in itself, is to us entirely secondary. We receive the book from God. This is enough for us. We heartily own it to be an inspired document, and we do not feel it to be our province to discuss the question as to where, when, or by whom it was penned. In short, we purpose, with the Lord's help, to offer a few plain and practical remarks on a book which we consider needs to be more closely studied, that it may be more fully understood. May the Eternal Spirit, who indited the book, expound and apply it to our souls!

The opening page of this remarkable book furnishes us with a view of the patriarch Job, surrounded by every thing that could make the world agreeable to him, and make him of importance in the world. "There was a man in the land of Uz whose name was Job; and that man was perfect and upright, and one that feared God and eschewed evil." Thus much as to *what he was.* Let us now see *what he had.*

"And there were born unto him seven sons and three daughters. His substance also was seven thousand sheep, and three thousand camels, and five hundred yoke of oxen, and five hundred she-asses, and a very great household; so that this man was the greatest of all the children of the east. And his sons went and feasted in their houses every one his day; and sent and called for their three sisters, to eat and to drink with them." Then, to complete the picture, we have the record of *what he did.*

"And it was so, when the days of their feasting were gone about, that Job sent and sanctified them, and rose up early in the morning, and offered burnt-offerings according to the number of them all; for Job said, 'It may be that my sons have sinned, and cursed God in their hearts.' Thus did Job continually."

Here, then, we have a very rare specimen of a man. He was perfect, upright, God-fearing, and eschewed evil. Moreover, the hand of God had hedged him round about on every side, and strewed his path with richest mercies. He had all that heart could wish, children and wealth in abundance, honor and distinction from all around. In short, we may almost say, his cup of earthly bliss was full.

But Job needed to be tested. There was a deep moral root in his heart which had to be laid bare. There was self-righteousness which had to be brought to the surface and judged. Indeed, we may discern this root in the very words which we have just quoted. He says, "It may be that my sons have sinned." He does not seem to contemplate the possibility of sinning himself. A soul really self-judged, thoroughly broken before God, truly sensible of its own state, tendencies, and capabilities, would think of his own sins, and his own need of a burnt-offering.

Now, let the reader distinctly understand that Job was a real saint of God,—a divinely quickened soul, a possessor of divine and eternal life. We cannot too strongly insist upon this. He was just as truly a man of God in the first chapter as he was in the forty-second. If we do not see this, we shall miss one of the grand lessons of the book. The eighth verse of chap. 1, establishes this point beyond all question. "And the Lord said unto Satan, 'Hast thou considered *My servant* Job, that there is none like him in the earth, a perfect and an upright man, one that feareth God and escheweth evil?'"

But, with all this, Job had never sounded the depths of his own heart. He did not know himself. He had never really grasped the truth of his own utter ruin and total depravity. He had never learnt to say, "I know that in me, that is in my flesh, dwelleth no good thing." This point must be seized, or the book of Job will not be understood. We shall not see the specific object of all those deep and painful exercises through which Job was called to pass unless we lay hold of the solemn fact that his conscience had never been really in the divine presence, that he had never seen himself in the light, never measured himself by a divine standard, never weighed himself in the balances of the sanctuary.

If the reader will turn for a moment to chap. 29, he will find a striking proof of what we assert. He will there see distinctly what a strong and deep root of self-complacency there was in the heart of this dear and valued servant of God, and how this root was nourished by the very tokens of divine favor with which he was surrounded. This chapter is a pathetic lament over the faded light of other days; and the very tone and character of the lament prove how necessary it was that Job should be stripped of every thing, in order that he might learn himself in the searching light of the Divine Presence.

Let us harken to his words.

"Oh that I were as in months past, as in the days when God preserved me; when His candle shined upon my head, and when by His light I walked through darkness; as I was in the days of my youth, when the secret of God was upon my tabernacle; when the Almighty was yet with me, when my children were about me; when I washed my steps with butter, and the rock poured me out rivers of oil; when I went out to the gate through the city; when I prepared my seat in the street! The young men saw me and hid themselves, and the aged arose and stood up. The princes refrained talking, and laid their hand on their mouth. The nobles held their peace, and their tongue cleaved to the roof of their mouth. When the ear heard me, then it blessed me; and when the eye saw me, it gave witness to me: because I delivered the poor that cried, and the fatherless, and him that had none to help him. The blessing of him that was ready to perish came upon me, and I caused the widow's heart to sing for joy. I put on righteousness, and it clothed me: my judgment was as a robe and a diadem. I was eyes to the blind, and feet was I to the lame. I was a father to the poor, and the cause which I knew not I searched out. And I brake the jaws of the wicked, and plucked the spoil out of his teeth. Then I said, 'I shall die in my nest, and I shall multiply my days as the sand.' My root was spread out by the waters, and the dew lay all night upon my branch. My glory was fresh in me, and my bow was renewed in my hand. Unto me men gave ear, and waited, and kept silence at my counsel. After my words they spake not again, and my speech dropped upon them. And they waited for me as for the rain, and they opened their mouth wide as for the latter rain. If I laughed on them, they believed it not; and the light of my countenance they cast not down. I chose out their way, and sat chief, and dwelt as a king in the army, as one that comforteth the mourners. But now, they that are younger than I have me in derision, whose fathers I would have disdained to have set with the dogs of my flock."

This, truly, is a most remarkable utterance. We look in vain for any breathings of a broken and a contrite spirit here. There are no evidences of self-loathing, or even of self-distrust. We cannot find so much as a single expression of conscious weakness and nothingness. In the course of this single chapter, Job refers to himself more than forty times, while the references to God are but five. It reminds us of the seventh of Romans, by the predominance of "I"; but there is this immense difference, that, in the seventh of Romans, "I" is a poor, weak, good-for-nothing, wretched creature in the presence of the holy law of God; whereas, in Job 29, "I" is a most important, influential personage, admired and almost worshiped by his fellows.

Now Job had to be stripped of all this; and when we compare chap. 29 with chap. 30 we can form some idea of how painful the process of stripping must have been. There is peculiar emphasis in the words, "*But now.*" Job draws a most striking contrast between his past and his present. In chap. 30 he is still occupied with himself. It is still "I"; but ah, how changed! The very men who flattered him in the day of his prosperity, treat him with contempt in the day of his adversity. Thus it is ever in this poor, false, deceitful world, and it is well to be made to prove it. All must, sooner or later, find out the hollowness of the world—the fickleness of those who are ready to cry out "hosanna" today, and "crucify Him" tomorrow. Man is not to be trusted. It is all very well while the sun shines; but wait till the nipping blasts of winter come, and then you will see how far nature's fair promises and professions can be trusted. When the prodigal had plenty to spend, he found plenty to share his portion; but when he began to be in want, "no man gave unto him."

Thus it was with Job in chap. 30. But be it well remembered that there is very much more needed than the stripping of self, and the discovery of the hollowness and deceitfulness of the world. One may go through all these, and the result be merely chagrin and disappointment. Indeed, it can be nothing more if God be not reached. If the heart be not brought to find its all-satisfying portion in God, then a reverse of fortune leaves it desolate; and the discovery of the fickleness and hollowness of men fills it with bitterness. This will account for Job's language in chap. 30: "But now they that are younger than I have me in derision, whose fathers I would have disdained to have set with the dogs of my flock." Was this the spirit of Christ? Would Job have spoken thus at the close of the book? He would not. When once Job got into God's presence, there was an end of the egotism of chap. 29 and the bitterness of chap. 30.*

But hear Job's further outpourings: "They were children of fools, yea, children of base men; they were viler than the earth. And now am I their song, yea, I am their by-word. They abhor me, they flee far from me, and spare not to spit in my face. Because He hath loosed my cord, and afflicted me, they also let loose the bridle before me. Upon my right hand rise the youth; they push away my feet, and they raise up against me the ways of their destruction. They mar my path, they set forward my calamity, they have no helper. They came upon me as a wide breaking in of waters: in the desolation they rolled themselves upon me."

Now, all this, we may truly say, is very far short of the mark. Lamentations over departed greatness, and bitter invectives against our fellow-men, will not do the heart much good; neither do they display aught of the spirit and mind of Christ, nor bring glory to His holy name. When we turn our eyes toward the blessed Lord Jesus we see something wholly different. That meek and lowly One met all the rebuffs of this world, all the disappointments in the midst of His people Israel, all the unbelief and folly of His disciples, with an, "Even so, Father." He was able to retire from the rebuffs of men into His resources in God, and then to come forth with those balmy words, "Come unto Me . . . and I will give you rest." No chagrin, no bitterness, no harsh invectives, nothing rough or unkind, from that gracious Saviour who came down into this cold and heartless world to manifest the perfect love of God, and who pursued His path of service spite of all man's perfect hatred.

But the fairest and best of men must retire into the shade when tested by the perfect standard of the life of Christ. The light of His moral glory makes manifest the defects and blemishes of even the most perfect of the sons of men. "In all things He must have the pre-eminence." He stands out in vivid

---

* The reader will bear in mind that, while it is the Holy Ghost who records what Job and his friends said, yet we are not to suppose that they *spoke* by inspiration.

contrast with even a Job or a Jeremiah in the matter of patient submission to all that He was called upon to endure. Job completely breaks down under his heavy trials. He not only pours forth a torrent of bitter invective upon his fellows, but actually curses the day of his birth. "After this opened Job his mouth and cursed his day. And Job spake and said, 'Let the day perish wherein I was born, and the night in which it was said, There is a man-child conceived' " (chap. 3:1-3).

We notice the selfsame thing in Jeremiah— that blessed man of God. He, too, gave way beneath the heavy pressure of his varied and accumulated sorrows, and gave vent to his feelings in the following bitter accents: "Cursed be the day wherein I was born; let not the day wherein my mother bare me be blessed. Cursed be the man who brought tidings to my father, saying, 'A man-child is born unto thee'; making him very glad. And let that man be as the cities which the Lord overthrew, and repented not; and let him hear the cry in the morning, and the shouting at noontide. *Because He slew me not from the womb;* or that my mother might have been my grave, and her womb to be always great with me. Wherefore came I forth out of the womb to see labor and sorrow, that my days should be consumed with shame?" (Jer. 20:14-18)

What language is here! Only think of cursing the man that brought tidings of his birth! cursing him because he had not slain him! All this, both in the prophet and the patriarch, contrasts strongly with the meek and lowly Jesus of Nazareth. That spotless One passed through deeper sorrows and more in number than all His servants put together; but not one murmuring word ever escaped His lips. He patiently submitted to all; and met the darkest hour with such words as these, "The cup which My Father hath given Me, shall I not drink it?" Blessed Lord Jesus, Son of the Father, we adore Thee! We bow down at Thy feet, lost in wonder, love, and praise, and own Thee Lord of all—the fairest among ten thousand, and the altogether lovely!

There is no more fruitful field of study than that which is opened before us in the history of God's dealings with souls. It is full of interest, and abounds in instruction and profit. One grand object in those dealings is to produce real brokenness and humility—to strip us of all false righteousness, empty us of all self-confidence, and teach us to lean wholly upon Christ. All have to pass through what may be called the process of stripping and emptying. With some this process precedes, with others it follows, conversion or the new birth. Many are brought to Christ through deep plowings and painful exercises of heart and conscience—exercises extending over years, often over the whole lifetime. Others, on the contrary, are brought with comparatively little exercise of soul. They lay hold, speedily, of the glad tidings of forgiveness of sins through the atoning death of Christ, and are made happy at once. But the stripping and emptying come afterward, and, in many cases, cause the soul to totter on its foundation, and almost to doubt its conversion.

This is very painful, but very needful. The fact is, self must be learnt and judged, sooner or later. If it be not learnt in communion with God, it must be learnt by bitter experience in failures and falls. "No flesh shall glory in His presence;" and we must all learn our utter powerlessness, in every respect, in order that we may taste the sweetness and comfort of the truth, that Christ is made of God unto us wisdom, righteousness, sanctification, and redemption. God will have *broken material.* Let us remember this. It is a solemn and necessary truth, "Thus saith the high and lofty One that inhabiteth eternity, whose name is Holy: I dwell in the high and holy place, with him also that is of a contrite and humble spirit, to revive the spirit of the humble, and to revive the heart of the contrite ones." And again, "Thus saith the Lord, 'The heaven is My throne, and the earth is My footstool: where is the house that ye build unto Me? and where is the place of My rest? For all those things hath Mine hand made, and all those things have been, saith the Lord: but to this man will I look, even to him that is poor and of a contrite spirit, and trembleth at My word' " (Isa. 57:15; 66:1-2).

These are seasonable words for all of us.

One special want of the present moment is brokenness of spirit. Nine-tenths of our trouble and difficulty may be traced to this want. It is marvelous how we get on from day to day—in the family, in the assembly, in the world, in our entire practical life, when *self* is subdued and mortified. A thousand things which else would prove more than a match for our hearts are esteemed as nothing, when our souls are in a truly contrite state. We are enabled to bear reproach and insult, to overlook slights and affronts, to trample upon our crotchets, predilections, and prejudices, to yield to others where weighty principle is not involved, to be ready to every good work, to exhibit a genial large-heartedness in all our dealings, and an elasticity in all our moral movements which so greatly tend to adorn the doctrine of God our Saviour. How often it is otherwise with us. We exhibit a stiff, unyielding temper; we stand up for our rights; we maintain our interests; we look after our own things; we contend for our own notions. All this proves, very clearly, that self is not habitually measured and judged in the presence of God.

But we repeat—and with emphasis—God will have broken material. He loves us too well to leave us in hardness and unsubduedness; and hence it is that He sees fit to pass us through all sorts of exercises in order to bring us into a condition of soul in which He can use us for His own glory. The will must be broken; self-confidence, self-complacency, and self-importance must be cut up by the roots. God will make use of the scenes and circumstances through which we have to pass, the people with whom we are associated in daily life, to discipline the heart and subdue the will. And further, He will deal with us directly Himself, in order to bring about these great practical results.

All this comes out with great distinctness in the book of Job, and gives a wonderful interest and charm to its pages. It is very evident that Job needed a severe sifting. Had he not needed it, we may rest assured the gracious, loving Lord would not have passed him through it. It was not for nothing that He let Satan loose upon His dear servant. We may say, with fullest confidence, that nothing but the most stern necessity would have led Him to adopt such a line of action. God loved Job with a perfect love; but it was a wise and faithful love; a love that could take account of every thing, and, looking below the surface, could see the deep moral roots in the heart of His servant—roots which Job had never seen, and, therefore, never judged. What a mercy to have to do with such a God! to be in the hands of One who will spare no pains in order to subdue every thing in us which is contrary to Himself, and to bring out in us His own blessed image!

But is there not something profoundly interesting in the fact that God can even make use of Satan as an instrument in the discipline of His people? We see this in the case of the Apostle Peter, as well as in that of the Patriarch Job. Peter had to be sifted, and Satan was used to do the work. "Simon, Simon, behold Satan hath desired to have you, that he may sift you as wheat." Here, too, there was a stern necessity. There was a deep root to be reached in Peter's heart—the root of self-confidence; and his faithful Lord saw it absolutely needful to pass him through a most severe and painful process in order that this root should be exposed and judged; and therefore Satan was permitted to sift him thoroughly, so that he might never again trust his own heart, but walk softly all his days. God will have broken material, whether it be in a patriarch or an apostle. All must be mellowed and subdued in order that the divine glory may shine forth with an ever brightening lustre.

Had Job understood this great principle—had he apprehended the divine object, how differently he would have carried himself! But, like ourselves, he had to learn his lesson; and the Holy Ghost has furnished us with the record of the mode in which the lesson was learnt, so that we may profit by it also.

Let us pursue the narrative.

"Now there was a day when the sons of God came to present themselves before the Lord, and Satan came also among them. And the Lord said unto Satan, 'Whence comest thou?' Then Satan answered the Lord and said, 'From going to and fro in the earth, and from walking up and down in it.' And the Lord said unto Satan, 'Hast thou considered My servant Job, that there is none like him in the earth, a perfect and an upright man, one that feareth God and escheweth evil?' Then Satan answered the Lord, and said, 'Doth Job fear God for naught? Hast not Thou made a hedge about him, and about his house, and about all that he hath on every side? Thou hast blest the work of his hands, and his substance is increased in the land. But put forth Thine hand now, and touch all that he hath, and he will curse Thee to Thy face.' " What a view we have here of Satan's malignity! What a striking proof of the way in which he watches and considers the ways and works of God's people! What insight into human character! What an intimate knowledge of man's mental and moral constitution! What a terrible thing to fall into his hands! He is ever on the watch; ever ready, if permitted of God, to put forth all his malignant energy against the Christian.

The thought of this is most solemn, and should lead us to walk humbly and watchfully through a scene where Satan rules. He has no power whatever over a soul who abides in the place of dependence and obedience; and, blessed be God, he cannot, in any case, go one hair's breadth beyond the limit prescribed by divine command. Thus, in Job's case, "The Lord said unto Satan, 'Behold, all that he hath is in thy power; only upon himself put not forth thine hand.' "

Here Satan was permitted to lay his hand on Job's possessions—to bereave him of his children, and despoil him of all his wealth. And truly he lost no time in despatching his business. With marvelous rapidity he executed his commission. Blow after blow fell, in quick succession, on the devoted head of the patriarch. Hardlly had one messenger told his melancholy tale, ere another arrived with still heavier tidings, until, at length, the afflicted servant of God "arose and rent his mantle, and shaved his head, and fell down upon the ground, and worshiped, and said, 'Naked came I out of my mother's womb, and naked shall I return thither: the Lord gave, and the Lord hath taken away; blessed be the name of the Lord.' In all this, Job sinned

not, nor charged God foolishly" (chap. 1:20-22).

All this is deeply touching. To speak after the manner of men, it was enough to make reason totter, to be thus, in a moment, bereft of his ten children, and reduced from princely wealth to absolute penury. What a striking contrast between the opening and the closing lines of our first chapter! In the former, we see Job surrounded by a numerous family, and in the enjoyment of vast possessions; in the latter, we see him left alone, in poverty and nakedness. And to think of Satan's being allowed—yea, commissioned of God—to bring about all this! And for what? For the deep and permanent profit of Job's precious soul. God saw that His servant needed to be taught a lesson; and, moreover, that, in no other way, by no other means could this lesson be taught than by passing him through an ordeal the bare record of which fills the mind with solemn awe. God *will* teach His children, even though it be by stripping them of all that the heart clings to in this world.

But we must follow our patriarch into still deeper waters.

"Again there was a day when the sons of God came to present themselves before the Lord, and Satan came also among them to present himself before the Lord. And the Lord said unto Satan, 'From whence comest thou?' And Satan answered the Lord, and said, 'From going to and fro in the earth, and from walking up and down in it.' And the Lord said unto Satan, 'Hast thou considered My servant Job, that there is none like him in the earth, a perfect and an upright man, one that feareth God and escheweth evil? and still he holdeth fast his integrity, although thou movedst Me against him, to destroy him without cause.' And Satan answered the Lord, and said, 'Skin for skin, yea, all that a man hath will he give for his life. But put forth Thine hand now, and touch his bone and his flesh, and he will curse Thee to Thy face.' And the Lord said unto Satan, 'Behold, he is in thy hand; but save his life.' So went Satan forth from the presence of the Lord, and smote Job with sore boils from the sole of his foot unto his crown. And he took him a potsherd to scrape himself withal; and he sat down among the ashes. Then said his wife unto him, 'Dost thou still retain thine integrity? curse God, and die.' But he said unto her, 'Thou speakest as one of the foolish women speaketh. What? shall we receive good at the hand of God, and shall we not receive evil?' In all this did not Job sin with his lips" (chap. 2:1-10).

This is a very remarkable passage. It instructs us as to the place which Satan occupies in respect to God's government. He is a mere instrument, and, though ever ready to accuse the Lord's people, can do nothing save as he is allowed of God. So far as Job was concerned, the efforts of Satan proved abortive; and having done his utmost, he goes away, and we hear nothing more of his actings, whatever may have been his inward temptations. Job was enabled to hold fast his integrity; and, had matters ended here, his patient endurance would only have strengthened the platform of his righteousness, and ministered to his self-complacency. "Ye have heard," says James, "of the patience of Job." And what then? "Ye have seen *the end of the Lord;* that the Lord is very pitiful, and of tender mercy." Had it been simply a question of Job's patience, it would have proved an additional ground of self-confidence, and thus "the end of the Lord" would not have been reached. For, be it ever remembered, the Lord's pity and tender mercy can only be tasted by those who are truly penitent and broken-hearted. Now Job was not this, even when he lay amid the ashes. He was not yet thoroughly broken down before God. He was still the great man—great in his misfortunes as he had been in his prosperity—great beneath the keen and withering blasts of adversity as he had been in the sunshine of brighter and better days. Job's heart was still unreached. He was not yet prepared to cry out, "Behold, I am vile." He had not yet learnt to "abhor" himself, "and repent in dust and ashes."

We are anxious that the reader should distinctly seize this point. It is, to a very great extent, the key to the entire book of Job. The divine object was to expose to Job's view the depths of his own heart, in order that he might learn to delight in the grace and mercy of God, and not in his own goodness, which was as a morning cloud and the early dew, that passeth away. Job was a true saint of God; and all Satan's accusations were flung back in his face; but, all the while, Job was unbroken material, and therefore unprepared for "the end of the Lord"—that blessed end for every contrite heart—that end which is marked by "pity and tender mercy." God, blessed and praised be His name! will not suffer Satan to accuse us; but He will expose us to ourselves, so that we may judge ourselves, and thus learn to mistrust our own hearts, and rest in the eternal stability of His grace.

Thus far, then, we see Job "holding fast his integrity." He meets with calmness all the heavy afflictions which Satan is allowed to bring upon him; and, moreover, he refuses the foolish counsel of his wife. In a word, he accepts all as from the hand of God, and bows his head in the presence of His mysterious dispensations.

All this is well. But the arrival of Job's three friends produces a marked change. Their very presence—the bare fact of their being eyewitnesses of his trouble—affects him in a very remarkable manner. "Now when Job's three friends heard of all this evil that was come upon him, they came every one from his own place, Eliphaz the Temanite, and Bildad the Shuhite, and Zophar the Naamathite; for they had made an appointment together to come to mourn with him and to comfort him. And when they lifted up their eyes afar off, and knew him not, they lifted up their voices and wept; and they rent every one his mantle, and sprinkled dust upon their heads toward heaven. So they sat down with him upon the ground seven days and seven nights, and none spake a word unto him; for they saw that his grief was very great" (chap. 2:11-13).

Now, we can fully believe that those three men were governed, in the main, by kindly feelings toward Job; and it was no small sacrifice on their part to leave their homes and come to condole with their bereaved and afflicted friend. All this we can easily believe. But it is very evident that their presence had the effect of stirring up feelings and thoughts in his heart and mind which had hitherto lain dormant. He had borne submissively the loss of children, property, and of bodily health. Satan had been dismissed, and the wife's counsel rejected; but the presence of his friends caused Job to break down completely. "After this, Job opened his mouth, and cursed his day."

This is very remarkable. It does not appear that the friends had spoken a single sentence. They sat in total silence, with rent garments, and covered with dust, gazing on a grief too profound for them to reach. It was Job himself who first broke silence; and the whole of the third chapter is an outpouring of the most bitter lamentation, affording melancholy evidence of an unsubdued spirit. It is, we may confidently assert, impossible that any one who had learnt, in any little measure, to say, "Thy will be done," could ever curse his day, or use the language contained in the third chapter of Job. It may doubtless be said, "It is easy for those to speak who have never been called to endure Job's heavy trials." This is quite true; and it may further be added that no other man would have done one whit better under the circumstances. All this we can fully understand; but it in no wise touches the great moral of the book of Job—a moral which it is our privilege to seize. Job was a true saint of God; but he needed to learn himself, as we all do. He needed to have the roots of his moral being laid bare in his own sight, so that he might really abhor himself, and repent in dust and ashes. And furthermore, he needed a truer and deeper sense of what God was, so that he might trust Him and justify Him under all circumstances.

But we look in vain for aught of this in Job's opening address. "Job spake and said, 'Let the day perish wherein I was born, and the night in which it was said, There is a man child conceived . . . . Why died I not from the womb?' " These are not the accents of a broken and a contrite spirit, or of one who had learnt to say, "Even so, Father, for so it seemed good in Thy sight." It is a grand point in the soul's history when one is enabled to bow with meekness to all the dispensations of our Father's hand. A broken will is a rich and rare endowment. It is a high attainment in

the school of Christ to be able to say, "I have learnt, in whatsoever state I am, to be content" (Phil. 4:11). Paul had to *learn* this. It was not natural to him; and, most surely, he never learnt it at the feet of Gamaliel. He had to be thoroughly broken down at the feet of Jesus of Nazareth, ere he could say from his heart, "I am content." He had to ponder the meaning of those words, "My grace is sufficient for thee," ere he could "take pleasure in infirmities." The man who could use such language was standing at the very antipodes of the man who could curse his day, and say, "Why died I not from the womb?" Only think of a saint of God, and heir of glory, saying, "Why died I not from the womb?" If Job had been in the presence of God he never could have uttered such words. He would have known full well why he had not died. He would have had a soul-satisfying sense of what God had in store for him. He would have justified God in all things. But Job was not in the presence of God, but in the presence of his friends; who proved, very distinctly, that they understood little or nothing of the character of God or the real object of His dealings with His dear servant Job.

It is not, by any means, our purpose to enter minutely into the lengthened discussion between Job and his friends—a discussion extending over twenty-nine chapters. We shall merely quote a few sentences from the opening address of each of the friends which will enable the reader to form an idea of the real ground occupied by these mistaken men.

Eliphaz was the first speaker. "Then Eliphaz the Temanite answered and said, 'If we essay to commune with thee wilt thou be grieved? but who can withhold himself from speaking? Behold, thou hast instructed many, and thou hast strengthened the weak hands. Thy words have upholden him that was falling, and thou hast strengthened the feeble knees. But now it is come upon thee, and thou faintest; it toucheth thee, and thou art troubled. Is not this thy fear, thy confidence, thy hope, and the uprightness of thy ways? Remember, I pray thee, who ever perished, being innocent? or where were the righteous cut off? *Even as I have seen*, they that plow iniquity, and sow wickedness, reap the same'" (chap. 4:1-8). And again, "*I have seen* the foolish taking root; but suddenly I cursed his habitation" (chap. 5:3; see also chap. 15:17).

From these sentences it seems very evident that Eliphaz belonged to that class of people who argue very much from their own *experience*. His motto was, "As I have seen." Now, what we have seen may be all true enough, so far as we are concerned. But it is a total mistake to found a general rule upon individual experience, and yet it is a mistake to which thousands are prone. What, for instance, had the experience of Eliphaz to do with Job? It may be he had never met a case exactly similar; and if there should happen to be a single feature of dissimilarity between the two cases, then the whole argument based on experience must go for nothing. And that it went for nothing in Job's case is evident, for no sooner had Eliphaz ceased speaking, than, without the slightest attention to his words, Job proceeded with the tale of his own sorrows, intermingled with much self-vindication and bitter complaints against the divine dealings (chap. 6:7).

Bildad is the next speaker. He takes quite different ground from that occupied by Eliphaz. He never once refers to his own experience, or to what had come under his own observation. He appeals to antiquity. "Inquire, I pray thee, of *the former age*, and prepare thyself to the search of their *fathers*. (For we are but of yesterday, and know nothing, because our days upon earth are a shadow.) Shall not they teach thee, and tell thee, and utter words out of their heart?" (chap. 8—10)

Now, it must be admitted that Bildad conducts us into a much wider field than that of Eliphaz. The authority of a number of "fathers" has much more weight and respectability than the experience of a single individual. Moreover, it would argue much more modesty to be guided by the voice of a number of wise and learned men than by the light of one's own experience. But the fact is that neither experience nor tradition will do. The former may be true so far as it goes, but

you can hardly get two men whose experience will exactly correspond; and as to the latter, it is a mass of confusion, for one father differs from another; and nothing can be more slippery or uncertain than the voice of tradition—the authority of the fathers.

Hence, as might be expected, Bildad's words had no more weight with Job than those of Eliphaz. The one was as far from the truth as the other. Had they appealed to divine revelation it would have been a different matter altogether. *The truth of God* is the only standard—the one grand authority. By that, all must be measured; to that all must, sooner or later, bow down. No man has any right to lay down his own experience as a rule for his fellows; and if no man has a right, neither have any number of men. In other words, it is not the voice of man, but the voice of God which must govern us all. It is not experience or tradition which shall judge at the last day, but the Word of God. Solemn and weighty fact! May we consider it! Had Bildad and Eliphaz understood it, their words would have had much more weight with their afflicted friend.

Let us now very briefly refer to the opening address of Zophar the Naamathite.

He says, "Oh, that God would speak, and open His lips against thee, and that He would show thee the secrets of wisdom, that they are double to that which is! Know, therefore, that God exacteth of thee less than thine iniquity deserveth." And again, "*If* thou prepare thy heart, and stretch out thy hands toward Him; if iniquity be in thy hand, put it far away, and let not wickedness dwell in thy tabernacles. For then shalt thou lift up thy face without spot: yea, thou shalt be stedfast, and shalt not fear" (chap. 11:5-6, 13-15).

These words savor strongly of *legality*. They prove very distinctly that Zophar had no right sense of the divine character. He did not know God. No one possessing a true knowledge of God could speak of Him as opening His lips against a poor afflicted sinner, or as exacting aught from a needy, helpless creature. God is not against us, but for us, blessed forever be His name! He is not a legal exactor, but a liberal giver. Then, again, Zophar says, "If thou prepare thy heart." But if not, what then? No doubt a man ought to prepare his heart,—and if he were right, he would; but then, he is not right, and hence, when he sets about preparing his heart, he finds nothing there but evil. He finds himself perfectly powerless. What is he to do? Zophar cannot tell. No; nor can any of his school. How can they? They only know God as a stern exactor—as One who, if He opens His lips, can only speak against the sinner.

Need we marvel, therefore, that Zophar was as far from convincing Job as either of his two companions? They were all wrong. Legality, tradition, experience, were alike defective, one-sided, false. Not any one of them, or all of them put together, could meet Job's case. They only darkened counsel by words without knowledge. Not one of the three friends understood Job; and what is more, they did not know God's character or His object in dealing with His dear servant. They were wholly mistaken. They knew not how to present God to Job; and, as a consequence, they knew not how to lead Job's conscience into the presence of God. In place of leading him to self-judgment, they only ministered to a spirit of self-vindication. They did not introduce God into the scene. They said some *true things*, but they had not *the truth*. They brought in experience, tradition, legality, but not the truth.

Hence the three friends failed to convince Job. Their ministry was one-sided, and instead of silencing Job, they only led him forth into a field of discussion which seemed almost boundless. He gives them word for word, and far more. "No doubt," he says, "but ye are the people, and wisdom shall die with you. But *I have understanding as well as you; I am not inferior to you:* yea, who knoweth not such things as these?" "What ye know, the same do I know also; I am not inferior to you." "Ye are forgers of lies, ye are all physicians of no value. Oh that ye would altogether hold your peace! and it should be your wisdom." "I have heard many such things: miserable comforters are ye all. Shall vain words have an end? or what emboldeneth thee that thou answerest? I also could speak as ye do: if your soul were in my soul's stead, I could heap up words against you, and shake my head at you." "How long will ye vex my soul, and break me in pieces with words? These ten times have ye reproached me; ye are not ashamed that ye make yourselves strange to me." "Have pity upon me, have pity upon me, O ye my friends; for the hand of God hath touched me."

All these utterances prove how far Job was from that true brokenness of spirit and humility of mind which ever flow from being in the Divine Presence. No doubt the friends were wrong—quite wrong in their notions about God, wrong in their method of dealing with Job; but their being wrong did not make him right. Had Job's conscience been in the presence of God, he would have made no reply to his friends, even though they had been a thousand times more mistaken and severe in their treatment. He would have meekly bowed his head, and allowed the tide of reproof and accusation to roll over him. He would have turned the very severity of his friends to profitable account, by viewing it as a wholesome moral discipline for his heart. But no; Job had not yet reached the end of himself. He was full of self-vindication, full of invective against his fellows, full of mistaken thoughts about God. It needed another ministry to bring him into a right attitude of soul.

The more closely we study the lengthened discussion between Job and his three friends, the more clearly we must see the utter impossibility of their ever coming to an understanding. He was bent upon vindicating himself; and they were bent upon the very reverse. He was unbroken and unsubdued, and their mistaken course of treatment only tended to render him more so. Had they changed sides, they would have reached a different issue altogether. If Job had condemned himself, had he taken a low place, had he owned himself nothing and nobody, he would have left his friends nothing to say. And, on the other hand, had they spoken softly, tenderly, and soothingly to him, they would have been far more likely to melt him down. As it was, the case was hopeless. He could see nothing wrong in himself; and they could see nothing right. He was determined to maintain his integrity; and they were quite as determined to pick holes and find out flaws. There was no point of contact whatever—no common ground of understanding. He had no penitential breathings for them, and they had no tender compassions for him. They were traveling in entirely opposite directions, and never could meet. In a word, there was a demand for another kind of ministry altogether, and that ministry is introduced in the person of Elihu.

"So these three men ceased to answer Job [high time they should], because he was righteous in his own eyes. Then was kindled the wrath of Elihu, the son of Barachel the Buzite, of the kindred of Ram: against Job was his wrath kindled, because he justified himself rather than God. Also against his three friends was his wrath kindled, because they had found no answer, and yet had condemned Job" (chap. 32:1-3).

Here Elihu, with remarkable force and clearness, seizes upon the very root of the matter on each side. He condenses, in two brief sentences, the whole of the elaborate discussion contained in twenty-nine chapters. Job justified himself instead of justifying God: and they had condemned Job, instead of leading him to condemn himself.

It is of the very last moral importance to see that whenever we justify ourselves, we condemn God; and on the other hand, when we condemn ourselves, we justify God. "Wisdom is justified of all her children." This is a grand point. The truly broken and contrite heart will vindicate God at all cost. "Let God be true, but every man a liar; as it is written, That thou mightest be justified in thy sayings, and mightest overcome when thou art judged" (Rom. 3:4). God must have the upper hand in the end; and it is the path of true wisdom to give Him the upper hand now. The very moment the soul is broken down in true self-judgment, God rises before it in all the majesty of His grace as a Justifier. But so long as we are ruled by a spirit of self-vindication or self-complacency, we must be total strangers to the deep blessedness of the man to whom God imputeth righteousness without works. The

greatest folly that any one can be guilty of is to justify himself; inasmuch as God must then impute sin. But the truest wisdom is to condemn one's self utterly; for in that case God becomes the Justifier.

But Job had not yet learnt to tread this marvelously blessed path. He was still built up in his own goodness, still clothed in his own righteousness, still full of self-complacency. Hence the wrath of Elihu was kindled against him. Wrath must assuredly fall upon self-righteousness. It cannot be otherwise. The only true ground for a sinner to occupy is the ground of genuine repentance. Here there is naught but that pure and precious grace that reigns through righteousness by Jesus Christ our Lord. Thus it stands ever. There is nothing but wrath for the self-righteous—nothing but grace for the self-judged.

Reader, remember this. Pause for a moment, and consider it. On what ground dost thou, at this moment, stand? Hast thou bowed before God in true repentance? Hast thou ever really measured thyself in His holy presence? Or, art thou on the ground of self-righteousness, self-vindication, and self-complacency? Do, we entreat you, weigh these solemn questions. Do not put them aside. We are most anxious to deal with the heart and conscience of the reader. We do not write merely for the understanding, for the mind, for the intelligence. No doubt it is well to seek to enlighten the understanding, by the Word of God; but we should exceedingly regret if our work were to end here. There is far more than this. God wants to deal with the heart, with the moral being, with the inward man. He will have us real before Him. It is of no possible use to build ourselves up in self-opinionativeness; for nothing is surer than that every thing of that kind must be broken up. The day of the Lord will be against every thing high and lifted up; and hence it is our wisdom now to be low and broken down; for it is from the low place that we get the very best view of God and His salvation. May the reader be led by God's Spirit into the reality of all this! May we all remember that God delights in a broken and contrite spirit—that He ever finds His abode with such; but the proud He knoweth afar off.

Thus, then, we may understand why Elihu's wrath was kindled against Job. He was entirely on God's side. Job was not. We hear nothing of Elihu until chap. 32, though it is very evident that he had been an attentive listener to the whole discussion. He had given a patient hearing to both sides, and he found that both were wrong. Job was wrong in seeking to defend himself; and the friends were wrong in seeking to condemn him.

How often is this the case in our discussions and controversies! And oh, what sorrowful work it is! In ninety-nine cases out of a hundred in the which persons are at issue, it will be found to be very much as it was with Job and his friends. A little brokenness on one side, or a little softness on the other, would go a great way toward settling the question. We speak not, of course, of cases in which the truth of God is concerned. There, one must be bold, decided, and unyielding. To yield where the truth of God or the glory of Christ is concerned, would be disloyalty to the One to whom we owe every thing. Plain decision and unflinching firmness alone become us in all cases in which it is a question of the claims of that blessed One who, when our interests were concerned, surrendered every thing, even life itself, in order to secure them.

God forbid we should drop a sentence or pen a line which might have the effect of relaxing our grasp of truth, or abating our ardor in contending earnestly for the faith once delivered to the saints. Ah, no, this is not the moment for ungirding the loins, laying aside the harness, or lowering the standard. Quite the reverse. Never was there more urgent need of having the loins girt about with truth, of having firm footing, and of maintaining the standard of divine principle in all its integrity. We say this advisedly. We say it in view of all the efforts of the enemy to drive us off the platform of pure truth by referring us to those who have failed in the maintenance of pure morals. Alas! there is failure—sad, humiliating failure. We do not deny it. Who could? It is too patent—too flagrant—too gross. The

heart bleeds as we think of it. Man fails always and every where. His history, from Eden to the present hour, is stamped with failure.

All this is undeniable. But, blessed be God! His foundation standeth sure, nor can human failure ever touch it. God is faithful. He knoweth them that are His; and let every one that nameth the name of Christ depart from iniquity. We have yet to learn that the way to improve *our* morals is to lower God's standard. We do not and cannot believe it. Let us humble ourselves in view of our failure; but never surrender the precious truth of God.

But all this is a digression into which we have allowed ourselves to be drawn in order to guard against the thought that, in urging upon the reader the importance of cultivating a broken, yielding spirit, we would have him to yield a single jot or tittle of divine revelation. We must now return to our subject.

There is something peculiarly marked and striking in the ministry of Elihu. He stands in vivid contrast with the three friends. His name signified "God is he," and no doubt we may view him as a type of our Lord Jesus Christ. He brings God into the scene, and puts a complete stop to the weary strife and contention between Job and his friends. Elihu argues not on the ground of experience; he appeals not to tradition; he breathes not the accents of legality; he brings in God. This is the only way of putting a stop to controversy, of hushing strife, of ending a war of words. Let us hearken to the words of this remarkable personage.

"Now Elihu had waited till Job had spoken, because they were elder than he. When Elihu saw that there was no answer in the mouth of these three men, then his wrath was kindled." Note this: *There was no answer.* In all their reasonings, in all their arguments, in all their references to experience, tradition, and legality, there was "no answer." This is very instructive. Job's friends had traveled over a very wide range, had said many true things, had attempted many replies; but, be it carefully noted, they found "no answer." It is not in the range of earth or of nature to find an answer for a self-righteous heart. God alone can answer it, as we shall see in the sequel. To all else but God the unbroken heart can find a ready reply.

This is most strikingly proved in the history now before us. Job's three friends found no answer. "And Elihu, the son of Barachel the Buzite, answered and said, 'I am young, and ye are very old; wherefore I was afraid, and durst not show mine opinion. I said, Days should speak [but, alas! they either do not speak at all or they speak a quantity of error and folly], and multitude of years should teach wisdom. But there is a spirit in man, and the inspiration of the Almighty giveth him understanding." Here divine light, the light of inspiration, begins to stream in upon the scene, and to roll away the thick clouds of dust raised by the strife of tongues. We are conscious of moral power and weight the very moment this blessed servant opens his lips. We feel we are listening to a man who speaks as the oracles of God—a man who is sensibly standing in the divine presence. It is not a man drawing from the meagre store of his own narrow and one-sided experience; nor yet a man appealing to hoary antiquity, or to a bewildering tradition, or the ever-conflicting voices of the fathers. No; we have before us now a man who introduces us at once into the very presence of "the inspiration of the Almighty."

This is the only sure authority—the only unerring standard. " 'Great men are not always wise, neither do the aged understand judgment.* Therefore I said, Hearken to me; I also will show mine opinion. Behold, I waited for your words; I gave ear to your reasons, whilst ye searched out what to say. Yea, I attended unto you, and, behold, there was none of you that convinced Job, or that answered his words: lest ye should say, We have found out wisdom: God thrusteth him down, not man. Now he hath not directed his

words against me, neither will I answer him with your speeches.' They were amazed; they answered no more; they left off speaking." Experience, tradition, and legality are all swept off the platform to leave room for the "inspiration of the Almighty"—for the direct and powerful ministry of the Spirit of God.

The ministry of Elihu breaks upon the soul with peculiar power and fullness. It stands in vivid contrast with the one-sided and most defective ministry of the three friends. Indeed, it is quite a relief to reach the close of a controversy which seemed likely to prove interminable—a controversy between intense egotism on the one hand and experience, tradition, and legality on the other—a controversy barren of any good, so far as Job was concerned, and leaving all parties at the close very much where they were at the beginning.

Still, however, the controversy is not without its value and interest to us. It teaches us very distinctly that when two parties join issue, they never can reach an understanding unless there be a little brokenness and subduedness on one side or the other. This is a valuable lesson, and one to which we all need to give attention. There is a vast amount of headiness and and highmindedness abroad, not only in the world, but in the Church. There is a great deal of self-occupation—a quantity of "I, I, I"—and that, too, even where we least suspect it, and where it is, most of all, unsightly, namely, in connection with the holy service of Christ. Never, we may safely assert, is egotism more truly detestable than when it shows itself in the service of that blessed One who made Himself of no reputation—whose whole course was one of perfect self-surrender, from first to last—who never sought His own glory in any thing, never maintained His own interest, never pleased Himself.

And yet, for all that, is there not a most deplorable amount of hateful, unsubdued self

---

* What would Elihu have said to the recent dogma of the infallibility of a man—a dogma accepted by over five hundred rational beings sitting in solemn conclave?

And this is to be henceforth part and parcel of the faith of Christians! Not long since, men were called upon to believe in *an immaculate woman*; now they are called upon to believe in *an infallible man!* What is to come next? Surely the "strong delusion" must soon set in, when men will be compelled, by God's judicial dealings, to believe a lie, because they *would* not believe the truth. May the eternal Spirit put forth His mighty energy in the conversion of precious souls ere the day of vengeance sets in!

displayed on the platform of Christian profession and Christian service? Alas! we cannot deny it. We are disposed to marvel, as the eye scans the record of the remarkable discussion between Job and his friends; we are amazed to find close upon a hundred references to himself in Job 29—31 alone. In short, it is all "I" from beginning to end.

But let us look to ourselves. Let us judge our own hearts in their deeper workings. Let us review our ways in the light of the divine presence. Let us bring all our work and service, and have it weighed in the holy balances of the sanctuary of God. Then shall we discover how much of hateful self is insinuated, like a dark and defiling tissue, into the whole web of our Christian life and service. How, for example, comes it to pass that we are so ready to mount the high horse when self is touched, even in the most remote degree? Why are we so impatient of reproof, be it clothed in language ever so refined and gentle? Why so ready to take offense at the slightest disparagement of self? And, further, why is it that we find our sympathies and our regards and our predilections going out, with special energy, after those who think well of us,—who value our ministry, agree with our opinions, and adopt our *cue?*

Do not all these things tell a tale? Do they not prove to us that, ere we condemn the egotism of our ancient patriarch, we should seek to get rid of a vast amount of our own? It is not, surely, that he was right; but we are far more wrong. It is far less to be wondered at that a man, amid the dim twilight of the farback patriarchal age, was entangled in the snare of self-occupation, than that we, in the full blaze of Christianity, should fall thereinto. Christ had not come. No prophetic voice had fallen on the ear. Even the law had not been given when Job lived and spoke and thought. We can form a very poor conception indeed of the tiny ray of light by which men had to walk in the days of Job. But to us pertain the high privilege and holy responsibility of walking in the very meridian light of a full-orbed Christianity. Christ has come. He has lived, died, risen, and gone back to Heaven. He has sent down the Holy Ghost to dwell in our hearts, as the witness of

His glory, the seal of accomplished redemption, and the earnest of the inheritance, until the redemption of the purchased possession. The canon of Scripture is closed. The circle of revelation is complete. The Word of God is filled up. We have before us the divine record of the self-emptied One who went about doing good—the marvelous story of what He did, and how He did it, of what He said, and how He said it, of who He was and what He was. We know that He died for our sins according to the Scriptures; that He condemned sin and put it away; that our old nature—that odious thing called self, sin, the flesh—has been crucified and buried out of God's sight—made an end of forever, so far as its power over us is concerned. Moreover, we are made partakers of the divine nature; we have the Holy Ghost dwelling in us; we are members of Christ's body, of His flesh, and of His bones; we are called to walk, even as He walked; we are heirs of glory—heirs of God and joint-heirs with Christ.

What did Job know of all this? Nothing. How could he know what was not revealed till fifteen centuries after his time? The full extent of Job's knowledge is poured upon us in those few glowing and impassioned words at the close of chap. 19. "Oh, that my words were now written! Oh, that they were printed in a book! That they were graven with an iron pen and lead in the rock forever! For I know that my Redeemer liveth, and that He shall stand at the latter day upon the earth. And though, after my skin worms destroy this body yet in my flesh shall I see God: whom I shall see for myself, and my eyes shall behold, and not another; though my reins be consumed within me."

This was Job's knowledge—this was his creed. There was a great deal in it, in one sense; but very little indeed when compared with the mighty circle of truths in the midst of which we are privileged to move. Job looked forward, through the dim twilight, to something that was to be done in the far-off future. We look back, from amid the full flood-tide of divine revelation, to something that has been done. Job could say of his Redeemer that "He *shall* stand in the latter day upon the *earth.*" We know that our

Redeemer sitteth on the throne of the Majesty in the heavens, after having lived and labored and died on the earth.

In short, the measure of Job's light and privilege admits of no comparison with that which we enjoy; and for this reason it is the less excusable in us to indulge in the varied forms of egotism and self-occupation. Our self-abnegation should be in proportion to the measure of our spiritual privilege. But alas! it is not so. We profess the very highest truths; but our character is not formed, nor is our conduct governed, by them. We speak of the heavenly calling; but our ways are earthly, sometimes sensual, or worse. We profess to enjoy the very highest standing; but our state does not comport therewith. Our real condition does not answer to our assumed position. We are high-minded, touchy, tenacious, and easily provoked. We are quite as ready to embark in the business of self-vindication as our patriarch Job.

And then, on the other hand, when we feel called upon to approach another in the attitude and tone of reproof, with what rudeness, coarseness, and harshness we discharge the necessary work! How little softness of tone or delicacy of touch! How little of the tender and the soothing! How little of the "excellent oil"! How little of the broken heart and weeping eye! What slender ability to bring our erring brother down into the dust! Why is this? Simply because we are not habitually in the dust ourselves. If, on the one hand, we fail quite as much as Job in the matter of egotism and self-vindication, so on the other, we prove ourselves fully as incompetent as Job's friends to produce self-judgment in our brother. For example, how often do we parade our own experience, like Eliphaz; or indulge in a legal spirit, like Zophar; or introduce human authority, like Bildad! How little of the spirit and mind of Christ! How little of the power of the Holy Ghost, or the authority of the Word of God!

It is not pleasant to write thus. Quite the contrary. But it is pressed upon us, and we must write. We feel most solemnly, the growing laxity and indifference of the day in which we live. There is something perfectly appalling in the disproportion between our profession and practice. The highest truths are professed in immediate connection with gross worldliness and self-indulgence. Indeed, it would appear as though, in some cases, the higher the doctrines professed, the lower the walk. There is a wise diffusion of truth in our midst; but where is its formative power? Floods of light are poured upon the intelligence; but where are the profound exercises of heart and conscience in the presence of God? The rigid rule of precise and accurate statement is attended to; but where is the true practical result? Sound doctrine is unfolded in the letter; but where is the spirit? There is the form of words; but where is the living exponent?

Is it that we do not prize sound doctrine and accurate statement? Is it that we undervalue the wide diffusion of precious truth, in its very highest forms? Far, far away be the thought! Human language would utterly fail to set forth our estimate of these things. God forbid we should pen a line which might tend in any wise to lower in the mind of the reader the sense of the unspeakable value and importance of a lofty—yea, the very loftiest—standard of truth and sound doctrine. We are most thoroughly convinced that we shall never improve our morals by lowering, the breadth of a hair, the standard of principle.

But, Christian reader, we would lovingly and solemnly ask you, Does it not strike you that there is in our midst a most melancholy lack of the tender conscience and the exercised heart? Does our practical piety keep pace with our profession of principle? Is the standard of morals at all up to the standard of doctrine?

Ah! we anticipate the reply of the grave and thoughtful reader. We know too well the terms in which that reply must be couched. It is but too plain that the truth does not act on the conscience—that the doctrine does not shine in the life—that the practice does not correspond with the profession.

We speak for ourselves. As God is our witness, we pen these lines, in His presence, in a spirit of self-judgment. It is our hearty desire that the knife should enter into our own soul, and reach the deep roots of things there. The Lord knows how much we should prefer laying the ax to the root of self and there leave it to do its work. But we feel we have a sacred duty to discharge to the individual reader and to the Church of God; and, moreover, we feel that that duty would not be discharged were we merely to set forth the precious and the beautiful and the true. We are convinced that God would have us not only to be exercised in heart and conscience ourselves, but also to seek to exercise the hearts and consciences of all with whom we have to do.

True it is (a truth often stated and proved) that worldliness and carnality, and self-indulgence in all its phases—in the wardrobe, the library, the equipage, and the table—that fashion and style, folly and vanity, pride of *caste*, of intellect, and of purse—none of these things can be talked down, written, lectured, or scolded down. This we fully believe. But must not conscience be addressed? Must not the voice of holy exhortation fall on the ear? Shall we suffer laxity, indifferentism, and Laodicean lukewarmness to pave the way for a universal skepticism, infidelity, and practical atheism, and not be roused in conscience ourselves, and seek to rouse others? God forbid! No doubt, the higher and the better way is to have the evil expelled by the good, to have the flesh subdued by the Spirit, to have self displaced by Christ, to have the love of the world supplanted by the love of the Father: all this we fully feel and freely admit; but, while feeling and admitting all this, we must still press upon our own conscience and that of the reader the urgent demand for solemn and searching review—for deep searchings of heart in the secret of the presence of God—for profound self-judgment, in reference to our whole career. Blessed be God! we can carry on these exercises before the throne of grace, the precious mercy-seat. "Grace reigns." Precious consoling sentence! Should it prevent exercise of soul? Nay, it should only impart the right tone and character thereto. We have to do with victorious grace, not that we may indulge self, but mortify it all the more thoroughly.

May the Lord make us really humble, earnest, and devoted! May the deep utterance of the heart both of the writer and the reader be, "Lord, I am Thine—Thine only, Thine wholly, Thine forever!"

This may seem to some a digression from our special theme; but we trust the digression may not be in vain, but that, by the grace of God, it will yield something for the heart and conscience of both the writer and the reader; and thus we shall be better prepared to understand and appreciate the powerful ministry of Elihu, to which we shall now turn our attention, in dependence upon divine guidance.

The reader cannot fail to notice the double bearing of this remarkable ministry—its bearing upon our patriarch and its bearing upon his friends. This is only what we might expect. Elihu, as we have already remarked, had patiently listened to the arguments on both sides. He had, as we say, heard both parties out. He had allowed them to exhaust themselves—to say all they had to say: "Elihu had waited till Job had spoken, because they were older than he." This is in lovely moral order. It was, most surely, the way of the Spirit of God. Modesty in a young man is most graceful. Would there were more of it in our midst! Nothing is more attractive in the young than a quiet, retiring spirit. When real worth lies concealed beneath a modest and humble exterior, it is sure to draw the heart with irresistible power. But on the other hand, nothing is more repulsive than the bold self-confidence, the pushing forwardness, and self-conceit of many of the young men of the present day. All such persons would do well to study the opening words of Elihu, and to imitate his example.

"And Elihu, the son of Barachel the Buzite, answered and said, 'I am young, and ye are very old; wherefore I was afraid, and durst not show you mine opinion. I said, Days should speak, and multitude of years should teach wisdom.' " This is the natural order. We expect hoary heads to contain wisdom; and hence it is but right and comely for young men to be swift to hear, slow to speak, in the presence of their elders. We may set it down as an almost fixed principle that a forward young man is not led by the Spirit of God—that he has never measured himself in the divine presence—that he has never been thoroughly broken down before God.

No doubt it may often happen, as in the case of Job and his friends, that old men give utterance to very foolish things. Gray hairs and wisdom do not always go together; and it not unfrequently happens that aged men, relying upon the mere fact of their years, assume a place for which they have no sort of power, either moral, intellectual, or spiritual. All this is perfectly true, and it has to be considered by those whom it may concern. But it leaves wholly untouched the fine moral sentiment contained in Elihu's opening address: "I am young, and ye are very old; wherefore I was afraid, and durst not show you mine opinion." This is always right. It is always comely for a young man to be afraid to show his opinion. We may rest assured that a man who possesses inward moral power—who, as we say, *has it in him*—is never in haste to push himself forward; but yet, when he does come forward, he is sure to be heard with respect and attention. The union of modesty and moral power imparts an irresistible charm to the character; but the most splendid abilities are marred by a self-confident style.

"But," continues Elihu, "there is a spirit in man; and the inspiration of the Almighty giveth him understanding." This introduces another element altogether. The moment the Spirit of God enters the scene, it ceases to be a question of youth or old age, inasmuch as he can speak by old or young. "Not by might or by power; but by My Spirit, saith the Lord of hosts." This holds good always. It was true for the patriarchs; true for the prophets; true for apostles; true for us; true for all. It is not by human might or power, but by the eternal Spirit.

Here lay the deep secret of Elihu's quiet power. He was filled with the Spirit, and hence we forget his youth, while hearkening to the words of spiritual weight and heavenly wisdom that proceed out of his mouth; and we are reminded of Him who spake as one having authority, and not as the scribes.

There is a striking difference between a man who speaks as an oracle of God, and one who speaks in mere official routine—between one who speaks from the heart, by the Spirit's holy unction, and one who speaks from the intellect by human authority. Who can duly estimate the difference between these two? None but those who possess and exercise the mind of Christ.

But let us proceed with Elihu's address.

"Great men," he tells us, "are not always wise." How true! "Neither do the aged understand judgment. Therefore I said, Hearken to me; I also will show mine opinion. Behold, I waited for your words; I gave ear to your reasons, whilst ye searched out what to say. Yea, I attended unto you, and, behold, there was none of you that convinced Job, or that answered his words."

Let us specially note this. "There was none of you that convinced Job." This was clear enough. Job was just as far from being convinced at the close of the discussion as he was at the commencement. Indeed we may say that each fresh argument drawn from the treasury of experience, tradition, and legality only served to stir some fresh and deeper depth of Job's unjudged, unsubdued, unmortified nature. This is a grand moral truth, illustrated on every page of the book which lies open before us.

But how instructive the reason for all this! "Lest ye should say, We have found out wisdom; God thrusteth him down, not man." No flesh shall glory in the presence of God. It may boast itself outside. It may put forth its pretensions, and glory in its resources, and be proud of its undertakings, so long as God is not thought of. But only introduce Him, and all the vauntings, the boastings, the vain-gloryings, the lofty pretensions, and the self-complacency, and the self-conceit will be withered up in a moment.

Let us remember this. "Boasting is excluded." Yes; all boasting—the boasting of Job, the boasting of his friends. If Job had succeeded in establishing his cause, he would have boasted. If, on the other hand, his friends had succeeded in silencing him, they might have boasted. But no; "God thrusteth him down, not man."

Thus it was; thus it is; and thus it must ever be. God knows how to humble the proud heart and subdue the stubborn will. It is utterly vain for any one to set himself up; for we may rest assured that every one who is set up must, sooner or later, be upset. The moral government of God has so ordered and enacted that all that is high and lifted up must come down. This is a salutary truth for us all; but especially for the young, the ardent, and the aspiring. The humble, retired, shady path is, unquestionably, the safest, the happiest, and the best. May we ever be found treading it, until we reach that bright and blessed scene where pride and ambition are unknown?

The effect of Elihu's opening words upon Job's three friends was most striking. "They were amazed; they answered no more; they left off speaking. When I had waited—for they spake not, but stood still, and answered no more—I said, I will answer also my part; I also will show mine opinion." And then, lest any should suppose that he was speaking his own words, he adds, "For I am full of matter; the spirit within me constraineth me." This is the true spring and power of all ministry, in all ages. It must be "the inspiration of the Almighty," or it is worth absolutely nothing.

We repeat, this is the only true source of ministry, at all times and in all places. And in saying this, we do not forget that a mighty change took place when our Lord Christ ascended to Heaven and took His seat at the right hand of God, in virtue of accomplished redemption. To this glorious truth we have often referred the readers of our magazine, *Things New and Old;* and hence shall not now permit ourselves to dwell upon it. We merely touch upon it in this place, lest the reader might imagine that, when we speak of the true source of ministry in all ages, we were forgetting what is marked and distinctive in the Church of God now, in consequence of the death and resurrection of Christ, the presence and indwelling of the Holy Ghost, in the individual believer, and in the Church, which is the body of Christ on earth. Far from it. Thanks and praise be to God! we have too deep a sense of the value, importance, and practical weight of that grand and glorious truth ever to lose sight of it for a moment. Indeed, it is just this deep sense, together with the remembrance of Satan's ceaseless effort to ignore the truth of the presence of the Holy Ghost in the Church, that leads us to pen this cautionary paragraph.

Still, Elihu's principle must ever hold good. If any man is to speak with power and practical effect, he must be able, in some measure, to say, "I am full of matter; the spirit within me constraineth me.* Behold, my belly is as wine which hath no vent; it is ready to burst like new bottles. I will speak, that I may be refreshed: I will open my lips and answer." Thus it must ever be, in measure at least, with all who will speak with real power and effect to the hearts and consciences of their fellows. We are forcibly reminded, by Elihu's glowing words, of that memorable passage in the seventh of John, "He that believeth on Me, as the Scripture hath said, out of his belly shall flow rivers of living water." True it is that Elihu knew not the glorious truth set forth in these words of our Lord, inasmuch as they were not made good till fifteen centuries after his time. But then he knew the principle—he possessed the germ of what was afterward to come out in full blown and rich mellow fruit. He knew that a man, if he is to speak with point, pungency, and power, must speak by the inspiration of the Almighty. He had listened till he was tired to men talking a quantity of powerless matter—saying some truisms—drawing from their own experience, or from

---

* Let the reader distinctly understand that Elihu, in the above quotation, speaks, not of the indwelling of the Holy Ghost, as believers now know it. This was wholly unknown to saints in Old Testament times, and was the direct result of accomplished redemption—the special fruit of the glorification of Christ at the right hand of the Majesty in the heavens. This important truth has been repeatedly referred to and dwelt upon at other times, and hence we shall not go into it now; but we would request the reader to turn to John 7:39 and 16:7, and meditate upon the doctrine there taught, apart from all preconceived thoughts of his own, and irrespective of all the opinions of men. From these Scriptures, he will see distinctly that the Holy Ghost did not and could not come until Jesus was glorified. This is not a mere speculation—a human theory—the dogma of a certain school. It is a grand foundation-truth of Christianity, to be reverently received, tenaciously held, and faithfully confessed by every true Christian. May all the Lord's people be led to see and believe it!

the musty stores of human tradition. He was well-nigh wearied out with all this, and he rises, in the mighty energy of the Spirit, to address his hearers as one fitted to speak like an oracle of God.

Here lies the deep and blessed secret of ministerial power and success. "If any man speak," says Peter, "let him speak as the oracles of God." It is not, be it carefully observed, merely speaking according to Scripture—an all-important and essential matter, most surely. It is more. A man may rise and address his fellows for an hour, and, from beginning to end of his discourse, he may not utter so much as a single unscriptural sentence; and all the while, he may not have been God's oracle at the time—he may not have been God's mouth-piece, or the present exponent of His mind to the souls before him.

This is peculiarly solemn, and demands the grave consideration of all who are called to open their lips in the midst of God's people. It is one thing to utter a certain amount of true sentiment, and quite another to be the living channel of communication between the very heart of God and the souls of God's people. It is this latter, and this alone, that constitutes true ministry. A man who speaks as an oracle of God will bring the conscience of the hearer so into the very light of the divine presence that every chamber of the heart is laid open, and every moral spring touched. This is true ministry. All else is powerless, valueless, fruitless. Nothing is more deplorable and humiliating than to listen to a man who is evidently drawing from his own poor and scanty resources, or trafficking in second-hand truth—in borrowed thoughts. Better far for such to be silent—better for their hearers, better for themselves. Nor this only. We may often hear a man giving forth to his fellows that on which his own mind has been dwelling in private with much interest and profit. He may utter truth, and important truth; but it is not *the* truth for the souls of the people—*the* truth for the moment. He has spoken according to Scripture so far as his matter is concerned, but he has not spoken as an oracle of God.

Thus, then, may all learn a valuable lesson

from Elihu; and, most surely, it is a needed lesson. Some may feel disposed to say it is a difficult lesson—a hard saying. But no; if we only live in the Lord's presence, in the abiding sense of our own nothingness and of His all-sufficiency, we shall know the precious secret of all effective ministry; we shall know how to lean upon God alone, and thus be independent of men, in the right sense; we shall be able to enter into the meaning and force of Elihu's further words, "Let me not, I pray you, accept any man's person; neither let me give flattering titles unto man. For I know not to give flattering titles; in so doing, my Maker would soon take me away" (Job 32:21-22).

In studying the ministry of Elihu, we find in it two grand elements, namely, "grace and truth." Both these were essential in dealing with Job; and, consequently, we find both coming out with extraordinary power. He tells Job and his friends very distinctly that he knows not how to give flattering titles unto man. Here the voice of "truth" falls with great clearness on the ear. Truth puts every one in his right place; and, just because it does so, it cannot bestow titles of flattery upon a poor guilty mortal, however much that mortal might be gratified by them. Man must be brought to know himself, to see his true condition, to confess what he really is. This was precisely what Job needed. He did not know himself, and his friends could not give him that knowledge. He needed to be led down into the depths; but his friends could not conduct him thither. He needed self-judgment; but his friends were wholly unable to produce it.

But Elihu begins by telling Job the truth. He introduces God into the scene in His true character. This was just what the three friends had failed to do. No doubt they had referred to God; but their references were cloudy, distorted, and false. This is plain from chap. 42:7-8, where we are told that "the Lord said to Eliphaz the Temanite, My wrath is kindled against thee, and against thy two friends; for *ye have not spoken of Me the thing* that is right, as My servant Job hath. Therefore take unto you now seven bullocks and seven rams, and go to My servant Job, and offer up for yourselves a burnt-offering; and My servant Job shall pray for you, for him will I accept; lest I deal with you after your folly, in that ye have not spoken of Me the thing which is right, like My servant Job."* They had utterly failed to bring God before the soul of their friend, and there they failed in producing the needed self-judgment.

Not so Elihu. He pursues a totally different line of things. He brings the light of "truth" to bear upon Job's conscience; and at the same time he administers the precious balm of "grace" to his heart. Let us quote his further sayings, "Wherefore, Job, I pray thee, hear my speeches, and hearken to all my words. Behold, now I have opened my mouth, my tongue hath spoken in my mouth. My words shall be of the uprightness of my heart, and my lips shall utter knowledge clearly. The Spirit of God hath made me, and the breath of the Almighty hath given me life. If thou canst answer me, set thy words in order before me, stand up. Behold, I am according to thy wish in God's stead: I am also formed out of clay. Behold, my terror shall not make thee afraid, neither shall my hand be heavy upon thee."

In these accents, the ministry of "grace" unfolds itself, sweetly and powerfully, to the heart of Job. Of this most excellent ingredient there was a total absence in the ministry of the three friends. They showed themselves only too ready to bear down upon Job with "a heavy hand." They were stern judges, severe censors, false interpreters. They could fix their cold, gray eye upon the wounds of their poor afflicted friend, and wonder how they came there. They looked on the crumbling ruins of his house, and drew the harsh inference that the ruin was but the result of his bad behavior. They beheld his fallen fortunes, and, with unmitigated severity, concluded that those fortunes had fallen because of his faults. They had proved themselves to be entirely one-sided judges. They had wholly misunderstood the dealings of God. They had never seized the full moral force of that one weighty sentence, "*God trieth the righteous.*" In a word, they were utterly astray. Their standpoint was false, and hence their whole range of vision was defective. There was neither "grace" nor "truth" in their ministry, and therefore they failed to convince Job. They condemned him without convincing him, whereas they ought to have convinced him and made him condemn himself.

Here it is that Elihu stands out in vivid contrast. He tells Job the truth; but he lays no heavy hand upon him. Elihu has learnt the mighty mysterious power of "the still small voice"—the soul-subduing, heart-melting virtue of grace. Job had given utterance to a quantity of false notions about himself, and those notions had sprouted from a root to which the sharp ax of "truth" had to be applied. "Surely," says Elihu, "thou hast spoken in my hearing, and I have heard the voice of thy words, saying, 'I am clean without transgression, I am innocent; neither is there iniquity in me.'"

What words for any poor sinful mortal to utter! Surely, though "the true light" in which we may walk had not shone on the soul of this patriarch, we may well marvel at such language. And yet, mark what follows. Although he was so clean, so innocent, so free from iniquity, he nevertheless says of God, that "He findeth occasions, he counteth me for His enemy. He putteth my feet in the stocks. He marketh all my paths." Here is a palpable discrepancy. How could a holy, just, and righeous Being count a pure and innocent man His enemy? Impossible. Either Job was self-deceived, or God was unrighteous; and Elihu, as the minister of truth, is not long in pronouncing a judgment, and telling us which is which. "Behold, in this thou art not just: I will answer thee, that God is greater than man." What a simple truth! And yet how little understood! If God is greater than man, then obviously He, and not man, must be the judge of what is right. This, the infidel heart refuses; and hence the constant tendency to sit in judgment upon the works and ways and Word of God—upon God Himself. Man, in his impious and infidel folly, undertakes to

---

* The reader will bear in mind that the above words were spoken after Job's repentance. It is of the very last importance to see this.

pronounce judgment upon what is and what is not worthy of God; to decide upon what God ought and what He ought not to say and to do. He proves himself utterly ignorant of that most simple, obvious necessary truth, that "God is greater than man."

Now, it is when the heart bows under the weight of this great moral truth, that we are in a fit attitude to understand the object of God's dealings with us. Assuredly He must have the upper hand. "Why dost thou strive against Him? for He giveth not account of any of His matters. For God speaketh once, yea, twice, yet man perceiveth it not. In a dream, in a vision of the night, when deep sleep falleth upon men, in slumberings upon the bed; then He openeth the ears of men, and sealeth their instruction, *that He may withdraw man from his purpose, and hide pride from man. He keepeth back* his soul from the pit, and his life from perishing by the sword."

The real secret of all Job's false reasoning is to be found in the fact that he did not understand the character of God, or the object of all His dealings. He did not see that God was trying him, that He was behind the scenes and using various agents for the accomplishment of His wise and gracious ends. Even Satan himself was a mere instrument in the hand of God; nor could he move the breadth of a hair beyond the divinely prescribed limit; and moreover, when he had executed his appointed business, he was dismissed, and we hear no more about him. God was dealing with Job. He was trying him in order that He might instruct him, withdraw him from his purpose, and hide pride from him. Had Job seized this grand point, it would have saved him a world of strife and contention. Instead of getting angry with people and things, with individuals and influences, he would have judged himself and bowed low before the Lord in meekness and brokenness and true contrition.

This is immensely important for us all. We are all of us prone to forget the weighty fact that "God trieth the righteous." "He withdraweth not His eyes from them." We are in His hands, and under His eye

continually. We are the objects of His deep, tender, and unchanging love; but we are also the subjects of His wise moral government. His dealings with us are varied. They are sometimes preventive; sometimes corrective; always instructive. We may be bent on some course of our own, the end of which would be moral ruin. He intervenes and withdraws us from our purpose. He dashes into fragments our air-built castles, dissipates our golden dreams, and interrupts many a darling scheme on which our hearts were bent, and which woud have proved to be certain destruction. "Lo, all these things worketh God oftentimes with man, to bring back his soul from the pit, *to be enlightened with the light of the livng.*"

If the reader will turn for a moment to Hebrews 12:3-12, he will find much precious instruction on the subject of God's dealings with His people. We do not attempt to dwell upon it, but would merely remark that it presents three distinct ways in which we may meet the chastening of our Father's hand. We may "*despise*" it, as though His hand and His voice were not in it; we may "*faint*" under it, as though it were intolerable, and not the precious fruit of His love; or lastly, we may be "*exercised* by it," and thus reap in due time, "the peaceable fruits of righteousness."

Now if our patriarch had only seized the great fact that God was dealing with him; that He was trying him for his ultimate good; that He was using circumstances, people, the Sabeans, Satan himself, as His instruments; that all his trials, his losses, his bereavements, his sufferings, were but God's marvelous agency in bringing about His wise and gracious end; that He would assuredly perfect that which concerned His dear and much-loved servant, because His mercy endureth forever; in a word, had Job only lost sight of all second causes, and fixed his thoughts upon the living God alone, and accepted all from His loving hand, he would have more speedily reached the divine solution of all his difficulties.

But it is precisely here that we are all apt to break down. We get occupied with men and things; we view them in reference to ourselves. We do not walk with God through, or rather above, the circumstances; but on the contrary, we allow the circumstances to get power over us. In place of keeping God between us and our circumstances, we permit these latter to get between us and God. Thus we lose the sense of His presence, the light of His countenance, the holy calmness of being in His loving hand, and under His fatherly eye. We become fretful, impatient, irritable, fault-finding. We get far away from God, out of communion, thoroughly astray, judging every one except ourselves, until at length God takes us in hand, and by His own direct and powerful ministry, brings us back to Himself in true brokenness of heart and humbleness of mind. This is "the end of the Lord."

We must, however, draw this paper to a close. Gladly would we expatiate further on Elihu's remarkable ministry; with pleasure and profit could we quote his further appeals to Job's heart and conscience, his pungent arguments, his pointed questions. But we must forbear, and leave the reader to go through the remaining chapters for himself. In so doing, we will find that when Elihu closes his ministry, God Himself begins to deal directly with the soul of His servant (chap. 38–41). He appeals to His works in creation as the display of a power and wisdom which ought assuredly to make Job feel his own littleness. We do not attempt to cull passages from one of the most magnificent and sublime sections of the inspired canon. It must be read as a whole. It needs no comment. The human finger could but tarnish its lustre. Its plainness is only equaled by its moral grandeur. All we shall attempt to do is to call attention to the powerful effect produced upon the heart of Job by this the most marvelous ministry surely under which mortal man was ever called to sit—the immediate ministry of the living God Himself.

This effect was threefold. It had reference to God, to himself, and to his friends—the very points on which he was so entirely astray. As to God, Elihu had declared Job's mistake in the following words: "Job hath spoken without knowledge, and his words were without wisdom. My desire is that Job

may be tried unto the end, because of his answers for wicked men. For he addeth rebellion unto his sin; he clappeth his hands among us, and multiplieth his words against God . . . . Thinkest thou this to be right, that thou saidst, 'My righteousness is more than God's' "? But mark the change. Harken to the breathings of a truly repentant spirit; the brief yet comprehensive statement of a corrected judgment. "Then Job answered the Lord, and said, 'I know that Thou canst do every thing, and that no thought can be withholden from Thee. Who is he that hideth counsel without knowledge? therefore have I uttered that I understood not; things too wonderful for me, which I knew not. Hear, I beseech Thee, and I will speak. I will demand of Thee, and declare Thou unto me. I have heard of Thee by the hearing of the ear, *but now mine eye seeth Thee*' " (chap. 42:1-9).

Here, then, was the turning-point. All his previous statements as to God and His ways are now pronounced to be "words without knowledge." What a confession! What a moment in man's history when he discovers that he has been all wrong! What a thorough break-down! What profound humiliation! It reminds us of Jacob getting the hollow of his thigh touched, and thus learning his utter weakness and nothingness. There are weighty moments in the history of souls—great epochs, which leave an indelible impress on the whole moral being and character. To get right thoughts about God is to begin to get right about every thing. If I am wrong about God, I am wrong about myself, wrong about my fellows, wrong about all.

Thus it was with Job. His new thoughts as to God were immediately connected with new thoughts of himself; and hence we find that the elaborate self-vindication, the impassioned egotism, the vehement self-gratulation, the lengthened arguments in self-defense—all is laid aside; all is displaced by one short sentence of three words,—"*I am vile.*" And what is to be done with this vile self? Talk about it? Set it up? Be occupied with it? Take counsel for it? Make provision for it? Nay, "*I abhor it.*"

This is the true moral ground for every one

of us. Job took a long time to reach it, and so do we. Many of us imagine that we have reached the end of self when we have given a nominal assent to the doctrine of human depravity, or judged some of those sprouts which have appeared above the surface of our practical life. But, alas! it is to be feared that very few of us indeed really know the full truth about ourselves. It is one thing to say, *"We* are all vile,*"* and quite another to feel, deep down in the heart, that *"I* am vile.*"* This latter can only be known and habitually realized in the immediate presence of God. The two things must ever go together, "Mine eye seeth *Thee,"* "wherefore I abhor *myself."* It is as the light of what God is shines in upon what I am that I abhor myself. And then my self-abhorrence is a real thing. It is not in word, neither in tongue, but in deed and in truth. It will be seen in a life of self-abnegation, a humble spirit, a lowly mind, a gracious carriage in the midst of the scenes through which I am called to pass. It is of little use to profess very low thoughts of self while, at the same time, we are quick to resent any injury done to us,—any fancied insult, slight, or disparagement. The true secret of a broken and contrite heart is, to abide ever in the Divine Presence, and then we are able to carry ourselves right toward those with whom we have to do.

Thus we find that when Job got right as to God and himself, he soon got right as to his friends, for he learned to pray for them. Yes, he could pray for the "miserable comforters," the "physicians of no value," the very men with whom he had so long, so stoutly, and so vehemently contended! "And the Lord turned the captivity of Job when he prayed for his friends."

This is morally beautiful. It is perfect. It is

the rare and exquisite fruit of divine workmanship. Nothing can be more touching than to see Job's three friends exchanging their experience, their tradition, and their legality for the precious "burnt-offering;" and to see our dear patriarch exchanging his bitter invectives for the sweet prayer of charity. In short, it is a most soul-subduing scene altogether. The combatants are in the dust before God and in each other's arms. The strife is ended; the war of words is closed; and instead thereof, we have the tears of repentance, the sweet odor of the burnt-offering, the embrace of love.

Happy scene! Precious fruit of divine ministry! What remains? What more is needed? What but that the hand of God should lay the top-stone on the beauteous structure? Nor is this lacking, for we read, "The Lord gave Job twice as much as he had before." But how? By what agency? Was it by his own independent industry and clever management? No; all is changed. Job is on new moral ground. He has new thoughts of God, new thoughts of himself, new thoughts of his friends, new thoughts of his circumstances; all things are become new. "Then came there unto him all his brethren, and all his sisters, and all they that had been of his acquaintance before, and did eat bread with him in his house; and they bemoaned him, and comforted him over all the evil that the Lord had brought upon him; *every man also gave him a piece of money, and every one an earring of gold.* So the Lord blessed the latter end of Job more than his beginning . . . . After this lived Job a hundred and forty years, and saw his sons, and his sons' sons, even four generations. So Job died, being old and full of days."

DISCIPLESHIP IN AN EVIL DAY

DANIEL 1—3

THE FIRST THREE CHAPTERS of the book of Daniel furnish a most seasonable and important lesson at a time like the present, in which the disciple is in such danger of yielding to surrounding influences, and of lowering his standard of testimony and his tone of discipleship, in order to meet the existing condition of things.

At the opening of chapter 1, we have a most discouraging picture of the state of things, in reference to the ostensible witness of God on the earth. "In the third year of the reign of Jehoiakim, king of Judah, came Nebuchadnezzar, king of Babylon, unto Jerusalem, and besieged it. And the Lord gave Jehoiakim, king of Judah, into his hand, with part of the vessels of the house of God, which he carried into the land of Shinar, to the house of his god; and he brought the vessels into the house of his god" (chap. 1: 1-2). Here then we have an aspect of things quite sufficient, if looked at from nature's point of view, to discourage the heart, to damp the spirit, and paralyse the energies. Jerusalem in ruins, the temple trodden down, the Lord's vessels in the house of a false god, and Judah carried away captive. Surely the heart would feel disposed to say, There is no use in seeking to hold up the standard of practical discipleship and personal devoted ness any longer. The spirit must droop, the heart must faint, and the hands must hang down, when such is the condition of the people of God. It could be nought but the greatest presumption for any of Judah's sons to think of taking up a true Nazarite's position at such a time.

Such would be nature's reasoning; but such was not the language of faith. Blessed be God! there is always a wide sphere in which the spirit of genuine devotedness can develop itself—there is always a path along which the true disciple can run, even though he should have to run in solitude. It matters not what the outward condition of things may be, it is faith's privilege to hang as much on God, to feed as much on Christ, and to breathe as much of the air of Heaven, as though all were in perfect order and harmony.

This is an unspeakable mercy to the faithful heart. All who desire to walk devotedly can always find a path to walk in; whereas, on the contrary, the man who draws a plea, from outward circumstances, for relaxing his energy, would not be energetic, though most favoraby situated.

If ever there was a time in which one might be excused for taking a low ground, it was the time of the Babylonish captivity. The entire framework of Judaism was broken up; the kingly power had passed out of the hand of David's successor, and into the hand of Nebuchadnezzar; the glory had departed from Israel; and, in one word, all seemed faded and gone, and naught remained for the exiled children of Judah, save to hang their harps upon the willows, and sit down by the rivers of Babylon, there to weep over departed glory, faded light, and fallen greatness.

Such would be the language of blind unbelief; but, blessed be God! it is when everything appears sunk to the lowest possible point, that then faith rises in holy triumph; and faith, we know, is the only true basis of effective discipleship. It asks for no props from the men and things around it; it finds "*all* its springs" in God; and hence it is that faith never shines so brightly as when all around is dark. It is when nature's horizon is overcast with the blackest clouds, that faith basks in the sunshine of the divine favor and faithfulness.

Thus it was that Daniel and his companions

were enabled to overcome the peculiar difficulties of their time. They judged that there was nothing to hinder their enjoying as elevated a Nazariteship in Babylon as ever had been known in Jerusalem; and they judged rightly. Their judgment was the judgment of a pure and well-founded faith. It was the selfsame judgment on which the Baraks, the Gideons, the Jephthahs, and the Samsons of old had acted. It was the judgment of which Jonathan gave utterance, when he said, "There is no restraint with the Lord to save by many or by few" (1 Sam. 14). It was the judgment of David, in the valley of Elah, when he called the poor trembling host of Israel "the army of the living God" (1 Sam. 17). It was the judgment of Elijah, on mount Carmel, when he built an altar with "twelve stones according to the number of the tribes of the sons of Jacob" (1 Kings 18). It was the judgment of Daniel himself when, at a further stage of his history, he opened his window and prayed toward Jerusalem (Dan. 6). It was the judgment of Paul when, in view of the overwhelming tide of apostasy and corruption which was about to set in, he exhorts his son Timothy to "hold fast the form of sound words" (2 Tim. 1:13). It was the judgment of Peter when, in prospect of the dissolution of the entire framework of creation, he encourages believers to "be diligent, that they be found of Him in peace, without spot and blameless" (2 Peter 3:14). It was the judgment of John when, amid the actual breaking up of everything ecclesiastical, he exhorts his well-beloved Gaius to "follow not that which is evil, but that which is good" (3 John 2). And it was the judgment of Jude when, in the presence of the most appalling wickedness, he encourages a beloved remnant to "build themselves up in their most holy faith, praying in the Holy Ghost, to keep themselves in the love of God, looking for the mercy of our Lord Jesus Christ unto eternal life" (Jude 20-21). In one word, it was the judgment of the Holy Ghost, and, therefore, it was the judgment of faith.

Now, all this attaches immense value and interest to Daniel's determination, as expressed in the first chapter of this book. "But Daniel purposed in his heart that he would not defile himself with the portion of the king's meat, nor with the wine which he drank; therefore he requested of the prince of the eunuchs that he might not defile himself" (ver. 8). He might, very naturally, have said to himself, "There is no use in one poor feeble captive seeking to maintain a place of separation. Everything is broken up. It is impossible to carry out the true spirit of a Nazarite amid such hopeless ruin and degradation. I may as well accommodate myself to the condition of things around me."

But no; Daniel was on higher ground than this. He knew it was his privilege to live as close to God in the palace of Nebuchadnezzar, as within the gates of Jerusalem. He knew that, let the outward condition of the people of God be what it might, there was a path of purity and devotedness opened to the individual saint, which he could pursue independently of everything.

And may we not say, that the Nazariteship of Babylon possesses charms and attractions fully as powerful as the Nazariteship of Canaan? Unquestionably. It is unspeakably precious and beautiful, to find one of the captives in Babylon breathing after, and attaining unto, so elevated a standard of separation. It teaches a powerful lesson for every age. It holds up to the view of believers, under every dispensation, a most encouraging and soul-stirring example. It proves that, amid the darkest shades, a devoted heart can enjoy a path of cloudless sunshine.

But how is this? Because "Jesus Christ is the same yesterday, to-day, and forever" (Heb. 13). Dispensations change and pass away. Ecclesiastical institutions crumble and moulder into ashes. Human systems totter and fall; but the name of Jehovah endureth forever, and His memorial unto all generations. It is upon this holy elevation that faith plants its foot. It rises above all vicissitude, and enjoys sweet converse with the unchangeable and eternal Source of all real good.

Thus it was that, in the days of the judges, individual faith was manifested and achieved more glorious triumphs than ever were known in the days of Joshua. Thus it was that

Elijah's altar on mount Carmel was surrounded by a halo fully as bright as that which crowned the altar of Solomon.

This is truly encouraging. The poor heart is so apt to sink, and be discouraged, by looking at the failure and unfaithfulness of man, instead of at the infallible faithfulness of God. "The foundation of God standeth sure, having this seal, The Lord knoweth them that are His. And, Let every one that nameth the name of Christ depart from iniquity" (2 Tim. 2:19). What can ever touch this enduring truth? Nothing! And, therefore, nothing can touch the faith which lays hold of it, or the superstructure of practical devotedness which is erected on the foundation of that faith.

And then look at the glorious results of Daniel's devotedness and separation. In the three opening chapters we observe three distinct things, resulting from the position assumed by Daniel and his companions, in reference to "the king's meat." 1, They were let into the secret of "*the king's dream.*" 2, They withstood the seductions of "*the king's image.*" And, 3, They were brought unscathed through "*the king's furnace.*"

1. "The secret of the Lord is with them that fear Him." This is beautifully exemplified in the case before us. "The magicians, and the astrologers, and the sorcerers, and the Chaldeans," who were breathing the atmosphere of the royal presence, were all in the dark as to the royal dream. "The Chaldeans answered before the king, and said, There is not a man upon the earth that can shew the king's matter." Very likely; but there was a God in Heaven who knew all about it; and who, moreover, could unfold it to those who had faith enough, and devotedness enough, and self-denial enough, to separate themselves from Babylonish pollutions, though involved in the Babylonish captivity. The mazes, the labyrinths, and the enigmas of human things are all plain to God; and He can and does make them plain to those who walk with Him, in the sanctity of His holy presence.

God's Nazarites can see farther into human affairs than the most profound philosophers of this world. And how is this? How can they so readily unravel the world's mysteries? Because they are above the world's mists. They are apart from the world's defilements. They are in the place of separation, the place of dependence, the place of communion. "Then Daniel went to his house, and made the thing known to Hananiah, Mishael, and Azariah, his companions: that they would desire mercies of the God of heaven, concerning this secret" (chap. 2:17-18). Here we have their place of strength and intelligence. They had only to look up to Heaven, in order to be endowed with a clear understanding as to all the destinies of earth.

How real and simple is all this? "God is light, and in Him is no darkness at all;" and, hence, if we want light, we can find it only in His presence; and we can only know the power of His presence as we are practically taking the place of separation from all the moral pollutions of earth.

And, observe, a further result of Daniel's holy separation. "Then the king Nebuchadnezzar fell upon his face and worshipped Daniel, and commanded that they should offer an oblation and sweet odors unto him." Here we have earth's proudest and most powerful monarch at the feet of the captive exile. Magnificent fruit of faithfulness! Precious evidence of the truth that God will always honor the faith that can, in any measure, rise to the height of His thoughts! He will not, He cannot, dishonor the draft which confidence presents at His exhaustless treasury. Daniel, on this memorable occasion, realized, in his own person, as fully as ever it was realized, God's ancient promise: "And all people of the earth shall see that thou art called by the name of the Lord; and they shall be afraid of thee . . . . And the Lord shall make thee the head, and not the tail; and thou shalt be above only, and thou shalt not be beneath" (Deut. 28: 10,13).

Assuredly Daniel was, in the above scene, "the head," and Nebuchadnezzar "the tail," as looked at from the divine point of view. Witness, also, the bearing of this holy Nazarite, in the presence of the impious Belshazzar (Dan. 5:17-29). Have we not, here, as magnificent a testimony to the destined pre-eminence of the seed of

Abraham, as when Joshua's victorious captains placed their feet on the necks of the kings of Canaan (Joshua 10: 24); or, when "all the earth sought to Solomon, to hear his wisdom, which God had put in his heart"? (1 Kings 10:24) Unquestionably; and, in a certain sense, it is a more magnificent testimony. It is natural to expect such a scene in the history of Joshua, or of Solomon; but to find the haughty king of Babylon prostrate at the feet of one of his captives, is something far beyond the utmost stretch of nature's expectation.

There it is, however, as a most striking and soul-stirring proof of the power of faith to triumph over all manner of difficulties, and to produce the most extraordinary results. Faith is the same mighty principle, whether it act on the plains of Palestine, on the top of Carmel, by the rivers of Babylon, or amid the ruins of the professing Church. No fetters can bind it, no difficulties deter it, no pressure damp it, no changes affect it. It ever rises to its proper object, and that object is God Himself, and His eternal revelation. Dispensations may change, ages may run their course, the wheels of time may roll on, and crush beneath their ponderous weight the fondest hopes of the poor human heart; but there stands faith, that immortal, divine, eternal reality, drinking at the fountain of pure truth, and finding all its springs in Him, who is "the way, the truth, and the life."

By this "precious faith" it was that Daniel acted, when he "purposed that he would not defile himself with the king's meat." True, he could no longer ascend to that holy and beautiful house, where his fathers had worshiped. The rude foot of a foreign foe had trodden down the holy city. The fire no longer burned on the altar of the God of Israel. The golden candlestick no longer enlightened, with its seven lamps, the holy place. But there was faith in Daniel's heart, and that faith carried him beyond every surrounding influence, and enabled him to appropriate, and act in the power of, "all the promises of God," which are "Yea, and Amen in Christ Jesus." Faith is not affected by ruined temples, fallen cities, faded lights, or departed glories. Why not? Because God is not affected by them. God is always to be found; and faith is always sure to find Him.

2. But the same faith which enabled those holy men of old to refuse the king's meat, enabled them, also, to despise the king's image. They had separated themselves from defilement, in order that they might enjoy a more intense communion with the true God; and they could not, therefore, bow down to an image of gold, even though it were ever so high. They knew that God was not an image. They knew He was a reality. They could only present worship to Him, for He alone was the true object thereof.

Nor did it make any matter to them that all the world was against them. They had only to live and act for God. It might seem as if they were setting up to be wiser than their neighbors. It might savor of presumption to stand against the tide of public opinion. Some might feel disposed to ask if truth lay only with them? Were all "the princes, the governors, and captains, the judges, the treasurers, the counsellors, the sheriffs, and all the rulers of the provinces," sunk in darkness and error? Could it be possible that so many men of rank, of intelligence, and of learning were in the wrong, and only a few strangers of the captivity in the right?

With such questions our Nazarites had nothing to do. Their path lay right onward. Should they bow down and worship an image, in order to avoid the appearance of condemning other people? Assuredly not. And yet how often are those who desire to keep a conscience void of offence in the sight of God, condemned for setting themselves up and judging others! Doubtless Luther was condemned by many for setting himself up in opposition to the doctors, the cardinals, and the pope. Should he, in order to avoid such condemnation, have lived and died in error? Who would say so?

"Ah! but," some will reply, "Luther had to deal with palpable error." So thought Luther; but thousands of learned and eminent men thought otherwise. So also in the case of "Shadrach, Meshach, and Abednego," they had to do with positive idolatry; but the whole world differed from them. What then? "We must obey God rather than man." Let others do as they will; "as for me and my house, we will serve the Lord." If people were to remain in error and continue to do what they, at least, feel to be wrong, in order to avoid the appearance of judging others, where should we be?

Ah! no; my reader, do you seek to pursue the steady, onward, upward path of pure and elevated discipleship. And, whether or not you thereby condemn others, is no concern of yours. *"Cease to do evil."* This is the first thing for the true disciple to do. When he has yielded obedience to this golden precept, he may expect to "learn to do well." "If thine eye be single, thy whole body shall be full of light." When God speaks, I am not to turn round to see how my obedience to His voice will affect my neighbors, or to consider what they will think about me. When the voice of the risen and glorified Jesus fell upon the ear of the prostrate Saul of Tarsus, he did not begin to inquire what the chief priests and Pharisees would think of him were he to obey. Surely not. "Immediately," he says, "I conferred not with flesh and blood" (Gal. 1: 16). "Whereupon, O king Agrippa, I was not disobedient unto the heavenly vision" (Acts 26: 19). This is the true spirit and principle of discipleship. "Give glory to God, before He cause darkness, and your feet stumble upon the dark mountains." Nothing can be more dangerous than to hesitate, when divine light shines upon the path. If you do not act upon the light, when you get it, you will, assuredly, be involved in thick darkness. Hence, therefore, as another has said, "Never go before your faith, nor lag behind your conscience."

3. But, we have said, if our Nazarites refused to bow before the king's image, they had to encounter the king's rage, and the king's furnace. For all this they were, by the grace of God, prepared: their Nazariteship was a real thing; they were ready to suffer the loss of all things, and even life itself, in defence of the true worship of the God of Israel. "They worshipped and served their own God," not merely beneath the peaceful vine and fig-tree in the land of Canaan, but in the very face of "a burning fiery furnace." They acknowledged Jehovah, not merely in the midst of a congregation of true worshipers, but in the presence of an opposing world. Theirs was a true discipleship in an evil day. They loved the Lord; and therefore, for His sake, they abstained from the king's luxuries, they withstood the king's rage, and they endured the king's furnace.

"O Nebuchadnezzar, we are not careful to answer thee in this matter. If it be so, our God whom we serve is able to deliver us from the burning fiery furnace; and He will deliver us out of thine hand, O king. But if not, be it known unto thee, O king, that we will not serve thy gods, nor worship the golden image which thou hast set up." This was the language of men who knew whose they were, and where they were—of men who had calmly and deliberately counted the cost—of men to whom the Lord was everything, the world nothing. All that the world could offer, together with life itself, was at stake; but what of that? "They endured as seeing Him who is invisible." Eternal glory lay before them; and they were quite prepared to reach that glory by a fiery pathway. God can take His servants to Heaven by a chariot of fire, or by a furnace of fire, as seems good to Him. Whatever be the mode of going, it is well to get there.

But could not the Lord have preserved His beloved servants from being cast into the furnace? No doubt. This would have been but a very small matter to Him. He did not, however, do so: it was His will that the faith of His servants should be put to the test—should be tried in the furnace—should be passed through the most searching crucible, in order that it "might be found to praise and honor and glory." Is it because the refiner sets no value on the wedge of gold, that he puts it into the furnace? No; but because he does. And, as some one has beautifully remarked, "His object is not merely to remove the dross, but to brighten the metal."

It is very evident that had the Lord, by an act of *power*, kept His servants out of the furnace, there would have been less glory to Him and as a consequence, less blessing to them. It was far better to have His presence and sympathy in the furnace, than His power to keep them out of it. What glory to Him in this! And what unspeakable privilege to them! The Lord went down and walked *with* His Nazarites in the furnace into which their faithfulness had brought them. They had walked with God in the king's palace; and God walked with them in the king's furnace. This was the most elevated moment in the entire career of Shadrach, Meshach, and Abednego.

How little had the king imagined the lofty position in which he was placing the objects of his rage and fury! Every eye was turned from the great image of gold, to gaze, in astonishment, upon the three captives. What could it mean? "Three men *bound!*" "Four men *loose!*" Could it be real? Was the furnace real? Alas, "the most mighty men in the king's army" had proved it to be real. And, had Nebuchadnezzar's image been cast into it, it would have proved its reality also. There was no material for the skeptic or the infidel to work upon. It was a real furnace, and a real flame, and the "three men" were "bound in their coats, their hosen, and their hats, and their other garments." All was reality.

But there was a deeper reality: *God was there.* This changed everything: it "changed the king's word," changed the furnace into a place of high and holy fellowship—changed Nebuchadnezzar's bondmen into God's freemen.

God was there!—there, in his power, to write contempt upon all man's opposition—there, in His deep and tender sympathy with His tried and faithful servant—there, in His matchless grace, to set the captives free, and to lead the hearts of His Nazarites into that deep fellowship with Himself for which they so ardently thirsted.

And is it not worth passing through a fiery furnace to enjoy a little more of the presence of Christ, and the sympathy of His loving heart? Are not fetters, with Christ, better than jewels without Him? Is not a furnace where He is better than a palace where He is not? Nature says, "*No!*" Faith says, "*Yes!*"

It is well to bear in mind that this is not the day of Christ's *power;* but it is the day of His *sympathy.* When passing through the deep waters of affliction, the heart may, at times, feel disposed to ask, "Why does not the Lord display His power, and deliver me?" The answer is, This is not the day of His power. He could avert that sickness—He could remove that difficulty—He could take off that pressure—He could prevent that catastrophe—He could preserve that beloved and fondly-cherished object from the cold grasp of death. But, instead of putting forth His power to deliver, He allows things to run their course, and pours His own sweet sympathy into the oppressed and riven heart, in such a way as to elicit the acknowledgment that we would not, for worlds, have missed the trial, because of the abundance of the consolation.

Such is the manner of our Jesus just now. By and by He will display His power; He will come forth as the Rider on the white horse; He will unsheath His sword; He will make bare His arm; He will avenge His people, and right their wrongs forever. But now His sword is sheathed, His arm covered. This is the time for making known the deep love of His heart, not the power of His arm, nor the sharpness of His sword. Are you satisfied to have it so? Is Christ's sympathy enough for your heart, even amid the keenest sorrow and the most intense affliction? The restless heart, the impatient spirit, the unmortified will, would lead one to long for escape from the trial, the difficulty, or the pressure; but this would never do. It would involve incalculable loss. We must pass from form to form in the school; but the Master accompanies us, and the light of His countenance, and the tender sympathy of His heart, sustain us under the most severe exercises.

And, then, see what glory redounds to the name of the Lord, when His people are enabled, by His grace, to pass, triumphantly, through a trial! Read Daniel 3: 26-28, and say where you could find richer or rarer fruits of a faithful discipleship. The king and all his nobles, who, just before, had been wholly engrossed with the bewitching music and the false worship, are now occupied with the amazing fact that the fire, which had slain the mighty men, had taken no effect whatever upon the worshipers of the true God, save to consume their fetters and let them walk free, in company with the Son of God. "Then Nebuchadnezzar came near to the mouth of the burning fiery furnace, and spake and said, Shadrach, Meshach, and Abednego, *ye servants of the Most High God*, come forth and come hither. Then Shadrach, Meshach, and Abednego, came forth of the midst of the fire. And the princes, governors, and captains, and the king's counsellors, being gathered together, *saw these men*, upon whose bodies the fire had no power, nor was a hair of their head singed, neither were their coats changed, nor the smell of fire had passed on them."

Here, then, was a noble testimony—such a testimony as would never have been rendered, had the Lord, by a mere act of power, preserved His servants from being cast into the furnace. Nebuchadnezzar was furnished with a striking proof that his furnace was no more to be dreaded than his image was to be worshiped by "the servants of the most high God." In a word, the enemy was confounded; God was glorified; and His dear servants brought forth unscathed from "the burning fiery furnace." Precious fruits, these, of a faithful Nazariteship!

And, observe further, the honor put upon our Nazarites. "Then Nebuchadnezzar spake and said, Blessed be *the God of Shadrach, Meshach, and Abednego*." Their names are intimately associated with the God of Israel. This was a high honor. They had identified themselves with the true God when it was a matter of life and death to do so; and, therefore, the true God identified Himself with them, and led them forth into a large and wealthy place. He set their feet upon a rock, and lifted their heads up above all their enemies round about them. How true it is that "them that honor Me I will honor!" And it is equally true that "they that despise Me shall be lightly esteemed" (1 Sam. 2: 30).

My beloved reader, have you found settled, divine peace for your guilty conscience, in the perfected atonement of the Lord Jesus Christ? Have you simply taken God at His word? Have you set to your seal that God is true? If so, you are a child of God; your sins are *all* forgiven, and you are accepted as righteous in Christ; Heaven, with all its untold glories, is before you; you are as sure of being in the glory as Christ Himself, inasmuch as you are united to Him.

Thus, everything is settled for you for time and eternity, according to the very utmost desire of your heart. Your need is met, your guilt removed, your peace established, your title sure. You have nought to do for yourself. All is divinely finished.

What remains? Just this: *live for Christ!* You are left here for "a little while," to occupy for Him, and wait for His appearing. Oh! seek to be faithful to your blessed Master. Be not discouraged by the fragmentary state of everything around you. Let the case of Daniel and his honored companions encourage your heart to seek after an elevated course here below. It is your privilege to enjoy as much of companionship with the blessed Lord Jesus, as if you were cast amid the palmy days of apostolic testimony.

May the Holy Ghost enable the writer and the reader of these lines to drink into the spirit—walk in the footsteps—manifest the graces—and wait for the coming of the Lord Jesus Christ!

The Christian Life

NOW AND THEN
OR, TIME AND ETERNITY

THE PRINCIPLES OF TRUTH laid down in Luke 12 are of the most solemn and searching character. Their practical bearing is such as to render them, in a day like the present, of the deepest importance. Worldly-mindedness and carnality cannot live in the light of the truth here set forth. They are withered up by the roots. If one were asked to give a brief and comprehensive title to this most precious section of inspiration, it might be entitled "Time in the light of eternity." The Lord evidently designed to set His disciples in the light of that world where every thing is the direct opposite of that which obtains here—to bring their hearts under the holy influence of unseen things, and their lives under the power and authority of heavenly principles. Such being the faithful purpose of the Divine Teacher, He lays the solid foundation for His superstructure of doctrine with these searching words: "Beware of the leaven of the Pharisees, which is hypocrisy." There must be no undercurrent in the soul. The deep springs of thought must be laid bare. We must allow the pure beams of heaven's light to penetrate to the depths of our moral being. We must not have any discrepancy between the hidden judgment of the soul and the style of our phraseology—between the bent of the life and the profession of the lips. In a word, we specially need the grace of "an honest and a good heart," in order to profit by this wondrous compendium of practical truth.

We are too apt to give an indifferent hearing or a cold assent to *home truth*. We do not like it. We prefer interesting speculations about the mere letter of Scripture, points of doctrine, or questions of prophecy, because we can indulge these in immediate connection with all sorts of worldly-mindedness, covetous practices, and self-indulgence. But ponderous principles of truth, bearing down upon the conscience in all their magnitude and flesh-cutting power, who can bear, save those who, through grace, are seeking to purge themselves from "the leaven of the Pharisees, which is hypocrisy"? This leaven is of a most specious character, takes various shapes, and is therefore most dangerous. Indeed, wherever it exists, there is a most positive and insurmountable barrier placed before the soul in its progress in experimental knowledge and practical holiness. If I do not expose my *whole soul* to the action of divine truth, if I am closing up some corner or crevice from the light thereof, if I am cherishing some secret reserve, if I am dishonestly seeking to accommodate the truth to my own standard of practice, or parry its keen edge from my conscience, then, assuredly, I am defiled by the leaven of hypocrisy, and my growth in likeness to Christ is a moral impossibility. Hence, therefore, it is imperative upon every disciple of Christ to search and see that nothing of this abominable leaven is allowed in the secret chambers of his heart. Let us, by the grace of God, put and keep it far away, so that we may be able on all occasions to say, "Speak, Lord, for Thy servant heareth."*

But not only is hypocrisy utterly subversive of spiritual progress, it also fails in attaining the object which it proposes to itself; "for there is nothing covered that shall not be revealed; neither hid, that shall not be known." Every man will find his level, and every thought will be brought to light. What

---

* The meaning which is generally attached to hypocrisy is a false profession of religion. It assuredly means this, but it means much more. A tacit assent to principles which do not govern the conduct deserves the appellation of hypocrisy. Looking at the subject in this point of view, we may all find occasion of deep humiliation before the Lord.

the truth would do *now*, the judgment-seat will do *then*. Every grade and shade of hypocrisy will be unmasked by the light which shall shine forth from the judgment-seat of Christ. Nothing will be allowed to escape. All will be reality *then*, though there is so much fallacy *now*. Moreover, every thing will get its proper name *then*, though it be misnamed *now*. Worldly-mindedness is called prudence; a grasping, covetous spirit is called foresight; and self-indulgence and personal aggrandizement are called judicious management and laudable diligence in business. Thus it is *now*; but *then* it will be quite the reverse. All things will be seen in their true colors, and called by their true names, before the judgment-seat. Wherefore it is the wisdom of the disciple to act in the light of that day, when the secrets of all hearts shall be disclosed. As to this, he is placed on a vantage-ground, for, says the apostle, "we must all [saints and sinners— though not at the same time, nor on the same ground] be manifested [φανερωθῆναι] before the judgment-seat of Christ." Should this disturb the disciple's mind? Assuredly not, if his heart be so purged of the leaven of hypocrisy and his soul so thoroughly grounded, by the teaching of God the Holy Ghost, in the great foundation-truth set forth in this very chapter (2 Cor. 5), namely, that Christ is his life, and Christ his righteousness; that he can say, "We are manifested [πεφανερώμεθα,—an inflection of the same word as is used at verse 10,] unto God, and I trust also are manifested in your consciences."

But if he be deficient in this peace of conscience and transparent honesty of heart, there is no doubt but that the thought of the judgment-seat will disturb his spirit. Hence we see that the Lord, in Luke 12, sets the consciences of His disciples directly in the light of the judgment-seat. "And I say unto you, *My friends*, Be not afraid of them that kill the body, and after that have no more that they can do. But I will forewarn you whom ye shall fear: Fear Him, which after He hath killed hath power to cast into hell; yea, I say unto you, Fear Him." "The fear of man bringeth a snare," and is closely connected with "the leaven of the Pharisees"; but "the fear of the Lord is the beginning of wisdom," and causes a man always so to carry himself—so to think, speak, and act—as in the full light of Christ's judgment-seat. This would impart immense dignity and elevation to the character, while it would effectually nip, in the earliest bud, the spirit of haughty independence, by keeping the soul under the searching power of divine light, the effect of which is to make every thing and every one manifest.

There is nothing that so tends to rob the disciple of Christ of the proper dignity of his discipleship as walking before the eyes or thoughts of men. So long as we are doing so, we cannot be unshackled followers of our heavenly Master. Moreover, the evil of walking before men is morally allied with the evil of seeking to hide our ways from God. Both partake of the "leaven of the Pharisees," and both will find their proper place before the judgment-seat. Why should we fear men? why should we regard their opinions? If their opinions will not bear to be tried in His presence who has power to cast into hell, they are worth nothing; for it is with Him we have to do. "With me it is a very small thing that I should be judged of you, or man's judgment." Man may have a judgment-seat *now*, but he will not have it *then*;—he may set up his tribunal in time, but he will have no tribunal in eternity. Why, therefore, should we shape our way in reference to a tribunal so frail and evanescent? Oh, let us challenge our hearts as to this. God grant us grace to act *now* in reference to *then*—to carry ourselves here with our eye on hereafter—to look at time in the light of eternity.

The poor unbelieving heart may however inquire, If I thus rise above human thoughts and human opinions, how shall I get on in a scene where those very thoughts and opinions prevail? This is a very natural question, but it meets its full and satisfactory answer from the Master's lips; yea, it would even seem as though He had graciously anticipated this rising element of unbelief, when, having carried His disciples above the hazy mists of time, and set them in the clear, searching, powerful light of eternity, He added, "Are not five sparrows sold for two farthings? and not one of them is forgotten before God. But even the very hairs of your head are all numbered. Fear not, therefore; ye are of more value than many sparrows" (ver. 6-7). Here the heart is taught not only to *fear* God, but also to *confide* in Him; it is not only warned, but also tranquilized. "Fear" and "fear not" may seem a paradox to flesh and blood, but to faith it is no paradox. The man who fears God most will fear circumstances least. The man of faith is at once the most dependent and independent man in the world—dependent upon God, independent upon circumstances. The latter is the consequence of the former.

And mark the ground of the believer's peace. The One who has power to cast into hell, the only One whom he is to fear, has actually taken the trouble to count the hairs of his head. He surely has not taken the trouble for the purpose of letting him perish here or hereafter. The minuteness of our Father's care should silence every doubt that might arise in our hearts. There is nothing too small and there can be nothing too great for Him. The countless orbs that move through infinite space and a falling sparrow are alike to Him. His infinite mind can take in with equal facility the course of everlasting ages and the hairs of our head. This is the stable foundation on which Christ founds His "fear not" and "take no thought." We frequently fail in the practical application of this divine principle. We may admire it as a principle, but it is only in the application of it that its real beauty is seen or felt. If we do not put it in practice, we are but painting sunbeams on canvas, while we famish beneath the chillling influences of our own unbelief.

Now, we find in this Scripture before us that bold and uncompromising testimony for Christ is connected with this holy elevation above men's thoughts and this calm reliance upon our Father's minute and tender care. If my heart is lifted above the influence of the fear of man, and sweetly tranquilized by the assurance that God takes account of the hairs of my head, then I am in a condition of soul to confess Christ before men (see verses 8-10). Nor need I be careful as to the result of this confession, for so long as God wants me here He will maintain me here. "And when they bring you unto the synagogues, and unto magistrates and powers, take ye no thought how or what thing ye shall answer, or what ye shall say; for the Holy Ghost shall teach you in the same hour what ye ought to say." The only proper ground of testimony for Christ is to be fully delivered from human influence, and established in unqualified confidence in God. So far as I am influenced by or a debtor to men, so far am I disqualified for being a servant of Christ; but I can only be effectually delivered from human influence by a lively faith in God. When God fills the heart, there is no room for the creature; and we may be perfectly sure of this, that no man has ever taken the trouble to count the hairs of our head; we have not even taken that trouble ourselves; but God has, and therefore I can trust God more than any one. God is perfectly sufficient for every exigency, great or small, and we only want to trust Him to know that He is.

True, He may and does use men as instruments; but if we lean on men instead of God, if we lean on instruments instead of on the hand that uses them, we bring down a curse upon us, for it is written, "Cursed be the man that trusteth in man, and maketh flesh his arm, and whose heart departeth from the Lord" (Jer. 17:5). The Lord used the ravens to feed Elijah, but Elijah never thought of trusting in the ravens. Thus it should be ever. Faith leans on God, counts on Him, clings to Him, trusts in Him, waits for Him, ever leaves a clear stage for Him to act on, does not obstruct His glorious path by any creature-confidence, allows Him to display Himself in all the glorious reality of what He is, leaves every thing to Him; and, moreover, if it gets into deep and rough waters, it will always be seen upon the crest of the loftiest billow, and from thence gazing in perfect repose upon God and His powerful actings. Such is faith—that precious thing—the only thing in this world that gives God and man their respective places.

While the Lord Jesus was in the act of

pouring forth these unearthly principles, a true child of earth intrudes upon Him with a question about property. "And one of the company said unto Him, 'Master, speak to my brother, that he divide the inheritance with me.'" How marvelously little did he know of the true character of that heavenly Man who stood before him! He knew nothing of the profound mystery of His being, or the object of His heavenly mission. He surely had not come from the bosom of the Father to settle lawsuits about property, nor to arbitrate between two covetous men. The spirit of covetousness was manifestly in the whole affair. Both defendant and plaintiff were governed by covetousness. One wanted to grasp and the other wanted to keep; what was this but covetousness? "And He said unto him, 'Man, who made Me a judge or a divider over you?'" It was not a question of which was right or which was wrong as to the property. According to Christ's pure and heavenly doctrine they were both wrong. In the light of eternity a few acres of land were little worth; and as to Christ Himself, He was only teaching principles entirely hostile to all questions of earthly possession; but in His own person and character He set an example of the very opposite. He did not go to law about the inheritance. He was "Heir of all things." The land of Israel, the throne of David, and all creation belonged to Him; but man would not own Him, or give Him possession. "The husbandmen said among themselves, 'This is the heir; come, let us kill him, and seize upon the inheritance.'" To this the Heir submitted in perfect patience, but [eternal homage to His glorious name!] by submitting unto death He crushed the enemy's power, and brought "many sons to glory."

Thus we see in the doctrine and practice of the Heavenly Man the true exhibition of the principles of the kingdom of God. He would not arbitrate, but yet He taught truth which would entirely do away with the need of arbitration. If the principles of the kingdom of God were dominant, there would be no need for courts of law; for inasmuch as people would not be wronged of their rights, they could have no wrongs to be righted. This would be admitted by all. But then the Christian, being in the kingdom, is bound to be governed by the principles of the kingdom, and to carry them out at all cost; for, in the exact proportion that he fails to exhibit those principles, he is robbing his own soul of blessing, and marring his testimony.

Hence, then, a person going to law is not governed, in so doing, by the principles of the kingdom of God, but by the principles of the kingdom of Satan, who is the prince of this world. It is not a question as to his being a Christian, but simply a question as to the principle by which he is governed in the act of going to law under any circumstances.* I say nothing of the moral instincts of the divine nature, which would surely lead one to apprehend with accuracy the gross inconsistency of a man who professes to be saved by *grace* going to *law* with a fellow-man—of one who, while he owns that if he had his *right* from the hand of God, he would be burning in hell, nevertheless insists upon exacting his rights from his fellow-man—of one who has been forgiven ten thousand talents, but yet seizes his fellow by the throat for a paltry hundred pence. Upon these things I shall not dwell. I merely look at the question of going to law in the light of the kingdom, in the light of eternity; and if it be true that in the kingdom of God there is no need for courts of law, then I press it solemnly upon my reader's conscience, in the presence of God, that he, as a subject of that kingdom, is totally wrong in going to law. True, it will lead to loss and suffering; but who is "worthy of the kingdom of God" who is not prepared to "suffer for it"? Let those who are governed by the things of *time* go to law; but the Christian is, or ought to be, governed by the things of *eternity*. People go to law *now*, but it will not be so *then*; and the Christian is to act *now* as if it were *then*. He belongs to the kingdom; and it is just because the kingdom of God is not dominant, but the King rejected, that the subjects of the kingdom are called to suffer. Righteousness

---

* How often, alas! does it happen that people go to law to be *righted* of their *wrongs*, and in the end find themselves *wronged* of their *rights!*

"suffers" *now;* it will "reign" in the millennium, and it will "dwell" in the new heavens and the new earth. Now, in going to law, the Christian anticipates the millennial age. He is going before his Master in the assertion of his rights. He is called to suffer patiently all sorts of wrongs and injuries. To resent them is to deny the truth of that kingdom to which he professes to belong. I press this principle upon my reader's conscience. Let him not trifle with its truth. There is nothing which tends so to hinder the freshness and power, growth and prosperity, of the kingdom of God in the heart as the refusal to carry out the principles of that kingdom in the conduct.*

But some may say that it is bringing us down from the high ground of the Church, as set forth in Paul's Epistles, to press thus the principles of the kingdom. By no means. We belong to the Church, but we are in the kingdom; and while we must never confound the two, it is perfectly plain that the ethics—the moral habits and ways—of the Church can never be below those of the kingdom. If it be contrary to the spirit and principles of the kingdom to assert my rights and go to law, it must, if possible, be still more contrary to the spirit and principles of the Church. This cannot be questioned. The higher my position, the higher should be my code of ethics and tone of character. I fully believe, and desire firmly to hold, experimentally to enter into, and practically to exhibit the truth of the Church as the body and bride of Christ—the possessor of a heavenly standing, and the expectant of heavenly glory, by virtue of her oneness with Christ; but I cannot see how my being a member of that highly privileged body can make my practice lower than if I were merely a subject or member of the kingdom. What is the difference, as regards present conduct and character, between belonging to the body of a rejected Head and belonging to the kingdom of a rejected King? Assuredly it cannot be to lower the tone in the former case. The higher and more intimate my relationship to the rejected One, the more intense should be my separation from that which rejects Him, and the more complete should be my assimilation to His character, and the more precise and accurate my walk in His footsteps in the midst of that scene from which He is rejected.

But the simple fact is, *we want conscience.* Yes, a tender, exercised, honest conscience, which will truly and accurately respond to the appeals of God's pure and holy Word, is, I verily believe, the grand desideratum—the pressing want of the present moment. It is not so much principles we want, as the grace, the energy, the holy decision, that will carry them out, cost what it may. We admit the truth of principles which most plainly cut at the very things which we ourselves are either directly or indirectly doing. We admit the principle of grace. And yet we live by the strict maintenance of righteousness. For example, how often does it happen that persons are preaching, teaching, and professing to enjoy grace, while at the very moment they are insisting upon their rights in reference to their tenants; and, either directly themselves or indirectly by means of their agents, dispossessing poor people, unroofing their houses, and sending them out, in destitution and misery, upon a cold, heartless world! This is a plain, palpable case, of which, alas! there have been too many

---

* The Christian should be governed by the principles of the kingdom in every thing. If he is engaged in business, he should conduct his business as a child of God, and a servant of Christ. He should not have a Christian character on Lord's day and a commercial character on Monday. I should have the Lord with me in my shop, my warehouse, and my counting-house. It is my privilege to depend upon God in my business; but in order to depend upon Him, my business must be of such a nature, and conducted upon such a principle as He can own. If it is not so, I must leave the Lord out, and I am then on the same footing as the men of the world, and left to fall into their ways and manner of doing business.

Of course, everything depends upon the motive which actuates the mind. What, then, is my motive in my daily labor? Is it to provide food and raiment, or is it to lay up treasures upon earth? If the former, God has pleasure in it, and is with it; so that, if you are in the way of His appointment, you have only to depend upon Him.

Faith always puts the soul on a totally different ground from that occupied by the world, no matter where or what our calling may be. Take, for example, David in the valley of Elah. Why did he not fight, like other men? Because he was on the ground of faith. So also Hezekiah. Why did he put on sackcloth when other men put on armor? Because he was on the ground of simple dependence upon God. Just so in the case of a man in trade; he must carry on his trade as a Christian, else he will mar the testimony and rob his own soul of blessing.

painful illustrations in the world within the last ten years.

And why put cases? Because one finds such melancholy deficiency in sensibility of conscience at the present day, that unless the thing is brought home plainly to one's self it will not be understood. Like David, our indignation is wrought up to the highest pitch by a picture of moral turpitude, so long as we do not see *self* in that picture. It needs some Nathan to sound in our ears, "Thou art the man," in order to prostrate us in the dust, with a smitten conscience, and true self-abhorrence. Thus, at the present day, eloquent sermons are preached, eloquent lectures delivered, and elaborate treatises written about the principles of grace, and yet the courts of law are frequented, attorneys, lawyers, sheriffs, agents, and sub-agents are called into requisition, with all their terrible machinery, in order to assert our rights; but we feel it not, because we are not present to witness the distress, and hear the groans and execrations of houseless mothers and children. Need we wonder, therefore, that true practical Christianity is at a low ebb amongst us? Is it any marvel that leanness, barrenness, drought and poverty, coldness and deadness, darkness, ignorance, and spiritual depression should be found amongst us? What else could be expected, when the principles of the kingdom of God are openly violated?

But is it unrighteous to seek to get our own, and to make use of the machinery within our reach in order to do so? Surely not. What is here maintained is, that no matter how well defined and clearly established the right may be, the assertion thereof is diametrically opposed to the kingdom of God. The servant in Matthew 18 was called "a wicked servant," and "delivered to the tormentors," not because he acted unrighteously in enforcing the payment of a lawful debt, but because he did not act in grace and remit that debt. Well, therefore, might the Lord Jesus sound in His disciples' ears this warning voice, "Take heed and beware of covetousness; for a man's life consisteth not in the abundance of the things which he possesseth."

But how difficult to define this "covetous-ness"! how hard to bring it home to the conscience! It is, as some one has said of worldliness, "shaded off gradually from white to jet black;" so that it is only as we are imbued with the spirit and mind of heaven, and thoroughly schooled in the principles of eternity, that we shall be able to detect its working. And not only so, but our hearts must, in this also, be purged from the leaven of the Pharisees, which is hypocrisy. The Pharisees were covetous, and could only turn Christ's doctrine into ridicule (see Luke 16: 14); and so will it be with all those who are tainted by their leaven. They *will* not see the just application of truth, either as to covetousness or any thing else. They will seek to define it in such a way as will suit themselves. They will interpret, modify, pare down, accommodate, until they have fully succeeded in getting their conscience from under the edge of God's truth; and thus they get into the power and under the influence of the enemy. I must either be governed by the pure truth of the Word or by the impure principles of the world, which, as we very well know, are forged in Satan's workshop, and brought into the world to be used in doing his work.

In the parable of the rich man, which the Lord here puts forth in illustration of covetousness, we see a character which the world respects and admires. But in this, as in every thing else brought forward in this searching chapter, we see the difference between *now* and *then*—between "time and eternity." All depends upon the light in which you look at men and things. If you merely look at them *now*, it may be all very well to get on in trade, and enlarge one's concerns, and make provision for the future. The man who does this is counted wise *now*, but he will be a "fool" *then*. But let us remember that we must make God's *then* to be our *now*; we must look at the things of time in the light of eternity—the things of earth in the light of Heaven. This is true wisdom, which does not confine the heart to that system of things which obtains "under the sun," but conducts it into the light, and leaves it under the power of "that world" where the principles of the kingdom of God bear sway. What should we think of courts of law and insurance offices if we look at them in the light of eternity?* These things do very well for men who are only governed by *now*, but the disciple of Christ is to be governed by *then*. This makes all the difference; and truly it is a serious difference.

"The ground of a certain rich man brought forth plentifully." What sin is there in being a successful agriculturist or merchant? If God bless a man's labor, should he not rejoice? Truly so; but mark the moral progress of a covetous heart. "He thought *within himself*." He did not think in the presence of God, he did not think under the mighty influences of the eternal world; no, "he thought within himself"—within the narrow compass of his selfish heart. Such was his range; and therefore we need not marvel at his practical conclusion. "What shall I do, because I have no room where to bestow my fruits?" What! Was there no way of using his resources with a view to God's future? Alas! no. Man has a future (or thinks he has) on which he counts, and for which he makes provision; but self is the only object which figures in that future—self, whether in my own person or that of my wife or child, which is morally the same thing.

The grand object in God's future is Christ; and true wisdom will lead us to fix our eye on Him, and make Him our undivided object for time and eternity—*now* and *then*. But this, in the judgment of a worldly man, is nonsense. Yes, Heaven's wisdom is nonsense in the judgment of earth. Hearken to the wisdom of earth, and the wisdom of those who are under the influence of earthly maxims and habits. "And he said, 'This will I do: I will pull down my barns, and build greater; and *there* will I bestow *all* my fruits and my goods.' " Thus we have what he "thought," what he "said," and what he "did;" and there is a melancholy consistency between his thoughts, his words,

and his acts. "*There*," in my self-built storehouse, "will I bestow *all*." Miserable treasure-house to contain the "all" of an immortal soul! God was not an item in the catalogue. God was neither his treasury nor his treasure. This is plain; and it is always thus with a mere man of the world. "And I will say to my soul, Soul, thou hast much goods laid up for many years; take thine ease, eat, drink, and be merry." Thus we see that a worldly man's provision is only "for many years." Make the best of it, it cannot go beyond that narrow limit. It cannot, even in his own thought about it, reach into that boundless eternity which stretches beyond this contracted span of time. And this provision he offers to his never-dying soul as the basis of its "ease and merriment." Miserable fatuity! Senseless calculation!

How different is the address which a believer may present to his soul! He too may say to his soul, "Soul, take thine ease; eat, drink, and be merry; eat of the fatness of God's storehouse, and drink of the river of His pleasures, and of the wine of His kingdom; and be glad in His accomplished salvation; for thou hast much goods, yea, unsearchable riches, untold wealth, laid up, not merely for many years, but for eternity. Christ's finished work is the ground of thine eternal peace, and His coming glory the sure and certain object of thy hope." This is a different character of address. This shows the difference between *now* and *then*. It is a fatal mistake not to make Christ the Crucified, Christ the Risen, Christ the Glorified, the Alpha and Omega of all our calculations. To paint a future, and not to place Christ in the foreground, is extravagance of the wildest character; for the moment God enters the scene, the picture is hopelessly marred.

"But God said unto him, 'Thou fool! this night thy soul shall be required of thee: *then*

---

* It should be a serious question with a child of God, ere he avails himself of an assurance company, whether in the matter of fire or life, "Am I hereby distrusting God? or am I seeking by human agency to counteract divine visitations?" There is something sadly anomalous in a Christian's insuring his life. He professes to be *dead*, and that Christ is his *life*; why then talk of insuring his life? But many will say, "We cannot bring Christianity into such things." I ask, Where are we to leave it? Is Christianity a convenient sort of garment, which we put on on Lord's day, and at the close of that day take it off, fold it carefully up, and lay it on the shelf till the following Lord's day? It is too often thus. People have two characters; and what is this but the leaven of the Pharisees, which is hypocrisy? Insurance offices are all very well for the men of this world, who should certaining avail themselves of them, inasmuch as every thing around and within is so uncertain. But to the child of God *all is sure*. God has insured his life forever, and hence he should regard insurance offices as so many depots of unbelief.

whose shall those things be which thou hast provided?' " And then mark the moral of all this. "So is he," no matter who—saint or sinner, "that layeth up *treasure for himself*, and is not rich toward God." The man who hoards up is virtually making a god of his hoard. His mind is tranquilized as to the future when he thinks of his hoard, for if he had not that hoard he would be uneasy. It is sufficient to put a natural man entirely out of his reason to give him naught but God to depend upon. Any thing but that for him. Give him old pieces of parchment in the shape of title-deeds, in which some clever lawyer will finally pick a hole, and prove worthless. He will lean on them—yea, die in peace, if he can leave such to his heirs. Give him an insurance policy,—any thing, in short, but God for the natural heart. *All is reality save the only reality*, in the judgment of nature. This proves what nature's true condition is. It cannot trust God. It *talks* about Him, but it cannot *trust* Him. The very basis of man's moral constitution is distrust of God; and one of the fairest fruits of regeneration is the capacity to confide in God for every thing. "They that know Thy name will put their trust in Thee." None else can.

However, my main object in this paper is to deal with Christian consciences. I ask the Christian reader, therefore, in plain terms, is it in keeping with Christ's doctrine, as set forth in the gospel, for His disciples to lay up for themselves treasure on the earth? It seems almost an absurdity to put such a question, in the face of Luke 12 and parallel Scriptures. "Lay not up for yourselves treasure on the earth, where moth and rust doth corrupt, and where thieves break through and steal; but lay up for yourselves treasure in heaven, where neither moth nor rust doth corrupt, and where thieves do not break through and steal." This is plain enought, and only wants an honest conscience to apply it, in order to produce its proper results. It is directly contrary to the doctrine of the kingdom of God, and perfectly incompatible with true discipleship, to lay up "treasure," in any shape or form, "on the earth." In this, as in the matter of going to law, we have only to remember that we are in the kingdom of God, in order to know how we should act. The principles of that kingdom are eternal and binding upon every disciple of Christ.

"And He said unto His disciples, 'Therefore I say unto you, Take no thought for your life, what ye shall eat; neither for the body, what ye shall put on. The life is more than meat, and the body is more than raiment.' " "Be careful for nothing," says the Spirit by the apostle. Why? Because God is caring for you. There is no use in two thinking about the same thing, when One can do every thing and the other can do nothing. "In every thing by prayer and supplication with thanksgiving let your requests be made known to God. And the peace of God, which passeth all understanding, shall garrison [φρουρησει] your hearts and minds through Christ Jesus." This is the solid foundation of peace of heart, which so few really enjoy. Many have gotten peace of conscience through faith in the sufficiency of Christ's work, who do not enjoy peace of heart through faith in the sufficiency of God's care. And oftentimes we go to pray about our difficulties and trials, and we rise from our knees as troubled as we knelt down. We profess to put our affairs into the hands of God, but we have no notion of *leaving them* there; and consequently we do not enjoy peace of heart. Thus it was with Jacob, in Genesis 32. He asked God to deliver him from the hand of Esau; but no sooner did he rise from his knees than he set forth the real ground of his soul's dependence, by saying, "I will appease him by a present." It is clear he had much more confidence in the "present" than in God. This is a common error amongst the children of God. We profess to be looking to the Eternal Fountain; but the eye of the soul is askance upon some creature-stream. Thus God is practically shut out; our souls are not delivered, and we have not got peace of heart.

The apostle then goes on, in Philippians 4: 8, to give a catalogue of those things about which we ought to think; and we find that *self* or its affairs is not once alluded to. "Whatsoever things are true, whatsoever things are venerable [σεμνα], whatsoever things are just, whatsoever things are pure, whatsoever things are lovely, whatsoever things are of good report; if there be any virtue, and if there be any praise, think on these things . . . . And the God of peace shall be with you." Thus, when I know and believe that God is thinking about me, I have "*the peace of God*"; and when I am thinking about Him and the things belonging to Him, I have "*the God of peace.*" This, as might be expected, harmonizes precisely with Christ's doctrine in Luke 12. After relieving the minds of His disciples in reference to present supplies and future treasure, He says, "But rather seek ye the kingdom of God, and all these things shall be added unto you." That is, I am not to seek the kingdom with the latent thought in my mind that my wants will be supplied in consequence. That would not be true discipleship. A true disciple never thinks of aught but the Master and His kingdom; and the Master will assuredly think of him and his wants. Thus it stands between a faithful servant and an all-powerful and all-gracious Master. That servant may therefore be free, perfectly free, from care.

But there is another ground on which we are exhorted to be free from care, and that is the utter worthlessness of that care. "Which of you, with taking thought, can add to his stature one cubit? If ye then be not able to do that thing which is least, why take ye thought for the rest?" We gain nothing by our care; and by indulging therein we only unfit ourselves for seeking the kingdom of God, and place a barrier, by our unbelief, in the way of His acting for us. It is always true in reference to us, "He could there do no mighty work, because of their unbelief." Unbelief is the great hindrance to the display of God's mighty works on our behalf. If we take our affairs into our own hands, it is clear that we do not want God. Thus we are left to the depressing influence of our own perplexing thoughts, and finally we take refuge in some human resource, and make shipwreck of faith.

It is important to understand that we are either leaning on God or on circumstances. It will not do, by any means, to say that we are leaning on God *and* circumstances. It must be God *only*, or not at all. It is all very well to talk of faith when our hearts are, in reality, leaning on the creature in some shape or form. We should sift and try our ways closely as to this; for inasmuch as absolute dependence upon God is one of the special characteristics of the divine life, and one of the fundamental principles of the kingdom, it surely becomes us to look well to it that we are not presenting any barrier to our progress in that heavenly quality. True, it is most trying to flesh and blood to have no settled thing to lean upon. The heart will quiver as we stand upon the shore of circumstances, and look forth upon that unknown ocean—unknown to all but faith, and where naught but simple faith can live for an hour. We may feel disposed, like Lot, to cry out, "Is it not a little one? and my soul shall live." The heart longs for some shred of the creature, some plank from the raft of circumstances—any thing but absolute dependence upon God. But oh! let God only be known, and He must be trusted; let Him be trusted, and He must be known.

Still the poor heart will yearn after something settled, something tangible. If it be a question of maintenance, it will earnestly desire some settled income, a certain sum in the funds, a certain amount of landed property, or a fixed jointure or annuity of some kind or other. Then, if it be a question of public testimony or ministry of any kind, it will be the same thing. If a man is going to preach or lecture, he will like to have something to lean upon; if not a written sermon, at least some notes, or some kind of previous preparation—any thing but unqualified, self-emptied dependence upon God. Hence it is that worldliness prevails to such a fearful extent amongst Christians. Faith alone can overcome the world and purify the heart. It brings the soul from under the influence of time, and keeps it habitually in the light of eternity. It is occupied not with *now*, but with *then*, not with *here*, but *hereafter*; not with earth, but with Heaven. Thus it overcomes the world and purifies the heart. It hears and believes Christ's word, "Fear not, little flock, for it is your Father's good pleasure to give you the kingdom." Now, if "the kingdom" fills my soul's vision, I have no room for aught beside. I can let go present shadows, in the prospect of future realities; I can give up an evanescent *now*, in the prospect of an eternal *then*.

Wherefore the Lord immediately adds, "Sell that ye have, and give alms: provide yourselves bags which wax not old, a treasure in the heavens that fadeth not, where no thief approacheth, neither moth corrupteth. For where your treasure is, there will the heart be also." If I have treasure on earth, no matter in what shape, my *heart* will be there also, and I shall be a downright worldly man. How shall I most effectually empty my heart of the world? By getting it filled with Christ. He is the true treasure which neither the world's "bags" nor its "storehouses" can contain. The world has its "barns" and its "bags," in which it hoards its "goods." But its barns will fall and its bags will wax old, and then what will become of the treasure? Truly "they build too low that build beneath the skies."

Yet people will build and hoard up, if not for themselves, at least for their children, or in other words, their second selves. If I hoard for my children, I am hoarding for myself; and not only so, but in numberless cases, the hoard, in place of proving a blessing, proves a positive curse to the child, by taking him off the proper ground appointed for him, as well as for all, in God's moral government, namely, "working with his hands the thing which is good, that he may have [not to hoard up for himself, or for his second self, but] to give to him that needeth." This is God's appointed ground for every man; and therefore if I hoard for my child, I am taking both myself and him off the divine ground, and the consequence will be a forfeiture of blessing. Do I taste the surpassing sweetness of obedience to and dependence upon God, and shall I deprive my child thereof? Shall I rob him, virtually, and so far as in me lies, of God, and give him, as a substitute, a few "old bags," an insurance policy, or some musty parchments?

But why need I hoard up for my children? If I can trust God for myself, why not trust Him for them likewise? Cannot the One who has fed and clothed me feed and clothe them

also? Let not the truth be misunderstood or misinterpreted. I am bound, by the powerful obligations of the Word and example of God, to provide for my own; for, "if any provide not for his own, and especially for those of his own house, he hath denied the faith, and is worse than an infidel" (1 Tim. 5: 8). This is plain enough. And, moreover, I am bound to fit my children, so far as God's principles admit, and my province extends, for any service to which He may be graciously pleased to call them. But I am no where instructed in the Word of God to give my children a hoard in place of an honest occupation, with simple dependence upon a heavenly Father. As a matter of actual fact, few children ever thank their fathers for inherited wealth; whereas they will ever remember, with gratitude and veneration, having been led, by parental care and management, into a godly course of action for themselves.

I do not, however, forget a passage which has often been used, or rather abused, to defend the worldly, unbelieving practice of hoarding up. I allude to 2 Corinthians 12:14: "Behold, the third time I am ready to come to you; and I will not be burdensome to you: for I seek not yours, but you: for the children ought not to lay up for the parents, but the parents for the children." How glad people are when they get a semblance of Scripture-authority for their worldliness! In this passage it is but a semblance of authority; for the apostle is certainly not teaching Christians to hoard up—he is not teaching heavenly men to lay up treasure upon the earth, for any object. He simply refers to a common practice *in the world*, and to a common feeling *in nature*, in order to illustrate his own mode of dealing with the Corinthians, who were his children in the faith. He had not burdened them, and he would not burden them, for he was the parent. Now, if the saints of God are satisfied to go back to the world and its maxims, to nature and its ways, then let them hoard up with all diligence—let them "heap treasure together for the last days;" but let them "remember that the moth, the canker-worm, and the rust" will be the end of it all. Oh for a heart to value those immortal "bags" in which faith lays up its "unfading treasure," those heavenly storehouses where faith "bestows all its fruits and its goods"! Then shall we pursue a holy and elevated path through this present evil world—then, too, shall we be lifted upon faith's vigorous pinion above the dark atmosphere which inwraps this Christ-rejecting, God-hating world, and which is impregnated and polluted by those two elements, namely, *hatred of God, and love of gold.*

I shall only add, ere closing this paper, that the Lord Jesus—the Adorable, the Divine, the Heavenly Teacher, having sought to raise, by His unearthly principles, the thoughts and affections of His disciples to their proper centre and level, gives them two things to do; and these two things may be expressed in the words of the Holy Ghost— "To serve the living and true God, and wait for His Son from heaven." The entire of the teaching of Luke 12, from verse 35 to the end, may be ranged under the above comprehensive heads, to which I call the Christian reader's prayerful attention. We have no one else to serve but "the living God," and nothing to wait for—nothing worth waiting for but "His Son." May the Holy Ghost clothe His own Word with heavenly power, so that it may come home to the heart and conscience, and tell upon the life of every child of God, that the name of the Lord Christ may be magnified, and His truth vindicated in the conduct of those that belong to Him. May the grace of an honest heart, and a tender, upright, well-adjusted conscience, be largely ministered to each and all of us, so that we may be like a well-tuned instrument, yielding a true tone when touched by the Master's hand, and harmonizing with His heavenly voice.

Finally, if this paper should fall into the hands of one who has not yet found rest of conscience in the perfected atonement of the Son of God, I would say to such an one, You will surely lay this paper down and say, "This is a hard saying, who can hear it?" You may be disposed to ask, "What would the world come to, if such principles were universally dominant?"

I reply, It would cease to be governed by Satan, and would be "the kingdom of God." But let me ask you, "To which kingdom do you belong? Which is it—*now,* or *then*—with you? Are you living for time, or eternity—earth, or heaven,—Satan, or Christ?" Do, I affectionately implore of you, be thoroughly honest with yourself in the presence of God. Remember, "there is *nothing* covered that shall not be revealed." The judgment-seat will bring *all* to light. Therefore I say, Be honest with yourself, and now ask your heart, "Where am I? How do I stand? What is the ground of my peace? What are my prospects for eternity?" Do not imagine that God wants *you* to buy Heaven with a surrender of earth. No; He points you to Christ, who, by bearing sin in His own body on the cross, has opened the way for the believing sinner to come into the presence of God in the power of divine righteousness. You are not asked to do or to be any thing; but the gospel tells you what Jesus is, and what He has done; and if you believe this in your heart, and confess it with your mouth, you shall be saved. Christ—God's Eternal Son—God manifest in the flesh—co-equal with the Father, being conceived by the Holy Ghost, was born of a woman, took upon Him a body prepared by the power of the Highest, and thus became a *real man*—very God and very man—He, having lived a life of perfect obedience, died upon the cross, being made sin and a curse, and having exhausted the cup of Jehovah's righteous wrath, endured the sting of death, spoiled the grave of its victory, and destroyed him that had the power of death, He went up into Heaven, and took His seat at the right hand of God. Such is the infinite merit of His perfect sacrifice, that all who believe are justified from *all things*—yea, are accepted in Him—stand in His acceptableness before God, and can never come into condemnation, but have passed from death into life. This is the gospel!—the glad tidings of salvation, which God the Holy Ghost came down from Heaven to preach to every creature. Let me exhort you, in this concluding line, to "behold the Lamb of God that taketh away the sin of the world." *Believe and live!*

SIMON PETER

HIS LIFE AND ITS LESSONS

Part 1

WE PROPOSE, in dependence upon the Spirit's guidance, to write a few papers on the life and ministry of the blessed servant of Christ whose name stands at the head of this paper. We shall trace him through the Gospels, through the Acts, and through the Epistles, for he appears in all the three grand divisions of the New Testament. We shall meditate upon his call, upon his conversion, his confession, his fall, his restoration; in a word, we shall glance at all the scenes and circumstances of his remarkable history, in which we shall find, if we mistake not, many valuable lessons which we may well ponder. May the Lord the Spirit be our Guide and Teacher!

For the earliest notice of Simon Peter, we must turn to the first chapter of the Gospel of John. Here we find, at the very outset, a scene full of interest and instruction. Amongst those who had been gathered by the powerful ministry of John the Baptist there were two men who heard him deliver his glowing testimony to the Lamb of God. We must quote the words: "Again the next day after John stood, and two of his disciples; and looking upon Jesus as He walked, he saith, Behold the Lamb of God."

There words fell with peculiar power upon the hearts of two of John's disciples. Not that the words were specially addressed to them; at least, we are not told so. But they were words of life, freshness, and power—words welling up from the depths of a heart that had found an object in the Person of Christ. On the preceding day, John had spoken of the work of Christ. "Behold the Lamb of God, which taketh away the sin of the world." And again, "The same is He which baptizeth with the Holy Ghost."

But note particularly John's testimony to the *person* of the Lamb of God. "John stood," riveted, no doubt, by the object which filled the vision of his soul. "And looking upon Jesus, as He walked, he said, Behold the Lamb of God." It was this that went right to the very heart of the two disciples who stood beside him, and so affected them that they left their master to follow this new and infinitely more glorious Object that had been presented to their notice.

There is always immense moral power in the testimony that emanates from an absorbed heart. There is nothing formal, official, or mechanical, in such testimony. It is the pure fruit of heart communion; and there is nothing like it. It is not the mere statement of true things about Christ. It is the heart occupied and satisfied with Christ. It is the eye riveted, the heart fixed, the whole moral being centred and absorbed in that one commanding object that fills all Heaven with His glory.

This is the kind of testimony we so much want both in our private life and in our public reunions. It is this that tells, with such marvelous power, on others. We never can speak effectively for Christ, unless our hearts are filled with Him. And so it is also, in reference to our meetings. When Christ is the one absorbing object of every heart, there will be a tone and an atmosphere which must tell in some way or other on all who enter the place. There may not be much gift, not much teaching—very little charm in the singing, for persons of musical taste; but oh! there is heart-enjoyment of Christ. His name is as ointment poured forth. Every eye is fixed on Him; every heart is centred in Him; He is the commanding object—the satisfying portion. The unanimous voice of the assembly seems to say, "Behold the Lamb of

God," and this must produce its own powerful effect, either in attracting souls to Him, or in convincing them that the people in that assembly have gotten something of which they know nothing at all.

But let us note particularly the effect produced on the two disciples of John. "They heard him speak and they followed Jesus. Then Jesus turned, and saw them following, and saith unto them, What seek ye? They said unto Him, Rabbi—which is to say, being interpreted, Master—where dwellest Thou? He said unto them, Come and see. They came and saw where He dwelt, and abode with Him that day; for it was about the tenth hour." Thus the blessed testimony of the Baptist led them to follow Jesus, and as they followed on, fresh light was poured upon their path, and they found themselves at length, in the very abode of that One of whom they had heard their master speak.

Nor was this all, though it was much—with their own hearts' deepest longings satisfied. There was now that delightful going out after others which must, in every instance, be the result of close personal acquaintance and occupation with the Person of Christ. "One of the two which heard John, and followed Jesus, was Andrew, Simon Peter's brother. He first findeth his own brother Simon, and saith unto him, We have found the Messias, which is, being interpreted, the Christ. And he brought him to Jesus."

Here is something which we may well ponder. See how the circle of blessing widens! See the result of a single sentence uttered in truth and reality! It might seem to a carnal observer as though John had lost by his testimony. Far from it. That honored servant found his joy in pointing souls to Jesus. He did not want to link them on to himself, or to gather a party round himself. "John bare witness of Him, and cried saying, This was He of whom I spake, He that cometh after me is preferred before me."

And again, "This is the record of John, when the Jews sent priests and Levites from Jerusalem to ask him, Who art thou? And he confessed, and denied not; but confessed, I am not the Christ. And they ask him, What then? Art thou Elias? And he saith, I am not.

Art thou that prophet? And he answered, No. Then said they unto him, Who art thou? that we may give an answer to them that sent us. What sayest thou of thyself? He said, I am the voice of one crying in the wilderness, Make straight the way of the Lord, as said the prophet Esaias. And they which were sent were of the Pharisees."

What a fine moral lesson for Pharisees to be set down to! "And they asked him, and said unto him, Why baptizest thou then, if thou be not that Christ, nor Elias, neither that prophet? John answered them, saying, I baptize with water: but there standeth One among you, whom ye know not. He it is, who coming after me is preferred before me, whose shoe's latchet I am not worthy to unloose."

It is not very likely that the man who could give such answers, and bear such a testimony, would be, in the smallest degree, affected by the loss of a few disciples. But, in good truth it was not losing them when they followed Jesus and found their abode with Him. Of this we have the very finest evidence that could be furnished, from John's own lips, in reply to those who evidently thought that their master might possibly feel at being left in the shade. "They came unto John, and said unto him, Rabbi, He that was with thee beyond Jordan, to whom thou barest witness, behold, the same baptizeth, and all come to Him. John answered and said, *A man can receive nothing, except it be given him from heaven.* Ye yourselves bear me witness, that I said, I am not the Christ, but that I am sent before Him. He that hath the bride is the bridegroom; but the friend of the bridegroom, which standeth and heareth him, rejoiceth greatly because of the bridegroom's voice: *this my joy therefore is fulfilled. He must increase, but I must decrease*" (John 3:26-30).

Noble words! It was the joy of this most illustrious servant—this greatest of woman-born, to hide himself behind his Master, and find all his personal springs in Him. As to himself, he was but a voice. As to his work, he was only baptizing with water, he was not worthy to loose the latchet of his Master's shoe.

Such was John. Such the man whose glowing testimony led the brother of Simon Peter to the feet of the Son of God. The testimony was clear and distinct, and the work deep and real in the souls of those who received it.

It does the heart good to note the simple, earnest, forcible words of Simon's brother, Andrew. He is able to say, without reserve or hesitation, "*We have found* the Messias." It was this that led him to look after his brother. He lost no time. Saved and blessed himself, he would, at once, begin to lead his brother into the same blessing.

How simple! How morally lovely! How divinely natural! No sooner had he found the Messias, than he went in search of his brother to tell him of his joy. It must ever be thus. We cannot doubt for a moment, that the actual finding Christ for ourselves is the true secret of looking after others. There is no uncertainty in Andrew's testimony—no wavering—no doubting or fearing. He does not even say, "I hope I have found." No; all is clear and distinct; and, we may say, with all possible assurance, it would not have done Simon Peter much good had it been anything else. An uncertain sound is not much use to any one.

It is a grand point to be able to say, "*I have found Christ.*" Can you say it? Doubtless, you have heard of Him. It may be you have heard from the lips of some ardent lover of Jesus, "Behold the Lamb of God." But have you followed that blessed One? If so, you will long to find some one to whom you can speak of your newly found treasure, and bring him to Jesus. Begin at home, Get hold of your brother or your sister, or your companion, your fellow-student, your fellow-shopman, your fellow-workman, your fellow-servant, and whisper lovingly, but clearly and decidedly, into his ear, "I have found Jesus. Do come, taste and see how gracious He is. Come! oh do come to Jesus." Remember this was the way that the great Apostle Peter was first called. He first heard of Jesus from the lips of his own brother Andrew. This mighty workman—this great preacher who was blessed, on one occasion, to three thousand souls—who opened the kingdom of Heaven to

the Jew in Acts 3 and to the Gentile in Acts 10—this blessed servant was brought to Christ by the hand of his own brother in the flesh.

Part 2

The notice which we have of our apostle, in John 1, is very brief indeed, though, doubtless, there is much wrapped up in it. "Andrew first findeth his own brother, Simon, and saith unto him, We have found the Messias, which is, being interpreted, the Christ. And he brought him to Jesus. And when Jesus beheld him, He said, Thou art Simon, the son of Jonas: thou shalt be called Cephas, which is by interpretation, A stone."

Now, we have no record here of any deep spiritual work in the soul of Simon. We are told his name in the old creation, and his name in the new; but there is no allusion whatever to those deep exercises of soul of which we know he was the subject. For these we must ask the reader to turn for a few moments to Luke 5, where we have a marvelous piece of divine workmanship.

"And it came to pass that, as the people pressed upon Him to hear the word of God, He stood by the lake of Gennesaret, and saw two ships standing by the lake; but the fishermen were gone out of them, and were washing their nets. And He entered into one of the ships, which was Simon's, and prayed him that he would thrust out a little from the land. And He sat down, and taught the people out of the ship."

Mark especially the moral grace that shines here. "He *prayed* him that he would thrust out *a little* from the land." Though Lord of all creation—Possessor of Heaven and earth—He nevertheless, as the lowly, gracious Man, courteously owns Simon's proprietorship, and asks, as a favor, that he would thrust out *a little* from the shore. This was morally lovely, and we may rest assured it produced its own effect upon the heart of Simon.

"Now when He had left speaking, He said unto Simon, Launch out into the deep, and let down your nets for a draught." Simon was about to be well paid for the loan of his boat.

"And Simon, answering, said unto Him, Master, we have toiled all the night, and have taken nothing; nevertheless, at Thy word, I will let down the net." There was power, as well as grace, in that word! "And when they had this done, they enclosed a great multitude of fishes; and their net brake. And they beckoned unto their partners, which were in the other ship, that they should come and help them. And they came, and filled both the ships, so that they began to sink." Neither their nets nor their ships were able to sustain the fruit of divine power and goodness. "When Simon Peter saw it, he fell down at Jesus' knees, saying, Depart from me; for I am a sinful man, O Lord."

Here, then, we have the great practical effect produced in Peter's soul by the combined action of grace and power. He is brought to see himself in the light of the divine presence, where alone self can be truly seen and judged. Simon had heard the word of Jesus addressed to the multitude on the shore. He had felt the sweet grace and moral beauty of His way towards himself. He had marked the display of divine power in the astonishing draught of fish. All told powerfully upon his heart and conscience, and brought him on his face before the Lord.

Now this is what we may call a genuine work of conviction. Simon is in the place of true self-judgment—a very blessed place indeed—a place from which all must start if they are to be much used in the Lord's work, or if, indeed, they are ever to exhibit much depth or stability in the divine life. We need never look for any real power or progress unless there is a deep and solid work of the Spirit of God in the conscience. Persons who pass rapidly into what they call peace, are apt to pass as rapidly out of it again.

It is a very serious thing indeed to be brought to see ourselves in the light of God's presence, to have our eyes opened to the truth of our past history, our present condition, and our future destiny. Simon Peter found it so in his day, and so have all those who have been brought to a saving knowledge of Christ. Hearken to Isaiah's words, when he saw himself in the powerful light of the divine glory. "Woe is me! for I am undone; because I am a man of unclean lips, and I dwell in the midst of a people of unclean lips: *for mine eyes have seen the King, the Lord of hosts*." So also in the case of the patriarch, Job. "I have heard of Thee by the hearing of the ear; but now *mine eye seeth Thee*. Wherefore *I abhor myself*, and repent in dust and ashes."

These glowing utterances reveal a deep and genuine work in both the patriarch and the prophet. And surely our apostle occupied the same moral ground when he exclaimed, from the very depths of a broken heart, "Depart from me; for I am a sinful man, O Lord." If Simon is to be called Cephas, he must be thoroughly broken up, and brought to the end of himself. If he is to be used to catch men, he must learn, in a divine way, man's true condition. If he is to teach others that "all flesh is as grass," he must learn the application of this great truth to his own heart.

Thus it is in every case. Look at Saul of Tarsus. What mean those three days of blindness, during which he neither did eat nor drink? May we not confidently affirm that they were serious days, perhaps the most serious in the entire history of that remarkable man? They were, doubtless, days in the which he was led down to the most profound depths of his moral being, the deepest roots of his history, his nature, his character, his conduct, his religion. He was led to see that his whole life had been a terrible mistake, an awful lie; that his very career as a religious man had been one of mad rebellion against the Christ of God.

All this, we may feel assured, passed in solemn and soul-subduing review before the soul of this deeply, because divinely, convicted man. His repentance was no superficial work; it was deep and thorough; it left its impress upon the whole of his after course, character, and ministry. He, too, like Simon, was brought to the end of himself, and there he found an Object that not only met his deepest need, but also perfectly satisfied all the cravings and aspirations of his renewed being.

Now, we must confess we delight in

contemplating a spiritual work of this kind. It is truly refreshing to dwell upon conversions of this type. We greatly fear that in much of the work of our time there is a sad lack of depth and spiritual power, and, as a consequence, a lack of stability in the Christian character, of depth and permanency in the Christian course. It may be that those of us who are engaged in the work of evangelization are feeble and shallow in the divine life ourselves, that we are not near enough to Christ to understand how to deal with souls; that we do not know how to present the truth from God's side of it; that we are more desirious of showing out how the sinners need is met, than how the glory of God is secured and maintained.

We do not, perhaps, sufficiently press the claims of truth and holiness upon the consciences of our hearers. There is a want of fulness in the presentation of the truth of God, too much harping upon one string; there is a barrenness and dreary monotony in the preaching, arising from lack of abiding near the fountain head, and drinking into our own souls from the inexhaustible springs of grace and truth in the Person and work of Christ. Perhaps, too, we are more occupied with ourselves and our preaching than with Christ and His glory; more anxious to be able to parade the results of our work, than to be a sweet savour of Christ to Godward.

We cannot but feel the weight and seriousness of these considerations for all who take part in the work of the gospel. We certainly do need to be more in the presence of God in reference to our service, for we cannot, by any possibility, hide from ourselves the fact, in reference to the preaching of this our day, that the fruit is small in quantity, and poor in quality. We desire to bless God for any display of His grace and power in souls; though we are by no means able to accredit as genuine much that is boastfully paraded in the way of conversion. What we long for is a deep, genuine unmistakable work of the Holy Ghost; a work which will prove itself, beyond all contradiction, by its permanent results in the life and character.

It is one thing to reckon up and publish a number of cases of conversion, and quite another to see these cases made good in actual fact. The Holy Ghost can, and does, tell us at times in the page of inspiration the number of souls converted. He tells us of three thousand on one occasion. He can do so, because He knows perfectly all about it. He can read the heart. He can distinguish between the spurious and the genuine. But when men undertake to count up and publish the number of their converts, we must receive their statement with considerable reserve and caution.

Not that we would be suspicious. God forbid; yea, we would earnestly cultivate a hopeful temper of soul. Still, we cannot but feel that it is better, in every case, to let the work speak for itself. All that is really divine is sure to be found, even though it be after many days; whereas, on the other hand, there is immense danger, both for the workman and his work, in an eager and hasty reckoning up and publishing of results.

But we must return to the lake of Gennesaret, and dwell for a moment on the lovely grace that shines forth in our Lord's dealing with Simon Peter. The work of conviction was deep and real. There could be no mistaking it. The arrow had entered the heart, and gone right to its very centre. Peter felt and owned that he was a man full of sin. He felt he had no right to be near such an one as Jesus; and yet we may truly say he would not for worlds have been anywhere else. He was perfectly sincere in saying, "Depart from me," though we cannot but believe he had an inward conviction that the blessed One would do nothing of the kind. And if he had, he was right. Jesus could never depart from a poor broken-hearted sinner—no, never. It was His richest, deepest, joy to pour the healing balm of His love and grace into a wounded soul. It was His delight to heal the broken heart. He was anointed for that work, and it was His meat and His drink to do it, blessed forever be His holy name!

"And Jesus said unto Simon, Fear not; from henceforth thou shalt catch men." Here was the divine response to the cry of a contrite heart. The wound was deep, but the grace was deeper still. The soothing hand of a Saviour-God applied the precious balm. Simon was not only convicted, but converted. He saw himself to be a man full of sin, but he saw the Saviour full of grace; nor was it possible that his sin could be beyond the reach of that grace. Oh, no, there is grace in the heart of Jesus, as there is power in His blood, to meet the very chief of sinners. "Fear not; from henceforth thou shalt catch men. And when they had brought their ships to land, they forsook *all*, and followed Him."

This was real work. It was a *bona fide* case, as to which there could be no question; a case of conviction, conversion, and consecration.

Part 3

We closed our last paper with these suggestive words, "*They forsook all, and followed Him*"—words expressive, at once, of thorough separation from the things of time and of nature, and of wholehearted consecration to Christ and His interests.

Both these we see in Simon Peter. There was a deep and blessed work wrought in his soul at the lake of Gennesaret. He was given to see himself, in the light of the divine presence, where alone self can be really seen and judged. We have no reason to suppose that, viewed from a human standpoint, Simon was worse than his neighbors. On the contrary, it is more than probable, that so far as his outward life was concerned, it was more blameless than that of many around him. He was not, like the great apostle of the Gentiles, arrested at the very height of a mad career of rebellion against Christ and His cause. He is introduced to us, by the inspired historian, in the pursuit of his quiet and honest calling as a fisherman.

But then Scripture expressly informs us that, "There is no difference, for all have sinned, and come short of the glory of God" (Rom. 3). And it repeats this statement, in chap. 10 of the same Epistle, basing it upon another footing, "There is no difference between the Jew and the Greek: for the same Lord over all is rich unto all that call upon Him."

See that you really understand this most important doctrine. It is not that there are not broad lines of distinction, in a moral and social point of view, between men. Most assuredly there are such. There is, for example, a vast difference between the wretched drunkard who comes home, or is carried home, night after night, worse than a beast, to his poor broken-hearted wife and squalid, starving children, and a sober, industrious man, who realizes his responsibility as a husband and a father, and seeks to fulfil the duties attaching to such relationships.

Now, we judge it would be a very great mistake indeed to ignore such a distinction as this. We believe that God, in His moral government of the world, recognizes it. Contrast, for a moment, the drunkard's home with that of the sober man. Yea, contrast their whole career, their social position, their course and character. Who can fail to recognize the amazing difference between the two? There is a certain way of presenting what is called, "the no-difference doctrine" which, to say the least of it, is far from judicious. It does not allow the margin which, as we believe, Scripture suggests, wherein to insert great social and moral distinctions between men and men—distinctions which only blindness itself can refuse to see.

If we look at the present government of God, we cannot but see that there is a very serious difference indeed between one man and another. Men reap as they sow. The drunken spendthrift reaps as he sows; and the sober, industrious, honest man reaps as he sows. The enactments of God's moral government are such as to render it impossible for men to escape, even in this life, the consequences of their ways.

Nor is this all. Not only does God's present government take cognizance of the conduct of men, causing them to reap, even here, the due reward of their deeds, but when Scripture opens to our view, as it does in manifold places, the awful judgment to come, it speaks of "books being opened." It tells us that men "shall be judged *every man according to their works*." In short, we have close and accurate discrimination, and not a promiscuous huddling of men and things.

And further, be it remembered, that the Word of God speaks of degrees of punishment. It speaks of "few stripes" and "many stripes." It uses such words as "more tolerable" for one than another.

What mean such words, if there be not varied grounds of judgment, varied characters of responsibility, varied measures of guilt, varied degrees of punishment? Men may reason; but "the Judge of all the earth will do right." It is of no possible use for people to argue and discuss. Every man will be judged and punished according to his deeds. This is the teaching of Holy Scripture; and it would be much better and safer and wiser for men to submit to it than to reason against it, for they may rest fully assured of it that the judgment-seat of Christ will make very short work of their reasonings.

Impenitent sinners will be judged and punished according to their works: and, although men may affect to believe that it is inconsistent with the idea of a God of love that any of His creatures should be condemned to endure eternal punishment in hell, still sin must be punished; and those who reason against its punishment have only a one-sided view of God's nature and character. They have invented a god of their own who will connive at sin. But it will not do. The God of the Bible, *the God whom we see at the cross*, the God of Christianity will, beyond all question, execute judgment upon all who reject His Son; that judgment will be according to every man's works; and the result of that judgment will, inevitably, be "The lake that burneth with fire and brimstone," forever and forever.

We deem it of the utmost importance to press on all whom it may concern the line of truth on which we have been dwelling. It leaves wholly untouched the real truth of the no-difference doctrine; but, at the same time, it qualifies and adjusts the mode of presenting the truth. It is always well to avoid an ultra one-sided way of stating things. It damages truth and stumbles souls. It perplexes the anxious, and gives a plea to the caviler. The full truth of God should always be unfolded, and thus all will be right. Truth puts men and things in their right places, and maintains a holy moral balance which is absolutely priceless.

Is it then asserted that there is a difference? Not as regards the question of righteousness before God. On this ground, there is not a shadow of difference, for "all have sinned and come short of the glory of God." Looked at in the light of that glory, all human distinctions vanish. All are lost, guilty and condemned. From the very lowest strata of society—its deepest dregs, up to the loftiest heights of moral refinement, men are seen, in the light of the divine glory, to be utterly and hopelessly lost. They all stand on one common ground, are all involved in the one common ruin. And not only so, but those who plume themselves on their morality, refinement, orthodoxy, and religiousness, are further from the kingdom of God than the vilest of the sons and daughters of men, as our Lord said to the chief priests and elders, "Verily I say unto you, that the publicans and the harlots go into the kingdom of God before you" (Matt. 21).

This is very humbling to human pride and pretension. It is a doctrine to which none will ever submit until they see themselves as Simon Peter saw himself in the immediate presence of God. All who have ever been there will fully understand those self-condemning words, "Depart from me; for I am a sinful man, O Lord." These were accents flowing from the depths of a truly penitent and contrite soul. There is what we may venture to call a lovely inconsistency in them. Simon had no such thought as that Jesus would depart from him. He had, we may feel assured, an instinctive sense that that blessed One who had spoken such words to him, and shown such grace, could not turn away from a poor broken-hearted sinner. And he judged rightly.

Jesus had not come down from Heaven to turn His back upon any one who needed Him. "He came to seek and to save that which is lost." "This is a faithful saying, and worthy of all acceptation, that Christ Jesus came into the world to save sinners." "Him that cometh unto Me, I will *in no wise* cast out." A Saviour-God had come down into this world, not, surely, to turn away from a lost sinner, but to save him and bless him, and make him a blessing. "Fear not; from henceforth thou shalt catch men."

Such was the grace that shone upon the soul of Simon Peter. It removed his guilt, hushed his fears, and filled him with joy and peace in believing. Thus it is in every case. Divine pardon follows human confession— follows it with marvelous rapidity. "I said, I will confess my transgressions unto the Lord: and Thou forgavest the iniquity of my sin." God delights to pardon. It is the joy of His loving heart to cancel our guilt, and fill our souls with His own blessed peace, and to make us the messengers of His grace to others.

Not that we are called in the same way, or to the same work, as our apostle; but surely we are called to follow the Lord, and cleave to Him, with purpose of heart. This is the blessed privilege and sacred duty of every saved soul on the face of the earth; we are imperatively called upon to break with the world, and follow Christ.

It is not a question of abandoning our proper calling in life, as in Simon's case. Few indeed and far between are the cases in which such a course of action is fitting. Many, alas! have assayed to do this, and have entirely broken down, simply because they were not called of God *to* it, or sustained of God *in* it. We are convinced that, as a rule, it is better for every man to work with his hands or his brains at some bread-winning calling, and preach and teach as well, if gifted to do so. There are exceptions, no doubt, to the rule. There are some who are so manifestly called, fitted, used, and sustained of God, that there can be no possible mistake as to their course. Their hands are so full of work, their every moment so engrossed with ministry in speaking or writing, teaching publicly and from house to house, that it would be a simple impossibility for them to take up what is termed a secular calling—though we like not the phrase. All such have to go on with God, looking only to Him, and He will infallibly maintain them unto the end.

Still, admitting, as we are bound to do fully, the exceptions to the rule, we are nevertheless convinced that, as a rule, it is better in every way for men to be able to preach and teach without being chargeable to any. It gives moral weight, and it furnishes a fine testimony against the wretched hirelingism of Christendom so demoralizing to souls, and so damaging, in every way, to the cause of Christ.

But we have to distinguish between abandoning our lawful calling and breaking with the world. The former may be quite wrong; the latter is our bounden duty. We are called to rise up, in the spirit of the mind and in the firm purpose of the heart, out of all merely worldly influences, to break every worldly link, and lay aside every weight, in order to follow our blessed Lord and Master. We are to be absolutely and completely for Him in this world, as He is for us in the presence of God. When this is really the case with us, it matters not whether we are sweeping a crossing or evangelizing a continent. All is done to Him. This is the one grand point. If Christ has His due place in our hearts, all will be right. If He has not, nothing will be right. If there is any under-current in the soul, any secondary object, any worldly motive, any selfish aim or end, there can be no progress. *We must make Christ and His cause our absorbing object.*

Part 4

The more deeply we ponder the history of professing Christians, whether as furnished by the pen of inspiration, or as coming within the range of personal observation, the more fully we must see the vast importance of a complete break with the world, at the outset. If there be not this, it is vain to look for inward peace, or outward progress. There may be a measure of clearness as to the doctrines of grace, the plan of salvation, as it is called, justification by faith, and the like. But unless there is the thorough judgment of self, and the complete surrender of this present evil world, peace and progress must be out of the question.

How can there be peace where *self*, in some one or other of its thousand shapes, is fostered? And how can there be progress where the heart is hankering after the world, halting between two opinions, and vacillating between Christ and present things? Impossible. As well might a racer expect to get on in the race while still lingering about the starting post, and encumbering himself with heavy weights.

Is it then, that peace is to be found by denying self and giving up the world? Most certainly not. But neither can peace ever be found while self is indulged and the world retained. True peace is found *only* in Christ—peace of conscience in His finished work—peace of heart in His blessed Person.

All this is clear enough. But how comes it to pass that hundreds of people who know, or profess to know, these things have no settled peace, and never seem to take a single step in advance? You meet them, week after week, month after month, year after year, and there they are in the same position, in the same state, and with the same old story, chronic cases of self-occupation, stereotyped world-borderers, "ever learning, and never able to come to the knowledge of the truth." They seem to delight in hearing the gospel clearly preached, and truth fully unfolded. In fact, they cannot endure anything else. But, for all that, they are never clear, bright, or happy. How can they be? They are halting between two opinions; they have never broken with the world; they have never surrendered a whole heart to Christ.

Here, we are persuaded, lies the real secret of the whole matter as regards that class of persons now before us. "A double-minded man is unstable in all his ways." A man who tries to keep one eye on the world, and the other on Christ, will be found to have no eye for Christ, but both eyes for the world. It must be so: Christ must be all or nothing; and hence it is the very height of absurdity to talk of peace or progress, where Christ is not the absorbing object of the soul. Where He is, there will never be any lack of settled peace; and there will be progress.

The Holy Ghost is jealous for the glory of Christ, and He can never minister comfort, consolation, or strength to a heart divided between Him and the world. It could not be.

He is grieved by such unfaithfulness; and instead of being the minister of comfort, He must be the stern reprover of indulged selfishness, worldliness, and vacillation.

Let us look at the case of our apostle. How refreshing it is to contemplate his thoroughgoing style! His starting was of the right sort. "He forsook all and followed Christ." There was no halting here, at all events; no vacillating between Christ and present things. Boats, nets, fish, natural ties, all are unhesitatingly and unreservedly surrendered, not as a matter of cold duty or legal service, but as the grand and necessary result of having seen the glory and heard the voice of the Son of God.

Thus it was with Simon Peter, at the opening of his remarkable career. All was clear and unequivocal, whole-hearted and decided, so far as the starting was concerned; and we must bear this in mind, as we pursue his after history. No doubt, we shall find mistakes and stumblings, failure, ignorance, and sin; but, underneath, and in spite of all this, we shall find a heart true to Jesue—a heart divinely taught to appreciate the Christ of God.

This is a grand point. Blunders may well be borne with, when the heart beats true to Christ. Some one has remarked that, "The blunderers do all the work." If this be so, the reason is that those blunderers have real affection for their Lord; and that is precisely what we all want. A man may make a great many mistakes, but if he can say when challenged by his Lord, "Thou knowest that I love Thee," he is sure to come right in the end; and not only so, but, even in the very midst of his mistakes, our hearts are much more drawn to him than to the cold, correct, sleek professor, who thinks of himself, and seeks to make the best of both worlds.

Simon Peter was a true lover of Christ. He had a divinely given sense of His preciousness, of the glory of His Person, and the heavenly character of His mission. All this comes out, with much force and freshness, in his varied confessions of Christ, even before the day of Pentecost. We shall glance at one or two of these, not with any view to chronological order, but simply to illustrate and prove the lovely devotedness of this true-hearted servant of Christ.

Let us turn to Matt. 16, "When Jesus came into the coasts of Caesarea Philippi, he asked His disciples, saying, Whom do men say that I, the Son of man, am?" Weighty question! Upon the answer to this question hangs the whole moral condition and future destiny of every human being under the sun.

All really depends upon the heart's estimate of Christ. This it is, which like a great moral indicator, reveals a man's true state, character, bent and object, in all things. It is not merely a question of his outward life, or of his profession of faith. The former may be blameless, and the latter orthodox; but, if underneath all this blameless morality and orthodox profession, there be not one true pulsation of the heart for Christ, no divinely wrought sense of what, and who, and whence He is, then verily all the morality and the orthodoxy are but the trappings with which a guilty, hell-deserving sinner adorns himself in the eyes of his fellows, or with which he deceives himself as to the awful eternity which lies before him. "What think ye of Christ?" is the all-deciding question; for God the Holy Ghost has emphatically declared that, "If any man"—no matter who or what he be—"love not the Lord Jesus Christ, let him be Anathema Maranatha" (1 Cor. 16: 22).

How awful is this! And how remarkable to find it at the close of such an Epistle as the first to the Corinthians! How forcibly it declares to all who will only bend their ears to listen, that love to Christ is the basis of all sound doctrine, the motive spring of all true morality! If that blessed One be not enthroned at the very centre of the heart's affections, an orthodox creed is an empty delusion; and an unblemished reputation is but dust cast in a man's eyes to prevent him seeing his true condition in the sight of God. The Christians at Corinth had fallen into many doctrinal errors and moral evils, all needing rebuke and correction; but when the inspiring Spirit pronounces His awful anathema, it is levelled, not at the introducers of any one special error, or moral pravity, but at "any man who loves not the Lord Jesus Christ."

This is peculiarly solemn at all times; but specially so for the day in which our lot is cast, when the Person and glory of Christ are so little thought of or cared for. A man may actually blaspheme Christ, deny His deity or His eternal Sonship, and yet be received into professing Christian circles, and allowed to preside at so-called religious meetings. Surely all this must be dreadful in the sight of God, whose purpose it is "that all men should honor the Son even as they honor the Father"; and that every knee should bow, and every tongue confess to Jesus as Lord of all. God is jealous for the honor of His Son; and the man that neglects, rejects, and blasphemes that blessed One will yet have to learn and own the eternal justice of that most solemn decree, "If any man love not the Lord Jesus Christ, let him be Anathema Maranatha."

How momentous, therefore, the question put by our Lord Christ to His disciples, "Whom do *men* say that I, the Son of man, am?" Alas, "men" knew nothing, cared nothing about Him. They knew neither who He was, what He was, nor whence He was. "Some say that thou art John the Baptist; some, Elias; and others, Jeremias, or one of the prophets." In a word, there was endless speculation, because there was utter indifference and thorough heartlessness. The human heart has not so much as a single true thought about Christ, not one atom of affection for Him.

Such is the awful condition of the very best of men until renewed by divine grace. They know not, they love not, they care not for the Son of God—the Beloved of the Father's heart—the Man on the throne of Heaven's majesty. Such is their moral condition, and hence their every thought, word, and act is contrary to God. They have not a single feeling in common with God, for the most distinct of all reasons, that the One who is everything to Him is nothing to them.

Christ is God's standard, and every one and everything must be measured by Him. The heart that does not love Christ has not a single pulsation in unison with the heart of

God; and the life that does not spring from love to Christ however blameless, respectable, or splendid in the eyes of men, is a worthless, objectless, misspent life in the judgment of God.

But how truly delightful to turn from all the heartlessness and indifference of "men," and harken to the testimony of one who was taught of God to know and own who the Son of man was! "Simon Peter answered and said, Thou art the Christ, the Son of the living God." Here was the true answer. There was no vain speculation here, no uncertainty, no may be this, or may be that. It was divine testimony flowing from divinely given knowledge. It was not yea and nay, but yea and amen to the glory of God. We may rest fully assured that these glowing words of Simon Peter went up, like fragrant incense, to the throne of God, and refreshed the heart of the One who sat there. There is nothing in all the world so precious to God as a heart that, in any measure, appreciates Christ. Let us never forget this!

"And Jesus answered and said unto him, Blessed art thou, Simon Barjona; for flesh and blood hath not revealed it unto thee, but My Father which is in heaven. And I say also unto thee, that thou art Peter; and upon this Rock I will build My Church; and the gates of hell shall not prevail against it."

Here we have the very first direct allusion to the Church, or assembly of Christ; and the reader will note that our Lord speaks of it as yet future. He says, "I *will* builld My church." He was the Rock, the divine foundation; but ere a single stone could be built on Him, He must die.

This is a grand cardinal truth of Christianity—a truth which our apostle had yet to learn, notwithstanding his brilliant and beautiful confession. Simon Peter was not yet prepared for the profound mystery of the cross. He loved Christ, and he had been taught of God to own Him in a very full and blessed manner; but he had yet much to learn ere he could take in the soul-subduing truth that this blessed Son of the living God must die, ere even he, as a living stone, could be built upon Him. "From that time forth began Jesus to show unto His disciples, how that He must go unto Jerusalem, and suffer many things of the elders and chief priests and scribes, and be killed, and be raised again the third day."

Here the solemn truth begins to break through the clouds. But Simon Peter is not prepared for it. It withered up all his Jewish hopes and earthly expectations. What! The Son of the living God must die! How could it be? The glorious Messiah be nailed to a cross! "Then Peter took Him, and began to rebuke Him, saying, Be it far from Thee, (or pity Thyself) Lord, this shall not be unto Thee."

Such is man! Such was even Simon Peter! He would fain turn the blessed Lord away from the cross! He would, in his ignorance, frustrate the eternal counsels of God, and play into the hands of the devil! Poor Peter! What a rock he would be for the Church to be built upon! "The Lord turned, and said unto Peter, Get thee behind Me, Satan, thou art an offence unto Me; for thou savorest not the things that be of God, but those that be of men."

Withering words? Who would have thought that "Blessed art thou, Simon Barjona," should so speedily be followed by, "Get thee behind Me, Satan"?

Part 5

We must still linger a little over the deeply interesting and instructive scene in the sixteenth chapter of Matthew. It brings before us two great subjects, namely, "the Church," and "the kingdom of Heaven." These things must never be confounded. As to the first, it is only to be found in the New Testament. Indeed, as has often been remarked, verse 18 of our chapter contains the very first direct allusion in the volume of God to the subject of the Church, or assembly, of Christ.

This, though familiar to many of our readers, may present a difficulty to others. Many Christians and Christian teachers strongly maintain that the doctrine of the Church is distinctly unfolded in Old Testament Scripture. They consider that the saints of the Old Testament belonged to the Church; in fact, that there is no difference whatever; all form one body; all stand on one common ground; and that to represent the Lord's people in New Testament times as in a higher position, or endowed with higher privileges than Abraham, Isaac, and Jacob, is a delusion.

It seems strange to such to assert that Enoch, Noah, Abraham, and Moses did not belong to the Church—were not members of the body of Christ—were not endowed with the selfsame privileges as believers now. Trained from their earliest days to believe that all God's people, from the beginning to the end of time, stand on the same ground, and form one common body, they find it impossible to admit of any difference. It seems to them presumption on the part of Christians to assert that they are in any respect different from God's beloved people of old—those blessed worthies of whom we read in Hebrews 11, who lived a life of faith and personal devotedness, and who are now in Heaven with their Lord.

But the all-important question is, "What saith the Scripture?" It can be of no possible use to set up our own thoughts, our own reasonings, our own conclusions, in opposition to the Word of God. It is a very easy matter for men to reason, with great apparent force, point, and cleverness, about the absurdity and presumption of the notion that Christians are in a better and higher place, and more privileged, than God's people of old.

But this is not the proper way in which to approach this great subject. It is not a question of the difference *personally* between the Lord's people at different periods. Were it so, where should we find, amongst the ranks of Christian professors, any one to compare with an Abraham, a Joseph, a Moses, or a Daniel? Were it a question of simple faith, where could we find in the entire history of the Church a finer example than the father of the faithful? Were it a question of personal holiness, where could we find a brighter illustration than Joseph? For intimacy with God, and acquaintance with His ways and mind, who could go beyond Moses? For unswerving devotedness to God and His truth, could we find a brighter example than the man who went down into the lions' den rather than not pray toward Jerusalem?

However, let it be distinctly understood that it is not by any means a personal question, or a comparison of people, but of dispensational position. If this be clearly seen, it will, we doubt not, remove out of the way a great deal of the difficulty which many pious people seem to feel in reference to the truth of the Church.

But above and beyond all this stands the question, What does Scripture teach on the subject? If any one had spoken to Abraham about being a member of the body of Christ, would he have understood it? Could that honored and beloved saint of God have had the most remote idea of being linked by an indwelling Spirit to a living Head in Heaven? Utterly impossible. How could he be a member of a body which had no existence? And how could there be a body without a Head? And when do we first hear of the Head? When the Man Christ Jesus, having passed through death and the grave, ascended into the heavens, and took His seat at the right hand of the Majesty on high. Then, and not until then, did the Holy Ghost come down to form the body, and link it by His presence to the glorified Head above.

This, however, is rather anticipating a line of argument which is yet to come before us. Let us here put another question to the reader. If any one had spoken to Moses about a body composed of Jews and Gentiles—a body whose constituent parts had been drawn from among the seed of Abraham and the cursed race of the Canaanites—what would he have said? May we not safely assert that his whole moral being would have shrunk with horror from the thought? What! Jews and Canaanites—the seed of Abraham and uncircumcised Gentiles—united in one body? Impossible for the lawgiver to take in such an idea. The fact is, if there was one feature which more strongly than another marked the Jewish economy, it was the rigid separation by divine appointment of Jew and Gentile. "Ye know," says Simon Peter, "how that it is an unlawful thing for a man that is a Jew to keep company, or to come unto one of another nation."

Such was the order of things under the Mosaic economy. It would have been a flagrant transgression on the part of a Jew to climb over that middle wall of partition which separated him from all the nations around; and hence the thought of a union between Jew and Gentile could not possibly have entered into any human mind; and the more faithful a man was to the existing order of things under the law, the more opposed he must have been to any such thought.

Now, in the face of all this, how can any one seek to maintain that the truth of the Church was known in Old Testament times, and that there is no difference whatever between the position of a Christian and that of an Old Testament believer? The fact is that even Simon Peter himself found it extremely difficult to take in the idea of admitting the Gentiles into the kingdom of Heaven. Though he was entrusted with the keys of that kingdom, he was very reluctant indeed to use them for the admission of the Gentiles. He had to be expressly taught by a heavenly vision, ere he was prepared to fulfil the commission with which he was charged by his Lord in Matthew 16.

No, it is of no possible use to stand against the plain testimony of Scripture. The truth of the Church was not—could not—be known in Old Testament times. It was, as the inspired apostle tells us, "hid in God"—hid in His eternal counsels—"not made known to the sons of men, as it is now revealed unto His holy apostles and prophets by the Spirit,* that the Gentiles should be *fellow-heirs*, and of *the same body*, and partakers of His promise in Christ by the gospel" (Eph. 3).

We can only reach the great mystery of the Church by walking over the broken-down middle wall of partition. "Wherefore remember, that ye being in time past Gentiles in the flesh, who are called Uncircumcision by that which is called the Circumcision in the flesh made by hands; that at that time ye were without Christ, being aliens from the commonwealth of Israel, and strangers from the covenants of promise, having no hope, and without God in the world. But now, in Christ Jesus, ye who sometimes were far off are made nigh *by the blood of Christ*. For He is our peace, who hath made both one, and hath broken down the middle wall of partition, having abolished in His flesh the enmity, the law of commandments in ordinances, for to make in Himself of twain one new man, making peace; and that He might reconcile both unto God in one body by the cross, having slain the enmity thereby; and came and preached peace to you which were afar off, and to them that were nigh. For through Him we both have access by one Spirit unto the Father" (Eph. 2: 11-18).

Thus, from all that has passed before us, the reader will, we trust, fully see why it is that our Lord in His word to Simon Peter speaks of the Church as a future thing. "Upon this rock *I will build* My Church." He does not say, "I have been," or, "I am, building My Church." Nothing of the kind. It could not be. It was still "hid in God." The Messiah had to be cut off and have nothing—nothing, for the present, as regards Israel and the earth. He must be rejected, crucified, and slain, in order to lay the foundation of the Church. It was utterly impossible that a single stone could be laid in this new, this wondrous building until "the chief Corner-stone" had passed through death and taken His place in the Heavens. It was not in incarnation, but in resurrection, that our Lord Christ became Head of a body.

Now our apostle was not in the least

---

* The "prophets," in this passage, are those of the New Testament. This is evident from the expression, "*Now revealed*." He could not speak of a thing being "now revealed" to men who had been dead for hundreds of years. Besides, had the apostle meant Old Testament prophets, the order would assuredly have been "Prophets and apostles." We have a similar expression in Eph. 2: 20: "Built upon the foundation of the apostles and prophets." He does not say, "prophets and apostles." The truth is that the apostles and prophets formed the first layer of the foundation of the Church of which Jesus Christ is the chief Corner-stone; and this is an additional proof that the Church had no existence save in the secret counsels of God until our Lord Christ, having accomplished the work of redemption, ascended into the heavens, and sent down the Holy Ghost to baptize believers—Jews and Gentiles—into one body.

The reader may also refer with real profit and interest to Rom. 16:25-26: "Now to Him that is of power to stablish you according to my gospel, and the preaching of Jesus Christ, according to *the revelation of the mystery, which was kept secret since the world began*, but *now is made manifest*, and by the scriptures of the prophets [literally, by the prophetic writings, that is, of the New Testament], according to the commandment of the everlasting God, made known to all nations for the obedience of faith."

prepared for this. He did not understand one jot or tittle of it. That Messiah should set up a kingdom in power and glory—that He should restore Israel to their destined pre-eminence in the earth—all this he could understand and appreciate—he was looking for it. But a suffering Messiah—a rejected and crucified Christ—of this he could not hear just then. "Be it far from Thee, Lord; this shall not be unto Thee." These were the words which drew forth that withering rebuke with which we closed our last paper, "Get thee behind Me, Satan; thou art an offence unto Me; for thou savorest not the things that be of God, but those that be of men."

We may gather the gravity of his error from the severity of the rebuke. Peter had much to learn, much to go through, ere he could grasp the great truth which His Lord was putting before him. But he did grasp it, by the grace of God, and confess it, and teach it with power. He was led to see not only that Christ was the Son of the living God, but that He was a rejected Stone, disallowed of men, but chosen of God and precious; and that all who through grace come to Him must share His rejection on earth as well as His acceptance in Heaven. They are perfectly identified with Him.

Part 6

At the close of John 6 we have a very clear and beautiful confession of Christ from the lips of our apostle—a confession rendered all the more touching and forcible by the circumstances under which it was delivered.

Our blessed Lord, in His teachings in the synagogue at Capernaum, had unfolded truth which puts the poor human heart to the test, and withers up all the pretensions of man in a very remarkable manner. We cannot here attempt to enter upon the subject of our Lord's discourse, but the effect of it is thus recorded: "From that time many of His disciples went back, and walked no more with Him." They were not prepared for the reception of such heavenly doctrine. They were offended by it, and they turned their backs upon that blessed One who alone was worthy of all the affections of the heart, and

of the homage and devotion of the whole moral being. "*They went back, and walked no more with Him.*"

Now we are not told what became of these deserters, or whether they were saved or not. No such question is raised. We are simply told that they abandoned Christ, and ceased to be any longer publicly identified with His name and His cause. How many, alas! have since followed their sad example! It is one thing to profess to be the disciples of Christ, and another thing altogether to stand with firm purpose of heart on the ground of public testimony for His name, in thorough identification with a rejected Lord. It is one thing for people to flock to Christ because of the benefits which He bestows, and it is quite another to cleave to Him in the face of the world's scorn and contempt. The application of the doctrine of the cross very speedily thins the ranks of professors. In the chapter before us we see at one moment multitudes thronging enthusiastically around the Man who could so marvelously supply their need, and the next moment abandoning Him, when His teaching offended their pride.

Thus it has been, thus it is, and thus it will be until that day in the which the despised Stranger of Nazareth shall reign from pole to pole, and from the river to the ends of the earth. We are ready enough to avail ourselves of the benefits and blessings which *a loving Saviour* can bestow upon us, but when it becomes a question of following *a rejected Lord* along that rough and lonely path which He has trodden for us in this sinful world, we are disposed, like those of old, to go back, and walk no more with Him.

This is very sad and very humiliating. It proves how little we know of His heart, or of what that heart desires from us. Jesus longs for fellowship. He does not want patronage. It does not meet the desire of His heart to be followed, or admired, or gazed at, because of what He can do or give. He delights in a heart taught of God to appreciate His Person, for this glorifies and gratifies the Father. He retired from the gaze of an excited and tumultuous throng who would fain make Him a king, because they had eaten of the loaves and were filled; but He could turn, with touching earnestness, to the little band of followers who still remained, and challenge their hearts with the question, "Will ye also go away?"

How deeply affecting! How it must have touched the hearts of all, save that one who had no heart for aught but money—who was "a thief" and "a devil"! Alas! a moment was approaching when all were to forsake Him and fly—when He was to be left absolutely *alone*, forsaken of men, forsaken of God—utterly and awfully deserted.

But that moment was yet future; and it is peculiarly refreshing to harken to the fine confession of our beloved apostle, in reply to the deeply affecting inquiry of his Lord. "Then Simon Peter answered Him, Lord, to whom shall we go? Thou hast the words of eternal life. And we believe and are sure that Thou art that Christ, the Son of the living God."

Well indeed might he say, "To whom shall we go?" There was not another throughout the wide universe of God to whom the heart could turn. He alone could meet their every need, satisfy their every right desire, fill up every chamber of the heart. Simon Peter felt this, and hence, with all his mistakes, his failures, and his infirmities, his loving and devoted heart turned with earnest affection to his beloved Lord. He would not abandon Him, though little able to rise to the height of His heavenly teaching. There was a link binding him to Jesus Christ which nothing could snap. "Lord, to whom shall we go?"—whither shall we betake ourselves?—on whom could we reckon beside?

True, there may be trial and difficulty in the path of true discipleship. It may prove a rough and a lonely path. The heart may be tried and tested in every possible way. There may be deep and varied sorrow—deep waters, dark shadows; but in the face of all we can say, "To whom shall we go?"

And mark the singular fulness of Peter's confession. "Thou *hast* the words of eternal life;" and then, "Thou *art* that Christ, the Son of the living God." We have the two things, namely, what He *has*, and what He *is*. Blessed be His name, Christ has all we can possibly want for time and eternity. Words of

eternal life flow from His lips into our hearts. He causes those who follow Him to "inherit substance." He bestows upon them "durable riches and righteousness." We may truly say that, in comparison of what Christ has to give, all the riches, honors, dignities, and pleasures of this world are but dross. They all pass away as the vapors of the morning, and leave only an aching void behind.

Nothing that this world has to offer can possibly satisfy the cravings of the human soul. "All is vanity and vexation of spirit." And not only so—it must be given up. If one had all the wealth of Solomon, it lasts but a moment in comparison with that boundless eternity which lies before every one of us. When death approaches, all the riches of the universe could not purchase one moment's respite. The last great enemy gives no quarter. He ruthlessly snaps the link that connects man with all that his poor heart prizes and loves upon earth, and hurries him away into eternity.

And what then? Yes, this is the question. Who can answer it? Who can attempt to picture the future of a soul that passes into eternity without God, without Christ, without hope? Who can describe the horrors of one who, all in a moment, opens his eyes to the fact—the tremendous fact—that he is lost, lost forever—hopelessly, eternally, lost? It is positively too dreadful to dwell upon it. And yet it must be looked at; and if the reader is still of the world, still unconverted, careless, thoughtless, unbelieving, we would earnestly entreat of him now, just now, to give his earnest attention to the weighty and all-important question of his soul's salvation —a question, in comparison with which all other questions dwindle into utter insignificance.

"What shall it profit a man, if he should gain the whole world, and lose his own soul? or what shall a man give in exchange for his soul?" It is, beyond all question, the most egregious folly that any one can be guilty of to put off the grand business of his soul's salvation.

And if any one inquire what he has to do in this business, the answer is *Nothing*— "nothing, either great or small." Jesus has the words of eternal life. He it is who says, "Verily, verily, I say unto you, he that heareth My word, and believeth on Him that sent Me, *hath* everlasting life, and shall not come into judgment, but *is passed* from death unto life."

Here is the hinge on which the whole matter moves. Harken to the words of Christ. Believe in Him that sent His blessed Son. Put your trust in God, and you shall be saved; you shall have eternal life, and never come into judgment.

Nor is this all. Simon Peter, in his lovely confession, does not confine himself to what Christ has to give, precious and blessed as that is, but he also speaks of what He is. "Thou art that Christ, the Son of the living God." This is full of deepest interest for the heart. Christ not only gives us eternal life, but He also becomes the object of our heart's affections—our satisfying portion, our unfailing resource, our infallible Guide and Counselor, our constant reference, in all our need, in all our pressure, in all our sorrows and difficulties. We need never go to any one else for succor, sympathy, or guidance. We have all we want in Him. He is the eternal delight of the heart of God, and He may well be the delight of our hearts here and hereafter, now and forever.

Part 7

The close of Matt. 14 presents a scene in the life of our apostle on which we may dwell with profit for a few moments. It furnishes a very fine illustration of his own touching inquiry, "Lord, to whom shall we go?"

Our Lord having fed the multitude, and sent His disciples across the sea, retired into a mountain, to be alone in prayer. In this we have a striking foreshadowing of the present time. Jesus has gone on high. Israel is for the present set aside, but not forgotten. Days of trouble will come—rough seas and stormy skies will fall to the lot of the remnant; but their Messiah will return, and deliver them out of all their troubles. He will bring them to their desired haven, and all will be peace and joy for the Israel of God.

All this is fully unfolded on the page of prophecy, and is of the deepest interest to every lover of God and His Word; but for the present we can merely dwell upon the inspired record concerning Simon Peter, and seek to learn the lesson which that record so forcibly teaches.

"And straightway Jesus constrained His disciples to get into a ship, and to go before Him unto the other side, while He sent the multitudes away. And when He had sent the multitudes away, He went up into a mountain apart to pray; and when the evening was come, He was there alone. But the ship was now in the midst of the sea, tossed with waves, for the wind was contrary. And in the fourth watch of the night Jesus went unto them, walking on the sea. And when the disciples saw Him walking on the sea, they were troubled, saying, It is a spirit; and they cried out for fear. But straightway Jesus spake unto them, saying, Be of good cheer; it is I; be not afraid. And Peter answered Him, and said, Lord, if it be Thou, bid me come unto Thee on the water. And He said, Come. And when Peter was come down out of the ship, he walked on the water to go to Jesus. But when he saw the wind boisterous, he was afraid; and beginning to sink, he cried, saying, Lord, save me. And immediately Jesus stretched forth His hand, and caught him, and said unto him, O thou of little faith, wherefore didst thou doubt?"

This brief passage presents to our view in a very forcible way some of the leading features of Simon Peter's character. His zeal, his energy, his real devotedness of heart, no one can for a moment call in question; but these very qualities—beautiful as they surely are—led him not unfrequently into a position of such prominence as to render his weak points all the more conspicuous. A man of less zeal, less energy, would have remained on board the ship, and thus avoided Peter's failure and breakdown. Perhaps, too, men of cooler temperament would condemn as unwarrantable rashness Peter's act in leaving the ship, or pronounce it a piece of forwardness which justly deserved a humiliating rebuff.

All this may be so; but we are free to confess that the zeal, energy and devotedness of this beloved servant of Christ have far more powerful charms for the heart than the cool, calculating, self-considering spirit which, in order to avoid the shame and humiliation of a defeat, refuses to take a bold and decided step for Christ. True it is that Peter in the interesting scene now before us completely broke down. But why did he? Was it because he left the ship? No; but because he ceased to look in simple faith to Jesus. Here lay the root of his failure. Had he only kept his eye on the Master, he could have walked on the water though ever so rough.

Faith can walk on rough water as easily as on smooth. Nature cannot walk on either. It is not a question of the state of the water, but the state of the heart. Circumstances have nothing to do with faith, except, indeed, that when difficult and trying, they develop its power and brightness. There was no reason whatever, in the judgment of faith, why Peter should have failed in his walk on the water. Faith looks not at the things that are seen and temporal, but at the things which are unseen and eternal. It endures as seeing Him who is invisible. "Faith is the evidence of things *not seen*." It lifts the heart above the winds and waves of this rough world, and keeps it in perfect peace, to the praise of Him who is the Giver of faith, as of "every good and perfect gift."

But our beloved apostle utterly failed in faith on the occasion now before us. He, as we, alas! so often do, took his eye off the Lord and fixed it on his surroundings, and as a consequence he immediately began to sink. It must ever be so. We cannot get on for a single moment save as we have the living God as a covering for our eyes. The grand motto for the life of faith is, "Looking off unto Jesus." It is this alone which enables us to "run the race set before us," be the way rough or smooth. When Peter came down out of the ship, it was either Christ or drowning. He might well say at such a moment, "Lord, to whom shall I go?" Whither could he turn? When on board the ship, he had its timbers between him and death, but when on the water he had nothing but Jesus.

And was not He enough? Yes, verily, if only Peter could have trusted Him. This is the point. All things are possible to him that believeth. Storms are hushed into a perfect calm, rough seas become like glass, lofty mountains are leveled, when faith brings the power of God to bear. The greater the difficulties, the brighter the triumphs of faith. It is in the furnace that the real preciousness of faith is displayed. Faith has to do with God, and not with men or things. If we cease to lean on God, we have nothing but a wild, watery waste—a perfect chaos—around us, where nature's resources must hopelessly fail.

All this was proved by Simon Peter when he came down out of the ship to walk on the water; and every child of God and every servant of Christ must prove it in his measure, for Peter's history is full of great practical lessons for us all. If we want to walk above the circumstances of the scene through which we are passing—if we would rise superior to its influences—if we would be able to give an answer, clear, distinct, and decided, to the skepticism, the rationalism and infidelity of the day in which we live—then, assuredly, we must keep the eye of faith firmly fixed on "the Author and Perfecter of faith." It is not by logical skill or intellectual power we shall ever meet the arguments of the infidel, but by an abiding sense, a living and soul-satisfying apprehension, of the all-sufficiency of Christ—Himself —His work—His Word—to meet our every need, our every exigence.

But it may be the reader feels disposed to condemn Peter for leaving the ship. He may think there was no need for his taking such a step. Why not abide with his brethren on board the vessel? Was it not possible to be quite as devoted to Christ in the ship as on the water? And, further, did not the sequel prove that it would have been far better, and safer, and wiser, for Peter to remain where he was, than to venture forth on a course which he was not able to pursue?

To all this we reply that our apostle was evidently governed by an earnest desire to be nearer to his Lord. And this was right. He saw Jesus walking on the water, and he longed to be with Him. And, further, he had the direct authority of his Lord for leaving the ship. We fully and freely grant that without this it would have been a fatal mistake to leave his position; but the moment that word "Come" fell on his ear he had a divine warrant for going forth upon the water—yea, to have remained would have been to miss great blessing.

Thus it is in every case. We must have authority before we can act in anything. Without this, the greater our zeal, energy, and apparent devotedness, the more fatal will be our mistake, and the more mischief we shall do to ourselves, to others, and to the cause of Christ. It is of the very last possible importance in every case, but especially where there is a measure of zeal, earnestness, and energy, that there should be sober subjection to the authority of the Word. If there be not this, there is no calculating the amount of mischief which may be done. If our devotedness flow not in the channel of simple obedience, if it rush over the embankments formed by the Word of God, the consequences must be most disastrous.

But there is another thing which stands next in importance to the authority of the *divine Word*, and that is the abiding realization of the *divine presence*. These two things must never be separated if we want to walk on the water. We may be quite clear and settled in our own minds, having distinct authority for any given line of action; but if we have not with equal distinctness the sense of the Lord's presence with us—if our eyes are not continually on the living God—we shall most assuredly break down.

This is very serious, and demands the gravest consideration of the Christian reader. It was precisely here that Peter failed. He did not fail in obedience, but in realized dependence. He acted on the word of Jesus in leaving the ship, but he failed to lean on the arm of Jesus in walking on the water; hence his terror and confusion. Mere authority is not enough; we want power. To act without authority is wrong. To act without power is impossible. The authority for starting is the Word. The power to proceed is the divine presence. The combination of the two must ever yield a successful career. It matters not in the smallest degree what the difficulties are if we have the stable authority of Holy Scripture for our course, and the blessed support of the presence of God in pursuing it. When God speaks, we must obey; but in order to do so, we must lean on His arm. "Have not I commanded you?" "Lo, I am with you."

Here are the two things so absolutely essential to every child of God and every servant of Christ. Without these, we can do nothing; with them, we can do all things. If we have not a "Thus saith the Lord," or "It is written," we cannot enter upon a path of devotedness; and if we have not His realized presence, we cannot pursue it. It is quite possible to be right in setting out, and yet to fail in going on.

It was so in the case of Simon Peter, and it has been so in the case of thousands since. It is one thing to make a good start, and another thing to make good progress. It is one thing to leave the ship, and another thing to walk on the water. Peter did the former, but he failed in the latter. This beloved servant of Christ broke down in his course; but where did he find himself? In the arms of a loving Saviour. "Lord, save me!" How touching! How deeply affecting! He casts himself upon a well-known love—a love which was yet to meet him in far more humiliating circumstances. Nor was he disappointed. Ah, no! Blessed be God, no poor failing creature can ever appeal to that love in vain.

"And immediately Jesus stretched forth His hand, and caught him, and said unto him, O thou of little faith, wherefore didst thou doubt?" Exquisite grace! If Peter failed to reach his Lord, his Lord did not fail to reach him. If Peter failed in faith, Jesus could not fail in grace. Impossible. The grace of our Lord Jesus is exceeding abundant. He takes occasion from our very failures to display His rich and precious love. Oh, how blessed to have to do with such a tender, patient, loving Lord! Who would not trust Him and praise Him, love Him and serve Him?

Part 8

We have now to follow our beloved apostle into the darkest and most humbling scene in his entire history—a scene which we could hardly understand or account for if we did not know something of the infinite depths of divine grace on the one hand, and, on the other hand, of the terrible depths into which even a saint of God or an apostle of Christ is capable of plunging if not kept by divine power.

It seems very wonderful to find on the page of inspiration the record of the fall of such an eminent servant of Christ as Simon Peter. We, in our wisdom, would judge it best to draw the curtain of silence over such an event. Not so the Holy Ghost. He has seen fit to tell us plainly of the errors, and failures, and sins, of such men as Abraham, Moses, David, Peter, and Paul, in order that we may learn holy lessons from such records—lessons of human frailty, lessons of divine grace, lessons full of solemn warning, and yet of most precious consolation and encouragement. We learn what we are, and we learn what God is. We learn that we cannot trust ourselves for a single moment; for, if not kept by grace, there is no depth of sin into which we are not capable of falling; but we learn to trust the eternal stability of that grace which has dealt with the erring ones and sinning ones of other days, and to lean with ever-growing confidence on the One who is "the same yesterday, to-day, and for ever."

Not one of the four evangelists omits the fall of Peter. Let us open at Matt. 26; "And when they had sung a hymn they went out into the mount of Olives. Then saith Jesus unto them, All ye shall be offended because of Me this night: for it written, I will smite the Shepherd, and the sheep of the flock shall be scattered abroad. But after I am risen again I will go before you into Galilee. Peter answered and said unto Him, Though all shall be offended because of Thee, yet will I never be offended."

In these few words Peter lets out the real root of the whole matter. That root was self-confidence—alas! alas! no uncommon root amongst us. We do not in the least question Peter's sincerity. We feel perfectly sure he meant all he said; and, further, that he had not the most remote idea of what he was about to do. He was ignorant of himself, and we generally find that ignorance and self-

confidence go together. Self-knowledge destroys self-confidence. The more fully self is known, the more it must be distrusted. If Peter had known himself, known his tendencies and capabilities, he never would have uttered the words which we have just penned. But so full was he of self-confidence, that when his Lord told him expressly what he was about to do, he replied, "Though I should die with Thee, yet will I not deny Thee."

This is peculiarly solemn. It is full of instruction for us all. We are all so ignorant of our own hearts that we deem ourselves incapable of falling into certain gross sins. But we should, every one of us, bear in mind that if not kept each moment by the grace of God, we are capable of anything. We have materials in us for any amount or character of evil; and whenever we hear any one saying, "Well, I certainly am a poor, failing, stumbling creature, but I am not capable of doing the like of that," we may feel assured he does not know his own heart; and not only so, but he is in imminent danger of falling into some grievous sin. It is well to walk humbly before our God, distrusting self, and leaning on Him. This is the true secret of moral safety at all times. Had Peter realized this, it would have saved him his terrible downfall.

But Peter was self-confident, and, as a consequence, he failed to watch and pray. This was another stage in his downward journey. Had he only felt his utter weakness, he would have sought for strength divine. He would have cast himself on God for grace to help in time of need. Look at the blessed Master! He, though God over all, blessed forever, yet being a Man, having taken the place of the creature, and fully entering into His position, was agonizing in prayer while Peter was fast asleep. Yes, Peter slept in the garden of Gethsemane while his Lord was passing through the deepest anguish He had yet tasted, though deeper still lay before Him.

"Then cometh Jesus with them unto a place called Gethsemane, and saith unto the disciples, Sit ye here, while I go and pray yonder. And He took with Him Peter and the sons of Zebedee, and began to be sorrowful and very heavy. Then saith He unto them,

My soul is exceeding sorrowful, even unto death; tarry ye here, and watch with Me. And He went a little further, and fell on His face, and prayed, saying, O My Father, if it be possible, let this cup pass from Me: nevertheless, not as I will, but as Thou wilt. And He cometh unto the disciples, and findeth them asleep, and *saith unto Peter,* What! could ye not watch with Me one hour? Watch and pray, that ye enter not into temptation: the spirit indeed is willing, but the flesh is weak."

What tender grace! What readiness to make allowance! What moral elevation! And yet He felt the sad want of sympathy, the cold indifference to His sore agony. "I looked for some to take pity, but there was none; and for comforters, but I found none." How much is involved in these words! He looked for comforters. That perfect human heart craved sympathy; but, alas! there was none for Him. Even Peter, who declared himself ready to die with Him, fell asleep in view of the agonies of Gethsemane.

Such is man—yea, the very best of men! Self-confident, when he ought to be self-distrusting—sleeping, when he ought to be watching; and, we may add, fighting, when he ought to be submitting. "Then Simon Peter, having a sword, drew it, and smote the high priest's servant, and cut off his right ear. The servant's name was Malchus." How incongruous, how utterly out of place, was a sword in compnay with the meek and lowly Sufferer!

"Then said Jesus unto Peter, Put up thy sword into the sheath: the cup which My Father hath given Me, shall I not drink it?" Peter was entirely out of the current of his Master's spirit. He had not a thought in common with Him in reference to His path of suffering. He would fain defend Him with carnal weapons, forgetting that His kingdom was not of this world.

All this is peculiarly solemn. To find a dear and honored servant of Christ failing so grievously is surely sufficient to teach us to walk very softly. But, alas! we have not yet reached the lowest point in Peter's downward course. Having used his sword in defense of his Master, we next find him

"following afar off." "Then took they Jesus, and led Him, and brought Him to the high priest's house. And *Peter followed afar off.* And when they had kindled a fire in the midst of the hall, and were set down together, *Peter sat down among them.*"

What company for an apostle of Christ! "Can a man touch pitch, and not be defiled by it? Can one walk on burning coals, and his feet not be burned?" It is terribly dangerous for the Christian to sit down among the enemies of Christ. The very fact of his doing so proves that decline has set in, and made serious progress. In Peter's case the stages of decline are strongly marked. First, boasting in his own strength; secondly, sleeping when he ought to have been praying; thirdly, drawing his sword when he ought to have been meekly bowing his head; fourthly, following afar off; fifthly, making himself comfortable in the midst of the open enemies of Christ.

Then comes the last sad scene in this terrible drama. "And as Peter was beneath in the palace, there cometh one of the maids of the high priest; and when she saw Peter warming himself, she looked upon him, and said, And thou also wast with Jesus of Nazareth. But he denied, saying, *I know not, neither understand I, what thou sayest.* And he went out into the porch; and the cock crew. And a maid saw him again, and began to say to them that stood by, This is one of them. *And he denied it again.* And a little after, they that stood by said again to Peter, Surely thou art one of them, for thou art a Galilean, and thy speech agreeth thereto. But *he began to curse and to swear, I know not this man of whom ye speak.* And the second time the cock crew. And Peter called to mind the word that Jesus said unto him, Before the cock crow twice thou shalt deny Me thrice. And when he thought thereon, he wept" (Mark 14: 66-72).

Luke adds a most touching clause: "*And the Lord turned and looked upon Peter.* And Peter remembered the word of the Lord, how He had said unto him, Before the cock crow, thou shalt deny Me thrice. And Peter went out, and wept bitterly."

How deeply affecting is all this! Only think

of a saint of God, and an apostle of Christ, cursing and swearing that he did not know his Lord! Does the reader feel disposed to question the fact that Peter was, spite of all this, a genuine saint of God? Some do question it, but their questioning is a gross mistake. They find it hard to conceive such a thing as a true child of God falling so terribly. It is because they have not yet thoroughly learnt what flesh is. Peter was as really a saint of God in the palace of the high priest as he was on the mount of transfiguration. But he had to learn himself, and that, too, by as humiliating and painful a process as any soul could well be called to pass through.

Doubtless, if any one had told Peter, a few days before, that he would ere long curse and swear that he did not know his Lord, he would have shrunk with horror from the thought. He might have said, like one of old, "Is thy servant a dog that he should do this thing?" Yet so it was. We know not what we may do until we are in the circumstances. The great thing for us all is to walk humbly with our God day by day, deeply sensible of our own utter weakness, and clinging to Him who is able to keep us from falling. We are safe only in the shelter of His presence. Left to ourselves, we are capable of anything, as our apostle found to his deep sorrow.

But the Lord was watching over His poor erring servant. He never lost sight of him for a single moment, He had His eye upon the whole process. The devil would have smashed the vessel in hopeless fragments if he could. But he could not. He was but an instrument in the divine hand to do a work for Peter which Peter had failed to do for himself. "Simon, Simon, behold Satan hath desired to have you, that he may sift you as wheat; but I have prayed for thee, that thy faith fail not; and when thou art converted (or restored), strengthren thy brethren."

Here we are permitted to see the root of the matter. Peter needed to be sifted, and Satan was employed to do the work—just as in the case of Job, and the man in 1 Cor. 5. It seems very wonderful, very mysterious, very solemn, that Satan should be so used. Yet so it is. God uses him "for the destruction of the flesh." He cannot touch the spirit. That is

eternally safe. But it is terrible work to get into Satan's sieve. Peter found it so, and so did Job, and so did that erring Corinthian.

But oh, the *grace* of those words! "I have prayed for thee"—not that he might not fall, but, having fallen, that his faith might not fail, his confidence might not give way. Nothing can surpass the grace that shines out here. The blessed One knew all that was to happen—the shameful denial—the cursing and swearing; and yet, "I have prayed for thee that thy faith fail not"—that thy confidence in the eternal stability of My grace may not give way.

Perfectly marvelous! And then, the *power* of that look! "The Lord turned, and looked upon Peter." It was this that broke Peter's heart, and drew forth a flood of bitter, penitential tears.

Part 9

We are now called to consider the intensely interesting subject of Simon Peter's restoration, in which we. shall find some points of the utmost practical importance. If in his fall we learn the frailty and folly of man, in his restoration we learn the grace, wisdom, and faithfulness of our Lord Jesus Christ. The fall was, indeed, deep, terrible, and humiliating. The restoration was complete and marvelous. We may rest assured that Simon Peter will never forget either the one or the other; nay, he will remember them with wonder, love, and praise, throughout the countless ages of eternity. The grace that shines in Peter's restoration is the same which is displayed in his conversion. Let us glance at some of the salient points. It can be but the merest glance, as our space is limited.

And first let us look at *the procuring cause.* This we have given us with peculiar force by the pen of the inspired evangelist Luke. "And the Lord said, Simon, Simon, behold Satan hath desired to have thee, that he may sift thee as wheat." If Satan had been suffered to have his way, poor Simon would have been hopelessly ruined. But no; he was merely employed as an instrument, as he had been in Job's case, to do a needed work, and, when that work was done, he had to retire. He dare not go one hair's breadth beyond his appointed sphere.

It is well to remember this. Satan is but a creature—crafty, wily, powerful, no doubt, but a creature who can only go as far as he is permitted by God. Had Peter walked softly, had he humbly and earnestly looked for divine help, had he been judging himself in secret, there would have been no need of Satan's sifting. Thanks be to God, Satan has no power whatever with a soul that walks humbly with God. There is perfect shelter, perfect safety, in the divine presence; and there is not an arrow in the enemy's quiver that can reach one who leans in simple confidence upon the arm of the living God. Here our apostle failed, and hence he had to pass through a very severe process indeed, in order that he might learn himself.

But, oh, the power and preciousness of those words, "*I have prayed for thee!*" Here assuredly lay the secret—here was the procuring cause of Simon's restoration. The prayer of Jesus sustained the soul of His erring servant in that terrible hour when the enemy would fain have crushed him to powder. What could Satan do in opposition to the all-powerful intercession of Christ? Nothing. That wonderful prayer was the ground of Peter's safety, when, to human view, all seemed hopelessly gone.

And for what did our Lord pray? Was it that Peter might not commit the awful sin of denying Him? Was it that he might not curse and swear? Clearly not. What then? "I have prayed for thee that thy faith fail not."

Can aught exceed the grace that shines here? That gracious, loving, faithful Lord, in view of Peter's terrible sin—knowing all he was about to do, all the sad forgetfulness—could actually plead for him that, spite of all, his confidence might not give way—that he might not lose the sense of the eternal stability of that grace which had taken him up from the depth of his ruin and guilt.

Matchless grace! Nothing can surpass it in brightness and blessedness. Had it not been for this prayer, Peter's confidence must have given way. He never could have survived the awful struggle through which his soul passed when thinking of his dreadful sin. When he came to himself, when he reflected upon the whole scene, his expressions of devotedness, "Though all should deny Thee, yet will I never deny Thee"—"Though I should die with Thee, yet will I not deny Thee"—"I am ready to go with Thee to prison and to death"—to think of all these words, and yet that he should deny his beloved Lord with cursing and swearing, was overpowering.

It is a dreadful moment in the soul's history when one wakes up to the consciousness of having committed sin—sin against light, knowledge, and privilege—sin against divine grace and goodness. Satan is sure to be specially busy at such a crisis. He casts in the most terrible suggestions—raises all manner of questions—fills the heart with legal reasonings, doubts, and fears—causes the soul to totter on the foundation.

But, thanks and praise to our God, the enemy cannot prevail. "Hitherto shalt thou come, and no further." The all-prevailing intercession of our divine Advocate sustains the faith so sorely tried, carries the soul through the deep and dark waters, restores the broken link of communion, heals the spiritual wounds, lifts up the fallen one, brings back the wanderer, and fills the heart with praise and thanksgiving. "I have prayed for thee that thy faith fail not; and when thou art restored, strengthen thy brethren." Here we have set before us in the most touching way *the procuring cause* of Simon Peter's restoration.

We shall now look for a moment at *the producing means.* For this, too, we are indebted to the evangelist Luke. Indeed it is through him the inspiring Spirit has given us so much of what is exquisitely human—so much of what goes straight to our very hearts, in subduing power—so much of God coming out in loveliest human form.

We have already noticed Peter's gradual descent—his sad progress, from one stage to another, in moral distance and culpable decline—forgetting to watch and pray—following afar off—warming himself at the enemy's fire—the cowardly denial—the cursing and swearing. All this was down! down! down! shamefully and awfully down. But when the erring, straying, sinning one had reached the very lowest point, then comes out, with heavenly lustre, the grace that shines in the procuring cause and the producing means of his restoration. The former we have in Christ's *prayer;* the latter in Christ's *look.* "The Lord turned, and looked upon Peter. And Peter remembered the Word of the Lord, how He had said unto him, Before the cock crow, thou shalt deny Me thrice. And Peter went out, and wept bitterly."

Yes, here it is; "The Lord *looked"*—"Peter remembered"—Peter wept—"wept bitterly." What a look! What a remembrance! What a weeping! What human heart can conceive, what tongue express, what pen portray, all that is wrapped up in that one look? We can well believe that it went right home to the very centre of Peter's soul. He will never forget that marvelous look, so full of mighty moral power—so penetrating—so melting—so soul-subduing.

"Peter went out, and wept bitterly." This was the turning point. Up to this all was darkly downward. Here divine light breaks in upon the deep moral gloom. Christ's most precious prayer is having its answer, His powerful look is doing its work. The fountain of the heart is broken up, and penitential tears flow copiously forth, demonstrating the depth, reality, and intensity of the work within.

Thus it must ever be, and thus it will ever be when the Spirit of God works in the soul. If we have sinned, we must be made to feel, to judge, and to confess our sin—to feel it deeply, judge it thoroughly, and confess it fully. It will not do merely to say, in levity, flippancy, or mere formality, "I have sinned." There must be reality, uprightness, and sincerity. God desires truth in the inward parts. There was nothing light, flippant, or formal about our beloved apostle in the hour of his fall and repentance. No, all was intensely real. It could not but be so with such a procuring cause, and such a producing means. The prayer and look of Peter's Lord displayed their precious results in Peter's restoration.

Now the reader will do well to notice that the prayer and look of our Lord Jesus Christ set forth, in a very striking and beautiful manner, the two grand aspects of Christ's present ministry as our Advocate with the Father. We have the value and prevalency of His intercession, and the power and efficacy of His Word in the hands of the Holy Ghost, that "other Advocate." Christ's *prayer* for Peter answers to His intercession for us. His *look* upon Peter answers to His Word brought home to us in the power of the Holy Ghost. When we sin—as, alas! we do in thought and deed—our blessed and adorable Advocate speaks to God on our behalf. This is the procuring cause of our repentance and restoration. But He speaks to us on God's behalf. This is the producing means.

We shall not dwell upon the great subject of the advocacy here, having recently sought to unfold it in our papers on "The All-sufficiency of Christ." We shall close this paper with a brief reference to two or three of the moral features of Peter's restoration—features which, be it well remembered, must be looked for in every case of true restoration.

In the first place there is *the state of the conscience.* Now, as to the full and complete restoration of Peter's conscience after his terrible fall, we have the most unquestionable evidence afforded in his after history. Take the touching scene at the sea of Tiberias, as given in John 21.* Look at that dear, earnest, thorough man, girding his fisher's coat around him, and plunging into the sea, in order to get to the feet of his risen Lord! He waits neither for the ship nor for his companions, but in all the lovely freshness and liberty of a divinely restored conscience, he rushes to his Saviour's feet. There is no tormenting fear, no legal bondage, no doubt, darkness, or distance. His conscience is perfectly at rest. The prayer and the look—the two grand departments of the work of advocacy—had proved effectual. Peter's conscience was all right, sound, and good; and hence he could find his home in the presence of his Lord—his holy, happy home.

Take another striking and beautiful evidence of a restored conscience. Look at

* We have no record of Peter's first meeting with his Lord, after the resurrection.

Peter in Acts 3. There he stands in the presence of assembled thousands of Jews, and boldly charges them with having "denied the Holy One and the Just"—the very thing which he himself had done though under circumstances very different. How could Peter do this? How could he have the face to speak so? Why not leave it to James or John to prefer this heavy charge?

The answer is blessedly simple. Peter's conscience was so thoroughly restored, so perfectly at rest, because perfectly purged, that he could fearlessly charge the house of Israel with the awful sin of denying the Holy One of God. Was this the fruit of moral insensibility? Nay, it was the fruit of divine restoration. Had any one of the congregation gathered in Solomon's porch undertaken to challenge our apostle as to his own shameful denial of his Lord, we can easily conceive his answer. The man who had "wept bitterly" over his sin would, we feel assured, know how to answer such a challenge. Not that his bitter weeping was the meritorious ground of his restoration; nothing of the kind, it only proved the reality of the work of repentance in his soul. Moral insensibility is one thing, and a restored conscience, resting on the blood and advocacy of Christ, is quite another.

But there is another thing involved in a true work of restoration, and that is *the state of the heart.*

This is of the very utmost importance in every instance. No restoration can be considered divinely complete which does not reach the very depths of the heart. And hence, when we turn back to the scenes on the shore of the sea of Tiberias, we find the Lord dealing very closely and very powerfully with the state of Peter's heart. We cannot attempt to expatiate, much as we should like to do so, on one of the most affecting interviews in the entire volume of God. We can do little more than quote the inspired record, but that is quite enough.

It is deeply interesting to notice that there is no allusion—not the most remote—to past scenes, during that wonderful dinner, provided, cooked, and dispensed by the risen Lord! But "when they had dined, Jesus saith

to Simon Peter, Simon, son of Jonas, lovest thou Me more than these?" Here Simon is recalled by the words of his faithful Lord to his self-confident profession. He had said, "Though all shall be offended, yet will not I." Then the searching question, three times repeated, evidently calls back the threefold denial.

Peter's *heart* is touched—the moral *root* of the whole matter is reached. This was absolutely necessary in Peter's case, and it is absolutely necessary in every case. The work of restoration can never be thorough unless the roots of things are reached and judged. Mere surface work will never do. It is of no use to crop the sprouts; we must get down to the depths, the hidden springs, the moral sources, and judge them in the very light of the divine presence.

This is the true secret of all genuine restoration. Let us ponder it deeply. We may rest assured it demands our most solemn consideration. We are all too apt to rest satisfied with cropping off the sprouts that appear above the surface of our practical daily life, without getting at the roots; and the sad consequence is that the sprouts quickly appear again, to our sorrow and shame, and the dishonor of our Lord's name. The work of self-judgment must be more profound if we would really make progress. We are terribly shallow, light, and flippant. We greatly lack depth, seriousness, and moral gravity. We want more of that heart-work which was wrought in Simon the son of Jonas on the shore of the sea of Tiberias.

"Peter was grieved because He said unto him the third time, Lovest thou Me?" The knife of the divine Operator had reached the root of the moral disease, and that was enough. It was needful, but it was enough; and the grieved and self-judged Simon Peter has only to fall back upon the great fact that his Lord knew all things. "Lord, Thou knowest all things, Thou knowest that I love Thee." It is as though he had said, "Lord, it demands the eye of Omniscience itself to discern in the heart of the poor erring one a single spark of affection for Thee."

This truly is real work. We have before us

a thoroughly restored soul—restored in conscience, restored in heart. And if it be asked, "What remains?" the answer is, We see a servant *restored to his work*.

Some would tell us that if a man falls, he can never recover his position; and no doubt, under *government*, we must reap as we sow. But *grace* is another thing altogether. Government drove Adam out of Eden, and never replaced him there, but grace announced the victorious Seed of the woman. Government kept Moses out of Canaan, but grace conducted him to Pisgah's top. Government sent a perpetual sword upon David's house, but grace made the son of Bathsheba the wisest and wealthiest of Israel's kings.

This distinction must never be lost sight of. To confound grace and government is to commit a very grave mistake indeed. We cannot attempt to enter upon this weighty subject here, having done so in one of our earlier volumes. But let the reader seek to understand it, and bear it ever in mind.

As to Simon Peter, we not only see him restored to the work to which he was called at the first, but to something even higher. "Feed My lambs—shepherd My sheep"—is the new commission given to the man who had denied his Lord with an oath. Is not this something beyond "catching men"? "When thou art restored, strengthen thy brethren." Can anything in the way of service be more elevated than shepherding sheep, feeding lambs, and strengthening brethren? There is nothing in all this world nearer or dearer to the heart of Christ than His sheep, His lambs, His brethren: and hence He could not have given Simon Peter a more affecting proof of His confidence than by committing to his care the dearest objects of His deep and tender love.

And then mark the closing words, "Verily, verily, I say unto thee, when thou wast *young*, thou girdedst thyself, and walkedst whither thou wouldest; but when thou shalt be *old*, thou shalt stretch forth thy hands, and another shall gird thee, and carry thee whither thou wouldest not. This spake He, signifying by what death he should glorify God. And when He had spoken this, He saith unto him, *Follow Me*."

What weighty words are these! Who can tell their depth, power, and significance? What a contrast between Simon, "*young*," restless, forward, blundering, boastful, self-confident; and Peter, "*old*," subdued, mellowed, passive, crucified! What a difference between a man walking whither he would, and a man following a rejected Lord along the dark and narrow pathway of the cross, home to glory!

Conclusion

We could not close this series of papers without glancing, however cursorily, at the way in which our apostle discharged his various commissions. We see him "catching men"; opening the kingdom of Heaven to the Jew and to the Gentile; and, finally, feeding and shepherding the lambs and sheep of the flock of Christ.

Elevated services these, for any poor mortal to be called to, and more especially for one who had fallen so deeply as Simon Peter. But the remarkable power with which he was enabled to fulfil his blessed service proved beyond all question the reality and completeness of his restoration. If, at the close of the Gospels, we see Peter restored in heart and conscience, in the Acts and in his Epistles we can see him restored to his work.

We cannot attempt to go into details; but a point or two must be briefly noticed. There is something uncommonly fine in Peter's address in the third chapter of Acts. We can only quote a sentence or two: "The God of Abraham, and of Isaac, and of Jacob, the God of our fathers, hath glorified His Son Jesus; whom ye delivered up, and *denied Him* in the presence of Pilate, when he was determined to let Him go. But *ye denied the Holy One and the Just*."

What a splendid evidence we have here of Peter's complete restoration! It would have been utterly impossible for him to charge his audience with having denied the Holy One if his own soul had not been fully and blessedly restored. Alas! he, too, had denied his Lord; but he had repented, and wept bitterly. He had been down in the depths of self-judgment, just where he desired to see every one of his hearers. He had been face to face with his Lord, just where he longed to see them. He had been given to taste the sweetness, the freeness, the fulness, of the pardoning love of God, to prove the divine efficacy of the atonement and the prevalency of the advocacy of Christ. He was pardoned, healed, restored; and as such he stood in their presence a living and striking monument of that grace which he was unfolding to them, and which was amply sufficient for them as it had proved for him. "Repent ye, therefore, and be converted, that your sins may be blotted out."

Who could more distinctly and emphatically utter such precious words than the erring, restored and forgiven Peter? If any one of his audience had ventured to remind the preacher of his own history, what would he have said in reply? Doubtless he would have had little to say about himself, but much, very much, to say about that rich and precious grace which had triumphed over all his sin and failure—much, very much, about that precious blood which had canceled forever all his guilt, and given perfect peace to his conscience—much, very much, about that all-prevailing advocacy to which he owed his full and perfect restoration.

Peter was just the man to unfold to others those glorious themes in which he had so thoroughly learnt to find his strength, his comfort, and his joy. He had proved in no ordinary way the reality and stability of the grace of our Lord Jesus Christ. It was no mere empty theory, no mere doctrine or opinion, with him. It was all intensely real to him. His very life and salvation were bound up in it. He knew the heart of Christ in a very intimate way. He knew its infinite tenderness and compassion, its unswerving devotedness in the face of many stumbles, shortcomings, and sins; and hence he could bear the most distinct and powerful testimony to the whole house of Israel to the power of the name of Jesus, the efficacy of His blood, and the deep and infinite love of His heart. "His name, through faith in His name, hath made this man strong, whom ye see and know; yea, the faith which is by Him hath given him *this perfect soundness* in the presence of you all."

What power in these words! How refreshing is the testimony to the peerless name of Jesus! It is perfectly delightful at all times, but specially so in this infidel day in which our lot is cast—a day so marked by the determined and persistent effort of the enemy to exclude the name of Jesus from every department.

Look where you will, whether it be in the domain of science, of religion, of philanthropy, or moral reform, and you see the same sedulous and diligently pursued purpose to banish the name of Jesus. It is not said so in plain terms, but it is so nevertheless. Scientific men, the professors and lecturers in our universities, talk and write about "the forces of nature" and the facts of science in such a way as practically to exclude the Christ of God from the whole field of nature. Scripture tells us, blessed be God, that by the Son of His love "All things were created that are in heaven, and that are in earth, visible and invisible, whether thrones or dominions, or principalities or powers: all things were created by Him and for Him: and He is before all things, and *by Him all things consist.*" And again, speaking of the Son, the inspiring Spirit says, "Who being the brightness of God's glory, and the express image of His person, and *upholding all things by the word of His power*, when He had by Himself purged our sins, sat down on the right hand of the Majesty on high" (Col. 1, Heb. 1).

These passages lead us to the divine root of the matter. They speak not of "the forces of nature," but of the glory of Christ, the power of His hand, the virtue of His Word. Infidelity would rob us of Christ, and give us, instead, "the forces of nature." We vastly prefer our own beloved Lord. We delight to see His name bound up, indissolubly, with creation in all its vast and marvelous fields. We vastly prefer the eternal record of the Holy Ghost to all the finely-spun theories of infidel professors. We rejoice to see the name of Jesus bound up in every department of religion and philanthropy.

We shrink with ever-increasing horror from every system, every club, every order, every association, that dares to shut out the glorious name of Jesus from its schemes of religion and moral reform. We do solemnly declare that the religion, the philanthropy, the moral reform, which does not make the name of Jesus its Alpha and its Omega, is the religion, the philanthropy and the moral reform of hell. This may seem strong, severe, ultra, and narrow-minded, but it is our deep and thorough conviction, and we utter it fearlessly, in the presence of all the infidelity and superstition of the day.

But we must return to our apostle's discourse, which has wakened up those glowing sentiments in the very depths of the soul.

Having charged home their terrible sin upon the consciences of his hearers, he proceeds to apply the healing, soothing balm of the gospel, in words of marvelous power and sweetness: "And now, brethren, I wot that through ignorance ye did it, as did also your rulers. But those things which God before had showed by the mouth of all His prophets that Christ should suffer, *He hath so fulfilled.*" Nothing can exceed the grace of this. It recalls the words of Joseph to his troubled brethren: "It was not you that sent me hither, but God." Such is the exquisite grace of our Lord Jesus Christ, such the infinite love and goodness of our God.

"Repent ye, therefore, and be converted, that your sins may be blotted out, when the time of refreshing shall come from (or by) the presence of the Lord; and He shall send Jesus Christ, which before was preached unto you; whom the heaven must receive until the times of restitution of all things, which God had spoken by the mouth of all His holy prophets since the world began. For Moses truly said unto the fathers, A Prophet shall the Lord your God raise up unto you of your brethren, like unto me; Him shall ye hear in all things whatsoever He shall say unto you. And it shall come to pass that every soul which will not hear that Prophet shall be destroyed from among the people. Yea, and all the prophets from Samuel, and those that follow after, as many as have spoken, have likewise foretold of these days. Ye are the children of the prophets, and of the covenant which God made with our fathers, saying unto Abraham, And in thy seed shall all the kindreds of the earth be blessed. *Unto you first* God, having raised up His Son Jesus, *sent Him to bless you*, in turning away every one of you from his iniquities."

Thus did this dear and honored apostle, in the power of the Holy Ghost, throw wide open the kingdom of Heaven to the Jews, in pursuance of his high commission as recorded in the sixteenth chapter of the Gospel of Matthew. It is what we may well call a splendid testimony, from first to last. Most gladly would we linger over it; but our limited space forbids. We can only commend it to the earnest study of the reader, and pass on, for a few moments, to the tenth chapter of Acts which records the opening of the kingdom to the Gentile.

We assume that the reader understands the truth in reference to the keys of the kingdom of Heaven being committed to Peter. We shall not therefore occupy his time or our own in combating the ignorant superstition which attributes to our apostle what we may rest assured he would have rejected with intense and holy horror, namely, the power to let souls into Heaven. Detestable folly! which, while it obstinately refuses Christ, who is God's *only* way to Heaven, will blindly build upon some poor sinful mortal like ourselves who himself was a debtor to the sovereign grace of God and the precious blood of Christ for his entrance into the Church on earth and into Heaven above.

But enough of this. All intelligent Christians understand that the apostle Peter was commissioned, by his Lord and ours, to open the kingdom of Heaven to both Jew and Gentile. To him were committed the keys, not of the Church, nor yet of Heaven, but of "the kingdom of heaven"; and we find him using them in Acts 3 and 10.

But he was by no means so alert in taking up the latter as he was in taking up the former. Prejudice—that sad hindrance then, now, and always—stood in the way. He needed to have his mind enlarged to take in the divine purpose in respect to the Gentiles. To one trained amid the influences of the Jewish system, it seemed one thing to admit Jews into the kingdom, and quite another to admit Gentiles. Our apostle had to get further instruction in the school of Christ ere his mind could take in the "no difference" doctrine.

"Ye know," he said to Cornelius, "how that it is an unlawful thing for a man that is a Jew to keep company or come unto one of another nation." Thus had it been in days gone by; but now all was changed. The middle wall was broken down—the barriers were swept away; "God hath shewed me that I should not call any man common or unclean." He had seen, in a vessel which came from Heaven, and returned thither, "*all manner* of fourfooted beasts," and a voice from Heaven had commanded him to slay and eat. This was something new to Simon Peter. It was a wonderful lesson he was called to learn on the housetop of Simon the tanner. He was there, for the first time, taught that "God is no respecter of persons," and that what God hath cleansed no man may call common.

All this was good and healthful for the soul of our apostle. It was well to have his heart enlarged to take in the precious thoughts of God—to see the old barriers swept away before the magnificent tide of grace flowing from the heart of God over a lost world—to learn that the question of "clean" or "unclean" was no longer to be decided by an examination of hoofs and habits (Lev. 11)—that the same precious blood of Christ which could cleanse a Jew could cleanse a Gentile also; and, moreover, that the former needed it just as much as the latter.

This, we repeat, was most valuable instruction for the heart and understanding of Simon Peter; and if the reader wants to know how far he took it in and appreciated it, he has but to turn to Acts 15 and read the apostle's own commentary upon the matter. The Church had reached a solemn crisis. Judaizing teachers had begun their terrible work. They would fain bring the Gentile converts under the law. The occasion was intensely interesting and deeply important— yea, solemnly momentous. The very foundations were at stake. If the enemy could but succeed in bringing the Gentile believers under the law, all was gone.

But, all praise to our ever-gracious God, He did not abandon His Church to the power or wiles of the adversary. When the enemy came in like a flood, the Spirit of the Lord raised up a standard against him. A great meeting was convened—not in some obscure corner, but at Jerusalem, the very centre and source of all the religious influence of the moment—the very place, too, from whence the evil had emanated. God took care that the great question should not be decided at Antioch by Paul and Barnabas, but at Jerusalem itself, by the unanimous voice of the apostles, elders, and the whole Church, governed, guided and taught by God the Holy Ghost.

At this great meeting our apostle delivered himself in a style that stirs the very deepest springs of our spiritual life. Hear his words: "And when there had been much disputing" —Alas! how soon the miserable disputing began—"Peter rose up and said unto them, Men, brethren, ye know how that a good while ago God made choice among us that the Gentiles by my mouth should hear the word of the gospel, and believe. And God, which knoweth the hearts, bare them witness, giving them the Holy Ghost even as He did unto us, and put *no difference between us and them*, purifying their hearts by faith. Now, therefore, *why tempt ye God* to put a yoke upon the neck of the disciples which neither our fathers nor we were able to bear? But we believe that by the grace of our Lord Jesus Christ we shall be saved *even as they*."

This is morally grand. He does not say, "They shall be saved even as we." No; but "We shall be saved even as they"—on the same ground, after the same model, in the same way. The Jew comes down from his lofty dispensational position, only too thankful to be saved, just like the poor Gentile, by the precious grace of our Lord Jesus Christ.

How those words of the apostle of the circumcision must have refreshed and delighted the heart of Paul as he sat at this never-to-be-forgotten meeting! Not that Paul sought in any way the countenance, the support, or authority of man. He had received his gospel and his commission, not from Peter, but from Peter's Lord; and from

Him, too, not as the Messiah on earth, but as the risen and glorified Son of God in Heaven. Still, we cannot doubt that the testimony of his beloved fellow-laborer was deeply interesting and cordially welcome to the apostle of the Gentiles. We can only say, Alas! that there should have been aught in the after-course of that fellow-laborer in the smallest degree inconsistent with his splendid testimony at the conference. Alas! that Peter's conduct at Antioch should vary so much from his words at Jerusalem. See Gal. 2.

But such is man, even the best of men, if left to himself. And the higher the man is, the more mischief he is sure to do if he makes a stumble. We shall not, however, dwell on the sad and painful scene at Antioch, between those two most excellent servants. They are both now in Heaven, in the presence of their beloved Lord, where the remembrance of past failure and sin only enhances the value of that blood which cleanseth from all sin, and of that grace which reigns, through righteousness, unto eternal life, by Jesus Christ our Lord.

The Holy Ghost has thought proper to record the fact that our apostle failed in frankness and integrity at Antioch; and

further, that the blessed apostle of the Gentiles had to withstand him to the face; but we are not going to expatiate upon it. We would profit by it, as well we may, for it is full of deep instruction and solemn warning. If such a one as the apostle Peter, after all his experience, his fall and restoration, his long course of service, his intimate acquaintance with the heart of Christ, all the instruction he had received, all his gifts and knowledge, all his powerful preaching and teaching—if such a one as this could, after all, dissemble through fear of man, or to hold a place in man's esteem, what shall we say for ourselves? Simply this:

O Lamb of God, still keep me close to
　　Thy pierced side;
'Tis only there in safety and peace I can abide.
When foes and snares surround me, when
　　lusts and fears within,
The grace that sought and found me, alone
　　can keep me clean.

May the Lord greatly bless to our souls our meditation on the history of Simon Peter! May his life and its lessons be used of the Holy Ghost to deepen in our souls the sense of our own utter weakness and of the matchless grace of our Lord Jesus Christ.

GRACE AND GOVERNMENT

THIS TITLE may possibly present a theme to which some of our readers have not given much of their attention; and yet few themes are more important. Indeed, we believe that the difficulty felt in expounding many passages of Holy Scripture, and in interpreting many acts of divine providence, is justly traceable to a want of clearness as to the vast difference between God in grace and in government. Now, as it is our constant aim to meet the actual need of our readers, we purpose, in dependence upon the Spirit's teaching, to unfold a few of the leading passages of Scripture in which the distinction between grace and government is fully and clearly presented.

In the third chapter of the book of Genesis we shall find our first illustration—the first exhibition of divine grace and divine government. Here, we find man a sinner—a ruined, guilty, naked sinner. But here, too, we find God in grace, to remedy the ruin, to cleanse the guilt, to clothe the nakedness. All this He does in His own way. He silences the serpent, and consigns him to eternal ignominy. He establishes His own eternal glory, and provides both life and righteousness for the sinner—all through the bruised Seed of the woman.

Now, this was grace—unqualified grace— free, unconditional, perfect grace—the grace of God. The Lord God gives His Son to be, as "the Seed of the woman," bruised for man's redemption—to be slain to furnish a robe of divine righteousness for a naked sinner. This, I repeat, was grace of the most unmistakable nature. But then, be it carefully noted, that in immediate connection with this first grand display of grace, we have the first solemn act of divine government. It was grace that clothed the man. It was government that drove him out of Eden. "Unto Adam also, and to his wife, did the Lord God make coats of skins, and clothed them." Here we have an act of purest grace. But then we read: "So He drove out the man: and He placed at the east of the garden of Eden Cherubim, and a flaming sword which turned every way, to keep the way of the tree of life."

Here we have a solemn, soul-subduing act of government. The coat of skin was the sweet pledge of grace. The flaming sword was the solemn ensign of government. Adam was the subject of both. When he looked at the coat, he could think of divine grace—how God provided a robe to cover his nakedness; when he looked at the sword, he was reminded of divine, unflinching government.

Hence, therefore, the "coat" and the "sword"* may be regarded as the earliest expression of "grace" and "government." True, these things appear before us in new forms as we pass down along the current of inspiration. Grace shines in brighter beams, and government clothes itself in robes of deeper solemnity. Moreover, both grace and government assume an aspect less enigmatical, as they develop themselves in connection with the personal history of the people of God from age to age; but still it is deeply interesting to find these grand realities so distinctly presented under the early figures of the coat and the sword.

The reader may perhaps feel disposed to ask, "How was it that the Lord God drove out the man, if He had previously forgiven him?" The same question may be asked in connection with every scene, throughout the entire book of God and throughout the entire history of the people of God, in which the combined action of grace and government is exemplified. Grace forgives; but the wheels of government roll on in all their terrible majesty. Adam was perfectly forgiven, but his sin produced its own results. The guilt of his conscience was removed, but not the "sweat of his brow." He went out pardoned and clothed; but it was into the midst of "thorns and thistles" he went. He could feed in secret on the precious fruits of grace, while he recognized in public the solemn and unavoidable enactments of government.

Thus it was with Adam; thus it has been ever since; and thus it is at this moment. We should seek to get a clear understanding of this subject in the light of Scripture. It is well worthy of prayerful attention. It too frequently happens that grace and government are confounded, and, as a necessary consequence, grace is robbed of its charms, and government is shorn of its solemn dignities: the full and unqualified forgiveness of sins, which the sinner might enjoy on the ground of free grace, is rarely apprehended, because the heart is occupied with the stern enactments of government.

The two things are as distinct as any two things can be; and this distinctness is as clearly maintained in the third chapter of Genesis as in any other section of the inspired volume. Did the "thorns and thistles" with which Adam found himself surrounded on his expulsion from Eden interfere with that full forgiveness of which grace had previously assured him? Clearly not. His heart had been gladdened by the bright beams of the lamp of promise, and his person clothed in the robe which grace had fashioned for him ere he was sent forth into a cursed and groaning earth, there to toil and struggle by the just decree of the throne of government. God's government "drove out the man"; but not until God's grace had pardoned and clothed him. That sent him forth into a world of gloom; but not until this had placed in his hand the lamp of promise to cheer him through the gloom. He could bear the solemn decree of government in proportion as he

---

* The "sword" is the ensign of divine government; the cherubim are the invariable companions thereof. Both symbols are frequently used throughout the Word of God.

experienced the rich provision of grace.

Thus much as to Adam's history in so far as it illustrates our thesis. We shall now pass on to the ark and deluge, in the days of Noah, which, like the coat of skin and the flaming sword, exemplify in a striking way divine grace and divine government.

The inspired narrative of Cain and his posterity presents, in lines of unflinching faithfulness, the progress of *man* in his fallen condition; while the history of Abel and his immediate line unfolds to us, in glowing contrast, the progress of those who were called to live a life of faith in the midst of that scene into which the enactments of the throne of government had driven our first parents. The former pursued with headlong speed the downward course until their consummated guilt brought down the heavy judgment of the throne of government. The latter, on the contrary, pursued, through grace, an upward course, and were safely borne, through the judgment, into a restored earth.

Now, it is interesting to see that, before ever the governmental act of judgment proceeded, the elect family, and all with them, were safely shut in the ark, the vessel of grace. Noah, safe in the ark, like Adam clad in the coat, was the witness of Jehovah's unqualified grace; and, as such, he could contemplate the throne of government, as it poured its appalling judgment upon a defiled world. God in grace saved Noah, ere God in government swept the earth with the besom of judgment. It is grace and government over again. That, acts in salvation; this, in judgment. God is seen in both. Every atom of the ark bore the sweet impress of grace; every wave of the deluge reflected the solemn decree of government.

We shall just select one case more from the book of Genesis—a deeply practical one—one in which the combined action of grace and government is seen in a very solemn and impressive way. I allude to the case of the patriarch Jacob. The entire history of this instructive man presents a series of events illustrative of our theme. I shall merely refer to the one case of his deceiving his father for the purpose of supplanting his brother. The

sovereign grace of God had, long before Jacob was born, secured to him a preeminence of which no man could ever deprive him; but, not satisfied to wait for God's time and way, he set about managing matters for himself.

What was the result? His entire after-life furnishes the admonitory reply. Exile from his father's house; twenty years of hard servitude; his wages changed ten times; never permitted to see his mother again; fear of being murdered by his injured brother; dishonor cast upon his family; terror of his life from the Shechemites; deceived by his ten sons; plunged into deep sorrow by the supposed death of his favorite Joseph; apprehension of death by famine; and, finally, death in a strange land.

What a lesson is here! Jacob was a subject of grace—sovereign, changeless, eternal grace. This is a settled point. But then, he was a subject of government likewise; and be it well remembered that no exercise of grace can ever interfere with the onward movement of the wheels of government. That movement is resistless. Easier would it be to stem the ocean's rising tide with a feather, or to check the whirlwind with a spider's web, than to stay by any power, angelic, human, or diabolical, the mighty movement of Jehovah's governmental chariot.

All this is deeply solemn. Grace pardons; yes, freely, fully and eternally pardons; but what is sown must be reaped. A man may be sent by his master to sow a field with wheat, and through ignorance, dulness, or gross inattention, he sows some noxious weed. His master hears of the mistake, and, in the exercise of his grace, he pardons it—pardons it freely and fully. What then? Will the gracious pardon change the nature of the crop? Assuredly not; and hence, in due time, when golden ears should cover the field, the servant sees it covered with noxious weeds. Does the sight of the weeds make him doubt his master's grace? By no means. As the master's grace did not alter the nature of the crop, neither does the nature of the crop alter the master's grace and pardon flowing therefrom. The two things are perfectly distinct; nor would the principle be infringed even though the master were, by the application of extraordinary skill, to extract from the weed a drug more valuable than the wheat itself. It would still hold good that "whatsoever a man soweth, that shall he also reap."

This will illustrate, in a feeble way, the difference between grace and government. The passage just quoted from the sixth of Galatians is a brief but most comprehensive statement of the great governmental principle—a principle of the gravest and most practical nature—a principle of the widest application. "Whatsoever a man soweth." It matters not who he is: as is your sowing, so will be your reaping. Grace pardons; nay, more, it may make you higher and happier than ever; but if you sow weeds in spring, you will not reap wheat in harvest. This is as plain as it is practical. It is illustrated and enforced both by Scripture and experience.

Look at the case of Moses. He spoke unadvisedly with his lips at the waters of Meribah (Num. 20). What was the result? Jehovah's governmental decree prohibited his entrance into the promised land. But be it noted, while the decree of the throne kept him out of Canaan, the boundless grace of God brought him up to Pisgah (Deut. 34), where he saw the land, not as it was taken by the hand of Israel, but as it had been given by the covenant of Jehovah. And what then? Jehovah buried His dear servant! What grace shines in this!

Truly, if the spirit is overawed by the solemn decree of the throne at Meribah, the heart is enraptured by the matchless grace on the top of Pisgah. Jehovah's government kept Moses out of Canaan. Jehovah's grace dug a grave for Moses in the plains of Moab. Was there ever such a burial? May we not say that the grace that dug the grave of Moses is only outshone by the grace that occupied the grave of Christ? Yes; Jehovah can dig a grave or make a coat; and, moreover, the grace that shines in these marvelous acts is only enhanced by being looked at in connection with the solemn enactments of the throne of government.

But again: look at David "in the matter of Uriah the Hittite." Here we have a most striking exhibition of grace and government.

In an evil hour David fell from his holy elevation. Under the blinding power of lust, he rushed into a deep and horrible pit of moral pollution. There, in that deep pit, the arrow of conviction reached his conscience, and drew forth from his broken heart those penitential accents, "I have sinned against the Lord." How were those accents met? By the clear and ready response of that free grace in which our God ever delights: "The Lord hath put away thy sin." This was absolute grace. David's sin was perfectly forgiven. There can be no question as to this. But whilst the soothing accents of grace fell on David's ears upon the confession of his guilt, the solemn movement of the wheels of government was heard in the distance. No sooner had mercy's tender hand removed the guilt, than "the sword" was drawn from the scabbard to execute the necessary judgment. This is deeply solemnizing. David was fully pardoned, but Absalom rose in rebellion.

"Whatsoever a man soweth, that shall he also reap." The sin of sowing weeds may be forgiven, but the reaping must be according to the sowing. The former is grace, the latter is government. Each acts in its own sphere, and neither interferes with the other. The lustre of the grace and the dignity of the government are both divine. David was permitted to tread the courts of the sanctuary as a subject of grace (2 Sam. 12:20) ere he was called to climb the rugged sides of mount Olivet as a subject of government (2 Sam. 15:30); and we may safely assert that David's heart never had a deeper sense of divine grace than at the very time in which he was experiencing the righteous action of divine government.

Sufficient has now been said to open to the reader a subject which he can easily pursue for himself. The Scriptures are full of it; and human life illustrates it every day. How often do we see men in the fullest enjoyment of grace, knowing the pardon of all their sins, walking in unclouded communion with God, and all the while suffering in body or estate the consequences of past follies and excesses. Here, again, you have grace and government. This is a deeply important and practical subject; it will be found to aid the soul very effectively in its study, not only of the page of inspiration, but also of the page of human biography.

A passage which is often erroneously adduced as an exhibition of grace is entirely an exhibition of government: "And the Lord passed by before him, and proclaimed, The Lord, The Lord God, merciful and gracious, long-suffering, and abundant in goodness and truth, keeping mercy for thousands, forgiving iniquity and transgression and sin, and that will by no means clear the guilty; visiting the iniquity of the fathers upon the children, and upon the children's children, unto the third and to the fourth generation" (Exod. 34:6-7). Were we to regard this passage as a presentation of God in the gospel, we should have a very limited view indeed of what the gospel is. The gospel speaketh on this wise: "God was in Christ, *reconciling* the world unto Himself, *not imputing* their trespasses unto them" (2 Cor. 5:19). "Visiting iniquity" and "not imputing" it are two totally different things. The former is God in government; the latter is God in grace. It is the same God, but a different manifestation.

RESTORATION

Genesis 35

THE WORDS "Arise, go up to Bethel" contain a great practical truth to which we desire to call the reader's attention.

It has been well remarked by some one that "God, in His dealings with us, always keeps us up to the original terms." This is true; but some may not exactly understand it. It may, perhaps, savor of the legal element. To speak of God as keeping us up to certain terms may seem to militate against that free grace in which we stand, and which has reigned through righteousness unto eternal life by Jesus Christ our Lord. Many, we are aware, have a kind of horror of everything bordering, in the most remote way, upon the legal system; and we may say we sympathize with such.

At the same time, we must take care not to carry that feeling to such an extent as would lead us to throw overboard aught that is calculated to act in a divine way upon the heart and conscience of the believer. We really want practical truth. There is a vast amount of what is called abstract truth in circulation among us, and we prize it, and would prize it more. We delight in the unfolding of truth in all its departments. But then we must remember that truth is designed to act on hearts and consciences, and that there are hearts and consciences to be acted upon. We must not cry out, "Legal! legal!" whenever some great practical truth falls upon our ears, even though that truth may come before us clothed in a garb which at first sight seems strange.

We are called to "suffer the word of exhortation"—to listen to wholesome words —to apply our hearts diligently to everything tending to promote practical godliness and personal holiness. We know that the pure and precious doctrines of grace—those doctrines which find their living centre in the person of Christ, and their eternal foundation in His work—are the means which the Holy Ghost uses to promote holiness in the life of the Christian; but we know also that those doctrines may be held in theory, and professed with the lips, while the heart has never felt their power, and the life never exhibited their moulding influence.

Yes, we frequently find that the loud and vehement outcry against everything that looks like legality proceeds from those who, though they profess the doctrines of grace, do not realize their sanctifying influence; whereas those who really understand the meaning of grace, who feel its power to mould and fashion, to purify and elevate, are ever ready to welcome the most pungent appeals to the heart and conscience.

But the pious reader may want to know what is meant by the expression quoted above, namely, "God always keeps us up to the original terms." Well, it simply means this, that when God calls us to any special position or path, and we fall short of it, or wander from it, He will recall us to it again and again. And further, when we set out under some special principle of action or standard of devotedness, and swerve from it, or fall below it, He will remind us of it, and bring us back to it. True, He bears with us patiently, and waits on us graciously; but "He always keeps us up to the original terms."

And can we not praise Him for this? Assuredly we can. Could we endure the thought of His allowing us to fall short of His holy standard, or to wander hither and thither without His uttering a word to urge us on or call us back? We trust not. Well, then, if He does speak, what must He say? He must just remind us of "the old terms." Thus it is, and thus has ever been. When Peter was converted at the lake of Gennesaret he forsook all and followed Jesus, and the last words that fell on his ear from the lips of his risen Lord were, "Follow thou Me." This was simply keeping him to the original terms. The heart of Jesus could not be satisfied with less, and neither should the heart of His servant.

By the lake of Gennesaret, Peter set out to follow Jesus. What then? Years rolled on; Peter had stumbled; he had denied his Lord; he had gone back to his boats and nets. What then? After the Lord's resurrection, as Peter, restored in soul, stood by the side of his loving Lord at the sea of Tiberias, he was called to listen to that one brief, pointed utterance, "Follow Me"—an utterance embracing in its comprehensive grasp all the details of a life of active service and of patient suffering. In a word, Peter was brought back to the original terms—the terms between his soul and Christ. He was brought to learn that the heart of Jesus had undergone no change toward him—that the love of that heart was inextinguishable and unaltered; and, because it was so, it could not tolerate any change in Peter's heart—neither decline nor departure from the original terms.

Now we see the same thing precisely in the history of the patriarch Jacob. Let us just turn to it for a moment. At the close of Gen. 28 we have the record of the original terms between the Lord and Jacob. We shall quote it at length.

"And Jacob went out from Beersheba, and went toward Haran. And he lighted upon a certain place, and tarried there all night, because the sun was set; and he took of the stones of that place, and put them for his pillows, and lay down in that place to sleep. And he dreamed, and behold a ladder set up on the earth, and the top of it reached to heaven: and behold the angels of God ascending and descending on it. And, behold, the Lord stood above it, and said, I am the Lord God of Abraham thy father, and the God of Isaac: the land whereon thou liest, to thee will I give it, and to thy seed: and thy seed shall be as the dust of the earth; and thou shalt spread abroad to the west, and to the east, and to the north, and to the south: and in thee and in thy seed shall all the families of the earth be blessed. And, behold, I am with thee, and will keep thee in all places whither thou goest, and will bring thee again into this land; for I will not leave thee, until I have done that which I have spoken to thee of."

Here, then, we have the blessed statement of what the God of Abraham, Isaac, and Jacob undertook to do for Jacob and for his seed—a statement crowned by these memorable words, *"I will not leave thee, until I have done that which I have spoken to thee of."* Such are the terms by which God binds Himself to Jacob; which terms, blessed be His name, have been and will be fulfilled to the letter, though earth and hell should interpose to prevent. Jacob's seed shall yet possess the whole land of Canaan as an everlasting inheritance, for who shall prevent Jehovah Elohim, the Lord God Almighty, from accomplishing His promise?

Let us now harken to Jacob. "And Jacob awaked out of his sleep, and he said, Surely the Lord is in this place; and I knew it not. And he was afraid, and said, How dreadful is this place! this is none other but the house of God, and this is the gate of heaven. And

Jacob rose up early in the morning, and took the stone that he had put for his pillows, and set it up for a pillar, and poured oil upon the top of it. And he called the name of that place Bethel. . . . And Jacob vowed a vow, saying, If God will be with me, and will keep me in this way that I go, and will give me bread to eat, and raiment to put on, so that I come again to my father's house in peace; then shall the Lord be my God: and this stone, which I have set for a pillar, shall be God's house: and of all that Thou shalt give me I will surely give the tenth unto Thee."

Thus much as to Bethel and the terms entered into there. God pledged Himself to Jacob; and though Heaven and earth should pass away, that pledge must be maintained in all its integrity. He revealed Himself to that poor lonely one who lay sleeping on his stony pillow; and not only revealed Himself to him, but linked Himself with him in a bond which no power of earth or hell can ever dissolve.

And what of Jacob? Why, he dedicated himself to God, and vowed that the spot where he had enjoyed such a revelation and harkened to such exceeding great and precious promises, should be God's house. All this was deliberately uttered before the Lord, and solemnly recorded by Him; and then Jacob went on his journey. Years passed—twenty long and eventful years—years of trial and exercise, during which Jacob experienced many ups and downs, changes, and varied trials; but the God of Bethel watched over His poor servant, and appeared unto him in the midst of his pressure, and said unto him, "I am the God of Bethel, *where thou anointedst the pillar*, and *where thou vowedst a vow unto Me:* now arise, get thee out from this land, and return unto the land of thy kindred."

God had not forgotten the original terms, neither would He let His servant forget them. Is this legality? Nay; it is the exhibition of divine love and faithfulness. God loved Jacob, and He would not suffer him to stop short of the old standard. He jealously watched over the state of His servant's heart; and, lest it should by any means remain below the Bethel mark, He gently reminds him by those touching and significant words, "I am the God of Bethel, where thou anointedst the pillar, and where thou vowedst a vow." This was the sweet expression of God's unchanging love, and of the fact that He counted on Jacob's remembrance of Bethel scenes.

How amazing that the High and Mighty One, who inhabiteth eternity, should so value the love and remembrance of a poor worm of the earth! Yet so it is, and we ought to bear it more in mind. Alas, we forget it! We are ready enough to take mercies and blessings from the hand of God, and most surely He is ready enough to bestow them.

But then we ought to remember that He looks for the loving devotion of our hearts to Him; and if we, in the freshness and ardor of other days, set out to follow Christ, give up all for Him, can we suppose for a moment that He could coldly and indifferently forego His claim upon our heart's affections? Should we like Him to do so? Could we endure the thought of its being a matter of indifference to Him whether we loved Him or not? God forbid! Yea, it should be the joy of our hearts to think that our blessed Lord seeks the loving devotion of our souls to Him; that He will not be satisfied without it; that when we wander hither and thither, He calls us back to Himself, in His own gentle, gracious, touching way.

> When, weary of His rich repast,
> I've sought, alas, to rove;
> He has recalled His faithless guest,
> And showed His banner, Love.

Yes, His banner ever floats, bearing its own inscription upon it to win back our vagrant hearts, and remind us of the original terms. He says to us, in one way or another, as He said to Jacob, "I am the God of Bethel, where thou anointedst the pillar, and where thou vowedst a vow." Thus he deals with us, in the midst of all our wanderings, our haltings, and our stumblings. He makes us to know, that as we cannot do without His love, so neither can He do without ours. It is truly wonderful; yet so it is. He will keep the soul up to the old terms. Harken to those touching appeals of the Spirit of Christ to His saints in other days: "Thou hast *left thy first love*";

"Remember from whence thou art fallen; and repent, and *do thy first works*" (Rev. 2); "Call to remembrance *the former times*" (Heb. 10:32); "Where is the blessedness ye spake of?" (Gal. 4:15)

What is all this but calling His people back to the old point from which they had declined? It may be said, they ought not to have needed this. No doubt; yet they did need it; and because they needed it, Jesus did it. It may be said, further, that tried love is better than first love. Granted; but do we not find, as a matter of fact in our spiritual history, that upon our first setting out to follow Jesus there is a simplicity, an earnestness, a freshness, fervor and depth of devotion, which, from various reasons, we fail to keep up? We become cold and careless; the world gets in upon us and eats up our spirituality; nature gains the upper hand, in one way or another, and deadens our spiritual sensibility, damps our ardor, and dims our vision.

Is the reader conscious of anything like this? If so, would it not be a peculiar mercy if at this very moment he were called back to the old terms? Doubtless. Well, then, let him be assured that the heart of Jesus is waiting and ready. His love is unchanging; and not only so, but He would remind you that He cannot be satisfied without a true response from you. Wherefore, beloved friend, whatever has drawn you away from the measure of your earliest dedication to Him, let your heart now spring up and get back at once to Him. Do not hesitate. Linger not. Cast yourself at the feet of your loving Lord—tell Him all—and let your heart fully turn to Him, and let it be only for Him.

This is the secret spring of all true service. If Christ has not the love of your heart, He does not want the labor of your hands. He does not say, "Son, give Me thy money, thy time, thy talents, thine energies, thy pen, thy tongue, thy head." All these are unavailing, unsatisfying to Him. What He says to you is, "My son, give Me thy *heart*." Where the heart is given to Jesus, all will come right. Out of the heart come all the issues of life; and if only Christ have His right place in the heart, the work and the ways, the walk and the character, will be all right.

But we must return to Jacob, and see further how our subject is illustrated in his fruitful history. At the close of Genesis 38 we find him settling down at Shechem, where he gets into all sorts of trouble and confusion. His house is dishonored, and his sons in avenging the dishonor endanger his life. All this Jacob feels keenly, and he says to his sons Simeon and Levi, "Ye have troubled me . . . among the inhabitants of the land, among the Canaanites and the Perizzites; and I being few in number, they shall gather themselves together against me; and I shall be destroyed, I and my house."

All this was most deplorable; but it does not appear to have once occurred to Jacob that he was in a wrong place. The defilement and confusion of Shechem failed to open his eyes to the fact that he was not up to the old terms. How often is this the case! We fall short of the divine standard in our practical ways; we fail in walking up to the height of the divine revelation; and although the varied fruits of our failure are produced on every side, yet our vision is so dimmed by the atmosphere around us, and our spiritual sensibilities so blunted by our associations that we do not discern how low we are, and how very far short of the proper mark.

However, in Jacob's case we see the divine principle again and again illustrated. "And God said unto Jacob, "Arise, *go up to Bethel*, and *dwell there;* and make there an altar unto God, that appeared unto thee when thou fleddest from the face of Esau thy brother."

Note this. We have here a most exquisite feature in the divine method of dealing with souls. There is not one word said about Shechem, its pollutions and its confusions. There is not a word of reproof for having settled down there. Such is not God's way. He employs a far more excellent mode. Had we been dealing with Jacob we should have come down upon him with a heavy hand, and read him a severe lecture about his folly in settling at Shechem, and about his personal and domestic habits and condition. But oh, how well it is that God's thoughts are not as our thoughts, nor His ways like ours!

Instead of saying to Jacob, "Why have you settled down in Shechem?" He simply says,

"Arise, go up to Bethel"; and the very sound of the word sent a flood of light into Jacob's soul by which he was enabled to judge himself and his surroundings. "Then Jacob said unto his household, and to all that were with him, Put away the strange gods that are among you, and be clean, and change your garments: and let us *arise, and go up to Bethel;* and I will make there an altar unto God, who answered me in the day of my distress, and was with me in the way which I went."

This was, assuredly, getting back to the original terms. It was the restoring of a soul and a leading in the paths of righteousness. Jacob felt that he could not bring false gods and defiled garments to Bethel: such things might pass at Shechem, but they would never do for Bethel. "And they gave unto Jacob all the strange gods which were in their hand, and all their earrings which were in their ears; and Jacob hid them under the oak which was by Shechem. . . . So Jacob came to Luz, which is in the land of Canaan, that is, Bethel, he and all the people that were with him. And he built there an altar, and called the place El-beth-el; because there God appeared unto him, when he fled from the face of his brother."

"EL-beth-EL" Precious title, which had God for its Alpha and its Omega! At Shechem, Jacob called his altar "El-elohe-Israel," That is, "God, the God of Israel"; but at Bethel, the true standpoint, he called his altar "El-beth-el," that is God—the house of God. This was true restoration. Jacob was brought back, after all his wanderings, to the very point from which he had started. Nothing less than this could ever satisfy God in reference to His servant. He could wait patiently on him—bear with him—minister to him—care for him—look after him; but He never could rest satisfied with anything short of this—"Arise, go up to Bethel."

We want to ask you a question. Are you conscious of having wandered from Jesus? Has your heart declined, and grown cold? Have you lost the freshness and ardor which once marked the tone of your soul? Have you allowed the world to get in upon you? Have you, in the moral condition of your soul, got

down into Shechem? Has your heart gone after idols, and have your garments become defiled? If so, let us remind you of this, that *the Lord wants you back to Himself.* Yes, this is what He wants; and He wants it now. He says to you at this moment, "Arise, go up to Bethel."

You will never be happy, you will never be right, until you yield a full response to this blessed and soul-stirring call. O yield it now, we beseech you. Rise up, and fling aside every weight and every hindrance; put away the idols and change your garments, and get back to the feet of your Lord, who loves you with a love which many waters cannot quench, neither can the floods drown; and who cannot be satisfied until He has you with Himself, according to the original terms. Say not this is legal; it is nothing of the sort. It is the love of Jesus—His deep, glowing, earnest love—love which is jealous of every rival affection—love which gives the whole heart, and must have a whole heart in return. May God the Holy Ghost bring back every wandering heart to the true standard! May He visit with fresh power every soul that has gone down to Shechem, and give no rest until a full response has been yielded to the call, "*Arise, go up to Bethel.*"

John 21: 1-19

A careful study of these verses will enable us to trace in them three distinct kinds of restoration, namely, restoration of conscience, restoration of heart, and restoration of position.

1. The first of these, restoration of conscience, is of all-importance. It would be utterly impossible to overestimate the value of a sound, clear, uncondemning conscience. A Christian cannot get on if there is a single soil on his conscience. He must walk before God with a pure conscience—a conscience without stain or sting. Precious treasure! May my reader ever possess it! but in each it must be a restoration to the original terms.

It is very obvious that Peter possessed it in the touching scene "at the sea of Tiberias." And yet he had fallen—shamefully, grievously fallen. He had denied his Lord with an oath; but he was restored. One look from Jesus had broken up the deep fountains of his heart, and drawn forth floods of bitter tears. And yet it was not his tears, but the love that drew them forth, which formed the ground of his thorough restoration of conscience. It was the changeless and everlasting love of the heart of Jesus—the divine efficacy of the blood of Jesus—and the all-prevailing power of the advocacy of Jesus, that imparted to Peter's conscience the boldness and liberty so strikingly and beautifully exhibited on the memorable occasion before us.

The risen Saviour is seen in these closing chapters of John's Gospel watching over His poor, feeble, erring disciples—hovering about their path—presenting Himself in various ways before them—taking occasion from their very necessities to make Himself known in perfect grace to their hearts. Was there a tear to be dried, a difficulty to be solved, a fear to be hushed, a bereaved heart to be soothed, an unbelieving mind to be corrected? Jesus was present, in all the fulness and variety of His grace, to meet all these things.

So also when, under the guidance of the ever forward Peter, they had gone forth to spend a night in fruitless toil, Jesus had His eye upon them. He knew all about the darkness, and the toil, and the empty net; and there He was on the shore to prepare a dinner for them. Yes, the self-same Jesus who had died on the cross to put away their sins, now stood on the shore to restore them from their wanderings, gather them round Himself, and minister to all their need. "Have ye any meat?" developed the fruitlessness of their night's toil. "Come and dine" was the touching expression of the tender, thoughtful, all-providing love of the risen Saviour.

But let us note particularly the evidences of a thoroughly restored conscience as exhibited by Simon Peter. "Therefore that disciple whom Jesus loved saith unto Peter, It is the Lord. Now when Simon Peter heard that it was the Lord, he girt his fisher's coat unto him, (for he was naked,) and did cast himself into the sea." He could not wait for the ships or for his fellow-disciples, so eager was he to get to the feet of his risen Lord.

In place of saying to John or to the others,

"You know how shamefully I have fallen; and although I have since then seen the Lord, and heard Him speak peace to my soul, yet I think it more becoming in one that has so fallen to keep back; do you therefore go first and meet the blessed One, and I shall follow after." In place of aught in this style, he flings himself boldly into the sea—as much as to say, "I must be the very first to get to my risen Saviour; none has such a claim on Him as poor, stumbling, failing Peter."

Now, here was a perfectly restored conscience—a conscience basking in the sunlight of unchanging love; and is not this the true, original terms for every Christian? Peter's confidence in Christ was unclouded, and this, we may boldly affirm, was grateful to the heart of Jesus. Love likes to be trusted. Let us ever remember this. No one need imagine that he is honoring Jesus by standing afar off on the plea of unworthiness; and yet it is very hard for one who has fallen, or backslidden, to recover his confidence in the love of Christ. Such a one can see clearly that a sinner is welcome to Jesus, no matter how great or manifold his sins may have been; but then, he thinks, the case of a backsliding, or stumbling, Christian is entirely different.

Should these lines be scanned by one who has backslidden, or fallen, we would press upon him most earnestly the importance of immediate return to Jesus. "Return, ye backsliding children, and I will heal your backslidings." What is the response to this pathetic appeal? "Behold, we come *unto Thee;* for Thou art the Lord our God." "If thou wilt return, O Israel, saith the Lord, return *unto Me*" (Jer. 3: 22; 4: 1). The love of the heart of Jesus knows no change. We change; but He is "the same yesterday, and to-day, and forever"; and He delights to be trusted. The confidence of Peter's heart was precious to the heart of Christ. No doubt it is sad to fall, to err, to backslide; but it is sadder still, when we have done so, to distrust the love of Jesus, or His gracious readiness to take us to His bosom again.

Have you fallen? Have you erred? Have you backslidden? Have you lost the sweet sense of divine favor, the happy consciousness of acceptance with God? If so, what are you to do? Simply this—"*Return.*" This is God's own special word to the backslider. Return in full confession, in self-judgment, and in the fullest confidence in the boundless, changeless love of the heart of Christ. Do not, we beseech you, keep away in the distance of your own unbelief. Do not measure the heart of Jesus by your own thoughts. Let Him tell you what is in His heart toward you.

You have sinned, you have failed, you have turned aside; and now, it may be, you are afraid or ashamed to turn your eyes toward the One whom you have grieved, or dishonored. Satan too is suggesting the darkest thoughts; for he would fain keep you at a chilling distance from that precious Saviour who loves you with an everlasting love.

But you have only to fix your gaze upon the blood, the advocacy, the heart of Jesus, to get a triumphant answer to all the enemy's terrible suggestions, and to all the infidel reasonings of your own heart. Do not, therefore, go on another hour without seeking to get a thorough settlement of the question between your soul and Christ. Remember, "His is an unchanging love, free and faithful, strong as death." Remember, also, His own words, "Return, ye backsliding children"—"Return *to Me.*" Christ, and He alone, is the centre and circumference of all the terms to which our souls are bound. And, finally, remember that Jesus loves to be trusted.

2. But the heart has to be restored as well as the conscience. Let this not be forgotten. It often happens, in the history of souls, that though the conscience may be perfectly clear as to certain *acts* which we have done, yet the *roots* from whence those acts have sprung have not been reached. The acts appear on the surface of daily life, but the roots are hidden down deep in the heart, unknown, it may be, to ourselves and others, but thoroughly exposed to the eye of Him with whom we have to do.

Now, these roots must be reached, exposed, and judged, ere the heart is in a right condition in the sight of God. Look at Abraham. He started on his course with a certain root in his heart, a root of unbelieving reserve in reference to Sarah. This thing led him astray when he went down to Egypt; and although his conscience was restored, and he got back to his altar at Bethel, yet the root was not reached for years afterwards, as seen in the affair of Abimelech, king of Gerar.

All this is deeply practical, and most solemn. It finds its illustration in Peter as well as in Abraham. But now mark the exquisitely delicate way in which our blessed Lord proceeds to reach the roots in the heart of His dear and honored servant. "So when they had dined." Not till then. There was no allusion to the past, nothing that might cause a chill to the heart, or bring a cloud over the spirit, while a restored conscience was feasting in company with a love that knows no change. This is a fine moral trait. It characterizes the dealings of God with all His saints. The conscience is set at rest in the presence of infinite and everlasting love.

But there must be the deeper work of reaching the root of things in the heart. When Simon Peter, in the full confidence of a restored conscience, flung himself at the feet of His risen Lord, he was called to listen to that gracious invitation, "Come and dine." But "when they had dined," Jesus, as it were, takes Peter apart, in order to let in upon his soul the light of truth, so that by it he might discern the root from whence all his failure had sprung. That root was self-confidence, which had led him to place himself in advance of his fellow-disciples, and say, "Though all should deny Thee, yet will not I."

This root had to be exposed, and therefore, "When they had dined, Jesus saith to Simon Peter, Simon, son of Jonas, lovest thou Me more than these?" This was a pointed and pungent question, and it went right to the very bottom of Peter's heart. Three times Peter had denied his Lord, and three times his Lord now challenges the heart of Peter—*for the roots must be reached if any permanent good is to be done*. It will not do merely to have the conscience purged from the effects which have been produced in practical life; there must also be the moral judgment of that which produced them. This is not sufficiently understood and attended to, and hence it is that again and again the roots spring up and bear forth their fruit with increasing power, thus cutting out for us the most bitter and sorrowful work, which might all be avoided if the roots of things were thoroughly judged and kept under judgment.

Our object is entirely practical. Let us therefore exhort one another to judge our roots, whatever they may be. Do we know our roots? Doubtless it is hard, very hard, to know them. They are deep and manifold: pride, personal vanity, covetousness, irritability, ambition—these are some of the roots of character, the motive springs of action, over which a rigid censorship must ever be exercised. We must let nature know that the eye of self-judgment is continually upon it. We have to carry on the struggle without cessation. We may have to lament over occasional failure; but we must maintain the struggle, for struggle bespeaks *life*. We must remember that the original terms are that in the flesh dwelleth *no* good thing. May God the Holy Ghost strengthen us for this vigilance against the flesh!

3. We shall close with a brief reference to restoration as bearing upon the soul's position, or path. The conscience being thoroughly purged, and the heart, with its varied roots, judged, there is moral preparedness for our proper path. The perfect love of Jesus had expelled all fear from Peter's conscience; and his threefold question had opened up the roots in Peter's heart, and now He says to him, "Verily, verily, I say unto thee, When thou wast young, thou girdedst thyself, and walkedst whither thou wouldest: but when thou shalt be old, thou shalt stretch forth thy hands, and another shall gird thee, and carry thee whither thou wouldest not. This spake He, signifying by what death he should glorify God. And when He had spoken this, He saith unto him, Follow Me." And this is exactly the original terms by which our Lord began with Peter as His disciple. It was then also, "Follow Me."

Here, then, we have in two words the path of the servant of Christ—"*Follow Me*." The Lord had just given Peter the sweetest pledges of His love and confidence. He had,

notwithstanding all past failure, entrusted him with the care of all that was dear to His loving heart in this world, even the lambs and sheep of His flock. He had said to him, "If you have affection for Me, feed My lambs, shepherd My sheep"; and now, in one brief but comprehensive utterance, He opens before him his proper path—"Follow Me." This is enough. It includes all besides.

If we want to follow Jesus, we must keep the eye continually upon Him; we must mark His footprints and tread therein. Yes, mark them, and walk in them; and when tempted, like Peter, to "turn about," in order to see what this one or that one has to do, or how he does it, we may hear the correcting words, "What is that to thee? follow thou Me." This is to be our one grand and all-absorbing business, come what may. A thousand things may arise to distract and hinder. The devil will tempt us to look hither and thither, to look at this one and that one; to imagine we could do better here than there, or there than here; to be occupied with, and imitating, the work of some fellow-servant. All this is met by those pointed words, "Follow Me."

There is immense danger of following in the wake of others, of doing certain things because others do them, or doing things as others do them. All this has to be carefully guarded against. It will be sure to come to nothing. What we really want is a broken will—the true spirit of a servant that waits on the Master to know His mind. Service does not consist in doing this or that, or running hither and thither; it is simply doing the Master's will, whatever that may be. "They serve who stand and wait."

It is easier to be busy than to be quiet. When Peter was "*young*," he went whither he would; but when he got "*old*," he went whither he would not. What a contrast between the young, restless, ardent, energetic Peter, going whither he would, and the old, matured, subdued, experienced Peter, going whither he would not! What a mercy to have the will broken!—to be able to say from the heart. "*What* Thou wilt—*as* Thou wilt—*where* Thou wilt—*when* Thou wilt"—"not my will, but Thine, O Lord, be done"!

"Follow Me!" Precious words! May they be engraved on our hearts! Then shall we be steady in our course and effective in our service. We shall not be distracted or unhinged by the thoughts and opinions of men. It may happen that we shall get very few to understand us or to sympathize with us—few to approve or appreciate our work. It matters not. The Master knows all about it. If a master tells one of his servants distinctly to go and do a certain thing, or occupy a certain post, it is his business to go and do that thing, or occupy that post, no matter what his fellow-servants may think. They may tell him that he ought to be somewhere else, or to do something else. A proper servant will heed them not; he knows his master's mind, and has to do his master's work.

Would it were more thus with all the Lord's servants! Would that we all knew more distinctly, and carried out more decidedly, the Master's will respecting us! Peter had his path, and John had his. James had his work, and Paul had his. So it was of old: the Gershonite had his work, and the Merarite had his; and if the one had interferred with the other, the work would not have been done. The tabernacle was carried forward, or set up, by each man doing his own proper work.

Thus it is in this our day. God has varied workmen in His house and in His vineyard; and the original terms of service are that the Holy Spirit divideth to every one as *He* will. He has quarrymen, stone-squarers, masons, and builders. Are all quarrymen? Surely not. But each has his work to do, and the building is carried forward by each one doing his own appointed work. Should a quarryman despise a builder, or a builder look down with contempt upon a quarryman? Assuredly not. The Master wants them both; and whenever the one would interfere with the other (as, alas, we are apt to do), the faithful correcting word falls on the ear, "*What is that to thee? follow thou Me.*"

LEGALITY AND LEVITY

FEELING, as we trust we do, in some little measure our responsibility to the souls of our readers, as well as to the truth of God, we desire to offer a brief but pointed word of warning against two opposite evils which we can plainly see working among Christians at the present moment. These are legality on the one hand, and levity on the other.

As to the first of these evils, we have sought in many of our former papers to deliver precious souls out of a legal state, as being, at once, dishonoring to God and utterly subversive of their own peace and liberty. We have endeavored to set forth the free grace of God, the value of the blood of Christ, the standing of the believer before God in perfect righteousness and acceptance in Christ. These precious truths, when applied to the heart in the power of the Holy Ghost, must deliver it from all legal influences.

But then it frequently happens that persons, when apparently delivered from legality, run into the opposite evil of levity. This may arise from the fact that the doctrines of grace are only taken up intellectually, instead of being wrought into the soul by the power of the Spirit of God. A great amount of evangelical truth may be taken up in a very light way, in cases where there has been no deep work of conscience, no real breaking down of nature, no thorough subjugation of the flesh in the presence of God. When this is the case there is sure to be levity of spirit in some form or another. There will be a very wide margin allowed for worldliness of various kinds—a liberty given to nature wholly incompatible with practical Christianity.

In addition to these things, there will be exhibited a very deplorable want of conscience in the practical details of daily life—duties neglected, work badly done, engagements not faithfully observed, sacred obligations trifled with, debts contracted, extravagant habits indulged. All these things we place under the head of levity, and they are, alas! too common amongst the very highest professors of what is termed evangelical truth.

Now we deeply deplore this, and would desire to have our own souls, as well as the souls of all our Christian readers, really exercised before God about it. We fear there is a great deal of hollow profession amongst us, a great want of earnestness, truthfulness and reality in our ways. We are not sufficiently permeated by the spirit of genuine Christianity, or governed in all things by the Word of God. We do not give sufficient attention to "the girdle of truth," or "the breastplate of righteousness."

In this way the soul gets into a very bad state indeed; conscience does not act. The moral sensibilities become blunted. The claims of truth are not duly responded to. Positive evil is trifled with. Moral relaxation is allowed. So far from there being the *con*straining power of the love of Christ, leading forth in the activities of goodness, there is not even the *re*straining power of the fear of God keeping back from the activities of evil.

We appeal solemnly to the consciences of our readers as to these things. The present is a deeply solemn time for Christians. There is a demand for earnest, deep-toned devotedness to Christ, but this cannot possibly exist where the common claims of practical righteousness are neglected. We must ever remember that the self-same grace which effectually delivers the soul from legality is the only safeguard against all levity. We have done very little for a man, if anything at all, if we bring him out of a legal state into a light, easy-going, careless, unconscientious condition of heart.

And yet we have frequently marked the history of souls, and noticed this sad fact respecting them, that when they were delivered out of darkness and bondage they became far less tender and sensitive. The flesh is ever ready to turn the grace of God

into lasciviousness, and therefore it must be subdued.

It needs that the power of the Cross be applied to all that is of the flesh. We want to mingle the "bitter herbs" with our paschal feast. In other words, we want those deep spiritual exercises which result from positive entrance into the power of the sufferings of Christ. We need to meditate more profoundly upon the death of Christ—His death as a victim under the hand of God, His death as a martyr under the hand of man.

This is at once the cure for legality and levity. The Cross, in its double aspect, delivers from both. Christ "gave Himself for our sins, that He might deliver us from this present evil world, according to the will of God and our Father" (Gal 1:4). By the Cross the believer is as completely delivered from this present evil world as he is forgiven his sins. He is not saved in order that he may enjoy the world, but that he may get done with it entirely.

We know few things more dangerous for the soul than the combination of evangelical truth with worldliness, ease and self-indulgence—the adoption of a certain phraseology of truth where the conscience is not in the presence of God—a merely intellectual apprehension of *standing* without any earnest dealing with the practical *state*—clearness in doctrine as to title, without any conscientious reference to the moral condition.

We trust our reader will suffer the word of exhortation. We should deem ourselves deficient in faithfulness were we to withhold it. True, it is not an agreeable task to call attention to practical evils—to urge the solemn duty of self-judgment—to press upon the conscience the claims of practical godliness. It were far more grateful to the heart to unfold abstract truth, to dwell upon free grace and what it has done for us, to expatiate upon the moral glories of the inspired volume, in a word, to dwell upon the privileges which are ours in Christ.

But there are times when the true, practical condition of things among Christians weighs heavily upon the heart and rouses the soul to make an urgent appeal to conscience in reference to matters of walk and conduct; and we believe the present to be such a time. The devil is ever busy, and on the alert. The Lord has granted much light upon His Word for some years past. The gospel has been brought out with peculiar clearness and power. Thousands have been delivered from a legal state; and now the enemy is seeking to hinder the testimony by leading souls into a light, careless, carnal condition—leading them to neglect the wholesome and indispensable exercise of self-judgment. It is the deep sense of this that

has suggested a word of warning on *"Legality and Levity."*

"For the grace of God that bringeth salvation hath appeared to all men, teaching us that, denying ungodliness and worldly lusts, we should live soberly, righteously, and godly, in this present world; looking for that blessed hope, and the glorious appearing of the great God and our Saviour Jesus Christ; who gave Himself for us, that He might redeem us from all iniquity, and purify unto Himself a peculiar people, zealous of good works" (Titus 2:11-14).

THE THRONE AND THE ALTAR

Isaiah 6:1-8

IN THIS SUBLIME PASSAGE of Scripture we notice two prominent objects, namely, the throne and the altar; and, moreover, we perceive the action of these two objects upon the soul of the prophet. The entire scene is full of interest and instruction. May we gaze upon it aright!

"In the year that king Uzziah died, I saw also the Lord sitting upon *a throne, high* and *lifted up,* and His train filled the temple." This was a solemn and soul-subduing sight. It is ever a serious matter for a sinner to find himself standing before the throne of God with the unanswered claims of that throne bearing down upon his conscience. Isaiah found it to be so. The light of the throne revealed to him his true condition. And what was that light? It was the moral glory of Christ, as we read in the Gospel of John, "These things said Esaias, when he saw His glory, and spake of Him" (chap. 12:41).

Christ is the perfect standard by which every one must be measured. It matters not what I may think of myself, nor yet what others may think about me: the question is, What am I as viewed in the presence of Christ? The law may tell me what I ought to

be; conscience may tell me I am not that; but it is only when the bright beams of Christ's moral glory pour themselves around me that I am enabled to form a just estimate of what I am. Then it is that the hidden chambers of my heart are laid open, the secret springs of action are revealed, the real condition is laid bare.

But perhaps my reader may ask, What do you mean by the moral glory of Christ? I mean the light which shone forth from Him in all His ways when He was down here in this dark world. It was this light that detected man, that disclosed what he was, that brought to light *all* that was in him. It was impossible for any one to escape the action of that light. It was a perfect blaze of divine purity, in view of which the seraphim could only cry out, "Holy, holy, holy!"

Need we marvel then if when Isaiah saw himself in the light of that glory he cried out, "Woe is me! for I am undone"? Nay; this was the proper utterance of one whose heart had been penetrated to its very centre by a light which makes all things perfectly manifest.

We have no reason to suppose that Isaiah was in any respect worse than his neighbors.

We are not told that the catalogue of his sins was heavier or darker than that of thousands around him. He may have been to all human appearance just like others. But ah! only remember, I pray you, where the prophet stood when he exclaimed, "Woe is me!" It was not at the foot of the burning mount when "the ministration of death and condemnation" was given forth amid thunderings and lightnings, blackness, darkness, and tempest. It was not there he stood, though even there a Moses had to say, "I exceedingly fear and quake"; but it was in the presence of the glory of Christ, the Lord God of Israel, that our prophet stood when he saw himself to be "unclean" and "undone." Such was his condition when seen in the light which reveals men and things just as they are.

"*I am undone.*" He does not say, "Woe is me! I am not what I ought to be." No; he saw deeper than this. He stood revealed in the power of a light which reaches to the most profound depths of the soul and discloses "the thoughts and intents of the heart."

Isaiah had never before seen himself in such a light—measured himself by such a rule—weighed himself in such a balance. He now saw himself standing in the presence of Jehovah's throne without any ability whatever to meet the claims of that throne. He "saw Jehovah sitting upon a throne, high and lifted up." He saw himself a helpless, ruined, guilty sinner at an immeasurable distance from that throne and from the blessed One who sat thereon. He heard the cry of the seraphim, "Holy, holy, holy"; and the only response which he could send back from the depths of a broken heart was, "Unclean, unclean, unclean." He beheld a gulf of guilt and uncleanness separating him from Jehovah which no effort of his could ever bridge.

Thus it was with him in that solemn moment when he gave forth that cry of a truly convicted soul, "Woe is me!" He was wholly engrossed with one thought, namely, *his own utter ruin.* He felt himself *a lost man.* He thought not of comparing himself with others, nor of seeking out some fellow-sinner worse than he. Ah, no! a divinely-convicted soul never thinks of such things. There is one grand, all-pervading idea, and that idea is embodied in the words, "I am undone."

And be it carefully noted that the prophet when under the convicting light of the throne is not occupied with what he had done or left undone. The question before his soul was not as to the evil he had done or the good he had left undone. No; it was something far deeper than this. In a word, he was occupied not with his *acts* but with his *condition.* He says, "*I am*" what? Defective in many things? Far behind in my duty? Deplorably short of what I ought to be? No. These and such-like confessions could never embody the experience of a heart on which the bright beams of Jehovah's throne had fallen in convicting power.

True it is "we have done that which we ought not to have done, and left undone that which we ought to have done." But all this is merely the fruit of a nature which is radically corrupt, and when divine light breaks in upon us it will always lead us to the *root.* It will not merely conduct us from leaf to leaf or from branch to branch, but passing down along the trunk it will lay bare the hidden roots of that nature which we inherit by birth from our first parents, and cause us to see that the whole thing is irremediably ruined. Then it is we are constrained to cry out, "Woe is me!" Not because my *conduct* has been defective, but my nature is undone.

Thus it was that Isaiah stood before Jehovah's throne. And oh, what place for a sinner to stand in! There are no excuses there—no palliating circumstances there—no qualifying clauses there—no blaming of men or things there. There is but one object seen there—seen in its guilt, its wretchedness and its ruin, and that object is *self,* and as to that object the tale is easily told. It is all summed up in that most solemn, weighty, suggestive word, "*undone.*" Yes; self is undone. That is all that can be said about it. Do what you will with it, and you cannot make it out to be aught but a hopeless, undone thing; and the more speedily and thoroughly this is understood the better.

Many take a long time to learn this foundation truth. They have not, as it were, stood in the full blaze of the throne, and as a consequence they have not been led to cry out with sufficient depth, emphasis or intensity, "I am undone!" It is the glory that shines from the throne which evokes the cry from the very depths of the soul.

All who have ever stood before that throne have given utterance to the same confession, and it will ever be found that just in proportion to our experience of the *light* of the *throne* will be our experience of the *grace* of the *altar*. The two things invariably go together. In this day of *grace* the throne and the altar are connected. In the day of *judgment* "the great white throne" will be seen without any altar. There will be no grace then. The *ruin* will then be seen without the *remedy*, and as for the *result*, it will be eternal perdition. Awful reality! O beware of having to meet the light of the throne without the provision of the altar!

This conducts us, naturally, to the second object in the interesting scene before us, namely, *the altar*. The very moment Isaiah gave utterance to the deep conviction of what he was, he was introduced to the divine provisions of God's altar. "Then flew one of the seraphims unto me, having a live coal in his hand, which he had taken with the tongs from off the altar: and he laid it upon my mouth, and said, Lo, this hath touched thy lips; and thine iniquity is taken away, and thy sin purged."

Here, then, we have the rich provisions of Jehovah's altar, which, be it well remembered, is seen in immediate connection with Jehovah's throne. The two things are intimately connected in the history and experience of every convicted and converted soul. The guilt which the throne detects, the altar removes. If in the light of the throne one object is seen, namely, ruined, guilty, undone self; then, in the light of the altar, one object is seen, namely, a full, precious all-sufficient Christ. The remedy reaches to the full exent of the ruin, and the same light that reveals the one reveals the other likewise. This gives settled repose to the conscience.

God Himself has provided a remedy for all the ruin which the light of His throne has revealed. "This *hath touched* thy lips; and

thine iniquity *is* taken away, and thy sin purged." Isaiah was brought into personal contact with the sacrifice, and the immediate result was the perfect removal of *all* his iniquity—the perfect purgation of *all* his sin.

Not a single spot remained. He could now stand in the light of that throne which had just detected and exposed his uncleanness, and know assuredly by that self-same light that not a speck of uncleanness remained. The very same light which manifested his sin, made manifest also the purging efficacy of the blood.

Such, then, is the precious and beautiful connection between the throne and the altar—a connection which may be easily traced through the inspired volume from Genesis to Revelation, and through the history of God's redeemed from Adam down to the present moment. All who have been really brought to Jesus have experienced the convicting light of the throne and the peace-giving virtues of the altar. All have been made to feel their ruin and cry out, "I am undone!" and all have been brought into personal contact with the sacrifice, and had their sin purged.

God's work is perfect. He convicts perfectly, and He purges perfectly. There is nothing superficial when He carries on His mighty work. The arrow of conviction penetrates to the very centre of the soul, only to be followed by the divine application of that blood which leaves not a stain upon the conscience; and the more deeply we are penetrated by the arrow, the deeper and more settled is our experience of the power of the blood. It is well to be thoroughly searched at the first—well to let the chambers of the heart be fully thrown open to the convicting action of the throne, for then we are sure to get a bolder grasp of that precious atoning blood that speaks peace to every believing heart.

Let me ask you to pause here for a moment and mark the peculiar *style* of the divine action in the case of the prophet.

We all know how much depends upon the way in which a thing is done. A person may do me a favor, but he may do it in such a style as to do away with all the good of it.

Now in the scene before us we not only see a marvelous favor conferred, but conferred after such a fashion as to let us into the very secrets of the bosom of God. The divine remedy was not only applied to Isaiah's felt ruin, but applied in such a way as to let him know assuredly that the whole heart of God was in the application. "Then *flew* one of the seraphims unto me." The rapidity of the movement speaks volumes. It tells us distinctly of Heaven's intense desire to tranquilize the convicted conscience, bind up the broken heart and heal the wounded spirit. The energy of divine love gave swiftness to the seraphic messenger as he winged his way down from Jehovah's throne to where a convicted sinner stood confessing himself "undone."

What a scene! One of those very seraphims that with veiled face stood above Jehovah's throne crying, "Holy, holy, holy," passes from that throne to the altar, and from the altar away down to the deep depths of a convicted sinner's heart, there to apply the balmy virtues of a divine sacrifice. No sooner had the arrow from the throne wounded the heart than the seraph from the altar "flew" to heal the wound. No sooner had the throne poured forth its flood of living light to reveal to the prophet the blackness of his guilt than a tide of love rolled down upon him from the altar and bore away upon its bosom every trace of that guilt. Such is the style—such the manner of the love of God to sinners! Who would not trust Him?

Whosoever you are, in earnest desire for the welfare of your immortal soul, permit me to ask you if you have experienced the action of the throne and the altar? Have you ever retired from all that false light which the enemy of your precious soul would fling around you in order to prevent your getting a true insight into your total ruin? Have you ever stood where Isaiah found himself when he cried out, "Woe is me! for I am undone"? Have you ever been brought to own from your heart, "I have sinned"? (Job 33) If so, it is your privilege to enter this moment into the rich enjoyment of all that Christ has done for you on the cross.

You do not need to see any vision. You do not require to see a throne, an altar, a flying seraph. You have the Word of God to assure you "Christ suffered for sins, the just for the unjust, that He might bring us to God" (1 Pet. 3:18). That same Word also assures you that "all that believe *are* justified from *all* things" (Acts 13:39).

And is not this far better than many visions or many seraphim? Isaiah believed that his "iniquity was taken away, and his sin purged," when the angelic messenger told him so. And should you not believe that Jesus died for you when the Word of God tells you so?

But perhaps you say, "How can I know that Jesus died for *me?* I reply, In the way that any one may know it—simply by the Word of God. There is no other way of knowing it. But you still object, "I do not see my name in the Word of God." No; and even though your name were mentioned this would in no wise satisfy you, inasmuch as there might be hundreds bearing your name. But you see your state, your character, your condition. You see your photograph flung, with divine precision, upon the page of inspiration by the action of that light which makes all things manifest.

Do you not own yourself to be a sinner?—a deep-dyed and ruined sinner? If so the death of Christ applies itself as perfectly to you as the "live coal" did to Isaiah when the seraph declared to him, "This hath touched thy lips." The word is, "If any say I haved sinned"—What then? He will send him to hell? No; but "he will deliver him." The very moment you take your true place, and cry out, "Undone!" all that Christ has done, and all that He is becomes yours—yours now—yours for ever. You need not make any effort to improve your condition. Do what you will, and you cannot make yourself anything but undone.

A single effort at improvement is but the evidence that you know not yet how bad, how *incurably* bad you are. You are "undone," and, as such, you have to stand still and see the salvation of God—a salvation the foundation of which was wrought out through the cross of Christ—a salvation which the Holy Ghost reveals on the authority of that Word which is settled for ever in Heaven, and which God "has exalted according to all His name." May the blessed Spirit lead you *now* to put your trust in the name of Jesus, that so, ere you lay down this page, you may know that your "iniquity *is* taken away, and your sin purged"! Then you will be able to follow me while, in a few closing words, I seek to unfold the practical result of all that has been engaging our attention.

We have seen the complete *ruin* of the sinner; we have seen the complete *remedy* in Christ; let us now look at the *result*, as exhibited in whole-hearted consecration to the service of God. Isaiah had nothing to do for salvation, but he had plenty to do for his Saviour. He had nothing to do to get his sins purged, but plenty to do for the One who had purged them. Now he gave the willing, ready expression of obedience to God when, on hearing that a messenger was needed, he answered, "Here am I; send me." This puts works in their proper place. The order is absolutely perfect. No one can do good works until he has experienced, in some degree, the action of the "throne" and the "altar." The light of the former must shew him what he is, and the provisions of the latter must shew him what Christ is ere he can say, "Here am I; send me."

This is a settled, universal truth, established in every section of inspiration, and illustrated in the biography of the saints of God and of the servants of Christ in every age, in every condition. All have been brought to see their *ruin* in the light of the throne, to see the *remedy* in the provisions of the altar ere they could exhibit the *result* in a life of practical devotedness. All this is from God the Father, through God the Son, by God the Holy Ghost—to whom be all the glory, world without end! Amen and Amen!

"PEACE"

John 20:19-21

IN THE PASSAGE which stands at the head of this paper we have the word "peace," in a twofold sense, first, as applied to the inner life; and, secondly, to the outer life of the Christian disciple. "Then the same day at evening, being the first day of the week, when the doors were shut where the disciples were assembled for fear of the Jews, came Jesus, and stood in the midst, and saith unto them, *Peace unto you.* And when He had so said, He shewed unto them His hands and His side."

Here we have peace in its blessed application to the inner life. All was finished. The battle was fought, the victory gained. The Conqueror was in their midst—the true David, with the head of the Philistine in His hand. All possible ground of anxiety was for ever removed. Peace was made, and established on a basis which could never be moved. It was utterly impossible that any power of earth or hell could ever touch the foundation of that peace which a risen Saviour was now breathing into the souls of His gathered disciples. He had made peace by the blood of His cross. He had met every foe. He had encountered the marshalled hosts of hell, and made a show of them openly. The full tide of Jehovah's righteous wrath against sin had rolled over Him. He had taken the sting from death, and spoiled the grave of its victory. In a word, the triumph was gloriously complete; and the blessed Victor at once presents Himself to the eyes and to the hearts of His beloved people, and sounds in their ears the precious word "*peace.*"

And then mark the significant action. "He shewed them His hands and His side." He brings them into immediate contact with Himself. He reveals His Person to their souls, and shews them the unequivocal tokens of His cross and passion—the wondrous marks of accomplished atonement. It is a risen Saviour, bearing in His body the marks of that death through which He had passed for His people.

Now this is the secret of peace. It is a great deal more than knowing that our sins are forgiven, and that we are justified from all things, blessed as all this assuredly is. It is having before our souls—before the eyes of our faith—the Person of a risen Christ, and receiving from His own lips the sweet message of "peace." It is having in our hearts that holy sense of deliverance which springs from having the Person of the Deliverer distinctly presented to our faith. It is not merely that we know we are forgiven and delivered, but our hearts are livingly engaged with the One who has done it all, and we gaze by faith upon the mysterious marks of His accomplished work. *This is peace for the inner life.*

But this is not all. "Then were the disciples glad when they saw the Lord. Then said Jesus to them again, Peace unto you. As My Father hath sent Me, even so send I you." Here we have the outer life of the Christian. It is all, from first to last, wrapped up in this one grand fact, he is sent into the world, as Jesus was sent by the Father. It is not a question of what he has to do, or where he has to go. He is one sent by Jesus, even as Jesus was sent by the Father; and ere he starts on this high and holy mission, his risen Lord ensures him perfect peace as to every scene and circumstance of his whole career.

What a mission! What a view of the life of a Christian! Do we at all enter into it? Let no one suppose for a moment that all this applies only to apostles. This would be a grand mistake. The passage on which we are dwelling does not speak of apostles. It speaks of "disciples," a term which surely applies to all the children of God. The very feeblest disciple is privileged to know himself as one sent into this world as Jesus was sent of the Father. What a model to study! What a place it gives us! What an object to live for! How it settles everything! It is not a question of "views"—of opinions, dogmas, or principles—of ordinances or ceremonies. No, thank God; it is something quite different. It is life and peace—life in a risen Saviour, and peace for that life, both inward and outward. It is gazing upon a risen Saviour, and starting from His feet to serve Him in this world, as He served the Father.

And be it remembered that all this has a direct bearing upon the very youngest disciple in all the Church of God. We earnestly press this upon the reader, because some would have us to believe that it is something official, something which applied only to the apostles. Those who urge this idea build much on verse 23. But the fact is, the apostles never undertook to forgive sins in an official way. This passage has no such bearing; it refers to the discipline of an assembly of disciples, acting by the Holy Ghost, in the name and on the authority of the Lord Jesus Christ. For example, when the assembly at Corinth put away from among them the evil-doer, it was retaining of sins. And when they received him back, on the ground of his repentance, it was a remitting of sins.

Such is the simple meaning of John 20:23. It does not touch the soul's eternal relation to God, but only its present relation to the assembly. Hence we should not allow ourselves to be robbed of the precious teaching of the entire passage through any false application of a particular clause.

SIN IN THE FLESH
AND SIN ON THE CONSCIENCE

IT IS OF THE UTMOST IMPORTANCE that we accurately distinguish between sin *in the flesh*, and sin *on the conscience*. If we confound these two, our souls must necessarily be unhinged, and our worship marred. An attentive consideration of 1 John 1:8-10 will throw much light upon this subject, the understanding of which is so essential.

There is no one who will be so conscious of indwelling sin, as the man who walks in the light. "If we say that we have *no sin*, we deceive ourselves, and the truth is not in us." In the verse immediately preceding, we read, "the blood of Jesus Christ His Son cleanseth us from *all sin*." Here the distinction between sin *in* us, and sin *on* us, is fully brought out and established. To say that there is sin on the believer, in the presence of God, is to call in question the purging efficacy of the blood of Jesus, and to deny the truth of the divine record. If the blood of Jesus can perfectly purge, then the believer's conscience is perfectly purged. The Word of God thus puts the matter; and we must ever remember that it is from God Himself we are to learn what the true condition of the believer is, in His sight. We are more disposed to be occupied in telling God what we are in ourselves, than to allow Him to tell us what we are in Christ. In other words, we are more taken up with our own self-consciousness, than with God's revelation of Himself. God speaks to us on the ground of what He is in Himself, and of what He has accomplished in Christ. Such is the nature and character of His revelation, of which faith takes hold, and thus fills the soul with perfect peace. God's revelation is one thing; my consciousness is quite another.

But the same word which tells us we have no sin *on* us, tells us, with equal force and clearness, that we have sin *in* us. "If we say we have no sin, we deceive ourselves, and

the truth is not in us." Every one who has "truth" in him, will know that he has "*sin*" in him, likewise; for truth reveals everything as it is. What, then, are we to do? It is our privilege so to walk in the power of the new nature (that is, the Holy Ghost), that the "*sin*" which dwells in us may not manifest itself in the form of "*sins*." The Christian's position is one of victory and liberty. He is not only delivered from the guilt of sin, but also from sin as a ruling principle in his life. "Knowing this, that our old man is crucified with Him, that the body of sin might be destroyed, that henceforth we should not serve sin. For he that is dead is freed from sin. . . . Let not sin therefore *reign* in your mortal body, that ye should *obey* it in the lusts thereof. . . . For sin shall not have dominion over you; for ye are not under the law, but under grace" (Rom. 6:6-14). Sin is there in all its native vileness, but the believer is *dead* to it. How? He died in Christ. By nature he was dead *in* sin. By grace he is dead *to* it. What claim can anything or any one have upon a dead man? None whatever. Christ "died unto sin once," and the believer died in Him. "Now if we be dead with Christ, we believe that we shall also live with Him; knowing that Christ, being raised from the dead, dieth no more; death hath no more dominion over Him. For in that He died, He died unto sin once; but in that He liveth, He liveth unto God. What is the result of this, in reference to believers? "*Likewise* reckon ye also yourselves to be *dead indeed unto sin*, but alive unto God through Jesus Christ our Lord." Such is the believer's unalterable position before God, so that it is his holy privilege to enjoy freedom from sin as a *ruler* over him, though it be a *dweller* in him.

But then, "if any man sin," what is to be done? The inspired apostle furnishes a full and most blessed answer: "If we confess our sins, He is faithful and just to forgive us our sins, and to cleanse us from all unrighteousness" (1 John 1:9). Confession is the mode in which the conscience is to be kept free. The apostle does not say, "If we pray for pardon, He is gracious and merciful to forgive us." No doubt, it is ever happy for a child to breathe the sense of need into his father's ear—to tell him of feebleness, to confess folly, infirmity, and failure. All this is most true; and, moreover, it is equally true that our Father is most gracious and merciful to meet His children in all their weakness and ignorance; but, while all this is true, the Holy Ghost declares, by the apostle, that "if we *confess*," God is "*faithful* and *just* to forgive." Confession therefore is the divine mode. A Christian, having erred in thought, word, or deed, might pray for pardon for days and months together, and not have any assurance, from 1 John 1:9, that he was forgiven; whereas, the moment he truly confesses his sin before God, it is a simple matter of faith to know that he is perfectly forgiven, and perfectly cleansed.

There is an immense moral difference between praying for forgiveness, and confessing our sins, whether we look at it in reference to the character of God, the sacrifice of Christ, or the condition of the soul. It is quite possible that a person's prayer may involve the confession of his sin, whatever it may happen to be, and thus come to the same thing. But then, it is always well to keep close to Scripture, in what we think, and say, and do. It must be evident that when the Holy Ghost speaks of *confession*, He does not mean *praying*. And it is equally evident that He knows there are moral elements in, and practical results flowing out of, confession, which do not belong to prayer. In point of fact, one has often found that a habit of importuning God for the forgiveness of sins, displayed ignorance as to the way in which God has revealed Himself in the Person and work of Christ; as to the relation in which the sacrifice of Christ has set the believer; and as to the divine mode of getting the conscience relieved from the burden, and purified from the evil of sin.

God has been perfectly satisfied, as to all the believer's sin, in the cross of Christ. On that cross a full atonement was presented for every jot and tittle of sin, in the believer's nature and on his conscience. Hence, therefore, God does not need any further propitiation. He does not need aught to draw His heart toward the believer. We do not require to supplicate Him to be "faithful and just," when His faithfulness and justice have been so gloriously displayed, vindicated, and answered, in the death of Christ. Our sins can never come into God's presence, inasmuch as Christ, who bore them all, and put them away, is there instead. But if we sin, conscience will feel it, must feel it; yea, the Holy Ghost will make us feel it. He cannot allow so much as a single light thought to pass unjudged. What then? Has our sin made its way into the presence of God? Has it found its place in the unsullied light of the inner sanctuary? God forbid! The "Advocate" is there—"Jesus Christ the righteous"—to maintain, in unbroken integrity, the relationship in which we stand.

But though sin cannot affect God's thoughts in reference to us, it can, and does affect our thoughts in reference to Him. Though it cannot make its way into God's presence, it can make its way into ours, in a most distressing and humiliating manner. Though it cannot hide the Advocate from God's view, it can hide Him from ours. It gathers, like a thick dark cloud, on our spiritual horizon, so that our souls cannot bask in the blessed beams of our Father's countenance. It cannot affect our relationship with God, but it can very seriously affect our enjoyment thereof. What, therefore, are we to do? The Word answers, "If we confess our sins, He is faithful and just to forgive us our sins, and to cleanse us from all unrighteousness." By confession, we get our conscience cleared; the sweet sense of our relationship restored; the dark cloud dispersed; the chilling, withering influence removed; our thoughts of God set straight. Such is the divine method; and we may truly say that the heart that knows what it is to have ever been in the place of confession, will feel the divine power of the apostle's words, "My little children, these things write I unto you, *that ye sin not*" (1 John 2:1).

Then again, there is a style of praying for forgiveness which involves a losing sight of the perfect ground of forgiveness, which has been laid in the sacrifice of the cross. If God forgives sins, He must be "faithful and just" in so doing. But it is quite clear that our prayers, be they ever so sincere and earnest, could not form the basis of God's faithfulness and justice in forgiving us our sins. Naught save the work of the cross could do this. There the faithfulness and justice of God have had their fullest establishment, and that, too, in immediate reference to our actual sins, as well as to the root thereof, in our nature. God has already judged our sins, in the Person of our Substitute, "on the tree"; and, in the act of confession, we judge ourselves. This is essential to divine forgiveness and restoration.

The very smallest unconfessed, unjudged sin, on the conscience, will entirely mar our communion with God. Sin *in* us need not do this; but if we suffer sin to remain *on* us, we cannot have fellowship with God. He has put away our sins in such a manner as that He can have us in His presence; and so long as we abide in His presence, sin does not trouble us. But if we get out of His presence, and commit sin, our communion must of necessity be suspended until, by confession, we have got rid of the sin. All this, I need hardly add, is founded exclusively upon the perfect sacrifice and righteous advocacy of the Lord Jesus Christ.

Finally, as to the difference between prayer and confession, as respects the condition of the heart before God, and its moral sense of the hatefulness of sin, it cannot possibly be overestimated. It is a much easier thing to ask in a general way for the forgiveness of our sins, than to confess those sins. Confession involves *self-judgment;* asking for forgiveness may not, and in itself does not. This alone would be sufficient to point out the difference. Self-judgment is one of the most valuable and healthful exercises of the Christian life; and therefore anything which produces it must be highly esteemed by every earnest Christian.

The difference between asking for pardon, and confessing the sin, is continually exemplified in dealing with children. If a child has done anything wrong, he finds much less difficulty in asking his father to forgive him, than in openly and unreservedly confessing the wrong. In asking for forgiveness, the child may have in his mind a number of things which tend to lessen the sense of the evil; he may be secretly thinking that he was not so much to blame after all, though, to be sure, it is only proper to ask his father to forgive him; whereas, in confessing the wrong, there is just one thing, and that is self-judgment. Further, in asking for forgiveness, the child may be influenced mainly by a desire to escape the consequences of his wrong; whereas a judicious parent will seek to produce a just sense of its moral evil, which can only exist where there is the full confession of the fault in connection with self-judgment.

Thus it is in reference to God's dealing with His children, when they do wrong. He must have the whole thing brought out and thoroughly judged. He will make us not only dread the consequences of sin—which are unutterable—but hate the thing itself, because of its hatefulness in His sight. Were it possible for us, when we commit sin, to be forgiven merely for the asking, our sense of sin, and our shrinking from it, would not be nearly so intense, and, as a consequence, our estimate of the fellowship with which we are blessed would not be nearly so high. The moral effect of all this upon the general tone of our spiritual constitution, and also upon our whole character and practical career, must be obvious to every experienced Christian.

GOD'S WAY, AND HOW TO FIND IT

Job 28; Luke 11:34-36

"THERE IS A PATH which no fowl know-eth, and which the vulture's eye hath not seen: the lion's whelps have not trodden it, nor the fierce lion passed by it." What an unspeakable mercy for one who really desires to walk with God, to know that there is a way for him to walk in! God has prepared a pathway for His redeemed in which they may walk with all possible certainty, calmness and fixedness. It is the privilege of every child of God, and every servant of Christ, to be as sure that he is in God's way as that his soul is saved. This may seem a strong statement; but the question is, Is it true? If it be true, it cannot be too strong. No doubt it may, in the judgment of some, savor a little of self-confidence and dogmatism to assert, in such a day as that in which we live, and in the midst of such a scene as that through which we are passing, that we are sure of being in God's path. But what saith the Scripture? It declares "there is a way," and it also tells us how to find and how to walk in that way. Yes; the self-same voice that tells us of God's salvation for our souls, tells us also of God's pathway for our feet;—the very same authority that assures us that "he that believeth on the Son of God hath everlasting life," assures us also that there is a way so plain that "the wayfaring men though fools shall not err therein."

This, we repeat, is a signal mercy—a mercy at all times, but especially in a day of confusion and perplexity like the present. It is deeply affecting to notice the state of uncertainty in which many of God's dear people are found at the present moment. We do not refer now to the question of salvation, of this we have spoken largely elsewhere; but that which we have now before us is the path of the Christian—what he ought to do, where

he should be found, how he ought to carry himself in the midst of the professing Church. Is it not too true that multitudes of the Lord's people are at sea as to these things? Are there not many who, were they to tell out the real feelings of their hearts, would have to own themselves in a thoroughly unsettled state—to confess that they know not what to do, or where to go, or what to believe? Now, the question is, Would God leave His children, would Christ leave His servants, in such darkness and confusion?

> No; my dear Lord, in following Thee,
> And not in dark uncertainty,
> This foot obedient moves.

May not a child know the will of his father? May not a servant know the will of his master? And if this be so in our earthly relationships, how much more fully may we count upon it in reference to our Father and Master in Heaven. When Israel of old emerged from the Red Sea, and stood upon the margin of that great and terrible wilderness which lay between them and the land of promise, how were they to know their way? The trackless sand of the desert lay all around them. It was in vain to look for any footprint there. It was a dreary waste in which the vulture's eye could not discern a pathway. Moses felt this when he said to Hobab, "Leave us not, I pray thee; forasmuch as thou knowest how we are to encamp in the wilderness, and thou mayest be to us instead of eyes" (Num. 10:31). How well our poor unbelieving hearts can understand this touching appeal! How one craves a human guide in the midst of a scene of perplexity! How fondly the heart clings to one whom we deem competent to give us guidance in moments of darkness and difficulty!

And yet, we may ask, what did Moses want with Hobab's eyes? Had not Jehovah graciously undertaken to be their guide? Yes, truly; for we are told that "on the day that the tabernacle was reared up, the cloud covered the tabernacle, namely, the tent of the testimony; and at even, there was upon the tabernacle as it were the appearance of fire, until the morning. So it was alway: the cloud covered it by day, and the appearance of fire by night. And when the cloud was taken up from the tabernacle, then after that the children of Israel journeyed; and in the place where the cloud abode, there the children of Israel pitched their tents. At the commandment of the Lord the children of Israel journeyed, and at the commandment of the Lord they pitched: as long as the cloud abode upon the tabernacle, they rested in their tents. And when the cloud tarried long upon the tabernacle many days, then the children of Israel kept the charge of the Lord, and journeyed not. And so it was, when the cloud was a few days upon the tabernacle; according to the commandment of the Lord they abode in their tents, and according to the commandment of the Lord, and journeyed not. And so it was, when the cloud abode from even unto the morning, and that the cloud was taken up in the morning, then they journeyed; whether it was by day or by night that the cloud was taken up, they journeyed; or whether it were two days, or a month, or a year, that the cloud tarried upon the tabernacle, remaining thereon, the children of Israel abode in their tents and journeyed not, but when it was taken up they journeyed. At the commandment of the Lord they rested in their tents, and at the commandment of the Lord they journeyed: they kept the charge of the Lord at the commandment of the Lord by the hand of Moses" (Num. 9:15-23).

Here was divine guidance—a guidance, we may surely say, quite sufficient to render them independent of their own eyes, of Hobab's eyes, and the eyes of any other mortal. It is interesting to note that in the opening of the book of Numbers, it was arranged that the ark of the covenant was to find its place in the very bosom of the congregation; but in chapter 10 we are told that when "they departed from the mount of the Lord three days' journey, the ark of the covenant of the Lord *went before them*, in the three days' journey, to search out a resting-place for them." Instead of Jehovah finding a resting-place in the bosom of His redeemed people, He becomes their traveling Guide, and goes before them to seek out a resting-place for them. What touching grace is here! and what faithfulness! If Moses will ask Hobab to be their guide, and that, too, in the very face of God's provision—even the cloud and the silver trumpet, then will Jehovah leave His place in the centre of the tribes, and go before them to search them out a resting-place. And did not He know the wilderness well? Would not He be better for them than ten thousand Hobabs? Might they not fully trust Him? Assuredly. He would not lead them astray. If His grace had redeemed them from Egypt's bondage, and conducted them through the Red Sea, surely they might confide in the same grace to guide them across that great and terrible wilderness, and bring them safely into the land flowing with milk and honey.

But it must be borne in mind that, in order to profit by divine guidance, there must be the abandonment of our own will, and of all confidence in our own reasonings, as well as all confidence in the thoughts and reasonings of others. If I have Jehovah as my Guide, I do not want my own eyes or the eyes of a Hobab either. God is sufficient: I can trust Him. He knows all the way across the desert; and hence, if I keep my eye upon Him, I shall be guided aright.

But this leads us on to the second division of our subject, namely, How am I to find God's way? An all-important question, surely. Whither am I to turn to find God's pathway? If the vulture's eye, so keen, so powerful, so far-seeing, hath not seen it—if the young lion, so vigorous in movement, so majestic in mien, hath not trodden it—if man knoweth not the price of it, and if it is not to be found in the land of the living—if the depth saith, It is not in me, and the sea saith, It is not with me—if it cannot be gotten for gold or precious stones—if the wealth of the universe cannot equal it, and no wit of man discover it—then whither am I to turn? where shall I find it?

Shall I turn to those great standards of orthodoxy which rule the religious thought and feeling of millions throughout the length and breadth of the professing Church? Is this wondrous pathway of wisdom to be found with them? Do they form any exception to the great, broad, sweeping rule of Job 28? Assuredly not.

What, then, am I to do? I know there is a way. God, who cannot lie, declares this, and I believe it; but where am I to find it? "Whence, then, cometh wisdom? and where is the place of understanding? seeing it is hid from the eyes of all living, and kept close from the fowls of the air. Destruction and Death say, We have heard the fame thereof with our ears." Does it not seem like a hopeless case for any poor ignorant mortal to search for this wondrous pathway? No, blessed be God, it is by no means a hopeless case, for "He understandeth the way thereof, and He knoweth the place thereof. For He looketh to the ends of the earth, and seeth under the whole heaven; to make the weight for the winds; and He weigheth the waters by measure. When He made a decree for the rain, and a way for the lightning of the thunder, then did He see it and *declare* it; He prepared it, yea, and searched it out. And unto man He said, 'Behold, *the fear of the Lord*, that is wisdom; and *to depart from evil* is understanding.'"

Here, then, is the divine secret of wisdom: "The fear of the Lord." This sets the conscience directly in the presence of God, which is its only true place. The object of Satan is to keep the conscience out of this place—to bring it under the power and authority of man—to lead it into subjection to the commandments and doctrines of men—to thrust in something between the conscience and the authority of Christ the Lord, it matters not what it is; it may be a creed or a confession containing a quantity of truth—it may be the opinion of a man or a set of men—the judgment of some favorite teacher—anything, in short, to come in and usurp, in the heart, the place which belongs to God's Word alone. This is a terrible snare,

and a stumbling-block—a most serious hindrance to our progress in the ways of the Lord. God's Word must rule me—God's pure and simple Word, not man's interpretation thereof. No doubt, God may use a man to unfold that Word to my soul; but then it is not man's unfolding of God's Word that rules me, but God's Word by man unfolded. This is of all importance.

We must be exclusively taught and exclusively governed by the Word of the living God. Nothing else will keep us straight, or give solidity and consistency to our character and course as Christians. There is a strong tendency within and around us to be ruled by the thoughts and opinions of men—by those great standards of doctrine which men have set up.

Those standards and opinions may have a large amount of truth in them—they may be all true so far as they go; that is not the point in question now. What we want to impress upon the Christian reader is, that he is not to be governed by the thoughts of his fellow-man, but simply and solely by the Word of God. It is of no value to hold a truth from man; I must hold it directly from God Himself. God may use a man to communicate His truth; but unless I hold it as from God, it has no divine power over my heart and conscience; it does not bring me into living contact with God, but actually hinders that contact by bringing in something between my soul and His holy authority.

We should greatly like to enlarge upon and enforce this great principle; but we must forbear, just now, in order to unfold to the reader one or two solemn and practical points set forth in the eleventh chapter of Luke, points which, if entered into, will enable us to understand a little better how to find God's way. We shall quote the passage at length. "The light of the body is the eye: therefore when thine eye is single, thy whole body also is full of light; but when thine eye is evil, thy body also is full of darkness. Take heed, therefore, that the light which is in thee be not darkness. If thy whole body therefore be full of light, having no part dark, the whole shall be full of light, as when the bright shining of a candle doth give thee light."

Here, then, we are furnished with the true secret of discerning God's way. It may seem very difficult, in the midst of the troubled sea of christendom, to steer one's course aright. So many conflicting voices fall on the ear. So many opposing views solicit our attention, men of God differ so in judgment, shades of opinion are so multiplied, that it seems impossible to reach a sound conclusion. We go to one man who, so far as we can judge, seems to have a single eye, and he tells us one thing; we go to another man who also seems to have a single eye, and he tells the very reverse. What, then, are we to think?

Well, one thing is certain, that our own eye is not single when we are running, in uncertainty and perplexity, from one man to another. The single eye is fixed on Christ alone, and thus the body is filled with light. The Israelite of old had not to run hither and thither to consult with his fellow as to the right way. Each had the same divine guide, namely, the pillar of cloud by day, and the pillar of fire by night. In a word, Jehovah Himself was the infallible Guide of each member of the congregation. They were not left to the guidance of the most intelligent, sagacious, or experienced man in the assembly; neither were they left to follow their own way; each was to follow the Lord. The silver trumpet announced to all alike the mind of God; and no one whose ear was open and attentive was left at any loss. The eye and the ear of each were to be directed to God *alone*, and not to a fellow-mortal. This was the secret of guidance in the trackless desert of old, and this is the secret of guidance in the vast moral wilderness through which God's redeemed are passing now. One man may say, Listen to me; and another may say, Listen to me; and a third may say, Let each one take his own way. The obedient heart says, in opposition to all, I must follow my Lord.

This makes all so simple. It will not, by any means, tender to foster a spirit of haughty independence; quite the reverse. The more I am taught to lean on God alone for guidance, the more I shall distrust and look off from myself; and this, assuredly, is not independence. True, it will deliver me from servile following of any man, but giving me to feel my responsibility to Christ alone; but this is precisely what is so much needed at the present moment. The more closely we examine the elements that are abroad in the professing Church, the more we shall be convinced of our personal need of this entire subjection to divine authority, which is only another name for "the fear of the Lord," or, "a single eye."

There is one brief sentence, in the opening of the Acts of the Apostles, which furnishes a perfect antidote to the self-will and the servile fear of man so rife around us, and that is, "We must obey God." What an utterance! "We must *obey*." This is the cure for self-will. "We must obey *God*." This is the cure for servile subjection to the commandments and doctrines of men. There must be obedience; but obedience to what? To God's authority, and to that alone. Thus the soul is preserved from the influence of infidelity on the one hand, and superstition on the other. Infidelity says, Do as you like. Superstition says, Do as man tells you. Faith says, "We must obey God."

Here is the holy balance of the soul in the midst of the conflicting and confounding influences around us in this our day. As a servant, I am to obey my Lord; as a child, I am to hearken to my Father's commandments. Nor am I the less to do this although my fellow-servants and my brethren may not understand me. I must remember that the immediate business of my soul is with God Himself.

> He before whom the elders bow,
> With Him is *all* my business now.

It is my privilege to be as sure that I have my Master's mind as to my path as that I have His Word for the security of my soul. If not, where am I? Is it not my privilege to have a single eye? Yes, surely. And what then? "A body full of light." Now, if my body is full of light, can my mind be full of perplexity? Impossible. The two things are wholly incompatible; and hence, when one is plunged "in dark uncertainty," it is very plain his eye is not single. He may seem very sincere, he may be very anxious to be guided aright; but he may rest assured there is the lack of a single eye—that indispensable prerequisite to divine guidance. The Word is plain, "If thine eye is single, thy whole body also is full of light."

God will ever guide the obedient, humble soul; but, on the other hand, if we do not walk according to the light communicated, we shall get into darkness. Light not acted upon becomes darkness, and oh, "how great is that darkness"! Nothing is more dangerous than tampering with the light which God gives. it must, sooner or later, lead to the most disastrous consequences. "Take heed, therefore, that the light which is in thee be not darkness." "Hear, ye, and give ear: be not proud; for the Lord hath spoken. Give glory to the Lord your God, before *He* cause darkness, and before your feet stumble on the dark mountains, and while ye look for light, *He* turn it into the shadow of death, and make it gross darkness" (Jer. 13:15-16).

This is deeply solemn. What a contrast between a man having a single eye, and a man not acting on the light which God has given him! The one has his body full of light; the other has his body full of darkness: the one has no part dark; the other is plunged in gross darkness: the one is a light-bearer for others; the other is a stumbling-block in the way. We know nothing more solemn than the judicial acting of God, in actually turning our light into darkness, because we have refused to act on the light which He has been pleased to impart.

Christian reader, art thou acting up to thy light? Has God sent a ray of light into thy soul? Has He shown thee something wrong in thy ways or associations? Art thou persisting in any line of action which conscience tells thee is not in full accordance with thy Master's will? Search and see. "Give glory to the Lord thy God." Act on the light. Do not hesitate. Think not of consequences. Obey, we beseech thee, the Word of thy Lord. This very moment, as thine eye scans these lines, let the purpose of thy soul be to depart from iniquity wherever thou findest it. Say not, Whither shall I go? What shall I do next? There is evil everywhere. It is only escaping from one evil to plunge into another. Say not these things; do not argue or reason; do not look at results; think not of what the world or the world-church will say of thee; rise above all these things, and tread the path of light—that path which shineth more and more unto the perfect day of glory.

Remember, God never gives light for two steps at a time. If He has given thee light for one step, then, in the fear and love of His Name, take that one step, and thou wilt assuredly get more light—yes, "more and more." But if there be the refusal to act, the light which is in thee will become gross darkness, thy feet will stumble on the dark mountains of error which lie on either side of the straight and narrow path of obedience; and thou wilt become a stumbling-block in the path of others.

Some of the most grievous stumbling-blocks that lie, at this moment, in the pathway of anxious inquirers are found in the persons of those who once seemed to possess the truth, but have turned from it. The light which was in them has become darkness, and oh, how great and how appalling is that darkness! How sad it is to see those who ought to be light-bearers, acting as a positive hindrance to young and earnest Christians! But let not young Christians be hindered by them. The way is plain. "The fear of the Lord, that is wisdom; and to depart from evil is understanding." Let each one hear and obey for himself the voice of the Lord. "My sheep hear My voice, and I know them, and they follow Me." The Lord be praised for this precious Word! It puts each one in the place of direct responsibility to Christ Himself; it tells us plainly what is *God's way*, and, just as plainly, *how to find it.*

GOD'S FULNESS FOR AN EMPTY VESSEL

1 Samuel 4 and 7

THE TWO CHAPTERS given above furnish a most impressive illustration of a principle which runs all through the inspired volume, namely, that the moment man takes his right place, God can meet him in perfect grace—free, sovereign, unqualified grace: the fulness of God waits on an empty vessel. This great principle shines everywhere from Genesis to Revelation. The word "principle" hardly expresses what is meant; it is too cold. We would speak of it as a grand, living, divine fact, which shines with heavenly lustre in the gospel of the grace of God and in the history of God's people collectively and individually, both in the Old and New Testament times.

But man must be in his right place. This is absolutely essential. It is only there he can get a right view of God. When man as he is, meets God as He is, there is a perfect answer to every question, a divine solution of every difficulty. It is from the standpoint of utter and hopeless ruin that man gets a full, clear, delivering view and sense of God's salvation. It is when man gets to the end of himself in every shape and form—his bad self and his good self, his guilty self and his righteous self—that he begins with a Saviour-God. This is true at the starting-post, and true all along the way. The fulness of God ever waits on an empty vessel. The great difficulty is to get the vessel empty: when that is done, the whole matter is settled, because the fulness of God can then flow in.

This surely is a grand, fundamental truth; and in the chapters which stand at the head of this paper we see it in its application to the Lord's earthly people of old. Let us turn to them for a moment.

In the opening of 1 Samuel 4 we find Israel defeated by the Philistines; but instead of humbling themselves before the Lord, in true contrition and self-judgment because of their terrible condition, and accepting their defeat as the just judgment of God, there is utter insensibility and hardness of heart.

"And when the people were come into the camp, the elders of Israel said, Wherefore hath the Lord smitten us to-day before the Philistines?" Now it is very evident from these words that the elders were not in their right place. The word "wherefore" would never have dropped from their lips had they but realized their moral condition. They would have known too well why it was. There was shameful sin in their midst—the vile conduct of Hophni and Phinehas. "Wherefore the sin of the young men was very great before the Lord; for men abhorred the offering of the Lord" (chap. 2:17).

But alas! the people had no true sense of their terrible condition, and, as a consequence, they had no true sense of the remedy. Hence they say, "Let us fetch the ark of the covenant of the Lord out of Shiloh unto us, that, when *it* cometh among us, *it* may save us out of the hand of our enemies." What a delusion! What utter blindness! There is no self-judgment, no confession of the dishonor done to the name and worship of the God of Israel, no looking to Jehovah in true brokenness and contrition of heart. No; there is the vain notion that the ark would save them out of the hand of their enemies.

"So the people sent to Shiloh, that they might bring from thence the ark of the covenant of the Lord of hosts, which dwelleth between the cherubim: and the two sons of Eli, Hophni and Phinehas, were there with the ark of the covenant of God." What a fearful condition of things! The ark of God associated with those ungodly men whose wickedness was about to bring down upon the whole nation the just judgment of a holy and righteous God. Nothing can be more dreadful, nothing more offensive to God, than the daring attempt to connect His name, His truth, with wickedness.

Moral evil, under any circumstances, is bad enough; but the attempt to combine moral evil with the name and service of Him who is holy and true, is the very highest and darkest form of wickedness, and can only bring down the heavy judgment of God. Those ungodly priests, the sons of Eli, had dared to defile the very precincts of the sanctuary with their abominations; and yet these were the men who accompanied the ark of God into the field of battle. What blindness and hardness of heart! That one sentence, "Hophni and Phinehas were there with the ark of the covenant of God," embodies in its brief compass the terrible reflection of Israel's moral condition.

"And when the ark of the covenant of the Lord came into the camp, *all Israel shouted with a great shout*, so that the earth rang again." How vain was the shout!—how hollow the boast!—how empty the pretension! Alas! it was followed, as must ever be the case, by humiliating defeat. "The Philistines fought, and Israel was smitten, and they fled every man into his tent: and there was a very great slaughter; for there fell of Israel thirty thousand footmen. And the ark of God was taken, and the two sons of Eli, Hophni and Phinehas, were slain."

What a condition of things! The priests slain; the ark taken; the glory departed. The ark in which they boasted, and on which they confidently built their hope of victory, was actually in the hands of the uncircumcised Philistines. All was gone. That one terrible fact—the ark of God in the house of Dagon—told the melancholy tale of Israel's complete failure and ruin. God must have reality, truth and holiness in those with whom He deigns to dwell. "Holiness becometh Thy house, O Lord, forever."

It was a privilege of the very highest order to have Jehovah dwelling in their midst; but it demanded holiness. He could not connect His name with unjudged sin. Impossible. It would be a denial of His nature, and God cannot deny Himself. He must have the place

where He dwells suited to His nature and character. "Be ye holy, for I am holy." This is a grand, fundamental truth, which must be tenaciously held and reverently confessed. It must never be surrendered.

But let us glance for a moment at the history of the ark in the land of the Philistines. It is at once solemn and instructive. Israel had signally failed and shamefully sinned. They had proved themselves wholly unworthy of the ark of the covenant of the Lord; and the Philistines had laid their uncircumcised hands upon it, and actually presumed to bring it into the house of their false god, as if the Lord God of Israel and Dagon could be in the same house! Blasphemous presumption! But the glory which had departed from Israel was vindicated in the darkness and solitude of the temple of Dagon.

God will be God, however His people may fail; and hence we see that when Israel had utterly failed to guard the ark of His testimony, and allowed it to pass into the hands of the Philistines,—when all was lost in man's hand,—then the glory of God shone out in power and splendor: Dagon fell, and the whole land of the Philistines was made to tremble beneath the hand of Jehovah. His presence was intolerable to them, and they sought to get rid of it as soon as possible. It was proved beyond all question to be utterly impossible that Jehovah and the uncircumcised could go on together. Thus it was, thus it is, and thus it ever must be. "What concord hath Christ with Belial? . . . And what agreement hath the temple of God with idols?" None whatever.

Let us now turn for a few moments to chap. 7. Here we find another condition of things altogether. Here we shall find something of the empty vessel, and, as is ever the case, the fulness of God waiting upon it. "And it came to pass, while the ark abode in Kirjath-jearim, that the time was long; for it was twenty years: and *all the house of Israel lamented after the Lord*." In chaps. 5 and 6 we see that the Philistines could not do *with* Jehovah. In chap. 7 we see that Israel could not do *without* Him. This is striking and instructive. The world cannot endure the very thought of the presence of God. We see this from the very moment of the fall, in Gen. 3. Man fled away from God ere God drove him out of Eden. He could not endure the divine presence. "I heard Thy voice in the garden, and I was afraid, because I was naked; and I hid myself."

Thus it has ever been, from that moment to the present. As some one has said, "If you could put an unconverted man into Heaven, he would get out of it as soon as possible." What a telling fact! How it stamps the whole human race, and accounts for any depth of moral pravity into which a member of that race may sink! If man cannot endure the presence of God, where is he fit for, and what is he capable of? Weighty and solemn questions!

But "all the house of Israel lamented after the Lord." Twenty long, dreary years had rolled on without the blessed sense of His presence; "And Samuel spake unto all the house of Israel, saying, If ye do return unto the Lord *with all your hearts*, then put away the strange gods, and Ashtaroth, from among you, and *prepare your hearts* unto the Lord, and serve Him *only*, and *He*"—not the ark—"will deliver you out of the hand of the Philistines. Then the children of Israel did put away Baalim and Ashtaroth, and served the Lord only. And Samuel said, Gather all Israel to Mizpeh, and I will pray for you unto the Lord. And they gathered together to Mizpeh, and drew water, and poured it out before the Lord, and fasted on that day, and said there, We have sinned against the Lord" (chap. 7:2-6.)

Here we have a different condition of things altogether from that presented in chap. 4. Here we see the empty vessel getting ready to receive the fulness of God. There is no hollow assumption, no looking to an outward form for salvation. All is reality, all heart-work here. Instead of the boastful shout, there is the outpoured water—the striking and expressive symbol of utter weakness and good-for-nothingness. In a word, man is taking his right place; and that, as we know, is the sure precursor of God taking His place. This great principle runs like a beauteous golden line all through the

divine volume, all through the history of God's people, all through the history of souls. It is wrapped up in that brief but comprehensive clause, "Repentance and remission of sins." Repentance is man's true place. Remission of sins is God's response. The former is the empty vessel; the latter, the fulness of God. When these meet, all is settled.

This is very strikingly presented in the scene now before us. Israel having taken their true place, God is free to act on their behalf. They had confessed themselves to be as water poured upon the ground—perfectly helpless, perfectly worthless. This was all they had to say for themselves, and this was enough. God can now enter the scene and make short work with the Philistines. "If God be for us, who can be against us?"

"And Samuel took a sucking lamb, and offered it for a burnt offering wholly unto the Lord: and Samuel cried unto the Lord for Israel; and the Lord heard him. And as Samuel was offering up the burnt offering, the Philistines drew near to battle against Israel"—How little they knew whom they were coming against, or who was about to meet them! "But the Lord thundered with a great thunder on that day upon the Philistines, and discomfited them; and they were smitten before Israel. . . . Then Samuel took a stone, and set it between Mizpeh and Shen, and called the name of it Eben-ezer (the stone of help), saying, Hitherto hath the Lord helped us."

What a contrast between Israel's boastful shout in chap. 4 and Jehovah's thunder in chap. 7! The former was human pretension; the latter, divine power. *That* was instantly followed by humiliating defeat; *this*, by splendid triumph. The Philistines knew nothing of what had taken place—the water poured out, the penitential cry, the offering up of the lamb, the priestly intercession. What could uncircumcised Philistines know about these precious realities? Just nothing. When the earth rang with Israel's pretentious shout, they could take cognizance of that. The men of the world can understand and appreciate self-assertion and self-confidence; but these are the very things that shut out God.

On the other hand, a broken heart, a contrite spirit, a lowly mind, are His delight. When Israel took the low place, the place of self-judgment and confession, then Jehovah's thunder was heard, and the host of the Philistines was scattered and confounded. The fulness of God ever waits on an empty vessel. Blessed, precious truth! May we enter more fully into its depth, fulness, power, and scope!

Ere closing this brief paper, I would just observe that 1 Sam. 4 and 7 remind us of the churches of Laodicea and Philadelphia, in Rev. 3. The former presents to us a condition which we should sedulously avoid; the latter, a condition which we should diligently and earnestly cultivate. In that, we see miserable self-complacency, and Christ left outside. In this, we see conscious weakness and nothingness, but Christ exalted, loved, and honored; His Word kept, and His Name prized.

And be it remembered that these things run on to the end. It is very instructive to see that the last four of the seven churches give us four phases of the Church's history right on to the end. In Thyatira, we find Romanism; in Sardis, Protestantism. In Philadelphia, as we have said, we have that condition of soul, that attitude of heart, which every true believer and every assembly of believers should diligently cultivate and faithfully exhibit. Laodicea, on the contrary, presents a condition of soul and an attitude of heart from which we should shrink with godly fear. Philadelphia is as grateful as Laodicea is loathsome to the heart of Christ. The former, He will make a pillar in the temple of His God; the latter, He will spew out of His mouth, and Satan will take it up and make it a cage of every unclean and hateful bird—Babylon! An awful consideration for all whom it may concern. And let us never forget that for any to pretend to be Philadelphia is really the spirit of Laodicea. Wherever you find pretension, assumption, self-assertion or self-complacency, there you have, in spirit and principle, Laodicea—from which may the good Lord deliver all His people!

Let us be content to be nothing and nobody in this scene of self-exaltation. Let it be our aim to walk in the shade, as far as human thoughts are concerned, yet never be out of the sunshine of our Father's countenance. In a word, let us ever bear in mind that *"the fulness of God ever waits on an empty vessel."*

CHRIST IN THE VESSEL

Mark 4:35-41

MAN'S EXTREMITY IS GOD'S opportunity." This is a very familiar saying. It often passes among us; and, no doubt, we fully believe it; but yet, when we find ourselves brought to *our* extremity, we are often very little prepared to count on *God's* opportunity. It is one thing to utter or hearken to a truth, and another thing to realize the power of that truth. It is one thing, when sailing over a calm sea, to speak of God's ability to keep us in the storm, and it is another thing altogether to prove that ability when the storm is actually raging around us. And yet God is ever the same. In the storm and in the calm, in sickness and in health, in pressure and in ease, in poverty and in abundance, "the same yesterday, and to-day, and forever"—the same grand reality for faith to lean upon, cling to and draw upon, at all times and under all circumstances.

But alas, we are unbelieving! Here lies the source of weakness and failure. We are perplexed and agitated, when we ought to be calm and confiding; we are casting about, when we ought to be counting on God; we are "beckoning to our partners," when we ought to be "looking unto Jesus." Thus it is we lose immensely, and dishonor the Lord in our ways. Doubtless there are few things for which we have to be more deeply humbled than our tendency to distrust the Lord when difficulties and trials present themselves; and assuredly we grieve the heart of Jesus by thus distrusting Him, for distrust must always wound a loving heart. Look, for example, at the scene between Joseph and his brethren in Gen. 50.

"And when Joseph's brethren saw that their father was dead, they said, Joseph will peradventure hate us, and will certainly requite us all the evil which we did unto him. And they sent a messenger unto Joseph, saying, Thy father did command before he died, saying, So shall ye say unto Joseph, Forgive, I pray thee now, the trespass of thy brethren, and their sin; for they did unto thee evil: and now, we pray thee, forgive the trespass of the servants of the God of thy father. And Joseph wept when they spake unto him."

It was a sad return for the love and tender care which Joseph had exercised towards them. How could they suppose that one who had so freely and fully forgiven them, and spared their lives when they were entirely in his power, would, after so many years of kindness, turn upon them in anger and revenge? It was indeed a grievous wrong, and it was no marvel that "Joseph wept when they spake unto him." What an answer to all their unworthy fear and dark suspicion! A flood of tears! Such is love! "And Joseph said unto them, Fear not: for am I in the place of God? But as for you, ye thought evil against me; but God meant it unto good, to bring to pass, as it is this day, to save much people alive. Now therefore, fear ye not: *I will nourish you, and your little ones.* And he comforted them, and spake kindly unto them."

Thus was it with the disciples on the occasion to which our paper refers. Let us meditate a little on the passage.

"And the same day, when the even was come, Jesus saith unto them, Let us pass over unto the other side. And when they had sent away the multitude, they took Him even

as He was in the ship; and there were also with Him other little ships. And there arose a great storm of wind, and the waves beat into the ship, so that it was now full. And He was in the hinder part of the ship, asleep on a pillow."

Here, then, we have an interesting and instructive scene. The poor disciples are brought to their extremity. They are at their wits' end. A violent storm—the ship full of water—the Master asleep. This was a trying moment indeed, and assuredly we, if we look at ourselves, need not marvel at the fear and agitation of the disciples. It is not likely that we should have done better had we been there. Still, we cannot but see wherein they failed. The narrative has been penned for our learning, and we are bound to study it, and seek to learn the lesson which it reads out to us.

There is nothing more absurd and irrational than unbelief when we come to look at it calmly. In the scene before us this absurdity is very apparent; for what could be more absurd than to suppose that the vessel could possibly sink with the Son of God on board? And yet this was what they feared. It may be said they did not just think of the Son of God at that moment. True, they thought of the storm, the waves, the filling vessel, and, judging after the manner of men, it seemed a hopeless case. Thus it is the unbelieving heart ever reasons. It looks only at the circumstances, and leaves God out. Faith, on the contrary, looks only at God, and leaves circumstances out.

What a difference! Faith delights in man's extremity, simply because it is God's opportunity. It delights in being "shut up" to God—in having the platform thoroughly cleared of the creature, in order that God may display His glory—in the multiplying of "empty vessels," in order that God may fill them. Such is faith. It would, we may surely say, have enabled the disciples to lie down and sleep beside their Master in the midst of the storm. Unbelief, on the other hand, rendered them uneasy; they could not rest themselves, and they actually aroused the blessed Lord out of His sleep by their unbelieving apprehensions. He, weary with incessant toil, was snatching a few moments' repose while the vessel was crossing the sea. He knew what fatigue was; He had come down into all our circumstances. He made Himself acquainted with all our feelings and all our infirmities, being in all points tempted like as we are, sin excepted.

He was found as a man in every respect, and as such He slept on a pillow, rocked by the waves of the sea. The storm and the billows beat upon the vessel, although the Creator was on board, in the person of that weary, sleeping Workman.

Profound mystery! The One who made the sea, and could hold the winds in His almighty grasp, lay sleeping in the hinder part of the ship, and allowed the sea and the wind to treat Him as unceremoniously as though He were an ordinary man. Such was the reality of the human nature of our blessed Lord. He was weary—He slept, being tossed on the bosom of that sea which His hands had made. O pause and meditate on this wondrous sight. Look closely, think upon it. We cannot expatiate upon the scene; we can only muse and worship.

But, as we have said, unbelief roused the blessed Lord out of His sleep. "They awake Him, and say unto Him, Master, *carest Thou not* that we perish?" What a question! "*Carest Thou not?*" How it must have wounded the sensitive heart of the Lord! How could they ever think that He was indifferent to their trouble and danger? How completely must they have lost sight of His love, to say nothing of His power, when they could bring themselves to say, "Carest Thou not?"

And yet, have we not in all this a mirror in which to see ourselves reflected? Assuredly we have. How often, in moments of pressure and trial, do our hearts conceive, if our lips do not utter the question, "Carest Thou not?" It may be we are laid on a bed of sickness and pain, and we know that one word from the God of all power and might could chase away the malady and raise us up; and yet the word is withheld. Or perhaps we are in need of temporal supplies, and we know that the silver and gold, and the cattle upon a thousand hills, belong to God—yea, that the

treasures of the universe are under His hand—and yet day after day rolls on, and our need is not supplied. In a word, we are passing through deep waters, in some way or another; the storm rages, wave after wave rolls over our tiny vessel, we are brought to our extremity, we are at our wits' end, and our hearts often feel ready to send up the terrible question, "Carest Thou not?" The thought of this is deeply humbling. To think of our grieving the loving heart of Jesus by our unbelief and suspicion should fill us with the deepest contrition.

And then the absurdity of unbelief! How can that One who gave His life for us—who left His glory and came down into this world of toil and misery and died a shameful death to deliver us from eternal wrath—how can such a One ever fail to care for us? But yet we are ready to doubt, or we grow impatient under the trial of our faith, forgetting that the very trial from which we so shrink and under which we so wince is far more precious than gold, for the former is an imperishable reality, whereas the latter must perish in the using. The more genuine faith is tried, the brighter it shines; and hence the trial, however severe, is sure to issue in praise and honor and glory to Him who not only implants the faith, but also passes it through the furnace and sedulously watches it therein.

But the poor disciples failed in the moment of trial. Their confidence gave way, they roused their Master from His slumber with that most unworthy question, "Carest Thou not that we perish?" Alas, what creatures we are! We are ready to forget ten thousand mercies in the presence of a single difficulty. David could say, "I shall one day perish by the hand of Saul"; and how did it turn out? Saul fell on mount Gilboa, and David was established on the throne of Israel. Elijah fled for his life at the threat of Jezebel; and what was the issue? Jezebel was dashed to pieces on the pavement, and Elijah was taken to Heaven in a chariot of fire. So here, the disciples thought they were going to be lost, with the Son of God on board; and what was the result? The storm was hushed into silence, and the sea became as glass, by that

Voice which of old had called worlds into existence. "And He arose and rebuked the wind, and said unto the sea, Peace, be still. And the wind ceased, and there was a great calm."

What a combination of grace and majesty is here! Instead of rebuking them for having disturbed His repose, He rebukes those elements which had terrified them. It was thus He replied to their question, "Carest Thou not?" Blessed Master! Who would not trust Thee? Who would not adore Thee for Thy patient grace and unupbraiding love?

There is something perfectly beautiful in the way in which our blessed Lord rises, without an effort, from the repose of perfect humanity into the activity of essential deity. As man, wearied with His work, He slept on a pillow; as God, He rises, and, with His almighty voice, hushes the storm and calms the sea.

Such was Jesus—very God and very man—and such He is now, ever ready to meet His people's need, to hush their anxieties and remove their fears. Oh that we trusted Him more simply! We have little idea of how much we lose by not leaning more on the arm of Jesus, day by day. We are so easily terrified. Every breath of wind, every wave, every cloud, agitates and depresses us. Instead of calmly lying down and reposing beside our Lord, we are full of terror and perplexity. Instead of using the storm as an occasion for trusting Him, we make it an occasion for doubting Him. No sooner does some trifling trouble arise than we think we are going to perish, although He assures us that He has numbered the very hairs of our head. Well may He say to us as He said to His disciples, "Why are ye so fearful? How is it that ye have no faith?"

It would indeed seem at times as though we had *no* faith. But oh, *His* tender love! He is ever near to shield and succor us, even though our unbelieving hearts are so ready to doubt His Word. He does not deal with us according to our poor thoughts of Him, but according to His own perfect love toward us. This is the solace and stay of our souls in passing across life's stormy sea homeward to our eternal rest. Christ is in the vessel. Let this ever suffice. Let us calmly rely on Him. May there ever be, at the very centre of our hearts, that deep repose which springs from real trust in Jesus! and then, though the storm rage and the sea run mountains high, we shall not be led to say, "Carest Thou not that we perish?" Is it possible we can perish with the Master on board? or can we ever think so with Christ in our hearts? May the Holy Spirit teach us to make a fuller, freer, bolder use of Christ! We really want this just now, and shall want it more and more. It must be Christ Himself, laid hold of and enjoyed in the heart by faith. Thus may it be to His praise and our abiding peace and joy!

We may just notice, in conclusion, the way in which the disciples were affected by the scene on which we have been dwelling. Instead of the calm worship of those whose faith had been answered, they manifest the amazement of those whose fears had been rebuked. "They feared exceedingly, and said one to another, What manner of man is this, that even the wind and the sea obey Him?" Surely they ought to have known Him better. Yes, and so should we.

PRAYER IN ITS PROPER PLACE

THERE IS A STRONG TENDENCY in the human mind to take a one-sided view of things. This should be carefully guarded against. It would ever be our wisdom to view things as God presents them to us, in His holy Word. We should put things where He puts them, and leave them there. Were this more faithfully attended to, the truth would be much more clearly understood, and souls much better instructed. There is a divinely appointed place for everything, and we should avoid putting right things in wrong places, just as carefully as we would avoid setting them aside altogether. The one may do as much damage as the other. Let any divine institution be taken out of its divinely-appointed place, and it must necessarily foil of its divinely-appointed end. This, I imagine, will hardly be questioned by any enlightened or well-regulated mind. It will be admitted on all hands, to be wrong to put things in any place but just where God intended them to be.

And in proportion to the importance of a right thing is the importance of having it in its right place. This remark holds good, in a special manner, with respect to the hallowed and most precious exercise of prayer. It is hard to imagine how any one, with the Word of God in his hand, could presume to detract from the value of prayer. It is one of the very highest functions, and most important privileges of the Christian life. No sooner has the new nature been communicated by the Holy Ghost, through faith in Christ, than it expresses itself in the sweet accents of prayer.

Prayer is the earnest breathing of the new man, drawn forth by the operation of the Holy Ghost, who dwells in all true believers. Hence, to find any one praying is to find him manifesting divine life in one of its most touching and beauteous characteristics, namely, dependence. There may be a vast amount of ignorance displayed in the prayer, both in its character and object; but the *spirit* of prayer is, unquestionably, divine. A child may ask for a great many foolish things; but, clearly, he could not ask for any thing if he had not life. The ability and desire to ask are the infallible proofs of life. No sooner had Saul of Tarsus passed from death unto life, than the Lord says of him, "*Behold he prayeth!*" (Acts 9) Doubtless he had, as "a Pharisee of the Pharisees," said many "long prayers"; but not until he "saw that Just One, and heard the voice of His mouth," could it be said of him, "behold, *he prayeth.*"

Saying prayers and praying are two totally different things. A self-righteous Pharisee may excel in the former; none but a converted soul can enjoy the latter. The spirit of prayer is the spirit of the new man; the language of prayer is the distinct utterance of the new life. The moment a spiritual babe is born into the new creation, it sends up its cry of dependence and of trust toward the Source of its birth. Who would dare to hush or hinder that cry? Let the babe be gently satisfied and encouraged, not ignorantly hindered or rudely silenced. The very cry which ignorance would seek to stifle, falls like sweetest music on the parent's ear. It is the proof of life. It evidences the existence of a new object around which the affections of a parent's heart may entwine themselves.

All this is plain enough. It commends itself to every renewed mind. The man who could think of hushing the accents of prayer must be wholly ignorant of the precious and beautiful mysteries of the new creation. The understanding of the praying one may need to be instructed; but oh! let not the spirit of prayer be quenched. Let the beams of divine revelation, in all their emancipating power, shine in upon the struggling conscience, but let not the breathings of the new life be interrupted.

The newly-converted soul may be in great darkness. The chilling mists of legalism may enwrap his spirit. He may not, as yet, be able to rest fully in Christ and His accomplished work. His awakened conscience may not, as yet, have found its peace-giving answer in the precious blood of Jesus. Doubts and fears may sorely beset him. He may not know about the important doctrine of the two natures, and the continual conflict between them. He is bowed down beneath the humiliating sense of indwelling sin, and sees not, as yet, the ample provision which redeeming love has made for that very thing, in the sacrifice and priesthood—the blood and advocacy of the Lord Jesus Christ. The joyous emotions which attended upon the first moments of his conversion may have passed away. The beams of the Sun of Righteousness may be hidden by the heavy clouds which arise from within and around him. It is not with him as in days past. He marvels at the sad change which has come over him, and well nigh doubts if he were ever converted at all.

Need we wonder that such an one should cry mightily to God? Yea, the wonder would be if he could do aught else. How, then, should we treat him? Should we teach him not to pray? God forbid. This would be to do the work of Satan, who, assuredly, hates prayer most cordially. To drop a syllable which could even be understood as making little of an exercise so entirely divine, would be to fly in the face of the entire book of God, to deny the very example of Christ, and hinder the utterance of the Holy Ghost in the new-born soul.

The Old and New Testament Scriptures literally teem with exhortations and encouragements to pray. To quote the passages would fill a volume. The blessed Master Himself has left His people an example as to the unceasing exercise of a spirit of prayer. He both prayed Himself and taught His disciples to pray. The same is true of the Holy Ghost in the apostles. (See the following passages; Luke 3:21; 6:12; 9:28-29; 11:1-13; 18:1-8; Acts 1:14; 4:31; Rom. 12:12; 15:30; Eph. 6:18; Phil. 4:6; Col. 4:2-4; 1 Thess. 5:17; 2 Thess. 3:1-2; 1 Tim. 2:1-3; Heb. 13:18; James 5:14-15.)

If my reader will look out and ponder the foregoing passages, he will have a just view of the place which prayer occupies in the Christian economy. He will see that disciples are exhorted to pray; and that it is only disciples who are so exhorted. He will see that prayer is a grand prominent exercise of the household of God, and that he must be of that household to engage in it. He will see that prayer is the undoubted utterance of the new life; and that the life therefore must be there to utter itself. He will see that prayer is an important part of the Christian's privilege; and that it enters in no wise in the foundation of the Christian's peace.

Thus, he will be able to put prayer in its proper place; and how important it is that it should be so put! How important it is that the anxious inquirer should see that the deep and solid foundations of his present and everlasting peace were laid in the work of the Cross, nineteen centuries ago! How important that the blood of Jesus should stand out before the soul in clear and bold relief, in its solitary grandeur, as the alone foundation of the sinner's rest! A soul may be earnestly seeking and crying for salvation, and all the while be ignorant of the great fact that it is ready to his hand—that he is actually commanded to accept a free, full, present, personal, and eternal salvation—that Christ has done all—that a brimming cup of salvation is set before him, which faith has only to take and drink for its everlasting satisfaction. The gospel of God's free grace points to the rent vail—the empty tomb—the occupied throne above (Matt. 28; Heb. 1 and 10). What do these things declare? What do they utter in the anxious sinner's ear? Salvation! salvation! The rent vail, the empty tomb, the occupied throne, all cry out, salvation!

Do you really want salvation? Then why not take it, as God's free gift? Are you looking to your own heart or to Christ's finished work for salvation? Is it needful, think you, to wait that God should do something more for your salvation? If so, then Christ's work were not finished; the ransom were not paid. But Christ said, *"It is finished,"* and God says, "I have found a ransom" (Job 33; John 19). And if *you* have to do, say, or think aught, to complete the work of salvation, then Christ would not be a whole, a perfect Saviour.

And, further, it would be a plain denial of Rom. 4:5, which says, "To him that *worketh not*, but believeth on Him that *justifieth the ungodly*, his faith is counted for righteousness." Take heed that you are not mixing up your poor prayers with the glorious work of redemption, completed by the Lamb of God on the cross. Prayer is most precious; but, remember, "without faith it is impossible to please God" (Heb. 11:6); and if you have faith, you have Christ; and having Christ, you have *all*. If you say you are crying for mercy, the Word of God points you to mercy's copious stream flowing from the finished sacrifice. You have all your anxious heart can want in Jesus, and He is God's free gift to you just as you are, where you are, *now*. If you had *to be* aught else but what you are, or *to go* anywhere else from where you are, then salvation would not be "by grace, through faith" (Eph. 2:8). If you are anxious to get salvation, and God desires you should have it, why need you be another moment without it? It is all ready. Christ died and rose again. The Holy Ghost testifies. The Word is plain. "*Only believe.*"

Oh, may the Spirit of God lead any anxious soul to find settled repose in Jesus. May He lead you to look away from all besides, straight to an all-sufficient atonement. May He give clearness of apprehension, and simplicity of faith to all; and may He

especially endow all who stand up to teach and preach with the ability "rightly to divide the word of truth," so that they not apply to the unregenerate sinner, or the anxious inquirer, such passages of Scripture as refer only to the established believer. Very serious damage is done both to the truth of God, and to the souls of men, by an unskilful division and application of the Word.

There must be spiritual life, before there can be spiritual action; and the *only* way to get spiritual life is by *believing* on the name of the Son of God* (John 1:12-13; 3:14-16, 36; 5:24; 20:31). If, therefore, the precepts of God's Word be applied to persons who have not the spiritual life to act in them, confusion must be the result. The precious privileges of the Christian are turned into a heavy yoke for the unconverted. A strange system of half-law half-gospel is propounded, whereby true Christianity is robbed of its characteristic glory, and the souls of men are plunged in mist and perplexity. There is urgent need for clearness in setting forth the true ground of a sinner's peace. When souls are convicted of sin, and have life, but not liberty, they want a full, clear, unclouded gospel. The claims of a divinely-awakened conscience can only be answered by the blood of the Cross. If anything, no matter what, be added to the finished work of Christ, the soul must be filled with doubt and darkness.

May God grant us to know more fully the true place and value of simple faith in the Lord Jesus Christ, and of earnest prayer in the Holy Ghost.

---

* When the jailer at Philippi inquired of Paul and Silas, "What must I do to be saved?" they simply replied, "*Believe* on the Lord Jesus Christ and thou shalt be saved, and thy house" (Acts 16:30-31). It would, surely, be well if this method of dealing with an anxious inquirer were more faithfully adopted.

EPAPHRAS
THE SERVICE OF PRAYER

Colossians 4:12

THERE IS A VERY STRIKING difference between the inspired records of the people of God and all human biographies. The former may truly be said to be "*much in little*"; while many of the latter may as truly be said to be "*little in much*." The history of one of the Old Testament saints—a history stretching over a period of 365 years—is summed up in two short clauses—"Enoch walked with God; and he was not, for God took him" (Gen. 5:24). How brief! but yet how full, how comprehensive! How many volumes would man have filled with the records of such a life! And yet, what more could he have said? To walk with God comprehends all that could possibly be said of any one.

A man may travel round the globe; he may preach the gospel in every clime; he may suffer in the cause of Christ; he may feed the hungry, clothe the naked, visit the sick; he may read, write, print and publish; in short, he may do all that ever man could or did do; and yet it may be all summed up in that brief clause, "He walked with God." And right well it will be for him if it can be so summed up. One may do nearly all that has been enumerated and yet never walk with God one hour; yea, one may not even know the meaning of a walk with God. The thought of this is deeply solemnizing and practical. It should lead us to the earnest cultivation of the hidden life, without which the most showy services will prove to be but mere flash and smoke.

There is something peculiarly touching in the mode in which the name of Epaphras is introduced to our notice in the New Testament. The allusions to him are very brief, but very pithy. He seems to have been the very stamp of man which is so much needed at the present moment. His labors, so far as the inspired penman has recorded them, do not seem to have been very showy or attractive. They were not calculated to meet the human eye or elicit human praise. But oh, they were most precious labors— peerless, priceless labors! They were the labors of the closet, labors within the closed door, labors in the sanctuary, labors without which all beside must prove barren and worthless. He is not placed before us by the sacred biographer as a powerful preacher, a laborious writer, a great traveler, which he may have been, and which are all truly valuable in their place.

The Holy Ghost, however, has not told us that Epaphras was any of the three; but then, He has placed this singularly interesting character before us in a manner calculated to stir the depths of our moral and spiritual being. He has presented him to us as *a man of prayer*—earnest, fervent, agonizing prayer; prayer not for himself, but for others. Let us harken to the inspired testimony:

"Epaphras, who is one of you, a servant of Christ, saluteth you, always laboring fervently [agonizing] for you in prayers, that ye may stand perfect and complete in all the will of God. For I bear him record, that he hath a great zeal for you, and them that are in Laodicea, and them in Hierapolis" (Col. 4:12-13). Such was Epaphras! Would there were hundreds like him in this our day! We are thankful for preachers, thankful for writers, thankful for travelers in the cause of Christ; but we want men of prayer, men of the closet, men like Epaphras.

We are happy to see men on their feet preaching Christ; happy to see them able to ply the pen of a ready writer in the noble cause; happy to see them making their way, in the true evangelistic spirit, into "the regions beyond"; happy to see them, in the true pastoral spirit, going again and again to visit their brethren in every city. God forbid that we should undervalue or speak disparagingly of such honorable services; yea, we prize them more highly than words could convey.

But then, at the back of all we want a spirit of prayer—fervent, agonizing, persevering prayer. Without this, nothing can prosper. A prayerless man is a sapless man. A prayerless preacher is a profitless preacher. A prayerless writer will send forth barren pages. A prayerless evangelist will do but little good. A prayerless pastor will have but little food for the flock. We want men of prayer, men like Epaphras, men whose closet walls witness their agonizing labors. These are, unquestionably, the men for the present moment.

There are immense advantages attending the labors of the closet, advantages quite peculiar, advantages for those who engage in them, and advantages for those who are the subjects of them. They are quiet, unobtrusive labors. They are carried on in retirement, in the hallowed, soul-subduing solitude of the divine presence, outside the range of mortal vision.

How little would the Colossians have known of the loving, earnest labors of Epaphras had the Holy Ghost not mentioned them! It is possible that some of them might have deemed him deficient in zealous care on their behalf: it is probable that there were persons then, as there are those now, who would measure a man's care or sympathy by his visits or letters. This would be a false standard. They should see him on his knees to know the amount of his care and sympathy. A love of travel *might* take me from London to Edinburgh to visit the brethren. A love of scribbling might lead me to write letters by every mail. Naught save a love for souls, a love for Christ, could ever lead me to agonize as Epaphras did, on behalf of the people of God, "that they may stand perfect and complete in all the will of God."

Again, the precious labors of the closet demand no special gift, no peculiar talents, no preeminent mental endowments Every Christian can engage in them. A man may not have the ability to preach, teach, write, or travel; but every man can pray. One sometimes hears of a *gift* of prayer. It is not a pleasant expression. It falls gratingly on the ear. It often means a mere fluent utterance of certain known truths which the memory retains and the lips give forth. This is poor work to be at. This was not the way with Epaphras. This is not what we want and long for. We want a real *spirit* of prayer. We want a spirit that enters into the present need of the Church, and bears that need in persevering, fervent, believing intercession before the throne of grace. This spirit may be exercised at all times, and under all circumstances. Morning, noon, eventide, or midnight will answer for the closet laborer.

The heart can spring upward to the throne in prayer and supplication at any time. Our Father's ear is ever open, His presence-chamber is ever accessible. Come when or with what we may, He is always ready to hear, ready to answer. He is the Hearer, the Answerer and the Lover of importunate prayer. He Himself has said, "Ask ... Seek ... Knock"; "Men ought *always* to pray, and not to faint"; "All things whatsoever ye shall ask in prayer, believing, ye shall receive"; "If any man lack wisdom, let him ask of God." These words are of universal application. They are intended for all God's children. The feeblest child of God can pray, can watch, can get an answer, and return thanks.

Furthermore, nothing is so calculated to give one a deep interest in people as the habit of praying constantly for them. Epaphras would be intensely interested in the Christians at Colosse, Laodicea, and Hierapolis. His interest made him pray, and his prayers made him interested. The more we are interested for any one, the more we shall pray for him; and the more we pray, the more interested we become. Whenever we are drawn out in prayer for people, we are sure to rejoice in their growth and prosperity. So, also, in reference to the unconverted. When we are led to wait on God about them, their conversion is looked for with the deepest anxiety, and hailed, when it comes, with unfeigned thankfulness. The thought of this should stir us up to imitate Epaphras, on whom the Holy Ghost has bestowed the honorable epithet of "a servant of Christ," in connection with his fervent prayers for the people of God.

Finally, the highest inducement that can be presented to cultivate the spirit of Epaphras is the fact of its being so directly in unison with the spirit of Christ. This is the most elevated motive. Christ is engaged on behalf of His people. He desires that they should "stand perfect and complete in all the will of God;" and those who are led forth in prayer in reference to this object are privileged to enjoy high communion with the great Intercessor. How marvelous that poor, feeble creatures down here should be permitted to pray about that which engages the thoughts and interests of the Lord of glory! What a powerful link there was between the heart of Epaphras and the heart of Christ when the former was laboring for his brethren at Colosse!

Let us ponder the example of Epaphras. Let us imitate it. Let us fix our eyes on some Colosse or other, and labor fervently in prayer for the Christians therein. The present is a deeply solemn moment. Oh for men like Epaphras—men who are willing to labor on their knees for the cause of Christ, or to wear, if it should be so, the noble bonds of the gospel. Such was Epaphras. We see him as a man of prayer (Col. 4:12), and as a companion in bonds with the devoted apostle of the Gentiles (Philem. 23).

May the Lord stir up amongst us a spirit of earnest prayer and intercession. May He raise up many of those who shall be cast in the same spiritual mould as Epaphras. These are the men for the present need.

PRAYER AND THE PRAYER MEETING

Part 1

IN CONSIDERING the deeply important subject of prayer, two things claim our attention; first, the moral basis of prayer; secondly, its moral conditions.

1. The basis of prayer is set forth in such words as the following: "*If ye abide in Me, and My words abide in you,* ye shall ask what ye will, and it shall be done unto you" (John 15:7). Again, "Beloved, *if our heart condemn us not,* then have we confidence toward God. And whatsoever we ask, we receive of Him, *because we keep His commandments,* and do those things that are pleasing in His sight" (1 John 3:21-22). So also, when the blessed apostle seeks an interest in the prayers of the saints, he sets forth the moral basis of his appeal—"Pray for us; *for we trust we have a good conscience,* in all things willing to live honestly" (Heb. 13:18).

From these passages, and many more of like import, we learn that, in order to have effectual prayer, there must be an obedient heart, an upright mind, a good conscience. If the soul be not in communion with God—if it be not abiding in Christ—if it be not ruled by His holy commandments—if the eye be not single, how could we possibly look for answers to our prayers? We should, as the apostle James says, be "asking amiss, that we may consume it upon our lusts." How could God, as a holy Father, grant such petitions? Impossible.

How very needful, therefore, it is to give earnest heed to the moral basis on which our prayers are presented. How could the apostle have asked the brethren to pray for him, if he had not a good conscience, a single eye, an upright mind—the moral persuasion that in all things he really wished to live honestly? We may safely assert, he could do no such thing.

But may we not often detect ourselves in the habit of lightly and formally asking others to pray for us? It is a very common formulary amongst us—"Remember me in your prayers," and most surely nothing can be more blessed or precious than to be borne upon the hearts of God's dear people in their approaches to the mercy-seat; but do we sufficiently attend to the moral basis? When we say, "Brethren pray for us," can we add, as in the presence of the Searcher of hearts, "For we trust we have a good conscience, in all things willing to live honestly"? and when we ourselves bow before the throne of grace, is it with an uncondemning heart—an upright mind—a single eye—a soul really abiding in Christ, and keeping His commandments?

These are searching questions. They go right to the very centre of the heart—down to the very roots and moral springs of our being. But it is well to be thoroughly searched—searched in reference to every thing, but especially in reference to prayer. There is a terrible amount of unreality in our prayers—a sad lack of the moral basis—a vast amount of "asking amiss."

Hence, the want of power and efficacy in our prayers—hence, the formality—the routine—yea, the positive hypocrisy. The Psalmist says, "If I regard iniquity in my heart, the Lord will not hear me." How solemn this is! Our God will have reality; He desireth truth in the inward parts. He, blessed be His name, is real with us, and He will have us real with Him. He will have us coming before Him as we really are, and with what we really want.

How often, alas! it is otherwise, both in private and in public! How often are our prayers more like orations than petitions—more like statements of doctrine than utterances of need! It seems, at times, as though we meant to explain principles to God, and give Him a large amount of information.

These are the things which cast a withering influence over our prayer-meetings, robbing them of their freshness, their interest, and their value. Those who really know what prayer is—who feel its value, and are conscious of their need of it, attend the prayer-meeting in order to pray, not to hear orations, lectures, and expositions from men on their knees. If they want lectures, they can attend at the lecture-hall or the preaching-room; but when they go to the prayer-meeting, it is to pray. To them, the prayer-meeting is the place of expressed need and expected blessing—the place of expressed weakness and expected power.

Such is their idea of "the place where prayer is wont to be made"; and therefore when they flock thither, they are not disposed or prepared to listen to long preaching prayers, which would be deemed barely tolerable if delivered from the desk, but which are absolutely insufferable in the shape of prayer.

We write plainly, because we feel the need of great plainness of speech. We deeply feel our want of reality, sincerity, and truth in our prayers and prayer-meetings. Not unfrequently it happens that what we call prayer is not prayer at all, but the fluent utterance of certain known and acknowledged truths and principles, to which one has listened so often that the reiteration becomes tiresome in the extreme. What can be more painful than to hear a man on his knees explaining principles and unfolding doctrines? The question forces itself upon us. "Is the man speaking to God, or to us?" If to God, surely nothing can be more irreverent or profane than to attempt to explain things to Him; but if to us, then it is not prayer at all, and the sooner we rise from the attitude of prayer the better, inasmuch as the speaker will do better on his legs and we in our seats.

And, having referred to the subject of attitude, we would very lovingly call attention to a matter which, in our judgment, demands a little serious consideration; we allude to the habit of sitting during the holy and solemn exercise of prayer. We are fully aware, of course, that the grand question in prayer is, to have the *heart* in a right attitude. And further, we know, and would ever bear in mind, that many who attend our prayer-meetings are aged, infirm, and delicate people, who could not possibly kneel for any length of time—perhaps not at all. Then again, it often happens that, even where there is not physical weakness, and where there would be real desire to kneel down, as feeling it to be the proper attitude, yet, from actual want of space, it is impossible to change one's position.

All these things must be taken into account; but, allowing as broad a margin as possible in which to insert these modifying clauses, we must still hold to it that there is a very deplorable lack of reverence in many of our public reunions for prayer. We frequently observe young men, who can neither plead physical weakness nor want of space, sitting through an entire prayer-meeting. This, we confess, is offensive, and we cannot but believe it grieves the Spirit of the Lord. We ought to kneel down when we can; it expresses reverence and prostration. The blessed Master "kneeled down and prayed" (Luke 22:41). His apostle did the same, as we read in Acts 20:36, "When he had thus spoken, he kneeled down and prayed with them all."

And is it not comely and right so to do? Assuredly it is. And can aught be more unseemly than to see a number of people sitting, lolling, lounging, and gaping about while prayer is being offered? We consider it perfectly shocking, and we do here most earnestly beseech all the Lord's people to give this matter their solemn consideration, and to endeavor, in every possible way, both by precept and example, to promote the godly habit of kneeling at our prayer-meetings. No doubt those who take part in the meeting would greatly aid in this matter by short and fervent prayers; but of this, more hereafter.

Part 2

We shall now proceed to consider, in the light of holy Scripture, the moral conditions or attributes of prayer. There is nothing like having the authority of the divine Word for every thing in the entire range of our practical Christian life. Scripture must be our one grand and conclusive referee in all our questions. Let us never forget this.

What, then, saith the Scripture as to the necessary moral conditions of prayer? Turn to Matthew 18:19—"Again I say unto you, that *if two of you shall agree* on earth as touching any thing that they shall ask, it shall be done for them of My Father which is in heaven."

Here we learn that one necessary condition of our prayers is, *unanimity*—cordial agreement—thorough oneness of mind. The true force of the words is, "If two of you shall symphonize"—shall make one common sound. There must be no jarring note, no discordant element.

If, for example, we come together to pray about the progress of the gospel—the conversion of souls, we must be of one mind in the matter—we must make one common sound before our God. It will not do for each to have some special thought of his own to carry out. We must come before the throne of grace in holy harmony of mind and spirit, else we cannot claim an answer, on the ground of Matthew 18:19.

Now, this is a point of immense moral weight. Its importance, as bearing upon the tone and character of our prayer-meetings, cannot possibly be overestimated. It is very questionable indeed whether any of us have given sufficient attention to it. Have we not to deplore the objectless character of our prayer-meetings? Ought we not to come together more with some definite object on our hearts, as to which we are going to wait together upon God? We read in the first chapter of Acts, in reference to the early disciples, "These all continued *with one accord* in prayer and supplication, with the women, and Mary the mother of Jesus, and with His brethren."* And again, in the second chapter, we read, "When the day of Pentecost was fully come, they were *all with one accord in one place.*"

They were waiting, according to our Lord's instructions, for the promise of the Father—the gift of the Holy Ghost. They had the sure word of promise. The Comforter was, without fail, to come; but this, so far from dispensing with prayer, was the very ground of its blessed exercise. They prayed; they prayed in one place; they prayed with one accord. They were thoroughly agreed. They all, without exception, had one definite object before their hearts. They were waiting for the promised Spirit; they continued to wait; and they waited with one accord, until He came. Men and women, absorbed with one object, waited in holy concord, in happy

---

* How interesting to find "Mary the mother of Jesus" named here, as being at the prayer-meeting! What would she have said if any one had told her that millions of professing Christians would yet be praying to her?

symphony—waited on, day after day, earnestly, fervently, harmoniously waited until they were indued with the promised power from on high.

Should not we go and do likewise? Is there not a sad lack of this "one accord," "one place" principle in our midst? True it is, blessed be God, we have not to ask for the Holy Ghost to come—He has come; we have not to ask for the outpouring of the Spirit,—He has been poured out: but we have to ask for the display of His blessed power in our midst. Supposing our lot is cast in a place where spiritual death and darkness reign. There is not so much as a single breath of life—not a leaf stirring. The Heaven above seems like brass; the earth beneath, iron. Such a thing as a conversion is never heard of. A withering formalism seems to have settled down upon the entire place. Powerless profession, dead routine, stupefying mechanical religiousness, are the order of the day. What is to be done? Are we to allow ourselves to fall under the fatal influence of the surrounding malaria? are we to yield to the paralyzing power of the atmosphere that inwraps the place? Assuredly not.

If not, what then? Let us, even if there be but two who really feel the condition of things, get together, with one accord, and pour out our hearts to God. Let us wait on Him, in holy concord, with united, firm purpose, until He send a copious shower of blessing upon the barren spot. Let us not fold our arms and vainly say, "The time is not come." Let us not yield to that pernicious offshoot of a one-sided theology, which is rightly called fatalism, and say, "God is sovereign, and He works according to His own will. We must wait His time. Human effort is in vain. We cannot get up a revival. We must beware of mere excitement."

All this seems very plausible; and the more so because there is a measure of truth in it; indeed it is all true, so far as it goes: but it is only one side of the truth. It is truth, and nothing but the truth; but it is not *the whole truth*. Hence its mischievous tendency. There is nothing more to be dreaded than one-sided truth; it is far more dangerous than positive, palpable error. Many an earnest soul has been stumbled and turned completely out of the way by one-sided or misapplied truth. Many a true-hearted and useful workman has been chilled, repulsed, and driven out of the harvest-field by the injudicious enforcement of certain doctrines having a measure of truth, but not *the* full truth of God.

Nothing, however, can touch the truth, or weaken the force of Matthew 18:19. It stands in all its blessed fullness, freeness, and preciousness before the eye of faith; its terms are clear and unmistakable. "If two of you shall agree upon earth, as touching *any thing* that they shall ask, it shall be done for them of My Father which is in heaven." Here is our warrant for coming together to pray for any thing that may be laid on our hearts. Do we mourn over the coldness, barrenness, and death around us? Are we discouraged by the little apparent fruit from the preaching of the gospel—the lack of power in the preaching itself, and the total absence of practical result? Are our souls cast down by the barrenness, dullness, heaviness, and low tone of all our reunions, whether at the table of our Lord, before the mercy-seat, or around the fountain of holy Scripture?

What are we to do? Fold our arms in cold indifference? give up in despair? or give vent to complaining, murmuring, fretfulness, or irritation? God forbid! What then? Come together, "with one accord in one place"; get down on our faces before our God, and pour out our hearts, as the heart of one man, pleading Matthew 18:19.

This, we may rest assured, is the grand remedy—the unfailing resource. It is perfectly true that "God is sovereign," and this is the very reason why we should wait on Him; perfectly true that "human effort is in vain," and that is the very reason for seeking divine power; perfectly true that "we cannot get up a revival," and that is the very reason for seeking to get it *down*; perfectly true that "we must beware of mere excitement"; equally true that we must beware of coldness, deadness, and selfish indifference.

The simple fact is, there is no excuse whatever—so long as Christ is at the right hand of God—so long as God the Holy Ghost is in our midst and in our hearts—so long as we have the Word of God in our hands—so long as Matthew 18:19 shines before our eyes—there is, we repeat, no excuse whatever for barrenness, deadness, coldness, and indifference—no excuse for heavy and unprofitable meetings—no excuse whatever for lack of freshness in our reunions or of fruitfulness in our service. Let us wait on God, in holy concord, and the blessing is sure to come.

Part 3

If we turn to Matthew 21: 22, we shall find another of the essential conditions of effectual prayer. "And all things whatsover ye shall ask in prayer, *believing,* ye shall receive." This is a truly marvelous statement. It opens the very treasury of Heaven to faith. There is absolutely no limit. Our blessed Lord assures us that we shall receive whatsoever we ask in simple faith.

The apostle James, under the inspiration of the Holy Ghost, gives us a similar assurance in reference to the matter of asking for wisdom. "If any of you lack wisdom, let him ask of God, that *giveth to all liberally,* and upbraideth not; and it shall be given him. But"—here is the moral condition—"let him ask *in faith, nothing wavering.* For he that wavereth is like a wave of the sea, driven with the wind and tossed. For let not that man think that he shall obtain any thing of the Lord."

From both these passages we learn that if our prayers are to have an answer, they must be prayers of faith. It is one thing to utter words in the form of prayer, and another thing altogether to pray in simple faith, in the full, clear, and settled assurance that we shall have what we are asking for. It is greatly to be feared that many of our so-called prayers never go beyond the ceiling of the room. In order to reach the throne of God, they must be borne on the wings of faith, and proceed from hearts united and minds agreed, in holy purpose, to wait on our God for the things which we really require.

Now, the question is, are not our prayers and prayer-meetings sadly deficient on this point? Is not the deficiency manifest from the fact that we see so little result from our prayers? Ought we not to examine ourselves as to how far we really understand these two conditions of prayer, namely, unanimity and confidence? If it be true—and it is true, for Christ has said it—that two persons agreed to ask in faith can have whatsoever they ask, why do we not see more abundant answers to our prayers? Must not the fault be in us?—are we not deficient in concord and confidence?

Our Lord, in Matthew 18:19, comes down, as we say, to the very smallest plurality—the smallest congregation—even to "two"; but of course the promise applies to dozens, scores, or hundreds. The grand point is, to be thoroughly agreed and fully persuaded that we shall get what we are asking for. This would give a different tone and character altogether to our reunions for prayer. It would make them very much more real than our ordinary prayer-meeting, which, alas! alas! is often poor, cold, dead, objectless, and desultory, exhibiting any thing but cordial agreement and unwavering faith.

How vastly different it would be if our prayer-meetings were the result of a cordial agreement on the part of two or more believing souls, to come together and wait upon God for a certain thing, and to persevere in prayer until they receive an answer! How little we see of this! We attend the prayer-meeting from week to week—and very right we should—but ought we not to be exercised before God as to how far we are agreed in reference to the object or objects which are to be laid before the throne? The answer to this question links itself on to another of the moral conditions of prayer.

Let us turn to Luke 11. "And He said unto them, 'Which of you shall have a friend, and shall go unto him at midnight, and say unto him, Friend, lend me three loaves; for a friend of mine in his journey is come to me, and I have nothing to set before him? And he from within shall answer and say, Trouble me not; the door is now shut, and my children are with me in bed; I cannot rise and give thee. I say unto you, though he will not rise and give him because he is his friend, yet because of his *importunity* he will rise and give him as many as he needeth. And I say unto you, Ask, and it shall be given you; seek, and ye shall find; knock, and it shall be opened unto you. For every one that asketh receiveth; and he that seeketh findeth: and to him that knocketh it shall be opened' " (ver. 5-10).

These words are of the very highest possible importance, inasmuch as they contain part of our Lord's reply to the request of His disciples, "Lord, teach us to pray." Let no one imagine for a moment that we would dare to take it upon ourselves to teach people how to pray. God forbid! Nothing is further from our thoughts. We are merely seeking to bring the souls of our readers into direct contact with the Word of God—the veritable sayings of our blessed Lord and Master—so that, in the light of those sayings, they may judge for themselves as to how far our prayers and our prayer-meetings come up to the divine standard.

What, then, do we learn from Luke 11? what are the moral conditions which it sets before us? In the first place, it teaches us to be *definite* in our prayers. "Friend, lend me three loaves." There is a positive need felt and expressed; there is the one thing before the mind and on the heart, and to this one thing he confines himself. It is not a long, rambling, desultory statement about all sorts of things: it is distinct, direct, and pointed—I want three loaves, I cannot do without them, I must have them, I am shut up, the case is urgent, the time of night—all the circumstances give definiteness and earnestness to the appeal. He cannot wander from the one point, "Friend, lend me three loaves."

No doubt it seems a very untoward time to come—"midnight." Every thing looks discouraging. The friend has retired for the night, the door is shut, his children are with him in bed, he cannot rise. All this is very depressing; but still the definite need is pressed: he must have the three loaves.

Now, we cannot but judge that there is a great practical lesson here which may be applied, with immense profit, to our prayers and our prayer-meetings. Must we not admit that our reunions for prayer suffer sadly from long, rambling, desultory prayers? Do

we not frequently give utterance to a whole host of things of which we do not really feel the need, and which we have no notion of waiting for at all? Should we not sometimes be taken very much aback were the Lord to appear to us at the close of our prayer-meeting and ask us, What do you really want Me to give or to do?

We feel most thoroughly persuaded that all this demands our serious consideration. We believe it would impart great earnestness, freshness, glow, depth, reality, and power to our prayer-meetings were we to attend with something definite on our hearts, as to which we could invite the fellowship of our brethren. Some of us seem to think it necessary to make one long prayer about all sorts of things—many of them very right and very good, no doubt—but the mind gets bewildered by the multiplicity of subjects. How much better to bring some one object before the throne, earnestly urge it, and pause, so that the Holy Spirit may lead out others, in like manner, either for the same thing or something else equally definite.

Long prayers are often wearisome; indeed, in many cases, they are a positive infliction. It will perhaps be said that we must not prescribe any time to the Holy Spirit. True indeed; away from us be the thought! Who would venture upon such a piece of daring blasphemy? We are simply comparing what we find in Scripture (where their brief pointedness is characteristic—see Matt. 6; John 17; Acts 4:24-30; Eph. 1; 3; etc.) with what we too often—not always, thank God!—find in our prayer-meetings.

Let it, then, be distinctly borne in mind that "long prayers" are not the rule in Scripture. They are referred to in Mark 12:40, etc., in terms of withering disapproval. Brief, fervent, pointed prayers impart great freshness and interest to the prayer-meeting; but on the other hand, as a general rule, long and desultory prayers exert a most depressing influence upon all.

But there is another very important moral condition set forth in our Lord's teaching in Luke 11, and that is, "*importunity*." He tells us that the man succeeds in gaining his object simply by his importunate earnestness. He is not to be put off; he must get the three loaves. Importunity prevails even where the claims of friendship prove inoperative. The man is bent on his object; he has no alternative. There is a demand, and he has nothing to meet it—"I have nothing to set before my traveling friend." In short, he will not take a refusal.

Now, the question is, how far do we understand this great lesson? It is not, blessed be God, that He will ever answer us "from within." He will never say to us, "Trouble me not"—"I cannot rise and give thee." He is ever our true and ready "Friend"—"a cheerful, liberal, and unupbraiding Giver." All praise to His holy name! Still, He encourages importunity, and we need to ponder His teaching. There is a sad lack of it in our prayer-meetings. Indeed, it will be found that in proportion to the lack of definiteness is the lack of importunity. The two go very much together. Where the thing sought is as definite as the "three loaves," there will generally be the importunate asking for it, and the firm purpose to get it.

The simple fact is, we are too vague and, as a consequence, too indifferent in our prayers and prayer-meetings. We do not seem like people *asking for what they want, and waiting for what they ask*. This is what destroys our prayer-meetings, rendering them pithless, pointless, powerless; turning them into teaching or talking-meetings, rather than deep-toned, earnest prayer-meetings. We feel convinced that the whole Church of God needs to be thoroughly aroused in reference to this great question; and this conviction it is which compels us to offer these hints and suggestions, with which we are not yet done.

Part 4

The more deeply we ponder the subject which has been for some time engaging our attention, and the more we consider the state of the entire Church of God, the more convinced we are of the urgent need of a thorough awakening every where in reference to the question of prayer. We cannot—nor do we desire to—shut our eyes

to the fact that deadness, coldness, and barrenness seem, as a rule, to characterize our prayer-meetings. No doubt we may find here and there a pleasing exception, but speaking generally, we do not believe that any sober, spiritual person will call in question the truth of what we state, namely, that the tone of our prayer-meetings is fearfully low, and that it is absolutely imperative upon us to inquire seriously as to the cause.

In the papers already put forth on this great, all-important, and deeply practical subject, we have ventured to offer to our readers a few hints and suggestions. We have briefly glanced at our lack of confidence, our failure in cordial unanimity, the absence of definiteness and importunity. We have referred in plain terms—and we must speak plainly if we are to speak at all—to many things which are felt by all the truly spiritual amongst us to be not only trying and painful, but thoroughly subversive of the real power and blessing of our reunions for prayer. We have spoken of the long, tiresome, desultory, preaching prayers which, in some cases, have become so perfectly intolerable, that the Lord's dear people are scared away from the prayer-meetings altogether. They feel that they are only wearied, grieved, and irritated, instead of being refreshed, comforted, and strengthened; and hence they deem it better to stay away. They judge it to be more profitable, if they have an hour to spare, to spend it in the privacy of their closet, where they can pour out their hearts to God in earnest prayer and supplication, than to attend a so-called prayer-meeting, where they are absolutely wearied out with incessant, powerless, hymn-singing, or long preaching prayers.

Now, we more than question the rightness of such a course. We seriously doubt if this be at all the way to remedy the evils of which we complain. Indeed, we are thoroughly persuaded it is not. If it be right to come together for prayer and supplication—and who will question the rightness?—then surely it is not right for any one to stay away merely because of the feebleness, failure, or even the folly of some who may take part in the meeting. If all the really spiritual members were to stay away on such a ground, what would become of the prayer-meeting? We have very little idea of how much is involved in the elements which compose a meeting. Even though we may not take part audibly in the action, yet if we are there in a right spirit—there really to wait upon God, we marvelously help the tone of a meeting.

Besides, we must remember that we have something more to do in attending a meeting than to think of our own comfort, profit, and blessing. We must think of the Lord's glory; we must seek to do His blessed will, and try to promote the good of others in every possible way; and neither of these ends, we may rest assured, can be attained by our deliberately absenting ourselves from the place where prayer is wont to be made.

We repeat, and with emphasis, the words, "*deliberately* absenting ourselves"—staying away because we are not profited by what takes place there. Many things may crop up to hinder our being present—ill-health, domestic duties, lawful claims upon our time if we are in the employment of others—all these things have to be taken into account; but we may set it down as a fixed principle that *the one who can designedly absent himself from the prayer-meeting is in a bad state of soul.* The healthy, happy, earnest, diligent soul will be sure to be found at the prayer-meeting.

But all this conducts us, naturally and simply, to another of those moral conditions at which we have been glancing in this series of papers. Let us turn for a moment to the opening lines of Luke 18. "And He spake a parable unto them to this end, *that men ought always to pray, and not to faint:* saying, 'There was in a city a judge, which feared not God, neither regarded man. And there was a widow in that city, and she came unto him, saying, Avenge me of mine adversary. And he would not for a while; but afterward he said within himself, Though I fear not God, nor regard man, yet, because this widow troubleth me, I will avenge her, lest by her continual coming she weary me.' And the Lord said, 'Hear what the unjust judge saith. And shall not God avenge His own elect, which cry day and night unto Him, though He bear long with them? I tell you that He will avenge them speedily' " (ver. 1-8).

Here, then, we have pressed upon our attention the important moral condition of *perseverance.* "Men ought *always* to pray, and *not to faint.*" This is intimately connected with the definiteness and importunity to which we have already referred. We want a certain thing; we cannot do without it. We importunately, unitedly, believingly, and perseveringly wait on our God until He graciously send an answer, as He most assuredly will, if the moral basis and the moral conditions be duly maintained.

But we must persevere. We must not faint, and give up, though the answer does not come as speedily as we might expect. It may please God to exercise our souls by keeping us waiting on Him for days, months, or perhaps years. The exercise is good. It is morally healthful; it tends to make us real; it brings us down to the roots of things. Look, for example, at Daniel. He was kept for "three full weeks" waiting on God, in profound exercise of soul. "In those days I Daniel was mourning three full weeks. I ate no pleasant bread, neither came flesh nor wine in my mouth, neither did I anoint myself at all, till three full weeks were fulfilled."

All this was good for Daniel. There was deep blessing in the spiritual exercises through which this beloved and honored servant of God was called to pass during those three weeks. And what is specially worthy of note is, that the answer to Daniel's cry had been despatched from the throne of God at the very beginning of his exercise, as we read at Daniel 10:12, "Then said he unto me, 'Fear not Daniel; for *from the first day that thou didst set thine heart to understand, and to chasten thyself before thy God, thy words were heard, and I am come for thy words.* But"—how marvelous and mysterious is this! —"the prince of the kingdom of Persia withstood me one and twenty days; but, lo, Michael, one of the chief princes, came to help me; and I remained there with the kings of Persia. Now I am come to make thee understand what shall befall thy people in the latter days."

All this is full of interest. Here was the beloved servant of God mourning, chastening himself, and waiting upon God. The angelic messenger was on his way with the answer. The enemy was permitted to hinder; but Daniel continued to wait: he prayed, and fainted not; and in due time the answer came.

Is there no lesson here for us? Most assuredly there is. We, too, may have to wait long in the holy attitude of expectancy, and in the spirit of prayer; but we shall find the time of waiting most profitable for our souls. Very often our God, in His wise and faithful dealing with us, sees fit to withhold the answer, simply to prove us as to the reality of our prayers. The grand point for us is, to have an object laid upon our hearts by the Holy Ghost—an object as to which we can lay the finger of faith upon some distinct promise in the Word, and to persevere in prayer until we get what we want. "Praying *always* with all prayer and supplication in the Spirit, and *watching* thereunto *with all perseverance* and supplication for all saints" (Eph. 6:18).

All this demands our serious consideration. We are as sadly deficient in perseverance as we are in definiteness and importunity. Hence the feebleness of our prayers and the coldness of our prayer-meetings. We do not come together with a definite object, and hence we are not importunate, and we do not persevere. In short, our prayer-meetings are often nothing but a dull routine—a cold, mechanical service—something to be gone through—a wearisome alternation of hymn and prayer, hymn and prayer, causing the spirit to groan beneath the heavy burden of mere profitless bodily exercise.

We speak plainly and strongly: we speak as we feel. We must be permitted to speak without reserve. We call upon the whole Church of God, far and wide, to look this great question straight in the face—to look to God about it—to judge themselves about it. Do we not feel the lack of power in all our public reunions? Why those barren seasons at the Lord's table? Why the dullness and feebleness in the celebration of that precious feast which ought to stir the very deepest depths of our renewed being? Why the lack of unction, power, and edification in our public readings—the foolish speculations and the silly questions which have been advanced and answered for the last forty years? Why those varied evils on which we have been dwelling, and which are being mourned over almost every where by the truly spiritual? Why the barrenness of our gospel services? Why are souls not smitten down under the Word? Why is there so little gathering-power?

Brethren, beloved in the Lord, let us rouse ourselves to the solemn consideration of these weighty matters. Let us not be satisfied to go on with the present condition of things. We call upon all those who admit the truth of what we have been putting forth in these pages on "Prayer and the Prayer-Meeting," to unite in cordial, earnest, united prayer and supplication. Let us seek to get together according to God; to come as one man and prostrate ourselves before the mercy-seat, and perseveringly wait upon our God for the revival of His work, the progress of His gospel, the ingathering and upbuilding of His beloved people. Let our prayer-meetings be really prayer-meetings, and not occasions for giving out our favorite hymns, and starting our fancy tunes. The prayer-meeting ought to be the place of expressed need and expected blessing—the place of expressed weakness and expected power—the place where God's people assemble with one accord, to take hold of the very throne of God, to get into the very treasury of Heaven, and draw thence all we want for ourselves, for our households, for the whole Church of God, and for the vineyard of Christ.

Yes, there's a power which man can wield,
  When mortal aid is vain:
That eye, that arm, that love to reach,
  That list'ning ear to gain.

That power is prayer, which soars on high,
  Through Jesus, to the throne,
And moves the hand which moves the world
  To bring deliverance down.

Such is the true idea of a prayer-meeting, if we are to be taught by Scripture. May it be more fully realized amongst the Lord's people every where. May the Holy Spirit stir us all up, and press upon our souls the value, importance, and urgent necessity of unanimity, confidence, definiteness, impor-

tunity, and perseverance in all our prayers and prayer-meetings.*

* NOTE.—It may perhaps be useful to notice that in the foregoing most needful pages, the beloved author has been speaking of the *prayer meeting* and the moral basis and conditions of prayer in general, not of personal, secret prayer. The importance of it can hardly be overestimated. The lack or neglect of this soon tells in the spiritual life of the Christian. Is not the lack of this the explanation of much leanness of soul, from which knowledge alone is not able to lift us up? Is it, as it were, the spiritual gauge of our soul's condition. There, in the secret of the closet, the godly soul ever loves to pour out in its Father's ear its trials, its fears, its desires, its wants, its thanksgivings, in all their details. And what comfort, what joy, what godly strength and purpose, the soul carries from thence! what preparation to go through the daily toil, and testings of the day! Beloved of the Lord, let us wait on God, that we may know more of this secret power, gotten in our closet with Him. [Ed.]

"THE MAN OF GOD"

2 Timothy 3:17

Part 1

THE SENTENCE which we have just penned occurs in Paul's Second Epistle to his beloved son Timothy—an Epistle marked, as we know, by intense individuality. All thoughtful students of Scripture have noticed the striking contrast between the two Epistles of Paul to Timothy. In the first, the Church is presented in its order, and Timothy is instructed as to how he is to behave himself therein. In the second, on the contrary, the Church is presented in its ruin. The house of God has become the great house, in the which there are vessels to dishonor as well as vessels to honor; and where, moreover, errors and evils abound—heretical teachers and false professors, on every hand.

It is in this Epistle of individuality, then, that the expression, "The man of God," is used with such obvious force and meaning. It is in times of general declension, of ruin and confusion that the faithfulness, devotedness, and decision of the individual man of God are specially called for. And it is a signal mercy for such an one to know that, spite of the hopeless failure of the Church as a responsible witness for Christ, it is the privilege of the individual to tread as holy a path, to taste as deep communion, and to

enjoy as rich blessings, as could be known in the Church's brightest days.

This is a most encouraging and consolatory fact—a fact established by many infallible proofs, and set forth in the very passage from which our heading is taken. We shall here quote at length this passage of singular weight and power: "But continue thou in the things which thou hast learned and hast been assured of, knowing of whom thou hast learned them; and that from a child thou hast known the Holy Scriptures, which are able to make thee wise unto salvation through faith which is in Christ Jesus. All Scripture is given by inspiration of God, and is profitable for doctrine, for reproof, for correction, for instruction in righteousness, that the man of God may be *perfect*, throughly *furnished unto all good works*"* (2 Tim. 3:14-17).

Here we have "the man of God," in the midst of all the ruin and confusion, the heresies and moral pravities of the last days, standing forth in his own distinct individuality, "perfect, throughly furnished unto all good works." And, may we not ask, what more could be said in the Church's brightest days? If we go back to the day of Pentecost itself, with all its display of power and glory, have we anything higher, or better, or more solid than that which is set forth in the words

* The reader should be informed that the word which is rendered "perfect," in the above passage, occurs but this once in the entire New Testament. It is $\alpha\rho\tau\iota\sigma\varsigma$ (*artios*) and signifies ready, complete, well fitted; as an instrument with all its strings, a machine with all its parts, a body with all its limbs, joints, muscles, and sinews. The usual word for "perfect" is $\tau\epsilon\lambda\epsilon\iota\sigma\varsigma$ (*teleios*) which signified the reaching of the moral *end*, in any particular thing.

"perfect, throughly furnished unto all good works"?

And is it not a signal mercy for anyone who desires to stand for God, in a dark and evil day, to be told that, spite of all the darkness, the evil, the error and confusion, he possesses that which can make a child *wise* unto salvation, and make a man *perfect* and thoroughly furnished unto all good works? Assuredly it is; and we have to praise our God for it, with full and overflowing hearts. To have access, in days like these, to the eternal fountain of inspiration, where the child and the man can meet and drink and be satisfied—that fountain so clear that the honest, simple soul can understand; and so deep that you cannot reach the bottom—that peerless, priceless volume which meets the child at his mother's knee, and makes him wise unto salvation; and meets the man in the most advanced stage of his practical career and makes him perfect and fully furnished for the exigence of every hour.

However, we shall have occasion, ere we close this paper, to look more particularly at "the man of God," and to consider what is the special force and meaning of this term. That there is very much more involved in it than is ordinarily understood, we are most fully persuaded.

There are three aspects in which man is presented in Scripture: in the first place, we have *man in nature*; secondly, *a man in Christ*; and, thirdly, we have, *the man of God*. It might perhaps be thought that the second and third are synonymous; but we shall find a very material difference between them. True, I must be a man in Christ before I can be a man of God; but they are by no means interchangeable terms.

Let us then, in the first place, consider *man in nature*.

This is a very comprehensive term indeed. Under this title, we shall find every possible shade of character, temperament, and disposition. Man, on the platform of nature, graduates between two extremes. You may view him at the very highest point of cultivation, or at the very lowest point of degradation. You may see him surrounded with all the advantages, the refinements and the so-called dignities of civilized life; or you may find him sunk in all the shameless and barbarous customs of savage existence. You may view him in the almost numberless grades, ranks, classes, and *castes* into which the human family has distributed itself.

Then again, in the self-same class, or caste, you will find the most vivid contrasts, in the way of character, temper, and disposition. There, for example, is a man of such an atrocious temper that he is the very horror of every one who knows him. He is the plague of his family circle, and a perfect nuisance to society. He can be compared to a porcupine with all his quills perpetually up; and if you meet him once you will not wish to meet him again. There, on the other hand, is a man of the sweetest disposition and most amiable temper. He is just as attractive as the other is repulsive. He is a tender, loving, faithful husband; a kind, affectionate, considerate father; a thoughtful, liberal master; a kindly, genial neighbor; a generous friend, beloved by all, and justly so: the more you know him the more you must like him, and if you meet him once you are sure to wish to meet him again.

Further, you may meet on the platform of nature, a man who is false and deceitful to the very heart's core. He delights in lying, cheating, and deception. He is mean and contemptible in his thoughts, words and ways; a man to whom all who know him would like to give as wide a berth as possible. And, on the other hand, you may meet a man of high principle, frank, honorable, generous, upright; one who would scorn to tell a lie, or do a mean act; whose reputation is unblemished, his character unexceptionable. His word would be taken for any amount; he is one with whom all who know him would be glad to have dealings; an almost perfect natural character; a man of whom it might be said, he lacks but one thing.

Finally, as you pass to and fro on nature's platform, you may meet the atheist who affects to deny the existence of God; the infidel who denies God's revelation; the skeptic and the rationalist who disbelieves everything. And, on the other hand, you will meet the superstitious devotee who spends his time in prayers and fastings, ordinances, and ceremonies; and who feels sure he is earning a place in Heaven by a wearisome round of religious observances that actually *un*fit him for the proper functions and responsibilities of domestic and social life. You may meet men of every imaginable shade of religious opinion, high church, low church, broad church, and no church; men who, without a spark of divine life in their souls, are contending for the powerless forms of a traditionary religion.

Now, there is one grand and awfully solemn fact common to all these various classes, castes, grades, shades, and conditions of men who occupy the platform of nature, and that is there is not so much as a single link between them and Heaven—there is no link with the Man who sits at the right hand of God—no link with the new creation. They are unconverted, and without Christ. As regards God, and Christ, and eternal life, and Heaven, they all—however they may differ morally, socially, and religiously—stand on one common ground; they are far from God—they are out of Christ—they are in their sins—they are in the flesh—they are of the world—they are on their way to hell.

There is really no getting over this, if we are to listen to the voice of Holy Scripture. False teachers may deny it. Infidels may pretend to smile contemptuously at the idea; but Scripture is plain as can be. It speaks in manifold places of a fire that *never* shall be quenched, and of a worm that shall never die.

It is the very height of folly for anyone to seek to set aside the plain testimony of the Word of God on this most solemn and weighty subject. Better far to let that testimony fall, with all its weight and authority, upon the heart and conscience—infinitely better to flee from the wrath to come than to attempt to deny that it is coming, and that, when it does come, it will abide forever—yes, forever, and forever, and forever! Tremendous thought!—overwhelming consideration! May it speak with living power to the soul of the unconverted reader, leading him to cry out in all sincerity, "What is to be done?"

Yes, here is the question, "What must I do to be saved?" The divine answer is wrapped up in the following words which dropped from the lips of two of Christ's very highest and most gifted ambassadors. "Repent and be converted," said Peter to the Jew. "Believe on the Lord Jesus Christ, and thou shalt be saved and thy house," said Paul to the Gentile. And again, the latter of these two blessed messengers, in summing up his own ministry, thus defines the whole matter, "Testifying both to the Jews, and also to the Greeks, repentance toward God, and faith toward our Lord Jesus Christ."

How simple! But how real! How deep! How thoroughly practical! It is not a nominal, national head belief. It is not saying, in mere flippant profession, "I believe." Ah! no; it is something far deeper and more serious than this. It is much to be feared that a large amount of the professed faith of this our day is deplorably superficial, and that many who throng our preaching rooms and lecture halls are, after all, but wayside and stony ground hearers. The plough of conviction and repentance has not passed over them. The fallow ground has never been broken up. The arrow of conviction has never pierced them through and through. They have never been broken down, turned inside out—thoroughly revolutionized. The preaching of the gospel to all such is just like scattering precious seed on the hard pavement or the beaten highway. It does not penetrate. It does not enter into the depths of the soul; the conscience is not reached; the heart is not affected. The seed lies on the surface, it has not taken root, and is soon carried away.

Nor is this all. It is also much to be feared that many of the preachers of the present day, in their efforts to make the gospel simple, lose sight of the abiding necessity of repentance, and the essential necessity of the action of the Holy Ghost, without which so-called faith is a mere human exercise and passes away like the vapors of the morning, leaving the soul still in the region of nature, satisfied with itself, daubed with the untempered mortar of a merely human gospel that cries peace, peace, where there is no peace, but the most imminent danger.

All this is very serious, and should lead the soul into profound exercise. We want the reader to give it his grave and immediate consideration. We would put this pointed question to him, which we entreat him to answer, now, *"Have you got eternal life?"* Say, *have you?* "He that believeth on the Son of God hath eternal life." Grand reality! If you have not got this, you have nothing. You are still on that platform of nature of which we have spoken so much. Yes, you are still there; no matter though you were the very fairest specimen to be found there—amiable, polished, affable, frank, generous, truthful, upright, honorable, attractive, beloved, learned, cultivated, and even pious after a merely human fashion. You may be all this, and yet not have a single pulsation of eternal life in your soul.

This may sound harsh and severe. But it is true; and you will find out its truth sooner or later. We want you to find it out *now*. We want you to see that you are a thorough bankrupt, in the fullest sense of that word. A deed of bankruptcy has been filed against you in the high court of Heaven. Here are its terms, *"They that are in the flesh cannot please God."* Have you ever pondered these words? Have you ever seen their application to yourself? So long as you are unrepentant, unconverted, unbelieving, you cannot do a single thing to please God—not one. "In the flesh" and "on the platform of nature" mean one and the same thing; and so long as you are there, you cannot please God. "You must be born again"—must be renewed in the very deepest springs of your being: unrenewed nature is wholly unable to see, and unfit to enter, the kingdom of God. You must be born of water and of the Spirit—that is by the living Word of God, and of the Holy Ghost. There is no other way by which to enter the kingdom. It is not by self-improvement, but by new birth we reach the blessed kingdom of God. "That which is born of the flesh is flesh;" and "the flesh profiteth nothing," for "they that are in the flesh cannot please God."

How distinct is all this! How pointed! How personal! How earnestly we desire that the unawakened or undecided reader should, just now, take it home to himself, as though he were the only individual upon the face of the earth. It will not do to generalize—to rest satisfied with saying, "We are all sinners." No; it is an intensely individual matter. "You *must* be born again." If you again ask, "How?" hear the divine response from the lips of the Master Himself, "As Moses lifted up the serpent in the wilderness, even so must the Son of man be lifted up; that whosoever believeth in Him should not perish, but have eternal life."

Here is the sovereign remedy, for every poor broken-hearted, conscience-smitten, hell-deserving sinner—for every one who owns himself lost—who confesses his sins, and judges himself—for every weary, heavy laden, sin-burdened soul—here is God's own blessed promise: Jesus died, that you might live. He was condemned, that you might be justified. He drank the cup of wrath, that you might drink the cup of salvation. Behold Him hanging on yonder cross for thee. See what He did for thee. Believe that He satisfied, on your behalf, *all* the claims of justice before the throne of God. See all your sins laid on Him—your guilt imputed to Him—your entire condition represented and disposed of by Him. See His atoning death answering perfectly for all that was or ever could be brought against you. See Him rising from the dead, having accomplished all. See Him ascending into the Heavens, bearing in His divine Person the marks of His finished atonement. See Him seated on the throne of God, in the very highest place of power. See Him crowned with glory and honor. Believe in Him, and you will receive remission of sins, the gift of eternal life, the seal of the Holy Ghost. You will pass off the platform of nature—you will be *"a man in Christ."*

Part 2

To all whose eyes have been opened to see their true condition by nature, who have been brought under the convicting power of the Holy Ghost, who know something of the real meaning of a broken heart and a contrite spirit—to all such it must be of the deepest possible interest to know the divine secret of rest and peace. If it be true—and it is true, because God says it—that "they that are *in the flesh* cannot please God," then how is any one to get *out of the flesh?* How can he pass off the platform of nature? How can he reach the blessed position of those to whom the Holy Ghost declares, "Ye are not in the flesh but in the Spirit"?

These are momentous questions, surely. For, be it thoroughly known and ever remembered, that no improvement of our old nature is of any value whatsoever as to our standing before God. It may be all very well, so far as this life is concerned, for a man to improve himself by every means within his reach, to cultivate his mind, furnish his memory, elevate his moral tone, advance his social position. All this is quite true, so true as not to need a moment's argument.

But, admitting in the fullest manner the truth of all this, it leaves wholly untouched the solemn and sweeping statement of the inspired apostle that, "they that are in the flesh cannot please God." There *must* be a new standing altogether, and this new standing cannot be reached by any change in the old nature—by any doings or formalities, feelings, ordinances of religion, prayers, alms or sacraments. Do what you will with nature and it is nature still. "That which is born of the flesh is flesh"; and do what you will with flesh you cannot make it spirit. There must be a new life—a life flowing from the new man, the last Adam, who had become, in resurrection, the Head of a new race.

How is this most precious life to be had? Hear the memorable answer—hear it and live. "Verily, verily, I say unto you, he that heareth My word, and believeth on Him that sent Me, *hath* everlasting life, and shall not come into judgment; but *is passed* from death unto life" (John 5: 24).

Here we have a total change of standing; a passing from death to life; from a position in which there is not so much as a single link with Heaven, with the new creation, with the risen Man in glory, into a position in which there is not a single link with the first man, with the old creation, and this present evil world. And all this is through believing on the Son of God—not *saying* we believe, but really, truly, heartily, believing on the Son of God; not by a mere intellectual faith, but believing with the heart.

Thus only does any one become *a man in Christ.*

Every true believer is a man in Christ. Whether it be the convert of yesterday or the hoary-headed saint of fifty or sixty years' standing as a Christian, each stands in precisely the same blessed position—he is in Christ. There can be no difference here. The practical *state* may differ immensely; but the positive standing is one and the same. As on the platform of nature, you may meet with every imaginable shade, class, grade, and condition (though all having one common standing) so on the new, the divine, the heavenly platform, you may meet with every possible variety of practical condition: the greatest possible difference in intelligence, experience, and spiritual power, while all possessing the same standing before God, all being in Christ. There can be no degrees as to standing, whatever there may be as to state. The convert of yesterday, and the hoary-headed father in Christ are both alike as to standing. Each is a man in Christ, and there can be no advance upon this. We sometimes hear of, "The higher Christian life": but, strictly speaking, there is no such thing as a higher or a lower Christian life, inasmuch as Christ is the life of every believer. It may be that those who use the term mean a right thing. They probably refer to the higher stages of the Christian life—greater nearness to God, greater likeness to Christ, greater power in the Spirit, more devotedness, more separation from the world, more entire consecration of heart to Christ. But all these things belong to the question of our *state*, not to our standing. This latter is absolute, settled, unchangeable. It is in Christ—nothing less, nothing more, nothing different. If we are not in Christ, we are in our sins; but if we are in Christ, we cannot possibly be higher, as to standing.

If the reader will turn with us, for a few moments, to 1 Cor. 15:45-48, he will find some powerful teaching on this great foundation truth. The apostle speaks here of two men, "The first and the second." And let it be carefully noted that the Second Man is by no means federally connected with the first, but stands in contrast with him—a new, independent, divine, heavenly source of life in Himself. The first man has been entirely set aside, as a ruined, guilty, outcast creature. We speak of Adam federally, as the head of a race. Personally, Adam was saved by grace; but if we look at him from a federal standpoint, we see him a hopeless wreck.

The first man is an irremediable ruin. This is proved by the fact of a *second* Man; for truly we may say of the men as of the covenants, "If the first had been found faultless, then should no place have been sought for the Second." But the very fact of a second Man being introduced demonstrates the hopeless ruin of the first. Why a second, if aught could be made of the first? If our old Adam nature was, in any wise, capable of being improved, there was no need of something new. But "they that are in the flesh cannot please God." "For in Christ Jesus neither circumcision availeth anything, nor uncircumcision, but a new creation" (Rom. 8: Gal. 6).

There is immense moral power in all this line of teaching. It sets forth Christianity in vivid and striking contrast with every form of religiousness under the sun. Take Judaism or any other *ism* that ever was known or that now exists in this world, and what do you find it to be? Is it not invariably something designed for the testing, or experimenting for the improvement, or advancement of the first man? Unquestionably.

But what is Christianity? It is something entirely new—heavenly, spiritual, divine. It is based upon the cross of Christ, in the which the first man came to his end, where sin was put away, judgment borne, the old man crucified and put out of God's sight forever, so far as all believers are concerned. The cross closes, for faith, the history of the first man. "I am crucified with Christ," says the apostle. And again, "They that are Christ's have crucified the flesh with its affections and lusts."

Are these mere figures of speech, or do they set forth, in the mighty words of the Holy Ghost, the grand fact of the entire setting aside of the first man, as utterly worthless and condemned? The latter, most assuredly. Christianity starts, as it were, from the open grave of the Second Man, to pursue its bright career onward to eternal glory. It is, emphatically, a new creation in which there is not so much as a single shred of the old thing—for in this "all things are of God." And if "*all things*" are of God, there can be nothing of man.

What rest! What comfort! What strength! What moral elevation! What sweet relief for the poor burdened soul that has been vainly seeking, for years perhaps, to find peace in self-improvement! What deliverance from the wretched thraldom of legality, in all its phases, to find out the precious secret that my guilty, ruined, bankrupt self—the very thing that I have been trying by every means in my power to improve, has been completely and forever set aside—that God is not looking for any amendment in it—that He has condemned it and put it to death in the cross of His Son! What an answer is here to the monk, the ascetic, and the ritualist! Oh, that it were understood in all its emancipating power! This heavenly, this divine, this spiritual Christianity. Surely were it only known in its living power and reality, it would deliver the soul from the thousand and one forms of corrupt religion whereby the arch-enemy and deceiver is ruining the souls of untold millions. We may truly say that Satan's most successful effort against the truth of the gospel, against the Christianity of the New Testament, is seen in the fact of his leading unconverted people to take and apply to themselves ordinances of the Christian religion, and to profess many of its doctrines. In this way he blinds their eyes to their own true condition, as utterly ruined, guilty, and undone; and strikes a deadly blow at the pure gospel of Christ. The best piece that was ever put upon the "old garment" of man's ruined nature is the profession of Christianity; and, the better the piece, the worse the rent. See Mark 2:21.

Let us bend an attentive ear to the following weighty words of the greatest teacher and best exponent of true Christianity the world ever saw. "For *I* through the law *am dead* to the law, that I might live to God. *I am crucified* with Christ; nevertheless I live; yet *not I,* but Christ liveth in me." Mark this, "I—not I—but Christ." The old "I"—"crucified." The new "I"—Christ. "And the life which I now live in the flesh, I live by the faith of the Son of God, who loved me and gave Himself for me" (Gal. 2:19-20).*

This, and nothing else, is Christianity. It is not "the old man," the first man, becoming religious, even though the religion be the profession of the doctrines, and the adopting of the ordinances of Christianity. No; it is the death and burial of the old man—the old I--and becoming a new man in Christ. Every true believer is a new man in Christ. He has passed clean out of the old creation-standing—the old estate of sin and death, guilt and condemnation; and he has passed into a new creation-standing—a new estate of life and righteousness in a risen and glorified Christ, the Head of the new creation, the last Adam.

Such is the position and unalterable standing of the feeblest believer in Christ. There is absolutely no other standing for any Christian. I must either be in the first man or in the Second. There is no *third* man, for the Second Man is the last Adam. There is no middle ground. I am either *in Christ,* or I am *in my sins.* But if I am in Christ, I am as He is before God. "As *He is* so *are we,* in this world." He does not say, "As He *was*" but "as He *is.*" That is, the Christian is viewed by God as one with Christ—the Second Man, in whom He delights. We do not speak of His deity, of course, which is incommunicable. That blessed One stood in the believer's stead—bore his sins, died his death, paid his penalty, represented him in every respect; took all his guilt, all his liabilities, all that pertained to him as a man in nature, stood as his substitute, in all the verity and reality of that word, and having divinely met his case, and borne his judgment, He rose from the dead, and is now the Head, the Representative, and the only true definition of the believer before God.

To this most glorious and enfranchising truth, Scripture bears the amplest testimony. The passage which we have just quoted from Galatians is a most vivid, powerful, and condensed statement of it. And if the reader will turn to Rom. 6, he will find further evidence. We shall quote some of the weighty sentences.

"What shall we say then? Shall we continue in sin, that grace may abound? Far be the thought. How shall *we that are dead* to sin, live any longer therein? Know ye not, that so many of us as were baptized to Jesus Christ were baptized to His death? Therefore we are buried with Him by baptism unto death; that *like as Christ* was raised up from the dead by the glory of the Father, *even so we also* should walk in newness of life. For if we have been planted together in the likeness of His death, we shall be also of resurrection. Knowing this that *our old man is crucified with Him,* that the body of sin might be destroyed, that henceforth we should not serve sin. For he that is dead is freed from sin. Now if we *be dead with Christ,* we believe that we shall also live with Him. Knowing that Christ being raised from the dead, dieth no more; death hath no more dominion over Him. For in that He died, He died unto sin once; but in that He liveth He liveth unto God. Likewise reckon ye also yourselves to be dead indeed unto sin, but alive unto God, through Jesus Christ our Lord" (Rom. 6:1-11).

Mark especially these words in the foregoing quotation—"We that *are dead*"—"We are buried with Him"—"*Like as Christ* was raised . . .*even so* we also"—"Our old man is crucified with Him"—"Dead with Christ"—"Dead indeed unto sin." Do we really understand such utterances? Have we entered into their real force and meaning? Do we, in very deed, perceive their application to ourselves? These are searching questions for the heart, and needful. The real doctrine of Rom. 6 is but little apprehended. There are thousands who profess to believe in the atoning virtue of the death of Christ, but who

---

* The reader will distinguish between the expression "in the flesh" as used in Gal. 2:20, and in Rom. 8:8-9. In the former, it simply refers to our condition as in the body. In the latter, it sets forth the principle or ground of our standing. The believer is in the body, as to the fact of his condition; but he is not in the flesh as to the principle of his standing.

do not see aught therein beyond the forgiveness of their *sins*. They do not see the crucifixion, death, and burial of the old man—the destruction of the body of sin—the condemnation of sin—the entire setting aside of the old system of things belonging to their first Adam condition—in a word their perfect identification with a dead and risen Christ. Hence it is that we press this grand and all-important line of truth upon the attention of the reader. It lies at the very base of all true Christianity, and forms an integral part of the truth of the gospel.

Let us hearken to further evidence on the point. Hear what the apostle said to the Colossians: "Wherefore, if ye be *dead with Christ* from the rudiments of the world, why, *as though living in the world*, are ye subject to ordinances, after the commandments and doctrines of men [such as] touch not, taste not, handle not"?—thus it is that human ordinances speak to us, telling us not to touch this, not to taste that, not to handle the other, as if there could possibly be any divine principle involved in such things—"which all are to perish with the using"; and "which, have indeed a show of wisdom in will worship, and humility, and neglecting of the body—not in any honor—to the satisfying of the flesh. If ye then be risen with Christ, seek those things which are above, where Christ sitteth on the right hand of God. Set your mind on things that are above, not on things on the earth. For *ye have died* and your life is hid with Christ in God" (Col. 2; 3:2).

Here, again, let us inquire how far we enter into the true force, meaning, and application of such words as these—"Why as though *living in the world*," etc.? Are we living in the world or living in Heaven—which? The true Christian is one who has died out of this present evil world. He has no more to do with it than Christ. "Like as Christ . . . even so we." He is dead to the law—dead to sin: alive in Christ—alive to God—alive in the new creation. He belongs to Heaven. He is enrolled as a citizen of Heaven. His religion, his politics, his morals are all heavenly. He is a heavenly man walking on the earth, and fulfilling all the duties which belong to the varied relationships in which the hand of God has placed him, and in which the Word of God most fully recognizes him, and amply guides him, such as husband, father, master, child, servant, and such like. The Christian is not a monk, an ascetic, or a hermit. He is, we repeat, a heavenly, spiritual man, *in* the world, but not *of* it. He is like a foreigner, so far as his residence here is concerned. He is in the body, as to the fact of his condition; but not in the flesh as to the principle of his standing. He is *a man in Christ*.

Ere closing this article, we should like to call the reader's attention to 2 Cor. 12. In it he will find, at once, the *positive standing* and the *possible state* of the believer. The standing is fixed and unalterable, as set forth in that one comprehensive sentence—"A man in Christ." The state may graduate between the two extremes presented in the opening and closing verses of this chapter. A Christian may be in the third heaven, amid the seraphic visions of that blessed and holy place; or he may, if not watchful, sink down into all the gross and evil things named in vers. 20-21.

It may be asked, "Is it possible that a true child of God could ever be found in such a low moral condition?" Alas! it is indeed possible. There is no depth of sin and folly into which a Christian is not capable of plunging, if not kept by the grace of God. Even the blessed apostle himself, when he came down from the third heaven, needed "a thorn in the flesh" to keep him from being "exalted above measure." We might suppose that a man who had been up in that bright and blessed region could never again feel the stirrings of pride. But the plain fact is that even the third heavens cannot cure the flesh. It is utterly incorrigible and must be judged and kept under, day by day, hour by hour, moment by moment, else it will cut out plenty of sorrowful work for us.

Still, the believer's standing is in Christ, forever justified, accepted, perfect in Him. And, moreover, he must ever judge his state by his standing, never his standing by his state. To attempt to reach the standing by my state is *legalism;* to refuse to judge my state by the standing is *antinomianism.* Both—though so diverse one from the other—are alike false, alike opposed to the truth of God, alike offensive to the Holy Ghost, alike removed from the divine idea of "a man in Christ."

Part 3

Having considered the deeply interesting questions of "a man in nature" and "a man in Christ," it remains for us now to consider, in this third and last part, the deeply practical subject of the title of this paper, namely, *the man of God.*

It would be a great mistake to suppose that every Christian is a man of God. Even in Paul's day—in the days of Timothy, there were many who bore the Christian name who were very far indeed from acquitting themselves as men of God, that is, as those who were really God's men, in the midst of the failure and error which, even then, had begun to creep in.

It is the perception of this fact that renders the Second Epistle to Timothy so profoundly interesting. In it we have what we may call ample provision for the man of God, in the day in which he is called to live—a dark, evil, and perilous day, most surely, in which all who will live godly must keep the eye steadily fixed on Christ Himself—His name—His person—His Word, if they would make any headway against the tide.

It is hardly possible to read Second Timothy without being struck with its intensely individual character. The very opening address is strikingly characteristic. "I thank God, whom I serve from my forefathers with pure conscience, that without ceasing I have remembrance of thee in my prayers night and day."

What glowing words are these! How affecting to harken thus to one man of God pouring the deep and tender feelings of his great, large, loving heart into the heart of another man of God! The dear apostle was beginning to feel the chilling influence that was fast creeping over the professing Church. He was tasting the bitterness of disappointed hopes. He found himself deserted by many who had once professed to be his friends and associates in that glorious work to which he had consecrated all the energies of his great soul. Many were becoming "ashamed of the testimony of our Lord, and of His prisoner." It was not that they altogether ceased to be Christians, or abandoned the Christian profession; but they turned their backs upon Paul, and left him alone in the day of trial.

Now, it is under such circumstances that the heart turns, with peculiar tenderness, to individual faithfulness and affection. If one is surrounded, on all hands, by true hearted confessors—by a great cloud of witnesses—a large army of good soldiers of Jesus Christ—if the tide of devotedness is flowing around one and bearing him on its bosom, he is not so dependent upon individual sympathy and fellowship.

But, on the other hand, when the general condition of things is low, when the majority prove faithless, when old associates are dropping off, it is then that personal grace and true affection are specially valued. The dark background of general declension throws individual devotedness into beauteous relief.

Thus it is in this exquisite Epistle which now lies open before us. It does the heart good to harken to the breathings of the aged prisoner of Jesus Christ, who can speak of serving God from his forefathers with pure conscience, and of unceasing remembrance of his beloved son and true yoke-fellow.

It is specially interesting to notice that, both in reference to his own history and that of his beloved friend, Paul goes back to facts of very early date—facts in their own individual paths, facts prior to their meeting one another, and prior to what we may call their church associations—important and interesting as these things surely are in their place. Paul had served God, from his forefathers, with pure conscience, before he had known a fellow-Christian. This he could continue to do though deserted by all his Christian companions. So also, in the case of his faithful friend, he says, "I call to remembrance the unfeigned faith that is in thee, which dwelt in thy grandmother Lois, and thy mother Eunice: and I am persuaded that is in thee also."

This is very touching and very beautiful. We cannot but be struck with such references to the previous history of those beloved men of God. The "pure conscience" of the one, and "the unfeigned faith" of the other, indicate two grand moral qualities which all must possess if they would prove true men of God in a dark and evil day. The former has its immediate references, in all things, to the one living and true God; the latter draws all its springs from Him. That, leads us to walk *before* God; this, enables us to walk *with* Him. Both together are indispensable in forming the character of the true man of God.

It is utterly impossible to over-estimate the importance of keeping a pure conscience before God, in all our ways. It is positively invaluable. It leads us to refer everything to God. It keeps us from being tossed hither and thither by every wave and current of human opinion. It imparts stability and consistency to the entire course and character. We are all in imminent danger of falling under human influence—of shaping our way according to the thoughts of our fellow-man, adopting his cue, or mounting his hobby.

All this is destructive of the character of the man of God. If you take your tone from your fellow, if you suffer yourself to be formed in a merely human mould, if your faith stands in the wisdom of man, if your object is to please men, then instead of being a man of God, you will become a member of a party or clique. You will lose that lovely freshness and originality so essential to the individual servant of Christ, and become marked by the peculiar and dominant features of a sect.

Let us carefully guard against this. It has ruined many a valuable servant. Many who might have proved really useful workmen in the vineyard, have failed completely through not maintaining the integrity of their individual character and path. They began with God. They started on their course in the exercise of a pure conscience, and in the pursuit of that path which a divine hand had

marked out for them. There was a bloom, a freshness, and a verdure about them, most refreshing to all who came in contact with them. They were taught of God. They drew near to the eternal fountain of Holy Scripture and drank for themselves. Perhaps they did not know much; but what they did know was real because they received it from God, and it turned to good account for "there is much food in the tillage of the poor."

But, instead of going on with God, they allowed themselves to get under human influence; they got truth secondhand, and became the vendors of other men's thoughts; instead of drinking at the fountain head, they drank at the streams of human opinion; they lost originality, simplicity, freshness, and power, and became mere copyists, if not miserable caricatures. Instead of giving forth those "rivers of living water" which flow from the true believer in Jesus, they dropped into the barren technicalities and cut and dry common-places of mere systematized religion.

All this must be sedulously guarded against. We must watch against it, pray against it, believe against it, and live against it. Let us seek to serve God, with a pure conscience. Let us live in His own immediate presence, in the light of His blessed countenance, in the holy intimacy of personal communion with Him, through the power of the Holy Ghost. This, we may rest assured, is the true secret of power for the man of God, at all times, and under all circumstances. We must walk with God, in the deep and cherished sense of our own personal responsibility to Him. This is what we understand by "a pure conscience."

But will this tend, in the smallest degree, to lessen our sense of the value of true fellowship, of holy communion with all those who are true to Christ? By no means; indeed it is the very thing which will impart power, energy, and depth of tone to the fellowship. If every "man in Christ" were only acquitting himself thoroughly as "a man of God," what blessed fellowship there would be! what heart work! what glow and unmistakable power! How different from the dull formalism of a merely nominal assent to certain accredited dogmas of a party, on the one hand, and from the mere *esprit de corps* of cliquism, on the other.

There are few terms in such common use and so little understood as "fellowship." In numberless cases, it merely indicates the fact of a nominal membership in some religious denomination—a fact which furnishes no guarantee whatsoever of living communion with Christ, or personal devotedness to His cause. If all who are nominally "in fellowship" were acquitting themselves thoroughly as men of God, what a very different condition of things we should be privileged to witness!

But what is fellowship? It is, in its very highest expression, having one common object with God, and taking part in the same portion; and that object, that portion, is Christ—Christ known and enjoyed through the Holy Ghost. This is fellowship with God. What a privilege! What a dignity! What unspeakable blessedness! To be allowed to have a common object and a common portion with God Himself! To delight in the One in whom He delights! There can be nothing higher, nothing better, nothing more precious than this. Not even in Heaven itself shall we know aught beyond this. Our own condition will, thank God, be vastly different. We shall be done with a body of sin and death, and be clothed with a body of glory. We shall be done with a sinful, sorrowful, distracting world, where all is directly opposed to God and to us, and we shall breathe the pure, invigorating atmosphere of that bright and blessed world above.

For, in so far as our fellowship is real, it is now as it shall be then, "with the Father and with His Son Jesus Christ"—"in the light," and by the power of the Holy Ghost.

Thus much as to our fellowship with God. And, as regards our fellowship one with another, it is simply as we walk in the light; as we read, "If we walk in the light, as He is in the light, we have fellowship one with another, and the blood of Jesus Christ His Son cleanseth us from all sin" (1 John 1:7). We can only have fellowship one with another as we walk in the immediate presence of God. There may be a vast amount of mere intercourse without one particle of divine fellowship. Alas! a great deal of what passes for Christian fellowship is nothing more than the merest religious gossip—the vapid, worthless, soul-withering chitchat of the religious world, than which nothing can be more miserably unprofitable. True Christian fellowship can only be enjoyed in the light. It is when we are individually walking with God, in the power of personal communion, that we really have fellowship one with another, and this fellowship consists in real heart enjoyment of Christ as our one object, our common portion. It is not heartless traffic in certain favorite doctrines which we receive to hold in common. It is not morbid sympathy with those who think, and see, and feel with us in some favorite theory or dogma. It is something quite different from all this. It is delighting in Christ, in common with all those who are walking in the light. It is attachment to Him, to His person, His name, His Word, His cause, His people. It is joint consecration of heart and soul to that blessed One who loved us and washed us from our sins in His own blood, and brought us into the light of God's presence, there to walk with Him and with one another. This, and nothing less, is Christian fellowship; and where this is really understood it will lead us to pause and consider what we say when we declare, in any given case, "such an one is in fellowship."

But we must proceed with our Epistle, and there see what full provision there is for the man of God, however dark the day may be in which his lot is cast.

We have seen something of the importance—yea, rather, we should say the indispensable necessity of "a pure conscience," and "unfeigned faith," in the moral equipment of God's man. These qualities lie at the very base of the entire edifice of practical godliness which must ever characterize the genuine man of God.

But there is more than this. The edifice must be erected as well as the foundation laid. The man of God has to work on amid all sorts of difficulties, trials, sorrows, disappointments, obstacles, questions and controversies. He has his niche to fill, his path to tread, his work to do. Come what may, he must serve. The enemy may oppose; the world may frown; the Church may be in ruins around him; false brethren may thwart, hinder, and desert; strife, controversy, and division may arise and darken the atmosphere; still the man of God must move on, regardless of all these things, working, serving, testifying, according to the sphere in which the hand of God has placed him, and according to the gift bestowed upon him. How is this to be done? Not only by keeping a pure conscience and the exercise of an unfeigned faith—priceless, indispensable qualities! but, further, he has to harken to the following weighty word of exhortation— "Wherefore I put thee in remembrance that thou stir up the gift of God, which is in thee by the putting on of my hands."

The gift must be stirred up, else it may become useless if allowed to lie dormant. There is great danger of letting the gift drop into disuse through the discouraging influence of surrounding circumstances. A gift unused will soon become useless; whereas, a gift stirred up and diligently used grows and expands. It is not enough to possess a gift, we must wait upon the gift, cultivate it, and exercise it. This is the way to improve it.

And observe the special force of the expression, "the gift of God." In Eph. 4 we read of "the gift of Christ," and there, too, we find all the gifts, from the highest to the lowest range, flowing down from Christ the risen and glorified Head of His body, the Church. But in Second Timothy, we have it defined as "the gift of God." True it is—blessed be His holy name!—our Lord Christ is God over all, blessed forever, so that the gift of Christ is the gift of God. But we may rest assured there is never any distinction in Scripture without a difference; and hence there is some good reason for the expression "gift of God." We doubt not it is in full harmony with the nature and object of the Epistle in which it occurs. It is "the gift of God" communicated to "the man of God" to be used by him notwithstanding the hopeless ruin of the professing church, and spite of all the difficulty, darkness, and discouragement of the day in which his lot is cast.

The man of God must not allow himself to be hindered in the diligent cultivation and exercise of his gift, though everything seems to look dark and forbidding, for "God hath not given us the spirit of fear; but of power and of love, and of a sound mind." Here we have "God" again introduced to our thoughts, and that, too, in a most gracious manner, as furnishing His man with the very thing he needs to meet the special exigence of his day—"The spirit of power, and of love, and of a sound mind."

Marvelous combination! Truly, an exquisite compound after the art of the apothecary! Power, love, and wisdom! How perfect! Not a single ingredient too much. Not one too little. If it were merely a spirit of power, it might lead one to carry things with a high hand. Were it merely a spirit of love, it might lead one to sacrifice truth for peace' sake; or indolently to tolerate error and evil, rather than give offence. But the power is softened by the love; and the love is strengthened by the power; and, moreover, the spirit of wisdom comes in to adjust both the power and the love. In a word, it is a divinely perfect and beautiful provision for the man of God—the very thing he needs for "the last days" so perilous, so difficult, so full of all sorts of perplexing questions and apparent contradictions. If one were to be asked what he would consider most necessary for such days as these? surely he should, at once, say, "power, love, and soundness of mind." Well, blessed be God, these are the very things which He has graciously given to form the character, shape the way, and govern the conduct of the man of God, right on to the end.

But there is further provision and further exhortation for the man of God. "Be not thou therefore ashamed of the testimony of our Lord, nor of me His prisoner; but be thou partaker of the afflictions of the gospel according to the power of God." In pentecostal days, when the rich and mighty tide of divine grace was flowing in, and bearing thousands of ransomed souls upon its bosom; when all were of one heart and one mind; when those outside were overawed by the extraordinary manifestations of divine power, it was rather a question of partaking of the *triumphs* of the gospel, than its afflictions. But in the days contemplated in Second Timothy, all is changed. The beloved apostle is a lonely prisoner at Rome; all in Asia had forsaken him; Hymeneus and Philetus are denying the resurrection; all sorts of heresies, errors, and evils are creeping in; the landmarks are in danger of being swept away by the tide of apostasy and corruption.

In the face of all this, the man of God has to brace himself up for the occasion. He has to endure hardness; to hold fast the form of sound words; he has to keep the good thing committed to him; to be strong in the grace that is in Christ Jesus; to keep himself *disentangled*—however he may be *engaged;* he must keep himself free as a soldier; he must cling to God's sure foundation; he must purge himself from the dishonorable vessels in the great house; he must *flee* youthful lusts, and *follow* righteousness, faith, love, peace, with them that call on the Lord out of a pure heart. He must avoid foolish and unlearned questions. He must turn away from formal and heartless professors. He must be thoroughly furnished for all good works, perfectly equipped through a knowledge of the Holy Scriptures. He must preach the Word; be instant in season and out of season. He must watch in all things; endure afflictions; and do the work of an evangelist.

What a category for the man of God! Who is sufficient for these things? Where is the spiritual power to be had for such works? It is to be had at the mercy-seat. It is to be found in earnest, patient, believing, waiting upon the living God, and in no other way. All our springs are in Him. We have only to draw upon Him. He is sufficient for the darkest day. Difficulties are nothing to Him, and they are bread for faith. Yes, difficulties of the most formidable nature are simply bread for faith, and the man of faith will develop and grow strong thereby. Unbelief says, "There is a lion in the way;" but faith slays the lion that roars along the path of the nazarite of God. It is the privilege of the true believer to rise above all the hostile influences which surround him, no matter what they are, or from whence they spring; and, in the calmness and brightness of the divine presence, enjoy as high communion, and taste as rich and rare privileges as ever were known in the Church's brightest days.

Let us remember this—every man of God needs to remember it: there is no comfort, no peace, no strength, no moral power, no true elevation to be derived from looking at the ruins. We must look up out of the ruins to the place where our Lord Christ has taken His seat, at the right hand of the Majesty in the heavens. Or rather, to speak more according to our true position, we should look down from our place in the heavens upon all the ruins of earth. To realize our place in Christ, and to be occupied in heart and soul with Him, is the true secret of power to carry ourselves as men of God. To have Christ ever before us—His work for the conscience, His person for the heart, His Word for the path, is the one grand, sovereign, divine remedy for a ruined self, a ruined world, a ruined Church.

But we close. Very gladly would we linger over the contents of this most precious Second Timothy. Truly refreshing would it be to dwell upon all its touching allusions, its earnest appeals, its weighty exhortations. But this would demand a volume, and hence we must leave the Christian reader to study the Epistle for himself, praying that the eternal Spirit who indited it may unfold and apply it in living power to his soul, so that he may be enabled to acquit himself as an earnest, faithful, whole-hearted man of God and servant of Christ, in the midst of a scene of hollow profession, and heartless worldly religiousness.

May the good Lord stir us all up to a more thorough consecration of ourselves, in spirit, soul, and body—all we are and all we have—to His service! We think we can really say we long for this—long for it, in the deep sense of our lack of it—long for it, more intensely, as we grow increasingly sick of the unreal condition of things within and around us.

Let us earnestly, believingly, and perseveringly cry to our own ever gracious God to make us more real, more whole-hearted, more thoroughly devoted to our Lord Jesus Christ in all things.

"THYSELF AND THE DOCTRINE"

A WORD FOR THE WORKMAN

"TAKE HEED UNTO THYSELF, and unto the doctrine [or teaching]; continue in them: for in doing this thou shalt both save thyself, and them that hear thee" (1 Tim. 4:16).

These are solemn and weighty words for all those who labor in the Word and doctrine. They were addressed by the inspired apostle to his beloved son Timothy, and contain most precious instruction for every one who is called of God to minister in the assembly, or to preach the gospel. It is assuredly a very high and holy privilege to be permitted to take part in such a ministry; but it involves a most serious responsibility; and the passage just quoted sets before the workman two deeply important duties—yea, absolutely essential duties, to which he must give his diligent, constant, prayerful attention, if he would be an efficient workman in the Church of God—"a good minister of Jesus Christ." He must take heed to himself; and he must take heed to the teaching.

1. And first, then, let us consider the solemn clause, *"Take heed to thyself."* We cannot adequately set forth the moral importance of this. It is, of course, important for all Christians; but for the workman preeminently so; for to such it is here particularly addressed. He, above all, will need to take heed to himself. He must guard the state of his heart, the state of his conscience, his whole inward man. He must keep himself pure. His thoughts, his affections, his spirit, his temper, his tongue, must all be kept under the holy control of the Spirit and Word of God. He must wear the girdle of truth and the breastplate of righteousness. His moral condition and his practical walk must answer to the truth ministered, else the enemy will most assuredly get an advantage over him.

The teacher ought to be the living exponent of what he teaches. At least this should be his honest, earnest, constant aim. He should ever keep this holy standard before "the eyes of his heart." Alas, the best will fail and come short; but where the heart is true, the conscience tender, and the fear of God and the love of Christ have their due place, the workman will never be satisfied with anything short of the divine standard for his inward state and his outward walk. It will ever be his earnest desire to exhibit the practical effect of his teaching, and to be "an example of the believers, in word, in conversation, in love, in spirit, in faith, in purity" (1 Tim. 4:12). With this he should ever remember that "we preach not ourselves, but Christ Jesus the Lord; and ourselves your servants, for Jesus' sake."

We must never for a moment lose sight of the weighty moral fact that the teacher ought to *live* the truth which he teaches. It is morally dangerous, in the extreme, for a man to teach in public what he does not live in private—dangerous for himself, most damaging to the testimony, and injurious to those with whom he has to do. What can be more deplorable or humiliating than for a man to be characterized by contradicting in his personal history and in his domestic life the truth which he utters in the public assembly? It is simply fearful, and must inevitably lead to the most disastrous results.

Hence, then, may it be the deep-seated, earnest purpose and aim of all those who minister in the Word and doctrine to feed upon the precious truth of God; to make it their own; to live and move and have their being in the very atmosphere of it; to have the inward man strengthened and formed by it; to have it dwelling richly in them, that thus it may flow out in living power, savor, unction and fulness to others.

It is a very poor, yea, a very dangerous

thing to sit down to the Word of God as a mere student, for the purpose of preparing lectures or sermons for other people. Nothing can be more deadening or withering to the soul. Mere intellectual traffic in the truth of God, storing up certain doctrines, views and principles in the memory, and giving them out with a certain fluency of speech, is at once deluding and demoralizing. We may be drawing water for other people, and all the while be like rusty pipes ourselves. How miserable this is!

"If any man thirst, let him come unto Me and *drink*," said our blessed Lord. He did not say *"draw."* The true spring and power of all ministry in the Church will ever be found in drinking for our own souls, not in drawing for others. "He that believeth on Me, as the Scripture hath said, out of his belly shall flow rivers of living water." We must abide close to the eternal fountain, the heart of Christ; drink deeply, drink continually. Thus our own souls shall be refreshed and enriched; rivers shall flow for the refreshment of others, and streams of praise ascend to the throne and to the heart of God by Jesus Christ. This is Christian ministry—yea, this is Christianity; all else is utterly worthless.

2. We shall now dwell for a few moments on the second point in our subject, namely, the doctrine, or teaching—for such is the true force of the original word. And oh, how much is involved in this! "Take heed to the teaching." Solemn admonition! What care is needed! What holy watchfulness! What earnest, prayerful, constant waiting upon God for the right thing to say, and the right way to say it! God only knows the state and the need of souls. He knows their capacity. We do not. We may be offering "strong meat" to those who can only bear "milk," and thus do positive mischief. "If any man speak, let him speak as oracles of God." He does not say, *"according* to the oracles of God." A man may rise and speak for an hour in the assembly, and every word he says may be in strict accordance with the letter of Scripture, and yet he may not at all speak as an oracle of God—as God's mouthpiece to the people. He may minister truth, but not the needed truth, at the time.

How solemn is all this! How it makes us feel the seriousness of the apostle's admonition, "Take heed to the teaching"! How it sets before us the urgent need of self-emptied dependence upon the power and guidance of the Holy Ghost! Here lies the precious secret of all effective ministry, whether oral or written. We may talk for hours, and write volumes,—and talk and write nothing unscriptural,—but if it be not in the power of the Spirit, our words will prove but as sounding brass and a tinkling cymbal, and our volumes as so much waste paper. We want to lie much at the Master's feet, to drink deeply into His Spirit, to be in fellowship with His heart of love for the precious lambs and sheep of His flock. Then shall we be in a condition of soul to give the portion of meat in due season.

He alone knows exactly what His beloved people really need at all times. We may perhaps feel deeply interested in some special line of truth, and we may judge it to be the right thing for the assembly; but this might be quite a mistake. It is not the truth which interests us, but the truth which the assembly needs, that should be given out; and for this we should ever wait upon our gracious Lord. We should look simply and earnestly to Him, and say, "Lord, what wouldest Thou have me to say to Thy beloved people? Give me the suited message for them." Then would He use us as His channels; and the truth would flow down from His loving heart into our hearts, and forth from us, in the power of His Spirit, into the hearts of His people.

Oh that it were thus with all who speak and write for the Church of God! What results we might look for!—what power!—what manifest progress in the divine life! The true interests of the flock of Christ would then be thought of in all that was spoken or written. Nothing equivocal, nothing strange or startling, would then be sent forth. Nothing but what is sound and seasonable would flow from the lips or the pen. Sound speech that cannot be condemned, that which is good for the use of edifying, would alone be sent forth.

May every beloved workman throughout the length and breadth of the Church of God take home to himself the apostolic admonition, "Take heed to thyself, and to the teaching . . . for in doing this thou shalt both save thyself, and them that hear thee"!

"Of these things put them in remembrance, testifying earnestly before the Lord, not to have disputes of words, profitable for nothing, to the subversion of the hearers. Strive diligently to present thyself *approved to God*, a workman that needeth not to be ashamed, rightly dividing the word of truth" (2 Tim. 2:14-15).

THE TRUE WORKMAN

HIS REBUFFS, HIS RESOURCES, HIS RETURNS

Matthew 11

THERE IS A NEVER-FAILING freshness in every part of the Word of God, but especially in those portions of it which present to us the blessed Person of the Lord Jesus; which tell us what He was, what He did, what He said, how He did it, and how He said it; which present Him to our hearts in His comings and goings, and matchless ways; in His spirit, tone, and manner, yea, in His very look. There is something in all this that commands and charms the heart. It is far more powerful than the mere statement of doctrines, however important, or the establishment of principles, however profound. These have their value and their place, most assuredly; they enlighten the understanding, instruct the mind, form the judgment, govern the conscience, and, in so doing, render us invaluable service.

But the presentation of the Person of Christ draws the heart, rivets the affections, satisfies the soul, commands the whole being. In short, nothing can exceed the occupation of heart with Christ Himself as the Holy Ghost has unfolded Him to us in the Word, and especially in the inimitable narratives of the Gospels. May it be given us to prove this, as we hang together over the eleventh chapter of the Gospel of Matthew, in which we shall get a view of Christ, the true Workman, in His rebuffs, His resources and His returns—the rebuffs which He met with in His ministry; the resources which He found in God; and the returns which He makes to us.

And first, let us look at *the rebuffs*.

There never yet was one who stood as a workman for God in this world, that had not to encounter rebuffs in some shape or form, and the only perfect Workman is no exception to the general rule. Jesus had His rebuffs and disappointments; for had it been otherwise with Him, He could not sympathize with those who have to meet them at every stage of their career. He, as man, perfectly entered into everything that man is capable of feeling—sin excepted. "He was in all points tempted like as we are, except sin." "He is touched with the feeling of our infirmities." He perfectly understands, and fully enters into, all that His servants have to pass through in their work.

Now, in this eleventh chapter, the Spirit has grouped together a series of those rebuffs or disappointments which the perfect Workman, the true Servant, the divine Minister had to encounter in the discharge of His ministry. The first of these came from a quarter from which we should not have expected it, namely, from John the Baptist himself. "Now, when John had heard in the prison the works of Christ, he sent two of his disciples, and said unto Him, Art Thou He that should come, or do we look for another?"

It is very evident that at the moment in which the Baptist sent this message to his Master, his spirit was under a cloud. It was a dark season in his experience. This was nothing uncommon. The very best and truest of Christ's servants have had their spirits overcast at times by the dark shadows of unbelief, despondency, and impatience. Moses, that highly honored, faithful servant of God, gave forth on one occasion such accents as these, "Wherefore hast Thou afflicted Thy servant, and wherefore have I not found favor in Thy sight, that Thou layest the burden of all this people upon me . . . I am not able to bear all this people alone, because it is too heavy for me. And if Thou deal thus with me, kill me, I pray Thee, out of hand, *if* I have found favor in Thy sight, and let me not see my wretchedness" (Num. 11:11-15).

Such was the language of the meekest man upon the face of the earth—language drawn forth, no doubt, by very aggravating circumstances, even by the murmuring voices of six hundred thousand footmen—but still it was the language of Moses; and surely it would ill become us to marvel, for where is the mere mortal who could have endured the intense pressure of such a moment? What merely human embankment could have resisted the violence of such a mighty tide?

Again, we find Elijah the Tishbite, in a moment of heavy pressure, when a dark cloud was passing over his soul, flinging himself down under a juniper tree, and requesting for himself that he might die. "It is enough; now, O Lord, take away my life; for I am not better than my fathers" (1 Kings 19:4). This was the language of Elijah, one of the most highly honored of the servants of Christ—language evoked, no doubt, by a combination of the most discouraging influences—but still it was the language of Elijah the Tishbite; and let no one blame him until he himself has passed, without a wavering feeling or a faltering word, through like conditions.

In like manner also we find Jeremiah, another of Christ's high-favored workmen, when under the smitings of Pashur, and the derisive insults of the ungodly around him, giving vent to his feelings in such language as this, "O Lord, Thou hast deceived me, and I was deceived: Thou art stronger than I, and hast prevailed; I am in derision daily, every one mocketh me. For since I spake, I cried out, I cried violence and spoil; because the word of the Lord was made a reproach unto me, and a derision, daily. Then I said, I will not make mention of Him, nor speak any more in His name."

And, again, "Cursed be the day wherein I was born: let not the day wherein my mother bare me be blessed. Cursed be the man who brought tidings to my father, saying, A man child is born unto thee; making him very glad. And let that man be as the cities which the Lord overthrew, and repented not: and let him hear the cry in the morning, and the shouting at noontide, because he slew me not from the womb; or that my mother might have been my grave, and her womb to be always great with me. Wherefore came I forth out of the womb to see labor and sorrow, that my days should be consumed with shame?" (Jer. 20:7-9,14-18) Such was the language of the weeping prophet— language drawn forth, no doubt, by sharp rebuffs and sore disappointments in his prophetic ministry, but still the language of Jeremiah; and, ere we condemn him, let us see if we could acquit ourselves better under similar pressure.

Need we wonder, then, after reading such records as the above, when we find the Baptist, amid the gloom of Herod's dungeon, faltering for a moment? Should we be greatly astonished to discover that he was made of no better material than the workmen of former generations? If Israel's lawgiver, Israel's reformer, and Israel's weeping prophet had, each in his day and generation, tottered beneath the ponderous weight of his burden, are we to be surprised to find "John, the son of Zacharias," giving way to a momentary feeling of impatience and unbelief beneath the dark shadow of his prison walls? Assuredly, not until we ourselves have sat unmoved amid similar influences.

And yet we have ventured to assert, that John's message was a rebuff and a disappointment to the spirit of his Master. Yes, that is just what we assert; and we find the authority for our assertion in the style of Christ's answer. "Jesus answered and said unto them, Go and shew John again those things which ye do hear and see. The blind receive their sight, and the lame walk, the lepers are cleansed, and the deaf hear, the dead are raised up, and the poor have the gospel preached to them. And blessed is he whosoever shall not be offended in Me."

It is very possible, nay probable, that the Baptist, under a passing shadow of unbelief, had been tempted to wonder if indeed Jesus was the One to whom he had, in the discharge of his ministry, borne such full and unqualified testimony. He was, doubtless, stumbled for the moment, when he saw himself in the iron grasp of Herod, and heard of the works of Christ. His poor heart might indulge itself in such reasoning as this, "If indeed this be the glorious Messiah for whom we looked, whose kingdom was to be set up in power, then why is it thus with me His servant and witness? Why am I here in the gloom of this prison? Why is not the strong hand of power stretched forth to free me from these bonds and fling open these prison doors?"

If such were the reasonings of the captive Baptist, and we can easily believe it, what a powerful, pointed, pungent answer lay folded up in his Master's reply! He points him to those grand moral evidences of His divine mission, which were amply sufficient to carry conviction to every one that was taught of God. Was it not to be expected that if the God of Israel appeared in the midst of His people, He should address Himself to their actual condition? Was that the moment for the display of mere power? Could the Son of David set up His throne amid disease and misery? Was there not a demand for the exercise of patient, lowly grace and mercy in the midst of the varied and multiplied fruits of sin?

True, mere power could have burst open Herod's prison, and set the captive free; but then what about the lame, the blind, the deaf, the leper, the dead, the poor, the wretched? Could the display of royalty alleviate their condition? Was it not plain that something else was needed? And was it not equally plain that that something was being supplied by the gracious, tender, soothing ministrations of the lowly Jesus of Nazareth?

Yes, and the Baptist ought to have known this. But ah! you and I may well tread softly in the prison-chamber of this honored servant

of Christ, not only because grace would have us so to do, but also because of the conviction which assuredly must possess our souls that, had *we* been in his position, the foundations of our personal faith, if not sustained by grace, would have given way far more deplorably.

Still, it is important that we should fully comprehend the failure of John the Baptist, and sedulously gather up the seasonable instruction furnished by his temporary depression. We shall do well to see, with distinctness, what was lacking in his faith, in order that we ourselves may profit by this touchingly interesting narrative. It would have greatly helped the Baptist had he only understood and remembered that this is the day of Christ's *sympathy* and not the day of His *power*. Were it the day of His power, there would be no dungeon, no block, no stake, no trial or sorrow of any sort for the saints of God. There would then be no tumultuous waves of the ocean, no cloud in the sky, no storm to brave, no roughness to endure.

But this is the day of Christ's sympathy; and the question for the tried and tempted, the harassed and oppressed, is this, "Which would you rather have, the *power* of Christ's *hand* in deliverance *from* the trial, or the *sympathy* of Christ's *heart* in the trial?" The carnal mind, the unsubdued heart, the restless spirit, will, no doubt, at once exclaim, "Oh! let Him only put forth His power and deliver me from this insupportable trial, this intolerable burden, this crushing difficulty. I sign for deliverance. I only want deliverance."

Some of us can well understand this. We are so often like a bullock unaccustomed to the yoke, restlessly struggling, instead of patiently submitting; rendering the yoke all the more galling and grievous by our senseless and useless efforts to shake it off. But the spiritual mind, the subdued heart, the lowly spirit, will say, and that without a single particle of reserve, Let me only enjoy the sweet sympathy of the heart of Jesus in my trial, and I ask no more. I do not want even the power of His hand to deprive me of one drop of consolation supplied by the tender love and profound sympathy of His heart. I know, assuredly, that He could deliver me. I know that He could, in the twinkling of an eye, snap these chains, level these prison walls, rebuke that sickness, raise up that beloved object that lies before me in the cold grasp of death, remove this heavy burden, meet this difficulty, supply this need.

But if He does not see fit to do so, if it does not fall in with His unsearchable counsels, and harmonize with His wise and faithful purpose concerning me so to do, I know it is only to lead me into a deeper and richer experience of His most precious sympathy. If He does not see it right to take me off the rough path of trial and difficulty—that path which He himself, in perfection, and all His saints from age to age, in their measure, have trodden—it is His gracious purpose to come and walk with me along that path which, though rough and thorny, leads to those everlasting mansions of light and blessedness above.

We cannot, for a moment, doubt but that the knowledge and recollection of these things would greatly have relieved the heart of John the Baptist in the midst of his prison experiences; and surely they would serve to soothe and sustain our hearts amid the varied exercises through which we are called to pass in this wilderness scene. The moment has not yet arrived for Jesus to take to Himself His great power, and reign. It is the day of His patience with the world, of His sympathy with His people. We must ever remember this. He did not put forth the strong hand of power to avert aught of His own suffering. Nay, when Peter, in mistaken zeal, drew the sword in His defence, He said, "Put up thy sword into its place; for all they that take the sword shall perish by the sword. Thinkest thou that I cannot now pray to My Father, and He shall presently give Me more than twelve legions of angels? But how then shall the Scriptures be fulfilled that thus it must be?" (Matt. 26:52-54)

But while we fully recognize the momentary failure of John the Baptist, and while we clearly discern the points in which his faith proved itself defective, let us remember the pressure of his circumstances,

and the great practical difficulty of the lesson which he was called to learn within his prison walls. It is very hard for a workman to find himself laid aside. Indeed, there are few things more difficult for an active mind than to learn that we can be dispensed with. We are so apt to think that the work cannot get on without us. And yet the Lord can soon teach us our mistake. Paul's bonds advanced the cause of Christ. The imprisonment of one great preacher drew out a multitude of minor preachers. Luther's confinement in the Wartburg furthered the cause of the Reformation.

Thus it is always; and we have all to learn the wholesome lesson, that God can do without us; that the work can go on without us. This holds good in every case. It matters not, in the least, what our sphere of action may be. We may not be apostles or reformers, teachers or preachers; but whatever we are, it is well for us to learn that we can very easily be spared from the scene around us. The remembrance of this gives great rest to the heart. It tends amazingly to cure us of all that bustling self-importance which is so truly hateful, and it enables us to say, "The Lord be praised! The work is being done. I am satisfied."

The reader will discern a very marked difference between Christ's message *to* John and his testimony *of* John. In speaking to His servant, He lets him know, in a way not to be mistaken, that He *felt* his question. We can have no difficulty in seeing this. We feel persuaded that the Lord's answer to His servant contained a sharp arrow. True, that arrow was enclosed in a very delicate case; but it was an arrow, and a sharp one too.

"Blessed is he, whosoever shall not be offended in Me." John would, doubtless, understand this. It was designed to go right home to his very inmost soul. That dear servant had said, in reference to Jesus, "He must increase, but I must decrease," and he was called to enter practically into this, not merely in his ministry, but in his person. He had to be content to end his career by the sword of the executioner, after having spent his closing days in the gloom of a dungeon. How mysterious! What a profound lesson to be set down to! How difficult to flesh and blood! What need—what urgent need there was, at such a moment, for John to have whispered into his ear these words, afterwards uttered to Peter, "What I do, thou knowest not *now;* but thou shalt know *hereafter.*"

What pregnant words! *"Now"* and *"Hereafter!"* How much we all need to remember them! Often it happens with us that "Now" is involved in deep and impenetrable obscurity. Heavy clouds hang upon our path. The dealings of our Father's hand are perfectly inexplicable to us. Our minds are bewildered. There are circumstances in our path for which we cannot account—ingredients in our cup the object of which we cannot understand or appreciate. We are confounded and feel disposed to cry out, "Why am I thus?" We are wholly engrossed with "Now," and our minds are filled with dark and unbelieving reasonings until those precious words fall, in a still small voice upon the ear, "What I do thou knowest not now; but thou shalt know hereafter."

Then the reasonings are answered, the storm hushed, the dark and depressing "Now" is lighted up with the beams of a brilliant and glorious "Hereafter," and the subdued heart breathes forth, in accents of holy and intelligent acquiescence, "As Thou wilt, Lord." Would that we knew more of this! Assuredly, we need it, whatsoever may be our lot in this world. We may not be called, like the Baptist, to the prison and the block; but each has his "Now" which must be interpreted in the light of "Hereafter." We must look at the "seen and temporal" in the clear and blessed light of the "unseen and eternal."

But let us now turn, for a moment, and hearken to Christ's testimony of John. "And, as they departed, Jesus began to say unto the multitudes concerning John, What went ye out into the wilderness to see? A reed shaken with the wind? But what went ye out to see? A man clothed in soft raiment? behold they that wear soft clothing are in kings' houses. But what went ye out for to see? A prophet? Yea, I say unto you, and more than a prophet. For this is he of whom it is written, Behold, I send My messenger before Thy face, which shall prepare Thy way before Thee. Verily I say unto you, Among them that are born of women there hath not risen a greater than John the Baptist: notwithstanding, he that is least in the kingdom of heaven is greater than he."*

Such was the glowing testimony borne by Christ of His servant, John the Baptist. "Among them that are born of women there hath not risen a greater than he." There is a great principle in this—a principle which we may see illustrated, again and again, in the record of God's dealings with His people. If the Lord had a message to send *to* His servant, He would send it. He would speak to him, plainly and pointedly. But, the moment He proceeds to speak *of* him, the case is totally different.

Thus it is always, and blessed be God that it is so. We have our ways and God has His thoughts; and while He will deal with us faithfully as to the former, He can only speak of us according to the latter. What relief for the heart is here! What comfort! What moral power! What solid ground for self-judgment! God has given us a standing, and He thinks of us, and speaks of us, according to that. We have our practical ways, and He deals with us and speaks to us in reference to them. He will expose us to ourselves, and make us feel our

* In order fully to understand this last clause, we must distinguish John's personal character and walk, and his dispensational and official position. If we look at him, in his person and walk, few, even in the kingdom, could bear comparison with him, in separation and devotedness. But when we look at him, in his dispensational position, *i.e.*, in the place assigned him in the divine economy, the very weakest and least in the kingdom occupies a better and higher place. The same remark holds good with respect to the saints of Old Testament times. If we take Abraham, for example, and compare him with the best of the children of God of this dispensation, the "father of the faithful" might stand higher, as regards personal faith and devotedness; the feeblest member of the Church of God occupies, dispensationally, in the divine economy, a place which Abraham never thought of, because it was not revealed. Very many pious and godly people are prevented from seeing the dignities and privileges of the saints of this dispensation, by comparing themselves *personally* with Old Testament believers. But we must remember it is not a question of what we are in ourselves, but of the *place* which God, in the arrangement of His kingdom and household, has thought proper to assign us; and if He has been pleased to give us a higher place than that occupied by His people in Old Testament times, it is *not* true humility on our part to refuse it; yea, rather let us seek grace to occupy it aright, and to walk worthy of it.

ways and judge our doings; but the moment He begins to speak of us to others, He brings out the perfection of His own thoughts respecting us, and speaks of us according to the perfect standing which He has given us in His presence, the fruit of His own eternal counsels respecting us, and of His perfect work on our behalf.

Thus it was with Israel, in the plains of Moab. They had their ways, and God had His thoughts; and while He had, often and often, to reprove them for their ways, to speak plainly to them about their perverseness and stiff-neckedness, yet no sooner did the covetous prophet appear upon the scene, to curse Israel, than the Lord placed Himself right between His people and the enemy to turn the curse into a blessing, and pour forth the most sublime and marvelous strains of testimony on their behalf.

"God is not a man, that He should lie; neither the son of man that He should repent: hath He said, and shall He not do it? or hath He spoken, and shall He not make it good? Behold, I have received commandment to bless, and He hath blessed; and I cannot reverse it. He hath not beheld iniquity in Jacob, neither hath He seen perverseness in Israel: the Lord his God is with him, and the shout of a king is among them. God brought them out of Egypt: he hath, as it were, the strength of a unicorn. Surely there is no enchantment against Jacob, neither is there any divination against Israel; according to this time it shall be said of Jacob and of Israel, What hath God wrought!" (Num. 23: 19-23)

What grace is here! "I have not beheld iniquity, nor seen perverseness." What could the enemy say to this? "What hath God wrought!" It is not, "What hath Israel wrought!" They had wrought folly, many a time; but God had wrought salvation. He had wrought for His own glory, and that glory had shone out in the perfect deliverance of a crooked, perverse, and stiff-necked people. It was no use the enemy's talking of iniquity and perverseness, if Jehovah would not see either the one or the other. It is of very little consequence to us that Satan accuses, when God has acquitted; that Satan counts up our

sins, when God has blotted them all out for ever; that Satan condemns, when God has justified.

> I hear the accuser roar,
> Of ills that I have done;
> I know them well, and thousands more,
> Jehovah findeth none.

But some may feel disposed to ask, "Is there not danger in the statement of such a principle as this? Might it not lead us into the dark and perilous region of antinomianism?" Be thou well assured of this, thou art never further removed from that justly dreaded region than when thy soul is basking in the bright and blessed beams of God's eternal favor, and exulting in the stability of His unconditional and everlasting salvation. There never was a greater mistake than to imagine that God's free grace and full salvation could ever lead to unholy results. Man's notions of these things may have that effect, but wherever grace is fully known and salvation enjoyed, there you will most assuredly find "The fruits of righteousness which are by Jesus Christ, unto the glory and praise of God."

But we know it is an old habit of ignorant and self-exalting legality to attribute an antinomian tendency to the free grace of God. "Shall we continue in sin that grace may abound?" is no modern objection to the precious doctrines of grace; and yet those doctrines remain untouched in all their purity and power, and find their divine centre in the Person of Christ Himself, who, having died on the cross to put away our sins, has become our life and righteousness, our sanctification and redemption, our all in all. He has not only delivered us from the future consequences of sin, but from the present power thereof.

This is what God hath wrought, and this is the groundwork of the great principle on which we have been dwelling, and which we have seen variously illustrated in God's dealings with Israel in the plains of Moab, and in Christ's dealings with the Baptist in the dungeon of Herod. Jehovah was compelling Balaam to exclaim in the ears of Balak, "How goodly are thy tents, O Jacob, and thy tabernacles, O Israel," at the very moment when those tents and tabernacles were furnishing ample material for judgment. So also, Jesus was telling out in the ears of the multitude the greatness of John the Baptist, at the very moment when the messengers were on their way back to their master, carrying with them an arrow for his heart.

Now, we want the reader to get a clear view of this principle, and to bear it in constant remembrance. If we mistake not, it will greatly help him, not only in the understanding of God's Word, but also in the interpreting of His ways. God judges His people. He will not and cannot pass over a jot or a tittle in their ways. The splendid testimony of Balaam on Moab's heights, was followed by the sharp javelin of Phineas in Moab's plains. "*Our* God is a consuming fire." This is what *our* God is now. He cannot tolerate evil. He speaks of us, He thinks of us, He acts toward us according to the perfection of His own work; but He will judge our ways. Let an enemy come forth to curse, and what is it? Not a spot, not a stain, all perfect and comely and goodly. How could it be otherwise? How could the eye of God behold those sins which have been for ever obliterated by the blood of the Lamb? Utterly impossible.

What then? Does this make light of sin? Far be the thought. Does it open the door for a loose walk? Nay, it lays the only true foundation of personal holiness. "The Lord will judge His people." He will look after the ways of His children. He will take care of His holiness; and not only so, but He will make His people partakers of that holiness, and chasten them with the rod of faithful discipline for that very purpose. It was just because Israel's tents were goodly in the eyes of Jehovah, that He sent Phineas into those very tents with the javelin of righteous judgment in his hand.

And so, now, it is because His people are precious to Him, and comely in His eyes, that He will not suffer aught in them, or in their ways, contrary to His holiness. "The time is come that judgment must begin at the house of God" (1 Peter 4: 17. God is not judging the world now. He is judging His people now. He will judge the world by-and-by. But, be it remembered, that it is as a "holy Father" He judges His people; it is as a righteous God He will judge the world. The object of the former is practical holiness; the issue of the latter will be eternal perdition. Solemn thought!

But there is another point in connection with this, which we desire to press upon the attention of the Christian reader—a point of very great practical moment, namely this, we must not measure our standing by our state, but ever judge our state by our standing. Many err in reference to this, and their error leads to most disastrous results. The standing of the believer is settled, perfect, eternal, divine. His state is imperfect and fluctuating. He is partaker of the divine nature which cannot sin; but he bears about with him also his old nature which can do nothing else but sin.

Now his standing is in the new and not in the old. God sees him only in the new. He is not in the flesh, but in the Spirit. He is not under law, but under grace. He is in Christ. God sees him as such. This is his perfect and unalterable standing; his sins gone; his person accepted; all complete. His practical state can never touch his standing. It can very seriously affect his communion, his worship, his testimony, his usefulness, his spiritual enjoyment, his mental repose, the glory of Christ as involved in his practical career. These are grave consequences in the estimation of every sensitive conscience and well-regulated mind; but the standing of the true believer remains—ever remains *intact* and unalterable. The feeblest member of the family of God has this place of security, and is perfect in Christ. To deny this is to remove the true basis of self-judgment and practical holiness.

Hence, if the Christian sets about measuring his standing by his state, he must be miserable, and his mental misery must be commensurate with his honesty and intelligence. There may be cases in which ignorance, self-complacency, or want of sincerity, will lead to a sort of false peace; but where there is any measure of light, intelligence, and uprightness, there must be mental anguish if the standing is measured by the state.

On the other hand, let it never be forgotten—indeed the earnest Christian never could desire to forget—that the state must be judged by the standing. If this wholesome truth be lost sight of, we shall very speedily make shipwreck of faith and a good conscience. We have to keep the eye of faith steadily fixed on a risen Christ, and never be satisfied with anything short of perfect conformity to Him, in spirit, soul, and body.

A very few words will suffice to present the remainder of those rebuffs with which our blessed Lord had to deal, as recorded in our chapter. Having disposed of the question of the Baptist and his ministry, He turns to the men of that generation, and says, "But whereunto shall I liken this generation? It is like unto children sitting in the markets, and calling unto their fellows, and saying, We have piped unto you, and ye have not danced; we have mourned unto you, and ye have not lamented. For John came neither eating nor drinking, and they say, He hath a devil. The Son of man came eating and drinking, and they say, Behold a man gluttonous, and a winebibber, a friend of publicans and sinners. But wisdom is justified of her children."

The piping and the mourning were alike neglected by an unbelieving age. "John came unto you in the way of righteousness, and ye believed him not." The Lord Jesus came in perfect grace, and they would not have Him. The stern and distant minister of righteousness, with the ax of judgment in his hand, and the lowly, gentle Minister of divine grace, with words of tenderness and acts of goodness, were alike rejected by the men of that generation. But wisdom's children will ever justify her, in all her doings and in all her sayings. The Lord be praised for this rich mercy! What a privilege to be of the favored number of wisdom's children! To have an eye to see, an ear to hear, and a heart to understand and appreciate the ways and works and words of divine Wisdom! "Oh, to grace how great a debtor!"

"Then began He to upbraid the cities wherein most of His mighty works were done, because they repented not. Woe unto thee, Chorazin! Woe unto thee, Bethsaida! for if the mighty works which were done in you had been done in Tyre and Sidon, they would have repented long ago in sackcloth and ashes. But I say unto you, It shall be more tolerable for Tyre and Sidon at the day of judgment than for you. And thou, Capernaum, which art exalted unto heaven, shalt be brought down to hell; for if the mighty works which have been done in thee, had been done in Sodom, it would have remained until this day. But I say unto you, It shall be more tolerable for Sodom in the day of judgment than for thee."

With what deep and awful solemnity does the word "Woe!" fall upon the ear, as coming from the lips of the Son of God. It is the woe consequent upon rejected grace. It is no longer merely a question of law broken, ordinances dishonored and abused, divine institutions shamefully corrupted, prophets and wise men rejected and stoned.

All this there was, alas! But there was more. The Son Himself had come, in richest grace. He had spoken in their ears such words as none other had ever spoken. He had wrought His mighty miracles in their midst. He had healed their sick, cleansed their lepers, raised their dead, fed their hungry, opened the eyes of their blind. What had He not done? What had He not said? He longed to gather them beneath His sheltering wing; but they would not nestle there. They preferred the wings of the archenemy to the wings of Jehovah. He had opened His bosom to receive them; but they would not trust Him. All day long had He stretched forth His hands to them; but they would not have Him; and now, at length, after long forbearing, He pours forth His solemn woes upon them, and tells them of the appalling destiny awaiting them.

But, does it not occur to you that the "woe" of the eleventh of Matthew may have a wider range than even Chorazin, Bethsaida, and Capernaum? Should it not fall with still deeper emphasis, and more soul-subduing power, upon the ear of Christendom? For our part, we cannot doubt it for a moment. We cannot attempt to enter upon the circumstances which conspire to aggravate the guilt of the professing Church—the wide diffusion of scriptural knowledge and evangelical light—the numberless and nameless forms in which spiritual privileges lie scattered upon the pathway of this generation.

And what is the return? What the true practical condition of even those who occupy the very highest platform of Christian profession? Alas! who shall venture a reply? We look in one direction, and see the dark shadows of superstition enwrapping the minds of men. We turn the eye to another point, and there we see infidelity raising its bold and audacious front, and daring to lay its impious hand upon the sacred canon of inspiration. Combined with these, we see the poor heart eagerly grasping at everything that can possibly minister to ease and self-indulgence.

In a word, it may be safely affirmed that during the entire history of the world, there has not been exhibited a darker spectacle than that which professing Christianity presents at this very hour. Take Chorazin and its companion cities; take Sodom and Gomorrah and the cities of the plain; take Tyre and Sidon; put all these together into one scale, with all their guilt, and Christendom will outweigh them all. For if, in those cities, you find wickedness and infidelity, you do not find them, as in Christendom, tacked on to the name of Christ, or covered with the specious robes of Christian profession. No; this latter is the aggravated sin of Christendom, and hence the terrible "woe unto thee" is to be measured by the greatness of the privileges and consequent responsibility.

And if these lines should be scanned by one who up to this moment has rejected the testimony of the gospel, we would affectionately remind him that he should feel the solemnity of the words, "Woe unto thee." We fear that very few, comparatively, realize the awful responsibility of continually hearing and rejecting the gospel message. If it was a solemn thing for Capernaum to reject the light which shone upon it, how much more solemn it is for any one now to reject the still brighter light that shines upon him in

the gospel of the grace of God! Redemption is now accomplished, Christ is exalted to be a Prince and a Saviour, the Holy Ghost has come down, the canon of inspiration is complete, everything has been done that love could do.

If, therefore, in the face of all this accumulated light and privilege, a man is found still in unbelief, still living in his sins, surely he has much reason to fear lest this word be pronounced upon him at the last, "Woe unto thee, gospel rejector." "Because I have called, and ye refused; I have stretched out My hand, and no man regarded; but ye have set at nought all My counsel, and would none of My reproof; I also will laugh at your calamity; I will mock when your fear cometh; when your fear cometh as desolation, and your destruction cometh as a whirlwind; when distress and anguish cometh upon you. Then shall they call upon Me, but I will not answer; they shall seek Me early, but they shall not find Me" (Prov. 1:24-28). May these words be used by the Holy Ghost to awaken some careless reader, and lead him to the feet of Jesus!

Let us now turn, for a moment, to *the resources* which the true, the perfect, the divine Workman found in God. That blessed One had, most surely, His rebuffs in this wretched world; but He had His never-failing resources in God; and, hence, when everything seemed against Him, when He might say, "I have labored in vain, and spent My strength for nought and in vain"; when unbelief, hardness of heart, and rejection met His view on every side, "At that time Jesus answered and said, I thank thee, O Father, Lord of heaven and earth, because Thou hast hid these things from the wise and prudent, and hast revealed them unto babes. Even so, Father, for so it seemed good in Thy sight. All things are delivered unto Me of My Father; and no man knoweth the Son but the Father; neither knoweth any man the Father, save the Son, and he to whomsoever the Son will reveal Him."

Here, then, were the resources—the rich and varied resources of the true Workman, who could thank God in everything, and at all times. He was unmoved in the midst of all. If the testimony was rejected, if the message fell upon deaf ears and uncircumcised hearts, if the precious seed which was scattered by His loving hand fell upon the beaten highway and was borne off by the fowls of the air, He could bow His head and say, "I thank Thee, O Father. Even so, Father; for so it seemed good in Thy sight." There was no failure on His part. He ever walked and worked in the perfect line of the divine counsels.

Not so with us. If our testimony is rejected, if our work is unproductive, we may have to inquire as to the cause. We may have to judge ourselves in the matter. Perhaps we have not been faithful. The lack of result may be wholly attributable to ourselves. It might have been different had we been more single-eyed and devoted. We might have gathered golden sheaves in yonder corner of the field, had it not been for our own carnality and worldliness. We were self-indulgent when we ought to have been self-denying; we were governed by mixed motives. In short, there may be a thousand reasons, in ourselves and in our ways, why our labor has proved unproductive.

But with the only perfect Workman, this was not the case, and hence He could calmly retire from the rebuffs without into the resources within. It was all bright with Him there. "I thank *Thee*." He stayed His heart upon the eternal counsels of God. All things were delivered unto Him; and, as He says, elsewhere, "All that the Father giveth Me shall come to Me." It was all settled, and all right. The divine counsel shall stand, and the divine good pleasure shall be accomplished. What a sweet relief for the heart amid rebuffs and disappointments!

God will perfect that which concerneth His servants; and even where there are mistakes and failures, as alas! there are in abundance with all of us, the Lord's rich grace abounds over all, and actually takes occasion from our very mistakes to shine out all the more brightly—though, assuredly, the mistakes must produce their own painful and humiliating results. It is the remembrance of this which alone can give calm repose in the midst of the most discouraging circumstances. If we take the eye off God, our souls must soon be overwhelmed. It is our privilege to be able, in our little measure, to thank God in view of everything, and take refuge in His eternal counsels, which must be made good despite all the unbelief of man, and all the malice of Satan.

But we must draw this paper to a close, and shall do little more than quote the precious words which set forth *the returns* which our blessed Lord and Saviour makes to us. "Come unto Me, all ye that labor and are heavy-laden, and I will give you rest. Take My yoke upon you, and learn of Me; for I am meek and lowly in heart; and ye shall find rest unto your souls. For My yoke is easy and My burden is light."

These words are familiar to our readers, and we but introduce them here as completing the lovely picture presented in our chapter. We feel assured the spiritual reader will greatly enjoy the presentation of the divine Workman in His rebuffs, His resources, and His returns. It is a marvelous lesson indeed. The Lord Jesus retires from a scene of disappointments, and finds all His springs in God; He then comes forth into the midst of the very scene that had repulsed Him, and makes His gracious returns. It is all in perfect grace—grace unfailing—mercy inexhaustible—patience unwearied.

True, He had sent an answer to the Baptist; He had faithfully portrayed the men of that generation; He had denounced a solemn woe upon the impenitent cities; but He can come forth in all the divine freshness and fulness of the grace that was in Him, and say, to every heavy laden soul, "*Come unto Me.*"

All this is divine. It draws out our hearts in worship and thanksgiving. If *faithfulness* is constrained, in the view of aggravated impenitence, to say, "*Woe* unto thee," *grace* can address every burdened heart in the touching accents, "*Come* unto *Me*." Both are perfect. The Lord Jesus felt the rebuffs. He would not have been very man if He had not felt them. Yes, He felt the rebuffs. He could say, "I looked for some to take pity, but there was none; and for comforters, but I found none." Mark, "*I looked*." His loving human heart fondly "looked" for pity, but found it not. He looked for comforters, but looked in vain. There was no pity for Jesus—no comforters for Him. He was left alone.

Loneliness and desolation, thirst, ignominy and death—such was the portion of the Son of God and Son of man. "Reproach," says He, "hath broken My heart." It is a fatal mistake to suppose that the Lord Jesus did not feel in every respect, as man should feel, the varied exercises through which He passed. He felt everything that man is capable of feeling except sin, and this latter He bore and expiated on the cross, blessed be His name!

This is not only a great cardinal doctrine of the Christian faith, but a truth of infinite sweetness to the heart of every true believer. Jesus, as man, felt what it was to be neglected, to be disappointed, to be wounded and insulted. Blessed Jesus! thus it was with Thee, down here, because Thou wast very man, perfect in all that became a man, in the midst of this heartless world. Thy loving heart sought sympathy, but found it not. Loneliness was Thy portion while craving sweet companionship. This world had no pity, no comfort for Thee.

And yet, mark the grace which breathes in those words, "Come unto Me." How unlike us! If we, who so often deserve them, because of our ways, meet with rebuffs and disappointments, what returns do we make? Alas! for the answer. Chagrin and sourness, fault-finding and bitter complaints. And why is this? It may be said we are not perfect: certainly not in ourselves; but we may rest assured, that if we were more in the constant habit of retiring from the rebuffs of the world or of the professing Church, into our resources in God, we should be much better

able to come forth and make gracious returns in the midst of the scene which had repulsed us. But it too often happens that instead of being driven in upon God, we are driven in upon *self;* and the consequence is that, instead of returning grace, we return bitterness. It is impossible that we can make a right return if we fail to realize our right resource.

Oh, that we may really learn of Jesus, and take His yoke upon us! May we drink into His meek and lowly spirit! What words—"Meek and lowly!" How unlike nature! How unlike the world! How unlike us! How much pride, haughtiness, and self-sufficiency in us! What self-confidence, self-seeking, and self-exaltation! May the Lord give us to see ourselves as He sees us, so that we may be in the dust in His presence, and ever walk humbly before Him.

May it be given us to prove, in this day of headiness and high-mindedness, the moral security of a lowly mind and humble spirit—gladly bearing His yoke—the yoke of entire subjection to our Lord's will in all things. This is the secret of true peace and power. We can only taste of true rest of heart when the will is kept in subjection. It is when we can meet every dispensation of our Father's hand with an "Even so," that rest is our portion. If our will is active, rest must be out of the question. It is one thing to *receive* rest of conscience on coming to Jesus, at the first, and quite another thing to *find* rest of heart through taking His yoke and learning of Him. May it be given us to know very much more of the latter, in this day of restless activity.

JOHN THE BAPTIST—ONLY "A VOICE"

QUESTIONS AND HOW TO MEET THEM

I HAVE BEEN VERY MUCH interested of late in looking at the excellent way in which John the Baptist met the various questions which came before him; for, alas! there were questions in his day, as there are in ours.

What I specially refer to now is presented to us in chapters 1 and 3 of John's Gospel.

The first question which this dear and honoured servant of Christ was called to answer had respect to himself, and of this he makes very short work indeed. "This is the record of John, when the Jews sent priests and Levites from Jerusalem to ask him, Who art thou?"

It is ever welcome to any right-minded person to be asked to speak about himself. So, I doubt not, John found it. He readily told them that he was not the Messiah, that he was not Elias; yea, that he was not even the prophet. But they would have a positive answer. "They said unto him, Who art thou? that we may give an answer to them that sent us. What sayest thou of thyself?" Little indeed had he to say of himself. "I" had a very small place in John's thoughts. "A voice." Was this all? Yes; this was all. The Spirit in the prophet had spoken; John quotes the words, and there he leaves it. Blessed servant! Honoured witness! Would we had more of thy excellent spirit!—more of thy method of answering questions!

But these Pharisees were not satisfied. John's self-hiding spirit was entirely beyond them. "They asked him, and said unto him, Why baptizest thou then, if thou be not the Christ, nor Elias, neither the prophet?"

Here again the Baptist makes short work. "John answered them, saying, I baptize with water; but there standeth one among you whom ye know not. He it is who, coming after me, is preferred before me, whose shoe's latchet I am not worthy to unloose."

Thus, as to himself, he was merely a voice. And, as to his work, he baptized with water, and he was only too glad to retire behind that blessed One whose shoe's latchet he felt himself utterly unworthy to unloose.

This is uncommonly fine. I feel assured that the lovely spirit displayed by this most illustrious servant of Christ is to be coveted. I do long to know more and more of this self-hiding—this losing sight of self and its doings—this retiring spirit. Truly it is much needed in this day of egotistical boast and pretension.

But turn with me for a moment to John 3. Here we have another kind of question. It is not now about himself or his work, but about purifying. "There arose a question among some of John's disciples and the Jews about purifying. And they came to John, and said unto him, Rabbi, He that was with thee beyond Jordan, to whom thou bearest witness, behold, the same baptizeth, and all come to Him."

Now this was a mistake, for "Jesus Himself baptized not, but His disciples." But this is not the point here. What strikes me is John's mode of settling all questions, right or wrong. He finds a perfect solution for all in the presence of his Lord. "John answered and said, A man can receive nothing except it be given him from heaven."

How true! How simple! How perfectly obvious! What a complete settlement of every question! If a man has anything at all, whence did it, whence could it, come? Surely only from Heaven. What a perfect cure for strife, envy, jealous, and emulation! "Every good gift and every perfect gift is *from above*, and *cometh down* from the Father of lights." What a tale this tells of earth and of man! What a record it bears to Heaven and to God! Not one atom of good on earth but what comes from Heaven. Not an atom of good in man but what comes from God. Why, then, should any one boast, or be jealous, or envious? If all goodness is from above, let there be an end of all strife, and let all hearts go up in praise to "the Father of lights."

Thus it was the Baptist met the questions of his day. He let all the questioners know that their questions had but little interest for him. And, more than that, he let them know where all his interests lay. This blessed servant found all his springs in the Lamb of God, in His precious work—in His glorious Person. The voice of the Bridegroom was enough for him, and, having heard that, his joy was full. The question of purifying might be interesting enough in its place, and no doubt, like all other questions, it had its right and its wrong side; but for John, the Bridegroom's voice was enough. In His presence he found a divine answer to every question—a divine solution to every difficulty. He looked up to Heaven, and saw every good thing coming from thence. He looked into the Bridegroom's face, and saw every moral glory centred there. This was enough for him. Why trouble him with questions of any kind—questions about himself or his work, or about purifying? He lived far beyond the region of questions, in the blessed presence of his Lord, and there he found all his heart could ever need.

Now it seems to me that you and I would do well to take a leaf out of John's book as regards all this. I need not remind you that in this our day there are questions agitating men's minds. Yes, and some of us are called to account for not expressing ourselves more decidedly on some at least of these questions. But, for my part, I believe the devil is doing his utmost to alienate our hearts from Christ and from one another by questions. We ought not to be ignorant of his devices. He does not come openly, and say, "I am the devil, and I want to divide and scatter you by questions." Yet this is precisely what he is seeking to do.

Now, it matters not whether the question be right or wrong in itself; the devil can make use of a right question just as effectively as of a wrong one, provided he can succeed in raising that question into undue prominence, and causing it to come between our souls and Christ, and between us and our brethren. I can understand a difference in judgment, on various minor questions. Christians have differed about such for many long centuries, and they will continue to differ until the end of time. It is human weakness. But when any question is allowed to assume undue prominence, it ceases to be mere human weakness, and becomes a wile of Satan. I may have a very decided judgment on any given point, and so may you. But what I long for now is a thorough sinking of all questions, and a rejoicing together in hearing the Bridegroom's voice, and going on together in the light of His blessed countenance. This will confound the enemy. It will effectually deliver us from prejudice and partiality, from cliques and coteries. We shall then measure one another, not by our views of any particular question, but by our appreciation of the Person of Christ, and our devotion to His cause.

In a word, what I long for is that you and I, and all our dear brethren throughout the whole world, may be characterized by a deep-toned, thorough, devotion to the name, and truth, and cause of Christ. I long to cultivate broad sympathies, that can take in every true lover of Christ, even though we see not eye to eye on all minor questions. At best "we know but in part"; and we can never expect people to agree with us about questions. But if Christ be our one absorbing object, all other things will assume their right place, their relative value, their proper proportions. "Let us, therefore, as many as be perfect [as many as have Christ for their one object], be thus minded: and if *in anything* ye be otherwise [or differently, ἑτέρως] minded, God shall reveal even this unto you. *Nevertheless*, whereto we have already attained, let us walk by *the same rule* [Christ], and mind the same thing" (Christ). The moment anything else but Christ is introduced as a rule to walk by, it is simply the work of the devil. Of this I am as sure as that I hold this pen in my hand.

May the Lord keep us all close to Himself, walking together, not in sectarianism, but in true brotherly love, seeking the blessing and prosperity of all who belong to Christ, and promoting in every possible way His blessed cause, until He come!

"THOU AND THY HOUSE"

THE CHRISTIAN AT HOME

THERE ARE TWO HOUSES which occupy a very prominent place on the page of inspiration, and these are, the house of God and the house of God's servant. God attaches immense importance to His house; and justly so, because it is His. His truth, His honor, His character, His glory, are all involved in the character of His house; and hence it is His desire that the impress of what He is should plainly appear on that which belongs to Him. If God has a house, it assuredly should be a godly house, a holy house, a spiritual house, an elevated house, a pure and heavenly house. It should be all this, not merely in abstract position and principle, but practically and characteristically. Its abstract position is founded upon what God has made it, and where He has set it; but its practical character is founded upon the actual walk of those who form its constituent parts down here upon this earth.

Now, while many minds may be prepared to enter into the truth and importance of all the principles connected with God's house, there may be but few, comparatively, who are disposed to give a due measure of attention to those connected with the house of God's servant; although if one were asked the question, What house stands next in order to the house of God? he should undoubtedly reply, The house of His servant. However, as there is nothing like bringing the holy authority of God's Word to bear upon the conscience, I shall quote a few passages of Scripture, which will tend to show, in a clear and forcible point of view, what are God's thoughts about the house of one holding connection with Him.

When the iniquity of the antediluvian world had risen to a head, and the end of all flesh had come before a righteous God, who was about to roll the heavy tide of judgment over the corrupted scene, these sweet words fell upon Noah's ear: "Come thou and *all thy house* into the ark; for thee have I seen righteous before Me in this generation" (Gen. 7:1). Now, it will be said that Noah was a type of Christ—the righteous head of a saved family—saved in virtue of their association with him. All this is fully granted; but Noah's typical character does not in any wise interfere with the principle which I seek to deduce from this and kindred passages, which principle I shall here, at the outset, distinctly lay down—it is this: *the house of every servant of God is, in virtue of its connection with Him, brought into a position of privilege and consequent responsibility.* *

That this is a principle involving vast practical consequences we shall, with God's blessing and grace, see ere we close this paper; but we must first seek to establish its truth from the Word of God. Were we merely left to argue from analogy, our thesis might be easily proved; for it could never be supposed, by any mind at all acquainted with the character and ways of God, that He would attach such unspeakable importance to His own house, and attach none at all, or almost none, to that of His servant. This

---

* The reader will not, I trust, imagine that the necessity for the work of the Holy Ghost in the regeneration of the children of Christian parents is denied or interfered with. God forbid! "Except a man be born again, he cannot see the kingdom of God." This is as true of a Christian's child as of every one else. Grace is not hereditary. The sum of what I would press upon Christian parents is, that Scripture inseparably links a man with his house, and that the Christian parent is warranted in counting upon God for his children, and responsible to train his children for God. Let any one who denies this interpret Ephesians 6: 4.

were impossible; it would be utterly unlike God, and God must always act like Himself. But we are not left to analogy on this most important and deeply practical question; and the passage just quoted forms one of the first of a series of direct and positive proofs. In it we find those immensely significant words, "*Thou and thy house*" inseparably linked together. God did not reveal a salvation for Noah which was of no avail to Noah's house. He never contemplated such a thing. The same ark that lay open to him lay open to them also. Why? Was it because they had faith? No; but because *he* had, and they were connected with him. God gave him a blank check for himself and his family, and it devolved upon him to fill it up by bringing them in along with him. I repeat it, this does not in the least interfere with Noah's typical character. I look at him typically, but I look at him personally also. Nor can I, under any circumstances, separate a man from his house. The house of God is brought into blessing and responsibility because of its connection with Him; and the house of the servant of God is brought into blessing and responsibility because of its connection with him. This is our thesis.

The next passage to which I shall refer occurs in the life of Abraham. "And the Lord said, 'Shall I hide from Abraham that thing which I do? . . . For I know him, that he will command his children and his household after him, and they shall keep the way of the Lord, to do justice and judgment; that the Lord may bring upon Abraham that which He hath spoken of him' " (Gen. 18:17-19). Here it is not a question of salvation, but of communion with the mind and purposes of God; and let the Christian parent note and solemnly ponder the fact that when God was seeking out a man to whom He could disclose His secret counsels, He selected one possessing the simple characteristic of "commanding his children and his household."

This, to a tender conscience, cannot fail to prove a most pungent principle. If there is one point above another in which Christians have failed, it is in this very point of commanding their children and household. They surely have not set God before them in

this particular; for if I look at the entire record of God's dealings with His house, I find them invariably characterized by the exercise of power on the principle of righteousness. He has firmly established and unflinchingly carried out His holy authority. It matters not what the outward aspect or character of His house may be, the essential principle of His dealing with it is immutable. "Thy testimonies are very sure; holiness becometh Thy house, O Lord, *forever*." Now, the servant must ever take his Master as his model; and if God rules His house with power exercised in righteousness, so must I; for if I am in any one particular of my conduct different from Him, I must in that particular be wrong. This is plain.

But not only does God so rule His house; He likewise loves, approves of, and treats with His marked and honored confidence those who do the same. In the above passage, we find Him saying, "I cannot hide my purposes from Abraham." Why? Is it because of his personal grace or faith? No; but simply because "he will command his children and his household." A man who knows how to command his house is worthy of God's confidence. This is a stupendous truth, the edge of which should pierce the conscience of many a Christian parent. Many of us, alas! with our eye resting on Genesis 18:19, may well prostrate ourselves before the One who uttered and penned that word, and cry out, Failure! failure! shameful, humiliating failure! And why is this? Why have we failed to meet the solemn responsibility devolving upon us in reference to the due command of our households? I believe there is but one reply, viz, because we have failed to realize, by faith, the privilege conferred upon those households in virtue of their association with us. It is remarkable that our two earliest proofs should present to our view, with such accuracy, the two grand divisions of our question, namely, privilege and responsibility. In Noah's case, the word was, "Thou and thy house" in the place of salvation; in Abraham's case, it was "Thou and thy house" in the place of moral government. The connection is at once marked and beautiful, and the man who fails in faith to appropriate the privilege will fail in moral power to answer the responsibility. God looks upon a man's house as a part of himself, and he cannot, in the smallest degree, whether in principle or practice, disregard the connection without suffering serious damange, and also marring the testimony.

Now, the question for the Christian parent's conscience really is, *Am I counting upon God for my house, and ruling my house for God?* A solemn question, surely; yet it is to be feared very few feel its magnitude and power. And here, perhaps, my reader may feel disposed to demand fuller Scripture proof than has yet been adduced, as to our warrant for counting upon God for our houses. I shall therefore proceed with the Scripture-quotations. I give one from the history of Jacob. "And God said to Jacob, 'Arise, go up to Bethel.' " This would seem to have been addressed to Jacob personally; but he never thought for a moment of disconnecting himself from his family, either as to privilege or responsibility; wherefore it is immediately added, "Jacob said unto *his household*, and to all that were with him, 'Put away the strange gods that are among you, and be clean, and change your garments; and let *us* arise, and go up to Bethel' " (Gen. 35:1-3). Here we see that a call to Jacob put Jacob's house under responsibility. He was called to go up to God's house, and the question immediately suggested itself to his conscience, whether his own house were in a fit condition to respond to such a call.

We now turn to the opening chapters of the book of Exodus, where we find that one of Pharaoh's four objections to the full deliverance and separation of Israel had specific reference to "the little ones." "And Moses and Aaron were brought again unto Pharaoh; and he said unto them, 'Go, serve the Lord your God; but who are they that shall go?' And Moses said, 'We will go with our young and with our old, with our sons and with our daughters, with our flocks and with our herds will we go; *for* we must hold a feast unto the Lord' " (Exod. 10:8-9).

The reason why they should take the little ones and all with them was because they were going to hold a feast unto the Lord. Nature might say, Oh, what can these little creatures know about a feast unto the Lord? Are you not afraid of making them formalists? The reply of Moses is simple and decisive—"We will go with our young . . . *for we* must hold a feast unto the Lord." They had no idea of seeking one thing for themselves and another for their children. They dreamed not of Canaan for themselves and Egypt for their children. How could they taste the manna of the wilderness, or the old corn of the land, while their children were feeding upon the leeks, the onions, and the garlic of Egypt? Impossible. Moses and Aaron understood not such acting. They felt that God's call to them was a call to their little ones; and, moreover, were it not fully carried out, they would no sooner have gone forth from Egypt by one road than their children would draw them back by another. That such would have been the case Satan was but too well aware, and hence appears the reason of the objection, "Not so: go now *ye that are men.*" This is the very thing which so many professing Christians are doing (or attempting, rather, to do) at this present time. They profess to go forth themselves to serve the Lord, but their little ones are in Egypt. They profess to have taken "three days' journey into the wilderness;" in other words, they profess to have left the world, they profess to be dead to it, and risen with Christ, as the possessors of a heavenly life, and the heirs and expectants of a heavenly glory; but they leave their little ones behind, in the hands of Pharaoh, or rather of Satan.* They have

---

* It will be said that there cannot be any analogy between the actual removal of people from one country to another and the training of our children. I reply, the analogy only applies in principle. It is perfectly evident that we cannot take our children to Heaven in the sense in which the Israelites took theirs to Canaan. God alone can fit our children for Heaven, by implanting in them the life of His own Son; and He alone can bring them to Heaven, in His own time. But then, although we can neither fit our children for, nor bring them to, Heaven, we can, nevertheless, by faith, train them for it; and it is not merely our *duty* (a poor, cold, and unworthy expression), but our high and holy *privilege* so to do. Hence, therefore, if the principle on which, and the object with which, we train our children are manifestly worldly, we do, virtually, and so far as in us lies, leave them in the world. And on the other hand, if our principle and object are unequivocally heavenly, then do we, so far as in us lies, train them for Heaven. This, my beloved reader, is all that is meant in this tract by leaving our children in Egypt or taking them to Canaan. We are responsible to *train* our children, though we cannot *convert* them; and God will assuredly bless the faithful training of those whom He has graciously given us.

given up the world for themselves, but they cannot do so for their children. Hence, on Lord's day, the professed position of strangers and pilgrims is taken; hymns are sung, prayers uttered, and principles taught which bespeak a people far advanced in the heavenly life, and just on the borders of Canaan, in actual experience (in spirit, of course, they are already there); but alas! on Monday morning, every habit, every pursuit, every object, contradicts all this. The little ones are trained for the world. The scope, aim, object, and entire character of their education is worldly, in the truest and strictest sense of the word. Moses and Aaron would not have understood such actings, and neither indeed should any morally honest heart, or upright mind, understand them. I should have no other principle, portion, or prospect for my children but what I have for myself; nor should I train them with a view to any other. If Christ and heavenly glory are sufficient for me, they are sufficient for them likewise; but then the proof that they are really sufficient for me should be unequivocal. The tone of the parent's character should be such as to afford not a shadow of a doubt as to the real, deep-seated purpose and object of his soul.

But what shall my child say to me if I tell him that I am earnestly seeking Christ and Heaven for him, while at the same time I am educating him for the world? Which will he believe? Which will exert the more powerful practical influence on his heart and life—my words, or my acts? Let conscience reply; and oh, let it be an honest reply, a reply emanating from its deepest depths, a reply which will unanswerably demonstrate that the question is understood in all its pungency and power. I verily believe the time is come for plain dealing with one another's conscience. It must be apparent to every prayerful and attentive observer of the Christianity of the present day, that it wears a most sickly aspect; that the tone is

miserably low; and, in a word, that there must be something radically wrong. As to testimony for the Son of God, it is rarely—alas! how rarely!—thought of. Personal salvation seems to form the very highest object with ninty-nine out of every hundred professing Christians, as if we were left here to be saved; and not, as saved ones, to glorify Christ.

Now, I would affectionately, yet faithfully, suggest the question, whether much of the failure in practical testimony for Christ is not justly traceable to the neglect of the principle involved in the expression, "Thou and thy house." I cannot but think it has much to do with it. One thing is certain, that a quantity of worldliness, confusion, and moral evil has crept in amongst us through our little ones having been left in Egypt. We see many who, it may be, ten, fifteen, or twenty years ago, took a prominent place in testimony and service, and seemed to have their hearts much in the work, are now gone back, lamentably, not having power to keep their own heads above water, much less to help any one else. All this utters a warning voice for Christian parents having rising families; and the utterance is, *"Beware of leaving your little ones in Egypt."* Many a heart-broken father, at the present moment, is left to weep and groan over his fatal mistake in reference to his household. He left them in Egypt, in an evil hour, and under a gross delusion, and now when he ventures, it may be in real faithfulness and earnest affection, to drop a word into the ear of those who have grown up around him, they meet it with a deaf ear and an indifferent heart, while they cling with vigor and decision to that Egypt in which he faithlessly and inconsistently left them. This is a stern fact, the statement of which may send a pang to many a heart; but truth must be told, in order that, though it wounds some, it may prove a salutary warning to others. But I must proceed with the proofs.*

In the book of Numbers, "the little ones"

---

* There is, I should say, a very serious error involved in a Christian parent's committing the training of his children to unconverted persons, or even to those whose hearts are not one with him as to separation from the world. It is natural that a child should look up to, and follow the example of, one who has the training and management of him. Now, what can a teacher make of a child, save what he is himself? Whither can he lead him, but to where he is himself? What principles can he instill, save those which govern his own mind, and form the basis of his own character? Well, if I see a man governed by worldly principles—if I see

are again introduced to our notice. We have just seen that the real purpose of a soul in communion with God was to go up with the little ones out of Egypt. They must be brought forth from thence at all cost; but neither faith nor faithfulness will rest here. We must not only count upon God to bring them up out of Egypt, but also to bring them on into Canaan. Here Israel signally failed. After the return of the spies, the congregation, on hearing their discouraging report, gave utterance to these fatal accents, "Wherefore hath the Lord brought us unto this land, to fall by the sword, that our wives and our children should be a prey? Were it not better for us to return into Egypt?" (Num. 14) This was terrible. It was, in reality, so far as in them lay, verifying Pharaoh's wily prediction in reference to these very little ones, "Look to it now, for evil is before you." Unbelief always justifies Satan and makes God a liar, while faith always justifies God and proves Satan a liar; and as it is invariably true that according to your faith so shall it be unto you, so we find, on the other hand, that unbelief reaps as it sows. Thus it was with unhappy, because unbelieving, Israel. "As truly as I live, saith the Lord, *as ye have spoken in Mine ears, so will I do to you.* Your carcasses shall fall in this wilderness; and all that were numbered of you, according to your whole number, from twenty years old and upward, which have murmured against Me, doubtless ye shall not come into the land concerning which I sware to make you dwell therein, save Caleb the son of Jephunneh, and Joshua the son of Nun. *But your little ones*, which ye

said should be a prey, them will I bring in, and they shall know the land which ye have despised. But as for you, your carcasses, they shall fall in the wilderness" (ver. 28-32). "They limited the Holy One of Israel" as to their little ones. This was a grievous sin, and it has been recorded for our admonition. How constantly does the heart of the Christian parent reason, in reference to the mode of dealing with children, instead of simply taking God's ground about them. It may be said, We cannot make Christians of our children. This is not the question. We are not called to "make" any thing of them. This is God's work, and His only; but if He says, "Bring your little ones with you," shall we refuse? I would not make a formalist of my child, and I *could* not make him a real Christian; but if God, in infinite grace, says to me, "I look upon your house as part of yourself, and, in blessing you, I bless it." shall I, in gross unbelief of heart, refuse this blessing, lest I should minister to formalism, or because I cannot impart reality? God forbid. Yea, rather, let me rejoice, with deep unfeigned joy, that God has blessed me with a blessing so divinely rich and full that it extends not only to me, but also to all who belong to me; and, seeing that grace has given me the blessing, let faith take it up and appropriate it.*

But let us remember that the way to prove our entrance into the blessing is by fulfililng the responsibility. To say that I am counting upon God to bring my children to Canaan, and yet all the while educating them for Egypt, is a deadly delusion. My conduct proves my profession to be a lie, and I am not

---

plainly, from his whole course and character, that he is an unconverted person, shall I commit to him the training and instruction of my children, or the formation of their characters? It would be the height of folly and inconsistency so to do. As well might a man who desired to make an oval-shaped bullet cast the melted lead into a circular mould.

The same principle applies to the reading of books. A book is decidedly a *silent* teacher and former of the mind and character; and if I am called to look well to the character and principles of the living teacher, I am equally so to look to those of the silent teacher. I am quite convinced that in reference both to books and teachers we need to have our consciences stirred and instructed.

* Very many content themselves with the assurance that at some time or other their children will be converted. But this is not taking God's ground with them now. If we have the assurance that they are within the range of God's purpose, why do we not act upon that assurance? If we are waiting to see certain evidences of conversion in them before we act as Scripture directs, it is plain that we are looking at something besides God's promise. This is not faith. The Christian parent is privileged to look upon his child *now* as one to be trained for the Lord. He is bound to take this ground, in faith, and train him thus, looking to God, in the fullest assurance, for the result. If I wait to *see* fruits, this is not faith. Besides, the question arises, What are my children now? They may be going about like idle, willful vagrants, bringing sad dishonor on the name and truth of Christ, and yet all the while I satisfy myself by saying, I know they will be converted yet. This will never do. My children should be *now* a testimony for God; and they can only be this by my taking God's ground with them, and going on with Him about them.

to wonder if, in the righteous dealings of God, I am allowed to be filled with the fruit of my own doings. Conduct will ever prove the reality of our convictions; and in this, as in every thing else, that Word of the Lord is most solemnly true, "If any man will do His will, he shall know of the doctrine." We often want to know the doctrine before we do the will, and the consequence is, we are left in the most profound ignorance.

Now, to do the will of God in reference to our children, is to treat them as He does, by regarding them as part of ourselves, and training them accordingly. It is not merely by hoping they may ultimately prove to be the children of God, but by regarding them as those who are already brought into a place of privilege, and dealing with them upon this ground in reference to every thing. According to the thoughts and actings of many parents, it would seem as though they regarded their children in the light of heathens, who had no present interest in Christ, or relationship to God at all. This is, assuredly, falling grievously short of the divine mark. Nor is this a question, as it is too often made, of infant or adult baptism. No; it is simply and entirely a question of faith in the power and extent of that peculiarly gracious word. "Thou and thy house"—a word the force and beauty of which we shall see more and more fully as we proceed.

Throughout the book of Deuteronomy, the children of Israel are again and again instructed to set the commandments, the statutes, the judgments, and precepts of the law before their little ones; and these same little ones are contemplated as inquiring into the nature and object of various ordinances and institutions. The reader can easily run through the various passages.

I now pass on to that truly memorable resolution of Joshua, "Choose you this day whom ye will serve . . . . but as for me and my house, we will serve the Lord" (Josh. 24:15). Observe, "Me and my house." He felt it was not sufficient that he himself should be personally pure from all contact with the defilements and abominations of idolatry; he had also to look well to the moral character

and practical condition of his house. Though Joshua were not to worship idols, yet if his children did so, would he be guiltless? Certainly not. Moreover, the testimony of the truth would have been as effecutally marred by the idolatry of Joshua's house as by the idolatry of Joshua himself; and judgment would have been executed accordingly. It is well to see this distinctly. The opening of the first book of Samuel affords most solemn demonstration of the truth of this—"And the Lord said to Samuel, 'Behold, I will do a thing in Israel, at which both the ears of every one that heareth it shall tingle. In that day I will perform against Eli all things which I have spoken concerning *his house:* when I begin, I will also make an end. For I have told him that I will judge his house forever for the iniquity which he knoweth; *Because his sons made themselves vile and he restrained them not'* " (1 Sam. 3:11-13).

Here we see that no matter what the personal character of the servant of God may be, yet if he fail in the due regulation of his house, God will not hold him guiltless. Eli should have restrained his sons. It was his privilege, as it is ours, to be able to count upon the specific power of God in the subjugation of every element in his house which was calculated to mar the testimony; but he did not do this, and hence his terrible end was that he broke his neck about the house of God, because he had not broken his heart about his own house. Had he waited upon God about his willful sons—had he acted faithfully—had he discharged the holy responsibilities devolving upon him, the house of God would never have been desecrated, and the ark of God would not have been taken. In a word, had he treated his house as part of himself, and made it what it ought to be, he would not have called down upon himself the heavy judgment of Him whose principle it is never to separate the words, *"Thou and thy house."*

But how many parents have since trodden in Eli's footsteps! Through an utterly false idea in reference to the entire basis and character of parental relationship, they have allowed their children, from infancy to boyhood, and from boyhood to manhood, in the unrestrained indulgence of the will. Not having faith to take divine ground, they have failed in moral power to take even the human ground of making their children respect and obey them, and the issue has presented to view the most fearful picture of lawless extravagance and wild confusion. The highest object for the servant of God to set before him in the management of his house is the testimony therein afforded to the honor of Him to whose house he himself belongs. This is really the proper ground of action. I must not seek to have my children in order because it would be an annoyance and inconvenience to *me* to have them otherwise, but because the honor of God is concerned in the godly order of the households of all those who form constituent parts of His house.

Here, however, it may be objected that up to this point we have been breathing only the atmosphere of Old Testament Scripture, and that the principles and proofs have been only thence deduced; now, on the contrary, God's principle of action is grace according to election, and this leads to the calling out of a man, irrespective of all domestic ties and relationships, so that you may find a godly, devoted, heavenly-minded saint at the head of a most ungodly, irregular, worldly family. I maintain, in opposition to this, that the principles of God's moral government are eternal, and therefore, whether developed in one age or another, they must be the same. He cannot at one time teach that a man and his house are one, and commend him for ruling it properly, and at another time teach that they are not one, but permit him to rule his house as he pleases. This is impossible.

God's approval and disapproval of things flows out of what He is in Himself; and in this matter in particular, inasmuch as God rules His own house according to what He is Himself, He commands His servants to rule their houses upon the same principle. Has the dispensation of grace, or of Christianity, come in to upset this lovely moral order? God forbid! Nay, it has rather, if possible, added new traits of beauty thereto. Was the house of a Jew looked at as part of himself, and shall the house of a Christian be different?

Truly not. It would be a sad abuse, and an anomalous application of that heavenly word, "grace," to apply it to the misrule and demoralization that prevail in the houses of numberless Christians of the present day. Is it grace to allow the will to ride rampant? Is it grace to have all the passions, tempers, whims, and appetites of a corrupt nature indulged? Alas! call it not grace, lest our souls should lose the real meaning of the word, and begin to imagine it to be what we have called it. Call it by its proper names—a monstrous abuse—a denial of God, not only as the Ruler of His own house, but as the moral Administrator of the universe—a flagrant contradiction of all the precepts of inspiration on this deeply important subject.

But let us turn to the New Testament and see if we cannot find in its sacred pages ample proof of our thesis. Does the Holy Ghost, in this grand section of His book, exclude a man's house from the privileges and responsibilities attached thereto in the Old Testament? We shall see very plainly that He does no such thing. Let us have the proofs. In Christ's commission to His apostles, we find these words: "And into whatsoever city or town ye shall enter, inquire who in it is worthy; and there abide till ye go thence. And when ye come into a house, salute it. And if the house [not merely the master] be worthy, let your peace come upon *it;* but if it be not worthy, let your peace return to you again" (Matt. 10:11-13). Again, "And Jesus said unto Zacchaeus, 'This day is salvation come to *this house*, forasmuch as he also is a son of Abraham. For the Son of Man is come to seek and to save that which was lost ' " (Luke 19:9-10). So in the case of Cornelius—"Send men to Joppa, and call for Simon, whose surname is Peter; who shall tell thee words whereby *thou and all thy house* shall be saved" (Acts 11:13-14). So also to the jailer at Philippi—"Believe on the Lord Jesus Christ, and *thou shalt be saved and thy house*" (Acts 16:31). Then we have the practical result—"And when he had brought them into his house, he set meat before them, and rejoiced, believing in God *with all his house*" (ver. 34). In the same chapter, Lydia says, "If ye have judged me to be faithful to the Lord, come into *my house* and abide" (ver. 15). "The Lord give mercy unto *the house* of Onesiphorus." Why? was it because of its actings toward him? No; but "because *he* oft refreshed me, and was not ashamed of my chain" (2 Tim. 1:16). "A bishop must be one that ruleth well his own house, having his children in subjection with all gravity. For if a man know not how to rule his own house, how shall he take care of the Church of God?"

Now, under the term "house," three things are included, viz., the house itself, the children, and the servants. All these, whether taken together or separately, should bear the distinct stamp of God. The house of a man of God should be ruled for God, in His name and for His glory. The head of a Christian household is the representative of God. Whether as a father or as a master, he is to his household an expression of the power of God; and he is bound to walk in the intelligent recognition and practical development of this fact. It is on this principle he is to provide for and govern the whole. Hence, "if any provide not for his own house, he hath denied the faith, and is worse than an infidel." By neglecting the sphere over which God has set him, he proves his ignorance of and unlikeness to the One whom he is called to represent.

This is plain enough. If I want to know how I am to provide for and rule my house, I have only carefully to study the way in which God provides for and rules His house. This is the true way to learn. Nor is it here a question as to the actual conversion of the constituent parts of the household. Not at all. What I desire to press upon all Christian heads of houses is, that the whole affair, from one end to the other, should distinctly wear the stamp of God's presence and God's authority,—that there should be a clear acknowledgment of God on the part of every member. That every thing should be so conducted as to elicit the confession, "*God is here*"; and all this, not that the head of the house may be praised for his moral influence and judicious management, but simply that God may be glorified. This is not too much to aim at; yea, we should never rest satisfied with any thing less. A Christian's house

should be but a miniature representation of the house of God, not so much in the actual condition of individual members as in the moral order and godly arrangement of the whole.

Some may shake their heads and say, This is all very fine, but where will you get it? I only ask, Does the Word of God teach a Christian man so to rule his house? If so, woe be to me if I refuse or fail to do so. That there has been the most grievous failure in the management of our houses every honest conscience must admit, but nothing can be more shameful than for a man calmly and deliberately to sit down satisfied with a disordered condition of his house because he cannot attain to the standard which God has set before him. All I have to do is to follow the line which Scripture has laid down, and the blessing must assuredly follow, for God cannot deny Himself. But if I, in unbelief of heart, say I cannot reach the blessing, of course I never shall. Every field of blessing or privilege which God opens before us demands an energy of faith to enter. Like Canaan of old to the children of Israel; there it lay, but they had to go thither, for the word was, "Every place that thy foot shall tread upon." Thus it is ever. Faith takes possession of what God gives. We should aim at every thing which tends to glorify Him who has made us all we are or ever shall be.

But what can be more dishonoring to God than to see the house of His servant the very reverse of what He would have it? And yet were we to judge from what constantly meets our view, it would seem as if many Christians thought that their houses had nothing whatever to do with their testimony. Most humbling it is to meet with some who, so far as they are personally concerned, seem nice Christians, but who entirely fail in the management of their houses. They speak of separation from the world, but their houses present the most distressingly worldly appearance; they speak of the world being crucified to them and of their being crucified to the world, and yet the world is stamped on the very face of their whole establishment. Every thing seems designed to minister to the lust of the flesh, the lust of the eye, and the pride of life. Magnificent pier glasses to reflect the flesh; sumptuous carpets, sofas, and loungers for the ease of the flesh; glittering chandeliers for the pride and vanity of the flesh. But it may be said, It is taking low ground to descend to such particulars. I reply, The daughters of Zion might just as well have passed the same comment upon the following solemn appeal: "In that day the Lord will take away the bravery of their tinkling ornaments about their feet, and their cauls, and their round tires like the moon, the chains and the bracelets and the mufflers, the bonnets and the ornaments of the legs and the headbands and the tablets and the earrings, the rings, and nose-jewels, the changeable suits of apparel and the mantles and the wimples and the crisping-pins, the glasses and the fine linen and the hoods and the vails" (Isa. 3:18-23).

This was descending to very minute particulars. The same might be said of the following passage from Amos: "Woe to them that are at ease in Zion . . . that lie upon beds of ivory, and stretch themselves upon their couches, and eat the lambs out of the flock, and the calves out of the midst of the stall; that chant to the sound of the viol, and invent to themselves instruments of musick, like David" (chap. 6:1-5). The Spirit of God can descend to particulars when the particulars are there to be descended to. But it may be further objected, We must furnish our houses according to our rank in life. Wherever his objection is urged, it reveals very fully the real ground of the objector's soul. That ground is the world, unquestionably. *"Our rank in life"*!—what does this really mean, as applied to those who profess to be *dead?* To talk of our rank in life is to deny the very foundations of Christianity. If we have rank in life, then it follows that we must be alive as men in the flesh—men according to nature, and then the law has its full force against us, "for the law hath dominion over a man as long as he liveth." Hence this rank in life becomes a serious matter.

But, let me ask, how did we get rank in life? or, in what life is it? If it be in this life, then we are liars whenever we talk of being "crucified with Christ"—"dead with Christ" —"buried with Christ"—"risen with Christ" —"outside the camp with Christ"—"not in the flesh"—"not of the world which fadeth away." All these are so many splendid lies to those possessing, or pretending to, a rank in this life. This is the real truth of the matter; and we must allow the truth to reach and act upon our consciences, that it may influence our lives. What, then, is the only life in which we have a rank? The resurrection-life of Christ.

Redeeming love has given us a rank in this life, and truly we know that worldly furniture, costly array, ridiculous parade and retinue, have nothing to do with rank in this life. Ah, no; the circumstances which comport with rank in heavenly life are, holiness of character, purity of life, spiritual power, profound humility, separation from everything which directly savors of the flesh and the world. To furnish our persons and our houses with these things would be furnishing them "according to our rank in life." But in point of fact, this objection does really bring out the true principle at the heart's core. It has already been remarked that the house reveals the moral condition of the man, and this objection confirms that statement. People who talk, or even think, of rank in life have, "in their hearts, turned back again into Egypt." And what does God say will be the end of such? "I will carry you away beyond Babylon." Yes, it is greatly to be feared that the great millstone of Revelation 18 presents but too true a picture of the end of much of the sickly, spurious, hollow Christianity of the present day.

It may, however, be further urged that Christianity affords no warrant for filthy and irregular houses. This is most true. I know few things more distressing and dishonoring than to see the house of a Christian characterized by filth and confusion. Such things could never exist in connection with a really spiritual or even a well-adjusted mind. You may set it down that there must be something radically wrong wherever such things exist. Here, in an especial manner, the house of God presents itself before us as a blessed model. Over the door of that house may be seen inscribed this wholesome motto: "Let all things be done decently and in order;" and all who love God and His house will desire to carry out this precept at home.

The next point suggested by the expression, "thou and thy house," is the management of our children. This is a sore and deeply humbling point to many of us, inasmuch as it discloses a fearful amount of failure. The condition of the children tends, more than any thing, to bring out the condition of the parent. The real measure of my surrender of the world, and my subjugation of nature, will constantly be shown in my thoughts about and treatment of my children. I profess to have given up the world, so far as I am personally concerned; but then I have children. Have I given up the world for them as well? Some may say, How can I? They are in nature, and must have the world. Here again the true moral condition of the heart is revealed. The world is really not given up, and my children are made an excuse for grasping again what I professed to have given up, but my heart retained all the while. Are my children part of myself, or are they not? Part of myself, assuredly. Well, then, if I profess to have relinquished the world for myself and yet am seeking it for them, what is it but the wretched anomaly of a man half in Egypt and half in Canaan? We know where such an one is wholly and in reality. He is wholly and really in Egypt. Yes, my brethren, here is where we have to judge ourselves. Our children tell a tale. The music-master and the dancing-master are surely not the agents which the Spirit of God would select to help our children along, nor do they, by any means, comport with that high-toned Nazariteship to which we are called. These things prove that Christ is not the chosen and amply sufficient portion of our souls. What is sufficient for me is sufficient for those who are part of me. And shall I be so base as to train my children for the devil and the world? Shall I minister to and pamper that in them which I profess to mortify in myself? It is a grievous mistake, and we shall find it so. If my children are in Egypt, I am there myself. If my children savor of Babylon, I savor of it myself. If my children belong to a corrupt worldly religious system, I belong to it myself, in principle. "Thou and thy house" are one; God has made them one; and "what He has joined together, let no man put asunder."

This is a solemn and searching truth, in the light of which we may clearly see the evil of urging our children along a path upon which we profess to have forever turned our backs, as believing firmly that it terminates in hell fire. We profess to count the world's literature, its honors, its riches, its distinctions, its pleasures, all "dung and dross," yet these very things, which we have declared to be only hindrances to us in our Christian course and which, as such, we have professed to cast aside, we are diligently setting before our children as things perfectly essential to their progress.

In so doing, we entirely forget that things which act as clogs to us cannot possibly act as helps to our children.* It were infinitely better to throw off the mask, and declare plainly that we have not given up the world at all; and nothing ever made this thoroughly manifest but our children. The Lord, I believe, in righteous judgment, is taking up the families of brethren, to show in them the actual condition of the testimony amongst us. In many cases it is well known that the children of Christians are the wildest and most ungodly in the neighborhood. Should this be so? Would God accept a testimony at the hand of those who have it so? Would it be thus if we were walking faithfully before God as to our houses? These inquiries must be

---

* The Christian parent may ask, What am I to teach my child? The answer is simple. Teach him only such things as will prove useful to him as a servant of Christ. Do not teach him aught which you know would prove a positive source of defilement or weakness to him should he remain here. We are seldom at a loss to know what kind of food to give our children. We are tolerably well aware of what would prove nourishing and what would prove the reverse. Now, were the instincts of the new nature as true and as energetic in us as those of the old, we should, I am persuaded, be at as little loss to decide in reference to what we should teach our children. In this, as in every thing else, it may be said, "If thine eye be single, thy whole body shall be full of light." If we have a deep sense of Christ's glory, and a sincere desire to promote it, we shall not be left in perplexity; but if our body is not "full of light," we may be assure our "eye" is not "single."

answered in the negative. If only I get the principle of "Thou and thy house" firmly fixed in my conscience, and intelligently wrought into my mind, I shall see it to be my place to count upon God, and cry to Him, just as much for the testimony of my house as for my own testimony. In reality, I cannot separate them. I may attempt it, but it is vain.

How often has one felt a pang at hearing such words as these: "Such an one is a very dear, godly, devoted brother; but, oh! he has the boldest and wildest children in the neighborhood, and his house is a sad mess of misrule and confusion." I ask, what is the testimony of such an one worth in the judgment of God? Little indeed. Saved he may be; but is salvation all we want? Is there no testimony to be given? and if there is, what is it? and where is it to be seen? Is it confined to the benches of a meeting room, or is it to be seen in the midst of a man's house? The heart can answer.

But it may be urged, Our children will crave a little worldly enjoyment, and we must indulge them. We cannot put old heads upon young shoulders. I reply, Our own hearts often crave a little of the world likewise. Shall we indulge their craving? No; but judge it. Exactly so. Do the same in reference to your children's craving. If I find my children going out after the world, I should immediately judge and chasten myself before God, crying to Him to enable me to put it down, so that the testimony may not suffer. But I cannot but believe that if the parent's heart is, from its centre to its circumference, purged of the world, its principles, and its lusts, it will exert a mighty influence upon his whole house. This is what makes this entire question one of such vast magnitude and practical weight. Is my house a just criterion by which to judge of my real condition? I believe the whole teaching of Scripture is in favor of an affirmative. This makes the matter peculiarly solemn. How am I walking before my family? Is my whole course and character so unequivocal that all can see that my one supreme object is Christ, and that I would just as soon, if I could, unlock the portals of hell, and let my children in, as

educate them for the world, or seek the world for them?

This I feel to be a startling inquiry; yet it is one which we are bound to follow up to the uttermost. What has called into existence, in many cases, that awful profanity, that disposition to scoff at sacred things, that utter distaste for the Scriptures, and for meetings where the Scriptures are brought forward, that skeptical and infidel spirit so sadly apparent in the children of Christian professors? Will any one undertake to say that the parents have nothing to do with this, in the judgment of God? May not much of this be justly traced to the sad incongruity between the professed principles and the actual practices of the parents? I believe it may. Children are shrewd observers. They very soon begin to discover what their parents are really at.

They will gather this, too, much more speedily and accurately from their *doings* than from their *prayings* or their *sayings;* and although the parents may teach that the world and its ways are bad, and though they may pray that their children may know the Lord, yet inasmuch as they are educating them for the world, and seeking most industriously to push them on in it, grasping at and getting in by every opening, and congratulating themselves when they have succeeded in settling them there, it necessarily follows that the children begin to say in their hearts, "The world is a good place after all, for my parents thank God on getting me a berth in it, and look upon it as a most marked opening of Providence. All that peculiar talk of theirs, therefore, about being dead to the world, and being risen with Christ—the world's being under judgment, and their being strangers and pilgrims therein—all this must be rank nonsense, or else Christians, so called, must be rank deceivers." Will any one say that such reasoning as this has not passed through the mind of many a professor's child? I cannot doubt it. The grace of God, no doubt, is sovereign, and often triumphs over all our errors and failures; but oh! let us think of the testimony, and let us see that our houses are really ordered for God and not for Satan.*

But it will be said, How are our children to get on? Must they not earn their bread? Unquestionably. God formed us for work. The very fact of my having a pair of hands proves that I am not to be idle. But I need not push my son back into that world which I have left, in order to give him employment. The Most High God, the Possessor of Heaven and earth, had one Son, His only begotten, the Heir of all things, by whom also He made the worlds; He did not take up any of the learned professions, but was known as "the carpenter." Has this no voice for us? Christ has gone up on high and taken His seat at God's right hand. As thus risen, He is our Head, Representative, and Model; but He has left us an example that we should follow His steps.

Are we following His steps in seeking to push our children on in that very world which crucified Him? Surely not: we are adopting the very opposite course, and the end will be accordingly. "Be not deceived; God is not mocked; for whatsoever a man soweth, that shall he also reap." As we sow, in reference to our children, so shall we also reap. If we sow to the flesh and the world, we cannot expect to reap otherwise. But I would not, by any means, be understood to teach that a Christian parent ought to place his child below the level on which the Lord has placed himself. I do not believe he would be warranted in so doing. If my calling be a godly one, it may suit my child as well as it suits myself. All cannot be carpenters, it is true; yet one feels that, in an age of progress like the present, where "onward and upward in the world" seems to be the great motto, there is a deep moral for the heart in the fact that the Son of God—the Creator and Sustainer of the universe—was only known amongst men as "the carpenter." It assuredly teaches that Christians should not be found

seeking "great things" for their children.

However, it is not merely in reference to the object set forth in our children's education that we have failed, and so marred the testimony; but also in the matter of keeping them in general subjection to parental authority. On this point there has been great deficiency amongst Christian parents. The spirit of the present age is that of insubordination. "Disobedient to parents" forms a trait in the apostasy of the last days; and we have specially helped on its development by an entirely false application of the principle of grace, as also by not seeing that there is involved in the parental relationship a principle of power exercised in righteousness, without which our houses must prove to be scenes of lawlessness and wild confusion. It is no grace to pamper an unsanctified will.

We mourn over our own lack of a broken will, and yet we are strengthening the will in our children. It is always, to my mind, a manifest proof of the weakness of parental authority, as well as of ignorance of the way in which the servant of God should rule his house, to hear a parent say to a child. "*Will* you do so and so?" This question, simple as it seems, tends directly to create or minister to the very thing which you ought to put down, by every means in your power, and that is, the exercise of the child's *will*. Instead, therefore, of asking the child, "Will you do?" just tell him what he is to do, and let there not be in his mind the idea of calling in question your authority. The parent's will should be supreme with a child, because the parent stands in the place of God. All power belongs to God, and He has invested His servant with power, both as a father and a master. If, therefore, the child or the servant resist this power, it is resistance of God.**

"Let as many servants as are under the

* I would, however, desire to remind the children of Christian parents that they are solemnly responsible to harken to God's holy Word, quite irrespective of the conduct of their parents. God's truth is not affected by the actings of men; and wherever one has heard the testimony of God's love, in the death and resurrection of Christ, he is responsible for the use he makes thereof, even though he should not have seen its sacred influence and power exemplified in the life of his parents. I would press these facts upon the serious attention of all children of Christian parents.

** "And ye fathers, provoke not your children to wrath; but bring them up in the nurture and admonition of the Lord" (Eph. 6:4). There is great danger of provoking our children to wrath by inordinate strictness and arbitrary treatment. We may constantly find ourselves seeking to mould and fashion our children according to our own tastes and peculiarities, rather than to "bring them yoke count their own masters worthy of all honor, that the name of *God* and His doctrine be not blasphemed." Observe, it is "God and His doctrine." Why? Because it is a question of power. The name of Christ and His doctrine would put the master and servant on a level, as members of one body. In Christ Jesus there is no distinction; but when I go abroad in the world, I encounter God's moral government, which makes one a master and another a servant; and any infringement upon that government will meet with certain judgment.

Now, it is of immense importance to have a clear understanding of the doctrine of God's moral government. It would settle many a difficulty, and solve many a question. This government is carried on with a righteous decision, which is peculiarly solemnizing. If we look through Scripture in reference to this subject, we shall find that in every instance in which there has been error or failure, it has inevitably produced its own results. Adam took of the forbidden fruit, and he was instantly thrust forth from the garden, into a world groaning beneath the curse and weight of his sin. Nor was he ever placed in paradise. True, grace came in, and gave him a promise of a Deliverer; moreover, it clothed his naked shoulders. Nevertheless,

his sin produced its own result. He made a false step, and he never recovered it.

Again, Moses, at the waters of Meribah, uttered a hasty word, and immediately a righteous God forbad his entrance into Canaan. In his case likewise grace came in, and gave him something better; for it was much better, from the top of Pisgah, to inspect the plains of Palestine in company with Jehovah than to inhabit them in company with Israel. So also in David's case. He committed a sin, and the solemn denunciation was immediately issued, "The sword shall never depart from thy house." In this case too grace abounded, and he enjoyed a more profound sense of grace as he ascended the side of mount Olivet with bare feet and covered head than he ever had enjoyed amid the splendors of a throne; nevertheless, his sin produced its own result. He made a false step, and he never recovered it.

Nor is the exemplification of this principle confined merely to Old Testament times. By no means. Look at the case of Barnabas. He gave utterance to the seemingly amiable desire to have the company of his nephew Mark, and, from that moment, he loses his honorable place in the records of the Holy Ghost. He is never heard of afterward, and

up in the nurture and admonition of the Lord." This is a very great mistake, and will surely issue in failure and confusion. We shall gain nothing, in the way of testimony for Christ, by moulding and fashioning nature into the most exquisite shapes. Moreover, it does not require faith to train and cultivate nature; but it does require it to bring up in the nurture and admonition of the Lord.

Some, however, may say that the apostle, in the above passage, is speaking of converted children. To this I reply, that there is nothing about conversion in the passage. It is not said, Bring up your converted children, etc. Were it thus, it would settle the whole question. But it is simply said, "*your children,*" which surely must mean *all* our children. Now, if I am to bring up all my children in the nurture and admonition of the Lord, when am I to commence? Am I to wait till they grow up to be almost men and women? or am I to begin where all right-minded people begin their work, namely, at the *beginning?* Am I to allow them to run on in nature's folly and wildness, during the most important part of their career, without ever seeking to bring their consciences into the presence of God, as to their solemn responsibilities? Am I to suffer them to spend in utter thoughtlessness that period of life in which the elements of their future character are imparted? This would be the most refined cruelty. What should we say to a gardener who would allow the branches of his fruit-trees to assume all sorts of crooked and fantastic shapes ere he thought of commencing a proper system of training? We should doubtless pronounce him a fool and a madman. And yet such an one is wise in comparison with a parent who suspends the nurture and admonition of the Lord until his children have made manifest progress in the nurture and admonition of the enemy.

But, it may be said, we must wait for evidences of conversion. To this I reply, that faith never waits for evidences, but acts on God's Word, and the evidences are sure to follow. It is always a manifest proof of infidelity to wait for signs when God gives a command. If Israel had waited for a sign when God said, "Go forward," it would have been plain disobedience; and if the man with the withered hand had waited for some evidence of strength when Christ commanded him to stretch forth his hand, he might have carried his withered hand to the grave with him. So is it with parents. If they wait for signs and evidences before they obey God's word in Ephesians 6: 4, they are certainly not walking by faith, but by sight. Besides, if we are to begin at the beginning to train our children, we must evidently begin before they are capable of giving what we might regard as evidences of conversion.

In this, as in every thing else, our place is to obey, and leave results with God. The moral condition of the soul may be tested by the command; but where there is the disposition to obey, the power to do so will surely accompany the command, and the fruits of obedience will follow "*in due season, if we faint not.*"

his place was supplied with a more wholly devoted heart.* Hence God's moral government is a most momentous truth. It is such, that as surely as one does wrong, he will reap the fruit of it, no matter who he is—believer or unbeliever, saint or sinner. Grace may forgive the sin, and will, where it is confessed and judged; but inasmuch as the principles of God's moral government have been interfered with, the offender must be made to feel his mistake. He has missed a step of the wheel, and he shall assuredly feel the consequences. This is a most solemn but specially wholesome truth, the action of which has been sadly clogged by false notions about grace. God never allows His grace to interfere with His moral government. He could not do so, because it would produce confusion, and "God is not the author of confusion."

It is here there has been so much failure in the management of our houses. We have forgotten the principle of righteous rule which God has set before us, and in the exercise of which He has given us an example. My reader must not confound the principle of God's government with the aspect of His character.** These two things are distinct. The former is righteousness, the latter is grace; but what I here desire to bring out is, the fact that there is a principle of righteousness involved in the relationship of father and master, and if this principle receive not its due place in the management of the family, there must be confusion. If I see a *strange* child doing wrong, I have no divine authority to exercise righteous discipline toward him; but the moment I see my own child doing so, I put him under discipline. Why? because I am his father.

But it may be said, The parental relationship is one of love. True; it is founded in love: "Behold, what manner of love the Father hath bestowed upon us, that we should be called the sons of God." But although the relationship is founded in love,

---

* It was nature in Barnabas that led him to wish for the company of one who "departed from them from Pamphylia, and went not with them to the work." It was amiable nature, yet it was nature, and it triumphed, for he took Mark and sailed to Cyprus, his native country, where, in the freshness of his Christian course, he had sold his property, in order to be a more unshackled follower of Him who had not where to lay His head (See Acts 4:36-37). This is no uncommon case. Many set out with a surrender of earth and nature with their respective claims. The blossom on the tree of Christian profession looks fair, and emits a fragrant perfume; but alas! it is not followed by the rich and mellow fruit of autumn. The influences of earth and nature gather around the soul and nip its beauteous blossoms, and all ends in barrenness and disappointment. This is very sad, and is always attended with the very worst moral effect upon the testimony. It is not at all a question of ceasing to be a saved person. Barnabas was a saved person. The influences of Mark and Cyprus could not blot out his name from the Lamb's book of life, but they did most thoroughly blot out his name from the records of testimony and service here below. And was not this something to be lamented? Is there naught to be deplored or dreaded save the loss of personal salvation? Most despicable is the selfishness that can think so. For what purpose does the blessed God take so much pains and trouble in maintaining His people here? Is it that they may be saved and made meet for glory? No such thing. Saved they are already, by the accomplished redemption of Christ, and therefore meet for glory. There is no middle step between justification and glory, for "whom He justified, them He also glorified." Why, therefore, does God leave us here? That we may be a testimony for Christ. Were it not for this, we might just as well be taken to Heaven the moment of our conversion. May we have grace to understand this point, in all its fullness and practical power.

** The Epistles of Peter develop the doctrine of God's moral government. He it is who asks the question, "Who is he that will harm you, if ye be followers of that which is good?" Now, some may find a difficulty in reconciling this inquiry with Paul's statement, "All that will live godly in Christ Jesus shall suffer persecution." It were needless to say that the two ideas are in perfect and beautiful harmony. The Lord Jesus Himself, who was the only perfect and unwavering follower of that which is good, who, from first to last, "went about doing good," found, in the end, the cross, the spear, the borrowed grave. The apostle Paul, who, beyond all other men, kept close to the Great Original which was set before him, was called to drink an unusually large cup of privation and persecution. And to this moment, the more like Christ, and the more devoted to Him any one is, the more privation and persecution he will suffer. Were any one, in true devotedness to Christ and love to souls, to take his stand publicly in some Roman Catholic district, and there preach Christ, his life would be in imminent danger. Do all these facts interfere with Peter's inquiry? By no means. The direct tendency of God's moral government is to protect from injury all who are "followers of that which is good," and to bring down punishment upon all who are the reverse; but it never interferes with the higher path of ardent discipleship, or deprives any one of the privilege and dignity of being as like Christ as he will, for unto you *it is given*, on behalf of Christ [$\tau o\ \upsilon\pi\varepsilon\rho\ X\rho\iota\sigma\tau o\upsilon$] , not only to believe on Him, but also to suffer for Him [$\upsilon\pi\varepsilon\rho\ \alpha\upsilon\tau o\upsilon$] ; having the same conflict which ye saw in me, and now hear in me" (Phil. 1:29-30). Here we are taught that it is an actual gift conferred upon us to be allowed to suffer for Christ, and this in the midst of a scene in which, on the ground of God's moral government, it can be said, "Who is he that will harm you, if ye be followers of that which is good?" To recognize and be a subject of God's government is one thing, and to be a follower or a rejected and crucified Christ is quite another. Even in Peter's Epistle, which, as we have remarked, has as its special theme the doctrine of God's government, we read, "But if, doing well and suffering for it, yet take it patiently, this is acceptable to God. For unto this were ye called, because Christ also suffered for us, leaving us an example, that we should follow His steps." And again, "If any suffer *as a Christian* [from being morally like Christ], let him not be ashamed; but let him glorify God in this matter."

it is exercised in righteousness, for "the time is come when judgment must begin at the house of God." So also, in Hebrews 12, we are taught that the very fact of our being genuine sons brings us under the righteous discipline of the Father's hand. In John 17, too, the Church is committed to the care of the Holy Father, to be kept by Him through His own name.

Now, in every case in which this great truth has been lost sight of by Christian parents, their houses have been thrown into confusion. They have not governed their children, and as a consequence, their children have, in process of time, governed them, for there will be government somewhere; and if those into whose hands God has put the reins do not hold them properly, they will speedily fall into bad hands; and can there be a more melancholy sight than to see parents governed by their children? I believe, in God's sight, it presents a fearful moral blot, which must bring down His judgment. A parent who lets the reins of government drop from his hands, or who does not hold them steadily, has grievously failed in his high and holy position as the representative of God, and the depositary of His power; nor do I believe that any one so failing can ever thoroughly regain his place, or be a proper witness for God in his day and generation. A subject of grace he may be; but then, a subject of grace and a witness for God are two widely different things. This will account for the sorrowful condition of many brethren. They have utterly failed to govern their houses, and hence they have lost their true position and moral influence—their energies are paralyzed, their mouths closed, their testimony hushed; and if such do lift the voice in some feeble way, the finger of scorn is instantly pointed at their families, and this cannot but send a blush to the cheek and a pang to the conscience.

Nor do people always take a correct view of this matter, and trace the failure up to its legitimate source. Many are too ready to look upon it as a natural and necessary thing that their children are to grow up willful and worldly. They say, It is all very well while your children are young, but wait till they grow older, and you will see that you must let them go into the world. Now, I want to know, is it the mind of God that the children of His servants must necessarily grow up willful and worldly? I never could believe any such thing. Well, then, if it be not His mind that they should so grow up, if He has graciously opened the same path to my house as He has opened to myself, if He has permitted me to select the same portion for my children as I have, through His grace, selected for myself—if, after all this, my children grow up willful and worldly, what am I to infer? Why, that I have grievously sinned and failed in my parental relationship and responsibilities—that I have wronged my children and dishonored the Lord.

Shall I go and make a general principle of this, and set it down that all the children of Christians must grow up as mine have? Shall I go and discourage young parents from taking God's ground in reference to their dear children, by setting before them my abominable failure, instead of encouraging them by setting before them God's infallible faithfulness to all who seek Him in the way of His appointment? To act thus would be to follow in the steps of the old prophet of Bethel, who, because he was in the midst of evil himself, sought to drag his brother in also, and had him slain by a lion for disobeying the Word of the Lord.

But the sum of the matter is this: The willfulness of my children reveals the willfulness of my own heart, and a righteous God is using them to chasten me, because I have not chastened myself. This is a peculiarly solemn view of the case, and one that calls for deep searching of heart. To save myself trouble, I have let things take their course in my family, and now my children have grown up around me to be thorns in my side, because I trained them not for God. This is the history of thousands. We should ever bear in mind that our children, as well as ourselves, should be "set for the defense and confirmation of the gospel." I feel persuaded that, could we only be led to regard our houses as a testimony for God, it would produce an immense reformation in our mode of ruling them. We should then seek a high tone of moral order, not that we might be spared any trouble or vexation, but rather that the testimony might not suffer through any confusion in our families. But let us not forget, that in order to subdue nature in our children, we must subdue it in ourselves. We can never subdue nature by nature. It is only as we have crushed it in ourselves that we are in a position to crush it in our children.

Moreover, there must be the clearest understanding and the fullest harmony between the father and mother. Their voice, their will, their authority, their influence, should be essentially one—one in the strictest sense of that word. Being themselves "no more twain, but one flesh," they should ever appear before their children in the beauty and power of that oneness. In order to this, they must wait much upon God together—they must be much in His presence, opening up all their hearts, and telling out all their need. Christians do frequently injure one another in this respect.

It sometimes happens that one partner really desires to give up the world and subdue nature to an extent for which the other is not prepared, and this produces sad results. It sometimes leads to reserve, to shuffling, to management and generalship, to positive antagonism in the views and principles of husband and wife, so that they cannot really be said to be joined in the Lord. The effect of all this upon the children as they grow up is pernicious beyond all conception; and the influence which it exerts in deranging the entire house is quite incalculable. What the father commands, the mother remits; what the father builds up, the mother pulls down. Sometimes the father is represented as stern, severe, arbitrary, and exacting. The maternal influence acts outside and independent of the paternal; sometimes,

even, it sets it aside altogether; so that the father's position becomes wretched in the extreme, and the whole family presents a most demoralized and ungodly appearance* This is terrible. Children never could be properly trained under such circumstances; and as to testimony for Christ, the bare thought of it is monstrous. Wherever such a state of things prevails, there should be the deepest sorrow of heart before the Lord on account of it. His mercy is exhaustless, and His tender compassions fail not; and surely we may hope that, where there is true contrition and confession, God will graciously come in with healing and restoration. One thing is certain, that we should not go on content to have things so; therefore, let the one who feels the sorrow of heart cry mightily to God, day and night—cry to Him on the ground of His own truth and name, which are blasphemed by such things; and, be assured, He will hear and answer.

But let all be viewed in the light of testimony for God's Son. It is to further this we are left here. We are surely not left here merely to bring up families. We are left here to bring them up for God, with God, by God, and before God. To do all this, we must be much in His presence. A Christian parent should take great care not to punish his children merely to gratify his whims and tempers. He is to represent God in the midst of his family. This, when properly understood, will regulate every thing. He is God's steward, likewise, and in order rightly and intelligently to discharge the functions of his stewardship, he must have frequent—yea, unbroken—intercourse with his Master. He must be constantly betaking himself to His feet, to know what he is to do, and how he is to do it. This will make every thing easy and happy.

It is often the desire of one's heart to get an

---

* Nothing can be more melancholy than to hear a mother say to a child, "We must not let your father know any thing about this." Where such a course of reserve and double dealing is adopted, there must be something radically and awfully wrong, and it is a moral impossibility that any thing like godly order can prevail, or right discipline be carried out. Either the father must, by inordinate severity or unwarrantable strictness, be "provoking his children to wrath," or the mother must be pampering the child's will at the expense of the father's character and authority. In either case, there is an effectual barrier to the testimony, and the children suffer grievous injury. Hence, Christian parents should see well to it that they always appear before their children, and also before their servants, in the power of that unity which flows from their being perfectly joined together in the Lord. If, unhappily, any shade of difference should arise in reference to the details of domestic government, let it be made a matter of private conference, prayer, and self-judgment in the presence of God; but never let the subjects of government see such a manifest proof of moral weakness, for it will surely cause them to despise the government.

abstract rule for this, that, and the other thing, in the details of family arrangement. One may ask what sort of punishments, what sort of rewards, what sort of amusements, should a Christian parent adopt. Actual punishment will, I believe, rarely be called for, if the divine principle of government be carried out from the earliest date; and as to rewards, it would be better to put them in the light of expressions of love and approval. A child must be obedient—unqualifiedly and unhesitatingly obedient—not to get a reward, which is apt to feed emulation, a fruit of the flesh; but because God would have him so; and then, of course, it is quite allowable for the parent to express his approval in the shape of some little present. As to amusement, let it always, if possible, assume the character of some useful occupation. This is most salutary. It is a bad thing to cherish the thought in the mind of a child that painted toys and gilded baubles minister pleasure. With very young children, I have constantly found that they derived more real, and certainly much more simple pleasure from a piece of stick or paper made out by themselves, than from the most expensive toy. Finally, let us, in all things, whether punishment, reward, or amusement, keep the eye on Christ, and earnestly seek the subjugation of the flesh in every shape and form. So shall our houses be a testimony for God, and all who enter them be constrained to say, *"God is here."*

As to the management of servants in a Christian household, the principle is equally simple. The master, as the head of the house, is the expression of the power of God, and as such, he must insist upon subjection and obedience. It is not a question of the Christianity of the servants, but simply of the order which should ever be maintained in a Christian household. Here, too, we must be on our guard against the mere indulgence of

our own arbitrary temper. We have to remember that we have a Master in Heaven, who has taught us to "give unto our servants that which is just and equal." If only we set the Lord before us from day to day, and seek to exhibit Him in all our dealings with our servants, we shall be kept from error on every side.

I must now close. I have not written, the Lord knows, to wound anyone. I feel the truth, importance, and deep solemnity of the points here put forward, and also my own lack of ability to bring them out with sufficient distinctness and power. However, I look to God to make them influential; and where He works, the very weakest agency will answer His end. To Him I now commend these pages, which have, I trust, been begun, continued, and ended in His holy presence. The thought has comforted me not a little, that at the very moment in which it was laid on my conscience to prepare this paper, a number of beloved brethren were actually assembled for humiliation, confession, and prayer, in immediate connection with the testimony of God's Son in these last days. I doubt not that a very leading point of confession has been failure in the government of the house; and if these pages should be used of God's Spirit to produce, even in one conscience, a deeper sense of this failure, and in one heart, a more earnest desire to meet the failure in God's own way, I shall rejoice, and feel I have not written in vain.

May God Almighty, in His great grace, produce, by His Holy Spirit, in the hearts of all His beloved saints, a more ardent purpose of soul to raise, in this closing hour, a fuller, brighter, more vigorous and decided testimony for Christ, that so, ere the shout of the archangel and the trump of God are heard in the air, there may be a people prepared to meet and welcome the heavenly Bridegroom.

THE UNEQUAL YOKE

NO ONE who sincerely desires to attain, in his own person, or promote in others, a purer and more elevated discipleship, can possibly contemplate the Christianity of the present day without an indescribable feeling of sadness and heaviness. Its tone is so excessively low, its aspect so sickly, and its spirit so enfeebled, that one is, at times, tempted to despair of any thing like a true and faithful witness for an absent Lord. All this is the more truly deplorable when we remember the commanding motives by which it is our special privilege ever to be actuated. Whether we look at the Master whom we are called to follow, the path which we are called to tread, the end which we are called to keep in view, or the hopes by which we are to keep in view, or the hopes by which we are to be animated, we cannot but own that, were all these entered into and realized by a more simple faith, we should assuredly exhibit a more ardent discipleship. "The love of Christ," says the apostle, "constraineth us." This is the most powerful motive of all. The more the heart is filled with Christ's love, and the eye filled with His blessed person, the more closely shall we seek to follow in His heavenly track. His footmarks can only be discovered by "a single eye"; and unless the will is broken, the flesh mortified, and the body kept under, we shall utterly fail in our discipleship, and make shipwreck of faith and a good conscience.

Let not my reader misunderstand me. It is not here, by any means, a question of personal salvation. It is quite another thing. Nothing can be more basely selfish than, having received salvation as the fruit of Christ's agony and bloody sweat, His cross and passion, to keep at as great a distance from His sacred person as we can without forfeiting our personal safety. This is, even in the judgment of nature, deemed a character of selfishness worthy of unmingled contempt; but when exhibited by one who professes to owe his present and his everlasting all to a rejected, crucified, risen, and absent, Master, no language can express its moral baseness. "Provided I escape hell fire, it makes little matter as to the discipleship."

Do you not, in your inmost soul, abhor this sentiment? If so, then earnestly seek to flee from it, to the very opposite point of the compass; and let your truthful language be, Provided that blessed Master is glorified, it makes little matter, comparatively, about my personal safety. Would to God that this were the sincere utterance of many hearts in this day, when, alas, it may be too truly said that, "All seek their own, not the things which are Jesus Christ's (Phil. 2:21). Would that the Holy Ghost would raise up, by His own resistless power, and send forth, by His own heavenly energy, a band of separated and consecrated followers of the Lamb, each one bound, by the cords of love, to the horns of the altar—a company, like Gideon's three hundred of old, able to confide in God and deny the flesh. How the heart longs for this! How the spirit, bowed down at times beneath the chilling and withering influence of a cold and uninfluential profession, earnestly breathes after a more vigorous and whole-hearted testimony for that One who emptied Himself and laid aside His glory, in order that we, through His precious bloodshedding, might be raised to companionship with Him in eternal blessedness!

Now, amongst the numerous hindrances to this thorough consecration of heart to Christ which I earnestly desire for myself and my reader, "the unequal yoke" will be found to occupy a very prominent place indeed. "Be ye not unequally yoked together[ετεροζυγουντες] with unbelievers: for what partnership [μετοχη] hath righteousness with unrighteousness [or rather lawlessness—$\alpha\nu o\mu\iota\alpha$]? and what communion [$\varkappa o\iota\nu\omega\nu\iota\alpha$] hath light with darkness? And what concord hath Christ with Belial? or what part hath a believer with an unbeliever [$\alpha\pi\iota\delta\tau o\upsilon$]? And what agreement hath the temple of God with idols? for ye are the temple of the living God; as God hath said, 'I will dwell in them, and walk in them; and I will be their God, and they shall be My people.' 'Wherefore come out from among them, and be ye separate, saith the Lord, and touch not the unclean thing; and I will receive you, and will be a Father unto you, and ye shall be My sons and daughters, saith the Lord Almighty' " (2 Cor. 6: 14-18).

Under the Mosaic economy, we learn the same moral principle. "Thou shalt not sow thy vineyard with divers seeds: lest the fruit of thy seed which thou hast sown, and the fruit of thy vineyard, be defiled. Thou shalt not plow with an ox and an ass together. Thou shalt not wear a garment of divers sorts, as of woolen and linen together" (Deut. 22: 9-11; Lev. 19: 19).

These Scriptures will suffice to set forth the moral evil of an unequal yoke. It may, with full confidence, be asserted that no one can be an unshackled follower of Christ who is, in any way, "unequally yoked." He may be a saved person, he may be a true child of God—a sincere believer, but he cannot be a thorough disciple; and not only so, but there is a positive hindrance to the full manifestation of that which he may really be, notwithstanding his unequal yoke. "Come out . . . and I will receive you . . . and ye shall be My sons and daughters, saith the Lord Almighty." That is to say, Get your neck out of the unequal yoke, and I will receive you, and there shall be the full, public, practical manifestation of your relationship with the Lord Almighty.

The idea here is evidently different from that set forth in James—"Of His own will begat He us, by the word of truth." And also in Peter—"Being born again, not of corruptible seed, but of incorruptible, by the Word of God, which liveth and abideth forever." And again in 1 John—"Behold what manner of love the Father hath bestowed upon us, that we should be called the sons of God." So also in John's Gospel—"But as many as received Him, to them gave He power to become the sons of God, even to them that believe on His name; which were born, not of blood, nor of the will of the flesh, nor of the will of man, but of God." In all these passages, the relationship of sons is founded upon the divine counsel and the divine operation, and is not set before us as the consequence of any acting of ours; whereas in 2 Corinthians 6 it is put as the result of our getting out of the unequal yoke. In other words, it is entirely a practical question.

Thus in Matthew 5 we read, "But I say unto you, 'Love your enemies, bless them that curse you, do good to them that hate you, and pray for them which despitefully use you, and persecute you; in order that [$\ddot{o}\pi\omega\varsigma$] ye may be the sons of your Father which is in heaven; because He causeth His sun to rise upon the evil and the good, and sendeth rain upon the just and the unjust." Here too it is the practical establishment and public declaration of the relationship, and its moral influence.

It becomes the sons of such a Father to act in such a way. In short, we have the abstract position or relationship of sons founded on God's sovereign will and operation; and we have the moral character consequent upon and flowing out of this relationship which affords just ground for God's public acknowledgment thereof. God cannot fully and publicly own those who are unequally yoked together with unbelievers, for, were He to do so, it would be an acknowledgment of the unequal yoke. He cannot acknowledge "darkness," "unrighteousness," "Belial," "idols," and "an infidel." How could He? Hence, if I yoke myself with any of these, I am morally and publicly identified with them, and not with God at all. I have put myself into a position which God cannot own, and, as a consequence, He cannot own me; but if I withdraw myself from that position—if I "come out and be separate"—if I take my neck out of the unequal yoke—then, but not until then, can I be publicly and fully received and owned as a "son or daughter of the Lord Almighty."

This is a solemn and searching principle for all who feel that they have unhappily gotten themselves into such a yoke. They are not walking as disciples, nor are they publicly or morally on the ground of sons. God cannot own them. Their secret relationship is not the point; but they have put themselves thoroughly off God's ground. They have foolishly thrust their neck into a yoke which, inasmuch as it is not Christ's yoke, must be Belial's yoke; and until they cast off that yoke, God cannot own them as His sons and daughters. God's grace, no doubt, is infinite, and can meet us in all our failure and weakness; but if our souls aspire after a higher order of discipleship, we must at once cast off the unequal yoke, cost what it may; that is, if it can be cast off; but if it cannot, we must only bow our heads beneath the shame and sorrow thereof, looking to God for full deliverance.

Now, there are four distinct phases in which "the unequal yoke" may be contemplated, viz, the domestic, the commercial, the religious, and the philanthropic. Some may be disposed to confine 2 Corinthians 6:14 to the first of these; but the apostle does not so confine it. The words are, "Be not unequally yoked together with unbelievers." He does not specify the character or object of the yoke, and therefore we are warranted in giving the passage its widest application, by bringing its edge to bear directly upon every phase of the unequal yoke; and we shall see the importance of so doing ere we close these remarks, if the Lord permit.

1. And first, then, let us consider the domestic or marriage yoke. What pen can portray the mental anguish, the moral misery, together with the ruinous consequences as to spiritual life and testimony, flowing from a Christian's marriage with an unconverted person? I suppose nothing can be more deplorable than the condition of one who discovers, when it is too late, that he has linked himself for life with one who cannot have a single thought or feeling in common with him. One desires to serve Christ; the other can only serve the devil: one breathes after the things of God; the other sighs for the things of this present world: the one

earnestly seeks to mortify the flesh, with all its affections and desires; the other only seeks to minister to and gratify these very things. Like a sheep and a goat linked together, the sheep longs to feed on the green pasture in the field, while, on the other hand, the goat craves the brambles which grow in the ditch. The sad consequence is that both are starved. One *will* not feed on the pasture, and the other *cannot* feed upon the brambles, and thus neither gets what his nature craves, unless the goat, by superior strength, succeeds in forcing his unequally yoked companion to remain among the brambles. there to languish and die.

The moral of this is plain enough; and, moreover, it is, alas! of but too common occurrence. The goat generally succeeds in gaining his end. The worldly partner carries his or her point, in almost every instance. It will be found, almost without exception, that in cases of the unequal marriage yoke, the poor Christian is the sufferer, as is evidenced by the bitter fruits of a bad conscience, a depressed heart, a gloomy spirit, and a desponding mind. A heavy price, surely, to pay for the gratification of some natural affection, or the attainment, it may be, of some paltry worldly advantage. In fact, a marriage of this kind is the death-knell of practical Christianity, and of progress in the divine life. It is morally impossible that any one can be an unfettered disciple of Christ with his neck in the marriage yoke with an unbeliever.

As well might a racer in the Olympic or Isthmaean games have expected to gain the crown of victory by attaching a heavy weight or dead body to his person. It is enough, surely, to have one dead body to sustain, without attaching another. There never was a true Christian yet who did not find that he had abundant work to do in endeavoring to grapple with the evils of *one* heart, without going to burden himself with the evils of two; and, without doubt, the man who foolishly and disobediently marries an unconverted woman; or the woman who marries an unconverted man, is burdened with the combined evils of two hearts; and who is sufficient for these things? One can most fully count upon the grace of Christ for the subjugation of his own evil nature; but he certainly cannot count, in the same way, upon that grace in reference to the evil nature of his unequal yoke-fellow. If he have yoked himself ignorantly, the Lord will meet him personally, on the ground of full confession, with entire restoration of soul, but in the matter of his discipleship, he will never recover it.

Now, in considering the terribly evil consequences of the unequal marriage yoke, it is mainly as bearing upon our discipleship that we are looking at them. I say "mainly" because our entire character and experience are deeply affected thereby. I very much question if any one can give a more effectual blow to his prosperity in the divine life than by assuming an unequal yoke. Indeed, the very fact of so doing proves that spiritual decline has already set in, with most alarming symptoms; but as to his discipleship and testimony, the lamp thereof may be regarded as all but gone out; or if it does give an occasional faint glimmer, it only serves to make manifest the awful gloom of his unhappy position, and the appalling consequences of being "unequally yoked together with an unbeliever."

Thus much as to the question of the unequal yoke in its influence upon the life, the character, the testimony, and the discipleship of the child of God.

I would now say a word as to its moral effect as exhibited in the domestic circle. Here too the consequences are truly melancholy. Nor could they possibly be otherwise. Two persons have come together in the closest and most intimate relationship, with tastes, habits, feelings, desires, tendencies, and objects diametrically opposite. They have nothing in common; so that in every movement they can but grate one against the other. The unbeliever cannot, *in reality*, go with the believer; and if there should, through excessive amiability or downright hypocrisy, be a show of acquiescence, what is it worth in the sight of the Lord, who judges the true state of the heart in reference to Himself? But little indeed; yea, it is worse than worthless. Then, again, if the believer should unhappily go in any measure with his unequal yoke-fellow, it can only be at the expense of his discipleship, and the consequence is, a condemning conscience in the sight of the Lord; and this, again, leads to heaviness of spirit, and, it may be, sourness of temper in the domestic circle, so that the grace of the gospel is by no means commended, and the unbeliever is not attracted or won. Thus it is in every way most sorrowful. It is dishonoring to God, destructive of spiritual prosperity, utterly subversive of discipleship and testimony, and entirely hostile to domestic peace and blessing. It produces estrangement, coldness, distance, and misunderstanding; or, if it does not produce these, it will doubtless lead, on the part of the Christian, to a forfeiture of his discipleship and good conscience, both of which he may be tempted to offer as a sacrifice upon the altar of domestic peace. Thus, whatever way we look at it, an unequal yoke must lead to the most deplorable consequences.

Then, as to its effect upon children, it is equally sad. These are almost sure to flow in the current with the unconverted parent. "Their children spoke half in the speech of Ashdod, and could not speak in the Jews' language, but according to the language of each people." There can be no union of heart in the training of the children,—no joint and mutual confidence in reference to them. One desires to bring them up in the nurture and admonition of the Lord; the other desires to bring them up in the principles of the world, the flesh, and the devil: and as all the sympathies of the children, as they grow up, are likely to be ranged on the side of the latter, it is easy to see how it will end. In short, it is an unseemly, unscriptural, and vain effort to plow with an "unequal yoke," or to "sow the ground with mingled seed;" and all must end in sorrow and confusion.*

* There are many cases in which one finds persons united, who though they cannot exactly be said to be "unequally yoked," are, to say the least, very badly matched. Their tempers, tastes, habits, and views are totally different; and so different, that instead of maintaining a desirable balance (which opposite tempers, if properly arranged, might do), they keep up a perpetual jar, to the sad derangement of the domestic circle, and the dishonor of the Lord's name. All this might be very much obviated if Christians would only wait upon God, and make His glory more their object than personal interest or affection.

I shall, ere turning from this branch of our subject, offer a remark as to the reasons which generally actuate Christians in the matter of entering into the unequal marriage-yoke. We all know, alas! how easily the poor heart persuades itself of the rightness of any step which it desires to take, and how the devil furnishes plausible arguments to convince us of its rightness— arguments which the moral condition of the soul causes us to regard as clear, forcible, and satisfactory. The very fact of our thinking of such a thing, proves our unfitness to weigh, with a well-balanced mind and spiritually adjusted conscience, the solemn consequences of such a step.

If the eye were single (that is, if we were governed but by one object, namely, the glory and honor of the Lord Jesus Christ), we should never entertain the idea of putting our necks in an unequal yoke; and consequently we should have no difficulty or perplexity about the matter.

A racer, whose eye was resting on the crown, would not be troubled with any perplexity as to whether he ought to stop and tie a hundred-weight round his neck. Such a thought would never cross his mind: and not only so, but a thorough racer would have a distinct and almost intuitive perception of every thing which would be likely to prove a hindrance to him in running the race; and, of course, with such an one, to perceive would be to reject with decision.*

Now, were it thus with Christians in the matter of unscriptural marriage, it would save them a world of sorrow and perplexity; but it is not thus. The heart gets out of communion, and is morally incompetent to "try the things that differ"; and when in this condition, the devil gains an easy conquest, and speedy success in his wicked effort to induce the believer to yoke himself with "Belial"—with "unrighteousness"—with "darkness"—with "an infidel." When the soul is in full communion with God, it is entirely subject to His Word; it sees things as He sees them, calls them what He calls them, and not what the devil or his own carnal heart would call them. In this way, the believer escapes the insnaring influence of a deception which is very frequently brought to bear upon him in this matter, namely, a false profession of religion on the part of the person whom he desires to marry. This is a very common case. It is easy to show symptoms of leaning toward the things of God; and the heart is treacherous and base enough to make a profession of religion in order to gain its end; and not only so, but the devil, who is "transformed into an angel of light," will lead to this false profession, in order thereby the more effectually to entrap the feet of a child of God. Thus it comes to pass that Christians, in this matter, suffer themselves to be satisfied, or at least profess themselves satisfied, with evidence of conversion which under any other circumstances they would regard as utterly lame and flimsy.

But, alas! experience soon opens the eyes to the *reality*. It is speedily discovered that the profession was all a vain show, that the *heart* is entirely in and of the world. Terrible discovery. Who can detail the bitter consequences of such a discovery—the anguish of heart—the bitter reproaches and cuttings of conscience—the shame and confusion—the loss of power and blessing— the forfeiture of spiritual peace and joy—the sacrifice of a life of usefulness? Who can describe all these things? The man awakes from his delusive dream, and opens

---

* It is important for the Christian to bear in mind the words of our Lord Jesus Christ, "If thine eye be single, thy whole body shall be full of light." Whenever I am in perplexity as to my path, I have reason to suspect that my eye is not single; for, assuredly, perplexity is not compatible with a "body full of light." We frequently go to pray for guidance in matters with which, if the eye were single and the will subject, we would have nothing whatever to do, and hence we should have no need to pray about them. To pray about aught concerning which the Word of God is plain, marks the activity of a rebellious will. As a recent writer has well remarked, "We sometimes seek God's will, desiring to know how to act in circumstances *in which it is not His will that we should be found at all;* if conscience were in real healthful activity, its first effect would be to make us quit them. It is our own will which sets us there, and we should like, nevertheless, to enjoy the consolation of God's direction in a path which ourselves have chosen. Such is a very common case. Be assured that if we are near enough to God, we shall have no trouble to know His will. . . . However, 'if thine eye be single, thy whole body shall be full of light'; whence it is certain that if the whole body is not full of light, the eye is not single. You will say, That is poor consolation. I answer, It is a rich consolation for those whose sole desire is to have the eye single and *to walk with God.*"

his eyes upon the tremendous reality that he is yoked for life with "Belial"! Yes, this is what the Spirit calls it. It is not an inference, or a deduction arrived at by a process of reasoning; but a plain and positive statement of holy Scripture, that thus the matter stands in reference to one who, from whatever motive, or under the influence of whatever reasons, or deceived by whatever false pretences, has entered into an unequal marriage-yoke.

Oh, my beloved Christian reader, if you are in danger of entering into such a yoke, let me earnestly, solemnly, and affectionately entreat of you to pause first, and weigh the matter in the balances of the sanctuary, ere you move forward a single hair's breadth on such a fatal path! You may rest assured that you will no sooner have taken the step than your heart will be assailed by hopeless regrets, and your life embittered by unnumbered sorrows. *Let nothing induce you to yoke yourself with an unbeliever.* Are your affections engaged? Then, remember, they cannot be the affections of your new man; they are, be assured of it, those of the old or carnal nature, which you are called upon to mortify and set aside. Wherefore you should cry to God for spiritual power to rise above the influence of such affections; yea, to sacrifice them to Him. Again, are your interests concerned? Then remember that they are only *your* interests; and if they are promoted, Christ's interests are sacrificed by your yoking yourself with "Belial."

Furthermore, they are only your temporal, and not your eternal interests. In point of fact, the interests of the believer and those of Christ ought to be identical; and it is plain that His interests, His honor, His truth, His glory, must inevitably be sacrificed if a member of His body is linked with "Belial." This is the true way to look at the question. What are a few hundreds, or a few thousands, to an heir of Heaven? "God is able to give thee much more than this." Are you going to sacrifice the truth of God, as well as your own spiritual peace, prosperity, and happiness, for a paltry trifle of gold, which must perish in the using of it? Ah, no! God forbid! Flee from it, as a bird from the snare

which it sees and knows. Stretch out the hand of genuine, well-braced, whole-hearted discipleship, and take the knife and slay your affections and your interests on the altar of God, and then, even though there should not be an audible voice from Heaven to approve your act, you will have the invaluable testimony of an approving conscience and an ungrieved Spirit—an ample reward, surely, for the most costly sacrifice which you can make. May the Spirit of God give power to resist Satan's temptations.

It is hardly needful to remark here that in cases where conversion takes place after marriage, the complexion of the matter is very materially altered. There will then be no smitings of conscience, for example, and the whole thing is modified in a variety of particulars. Still, there will be difficulty, trial, and sorrow, unquestionably. The only thing is, that one can far more happily bring the trial and sorrow into the Lord's presence, when he has not deliberately and willfully plunged himself thereinto; and, blessed be God, we know how ready He is to forgive, restore, and cleanse from all unrighteousness the soul that makes full confession of its error and failure. This may comfort the heart of one who has been brought to the Lord after marriage. Moreover, to such an one the Spirit of God has given specific direction and blessed encouragement in the following passage: "If any brother have an unbelieving wife, and she think proper to dwell with him, let him not put her away: and if any woman have an unbelieving husband, and he think proper to dwell with her, let her not put him away (for the unbelieving husband is sanctified by the wife, and the unbelieving wife is sanctified by the husband, else were your children unclean, but now are they holy) . . . . For what knowest thou, O wife, if thou shalt save thy husband? or what knowest thou, O husband, if thou shalt save thy wife?" (1 Cor. 7:12-16)

2. We shall now consider "the unequal yoke" in its commercial phase, as seen in cases of partnership in business. This, though not so serious an aspect of the yoke as that which we have just been considering, will nevertheless be found a very positive

barrier to the believer's testimony. When a Christian yokes himself, for business purposes, with an unbeliever—whether that unbeliever be a relative or not—or when he becomes a member of a worldly firm, he virtually surrenders his individual responsibility. Henceforth the acts of the firm become his acts, and it is perfectly out of the question to think of getting a worldly firm to act on heavenly principles. They would laugh at such a notion, inasmuch as it would be an effectual barrier to the success of their commercial schemes. They will feel perfectly free to adopt a number of expedients in carrying on their business which would be quite opposed to the spirit and principles of the kingdom in which he is, and of the Church of which he forms a part. Thus he will find himself constantly in a most trying position. He may use his influence to Christianize the mode of conducting affairs, but they will compel him to do business as others do, and he has no remedy save to mourn in secret over his anomalous and difficult position, or else to go out at great pecuniary loss to himself and family. Where the eye is single, there will be no hesitation as to which of these alternatives to adopt; but alas! the very fact of getting into such a position proves the lack of a single eye; and the fact of being in it argues the lack of spiritual capacity to appreciate the value and power of the divine principles which would infallibly bring a man out of it. A man whose eye was single could not possibly yoke himself with an unbeliever for the purpose of making money. Such an one could only set, as an object before his mind, the direct glory of Christ; and this object could never be gained by a positive transgression of divine principle.

This makes it very simple. If it does not glorify Christ for a Christian to become a partner in a worldly firm, it must, without doubt, further the designs of the devil. There is no middle ground; but that it does not glorify Christ is manifest, for His Word says, "Be not unequally yoked together with unbelievers." Such is the principle, which cannot be infringed without damage to the testimony, and forfeiture of spiritual blessing. True, the conscience of a Christian who transgresses in this matter may seek relief in various ways—may have recourse to various subterfuges—may set forth various arguments to persuade itself that all is right. It will be said that "we can be very devoted and very spiritual, so far as we are personally concerned, even though we are yoked, for business purposes, with an unbeliever." This will be found fallacious when brought to the test of the actual practice. A servant of Christ will find himself hampered in a hundred ways by his worldly partnership. If in matters of service to Christ he is not met with open hostility, he will have to encounter the enemy's secret and constant effort to damp his ardor, and throw cold water on all his schemes. He will be laughed at and despised—he will be continually reminded of the effect which his enthusiasm and fanaticism will produce in reference to the business prospects of the firm. If he uses his time, his talents, or his pecuniary resources in what he believes to be the Lord's service, he will be pronounced a fool or a madman, and reminded that the true—the proper way for a commercial man to serve the Lord is to "attend to business, and nothing but business;" and that it is the exclusive business of clergymen and ministers to attend to religious matters, inasmuch as they are set apart and paid for so doing.

Now, although the Christian's renewed mind may be thoroughly convinced of the fallacy of all this reasoning—although he may see that this worldly wisdom is but a flimsy, threadbare cloak, thrown over the heart's covetous practices—yet who can tell how far the heart may be influenced by such things? We get weary of constant resistance. The current becomes too strong for us, and we gradually yield ourselves to its action, and are carried along on its surface. Conscience may have some death-struggles; but the spiritual energies are paralyzed, and the sensibilities of the new nature are blunted, so that there is no response to the cries of conscience, and no effectual effort to withstand the enemy; the worldliness of the Christian's heart leagues itself with the opposing influences from without—the outworks are stormed, and the citadel of the soul's affections vigorously assaulted; and finally, the man settles down in thorough worldliness, exemplifying in his own person the prophet's touching lament, "Her Nazarites *were* purer than snow, they *were* whiter than milk, they *were* more ruddy in body than rubies, their polishing *was* of sapphire: their visage *is* blacker than a coal; they *are* not known in the streets; their skin cleaveth to their bones; it is withered, it is become like a stick" (Lam. 4:7-8). The man who was once known as a servant of Christ—a fellow-helper unto the kingdom of God—making use of his resources only to further the interests of the gospel of Christ, is now, alas! settled down upon his lees, only known as a plodding, keen, bargain-making man of business, of whom the apostle might well say, "Demas hath forsaken me, having loved this present age [τον νυν αιωνα]."

But perhaps nothing so operates on the hearts of Christians, in inducing them to yoke themselves commercially with unbelievers, as the habit of seeking to maintain the two characters of a Christian and a man of business. This is a grievous snare. In point of fact, there can be no such thing. A man must be either the one or the other. If I am a Christian, my Christianity must show itself as a living reality in that in which I am; and if it cannot show itself there, I ought not to be there: for if I continue in a sphere or position in which the life of Christ cannot be manifested, I shall speedily possess naught of Christianity but the name without the reality—the outward form without the inward power—the shell without the kernel. I should be the servant of Christ, not merely on Sunday, but from Monday morning to Saturday night. I should not only be a servant of Christ in the public assembly, but also in my place of business, whatever it may happen to be.

But I cannot be a proper servant of Christ with my neck in the yoke with an unbeliever; for how could the servants of two hostile masters work in the same yoke? It is utterly impossible; as well might one attempt to link the sun's meridian beams with the profound darkness of midnight. It cannot be done; and I do therefore most solemnly appeal to my reader's conscience, in the presence of Almighty God, who shall judge the secrets of men's hearts by Jesus Christ, as to this important matter.

I would say to him, if he is thinking of getting into partnership with an unbeliever, *Flee from it!* yes, flee from it, though it promises you the gain of thousands. You will plunge yourself into a mass of sorrow and trouble. You are going to "plow" with one whose feelings, instincts, and tendencies are diametrically opposed to your own. "An ox and an ass" are not so unlike, in every respect, as a believer and an unbeliever. How will you ever get on? He wants to make money—to profit himself—to get on in the world; you want (at least you ought to want) to grow in grace and holiness—to advance the interests of Christ and His gospel on the earth, and to push onward to the everlasting kingdom of the Lord Jesus Christ. His object is money; yours, I trust, is Christ: he lives for this world; you, for the world to come; he is engrossed with the things of time; you, with those of eternity. How, then, can you ever take common ground with him? Your principles, your motives, your objects, your hopes, are all opposed. How is it possible you can get on? How can you have aught in common?

Surely, all this needs only to be looked at with a single eye in order to be seen in its true light. It is impossible that any one whose eye is filled and whose heart is occupied with Christ, could ever yoke himself with a worldly partner, for any object whatsoever. Wherefore, my beloved Christian reader, let me once more entreat you, ere you take such a tremendous step—a step fraught with such awful consequences—so pregnant with danger to your best interests, as well as to the testimony of Christ, with which you are honored—to take the whole matter, with an honest heart, into the sanctuary of God, and weigh it in His sacred balance. Ask Him what He thinks of it, and harken, with a subject will and a well-adjusted conscience, to His reply. It is plain and powerful—yea, as plain and as powerful as though it fell from the open heavens—"*Be not unequally yoked together with unbelievers.*"

But if, unhappily, my reader is already in the yoke, I would say to him, disentangle yourself as speedily as you can. I am much mistaken if you have not already found the yoke a burdensome one. To you it were superfluous to detail the sad consequences of being in such a position; you doubtless know them all. It is needless to print them on paper, or paint them on canvas, to one who has entered into all their reality. My beloved brother in Christ, lose not a moment in seeking to throw off the yoke. This must be done before the Lord, on His principles, and by His grace.

It is easier to get into a wrong position than to get out of it. A partnership of ten or twenty years' standing cannot be dissolved in a moment. It must be done calmly, humbly, and prayerfully, as in the sight of the Lord, and with entire reference to His glory. I may dishonor the Lord as much in my way of getting out of a wrong position as by getting into it at the first. Hence, if I find myself in partnership with an unbeliever, and my conscience tells me I am wrong, let me honestly and frankly state to my partner that I can no longer go on with him; and having done that, my place is to use every exertion to wind up the affairs of the firm in an upright, a straightforward, and businesslike manner, so as to give no possible occasion to the adversary to speak reproachfully, and that my good may not be evil spoken of. We must avoid rashness, headiness, and highmindedness, when apparently acting for the Lord, and in defense of His holy principles. If a man gets entangeled in a net, or involved in a labyrinth, it is not by bold and violent plunging he will extricate himself. No; he must humble himself, confess his sins before the Lord, and then retrace his steps, in patient dependence upon that grace which can not only pardon him for being in a wrong position, but lead him forth into a right one.

Moreover, as in the case of the marriage yoke, the matter is very much modified by the fact of the partnership having been entered into previous to conversion. Not that this would, in the slightest degree, justify a continuance in it. By no means; but it does away with much of the sorrow of heart and defilement of conscience connected with such a position, and will also very materially affect the mode of escape therefrom. Besides, the Lord is glorified by, and He assuredly accepts, the moral bent of the heart and conscience in the right direction. If I judge myself for being wrong, and that the moral bent of my heart and conscience is to get right, God will accept of that, and surely set me right. But if He sets me right, He will not suffer me to do violence to one truth while seeking to act in obedience to another. The same Word that says "Be not unequally yoked together with unbelievers" says also "Render therefore to all their dues"—"owe no many any thing"—"provide things honest in the sight of all"—"walk honestly toward them that are without." If I have wronged God by getting into partnership with an unbeliever, I must not wrong any man in my way of getting out of it. Profound subjection to the Word of God, by the power of the Holy Ghost, will set all to rights, will lead us into straight paths, and enable us to avoid all dangerous extremes.

3. In glancing for a moment at the religious phase of the unequal yoke, I would assure my reader that it is by no means my desire to hurt the feelings of any one by canvassing the claims of the various denominations around me. Such is not my purpose. The subject of this paper is one of quite sufficient importance to prevent its being encumbered by the introduction of other matters. Moreover, it is too definite to warrant any such introduction. "The unequal yoke" is our theme, and to it we must confine our attention.

In looking through Scripture we find almost numberless passages setting forth the intense spirit of separation which ought ever to characterize the people of God. Whether we direct our attention to the Old Testament, in which we have God's relationship and dealings with His earthly people, Israel, or to the New Testament, in which we have His relationship and dealings with His heavenly people, the Church, we find the same truth prominently set forth, namely, the entire separation of those who belong to God.

Israel's position is thus stated in Balaam's parable, "Lo, the people shall *dwell alone*, and shall not be reckoned amongst the nations." Their place was outside the range of all the nations of the earth, and they were responsible to maintain that separation. Throughout the entire Pentateuch they were instructed, warned, and admonished as to this; and throughout the psalms and the prophets we have a record of their failure in the maintenance of this separation, which failure, as we know, has brought down upon them the heavy judgments of the hand of God. It would swell this little paper into a volume were I to attempt a quotation of all the passages in which this point is put forward. I take it for granted that my reader is sufficiently acquainted with his Bible, to render such quotations unnecessary. Should he not be so, however, a reference, in his concordance, to the words, "separate," "separated," and "separation" will suffice to lay before him at a glance the body of Scripture evidence on the subject. The passage just quoted from the book of Numbers is the expression of God's thoughts about His people Israel: "The people shall dwell *alone*."

The same is true, only upon a much higher ground, in reference to God's heavenly people, the Church—the body of Christ— composed of all true believers. They too are a separated people.

We shall now proceed to examine the ground of this separation. There is a great difference between being separate on the ground of what *we* are and of what *God* is. The former makes a man a *Pharisee;* the latter makes him a *saint.* If I say to a poor fellow-sinner, "Stand by thyself, I am holier than thou," I am a detestable Pharisee and a hypocrite; but if God, in His infinite condescension and perfect grace, says to me, I have brought you into relationship with Myself in the person of My Son Jesus Christ, therefore be separate and holy from all evil; come out from among them and be separate; I am bound to obey, and my obedience is the practical manifestation of my character as a saint—a character which I have, not because of any thing in myself, but simply because

God has brought me near unto Himself through the precious blood of Christ.

It is well to be clear as to this. Pharisaism and divine sanctification are two very different things; and yet they are often confounded. Those who contend for the maintenance of that place of separation which belongs to the people of God, are constantly accused of setting themselves up above their fellow-men, and of laying claim to a higher degree of personal sanctity than is ordinarily possessed. This accusation arises from not attending to the distinction just referred to. When God calls upon men to be separate, it is on the ground of what He has done for them upon the cross, and where He has set them, in eternal association with Himself, in the person of Christ. But if I separate myself on the ground of what I am in myself, it is the most senseless and vapid assumption, which will sooner or later be made manifest. God commands His people to be holy on the ground of what He is: "Be ye holy, for I am holy." This is evidently a very different thing from "Stand by thyself: I am holier than thou." If God brings people into association with Himself, He has a right to prescribe what their moral character ought to be, and they are responsible to answer thereto. Thus we see that the most profound humility lies at the bottom of a saint's separation. There is nothing so calculated to put one in the dust as the understanding of the real nature of divine holiness. It is an utterly false humility which springs from looking at ourselves—yea, it is, in reality, based upon pride, which has never yet seen to the bottom of its own perfect worthlessness. Some imagine that they can reach the truest and deepest humility by looking at self, whereas it can only be reached by looking at Christ.

> The more Thy glories strike mine eye,
> The humbler I shall be.

This is a just sentiment, founded upon divine principle. The soul that loses itself in the blaze of Christ's moral glory is truly humble, and none other. No doubt we have a right to be humble when we think of what poor creatures we are, but it only needs a moment's just reflection to see the fallacy of seeking to produce any practical result by looking at self. It is only when we find ourselves in the presence of infinite excellency that we are really humble.

Hence, therefore, a child of God should refuse to be yoked with an unbeliever, whether for a domestic, a commercial, or a religious object, simply because God tells him to be separate, and not because of his own personal holiness. The carrying out of this principle in matters of religion will necessarily involve much trial and sorrow; it will be termed intolerance, bigotry, narrow-mindedness, exclusiveness, and such like; but we cannot help all this. Provided we keep ourselves separate upon a right principle and in a right spirit, we may safely leave all results with God.

No doubt the remnant in the days of Ezra must have appeared excessively intolerant in refusing the co-operation of the surrounding people in building the house of God, but they acted upon divine principle in the refusal. "Now when the adversaries of Judah and Benjamin heard that the children of the captivity builded the temple unto the Lord God of Israel, then they came to Zerubbabel, and to the chief of the fathers, and said unto them, 'Let us build with you; for we seek your God as ye do; and we do sacrifice unto Him, since the days of Esar-haddon, king of Assur, which brought us up hither.'"

This might seem a very attractive proposal—a proposal evidencing a very decided leaning toward the God of Israel; yet the remnant refused, because the people, notwithstanding their fair profession, were, at heart, uncircumcised and hostile. "But Zerubbabel and Jeshua and the rest of the chief of the fathers of Israel said unto them, 'Ye have nothing to do *with us* to build a house unto *our* God; but *we ourselves together* will build unto the Lord God of Israel (Ezra 4:1-3). They would not yoke themselves with the uncircumcised—they would not "plow with the ox and ass"—they would not "sow their field with mingled seed" —they kept themselves separate, even though by so doing they exposed themselves to the charge of being a bigoted, narrow-minded, illiberal, uncharitable set of people.

So also in Nehemiah we read, "And the seed of Israel *separated themselves* from all strangers, and stood and confessed their sins, and the iniquities of their fathers" (chap. 9: 2). This was not sectarianism, but positive obedience. Their separation was essential to their existence as a people. They could not have enjoyed the divine presence on any other ground. Thus it must ever be with God's people on the earth. They must be separate, or else they are not only useless, but mischievous. God cannot own or accompany them if they yoke themselves with unbelievers, upon any ground or for any object whatsoever.

The grand difficulty is to combine a spirit of intense separation with a spirit of grace, gentleness, and forbearance; or, as another has said, "to maintain a *narrow circle* with a *wide heart*." This is really a difficulty. As the strict and uncompromising maintenance of *truth* tends to narrow the circle around us, we shall need the expansive power of *grace* to keep the heart wide, and the affections warm. If we contend for *truth* otherwise than in *grace*, we shall only yield a one-sided and most unattractive testimony. And on the other hand, if we try to exhibit grace at the expense of truth, it will prove, in the end, to be only the manifestation of a popular liberality at God's expense—a most worthless thing.

Then, as to the object for which real Christians usually yoke themselves with those who, even on their own confession, and in the judgment of charity itself, are not Christians at all, it will be found in the end that no really divine and heavenly object can be gained by an infringement of God's truth. *Per fas aut nefas* (by any means) can never be a divine motto. The means are not sanctified by the end; but both means and end must be according to the principles of God's holy Word, else all must eventuate in confusion and dishonor. It might have appeared to Jehoshaphat a very worthy object to recover Ramoth-Gilead out of the hand of the enemy; and moreover, he might have appeared a very liberal, gracious, popular, largehearted man, when, in reply to Ahab's proposal, he said, "I am as thou art, and my people as thy people; and *we will be with thee* in the war." It is easy to be liberal and largehearted at the expense of divine principle; but how did it end? Ahab was killed, and Jehoshaphat narrowly escaped with his life, having made total shipwreck of his testimony.

Thus we see that Jehoshaphat did not even gain the object for which he unequally yoked himself with an unbeliever; and even had he gained it, it would have been no justification of his course.* Nothing can ever warrant a believer's yoking himself with an unbeliever; and therefore however fair, attractive, and plausible the Ramoth expedition might seem in the eye of man, it was, in the judgment of God, "helping the ungodly, and loving them that hate the Lord" (2 Chron. 19:2). The truth of God strips men and things of the false colors with which the spirit of expediency would deck them, and presents them in their proper light; and it is an unspeakable mercy to have the clear judgment of God about all that is going on around us: it imparts calmness to the spirit, and stability to the course and character, and saves one from that unhappy fluctuation of thought, feeling, and principle which so entirely unfits him for the place of a steady and consistent witness for Christ.

We shall surely err if we attempt to form our judgment by the thoughts and opinions of men; for they will always judge according to the outward appearances, and not according to the intrinsic character and principle of things. Provided men can gain what they conceive to be a right object, they care not about the mode of gaining it. But the true servant of Christ knows that he must do his Master's work upon his Master's principles and in his Master's spirit. It will not satisfy such an one to reach the most praiseworthy end unless he can reach it by a divinely appointed road. The means and the end must both be divine. I admit it, for example, to be a most desirable end to circulate the Scriptures—God's own pure, eternal Word; but if *I could not* circulate them save by

yoking myself with an unbeliever, I should refrain, inasmuch as I am not to do evil that good may come.

But, blessed be God, His servant can circulate His precious book without violating the precepts contained in that book. He can, upon his own individual responsibility, or in fellowship with those who are really on the Lord's side, scatter the precious seed every where, without leaguing himself with those whose whole course and conduct prove them to be of the world. The same may be said in reference to every object of a religious nature. It can and should be gained on God's principles, and only thus. It may be argued, in reply, that we are told not to judge—that we cannot read the heart—and that we are bound to hope that all who would engage in such good works as the translation of the Bible, the distribution of tracts, and the aiding of missionary labors, must be Christians; and that therefore it cannot be wrong to link ourselves with them. To all this I reply that there is hardly a passage in the New Testament so misunderstood and misapplied as Matthew 7: 1: "Judge not, that ye be not judged." In the very same chapter we read, "Beware of the false prophets . . . by their fruits ye shall know them." Now, how are we to "beware" if we do not exercise judgment?

Again, in 1 Corinthians 5 we read, "For what have I to do to judge them also that are without? do not ye judge them that are within? But them that are without God judgeth. Therefore put away from among yourselves that wicked person." Here we are distinctly taught that those "within" come within the immediate range of the Church's judgment; and yet according to the common interpretation of Matthew 7:1 we ought not to judge anybody; that interpretation, therefore, must needs be unsound. If people take, even in profession, the ground of being "within," we are commanded to judge them. "Do not ye judge them that are within?" As to those "without" we have naught to do with them,

---

* The unequal yoke proved a terrible snare to the amiable heart of Jehoshaphat. He yoked himself with Ahab for a religious object; and notwithstanding the disastrous termination of this scheme, we find him yoking himself with Ahaziah for a commercial object, which likewise ended in loss and confusion; and lastly, he yoked himself with Jehoram for a military object (comp. 2 Chron. 18; 20:32-37; 2 Kings 3).

save to present the pure and perfect, the rich, illimitable, and unfathomable grace which shines, with unclouded effulgence, in the death and resurrection of the Son of God.

All this is plain enough. The people of God are told to exercise judgment as to all who profess to be "within;" they are told to "beware of false prophets;" they are commanded to "try the spirits:" and how can they do all this if they are not to judge at all? What, then, does our Lord mean, when He says, "Judge not"? I believe He means just what St. Paul, by the Holy Ghost, says, when he commands us to judge nothing before the time, until the Lord come, who both will bring to light the hidden things of darkness, and will make manifest the counsels of the heart: and then shall every man have praise of God" (1 Cor. 4:5). We have nothing to do with judging motives, but we have to judge conduct and principles; that is to say, the conduct and principles of all who profess to be "within." And, in point of fact, the very persons who say, "We must not judge," do themselves constantly exercise judgment. There is no true Christian in whom the moral instincts of the divine nature do not virtually pronounce judgment as to character, conduct, and doctrine; and these are the very points which are placed within the believer's range of judgment.

All, therefore, that I would press upon the Christian reader is, that he would exercise judgment as to those with whom he yokes himself in matters of religion. If he is at this moment working in yoke or in harness with an unbeliever, he is positively violating the command of the Holy Ghost. He may be ignorantly doing so up to this; and if so, the Lord's grace is ready to pardon and restore; but if he persist in disobedience after having been warned, he cannot possibly expect God's blessing and presence with him, no matter how valuable or important the object which he may seek to attain. "To obey is better than sacrifice, and to hearken than the fat of rams."

4. We have only to consider the philanthropic phase of the unequal yoke. Many will say, I quite admit that we ought not to mingle ourselves with positive unbelievers in the worship or service of God, but then we can freely unite with such for the furtherance of objects of philanthropy—such, for instance, as feeding the hungry, clothing the naked, reclaiming the vicious, in providing asylums for the blind and lunatic, hospitals and infirmaries for the sick and infirm, places of refuge for the homeless and houseless, the fatherless and the widow; and in short, for the furtherance of every thing that tends to promote the amelioration of our fellow creatures, physically, morally, and intellectually.

This, at first sight, seems fair enough; for I may be asked if I would not help a man by the roadside to get his cart out of the ditch. I reply, Certainly; but if I were asked to become a member of a mixed society for the purpose of getting carts out of ditches, I should refuse—not because of my superior sanctity, but because God's Word says, "Be not unequally yoked together with unbelievers." This would be my answer, no matter what were the object proposed by a mixed society. The servant of Christ is commanded "to be ready to every good work"—"to do good unto all"—"to visit the fatherless and the widows in their affliction;" but then it is as the servant of Christ, and not as the member of a society or a committee in which there may be infidels and atheists, and all sorts of wicked and godless men.

Moreover, we must remember that all God's philanthropy is connected with the cross of the Lord Jesus Christ. That is the channel through which God will bless—that the mighty lever by which He will elevate man, physically, morally, and intellectually. "After that the kindness and philanthropy [φιλανθρωπια] of God our Saviour toward man appeared, not by works of righteousness which we have done, but according to His mercy He saved us, by the washing of regeneration, and renewing of the Holy Ghost; which He shed on us abundantly through Jesus Christ our Saviour" (Titus 3: 4-6). This is God's philanthropy; this is His mode of ameliorating man's condition. With all who understand its worth the Christian can readily yoke himself, but with none other.

The men of the world know naught of this, care not for it. They may seek reformation, but it is reformation without Christ; they may promote amelioration, but it is amelioration without the cross. They wish to advance, but Jesus is neither the starting post nor the goal of their course. How, then, can the Christian yoke himself with them? They want to work without Christ, the very One to whom he owes every thing. Can he be satisfied to work with them? Can he have an object in common with them? If men come to me and say, "We want your co-operation in feeding the hungry, in clothing the naked, in founding hospitals and lunatic asylums, in feeding and educating orphans, in improving the physical condition of our fellow-mortals; but you must remember that a leading rule of the society, the board, or the committee formed for such objects is, that the name of Christ is not to be introduced, as it would only lead to controversy. Our objects being not at all religious, but undividedly philanthropic, the subject of religion must be studiously excluded from all our public meetings. We are met as *men*, for a benevolent purpose, and therefore infidels, atheists, Socinians, Arians, Romanists, and all sorts, can happily yoke themselves to move onward the glorious machine of philanthropy."

What should be my answer to such an application? The fact is, words would fail one who really loved the Lord Jesus, in attempting to reply to an appeal so monstrous. What! benefit mortals by the exclusion of Christ? God forbid! If I cannot gain the objects of pure philanthropy without setting aside that blessed One who lived and died, and lives eternally for me, then away with your philanthropy, for it assuredly is not God's, but Satan's. If it were God's, the word is, "He shed it on us abundantly *through* Jesus Christ," the very One whom your rule leaves entirely out. Hence your rule must be the direct dictation of Satan, the enemy of Christ. Satan would always like to leave out the Son of God; and when he can get men to do the same, he will allow them to be benevolent, charitable, and philanthropic.

But, in good truth, such benevolence and philanthropy ought to be termed malevolence and misanthropy, for how can you more effectually exhibit ill-will and hatred toward men than by leaving out *the only One* who can really bless them, for time or for eternity? But what must be the moral condition of a heart, in reference to Christ, who could take his seat at a board, or on a platform, on the condition that that name must not be introduced? It must be cold indeed; yea, it proves that the plans and operations of unconverted men are of sufficient importance, in his judgment, to lead him to throw his Master overboard, for the purpose of carrying them out. Let us not mistake matters. This is the true aspect in which to view the world's philanthropy. The men of this world can "sell ointment for three hundred pence, and give to the poor"; while they pronounce it *waste* to pour that ointment on the head of Christ! Will the Christian consent to this? Will he yoke himself with such? Will he seek to improve the world without Christ? Will he join with men to deck and garnish a scene which is stained with his Master's blood?

Peter could say, "Silver and gold have I none; but such as I have give I thee: in the name of Jesus Christ of Nazareth, rise up and walk." Peter would heal a cripple by the power of the name of Jesus, but what would he have said if asked to join a committee or society to alleviate cripples, on the condition of leaving that name out altogether? It requires no great stretch of imagination to conceive his answer. His whole soul would recoil from such a thought. He only healed the cripple for the purpose of exalting the name of Jesus, and setting forth its worth, its excellency, and its glory, in the view of men: but the very reverse is the object of the world's philanthropy; inasmuch as it sets aside His blessed name entirely, and banishes Him from its boards, its committees, and its platforms.

May we not therefore well say, Shame on the Christian who is found in a place from which his Master is shut out? Oh, let him go forth, and, in the energy of love to Jesus, and by the power of that name, do all the good he can; but let him not yoke himself with unbelievers, to counteract the effects of sin by excluding the cross of Christ. God's grand object is to exalt His Son—"that all should honor the Son even as they honor the Father." This should be the Christian's object likewise; to this end he should "do good unto all"; but if he join a society or a committee in order to do good, it is not "in the name of Jesus" he acts, but in the name of the society or committee, without the name of Jesus.

This ought to be enough for every true and loyal heart. God has no other way of blessing men but through Christ, and no other object in blessing them but to exalt Christ. As with Pharaoh of old, when the hungry Egyptians flocked to his presence, his word was, "Go to Joseph"; so God's word to all is, "Come to Jesus." Yes, for soul and body, time and eternity, we must go to Jesus; but the men of the world know Him not, and want Him not; what, therefore, has the Christian to do with such? How can he act in yoke with them? He can only do so on the ground of practically denying his Saviour's name. Many do not see this; but that does not alter the case for those who do. We ought to act honestly, as in the light; and even though the feelings and affections of the new nature were not sufficiently strong in us to lead us to shrink from ranking ourselves with the enemies of Christ, the conscience ought, at least, to bow to the commanding authority of that word, "*Be not unequally yoked together with unbelievers.*"

May the Holy Ghost clothe His own Word with heavenly power, and make its edge sharp to pierce the conscience, that so the saints of God may be delivered from every thing that hinders their "running the race that is set before them." Time is short. The Lord Himself will soon be here. Then many an unequal yoke will be broken in a moment: many a sheep and goat shall then be eternally severed. May we be enabled to purge ourselves from every unclean association and every unhallowed influence, so that when Jesus returns, we may not be ashamed, but meet Him with a joyful heart and an approving conscience.

THE CHRISTIAN'S MISSION
and HOW TO FULFIL IT*

IN THOSE DAYS the multitude being very great and having nothing to eat, Jesus called his disciples unto Him, and saith unto them, I have compassion on the multitude, because they have now been with Me three days, and have nothing to eat: and if I send them away fasting to their own houses, they will faint by the way; for divers of them came from far. And His disciples answered Him, From whence can a man satisfy these men with bread here in the wilderness? And He asked them, How many loaves have ye? And they said, Seven. And He commanded the people to sit down on the ground; and He took the seven loaves, and gave thanks, and brake, and gave to His disciples to set before them; and they did set them before the people. And they had a few small fishes; and He blessed, and commanded to set them also before them. So they did eat, and were filled; and they took up of the broken meat that was left, seven baskets. And they that had eaten were about four thousand, and He sent them away" (Mark 8:1-9).

* This little book is sent forth to the Church of God—"To all that, in every place, call on the name of our Lord Jesus Christ, both theirs and ours"—with earnest prayer that it may be used of the Holy Spirit to awaken in the hearts of all who may read it a true sense of the Christian's mission, and a fixed purpose to seek, by the grace of God, to fulfill it.

We need to be reminded, in days like the present, that every child of God, every member of the body of Christ, whatever be his position or sphere of action, has a mission to fulfil—a work to do for Christ. He may not be called to be an evangelist, a pastor, or a teacher; but he is called to live Christ—to represent Him—to be a channel of communication between His loving heart and every form of need, in this poor dark, cold, selfish world. This is the Christian's mission; may every Christian seek to fulfil it!

The foregoing passage presents a very striking and beautiful illustration of one special feature of the Christian's mission in this world, which the reader will do well to ponder. It is of immense importance, and of universal application. It concerns every child of God. We have each one to remember, that we are sent into this world to be a channel of communication between the heart of Christ and every form of need that may cross our path from day to day.

This is an interesting and lovely feature of the Christian's mission. True, it is only one of the many features, but it is one of exceeding preciousness and beauty. It is pre-eminently practical too, as we shall see.

Of course, of necessity, it assumes that I am a Christian. If I do not know that I have eternal life, if I am at all doubtful as to my eternal salvation, if I do not know Christ as my own precious Saviour and Lord—the portion, the object, and the resting-place of my heart—to occupy myself with the Christian's mission is simply to deceive myself, and blind my eyes to my true condition. A known and enjoyed salvation, and a known and enjoyed Saviour and Lord, are absolutely essential conditions for it.

Having said thus much, to guard the reader against self-deception, as also to guard our subject against any misapprehension, we shall look, for a few moments, at the lovely passage which stands at the head of this paper. May the blessed Spirit open and apply it to our hearts!

"In those days, the multitude being *very great*, and having *nothing to eat.*" Here was the state of the case—great need, and no apparent resources to meet it. But Jesus was there—blessed be His holy name!—in all the love of His heart, and the almighty power of His hand. He was there who, of old, had fed three millions of people, in a vast howling wilderness, for forty years. Yes, He was there, and, of course, He could at once, and directly, have met the need without calling His poor unbelieving and self-occupied disciples into the scene at all. He could have summoned angelic messengers from Heaven to wait upon those hungry thousands.

But He did neither the one nor the other, because it was His gracious purpose to use His disciples as channels of communication between Himself and that vast hungry multitude. Not merely as instruments of His *power*, which angels might be, but the very expression of His *heart*.

And let us note *how* He did this. Had He merely intended to use them as instruments of His power, it would have sufficed to put the ways and means into their hands. But no; He wanted to make them channels through which the tender compassion of His heart might flow out. And how was this to be done? Thus: "He called His disciples unto Him, and saith unto them, *I* have compassion on the multitude, because they have now been with Me three days, and have nothing to eat; and if I send them away fasting to their own houses they will faint by the way; for divers of them came from far."

Here, then, we have the true secret of preparation of our high and holy mission. Our blessed Lord first gathers His disciples round Himself, and seeks to fill their hearts with His own feelings and thoughts ere He fills their hands with the loaves and fishes. It is as if He had said, "I have compassion, and I want you to have it also. I want you to enter into all my thoughts and feelings, to think as I do, and feel as I do. I want you to look with mine eyes at this hungry multitude, in order that you may be in a moral condition to be My channels."

This is uncommonly fine. A person may say, "I long to be a channel, but it seems quite too high, quite beyond me. How could I ever attain to such a height?" The answer is, Get near enough to Christ to think as He thinks, to feel as He feels. Drink into His spirit. This, be assured of it, is the true, the only way to be a channel of communication. If I say, "I must try and be a channel," I shall make a fool of myself. But if I drink at the fountain of Christ's heart, I shall be filled to overflowing, my whole moral being will be permeated by His spirit, so that I shall be in a fit condition to be used by Him, and I shall be sure to make a right use of—that is, to use for Him—whatever ways and means He may put into my hands. If I get my hands full of means, before my heart is full of Christ, I shall not use the means for Him, I shall use them for my own glory, and not for the glory of God.

Let us ponder this. Let us consider our mission, and the true secret of fulfilling it. It is a grand point to have the heart impressed with the fact, that we are called to be channels through which the heart of Christ may flow out to His own, and to a needy world. It is wonderful, it seems too good to be true; but, blessed be God, it is as true as it is wonderful. Let us only seek to take it in—to believe it, to make it our own. Let us not content ourselves with admiring it as a beautiful theory, but seek to have it wrought into our souls by the mighty power of the Holy Spirit.

But mark how slow the disciples were in responding to the desire of the heart of Christ respecting them. It was His gracious purpose to use them as His channels, to bestow upon them this immense privilege; but they, like ourselves, were little able to appreciate it, simply because they failed to enter into His thoughts, and to apprehend the glory of His Person. "His disciples answered Him, From whence *can a man* satisfy these men with bread here in the wilderness?" On another occasion they said, "We have here but five loaves and two fishes."

Did they not know, or had they forgotten, that they were in the immediate presence of the Creator and Sustainer of the universe? True, He was there in the lowly form of Jesus of Nazareth. His divine glory was hidden from nature's view behind the veil of humanity. But they ought to have known better who and what He was, and how to avail themselves of His glorious presence, and of His unsearchable riches. Surely, had their hearts at all apprehended the glory of His Person, they could never have asked such a question as, "Whence can *a man* satisfy these men with bread here in the wilderness?" Moses, of old, had asked, "Whence should *I* have flesh to give to all this people?" God is shut out by the poor unbelieving heart. Did Jehovah ask Moses to provide flesh? Surely not. No mere man could do it. Neither could a mere man feed four thousand in a desert place.

But God was there. Yes, it was God, speaking through human lips, who had said, "I have compassion on the multitude." It was God who took account of all the circumstances of each individual in that vast multitude of hungry fainting people. He knew the exact distance each one had travelled, and the length of time each one had been fasting. He took account of the sure consequences of their being dismissed without food. It was God who gave utterance to those touching words, "I cannot send them away fasting, lest they faint by the way, for divers of them came from far."

Yes, God was there, in all the tenderness of a love, which could take account of the most minute details of a creature's weakness, and a creature's necessity. There, too, in His almighty power and exhaustless resources, and there to enable His poor disciples to be the depositaries of His thoughts, the vessels of His goodness, the channels of His grace. And what did they want, in order to be able to fulfil their mission? Did they want to be, or to do, anything? No; they simply want to see Him, and to use Him. They wanted to exercise that simple faith which counts on God for everything, and finds all its springs in Him.

Thus it was with the disciples, and thus it is with us. If we want to act as the channels of the grace of Christ, we must have to do with Him in the deep secret of our own souls. We must learn of Him; we must feed upon Him; we must know the meaning of communion with His heart; we must be near enough to Him to know the secrets of His mind, and carry out the purposes of His love. If we would reflect Him, we must gaze upon Him. If we would reproduce Him, we must feed upon Him, we must have Him dwelling in our hearts by faith.

We may depend upon it, that what is really in our hearts will come out in our lives. We may have a quantity of truth in our heads, and flippantly flowing from our lips, but if we really desire to be channels of communication between His heart and the needy ones in the scene through which we are passing, we must habitually drink into His love. It cannot possibly be in any other way. "He that believeth on Me, as the Scripture hath said, out of his belly shall flow rivers of living water" (John 8:38).

Here lies the grand secret of the whole matter: "If any man thirst, let him come unto Me and drink." If the rivers are to flow, we must drink. It cannot be otherwise. If every member of the Church of God were in the power of this great principle, what a very different state of things we should witness! And where lies the hindrance? We are not straitened in our adorable Lord and Saviour. It is His desire to use us, just as He used His disciples on the occasion before us. He gathered them round Himself, and graciously sought to pour into their hearts the compassion of His own heart, in order that they might feel with Him, as the moral qualification for acting *for Him*. We may always feel assured that where the heart is full of Christ, the power to act will not be lacking.

But, alas! as it was with the disciples, so it is with us. They failed in appreciating and using the power that was in their midst. They said, "Whence can a man?" when they ought to have said, "We have Christ." They practically ignored Him, and so do we. We make excuses for our poverty, our indolence, our coldness, our indifference, by the plea that we have not got this, and that, and the other; whereas, what we really want is a heart full of Christ—full of His thoughts, full of His love, full of His kindness, full of His tender consideration for others, full of His beautiful self-forgetfulness. We complain of our want of ways and means, when what we really want is the right condition of soul— the true moral attitude of the heart, and this can only spring from close intimacy with Christ, communion with his mind, and drinking into His spirit.

We would very earnestly press this subject upon the Church of God. We long to see every member of the body of Christ acting as a channel through which His precious grace may flow out in living streams to all around, shedding freshness and verdure in its course—and not a stagnant pool, so strikingly illustrative of a Christian out of communion.*

* Note.—We should ever remember, that we are not to be *expectants* from the scene around us, but *contributors*. A true contributor never complains of want of love. He walks in love and manifests love: and his language is, "I have all and abound." Oh, that it were thus with us all!

LIVING BY FAITH

THE *JUST SHALL LIVE BY HIS* faith." This weighty statement occurs in the second chapter of the prophet Habakkuk; and it is quoted by an inspired apostle in three of his Epistles, namely, Romans, Galatians, and Hebrews, with a distinct application in each. In Rom. 1:17 it is applied to the great question of righteousness. The blessed apostle declares himself not ashamed of the gospel; "for it is the power of God unto salvation to every one that believeth; to the Jew first, and also to the Greek. For therein is the righteousness of God revealed, on the principle of faith, to faith: as it is written, The just shall live by faith."**

Then, in the third of Galatians, where the apostle is seeking to recall those erring assemblies to the foundations of Christianity, he says, "But that no man is justified by the law in the sight of God, it is evident: for, The just shall live by faith."

Finally, in the tenth of Hebrews, where the object is to exhort believers to hold fast their confidence, we read, "Cast not away

** The phrase "from faith to faith" is quite unintelligible. We have given in the text the literal rendering of the Greek words ἐκ πίστεως εἰς πίστιν. They set forth the ground, or principle, on which righteousness is to be obtained. It is not on the ground of works, but of faith; and it is revealed to faith. Our apostle repeatedly contrasts ἐκ πίστεως with ἐξ ἔργων—the principle of faith, with the principle of works. Blessed contrast!

therefore your confidence, which hath great recompence of reward. For ye have need of patience, that, after ye have done the will of God, ye might receive the promise. For yet a little while, and He that shall come will come, and will not tarry. Now the just shall live by faith." Here we have faith presented not only as the ground of righteousness, but as the vital principle by which we are to live, day by day, from the starting-post to the goal of the Christian course. There is no other way of righteousness, no other way of living, but by faith. It is by faith we are justified, and by faith we live. By faith we stand, and by faith we walk.

Now this is true of all Christians, and all should seek to enter into it fully. Every child of God is called to live by faith. It is a very grave mistake indeed to single out certain individuals who happen to have no visible source of temporal supplies, and speak of them as though they alone lived by faith. According to this view of the question, ninety-nine out of every hundred Christians would be deprived of the precious privilege of living by faith. If a man has a settled income; if he has a certain salary; if he has what is termed a secular calling, by which he earns bread for himself and his family, is he not privileged to live by faith? Do none live by faith save those who have no visible means of support? Is the life of faith to be confined to the matter of trusting God for food and raiment?

What a lowering of the life of faith it is to confine it to the question of temporal supplies! No doubt it is a very blessed and a very real thing to trust God for everything; but the life of faith has a far higher and wider range than mere bodily wants. It embraces all that in any wise concerns us, in body, soul, and spirit. To live by faith is to walk with God; to cling to Him; to lean on Him; to draw from His exhaustless springs; to find *all* our resources in Him; and to have Him as a perfect covering for our eyes and a satisfying object for our hearts—to know Him as our *only* resource in all difficulties, and in all our trials. It is to be absolutely, completely, and continually shut up to Him; to be undividedly dependent upon Him, apart from and above every creature confidence, every human hope, and every earthly expectation.

Such is the life of faith. Let us see that we understand it. It must be a reality, or nothing at all. It will not do to talk about the life of faith; we must *live* it; and in order to live it, we must know God practically—know Him intimately, in the deep secret of our own souls. It is utterly vain and delusive to profess to be living by faith and looking to the Lord, while in reality our hearts are looking to some creature resource. How often do people speak and write about their dependence upon God to meet certain wants, and by the very fact of their making it known to a fellow-mortal they are, in principle, departing from the life of faith!

If I write to a friend, or publish to the church, the fact that I am looking to the Lord to meet a certain need, I am virtually off the ground of faith in that matter. The language of faith is this: "My soul, wait thou *only* upon God; for my expectation is from Him." To make known my wants, directly or indirectly, to a human being, is departure from the life of faith, and a positive dishonor to God. It is actually betraying Him. It is tantamount to saying that God has failed me, and I must look to my fellow for help. It is forsaking the living fountain and turning to a broken cistern. It is placing the creature between my soul and God, thus robbing my soul of rich blessing, and God of the glory due to Him.

This is serious work, and it demands our most solemn attention. God deals in realities. He can never fail a trusting heart. But then, He must be trusted. It is of no possible use to talk about trusting Him when our hearts are really looking to creature-streams. "What doth it profit, my brethren though a man *say* he hath faith?" Empty profession is but a delusion to the soul and a dishonor to God. The true life of faith is a grand reality. God delights in it, and He is glorified by it. There is nothing in all this world that so gratifies and glorifies God as the life of faith. "Oh how great is Thy goodness, which Thou hast laid up for them that fear Thee; which Thou hast wrought for them that trust in Thee before the sons of men!" (Psa. 31:19)

How is it with you in reference to this great question? Are you living by faith? Can you say, "The life that I live in the flesh, I live by the faith of the Son of God, who loved me and gave Himself for me?" Do you know what it is to have the living God filling the whole range of your soul's vision? Is He enough for you? Can you trust Him for everything—for body, soul, and spirit—for time and eternity? Or are you in the habit of making known your wants to man in any one way? Is it the habit of your heart to turn to the creature for sympathy, succor, or counsel?

These are searching questions; but we entreat you not to turn away from them. Be assured it is morally healthful for our souls to be tested faithfully, as in the very presence of God. Our hearts are so terribly treacherous, that when we imagine we are leaning upon God, we are really leaning upon some human prop. Thus God is shut out, and we are left in barrenness and desolation.

And yet it is not that God does not use the creature to help and bless us. He does so constantly; and the man of faith will be deeply conscious of this fact, and truly grateful to every human agent that God uses to help him. God comforted Paul by the coming of Titus; but had Paul been looking to Titus, he would have had but little comfort. God used the poor widow to feed Elijah; but Elijah's dependence was not upon the widow, but upon God. Thus it is in every case.

Doctrine

GLAD TIDINGS

"FOR GOD SO LOVED THE WORLD, that He gave His only-begotten Son, that whosoever believeth in Him should not perish, but have everylasting life" (John 3:16).

There are some passages of holy Scripture which seem to contain, in a line or two, an entire volume of most precious truth. The verse which we have just penned is one of such. It is part of our Lord's memorable discourse with Nicodemus, and it embodies, in a condensed form, a very full statement of gospel truth—a statement which may well be termed, "Glad Tidings."

It should ever be borne in mind, both by preachers and those to whom they preach, that one grand object of the gospel is to bring God and the sinner together in such a way as to secure the sinner's eternal salvation. It reveals a *Saviour God* to a *lost man*. In other words, it presents God to the sinner in the very character that meets the sinner's need. A Saviour is precisely what suits the lost, just as a life-boat suits a drowning man, or a physician a sick man, or bread a hungry man. They are fitted the one for the other; and when God as a Saviour, and man as a lost sinner, meet together, the whole question is settled forever. The sinner is saved, because God is a Saviour. He is saved according to the perfection which belongs to God, in every character He wears, in every office He fills, in every relationship He sustains.

To raise a question as to the full and everlasting salvation of a believing soul, is to deny that God is a Saviour. So it is in reference to justification. God has revealed Himself as a Justifier; and hence, the believer is justified according to the perfection which attaches to God in that character. If a single flaw could be detected in the title of the very weakest believer, it would be a dishonor to God as a Justifier. Grant me but this, that God is my Justifier,

and I argue, in the face of every opposer and every accuser, that I am, and must be, perfectly justified.

And, on the same principle, grant me but this, that God has revealed Himself as a Saviour, and I argue, with unclouded confidence and holy boldness, that I am, and must be, perfectly saved. It does not rest upon aught in me, but simply and entirely upon God's revelation of Himself. I know He is perfect in everything; and, therefore, perfect as my Saviour. Hence, I am perfectly saved, inasmuch as the glory of God is involved in my salvation. "There is no God else beside Me: a just God and a Saviour; there is none beside Me." What then? "*Look unto Me, and be ye saved, all the ends of the earth;* for I am God, and there is none else" (Isa. 45:21-22). One believing *look* from a lost sinner to a just God and a Saviour, secures eternal salvation. "*Look!*" How simple! It is not "Work"—"Do"—"Pray"—"Feel"—no; it is simply "Look."

And what then? Salvation—everlasting life. It must be so, because God is a Saviour; and the precious little word "look" fully implies all this, inasmuch as it expresses the fact that the salvation which I want is found in the One to whom I look. It is all there, ready for me, and one look secures it—secures it forever—secures it for *me*. It is not a thing of to-day or to-morrow; it is an eternal reality. The bulwarks of salvation behind which the believer retreats have been erected by God Himself—the Saviour-God, on the sure foundation of Christ's atoning work; and no power of earth or hell can ever shake them. "Wherefore also it is contained in the Scripture, Behold, I lay in Zion a chief Corner-stone, elect, precious; and he that believeth on Him shall not be confounded" (Isa. 28:16; 1 Pet. 2:6).

But let us now turn directly to the profound and comprehensive passage which forms the special subject of this paper. In it, most assuredly, we listen to the voice of a Saviour-God—the voice of Him who came down from Heaven to reveal God in such a way as He had never been revealed before. It is a marvelously blessed fact that God has been fully revealed in this world—revealed, so that we—the writer and the reader of these lines—may know Him, in all the reality of what He is—know Him, each for himself, with the utmost possible certainty, and have to do with Him, in all the blessed intimacy of personal communion.

Think of this! Think, we beseech you, of this amazing privilege. You may know God for yourself, as *your* Saviour, *your* Father, *your* own very God. You may have to do with Him; you may lean upon Him, cling to Him, walk with Him, live and move and have your being in His own most blessed presence, in the bright sunshine of His loving countenance, under His own immediate eye.

This is life and peace. It is far more than mere theology or systematic divinity. These things have their value, but, be it remembered, a man may be a profound theologian, an able divine, and yet live and die without God and perish eternally. Solemn, awful, overwhelming thought! A man may go down to hell, into the blackness and darkness of an eternal night, with all the dogmas of theology at his fingers' ends. A man may sit in the professor's chair, stand in the pulpit and at the desk; he may be looked up to as a great teacher and an eloquent preacher: hundreds may sit at his feet and learn, thousands may hang on his lips and be enraptured, and, after all, he himself may descend into the pit, and spend a dismal, miserable eternity in company with the most profane and immoral.

Not so, however, with one who knows God as He is revealed in the face of Jesus Christ. Such a one has gotten life eternal. "This," says Christ, "is life eternal, that they might know Thee the only true God, and Jesus Christ, whom Thou hast sent" (John 17:3). It is not life eternal to know theology or divinity. A man may sit down to the study of these, as he would to study law or medicine, astronomy or geology, and all the while know nothing of God, and therefore be without

divine life, and perish in the end.

So also as to mere religiousness. A man may be the greatest devotee in the world. He may most diligently discharge all the offices, and sedulously attend upon all the ordinances of systematic religion; he may fast and pray; hear sermons and say prayers; be most devout and exemplary; and all the while know nothing of God in Christ; yea, he may live and die without God, and sink into hell forever.

Look at Nicodemus. Where could you find a better sample of religious human nature than in him? A man of the Pharisees, a ruler of the Jews, a master in Israel; one, moreover, who seemed to discern in the miracles of our Lord the clear proofs of His divine mission; and yet the word to him was, "Ye must be born again." We have no need, surely, to go farther than this to prove that a man may be not only religious, but actually a guide and a teacher of others, and yet not have divine life in his soul.

But it is not so with one who knows God in Christ. Such a one has life and an object. He has God Himself for his priceless portion. This is divine. It lies at the very foundation of personal Christianity and true religion. It is above and beyond everything. It is not, we repeat, mere theology, divinity, or religiousness; it is God Himself, known, trusted, and enjoyed. It is a grand, unmistakable reality. It is the soul of theology, the groundwork of divinity, the life of true religion. There is nothing in all this world like it. It is something which must be *felt* in order to be known. It is acquaintance with God, confidence in Him, and enjoyment of Him.

Now, it may be that the reader is disposed to ask, "How can I possess this priceless treasure? How can I know God for myself, in this living, saving, powerful manner? If it be true that without this personal knowledge of God I *must* perish eternally, then how am I to obtain it? What am I to do, what am I to be, in order to know God?" The answer is, God has revealed Himself. If He had not, we may say with decision that nothing that we could do, nothing that we could be, nothing in us or of us, could possibly make us acquainted with God.

If God had not manifested Himself, we

should have remained forever in ignorance of Him and perished in our ignorance. But, seeing that He has come forth from the thick darkness and showed Himself, we may know Him according to the truth of His own revelation, and find, in that knowledge, everlasting life, and a spring of blessedness at which our ransomed souls shall drink throughout the golden ages of eternity.

We know of nothing which so clearly and forcibly proves man's utter incompetency to do aught towards procuring life, as the fact that the possession of that life is based upon the knowledge of God: and this knowledge of God must rest upon the *revelation* of God. In a word, to know God is life, to be ignorant of Him is death.

But where is He to be known? This is, in very deed, a grave question. Many a one has had to cry out, with Job, "Oh, that I knew where I might find Him." Where is God to be found? Am I to look for Him in creation? Doubtless, His hand is visible there; but ah! that will not do for me. A Creator-God will not suit a lost sinner. *The hand of power* will not avail for a poor, guilty wretch like me. I want *a heart of love*.

Yes, I want a heart that can love me in all my guilt and misery. Where can I find this? Shall I look into the wide domain of providence—the widely extended sphere of God's government? Has God revealed Himself there in such a way as to meet me, a poor lost one? Will providence and government avail for one who knows himself to be a hell-deserving sinner? Clearly not. If I look at these things, I may see what will perplex and confound me. I am short-sighted and ignorant, and wholly unable to explain the ins and outs, the bearings and issues, the why and the wherefore, of a single event in my own life, or in the history of this world.

Am I able to explain all about the loss of *The London?* Can I account for the fact that a most valuable life is suddenly cut short, and an apparently useless one prolonged? There is a husband and the father of a large family; he seems perfectly indispensable to his domestic circle and yet, all in a moment, he is cut down, and they are left in sorrow and destitution; while, on the other hand, yonder lies a poor bed-ridden creature, who has outlived all her relations, and is dependent on the parish, or on individual benevolence. She has lain there for years, a burden to some, no use to any. Can I account for this? Am I competent to interpret the voice of Providence in this deeply mysterious dispensation? Certainly not. I have nothing in or of myself wherewith to thread my way through the mazes of the labyrinth of what is called providence. I cannot find a Saviour-God there.

Well, then, shall I turn to the law—to the Mosaic economy—the Levitical ceremonial? Shall I find what I want there? Will a Lawgiver, on the top of a fiery mount, wrapped in clouds and thick darkness, sending forth thunders and lightnings, or hidden behind a veil—will such a One avail for me? Alas! I cannot meet Him—I cannot answer His demands nor fulfil the conditions. I am told to love Him with all my heart, with all my mind, and with all my strength; but I do not know Him. I am blind and cannot see. I am alienated from the life of God, an enemy by wicked works. Sin has blinded my mind, blunted my conscience, and hardened my heart. The devil has completely perverted my moral being, and led me into a state of positive rebellion against God.

I want to be renewed in the very source of my being ere I can do what the law demands. How can I be thus renewed? Only by the knowledge of God. But God is not revealed in the law. Nay, He is hidden—hidden behind an impenetrable cloud, an unrent veil. Hence I cannot know Him there. I am compelled to retire from that fiery mount, and from that unrent veil, and from the whole economy of which these were the characteristic features, the prominent objects, still crying out, "Oh! that I knew where I might find Him."

In a word, then, neither in creation, nor in providence, nor in the law, is God revealed as "a just God and a Saviour." I see a God of power in creation: a God of wisdom in providence; a God of justice in the law; a God of love *only* in the face of Jesus Christ. *"God was in Christ*, reconciling the world unto Himself"* (2 Cor. 5:19).

To this stupendous fact we call the reader's

earnest attention; that is, if he be one who does not yet know the Lord. It is of the very last possible importance that he be clear as to this. Without it there can be nothing right. To know God is the first step. It is not merely knowing some things about God. It is not unrenewed nature turning religious, trying to do better, endeavoring to keep the law. No; it is none of these things. It is God, known in the face of Jesus Christ.

"For God, who commanded the light to shine out of darkness, hath shined in our hearts, to give the light of the knowledge of the glory of God in the face of Jesus Christ." This is the deep and blessed secret of the whole matter.

The reader, so far as his natural condition is concerned, is in a state of darkness. There is not so much as a single ray of spiritual light. He is, spiritually and morally, just what creation was physically before that sublime and commanding utterance fell from the lips of the Almighty Creator, "Let there be light." All is dark and chaotic, for the "god of this world hath blinded the minds of them which believe not, lest the light of the glorious gospel of Christ, who is the image of God, should shine unto them" (2 Cor. 4:4-6).

Here are two things; namely, the god of this world blinding the mind, and seeking to hinder the inshining of the precious, life-giving beams of the light of God's glory; and, on the other hand, God, in His marvelous grace, shining in the heart, to give the light of the knowledge of His glory in the face of Jesus Christ. Thus all hinges upon the grand reality of the knowledge of God. Is there light? It is because God is known. Is there darkness? It is because God is not known.

No doubt there are various measures in the experience and exhibition of this light: but there is light, because there is the knowledge of God. So also there may be various forms of darkness; some more hideous than others; but there is darkness because God is not known. The knowledge of God is light and life. Ignorance of God is darkness and death. A man may enrich himself with all the treasures of science and literature; but if he does not know God, he is in the darkness of primeval night. But, on the other hand, a man may be profoundly ignorant of all human learning; but if he knows God, he walks in broad day-light.

In the passage of Scripture which is engaging our attention, namely, John 3:16, we have a very remarkable illustration of the character of the entire Gospel of John, and especially the opening chapters. It is impossible to meditate upon it without seizing this interesting fact. In it we are introduced to God Himself, in that wondrous aspect of His character and nature, as loving *the world*, and giving His Son. In it, too, we find, not only the "world" as a whole, but the individual sinner, under that most satisfactory title of "whosoever."

Thus God and the sinner are together—God, *loving* and *giving;* and the sinner, *believing* and *having.* It is not God judging and exacting; but God loving and giving. The former was law; the latter, grace; that was Judaism; this, Christianity. In the one, we see God demanding obedience in order to have life; in the other, we see God giving life as the only basis of obedience. In the one, we see man struggling for life, but never obtaining it; in the other, we see man receiving life as a free gift, through faith in the Lord Jesus Christ. Such is the contrast between the two systems—a contrast which cannot be too deeply pondered. "The law was given by Moses, but grace and truth came by Jesus Christ" (John 1:17).

But let us mark the way in which this is unfolded in our text. "God so loved the world." Here we have the wide aspect of the love of God. It is not confined to any particular nation, tribe, caste, or family. It embraces the whole world. God is love; and, being so, it is not a question of the fitness or worthiness of the object of His love. It is what He *is.* He is love, and He cannot deny Himself. It is the very energy and activity of His nature.

The heart may have many a question, many an exercise as to its state and condition before God, and very right it should have them. The Spirit Himself may produce such exercises and raise such questions; but, after all, the grand truth shines forth in all its lustre, "God is love." Whatever we are, whatever the world is, that is what God is; and we know that the truth as to God forms the deep and rich substratum which underlies the whole system of Christianity.

The soul may pass through deep and sore conflict, under the sense of its own wretchedness; there may be many doubts and fears; many dark and heavy clouds; weeks, months, or years may be spent under the law, in one's inward self-consciousness, and that, moreover, long after the mere intellect has yielded its assent to the principles and doctrines of evangelical truth. But, after all, we must be brought into direct personal contact with God Himself—with what He is—with His nature and character, as He has revealed Himself in the gospel. We have to acquaint ourselves with Him, and He is love.

Observe, it does not say merely that God is *loving*, but that He is *love*. It is not only that love is an attribute of His character, but it is the very activity of His nature. We do not read that God is justice, or holiness; He is just and He is holy; but it would not express the full and blessed truth to say that God is loving; He is much more, He is love itself. Hence, when the sinner—"whosoever" he be, it matters not—is brought to see his own total and absolute ruin, his hopeless wretchedness, his guilt and misery, the utter vanity and worthlessness of all within and around him, (and there is nothing in the whole world that can satisfy his heart, and nothing in his heart that can satisfy God, or satisfy even his own conscience) when these things are opened in any measure to his view, then is he met by this grand substantial truth that "God is love," and that He so loved the world as to give His only-begotten Son.

Here is life and rest for the soul. Here is salvation, full, free, and everlasting, for the poor, needy, guilty, lost one;—salvation resting not upon anything in man or of man, upon aught that he is or can be, aught that he has done or can do, but simply upon what God is and has done. God *loves* and *gives*, and the sinner *believes* and *has*. This is far beyond creation, government, or law. In creation, God spake and it was done. He called worlds into existence by the word of His mouth. But we hear nothing, throughout the entire record of creation, of God loving and giving.

So as to government, we see God ruling in unsearchable wisdom, amid the armies of Heaven, and among the children of men: but we cannot comprehend Him. We can only say, as to this subject, that:

> God moves in a mysterious way,
>   His wonders to perform;
> He plants His footsteps in the sea,
>   And rides upon the storm.
> Deep in unfathomable mines
>   Of never failing skill,
> He treasures up His bright designs,
>   And works His sovereign will.

Finally, as to the law, it is, from beginning to end, a perfect system of command and prohibition—a system perfect in its action as testing man, and making manifest his entire alienation from God. "The law worketh wrath." And again, "By the law is the knowledge of sin." But what could such a system do in a world of sinners? Could it give life? Impossible. Why? Because man could not fulfil its holy requirements. "If there had been a law given which could have given life, then verily, righteousness should have been by the law." But no; the law was a ministration of death and condemnation. (See 2 Cor. 3.) The only effect of the law, to anyone who is under it, is the pressure of death upon the soul, and of guilt and condemnation upon the conscience. It cannot possibly be otherwise with an honest soul under the law.

What, then, is needed? Simply this, the knowledge of the love of God, and of the precious gift which that love has bestowed. This is the eternal groundwork of all. Love, and the gift of love. For, be it observed and ever remembered, that God's love could never have reached us save through the medium of that gift. God is holy, and we are sinful. How could we come near Him? How could we dwell in His holy presence? How could sin and holiness ever abide in company? Impossible. Justice demands the condemnation of sin; and if love will save the sinner, it must do so at no less a cost than the gift of the only-begotten Son.

Darius loved Daniel, and labored hard to save him from the lions' den; but his love was powerless because of the unbending law of the Medes and Persians. He spent the night in sorrow and fasting. He could weep at the mouth of the den; but he could not save his friend. His love was not mighty to save. If he had offered himself to the lions instead of his friend, it would have been morally glorious; but he did not. His love told itself forth in unavailing tears and lamentations. The law of the Persian kingdom was more powerful than the love of the Persian king. The law, in its stern majesty, triumphed over an impotent love which had nothing but fruitless tears to bestow upon its object.

But the love of God is not like this—eternal and universal praise to His name! His love is mighty to save. It *reigns* through righteousness. How is this? Because "God *so* loved the world that He gave His only-begotten Son." The law had declared in words of awful solemnity. "The soul that sinneth it shall die." Was this law less stern, less majestic, less stringent, than the law of the Medes and Persians? Surely not. How then, was it to be disposed of? It was to be magnified and made honorable, vindicated and established. Not one jot or tittle of the law could ever be set aside. How, then, was the difficulty to be solved? Three things had to be done: the law had to be magnified; sin condemned; the sinner saved. How could these grand results be reached? We have the answer in two bold and vivid lines from one of our own poets:

On Jesus' cross this record's graved,
Let sin be damned, and sinners saved.

Precious record! May many an anxious sinner read and believe it! Such was the amazing love of God, that He spared not His own Son, but delivered Him up for us all. His love cost Him nothing less than the Son of His bosom. When it was a question of creating worlds, it cost Him but the word of His mouth: but when it was a question of loving a world of sinners, it cost His only-begotten Son. The love of God is a holy love, a righteous love, a love acting in harmony with all the attributes of His nature, and the claims of His throne.

"Grace *reigns*, through righteousness, unto eternal life, by Christ Jesus our Lord." The soul can never be set at liberty till this truth be fully laid hold of. There may be certain vague hopes in the mercy of God, and a measure of confidence in the atoning work of Jesus, all true and real so far as it goes; but true liberty of heart cannot possibly be enjoyed until it is seen and understood that God has glorified Himself in the manner of His love toward us. Conscience could never be tranquilized, nor Satan silenced, if sin had not been perfectly judged and put away. But "God *so* loved the world that He gave His only-begotten Son." What depth and power in the little word "so"!

It may here be needful to meet a difficulty which often occurs to anxious souls, in reference to the question of appropriation. Thousands have been harassed and perplexed by this question, at some stage or other of their spiritual history; and it is not improbable that many who shall read these pages may be glad of a few words on the subject.

Many may feel disposed to ask, "How am I to know that this love, and the gift of love, are intended for *me?* What warrant have *I* for believing that 'everlasting life' is for *me?* I know the plan of salvation; I believe in the all-sufficiency of the atonement of Christ for the forgiveness and justification of all who truly believe. I am convinced of the truth of all that the Bible declares. I believe we are all sinners, and moreover, that we can do nothing to save ourselves—that we need to be washed in the blood of Jesus, and to be taught and led by the Holy Ghost, ere we can please God here, and dwell with Him hereafter. All this I fully believe, and yet I have no assurance that I am saved, and I want to know on what authority I am to believe that my sins are forgiven and that I have everlasting life."

If the foregoing be, in any measure, the language of the reader—if it be, at all, the expression of his difficulty, we would, in the first place, call his attention to two words which occur in our precious test (John 3:16), namely, "*world*" and "*whosoever*." It seems utterly impossible for anyone to refuse the application of these two words. For what, let us ask, is the meaning of the term *"world"*? What does it embrace? or, rather, what does it not embrace? When our Lord declares that "God so loved the world," on what ground can the reader exclude himself from the range, scope, and application of this divine love? On no other ground whatever, unless he can show that he alone belongs not to the world, but to some other sphere of being. If it were declared that "the world" is hopelessly condemned, could anyone making a part of that world avoid the application of the sentence! Could he exclude himself from it? Impossible. How then can he—why should he—exclude himself, when it is a question of God's free love, and of salvation by Christ Jesus?

But, further, we would ask, What is the meaning, what is the force of the familiar word, *"whosoever"*? Assuredly it means *"anybody"*; and if anybody, why not the reader? It is infinitely better, infinitely surer, and more satisfactory to find the word "whosoever" in the gospel than to find my own name there, inasmuch as there may be a thousand persons in the world of the same name; but "whosoever" applies to me as distinctly as though I were the only sinner on the face of the earth.

Thus, then, the very words of the gospel message—the very terms used to set forth the glad tidings, are such as leave no possible ground for a difficulty as to their application. If we listen to our Lord in the days of His flesh, we hear such words as these: "God so loved the *world* that He gave His only-begotten Son, that *whosoever* believeth in Him might not perish, but have everlasting life." Again, if we listen to Him after His resurrection, we hear these words, "Go ye into *all the world*, and preach the gospel to *every creature*" (Mark 16). And lastly, if we listen to the voice of the Holy Ghost sent from a risen, ascended, and glorified Lord, we hear such words as these: "The same Lord over all is rich unto *all* that call upon Him. For *whosoever* shall call on the name of the Lord shall be saved" (Rom. 10:12-13).

In all the above-cited passages we have two terms used, one general, the other particular, and both together so presenting the message of salvation as to leave no room whatever for anyone to refuse its application. If "all the world" is the scope, and "every creature" is the object of the precious gospel of Christ, then, on what ground can anyone exclude himself? Where is there authority for any sinner out of hell to say that the glad tidings of salvation are not for him? There is none. Salvation is as free as the air we breathe—free as the dewdrops that refresh the earth—free as the sunbeams that shine upon our pathway; and if any attempt to limit its application, they are neither in harmony with the mind of Christ, nor in sympathy with the heart of God.

But it may be that some of our readers would, at this stage of the subject, feel disposed to ask us, "How do you dispose of the question of election?" We reply, "Very simply, by leaving it where God has placed it, namely, as a landmark in the inheritance of the spiritual Israel, and not as a stumbling-block in the pathway of the anxious inquirer." This we believe to be the true way of dealing with the deeply important doctrine of election.

The more we ponder the subject, the more thoroughly are we convinced that it is a mistake on the part of the evangelist or preacher of the gospel to qualify his message, hamper his subject, or perplex his hearers, by the doctrine of election or predestination. He has to do with lost sinners in the discharge of his blessed ministry. He meets men where they are, on the broad ground of our common ruin, our common guilt, our common condemnation. He meets them with a message of full, free, present, personal, and eternal salvation—a message which comes fresh, fervent, and glowing from the very bosom of God. His ministry is, as the Holy Ghost declares in 2 Cor. 5, "a ministry of reconciliation," the glorious characteristics of which are these, "God in Christ" . . . "reconciling the world unto Himself" . . . "not imputing their trespasses"; and the marvelous foundation of which is, that God has made Jesus who knew no sin to be sin for us, that we might become the righteousness of God in Him.

Does this trench, in the smallest degree, upon the blessed and clearly established truth of election? By no means. It leaves it, in all its integrity and in its full value, as a grand fundamental truth of Holy Scripture, exactly where God has placed it; not as a preliminary question to be settled ere the sinner comes to Jesus, but as a most precious consolation and encouragement to him when he has come. This makes all the difference.

If the sinner be called upon to settle beforehand the question of his election, how is he to set about it? Whither is he to turn for a solution? Where shall he find a divine warrant for believing that he is one of the elect? Can he find a single line of Scripture on which to base his faith as to his election? He cannot. He can find scores of passages declaring him to be lost, guilty and undone—scores of passages to assure him of his total inability to do aught in the matter of his own salvation—hundreds of passages unfolding the free love of God, the value and efficacy of the atonement of Christ, and assuring him of a hearty welcome to come *just as he is*, and make God's blessed salvation his own. But if it be needed for him to settle the prior question of his predestination and election, then is his case hopeless, and he must, in so far as he is in earnest, be plunged in black despair.

And is it not thus with thousands at this moment through the misapplication of the doctrine of election? We fully believe it is, and hence our anxiety to help our readers by setting the matter in what we judge to be the true light before their minds. We believe it to be of the utmost importance for the anxious inquirer to know that the standpoint from which he is called to view the cross of Christ is not the standpoint of election, but of conscious ruin. The grace of God meets him as a lost, dead, guilty sinner; not as an elect one. This is an unspeakable mercy, inasmuch as he knows he is the former, but cannot know that he is the latter until the gospel has come to him in power. "Knowing, brethren beloved, your election of God." How did he know it? "Because our gospel came not unto you in word only, but also in power, and in the Holy Ghost, and in much assurance" (1 Thess. 1:4-5). Paul preached to the Thessalonians as lost sinners; and when the gospel had laid hold of them as lost, he could write to them as elect.

This puts election in its right place. If the reader will turn for a moment to Acts 17, he will there see how Paul discharged his business as an evangelist amongst the Thessalonians: "Now when they had passed through Amphipolis and Apollonia, they came to Thessalonica, where was a synagogue of the Jews. And Paul, as his manner was, went in unto them, and three sabbath days reasoned with them out of the Scriptures, opening and alleging that Christ must needs have suffered, and risen again from the dead; and that this Jesus whom I preach unto you is Christ." So, also, in that passage at the opening of 1 Cor. 15: "Moreover, brethren, I declare unto you the gospel which I preached unto you, which also ye have received, and wherein ye stand; by which also ye are saved, if ye keep in memory what I preached unto you, unless ye have believed in vain. For I delivered unto you first of all that which I also received, how that Christ died for our sins according to the Scriptures; and that He was buried, and that He rose again the third day, according to the Scriptures" (ver. 1-4).

From this passage, and many others which might be quoted, we learn that the apostle preached not merely a doctrine, but a person. He did not preach election. He taught it to saints, but never preached it to sinners. This should be the evangelists's model at all times. We never once find the apostles preaching election. They preached Christ—they unfolded the goodness of God—His loving-kindness—His tender mercy—His pardoning love—His gracious readiness to receive all who come in their true character and condition as lost sinners. Such was their mode of preaching, or, rather, such was the mode of the Holy Ghost in them; and such, too, was the mode of the blessed Master Himself. "*Come unto Me*, all ye that labor and are heavy laden, and *I will give* you rest." "If *any man* thirst, let him come unto Me and drink." "Him that cometh to Me I will *in no wise* cast out" (Matt. 11; John 6—7).

Here are no stumbling-blocks in the way of anxious inquirers—no preliminary questions to be settled—no conditions to be fulfilled—no theological difficulties to be solved. No, the sinner is met on his own ground—met as he is—met just now. There is rest for the weary, drink for the thirsty, life for the dead, pardon for the guilty, salvation for the lost. Do these free invitations touch the doctrine of election? Assuredly not. And what is more, the doctrine of election does not touch them.

In other words, a full and free gospel leaves perfectly untouched the grand and all-important truth of election; and the truth of election, in its proper place, leaves the gospel of the grace of God on its own broad and blessed base, and in all its divine length, breadth, and fulness. The gospel meets us as lost, and saves us; and then, when we know ourselves as saved, the precious doctrine of election comes in to establish us in the fact that we can never be lost.

It never was the purpose of God that poor anxious souls should be harassed with theological questions or points of doctrine. No; blessed forever be His name, it is His gracious desire that the healing balm of His pardoning love, and the cleansing efficacy of the atoning blood of Jesus, should be applied to the spiritual wounds of every sin-sick soul.

And as to the doctrines of predestination and election, He has unfolded them in His Word to comfort His saints, not to perplex poor sinners. They shine like precious gems on the page of inspiration, but they were never intended to lie as stumbling-blocks in the way of earnest seekers after life and peace. They are deposited in the hand of the teacher to be unfolded in the bosom of the family of God; but they are not intended for the evangelist, whose blessed mission is to the highways and hedges of a lost world. They are designed to feed and comfort the children, not to scare and stumble the sinner.

We would say, and that with real earnestness, to all evangelists, Do not hamper your preaching with theological questions of any sort or description. Preach Christ. Unfold the deep and everlasting love of a Saviour-God. Seek to bring the guilty, conscience-smitten sinner into the very presence of a pardoning God. Thunder, if you please, if so led, at the conscience—thunder loud at sin—thunder forth the dread realities of the great white throne, the lake of fire, and everlasting torment; but see that you aim at bringing the guilt-stricken conscience to rest in the atoning virtues of the blood of Christ.

Then you can hand over the fruits of your ministry to the divinely qualified, to be instructed in the deeper mysteries of the faith of Christ. You may rest assured that the faithful discharge of your duty as an evangelist will never lead you to trespass on the domain of sound theology.

And to the anxious inquirer we would say with equal earnestness, Let nothing stand in your way in coming this moment to Jesus. Let theology speak as it may, you are to listen to the voice of Jesus, who says, "*Come unto Me.*" Be assured there is no hindrance, no difficulty, no hitch, no question, no condition. You are a lost sinner, and Jesus is a full Saviour. Put your trust in Him, and you are saved forever. Believe in Him, and you will know your place amongst the "elect of God" who are "predestinated to be conformed to the image of His Son." Bring your sins to Jesus and He will pardon them, cancel them by His blood, and clothe you in a spotless robe of divine righteousness. May God's Spirit lead you now to cast yourself simply and entirely upon that precious, all-sufficient Saviour!

We will now notice, very briefly, three distinct evils resulting from a wrong application of the doctrine of election, namely:

1. The discouragement of really earnest souls, who ought to be helped on in every possible way. If such persons are repulsed by the question of election, the result must be disastrous in the extreme. If they are told that the glad tidings of salvation are only for the elect—that Christ died only for such, and hence only such can be saved—that unless they are elect they have no right to apply to themselves the benefits of the death of Christ: if, in short, they are turned from Jesus to theology—from the heart of a

loving, pardoning God to the cold and withering dogmas of systematic divinity, it is impossible to say where they may end; they may take refuge either in superstition on the one hand, or in infidelity on the other. They may end in high church, broad church, or no church at all. What they really want is Christ, the living, loving, precious, all-sufficient Christ of God. He is the true food for anxious souls.

2. But, in the second place, careless souls are rendered more careless still by a false application of the doctrine of election. Such persons, when pressed as to their state and prospects, will fold their arms and say, "You know I cannot believe unless God give me the power. If I am one of the elect, I must be saved; if not, I cannot. I can do nothing, but must wait God's time." All this false and flimsy reasoning should be exposed and demolished. It will not stand for a moment in the light of the judgment-seat of Christ. Each one will learn there that election furnished no excuse whatever, inasmuch as it never was set up by God as a barrier to the sinner's salvation. The word is "*Whosoever* will, let him take the water of life *freely*." The very same form of speech and style of language which removes the stumbling-block from the feet of the anxious inquirer snatches the plea from the lips of the careless rejecter. No one is shut out. All are invited. There is neither barrier on the one hand, nor a plea on the other. All are made welcome; and all are responsible. Hence, if any one presumes to excuse himself for refusing God's salvation, which is as clear as a sunbeam, by urging God's decrees, which are entirely hidden, he will find himself fatally mistaken.

3. And now, in the third and last place, we have frequently seen with real sorrow of heart the earnest, loving, large-hearted evangelist damped and crippled by a false application of the truth of election. This should be most carefully avoided. We hold that it is not the business of the evangelist to preach election. If he is rightly instructed, he will *hold* it; but if he is rightly directed, he will not *preach* it.

In a word, then, the precious doctrine of election is not to be a stumbling-block to the anxious—a plea for the careless—a damper to the fervent evangelist. May God's Spirit give us to feel the adjusting power of truth!

Having thus briefly endeavored to clear away any difficulty arising from the misuse of the precious doctrine of election, and to show the reader, "whosoever" he be, that there is no hindrance whatever to his full and hearty acceptance of God's free gift, even the gift of His only-begotten Son, it now only remains for us to consider the result, in every case, of this acceptance, as set forth in the words of our Lord Jesus Christ: "God so loved the world, that He gave His only-begotten Son, that whosoever believeth in Him should not perish, but have everlasting life."

Here, then, we have the result in the case of every one who believes in Jesus. He shall never perish, but possesses everlasting life. But who can attempt to unfold all that is included in this word "perish"? What mortal tongue can set forth the horrors of the lake that burneth with fire and brimstone, "where their worm dieth not, and the fire is not quenched"? We believe, assuredly, that none but the One who used the Word, in speaking to Nicodemus, can fully expound it to anyone; but we feel called upon to bear our decided and unequivocal testimony as to what He has taught on the solemn truth of eternal punishment. We have occasionally referred to this subject, but we believe it demands a formal notice; and inasmuch as the word "*perish*" occurs in the passage which has been occupying our thoughts, we cannot do better than call the reader's attention to it.

It is a serious and melancholy fact that the enemy of souls and of the truth of God is leading thousands, both in Europe and America, to call in question the momentous fact of the everlasting punishment of the wicked. This he does on various grounds, and by various arguments, adapted to the habits of thought and moral condition and intellectual standpoint of individuals. Some he seeks to persuade that God is too kind to send anyone to a place of torment. It is contrary to His benevolent mind and His beneficent nature to inflict pain on any of His creatures.

Now, to all who stand, or affect to stand,

upon this ground of argument, we would suggest the important inquiry, "What is to be done with the sins of those who die impenitent and unbelieving?"

Whatever there may be in the idea that God is too kind to send sinners to hell, it is certain that He is too holy to let sin into Heaven. He is "of purer eyes than to behold evil, and cannot look on iniquity" (Hab. 1:13). God and evil cannot dwell together. This is plain. How, then, is the case to be met? If God cannot let sin into Heaven, what is to be done with the sinner who dies in his sins? He must perish! But what does this mean? Does it mean annihilation—that is, the utter extinction or blotting out of the very existence of body and soul? Nay, this cannot be. Many would like this, no doubt.

"Let us eat and drink, for to-morrow we die," would, alas, suit many thousands of the sons and daughters of pleasure who think only of the present moment, and who roll sin as a sweet morsel under their tongue. There are millions on the surface of the globe who are bartering their eternal happiness for a few hours of guilty pleasure, and the crafty foe of mankind seeks to persuade such that there is no such place as hell, no such thing as the lake that burneth with fire and brimstone; and in order to obtain a footing for this fatal suggestion, he bases it upon the plausible and imposing notion of the kindness of God.

Do not believe the arch-deceiver. Remember, God is holy. He cannot let sin into His presence. If you die in your sins you must perish, and this word "perish" involves, according to the clear testimony of Holy Scripture, eternal misery and torment in hell. Hear what our Lord Jesus Christ saith, in His solemn description of the judgment of the nations: "Then shall the King say also to them on His left hand, Depart from Me, ye cursed, into *everlasting* fire, prepared for the devil and his angels" (Matt. 25:41). And while you harken to these awfully solemn accents, remember that the word translated "everlasting" occurs seventy times in the New Testament, and is applied as follows: "Everlasting fire"—"eternal life"—"everlasting punishment"—"eternal damnation"—"everlasting habitations"—"the everlasting God"—"eternal weight of glory"—"everlasting destruction"—"everlasting consolation"—"eternal glory"—"eternal salvation"—"eternal judgment"—"eternal redemption"—"the eternal Spirit"—"eternal inheritance"—"everlasting kingdom"—"eternal fire."

Now, we ask any candid, thoughtful person, upon what principle can a word be said to mean *eternal* when applied to the Holy Ghost or to God, and only *temporary* when applied to hell-fire or the punishment of the wicked? If it means eternal in the one case, why not also in the other? We have just glanced at a Greek concordance, and we should like to ask, Would it be right to mark off some half-dozen passages in which the word "everlasting" occurs, and write opposite to each these words: "Everlasting here only means for a time"? The very thought is monstrous. It would be a daring and blasphemous insult offered to the volume of inspiration. No, be assured of it, you cannot touch the word "everlasting" in one case without touching it also in all the seventy cases in which it occurs.

It is a dangerous thing to tamper with the Word of the living God. It is infinitely better to bow down under its holy authority. It is worse than useless to seek to avoid the plain meaning and solemn force of that word "perish" as applied to the immortal soul of man. It involves, beyond all question, the awful, the ineffably awful reality of burning forever in the flames of hell. This is what Scripture means by "perishing."

The votary of pleasure, or the lover of money, may seek to forget this. They may seek to drown all thought of it in the glass or in the busy mart. The sentimentalist may rave about the divine benevolence; the skeptic may reason about the possibility of eternal fire; but we are intensely anxious that the reader should rise from this paper with the firm and deeply wrought conclusion and hearty belief that the punishment of all who die in their sins will be eternal in hell as surely as the blessedness of all who die in the faith of Christ will be eternal in the heavens. Were it not so, the Holy Ghost would most assuredly have used a different word, when speaking of the former, from that which He applies to the latter. This, we conceive, is beyond all question.

But there is another objection urged against the doctrine of eternal punishment. It is frequently said, "How can we suppose that God would inflict eternal punishment as a penalty for a few short years of sin?" We reply, It is beginning at the wrong end to argue in this way. It is not a question of time as viewed from man's standpoint, but of the gravity of sin itself as looked at from God's standpoint. And how is this question to be solved? Only by looking at the Cross.

If you want to know what sin is in God's sight, you must look at what it cost Him to put it away. It is by the standard of Christ's infinite sacrifice, and by that alone, that you can rightly measure sin. Men may compare their few years with God's eternity; they may compare their short span of life with that boundless eternity that stretches beyond; they may seek to put a few years of sin into one scale, and an eternity of woe and torment into the other, and thus attempt to reach a just conclusion: but it will never do to argue thus. The question is, Did it require an infinite atonement to put away sin? If so, the punishment of sin must be eternal. If nothing short of an infinite sacrifice could deliver from the consequences of sin, those consequences must be eternal.

In a word, then, we must look at sin from God's point of view, and measure it by His standard, else we shall never have a just sense of what it is or what it deserves. It is the height of folly for men to attempt to lay down a rule as to the amount or duration of the punishment due to sin. God alone can settle this. And, after all, what was it that produced all the misery and wretchedness, the sickness and sorrow, the death and desolation, of well-nigh six thousand years? Just *one act* of disobedience—the eating of a forbidden fruit. Can man explain this? Can human reason explain how one act produced such an overwhelming amount of misery? It cannot. Well, then, if it cannot do this, how can it be trusted when it attempts to decide the question as to what is due to sin? Woe be to all those who commit themselves to its guidance on this most momentous point!

Ah, you must see that God alone can estimate sin and its just deserts, and He alone can tell us all about it. And has He not done so? Yes, verily, He has measured sin in the cross of His Son; and there, too, He has set forth in the most impressive manner what it deserves. What, think you, must that be that caused the bitter cry, "My God, My God, why hast Thou forsaken Me?" If God forsook His only-begotten Son when He was made sin, must He not also forsake all who are found in their sins? But how can they ever get rid of them? We believe the conclusion is unavoidable. We consider that the infinite nature of the atonement proves unanswerably the doctrine of eternal punishment.

That peerless and precious sacrifice is at once the foundation of our eternal life and of our deliverance from eternal death. It delivers from eternal wrath and introduces to eternal glory. It saves from the endless misery of hell and procures for us the endless bliss of Heaven. Thus, whatever side of the Cross we look at, or from whatever side we view it, we see eternity stamped upon it. If we view it from the gloomy depths of hell or from the sunny heights of Heaven, we see it to be the same infinite, eternal, divine reality. It is by the Cross we must measure both the blessedness of Heaven and the misery of hell. Those who put their trust in that blessed One who died on the cross obtain everlasting life and felicity. Those who reject Him must sink into endless perdition.

We do not by any means pretend to handle this question theologically, or to adduce all the arguments that might be advanced in defence of the doctrine of eternal punishment; but there is one further consideration which we must suggest to the reader as tending to lead him to a sound conclusion, and that is the immortality of the soul. "God breathed into man's nostrils the breath of life, and man became a living soul." The fall of man in nowise touched the question of the soul's immortality.

If, therefore, the soul is immortal, annihilation is impossible. The soul must live forever. Overwhelming thought! Forever! Forever! Forever! The whole moral being sinks under the awful magnitude of the thought. It surpasses all conception and baffles all mental calculation. Human arithmetic can only deal with the finite. It has no figures by which to represent a never-ending eternity. But the writer and the reader must live throughout eternity either in that bright and blessed world above or in that terrible place where hope can never come.

May God's Spirit impress our hearts more and more with the solemnity of eternity, and of immortal souls going down into hell. We are deplorably deficient in feeling as to these weighty realities. We are daily thrown in contact with people, we buy and sell and carry on intercourse in various ways with those who must live forever, and yet how rarely do we seek occasion to press upon them the awfulness of eternity and the appalling condition of all who die without a personal interest in the blood of Christ!

Let us ask God to make us more earnest, more solemn, more faithful, more zealous in pleading with souls, in warning others to flee from the wrath to come. We want to live more in the light of eternity, and then we shall be better able to deal with others.

It only remains for us now to ponder the last clause of the fruitful passage of Scripture which has been under consideration (John 3:16). It sets forth the positive result, in every case, of simple faith in the Son of God. It declares, in the simplest and clearest way, the fact that every one who believes in the Lord Jesus Christ is a possessor of everlasting life. It is not merely that his sins are blotted out; that is blessedly true. Nor is it merely that he is saved from the consequences of his guilt, which is equally true. But there is more. The believer in Jesus has a new life, and that life is in the Son of God. He is placed upon a new footing altogether. He is no longer looked at in the old Adam condition, but in a risen Christ.

This is an immense truth, and one of deepest possible moment. We earnestly pray the reader's calm and prayerful attention while we seek, in some feeble way, to present to him what we believe to be wrapped up in the last clause of John 3:16.

There is in the minds of many a very imperfect sense of what we get by faith in Christ. Some seem to view the atoning work of Christ merely as a remedial measure for the sins of our old nature—the payment of debts contracted in our old condition. That it is all this we need not say; blessed be God for the precious truth. But it is much more. It is not merely that the sins are atoned for, but the nature which committed them is condemned and set aside by the cross of Christ, and is to be "*reckoned*" dead by the believer. It is not merely that the debts contracted in the old condition are canceled, but the old condition itself is completely ignored by God, and is to be so accounted by the believer.

This great truth is doctrinally unfolded in 2 Cor. 5, where we read, "If any man be in Christ, he is a new creature: old things are passed away; behold, all things are become new" (ver. 17). The apostle does not say, "If any man be in Christ he is pardoned—his sins are forgiven—his debts paid." All this is divinely true; but the statement just quoted goes very much farther. It declares that a man in Christ is a new creation altogether. It is not the old nature pardoned, but completely set aside, with all its belongings, and a new creation introduced in which there is not a single shred of the old. "All things are become new; and all things are of God."

Now this gives immense relief to the heart. Indeed, we question if any soul can enter into the full liberty of the gospel of Christ until he lay hold, in some measure, of the truth of the "new creation." There may be a looking to Christ for pardon, a vague hope of getting to Heaven at the last, a measure of reliance on the goodness and mercy of God—there may be all this, and yet no just sense of the meaning of "everlasting life," no happy consciousness of being "a new creation"—no understanding of the grand fact that the old Adam nature is entirely set aside, the old condition in which we stood done away in God's sight.

But it is more than probable that some of our readers may be at a loss to know what is meant by such terms as "the old Adam nature"—"the old condition"—"the flesh"—"the old man," and such like. These expressions may fall strangely on the ears of those for whom we specially write; and we certainly wish to avoid shooting over the heads of our readers.

As God is our witness, there is one thing we earnestly desire, one object which we would ever keep before our minds, and that is the instruction and edification of our readers; and therefore we would rather run the risk of being tedious than make use of phrases which convey no clear or intelligible idea to the mind. Such terms as "the old man"—"the flesh," and the like, are used in Scripture in manifold places: for example, in Rom. 6 we read, "Our *old man* is crucified with Him [Christ], that *the body of sin* might be destroyed, that henceforth we should not serve sin" (ver. 6).

Now what does the apostle mean by the "old man"? We believe he means man as in that Adam nature which we inherited from our first parents. And what does he mean by "the body of sin"? We believe he means the whole system or condition in which we stood in our unregenerate, unrenewed, unconverted state. The old Adam, then, is declared to be crucified—the old condition of sin is said to be destroyed (annulled)—by the death of Christ. Hence the soul that believes on the Lord Jesus Christ is privileged to know that he—his sinful, guilty self—is looked upon by God as dead and set aside completely. He has no more existence as such before God. He is dead and buried.

Observe, it is not merely that our sins are forgiven, our debts paid, our guilt atoned for; but the man in the nature that committed the sins, contracted the debts, and incurred the guilt, is put forever out of God's sight. It is not God's way to forgive us our sins and yet leave us in the same relations in which we committed them. No; He has, in His marvelous grace and vast plan, condemned and abolished forever, for the believer, the old Adam relationship, with all its belongings, so that it is no longer recognized by Him. We are declared, by the voice of holy Scripture, to be "crucified"—"dead"—"buried"—"risen" with Christ. God tells us we are so, and we are to *"reckon"* ourselves to be so. It is a matter of faith, and not of feeling.

If I look at myself from *my* standpoint, or judge by my feelings, I shall never, can never understand this truth. And why? Because I feel myself to be just the same sinful creature as ever. I feel that there is sin in me; that in my flesh there dwelleth no good thing; that my old nature is in nowise changed or improved; that it has the same evil tendencies as ever, and, if not mortified and kept down by the gracious energy of the Holy Spirit, it will break out in its true character.

And it is just here, we doubt not, that so many sincere souls are perplexed and troubled. They are looking at themselves, and *reasoning* upon what they see and feel, instead of resting in the truth of God, and *reckoning* themselves to be what God tells them they are. They find it difficult, if not impossible, to reconcile what they feel in themselves with what they read in the Word of God—to make their inward self-consciousness harmonize with God's revelation.

But we must remember that faith takes God at His Word. It ever thinks with Him on all points. It believes what He says because He says it. Hence, if God tells me that my old man is crucified, that He no longer sees me as in the old Adam state, but in a risen Christ, I am to believe, like a little child, what He tells me, and walk in the faith of it from day to day. If I look in at myself for evidences of the truth of what God says, it is not faith at all. Abraham "considered not his own body, now dead, when he was about an hundred years old; neither yet the deadness of Sarah's womb; he staggered not at the promise of God through unbelief, but was strong in faith, giving glory to God" (Rom. 4:19-20).

This is the great principle which underlies the whole Christian system. "Abraham believed God," not something about God, but God Himself. This is faith. It is taking God's thoughts in place of our own. It is, in short, allowing God to think for us.

Now, when we apply this to the subject before us, it makes it most simple. He that believeth in the Son of God hath everlasting life. Mark, it is not he that believeth something about the Son of God. No, it is he that believeth in Himself. It is a question of simple faith in the person of Christ; and everyone that has this faith is the actual possessor of everlasting life. This is the direct and positive statement of our Lord in the Gospels. It is repeated over and over again.

Nor is this all. Not only does the believer thus possess eternal life, but by the further light which the Epistles throw upon this grand question he may see that his old self—that which he was in nature—that which the apostle designates "the old man"—is accounted by God dead and buried. This may be difficult to understand; but the reader must remember he must believe not because he understands, but because it is written in God's Word. It is not said, "Abraham understood God." No; but he "believed God." It is when the heart believes that light is poured in upon the understanding. If I wait till I understand in order to believe, I am leaning to my own understanding, instead of committing myself in childlike faith to God's Word.

Ponder this! You may say you cannot understand how your sinful self can be looked upon as dead and gone while you feel its workings, its heavings, its tossings, its tendencies, continually within you. We reply, or rather God's eternal Word declares, that if your heart believes in Jesus, then is all this true for you, namely, you *have* eternal life; you *are* justified from all things; you *are* a new creation; old things *are* passed away; *all* things *are* become new; and *all* things *are* of God. In a word, you are "*in Christ,*" and "*as* He is, so *are* you in this world*" (1 John 4:17).

And is not this a great deal more than the mere pardoning of your sins, the canceling of your debts, or the salvation of your soul from hell? Assuredly it is. And suppose we were to ask you on what authority you believe in the forgiveness of your sins. Is it because you feel, realize, or understand? Nay; but because it is written, "To Him give all the prophets witness, that through His name whosoever believeth in Him shall receive remission of sins" (Acts 10:43). "The blood of Jesus Christ, God's Son, cleanseth us from all sin" (1 John 1:7). Well, then, upon precisely the same authority you are to believe that your old man has been crucified, that you are not in the flesh, not in the old creation, not in the old Adam relation; but that, on the contrary, you are viewed by God as actually in a risen and glorified Christ—that He looks upon you as He looks upon Christ.

True it is—alas, how true!—the flesh is in you, and you are still here, as to the fact of your condition, in this old world, which is under judgment. But then, hear what your Lord saith, when speaking about you to His Father: "They are not of the world, even as I am not of the world." And again, "As Thou hast sent Me into the world, even so have I also sent them into the world."

Hence, therefore, if you will just bow to God's Word, if you will reason not about what you see in yourself, and feel in yourself, and think of yourself, but simply *believe* what God says, you will enter into the blessed peace and holy liberty flowing from the fact that you are not in the flesh, but in the Spirit; not in the old creation, but in the new; not under law, but under grace; not of the world, but of God. You have passed clean off the old platform which you occupied as a child of nature and a member of the first Adam, and you have taken your place on a new platform altogether as a child of God and a member of Christ.

All this is vividly prefigured by the deluge and the ark, in the days of Noah. (See Gen. 6—8.) "And God looked upon the earth, and behold, it was corrupt; for all flesh had corrupted his way upon the earth. And God said unto Noah, *The end of all flesh* is come before Me; for the earth is filled with violence through them; and behold, I will destroy them with the earth." Here, then, was, in type, the end of the old creation. All was to pass under the waters of judgment. What then? "Make thee an ark of gopher wood."

Here we have set forth a figure of the new thing. That ark, floating peacefully over the dark abyss of waters, was a type of Christ, and the believer in Him. The old world, together with man, was buried beneath the waves of judgment, and the only object that remained was the ark—the vessel of mercy and salvation, riding in safety and triumph over the billows.

Thus it is now, in truth and reality. There

is nothing before the eye of God but a risen, victorious and glorified Christ, and His people linked with Him. The end of *all* flesh has come before God. It is not a question of some very gross forms of "flesh," or of nature, of that merely which is "vile and refuse." No; it is "the *end* of *all*." Such is the solemn, sweeping verdict; and then—what? A risen Christ. Nothing else. All in Him are seen by God as He is seen. All out of Him are under judgment. It all hinges upon this one question. "Am I in or out of Christ?" What a question!

Are *you* in Christ? Do you believe in His name? Have you given Him the confidence of your heart? If so, you have "eternal life"— you are "a new creature"—"old things are passed away." God does not see a single shred of the old thing remaining for you. "All things are become new, and all things are of God." You may say you do not *feel* that old things are all passed away. We reply, God says they are, and it is your happy privilege to *believe* what He says, and "*reckon*" yourself to be what He declares you are.

God speaks according to that which is true of you in Christ. He does not see you in the flesh, but in Christ. There is absolutely nothing before the eye of God but Christ: and the very weakest believer is viewed as part of Christ, just as your hand is a part of your body. You have no existence before God apart from Christ—no life—no righteousness —no holiness—no wisdom—no power. Apart from Him, you have nothing, and can be nothing. In Him you have all and are all, He says; you are thoroughly identified with Christ. Marvelous fact! Profound mystery! Most glorious truth! It is not a question of attainment or of progress. It is the settled and absolute standing of the feeblest member of the Church of God.

True, there are various measures of intelligence, experience, and devotedness; but there is only one life, one standing, one position before God, and that is Christ. There is no such thing as a higher or lower Christian life. Christ is the believer's life, and you cannot speak of a higher or a lower Christ. We can understand the higher stages of Christian life; but there is no spiritual intel-

ligence in speaking of a higher Christian life.

This is a grand truth, and we earnestly pray that God the Spirit may open it fully to the mind of the reader. We feel assured that a clearer understanding thereof would chase away a thousand mists, answer a thousand questions, and solve a thousand difficulties. It would not only have the effect of giving settled peace to the soul, but also of determining the believer's position in the most distinct way. If Christ is my life—if I am in Him and identified with Him, then not only do I share in His acceptance with God, but also in His rejection by this present world. The two things go together. They form the two sides of the one grand question. If I am in Christ and as Christ before God, then I am in Christ and as Christ before the world: and it will never do to accept the result of this union before God and refuse the result of it as regards the world. If we have the one, we must have the other likewise.

All this is fully unfolded in John 17. There we read on the one hand, "The glory which Thou gavest Me I have given them; that they may be one, even as We are one: I in them, and Thou in Me, that they may be made perfect in one; and that the world may know that Thou hast sent Me, and *hast loved them as Thou hast loved Me*" (ver. 22-23).

And, on the other hand, we read, "I have given them Thy Word; and *the world hath hated them*, because they are not of this world, even as I am not of the world" (ver. 14). This is as plain and positive as anything can be. And be it remembered that, in this wondrous Scripture, our Lord is not speaking merely of the apostles, but, as He says, of "them also who shall believe on Me through their word," that is, of all believers. Hence it follows that all who believe in Jesus are one with Him as accepted above, and one with Him as rejected below. The two things are inseparable. The Head and the members share in one common acceptance in Heaven, and in one common rejection upon earth.

Oh that all the Lord's people entered more into the truth and reality of this! Would that we all knew a little more of the meaning of fellowship with a Heaven-accepted, earth-rejected Christ!

CHRISTIANITY
WHAT IS IT?

Philippians 3

WE HAVE ENDEAVORED to hold up the Bible as the Church's supreme and all-sufficient guide, in all ages, in all climes, and under all circumstances. We now desire to hold up Christianity in its divine beauty and moral excellence, as illustrated in this well-known passage of Holy Scripture.

And be it observed that, as it was the Bible itself, and not any special system of theology deduced therefrom, that we sought to present to our readers; so now, it is Christianity, and not any peculiar form of human religiousness, that we desire to place before them. We are deeply thankful for this. We dare not enter upon the defence of men or their systems. Men err in their theology and fail in their ethics; but the Bible and Christianity remain unshaken and unshakeable. This is an unspeakable mercy. Who can duly estimate it? To be furnished with a perfect standard of divinity and morals is a privilege for which we can never be sufficiently thankful. Such a standard we possess, blessed be God! in the Bible and in the Christianity which the Bible unfolds to our view. Men may err in their creed and break down in their conduct, but the Bible is the Bible still, and Christianity is Christianity still.

Now, we believe that this third chapter of Philippians gives us the model of a true Christian—a model on which every Christian should be formed. The man who is here introduced to our notice could say, by the Holy Ghost, "Brethren, be ye followers together of me." Nor is it as an apostle that he here speaks to us—nor as one endowed with extraordinary gifts, and privileged to see unspeakable visions. It is not to Paul, the apostle, nor Paul, the gifted vessel, that we

listen, in verse 17 of our chapter, but to Paul, the Christian. We could not follow him in his brilliant career, as an apostle. We could not follow him, in his rapture to Paradise; but we can follow him in his Christian course, in this world; and it seems to us that we have in our chapter a very full view of that course, and not only of the course itself, but also the starting-post and the goal. In other words, we have to consider, first, the Christian's *standing;* secondly, the Christian's *object;* and thirdly, the Christian's *hope.* May God the Holy Ghost be our teacher, while we dwell for a little on these most weighty and most interesting points! And first, as to *the Christian's Standing.*

The point is unfolded, in a double way, in our chapter. We are not only told what the Christian's standing is, but also what it is not. If ever there was a man who could boast of having a righteousness of his own in which to stand before God, Paul was the man. "If," says he, "any other man thinketh that he hath whereof to trust in the flesh, I more: circumcised the eighth day, of the stock of Israel, of the tribe of Benjamin, an Hebrew of the Hebrews; as touching the law, a Pharisee; concerning zeal, persecuting the church; touching the righteousness which is in the law, blameless."

This is a most remarkable catalog, presenting everything that one could possibly desire for the formation of a standing in the flesh. No one could excel Saul of Tarsus. He was a Jew, of pure pedigree, in orderly fellowship, of blameless walk, of fervid zeal and unflinching devotedness. He was, on principle, a persecutor of the Church. As a Jew, he could not but see that the very foundations of Judaism were assailed by the new economy of the Church of God. It was utterly impossible that Judaism and Christianity could subsist on the same platform, or hold sway over the same mind. One special feature of the former system was the strict separation of Jew and Gentile; a special feature of the latter was the intimate union of both in one body. Judaism erected and maintained the middle wall of partition; Christianity abolished that wall altogether.

Hence Saul, as an earnest Jew, could not but be a zealous persecutor of the Church of God. It was part of his religion—of that in which he "excelled many of his equals in his own nation"—of that in which he was "exceedingly zealous." Whatever was to be had, in the shape of religiousness, Saul would have it; whatever height was to be attained, he would attain. He would leave no stone unturned in order to build up the superstructure of his own righteousness— righteousness in the flesh—righteousness in the old creation. He was permitted to possess himself of all the attractions of legal righteousness in order that he might fling them from him amid the brighter glories of a righteousness divine. "But what things were gain to me, those I counted loss for Christ. Yea, doubtless, and I count all things but loss, for the excellency of the knowledge of Christ Jesus my Lord; for whom I have suffered the loss of all things, and do count them but dung, that I may win Christ, and be found in Him, not having mine own righteousness which is of the law, but that which is through the faith of Christ, the righteousness which is of God by faith."

And we should note here that the grand prominent thought, in the above passage, is not that of a guilty sinner betaking himself to the blood of Jesus for pardon, but rather of a legalist casting aside, as dross, his own righteousness, because of having found a better. We need hardly say that Paul was a sinner—"chief of sinners"—and that, as such, he betook himself to the precious blood of Christ, and there found pardon, peace, and acceptance with God. This is plainly taught us in many passages of the New Testament. But it is not the leading thought in the chapter now before us. Paul is not speaking

of his *sins*, but of his *gains*. He is not occupied with his necessities, as a sinner, but with his advantages, as a man—a man in the flesh—a man in the old creation—a Jew—a legalist.

True it is, most blessedly true, that Paul brought all his sins to the cross, and had them washed away in the atoning blood of the divine Sin-offering. But, in this passage, we see another thing. We see a legalist flinging far away from him his own righteousness, and esteeming it as a worthless and unsightly thing in contrast with a risen and glorified Christ, who is the righteousness of the Christian—the righteousness which belongs to the new creation. Paul had sins to mourn over, and he had a righteousness to boast in. He had guilt on his conscience, and he had laurels on his brow. He had plenty to be ashamed of, and plenty to glory in. But the special point presented in Phil. 3: 4-8 is not a sinner getting his sins pardoned, his guilt cleared, his shame covered, but a legalist laying aside his righteousness, a scholar casting away his laurels, and a man abandoning his vain glory, simply because he had found true glory, unfading laurels, and an everlasting righteousness in the Person of a victorious and exalted Christ. It was not merely that Paul, the sinner, *needed* a righteousness because, in reality, he had none of his own; but that Paul, the Pharisee, *preferred* the righteousness which was revealed to him in Christ, because it was infinitely better and more glorious than any other.

No doubt Paul as a sinner needed, like every other sinner, a righteousness in which to stand before God; but that is not what he is bringing before us in our chapter. We are anxious that the reader should clearly apprehend this point. It is not merely that my sins *drive* me to Christ; but His excellences *draw* me to Him. True, I have sins and therefore I need Christ; but even if I had a righteousness, I should cast it from me, and gladly hide myself "*in Him.*" It would be a positive "loss" to me to have any righteousness of my own, seeing that God has graciously provided such a glorious righteousness for me in Christ. Like Adam, in the garden of Eden, he was naked, and therefore he made himself an apron; but it would have been a "loss" to him to retain the apron after that the Lord God had made him a coat. It was surely far better to have a God-made coat than a man-made apron. So thought Adam, so thought Paul, and so thought all the saints of God whose names are recorded upon the sacred page. It is better to stand in the righteousness of God, which is by faith, than to stand in the righteousness of man, which is by works of law. It is not only mercy to get rid of our sins, through the remedy which God has provided, but to get rid of our righteousness, and accept, instead, the righteousness which God has revealed.

Thus, then, we see that the standing of a Christian is *in Christ*. "Found in Him." This is Christian standing. Nothing less, nothing lower, nothing different. It is not partly in Christ, and partly in law—partly in Christ and partly in ordinances. No; it is "found in Him." This is the standing which Christianity furnishes. If this be touched, it is not Christianity at all. It may be some ancient *ism*, or some mediaeval *ism*, or some modern *ism;* but most surely it is not the Christianity of the New Testament if it be aught else than this, "found in Him."

We do therefore earnestly exhort the reader to look well to this our first point, "In Christ it is we stand." He is our righteousness. He Himself, the crucified, risen, exalted, glorified Christ. Yes; He is our righteousness. To be found in Him is proper Christian standing. It is not Judaism, Catholicism, nor any other *ism*. It is not the being a member of this church, that church, or the other church. It is to be in Christ. This is the great foundation of true practical Christianity. In a word this is the standing of the Christian.

Let us now in the second place, look at *the Christian's Object.*

Here again, Christianity shuts us up to Christ: "That I may *know Him*," is the breathing of the true Christian. If to be "found in Him" constitutes the Christian's standing, then "to know Him" is the Christian's proper object. The ancient philosophy had a motto which it was constantly sounding in the ears of its votaries,

and that motto was, "Know thyself." Christianity, on the contrary, has a loftier motto, pointing to a nobler object. It tells us to know Christ—to make Him our object—to fix our earnest gaze on Him.

This, and this alone, is the Christian's object. To have any other object is not Christianity at all. Alas! Christians have other objects. And that is precisely the reason why we said, at the opening of this paper, that it is Christianity, and not the ways of Christians, that we desire to hold up to the view of our readers. It matters not in the least what the object is; if it is not Christ, it is not Christianity. The true Christian's desire will ever be embodied in these words, "That I may know Him, and the power of His resurrection, and the fellowship of His sufferings, being made conformable unto His death." It is not that I may get on in the world—that I may make money—that I may attain a high position—that I may aggrandize my family—that I may make a name—that I may be regarded as a great man, a rich man, a popular man. No; not one of these is a Christian object. It may be all very well for a man, who has got nothing better, to make such things his object. But the Christian has got Christ. This makes all the difference. It may be all well enough for a man, who does not know Christ as his righteousness, to do the best he can in the way of working out a righteousness for himself; but to one whose standing is in a risen Christ, the very fairest righteousness that could be produced by human efforts would be an actual loss. So is it exactly in the matter of an object. The question is not, What harm is there in this or that? but, is it a Christian object?

It is well to see this. We may depend upon it that one great reason of the low tone which prevails amongst Christians will be found in the fact that the eye is taken off Christ and fixed upon some lower object. It may be a very laudable object for a mere man of the world—for one who merely sees his place in nature, or in the old creation. But the Christian is not this. He does not belong to this world at all. He is in it, but not of it. "They," says our blessed Lord, "are not of the world, even as I am not of the world"

(John 17). "Our citizenship is in heaven;" and we should never be satisfied to propose to ourselves any lower object than Christ. It matters not in the least what a man's position may be. He may be only a scavenger, or he may be a prince, or he may stand at any one of the many gradations between these two extremes. It is all the same, provided Christ is his real, his only object. It is a man's object, not his position, that gives him his character.

Now Paul's one object was Christ. Whether he was stationary, or whether he traveled; whether he preached the gospel, or whether he gathered sticks; whether he planted churches, or made tents, Christ was his object. By night and by day, at home or abroad, by sea or by land, alone or in company, in public or private, he could say, "One thing I do." And this, be it remembered, was not merely Paul the laborious apostle, or Paul the raptured saint, but Paul the living, acting, walking Christian—the one who addresses us in these words, "Brethren, be ye followers together of me." Nor should we ever be satisfied with anything less than this. True, we fail sadly; but let us always keep the true object before us. Like the school-boy at his copy, he can only expect to succeed by keeping his eye fixed upon his head-line. His tendency is to look at his own last written line, and thus each succeeding line is worse than the preceding one. Thus it is in our own case. We take our eye off the blessed and perfect head-line, and begin to look at ourselves, our own productions, our own character, our interests, our reputation. We begin to think of what would be consistent with our own principles, our profession, or our standing, instead of fixing the eye steadily upon that one object which Christianity presents, even Christ Himself.

But some will say, "Where will you find this?" Well, if it be meant, where are we to find it amongst the ranks of Christians, now-a-days, it might be difficult indeed. But we have it in the third chapter of the Epistle to the Philippians. This is enough for us. We have here a model of true Christianity, and let us ever and only aim thereat. If we find our hearts going after other things let us judge them. Let us compare our lines with the head-line, and earnestly seek to produce a faithful copy thereof. In this way, although we may have to weep over constant failure, we shall always be kept occupied with our proper object, and thus have our character formed; for, let it never be forgotten, it is the object which forms the character. If money be my object, my character is covetous; if power, I am ambitious; if books, I am literary; if Christ, I am a Christian. It is not here a question of life and salvation, but only of practical Christianity. If we were asked for a simple definition of a Christian, we should at once say, a Christian is a man who has Christ for his object. This is most simple. May we enter into its power, and thus exhibit a more healthy and vigorous discipleship in this day, when so many, alas! are minding earthly things.

We shall close this hasty and imperfect sketch of a wide and weighty subject, with a line or two on *the Christian's Hope*.

This, our third and last point, is presented in our chapter in a manner quite as characteristic as the other two. The *standing* of the Christian is to be found in Christ; the *object* of the Christian is to know Christ; and the *hope* of the Christian is to be like Christ. How beautifully perfect is the connection between these three things. No sooner do I find myself in Christ as my righteousness, than I long to know Him as my object, and the more I know Him, the more ardently shall I long to be like Him, which hope can only be realized when I see Him as He is. Having a perfect righteousness, and a perfect object, I just want one thing more, and that is to be done with everything that hinders my enjoyment of that object. "For our conversation [or citizenship, $\pi o \lambda \iota \tau \nu \mu \alpha$ not $\alpha \nu \alpha \sigma \tau \rho o \varphi \eta$,Phil. 3:20], is in heaven; from whence also we look for the Saviour, the Lord Jesus Christ, who shall change our vile body, that it may be fashioned like unto His glorious body, according to the working whereby He is able even to subdue all things unto Himself."

Now putting all these things together, we get a very complete view of true

Christianity. We cannot attempt to elaborate any one of the three points above referred to; for, it may be truly said, each point would demand a volume to treat it fully. But we would ask the reader to pursue the marvelous theme for himself. Let him rise above all the imperfections and inconsistencies of Christians, and gaze upon the moral grandeur of Christianity as exemplified in the life and character of the model man presented to our view in this chapter. And may the language of his heart be, "Let others do as they will, as for me, nothing short of this lovely model shall ever satisfy my heart. Let me turn away my eye from men altogether, and fix it intently upon Christ Himself, and find all my delight in Him as my righteousness, my object, my hope." Thus may it be with the writer and the reader, for Jesus' sake.

FORGIVENESS OF SINS WHAT IS IT?

OH, THE BLESSEDNESS! transgression forgiven—sin covered! This truly is blessedness; and without this, blessedness must be unknown. To have the full assurance that my sins are all forgiven is the only foundation of true happiness. To be happy without this is to be happy on the brink of a yawning gulf, into which I may at any moment be dashed forever. It is utterly impossible that any one can enjoy solid happiness until he is possessed of the divine assurance that all his guilt has been canceled by the blood of the cross. Uncertainty as to this must be the fruitful source of mental anguish to any soul who has ever been led to feel the burden of sin. To be in doubt as to whether my guilt was all borne by Jesus, or is yet on my conscience, is to be miserable.

Now, before proceeding to unfold the subject of forgiveness, I should like to ask my reader a very plain, pointed, personal question, namely, Dost thou believe that thou canst have the clear and settled assurance that thy sins are forgiven? I ask this question at the outset, because there are many, now-a-days, who profess to preach the gospel of Christ, and yet deny that any one can be sure that his sins are forgiven. They maintain that it is presumption for any one to believe in the forgiveness of his sins; and, on the other hand, they look upon it as a proof of humility to be always in doubt as to this most momentous point. In other words, it is presumption to believe what God says, and humility to doubt it. This seems strange in the face of such passages as the following: "Thus it is written, and thus it behooved Christ to suffer, and to rise from the dead the third day; and that repentance and remission of sins should be preached in His name among all nations, beginning at Jerusalem" (Luke 24:46-47); "In whom *we have* redemption through His blood, *the forgiveness of sins*, according to the riches of His grace" (Eph. 1: 7; Col. 1: 14).

Here we have remission, or forgiveness, of sins (the word is the same in the three passages) preached in the name of Jesus, and possessed by those who believed that preaching. A proclamation was sent to the Ephesians and Colossians, as belonging to the "all nations," telling them of forgiveness of sins, in the name of Jesus. They believed this proclamation, and entered on the possession of the forgiveness of sins. Was this presumption on their part? or would it have been piety and humility to doubt the forgiveness of sins? True, they had been great sinners—"dead in trespasses and sins," "children of wrath," "aliens and foreigners," "enemies by wicked works." Some of them had doubtless bowed the knee to Diana. They had lived in gross idolatry and all manner of wickedness. But then, "forgiveness of sins" had been preached to them in the name of Jesus. Was this preaching true, or was it not?

Was it for them, or was it not? Was it all a dream—a shadow—a myth? Did it mean nothing? Was there nothing sure, nothing certain, nothing solid about it?

These are plain questions, demanding a plain answer from those who assert that no one can know for certain that his sins are forgiven. If, indeed, no one can know it now, then how could any one have known it in apostolic times? If it could be known in the first century, then why not in the nineteenth? "David describeth the blessedness of the man unto whom God imputeth righteousness without works, saying, Blessed are they whose iniquities are forgiven, and whose sins are covered. Blessed is the man to whom the Lord will not impute sin" (Rom. 4:6-8). Hezekiah could say, "Thou *hast cast all my sins* behind Thy back" (Isaiah 38:17). The Lord Jesus said to one, in His day, "Son, be of good cheer; thy sins be forgiven thee" (Matt. 9: 2).

Thus at all times forgiveness of sins was known with all the certainty which the Word of God could give. Any one of the cases adduced above is sufficient to overthrow the teaching of those who assert that *no one* can know that his sins are forgiven. If I find from Scripture that any one ever knew this marvelously precious blessing, that is quite enough for me. Now, when I open my Bible, I find persons who had been guilty of all manner of sins brought to the knowledge of forgiveness; and I therefore argue that it is possible for the very vilest sinner to know now, with divine certainty, that his sins are forgiven. Was it presumption in Abraham, in David, in Hezekiah, in the palsied man, and in numbers besides, to believe in the forgiveness of sins? Would it have been a sign of humility and true piety in them to doubt? It will perhaps be argued that these were all special and extraordinary cases. Well, it matters not, so far as our present question is concerned, whether they were ordinary or extraordinary. One thing is plain—they completely disprove the assertion that *no one* can know that his sins are forgiven. The Word of God teaches me that numbers, subject to like passions, like infirmities, like failures, and like sins as the writer and reader, were

brought to know and rejoice in the full forgiveness of sins; and hence those who maintain that no one can be sure on this momentous question have no scriptural foundation for their opinion.

But is it true that the cases recorded in the Holy Scriptures are so special and extraordinary as not to afford any precedent for us? By no means. If any case could be so regarded, it is surely that of Abraham, and yet of him we read that "it was not written for his sake alone, that righteousness was imputed to him: *but for us also,* to whom it shall be imputed, if we believe on Him that raised up Jesus our Lord from the dead; who was delivered for our offences, and was raised again for our justification" (Rom. 4:23-25). Abraham "believed in the Lord; and He counted it to him for righteousness" (Gen. 15:6). And the Holy Ghost declares that righteousness shall be imputed to us also if we believe—"Be it known unto you therefore, men and brethren, that through this man is preached unto you the forgiveness of sins; and by Him all that believe are justified from all things from which ye could not be justified by the law of Moses" (Acts 13:38-39); "To Him give *all the prophets* witness, that through His name *whosoever believeth* in Him shall receive remission of sins" (Acts 10:43).

Now, the question is, What did the apostles Peter and Paul mean when they so unreservedly preached the forgiveness of sins to those who listened to them? Did they really mean to convey to their hearers the idea that no one could be sure that he possessed this forgiveness of sins? When in the synagogue of Antioch, Paul said to his audience, "We declare unto you *glad tidings,*" did he entertain the notion that no one could be sure that his sins were forgiven? How could the gospel ever be called "glad tidings" if its only effect were to leave the soul in doubt and anxiety? If indeed it be true that no one can enjoy the assurance of pardon, then the whole style of apostolic preaching should be reversed. We might then expect to find Paul saying to his hearers, Be it known unto you therefore, men and brethren, that no one can ever know, in this life, whether his sins are forgiven or not. Is there aught like this in the entire range of apostolic preaching and teaching? Do not the apostles everywhere set forth, in the fullest and clearest manner, remission of sins as the necessary result of believing in a crucified and risen Saviour? Is there the most remote hint of that which is so much insisted upon by some modern teachers, namely, that it is a dangerous presumption to believe in the full forgiveness of all our sins, and that it argues a pious and humble frame of soul to live in perpetual doubt? Is there no possibility of ever enjoying, in this world, the comfortable certainty of our eternal security in Christ?

Can we not rely upon God's Word, or commit our souls to the sacrifice of Christ? Can it be possible that the only effect of God's glad tidings is to leave the soul in hopeless perplexity? Christ has put away sin; but I cannot know it! God has spoken; but I cannot be sure! The Holy Ghost has come down; but I cannot rely upon His testimony! It is piety and humility to doubt God's Word, to dishonor the atonement of Christ, and to refuse the faith of the heart to the record of the Holy Ghost! Alas! alas! if this is the gospel, then adieu to peace and joy in believing. If this is Christianity, then in vain has "the dayspring from on high visited us, to give the knowledge of salvation through the remission of our sins" (Luke 1). If no one can have this "knowledge of salvation," then to what end has it been given?

And bear in mind that the question before us is not whether a person may not deceive himself and others. This would be at once conceded. Thousands, alas! have deceived themselves, and thousands more have deceived others; but is that any reason why I cannot possess the absolute certainty that what God has said is true, and that the work of Christ has availed to put away all my sins?

Men have deceived themselves, and therefore I am afraid to trust Christ! Men have deceived others, and therefore I am afraid that God's Word will deceive me! This is really what it all amounts to, when put into plain language. And is it not well to have things thus put? Is it not needful, at times, to strip certain propositions of the dress in which legality and fleshly pietism would clothe them, so that we may see what they are? Does it not behove us, when men stand forth as the professed and authorized exponents of a sound and enlightened Christianity, to test what they say by the unerring standard of Holy Scripture? Assuredly it does. And if they tell us we can never be sure of salvation; and that it is presumption to think of such a thing; and, further, that the very utmost we can attain to in this life is a faint hope that, through the mercy of God, we may get to Heaven when we die; we must utterly reject such teaching, as being in direct opposition to the Word of God.

False theology tells me I can never be sure, God's Word tells me I can. Which am I to believe? The former fills me with gloomy doubts and fears; the latter imparts divine certainty. That casts me upon my own efforts; this, upon a finished work. To which shall I attend? Is there a shadow of foundation, throughout the entire volume of God, for the notion that no one can be sure of his eternal salvation? I most fearlessly assert there is not. So far from this, the Word of God, in every section of it, sets before us, in the clearest way, the privilege of the believer to enjoy the most unclouded certainty as to his pardon and acceptance in Christ.

And, let me ask, is it not due to God's faithful Word and Christ's finished work, that the soul confiding therein should enjoy the fullest assurance? True, it is by faith that any one can so confide, and this faith is wrought in the heart by the Holy Ghost. But all this in nowise affects our present question. What I desire is, that my reader should rise from the study of this paper with a full and firm conviction that it is possible for him to possess the present assurance that he is as safe as Christ can make him. If any sinner ever enjoyed this assurance, then why may not my reader now enjoy it? Is Christ's work finished? Is God's Word true? Yes, verily. Then, if I simply trust therein, I am pardoned, justified and accepted. All my sins were laid on Jesus when He was nailed to the cursed tree. Jehovah made them all meet on Him. He bore them and put them away, and now He is up in Heaven without them. This is enough for me. If the One who stood charged with *all* my guilt is now at the right hand of the Majesty in the heavens, then, clearly, there is nothing against me. All that divine justice had against me was laid on the Sin-bearer, and He endured the wrath of a sin-hating God that I might be freely and forever pardoned and accepted in a risen and glorified Saviour.

These are glad tidings. Does my reader believe them? Dost thou heartily believe in a dead and risen Christ? Hast thou come to Him as a lost sinner, and put thy heart's full confidence in Him? Dost thou believe that "He died for our sins according to the Scripture, and that He was buried and rose again the third day according to the Scriptures"? If so, thou art saved, justified, accepted, complete in Christ. True, thou art, in thyself, a poor feeble creature, having an evil nature to contend with every moment; but Christ is thy life, and He is thy wisdom, and thy righteousness, thy sanctification, thy redemption, thy all. He ever lives for thee up in Heaven. He died to make thee clean. He lives to keep thee clean. Thou art made as clean as His death can make thee, and thou art kept as clean as His life can keep thee. He made Himself responsible for thee. God sees thee to be what Christ has made thee to be. He sees thee in Christ and as Christ. Wherefore, then, I pray thee, tread no more those gloomy corridors of legalism, pietism, and false theology, which have resounded for ages with the sighs and groans of poor sin-burdened and misguided souls; but, seeing the fullness of thy portion, and the completeness of thy standing in a risen and victorious Christ, rejoice in Him all thy days upon earth, and live in the hope of being with Him forever in His own mansions of heavenly glory.

Having thus sought to establish the fact that it is possible for one to know, upon divine authority, that his sins are forgiven, we shall now, in dependence upon the teaching of the Spirit of God, proceed to consider the subject of forgiveness of sins, as unfolded in the Word, and, in doing so, we shall present it under the three following heads; namely,

First, the *ground* on which God forgives sins.

Secondly, the *extent* to which He forgives sins.

Thirdly, the *style* in which He forgives sins. There is value in this threefold presentation, as it gives clearness, fullness and precision to our apprehension of the subject as a whole. The more clearly we understand the ground of divine forgiveness, the more shall we appreciate the extent, and admire the style thereof.

May God the Spirit now be our guide while we ponder, for a little: *the Ground of Divine Forgiveness.*

It is of the very last importance that the anxious reader should understand this cardinal point. It is quite impossible that a divinely convicted conscience can enjoy true repose until the ground of forgiveness is clearly seen. There may be certain vague thoughts respecting the mercy and goodness of God, His readiness to receive sinners and pardon their sins, His unwillingness to enter the place of judgment, and His promptness to enter the place of mercy—all this there may be; but until the convicted soul is led to see how God can be just and yet the Justifier—how He can be a just God and yet a Saviour-God—how He has been glorified with respect to sin—how all the divine attributes have been harmonized, it must be a stranger to the peace of God which truly passeth all understanding. A conscience on which the light of divine truth has poured itself in convicting power, feels and owns that sin can never enter into the presence of God—that sin, wherever it is found, can only be met by the just judgment of a sin-hating God. Hence, until the divine method of dealing with sin is understood and believed, there must be intense anxiety. Sin is a reality, God's holiness is a reality, conscience is a reality, judgment to come is a reality. All these things must be looked at and duly considered. Justice must be satisfied; conscience, purged; Satan, silenced. How is all this to be done? Only by the cross of Jesus.

Here, then, we have the true ground of divine forgiveness. The precious atonement of Christ forms the base of that platform on which a just God and a justified sinner meet in sweet communion. In that atonement I see sin condemned, justice satisfied, the law magnified, the sinner saved, the adversary confounded. Creation never exhibited aught like this. There, the creature enjoyed the manifestation of power, wisdom, and goodness; but the fairest fields of the old creation presented nothing like "grace reigning through righteousness"—nothing like a glorious combination of "righteousness and peace, mercy and truth." It was reserved for Calvary to display all this. There, that grand and all-important question, How can God be just and the Justifier? received a glorious reply. The death of Christ furnishes the answer. A just God dealt with sin at the cross, in order that a justifying God might deal with the sinner on the new and everlasting ground of resurrection. God could not tolerate or pass over a single jot or tittle of sin; but He could put it away. He has condemned sin. He has poured out His righteous wrath upon sin, in order that He might pour the everlasting beams of His favor upon the believing sinner.

> On Jesus' cross this record's graved,
> Let sin be judged and sinners saved.

Precious record! may every anxious sinner read it with the eye of faith. It is a record which must impart settled peace to the heart. God has been satisfied as to sin. This is enough for me. Here my guilty, troubled conscience finds sweet repose. I have seen my sins rising like a dark mountain before me, threatening me with eternal wrath; but the blood of Jesus has blotted them all out from God's view. They are gone, and gone forever—sunk as lead into the mighty waters of divine forgetfulness, and I am free—as free as the One who was nailed to the cross for my sins, but who is now on the throne without them.

Such, then, is the ground of divine forgiveness. What a solid ground! Who or what can touch it? Justice *has* owned it. The troubled conscience *may* rest in it. Satan *must* acknowledge it. God has revealed Himself as a Justifier, and faith walks in the light and power of that revelation. Nothing

can be simpler, nothing clearer, nothing more satisfactory. If God reveals Himself as a Justifier, then I am justified through faith in the revelation. When the moral glories of the Cross shine upon the sinner, he sees and knows, believes and owns, that the One who has judged his sins in death, has justified him in resurrection.

Anxious reader, see, I beseech thee, that thou apprehendest the true ground of the forgiveness of sins. There is no use in our proceeding to consider the *extent* and *style* until thy poor troubled conscience has been led to rest upon the imperishable *ground* of forgiveness. Let me reason with thee. What is to hinder thee, from this very moment, resting on the foundation of accomplished atonement? Say, does thy conscience need something more to satisfy it than that which satisfied the inflexible justice of God? Is not the ground on which God reveals Himself as a righteous Justifier sufficiently strong for thee to stand upon as a justified sinner? What sayest thou, friend? Art thou satisfied? Is Christ sufficient for thee? Art thou still searching for something in thyself, thy ways, thy works, thy thoughts, thy feelings? If so, give up the search as utterly vain. Thou wilt never find any thing. And even though thou couldst find something, it would only be an encumbrance, a loss, a hindrance. Christ is sufficient for God, let Him be sufficient for thee likewise. Then—but not until then—wilt thou be truly happy.

May God the Holy Ghost cause thee to rest, this moment, upon an all-sufficient sacrifice, as the only ground of divine forgiveness, so that thou mayest be able to enter, with real intelligence and interest, upon the examination of the second point in our subject, namely: *the Extent of Divine Forgiveness*.

Very many are perplexed as to this. They do not see the fullness of the atonement; they do not grasp the emancipating fact of its application to all their sins; they do not enter into the full force of those lines, which perhaps they often sing,

> All thine iniquities who doth
> Most graciously forgive.

They seem to be under the impression that

Christ only bore some of their sins, namely, their sins up to the time of their conversion. They are troubled as to the question of their daily sins, as if these were to be disposed of upon a different ground from their past sins. Thus they are at times much cast down and sorely beset. Nor could it be otherwise with them until they see that in the death of Christ, provision was made for the full forgiveness of *all* their sins. True it is that the child of God who commits sin has to go to his Father and confess that sin. But what does the apostle say in reference to one so confessing his sins? "God is faithful and just to forgive us our sins and to cleanse us from all unrighteousness." Now, why does he say, "Faithful and just"? Why does he not say, "Gracious and merciful"? Because he speaks on the ground that the entire question of sin was gone into and settled by the death of Christ, who is now up in Heaven as the righteous Advocate. On no other ground could God be faithful and just in connection with the forgiveness of sins. The sins of the believer have *all* been atoned for on the cross. If one has been left out, he should be eternally lost, inasmuch as it is impossible that a single sin, however trifling, can ever enter the precincts of the sanctuary of God. And, further, let me add, if all the believer's sins were not atoned for in the death of Christ, then, neither by confession, nor by prayer, nor by fasting, nor by any other means, could they ever be forgiven. The death of Christ is the *only* ground on which God could, in faithfulness and justice, forgive sin; and we know He must either do it in faithfulness and justice, or not at all. This is to His praise and our exceeding comfort.

But I can imagine my reader exclaiming, "What! do you mean to say that my *future* sins were all atoned for?" To this I reply that all our sins were future when Christ bore them on the accursed tree. The sins of all believers, for the last eighteen centuries, were future when Christ died for them. Hence, if the idea of future sins presents a difficulty in reference to what we may commit, if left here, it presents just as great a difficulty in reference to what we have committed.* But, in truth, all this perplexity about future sins arises very much from the habit of looking at the cross from our own point of view instead of God's—looking at it from earth instead of from Heaven. Scripture never speaks of future sins. Past, present, and future are only human and earthly. All is an eternal now with God. All our sins were before the eye of infinite Justice at the cross, and all were laid on the head of Jesus, the Sin-bearer, who, by His death, laid the eternal foundation of forgiveness of sins, in order that the believer, at any moment of his life, at any point in his history, at any stage of his career, from the time at which the hallowed tidings of the gospel fall upon the ear of faith, until the moment in which he steps into the glory, may be able to say, with clearness and decision, without reserve, misgiving, or hesitation, "Thou hast cast all my sins behind Thy back." To say this, is but faith's response to God's own declaration, when He says, "Their sins and their iniquities will I remember no more;" "Jehovah hath made to meet on Him the iniquities of us all."

Let us, by way of illustration, take the case of the thief on the cross. When he, as a convicted sinner, cast the eye of faith upon that blessed One who hung beside him, was he not, then and there, rendered fit to enter the paradise of God? Was he not furnished with a divine title to pass from the cross of a malefactor into the presence of God? Unquestionably. Did he need anything more to be done for him, in him, or with him, in order to fit him for Heaven? By no means. Well, then, suppose that, instead of passing into Heaven, he had been permitted to come down from the cross—suppose the nails had been extracted and he allowed to go at liberty; he would have had sin in his nature, and, having sin in his nature, he would have been liable to commit sin, in thought, word, and deed. Now, could he ever lose his title, his fitness, his meetness? Surely not. His title was divine and everlasting. All his sins were

---

* Let it be remembered that all the value of the atoning sufferings of Christ on the cross are ever before God, and the soul of the believer will there find the unchanging foundation of the blessed words of Rom. 8:34: *"Who is he that condemneth? Is it Christ that died, yea rather, that is risen again, who is even at the right hand of God, who also maketh intercession for us."*

borne by Jesus. That which had fitted him to enter Heaven at the first, had fitted him once and forever, so that if he had remained on earth for fifty years, he would, at any moment, have been equally fit to enter Heaven.

True it is, if the pardoned sinner commits sin, his communion is interrupted, and there must be the hearty confession of that sin ere his communion can be restored. "If we say that we have fellowship with Him, and walk in darkness, we lie, and do not the truth." But this is obviously a different point altogether. My communion may be interrupted, but my title can never be forfeited. All was accomplished on the cross. Every trace of sin and guilt was atoned for by that peerless, priceless sacrifice. By that sacrifice, the believer is transferred from a position of guilt and condemnation into a position of justification and perfect favor. He is translated from a condition in which he had not a single trace of righteousness, into a condition in which he has not a single trace of guilt, nor ever can have. He stands in grace, he is under grace, he breathes the very atmosphere of grace, and he never can be otherwise, according to God's view. If he commits sin (and who does not?) there must be confession. And what then? Forgiveness and cleansing, on the ground of the faithfulness and justice of God which have had their divine answer in the cross. *All is founded on the cross.* The faithfulness and justice of God, the advocacy of Christ, our full confession, our full forgiveness, our perfect cleansing, the restoration of our communion, all rests upon the solid basis of the precious blood of Christ.

Bear in mind that we are, at present, occupied with the one point, namely, the extent of divine forgiveness. There are other points of great importance which might be looked at in connection, such as the believer's oneness with Christ, his adoption into the family of God, the indwelling of the Holy Ghost, all of which necessarily imply the full forgiveness of sins; but we must confine ourselves to our immediate theme, and having endeavored to set forth the ground and the extent, we shall close with a few words on: *the Style of Divine Forgiveness.*

We are all conscious of how much depends upon the style of an action. Indeed, there is frequently far more power in the style than in the substance. How often have we heard such words as these, "Yes, I own he did me a favor; but then he did it in such a way as to take away all the good of it." Now, the Lord has His style of doing things, blessed be His name. He not only does great things, but He does them in such a way as to convince us that His heart is in the doing of them. Not only is the substance of His acts good, but the style most charming.

Let us have a sample or two. Look, for instance, at Christ's touching word to Simon the Pharisee, in Luke 7. "When they had nothing to pay, he *frankly* forgave them both." Now, so far as the mere matter of the debt was concerned, the result would have been the same whatever style had been adopted. But what heart does not perceive the moral power of the word "frankly"? Who would part with it? Who could bear to see the substance stripped of its style? The creditor might forgive with a murmur about the amount. That murmur would, in the judgment of a sensitive heart, rob the act of all its charms. On the other hand, the frankness of the style enhances, beyond expression, the value of the substance.

Again, look, for a moment, at that familiar but ever fruitful section of inspiration, Luke 15. Each of the parables illustrates the power and beauty of style. When the man finds his sheep, what does he do? Does he complain of all the trouble, and commence to drive the sheep home before him? Ah, no! this would never do. What then? "He layeth it on His shoulders." How? Complaining of the weight or the trouble? Nay; but "*rejoicing.*" Here we have the lovely style. He showed that He was glad to get His sheep back again. The sheep would have been safe on the shoulder however it had been placed there; but who would part with the word "rejoicing"? Who would bear to see the substance of the action stripped of its charming style?

So, also, in the case of the woman and her lost piece of silver. "She lights a candle, sweeps the house, and seeks." How? With dullness, weariness and indifference? By no means; but "diligently," like one whose whole heart was in her work. It was quite manifest that she really wanted to find the lost piece of silver. Her style proved this.

Lastly, mark the style of the father in receiving the poor returning prodigal. "When he was yet a great way off, his father saw him, and had compassion, and *ran* and fell on his neck and kissed him." He does not send out a servant to tell the erring one to turn aside into one of the out-offices, or betake himself to the kitchen, or even to confine himself to his own room. No; he himself *runs*. He, as it were, lays aside his paternal dignity, in order to give expression to his fatherly affection. He is not satisfied with merely receiving the wanderer back: he must prove that his whole heart is in the reception; and this he does, not merely by the substance of the act, but by his style of doing it.

Various other passages might be adduced to illustrate the style of divine forgiveness, but the above will suffice to prove that God graciously recognizes the power which style has to act upon the human heart. I shall, therefore, in closing this paper, make an earnest appeal to my reader, as to what he now thinks of the ground, the extent, and the style of divine forgiveness.

Thou seest that the ground is as stable as the very throne of God itself, that the extent is infinite, and the style all that the heart could possibly desire. Say, therefore, art thou satisfied as to the great question of the forgiveness of sins? Can you any longer doubt God's willingness to forgive, when He has set before you, in such a way, the ground on which, the extent to which, and the style in which, He forgives sin? Can you hesitate when He actually

Opens His own heart to thee,
And shows His thoughts how kind they be?

He stands with open arms to receive thee. He points thee to the cross, where His own hand laid the foundation of forgiveness, and assures thee that all is done, and beseeches thee to rest now, henceforth and for evermore, in that which He has wrought for you. May the blessed Spirit lead thee to see these things in all their clearness and fullness, so that thou mayest not only believe in the forgiveness of sins, but believe also that all thy sins are frankly and forever forgiven.

THE TWO "MUSTS"

IN OUR LORD'S DISCOURSE with Nicodemus He twice makes use of the word "must"—a word of immense depth and moral power in both cases. Let us ponder it for a few moments; for, though but a word of one syllable, it contains a volume of most precious evangelical truth in whichever light we view it.

1. And first, then, we read, "Marvel not that I said unto thee, Ye must be born again." Here we have the total setting aside of man in his very best estate. If I must be born again, if I must have a new life, a new nature, then it matters not in the smallest degree what I can or cannot boast of. Man, as born of a woman, enters this world with the image of his fallen parent stamped upon him. Man, as he came from the hand of his Creator, was made in the "image of God."

Man, as he issues from the womb of his mother, bears the image and likeness of a fallen creature. Hence the force of our Lord's expression, "Ye *must* be born again." It is not said, Ye must mend, ye must try and be better, ye must alter your mode of living, ye must turn over a new leaf. Had it been thus, Nicodemus would never have asked, "How can these things be?" A man of the Pharisees would have understood any or all of these things.

A change of conduct, a change of character, any moral reform, any self-improvement, is perfectly intelligible to a Pharisee of every age; but to be told "Ye *must* be *born* again" can only be understood by one who has reached the end of himself and his doings; who has been brought to see that in him, that is in his flesh, dwelleth no good thing; who sees himself as a thorough bankrupt without a certificate, who can never again set up on his own account. He must get a new life to which the verdict of bankruptcy cannot apply, and he must trade in the wealth of another, on which creditors have no possible claim.

There is immense power in this little word "*must*." It bears upon all alike. It speaks to the drunkard, and says, "You must be born again." It addresses the most rigid teetotaler, and says, "You must be born again." It speaks to every class, to every condition, to every grade and shade of character, to man in every rank and every clime, to every creed and every denomination, in its own clear, emphatic, sweeping style, and says, "You *must* be born again." It bears down with far more weight upon the conscience than any appeal that could be made on the ground of moral conduct. It does not interfere in the least with the question of moral reform, in any one of its many phases. It allows as broad a margin as any philanthropist or moral reformer may desire. It does not disturb the various distinctions which society, public opinion, law or equity has established. It leaves all these things perfectly untouched, but it raises its clear and commanding voice above them all, and says to the sinner—to man as born of a woman—to the worst and to the best of men, "You *must* be born again." It demands not reformation, but regeneration; not amendment, but a new life.

2. What then, it may be asked, are we to do? Whither are we to turn? How are we to get this new life? Our Lord's second "must" furnishes the reply. "As Moses lifted up the serpent in the wilderness, even so *must* the Son of man be lifted up: that whosoever *believeth* in Him should not perish, but have eternal life." This makes all plain. A second Man has entered the scene. There are two *men* and two *musts*. As to the first man, he must be born again, and as to the second Man, He must be lifted up. In a word, the Cross is the grand solution of the difficulty, the divine answer to the "How?"

Am I completely struck down by the first "must"? Am I overwhelmed by the insuperable difficulty which it proposes to me? Am I on the very verge of despair as I contemplate the apparent impossibility of what, nevertheless, *must* be? Oh then, with what power does the second "must" fall on my heart! "The Son of man must be lifted up." Why must He? Because I must have new life, and this life is in the Son, but it could only be mine through His death. The death of the second Man is the only ground of life to the first—life to *me*. One look at Christ, as lifted up for me, is life eternal.

The soul that simply believes on the Son of God, as dead and risen, is "born of water and of the Spirit;" he *hath* everlasting life—he *is* passed from death unto life, from the old creation into the new, from the first man to the Second, from guilt to righteousness, from condemnation to favor, from darkness to light, from Satan to God. May God the Spirit unfold to the reader's heart the beauty and power, the depth, the comprehensiveness, and moral glory of the two "musts."

"Not by works of righteousness which we have done, but according to His mercy He saved us, by the washing of regeneration, and renewing of the Holy Ghost; which He shed on us abundantly through Jesus Christ our Saviour; that being justified by His grace, we should be made heirs according to the hope of eternal life" (Titus 3:5-7).

THE THREE CROSSES

Luke 23:39-43

TURN ASIDE WITH US for a few moments and meditate upon those three crosses. If we mistake not, we will find a very wide field of truth opened before us in the brief but comprehensive record given at the head of this article.

1. First of all, we must gaze at the centre cross, or rather at Him who was nailed thereon—Jesus of Nazareth—that blessed One who had spent His life in labors of love, healing the sick, cleansing the lepers, opening the eyes of the blind, raising the dead, feeding the hungry, drying the widow's tears, meeting every form of human need, ever ready to drop the tear of true sympathy with every child of sorrow; whose meat and drink it was to do the will of God, and to do good to man; a holy, spotless, perfectly gracious man; the only pure, untainted sheaf of human fruit ever seen in this world; "a man approved of God," who had perfectly glorified God on this earth and perfectly manifested Him in all His ways.

Such, then, was the One who occupied the centre cross; and when we come to inquire what it was that placed Him there, we learn a threefold lesson; or rather, we should say, three profound truths are unfolded to our hearts.

In the first place, we are taught, as nothing else can teach us, what man's heart is toward God. Nothing has ever displayed this—nothing could display it—as the cross has. If we want a perfect standard by which to measure the world, to measure the human heart, to measure sin, we must look at the cross of our Lord Jesus Christ. We cannot stop short of the cross, and we cannot go beyond it, if we want to know what the world is, inasmuch as it was there that the world fully uttered itself—there fallen humanity fully let itself out. When the human voice cried out, "Crucify Him! crucify Him!" that voice was the utterance of the human heart, declaring, as nothing else could declare, its true condition in the sight of God. When man nailed the Son of God to the cross, he reached the full height of his guilt, and the depth of moral turpitude. When man preferred a robber and murderer to Christ, he proved that he would rather have robbery and murder than light and love. The cross demonstrates this tremendous fact; and the demonstration is so clear as to leave not the shadow of a question.

It is well to seize this point. It is certainly not seen with sufficient clearness. We are very prone to judge of the world according to its treatment of ourselves. We speak of its hollowness, its faithlessness, its baseness, its deceitfulness, and such like; but we are too apt to make *self* the measure in all this, and hence we fall short of the real mark. In order to reach a just conclusion, we must judge by a perfect standard, and this can only be found in the cross. The cross is the only perfect measure of man, of the world, of sin. If we really want to know what the world is, we must remember that it preferred to robber to Christ, and crucified between two thieves the only perfect man that ever lived.

Such is the world in which we live. Such is its character—such its moral condition—such its true state as proved by its own deliberately planned and determinedly perpetrated act. And therefore we need not marvel at aught that we hear or see of the world's wickedness, seeing that in crucifying the Lord of glory, it gave the strongest proof that could be given of wickedness and guilt.

It will perhaps be said, in reply, the world is changed. It is not now what it was in the days of Herod and Pontius Pilate. The world of the nineteenth century is very different from the world of the first. It has made progress in every way. Civilization has flung its fair mantle over the scene; and, as respects a large portion of the world, Christianity has shed its purifying and enlightening influence upon the masses; so that it would be *very* unwarrantable to measure the world that *is* by the terrible act of the world that *was*.

Do you really believe that the world is changed? Is it really improved in the deep springs of its moral being—is it altered at its heart's core? We readily admit all that a free gospel and an open Bible have, by the rich mercy of God, achieved here and there. We think, with grateful hearts and worshiping spirits, of thousands and hundreds of thousands of precious souls converted to God. We bless the Lord, with all our hearts, for multitudes who have lived and died in the faith of Christ; and for multitudes who, at this very moment, are giving most convincing evidence of their genuine attachment to the name, the person, and the cause of Christ.

But, after allowing the broadest margin in which to insert all these glorious results, we return, with firm decision, to our conviction that the world is the world still, and if it had the opportunity, the act that was perpetrated in Jerusalem in the year 33, would be perpetrated in Christendom now.

This may seem severe and sweeping; but is it true? Is the Name of Jesus one whit more agreeable to the world to-day, than it was when its great religious leaders cried out, "Not this man, but Barabbas!" Only try it. Go and breathe that peerless and precious Name amid the brilliant circles that throng the drawing-rooms of the polite, the fashionable, the wealthy, and the noble of this our own day. Name Him in the steamboat saloon, in the railway carriage, or in the public hall, and see if you will not very speedily be told that such a subject is out of place. Any other name, any other subject will be tolerated. You may talk folly and nonsense in the ear of the world, and you will never be told it is out of place; but talk of Jesus, and you will very soon be silenced. How often have we seen our leading thoroughfares

literally blocked up by crowds of people looking at a puppet show, or listening to a ballad singer or a German band, and no policeman tells them to move on. Let a servant of Christ stand to preach in our thoroughfares and he will be summoned before the magistrates. There is room in our public streets for the devil, but there is no room for Jesus Christ. "Not this man, but Barabbas."

Can any one deny these things? Have they not been witnessed again and again? And what do they prove? They prove, beyond all question, the fallacy of the notion that the world is improved. They prove that the world of the nineteenth century is the world of the first. It has, in some places, changed its dress, but not its real *animus*. It has doffed the robes of paganism, and donned the cloak of Christianity; but underneath that cloak may be seen all the hideous features of paganism's spirit. Compare Romans 1:29-31 with 2 Timothy 3 and there you will find the very traits and lineaments of nature in darkest heathenism, reproduced in connection with "the form of godliness"—the grossest forms of moral pravity covered with the robe of Christian profession.

No; it is a fatal mistake to imagine that the world is improving. It is stained with the murder of the Son of God; and it proves its consent to the deed in every stage of its history, in every phase of its condition. The world is under judgment. Its sentence is passed; the awful day of its execution is rapidly approaching. The world is simply a deep, dark, rapid stream rushing onward to the lake of fire. Nothing but the sword of judgment can ever settle the heavy question pending between the God and Father of our Lord Jesus Christ and that world which murdered His Son.

Thus it is, if Scripture is to be our guide. Judgment is coming. It is at the very door. Eighteen hundred years ago, the inspired apostle penned the solemn sentence, that "God is *ready* to judge." If He was ready then, surely He is ready now. And why tarries He? In long-suffering mercy, not willing that *any* should perish, but that *all* should come to repentance. Precious words!

Words of exquisite tenderness and matchless grace! Words that tell out the large, loving, gracious heart of our God, and His intense desire for man's salvation.

But judgment is coming. The awful day of vengeance is at hand; and, meanwhile, the voice of Jesus, sounding through the lips of His dear ambassadors, may be heard on every side calling men to flee out of the terrible vortex, and make their escape to the stronghold of God's salvation.

2. But this leads us, in the second place, to look at the cross as the expression of God's heart toward man. If on the cross of our adorable Lord and Saviour Jesus Christ, we read, in characters deep, broad, and unmistakable, the true state of man's heart Godward; in the selfsame cross, we may read, with no less clearness surely, the state of God's heart toward man. The cross is the divinely perfect measure of both.

> The very spear that pierced Thy side,
> Drew forth the blood to save.

We behold, at the cross, the marvellous meeting of enmity and love—sin and grace. Man displayed at Calvary, the very height of his enmity against God. God, blessed for ever be His name, displayed the height of His love. Hatred and love met; but love proved victorious. God and sin met; God triumphed, sin was put away, and now, at the resurrection side of the cross, the eternal Spirit announces the glad tidings, that grace reigns through righteousness, unto eternal life by Jesus Christ our Lord. At the cross, the battle was fought and the victory won; and now the liberal hand of sovereign grace is scattering far and wide the spoils of victory.

Do you really desire to know what the heart of God is toward man? If so, go and gaze on that centre cross to which Jesus Christ was nailed, by the determinate counsel and foreknowledge of God. True it is, as we have already seen, man did, with wicked hands, crucify and slay the blessed One. This is the dark side of this question. But there is a bright side also, for God is seen in it. No doubt, man fully let himself out at the cross; but God was above him. Yes, above all the powers of earth and hell which were

there ranged in their terrible array.

As it was, in the case of Joseph and his brethren; they told out the enmity of their hearts in flinging him into the pit, and selling him to the Ishmaelites. Here was the dark side. But then, mark these words of Joseph: "Now therefore be not grieved, nor angry with yourselves, that ye sold me hither; for God did send me before you to preserve life."

Here was the bright side. But to whom were these wondrous words of grace addressed? To broken hearts and penitent spirits, and convicted consciences. To men who had learnt to say, "We are verily guilty." It is only such that can at all enter into the line of truth which is now before us. Those who have taken their true place, who have accepted the judgment of God against themselves, who truly own that the cross is the measure of their guilt—they can appreciate the cross as the expression of God's heart of love toward them; they can enter into the glorious truth that the selfsame cross which demonstrates man's hatred of God sets forth also God's love to man. The two things ever go together. It is when we see and own our guilt, as proved in the cross, that we learn the purifying and peace-speaking power of that precious blood which cleanseth us from all sin.

Yes; it is only a broken heart and a contrite spirit that can truly enter into the marvellous love of God as set forth in the cross of Christ. How could Joseph ever have said, "Be not grieved with yourselves," if he had not seen his brethren broken down in his presence? Impossible. And how can an unbroken heart, an unreached conscience, an impenitent soul enter into the value of the atoning blood of Christ, or taste the sweetness of the love of God? Utterly impossible. Joseph "spake roughly" to his brethren at the first, but the very moment those accents emanated from their broken hearts, "We are verily guilty," they were in a condition to understand and value the words, "Be not grieved with yourselves." It is when we are completely broken down in the presence of the cross, seeing it as the perfect measure of our own deep personal guilt, that we are prepared to see it as the glorious display of God's love towards us.

And then and there we escape from a guilty world. Then and there we are rescued completely from that dark and rapid current of which we have spoken, and brought within the hallowed and peaceful circle of God's salvation, where we can walk up and down in the very sunlight of a Father's countenance and breathe the pure air of the new creation. "Thanks be to God for His unspeakable gift!"

3. And now, one word, ere closing this branch of our subject on the cross as displaying the heart of Christ toward God. We can do little more than indicate this point, leaving the reader to prove its suggestive power, under the immediate ministry of the Holy Ghost.

It is an unspeakable comfort to the heart, in the midst of such a world as this, to remember that God has been perfectly glorified by One, at least. There has been One on this earth whose meat and drink was to do the will of God, to glorify Him, and finish His work. In life and death, Jesus perfectly glorified God. From the manger to the cross, His heart was perfectly devoted to *the* one great object, namely, to accomplish the will of God, whatever that will might be. "Lo, I come (in the volume of the book it is written of Me) to do Thy will, O God."

In the roll of Scripture it was written of the Son that, in due time, He should come into this world, according to God's eternal counsels, and accomplish the will of the Godhead. To this He dedicated Himself with all the energies of His perfect being. From this He never swerved a hair's breadth from first to last; and when we gaze on that centre cross which is now engaging our attention, we behold the perfect consummation of that which had filled the heart of Jesus from the very beginning, even the accomplishment of the will of God.

All this is blessedly unfolded to us in that charming passage in Philippians 2. "Let this mind be in you which was also in Christ Jesus; who being in the form of God, thought it not robbery to be equal with God; but made Himself of no reputation, and took upon Him the form of a servant, and was made in the likeness of men; and being found in fashion as a man, He humbled Himself, and became obedient unto death, even the death of the cross" (ver. 5-8).

How wonderful is all this! What profound depths there are in the mystery of the cross! What lines of truth converge in it! What rays of light emanated from it! What unfoldings of heart there! The heart of man to Godward—the heart of God to manward—the heart of Christ to God! All this we have in the cross. We can gaze on that One who hung there between two thieves, a spectacle to Heaven, earth, and hell, and see the perfect measure of every one and everything in the whole universe of God. Would we know the measure of the heart of God—His love to us—His hatred of sin? we must look at the cross. Would we know the measure of the heart of man, his real condition, his hatred of all that is divinely good, his innate love of all that is thoroughly bad? we must look at the cross. Would we know what the world is—what sin is—what Satan is? we must look at the cross.

Assuredly, then, there is nothing like the cross. Well may we ponder it. It shall be our theme throughout the everlasting ages. May it be, more and more, our theme now! May the Holy Ghost so lead our souls into the living depths of the cross, that we may be absorbed with the One who was nailed thereto, and thus weaned from the world that placed Him there. May the real utterance of our hearts ever be, "God forbid that I should glory save in the cross of our Lord Jesus Christ." God grant it, for Jesus Christ's sake!

Having dwelt, for a little, on that marvellous centre cross to which the Lord of glory was nailed, for our redemption, we shall now turn to the other two, and seek to learn some solemn and weighty lessons from the inspired record concerning the men who hung thereon. We shall find in these two men samples of the two great classes into which the human family is divided, from the beginning to the end of time, namely the receivers and the rejecters of the Christ of God—those who believe in Jesus, and those who believe not.

In the first place, it is of the utmost importance to see that there was no essential difference between those two men. In nature, in their recorded history, in their circumstances, they were one. Some have labored to establish a distinction between them; but for what object it is difficult to say, unless it be to dim the lustre of the grace that shines forth in the narrative of the penitent thief. It is maintained that there must have been some event in his previous history to account for his marvellous end—some redeeming feature—some hopeful circumstance on account of which his prayer was heard at the last.

But Scripture is totally silent as to aught of this kind. And not only is it silent as to any redeeming or qualifying circumstance, but it actually gives us the testimony of two inspired witnesses to prove that, up to the very moment in which Luke introduces him to our notice, he, like his fellow on the other side, was engaged in the terrible work of railing on the Son of God. In Matthew 27:44, we read that "The *thieves* also, which were crucified with Him, cast the same in His teeth." So also in Mark 15:32, "*They* that were crucified with Him reviled Him."

Now, this is divinely conclusive. It proves, beyond all question, that there was no difference between the two thieves. They were both condemned malefactors; and not only so, but when actually on the very confines of the eternal world, they were both occupied in the awful sin of reviling the blessed Son of God.

It is utterly vain, therefore, for any one to seek to establish a distinction between these two men, inasmuch as they were alike in their nature, in their guilt, in their criminality, and in their profane wickedness. There was no difference up to the moment in which the arrow of conviction entered the soul of him whom we call the penitent thief. The more clearly this is seen, the more the sovereign grace of God shines out in all its blessed brightness. "There is no difference; for all have sinned, and come short of the glory of God." And, on the other hand, "There is no difference, for the same Lord over all is rich unto all that call upon Him" (compare Rom. 3:22-23, with chapter 10:12).

The only standard by which men are to be measured is "the glory of God"; and inasmuch as all have come short of that—the best as

well as the worst of men—there is no difference. Were it merely a question of conscience, or of human righteousness, there might be some difference. Were the standard of measurement merely human, then indeed some shades of distinction might easily be established. But it is not so. All must be ruled by the glory of God; and, thus ruled, all are alike deficient. "There is no difference; for all have sinned, and come short of the glory of God."

But, blessed be God, there is another side to this great question. "The same Lord over all is rich unto all that call upon Him." The riches of the grace of God are such as to reach down to the very deepest depths of human ruin, guilt and misery. If the light of divine glory reveals—as nothing else could reveal—man's utter ruin; the riches of divine grace, as displayed in the person and work of Christ, have perfectly met that ruin, and provided a remedy in every way adequate to meet the claims of the divine glory.

But let us see how all this is illustrated in the striking and beautiful narrative of the penitent thief.

It is very evident that the Spirit of God, in the evangelist Luke, takes up this interesting case at that special point in the which a divine work had really begun. Matthew and Mark present him as a blaspheming malefactor. We can hardly conceive a deeper shade of moral turpitude than that which he, according to their inspired record, exhibits to our view! There is not so much as a single relieving tint. All is dark as midnight—dark almost as hell; yet not too dark to be reached by the light that was shining straight down from Heaven through the mysterious medium of that centre cross.

It is well to get a very profound sense of our true condition by nature. We cannot possibly go too deep in this line. The ruin of nature is complete—of nature in all its phases and in all its stages. If all have not gone to the same length as the thief on the cross—if all have not brought forth the same fruit—if all have not clothed themselves in forms equally hideous, it is no thanks to their nature. The human heart is a seed plot in which may be found the seed of every crime that has ever stained the page of human history. If the seed has not germinated and fructified, it is not owing to a difference in the soul, but a difference in surrounding circumstances and influences.

The testimony of Scripture on this great question, is distinct and conclusive, "There is no difference." Men do not like this. It is too leveling for them. Self-righteousness is cut out by the roots by this sweeping statement of inspiration. Man likes to establish distinctions. He cannot bear to be placed in the same category with the Magdalenes and the Samaritans, and such like. But it cannot be otherwise. Grace levels all distinctions now; and judgment will level them all by-and-by. If we are saved, it is in company with Magdalenes and Samaritans; and if we are lost, it will be in company with such likewise.

There will, no doubt, be degrees of glory; as there will be degrees of punishment; but as to the real nature and character of the human heart, "there is no difference." "The *heart* is deceitful above all things, and desperately wicked." What heart? Man's heart—the heart of the writer and the reader of these lines. "For out of *the heart* proceed evil thoughts, murders, adulteries, fornications, thefts, false witness, blasphemies." Out of what heart? Man's heart—the heart of the writer and the reader of these lines. These things could not come out of the heart if they were not there; and if they do not come out in action, it is not because they are not there, but that circumstances have operated to prevent.

Such is the clear and unvarying testimony of Holy Scripture; and whenever the Spirit of God begins to operate on the heart and conscience of a man He produces the deep sense and full confession of the truth of this testimony. Every divinely convicted soul is ready to adopt as his own these words, "In me, that is, in my flesh, dwelleth no good." Every truly contrite spirit owns the fact of his total ruin. All wisdom's children justify God and condemn themselves—there is no exception. All who are really brought under the convicting power of the Holy Spirit will, without any reserve, set their seal—the seal of their whole moral being to the inspired statement, "there is no difference."

Any who hesitate to own this have yet to learn themselves, in the light of the holiness of God. The most refined, polished and cultivated person, if enlightened by the Spirit of God, will readily take his place with the thief on the cross, inasmuch as the divine light shining in upon him, reveals the hidden springs of his being, leads him to see the profound depths of his nature—the roots and sources of things. Thus while relatives, friends and acquaintances—mere onlookers, judging from the surface, may think very highly of his character, he himself, knowing better, because of divine light, can only exclaim, "O wretched man that I am"—"Behold I am vile"—"Woe is me, I am undone"—"I am a sinful man, O Lord."

These are the proper utterances of a divinely convicted soul; and it is only when we can thus truly and heartily express ourselves that we are really prepared to appreciate the riches of the grace of God as unfolded in the gospel of Jesus Christ. Grace takes up real sinners. "The Son of man is come to seek and to save that which is lost;" and the more fully I realize my lost estate, my hopeless ruin, my utter wretchedness, the more fully I can enter into the fulness and freeness of God's salvation—a salvation purchased by the blood of the cross.

Hence we see how brightly grace shines in the salvation of the thief on the cross. There can be no possible mistake as to him. Clearly he had no good works to trust in. He had performed no deeds of charity. Of baptism and the Lord's Supper he knew nothing. The rites, ceremonies, and ordinances of religion had done—could do nothing for him. In a word, his case was a thoroughly hopeless one, so far as *he* was concerned. For what could *he* do? Whither could he turn? His hands and his feet were nailed fast to a malefactor's cross. It was useless to talk to him about doing or going. His hands, while he had the use of them, had been stretched forth in deeds of violence; and now they were nailed to the tree, and could do nothing. His feet, while he had the use of them, had trodden the terrible path of the transgressor; and now they were nailed to the tree, and could not carry him anywhere.

But, note this. Although the poor thief no longer had the use of his hands and his feet—so indispensable to a religion of works—his heart and his tongue were free; and these are the very things that are called into exercise in a religion of faith, as we read in that lovely tenth of Romans, "With the *heart* man believeth unto righteousness; and with the *mouth* confession is made unto salvation."

Precious words! How suited to the thief on the cross! How suited and seasonable for *every* poor helpless, hopeless, self-destroyed sinner! And we must all be saved in like manner as the thief on the cross. There are no two ways to Heaven. There is not one way for the religionist, the moralist, the Pharisee, and another way for the malefactor. There is but one way, and that way is marked from the very throne of God down to where the guilty sinner lies, dead in trespasses and sins, with the footprints of redeeming love; and from thence back to the throne by the precious atoning blood of Christ. This is the way to Heaven—a way paved with love, sprinkled with blood, and trodden by a happy holy band of redeemed worshipers gathered from all the ends of the earth, to chant the heavenly anthem, "Worthy is the Lamb that was slain."

We have said that the heart of the thief was free; yes, free under the mighty action of the Holy Ghost, to turn toward that blessed One who hung beside him—that One whom he had just been reviling, but on whom he could now fix his repentant gaze, and to whom he could now bear the noblest testimony ever uttered by men or angels.

But it is most instructive and interesting to mark the progress of the work of God in the soul of the dying thief. Indeed the work of God in any soul is ever of the deepest possible interest. The operations of the Holy Spirit *in us* must never be separated from the work of Christ *for us;* and, we may add, both the one and the other are founded upon, and inseparably linked with the eternal counsels of God with respect to us. This is what makes it all so real, so solid, so entirely divine. It is not of man. It is all of God, from first to last—from the first dawning of conviction in the soul until it is introduced into the full-orbed light of the glorious gospel of the grace of God. The Lord be praised that it is so! Were it otherwise—were there a single atom of the creature in it, from beginning to end, that one atom would neutralize and destroy the whole, and render it not worth having.

Now in the case of the penitent thief, we discern the first touch of the Eternal Spirit—the very earliest fruit of His sanctifying work, in the words addressed to his fellow, "Dost thou not fear God?" He does not say, "Dost thou not fear punishment?" The sanctification of the Spirit, in every case, is evidenced by the fear of the Lord, and a holy abhorrence of evil for its own sake. "The fear of the Lord is the beginning of wisdom." There may be a fear of judgment, a fear of hell, a fear of the consequences of sin, without the smallest particle of hatred of sin itself. But where the Spirit of God is really at work in the heart, He produces the real sense of sin and the judgment thereof in the sight of God.

This is repentance; let the reader ponder it deeply. It is a grand reality; an essential element, in every case. "God commandeth all men, everywhere, to repent" (Acts 17:30). There is no getting over this—no setting it aside. Some may seek to do away with man's responsibility on the plea of his inability to do anything right or good. They may seek to persuade us that it is useless, yea unsound, to call upon men to repent and believe, seeing that men can do nothing of themselves. But the question is, what is the meaning of the words which we have just culled from the apostle's address at Athens? Did Paul preach the truth? Was he sound in the faith? Was he sufficiently high in doctrine?

Well then Paul declares, in the clearest and most emphatic manner, that "God commandeth *all* men, *everywhere*, to repent." Will any turn around and say they cannot? Will any venture to deny man's responsibility to obey a divine command? If so, where are they? On very dangerous ground. If God commands all men to repent, woe be to those who refuse to do so; and woe be to those who teach that they are not responsible to do so.

But let us devote a few moments to the examination of this great practical question in the light of the New Testament. Let us see whether our Lord and His apostles called upon men—"all men, everywhere, to repent."

In the third chapter of Matthew's Gospel, we read, "In those days came John the Baptist, preaching in the wilderness of Judaea, and saying, Repent ye: for the kingdom of heaven is at hand."

It will, perhaps, be said that John addressed himself specially to Israel—a people in recognized relationship with Jehovah—and hence this passage cannot be adduced in proof of the universal and abiding necessity of repentance. Well, we merely quote it here in order to shew that man, whether Jew or Gentile, is responsible to repent, and that the very first voice which falls upon the ear, in the time of the New Testament, is heard calling sinners to repentance.

Was the Baptist right or wrong? Was he trespassing upon the domain of sound doctrine when he summoned men to repent? Would some of our modern theologians have called him aside, after he was done preaching, and taken him to task for deceiving men by leading them to suppose that they could repent? We should like to have heard the Baptist's reply.

But we have the example of a greater than John the Baptist, as our warrant for preaching repentance, for in Matthew 4 we read, "From that time, Jesus began to preach, and to say, Repent; for the kingdom of heaven is at hand." Dare any one turn round and say to the divine Preacher, "We cannot repent. We have no power. We are not responsible!"

Ah, no! men may argue and reason, and talk theology; but there stands the living record before us—Jesus called upon men to repent, and that, too, without entering, in any way, upon the question of man's ability here or there. He addressed man as a responsible being, as one who was imperatively called to judge himself and his ways, to confess his sins, and repent in dust

and ashes. The only true place for a sinner is the place of repentance; and if he refuses to take that place in the presence of divine grace, he will be compelled to take it in the presence of divine judgment, when repentance will be too late. "God commandeth all men, everywhere, to repent."

Passing on to the opening of the Acts of the Apostles, we are privileged to harken to Peter's address on the day of Pentecost—the most fruitful sermon ever preached in this world—crowned with the glorious result of three thousand souls! And what did Peter preach? He preached Christ, and he called upon men to repent. Yes, the great apostle of the circumcision insisted upon repentance—self-judgment—true contrition of heart before God. "Then said Peter unto them, Repent, and be baptized *every one of you* in the name of Jesus Christ, for the remission of sins, and ye shall receive the gift of the Holy Ghost" (Acts 2:38). And, again, "Repent ye therefore and be converted, that your sins may be blotted out" (chap. 3:19).

Was Peter right in calling upon men to repent and be converted? Would any one be justified in saying to him, at the close of his preaching, "How can men repent? How can they be converted? They can do nothing." We should vastly like to hear Peter's reply. One thing is certain, the power of the Holy Ghost accompanied the preaching. He set His seal to it, and that is enough. "God commandeth *all men, everywhere*, to repent." Woe to all who refuse.

We have already referred to the preaching of the blessed apostle of the Gentiles, and the great teacher of the Church of God. He himself, referring to his ministry at Ephesus, declares in the audience of the elders, "I kept back nothing that was profitable, but have shewed you, and have taught you publicly, and from house to house, testifying both to the Jews, and also to the Greeks, repentance toward God, and faith toward our Lord Jesus Christ" (Acts 20:20-21). So also, in his pungent address to Agrippa, he says, "I was not disobedient unto the heavenly vision; but shewed first unto them of Damascus, and at Jerusalem, and throughout all the coasts of Judaea, and then to the Gentiles, that they should repent and turn to God, and do works meet for repentance."

Thus we have a body of evidence, drawn from Scripture, such as cannot be gainsaid, proving the universal and abiding necessity of repentance. "God commandeth all men, everywhere, to *repent*." There is no avoiding this. Let men beware how they set it aside. No system of theology can be sound that denies the responsibility of the sinner to repent and turn to God, and do works meet for repentance.

We have digressed; but the digression was needful, and we now return to our theme.

The case of the penitent thief furnishes a very fine illustration of Peter's weighty sentence, "Repent and be converted." It teaches us in a clear and forcible manner, the true meaning of repentance and conversion— two subjects so little understood, so sadly clouded by false teaching.

The human heart is ever prone to take divine things by the wrong end; and when false theology combines with this tendency of the heart, by presenting things in a one-sided manner, the moral effect upon the soul is something terrible. Hence it is that, when men are called upon in the gospel message to repent and turn to God, they think it needful to set about doing something or other, in the shape of reading, praying, and attending upon the ordinances and offices of religion, so called. Thus they become occupied with thier doings instead of judging their state.

This is a fatal mistake—the result of the combined influence of self-righteousness and bad theology—these fruitful sources of darkness and misery to precious souls, and of serious damage to the truth of God.

It is perfectly marvellous to note the varied forms in which self-righteousness clothes itself. Indeed so varied are these forms that one would scarcely recognize it to be what it really is. Sometimes it looks like humility, and speaks largely of the evil and danger of being too presumptuous. Then again, it assumes the garb and adopts the language of what is called experimental religion, which, very often, is nothing more than intense self-occupation. At other times, it expresses itself in the threadbare

formularies of systematic divinity—that stumbling-block of souls and the sepulchre of divine revelation.

What then is repentance? It is, in one of its grand elements, the thorough judgment of self—of its history and its ways. It is the complete breaking up of the entire system of self-righteousness and the discovery of our complete wreck, ruin and bankruptcy. It is the sense of personal vileness, guilt, and danger—a sense produced by the mighty action of the Word and Spirit of God upon the heart and conscience. It is a hearty sorrow for sin, and a loathing of it for its own sake.

True, there are other features and elements in genuine repentance. There is a change of mind as to self, and the world, and God. And further, there are various degrees in the depths and intensity of the exercise. But, for the present, we confine ourselves to that deeply important feature of repentance illustrated in the touching narrative of the penitent thief, which we may term, in one word, self-judgment. This must be insisted upon constantly.

We greatly fear it is sadly lost sight of in much of our modern preaching and teaching. In our efforts to make the gospel simple and easy, we are in danger of forgetting that "God commandeth all men everywhere to repent." The sinner must be made to feel that he is a sinner, a lost sinner, a guilty sinner, a hell-deserving sinner. He must be made to feel that sin is a terrible thing in the sight of God; so terrible, that nothing short of the death of Christ could atone for it—so terrible, that all who die unpardoned must inevitably be damned—must spend a dreary, never-ending eternity in the lake that burneth with fire and brimstone.

Is there, then, anything meritorious in repentance? Is there anything to build upon or to boast in? Has it aught to do with the ground of our salvation, our righteousness, or our acceptance with God? As well might we inquire if the consciousness of bankruptcy could form the basis of a man's credit or future fortune. No, no, reader; repentance, in its deepest and most intensified form, has nothing to do with the ground of our pardon. How could the sense of guilt have aught to do with the ground of pardon? How could the feelings of a drowning man have aught to do with the life-boat that saves him? Or how could the agonies of a man in a house on fire have aught to do with the fire-escape by which he descends from the burning pile?

Look at the case of the thief on the cross. Harken to his words: "Dost thou not fear God, seeing thou art in the same condemnation: *And we indeed justly; for we receive the due reward of our deeds.*" Here are the accents of a genuine repentance, "we indeed justly." He felt and owned that he was justly condemned; that he was reaping only "the due reward of his deeds." Was there anything meritorious in this? By no means. It was the judgment of himself, the condemnation of his ways, the sense of his guilt. And this was right. It was the sure precursor of conversion to God. It was the fruit of the Spirit's work in his soul, and enabled him to appreciate God's salvation. It was the hearty acknowledgment of his own just condemnation; and, most surely, this could in no wise contribute to his righteousness before God. It is utterly impossible that the sense of guilt could ever form the basis of righteouness.

Still, there must be repentance; and the deeper the better. It is well that the plough should do its work in breaking up the fallow ground, and making deep the furrows in which the incorruptible seed of the Word may take root. We do not believe that any one had ever to complain that the ploughshare entered too deeply into the soul. Nay, we feel assured that the more we are led down into the profound depths of our own moral ruin, the more fully we shall appreciate the righteousness of God which is by faith of Jesus Christ, unto all, and upon all them that believe.

But, be it well understood, repentance is not doing this or that. What did the thief do? What could he do? He could not move hand or foot. And yet he was truly repentant. He is handed down, on the page of history, as "the penitent thief." Yes, he was penitent; and his penitence expressed itself in the unmistakable accents of self-judgment. Thus it must ever be. There must be the judgment of sin, sooner or later; and the sooner, the better; and the deeper, the better.

And what then? What is the divine order? "Repent, and be converted." "Repent, and turn to God." Beauteous order! It is conviction and conversion. It is the discovery of self and its ruin, and the discovery of God and His remedy. It is condemning myself and justifying God. It is finding out the emptiness of self, and finding out the fulness of Christ. It is learning the force and application of those few words, "Thou hast destroyed thyself; but in Me is thy help."

And see how all this comes out in the brief but comprehensive record of the thief. No sooner does he give expression to the sense of his own just condemnation, than he turns so that blessed One who was hanging beside him, and bears the sweet testimony, "This man hath done nothing amiss." Here he gives a flat contradiction to the whole world. He joins issue with the chief priests, elders, and scribes, who had delivered up the holy One as a malefactor. They had declared, "If He were not a malefactor, we would not have delivered Him up unto thee." But the dying thief declares, "This man hath done nothing amiss." Thus he stands forth in clear and decided testimony to the spotless humanity of the Lord Jesus Christ—that grand truth which lies at the very base of "the great mystery of godliness." He turns from a guilty self to a spotless Christ; and he tells the world that it had made a terrible mistake in crucifying the Lord of glory.

And was not this a good work? Yes, truly, the very best work that any one could do. To bear a full, clear, bold testimony to Christ, is the most acceptable and fragrant service that any mortal can render to God. Millions bestowed in charity, continents traversed in the interests of philanthropy, a lifetime spent in the dreary exercises of mechanical religiousness—all these things put together are as the small dust of the balance when compared with one word of heartfelt, genuine, Spirit-taught testimony to God's beloved Son. The poor thief could do nothing and give nothing; but oh, he was permitted to enjoy the richest and rarest privilege that could possibly fall to the lot of any mortal, even the privilege of bearing witness to Christ, when the whole world had cast Him out, when one of His own disciples had denied Him, another had sold Him, and all had forsaken Him. This, indeed, was service; this was work; a service and a work which shall live in the records and the memory of Heaven when the proudest monuments of human genius and benevolence shall have crumbled and sunk in eternal oblivion.

But we have some further lessons to learn from the lips of the dying malefactor. Not only does he bear a bright and blessed testimony to the spotless humanity of Christ, but he also owns Him as Lord and King; and this, too, at a moment, and amid a scene when, to nature's view, there was not a single trace of lordship or royalty. "He said unto Jesus, Lord, remember me when Thou comest into Thy kingdom."

Think of this! Think of one who had, as it were, a moment before, been railing on the dying Saviour, now owning Him as Lord and King! Truly this was divine work. Surely this was real conversion—a true turning to God. "Lord, remember *me*." Oh, how unspeakably precious is this golden chain with its three links! How lovely to see a poor worthless, guilty, hell-deserving "*me*" linked on to the divine Saviour by that one word, "*remember!*"

This was life eternal. A Saviour and a sinner linked together, is everlasting salvation. Nothing can be simpler. People may talk of works, of feelings, of experiences; but here we have the matter presented in its divine simplicity, and in its divine order. We have first the fruit of a genuine repentance, in the words, "We indeed justly"; and then the sweet result of spiritual conversion in the one simple but powerful utterance, "Lord, remember me." "Repent and be converted, that your sins may be blotted out." "Repent and turn to God."

What marvellous depth and power in those words! To repent is to see the utter ruin of self. To turn to God, is life, and peace, and everlasting salvation. We discover self and we loathe and abhor it. We discover God and turn to Him with the whole heart, and find in Him all we want for time and for eternity. It is all divinely simple and unspeakably blessed. Repentance and conversion are inseparably linked together. They are distinct, yet intimately connected. They must neither be separated nor confounded.

And, now, let us note the divine response to the appeal of the penitent thief. He had said, "Lord, remember me when Thou comest into Thy kingdom." What is the answer? "To-day shalt thou be with Me in Paradise." It is as though the blessed Saviour had said to him, "You need not wait for the *glory* of the *kingdom;* this very day thou shalt taste the *grace* of the *house*—the love of My Father's home above; I shall have you with Me in that bright paradise, to enjoy full communion with Me long before the glories of the kingdom shall be unfolded." Most blessed Saviour, such was Thy matchless grace!

And not one reproving word! Not a single reference to the past! Not even a glance at the recent heartless wickedness! Ah, no; there is never aught of this in the divine dealing with a penitent soul. The thief had said—said from the depths of a broken and contrite heart, "We indeed justly." This was enough. True, it was needful; but it was enough. "A broken and a contrite heart, O God, Thou wilt not despise." No; and not only will He not despise it, but He will pour into it the rich and precious consolation of His grace and pardoning love. It is the joy of God to pardon a penitent sinner; and none but a penitent sinner can truly enjoy the pardon of God.

"*To-day* shalt thou be *with Me* in paradise." Here the glories of a present, personal, and perfect salvation pour themselves in divine lustre upon the gaze of the astonished thief.

And, be it noted, that there is not one syllable about doing, or giving, or feeling, or aught else that might turn the eye in upon self. The eye had been turned in, and rightly so; and it had seen nothing but a deep, dark abyss of guilt and ruin. This was enough. The eye must henceforth and for evermore be turned outward and upward; it must be fixed on the precious Saviour who was bringing him to paradise, and on that bright paradise to which He was bringing him.

No doubt the thief could never forget what a sinner he had been—never forget his guilt and wickedness—he never could, he never shall; yea, throughout the countless ages of eternity, he and all the redeemed shall remember the past. How could it be otherwise? Shall we lose the power of memory in the future? Surely not. But every remembrance of the past shall only tend to swell the note of praise which the heart shall give forth as we think of the grace that shines in those precious words, "Their sins and their iniquities will I remember no more." Such is the style of divine forgiveness! God will never again refer to those sins which His own loving hand has cancelled by the blood of the cross. Never! No, never! He has cast them behind His back for ever. They have sunk as lead into the deep waters of His eternal forgetfulness. All praise to His glorious Name!

Let us now fix the eye, for a brief moment, upon the third cross. On it we behold—what? A guilty sinner? Not merely that. The penitent thief was that. They were in the same condemnation. No one need go to hell simply because he is a sinner, inasmuch as Christ Jesus came into the world to save sinners, "even the chief." There is not a sinner this day, outside the precincts of hell, who is not within the reach of God's salvation if he only feel his need of it. No one need be lost, merely because he is a ruined, guilty, hell-deserving sinner.

But what do we behold on that third cross? We behold an *unbelieving* sinner. This is the solemn point. We may, without any hesitation, declare that had the occupant of that cross, like his penitent companion, cast himself upon the grace of the dying Saviour, he would, most assuredly, have met with the same response. There was grace in the heart of Jesus to meet the one as well as the other. But he did not want it, would not have it. He remained impenitent and unbelieving until the dark shadows of death gathered round him, and the darker horrors of hell burst upon his guilty soul. He perished within arm's length of the Saviour and salvation.

Tremendous thought! what finite mind can take it in? Who can fully estimate the contrast between those two men? True, the contrast was in one point; but that one point involved consequences of eternal moment.

What was it? It was this—*the reception or rejection of the Son of God;* believing or not believing on that blessed One who was hanging between them—as near to the one as He was to the other. There was no difference in their nature; no difference in their condition; no difference in their circumstances. The grand and all-important difference lay in this, that one believed in Jesus, and the other did not; one was enabled to say, "Lord, remember me"; the other said, "If thou be the Christ."

What a contrast! What a broad line of demarcation! What an awful chasm between two men so like in other respects—so near to one another—so near to the divine Saviour! But it is just the same in all cases, everywhere, and at all times. The one simple but solemn question for each and for all is this, "What is my relation to Christ?" All hinges upon this—yes, for time and eternity. Have I received Christ? or have I not? Am I in Him? or am I not?

The two thieves represent the two great classes into which mankind has been divided, from the days of Cain and Abel down to this very moment. God's Christ is the one great and all-deciding test in every case. All the shades of moral character; all the grades of social life; all the castes, classes, sects and parties into which the human family has been, is, or ever shall be divided—all are absorbed in this one momentous point—*"In or out of Christ."*

The difference between the two thieves is just the difference between the saved and the lost; the Church and the world—the children of God and the children of God's great enemy. True it is that, in the case of the two thieves, the matter is brought to a point, so that we can see it at a glance; but it is the same in every case. The person of Christ is the one great boundary line that marks off the new creation from the old—the kingdom of God from the kingdom of Satan—the children of light from the children of darkness; and this boundary line stretches away into eternity.

What sayest thou to these things? On which side of this line art thou, at this moment, standing? Art thou, like the penitent thief, linked on to Christ by a simple faith?

Or dost thou, like his impenitent companion,* speak of Christ with an "if"? Do not put this question away from thee. Take it up and look it solemnly in the face. Your eternal weal or woe hangs on your answer to this question.

Turn to Jesus now! Come now! God commands thee! Delay not! Reason not! Come just as thou art to Jesus, who hung on that centre cross for us.

---

* NOTE.—The two thieves furnish a powerful answer to the ritualist and the rationalist. In one, we see a man going straight to paradise who had never been baptized, and never received what ritualists call "the holy communion." In the other, we see a man who perishes, within arm's length of a Saviour, through a skeptical, rationalistic, infidel "*if.*" Let all ritualists and rationalists ponder these *facts.*

CONVERSION
WHAT IS IT?

Part 1

THE FIRST CHAPTER of First Thessalonians presents a very striking and beautiful picture of what we may truly call *genuine conversion*. We propose to study the picture in company with the reader. If we are not much mistaken, we shall find the study at once interesting and profitable. It will furnish an answer, distinct and clear, to the question which stands at the head of this article, namely, What is conversion?

Nor is this by any means a small matter. It is well, in days like these, to have a divine answer to such a question. We hear a good deal now-a-days about cases of conversion; and we would heartily bless God for every soul truly converted to Him.

We need hardly say we believe in the absolute, the indispensable, the universal necessity of divine conversion. Let a man be what he may; be he Jew or Greek, barbarian, Scythian, bond or free, Protestant or Roman Catholic; in short, whatever be his nationality, his ecclesiastical position, or his theological creed, he *must* be converted, else he is on the broad and direct road to an everlasting hell.

There is no one born a Christian, in the true sense of that word. Neither can anyone be educated into Christianity. It is a fatal mistake, a deadly delusion, a deceit of the arch-enemy of souls, for anyone to think that he can be a Christian either by birth or education, or that he can be made a Christian by water baptism, or by any religious ceremony whatsoever. A man becomes a Christian only by being divinely converted. We would earnestly press on the attention of all whom it may concern, the urgent and absolute necessity in every case of true conversion to God.

This cannot be overlooked. It is the height of folly for anyone to attempt to ignore or to make light of it. For an immortal being—one who has a boundless eternity stretching away before him—to neglect the solemn question of his conversion, is the wildest fatuity of which anyone can possibly be guilty. In comparison with this most weighty subject, all other things dwindle into utter insignificance. The various objects that engage the thoughts and absorb the energies of men and women in the busy scene around us, are but as the small dust of the balance in comparison with this one grand, momentous question of the soul's conversion to God.

All the speculations of commercial life, all the schemes of money-making, the absorbing question of profitable investment, all the pursuits of the pleasure hunter—the theatre, the concert, the ball-room, the billiard-room, the card-table, the dice-box, the race-course, the hunting-ground, the drinking saloon—all the numberless and nameless things that the poor unsatisfied heart longs after, and grasps at—all are but as the vapor of the morning, the foam on the water, the smoke from the chimney-top, the withered leaf of autumn—all vanish away, and leave an aching void behind. The heart remains unsatisfied, the soul unsaved, because unconverted.

And what then? Tremendous question! What remains at the end of all this scene of commercial excitement, political strife and ambition, money-making and pleasure-hunting? Why, then the man has to face death! "It is appointed unto men once to die." There is no getting over this. There is no discharge in this war. All the wealth of the universe could not purchase one moment's respite at the hand of the ruthless foe. All the medical skill which earth affords, all the fond solicitude of affectionate relatives and friends, all their tears, all their sighs, all their entreaties cannot stave off the dreaded moment, or cause the king of terrors to sheathe his terrible sword.

Death cannot be disposed of by any art of man. The moment *must* come when the link is to be snapped which connects the heart with all the fair and fascinating scenes of human life. Fondly loved friends, charming pursuits, coveted objects, all must be given up. A thousand worlds could not avert the stroke. Death must be looked at straight in the face. It is an awful mystery—a tremendous fact—a stern reality. It stands full in front of every unconverted man, woman, and child beneath the canopy of Heaven; and it is merely a question of time—hours, days, months, or years—when the boundary line must be crossed which separates time, with all its empty, vain, shadowy pursuits, from eternity with all its stupendous realities.

And what then? Let Scripture answer. Nothing else can. Men would fain reply according to their own vain notions. They would have us believe that after death comes annihilation. "Let us eat and drink, for to-morrow we die." Empty conceit! Vain delusion! Foolish dream of the human imagination blinded by the god of this world! How could an immortal soul be annihilated? Man, in the garden or Eden, became the possessor of a never-dying spirit. "The Lord God breathed into his nostrils the breath of life, and man became a *living* soul"—not a

dying soul. The soul must live forever. Converted or unconverted, it has eternity before it. Oh, the overpowering weight of this consideration to every thoughtful spirit! No human mind can grasp its immensity. It is beyond our comprehension, but not beyond our belief.

Let us harken to the voice of God. What does Scripture teach? One line of holy Scripture is quite sufficient to sweep away ten thousand arguments and theories of the human mind. Does death annihilate? Nay! "It is appointed unto men once to die, but after this the judgment."

Mark these words, "*After this* the judgment." And this applies only to those who die in their sins, only to unbelievers. For the Christian, judgment is passed forever, as Scripture teaches in manifold places. It is important to note this, because men tell us that, inasmuch as there is eternal life only in Christ, therefore all who are out of Christ shall be annihilated.

Not so says the Word of God. There is judgment after death. And what will be the issue of the judgment? Again Scripture speaks in language as clear as it is solemn. "And I saw a great white throne, and Him that sat on it, from whose face the earth and the heaven fled away; and there was found no place for them. And I saw the dead, small and great, stand before God; and the books were opened; and another book, which is the book of life; and the dead were judged out of those things which were written in the books, *according to their works*. And the sea gave up the dead which were in it; and death and hades delivered up the dead which were in them; and *they were judged every man according to their works*. . . . This is the second death"—the lake of fire. "And whosoever was not found written in the book of life was cast into the lake of fire" (Rev. 20).

All this is as plain as words can make it. There is not the slightest ground for demur or difficulty. For all whose names are in the book of life there is no judgment at all. Those whose names are not in that book shall be judged according to their works. And what then? Annihilation? Nay; but "the lake of fire;" and that forever and forever.

How overwhelming is the thought of this! An unconverted person, whoever and whatever he is, has death, judgment, and the lake of fire before him, and every throb of his pulse brings him nearer and nearer to those awful realities. It is not more sure that the sun shall rise, at a certain moment, to-morrow morning, than that the reader must, ere long, pass into eternity; and if his name is not in the book of life—if he is not converted—if he is not in Christ, he will assuredly be judged according to his works, and the certain issue of that judgment will be the lake of fire, through the endless ages of eternity.

The reader may perhaps marvel at our dwelling at such length on this dreadful theme. He may feel disposed to ask, "Will this convert people?" If it does not convert them, it may lead them to see their need of conversion. It may lead them to see their imminent danger. It may induce them to flee from the wrath to come. Why did the blessed apostle reason with Felix on the subject of "judgment to come"? Surely that he might persuade him to turn from his evil ways and live. Why did our blessed Lord Himself so constantly press upon His hearers the solemn reality of eternity? Why did He so often speak of the deathless worm and the unquenchable fire? Surely it was for the purpose of rousing them to a sense of their danger, that they might flee for refuge to lay hold upon the hope set before them.

Are we wiser than He? Are we more tender? Have we found out some better mode of converting people? Are we to be afraid of pressing upon our readers the same solemn theme which our Lord so pressed upon the men of His time? Are we to shrink from offending polite ears by the plain declaration that all who die unconverted must inevitably stand before the great white throne, and pass into the lake of fire? God forbid! It must not be. We solemnly call upon the un-converted reader to give his undivided attention to the all-important question of his soul's vation. Let nothing induce him to neglect it. Let neither cares, pleasures, nor duties so occupy him as to hide from his view the magnitude and deep seriousness of this mat-

ter. "What shall it profit a man if he shall gain the whole world and lose his own soul? Or what shall a man give in exchange for his soul?"

O, if thou art unsaved, unconverted, let us earnestly entreat thee to ponder these things, and rouse thee to a sense of thy need of being savingly converted to God. This is the only way of entering His kingdom. So our Lord Christ distinctly tells us; and we trust you know this at least, that not one jot or tittle of His holy sayings can ever pass away. Heaven and earth shall pass away; but His Word can never pass away. All the power of earth and hell, men and devils, cannot make void the words of our Lord Jesus Christ. Either of two things for thee— *conversion here*, or *eternal damnation hereafter*.

Thus it stands, if we are to be guided by the Word of God; and, in view of this, is it possible for us to be too earnest, too vehement, too importunate in urging upon every unconverted soul with whom we may come in contact, either with voice or pen, the indispensable necessity, this very moment, of fleeing from the wrath to come, fleeing to that blessed Saviour who died on the cross for our salvation; who stands with open arms to receive all who come; and who declares in His own sweet and precious grace, *"Him that cometh unto Me, I will in no wise cast out"?*

Part 2

In our previous paper, we have sought to set forth the absolute need, in every case, of conversion. Scripture establishes this point in such a way as to leave no possible ground of doubt for anyone who bows to its holy authority. "Except ye be converted, and become as little children, ye shall not enter into the kingdom of heaven" (Matt. 18:3).

This applies, in all its moral force and deep solemnity, to every son and daughter of fallen Adam. There is not so much as a solitary exception, throughout the thousand millions that people this globe. Without conversion, there is—there can be—no entrance into the kingdom of God. Every unconverted soul is outside the kingdom of

God. It matters not, in the smallest degree, who I am, or what I am; if I am unconverted, I am in "the kingdom of darkness," under the power of Satan, in my sins, and on the way to hell.

I may be a person of blameless morals; of spotless reputation; a high professor of religion; a worker in the vineyard; a Sunday-school teacher; an office-bearer in some branch of the professing church; an ordained minister; a deacon, elder, pastor or bishop; a most charitable individual; a munificent donor to religious and benevolent institutions; looked up to, sought after, and reverenced by all because of my personal worth and moral influence. I may be all this and more; I may be, and I may have, all that it is possible for a human being to be or to have, and yet be unconverted, and hence outside the kingdom of God, and in the kingdom of Satan, in my guilt, and on the broad road that leads straight down to the lake that burns with fire and brimstone.

Such is the plain and obvious meaning and force of our Lord's words in Matt. 18:3. There is no possibility of evading it. The words are as clear as a sunbeam. We cannot get over them. They bear down, with what we may truly call tremendous solemnity, upon every unconverted soul on the face of the earth. "Except ye be converted, ye *cannot* enter the kingdom of heaven." This applies, with equal force, to the degraded drunkard that rolls along the street, worse than a beast, and to the unconverted Good Templar or teetotaler who prides himself on his sobriety, and is perpetually boasting of the number of days, weeks, months, or years during which he has refrained from all intoxicating drink. They are both alike outside the kingdom of God; both in their sins; both on the way to eternal destruction.

True it is that the one has been converted from drunkenness to sobriety—a *very great* blessing indeed, in a moral and social point of view—but conversion from drunkenness to a temperance, pluming himself upon his morality, and thus deceiving himself into the vain not entering the kingdom of God's dear Son. There is just this difference between the two, that the teetotaler may be building upon his

temperance, pluming himself upon his morality, and thus deceiving himself into the vain notion that he is all right, whereas, in reality, he is not. The drunkard is palpably and unmistakably wrong. Everybody knows that no drunkard can inherit the kingdom of God; but neither can an unconverted teetotaler. Both are outside. Conversion to God is absolutely indispensable for the one as well as the other; and the same may be said of all classes, all grades, all shades, all castes and conditions of men under the sun. There is no difference as to this great question. It holds good as to all alike, be their outward character or social status what it may— "Except ye be converted, *ye cannot* enter the kingdom of heaven."

How important, then—yea, how momentous the question for each one, "*Am I converted?*" It is not possible for human language to set forth the magnitude and solemnity of this inquiry. For any one to think of going on, from day to day, and year to year, without a clear and thorough settlement of this most weighty question, can only be regarded as the most egregious folly of which a human being can be guilty. If a man were to leave his earthly affairs in an uncertain, unsettled condition, he would lay himself open to the charge of the grossest and most culpable neglect and carelessness. But what are the most urgent and weighty temporal affairs when compared with the salvation of the soul? All the concerns of time are but as the chaff of the summer threshing-floor, when compared with the interests of the immortal soul—the grand realities of eternity.

Hence it is, in the very highest degree, irrational for any one to rest for a single hour without a clear and settled assurance that he is truly converted to God. A converted soul has crossed the boundary line that separates the saved from the unsaved—the children of light from the children of darkness—the Church of God from this present evil world. The converted soul has death and judgment behind him, and glory before. He can be as sure of Heaven as though he were already there; indeed as a man in Christ he belongs there already. He has a title without a blot, a prospect without a cloud. He knows Christ as his Saviour and Lord; God as his Father and Friend; the Holy Ghost as his blessed Comforter, Guide, and Teacher; Heaven as his bright and happy home. Oh! the unspeakable blessedness of being converted. Who can utter it? "Eye hath not seen, nor ear heard, neither have entered into the heart of man, the things which God hath prepared for them that love Him. But God hath revealed them unto us [believers] by His Spirit; for the Spirit searcheth all things, yea the deep things of God" (1 Cor. 2:9-10).

And now let us inquire what this conversion is, whereof we speak. Well, indeed, will it be for us to be divinely instructed as to this. An error here will prove disastrous in proportion to the interests at stake.

Many are the mistaken notions in reference to conversion. Indeed we might conclude, from the very fact of the vast importance of the subject, that the great enemy of our souls and of the Christ of God would seek, in every possible way, to plunge us into error respecting it. If he cannot succeed in keeping people in utter carelessness as to the subject of conversion, he will endeavour to blind their eyes as to its true nature. If, for example, a person has been roused, by some means or other, to a sense of the utter vanity and unsatisfactoriness of worldly amusements, and the urgent necessity of a change of life, the arch-deceiver will seek to persuade such an one to become religious, to busy himself with ordinances, rites and ceremonies, to give up balls and parties, theatres and concerts, drinking, gambling, hunting and horse-racing; in a word, to give up all sorts of gaiety and amusement, and engage in what is called a religious life, to be diligent in attending the public ordinances of religion, to read the Bible, say prayers, and give alms, to contribute to the support of the great religious and benevolent institutions of the country.

Now, this is not conversion. A person may do all this, and yet be wholly unconverted. A religious devotee whose whole life is spent in vigils, fastings, prayers, self-mortifications and alms deeds, may be as thoroughly unconverted, as far from the kingdom of God as the thoughtless pleasure hunter, whose whole life is spent in the pursuit of objects as worthless as the withered leaf or the faded flower. The two characters, no doubt, differ widely—as widely perhaps, as any two could differ. But they are both unconverted, both outside the blessed circle of God's salvation, both in their sins. True, the one is engaged in "wicked works," and the other in "dead works;" they are both out of Christ; they are unsaved; they are on the way to hopeless, endless misery. The one, just as surely as the other, if not savingly converted, will find his portion in the lake that burneth with fire and brimstone.

Again, conversion is not a turning from one religious system to another. A man may turn from Judaism, Paganism, Mahometanism, or Popery, to Protestantism, and yet be wholly unconverted. No doubt, looked at from a social, moral, or intellectual standpoint, it is much better to be a Protestant than a Mahometan; but as regards our present thesis, they are both on one common platform, both unconverted. Of one, just as truly as the other, it can be said, unless he is converted, he cannot enter the Kingdom of God. Conversion is not joining a religious system, be that system ever so pure, ever so sound, ever so orthodox. A man may be a member of the most respectable religious body in Christendom, and yet be an unconverted, unsaved man, on his way to eternal perdition.

So also as to the theological creeds. A man may subscribe to any of the great standards of religious belief, the Thirty-nine Articles, the Westminister Confession, John Wesley's sermons, Fox and Barclay, or any other creed, and yet be wholly unconverted, dead in trespasses and sins, and on his way to that place where a single ray of hope can never break in upon the awful gloom of eternity.

Of what use, we may lawfully inquire, is a religious system or a theological creed to a man who has not a single spark of divine life? Systems and creeds cannot quicken, cannot save, cannot give eternal life. A man may work on in religious machinery like a horse in a mill, going round and round, from one year's end to another, leaving off just where he began, in a dreary monotony of dead works. What is it all worth? what does it all come to? where does it all end? *Death!* Yes; and what then? Ah! that is the question. Would to God the weight and seriousness of this question were more fully realized!

But further, Christianity itself, in all its full-orbed light, may be embraced as a sytem of religious belief. A person may be intellectually delighted—almost entranced with the glorious doctrines of grace, a full, free gospel, salvation without works, justification by faith; in short, all that goes to make up our glorious New Testament Christianity. A person may profess to believe and delight in this; he may even become a powerful writer in defence of Christian doctrine, an earnest eloquent preacher of the gospel. All this may be true, and yet the man be wholly unconverted, dead in trespasses and sins, hardened, deceived and destroyed by his very familiarity with the precious truths of the gospel—truths that have never gone beyond the region of his understanding—never reached his conscience never touched his heart, never converted his soul.

This is about the most appalling case of all. Nothing can be more awful, more terrible, than the case of a man professing to believe and delight in, yea, actually preaching the gospel of God, and teaching all the grand characteristic truths of Christianity, and yet wholly unconverted, unsaved, and on his way to an eternity of ineffable misery—misery which must needs be intensified to the very highest degree, by the remembrance of the fact that he once professed to believe, and actually undertook to preach the most glorious tidings that ever fell on mortal ears.

O! reader, whoever thou art, do, we entreat of thee, give thy fixed attention to these things. Rest not, for one hour, until thou art assured of thy genuine, unmistakable conversion to God.

Part 3

Having thus far seen the absolute necessity, in every case, of conversion, and having, in some measure, sought to point out what conversion is *not*, we have now to inquire what it *is*. And here we must keep close to the veritable teaching of holy Scripture. We can accept nothing less, nothing different.

It is greatly to be feared that very much of what passes, now-a-days, for conversion is not conversion at all. Many so-called cases of conversion are published and talked of, which cannot stand the test of the Word of God. Many profess to be converted, and are accredited as such, who prove to be merely stony-ground hearers. There is no depth of spiritual work in the heart, no real action of the truth of God on the conscience, no thorough breaking with the world. It may be the feelings are wrought upon by human influence, and certain evangelical sentiments take possession of the mind; but *self* is not judged; there is a clinging to earth and nature; a lack of that deep-toned earnestness and genuine reality which so remarkably characterize the conversions recorded in the New Testament, and for which we may always look where the work of conversion is divine.

We do not here attempt to account for all these superficial cases; we merely refer to them in order that all who are engaged in the blessed work of evangelization may be led to consider the matter in the light of holy Scripture, and to see how far their own mode of working may call for holy correction. It may be there is too much of the merely human element in our work. We do not leave the Spirit of God to act. We are deficient in faith, in the power and efficacy of the simple work of Christ itself. There may be too much effort to work on the feelings, too much of the emotional and the sensational. Perhaps, too, in our desire to reach results—a desire which may be right enough in itself—we are too ready to accredit and announce, as cases of conversion, many which, alas! are merely ephemeral.

Will this lessen our earnestness? The very reverse; it will intensify our earnestness immensely. We shall be more earnest in pleading with God in secret, and in pleading with our fellows in public.

We shall feel more deeply the divine seriousness of the work, and our own utter insufficiency. We shall ever cherish the wholesome conviction that the work must be of God from first to last. This will keep us in our right place, that of self-emptied dependence upon God, who is the Doer of all the works that are done upon the earth. We shall be more on our faces before the mercy-seat, both in the closet and in the assembly, in reference to the glorious work of conversion; and then, when the golden sheaves and mellow clusters appear, when genuine cases of conversion turn up—cases which speak for themselves, and carry their own credentials with them to all who are capable of judging—then verily shall our hearts be filled with praise to the God of all grace who has magnified the name of His Son Jesus Christ in the salvation of precious souls.

How much better is this than to have our poor hearts puffed up with pride and self-complacency by reckoning up our cases of conversion! How much better, safer and happier to be bowed in worship before the throne, than to have our names heralded to the ends of the earth as great preachers and wonderful evangelists! No comparison, in the judgment of a truly spiritual person. The dignity, reality, and seriousness of the work will be realized; the happiness, the moral security, and the real usefulness of the workman will be promoted; and the glory of God secured and maintained.

Let us see how all this is illustrated in 1 Thessalonians 1. "Paul, and Silvanus, and Timotheus, unto the assembly of the Thessalonians in God the Father, and the Lord Jesus Christ: grace be unto you, and peace from God our Father, and the Lord Jesus Christ. We give thanks to God always for you all, making mention of you in our prayers: remembering without ceasing your work of *faith* and labor of *love*, and patience of *hope*"—the grand elements of true Christianity—"in our Lord Jesus Christ, in the sight of God and our Father; knowing, brethren, beloved of God, your election." How did he know it? By the clear and unquestionable evidence afforded in their practical life—the

only way in which the election of any one can be known. "For our gospel came not unto you in word only, but also *in power,* and in the Holy Ghost, and in much assurance; *as ye know what manner of men we were among you for your sake.*"

The blessed apostle was, in his daily life, the exponent of the gospel which he preached. He *lived* the gospel. He did not demand or exact aught of them. He was not burdensome to them. He preached unto them the precious gospel of God freely; and in order that he might do so, he wrought with labor and travail, night and day. He was as a loving, tender nurse, going in and out among them. There were with him no high-sounding words about himself, or his office, or his authority, or his gifts, or his preaching, or his wonderful doings in other places. He was the loving, lowly, unpretending, earnest, devoted workman, whose work spoke for itself, and whose whole life, his spirit, style, deportment, and habits, were in lovely harmony with his preaching.

How needful for all workmen to ponder these things! We may depend upon it that very much of the shallowness of our work is the fruit of the shallowness of the workman. Where is the power? Where is the demonstration of the Spirit? Where is the "much assurance"? Is there not a terrible lack of these things in our preaching? There may be a vast amount of fluent talking; a great deal of so-called cleverness; and much that may tickle the ear, act on the imagination, awaken a temporary interest, and minister to mere curiosity. But oh! where is the holy unction, the living earnestness, the profound seriousness? And then the living exponent in the daily life and habits—where is this? May the Lord revive His work in the hearts of His workmen, and then we may look for more of the results of the work.

Do we mean to teach that the work of conversion depends upon the workman? Far away be the monstrous notion! The work depends wholly and absolutely on the power of the Holy Ghost, as the very chapter now lying open before us proves beyond all question. It must ever hold good, in every department and every stage of the work, that it is "not by might nor by power; but by My Spirit, saith the Lord."

But what kind of instrument does the Spirit ordinarily use? Is not this a weighty question for us workmen? What sort of vessels are "meet for the Master's use"? Empty vessels—clean vessels. Are we such? Are we emptied of ourselves? Are we cured of our deplorable self-occupation? Are we "clean"? Have we clean hands? Are our associations, our ways, our circumstances, clean? If not, how can the Master use us in His holy service? May we all have grace to weigh these questions in the divine presence! May the Lord stir us all up, and make us more and more vessels such as He can use for His glory!

We shall now proceed with our quotation. The whole passage is full of power. The character of the workman on the one hand, and of the work on the other, demands our most serious attention.

"And ye became followers of us, and of the Lord, having received the word in much affliction, with joy of the Holy Ghost: so that ye were ensamples [or models] to all that believe in Macedonia and Achaia. For from you sounded out the word of the Lord, not only in Macedonia and Achaia, but also in every place of faith to Godward is spread abroad; so that we need not to speak anything, for they themselves show of us what manner of entering in we had unto you."

This was real work. It carried its own credentials with it. There was nothing vague or unsatisfactory about it—no occasion for any reserve in forming or expressing a judgment respecting it. It was clear, distinct, and unmistakable. It bore the stamp of the Master's hand, and carried conviction to every mind capable of weighing the evidence. The work of conversion was wrought, and the fruits of conversion followed in delightful profusion. The testimony went forth far and wide, so that the workman had no need to speak about his work. There was no occasion for him to reckon up and publish the number of conversions at Thessalonica. All was divinely real. It was a thorough work of God's Spirit as to which there could be no possible mistake, and about which it was superfluous to speak.

The apostle had simply preached the Word in the power of the Holy Ghost, in much assurance. There was nothing vague, nothing doubtful about his testimony. He preached as one who fully believed and thoroughly entered into what he was preaching about. It was not the mere fluent utterance of certain known and acknowledged truths—not the cut and dry statement of certain barren dogmas. No; it was the living outpouring of the glorious gospel of God, coming from a heart that felt profoundly every utterance, and falling upon hearts prepared by God's Spirit for its reception.

Such was the work at Thessalonica—a blessed divine work—all real, the genuine fruit of God's Spirit. It was no mere religious excitement, nothing sensational, no high pressure, no attempt to "get up a revival." All was beautifully calm. The workman, as we are told in Acts 17, "came to Thessalonica, where was a synagogue of the Jews; and as his manner was, he went in unto them, and three sabbath days reasoned with them out of the Scriptures"—Precious, powerful reasoning! would to God we had more of it in our midst!—"opening and alleging that Christ must needs have suffered, and risen again from the dead, and that this Jesus, whom I preach unto you, is Christ."

How simple! Preaching Jesus out of the Scriptures! Yes, here lay the grand secret of Paul's preaching. He preached a living Person, in living power, on the authority of a living Word, and this preaching was received in living faith, and brought forth living fruit, in the lives of the converts. This is the preaching that God has ordained and uses. It is not sermonizing, not religious talk, but the preaching of Christ by the Holy Ghost speaking through men who are themselves under the power of what they are preaching. God grant us more of this!

Part 4

The last two verses of our chapter (1 Thess. 1) demand our very special attention. They furnish a remarkable statement of the real nature of conversion. They show, very distinctly, the depth, clearness, fulness, and reality of the work of God's Spirit in those Thessalonian converts. There was no mistaking it. It carried its own credentials with it. It was no uncertain work. It did not call for any careful examination ere it could be accredited. It was a manifest, unmistakable work of God, the fruits of which were apparent to all. "They themselves shew of us what manner of entering in we had unto you, and how *ye turned to God from idols*, to serve the living and true God; and to wait for His Son from heaven, whom He raised from the dead, Jesus, who delivered us from the wrath to come" (vers. 9-10).

Here, then, we have a divine definition of conversion—brief, but comprehensive. It is a turning *from*, and a turning *to*. They turned from idols. There was a complete break with the past, a turning of the back, once and forever, on their former life and habits; a thorough surrender of all those objects that had ruled their hearts and commanded their energies.

Those dear Thessalonians were led to judge, in the light of divine truth, their whole previous course, and not only to judge it, but to abandon it unreservedly. It was no half-and-half work. There was nothing vague or equivocal about it. It was a marked epoch in their history—a grand turning-point in their moral and practical career. It was not a mere change of opinion, or the reception of a new set of principles, a certain alteration in their intellectual views. It was far more than any or all of these things. It was the solemn discovery that their whole past career had been one great, dark, monstrous lie. It was the real heart conviction of this. Divine light had broken in upon their souls, and in the power of that light they judged themselves and the entire of their previous history. There was an out-and-out surrender of that world which had hitherto ruled their hearts' affections; not a shred of it was to be spared.

And what, we may ask, produced this marvelous change? Simply the Word of God brought home to their souls in the mighty power of the Holy Ghost. We have referred to the inspired account of the apostle's visit to Thessalonica. We are told that "he reasoned with them out of the Scriptures." He sought to bring their souls into direct contact with the living and eternal Word of God. There was no effort to act on their feelings and imagination. All this the blessed workman judged to be utterly valueless. He had no confidence whatever in it. His confidence was in the Word and Spirit of God. He assured the Thessalonians of this very thing in the most touching manner, in chap. 2 of his Epistle. "For this cause," he says, "thank we God without ceasing, because, when ye received the word of God which ye heard of us, ye received it *not as the word of men*, but, as it is in truth, *the word of God*, which effectually worketh also in you that believe."

This is what we may call a vital and cardinal point. The Word of God, and that alone, in the mighty hand of the Holy Ghost, produced these grand results in the case of the Thessalonians, which filled the heart of the beloved apostle with unfeigned thanksgiving to God. He rejoiced that they were not linked on to him, but to the living God Himself, by means of His Word. This is an imperishable link. It is as enduring as the Word which forms it. The word of man is as perishable as himself; but the Word of the Lord endureth forever. The apostle, as a true workman, understood and felt all this, and hence his holy jealousy, in all his ministry, lest the souls to whom he preached should, in any way, lean upon him instead of on the One whose messenger and minister he was.

Hear what he says to the Corinthians: "And I, brethren, when I came unto you, came not with excellency of speech or of wisdom, declaring unto you *the testimony of God*. For I determined not to know anything among you, saving Jesus Christ, and Him crucified. And I was with you in weakness, and in fear, and in much trembling. And my speech and my preaching was not with enticing words of man's wisdom, but *in demonstration of the Spirit* and of power; that your faith should not stand in the wisdom of men, but *in the power of God*" (1 Cor. 2:1-5).

Here we have true ministry—"the testimony of God," and "the demonstration of the Spirit"—the Word and the Holy Ghost. Nothing else is of any value. All mere human influence, human power, and the results produced by human wisdom or energy, are perfectly worthless—yea, positively mischievous. The workman is puffed up by the apparent results of his work paraded and talked of, and the poor souls that are acted upon by this false influence are deceived, and led into an utterly false position and false profession. In a word, the whole thing is disastrous in the extreme.

Not so when the Word of God, in its mighty moral power, and the energy of the Holy Ghost, are brought to bear on the heart and conscience. Then it is we see divine results, as in the case of the Thessalonians. Then indeed it is made apparent, beyond all question, who is the workman. It is not Paul, or Apollos, or Cephas, but God Himself, whose work accredits itself, and shall stand forever; all homage to His holy name! The apostle had no need to reckon up and publish the results of his work at Thessalonica, or rather God's work by his means. It spoke for itself. It was genuine. It bore, with unmistakable distinctness, the stamp of God upon it, and this was quite enough for Paul; and it is quite enough for every true-hearted, self-emptied workman. Paul preached the Word, and that Word was brought home, in the quickening energy of the Holy Ghost, to the hearts of the Thessalonians. It fell into good ground, took root, and brought forth fruit in abundance.

And let us mark the fruit. "*Ye turned from idols.*" Here we have, in one word, the whole life of every unconverted man, woman, or child on the face of the earth. It is all wrapped up and presented to our view in the one expression, "*idols.*" It is not by any means necessary to bow down to a stock or a stone in order to be an idolater. Whatever commands the heart is an idol; the yielding of the heart to that thing is idolatry, and the one who so yields it is an idolater. Such is the plain, solemn truth in this matter, however unpalatable it may be to the proud human heart. Take that one great, crying, universal sin of "covetousness." What does the inspired apostle call it? He calls it "idolatry." How

many hearts are commanded by money! How many worshipers bow down before the idol of gold! What is covetousness? Either a desire to get more, or the love of what we have. We have both forms in the New Testament. The Greek has a word to represent both. But whether it be the desire to grasp, or the desire to hoard, in either case it is idolatry.

And yet the two things may be very unlike in their outward development. The former, that is, the desire to get more, may often be found in connection with a readiness to spend; the latter, on the contrary, is generally linked with an intense spirit of hoarding. There, for example, is a man of great business capacity—a thorough commercial genius—in whose hand everything seems to prosper. He has a real zest for business, an unquenchable thirst for making money. His one object is to get more, to add thousand to thousand, to strengthen his commercial foundation, and enlarge his sphere. He lives, thrives, and revels in the atmosphere of commerce.

He started on his career with a few pence in his pocket, and he has risen to the proud position of a merchant prince. He is not a miser. He is as ready to scatter as to obtain. He fares sumptuously, entertains with a splendid hospitality, gives munificently to manifold public objects. He is looked up to and respected by all classes of society.

But he loves to get more. He is a covetous man—an idolater. True, he despises the poor miser who spends his nights over his money-bags, "holding strange communion with his gold"; delighting his heart and feasting his eyes with the very sight of the fascinating dust, refusing himself and his family the common necessaries of life; going about in rags and wretchedness, rather than spend a penny of the precious hoard; who loves money, not for what it can get or give, but simply for its own sake; who loves to accumulate, not that he may spend, but that he may hoard; whose one ruling desire is to die worth so much wretched dust—strange, contemptible desire!

Now these two are apparently very different, but they meet in one point; they stand on one common platform; they are both covetous, and they are both idolaters.* This may sound harsh and severe, but it is the truth of God, and we must bow down before its holy authority. True it is that nothing is apparently more difficult to bring home to the conscience than the sin of covetousness—that very sin which the Holy Ghost declares to be idolatry. Thousands might see it in the case of the poor degraded miser, who nevertheless would be shocked by its application to a merchant prince.

It is one thing to see it in others, and quite another to judge it in ourselves. The fact is, that nothing but the light of the Word of God shining in upon the soul, and penetrating every chamber of our moral being, can enable us to detect the hateful sin of coveteousness. The pursuit of gain—the desire to have more—the spirit of commerce—the ability to make money—the desire to get on—all this is so "highly esteemed amongst men," that very few, comparatively, are prepared to see that it is positively "an abomination in the sight of God." The natural heart is formed by the thoughts of men. It loves, adores and worships the objects that it finds in this world; and each heart has its own idol. One worships gold, another worships pleasure, another worships power. Every unconverted man is an idolater; and even converted men are not beyond the reach of idolatrous influences, as is evident from the warning note raised by the venerable apostle, "Little children, keep yourselves from idols" (1 John 5:21).

Reader, will you permit us to put a plain, pointed question to you, ere we proceed further? Are you converted? Do you profess to be so? Do you take the ground of being a Christian? If so, have you turned from idols? Have you really broken with the world, and with your former self? Has the living Word of God entered your heart, and led you to judge the whole of your past life, whether it has been a life of gayety and thoughtless folly, a life of busy money-making, a life of abominable vice and wickedness, or a life of mere religious routine—Christless, faithless, worthless religion?

Say, how is it? Be thoroughly in earnest. Be assured there is an urgent demand for out-and-out earnestness in this matter. We cannot hide from you the fact that we are painfully conscious of the sad lack of thorough decision amongst us. We have not, with sufficient emphasis or distinctness, "turned from idols." Old habits are retained; former lusts and objects rule the heart. The temper, style, spirit and deportment do not bespeak conversion. We are sadly too like our former selves—too like the openly and confessedly worldly people around us.

All this is really terrible. We fear it is a sad hindrance to the progress of the gospel and the salvation of souls. The testimony falls powerless on the ears of those to whom we speak, because we do not seem as though we ourselves really believe what we are talking about. The apostle could not say to us, as he said to his dear Thessalonian converts, "From you sounded out the word of the Lord . . . so that we need not to speak anything." There is a want of depth, power and markedness in our conversion. The change is not sufficiently apparent. Even where there is a work, there is a tameness, feebleness and vagueness about it truly deplorable and discouraging.

Part 5

We are now called to consider what we may term the positive side of the great subject of conversion. We have seen that it is a turning *from* idols—a turning from all those objects which ruled our hearts and engaged our affections—the vanities and follies, the lusts and pleasures which made up the whole of our existence in the days of our darkness and blindness. It is, as we read in Acts 26:18, a turning *from* darkness, and from the power of Satan; and, as we read in Gal. 1:4, a turning *from* this present evil world.

But conversion is much more than all this. It would, in one sense, be but a poor thing if it were merely a turning "*from* sin, the world, and Satan." No doubt it is a signal mercy to

* The two Greek words to which we have alluded in the text are, $\pi\lambda\varepsilon o\nu\varepsilon\xi\iota\alpha$ (pleonexia—the desire to get more), and $\varphi\iota\lambda\alpha\rho\gamma\upsilon\rho\iota\alpha$ (philarguria—the love of money). Now it is the former that occurs in Col. 3:5—"Covetousness, which is idolatry"; and there it stands in the terrible category with some of the very vilest sins that stain the pages of human history.

be delivered, once and forever, from all the wretchedness and moral degradation of our former life; from the terrible thraldom of the god and prince of this world; from all the hollowness and vanity of a world that lieth in the arms of the wicked one; and from the love and practice of sin—the vile affections which once held sway over us. We cannot be too thankful for all that is included in this side of the question.

But, we repeat, there is very much more than this. The heart may feel disposed to inquire, "What have we gotten in lieu of all we have given up? Is Christianity merely a system of negations? If we have broken with the world and self—if we have given up our former pleasures and amusements—if, in short, we have turned our back upon what goes to make up life in this world, what have we instead?"

1 Thessalonians 1:9 furnishes, in one word, the answer to all these inquiries—an answer full, clear, distinct, and comprehensive. Here it is—"Ye turned to *God*."

Precious answer! Yes, unspeakably precious to all who know aught of its meaning. What have I got instead of my former "idols"? God! Instead of this world's vain and sinful pleasures? God! Instead of its riches, honors, and distinctions? God! Oh, blessed, glorious, perfect Substitute! What had the prodigal instead of the rags of the far country? The best robe in the father's house! Instead of the swine's husks? The fatted calf of the father's providing! Instead of the degrading servitude of the far country? The father's welcome, his bosom, and his table!

Is not this a blessed exchange? Have we not, in the familiar, but ever charming history of the prodigal a most touching and impressive illustration of true conversion in both its sides? May we not well exclaim, as we gaze on the inimitable picture, "What a conversion! What a turning from and turning to!" Who can utter it? What human tongue can adequately set forth the feelings of the returned wanderer when pressed to the father's bosom and bathed in the light and love of the father's house? The rags, the husks, the swine, the slavery, the cold selfishness, the destitution, the famine, the misery, the moral degradation—all gone, and gone forever; and instead thereof the ineffable delight of that bright and happy home, and, above all, the exquisite feeling that all that festive joy which surrounded him was wakened up by the very fact of his return—that it made the father glad to get him back!

But we shall, perhaps, be told that this is but a figure. Yes; but a figure of what? Of a precious, a divine reality; a figure of what takes place in every instance of true conversion, if only it be looked at from a heavenly standpoint. It is not a mere surrender of the world, with its thousand and one vanities and follies. It is this, no doubt; but it is very much more. It is being brought to God, *brought home*, brought to the Father's bosom, brought into the family; made—not in the language of a barren formulary, but in the power of the Spirit, and by the mighty action of the Word—a child of God, a member of Christ, and an heir of the kingdom.

This, and nothing less, is conversion. Let the reader see that he thoroughly understands it. Let him not be satisfied with anything short of this grand reality—this turning from darkness to light, from the power of Satan, and from the worship of idols, to God. The Christian is, in one sense, as really brought to God now as if he were actually in Heaven. This may seem strong, but it is blessedly true. Hear what the apostle Peter says as to this point: "Christ hath once suffered for sins, the Just for the unjust, to bring us to"—what? Heaven when we die? Nay; but "to bring us to God" *now*. So, also, in Rom. 5 we read, "For if, when we were enemies, we were reconciled to God by the death of His Son, much more, being reconciled, we shall be saved by His life! And not only so, but we also *joy in God*, through our Lord Jesus Christ, by whom we have now received the reconciliation."

This is an immense principle. It is not within the compass of human language to set forth all that is involved in being "turned," or "brought to God." Our adorable Lord Jesus Christ brings all who believe in His name into God's presence, in all His own perfect acceptability. They come in all the credit, and virtue, and value of the blood of Jesus, and in all the fragrance of His most excellent name. He brings us into the very same position with Himself. He links us with Himself, and shares with us all He has, and all He is, save His Deity, which is incommunicable. We are perfectly identified with Him.

"Yet a little while, and the world seeth Me no more; but ye see Me; *because I live, ye shall live* also." Again, "Peace I leave with you, *My peace I give unto you;* not as the world giveth, give I unto you. Let not your heart be troubled, neither let it be afraid." "These things have I spoken unto you, that *My joy might remain in you,* and that your joy might be full." "Henceforth I call you not servants, for the servant knoweth not what his lord doeth; but I have called you friends, for *all things that I have heard of My Father I have made known unto you."*

So, also, in that marvelous prayer in John 17, we read, "I have given unto them the words which Thou gavest Me; and they have received them, and have known surely that I came out from Thee, and they have believed that Thou didst send Me. I pray for them; I pray not for the world, but for them which Thou hast given Me; for they are Thine. And all Mine are Thine, and Thine are Mine, and I am glorified in them." "I have given them Thy word; and the world hath hated them, because *they are not of the world, even as I am not of the world." "As Thou hast sent Me into the world, even so have I also sent them into the world."*

"And the glory which Thou gavest Me I have given them; that they may be one, even as We are one: I in them, and Thou in Me, that they may be made perfect in one; and that the world may know that Thou hast sent Me, *and hast loved them as Thou hast loved Me.* Father, *I will that they also whom Thou hast given Me be with Me where I am;* that they may behold My glory which Thou hast given Me; for thou lovedst Me before the foundation of the world. O righteous Father, the world hath not known Thee, but I have known Thee, and these have known that Thou hast sent Me. And I have declared unto them Thy name, and will declare it; that *the love*

wherewith Thou hast loved Me may be in them, and I in them."

Now it is utterly impossible to conceive anything higher or more blessed than this. To be so thoroughly identified with the Son of God, to be so wholly one with Him as to share in the very same love wherewith He is loved by the Father, to partake of His peace, His joy, His glory—all this involves the very highest possible measure and character of blessing with which any creature could be endowed. To be saved from the everlasting horrors of the pit of hell; to be pardoned, washed, and justified; to be reinstated in all that Adam lost; to be let into Heaven on any ground or in any character whatsoever, would be marvelous mercy, goodness, and loving-kindness; but to be brought to God in all the love and favor of His own beloved Son, to be intimately associated with Him in all His position before God—His acceptability now—His glory by and by—this, truly, is something which only the heart of God could think of, and only His mighty power accomplish.

Well, all this is involved in the conversion whereof we speak. Such is the magnificent grace of God, such the love wherewith He loved us, even when we were dead in trespasses and sins, enemies in our minds by wicked works, serving divers lusts and pleasures, worshiping idols, the blind, degraded slaves of sin and Satan, children of wrath, and going straight to hell.

And the best of it all is, that it both glorifies the name and gratifies the heart of God to bring us into this place of inconceivable blessedness, love, and glory. It would not satisfy the love of His heart to give us any lower place than that of His own Son. Well might the inspired apostle exclaim, in view of all this stupendous grace, "Blessed be the God and Father of our Lord Jesus Christ, who hath blessed us with all spiritual blessings in heavenly places in Christ; according as He hath chosen us in Him before the foundation of the world, that we should be holy and without blame before Him in love; having predestinated us unto the adoption of children by Jesus Christ to Himself, according to the good pleasure of

His will, *to the praise of the glory of His grace, wherein He hath made us accepted in the Beloved,* in whom we have redemption through His blood, the forgiveness of sins, according to the riches of His grace" (Eph. 1).

What depth of love, what fulness of blessing, have we here! It is the purpose of God to glorify Himself, throughout the countless ages of eternity, in His dealings with us. He will display, in view of all created intelligences, the riches of His grace, in His kindness toward us, by Christ Jesus. Our forgiveness, our justification, our perfect deliverance, our acceptance—all the blessings bestowed upon us in Christ—are for the display of the divine glory throughout the vast universe forever. It would not meet the claims of God's glory, or answer the affections of His heart, to have us in any other position but that of His own well-beloved and only begotten Son.

All this is marvelous. It seems too good to be true. But it is worthy of God, and it is His good pleasure so to act toward us. This is enough for us. It may be, and most assuredly is, too good for us to get, but it is not too good for God to give. He acts toward us according to the love of His heart, and on the ground of the worthiness of Christ. The prodigal might ask to be made as one of the hired servants, but this could not be. It would not be according to the Father's heart to have him in the house as a servant. It must be as a son or not at all. If it were a question of desert, we do not deserve the place of a servant any more than that of a son. But, blessed be God, it is not according to our deserts at all, but according to the boundless love of His heart, and to the glory of His holy name.

This, then, is conversion. Thus we are *brought to God.* Nothing short of this. We are not merely turned from our idols, whatever they were, but we are actually brought into the very presence of God, to find our delight in Him, to joy in Him, to walk with Him, to find all our springs in Him, to draw upon His exhaustless resources, to find in Him a perfect answer to all our necessities, so that our souls are satisifed, and that forever.

Do we want to go back to the idols? Never! Have we any hankering after our former objects? Not if our hearts are realizing our place and portion in Christ. Had the prodigal any longings after the husks and the swine when folded in the father's bosom, clothed in the father's house, and seated at the father's table? We do not, and cannot, believe it. We cannot imagine his heaving a single sigh after the far country when once he found himself within the hallowed circle of that bright and blissful home of love.

We speak according to the divine standard. Alas! many profess to be converted, and seem to go on for a season; but ere long they begin to grow cold, and get weary and dissatisfied. The work was not real. They were not really brought to God. Idols may have been given up for a time, but God Himself was never reached. They never found in Him a satisfying portion for their hearts—never knew the real meaning of communion with Him—never tasted heart-satisfaction, heart-rest, in Christ. Hence, in process of time, the poor heart began to long once more for the world, and back they went, and plunged into its follies and vanities with greater avidity than ever.

Such cases are very sad, very disappointing. They bring great reproach on the cause of Christ, and are used as a plea for the enemy, and as a stumbling-block for anxious inquirers. But they leave the question of divine conversion just where it was. The soul that is truly converted is one who has not merely been turned from this present evil world, and all its promises and pretensions, but who has been led by the precious ministry of the Holy Ghost to find in the living God, and in His Son Jesus Christ, all he can possibly want for time and eternity. Such an one has divinely done with the world. He has broken with it forever. He has had his eyes opened to see, through and through, the whole thing. He has judged it in the light of the presence of God. He has measured it by the standard of the the cross of Christ. He has weighed it in the balances of the sanctuary, and turned his back upon it forever, to find an absorbing and a commanding object in the Person of that blessed One who was nailed to the accursed tree, in order to deliver him, not only from everlasting burnings, but also from this present evil world.

Part 6

The more we dwell on 1 Thess. 1:9, the more we are struck with its marvelous depth, fulness, and power. It seems like sinking a shaft into an inexhaustible mine. We have dwelt a little on that very fruitful and suggestive clause, "*Turned to God from idols.*" How much is wrapped up in it! Do we really understand the force and fulness of it? It is a wonderful thing for the soul to be brought to God—to know Him now as our resource in all our weakness and need—the spring of all our joys—our strength and shield—our Guide and Counsellor—our all in all—to be absolutely and completely shut up to Him, wholly dependent upon Him.

Do you know the deep blessedness of all this in your own soul? If you are a child of God, a truly converted soul, then it is your happy privilege to know it, and you ought not to be satisfied without it. If we are "turned to God," what is it for but to find in Him all we can possibly want for time and eternity? Nothing can ever satisfy the human soul but God Himself. It is not within the compass of earth to meet the cravings of the heart. If we had the wealth of the universe, and all that wealth could procure, the heart would still want more; there would still be an aching void which nothing under the sun could fill.

Look at the history of Solomon. Hear him recording his own experience. "I, the preacher, was king over Israel in Jerusalem; and I gave my heart to seek and search out by wisdom concerning all things that are done under heaven; this sore travail hath God given to the sons of men to be exercised therewith. I have seen all the works that are done under the sun, and, behold, all is vanity and vexation of spirit. That which is crooked cannot be made straight, and that which is wanting cannot be numbered. I communed with mine own heart, saying, Lo, I am come to great estate, and have gotten more widom than all they that have been before me in Jerusalem; yea, my heart had great experience of wisdom and knowledge. And I gave my heart to know wisdom, and to know madness and folly. I perceived that this also is vexation of spirit.

"For in much wisdom is much grief, and he that increaseth knowledge increaseth sorrow. I said in my heart, Go to, now, I will prove thee with mirth; therefore enjoy pleasure; and behold, this also is vanity. I said of laughter, it is mad, and of mirth, what doeth it? I sought in my heart to give myself to wine, yet acquainting ny heart with wisdom, and to lay hold on folly, till I might see what was that good for the sons of men, which they should do under the heaven all the days of their life. I made me great works; I builded me houses; I planted me vineyards; I made me gardens and orchards, and I planted trees in them of all kind of fruits; I made me pools of water, to water there with the wood that bringeth forth trees. I got me servants and maidens, and had servants born in my house; also, I had great possessions of great and small cattle, above all that were in Jerusalem before me. I gathered me also silver and gold, and the peculiar treasure of kings and of the provinces; I gat me men singers and women singers, and the delights of the sons of men, as musical instruments, and that of all sorts. So I was great, and increased more than all that were before me in Jerusalem; also, my wisdom remained with me. And whatsoever mine eyes desired I kept not from them; I withheld not my heart from any joy; for my heart rejoiced in all my labor; and this was my portion of all my labor. Then I looked on all the works that my hands had wrought, and on the labor that I had labored to do; and behold, *all was vanity and vexation of spirit, and there was no profit under the sun*" (Eccles. 1—2).

Such is the withering commentary upon all earth's resources as given by the pen of one who had all that earth could give—of one who was allowed to drain to the very dregs every cup of human and earthly pleasure. And what was it all? "Vanity and vexation of spirit." "All things are full of labor; man cannot utter it; the eye is not satisfied with seeing, nor the ear filled with hearing." The poor human heart can never be satisfied with the resources of earth. Creature streams can never quench the thirst of the immortal soul. Material things cannot possibly make us truly happy, even if they were permanent. "All is vanity and vexation of spirit."

The truth of this must be proved by every human heart. Sooner or later all must find it out. Men may turn a deaf ear to it now; they may refuse to listen to the Spirit's warning voice; they may vainly imagine that this poor world can yield them substantial comfort and happiness; they may eagerly grasp at its riches, its honors, its distinctions, its pleasures, its material comforts; but they will find out their mistake. And oh, how dreadful to find it out *too late!* How terrible to open one's eyes in hell, like the rich man in the parable! What human language can set forth the horrors of a soul shut out forever from the presence of God, and consigned to outer darkness, to the place of weeping, and wailing, and gnashing of teeth? It is overwhelming to think of it. What will it be to realize it? What will it be to find oneself in the tormenting flames of hell, at the other side of that impassable gulf where a single ray of hope can never break through the deep gloom of eternity?

Oh that men would think of all this in time! that they might flee from the wrath to come, and lay hold on the blessed hope set before them in the gospel; that they might "turn to God." But alas! the god of this world blinds their minds, lest the light of the gospel of the glory of Christ, who is the image of God, should shine into them. He engrosses them with present things—business, money-making, pleasures, cares, lusts, anything and everything but the one thing, in comparison with which all earthly things are but as the small dust of the balance.

But we have digressed from our special theme, to which we must return.

We are particularly anxious to press upon the Christian reader the immense importance of seeking to find all his resources in the living God. We have only for a moment turned aside from this point, in order to sound a warning note in the ear of any unconverted, careless one who may happen to take up this paper. We earnestly entreat the latter to turn to God. We entreat the former to seek a deeper acquaintance with the One to whom, by grace, he has turned. We have the two things before us in penning these papers on the great subject of "conversion." We can truly say, we long to see precious souls converted to God, and we long to see converted souls happy in God.

We are increasingly convinced of the practical importance of Christians proving in their daily life that they have found thorough rest of heart in God. It has immense weight with worldly people. It is a grand point gained when we are able, through grace, to tell the world that we are independent of it; and the only way to do this is to live in the abiding sense of what we have in God. This would impart a moral elevation to our entire course and character. It would deliver us completely from that strong tendency to lean on human props and to betake ourselves to creature streams which we have all more or less to lament, and which assuredly issue in disappointment to us and dishonor to God.

How prone we are on all occasions to look to our fellow-men for sympathy, succor and counsel instead of looking directly and exclusively to God! This is a serious mistake. It is in principle to forsake the Fountain of living waters, and hew out for ourselves broken cisterns which can hold no water. What can we expect? What must be the issue? Barrenness and desolation. Our God, in very faithfulness to us, will cause our fellow-man to fail us, in order that we may learn the folly of leaning upon an arm of flesh.

Hear what the prophet says on this great practical question: "Thus saith the Lord, Cursed be the man that trusteth in man, and maketh flesh his arm, and whose heart departeth from the Lord. For he shall be like the heath in the desert, and shall not see when good cometh, but shall inhabit the parched places in the wilderness, in a salt land, and not inhabited."

But mark the contrast. "Blessed is the man that trusteth in the Lord, and whose hope the Lord is. For he shall be as a tree planted by the waters, and that spreadeth out her roots by the river, and shall not see when heat cometh, but her leaf shall be green, and shall not be careful in the year of drought, neither shall cease from yielding fruit" (Jer. 17).

It is a grand reality to lean on the arm of the living God—to find in Him our relief and our resource at all times, in all places, and under all circumstances. He never fails a trusting heart. He will never disappoint us. He may see fit to keep us waiting for an answer to our call, but the time we spend in waiting is well spent, and when the answer comes our hearts are filled with praise, and we are able to say, "Oh, how great is Thy goodness, which Thou hast laid up for them that fear Thee, which Thou hast wrought for them that trust in Thee before the sons of men" (Psa. 31:19).

It is a great thing to be able to trust God before the sons of men, to confess His sufficiency for our every exigence. But it must be a reality, and not mere profession. It is no use to talk of leaning on God while at the same time we are, in one way or another, looking to some poor mortal to help us. This is a sad delusion. But, alas! how often we fall under its power! We adopt the language of dependence upon God, but in reality we are looking to man, and letting him know our wants. We deceive ourselves and dishonor God and the end is disappointment and confusion of face.

Let us look closely and honestly at this matter. Let us see to it that we understand the meaning of those precious words, "Turned to God." They contain the very essence of true happiness and true holiness. When the heart is really turned to God it has found the true, the divine secret of peace, rest and full satisfaction; it finds its all in God, and has no occasion whatever to turn to the creature. Am I in any perplexity? I can look to God for guidance. He has promised to guide me with His eye. What perfect guidance! Can man do better for me? Surely not. God sees the end from the beginning. He knows all the bearings, all the belongings, all the roots and issues of my case. He is an infallible guide. His wisdom is unerring, and, moreover, He loves me perfectly. Where could I find a better guide?

Am I in want? I can go to God about it. He is the Possessor of Heaven and earth. The treasures of the universe are at His disposal. He can help me if He sees it to be good for me; and if not, the pressure will be much better for me than the relief. "My God shall supply all your need, according to His riches

in glory, by Christ Jesus." Is not this enough? Why look to a creature stream? Why turn from such a God and go with our wants to a human being? It is in reality giving up, so far, the ground of faith, the life of simple dependence on God. It is actually dishonoring our Father.

If I apply to my fellow for help, it is tantamount to saying that God has failed me. It is really betraying my loving Father who has taken me up, body, soul, and spirit, to do for me for time and eternity. He has pledged Himself to provide for all my wants, be they ever so many, ever so great, ever so varied. "He that spared not His own Son, but delivered Him up for us all, how shall He not, with Him, also *freely* give us *all things?*" His Word is, "Call upon Me in the day of trouble; I will deliver thee, and thou shalt glorify Me."

True, God uses the creature to meet our need; but this is a totally different matter. The blessed apostle could say, "God who comforteth those that are cast down, comforted us by the coming of Titus." Paul was looking to God for comfort, and God sent Titus to comfort him. Had Paul been looking to Titus, he would have been disappointed.

Thus it is in every case. Our immediate and exclusive reference must be to God in all our need. "We have turned *to God* from idols," and hence in every exigence He is our sure resource. We can go to Him for counsel, for succor, for guidance, for sympathy, for all. "My soul, wait thou *only* upon God, for my expectation is from Him. He *only* is my rock and my salvation; He is my defence; I shall not be moved."

Will this most blessed habit of looking only to God lead us to undervalue the channels through which His precious grace flows to us? The very reverse. How could I undervalue one who comes to me directly from God, as His manifest instrument, to meet my need? Impossible. But I value him as a channel, instead of applying to him as a source. This makes all the difference. We must never forget that true conversion means our being brought to God; and most surely, if we are brought to God, it is in order that we should find in Him a perfect covering for our eyes, a perfect object for the heart, a perfect resource in all our exigencies, from first to last. A truly converted soul is one who is turned from all creature confidences, human hopes, and earthly expectations, to find all he wants in the living and true God, and that forever.

Part 7

We are now called to consider a deeply practical point in our subject. It is contained in the clause, "*To serve the living and true God.*" This is full of interest to every truly converted soul, every true Christian. We are called "to serve." Our whole life, from the moment of our conversion to the close of our earthly career, should be characterized by a spirit of true, earnest, intelligent service. This is our high privilege, not to say our hallowed duty. It matters not what our sphere of action may be, what our line of life, or what our calling; when we are converted, we have just got one thing to do, namely, to serve God. If there be anything in our calling which is contrary to the revealed will of God—contrary to the direct teaching of His Word—then we must at once abandon it, cost what it may. The very first step of an obedient servant is to step out of a false position, be it what it may.

We are called to serve God, and everything must be tried by this standard. The Christian has to ask himself this one question, "Can I fulfil the duties of this situation to the glory of God?" If not, he must abandon it. If we cannot connect the name of God with our calling in life, then, assuredly, if we want to walk with God, if we aim at serving Him, if it be our one desire to be found well-pleasing in His sight, then we must give up that calling and look to Him to open some path for us in which we can walk to His praise.

This He will do, blessed be His name. He never fails a trusting soul. All we have to do is to cleave to Him with purpose of heart, and He will make the way plain before us. It may seem difficult at first. The path may appear narrow, rough, lonely; but our simple business is to stand for God, and not to continue for one hour in connection with

anything contrary to His revealed will. A tender conscience, a single eye, a devoted heart, will settle many a question, solve many a difficulty, remove many a barrier. Indeed, the very instincts of the divine nature, if only they be allowed to act, will guide in many a perplexity. "The light of the body is the eye; therefore, when thine eye is single, thy whole body also is full of light."

When the purpose of the heart is true to Christ, true to His name and cause, true to the service of God, the Holy Spirit opens up the precious treasures of divine revelation to the soul, and pours a flood of living light upon the understanding, so that we see the path of service as clear as a sunbeam before us, and we have only got to tread it with a firm step.

But we must never, for one moment, lose sight of the grand fact that we are converted to the service of God. The outcome of the life which we possess must ever take the form of service to the living and true God. In our unconverted days we worshiped idols, and served divers lusts and pleasures; now, on the contrary, we worship God in the Spirit, and we are called to serve Him with all our ransomed powers. We have turned to God, to find in Him our perfect rest and satisfaction. There is not a single thing in the entire range of a creature's necessities, for time and eternity, that we cannot find in our own most gracious God and Father. He has treasured up in Christ, the Son of His love, all that can satisfy the desires of the new life in us. It is our privilege to have Christ dwelling in our hearts by faith, and to be so rooted and grounded in love as to be able to comprehend with all saints what is the breadth and length and depth, and height, and to know the love of Christ, which passeth knowledge, that we may be filled with all the fulness of God.

Thus filled, satisifed, and strengthened, we are called to dedicate ourselves, spirit, soul, and body, to the service of Christ; to be steadfast, unmovable, always abounding in the work of the Lord. We should have nothing else to do in this world. Whatever cannot be done as service to Christ ought not to be done at all. This simplifies the matter amazingly. It is our sweet privilege to do everything in the name of the Lord Jesus, and to the glory of God. We sometimes hear people speak of "a secular calling," as contrasted with what is "sacred." We question the correctness of such a distinction. Paul made tents and planted churches, but in both he served the Lord Christ.

All that a Christian does ought to be sacred, because it is done as service to God. If this were borne in mind, it would enable us to connect the very simplest duties of daily life with the Lord Himself, and to bring Him into them in such a way as to impart a holy dignity and interest to all that we have to do, from morning till night. In this way, instead of finding the duties of our calling a hindrance to our communion with God, we should actually make them an occasion of waiting on Him for wisdom and grace to discharge them aright, so that His holy name might be glorified in the most minute details of practical life.

The fact is that the service of God is a much simpler matter than some of us imagine. It does not consist in doing some wonderful things beyond the bounds of our divinely appointed sphere of action. Take the case of a domestic servant. How can she serve the living and true God? She cannot go about visiting and talking. Her sphere of action lies in the shade and retirement of her master's house. Were she to run about from house to house, she would be actually neglecting her proper work, her divinely appointed business. Harken to the following sound and wholesome words: "Exhort servants to be obedient unto their own masters, and to please them well in all things; not answering again: not purloining, but showing all good fidelity; that they may adorn the doctrine of God our Saviour in all things" (Titus 2:9-10).

Here we see that the servant, by obedience, humility, and honesty can adorn the doctrine of God just as effectually, according to her measure, as an evangelist ranging the world over in the discharge of his high and holy commission.

Again, we read, "Servants, be obedient to them that are your masters according to the flesh, with fear and trembling, in singleness of your heart, as unto Christ; not with eye-service as men-pleasers, but as *the servants of Christ*, doing the will of God from the heart; with good-will doing *service*, as to the Lord, and not to men; knowing that whatsoever good thing any man doeth, the same shall he receive of the Lord, whether he be bond or free" (Eph. 6).

How lovely is all this! What a fine field of service is opened up for us here! How beautiful this "fear and trembling"! Where do we see it nowadays? Where is the holy subjection to authority? Where the singleness of eye? Where the willing-hearted service? Alas! we see headiness and high-mindedness, self-will, self-pleasing, and self-interest. How must all these things dishonor the Lord, and grieve His Holy Spirit! How needful that our souls should be roused to a sense of what becomes us as those who are called to serve the living and true God! Is it not a signal mercy to every true Christian to know that he can serve and glorify God in the most commonplace domestic duties? If it were not so, what would become of ninety-nine out of every hundred Christians?

We have taken up the case of an ordinary domestic servant in order to illustrate that special line of practical truth now under our consideration. Is it not most blessed for us to know that our God graciously condescends to connect His name and His glory with the very humblest duties that can devolve upon us in our ordinary domestic life? It is this which imparts dignity, interest and freshness to every little act, from morning till night. "Whatsoever ye do, do it *heartily*, as unto the Lord, and not unto men." Here lies the precious secret of the whole matter. It is not working for wages, but serving the Lord Christ, and looking to Him to receive the reward of the inheritance.

Oh that all this were more fully realized and illustrated amongst us! What moral elevation it would give to the entire Christian life! What a triumphant answer it would furnish to the infidel! What a withering rebuke to all his sneers and cavils! Better by far than ten thousand learned arguments. There is no argument so forcible as an earnest, devoted, holy, happy, self-sacrificing

Christian life, and this life can be displayed by one whose sphere of action is bounded by the four walls of a kitchen.*

And not only does the practical life of a true Christian afford the very best possible answer to the skeptic and the infidel, but it also meets in a most satisfactory manner the objections of those who talk about works, and insist upon putting Christians under the law, in order to teach them how to live. When people challenge us as to our not preaching up works, we simply ask them, "For what should we preach works?" The unconverted man cannot do any works, save "wicked works," or "dead works." "They that are in the flesh"—unconverted people—"cannot please God." Of what possible use can it be to preach works to such? It can only cast dust in their eyes, blind their minds, deceive their hearts, and send them down to hell with a lie in their right hand.

There must be a genuine conversion to God. This is a divine work from first to last. And what has the converted man got to do? He certainly has not to work for life, because he has it, even life eternal, as God's free gift, through Jesus Christ our Lord. He has not to work for salvation, because he is saved already—"saved in the Lord with an everlasting salvation." What, then, is he called to do? "To serve the living and true God." How? When? Where? In everything; at all times, and in all places. The converted man has nothing else to do but to serve God. If he does anything else, he is positively untrue, unfaithful to that blessed Lord and Master who, ere ever He called him to serve, endowed him with the life, and the grace, and the power, whereby alone the service can be rendered.

Yes, the Christian is called to serve. Let us never forget this. He is privileged to "present his body as a living sacrifice, holy and acceptable to God, which is his reasonable [his intelligent] service." This settles the whole

question. It removes all difficulties; it silences all objections; it puts everything in its right place. It is not a question of what I am doing, but how I do it—not where I am, but how I conduct myself. Christianity as displayed in the New Testament is the outcome of the life of Christ in the believer; it is Christ reproduced in the Christian's daily life, by the power of the Holy Ghost. Everything the Christian touches, everything he does, everything he says, his whole practical life, from Lord's day morning till Saturday night, should bear the impress and breathe the spirit of that great practical clause on which we have been dwelling—"serving the living and true God." May it be so more and more! May all the Lord's beloved people, everywhere, be really stirred up to seek more earnest, out-and-out, whole-hearted devotedness to Christ and His precious service!

Part 8

The last words of our chapter—1 Thess. 1—now claim our attention. They furnish a very striking and forcible proof of the clearness, fulness, depth and comprehensiveness of the apostle's testimony at Thessalonica, and also of the brightness and reality of the work in the young converts in that place. It was not only that they turned from idols to God, to serve the living and true God. This, through grace, they did; and that, too, with uncommon power, freshness, and fervor.

But there was something more; and we may assert, with all possible confidence, that there would have been a grand defect in the conversion and in the Christianity of those beloved disciples if that had been lacking. *They were converted "to wait for the Son of God from the heavens."*

Let the reader give to this very weighty fact his most devout attention. The bright

---

* It is remarkable that both in Eph. 6 and Col. 3 the address to servants is far more elaborate than to any of the other classes. In Titus 2 servants are specially singled out. There is no address to husbands, none to masters, none to children. We do not attempt to account for this, but we cannot help noticing it as a very interesting fact; and most assuredly it teaches us what a very important place is assigned in Christianity to one who, in those early days of the Church's history, occupied the place of a slave. The Holy Ghost took special pains to instruct such an one as to how he was to carry himself in his most trying sphere of work. The poor slave might think himself shut out from the service of God. So far from this, he is sweetly taught that by simply doing his duty as in the sight of God he could adorn the doctrine of God his Saviour, and bring glory to the name of Jesus. Nothing can exceed the grace that shines in this.

and blessed hope of the Lord's coming formed an integral part of the gospel which Paul preached, and of the Christianity of those who were converted by his ministry. That blessed servant preached a full gospel. He not only declared that the Son of God had come into the world to accomplish the great work of redemption, and lay the everlasting foundation of the divine glory and counsels, but that He had gone back to the heavens, and taken His seat as the victorious, exalted and glorified Man, at the right hand of the throne of God; and that He is coming again; first, to receive His people to Himself, and conduct them into the very innermost circle of His Father's house—the place prepared for them: and then to come forth *with* them, to execute judgment upon His enemies—gather out of His kingdom all that offend, and all that do iniquity, and set up His glorious dominion from sea to sea, and from the river to the ends of the earth.

All this was included in the precious gospel which Paul preached, and which the Thessalonian converts received. We find an indirect but very interesting intimation of this in a passage in Acts 17, where the inspired writer records what the infidel Jews thought and said about the apostle's preaching. "But the Jews which believed not, moved with envy, took unto them certain lewd fellows of the baser sort, and gathered a company, and set all the city on an uproar, and assaulted the house of Jason, and sought to bring them out to the people. And when they found them not, they drew Jason and certain brethren unto the rulers of the city, crying, *These that have turned the world upside down* are come hither also; whom Jason hath received; and these all do contrary to the decrees of Caesar, *saying that there is another king, Jesus."*

Such were the ideas which these poor, ignorant, prejudiced unbelievers gathered from the preaching of the Lord's beloved servants; and we can see in them the elements of great and solemn truths—the complete upturning of the present system of things, and the establishment of the everlasting kingdom of our Lord and Saviour Jesus Christ. "I will overturn, overturn, overturn it; and it shall be no more, until He come whose right it is; and I will give it Him" (Ezek. 21:27).

But not only did the Lord's coming and kingdom occupy a prominent place in the *preaching* of the apostle, it also shines brilliantly forth in all his *teaching*. Not only were the Thessalonians converted to this blessed hope, they were built up, established, and led on in it. They were taught to live in the brightness of it every hour of the day. It was not a dry, barren dogma, to be received and held as part of a powerless, worthless creed; it was a living reality, a mighty moral power in the soul—a precious, purifying, sanctifying, elevating hope, detaching the heart completely from present things, and causing it to look out, moment by moment—yes, we repeat it with emphasis, moment by moment—for the return of our beloved Lord and Saviour Jesus Christ, who loved us, and gave Himself for us.

It is interesting to notice that in the two Epistles to the Thessalonians there is far more allusion to the Lord's coming than in all the other Epistles put together. This is all the more remarkable inasmuch as they were the very earliest of Paul's Epistles, and they were written to an assembly very young in the faith.

If the reader will just glance rapidly through these two most precious writings, he will find the hope of the Lord's return introduced in every one of the eight chapters, and in connection with all sorts of subjects. For example, in chap. 1 we have it presented as the grand object to be ever kept before the Christian's heart, let his position or his relationship be what it may—the brilliant light shining at the end of his long pilgrimage through this dark and toilsome world. "Ye turned to God from idols, to serve the living and true God; and to wait for"—what? The time of their death? No such thing, no allusion to such a thing. Death, for the believer, is abolished, and is never presented as the object of his hope. For what, then, were the Thessalonian disciples taught to wait? "For God's Son from heaven, whom He raised from the dead."

And then mark the beauteous addition!

"Jesus, which delivered us from the wrath to come." This is the Person for whom we are waiting our precious Saviour; our great Deliverer; the One who undertook our desperate case; who took, on our behalf, the cup of wrath from the hand of infinite Justice and exhausted it forever; who cleared the prospect of every cloud, so that we can gaze upward into Heaven, and onward into eternity, and see nothing but the brightness and blessedness of His own love and glory, as our happy home throughout the everlasting ages.

Oh, how blessed to be looking out, morning, noon, eventide, and midnight, for the coming of our gracious Deliverer! What a holy reality to be ever waiting for the return of our own loving and beloved Saviour and Lord! How separating and elevating, as we arise each morning to start on our daily course of duty—whatever that duty may be, whether the scrubbing of a floor or the preaching of the gospel—to cherish the bright and blessed hope that, ere the shades of evening gather round us, we may be summoned to ascend in the folds of the cloud of glory to meet our coming Lord!

Is this the dream of a wild fanatic or a visionary enthusiast? Nay, it is an imperishable truth, resting on the very same foundation that sustains the entire fabric of our most glorious Christianity. Is it true that the Son of God has trod this earth of ours in the person of Jesus of Nazareth? Is it true that He lived and labored here, amid the sins and sorrows of poor, fallen humanity? Is it true that He sighed, and wept, and groaned, under the sense of the widespread desolation which sin had wrought in this world?

Is it true that He went to the cross, and there offered Himself without spot to God, in order to vindicate the Divine Majesty; to answer all the claims of the throne of God; to destroy all the works of the devil; to make a public show of all the powers of hell; to put away sin by the sacrifice of Himself; to bear the sins of all those who, from the beginning to the end of time, should, through grace, believe in His name?

Is it true that He lay for three days and three nights in the heart of the earth, and on the first day of the week rose triumphant from the grave, as the Head of the new creation, and ascended into the heavens, after He had been seen by at least five hundred witnesses?

Is it true that fifty days after His resurrection He sent down the Holy Ghost, in order to fill and fit His apostles to be His witnesses to the ends of the earth? Is it true that from the day of Pentecost to this very hour He has been acting on His people's behalf as an Advocate with the Father, a great High Priest with God; interceding for us in all our failures, sins, and shortcomings, and sympathizing with us in all our infirmities and in all our sorrows; and presenting continually our sacrifices of prayer and praise, in all the fragrance of His own glorious Person?

Are all these things true? Yes, thank God, they are all divinely true, all set forth in the pages of the New Testament, with most marvelous fulness, clearness, depth, and power; all rest on the solid foundation of Holy Scripture—a foundation which not all the powers of earth and hell, men and devils, can ever touch.

Well, then, the blessed hope of the Lord's coming rests on precisely the same authority. It is not more true that our Lord Jesus Christ lay as a babe in a manger of Bethlehem, that He grew up to man's estate, that He went about doing good, that he was nailed to the cross and laid in the tomb, that He is now seated on the throne of the Majesty in the heavens, than that He will come again to receive His people to Himself. He may come tonight. No one can tell when He will come, but at any moment He may come. The only thing that detains Him is His long-suffering, not willing that any should perish, but that all should come to repentance. For eighteen long centuries has He waited in lingering love, mercy, and compassion; and during all that time salvation has been ready to be revealed, and God has been ready to judge; but He has waited, and He still waits, in long-suffering grace and patience.

But He will come, and we should ever live in the hope of His coming. Thus the apostle taught his beloved Thessalonians to live.

Thus he lived himself. The blessed hope was intimately bound up with all the habits and feelings of his daily life. Was it a question of reaping the fruit of his labors? Hear what he says: "For what is our hope, or joy, or crown or rejoicing? Are not even ye, in the presence of our Lord Jesus Christ, *at His coming?*" He would see them all then and there. No enemy will be allowed to hinder that meeting.

"We would have come unto you, even I Paul, once and again, but Satan hindered us." Very wonderful! Very mysterious! Yet so it was. Satan hindered an angel of God in the discharge of his business in the days of Daniel; and he hindered an apostle of Christ in the accomplishment of his loving desire to see his brethren at Thessalonica. But, thanks be to God, he will not be able to hinder the joyful meeting of Christ and His saints for which we wait. What a moment that will be! What precious reunions! What sweet recognitions! What affectionate greetings of dear old friends! But, far above all, Himself! His smile! His welcome! His soul-stirring "Well done!"

What a precious, soul-sustaining hope! Need we wonder at the prominent place it occupied in the thoughts and the teachings of the blessed apostle? He recurs to it on all occasions, and in connection with every subject. Is it a question of progress in the divine life and practical godliness? Thus he puts it: "And the Lord make you to increase and abound in love one toward another, and toward all, even as we do toward you; to the end He may establish your hearts unblameable in holiness before God, even our Father, *at the coming of our Lord Jesus Christ with all His saints.*"

Let the reader specially mark the last clause of this touching and beautiful quotation. "*With all His saints.*" What admirable wisdom shines here! The apostle was about to touch directly upon an error into which the Thessalonian believers had fallen in reference to their departed friends. They feared that those who had fallen asleep would not participate in the joy of the Lord's coming. This error is completely demolished by that brief sentence, "with *all* His saints." Not one will be absent from that joyous meeting, that festive scene. Blessed

assurance! Triumphant answer to all who would have us believe that none will share the joy of our Lord's coming save those who see this, that, and the other! "With *all* his saints," spite of their ignorance and their errors, their wanderings and their stumblings, their shortcomings and their failures. Our blessed Saviour, the everlasting Lover of our souls, will not shut any of us out at that blissful moment.

Is all this matchless grace to make us careless? God Forbid! Nay, it is the abiding sense of it which alone can keep us alive to our holy responsibility to judge everything in us and in our ways which is contrary to the mind of Christ. And not only so, but the hope of our Lord's return, if it be kept bright and fresh in the heart, *must* purify, sanctify and elevate our entire character and course as nothing elese can. "Every man that hath this hope in him purifieth himself, even as He is pure."

It is morally impossible for any one to *live* in the hope of seeing his Lord at any moment and yet have his heart set upon worldly things—upon money-making, self-indulgence, pleasure, vanity, folly. Let us not deceive ourselves. If we are daily looking out for the Son of God from Heaven, we must sit loose to the things of time and sense.

We may hold the doctrine of the Lord's coming as a mere dogma in the intellect; we may have the entire range of prophetic truth mapped out before our mind's eye, without its producing the smallest effect upon the heart, the character, or the practical life. But it is another thing altogether to have the whole moral being, the entire practical career, governed by the bright and blessed hope of seeing the One who loveth us and hath washed us from our sins in His own most precious blood.

Would there were more of this amongst us! It is to be feared that many of us have lost the freshness and power of our true and proper hope. The truth of the Lord's coming has become so familiar as a mere doctrine that we can flippantly speak of it, and discuss various points in connection with it, and argue with people about it, and all the while our ways, our deportment, our spirit and temper give the lie to what we profess to hold.

But we shall not pursue this sad and humbling side of the subject. May the Lord look upon us, and graciously heal, restore and lift up our souls! May He revive in the hearts of all His beloved people the proper Christian hope—the hope of seeing the bright and Morning Star. May the utterance of the whole heart and the utterance of the whole life be, "Even so, come, Lord Jesus!"

Here we must close this paper. We had hoped to turn through the two Epistles to the Thessalonians in company with our readers, in order to prove and illustrate the statement that the hope of the Lord's return was bound up in the heart of the apostle, with all the scenes, circumstances, and associations of Christian life. But we must allow the reader to do this for himself. Sufficient, we trust, has been said to show that true conversion, according to apostolic teaching, cannot stop short of the blessed hope of the Lord's coming.

A truly converted person is one who has turned from idols—has broken with the world—broken with his former self—turned to God, to find in Him all he can possibly want for time and eternity, to serve Him, and Him only—and, finally, "to wait for the Son of God from heaven." Such we conceive to be the true and proper answer to the question, "What is conversion?"

Art *thou* converted? If not, what then? If thou art, does thy life declare it?

LANDMARKS AND STUMBLINGBLOCKS

THE DOCTRINE OF ELECTION MISPLACED

"THOU SHALT NOT REMOVE thy neighbor's landmark, which they of old have set in thine inheritance" (Deut. 19:14).

"Take up the stumblingblock out of the way of My people" (Isa. 57:14).

What tender care, what gracious considerateness, breathe in the above passages! The ancient landmarks were not to be removed; but the stumblingblocks were to be taken up. The inheritance of God's people was to stand entire and unchanged, while the stumblingblocks were to be sedulously removed out of their pathway. Such was the grace and care of God for His people! The portion which God had given to each was to be enjoyed, while, at the same time, the path in which each was called to walk should be kept free from every occasion of stumbling.

Now, judging from recent communications, we believe we are called upon to give attention to the spirit of those ancient enactments. Some of our friends have, in their letters to us, opened their minds very freely as to their spiritual condition. They have told us of their doubts and fears, their difficulties and dangers, their conflicts and exercises. We are truly grateful for such confidence; and it is our earnest desire to be used of God to help our readers by pointing out the landmarks which He, by His Spirit, has set up, and thus remove the stumblingblocks which the enemy diligently flings in their path.

In pondering the cases which have lately been submitted to us, we have found some in which the enemy was manifestly using as a stumblingblock the doctrine of election *misplaced*. The doctrine of election, in its right place, instead of being a stumblingblock in the pathway of anxious inquirers, will be found to be a landmark set by them of old time, even by the inspired apostles of our Lord and Saviour Jesus Christ, in the inheritance of God's spiritual Israel.

But we all know that *misplaced* truth is more dangerous than positive error. If a man were to stand up, and boldly declare that the doctrine of election is false, we should without hesitation reject his words; but we might not be quite so well prepared to meet one who, while admitting the doctrine to be true and important, puts it out of its divinely appointed place. This latter is the very thing which is so constantly done, to the damaging of the truth of God, and the darkening of the souls of men.

What, then, is the true place of the doctrine of election? Its true, its divinely appointed place, is for those within the house—for the establishment of true *believers*. Instead of this, the enemy puts it *outside* the house, for the stumbling of anxious *inquirers*. Harken to the following language of a deeply exercised soul: "If I only knew that I was one of the elect I should be quite happy, inasmuch as I could then confidently apply to myself the benefits of the death of Christ."

Doubtless, this would be the language of many, were they only to tell out the feelings of their hearts. They are making a wrong use of the doctrine of election—a doctrine blessedly true in itself—a most valuable "landmark," but made a "stumblingblock" by the enemy. It is very needful for the anxious inquirer to bear in mind that it is *as a lost sinner*, and not as "one of the elect," that he can apply to himself the benefits of the death of Christ.

The proper stand-point from which to get a saving view of the death of Christ is not election, but *the consciousness of our ruin*. This is an unspeakable mercy, inasmuch as I *know* I am a lost sinner; but I do *not* know that I am one of the elect, until I have received, through the Spirit's testimony and teaching, the glad tidings of salvation through the blood of the Lamb. Salvation—free as the sunbeams, full as the ocean, permanent as the throne of the eternal God—is *preached* to me, *not* as one of the elect, but as one *utterly lost*, guilty, and undone; and when I have received this salvation there is conclusive evidence of my election.

"Knowing, brethren beloved, your election of God; for our gospel came not unto you in word only, but also in power, and in the Holy Ghost, and in much assurance" (1 Thess. 1: 4-5). Election is not my warrant for accepting salvation; but the reception of salvation is the proof of election. For how is any sinner to know that he is one of the elect? Where is he to find it? It must be a matter of divine

revelation, else it cannot be a matter of faith. But where is it revealed? Where is the knowledge of election made an indispensable prerequisite, an essential preliminary, to the acceptance of salvation? Nowhere, in the Word of God. My only title to salvation is, that I am a poor guilty, hell-deserving sinner. If I wait for any other title, I am only removing a most valuable landmark from its proper place, and putting it as a stumblingblock in my way. This, to say the least of it, is very unwise.

But it is more than unwise. It is positive opposition to the Word of God; not only to the quotations which stand at the head of this paper, but to the spirit and teaching of the entire volume. Harken to the risen Saviour's commission to His first heralds: "Go ye into *all* the world, and preach the gospel to *every* creature" (Mark 16:15). Is there so much as a single point, in these words, on which to base a question about election? Is any one, to whom this glorious gospel is preached, called to settle a prior question about his election? Assuredly not.

"All the world" and "every creature" are expressions which set aside every difficulty, and render salvation as free as the air, and as wide as the human family. It is not said, "Go ye into a given section of the world, and preach the gospel to a certain number." No; this would not be in keeping with that grace which was to be proclaimed to the wide, wide world. When the law was in question, it was addressed to a certain number, in a given section; but when the gospel was to be proclaimed, its mighty range was to be, "All the world," and its object, "Every creature."

Again, hear what the Holy Ghost saith, by the apostle Paul: "This is a faithful saying, and worthy of *all* acceptation, that Christ Jesus came into the world to save *sinners*" (1 Tim. 1:15). Is there any room here for raising a question as to one's title to salvation? None whatever. If Christ Jesus came into the world to save sinners, and if I am a sinner, then I am entitled to apply to my own soul the benefits of His precious sacrifice. Ere I can possibly exclude myself therefrom I must be something else than a sinner. If it were anywhere declared in Scripture that Christ

Jesus came to save only the elect, then clearly I should, in some way or another, prove myself one of that number, ere I could make my own the benefits of His death. But, thanks be to God, there is nothing the least like this in the whole gospel scheme.

"The Son of man is come to seek and to save that which was *lost*" (Luke 19:10). And is not that just what I am? Truly so. Well then, is it not from the standpoint of a lost one that I am to look at the death of Christ? Doubtless. And can I not, while contemplating that precious mystery from thence, adopt the language of faith, and say, "He loved *me*, and gave Himself for *me*"? Yes, as unreservedly and unconditionally as though I were the only sinner on the surface of the globe.

Nothing can be more soothing and tranquilizing to the spirit of an anxious inquirer than to mark the way in which salvation is brought to him in the very condition in which he is, and on the very ground which he occupies. There is not so much as a single stumblingblock along the entire path leading to the glorious inheritance of the saints—an inheritance settled by landmarks which neither men nor devils can ever remove.

The God of all grace has left nothing undone, nothing unsaid, which could possibly give rest, assurance, and perfect satisfaction to the soul. He has set forth the very condition and character of those for whom Christ died, in such terms as to leave no room for any demur or hesitation. Listen to the following glowing words: "For when we were yet *without strength*, in due time Christ died *for the ungodly*." "But God commendeth His love toward us, in that *while we were yet sinners*, Christ died for us." "For if, *when we were enemies*, we were reconciled to God by the death of His Son" (Rom. 5: 6, 8, 10).

Can aught be plainer or more pointed than these passages? Is there a single term made use of which could possibly raise a question in the heart of any sinner as to his full and undisputed title to the benefits of the death of Christ? Not one. Am I "ungodly?" It was for such Christ died. Am I "a sinner?" It is to such that God commendeth His love. Am I

"an enemy?" It is such God reconciles by the death of His Son.

Thus all is made as plain as a sunbeam; and as for the theological stumblingblock caused by misplacing the doctrine of election, it is entirely removed. It is as a sinner I get the benefit of Christ's death. It is as a lost one I get a salvation which is as free as it is permanent, and as permanent as it is free. All I want, in order to apply to myself the value of the blood of Jesus, is to know myself a guilty *sinner*. It would not help me the least in this matter to be told that I am one of the elect, inasmuch as it is not in that character God addresses me in the gospel, but in another character altogether, even as a *lost* sinner.

But then, some may feel disposed to ask, "Do you want to set aside the doctrine of election?" God forbid. We only want to see it in its right place. We want it as a landmark, not as a stumblingblock. We believe the evangelist has no business to *preach* election. Paul never preached election. He *taught* election, but he preached Christ. This makes all the difference. We believe that no one can be a proper evangelist who is, in any wise, hampered by the doctrine of election misplaced. We have seen serious damage done to two classes of people by preaching election instead of preaching Christ. Careless sinners are made more careless still, while anxious souls have had their anxiety intensified.

These, surely, are sad results, and they ought to be sufficient to awaken very serious thoughts in the minds of all who desire to be successful preachers of that free and full salvation which shines in the gospel of Christ, and leaves all who hear it without a shadow of an excuse. The grand business of the evangelist is to set forth, in his preaching, the perfect love of God, the efficacy of the blood of Christ, and the faithful record of the Holy Ghost. His spirit should be entirely untrammelled, and his gospel unclouded. He should preach a present salvation, free to all, and stable as the pillars which support the throne of God. The gospel is the unfolding of the heart of God as expressed in the death of His Son, recorded by the Holy Spirit.

Were this more carefully attended to, there would be more power in replying to the oft-repeated objection of the careless, as well as in hushing the deep anxieties of exercised and burdened souls. The former would have no just ground of objection; the latter, no reason to fear. When persons reject the gospel on the ground of God's eternal decrees, they are rejecting what is *revealed* on the ground of what is *hidden*. What can they possibly know about God's decrees? Just nothing. How then can that which is secret be urged as a reason for rejecting what is revealed? Why refuse what *can* be known, on the ground of what *cannot?* It is obvious that men do not act thus in cases where they wish to believe a matter. Only let a man be willing to believe a thing, and you will not find him anxiously looking for a ground of objection. But alas! men do not want to believe God. They reject His precious testimony which is as clear as the sun in meridian brightness, and urge, as their plea for so doing, His decrees which are wrapped in impenetrable darkness. What folly! What blindness! What guilt!

And then as to anxious souls who harass themselves with questions about election, we long to show them that it is not in accordance with the divine mind that they should raise any such difficulty. God addresses them in the exact state in which He sees them and in which they can see themselves. He addresses them as *sinners*, and this is exactly what they are. *There is nothing but salvation for any sinner, the moment he takes his true place as a sinner.* This is simple enough for any simple soul. To raise questions about election is sheer unbelief. It is, in another way, to reject what is revealed on the ground of what is hidden; it is to refuse what I *can* know, on the ground of what I *cannot.*

God has revealed Himself in the face of Jesus Christ, so that we may know Him and trust Him. Moreover, He has made full provision in the atonement of the cross for all our need and all our guilt. Hence, therefore instead of perplexing myself with the question, "Am I one of the elect?" it is my happy privilege to rest in the perfect love of God, the all-sufficiency of Christ, and the faithful record of the Holy Ghost.

We must close, though there are other stumblingblocks which we long to see removed out of the way of God's people, as well as landmarks which are sadly lost sight of.

ONE-SIDED THEOLOGY

CALVINISM AND ARMINIANISM

WE HAVE LATELY RECEIVED a long letter, furnishing a very striking proof of the bewildering effect of one-sided theology. Our correspondent is evidently under the influence of what is styled the high school of doctrine. Hence, he cannot see the rightness of calling upon the unconverted to "come," to "hear," to "repent," or to "believe." It seems to him like telling a crab-tree to bear some applies in order that it may become an apple-tree.

Now, we thoroughly believe that faith is the gift of God, and that it is not according to man's will or by human power. And further,

we believe that not a single soul would ever come to Christ if not drawn, yea, compelled by divine grace so to do; and therefore all who are saved have to thank the free and sovereign grace of God for it; their song is, and ever shall be, "Not unto us, O Lord, not unto us, but unto Thy name give glory, for Thy mercy, and for Thy truth's sake."

And this we believe not as part of a certain system of doctrine, but as the revealed truth of God. But, on the other hand, we believe, just as fully, in the solemn truth of man's moral responsibility, inasmuch as it is plainly taught in Scripture, though we do not find it amongst what are called "the five points of the faith of God's elect."

We believe these five points, so far as they go; but they are very far indeed from containing the faith of God's elect. There are wide fields of divine revelation which this stunted and one-sided system does not touch upon, or even hint at, in the most remote manner. Where do we find the heavenly calling? Where, the glorious truth of the Church as the body and bride of Christ? Where, the precious sanctifying hope of the coming of Christ to receive His people to Himself? Where have we the grand scope of prophecy opened to the vision of our souls, in that which is so pompously styled "the faith of God's elect"? We look in vain for a single trace of them in the entire system to which our friend is attached.

Now, can we suppose for a moment that the blessed apostle Paul would accept as "the faith of God's elect" a system which leaves out that glorious mystery of the Church of which he was specially made the minister? Suppose any one had shewn Paul "the five points" of Calvinism, as a statement of the truth of God, what would he have said? What! "The whole truth of God;" "the faith of God's elect;" "all that is essential to be believed;" and yet not a syllable about the real position of the Church—its calling, its standing, its hopes, its privileges!

And not a word about Israel's future! A complete ignoring, or at best a thorough alienation, of the promises made to Abraham, Isaac, Jacob, and David! The whole body of prophetic teaching subjected to a system of spiritualizing, falsely so called, whereby Israel is robbed of its proper portion, and Christians dragged down to an earthly level—and this presented to us with the lofty pretension of "The faith of God's elect!"

Thank God it is not so. He, blessed be His name, has not confined Himself within the narrow limits of any school of doctrine, high, low, or moderate. He has revealed Himself. He has told out the deep and precious secrets of His heart. He has unfolded His eternal counsels, as to the Church, as to Israel, the Gentiles, and the wide creation. Men might as well attempt to confine the ocean in buckets of their own formation as to confine the vast range of divine revelation within the feeble enclosures of human systems of doctrine. It cannot be done, and it ought not to be attempted. Better far to set aside the systems of theology and schools of divinity, and come like a little child to the eternal fountain of Holy Scripture, and there drink in the living teachings of God's Spirit.

Nothing is more damaging to the truth of God, more withering to the soul, or more subversive of all spiritual growth and progress than mere theology, high or low—Calvinistic or Arminian. It is impossible for the soul to make progress beyond the boundaries of the system to which it is attached. If I am taught to regard "the five points" as "the faith of God's elect," I shall not think of looking beyond them; and then a most glorious field of heavenly truth is shut out from the vision of my soul. I am stunted, narrowed, one-sided; and I am in danger of getting into that hard, dry state of soul which results from being occupied with mere points of doctrine instead of with Christ.

A disciple of the high school of doctrine will not hear of a world-wide gospel—of God's love to the world—of glad tidings to every creature under Heaven. He has only gotten a gospel for the elect. On the other hand, a disciple of the low or Arminian school will not hear of the eternal security of God's people. Their salvation depends partly upon Christ, and partly upon themselves. According to this system, the song of the redeemed should be changed. Instead of "Worthy is the Lamb," we should have to add, "and worthy are we." We may be saved to-day, and lost to-morrow. All this dishonors God, and robs the Christian of all true peace.

We do not write to offend the reader. Nothing is further from our thoughts. We are dealing not with persons, but with schools of doctrine and systems of divinity which we would, most earnestly, entreat our beloved readers to abandon, at once, and for ever. Not one of them contains the full, entire truth of God. There are certain elements of truth in all of them; but the truth is often neutralized by the error; and even if we could find a system which contains, so far as it goes, nothing but the truth, yet if it does not contain the whole truth, its effect upon the soul is pernicious, because it leads a person to plume himself on having the truth of God when, in reality, he has only laid hold of a one-sided system of man.

Then again we rarely find a mere disciple of any school of doctrine who can face Scripture as a whole. Favorite texts will be quoted and continually reiterated; but a large body of Scripture is left almost wholly unappropriated. For example, take such passages as the following, "But now God commandeth *all men* everywhere to repent" (Acts 17:30.) And again, "Who will have *all men* to be saved, and to come to the knowledge of the truth" (1 Tim. 2). So also, in 2 Peter, "The Lord . . . is long-suffering to usward, not willing that *any* should perish, but that *all* should come to repentance" (chap 3:9). And, in the very closing section of the volume, we read, "Whosoever will, let him take the water of life freely."

Are these passage to be taken as they stand, or are we to introduce qualifying or modifying words to make them fit in with our system? The fact is, they set forth the largeness of the heart of God, the gracious activities of His nature, the wide aspect of His love. It is not according to the loving heart of God that any of His creatures should perish. There is no such thing in Scripture as any decree of God consigning a certain number of the human race to eternal damnation.* Some may be judicially given over to blindness because of deliberate rejection of the light (see Rom. 9:17; Heb. 6:4-6; 10:26-27; 2 Thess. 2:11-12; 1 Pet. 2:8). But all who perish will have only themselves to blame. All who reach Heaven will have to thank God.

If we are to be taught by Scripture we must believe that every man is responsible according to his light. The Gentile is responsible to listen to the voice of creation.

The Jew is responsible on the ground of the law. Christendom is responsible on the ground of the full-orbed revelation contained in the whole Word of God. If God commands all men, everywhere to repent, does He mean what He says, or merely all the elect? What right have we to add to, or alter, to pare down, or to accommodate the Word of God? None whatever.

Let us face Scripture as it stands, and reject everything which will not stand the test. We may well call in question the soundness of a system which cannot meet the full force of the Word of God as a whole. If passages of Scripture seem to clash, it is only because of our ignorance. Let us humbly own this, and wait on God for further light. This, we may depend upon it, is safe moral ground to occupy. Instead of endeavoring to reconcile apparent discrepancies, let us bow at the Master's feet and justify Him in all His sayings. Thus shall we reap a harvest of blessing, and grow in the knowledge of God and His Word as a whole.

A few days since, a friend put into our hands a sermon recently preached by an eminent clergyman belonging to the high school of doctrine. We have found in this sermon, quite as much as in the letter of our correspondent, the effects of one-sided theology. For instance, in referring to that magnificent statement of the Baptist in John 1:29, the preacher quotes it thus, "The Lamb of God, which taketh away the sin of *the whole world of God's chosen people."*

But there is not a word about "God's chosen people" in the passage. It refers to the great propitiatory work of Christ, in virtue of which every trace of sin shall yet be obliterated from the wide creation of God. We shall only see the full application of that blessed Scripture in the new heavens and the new earth wherein dwelleth righteousness. To confine it to the sin of God's elect can only be viewed as the fruit of theological bias.

* NOTE.—It is deeply interesting to mark the way in which Scripture guards against the repulsive doctrine of reprobation. Look, for example, at Matthew 25:34. Here, the King, in addressing those on His right hand, says, "Come, *ye blessed of My Father*, inherit *the kingdom prepared for you* from the foundation of the world." Contrast with this the address to those on His left hand: "Depart from Me ye cursed [He does not say of 'My Father'] into everlasting fire, prepared [not for you, but] for the devil and his angels." So also, in Romans 9. In speaking of the "vessels of wrath," it says "fitted to destruction"—fitted not by God surely, but by themselves. On the other hand, when speaking of the "vessels of mercy," it says, "which *He had afore prepared* unto glory." The grand truth of *election* is fully established; the repulsive error of *reprobation*, sedulously avoided.

"GOD FOR US"

Romans 8:31

HOW MUCH IS WRAPPED UP in these few words, "God for us"! They form one of those marvelous chains of three links so frequently found in Scripture. We have "God" linked on to "us" by that precious little word "for." This secures every thing, for time and eternity. There is not a single thing within the entire range of a creature's necessities that are not included in the brief but comprehensive sentence which forms the heading of this paper. If God be for us, then it follows of necessity—blessed necessity—that neither our sins, nor our iniquities, nor our guilt, nor our ruined nature, nor Satan, nor the world, nor any other creature can possibly stand in the way of our present peace and our everlasting felicity and glory. God can dispose of all—has disposed of them, in such a way as to illustrate His own glory, and magnify His holy name, throughout the wide universe, forever and ever. All praise and adoration be to the eternal Trinity!

It may be, however, that the reader feels disposed, at the very outset, to inquire how he is to know his place amongst the "us" of our precious thesis. This, truly, is a most momentous question. Our eternal weal or woe hangs upon the answer. How, then, are we to know that God is for us? In reply to this most weighty question, we shall seek, by God's grace, to furnish the reader with five substantial proofs that God is for us, in all our need, our guilt, our misery, and our danger—for us, spite of all that we are, and all that we have done—for us, although there is no reason whatever, so far as we are concerned, why He should be for us, but every reason why He should be against us.

The first grand proof which we shall adduce is *the gift of His Son*. "For God so loved the world, that He gave His only begotten Son, that whosoever believeth in Him should not perish, but have everlasting life" (John 3:16).

Now we are glad, for various reasons, to commence our series of proofs with these memorable words. In the first place, they meet a difficulty which may suggest itself to the mind of the anxious reader—a difficulty based upon the fact that the sentence culled from Rom. 8:31 evidently applies primarily to believers, and only to such, as does the entire Epistle and every one of the Epistles.

But, blessed be God, no such difficulty can be started in reference to the all-embracing, and encouraging words of Him who spake as never man spake. When we have from the lips of our blessed Lord Himself, the eternal Son of God, such words as these, "God so loved *the world*," we have no ground whatever for questioning their application to each and all who come under the comprehensive word "world." Before any one can prove that the free love of God does not apply to him, he must first prove that he does not form a part of the world, but that he belongs to some other sphere of being. If indeed, our Lord had said, "God so loved a certain portion of the world," call it what you please, then verily it would be absolutely necessary to prove that we belong to that particular portion or class, ere we could attempt to apply His words to ourselves. If He had said that God so loved the predestinated, the elect, or the called, then we must seek to know our place amongst the number of such, before we can take home to ourselves the precious assurance of the love of God, as proved by the gift of His Son.

But our Lord used no such qualifying clause. He is addressing one who, from his earliest days, had been trained and accustomed to take a very limited view indeed of the favor and goodness of God. Nicodemus had been taught to consider that the rich tide of Jehovah's goodness, loving-kindness, and tender mercy could only flow within the narrow inclosure of the Jewish system and the Jewish nation. The thought of its rolling forth to the wide wide world had never, we may safely assert, penetrated the mind of one trained amid the contracting influences of the legal system. Hence, therefore, it must have sounded passing strange in his ear, to hear "a teacher come from God" giving utterance to the great fact that God loved not merely the Jewish nation, nor yet some special portion of the human race, but "the world." No doubt, such a statement would add not a little to the amazement felt by this master in Israel at being told that he himself, with all His religious advantages, needed to be born again in order to see or enter the kingdom of God.

Do we then deny or call in question the grand truth of predestination, election, or effectual calling? God forbid. We hold these things as amongst the fundamental principles of true Christianity. We believe in the eternal counsels and purposes of our God—His unsearchable decrees—His electing love—His sovereign mercy.

But do any or all of these things interfere, in the smallest degree, with the gracious activities of the divine nature, or the outgoings of God's love towards a lost world? In no wise. God is love. That is His blessed nature, and this nature must express itself toward all. The mistake lies in supposing that because God has His purposes, His counsels, His decrees—because He is sovereign in His grace and mercy—because He has chosen from all eternity a people for His own praise and glory—because the names of the redeemed, all the redeemed, were written down in the book of the slain Lamb, before the foundation of the world—that therefore God cannot be said to love all mankind—to love the world—and, moreover that the glad tidings of God's full and free salvation ought not to be proclaimed in the ears of every creature under Heaven.

The simple fact is that the two lines, though so perfectly distinct, are laid down with equal clearness, in the Word of God;

neither interferes, in the smallest degree, with the other, but both together go to make up the beauteous harmony of divine truth and to set forth the glorious unity of the divine nature.

Now, it is with the activities of the divine nature and the outgoings of divine love that the preacher of the gospel has specially to do. He is not to be cramped, crippled, or confined in his blessed work, by any reference to God's secret decrees or purposes, though fully aware of the existence of such. His mission is to the world—the wide wide world. His theme is salvation—a salvation as full as the heart of God, as permanent as the throne of God—as free as the air—free to all without any exception, limitation, or condition whatsoever. The basis of his work is the atoning death of Christ which has removed all barriers out of the way, and opened up the floodgates in order that the mighty tide of divine love may roll forth, in all its fulness, richness and blessedness, to a lost and guilty world.

And here, we may add, lies the ground of man's responsibility in reference to the gospel of God. If, indeed, it be true that God so loved the world as to give His only begotten Son—if "the righteousness of God is unto all" (Rom. 3:22)—if it be God's gracious will that "all should be saved and come to the knowledge of the truth" (1 Tim. 2:4)—if He is "not willing that any should perish but that all should come to repentance" (2 Pet. 3:9)—then verily is every man who hears this glorious gospel laid under the most solemn responsibility to believe it and be saved. No one can honestly and truthfully turn round and say, "I longed to be saved, but could not, because I was not one of the elect. I longed to flee from the wrath to come but was prevented by the insuperable barrier of the divine decree which irresistibly consigned me to an everlasting hell."

There is not, within the covers of the volume of God, in the entire range of His dealings with His creatures, in the aspect of His character, or in the enactments of His moral government, the very faintest shadow of a foundation for such an objection. Every man is left without excuse. God can say to all who have rejected His gospel, "I would, but ye would not." There is absolutely no such thing as reprobation in the Word of God, meaning thereby the consignment on God's part, of any number of His creatures to everlasting damnation. Everlasting fire is prepared for the devil and his angels (Matt. 25). Men *will* rush into it. "Vessels of wrath" are fitted, not by God, but by themselves, "to destruction" (Rom. 9). Everyone who gets to Heaven will have to thank God for it. Everyone who finds himself in hell will have to blame himself for it.

Furthermore, we have ever to remember that the sinner has nothing to do with God's unpublished decrees. What does he—what can he—know about such? Nothing whatever. But he has to do with God's published love—His proffered mercy—His free salvation—His glorious gospel. We may fearlessly assert that so long as these glowing and glorious words shine in the record of God, "*Whosoever will* let him take of the water of life *freely*," (Rev. 22:17) it is impossible for any son or daughter of Adam to say, "I longed to be saved, but could not. I thirsted for the living water, but could not reach it. The well was deep and I had nothing to draw with." Ah, no! such language will never be used, such an objection will never be urged by anyone in all the ranks of the lost. When men pass into eternity they will see with awful clearness what they now affect to think is so obscure and perplexing, namely, the perfect compatibility of God's electing sovereign grace and the free offer of salvation to all—the fullest harmony between divine sovereignty and human responsibility.

We fondly trust the reader sees these things, even now. It is of the very last possible importance to maintain the balance of truth in the soul—to allow the beams of divine revelation to act, with full power, on the heart and conscience, unimpeded by the murky atmosphere of mere human theology. There is imminent danger in taking up a certain number of abstract truths and forming them into a system. We want the adjusting power of *all truth*. The growth and practical sanctification of the soul are promoted, not by some truth, but by *the*

truth, in all its fullness, as embodied in the person of Christ, and set forth by the eternal Spirit in the holy Scriptures. We must get rid completely of all our own preconceived notions—all merely theological views and opinions—and come like a little child, to the feet of Jesus to be taught by His Spirit, from out His holy word. Thus only shall we find rest from conflicting dogmas. Thus shall all the heavy clouds and mists of human opinion be rolled away, and our enfranchised souls shall bask in the clear sunlight of a full divine revelation.

We shall now proceed with our proofs.

The second fact which proves that God is for us will be found in *the death of His Son*. It is only necessary for us to take up one feature in the atoning death of Christ, but that one feature is a cardinal one. We refer to the marvelous fact set forth by the Holy Ghost in the prophet Isaiah, "It pleased Jehovah to bruise Him. He hath put Him to grief" (chapter 53).

Our blessed Lord might have come into this world of sin and sorrow. He might have become a man. He might have been baptized in the Jordan—anointed by the Holy Ghost—tempted of Satan in the wilderness. He might have gone about doing good. He might have lived and labored, wept and prayed, and, at the close, gone back to Heaven again, thus leaving us involved in deeper gloom than ever. He might, like the priest or the Levite, in the parable, have come and looked upon us in our wounds and misery, passed by on the other side and returned alone to the place from whence He came.

And what if He had? what but the flames of an everlasting hell for thee and me? For, be it well remembered, that all the living labors of the Son of God—His amazing ministry—His days of toil and His nights of prayer—His tears, His sighs, His groans—the whole of His life-work, from the manger up to, but short of, the cross, could not have blotted out one speck of guilt from a human conscience. "Without shedding of blood is no remission." No doubt, the eternal Son had to become a man that He might die; but incarnation could not cancel guilt. Indeed, the life of Christ, as a man on this earth, only proved the human race more guilty still. "If I had not come and spoken to them, they had not had sin." The light that shone in His blessed ways only revealed the moral darkness of man—of Israel—of the world. Hence, therefore, had He merely come and lived and labored here for three-and-thirty years, and gone back to Heaven, our guilt and moral darkness would have been fully proved but no atonement made. "It is the blood that maketh atonement for the soul." "Without shedding of blood is no remission" (Heb. 9:22).

This is a grand foundation-truth of Christianity, and must be constantly affirmed, and tenaciously held. There is immense moral power in it. If it be true that all the life-labors of the Son of God—His tears, His prayers, His groans, His sighs—if all these things put together could not cancel one single speck of guilt; then, indeed, may we not lawfully inquire what possible value can there be in our works—our tears—our prayers—our religious services—our ordinances, sacraments and ceremonies—the whole range of religious activity and moral reform? Can such things avail to cancel our sins and give us a righteousness before God? The thought is perfectly monstrous. If any or all of these things could avail, then why the sacrificial, atoning death of Christ? Why that ineffable and inestimable sacrifice, if aught else would have done?

But, it will perhaps be said that, although none of these things could avail *without* the death of Christ, yet they must be added to it. For what? To make that peerless death—that precious blood—that priceless sacrifice of full avail? Is that it? Shall the rubbish of human doings, human righteousness, be flung into the scale to make the sacrifice of Christ of full avail in the judgment of God? The bare thought is positive and absolute blasphemy.

But are there not to be good works? Yes, verily; but what are they? Are they the pious doings, the religious efforts, the moral activities of unregenerate, unconverted, unbelieving nature? Nay. What then? What are the Christian's good works? They are *life-works*, not dead works. They are the precious fruits of life possessed—the life of

Christ in the true believer. There is not anything beneath the canopy of Heaven which God can accept as a good work save the fruit of the grace of Christ in the believer. The very feeblest expression of the life of Christ, in the daily history of a Christian, is fragrant and precious to God. But the most splendid and gigantic labors of an unbeliever are, in God's account, but "dead works."

All this, however, is a digression from our main line, to which we must now return.

We refer to one special point in the death of Christ, and that is the fact that it pleased Jehovah to bruise Him. Herein lies the striking and soul-subduing proof that God is for us. "He spared not His own Son, but delivered Him up for us all." He not merely *gave* Him but *bruised* Him, and that for us. That spotless, holy, perfect One—the only perfect Man that ever trod this earth—the One who ever did the things which pleased His Father—whose whole life from the manger to the tree was one continued sweet odor ascending to the throne and to the heart of God—whose every movement, every word, every look, every thought was well pleasing to God—whose one grand object, from first to last, was to glorify God and finish His work—this blessed One was delivered by the determinate counsel and foreknowledge of God—was nailed to the cursed tree, and there endured the righteous wrath of a sin-hating God; and all this because God was for us—even *us*.

What marvelous and matchless grace is here! The Just One bruised for the unjust—the sinless, spotless, holy Jesus, bruised by the hand of Infinite Justice in order that guilty rebels might be saved; and not only saved but brought into the position and relationship of sons—sons and daughters of the Lord Almighty—heirs of God and joint-heirs with Christ.

This surely is grace—rich, free, sovereign grace—grace abounding to the very chief of sinners—grace reigning, through righteousness, unto eternal life, by Jesus Christ. Who would not trust this grace? Who can look at the cross, and doubt that God is for the sinner—for any sinner—for him—for the reader of these lines? Who would not confide in that love that shines in the cross? Who can look at the cross and not see that God willeth not the death of any sinner? Why did He not allow us to perish in our guilt—to descend into that everlasting hell which we so richly deserved because of our sins? Why give His Only-begotten Son? Why bruise Him on that shameful cross? Why hide His face from the only perfect Man that ever lived—that Man His own Eternal Son? Why all this? Surely it was because God is for us, spite of all our guilt and sinful rebellion. Yes, blessed be His Name, He is for the poor self-destroyed, hell-deserving sinner, be he who or what he may; and each one whose eye scans these lines is now entreated to come and confide in the love that gave Jesus from the bosom and bruised Him on the cross.

Oh! do come, just now. Delay not! Waver not! Reason not! Listen not to Satan! Listen not to the suggestions and imaginings of your own heart; but listen to that Word which assures you that God is for you, and to that love which shines forth in the gift and the death of His Son.

In pursuing what we may truly call the golden chain of evidence in proof that God is for us, we have dwelt upon the two precious facts of the gift and the death of His Son. We have traveled from the bosom to the cross, along that mysterious and marvelous path which is marked by the footprints of divine and everlasting love. We have seen the blessed One not only giving His only begotten Son from His bosom, but actually bruising Him for us—making His spotless soul an offering for sin—bringing Him down into the dust of death—making Him to be sin for us—judging Him in our stead—thus affording the most unanswerable evidence of the fact that He is for us, that His heart is toward us, that He earnestly desires our salvation, seeing that He hath not withheld His Son, His only Son from us, but delivered Him up for us all.

Our third proof is furnished by *the raising of His Son*. And in speaking of the glorious fact of resurrection, we must confine ourselves to the one point therein, namely, the proof which it furnishes of God's being friendly to us. A passage or two of Scripture will suffice to unfold and establish this special point.

In Romans 4 the inspired apostle introduces God to our hearts as the One who raised Jesus our Lord from the dead. He is speaking of Abraham who, He tells us, "against hope believed in hope, that he might become the father of many nations, according to that which was spoken, So shall thy seed be. And being not weak in faith, he considered not his own body now dead, when he was about an hundred years old, neither yet the deadness of Sarah's womb. He staggered not at the promise of God through unbelief; but was strong in faith, giving glory to God; and being fully persuaded that what He had promised, He was able also to perform. And therefore it was imputed to him for righteousness. Now it was not written for his sake alone that it was imputed to him; but for us also, to whom it shall be imputed, if we believe on Him that"—what? That gave His Son? Nay. That bruised His Son upon the cross? Nay. What then? "That raised up Jesus our Lord from the dead"—the very same "who was delivered for our offences, and was raised again for our justification."

Weigh this great fact. What was it that brought the precious Saviour to the cross? What brought Him down to the dust of death? Was it not our offences? Truly so. "He was delivered for our offences." He was nailed to the cursed tree for us. He represented us on the cross. He was our Substitute, in all the full value and deep significance of that word. He took our place and was treated, in every respect, as we deserve to be treated. The hand of infinite justice dealt with our sins—all our sins, at the cross. Jesus made Himself responsible for all our offences, our iniquities, our transgressions, our liabilities, all that was or ever could be against us; He—blessed be His peerless and adorable name!—made Himself answerable for all, and died in our stead, under the full weight of our sins. He died, the just for the unjust.

Where is He now? The heart bounds with ineffable joy and holy triumph at the thought of the answer. Where is the blessed One who hung on yonder cross, and lay in yonder tomb? He is at the right hand of God, crowned with glory and honor. Who set Him there? Who put the crown upon His blessed brow? God Himself. The One who gave Him, and the One who bruised Him is the One who raised Him, and it is in Him we are to believe if we are to be counted righteous. This is the special point before the apostle's mind. Righteousness shall be imputed to us if we believe on God as the One who raised Jesus our Lord from the dead.

Mark the vital link. Seize the all-important connection. The selfsame One who hung upon the cross, charged with all our offences, is now on the throne without them. How did He get there? Was it in virtue of His eternal Godhead? No: for on that ground He was always there. He was God over all, blessed forever. Was it in virtue of His eternal Sonship? Nay; for He was ever there on that ground also.* Therefore, it could, in no wise, meet our need as guilty sinners, charged with innumerable offences, to be told that the eternal Son of the Father had taken His seat at the right hand of the majesty in the heavens, inasmuch as that place ever belonged to Him—yea, the very deepest and tenderest place in the bosom of the Father.

But, further, we may inquire, was it as the spotless, sinless, perfect Man that our adorable Lord took His seat on the throne? Nay; as such, He could, at any moment, between the manger and the cross, have taken His place there.

To what conclusion, then, are we absolutely shut up, in this matter? To that most precious, that tranquilizing conclusion, that the selfsame One who was delivered for our offences, bruised for our iniquities, judged in our stead, is now in Heaven; that the One who represented us on the cross, is now on the throne; that the One who stood charged with all our guilt, is now crowned with glory and honor; that, so perfectly, so absolutely and completely, has He disposed of the entire question of our sins, that infinite justice has raised Him from the dead, and placed a diadem of glory upon His sacred brow.

Reader, dost thou understand this? Dost thou see its bearing upon thyself? Dost thou believe in the One who raised up Jesus our Lord from the dead? Dost thou see that, in so doing, He has declared Himself friendly to thee? And dost thou believe that, in raising up Jesus, He set forth His infinite satisfaction in the great work of atonement, and furnished thee with a receipt in full for all thy debts—a receipt for the "ten thousand talents."

Here lies the gist, marrow, and substance of this magnificent argument of Romans 4. If the Man who was delivered for our offences is now in Heaven,—in Heaven, too, by the hand and act of God Himself; then, most surely, our offences are all gone, and we stand justified from all things, as free from every charge of guilt, and every breath of condemnation, as the blessed One Himself. It cannot possibly be otherwise, if we believe on Him who raised up Jesus our Lord from the dead. It is utterly impossible for a charge to be brought against the believer in the God of resurrection, for the simplest of all reasons that the One whom He raised was the One whom He bruised for the believer's sins. Why did He raise Him? Because the sins for which He bruised Him were all put away, and put away forever. The Lord Jesus, *having undertaken our cause, and made Himself answerable for us in every way,* could not be where He now is, if a single jot or tittle of our guilt remained. But on the other hand, being where He now is, and being there by God's own act, it is impossible—utterly impossible —for any question to be raised as to the full and complete justification and perfect righteousness of the soul that believes in Him. Thus, the moment that any one believes in God, in the special character of the raiser of Jesus, he is counted perfectly righteous before Him. This is most marvelous, but divinely and eternally true. May the reader feel its power, sweetness, and tranquilizing virtue! Yea, may the eternal Spirit give him the blessed sense of it, deep down in his heart! Then, indeed shall he have perfect peace in his soul; then, too, shall

* We rejoice in every opportunity for the setting forth of Christ's eternal Sonship. We hold it to be an integral and essentially necessary part of the Christian faith.

he understand how that, in raising, as well as in bruising and giving His Son, God has declared and proved Himself to be for us.

We had intended to bring under the special notice of the reader Hebrews 13:20, but we must allow him to dwell upon that lovely passage for himself, while we proceed to exhibit our fourth proof that God is for us, which will be found in *the descent of the Holy Ghost*. Here, too, we must confine ourselves to one point in that most glorious event, and that is the form in which that august witness, the eternal Spirit, descended.

Let the reader turn to the second chapter of the Acts. "And when the day of Pentecost was fully come, they were all with one accord in one place. And suddenly there came a sound from heaven, as of a rushing mighty wind, and it filled all the house where they were sitting. And there appeared unto them *cloven tongues*, like as of fire, and it sat upon each of them. And they were all filled with the Holy Ghost, and began to speak with *other tongues*, as the Spirit gave them utterance. And there were dwelling at Jerusalem, Jews, devout men, *out of every nation under heaven*. Now, when this was noised abroad, the multitude came together, and were confounded, because that every man heard them speak *in his own language*. And they were all amazed and marveled, saying one to another, Behold, are not all these which speak Galileans? And how hear we *every man in our own tongue wherein we were born?* Parthians, and Medes, and Elamites, and the dwellers in Mesopotamia, and in Judea, and Capadocia, in Pontus, and Asia, Phrygia, and Pamphylia, in Egypt, and in the parts of Libya about Cyrene, and strangers of Rome, Jews and proselytes, Cretes and Arabians, we do hear them speak *in our tongues*, the wonderful works of God."

Here then we mark one special fact—a fact of deepest interest—three times referred to in the foregoing quotation. It is this, the Holy Ghost came down to speak to every man "in his own dialect"—not the dialect in which he was *educated* merely, but *'in which he was born"*—the very dialect in which his mother first whispered into his infant ears, the sweet and tender accents of a mother's love. Such

was the medium, such the vehicle which the divine Messenger adopted for the blessed purpose of making known to man that God was for us. He did not speak to the Hebrew in Greek, or to the Greek in Latin. He spoke to each one in the language which he understood, in the plain vernacular—the mother tongue. If there was any peculiarity in that mother tongue, any idiom, any provincialism in the dialect of each, the blessed Spirit would make use of it for the purpose of reaching the heart with the sweet story of grace.

Contrast with this the giving of the law from mount Sinai. There Jehovah confined Himself absolutely to one language. If persons had been gathered there "from every nation under heaven," they would not have understood a single syllable. The law—the ten words—the record of *man's duty* to God and to his neighbor was sedulously wrapped up in one tongue. But when *"the wonderful works of God"* were to be published—when the blessed story of love was to be told out—when the heart of God towards poor guilty sinners was to be revealed, was one language enough? No! "Every nation under heaven" must hear, and hear, too, in their own mother tongue.

Is not this a telling fact? It will perhaps be said that those who heard Peter and the rest on the day of Pentecost, were Jews. Well, that in no wise robs our fact of its charm, its sweetness, and its power. Our fact is that when the eternal Spirit descended from Heaven, to tell of the resurrection of Christ, to tell of accomplished redemption—to publish the glad tidings of salvation—to preach repentance and remission of sins—He did not confine Himself to one language, but spoke in every dialect under Heaven!

And why? Because He desired to make man understand what He had to say to him—He desired to reach his heart with the sweet tidings of redeeming love—the soul-stirring message of full remission of sins. When the law was to be given—when Jehovah had to speak to man about his duty—when He had to address him in such terms as, "Thou shalt do this, and thou shalt not do that," He confined Himself to one solitary language. But when He would unfold the precious secret of His love—when He would prove to man that He was for him, He, blessed forever be His name, took care to speak in every language under Heaven, so that every man might hear, in his own dialect wherein he was born, the wonderful works of God.*

Thus, then, in our series of proofs—our golden chain of evidence, we have traveled from the bosom of God to the cross of Christ, and from that precious cross back to the throne—we have marked the giving, the bruising, and the raising of the Son; we have seen the very heart of God told out in deep and marvelous love, and tender compassion toward guilty perishing sinners. Moreover, we have marked the descent of the eternal Spirit, from the throne of God—His mission to this world to announce to every creature under Heaven the glad tidings of a full, free, and everlasting salvation, through the blood of the Lamb, and to announce these tidings not in an unknown tongue, but in the very tongue wherein each was born.

What more remains? Is there yet another link to be added to the chain? Yes; there is *the possession of the Holy Scriptures.* It may perhaps be said that our fifth proof is involved in our fourth, inasmuch as the fact of my possessing a copy of the Bible in my mother tongue is, in reality, the Holy Ghost speaking to me in the language in which I was born.

True; but still, so far as the reader is concerned, the fact that God has put into his hand or within his reach the sacred volume—the inestimable boon, the holy Scriptures—is an additional proof that He is for him. For why were we not left in ignorance and total darkness? Why was the divine book put into our hands? Why, each one may say, for himself and herself, was I thus favored? Why was I not left to live and die in heathen blindness? Why was the heavenly lamp allowed to cast its precious beams on me—even me?

Ah! the answer is, "Because God is for thee." Yes, for thee, notwithstanding all thy many sins—for thee, spite of all thy forgetfulness, ingratitude and rebellion—for thee, although as thou very well knowest, thou canst not shew a single reason why He should not be against thee. He gave His Son from His bosom, bruised Him on the cross, raised Him from the dead, sent down the Holy Ghost, put into your very hands His blessed book, all to shew you that He is for you, that His heart is toward you, that He earnestly desires your salvation.

And mark, we pray thee, thou canst not say, nor wilt thou ever dare to say, "I could not understand the Bible; it was beyond me; it was full of abstruse mysteries which I could not fathom; of difficulties which I could not solve; of discrepancies which I could not reconcile. And when I turned to those who professed to be Christians, I found them split up into almost innumerable sects, and divided into almost endless schools of doctrine. And, not only so, but I saw such utter hollowness, such gross inconsistency, such flagrant contradiction between profession and practice, that I was forced to abandon the whole subject of religion with a mingled feeling of perplexity, contempt, and disgust."

These objections will not stand in the judgment, nor keep thee out of the lake that burneth with fire and brimstone. Remember this. Yes, ponder it deeply. Let not the devil, let not thine own heart deceive thee. What does Abraham say to the rich man, in Luke 16? "They have Moses and the prophets, *let them hear them.*" Why does the rich man not reply, "They cannot understand them?" He dare not.

No; a child can understand the holy Scriptures, which are able to make us wise unto salvation through faith which is in Christ Jesus. There is not one beneath the canopy of God's Heaven, who possesses a copy of the holy Scriptures, who is not solemnly responsible before God for the use he makes of them. If professing Christians

---

* The reader will note with interest a fact alluded to elsewhere, that in Genesis 11 divers tongues were given as a judgment upon man's pride. In Acts 2 divers tongues were given in grace to meet man's need. And in Revelation 7 the various tongues are all found united in one song of praise to God and to the Lamb. Such are some of the wonderful works of God. May we praise Him with all our ransomed powers! May our hearts adore Him!

were split up into ten thousand times as many sects as they are; if they were ten thousand times as inconsistent as they are; if schools and doctors of divinity were ten thousand times more conflicting than they are—still the word to each possessor of the Bible is, "You have Moses and the prophets, and the New Testament, hear them."

Oh! that we could persuade the unconverted, the unawakened, the unbelieving reader to think of these things, to think of them now, to ponder them, in the very hidden depths of his moral being, to give them his heart's undivided attention, ere it be too late. We contemplate, with ever-deepening horror, the condition of a lost soul in hell—of one opening his eyes, in that place of endless torment, to the tremendous fact that God is against him and against him forever; that all hope is gone; that nothing can ever bridge the chasm that separates the region of the lost from the heaven of the redeemed; that "there is a great gulf *fixed*."

We cannot proceed. The thought is really overpowering. The heart is crushed by the appalling contemplation. Dear reader, do let us entreat of thee, ere we lay down the pen, to turn, this very hour, to a dear loving Saviour who stands with open arms and open bosom to receive all who come to Him, and who assures thee that "him that cometh unto Me I will in no wise case out." Do come and trust in God's faithful word and Christ's finished work.

Here lies the precious secret of the whole matter. Look away from self, look straight to Jesus, confide simply in Him, and in what He has done for thee on the cross, and all thy sins shall be blotted out, divine righteousness shall be thine, eternal life, sonship, an indwelling Spirit, an all-prevailing Advocate, a bright home in the heavens, a portion in Christ's eternal glory—yes, if thou wilt but believe in Jesus all shall be thine—Himself the best of all.

May the Holy Ghost lead thee, this moment, to the feet of Jesus, and enable thee to cry out, in holy triumph, "If God be for us, who can be against us?" God grant it for Jesus Christ's sake!

REGENERATION
WHAT IS IT?

THERE ARE FEW SUBJECTS which have given rise to more difficulty and perplexity than that of regeneration, or the new birth. Very many who are themselves the subjects of this new birth are at a loss to know what it is, and filled with doubt as to whether they have ever really experienced it. Many there are who, were they to clothe their desires in words, would say, "Oh, that I knew for certain that I had passed from death unto life. If only I were sure that I was born again, I should be happy indeed." Thus they are harassed with doubts and fears from day to day and from year to year. Sometimes they are full of hope that the great change has passed upon them; but, anon, something springs up within them which leads them to think their former hopes were a delusion. Judging from feeling experience rather than from the plain teaching of the Word of God, they are, of necessity, plunged into uncertainty and confusion as to the whole matter.

Now, I would desire to enter, in company with my reader, upon an examination, in the light of Scripture, of this most interesting subject. It is to be feared that very much of the misapprehension which prevails in reference thereto, arises from the habit of preaching regeneration and its fruits instead of Christ. The effect is put before the cause, and this must always produce derangement of thought.

Let us, then, proceed to consider this

question. What is regeneration? How is it produced? What are its results?

1. First, what is regeneration? Very many look upon it as a change of the old nature, produced, no doubt, by the influence of the Spirit of God. This change is gradual in its operation, and proceeds, from stage to stage, until the old nature is completely brought under. This view of the subject involves two errors; namely, first, an error as to the real condition of our old nature; and, secondly, as to the distinct personality of the Holy Ghost. It denies the hopeless ruin of nature, and represents the Holy Ghost more as an influence than as a Person.

As to our true state by nature, the Word of God presents it as one of total and irrecoverable ruin. Let us adduce the proofs. "And God saw that the wickedness of man was great in the earth, and that *every* imagination of the thoughts of his heart was *only* evil *continually*" (Gen. 6:5). The words "*every*," "*only*," and "*continually*," set aside every idea of a redeeming feature in man's condition before God. Again, "The Lord looked down from heaven upon the children of men, to see if there were any that did understand, and seek God. They are *all* gone aside, they are *all* together become filthy: there is *none* that doeth good; no, no one" (Ps. 14:2-3). Here, again, the expressions "*all*," "*none*," "*no, not one*," preclude the idea of a single redeeming quality in man's condition, as judged in the presence of God. Having thus drawn a proof from Moses and one from the Psalms, let us take one or two from the prophets. "Why should ye be stricken any more? Ye will revolt more and more: the *whole* head is sick, and the *whole* heart faint. From the sole of the foot even unto the head there is no soundness in it" (Isa. 1:5-6). "The voice said, 'Cry.' And he said, 'What shall I cry?' *All* flesh is grass, and all the goodliness thereof is as the flower of the field" (Isa. 40:6). "The heart is deceitful above all things, and desperately wicked: who can know it?" (Jer. 17:9)

The above will suffice from the Old Testament. Let us now turn to the New. "Jesus did not commit Himself unto them, because He knew all, and needed not that any should testify of man: for He knew what was in man" (John 2:24-25). "That which is born of the flesh is flesh" (John 3:6). Read, also, Romans 3:9-19. "Because the carnal mind is enmity against God: for it is not subject to the law of God; neither, indeed, can be" (Rom. 8:7). "Having no hope, and without God in the world" (Eph. 2:12). These quotations might be multiplied, but there is no need. Sufficient proof has been adduced to show forth the true condition of nature. It is "lost," "guilty," "alienated," "without strength," "evil only," "evil continually."

How, then, we may lawfully inquire, can that which is spoken of in such a way ever be changed or improved? "Can the Ethiopian change his skin, or the leopard his spots?" "That which is crooked cannot be made straight." The fact is, the more closely we examine the Word of God, the more we shall see that it is not the divine method to improve a fallen, ruined thing, but to bring in something entirely new. It is precisely thus in reference to man's natural condition—God is not seeking to improve it. The gospel does not propose, as its object, to better man's nature, but to give him a new one. It seeks not to put a new piece upon an old garment, but to impart a new garment altogether. The law looked for something in man, but never got it. Ordinances were given, but man used them to shut out God. The gospel, on the contrary, shows us Christ magnifying the law and making it honorable; it shows Him dying on the cross, and nailing ordinances thereto; it shows Him rising from the tomb, and taking His seat as a Conqueror, at the right hand of the Majesty in the heavens; and, finally, it declares that all who believe in His name are partakers of His own life, and are one with Him who is risen. (See, carefully, the following passages: John 20:31; Acts 13:39; Rom 6:4-11; Eph. 2:1-6; 3:13-18; Col. 2:10-15).

It is of the very last importance to be clear and sound as to this. If I am led to believe that regeneration is a certain change in my old nature, and that this change is gradual in its operation, then, as a necessary consequence, I shall be filled with continual anxiety and apprehension, doubt and fear, depression and gloom, when I discover, as I surely shall, that nature is nature, and will be nought else but nature to the end. No influence or operation of the Holy Ghost can ever make the flesh spiritual. "That which is born of the flesh is flesh," and can never be aught else but "flesh"; and "all flesh is as grass,"—as withered grass. The flesh is presented in Scripture not as a thing to be improved, but as a thing which God counts as "dead," and which we are called to "mortify"—subdue and deny—in all its thoughts and ways. In the cross of the Lord Jesus Christ we see the end of everything pertaining to our old nature. "They that are Christ's have crucified the flesh with the affections and lusts" (Gal. 5:24). He does not say, They that are Christ's are improving, or trying to improve, the flesh. No; but they "have crucified it." It is utterly unimprovable. How can they do this? By the energy of the Holy Ghost, acting not *on* the *old* nature, but *in* the new, and enabling them to keep the old nature where the cross has put it, namely, in the place of death. God expects nothing from the flesh; neither should we. He looks upon it as dead; so should we. He has *put* it out of sight, and we should *keep* it so. The flesh should not be allowed to show itself. God does not own it. It has no existence before Him. True, it is in us, but God gives us the precious privilege of viewing and treating it as dead. His word to us is, "Likewise reckon ye also yourselves to be dead indeed unto sin, but alive unto God through Jesus Christ our Lord" (Rom. 6:11).

This is an immense relief to the heart that has struggled for years in the hopeless business of trying to improve nature. It is an immense relief, moreover, to the conscience which has been seeking a foundation for its peace in the gradual improvement of a totally unimprovable thing. Finally, it is an immense relief to any soul that may, for years, have been earnestly breathing after holiness, but has looked upon holiness as consisting in the inprovement of that which hates holiness and loves sin. To each and all of such it is infinitely precious and important to understand the real nature of regeneration. No one who has not experienced it can conceive the intensity of anguish and the bitterness of the disappointment which a soul feels, who, vainly expecting some improvement in nature, finds, after years of struggling, that nature is nature still—ever the same. And just in proportion to the anguish and disappointment will be the joy of discovering that God is not looking for any improvement in nature—that He sees *it* as dead, and *us* as alive in Christ—one with Him, and accepted in Him, forever. To be led into a clear and full apprehension of this is divine emancipation to the conscience and true elevation for the whole moral being.

Let us, then, see clearly what regeneration is. It is a new birth—the imparting of a new life—the implantation of a new nature—the formation of a new man. The old nature remains in all its distinctness, and the new nature is introduced in all its distinctness. This new nature has its own habits, its own desires, its own tendencies, its own affections. All these are spiritual, heavenly, divine. Its aspirations are all upward. It is ever breathing after the heavenly source from which it has emanated. As in nature water always finds its own level, so in grace the new—the divine—nature always tends toward its own proper source. Thus regeneration is to the soul what the birth of Isaac was to the household of Abraham (Gen. 21). Ishmael remained the same Ishmael, but Isaac was introduced; so the old nature remains the same, but the new is introduced. "That which is born of the Spirit is spirit": it partakes of the nature of its source. A child partakes of the nature of its parents, and the believer is made "a partaker of the divine nature" (2 Peter 1:4). "*Of His own will* begat He us" (James 1:18).

In a word, then, regeneration is God's own work, from first to last. God is the Operator; man is the happy, privileged subject. His co-operation is not sought in a work which must ever bear the impress of one almighty hand. God was alone in creation, alone in redemption, and He must be alone in the mysterious and glorious work of regeneration.

2. Having endeavored to show, from various passages of Scripture, that regen-

eration, or the new birth, is not a change of man's fallen nature, but the imparting of a new—a divine—nature, we shall now, in dependence upon the blessed Spirit's teaching, proceed to consider how the new birth is produced,—how the new nature is communicated. This is a point of immense importance, inasmuch as its places the Word of God before us as the grand instrument which the Holy Ghost uses in quickening dead souls. "By the word of the Lord were the heavens made," and by the Word of the Lord are dead souls called into new life. The Word of the Lord is creative and regenerating. It called worlds into existence; it calls sinners from death to life. The same voice which, of old, said, "Let there be light" must, in every instance, say, "Let there be life."

In the third chapter of John's Gospel, in our Lord's interview with Nicodemus, there is much precious instruction in reference to the mode in which regeneration is produced. Nicodemus held a very high place in what would be termed the religious world. He was "a man of the Pharisees," "a ruler of the Jews," "a master of Israel." He could hardly have occupied a more elevated or influential position. But yet, it is very evident that this highly privileged man was ill at ease. Despite all his religious advantages, his heart felt a restless craving after something which neither his Pharisaism, nor yet the entire system of Judaism could supply. It is quite possible he might not have been able to define what he wanted; but he wanted something, else he never would have come to Jesus by night. It was evident that the Father was drawing him, by a resistless though most gentle hand, to the Son; and the way He took of drawing him was by producing a sense of need which nothing around him could satisfy. This is a very common case. Some are drawn to Jesus by a deep sense of guilt, some by a deep sense of need. Nicodemus, obviously, belongs to the latter class. His position was such as to preclude the idea of anything like gross immorality; and hence it would not, in his case, be so much guilt on his conscience as a void in his heart. But it comes to the same in the end: the guilty conscience and the craving heart must both be brought to Jesus, for He alone can perfectly meet both the one and the other. He can remove, by His precious sacrifice, every stain from the conscience; and He can fill up, by His peerless Person, every blank in the heart. The conscience which has been purged by the blood of Jesus is perfectly clean, and the heart which is filled with the Person of Jesus is perfectly satisfied.

However, Nicodemus had, like many beside, to unlearn a great deal ere he could really grasp the knowledge of Jesus. He had to lay aside a cumbrous mass of religious machinery ere he could apprehend the divine simplicity of God's plan of salvation. He had to descend from the lofty heights of Rabbinical learning and traditionary religion, and learn the alphabet of the gospel in the school of Christ. This was very humiliating to "a man of the Pharisees," "a ruler of the Jews," "a master of Israel." There is nothing of which man is so tenacious as his religion and his learning; and, in the case of Nicodemus, it must have sounded passing strange upon his ear when "a teacher come from God" declared to him, "Verily, verily, I say unto thee, Except a man be born again, he cannot see the kingdom of God." Being *by birth* a Jew, and, as such, entitled to all the privileges of a son of Abraham, it must have involved him in strange perplexity to be told that he must be born again, that he must be the subject of a *new birth*, in order to see the kingdom of God. This was a total setting aside of all his privileges and distinctions. It called him down at once from the very highest to the very "lowest step of the ladder." A Pharisee, a ruler, a master, was not one whit nearer to, or fitter for, this heavenly kingdom, than the most disreputable of the children of men. This was deeply humbling. If he could carry all his advantages and distinctions with him, so as to have them placed to his credit in this new kingdom, it would be something. This would secure for him a position in the kingdom of God far above that of a harlot or a publican. But then, to be told that he must be born again left him nothing to glory in. This was deeply humbling to a learned, religious, and influential man.

But it was puzzling as well as humbling. "Nicodemus saith unto Him, 'How can a man be born when he is old? Can he enter the second time into his mother's womb, and be born?' " Surely not. There would be no more gained by a second natural birth than by a first. If a natural man could enter ten thousand times into his mother's womb and be born, he would be naught but a natural man after all, for "that which is born of the flesh is flesh." Do what you will with flesh, with nature, and you cannot alter or improve it. Nothing could change flesh into spirit. You may exalt it to the rank of a Pharisee, a ruler of the Jews, a master of Israel, and you could hardly make it higher, but it will be flesh notwithstanding. If this were more generally and clearly apprehended, it would prove the saving of fruitless labor to hundreds. Flesh is of no value whatever. In itself it is but withered grass; and as to its most pious endeavors, its religious advantages and attainments, its works of righteousness, they have been pronounced by the pen of inspiration to be as "filthy rags" (Isaiah 44:6).

But let us see the mode in which our blessed Lord replies to the "how?" of Nicodemus. It is peculiarly interesting. Jesus answered, "Verily, verily, I say unto thee, Except a man be born of water and of the Spirit, he cannot enter into the kingdom of God. That which is born of the flesh is flesh, and that which is born of the Spirit is spirit. Marvel not that I said unto thee, 'Ye must be born again.' The wind bloweth where it listeth, and thou hearest the sound thereof, but canst not tell whence it cometh, and whither it goeth: so is every one that is born of the Spirit" (John 3:5-8). Here we are distinctly taught that regeneration, or the new birth, is produced by "water and the Spirit." A man must be born of water and of the Spirit ere he can see the kingdom of God, or enter into its profound and heavenly mysteries. The keenest mortal vision cannot "see" the kingdom of God, nor the most gigantic human intellect "enter" into the deep secrets thereof. "The natural man receiveth not the things of the Spirit of God; for they are foolishness unto him: neither can he know them, because they are spiritually

discerned" (1 Cor. 2:14). "Except a man be born of water and of the Spirit, he cannot enter the kingdom of God."

It may be, however, that many are at a loss to know what is meant by being "born of water." Certainly the expression has been made the ground of very much discussion and controversy. It is only by comparing Scripture with Scripture that we can ascertain the real sense of any particular passage. It is a special mercy for the unlettered Christian—the humble student of the inspired volume—that he need not travel outside the covers of that volume in order to interpret any passage contained therein.

What, then, is the meaning of being "born of water"? We must reply to this question by quoting two or three passages from the Word. In the opening of John's Gospel we read, "He came unto His own, and His own received Him not. But as many as received Him, to them gave He power to become the sons of God, even to *them that believe on His name: which were born*, not of blood, nor of the will of the flesh, nor of the will of man, but *of God"* (John 1:11-13). From this passage we learn that every one who believes on the name of the Lord Jesus Christ is born again, born of God. This is the plain sense of the passage. All who, by the power of God the Holy Ghost, believe on God the Son, are born of God the Father. The source of the testimony is divine; the object of the testimony is divine; the power of receiving the testimony is divine; the entire work of regeneration is divine. Hence, instead of being occupied with myself, and inquiring, like Nicodemus, "How can I be born again?" I have simply to cast myself, by faith, on Jesus; and thus I am born again. All who put their trust in Christ have gotten a new life—are regenerated.

Again, "Verily, verily, I say unto you, *He that heareth My word, and believeth on Him that sent Me*, HATH everlasting life, and shall not come into judgment; but is passed from death unto life" (John 5:24). "Verily, verily, I say unto you, He that believeth on Me hath everlasting life" (John 6:47). "But these are written that ye might believe that Jesus is the Christ, the Son of God; and that, *believing, ye might have life through His name"* (John 20:31). All these passages go to prove that the only way in which we can get this new and everlasting life is by simply receiving the record concerning Christ. All who believe the record, *have* this new, this eternal life. Mark, it is not those who merely *say* they believe, but those who actually *do believe*, according to the sense of the word in the foregoing passages. There is life-giving power in the Christ whom the Word reveals, and in the Word which reveals Him. "Verily, verily, I say unto you, The hour is coming, and now is, when the dead shall hear the voice of the Son of God; and they that hear shall live." And then, lest ignorance should marvel or skepticism sneer at the idea of dead souls hearing, it is added, "Marvel not at this: for the hour is coming, in the which all that are in the graves shall hear His voice, and shall come forth: they that have done good, unto the resurrection of life; and they that have done evil, unto the resurrection of judgment" (John 5:25,28-29). The Lord Christ can make dead souls, as well as dead bodies, hear His quickening voice. It is by His mighty voice that life can be communicated to either body or soul. If the infidel or the skeptic reasons and objects, it is simply because he makes his own vain mind the standard of what ought to be, and thus entirely shuts out God. This is the climax of folly.

What has all this to do with the word "water," in John 3:5? It has to do with it, inasmuch as it shows that the new birth is produced, the new life communicated, by the voice of Christ—which is really the Word of God, as we read in the first chapter of James, "Of His own will begat He us *with the word of truth*" (ver. 18). So also in 1 Peter, "*Being born again*, not of corruptible seed, but of incorruptible, *by the word of God*, which liveth and abideth for ever" (1 Peter 1:23). In both these passages the Word is expressly set forth as the instrument by which the new birth is produced. James declares that we are begotten "by the Word of truth"; and Peter declares that we are "born again by the word of God." If, then, our Lord speaks of being "born of water," it is obvious that He

represents the Word under the significant figure of "water"—a figure which "a master of Israel" might have understood, had he only studied aright Ezekiel 36:25-27.

There is a beautiful passage in the Epistle to the Ephesians, in which the Word is presented under the figure of water. "Husbands, love your wives, even as Christ also loved the Church, and gave Himself for it; that He might sanctify and cleanse it with *the washing of water by the Word*" (chap. 5:25-26). So also in the Epistle to Titus: "Not by works of righteousness which we have done, but according to His mercy He saved us, by the washing of regeneration, and renewing of the Holy Ghost; which He shed on us abundantly, through Jesus Christ our Saviour; that, being justified by His grace, we should be made heirs according to the hope of eternal life" (chap. 3:5-7).

From all these quotations we learn that the Word of God is the grand instrument of which the Holy Ghost makes use in calling dead souls into life. This truth is confirmed, in a peculiarly interesting manner, by our Lord's conversation with Nicodemus; for, instead of replying to the repeated inquiry, "How can these things be?" He sets this "master of Israel" down to learn the simple lesson taught by "the brazen serpent." The bitten Israelite of old was to be healed by simply *looking* at the serpent of brass on the pole: the dead sinner now is to get life by simply looking at Jesus on the cross and Jesus on the throne. The Israelite was not told to look at his wound, though it was the sense of his wound that made him look: the dead sinner is not told to look at his sins, though it is the sense of his sins that will make him look. One look at the serpent healed the Israelite: one look of faith at Jesus, who hung on the cross of Calvary, quickens the dead sinner. The former had not to look a second time to be healed: the latter has not to look a second time to get life. It was not the way he looked, but the object he looked at, that healed the Israelite: it is not the way he looks, but the object he looks at, that saves the sinner: "*Look* unto *Me*, and be ye saved, all the ends of the earth."

Such was the precious lesson which

Nicodemus was called to learn, such the reply to his "how?" If a man begins to reason about the new birth, he must be confounded; but if he believes in Jesus, he is born again. Man's reason can never understand the new birth; but the Word of God produces it. Many are astray as to this. They are occupied with the process of regeneration, instead of the Word which regenerates. Thus they are perplexed and confounded. They are looking at self instead of at Christ; and as there is no inseparable connection between the object at which we look and the effect of looking at it, we can easily see what must be the effect of looking in upon one's self. What could an Israelite have gained by looking at his wound? Nothing. What did he gain by looking at the serpent? Health. What does a sinner gain by looking at himself? Nothing. What does he gain by looking at Jesus? "Everlasting life."

3. We come now to consider, in the third and last place, the results of regeneration, a point of the deepest interest. Who can estimate aright the glorious results of being a child of God? Who can unfold those affections which belong to that high and hallowed relationship in which the soul is placed by being born again? Who can fully explain that precious fellowship which the child of God is privileged to enjoy with his heavenly Father? "Behold, what manner of love the Father hath bestowed upon us, that we should be called the sons of God: therefore the world knoweth us not, because it knew Him not. Beloved, now are we the sons of God, and it doth not yet appear what we shall be: but we know that, when He shall appear, we shall be like Him, for we shall see Him as He is. And every man that hath this hope in Him purifieth himself, even as He is pure" (1 John 3:1-3). "For as many as are led by the Spirit of God, they are the sons of God. For ye have not received the spirit of bondage again to fear; but we have received the Spirit of adoption, whereby we cry, Abba, Father. The Spirit itself beareth witness with our spirit, that we are the children of God: and if children, then heirs; heirs of God and *joint-heirs* with Christ; if so be that we suffer with Him, that we may be also glorified *together*" (Rom. 8:14-17).

It is most important to understand the distinction between *life* and *peace*. The former is the result of being linked with Christ's *Person;* the latter is the result of His *work*. "He that hath the Son hath *life*" (1 John 5:12); but "being *justified* by faith, we have *peace*" (Rom. 5:1), "having made peace through the blood of His cross" (Col. 1:20). The very moment a man receives into his heart the simple truth of the gospel, he becomes a child of God. The truth which he receives is the "incorruptible seed" of "the divine nature" (1 Pet. 1:23; 2 Pet. 1:4.) Many are not aware of all that is involved in thus simply receiving the truth of the gospel. As in nature, the child of a nobleman may not know the varied results of the relationship, so it is, likewise, in grace. I may be ignorant both as to the relationship and its results; but I am in it notwithstanding; and being in it, I have the affections which belong to it, and I ought to cultivate them, and allow them to entwine themselves artlessly around their proper object, even Him who has begotten me by the Word of truth (James 1:18). It is my privilege to enjoy the full flow of parental affection emanating from the bosom of God, and to reciprocate that affection, through the power of the indwelling Spirit. "Now *are* we the sons of God." He has made us such. He has attached this rare and marvelous privilege to the simple belief of the truth (John 1:12). We do not reach this position "by works of righteousness which we have done," or could do, but simply "according to His mercy He saved us, by the washing of regeneration, and renewing of the Holy Ghost; which He shed on us abundantly through Jesus Christ our Saviour; that being justified by His grace, we should be *made heirs* according to the hope of eternal life" (Titus 3:5-7). We are *"called sons"* and *"made* heirs," and all this simply by the belief of the truth of the gospel, which is God's "incorruptible seed."

Take the case of the very vilest sinner, who up to this moment has been living a life of gross wickedness. Let that person receive into his heart the pure gospel of God, let him heartily believe, "that Christ died for our sins according to the Scriptures; and that He was buried, and that He rose again the third day according to the Scriptures," and he there, then and thus becomes a child of God, a thoroughly, saved, perfectly, justified, and divinely accepted person. In receiving into his heart the simple record concerning Christ, he has received new life. Christ is the truth and the life; and when we receive the truth we receive Christ, and when we receive Christ we receive life, "he that believeth on the Son *hath* everlasting life" (John 3:36). When does he get this life? The very moment he believes—"*believing* ye might have life through His name" (John 20:31). The truth concerning Christ is the seed of eternal life, and when that truth is believed, life is communicated.

Observe, this is what the Word of God declares—it is a matter of divine testimony, not merely of human feeling. We do not get life by *feeling* something in ourselves, but by *believing* something about Christ; and that something we have on the authority of God's eternal Word—"the Holy Scriptures." It is well to understand this. Many are looking *in* for evidences of the new life, instead of looking *out* at the object which imparts that life. It is quite true that "he that believeth on the Son of God hath the witness in himself" (1 John 5:10); but, be it remembered, it is "the witness" of a life which is received by "*believing* on the Son of God," not by looking in upon one's self; and the more undividedly I am occupied with Christ, the more distinct and satisfactory will be "the witness" in myself. If I make the witness my object, I shall be plunged in doubt and uncertainty; but if I make Christ my object, I have the witness in all its divine integrity and power. There is special need of clearness as to this, because of the strong tendency of our hearts to make something *within* the ground of our peace and contentment, instead of building, absolutely and exclusively, upon Christ. The more simply we cling to Christ, apart from all beside, the more peaceful and happy we shall be; but directly we take the eye off Him, we become unhinged and unhappy.

In a word, then, we should seek to understand, with scriptural accuracy, the distinction between *life* and *peace*. The former is the result of the connection with Christ's *Person*; the latter is the result of believing in His finished *work*. We very frequently meet with quickened souls who are in sad trouble and disquietude as to their acceptance with God. They really do believe on the name of the Son of God, and, believing, they have life; but, from not seeing the fullness of the work of Christ as to their sins, they are troubled in conscience—they have no mental repose. Take an illustration. If you place a hundredweight upon the bosom of a dead man he does not feel it. Place another, and another, and another, he is wholly unconscious. Why? Because there is no *life*. Let us suppose, for a moment, the entrance in of life, and what will be the result? A most distressing sensation occasioned by the terrible weight upon the bosom. What then will be needful in order to the full enjoyment of the life which had been imparted? Clearly, the removal of the burden. It is somewhat thus with the sinner who receives life by believing on the Person of the Son of God. So long as he was in a state of spiritual death he had no spiritual sensations—he was unconscious of any weight pressing upon him. But the entrance of spiritual life has imparted spiritual sensibilities, and he now feels a burden pressing upon his heart and conscience, which he knows not exactly how to get rid of. He sees not as yet all that is involved in believing on the name of the only begotten Son of God. He does not see that Christ is at once his righteousness and his life. He needs a simple view of the finished atonement of Christ, whereby *all* his sins were plunged in the waters of eternal oblivion, and he himself introduced into the full favor of God. It is this, and this alone, that can remove the heavy burden off the heart, and impart that profound mental repose which nothing can ever disturb.

If I think of God as a judge, and myself as a sinner, I need the blood of the cross to bring me into His presence, in the way of righteousness. I must fully understand that every claim which God, the righteous Judge, had upon me, a guilty sinner, has been divinely answered and eternally settled by "the precious blood of Christ." This gives my soul peace. I see that, through that blood,

God can be "just and the justifier of him which believeth in Jesus" (Rom. 3:29). I learn that in the cross God has been glorified about my sins—yea, that the whole question of sin was fully gone into and perfectly settled between God and Christ amid the deep and awful solitudes of Calvary. Thus my load is taken off, my weight removed, my guilt canceled: I can breathe freely; I have perfect peace; there is literally nothing against me; I am as free as the blood of Christ can make me. The Judge has declared Himself satisfied as to sin by raising the sinner's Surety from the dead, and placing Him at the right hand of the Majesty in the heavens.

But, then, there comes another thing of immense value. I not only see myself as a guilty sinner provided with a way of access to God as a righteous Judge, but I see God, in pursuance of His eternal counsels of electing love, begetting me through the Word of truth, making me His child, adopting me into His family, and setting me before Him in such a way as that I can enjoy communion with Him as my Father in the midst of all the tender endearments of the divine family circle. This is obviously another phase of the believer's position and character. It is no longer a question of his coming to God in the full and settled consciousness that every just claim has been met—this in itself is ineffably precious to every sin-burdened heart—but there is far more than this: God is my Father and I am His child. He has a Father's heart, and I can count on the tender affections of that heart in the midst of all my feebleness and need. He loves me, not because of what I am enabled to do, but because I am His child.

Look at yonder tottering babe, the object of ceaseless care and solicitude, wholly unable to promote his father's interests in any one way, yet so loved by the father that he would not exchange him for ten thousand worlds; and if it be thus with an earthly father, what must it be with our heavenly Father? He loves us, not for aught that we are able to do, but because we are His children. He has begotten us of His own will, by the Word of truth (James 1:18). We could no more earn a place in the heart of the Father than we could satisfy the claims of the righteous Judge. All is of free grace. The Father has begotten us, and the Judge has found a ransom (Job 33:24). We are debtors to grace for both the one and the other.

But, be it remembered, while we are wholly unable to earn, by our works, a place in the Father's heart, or to satisfy the claims of the righteous Judge, we are, nevertheless, responsible to "believe the record which God has given of His Son" (1 John 5:9-11). I say this lest, by any means, my reader should be one of those who intrench themselves behind the dogmas of a one-sided theology, while refusing to believe the plain testimony of God. Many there are—intelligent people, too—who, when the gospel of the grace of God is pressed upon their acceptance, are ready to reply, I cannot believe unless God gives me power to do so; nor shall I ever be endowed with that power unless I am one of the elect. If I belong to the favored number, I *must* be saved; if not, I *can't.*

This is a thoroughly one-sided theology; and not only so, but its one side is turned the wrong way—yea, it is so turned as to wear the form of an absurd but most dangerous fatalism, which completely destroys man's responsibility, and casts dishonor upon God's moral administration. It sends man forth upon a wild career of reckless folly, and makes God the author of the sinner's unbelief. This is to add insult to injury. It is, first, to make God a liar, and then charge Him with being the cause of it. It is to reject His proffered love, and blame Him for the rejection. This is, in reality, the most daring wickedness, though based, as I have said, upon a one-sided theology.

Now, does any one imagine that an argument so flimsy will hold good for a moment in the presence of the king of terrors, or before the judgment-seat of Christ? Is there a soul throughout the gloomy regions of the lost that would ever think of charging God with being the author of its eternal perdition? Ah, no! it is only on earth that people argue thus. Such arguments are never breathed in hell. When men get to hell, they blame themselves. In Heaven they praise the Lamb. All who are lost will have to thank *self;* all who are saved will have to thank *God*. It is when the impenitent soul has passed through the narrow archway of time into the boundless ocean of eternity, that it will enter into the full depth and power of those solemn words, *"I would . . . but ye would not."*

In truth, human responsibility is as distinctly taught in the Word of God as is divine sovereignty. Man finds it impossible to frame a system of divinity which will give each truth its proper place; but he is not called upon to frame systems, but to believe a plain record, and be saved thereby.

Having said thus much by way of caution to any who may be in danger of falling under the power of the above line of argument, I shall proceed to unfold a little further the results of regeneration, as seen in the matter of the discipline of the Father's house.

As the children of God, we are admitted to all the privileges of His house; and in point of fact the discipline of the house is as much a privilege as anything else. It is on the ground of the relationship in which God has set us that He acts in discipline towards us. A father disciplines his children because they are his. If I see a strange child doing wrong, I am not called upon to chasten him. I am not in the relationship of a father to him, and as a consequence I neither know the affections nor the responsibilities of that relationship. I must be in a relationship in order to know the affections which belong to it. Now, as our Father, God, in His great grace and faithfulness, looks after us in all our ways, He will not suffer aught upon us or about us which would be unworthy of Him and subversive of our real peace and blessedness. "Furthermore, we have had fathers of our flesh which corrected us, and we gave them reverence: shall we not much rather be in subjection unto the Father of spirits, and live? For they verily for a few days chastened us after their own pleasure; but He for our profit, that we might be partakers of His holiness" (Heb. 12:9-10). Thus the discipline is a positive privilege, inasmuch as it is a proof of our Father's care, and has for its object our participation in the divine holiness.

But then, we must ever bear in mind that the discipline of our Father's hand is to be interpreted in the light of our Father's countenance, and the deep mysteries of His moral government to be contemplated through the medium of his tender love. If we lose sight of this, we shall be sure to get into a spirit of bondage as respects ourselves, and a spirit of judgment as respects others, both of which are in direct opposition to the spirit of Christ. All our Father's dealings with us are in perfect love. When He furnishes us with bread, it is in love; and when He takes down the rod, it is in love also. *"God is love."* It may frequently happen that we are at a loss to know the why and the wherefore of some special dispensation of our Father's hand. It seems dark and inexplicable. The mist which enwraps our spirits is so thick and heavy as to prevent our catching the bright and cheering beams from our Father's countenance. This is a trying moment—a solemn crisis in the soul's history. We are in great danger of losing the sense of divine love through inability to understand the profound secrets of divine government. Satan, too, is sure to be busy at such a time. He will ply his fiery darts, and throw in his dark and diabolical suggestions. Thus, between the filthy reasonings which spring up within and the horrible suggestions which come from without, the soul is in danger of losing its balance, and of getting away from the precious attitude of artless repose in divine love, let the divine government be what it may.

Thus much with reference to our own souls while under any special visitation of the hand of God. The effect as to others is equally bad. How often may we have detected ourselves in the habit of cherishing a spirit of judgment in reference to a child of God whom we found in circumstances of trial, either of "mind, body, or estate." This should be carefully guarded against. We ought not to imagine that every visitation of the hand of God must necessarily be on account of some special sin in the person. This would be an entirely false principle. The dealings of God are preventive as well as corrective.

Take a case in point. My child may be in the room with me, enjoying all the sweet intimacies which belong to our relationship.

A person enters who I know will utter things which I do not wish my child hear. I therefore, without assigning any reason, tell my child to go to his room. Now, if he has not the fullest confidence in my love, he may entertain all manner of false notions about my act; he may reason about the why and wherefore to such a degree as almost to question my affection. However, directly the visitor takes his leave, I call the child into my presence and explain the whole matter to him, and in the renewed experience of a father's love he gets rid of the unhappy suspicions of a few dark moments.

Thus it is often with our poor hearts in the matter of the divine dealings both with ourselves and others. We reason when we ought to repose: we doubt when we ought to depend. Confidence in our Father's love is the true corrective in all things.

We should ever hold fast the assurance of that changeless, infinite, and everlasting love which has taken us up in our low and lost estate, made us "sons of God," and will never fail us, never let us go, until we enter upon the unbroken and eternal communion of our Father's house above. May that love dwell more abundantly in our hearts, that so we may enter more fully into the meaning and power of regeneration—what it is, how it is produced, and what are its results.

SANCTIFICATION
WHAT IS IT?

TO MINISTER PEACE AND COMFORT to those who, though truly converted, have not laid hold of a full Christ, and who, as a consequence, are not enjoying the liberty of the gospel, is the object we have in view in considering the important and deeply-interesting subject of sanctification. We believe that very many of those, whose spiritual welfare we desire to promote, suffer materially from defective, or erroneous, ideas on this vital question. Indeed, in some cases, the doctrine of sanctification is so entirely misapprehended as to interfere with the faith of the believer's perfect justification and acceptance before God.

For example, we have frequently heard persons speak of sanctification as a progressive work, in virtue of which our old nature is to be made gradually better; and, moreover, that until this process has reached its climax, until fallen and corrupt humanity has become completely sanctified, we are not fit for Heaven.

Now, so far as this view of the question is concerned, we have only to say that both Scripture and the truthful experience of all believers are entirely against it. The Word of God never once teaches us that the Holy Spirit has for His object the improvement, either gradual or otherwise, of our old nature—that nature which we inherit, by natural birth, from fallen Adam. The inspired apostle expressly declares that, "The natural man receiveth not the things of the Spirit of God; for they are foolishness unto him: neither can he know them, because they are spiritually discerned" (1 Cor. 2:14). This one passage is clear and conclusive on the point. If "the natural man" can neither "receive" nor "know" "the things of the Spirit of God," then how can that "natural man" be sanctified by the Holy Ghost? Is it not plain that, to speak of "the sanctification of our nature" is opposed to the direct teaching of 1 Cor. 2:14?

Other passages might be adduced to prove that the design of the Spirit's operations is not to improve or sanctify the flesh, but there is no need to multiply quotations. An utterly ruined thing can never be sanctified. Do what you will with it, it is ruined; and, most assuredly, the Holy Ghost did not come down to sanctify a ruin, but to lead the ruined one to Jesus. So far from any attempt to sanctify the flesh, we read that "The flesh lusteth against the Spirit, and the Spirit against the flesh: and these are contrary the one to the other" (Gal. 5:17). Could the Holy Ghost be represented as carrying on a warfare with that which He is gradually improving and sanctifying? Would not the conflict cease so soon as the process of improvement had reached its climax? But does the believer's conflict ever cease so long as he is in the body?

This leads us to the second objection, to the erroneous theory of the progressive sanctification of our nature, namely, the objection drawn from the truthful experience of all believers. Is the reader a true believer? If so, has he found any improvement in his old nature? Is it a single whit better now than it was when he first started on his Christian course? He may, and should through grace, be able to subdue it more thoroughly; but it is nothing better. If it be not mortified, it is just as ready to spring up and show itself in all its vileness as ever. "The flesh" in a believer is in no wise better than "the flesh" in an unbeliever. And if the Christian does not bear in mind that *self* must be judged, he will soon learn, by bitter experience, that his old nature is as bad as ever; and, moreover, that it will be the very same to the end.

It is difficult to conceive how any one who is led to expect a gradual improvement of his nature, can enjoy an hour's peace, inasmuch as he cannot but see, if he only looks at himself in the light of God's holy Word, his old self—the flesh—is the very same as when he walked in the moral darkness of his unconverted state. His own condition and character are, indeed, greatly changed by the possession of a new, yea, a "divine nature" (2 Pet. 1:4), and by the indwelling of the Holy Ghost, to give effect to its desires; but the moment the old nature is at work, he finds it as opposed to God as ever.

We doubt not but that very much of the gloom and despondency, of which so many complain, may be justly traced to their misapprehension of this important point of sanctification. They are looking for what they can never find. They are seeking for a ground of peace in a sanctified nature instead of in a perfect sacrifice—in a progressive work of holiness instead of in a finished work of atonement. They deem it presumptuous to believe that their sins are forgiven until their evil nature is completely sanctified; and, seeing that this end is not reached, they have no settled assurance of pardon, and are therefore miserable. In a word, they are seeking for a "foundation" totally different from that which Jehovah says He has laid, and, therefore they have no certainty whatever. The only thing that ever seems to give them a ray of comfort is some *apparently* successful effort in the struggle for personal sanctity. If they have had a good day—if they are favored with a season of comfortable communion—if they happen to enjoy a peaceful, devotional frame, they are ready to cry out, "Thou hast made my mountain to stand strong; I shall never be moved" (Ps. 30).

But these things furnish a sorry foundation for the souls's peace. They are not Christ; and until we see that our standing before God is *in Christ*, there cannot be settled peace. The soul that has really got hold of Christ is desirous indeed of holiness; but if intelligent of what Christ is to him, he has done with all thoughts about sanctified nature. He has found his all in Christ, and the paramount desire of his heart is to grow into His likeness. This is true, *practical* sanctification.

It frequently happens that persons, in speaking of sanctification, mean a right thing, although they do not express themselves according to the teaching of holy Scripture. There are many also, who see one side of the truth as to sanctification, but not the other; and, although we should be sorry to make any one an offender for a word, yet it is always most desirable, in speaking of any point of truth, and especially of so vital a point as that of sanctification, to speak according to the divine integrity of the Word. We shall, therefore, proceed to quote for our readers a few of the leading passages from the New Testament in which this doctrine is unfolded. These passages will teach us two things, namely, what sanctification is, and how it is effected.

The first passage to which we would call

attention is 1 Cor. 1:30, "But of Him are ye in Christ Jesus, who of God is made unto us wisdom, and righteousness and *sanctification*, and redemption." Here we learn that Christ "is made unto us" all these things. God has given us, in Christ, a precious casket, and when we open that casket with the key of faith, the first gem that glitters in our view, in this wisdom of God, is "righteousness"; then, "sanctification"; and lastly, "redemption." We have them all *in Christ*. As we get one so we get all. And how do we get one and all? By faith.

But why does the apostle name redemption last? Because it takes in the final deliverance of the body of the believer from under the power of mortality, when the voice of the archangel and the trump of God shall either raise it from the tomb, or change it, in the twinkling of an eye. Will this act be progressive? Clearly not; it will be done "in the twinkling of an eye." The body is in one state now, and "in a moment" it will be in another. In the brief point of time expressed by the rapid movement of the eyelash, will the body pass from corruption to incorruption; from dishonor to glory; from weakness to power. What a change! It will be immediate, complete, eternal.

But what are we to learn from the fact that "sanctification" is placed in the group with "redemption"? We learn that what redemption *will be* to the body, that sanctification *is* now to the soul. In a word, sanctification, in the sense in which it is here used, is immediate, and complete, a divine work. The one is no more progressive than the other. The one is as immediate as the other. The one is as complete and as independent of man as the other. No doubt, when the body shall have undergone the glorious change, there will be heights of glory to be trodden, depths of glory to be penetrated, wide fields of glory to be explored. All these things shall occupy us throughout eternity. But, then, the work which is to fit us for such scenes will be done in a moment. So also is it, in reference to sanctification. The *practical* results of it will be continually developing themselves; but the thing itself, as spoken of in this passage, is done in a moment.

What an immense relief it would be to thousands of earnest, anxious, struggling souls to get a proper hold of Christ as their sanctification! How many are vainly endeavoring to work out a sanctification for themselves! They have come to Christ for righteousness after many fruitless efforts to get a righteousness of their own; but they are seeking after sanctification in a different way altogether. They have gotten "righteousness without works," but they imagine that they must get sanctification with works. They have gotten righteousness by faith, but they imagine they must get sanctification by effort. They do not see that we get sanctification in precisely the same way as we get righteousness, inasmuch as Christ "is made unto us" the one as well as the other. Do we get Christ by effort? No; by faith. It is "to him that worketh *not*" (Rom 4:5). This applies to all that we get in Christ.

We have no warrant whatever to single out from 1 Cor. 1:30, the matter of "sanctification," and place it upon a different footing from all the other blessings which it enfolds. We have neither wisdom, righteousness, sanctification, nor redemption in ourselves; nor can we procure them by aught that we can do; but God has made Christ to be unto us all these things. In giving us Christ, He gave us all that is in Christ. The fullness of Christ is ours, and Christ is the fullness of God.

Again, in Acts 26:18, the converted Gentiles are spoken of as "receiving forgiveness of sins and an inheritance among them which *are* sanctified by faith." Here, faith is the instrument by which we are said to be sanctified, because it connects us with Christ. The very moment the sinner believes on the Lord Jesus Christ he becomes linked to Him. He is made one with Him, complete in Him, accepted in Him. This is true sanctification and justification. It is not a process. It is not a gradual work. It is not progressive. The Word is very explicit. It says, "them which *are* sanctified by *faith* which is in Me." It does not say, "which *shall be* sanctified," or, "which are being sanctified." If such were the doctrine it would have been so stated.

No doubt, the believer grows in the

knowledge of this sanctification, in his sense of its power and value, its practical influence and results, the experience and enjoyment of it. As "the truth" pours its divine light upon his soul, he enters into a more profound apprehension of what is involved in being "set apart" for Christ, in the midst of this evil world. All this is blessedly true; but the more its truth is seen, the more clearly we shall understand that sanctification is not merely a progressive work, wrought in us by the Holy Spirit, but that it is one result of our being linked to Christ, by faith, whereby we become partakers of all that He is. This is an immediate, a complete, and an eternal work. "Whatsoever God doeth, it shall be forever: nothing can be put to it, nor anything taken from it" (Eccles. 3:14). Whether He justifies or sanctifies, "it shall be forever." The stamp of eternity is fixed upon every work of God's hand: "nothing can be put to it," and, blessed be His name, "nothing can be taken from it."

There are passages which present the subject in another aspect—the *practical result* in the believer of his sanctification in Christ, and which may require fuller consideration hereafter. In Thess. 5:23, the apostle prays for the saints whom he addresses, "And the very God of peace sanctify you wholly; and I pray God your whole spirit, and soul, and body, be preserved blameless unto the coming of our Lord Jesus Christ." Here, the word is applied to a sanctification admitting of degrees. The Thessalonians had, along with all believers, a perfect sanctification in Christ; but as to the practical enjoyment and display of this, it was only accomplished in part, and the apostle prays that they may be wholly sanctified.

In this passage, it is worthy of notice, that nothing is said of "the flesh." Our fallen, corrupt nature is always treated as a hopelessly ruined thing. It has been weighed in the balance and found wanting. It has been measured by a divine rule and found short. It has been tried by a perfect plummet and proved crooked. God has set it aside. Its "end has come before Him." He has condemned it and put it to death (Rom. 8:3). Our old man is crucified, dead, and buried (Rom. 6:8). Are

we, then, to imagine for a moment, that God the Holy Ghost came down from Heaven for the purpose of exhuming a condemned, crucified, and buried thing, so that He might sanctify it? The idea has only to be named, to be abandoned forever by every one who bows to the authority of Scripture. The more closely we study the Law, the Prophets, the Psalms, and the entire New Testament, the more closely we shall see that the flesh is wholly unmendable. It is, absolutely, good for nothing. The Spirit does not *sanctify* it, but he enables the believer to *mortify* it. We are told to "*put off* the old man." This precept would never have been delivered to us if the object of the Holy Ghost were the sanctification of that "old man."

We trust that no one will acuse us of entertaining a desire to lower the standard of personal holiness, or to weaken the soul's earnest aspirations after a growth in that purity for which every true believer must ardently long. God forbid! If there is one thing above another which we desire to promote in ourselves and others, it is a full personal purity—a godly practical sanctity—a wholehearted separation to God—from all evil—in every shape and form. For this we long, for this we pray, in this we desire to grow daily.

But then we are fully convinced that a superstructure of true, practical holiness can never be erected on a legal basis; and hence it is that we press 1 Cor 1:30, upon the attention of our readers. It is to be feared that many who have, in some measure, abandoned the legal ground, in the matter of "righteousness," are yet lingering thereon for "sanctification." We believe this to be the mistake of thousands, and we are most anxious to see it corrected. The passage before us would, if simply received into the heart by faith, entirely correct this serious mistake.

All intelligent Christians are agreed as to the fundamental truth of "righteousness without works." All freely and fully admit that we cannot, by any efforts of our own, work out a righteousness for ourselves before God. But it is not just so clearly seen that righteousness and sanctification are put upon precisely the same ground in the Word of God. We can no more work out a sanctification than we can work out a righteousness. We may try it, but we shall, sooner or later, find out that it is utterly vain. We may vow and resolve; we may labor and struggle; we may cherish the fond hope of doing better to-morrow than we have done to-day; but, in the end, we must be constrained to see, and feel, and own, that as regards the matter of sanctification, we are as completely "without strength" as we have already proved ourselves to be in the matter of righteousness.

And, oh! what sweet relief to the suffering one who has been seeking for satisfaction or rest in his own holiness to find, after years of unsuccessful struggle, that the very thing he longs for is treasured up in Christ for him,—his own this moment, even a complete sanctification to be enjoyed *by faith!* Such an one may have been battling with his habits, his lusts, his tempers, his passions; he has been making the most laborious efforts to subdue his flesh and grow in inward holiness, but alas! he has failed.* He finds, to his deep sorrow, that *he* is not holy, and he reads that "Without holiness no man shall see the Lord" (Heb. 12). Not, observe, without a certain measure, or attainment in holiness, but without the thing itself; which every Christian has, from the moment he believes, whether he knows it or not. Perfect sanctification is as fully included in the word "salvation" as is "righteousness, or redemption." He did not get Christ by effort, but by faith; and when he laid hold on Christ he received all that is in Christ. Hence, it is by abiding in Christ he finds power for the subjugation of his lusts, passions, tempers, habits, circumstances, and influences. He must look to Jesus for all.

All this is simple to faith. The believer's standing is in Christ, and if in Christ for one thing, he is in Christ for all. I am not in Christ for righteousness, and out of Christ for sanctification. If I am a debtor to Christ for righteousness, I am equally a debtor to Him for sanctification. I am not a debtor to legality for either the one or the other. I get both by grace, through faith, and all in Christ. Yes, all—all in Christ. The moment the sinner comes to Christ, and believes on Him, he is taken completely off the old ground of nature; he loses his old legal standing and all its belongings, and is looked at as in Christ. He is no longer "in the flesh" but "in the Spirit" (Rom. 8:9). God only sees him in Christ, and as Christ. He becomes one with Christ forever.

"As He is, so are we in this world" (1 John 4). Such is the absolute standing, the settled and eternal position, of the very feeblest babe in the family of God. There is but one standing for every child of God, every member of Christ. Their knowledge, experience, power, gift, and intelligence, may vary; but their standing is one. Whatever of righteousness or sanctification they possess, they owe it all to their being in Christ; consequently, if they have not gotten a perfect sanctification, neither have they gotten a perfect righteousness. But 1 Cor. 1:30, distinctly teaches that Christ "*is made*" both the one and the other to all believers. It does not say that we have righteousness and "*a measure* of sanctification." We have just as much Scripture authority for putting the word "measure" before righteousness as before sanctification. The Spirit of God does not put it before either. Both are perfect, and we have both in Christ.

God never does anything by halves. There is no such thing as a half justification. Neither is there such a thing as a half sanctification. The idea of a member of the family of God, or of the body of Christ, wholly justified, but only half sanctified, is at once opposed to Scripture, and revolting to all sensibilities of the divine nature.

It is not improbable that very much of the misapprehension which prevails, in reference to sanctification, is traceable to the habit of confounding two things which differ very materially, namely our *standing* and our *walk*, or position and condition. The believer's standing is perfect, because it is the gift of God in Christ. His walk, alas, may

* The divine picture of this experience and conflict is given us in the seventh chapter of Romans. For a full consideration of this subject, see the article entitled, "Deliverance, What is it?"

be very imperfect, fluctuating, and marked with personal infirmity. Whilst his position is absolute and unalterable, his practical condition may exhibit manifold imperfections, inasmuch as he is still in the body, and surrounded by various hostile influences which affect his moral condition from day to day. If, then, his standing be measured by his walk, his position by his condition, what he is in God's view by what he is in man's, the result must be false. If I reason from what I am in myself, instead of from what I am in Christ, I must, of necessity, arrive at a wrong conclusion.

We should look carefully to this. We are very much disposed to reason upward from ourselves to God, instead of downward from God to us. We should bear in mind that

> Far as Heaven's resplendent orbs
>   Beyond earth's spot extend,
> As far My thoughts, as far My ways,
>   Your ways and thoughts transcend.

God looks on His people, and acts toward them, too, according to their standing in Christ. He has given them this standing. He has made them what they are. They are His workmanship. Hence, therefore, to speak of them as half justified would be a dishonor cast upon God; and to speak of them as half sanctified would be just the same.

This train of thought conducts us to another weighty proof drawn from the authoritative and conclusive page of inspiration, namely, 1 Cor. 6:11. In the verses preceding, the apostle draws a fearful picture of fallen humanity, and he plainly tells the Corinthian saints that they had been just like that. "Such were some of you." This is plain dealing. There are no flattering words—no daubing with untempered mortar—no keeping back the full truth as to nature's total and irretrievable ruin. "Such were some of you: but ye *are* washed, but ye *are* sanctified, but ye *are* justified, in the name of the Lord Jesus, and by the Spirit of our God."

What a striking contrast between the two sides of the apostle's *"but"!* On the one side, we have all the moral degradation of man's condition; and, on the other side, we have all the absolute perfectness of the believer's standing before God. This, truly, is a marvelous contrast; and be it remembered that the soul passes in a moment, from one side to the other of this "but." "Such *were* some of you: but ye *are*," now, something quite different. The moment they received Paul's gospel, they were "washed, sanctified, and justified." They were fit for Heaven; and, had they not been so, it would have been a slur upon the divine workmanship.

> "Clean every whit," Thou saidst it, Lord;
>   Shall one suspicion lurk?
> Thine, surely, is a faithful word,
>   And Thine a *finished work*.

This is divinely true. The most inexperienced believer is "clean every whit," not as a matter of attainment, but as the necessary result of being in Christ. He will, no doubt, grow in the knowledge and experience of what sanctification really is. He will enter into its practical power; its moral effects upon his habits, thoughts, feelings, affections, and associations: in a word, he will understand and exhibit the mighty influence of divine sanctification upon his entire course, conduct, and character. But then, he was as completely sanctified, in God's view, the moment he became linked to Christ by faith, as he will be when he comes to bask in the sunlight of the divine presence, and reflect back the concentrated beams of glory emanating from the throne of God and of the Lamb. He is in Christ now; and he will be in Christ then. His sphere and his circumstances will differ. His feet shall stand upon the golden pavement of the upper sanctuary, instead of standing upon the arid sand of the desert. He will be in a body of glory, instead of a body of humiliation; but as to his standing, his acceptance, his completeness, his justification, and sanctification, all was settled the moment he believed on the name of the only begotten Son of God—as settled as ever it will be, because as settled as God could make it. All this seems to flow as a necessary and unanswerable inference from 1 Cor. 6:11.

It is of the utmost importance to

apprehend, with clearness, the distinction between a truth and the practical application and result of a truth. This distinction is ever maintained in the Word of God. "Ye *are* sanctified." Here is the absolute truth as to the believer, as viewed in Christ. The practical application of it, and its results in the believer, we find in such passages as these. "Christ loved the church, and gave Himself for it; that He might sanctify and cleanse it with the washing of water by the Word" (Eph. 5:25-26). And "the very God of peace sanctify you wholly" (1 Thess. 5:23).

But how is this application made, and this result reached? By the Holy Ghost, through the written Word. Hence we read, "Sanctify them through Thy truth" (John 17). And again, "God hath from the beginning chosen you to salvation, through sanctification of the Spirit and belief of the truth" (2 Thess. 2:13). So also, in Peter, "Elect according to the foreknowledge of God the Father, through sanctification of the Spirit" (1 Pet. 1:2). The Holy Ghost carries on the believer's practical sanctification on the ground of Christ's accomplished work; and the mode in which He does so is by applying to the heart and conscience the truth as it is in Jesus. He unfolds the truth as to our perfect standing before God in Christ, and, by energizing the new man in us, He enables us to put away everything incompatible with that perfect standing.

A man who is "washed, sanctified, and justified," ought not to indulge in any unhallowed temper, lust, or passion. He is separated to God and should "cleanse himself from all filthiness of the flesh and spirit." It is his holy and happy privilege to breathe after the very loftiest heights of personal sanctity. His heart and his habits should be brought and held under the power of that grand truth that he is perfectly "washed, sanctified, and justified."

This is true practical sanctification. It is not any attempt at the improvement of our old nature. It is not a vain effort to reconstruct an irretrievable ruin. No; it is simply the Holy Ghost, by the powerful application of "the truth," enabling the new man to live, and move, and have his being in

that sphere to which he belongs. Here there will, undoubtedly, be progress. There will be growth in the moral power of this precious truth—growth in spiritual ability to subdue and keep under all that pertains to nature—a growing power of separation from the evil around us—a growing meetness for that Heaven to which we belong, and toward which we are journeying—a growing capacity for the enjoyment of its holy exercises. All this there will be, through the gracious ministry of the Holy Ghost, who uses the Word of God to unfold to our souls the truth as to our standing in Christ, and as to the walk which *comports with* such standing. But let it be clearly understood that the work of the Holy Ghost in practical sanctification, day by day, is founded upon the fact that believers *"are"* sanctified through the offering of the body of Jesus Christ once" (Heb. 10:10). The object of the Holy Ghost is to lead us into the knowledge, the experience, and the practical exhibition of that which was true of us in Christ the very moment we believed. As regards this, there is progress; but our standing in Christ is eternally complete.

"Sanctify them through Thy truth; Thy Word is truth" (John 17:17). And again, "The very God of peace sanctify you wholly" (1 Thess. 5:23). In these passages, we have the grand practical side of this question. Here we see sanctification presented, not merely as something absolutely and eternally true of us in Christ, but also as wrought out in us, daily and hourly, by the Holy Ghost through the Word. Looked at from this point of view, sanctification is, obviously, a progressive thing. I should be more advanced in personal holiness next year than I was in this. I should, through grace, be advancing, day by day, in practical holiness. But what, let me ask, is this? What, but the working out in me of that which was true of me in Christ, the very moment I believed? The basis on which the Holy Ghost carries on the *subjective* work in the believer, is the *objective* truth of his eternal completeness in Christ.

Again, "Follow peace with all men, and holiness, without which no man shall see the Lord" (Heb. 12:14). Here is holiness presented as a thing to be "followed after"—to be attained by earnest pursuit—a thing which every true believer will long to cultivate.

May the Lord lead us into the power of these things. May they not dwell as doctrines and dogmas in the region of our intellect, but enter into and abide in the heart, as sacred and powerfully influential realities! May we know the sanctifying power of the truth (John 17:17); the sanctifying power of faith (Acts 26:18); the sanctifying power of the name of Jesus (1 Cor. 1:30; 6:11); the sanctifying of the Holy Ghost (1 Peter 1:2); the sanctifying grace of the Father (Jude 1).

ETERNAL PUNISHMENT VS. UNIVERSALISM AND ANNIHILATIONISM

I HAVE BEEN THINKING a good deal of late, on the last verse of the third chapter of John. It seems to me to furnish a most powerful answer to two of the leading heresies of this our day, namely, *Universalism* on the one hand, and *Annihilationism*, on the other: "He that believeth on the Son hath everlasting life; and he that believeth not the Son, *shall not see life;* but *the wrath of God abideth on him.*"

The deniers of eternal punishment, as you know, are divided into two classes, differing from each other very materially. The one professes to believe that all will utimately be restored and brought into everlasting felicity; these are the *Universalists.* The other is of the opinion that all who die out of Christ are annihilated, soul and body—made an end of thoroughly—will perish like the beast.

I think you will agree with me that John 3:36 completely demolishes both these fatal errors. It meets the Universalist by the sweeping and conclusive statement that the unbeliever "shall not see life." It entirely sets aside the notion of all being restored and eternally saved. Those who refuse to believe the Son, shall die in their sins, and never see life.

But, were this all, the Annihilationist might say, "Exactly so; that is just what I believe. None but those who believe in the Son shall live eternally. Eternal life is only in the Son, and hence, all who die out of Christ shall perish—soul and body shall be made an end of."

Not so, says the Holy Spirit. It is quite true they shall not see life; but—tremendous fact! "The wrath of God *abideth* on him." This, beyond all question, gives a flat contradiction to annihilationism. If the wrath of God is to abide upon the believer, it is utterly impossible he can be made an end of. Annihilation and abiding wrath are wholly incompatible. We must either erase the word "abiding" from the inspired page, or abandon completely the notion of annihilation. To hold the two is out of the question.

Of course, I am merely now referring to this one passage of Holy Scripture; and truly it is enough of itself to settle any mind that simply bows to the voice of God, as to the solemn question of eternal punishment. But here is just the point. Men *will* not submit to the teaching and authority of Holy Scripture. They presume to sit in judgment upon what is and what is not worthy of God to do. They imagine that people may live in sin, in folly, in rebellion against God, and in the neglect of His Christ, and after all go unpunished. They take upon them to decide that it is inconsistent with their idea of God to allow such a thing as eternal punishment. They attribute to the government of God what we should consider a weakness in any human government, namely, an inability to punish evil-doers.

But the Word of God is against them. It speaks of "*unquenchable* fire"—of an "*undying* worm"—of a "*fixed* gulf"—of "*abiding* wrath." What, I would ask, is the meaning of such words, in the judgment of any honest, unprejudiced mind? It may be said that these are figures. Granted that the "fire," the "worm," and the "gulf" are figures, but figures of what? Of something ephemeral—something which must, sooner or later, have an end? Nay; but something which is eternal, if anything is eternal.

If we deny eternal punishment, we must deny an eternal anything, inasmuch as it is the same word which is used in every instance to express the idea of endless continuance. There are about seventy passages in the Greek New Testament where the word "everlasting" occurs. It is applied, amongst many other things, to the life which believers possess, and to the punishment of the wicked, as in Matthew 25:46. Now, upon what principle can any one attempt to take out the six or seven passages in which it applies to the punishment of the wicked, and say that in all these instances it does not mean for ever; but that in all the rest it does? I confess this seems to be perfectly unanswerable. If the Holy Ghost, if the Lord Jesus Christ Himself had thought proper to make use of a different word, when speaking of the punishment of the wicked, from what He uses when speaking of the life of believers, I grant there might be some basis for an objection.

But no; we find the same word invariably used to express what everybody knows to be endless; and therefore if the punishment of the wicked be not endless, nothing is endless. They cannot, consistently, stop short with the question of punishment, but must go on to the denial of the very existence of God Himself.

Indeed, I cannot but believe that here lies the real root of the matter. The enemy desires to get rid of the Word of God, of the Spirit of God, the Christ of God, and God Himself; and he craftily begins by introducing the thin end of his fatal wedge, in the denial of eternal punishment; and when this is admitted, the soul has taken the first step on the inclined plane which leads down to the dark abyss of atheism.

This may seem strong, harsh, and ultra; but it is my deep and thorough conviction; and I feel most solemnly impressed with the necessity of warning all our young friends against the danger of admitting into their minds the very shadow of a question or doubt as to the divinely established truth of the endless punishment of the wicked in hell. The unbeliever cannot be restored, for Scripture declares "he shall not see life." Moreover, he cannot be annihilated, for Scripture declares that "the wrath of God abideth upon him."

How much better and wiser and safer it would be for our fellow men to flee from the wrath to come than to deny that it is coming; or that, when it does come, it will be eternal.

ETERNAL PUNISHMENT

WE HAVE RECEIVED a communication on the deeply solemn subject of eternal punishment, from a person who would seem to be the exponent of the feelings of a very numerous class. Our correspondent does not, by any means, write as an objector, or a caviler, but as an honest inquirer; and we are not sorry to be called upon to bear a clear and decided testimony on a point of such grave moment. He asks us to let him know "what the Holy Ghost has taught us on the subject," and we cheerfully comply.

We believe the Word of God most clearly and fully teaches the eternity of punishment. The word which is rendered "everlasting," or "eternal," occurs about seventy times in the New Testament. We shall give some examples. "To be cast into *everlasting* fire" (Matt. 18:8). "That I may have *eternal* life" (Matt. 19:16). "These shall go away into *everlasting* punishment" (Matt. 25:46). And in the same verse, "The righteous unto life *eternal*." "Is in danger of *eternal* damnation" (Mark 3:29). "They may receive you into everlasting habitations" (Luke 16:9). "In the world to come, life *everlasting*" (Luke 18:30).

"He that believeth on the Son hath *everlasting* life" (John 3:15-16,36;5:24). "The commandment of the *everlasting* God" (Rom. 16:26). "An exceeding and *eternal* weight of glory" (2 Cor. 4:17). "The things which are not seen are *eternal*" (2 Cor. 16:18). "A house not made with hands, *eternal* in the heavens" (2 Cor. 5:1). "They shall be punished with *everlasting* destruction" (2 Thess. 1:9). "Hath given us *everlasting* consolation" (2 Thess. 2:16). "In Christ Jesus with *eternal* glory" (2 Tim. 2:10). "The author of *eternal* salvation" (Heb. 5:9). "Having obtained *eternal* redemption" (Heb. 9:12). "Who through the *eternal* Spirit offered Himself without spot to God" (ver. 14). "The promise of *eternal* inheritance" (ver. 15). "Called us unto His *eternal* glory" (1 Pet. 5:10). "Into the *everlasting* kingdom of our Lord and Saviour" (2 Pet. 1:11). "This is the true God and *eternal* life" (1 John 5:20). "Suffering the vengeance of *eternal* fire" (Jude 7).

Now, we are aware that the opposers of the doctrine of eternal punishment endeavor to prove that the word "everlasting" does not mean everlasting in the Greek; and this is one reason why we have quoted such a number of passages in which the Greek word αιωνιος (*aionios*) occurs, and in which the Holy Ghost applies it in such a variety of ways. The word which is applied to the punishment of the wicked is also applied to the life which believers possess, to the salvation and redemption in which they rejoice, to the glory to which they look forward, to those mansions in which they hope to dwell, and to the inheritance which they expect to enjoy. Moreover, it is applied to God, and to the Spirit. If, therefore, it be maintained that the word "everlasting" does not mean everlasting when applied to the punishment of the wicked, what security have we that it means everlasting when applied to the life, blessedness, and glory of the redeemed? What warrant has any one, be he ever so learned, to single out seven instances from the seventy in which the Greek word αιωνιος is used, and say that in those seven it does not mean everlasting, but that in all the rest it does? They have none whatever.

Men may reason as they will about divine benevolence and goodness—about its being inconsistent with the mercy of God to permit such a thing as eternal punishment—as to the strange want of proportion between a few years of sin and an endless eternity of punishment; a single line of holy Scripture is amply sufficient, in our judgment, to sweep away ten thousand such reasonings, even though supported by the learned dogma that "everlasting" does not mean everlasting in the Greek. "Where their worm dieth not, and the fire is not quenched" (Mark 9:46). Solemn statement! Let men beware of trifling with it, or reasoning about it. Let them believe it, and flee from the wrath to come—flee now to Jesus, who died on Calvary's cursed tree to deliver us from everlasting burnings.

But not only is the eternity of punishment clearly laid down in Scripture—as clearly as the eternity of God Himself, or of any thing pertaining to Him; we believe it also flows as a necessary truth from other truths which are generally received without a single question. Take, for instance, the immortality of the soul. Did the fall of man touch this question? We believe not. Man was made the possessor of an immortal spirit, by the breath of the Almighty; and we have no authority whatsoever to say that his fall made any difference as to this. Immortal he was, as to his soul, immortal he is, and immortal he must be. Yes, he must live forever somewhere. Tremendous thought! Many do not like it. They would fain be able to say, "Let us eat and drink, for to-morrow we die." They would like to pass away as the beasts that perish; and this very desire, we doubt not, has been, in many cases, the parent of the notion that punishment is non-eternal. "The wish is father to the thought." But, ah! man must face that dreadful reality, *Eternity*. Saved or unsaved, there is no escaping that. He must either deny the immortality of the soul, or admit the eternity of punishment.

Again, take the doctrine of the atonement. If anything less than eternal punishment be due to sin, what need was there of an infinite sacrifice to give deliverance from that punishment? Could nothing less than the peerless, priceless, divine sacrifice of the Son of God deliver any one from hell fire, and that fire not be eternal? Did Jesus shed His precious blood to deliver us from the consequences of our guilt, and those consequences be only temporary? We can never admit any such proposition. Grant us the truth of an infinite sacrifice, and we argue from thence the truth of eternal punishment.

We attach no weight whatever to the argument drawn from the lack of proportion between a few years of sin and an eternity of woe. We do not believe that this is the true way to measure the matter. The cross is the only measure by which to reach a true result; and we believe the deniers of eternal punishment offer dishonor to the cross by lowering it into a means of deliverance from a doom which is not eternal in its duration.

And now, one word as to the idea of its being incompatible with the character of God to allow such a thing as eternal punishment. Many seem to attach great weight to this. They appear to think that eternal misery could never comport with divine mercy and goodness. But those who urge this plea seem to forget that there is another side of the question, which must be looked at if we would reach a sound conclusion on the point. What about divine justice, holiness, and truth? Are these things not to be taken into account? Can we base an argument on some of the divine attributes and leave others out? Surely not. We must look at them all. The cross of Christ has harmonized them all, in the view of all created intelligences. In that cross, God has set forth His perfect love to the sinner; but He also has set forth His perfect hatred of sin. Now, if a man deliberately rejects that only way of escape—that perfect remedy—that divine provision, what is to be done? God cannot let sin into His presence. He is of purer eyes than to behold evil, and cannot look on iniquity. Will the deniers of eternal punishment tell us what is to be done?

How is this question to be settled? They say, by annihilation—that is, by man's perishing like a beast. Ah, this will never do! "The Lord God breathed into his nostrils the breath of life, and man became a living soul" (Gen. 2:7). Was this ever revoked? Is there a

shadow of foundation in the entire book of God for the theory of annihilation? If there is, let it be produced. We look upon it as a most miserable subterfuge—a pitiable attempt to get rid of the awful thought of eternity. But it will not do. Let man but cast his eye on the page of inspiration, and there he sees that tremendous word, *"Eternity"! "Eternity"! "Eternity"!* Let him but lend his ear to the voice that issues from the depth of his moral being, and he will hear the same soul-subduing word, "Eternity"! "Eternity"! "Eternity"! He cannot get rid of it; he cannot shake it off. He is shut up to the stern fact that he must live forever.

Well, then, what about his sin? That cannot get into God's presence. God and sin can never be together. This is a fixed principle. God is good, no doubt, and the proof of His goodness is the gift of His Son. But then He is holy; and between holiness and sin there must be an eternal separation; so that we are forced to the same solemn conclusion, namely, that all who die in their sins—all who die in the rejection of God's infinite provision for the forgiveness of sins, will have to endure the consequences of those sins in the lake that burneth with fire and brimstone throughout the countless ages of eternity.

We would most earnestly beseech the unconverted reader to pause and seriously consider this most momentous question. Let him not be deceived by vain words; let him not harken to a false criticism, which would fain persuade him that "eternal" does not mean eternal in the Greek; for, oh, most assuredly, it does mean eternal, whether in Hebrew, Greek, Latin, or English. "Eternal" can never mean temporal, or "temporal" eternal, in any language under heaven. And furthermore, let him not harken to a false sentimentality, which would fain persuade him that God is too kind to consign any of His creatures to hell fire. God was so kind as to "give His only begotten Son, that whosoever believeth in Him might not perish, but have everlasting life."

But God is too holy to let sin into Heaven; and hence, instead of feeding himself with the vain hope (if hope it can be called,) of annihilation, let him build upon the sure

Word of God, which tells him of full, free, and everlasting salvation through the blood of the Lamb. Our God has no pleasure in the death of a sinner. His long-suffering is salvation, not willing that any should perish, but that all should come to repentance. There is no reason why the reader should perish. God waits to be gracious. Mercy's door stands wide open, and the sword of judgment is in the scabbard. But the moment is rapidly approaching when all shall be changed, and then all who die in their sins will prove, by bitter experience, that, notwithstanding all the arguments founded upon a false criticism and a false sentimentality, *the punishment of sin is and must be eternal.*

"And I say unto you My friends, Be not afraid of them that kill the body, and after that have no more that they can do. But I will forewarn you whom ye shall fear: Fear Him, which after He hath killed hath power to cast into hell; yea, I say unto you, Fear Him" (Luke 12: 4-5).

THE CONFIRMATION VOWS

"ALL THAT THE LORD HATH SPOKEN we will do." Such were the memorable words with which the people of Israel virtually abandoned the ground on which the blessed God had just been setting them, and on which, too, He had dealt with them in bringing them up out of the land of Egypt. "Ye have seen," said He, "what I did unto the Egyptians, and how I bare you on eagles' wings, and brought you unto Myself." All this was grace—pure, perfect, divine grace. He heard the groans and beheld the sorrows of the people amid the darkness and degradation of Egyptian bondage, and in His unmingled mercy He came down to deliver them. He sought not their aid, He looked not for aught from them. "His own arm brought salvation." He acted *for* them, *with* them, and *in* them; and that, too, in the solitariness and sovereignty of His own unfailing grace.

He said to Moses at the opening of the book of Exodus, *"I am come down to deliver them."* This was absolute and unqualified grace. There was no "if," no "but," no condition, no vow, no resolve. It was *free grace*, founded upon God's eternal counsels, and righteously displayed in immediate connection with "the blood of the Lamb." Hence, from first to last, the word to Israel was, *"stand still, and see the salvation of Jehovah."* They were not called to "resolve," or to "vow," or to "do." God was acting for them—He was doing *all*: He placed Himself between them and every enemy, and every evil. He spread forth the shield of His salvation that they might hide themselves behind its impenetrable defences, and abide there in peace.

But, alas, Israel made a vow—a strange, a singular vow indeed. Not satisfied with God's doings, they would fain talk of their own. They would be doing, as if God's salvation were incomplete; and in lamentable ignorance of their own weakness and nothingness, they said, "All that the Lord hath spoken we will do." This was taking a bold stand, a high ground. For a poor worm to make such a vow proved how little grace was really understood, or nature's true condition apprehended.

However, Israel having undertaken to "*do*," they were put to the test, and the most cursory view of Exod. 19 will be sufficient to show what a marked change took place the moment they had uttered the words "we will do." The Lord had just reminded them of how He "bare them on eagles' wings, and brought them unto Himself"; but now He says, "Set bounds unto the people round about, saying, Take heed to yourselves, that ye go not up into the mount, or touch the border of it: whosoever toucheth the mount shall be surely put to death." This was a very different aspect of things. It was the simple result of man's having said, "I will do." There is far more involved in those words than many might imagine. If we take our eyes off from God's actings, and fix them on our own, the consequences must be disastrous in the extreme. But we shall see this more fully ere we close this paper. Let us now inquire how the house of Israel fulfilled their singular vow. We shall see that it ended like human vows in every age.*

Did they do "*all*" that the Lord commanded? Did they "continue in all things which are written in the book of the law, to do them?" Alas, no. On the contrary, we find that ere the tables of testimony were given, they had broken the very first commandment in the decalogue, by making a golden calf, and bowing down thereto. This was the earliest fruit of their broken vow; and then, onward they went, from stage to stage, dishonoring the name of the Lord—breaking His laws, despising His judgments, trampling under foot His sacred institutions. Then followed the stoning of His messengers whom, in patient grace and long-suffering, He sent unto them.

Finally, when the only-begotten Son came forth from the bosom of the Father, they with wicked hearts rejected and with wicked hands crucified Him. Thus we pass from Sinai to Calvary: at the former we hear man undertaking to do all the Lord's commandments, and at the latter see him crucifying the Lord Himself. So much for man's vows, so much for man's "*I will do.*" The fragments of the tables of testimony scattered beneath the fiery mount told the first melancholy tale of the failure of man's audacious resolution: nor was there any real break in the narrative, which has its closing scene around the cross of Calvary. All was failure—gross, unmitigated failure. Thus it must ever be when man presumes to vow or resolve in the presence of God.

Now there is a very striking resemblance between Israel's vow at the foot of mount Sinai and the confirmation vow of the establishment. We have rapidly glanced at the former; let us now refer to the latter.

In "the ministration of public baptism of infants," after various prayers and the reading of the Gospel, the minister addresses the godfathers and godmothers on this wise: "Dearly beloved, ye have brought this child here to be baptized; ye have prayed that our Lord Jesus Christ would vouchsafe to receive him, to release him of his sins, to sanctify him with the Holy Ghost, to give him the kingdom of heaven and everlasting life. Ye have heard also that our Lord Jesus Christ hath promised in His gospel to grant all these things that ye have prayed for: which promise He, for His part, will most surely keep and perform. Wherefore, after this promise made by Christ, this infant must also faithfully, for his part, promise by you that are his sureties (until he come of age to take it upon himself), that *he will renounce* the devil and all his works, and constantly believe God's holy Word and *obediently keep His commandments*. I demand, therefore, Dost thou, in the name of this child, renounce the devil and all his works, the vain pomp and glory of the world, with all covetous desires of the same, and the carnal desires of the flesh, so that thou wilt not follow nor be led by them?" *Answer: "I renounce them all."* Again: "Wilt thou obediently keep God's holy will and commandments, and walk in the same all the days of thy life?" *Answer: "I will."*

Both the above vows the children, when come to years of discretion, deliberately and solemnly take upon themselves, as may be seen by reference to "The Order of Confirmation." Thus we have, in the first

---

* There is a passage in the book of Deuteronomy which, as it may present a difficulty to some minds, should be noticed here. "And the Lord heard the voice of your words, when ye spake unto me; and the Lord said unto me, I have heard the voice of the words of this people which they have spoken unto thee: *they have well said all that they have spoken*" (Deut. 5: 28). From this passage, it might seem as though the Lord approved of their making a vow; but if my reader will take the trouble of reading the entire context, from verse 24 to 27, he will see that it has nothing whatever to say to the vow, but that it contains the expression of their terror at the consequences of their vow. They were not able to endure that which was commanded. "If," said they, "we hear the voice of the Lord our God any more, then we shall die. For who is there of all flesh that hath heard the voice of the living God speaking out of the midst of the fire, as we have, and lived? Go thou near, and hear all that the Lord our God shall say; and speak thou unto us all that the Lord our God shall speak unto thee; and we will hear it and do it." It was the confession of their own inability to encounter Jehovah in that awful aspect which their proud legality had led Him to assume. It is impossible that the Lord could ever commend an abandonment of free and changeless grace for a sandy foundation of works of law. (See *Notes on the book of Exodus*, page 253; or C.H. Mackintosh's *Genesis to Deuteronomy: Notes on the Pentateuch*, page 228.)

place, people vowing and resolving, on behalf of unconscious infants, to "renounce the world, the flesh, and the devil," and to keep all God's commandments, all the days of their life; and, in the second place, we find those children, in due time, placing themselves under the weight of those awful vows; and all this, moreover, as a necessary condition to the fulfilment of Christ's promise. That is to say, if they allow aught of the world, the flesh or the devil to adhere to them; or if they fail in the faithful keeping of *all* God's commandments, then they cannot be saved, but must, so far as they are concerned, inevitably be condemned.

In short, salvation is here made to depend on a covenant to which man makes himself a party. Christ is represented as willing to do His part, provided always that man accomplishes his; but not otherwise. In other words, there is an "*if*" in the matter, and, as a consequence, there never is, and never can be, the certainty of salvation; yea, there can only be the constant terror of eternal condemnation hanging over the soul; that is, if there is any thought about the matter at all.

If the heart is not perfectly assured of the fact that Christ has in very deed done all; that He has put away our sin; that He has forever canceled our debt; that He has settled, by His perfect sacrifice, every question that could possibly arise, whether it be the charges of conscience, the accusings of Satan, or the claims of divine justice; that He has not left a cloud on the prospect; that all is perfectly done—in a word, that we stand before God in the power of divine righteousness, and in the same favor with His own Son; if, I say, there be any doubt in the soul as to the eternal truth of all these things—then there cannot be settled peace. And that there is not this settled peace in the case of those who have taken on themselves the above tremendous vows is but too evident from the clouds and darkness which hang around their spirits as they tread the next stage of their ecclesiastical journey.

We could hardly expect that persons who

boldly vow to renounce all evil, and perfectly to fulfil all good, could approach the Lord's table with any other acknowledgment than the following, namely: "The burden of our sins is intolerable." It would need an obtuse conscience to be able to shake off the conviction that those vows have been unfulfilled; and then, assuredly, the burden must be intolerable. If I have taken vows upon me, they will, without doubt, prove in the sequel to be dishonored vows; and thus the whole matter of my salvation comes to the ground, and I find myself, according to the terms of my own self-chosen covenant, righteously exposed to the curses of a broken law. I have undertaken to do everything; and yet I have in reality done nothing. Hence I am "cursed"; for the word is, "Cursed is every one that continueth not in all things which are written in the book of the law, to do them."

Nor will it at all alter the matter to say that those extraordinary vows are entered into in dependence upon divine grace; for there cannot be such a thing as dependence upon *grace* when people are placing themselves directly under the *law*. No two things can be more opposite than law and grace. They are put in direct contrast in Paul's Epistles to the Romans and Galatians. "Whosoever of you are justified by the law ($\dot{\varepsilon}\nu \ \nu\acute{o}\mu\omega$),* ye are fallen from grace" (Gal. 5: 4).

Hence, to think of depending upon grace when putting myself under law is precisely the same as if I were to look to God for grace to enable me to subvert the entire gospel of His Son Jesus Christ. "As many as are of works of law ($\dot{\varepsilon}\xi \ \ddot{\varepsilon}\rho\gamma\omega\nu \ \nu\acute{o}\mu\upsilon$)* are under the curse." Could I depend upon God's grace to enable me to abide under the curse? The thought is preposterous in the extreme. And be it observed that the apostle, in the last-quoted passage, does not merely say, "As many as fail to keep the law are under the curse." This he distinctly teaches, no doubt; but the special point is, that as many as attempt to stand before God on the ground of "works of law," are of necessity under the curse, for the simplest of all reasons, that they are not able to satisfy His claims.

---

* That is, as many as are on that principle—of "law," "works of law." [ED.]

In order for man to satisfy God's claims, he must be what in himself he cannot be; that is, without sin. The law demands, as its right, perfect obedience; and those who take upon them the confirmation vows promise perfect obedience. They promise to renounce all evil, and to fulfil all good, in the most absolute manner; and moreover, they make their salvation to depend upon their fulfilment of those vows, else why make them at all?

This, when looked at in the light of the apostolic teaching in Romans and Galatians, is the most complete denial of all the fundamental truths of the gospel. In the first place, it is a denial of man's total ruin, of his condition as one "dead in trespasses and sins," "alienated from the life of God," "without strength," "ungodly" "enmity against God." If I can undertake to renounce all evil, and to do all God's commandments, then, assuredly, I do not know myself to be a lost, ruined, helpless creature; and, as a consequence, I do not need a Saviour. If I can boldly undertake to "*renounce*" and to "*do*," to "keep" and to "walk," I am manifestly not lost, and hence I do not want salvation; I am not dead, and hence I do not want life; I am not "without strength," and hence I do not want the energy of that new, that divine life which is imparted by the Holy Ghost to all who, by His grace, believe in the Son of God. If I am capable of doing for myself, I do not want another, even the Lord Jesus Christ, to do all for me.

Again, as flowing out of what has already been stated, those vows do entirely set aside the essential glories, divine dignities and sacred virtues of the cross of Christ. If I can get a godfather and godmother to take vows on them on my behalf until I am capable of taking them on myself, then it is evident I cannot possibly know the deep blessedness of having all my vows, all my responsibilities and liabilities as a lost sinner, all my sins and shortcomings—everything, in short—fully and eternally answered in the Cross. If there is anything in my case which has not been perfectly settled in the Cross, then I must inevitably perish. I may make vows and resolutions, but they are as the morning cloud that passeth away. I may get a sponsor to renounce the devil on my behalf, and I may in due time talk of renouncing him for myself; but what if the devil all the while has fast hold of both my sponsor and myself? He will not renounce me, unless the chain by which he binds me has been snapped asunder by the Cross.

Again, I may get a sponsor to undertake to keep all God's commandments for me, and, in due time, I may undertake to keep them for myself; but what if neither my sponsor nor I really understand the true nature or spirituality, the majesty or stringency, of that law? Yea, more. What if both he and I are, by our very vows, made debtors to do the whole law, and thus shut up under its terrible curse? What then becomes of all our vows and resolutions? Is it not plain that I am throwing overboard the Cross of Christ? Truly so. That Cross must either be everything or nothing to me. If it is anything it must be everything; and if it is not everything it is nothing. Thus it stands. The gospel of the grace of God sets forth Christ as the great Sponsor and Surety of His people. The confirmation service sets one sinner to stand sponsor for another, or for himself. The gospel sets forth One, who is possessed of "unsearchable riches," as the security for His people; the confirmation service sets one bankrupt to stand security for another or for himself. What avails such security? Who would accept of it? It is perfectly valueless to God and man. If I am a bankrupt, I cannot promise to pay anything, and if I could promise, no one would accept of it—yea, it would be justly regarded in the light of an empty formality. The promissory note of a bankrupt is little worth; and truly the vows and resolutions of a poor ruined sinner are not merely an empty formality, but a solemn mockery, in the presence of Almighty God. No one who knows himself would presume to vow, or resolve, to keep all God's commandments—such an one would have the full conviction that he could never do anything of the kind.

But, as a further reply to the statement that those confirmation vows are made in entire dependence upon the grace of God, I would observe that grace can only be known or trusted by those who are His. "They that know Thy name will put their trust in Thee," and none else. Now, the Word of God connects eternal life with the knowledge of Him. "This is life eternal, that they might know Thee, the only true God, and Jesus Christ, whom Thou hast sent" (John 17:3). If, therefore, I have eternal life, I need not make vows to get it. If I am eternally saved, I need not make vows to get salvation. If my sins are all canceled by the precious blood of the Lamb, I need not make vows to get them canceled. Neither baptismal vows, confirmation vows, sacramental vows, nor any other vows are necessary for one who has found life, righteousness, wisdom, sanctification, redemption—yea, all things in Christ.

The comfort and peace of the feeblest believer are based upon the fact that Christ took all his vows, all his liabilities, all his sins, all his iniquities entirely upon Himself, and, by His death upon the cross, gloriously discharged them all. This sets him entirely free. Hence, it follows that if I am not a child of God, I cannot keep vows; and if I am, I need not make them. In either case, I deny man's fallen condition, and set aside the true glories of the Cross. It may be in ignorance—it may be with the most sincere intention—no doubt; but the most profound ignorance and the purest sincerity cannot alter the real principle which lies at the root of all manner of vows, promises, and resolutions. There is, beyond all question, involved therein a plain denial of the great foundation-truths of the Christian religion. A vow assumes the competency to fulfil. Well, then, if I vow to keep all God's commandments perfectly, all the days of my life, I am not lost or without strength. I must have strength, else I could not undertake such a ponderous responsibility.

And remark further the strange anomaly involved in this sytem of vows; that while it denies my lost estate, it robs me of everything approaching to a certainty of ever being saved. If I resolve to keep God's commandments as a necessary condition of my salvation, I never can be sure of being saved until I have fulfilled the condition; but inasmuch as I never can fulfil it, I, therefore,

never can be sure of my salvation; and thus I travel on, from stage to stage, from baptism to confirmation, from confirmation to communion, and from communion to the death-bed, in a state of miserable doubt and torturing uncertainty. This is not the gospel. It is "a different gospel which is not another."

The immediate effect of the work of Christ, when laid hold of by faith, is to give settled peace to the conscience; the effect of the system of vows, is to keep the heart in constant doubt and heaviness. How many have approached the ordinance of confirmation with trembling hearts, at the thought of having to take upon their own shoulders the solemn vows which, from the period of their baptism, had rested on their godfathers and godmothers. How could it be otherwise with an honest mind? If I am really sincere, the thought of having to take on myself those solemn baptismal vows, must fill me with horror. Some, alas! go through these things with thoughtless hearts and frivolous minds; but it is evident the confirmation service was never framed for such. It was designed for thoughtful, serious, earnest spirits; and all such must, assuredly, retire from the ceremony, with troubled hearts and burdened consciences.

With what different feelings we gaze upon the Cross of the Son of God! There, in good truth, Satan was renounced, and his works destroyed. There the law of God was magnified and made honorable, vindicated, and established. There the justice of God was fully answered. There Satan was vanquished; there conscience gets its full answer; there the cup of God's unmingled wrath against sin was drained to the dregs by His blessed Son. Where is the proof of all this? Not in the unaccomplished, dishonored vows of poor frail mortals; but in a risen, ascended, glorified Christ, seated at the right hand of the Majesty in the heavens.

Who that knows aught of the pure and most excellent grace of God, or that has tasted aught of the true blessedness of divinely-accomplished redemption, could tolerate such language as, "*Christ for His part*" and "*this infant for his part*"? Who that has listened, by faith, to those words, "It is finished," issuing, as they do, from amid the solemn scenes of Calvary, could endure a sinful mortal's *"I do,"* or *"I will"*? What a total setting aside of grace! What a tarnishing of the brightness of God's salvation! What an insult to the righteousness of God, which is by faith, and without works! What a manifest return to a religion of ordinances and the poor works of man! Christ and an infant, or the infant's sureties, are placed on the same platform to work out salvation. Is it not so? If not, what mean the words, "Christ for His part, and this infant for his part"? Is it not plain that salvation is made to depend upon something or some one besides Christ? Unquestionably. The vows must be fulfilled, or there is no salvation! Miserable condition! Christ's accomplished work abandoned for a sinner's unaccomplishable vows and resolutions! Man's "I do" substituted for Christ's "I have finished"!

Can you own such a fearful surrender of the truth of God? Are you content with such a sandy foundation? Whither, think you, will such a system lead you? To Heaven, or to Rome? Which? Be honest. Take the New Testament, search it from cover to cover, and see if you can find such a thing as infants making vows by proxy, to renounce the world, the flesh, and the devil, and to keep all God's commandments, in order to obtain salvation. There is not so much as a shadow of a foundation for such an idea. "By works of law shall no flesh living be justified." "But now the righteousness of God, without law, is manifested, being witnessed by the law and the prophets." "To him that worketh not, but believeth on Him that justified the ungodly, his faith is counted to him for righteousness." "For by grace are ye saved, through faith; and that not of yourselves it is the gift of God: not of works, lest any man should boast." "Not by works of righteousness which we have done, but according to His mercy He saved us." (See Rom. 3:20-28; 4:4-5; Eph. 2:8-9; Titus 3:5-7.)

These are but a very few of the numerous passages which might be adduced in proof of the fact that the confirmation vows are diametrically opposed to the truth of God—totally subversive of the grace of God. If my vows mean anything I must be miserable, because I am in imminent danger of being lost forever, inasmuch as I have *not* kept them, and never could keep them.

Oh! what sweet relief for the wearied heart and sin-burdened conscience in the atoning blood of Jesus! What full deliverance from my worthless and worse than worthless vows! *Christ has done all.* He has put away sin—made peace—brought in everlasting righteousness—brought life and immortality to light. In Him may you, my beloved reader, find abiding peace, unfading joy, and everlasting glory. To Him and His perfect work I now most affectionately commend you, body, soul, and spirit, fully assuring you my object in this paper is not to attack the prejudices, or wound the feelings of any, but simply to take occasion to show how the perfect work of the Lord Jesus Christ is thrown into full and blessed relief by being looked at in contrast with the "confirmation vows."

SAUL OF TARSUS

IN CONTEMPLATING the character of this most remarkable man, we may gather valuable principles of gospel truth. He seems to have been peculiarly fitted to show forth, in the first place, what the grace of God *can* do; and, in the second place, what the greatest amount of legal effort *cannot* do. If ever there was a man upon this earth whose history illustrates the truth that "salvation is by grace, without works of law," Saul of Tarsus was that man. Indeed, it is as though God had specially designed to present in this man a living example, first, of the depth from which His grace can rescue a *sinner;* and, secondly, the height from which a *legalist* is brought down to receive Christ. He was at once the very *worst* and the very *best* of men —the chief of sinners and the chief of legalists: as he hated and persecuted Christ in His saints, he was a sinner of sinners; and a Pharisee of the Pharisees in his moral conduct and pride.

Let us, then, in the first place, contemplate him as *the chief of sinners.*

"This is a faithful saying, and worthy of all acceptation, that Christ Jesus came into the world to save sinners; of whom *I am chief*" (1 Tim. 1:15). Now, note particularly what the Spirit of God declares concerning Saul of Tarsus: that he was the chief of sinners. It is not the expression of Paul's humility, though, no doubt, he was humble under the sense of what he had been. We are not to be occupied with the feelings of an inspired writer, but with the statements of the Holy Ghost who inspired him. It is well to see this.

Very many persons speak of the feelings of the various inspired writers in a way calculated to weaken the sense of that precious truth, the plenary inspiration of Holy Scripture. They may not mean to do so; but then, at a time like the present, when there is so much of reason, so much of human speculation, we cannot be too guarded against aught that might, even in appearance, militate against the integrity of the Word of God. We are anxious that our readers should treasure the Scriptures in their hearts' affections, not as the expression of human feelings, however pious and praiseworthy, but as the depository of the thoughts of God. "For the prophecy came not in old time by the will of man: but holy men of God spake as they were moved by the Holy Ghost" (2 Peter 1:21).

Hence, therefore, in reading 1 Tim. 1:15, we are not to think of the feelings of man, but of the record of God, which declares that Paul was "chief of sinners." It is never stated of any one else. No doubt, in a secondary sense, each convicted heart will feel and own itself the guiltiest within its own range of knowledge; but this is quite another matter. The Holy Ghost has declared this of Paul; nor does the fact that He has told us this by the pen of Paul himself interfere with or weaken the truth and value of the statement. No

matter how bad any one may be, Paul could say, "*I am chief.*" No matter how far from God any one may feel himself to be—no matter how deeply sunk in the pit of ruin—a voice rises to his ear from a deeper point still, "*I am chief.*"

But let us mark the *object* of all this dealing with the chief of sinners. "Howbeit for this cause I obtained mercy, that in *me first*, Jesus Christ might show forth *all* long-suffering, for a *pattern* to them who should hereafter believe on Him to life everlasting." The chief of sinners is in Heaven. How did he get there? Simply by the blood of Jesus; and moreover, he is Christ's "pattern" man. All may look at him and see how they too are to be saved; for in such wise as the "chief" was saved, must all the subordinate be saved. The *grace* that reached the chief can reach all. The blood that cleansed the chief can cleanse all. The title by which the chief entered Heaven is the title for all. Behold in Paul a "pattern of Christ's long-suffering"! There is not a sinner at this side the portal of hell, back-slider or aught else, beyond the reach of the love of God, the blood of Christ, or the testimony of the Holy Ghost.

We shall now turn to the other side of Saul's character, and contemplate him as *the chief of legalists.*

"Though I might also have confidence in the flesh. If any other man thinketh that he hath whereof he might trust in the flesh, *I more*" (Phil. 3:4). Here we have a most valuable point. Saul of Tarsus stood, as it were, on the loftiest height of the hill of legal righteousness. He reached the topmost step of the ladder of human religion. He would suffer no man to get above him. His religious attainments were of the very highest order. (See Gal. 1:14.) "If *any* other man thinketh that he hath whereof he might trust in the flesh, *I more.*" Is any man trusting in his temperance? Paul could say, "I *more.*" Is any man trusting in his morality? Paul could say, "I *more.*" Is any man trusting in ordinances, sacraments, religious services, or pious observances? Paul could say, "I *more.*"

All this imparts a peculiar interest to the history of Saul of Tarsus. In him we see, at one view, the power of the blood of Christ, and the utter worthlessness of the fairest robe of self-righteousness that ever decked the person of a legalist. Looking at him, no sinner need despair; looking at him, no legalist can boast. If the chief of sinners is in Heaven, I can get there too. If the greatest religionist, legalist, and doer, that ever lived had to come *down* from the ladder of self-righteousness, it is of no use for me to go *up*.

The guilt of Saul of Tarsus was completely covered by the blood of Christ; and his lofty religious pride and boasting was swept away by a sight of Jesus, and Saul found his place at the pierced feet of Jesus of Nazareth. His guilt was no hindrance, and his righteousness no use. The former was washed away by the blood, and the latter turned into dung and dross by the moral glory of Christ. It mattered not whether it was "*I chief*," or "*I more.*" The Cross was the only remedy.

"God forbid," says this chief of sinners and prince of legalists, "that I should glory, save in the cross of our Lord Jesus Christ, by whom the world is crucified unto me, and I unto the world" (Gal. 6:14). Paul had just as little idea of trusting in his righteousness as in his crimes. He was permitted to win the laurel of victory in the grand legal struggle with his "equals in his own nation," only that he might fling it, as a withered, worthless thing, at the foot of the Cross. He was permitted to outstrip all in the dark career of guilt, only that he might exemplify the power of the love of God and the efficacy of the blood of Christ. Saul was no nearer to Christ as the chief of legalists than he was as the chief of sinners. There was no more justifying merit in his noblest efforts in the school of legalism than in his wildest acts of opposition to the name of Christ. He was saved by grace, saved by blood, saved by faith. There is no other way for sinner or legalist.

There is another point in Paul's history at which we must briefly glance, in order to shew the practical results of the grace of Christ wherever that grace is known. This will present him to our notice as *the most laborious of apostles*.

If Paul learned to cease working for righteousness, he also learned to begin working for Christ. When we behold on Damascus' road the shattered fragments of this worst and best man—when we hear those pathetic accents emanating from the depths of a broken heart, "Lord, what wilt *Thou* have me to do?"—when we see that man who had left Jerusalem in the mad fury of a persecuting zealot, now stretching forth the hand of blind helplessness to be led like a little child into Damascus, we are led to form the very highest expectations as to his future career; nor are we disappointed.

Mark the progress of that most remarkable man, behold this gigantic labors in the vineyard of Christ; see his tears, his toils, his travels, his perils, his struggles; see him as he bears his golden sheaves into the heavenly garner, and lays them down at the Master's feet; see him wearing the noble bonds of the gospel, and finally laying his head on a martyr's block, and say if the gospel of God's free grace—the gospel of Christ's free salvation, does away with good works? Nay, that precious gospel is the only true basis on which the superstructure of good works can ever be erected.

Morality, without Christ, is an icy morality. Benevolence, without Christ, is a worthless benevolence. Ordinances, without Christ, are powerless and valueless. Orthodoxy, without Christ, is heartless and fruitless. We must get to the end of *self*, whether it be a guilty self or a religious self, and find Christ as the satisfying portion of our hearts, now and for ever. Then we shall be able to say, with truth,

> Thou, O Christ, art all I want,
> More than all in Thee I find.

And again:

> Love so amazing, so divine,
> Demands my soul, my life, my all.

Thus it was with Saul of Tarsus. He got rid of himself and found his all in Christ; and hence, as we hang over the impressive page of his history, we hear, from the depths of ruin, the words, "I am *chief*"—from the most elevated point in the legal system, the words, "I *more*"—and from amid the golden fields of apostolic labor, the words, "I labored *more abundantly* than they all."

FINAL PERSEVERANCE
WHAT IS IT?

DEAR FRIEND: The question of final perseverance, though in our judgment a very simple one, has perplexed a great many; and the questions which you introduce to our notice, and the passages of Scripture which you adduce, furnish abundant proof that your own mind is not quite clear or settled on the point.

In seeking, then, to reply to your interesting letter, we have three things to do, namely: first, to establish the doctrine of final perseverance, or, in other words, the eternal security of all Christ's members; secondly, to answer the questions which you have given us, and which we take to be those usually or frequently put by the opposers of the doctrine; and, thirdly, to expound those texts which you have quoted, and in which you seem to find considerable difficulty. May the Holy Spirit be our teacher, and may He give us minds entirely subject to Scripture, so that we may be able to form a sound judgment on the question now before us!

1. And first, as to the doctrine of final perseverance, it seems to us exceedingly clear and simple if only we look at it in immediate connection with Christ Himself. This indeed is the only true way to look at any doctrine. Christ is the soul, centre, and life of all doctrine. A doctrine separated from Christ becomes a lifeless, powerless, worthless dogma—a mere idea in the mind—a mere item in the creed. Hence, therefore, we must look at every truth as it stands connected with Christ. We must make Him our point of view. It is only as we keep near to Him, and look at all points from that one grand point, that we can have a correct view of any point. If for example, I make self my point of view, and look from thence at the subject of final perseverance, I shall be sure

to get a false view altogether, inasmuch as it then becomes a question of *my* perseverance, and anything of *mine* must necessarily be doubtful.

But if, on the other hand, I make Christ my viewing-point, and look at the subject from thence, I shall be sure to have a correct view, inasmuch as it then becomes a question of the world, the flesh, or the devil, can ever hinder His final perseverance in the salvation of the world, the flesh, or the evil, can ever hinder His final preservance in the salvation of those whom He has purchased with His own blood, seeing "He is able to save to *the uttermost* them that come unto God by Him." This, surely, is final perseverance. It matters not what the difficulty or what the hostile power may be, "He is able to save to the uttermost." The world, with its ten thousand snares, is against us, but "He is able." Indwelling sin, in its ten thousand workings, is against us, but "He is able." Satan, with his ten thousand devices, is against us, but "He is able." In a word, it is Christ's ability, not ours; it is Christ's faithfulness, not ours; it is Christ's final perseverance, not ours. All depends upon Him as to this weighty matter. He has purchased His sheep, and surely He will keep them to the best of His ability; and, seeing that "*all* power is given unto Him in heaven and on earth," His sheep must be perfectly and forever safe. If aught could touch the life of the feeblest lamb in all the flock of Christ, He could not be said to have "all power."

Thus it is immensely important to consider the question of final perseverance in inseparable connection with Christ. Difficulties vanish. Doubts and fears are chased away. The heart becomes established, the conscience relieved, the understanding enlightened. It is impossible that one who forms a part of Christ's body can ever perish; and the believer is this—"We are members of His body, of His flesh, and of His bones" (Eph. 5:30). Every member of the body of Christ was written in the book of the slain Lamb before the foundation of the world, nor can anything or any one ever obliterate that writing. Hear what our Lord Jesus Christ saith in reference to those that are His: "My sheep hear My voice, and I know them, and they follow Me; and I *give* unto them *eternal* life, and they shall never perish, neither shall *any* [man, devil, or any one else] pluck them out of My hand. My Father, which gave them Me, is greater than all; and no man is able to pluck them out of My Father's hand" (John 10:27-29).

Here, then, most assuredly, we have final perseverance; and that, moreover, not merely the perseverance of the saints, but of the Father and of the Son and of the Holy Ghost. Yes, this is the way we would have you view the matter. It is the final perseverance of the Holy Trinity. It is the perseverance of the Holy Ghost, in opening the ears of the sheep. It is the perseverance of the Son, in receiving all whose ears are thus opened. And, finally, it is the perseverance of the Father, in keeping, through His own name, the blood-bought flock in the hollow of His everlasting hand. This is plain enough. We must either admit the truth—the consolatory and sustaining truth—of final perseverance or succumb to the blasphemous proposition that the enemy of God and man can carry his point against the Holy and Eternal Trinity. We see no middle ground. "Salvation is of the Lord" from first to last. It is a free, unconditional, and everlasting salvation. It reaches down to where the sinner is in all his guilt, ruin, and degradation, and bears him up to where God is in all His holiness, truth, and righteousness; and it endures forever. God the Father is its source, God the Son is its channel, and God the Holy Ghost is the power of application and enjoyment. It is all of God from beginning to end, from foundation to topstone, from everlasting to everlasting. If it were not so, it would be presumptuous folly

to speak of final perseverance; but seeing it is so, it would be presumptuous unbelief to think of aught else.

True, there are great and manifold difficulties in the way—difficulties before and difficulties after conversion. There are many and powerful adversaries; but that is the very reason why we must keep the question of final perseverance entirely clear of self and all its belongings, and make it repose simply upon God. It matters not in the least what the difficulties or the adversaries may be, for faith can ever triumphantly inquire, "If God be for us, who can be against us?" And again, "Who shall separate us from the love of Christ? Shall tribulation, or distress, or persecution, or famine, or nakedness, or peril, or sword? As it is written, 'For Thy sake, we are killed all the day long; we are accounted as sheep for the slaughter.' Nay, in all these things we are more than conquerors through Him that loved us. For I am persuaded that neither death, nor life, nor angels, nor principalities, nor powers, nor things present, nor things to come, nor height, nor depth, nor *any other creature*, shall be able to separate us from the love of God, which is in Christ Jesus our Lord" (Rom. 8:35-39).

Here, again, we have final perseverance taught, in the clearest and strongest way possible—not any creature shall be able to separate us. Neither self, in all its forms; nor Satan, in all his wiles and machinations; nor the world, in all its allurements, or all its scorn, can ever separate the "us" of Romans 8:39 from the love of God, which is in Christ Jesus our Lord. No doubt persons may be deceived, and they may deceive others. Spurious cases may arise; counterfeit conversions may take place. Persons may seem to run well for a time, and then break down. The blossoms of springtime may not be followed by the mellow fruits of autumn. Such things may be; and, moreover, true believers may fail in many things; they may stumble and break down in their course. They may have ample cause for self-judgment and humiliation in the practical details of life. But, allowing the widest possible margin for all these things, the precious doctrine of final perseverance remains unshaken—yea, untouched—upon its own divine and eternal foundation—"I give unto My sheep *eternal* [not temporary or conditional] life, and they shall *never* perish."

Again: "Upon this rock I will build My church, and the gates of hell shall not prevail against it." People may argue as they will, and base their arguments on cases which come under their notice, from time to time, in the history of professing Christians; but, looking at the subject from a divine point of view, and basing our convictions on the sure and unerring Word of God, we maintain that all who belong to the "us" of Romans 8, the "sheep" of John 10, and the "church" of Matthew 16, are as safe as Christ can make them, and this we conceive to be the sum and substance of the doctrine of final perseverance.

2. And now, dear friend, we shall, in the second place, briefly and pointedly reply to the questions which you have put before us:

(1) "Will a believer be saved, no matter into what course of sin he may fall, and die in?" A true believer will, infallibly, be saved; but we consider that salvation includes, not only full deliverance from the future consequences of sin, but from the present power and practice thereof. And, hence, if we find a person living in sin, and yet talking about his assurance of salvation, we look upon him as an antinomian, and not a saved person at all. "If we say that we have fellowship with Him, and walk in darkness, we lie, and do not the truth." The believer may fall, but he will be lifted up; he may be overtaken, but he will be restored; he may wander, but he will be brought back, because Christ is able to save to the uttermost, and not one of His little ones shall perish.

(2) "Will the Holy Spirit dwell in a heart where evil and unholy thoughts are *indulged?*" The body of the believer is the temple of the Holy Ghost (1 Cor. 6:19). And this precious truth is the ground of exhortation to purity and holiness of heart and life. We are exhorted not to grieve the Holy Spirit. To "*indulge*" evil and unholy thoughts is not Christian walk at all. The Christian may be assaulted, grieved, and

harassed by evil thoughts, and in such a case he has only to look to Christ for victory. Proper Christian walk is thus expressed in John's first Epistle: "We know that whosoever is born of God sinneth not; but he that is begotten of God keepeth himself, and that wicked one toucheth him not" (chap. 5:18). This is the divine side of the question. Alas! we know there is the human side likewise; but we judge the human side by the divine. We do not lower the divine to meet the human, but ever aim at the divine notwithstanding the human. We should never be satisfied with anything lower than 1 John 5:18. It is by keeping up the true standard that we may expect to raise our moral tone. To talk of having the Spirit and yet "*indulge*" in evil and unholy thoughts is, in our judgment, the ancient Nicolaitanism (Rev. 2:6, 15), or modern antinomianism.

(3) "If it be so, then, will not people say, they may live as they like?" Well, how does a true Christian like to live? As like Christ as possible. If one had put this question to Paul, what would have been his answer? 2 Cor. 5:14-15, and Phil. 3:7-14, furnish the reply. It is to be feared that the persons who ask such questions know but little of Christ. We can quite understand a person getting entangled in the meshes of a one-sided theological system and being perplexed by the conflicting dogmas of systematic divinity; but we believe that the man who draws a plea from the freedom, sovereignty, and eternal stability of the grace of God to continue in sin, knows nothing of Christianity at all, has neither part nor lot in the matter, but is in a truly awful and dangerous condition.

As to the case which you adduce, of a young man who heard a minister state in his sermon that "once a child, always a child," and who took occasion from that to plunge into and continue in open sin, it is only one of thousands. We believe the minister was right in what he said, but the young man was wrong in what he did. To judge the words of the former by the acts of the latter is utterly false. What should I think of my son, if he were to say, Once a son, always a son, and therefore I may proceed to smash my father's windows and do all sorts of mischief? We judge the minister's statement by the Word of God, and pronounce it true. We judge the young man's conduct by the same rule, and pronounce it false. The matter is quite simple. We have no reason to believe that the unhappy young man ever really tasted the true grace of God; for it he had, he would love and cultivate and exhibit holiness. The Christian has to struggle with sin; but *struggling* with it and *wallowing* in it are two totally different ideas. In the one case we can count on Christ's sympathy and grace; in the other, we are actually blaspheming His name by implying that He is the minister of sin.

We consider it a very serious mistake to set about judging the truth of God by the actings of men. All who do so must reach a false conclusion. The true way is just to reverse the order. Get hold of God's truth first, and then judge everything by that. Set up the divine standard, and test everything thereby. Set up the public scales, and weigh every man's load therein. The scales must not be regulated by each man's load, but each man's load be tested by the scales. If ten thousand professors were to fall away, and live and die in open sin, it would not shake our confidence in the divine doctrine of final perseverance. The selfsame Word that proves the doctrine to be true, proves them to be false. "They went out from us, but they were not of us; for if they had been of us, they would no doubt have continued with us; but they went out, that they might be manifest that they were not all of us" (1 John 2:19). "The foundation of God standeth sure, having this seal, The Lord knoweth them that are His. And, let every one that nameth the name of Christ depart from iniquity" (2 Tim. 2:19).

3. We shall now proceed to examine the various passages of Scripture which, as you say, are generally adduced by those who seek to overthrow the doctrine of final perseverance. But before doing so, we deem it of importance to lay down the following fundamental principle, which will, in our judgment, be found most helpful in the interpretation of Scripture generally. The principle is very simple. No one passage of Holy Scripture can by any possibility contradict another. If therefore there be a

seeming contradiction, it must arise from our want of spiritual intelligence. Thus, for example, if any one were to quote James 2:24 in defense of the doctrine of justification by works, I might not be able to answer him. It is quite possible that thousands, like Luther, have been sadly perplexed by that passage. They may feel the fullest and clearest assurance that they are justified, and that not by any works that they have done, but simply "by faith of Jesus Christ," and yet be wholly unable to explain these words of James—"Ye see then how that by works a man is justified, and not by faith only."

Now, how is one to meet such a difficulty as this? He really does not understand the apostle James. He is involved in much perplexity by the apparent contradiction between James and Paul. What is he to do? Just to apply the principle above stated. No one passage of Scripture can possibly contradict another. As well might we apprehend a collision between two of the heavenly bodies while moving in their divinely appointed orbits, as that two inspired writers could possibly clash in their statements. Well, then, I read in Rom. 4:5 such plain words as these: "But to him that *worketh not*, but believeth on Him that justifieth the ungodly, his *faith* is counted for righteousness." Here I find works entirely excluded as a ground of justification, and faith alone recognized. So also in chapter 3 I read, "Therefore we conclude that a man is justified by faith without [or apart from] works of law." And, again, "Being justified by faith, we have peace with God." Exactly similar is the teaching in the Epistle to the Galatians, where we reach such plain words as these: "*Knowing* that a man is not justified by works of law, but by faith of Jesus Christ, even we [Jews] have believed in Jesus Christ, that we might be justified by faith of Christ, and not by works of law: for by works of law shall no flesh be justified" (chap. 2:16).

In all these passages, and many more which might be quoted, works are sedulously excluded as a ground of justification, and that too in language so plain that a wayfaring man, though a fool, need not err therein. If therefore we cannot explain James 2:24, we must either deny its inspiration or have recourse to our principle, namely, that no one passage of Holy Scripture can possibly contradict another, and so remain, with unshaken confidence and unruffled repose, rejoicing in the grand foundation truth of justification by faith alone, apart from law-works altogether.

Having called the reader's attention to the famous passage in James 2, it may not be amiss to offer him, in passing, a word or two of exposition which will help him in the understanding of it. There is a little word in verse 14 which will furnish the key to the entire passage. The inspired apostle inquires, "What doth it profit, my brethren, though a man *say* he hath faith?" Had he said, What doth it profit though a man *have* faith? the difficulty would be insuperable, the perplexity hopeless. But the important word "say" quite removes all difficulty, and unfolds in the simplest possible way the point which the apostle has in his mind. We might inquire, What doth it profit though a man *say* he hath ten thousand a year, if he have it not?

Now, we are aware that the word "say" is constantly left out in quoting James 2:14. Some have even ventured to assert that it is not in the original. But any one who can read Greek has only to look at the passage and he will see the word *legee* (*say*) placed there by the Holy Ghost, and left there by all our leading editors and Biblical critics; nor can we well conceive a word of more vital importance in a passage. Its influence, we believe, is felt throughout the entire context in which it occurs. There is no use in a man merely *saying* he has faith; but if he really has it, it "profits" him for time and eternity, inasmuch as it connects him with Christ, and puts him in full and inalienable possession of all that Christ has done and all that He is for us before God.

This leads us to another point, which will greatly tend to clear away the seeming contradiction between the two inspired apostles, Paul and James. There is a very material difference between *law-works* and *life-works*. Paul jealously excludes the former; James as jealously insists on the latter. But be it carefully noted that it is only

the former that Paul excludes, as it is only the latter that James insists on. The acts of Abraham and Rahab were not law-works, but life-works. They were the genuine fruits of faith, apart from which they would have possessed no justifying virtue whatever.

It is well worthy of note that with the history of four thousand years before Him, the Holy Ghost, in the apostle, should have fixed upon two such works as that of Abraham in Genesis 22 and that of Rahab in Joshua 2. He does not adduce some acts of charity or benevolence, though surely He might easily have selected many such from the vast mass of materials which lay before Him. But, as if anticipating the use that the enemy would make of the passage now before us, He takes care to select two such illustrations of His thesis to prove beyond all question that it is life-works and not law-works He is insisting upon, and leaves wholly untouched the priceless doctrine of justification by faith, apart from works of law.

Finally, if any should feel disposed to inquire as to the difference between law-works and life-works, it is simply this: law-works are such as are done in order to get life: life-works are the genuine fruits of life possessed. And how do we get life? By believing on the Son of God. "Verily, verily, I say unto you, He that heareth My words, and believeth on Him that sent Me, *hath* everlasting life" (John 5:24). We must have life before we can do anything; and we get life, not by "saying" we have faith, but by really having it; and when we have it, we shall manifest the precious fruits thereof, to the glory of God.

Thus, then, we not only implicitly believe that Paul and James *must* harmonize, but we can plainly see that they *do*.

Having thus sought to define and illustrate our principle, we shall leave you, dear friend, to apply it in the various cases of difficulty and perplexity which may come before you in the study of Scripture, while we endeavor to expound, as the Lord may enable us, the important passages of Scripture which you have laid before us.

(1) The first quotation is from the second

Epistle of Peter—"But there were false prophets also among the people, even as there shall be false teachers among you, who privily shall bring in damnable heresies, even denying the Lord that bought them, and bring upon themselves swift destruction" (chap. 2:1). The difficulty of this passage arises, we suppose, from the expression, "denying the Lord that bought them." But there is, in reality, no difficulty whatever in these words. The Lord has a double claim on every man, woman, and child beneath the canopy of Heaven. He has a claim founded on creation, and a claim founded on redemption. It is to the latter of these two that the apostle refers. The false teachers will not merely deny the Lord that *made* them, but even the Lord that *bought* them. It is of importance to see this. It will help to clear away many difficulties. The Lord Jesus has a purchased right over every member of the human family. The Father has given Him power over all flesh. Hence the sin of those who deny Him. It would be sin to deny Him as Creator; it is a greater sin to deny Him as Redeemer. It is not at all a question of regeneration. The apostle does not say, Denying the Lord that quickened them. This would indeed be a difficulty; but as the passage stands, it leaves wholly untouched the truth of final perseverance.

(2) The second passage occurs at the close of the same chapter (verses 20 and 22)—"For if after they have escaped the pollutions of the world, through the knowledge of the Lord and Saviour Jesus Christ, they are again entangled therein and overcome, the latter end is worse with them than the beginning. . . . But it is happened unto them according to the true proverb, 'The dog is turned to his own vomit again: and the sow that was washed, to her wallowing in the mire.' " The diffusion of scriptural knowledge and evangelical light may and does frequently exert an amazing influence upon the conduct and character of persons who have known the saving, quickening, emancipating power of the gospel of Christ. Indeed it is hardly possible for an open Bible to be circulated, or a free gospel to be preached, without producing very striking

results which, after all, will be found to fall far short of *the* grand result of regeneration. Many gross habits may be abandoned, many "pollutions" laid aside, under the influence of a merely intellectual "knowledge of the Lord and Saviour Jesus Christ"; while, at the same time, the *heart* has never really been savingly reached at all. Now, it will be invariably found that when persons shake off the influence of evangelical light—even though that influence never extended beyond their outward conduct—they are sure to plunge into greater depths of evil, and greater excesses of worldliness and folly than ever; "The latter end is worse with them than the beginning." The devil takes delight in dragging the *quondam* professor through deeper mire than that in which he wallowed in the days of his ignorance and thoughtless folly. Hence the urgent need of pressing on all with whom we have to do the importance of making sure work of it, so that the knowledge of truth may not merely affect their external conduct, but reach the heart, and impart that life which, when once possessed, can never be lost. There is nothing in this passage to terrify the sheep of Christ, but very much to warn those who, though they may for a time put on the outward appearance of sheep, have never been inwardly aught but as the dog and the sow.

(3) Ezekiel 18:24,26—"But when the righteous turneth away from his righteousness, and committeth iniquity, and doeth according to all the abominations that the wicked man doeth, shall he live? All his righteousness that he hath done shall not be mentioned: in his trespass that he hath trespassed, and in his sin that he hath sinned, in them shall he die. . . . When a righteous man turneth away from his righteousness and committeth iniquity, and dieth in them; for his iniquity, that he hath done, shall he die." With this we may connect your reference to 2 Chronicles 15:2—"The Lord is with you while ye be with Him: and if ye seek Him, He will be found of you: but if ye forsake Him, He will forsake you." We feel constrained, dear friend, to say that it evidences a sad want of spiritual intelligence to adduce such passages of Scripture as

bearing in any way upon the truth of the final perseverance of Christ's members. These, and numberless other Scriptures in the Old Testament, as well as many similar passages in the New Testament, unfold to us the deeply important subject of God's moral government. Now, to be merely a subject of God's government is one thing; to be a subject of His unchangeable grace is another. We should never confound them. To elaborate this point, and to refer to the various passages which illustrate and enforce it, would demand a volume: we would here only add our full persuasion that no one can understand the Word of God who does not accurately distinguish between man under government and man under grace. In the one case he is looked at as walking down here, in the place of responsibility and danger; in the other, he is looked at as associated with Christ above, in the place of inalienable privilege and eternal security. These two Old Testament Scriptures to which you have referred us are entirely governmental, and, as a consequence, have nothing whatever to do with the question of final perseverance.

(4) Matthew 12:45—"Then goeth he and taketh with him seven other spirits more wicked than himself, and they enter in and dwell there: and the last state of that man is worse than the first. Even so shall it be unto this wicked generation." The closing sentence of this passage quite explains the whole context. Our Lord is describing the moral condition of the Jewish people. The spirit of idolatry had gone out of them, but only for a time, and to return again in sevenfold energy and intensity, rendering their last state worse by far than aught that has yet appeared in their most marvelous history. This passage, taken in a secondary way, may be very intelligently applied to an individual who, having undergone a certain moral change, and exhibited a measure of improvement in his outward conduct, afterwards falls back and becomes more openly corrupt and vicious than ever.

5. 2 John 1:8-9—"Look to yourselves, that we lose not those things which we have wrought, but that we receive a full reward. Whoever transgresseth, and abideth not in the doctrine of Christ, hath not God. He that abideth in the doctrine of Christ, he hath both the Father and the Son." In verse 8 the apostle exhorts the elect lady and her children to look to themselves, lest by any means he should lose aught of the fruit of his ministry. They were to form part of his reward in the coming day of glory, and he longed to present them faultless in the presence of that glory, that his reward might be full. Verse 9 needs no explanation; it is solemnly plain. If one does not *abide* in the doctrine of Christ, he has got nothing. Let slip the truth as to Christ, and you have no security as to anything. The Christian most assuredly needs to walk watchfully in order to escape the manifold snares and temptations which surround him; but whether is that watchfulness better promoted by placing his feet upon the shifting sand of his own performances or by fixing them firmly upon the rock of God's eternal salvation? Whether am I in a more favorable position for the exercise of watchfulness and prayer while living in perpetual doubt and fear, or reposing in artless confidence in the unchangeable love of my Saviour-God? We think, dear friend, we may very safely anticipate your reply.

6. Rev. 3:11—"Behold, I come quickly; hold that fast which thou hast, that no man take thy crown." Two things are here to be considered, namely: first, this is an address to an assembly; and, secondly, it does not say, That no man take thy *life*. A *servant* may lose his *reward*; but a *child* can never lose his eternal *life*. Attention to this would remove a host of difficulties. Sonship is one thing; discipleship is quite another. Security in Christ is one thing; testimony for Christ is quite another. If our security were dependent upon our testimony—our sonship upon our discipleship, where should we be? True, the more I know my security and enjoy my sonship, the more effective will be my testimony and the more faithful my discipleship; but these things must never be confounded.

In conclusion, dear friend, you say that "All those texts which speak of enduring to the end, and overcoming, are thought to mean that, since there is a possibility of our not doing so, we may not be saved in the end." As to this, we would merely add that we shall be most happy at any time to enter with you upon the close examination of every one of those passages to which you in this general way refer, and to prove, by the grace of God, that not one of them, when rightly interpreted, militates in the smallest degree against the precious truth of final perseverance; but that, on the contrary, each passage contains within itself, or within its immediate context, that which will clearly prove its perfect harmony with the truth of the eternal security of the very feeblest lamb in all the blood-bought flock of Christ.*

May the Lord establish our souls, more and more firmly, in His own truth, and preseve us unto His heavenly kingdom, to the glory of His holy name!

* Paley observes that "we should never suffer what we know to be disturbed by what we know not." And Butler remarks nearly the same when he says, "If a *truth* be established, *objections* are nothing. The one is founded on our *knowledge*, and the other on our *ignorance.*" (See Jay's *Autobiography*, p. 170).

THE SABBATH, THE LAW, AND CHRISTIAN MINISTRY

THE SABBATH

IF IT WERE MERELY A QUESTION of the observance or non-observance of a day, it might be easily disposed of inasmuch as the apostle teaches us in Rom. 14:5-6, and also in Col. 2:16, that such things are not to be made a ground of judgment. But seeing there is a great principle involved in the Sabbath question, we deem it to be of the very last importance to place it upon a clear and scriptural basis.

We shall quote the fourth commandment at full length: "Remember the sabbath day, to keep it holy. Six days shalt thou labor, and do all thy work; but the seventh day is the sabbath of the Lord thy God: in it thou shalt not do any work, thou, nor thy son, nor thy daughter, thy manservant, nor thy maidservant, nor thy cattle, nor thy stranger that is within thy gates: for in six days the Lord made heaven and earth, the sea, and all that in them is, and rested the seventh day: wherefore the Lord blessed the sabbath day and hallowed it" (Exod. 20:8-11).

This same law is repeated in Exodus 31:12-17. And in pursuance thereof we find in Numbers 15 a man stoned for gathering sticks on the sabbath day. All this is plain and absolute enough. Man has no right to alter God's law in reference to the sabbath; no more than he has to alter it in reference to murder, adultery, or theft. This, we presume, will not be called in question. The entire body of Old Testament Scripture fixes the seventh day as the sabbath; and the fourth commandment lays down the mode in which that sabbath was to be observed.

Now where, we ask, is this precedent followed? Where is this command obeyed? Is it not plain that the professing church neither keeps the right day as the sabbath, nor does she keep it after the Scripture mode? The commandments of God are made of none effect by human traditions, and the glorious truths which hang around "the Lord's day" are lost sight of.

The Jew is robbed of his distinctive day and all the privileges therewith connected, which are only suspended for the present, while judicial blindness hangs over that loved and interesting, though now judged and scattered, people. And furthermore, the Church is robbed of her distinctive day and all the glories therewith connected, which if really understood would have the effect of lifting her above earthly things into the sphere which properly belongs to her, as linked by faith to her glorified Head in Heaven. In result, we have neither pure

Judaism nor pure Christianity, but an anomalous system arising out of an utterly unscriptural combination of the two.

However, we desire to refrain from all attempt at developing the deeply spiritual doctrine involved in this great question, and confine ourselves to the plain teaching of Scripture on the subject; and in so doing we maintain that if the professing church quotes the fourth commandment and parallel Scriptures in defense of keeping the sabbath, then it is evident that in almost every case the law is entirely set aside. Observe, the word is, "Thou shalt not do *any* work." This ought to be perfectly binding on all who take the Jewish ground.

There is no room here for introducing what we deem to be "works of necessity." We may think it necessary to kindle fires, to make servants harness our horses and drive us hither and thither. But the law is stern and absolute, severe and unbending. It will not, it can not, lower its standard to suit our convenience or accommodate itself to our thoughts. The mandate is, "Thou shalt not do *any* work," and that, moreover, on "the seventh day," which answers to our Saturday. We ask for a single passage of Scripture in which the day is changed, or in which the strict observance of the day is in the smallest degree relaxed.

We request the reader of these lines to pause and search out this matter thoroughly in the light of Scripture. Let him not be scared as by some terrible bugbear, but let him, in true Berean nobility of spirit, "search the Scriptures." By so doing he will find that from the second chapter of Genesis down to the very last passage in which the sabbath is named, it means the *seventh* day and none other; and further, that there is not so much as a shadow of divine authority for altering the mode of observing that day. Law is law, and if we are under the law we are bound to keep it or else be cursed; for "it is written, Cursed is every one that continueth not in all things which are written in the book of the law to do them" (Deut. 27:26; Gal. 3:10).

But it will be said, "We are not under the Mosaic law; we are the subjects of the Christian economy." Granted; most fully,

freely, and thankfully granted. All true Christians are, according to the teaching of Romans 7 and 8, and Galatians 3 and 4, the happy and privileged subjects of the Christian dispensation. But if so, what is the day which specially characterizes that dispensation? Not "the seventh day," but "the first day of the week"— *"The Lord's day."* This is pre-eminently the Christian's day. Let him observe this day with all the sanctity, the sacred reverence, the hallowed retirement, the elevated tone, of which his new nature is capable.

We believe the Christian's retirement from all secular things cannot possibly be too profound on the Lord's day. The idea of any one, calling himself a Christian, making the Lord's day a season of what is popularly called recreation, unnecessary traveling, personal convenience, or profit in temporal things, is perfectly shocking. We are of opinion that such acting could not be too severely censured. We can safely assert that we never yet came in contact with a godly, intelligent, right-minded Christian person who did not love and reverence the Lord's day; nor could we have any sympathy with any one who could deliberately desecrate that holy and happy day.

We are aware, alas, that some persons have through ignorance or misguided feelings said things in reference to the Lord's day which we utterly repudiate, and that they have done things on the Lord's day of which we wholly disapprove. We believe that there is a body of New Testament teaching on the important subject of the Lord's day quite sufficient to give that day its proper place in every well-regulated mind.

The Lord Jesus rose from the dead on that day (Matt. 28:1-6; Mark 16:1-2; Luke 24:1; John 20:1). He met His disciples once and again on that day (John 20:19, 26). The early disciples met to break bread on that day (Acts 20:7). The apostle, by the Holy Ghost, directs the Corinthians to lay by their contributions for the poor on that day (1 Cor. 16:2). And finally, the exiled apostle was in the Spirit and received visions of the future on the day (Rev. 1:10).

The above Scriptures are conclusive. They

prove that the Lord's day occupies a place quite unique, quite heavenly, quite divine. But they as fully prove the entire distinctness of the Jewish sabbath and the Lord's day. The two days are spoken of throughout the New Testament with fully as much distinctness as we speak of Saturday and Sunday. The only difference is that the latter are heathen titles, and the former divine. (Comp. Matt. 28:1; Acts 13:14, 17:2, 20:7; Col. 2:16).

Having said thus much as to the question of the Jewish sabbath and the Lord's day, we shall suggest the following questions to the reader, namely: Where in the Word of God is the sabbath said to be changed to the first day of the week? Where is there any repeal of the law as to the sabbath? Where is the authority for altering the day or the mode of observing it? Where in Scripture have we such an expression as "the Christian sabbath"? Where is the Lord's day ever called the sabbath?*

We would not yield to any of our dear brethren in the various denominations around us in the pious observance of the Lord's day. We love and honor it with all our hearts; and were it not that the gracious providence of God has so ordered it in these realms that we can enjoy the rest and retirement of the Lord's day without pecuniary loss, we should feel called upon to abstain from business, and give ourselves wholly up to the worship and service of God on that day—not as a matter of cold legality, but as a holy and happy privilege.

It would be the deepest sorrow to our hearts to think a true Christian should be found taking common ground with the ungodly, the profane, the thoughtless, and the pleasure-hunting multitude, in desecrating the Lord's day. It would be sad indeed if the child of the kingdom and the children of this world were to meet in an excursion train on the Lord's day. We feel persuaded that any who in any wise profane or treat with lightness the Lord's day act in direct opposition to the Word and Spirit of God.

THE LAW

As regards the law, it is looked at in two ways: first, as a round of justification; and secondly, as a rule of life. A passage or two of Scripture will suffice to settle both the one and the other: "Therefore by the deeds of the law there shall no flesh be justified in His sight: for by the law is the knowledge of sin" (Rom. 3:20). "Therefore we conclude that a man is justified by faith without the deeds of the law" (ver. 28). Again: "Knowing that a man is not justified by the works of the law, but by the faith of Jesus Christ, even we have believed in Jesus Christ, that we might be justified by the faith of Christ, and not by the works of the law; for by the works of the law shall no flesh be justified" (Gal. 2:16).

Then, as to its being a rule of life, we read, "Wherefore, my brethren, ye also are become dead to the law by the body of Christ; that ye should be married to another, even to Him that is raised from the dead, that we should bring forth fruit unto God" (Rom. 7:4). "But now are we delivered from the law, being dead to that wherein we were held: that we should serve in newness of spirit, and not in the oldness of the letter" (ver. 6).

Observe in this last-quoted passage two things: first, "we are delivered from the law;" second, not that we may do nature's pleasure, but "that we should *serve* in newness of spirit." Being delivered from bondage, it is our privilege to "serve" in liberty. Again we read, further on in the chapter, "And the commandment which was ordained to life, I found to be *unto death*" (ver. 10). It evidently did not prove as a rule of *life* to him. "I was *alive without the law* once; but *when the commandment came*, sin revived, and *I died*" (ver. 9). Whoever "I" represents in this chapter was alive until the law came, and then he died. Hence, therefore, the law could not have been a rule of life to him; yea, it was the very opposite, even a rule of death.

In a word, then, it is evident that a sinner cannot be justified by the works of the law;

---

* For a fuller exposition of the doctrine of the sabbath, see *Notes on Genesis* (chap. 2); also, *Notes on Exodus*" (Chap. 16 and 31), in his *Genesis to Deuteronomy: Notes on the Pentateuch*.

and it is equally evident that the law is not the rule of the believer's life. "For as many as are of the works of the law are under the curse" (Gal. 3:10). The law knows no such thing as a distinction between a regenerated and an unregenerated man: it curses all who attempt to stand before it. It rules and curses a man so long as he lives; nor is there any one who will so fully acknowledge that he cannot keep it as the true believer, and hence no one would be more thoroughly under the curse.

What, therefore, is the ground of our justification? and what is our rule of life? The Word of God answers, "We are justified by the faith of Christ," and Christ is our rule of life. He bore all our sins in His own body on the tree; He was made a curse for us; He drained on our behalf the cup of God's righteous wrath; He deprived death of its sting, and the grave of its victory; He gave up His life for us; He went down into death, where we lay, in order that He might bring us up in eternal association with Himself in life, righteousness, favor and glory, before our God and His God, our Father and His Father. (See carefully the following Scriptures: John 20:17; Rom. 4:25; 5:1-10; 6:1-11; 7 *passim*, 8:1-4; 1 Cor. 1:30-31; 6:11; 15:55-57; 2 Cor. 5:17-21; Gal. 3:13, 25-29; 4:31; Eph. 1:19-23; 2:1-6; Col. 2:10-15; Heb. 2:14-15; 1 Peter 1:23).

If the reader will prayerfully ponder all these passages of Scripture he will see clearly that we are not justified by the works of the law; and not only so, but he will see how we are justified. He will see the deep and solid foundations of the Christian's life, righteousness, and peace planned in God's eternal counsels, laid in the finished atonement of Christ, developed by God the Holy Ghost in the Word, and made good in the happy experience of all true believers.

Then, as to the believer's rule of life, the apostle does not say, To me to live is the law; but, "To me to live is Christ" (Phil. 1:21). Christ is our rule, our model, our touchstone, our all. The continual inquiry of the Christian should be, not is this or that according to law? but is it like Christ? The law never could teach me to love, bless, and pray for my enemies; but this is exactly what the gospel teaches me to do, and what the divine nature leads me to do. "Love is the fulfilling of the law;" and yet, were I to seek justification by the law, I should be lost; and were I to make the law my standard of action, I should fall far short of my proper mark. We are predestinated to be conformed, not to the law, but to the image of God's Son. We are to be like Him. (See Matt. 6:21-48; Rom. 8:29; 1 Cor. 13:4-8; Rom. 13:8-10; Gal. 5:14-26; Eph. 1:3-5; Phil. 3:20-21; 2:5; 4:8; Col. 3:1-17).

It may seem a paradox to some to be told that "the righteousness of the law is fulfilled in us" (Rom. 8:4), and yet that we cannot be justified by the law, nor make the law our rule of life. Nevertheless, thus it is if we are to form our convictions by the Word of God. Nor is there any difficulty to the renewed mind in understanding this blessed doctrine. We are by nature "dead in trespasses and sins," and what can a dead man do?

How can a man get life by keeping that which requires life to keep it—a life which he has not? And how do we get life? Christ is our life. We live in Him who died for us; we are blessed in Him who became a curse for us by hanging on a tree; we are righteous in Him who was made sin for us; we are brought nigh in Him who was cast out for us (Rom. 5:6-15; Eph. 2:4-6; Gal. 3:13).

Having thus life and righteousness in Christ, we are called to walk as He walked, and not merely to walk as a Jew. We are called to purify ourselves even as He is pure; to walk in His footsteps; to show forth His virtues; to manifest His spirit (John 13:14-15; 17:14-19; 1 Peter. 2:21; 1 John 2:6, 29; 3:3).

We shall close our remarks on this head by suggesting two questions to the reader, namely, Would the Ten Commandments without the New Testament be a sufficient rule of life for the believer? Is not the New Testament a sufficient rule without the Ten Commandments? Surely that which is insufficient cannot be our rule of life.

We receive the Ten Commandments as part of the canon of inspiration; and moreover, we believe that the law remains in full force to rule and curse a man as long as he liveth. Let a sinner only try to get life by it, and see where it will put him; and let a believer only shape his way according to it, and see what it will make of him. We are fully convinced that if a man is walking according to the spirit of the gospel, he will not commit murder nor steal; but we are also convinced that a man, confining himself to the standard of the law of Moses would fall very far short of the spirit of the gospel.

The subject of "the law" would demand much more elaborate exposition, but the limits of this paper do not admit of it, and we therefore entreat of the reader to look out the various passages of Scripture referred to and ponder them carefully. In this way we feel assured he will arrive at a sound conclusion, and be independent of all human teaching and influence. He will see how that a man is justified freely by the grace of God through faith in a crucified and risen Christ; that he is made a partaker of divine life, and introduced into a condition of divine and everlasting righteousness, and consequent exemption from all condemnation; that in this holy and elevated position Christ is his object, his theme, his model, his rule, his hope, his joy, his strength, his all; that the hope which is set before him is to be with Jesus where He is, and to be like Him forever.

And he will also see that if as a lost sinner he has found pardon and peace at the foot of the cross, he is not, as an accepted and adopted son, sent back to the foot of mount Sinai, there to be terrified and repulsed by the terrible anathemas of a broken law. The Father could not think of ruling with an iron law the prodigal whom He had received to His bosom in purest, deepest, richest grace. Oh no! "Being justified by faith, we have peace with God through our Lord Jesus Christ; by whom also we have access by faith into this *grace* wherein we stand, and rejoice in hope of the glory of God" (Rom. 5:1-2). The believer is justified not by works, but by *faith;* he stands not in law, but in *grace;* and he waits not for judgment, but for *glory.*

THE CHRISTIAN MINISTRY

In reference to the Christian ministry we have only to say, that we hold it to be a divine institution: its source, its power, its characteristics, are all divine and heavenly. We believe that the great Head of the Church received in resurrection gifts for His body. He, and not the Church, or any section of the Church, is the reservoir of the gifts. They are vested in Him, and not in the Church. He imparts them as, and to whom, He will. No man, nor body of men, can impart gifts. This is Christ's prerogative, and His alone; and we believe that when He imparts a gift, the man who receives that gift is responsible to exercise the same, whether as an evangelist, a pastor, or a teacher, quite independently of all human authority.

We do not by any means believe that all are endowed with the above gifts, though all have some ministry to fulfil. All are not evangelists, pastors, and teachers. Such precious gifts are only administered according to the sovereign will of the divine Head of the Church. Man has no right to interfere with them. Wherever they really exist, it is the place of the assembly to recognize them with devout thankfulness.

Christians are exhorted to remember them that are over them in the Lord, to know them that guide them, and those who addict themselves to the ministry of the saints, and those who have spoken to them the word of life. Were they to refuse to do so, they would only be forsaking and rejecting their own mercies, for all things are theirs. (See Rom. 12:3-8; 1 Cor. 3:21-23; 12; 14; 16:15; Gal. 1:11-17; Eph. 4:7-16; 1 Thess. 5:12-13; Heb. 13:7,17; 1 Peter 4:10-11.)

All this is simple enough. We can easily see where a man is divinely qualified for any department of ministry. It is not if a man *say* he has a gift, but if he in reality has it. A man may say he has a gift on the same principle as he may say he has faith (James 2:14), and it may only be, after all, an empty conceit of his own ill-adjusted mind, which a spiritual assembly could not recognize for a moment. God deals in realities. A divinely-gifted evangelist is a reality; a teacher is a reality; a pastor is a reality; and such will be duly recognized, thankfully received, and counted worthy of all esteem and honor for their work's sake.

Now we hold that unless a man has a *bona*

fide gift imparted to him by the Head of the Church, all the instruction, all the education, and all the training that men could impart to him would not constitute him a Christian minister. If a man has a gift, he is responsible to exercise, to cultivate, and to wait upon his gift.

But unless a man has a direct gift from Christ, though he had all the learning of a Newton, all the philosophy of a Bacon, all the eloquence of a Demosthenes, he is not a Christian minister. He may be a very gifted and efficient minister of religion, so called; but a minister of religion and a minister of Christ are two different things. And further, we believe that where the Lord Christ has bestowed a gift, that gift makes the possessor thereof a Christian minister, whom all true Christians are bound to own and receive, quite apart from all human appointment: whereas, though a man had all the human qualifications, human titles and human authority which it is possible to possess, and yet lacked that one grand reality, namely, Christ's gift, he is not a minister of Christ.

We thank God for Christian ministry; and we feel assured that there are many truly gifted servants of Christ in the various denominations around us; but they are ministers of Christ on the ground of possessing His gift, and not, by any means, on the ground of man's ordination. Man cannot add aught to a heaven-bestowed gift. As well might he attempt to add a shade to the rainbow, a tint to the violet, motion to the waves, height to the snow-capped mountains, or daub with a painter's brush the peacock's plumage, as attempt to render more efficient by his puny authority the gift which has come down from the risen and glorified Head of the Church.

Ah no! the vine, the olive and the fig-tree, in Jotham's parable (Judges 9) needed not the appointment of the other trees. God had implanted in each its specific virtue. It was only the worthless bramble which hailed with delight an appointment that raised it from the position of *a real nothing* to be *an official something*.

Thus it is with a divinely-gifted man. He

has what God has given him: he wants, he asks no more. He rises above the narrow enclosure which man's authority would erect around him, and plants his foot upon that elevated ground where prophets and apostles have stood. He feels that it lies not within the range of the schools and colleges of this world to open to him his proper sphere of action. It appertains not to them to provide a setting for the precious gem which sovereign grace has imparted. The hand which has bestowed the gem can alone provide the proper setting. The grace which has implanted the gift can alone throw open a proper sphere for its exercise.

What! can it be possible that those gifts which emanate from the Church's triumphant and glorious Lord are not available for her edification until they are dragged through the mire of a heathen mythology? Alas for the heart that can think so! As well might we say that the fatness of the olive and the pure blood of the grape must be mingled with the contents of a quagmire to render them available for human use.

But it will be asked, "Were there not elders and deacons in the early Church, and ought we not to have such likewise?" Unquestionably there were elders and deacons in the early Church. They were appointed by the apostles, or those whom the apostles deputed: that is to say, they were appointed by the Holy Ghost—the only One who could then, or can now, appoint them. We believe that none but God can make or appoint an elder, and therefore for man to set about such work is but a powerless form, an empty name. Men may, and do, point us to the shadows of their own creation, and call upon us to recognize in those shadows divine realities; but alas! when we examine them in the light of Holy Scripture, we cannot even trace the outline, to say nothing of the living, speaking features of the divine original.

We see divinely-appointed elders in the New Testament, and we see humanly-appointed elders in the professing Church; but we can by no means accept the latter as a substitute for the former. We cannot accept a mere shadow in lieu of the substance. Neither do we believe that men have any divine authority for their act when they set about making and appointing elders. We believe that when Paul, or Timothy, or Titus, ordained elders, they did so as acting by the power and under the direct authority of the Holy Ghost; but we deny that any man, or body of men, can so act now. We believe it was the Holy Ghost then, and it must be the Holy Ghost now. Human assumption is perfectly contemptible. If God raises up an elder or a pastor we thankfully own him. He both can and does raise up such. He does raise up men fitted by His Spirit to take the oversight of His flock, and to feed His lambs and sheep. His hand is not shortened that He cannot provide those blessings for His Church even amid its humiliating ruins. The reservoir of spiritual gift in Christ the Head is not so exhausted that He cannot shed forth upon His body all that is needed for the edification thereof.

We are of opinion that were it not for our impatient attempts to provide for ourselves by making pastors and elders of our own, we should be far more richly endowed with pastors and teachers after God's own heart. We need not marvel that He leaves us to our own resources when by our unbelief we limit Him in His. Instead of "proving" Him, we "limit" Him, and therefore we are shorn of our strength and left in barrenness and desolation; or, what is worse, we betake ourselves to the miserable provisions of human expediency.

However, we believe it is far better, if we have not God's reality, to remain in the position of real, felt, confessed weakness than to put forth the hollow assumption of strength; we believe it is better to be real in our poverty than to put on the appearance of wealth. It is infinitely better to wait on God for whatever He may be pleased to bestow, than to limit His grace by our unbelief, or hinder His provision for us by making provision for ourselves.

We ask, where is the Church's warrant for calling, making or appointing pastors? Where

have we an instance in the New Testament of a Church electing its own pastor? Acts 1:23-26 has been adduced in proof. But the very wording of the passage is sufficient to prove that it furnishes no warrant whatever. Even the eleven apostles could not elect a brother apostle, but had to commit it to higher authority. Their words are, "Thou, Lord, *which knowest the hearts of all,* show whether of these two *Thou hast chosen.*" This is very plain. They did not attempt to choose. God knew the heart. He had formed the vessel. He had put the treasure therein, and He alone could appoint it to its proper place.

It is very evident, therefore, that the case of the eleven apostles calling upon the Lord to choose a man to fill up their number affords no precedent whatever for a congregation electing a pastor: it is entirely against any such practice. God alone can make or appoint an apostle or an elder, an evangelist or a pastor. This is our firm belief, and we ask for Scripture proof of its unsoundness. Human opinion will not avail; tradition will not avail; expediency will not avail. Are we taught from the Word of God that the early Church ever elected its own pastors or teachers? We positively affirm that there is not so much as a single line of Scripture in proof of any such custom.

If we could only find direction in the Word of God to make and appoint pastors, we should at once seek to carry such direction into effect; but in the absence of any divine warrant we could only regard it as a mimicry on our part to attempt any such a thing. Why was not the church at Ephesus, or why were not the churches at Crete, directed to elect or appoint elders? Why was the direction given to Timothy and Titus without the slightest reference to the Church, or to any part of the Church? Because, as we believe, Timothy and Titus acted by the direct power and under the direct authority of God the Holy Ghost, and hence their appointment was to be regarded by the Church as divine.*

But where have we anything like this now?

---

* We would here offer a remark in reference to the appointment of deacons in Acts 6. This case has been adduced in proof of the rightness of a congregation electing its own pastor; but the proof fails in every particular. In the first place, the business of those deacons was "to serve tables." Their functions as deacons were temporal, not spiritual. They might possess spiritual gift independently altogether of their deaconship. Stephen did possess such.

But more than this. Although the disciples were called upon to look out for men competent to take charge of their temporal

Where is the Timothy or the Titus now? Where is there the least intimation in the New Testament that there should be a succession of men invested with the power to ordain elders or pastors? True, the apostle Paul, in his second Epistle to Timothy, says, "The things which thou hast heard of me among many witnesses, the same commit thou to faithful men, who shall be able to teach others also" (2 Tim. 2:2). But there is not a word here about a succession of men having power to ordain elders and pastors. Assuredly teaching is not ordination; still less is it imparting the power to ordain.

If the inspired apostle had meant to convey to the mind of Timothy that he was to commit to others authority to ordain, and that such authority was to descend by a regular chain of succession, he could and would have done so; and in that case the passage would have run thus: "The power which has been vested in you, the same do thou vest in faithful men, that they may be able also to ordain others." Such, however, is not the case; and we deny that there is any man or body of men now upon earth possessing power to ordain elders, nor was that power or authority ever committed to the Church.

We hold it to be absolutely divine; and therefore, when God sends an elder or a pastor, an evangelist or a teacher, we thankfully hail the heaven-bestowed gift;* but we desire to be delivered from all empty pretension. We will have God's reality or nothing. We will have Heaven's genuine coin, not earth's counterfeit. Like the Tirshatha of old, who said "that they should not eat of the most holy things till there stood up a priest with Urim and Thummim" (Ezra 2:63), so would we say, let us rather, if it must be so,

remain without office-bearers than substitute for God's realities the shadows of our own creation.

Ezra could not accept the pretensions of men. Men might *say* they were priests; but if they could not produce the divine warrant and the divine qualifications, they were utterly rejected. In order for a man to be entitled to approach the altar of the God of Israel, he should not only be descended from Aaron, but also be free from every bodily blemish. (See Lev. 21: 16-23.) So now, in order for any man to minister in the Church of God, he must be a regenerated man, and he must have the necessary spiritual qualifications. Even St. Paul, in his powerful appeal to the conscience and judgment of the church of Corinth, refers to his spiritual gifts and the fruits of his labor as the indisputable evidences of his apostleship. (See 2 Cor. 10, 12.)

Before dismissing the subject of the Christian ministry, we would offer a remark upon the practise of laying on of hands, which is presented in the New Testament in two ways. First, we find it connected with the communication of a positive gift. "Neglect not the gift that is in thee, which was given thee by prophecy, with the laying on of the hands of the presbytery" (1 Tim. 4:14). This is again referred to in the Second Epistle: "Wherefore I put thee in remembrance that thou stir up the gift of God which is in thee by the putting on of my hands" (2 Tim. 1:6). This latter passage fixes the import of the expression "presbytery," as used in the First Epistle. Both passages prove that the act of laying on of hands in Timothy's case was connected with the imparting of a gift.

But secondly, we find the laying on of hands

---

affairs, yet the apostles alone could appoint them. Their words are, "Whom *we* may appoint over this business." In other words, although there is a vast difference between a deacon and a pastor, between taking charge of money and taking the oversight of souls, yet even in the matter of a deacon the appointment in Acts 6 was entirely divine; and hence it affords no warrant for a church electing its own pastor.

We might further add that *office* and *gift* are clearly distinguished in the Word of God. There might be, and were, many elders and deacons in any given church, and yet the fullest and freest exercise of gift when the whole church came together into one place. Elders and deacons might or might not have the gift of teaching or exhortation. Such gift was quite independent of their special office. In 1 Cor. 14, where it is said, "Ye may all prophesy one by one," and where we have a full view of the public assembly, there is not a word about an elder or a president of any kind whatever.

* Let the reader carefully note that *gifts*, as evangelists, pastors, teachers, prophets, being given directly by the Head of the Church for the edification of His people on earth (see Eph. 4: 8-13) were never appointed or "licensed" by apostolic hands or any others. Elders and deacons were to act as guides and to serve in the assemblies in which they had their place. To this position or *office* they were appointed by an apostle, or one sent by him. (ED.)

adopted simply for the purpose of expressing full fellowship and identification, as in Acts 13:3. It could not possibly mean ordination in this passage, inasmuch as Paul and Barnabas had been in the ministry long before. It simply gave beautiful expression to the full identification of their brethren in that work unto which the Holy Ghost had called them, and to which He alone could send them forth.

Now we believe that the laying on of hands as expressing ordination, if there be not the power to impart a gift, is worth nothing, if indeed it be not mere assumption; but if it be merely adopted as the expression of full fellowship in any special work or mission, we should quite rejoice in it. For example, if two or three brethren felt themselves called of God to go on an evangelistic mission to some foreign land, and that those with whom they were in communion perceived in them the needed gift and grace for such a work, we should deem it exceedingly happy were they to set forth their unqualified approval and their brotherly fellowship by the act of laying on of hands. Beyond this we can see no value whatever in that act.

Having thus, so far as our limits would permit, treated of the questions of the Sabbath, the Law, and the Christian ministry; having shown that we honor and observe the Lord's day, that we give the Law its divinely appointed place, and finally, that we hold the sacred and precious institution of the Christian ministry, we might close this paper, did we not feel called upon to present a few other points.

In our general teaching and preaching we seek to set forth the fundamental truths of the gospel, such as the doctrine of the Trinity; the eternal Sonship; the personality of the Holy Ghost; the plenary inspiration of Holy Scripture; the eternal counsels of God in reference to His elect; the fullest and freest presentation of His love to a lost world; the solemn responsibility of every one who hears the glad tidings of salvation to accept the same; man's total ruin by nature and by practice; his inability to help himself in thought, word, or deed; the utter corruption of his will; Christ's incarnation, death, and resurrection; His absolute deity and perfect humanity in one person; the perfect efficacy of His blood to cleanse from all sin; perfect justification and sanctification by faith in Christ, through the operation of God the Holy Ghost; the eternal security of all true believers; the entire separation of the Church in calling, standing, and hope from this present world.

Then, again, we hold, in common with many of our brethren in the denominations, that the hope of the believer is set forth in these words of Christ: "I will come again and receive you unto Myself; that where I am, there ye may be also" (John 14:3). We believe that the early Christians were converted to "that blessed hope"—that it was the common hope of Christians in apostolic times. To adduce proofs would swell this paper into a volume.

Futhermore, we believe that all disciples should meet on the first day of the week to break bread (Acts 20:7); and when so met, they should look to the Head of the Church to furnish the needed gifts, and to the Holy Ghost to guide in the due administration of these gifts.

As to the scriptural ordinance of baptism, we look upon it as a beautiful exhibition of the truth of the believer's identification with Christ in death. (See Matt. 28:19; Mark 16:16; Acts 2:38,41; 8:38; 10:47-48; 16:33; Rom. 6:3-4.)

As regards the precious institution of the Lord's Supper, we believe that Christians should celebrate it on every Lord's day, and that in so doing they commemorate the Lord's death until He come. We believe that as baptism sets forth our death with Christ, so the Lord's Supper sets forth Christ's death for us. We do not see any authority in the Word of God for regarding the Lord's Supper as "a sacrifice," "a sacrament," or "a covenant." The word is, "This do in remembrance of Me." (See Matt. 26:26-28; Mark 14:22-24; Luke 22:19-20; 1 Cor. 11:23-26.)

The above is a very brief but explicit statement of what we hold, and preach, and practise. We meet in public: our worship meetings, our prayer meetings, our reading meetings, our lectures, our gospel preachings, are all open to the public.

But we have done. We would in this closing line entreat the reader to "search the Scriptures." Let him try everything by that standard. Let him see to it that he has plain Scripture for everything with which he stands connected. "To the law and to the testimony: if they speak not according to this word, it is because there is no light in them" (Isa. 8:20).

We can honestly say we love with all our hearts all those who love our Lord Jesus Christ in sincerity; and wherever there is one who preaches a full, free and an everlasting salvation to perishing sinners, through the blood of the Lamb, we wish him Godspeed in the name of the Lord.

We now commend the reader to the blessing of the Father, and of the Son, and of the Holy Ghost. If he be a true believer, we pray that in his course down here he may be a bright and faithful witness for his absent Lord. But if he be one who has not yet found peace in Jesus, we would say to him, with solemn emphasis and earnest affection, *"Behold the Lamb of God, which taketh away the sin of the world!"* (John 1:29)

LIFE-WORKS

"AS WE HAVE THEREFORE opportunity, let us do good unto all, especially unto them who are of the household of faith" (Gal. 6:10). If aught could enhance the value of these lovely words, it would be the fact of their being found at the close of the Epistle to the Galatians. In the progress of this very remarkable writing, the inspired apostle cuts up by the roots the entire system of legal righteousness. He proves, in the most unanswerable way, that by works of law, of any sort, moral or ceremonial, no man can be justified in the sight of God. He declares that believers are not under law in any way whatever, either for life, for justification, or for walk—that if we are under law, we must give up Christ; we must give up the Spirit of God; we must give up faith; we must give up the promises. In short, if we take up legal ground, in any shape whatever, we must give up Christianity and lie under the actual curse of the law.

We do not attempt to quote the passages, or to go into this side of the question at all, just now. We merely call the earnest attention of the Christian reader to the golden words which stand at the head of this paper—words which, we cannot but feel, come in with incomparable beauty and peculiar moral force at the close of an Epistle in which all human righteousness is withered up and flung to the winds. It is always needful to take in both sides of a subject. We are all so terribly prone to one-sidedness, that it is morally healthful for us to have our hearts brought under the full action of *all* truth. It is, alas, possible for grace itself to be abused; and we may sometimes forget that, while we are justified in the sight of God by faith alone, a real faith must be evidenced by works. We have, all of us, to bear in mind that while *law-works* are denounced and demolished, in the most unqualified manner, in manifold parts of Holy Scripture, yet that *life-works* are diligently and constantly maintained and insisted upon.

Yes, we have to bend our earnest attention to this. If we profess to have life, this life must express itself in something more tangible and forcible than mere words or empty lip-profession. It is quite true that law cannot give life, and hence it cannot produce life-works. Not a single cluster of living fruit ever was, or ever will be, culled from the tree of legality. Law can only produce "dead works," from which we need to have the conscience purged just as much as from "wicked works."

All this is most true. It is demonstrated in the pages of inspiration beyond all possibility of question or demur. But then there must be life-works, or else there is no life. Of what possible use is it to profess to have eternal life; to talk about faith; to advocate the doctrines of grace, while at the same time, the entire life, the whole practical career is marked by selfishness in every shape and form? "Whoso," says the blessed Apostle John, "hath this world's good, and seeth his brother have need, and shutteth up his bowels of compassion from him, how dwelleth the love of God in him?"

So also the Apostle James puts a very wholesome question to our hearts, "What doth it profit, my brethren, though a man *say* he hath faith, and have not works? Can faith save him? If a brother or sister be naked or destitute of daily food, and one of you say unto them, Depart in peace, be ye warmed and filled; notwithstanding ye give them not those things which are needful to the body; what doth it profit?"

Here we have life-works insisted upon in a way which ought to speak home, in the most solemn and forcible way, to our hearts. There is an appalling amount of empty profession—shallow, powerless, worthless talk in our midst. We have a wonderfully clear gospel—thanks be to God for it! We see very distinctly that salvation is by grace, through faith, not by works of righteousness, nor by works of law. Blessedly true, and our heart praises God for it. But when people are saved, ought they not to live as such? Ought not the new life to come out in fruits? It must come out if it be in; and if it does not come out, it is not there.

Mark what the Apostle Paul says, "For by grace are ye saved through faith; and that not of yourselves; it is the gift of God; not of works, lest any man should boast." Here we have what we may call the upper side of this great practical question. Then the other side, to which every true and earnest Christian will delight to give his attention. The apostle goes on to say, "We are His workmanship *created in Christ Jesus unto good works, which God hath before prepared that we should walk in them.*"

Here we have the whole subject fully and clearly before us. God has created us to walk in a path of good works, and He has prepared the path of good works for us to walk in. It is

all of God, from first to last; all through grace, and all by faith. Thanks and praise be to God that it is so! But, let us remember that it is utterly vain to talk about grace and faith, and eternal life, if the "good works" are not forthcoming. It is useless to boast of our high truth, our deep, varied, and extensive acquaintance with Scripture, our correct position, our having come out from this, that, and the other, if our feet are not found treading that "path of good works which God hath before prepared" for us.

God looks for reality. He is not satisfied with mere words of high profession. He says to us, "My little children, let us not love in word, neither in tongue, but in *deed* and in *truth.*" He, blessed be His name, did not love us in word or in tongue, but in deed and in truth; and He looks for a response from us—a response clear, full, and distinct; a response coming out in a life of good works, a life yielding mellow clusters of the "fruits of righteousness which are by Christ Jesus, to the glory and praise of God."

Do you not consider it to be our bounden duty to apply our hearts to this weighty subject? Ought we not diligently to seek to promote love and good works? And how can this be most effectually accomplished? Surely by walking in love ourselves, and faithfully treading the path of good works in our own private life. For ourselves, we confess we are thoroughly sick of hollow profession. High truth on the lips and low practice in daily life, is one of the crying evils of this our day. We talk of grace; but fail in common righteousness—fail in the plainest moral duties in our daily private life. We boast of our "*position*" and our "*standing;*" but we are deplorably lax as to our *condition* and *state*.

May the Lord, in His infinite goodness, stir up all our hearts to more thorough earnestness, in the pursuit of good works, so that we may more fully adorn the doctrine of God our Saviour in all things!

P.S.—It is very interesting and instructive to compare the teaching of Paul and James—two divinely inspired apostles—on the subject of "works." Paul utterly repudiates *law-works*. James jealously insists upon *life-works*. If this fact be seized, all difficulty vanishes; and the divine harmony is clearly seen. Many have failed to do this, and hence have been much perplexed by the seeming difference between Romans 4: 5, and James 2: 24. We need not say there is the most perfect and beautiful harmony. When Paul says, "To him that *worketh not*, but believeth on him that justifieth the ungodly, his faith is counted for righteousness," he refers to law-works. When James says, "Ye see then how that *by works* a man is justified, and not by faith only," he refers to life-works.

This is abundantly confirmed by the two cases adduced by James in proof of his thesis, namely, Abraham offering up his son and Rahab concealing the spies. If you abstract faith from these cases, they were bad works. Look at them as the fruit of faith, and they were life-works.

How marked is the far-seeing wisdom of the Holy Spirit in all this! He foresaw the use that would be made of this passage; and hence, instead of selecting works abstractedly good, He takes up two from the history of four thousand years, which, if they were not the fruit of faith, were bad works.

THE CHRISTIAN

HIS POSITION AND HIS WORK

Part 1

WHAT IS THE TRUE POSITION of a Christian? and what has he got to do? are questions of the very deepest practical importance. It is assumed, of course, that he has eternal life: without this, one cannot be a Christian at all. "He that believeth on the Son of God hath everlasting life." This is the common portion of all believers. It is not a matter of attainment, a matter of progress, a thing which some Christians have and others have not. It belongs to the very feeblest babe in the family of God, as well as to the most matured and experienced servant of Christ. All are possessed of eternal life, and can never by any possibility lose it.

But our present theme is not life, but position and work; and in considering it, we shall ask the reader to turn for a moment to a passage in Heb. 13. Perhaps we cannot do better than quote it for him. There is nothing like the plain and solid word of Holy Scripture.

"Be not carried about with divers and strange doctrines; for it is a good thing that the heart be established with grace; not with meats, which have not profited them that have been occupied therein. We have an altar, whereof they have no right to eat which serve the tabernacle. For the bodies of those beasts, whose blood is brought into the sanctuary by the high priest for sin are burned without the camp. Wherefore Jesus also, that He might sanctify the people with His own blood, suffered without the gate. Let us go forth therefore unto Him without the camp, bearing His reproach. For here have we no continuing city, but we seek one to come" (vers. 9-14).

Here, then, we have one grand aspect of the Christian's position. It is defined by the position of his Lord. This makes it divinely simple; and, we may add, divinely settled. The Christian is identified with Christ. Amazing fact! "As He is so *are* we in this world." It is not said, "As He is, so *shall* we be in the world to come." No; this would not come up to the divine idea. It is, "so are we *in this world*." The position of Christ defines the position of the Christian.

But this glorious fact tells in a double way: it tells upon the Christian's place before God; and it tells on his place as regards this present world. It is upon the latter that Heb. 13 instructs us so blessedly, and it is that which is now more especially before us.

Jesus suffered without the gate. This fact is the basis on which the apostle grounds his exhortation to the Hebrew believers to go forth without the camp. The cross of Christ closed his connection with the camp of Judaism; and all who desire to follow Him must go outside to where He is. The final breach with Israel is presented, morally, in the death of Christ; doctrinally, in the Epistle to the Hebrews; historically, in the destruction of Jerusalem. In the judgment of faith, Jerusalem was as thoroughly rejected when the Messiah was nailed to the cross, as it was when the army of Titus left it a smouldering ruin. The instincts of the divine nature, and the inspired teachings of Scripture, go before the actual facts of history.

"Jesus suffered without the gate." For what end? "That He might sanctify [or set apart to God] the people with His own blood." What follows? What is the necessary practical result? "Let us go forth therefore unto Him without the camp, bearing His reproach."

But what is "the camp?" Primarily, Judaism; but, most unquestionably, it has a moral application to every organized system of religion under the sun. If that system of ordinances and ceremonies which God Himself had set up—if Judaism, with its imposing ritual, its splendid temple, its priesthood and its sacrifices, has been found fault with, condemned, and set aside, what shall be said of any or all of those organizations which have rebuilt it? If our Lord Christ is outside of that, how much more out of these!

Yes, we may rest assured that the outside place, the place of rejection and reproach is that to which we are called, if we would know aught of true fellowship with our Lord Jesus Christ. Mark the words! "Let us go forth." Will any Christian say, "No; I cannot go forth. My place is inside the camp. I must work there?" If so, then, there must be moral distance between you and Jesus, for He is as surely outside the camp as He is on the throne of God. If your sphere of work lies inside the camp, when your Master tells you to go forth, what shall we say for your work?

Can it be "gold, silver, precious stones?" Can it have your Lord's approving smile? It may exhibit His overruling hand, and illustrate His sovereign goodness; but can it possibly have His unqualified approval while carried on in a sphere from which He commands you to go forth?

The all-important thing for every true servant is to be found exactly where his Master would have him. The question is not, Am I doing a great deal of work? but, Am I pleasing my Master? I may seem to be doing wonders in the way of work; my name may be heralded to the ends of the earth as a most laborious, devoted, and successful workman; and, all the while, I may be in an utterly false position, indulging my own unbroken will, pleasing myself, and seeking some personal end or object.

All this is very solemn indeed, and demands the consideration of all who really desire to be found in the current of God's thoughts. We live in a day of much wilfulness. The commandments of Christ do not govern all. We think for ourselves, in place of submitting ourselves absolutely to the authority of the Word. When our Lord tells us to go forth without the camp, we, instead of yielding a ready obedience, begin to reason as to the results which we can reach by remaining within. Scripture seems to have little or no power over our souls. We do not aim at simply pleasing Christ. Provided we can make great show of work, we think all is right. We are more occupied with results which, after all, may only tend to magnify ourselves, than with the earnest purpose to do what is agreeable to the mind of Christ.

But are we to be idle? Is there nothing for us to do in the outside place to which we are called? Is Christian life to be made up of a series of negations? Is there nothing positive? Let Heb. 13 furnish the clear and forcible answer to all these inquiries. We shall find it quite as distinct in reference to our *work* as it is in reference to our *position*.

What, then, have we got to do? Two things; and these two in their comprehensive range take in the whole of a Christian's life in its two grand aspects. They give us the inner and the outer life of the true believer. In the first place, we read, "By Him therefore let us offer the sacrifice of praise to God continually, that is, the fruit of our lips, giving thanks to His name."

Is not this something? Have we not here a very elevated character of work? Yes, verily, the most elevated that can possibly engage the energies of our renewed being. It is our privilege to be occupied, morning, noon, eventide, and midnight, in presenting the sacrifice of praise to God—a sacrifice which, He assures us, is ever most acceptable to Him. "Whoso offereth praise," He says, "glorifieth Me."

Let us carefully note this. Praise is to be the primary and continual occupation of the believer. We, in our fancied wisdom, would put work in the first place. We are disposed to attach chief importance to bustling activity. We have such an overweening sense of the value of *doing*, that we lose sight of the place which worship occupies in the thoughts of God.

Again, there are some who vainly imagine that they can please God by punishing their bodies. They think that He delights in their vigils, fastings, floggings, and flagellations. Miserable, soul-destroying, God-dishonoring delusion! Will not those who harbor it and act upon it bend their ears and their hearts to those gracious words which we have just penned, "Whoso offereth praise glorifieth Me"? True, it is, that those words are immediately followed by that grand practical statement, "And to him that ordereth his conversation aright, will I show the salvation of God." But still, here, as everywhere, the highest place is assigned to praise, not to work. And, most assuredly, no man can be said to be ordering his conversation aright who abuses his body and renders it unfit to be the vessel or instrument by which he can serve God.

No, if we really desire to please God, to gratify His heart and to glorify His name, we shall give our heart's attention to Heb. 13: 15, and seek to offer the sacrifice of praise *continually*. Yes, "continually." Not merely now and then, when all goes on smoothly and pleasantly. Come what may, it is our high and holy privilege to offer the sacrifice of praise to God. It does so glorify God when His people live in an atmosphere of praise. It imparts a heavenly tone to their character, and speaks more powerfully to the hearts of those around them than if they were preaching to them from morning till night. A Christian should "rejoice in the Lord alway," always reflecting back upon this dark world the blessed beams of his Father's countenance.

Thus it should ever be. Nothing is so unworthy of a Christian as a fretful spirit, a gloomy temper, a sour, morose-looking face. And not only is it unworthy of a Christian, but it is dishonoring to God, and it causes the enemies of truth to speak reproachfully. No doubt, tempers and dispositions vary; and allowance must be made in cases of weak bodily health, and of circumstances of sorrow. It is not easy to look pleasant when the body is in suffering; and, further, we should be very far indeed from the commending anything like levity or the everlasting smile of mere unsubdued nature.

But Scripture is clear and explicit. It tells us to "offer the sacrifice of praise to God continually, that is, the fruit of our lips giving thanks to His name." How simple! *"The fruit of our lips."* This is what our God delights in. It is His joy to be surrounded with the praises of hearts filled to overflowing with His abounding goodness. Thus it will be throughout eternity, in that bright home of love and glory to which we are so rapidly hastening.

Specially note the words, *"By Him."* We are to offer our sacrifice of praise by the hand of our Great High Priest, who is ever in the presence of God for us. This is most consolatory and assuring to our hearts. Jesus presents our sacrifice of praise to God. It must therefore be ever acceptable, coming thus by the priestly hand of the Great Minister of the sanctuary. It goes up to God, not as it proceeds from us, but as it is presented by Him. Divested of all the imperfection and failure attaching to us, it ascends to God in all the fragrance and acceptancy belonging to Him. The feeblest note of praise, the simple "Thank God!" is perfumed with the incense of Christ's infinite preciousness. This is unspeakably precious: and it should greatly encourage us to cultivate a spirit of praise. We should be "continually" praising and blessing God. A murmuring or fretful word should never cross the lips of one who has Christ for his portion, and who stands identified with that blessed One in His position and His destiny.

But we must draw this paper to a close by a rapid glance at the other side of the Christian's work. If it is our privilege to be continually praising and blessing God, it is also our privilege to be doing good to man. "But to do good and to communicate forget not; for with such sacrifices God is well pleased." We are passing through a world of misery, of sin and death and sorrow. We are surrounded by broken hearts and crushed spirits, if we would only look them out.

Yes; this is the point; *if we would only look them out.* It is easy for us to close our eyes to such things, to turn away from them, to forget that there are such things always within reach of us. We can sit in our easy chair, and speculate about truth, doctrines, and the letter of Scripture; we can discuss the theories of Christianity, and split hairs about prophecy and dispensational truth, and, all the while, be shamefully failing in the discharge of our grand responsibility as Christians.

We are in imminent danger of forgetting that Christianity is a living reality. It is not a set of dogmas, a number of principles strung together on a thread of systematized divinity, which unconverted people can have at their fingers' ends. Neither is it a set of ordinances to be gone through, in dreary formality, by lifeless, heartless professors. No; it is life—life eternal—life implanted by the Holy Ghost, and expressing itself in those two lovely forms on which we have been dwelling, namely, praise to God and doing good to man. Such was the life of Jesus when He trod this earth of ours. He lived in the atmosphere of praise; and He went about doing good.*

He is our life, and He is our model on which the life is to be formed. The Christian should be the living expression of Christ, by the power of the Holy Ghost. It is not a mere question of leading what is called a religious life, which very often resolves itself into a tiresome round of duties which neither yield "praise" to God nor one atom of "good" to man. There must be *life*, or it is perfectly worthless. "The kingdom of God is not meat or drink; but righteousness and peace and joy in the Holy Ghost. For he that in these things serveth Christ is acceptable to God, and approved of men" (Rom. 14: 17-18).

Let us earnestly apply our hearts to the consideration of these great practical truths. Let us seek to be Christians not merely in name but in reality. Let us not be distinguished as the mere vendors of peculiar "*views.*" Oh! how worthless are views! How utterly profitless is discussion! How wearisome are theological hair-splittings! Let us have life, light, and love. These are heavenly, eternal, divine. All else is vanity. How we do long for reality in this world of sham—for deep thinkers and earnest workers in this day of shallow talkers!

Part 2

We must ask the reader to open his Bible and read Heb. 10:7-24. In it he will find a very deep and marvelous view of the Christian's position and his work. The inspired writer gives us, as it were, three solid pillars on which the grand edifice of Christianity rests. These are, first, *the will of God;* secondly, *the work of Christ;* and, thirdly, *the witness of the Holy Ghost*, in Scripture. If these grand realities be laid hold of in simple faith, the soul *must* have settled peace. We may assert, with all possible confidence, that no power of earth or hell, men or devils, can ever disturb the peace which is founded upon Heb. 10: 7-17.

Let us then, in the first place, dwell, for a few moments, on the manner in which the

---

* Note: The reader will find it profitable to compare Heb. 13: 13-16 with 1 Peter 2: 4-9. "Let us go forth therefore unto Him," says Paul. "To whom coming," says Peter. Then we have "the holy priesthood" offering up spiritual sacrifices of praise. And "the royal priesthood" doing good and communicating—"showing forth the virtues of Him who hath called us out of darkness into His marvellous light." The two Scriptures give us a magnificent view of fundamental, devotional, and practical Christianity.

apostle unfolds, in this magnificent passage, *the will of God*. In the opening of the chapter, we are instructed as to the utter inadequacy of the sacrifices under the law. They could never make the conscience perfect—they could never accomplish the will of God—never fulfil the gracious desire and purpose of His heart. "The law, having a shadow of good things to come, and not the very image of the things, can never with those sacrifices which they offered year by year continually make the comers thereunto perfect. For then would they not have ceased to be offered? because *the worshipers once purged* should have had *no more conscience of sins*."

Carefully note this. "The worshipers once purged should have had no more conscience of sins." He does not say—"No more *consciousness of sins*." There is an immense difference between these two things; and yet, it is to be feared, they are often confounded. The Christian has, alas, the consciousness of *sin in him*, but he ought to have no conscience of *sins on him*, inasmuch as he is purged once and forever, by the precious blood of Christ.

Some of the Lord's people have a habit of speaking of their continual need of applying to the blood of Christ, which, to say the least of it, is by no means intelligent, or in accordance with the accurate teaching of Holy Scripture. It seems like humility; but, we may rest assured, true humility can only be found in connection with the full, clear, settled apprehension of the truth of God, and as to His gracious will concerning us. If it be His will that we should have "no more conscience of sins," it cannot be true humility, on our part, to go on from day to day, and year to year, with the burden of sins upon us. And, further, if it be true that Christ has borne our sins and put them away forever—if He has offered one perfect sacrifice for sins, ought we not assuredly to know that we are perfectly pardoned and perfectly purged?

Is it—can it be, true humility to reduce the blood of Christ to the level of the blood of bulls and of goats? But this is what is virtually done, though, no doubt, unwitting-ly, by all who speak of applying continually to the blood of Christ. One reason why God found fault with the sacrifices under the law was, as the apostle tells us, "In those sacrifices there is a remembrance again made of sins every year." This, blessed be His name, was not according to His mind. He desired that every trace of guilt and every remembrance of it should be blotted out, once and forever; and hence it cannot be His will that His people should be continually bowed down under the terrible burden of unforgiven sin. It is *contrary* to His will; it is subversive of their peace, and derogatory to the glory of Christ and the efficacy of His one sacrifice.

One grand point of the inspired argument, in Hebrews 10 is to show that the continual remembrance of sins and the continual repetition of the sacrifice go together; and therefore, if Christians now are to have the burden of sins constantly on the heart and conscience, it follows that Christ should be offered again and again—which were a blasphemy. His work is done, and hence our burden is gone—gone forever.

"It is not possible that the blood of bulls and goats should take away sin. Wherefore, when He cometh into the world, He saith, Sacrifice and offering Thou wouldest not, but a body hast Thou prepared Me. In burnt-offerings and sacrifices for sin Thou hast had no pleasure. Then said I, Lo, I come (in the volume of the book it is written of Me) to do Thy will, O God. Above, when He said, Sacrifice and offering and burnt-offerings and offerings for sin Thou wouldest not, neither hadst pleasure therein (which are offered by the law) then said He, Lo, I come to do Thy will, O God. He taketh away the first that He may establish the second. By the which will we are sanctified (or set apart) by the offering of the body of Jesus Christ *once*."

Here we are conducted, in the most distinct and forcible manner, to the eternal source of the whole matter, namely, the will of God—the purpose and counsel formed in the divine mind, before the foundation of the world, before any creature was formed, before sin or Satan existed. It was the will of

God, from all eternity, that the Son should, in due time, come forth and do a work which was to be the foundation of the divine glory and of all the counsels and purposes of the Trinity.

It would be a very grave error indeed to suppose that redemption was an after-thought with God. He had not, blessed be His holy name, to sit down and plan what He would do, when sin entered. It was all settled beforehand. The enemy, no doubt, imagined that he was gaining a wonderful victory when he meddled with man in the garden of Eden. In point of fact, he was only giving occasion for the display of God's eternal counsels in connection with the work of the Son. There was no basis for those counsels, no sphere for their display in the fields of creation. It was the meddling of Satan—the entrance of sin—the ruin of man, that opened a platform on which a Saviour-God might display the riches of His grace, the glories of His salvation, the attributes of His nature, to all created intelligences.

There is great depth and power in those words of the eternal Son, "In the volume of the book it is written of Me." To what "volume" does He here refer? Is it to Old Testament Scripture merely? Surely not; the apostle quotes from the Old Testament, but it is nothing less than the roll of God's eternal counsels in which the "vast plan" was laid, according to which, in the appointed time, the eternal Son was to come forth and appear on the scene, in order to accomplish the divine will, vindicate the divine glory, confound the enemy utterly, put away sin, and save ruined man in a manner which yields a richer harvest of glory to God than ever He could have reaped in the fields of an unfallen creation.

All this gives immense stability to the soul of the believer. Indeed it is utterly impossible for human language to set forth the preciousness and blessedness of this line of truth. It is such rich consolation to every pious soul to know that One has appeared in this world to do the will of God—whatever that will might be. "Lo, I come to do Thy will O God." Such was the one undivided purpose and object of that perfect human heart. He

never did His own will in anything. He says, "I came down from heaven, not to do Mine own will, but the will of Him that sent Me." It mattered not to Him what that will might involve to Himself personally. The decree was written down in the eternal volume that He should come and do the divine will; and, all homage to His peerless name! He came and did it perfectly. He could say, "A body hast Thou prepared Me." "Mine ears hast Thou opened."

"I clothe the heavens with blackness, and I make sackcloth their covering. The Lord God hath given Me the tongue of the learned, that I should know how to speak a word in season to him that is weary: He wakeneth morning by morning, He wakeneth Mine ear to hear as the learned. The Lord God hath opened Mine ear, and I was not rebellious, neither turned away back. I gave My back to the smiters, and My cheeks to them that plucked off the hair: I hid not My face from shame and spitting" (Isa. 1: 3-6).

But this leads us, in the second place, to contemplate *the work of Christ*.

It was ever the delight of the heart of Jesus to do His Father's will and finish His work. From the manger at Bethlehem to the cross of Calvary, the one grand object that swayed His devoted heart was the accomplishment of the will of God. He perfectly glorified God, in all things. This, blessed be God, perfectly secures our full and everlasting salvation, as the apostle in this passage, so distinctly states. "By the which will we are sanctified, through the offering of the body of Jesus Christ, once."

Here our souls may rest in sweetest peace and unclouded certainty. It was the will of God that we should be set apart to Himself, according to all the love of His heart, and all the claims of His throne; and our Lord Christ, in due time, in pursuance of the everlasting purpose as set forth "in the volume of the book," came forth from the glory which He had with the Father, before all worlds, to do the work which forms the imperishable basis of all the divine counsels and of our eternal salvation.

And—forever be His name adored!—He has finished His work. He has perfectly glorified God in the midst of the scene in which He has been so dishonored. At all cost He has vindicated Him and made good His every claim. He magnified the law and made it honorable. He vanquished every foe, removed every obstacle, swept away every barrier, bore the judgment and wrath of a sin-hating God; destroyed death and him that had the power of it, extracted its sting, and spoiled the grave of its victory. In a word, He gloriously accomplished all that was written in the volume of the book concerning Him; and now we see Him crowned with glory and honor, at the right hand of the Majesty in the heavens.

He traveled from the throne to the dust of death, in order to accomplish the will of God, and having done so, He has gone back to the throne, in a new character and on a new footing. His pathway from the throne to the cross was marked by the footprints of divine and everlasting love; and His pathway from the cross back to the throne is sprinkled by His atoning blood. He came from Heaven to earth to do the will of God, and, having done it, He returned to Heaven again, thus opening up for us "a new and living way" by which we draw nigh to God, in holy boldness and liberty, as purged worshipers.

All is done. Every question is settled. Every barrier is removed. The vail is rent. That mysterious curtain which, for ages and generations, had shut God in from man, and shut man out from God, was rent in twain, from top to bottom, by the precious death of Christ; and now we can look right up into the opened heavens and see on the throne the Man who bore our sins in His own body on the tree. A seated Christ tells out, in the ear of faith, the sweet emancipating tale that all that had to be done is done—done forever—done for God—done for us. Yes; all is settled now, and God can, in perfect righteousness, indulge the love of His heart, in blotting out all our sins and bringing us nigh unto Himself in all the acceptance of the One who sits beside Him on the throne.

Carefully note the striking and beautiful way in which the apostle contrasts *a seated Christ in Heaven* with *the standing priest on earth.* "Every priest standeth daily minis-

tering, and offering oftentimes the same sacrifices, which can never take away sins. But this Man, after He had offered one sacrifice for sins, forever [εἰς τὸ διηνεκὲς —in perpetuity] sat down on the right hand of God; from henceforth expecting till His enemies be made His footstool. For by one offering He hath perfected forever (in perpetuity) them that are sanctified."

This is exceedingly blessed. The priest, under the Levitical economy, could never sit down, for the obvious reason that his work was never done. There was no seat provided in the temple or in the tabernacle. There is remarkable force and significance in the manner in which the inspired writer puts this. "*Every priest*"—"standeth *daily*"—"offering *oftentimes*"—"*the same sacrifices*"—"which can *never take away sins.*" No human language could possibly set forth, more graphically, the utter inefficacy of the Levitical ceremonial. How strange that, in the face of such a passage of Holy Scripture, Christendom should have set up a human priesthood, with its daily sacrifice!—a priesthood moreover, not belonging to the tribe of Levi, not springing from the house of Aaron, and therefore having no sort of divine title or sanction. And, then as to the sacrifice, it is, according to their own admission, a sacrifice without blood, and therefore a sacrifice without remission, for, "Without the shedding of blood there is no remission" (Heb. 9:22).

Hence, this self-made priesthood is a daring usurpation, and her sacrifices a worthless vanity—a positive lie—a mischievous delusion. The priests of whom the apostle speaks in Heb. 10 were priests of the tribe of Levi and of the house of Aaron—the only house, the only tribe ever recognized of God as having any title to assume the office and the work of an earthly priest. And, further, the sacrifices which the Aaronic priests offered were appointed by God, for the time being, to serve as *figures* of Him that was to come; but they never gave Him any pleasure, inasmuch as they could never take away sins; and the true Priest having come, the true sacrifice having been offered, the figures have been forever abolished.

Now, in view of all this, what shall we say of Christendom's priests and Christendom's sacrifices? What will a righteous Judge say to them? We cannot attempt to dwell upon such an awful theme. We can merely say, alas! alas! for the poor souls that are deluded and ruined by such antichristian absurdities. May God in His mercy deliver them and lead them to rest in the one offering of Jesus Christ—that precious blood that cleanses from all sin. May many be led to see that a repeated sacrifice and a seated Christ are in positive antagonism.

If the sacrifice must be repeated, Christ has no right to His seat and to His crown—God pardon the very penning of the words! If Christ has a divine right to His seat and to His crown, then to repeat a sacrifice is simply a blasphemy against His cross, His name, His glory. To repeat in any way, or under any form whatsoever, the sacrifice, is to deny the efficacy of Christ's one offering, and to rob the soul of anything like an approach to the knowledge of remission of sins. A repeated sacrifice and perfect remission are an absolute contradiction in terms.

But we must turn, for a moment, to the third grand point in our subject, namely, *the witness of the Holy Ghost.*

This is of the deepest possible moment to understand. It gives great completeness to the subject. How are we to know that Christ has, by His work on the cross, absolutely and divinely accomplished the will of God? Simply by the witness of the Holy Ghost in Scripture. This is the third pillar on which the Christian's position rests, and it is as thoroughly divine and, therefore, as thoroughly independent of man as the other two. It is very evident that man had nothing to do with the eternal counsels of the Trinity—nothing to do with the glorious work accomplished on the cross. All this is clear; and it is equally clear that man has nothing to do with the authority on which our souls receive the joyful news as to the *will of God*, and *the work of Christ*, inasmuch as it is nothing less than *the witness of the Holy Ghost.*

We cannot be too simple as to this. It is not, by any means, a question of our feelings, our frames, our evidences, or our experiences—things interesting in their right place. We must receive the truth solely and simply on the authority of that august Witness who speaks to us in Holy Scripture. Thus we read, "Whereof the Holy Ghost also is a witness to us; for after that He had said before, This is the covenant that I will make with them after those days, saith the Lord; I will put My laws into their hearts, and in their minds will I write them; and their sins and iniquities will I remember no more."

Here, then, we have fully before us the solid foundation of the Christian's position and the Christian's peace. It is all of God, from first to last. The *will*, the *work*, and the *witness* are all divine. The Lord be praised for this glorious fact! What should we do, what would become of us, were it otherwise? In this day of confusion, when souls are tossed about by every wind of doctrine—when the beloved sheep of Christ are driven hither and thither, in bewilderment and perplexity—when ritualism with its ignorant absurdities, and rationalism with its impudent blasphemies, and spiritualism with its horrible traffic with demons, are threatening the very foundations of our faith, how important it is for Christians to know what those foundations really are, and that they should be consciously resting thereon!

Part 3

We would recall for a moment to the reader's attention the third point in our subject, namely, "The witness of the Holy Ghost in Scripture." We feel it to be of too much importance to be dismissed with such a cursory glance as we were able to give it at the close of our last paper.

It is absolutely essential to the enjoyment of settled peace that the heart should rest *solely* on the authority of Holy Scripture. Nothing else will stand. Inward evidences, spiritual experiences, comfortable frames, happy feelings, are all very good, very valuable, and very desirable; indeed we cannot prize them too highly in their right place. But, most assuredly, their right place is not at the foundation of the Christian position. If we look to such things as the ground of our peace, we shall very soon become clouded, uncertain, and miserable.

The reader cannot be too simple in his apprehension of this point. He must rest like a little child upon the testimony of the Holy Ghost in the Word. It is blessedly true that "He that believeth hath the witness in himself." And again, "The Spirit itself beareth witness with our spirit that we are the children of God." All this is essential to Christianity; but it must, in no wise, be confounded with the witness of the Holy Ghost, as given to us in Holy Scripture. The Spirit of God never leads any one to build upon His work as the ground of peace, but only upon the finished work of Christ, and the unchangeable Word of God; and we may rest assured that the more simply we rest on these the more settled our peace will be, and the clearer our evidences, the brighter our frames, the happier our feelings, the richer our experiences.

In short, the more we look away from self and all its belongings, and rest in Christ, on the clear authority of Scripture, the more spiritually minded we shall be; and the inspired apostle tells us that "to be spiritually minded [or, the minding of the Spirit] is life and peace." The best evidence of a spiritual mind is child-like repose in Christ and His Word. The clearest proof of an unspiritual mind is self-occupation. It is a poor affair to be trafficking in *our* evidences, or *our* anything. It looks like piety, but it leads away from Christ—away from Scripture—away from God; and this is not piety, or faith, or Christianity.

We are intensely anxious that the reader should seize, with great distinctness, the importance of committing his whole moral being to the divine authority of the Word of God. It will never fail him. All else may go, but "the word of our God shall stand forever." Heart and flesh may fail. Internal evidences may become clouded; frames, feelings, and experiences may all prove unsatisfactory; but the Word of the Lord, the testimony of the Holy Ghost, the clear voice of Holy Scripture, must ever remain unshaken. "And this is the Word which by the gospel is preached unto us."

Thus much, then, as to the divine and everlasting basis of the Christian's position, as set forth in the tenth chapter of the Epistle to the Hebrews. Let us, now, see what this same Scripture tells us of the Christian's work, and of the sphere in which that work is to be carried on.

The Christian is brought into the immediate presence of God, inside the veil, into the holiest of all. This is his proper place, if indeed we are to listen to the voice of Scripture. "Having therefore, brethren, boldness to enter into the holiest by the blood of Jesus, by a *new* and *living* way which He hath consecrated for us, through the veil, that is to say, His flesh; and having a high-priest over the house of God; *let us draw near* with a true heart, in full assurance of faith, having our hearts sprinkled from an evil conscience, and our bodies washed with pure water."

Our God, blessed be His holy name, would have us near unto Himself. He has made out for us a title clear and indisputable in *"the blood of Jesus."* Nothing more is needed. That precious blood stands out before the eye of faith in all its infinite value. In it alone we read our title. It is not the blood *and* something else—be that something what it may. The blood constitutes our exclusive title. We come before God in all the perfect efficacy of that blood which rent the veil, glorified God as to the question of sin, canceled our guilt according to all the demands of infinite holiness, silenced, forever, every accuser, every foe. We enter by a new and living way—a way which can never become old or dead. We enter by the direct invitation, yea, by the distinct command of God. It is positive disobedience not to come. We enter to receive the loving welcome of our Father's heart, it is an insult to that love not to come. He tells us to "come boldly"—to "draw near" with full, unclouded confidence—a boldness and confidence commensurate with the love that invites us; the word that commands us, and the blood that fits and entitles us. It is offering dishonor to the eternal Trinity not to draw near.

Is all this understood and taught in Christendom? Say, do Christendom's creeds, confessions, and liturgical services harmonize with apostolic teaching in Heb. 10? Alas! they do not. Nay, they are in direct antagonism; and the state of souls, accordingly, is the very reverse of what it ought to be. In place of "draw near," it is keep off. In place of liberty and boldness, it is legality and bondage. In place of a heart sprinkled from an evil conscience, it is a heart bowed down beneath the intolerable burden of unforgiven sin. In place of a great High Priest seated on the throne of God, in virtue of accomplished redemption, we have poor mortal—not to say sinful—priests standing from week to week, all the year round in wearisome routine, actually contradicting, in their barren formularies, the very foundation truths of Christianity.

How truly deplorable is all this! And then the sad condition of the Lord's dear people, the lambs and sheep of that precious flock for which He died! It is this that so deeply affects us. It is of little use attacking christendom. We quite admit this; but we yearn over the souls of God's people. We long to see them fully delivered from false teaching, from Judaism, legalism, and every other *ism* that robs them of a full salvation and precious Saviour. We long to reach them with the clear and soul-satisfying teachings of Holy Scripture, so that they may know and enjoy the things that are freely given to them of God.

We can truly say there is nothing which gives us such painful concern as the state of the Lord's dear people, scattered upon the dark mountains and desolate moors: and one special object for which we desire to live is to be the instrument of leading them into those green pastures and beside those still waters where the true Shepherd and Bishop of their souls longs to feed them, according to all the deep and tender love of His heart. He would have them near Himself, reposing in the light of His blessed countenance.

It is not according to His mind or His loving heart that His people should be kept at a dim cold distance from His presence, in doubt and darkness. Ah, no; His Word tells us to draw near—to come boldly—to appropriate freely —to make our very own all the precious privileges to which a Father's love invites us, and a Saviour's blood entitles us.

"Let us draw near." This is the voice of God to us. Christ has opened up the way. The veil is rent, our place is in the holiest of all, the conscience sprinkled, the body washed, the soul entering intelligently into the atoning value of the blood, and the cleansing, sanctifying power of the Word—its action upon our habits, our ways, our associations, our entire course and character.

All this is of the very utmost practical value to every true lover of holiness—and every true Christian is a lover of holiness. "The body washed with pure water" is a perfectly delightful thought. It sets forth the purifying action of the Word of God on the Christian's entire course and character. We must not be content with having the heart sprinkled by the blood; we must also have the body washed with pure water.

What then? *"Let us hold fast* the profession of our hope [$ελπιδος$] without wavering (for He is faithful that promised)." Blessed parenthesis! We may well hold fast, seeing He is faithful. Our hope can never make ashamed. It rests, in holy calmness, upon the infallible faithfulness of Him who cannot lie, whose word is settled for ever in Heaven, far above all the changes and chances of this mortal life, above the din of controversy, the strife of tongues, the impudent assaults of infidelity, the ignorant ravings of superstition —far away above all these things, eternally settled in Heaven is that Word which forms the ground of our "hope."

It well becomes us, therefore, to hold fast. We should not have a single wavering thought—a single question—a single misgiving. For a Christian to doubt is to cast dishonor upon the word of a faithful God. Let skeptics, and rationalists, and infidels doubt, for they have nothing to believe, nothing to rest upon, no certainty. But for a child of God to doubt, is to call in question the faithfulness of the divine Promiser. We owe it to His glory, to say nothing of our own peace, to "hold fast the confession of our hope without wavering." Thus may it be with every beloved member of the household of faith, until that longed-for moment "when faith and hope shall cease, and love abide alone."

But there is one more interesting branch of Christian work at which we must glance ere closing this paper. "*Let us consider one another*, to provoke unto love and to good works."

This is in lovely moral keeping with all that has gone before. The grace of God has so richly met all our personal need—setting before us such an array of precious privileges—an opened Heaven—a rent veil—a crowned and seated Saviour—a great High Priest—a perfectly purged conscience—boldness to enter—a hearty welcome—a faithful Promiser—a sure and certain hope: having all these marvelous blessings in full possession, what have we got to do? To consider ourselves? Nay verily; this were superfluous and sinfully selfish. We could not possibly do so well for ourselves as God has done for us. He has left nothing unsaid, nothing undone, nothing to be desired. Our cup is full and running over. What remains? Simply to "consider one another"; to go out in the activities of holy love, and serve our brethren in every possible way; to be on the lookout for opportunities of doing good; to be ready for every good work; to seek in a thousand little ways to make hearts glad; to seek to shed a ray of light on the moral gloom around us; to be a stream of refreshing in this sterile and thirsty wilderness.

These are some of the things that make up a Christian's work. May we attend to them! May we be found provoking one another, not to envy and jealousy, but to love and good works; exhorting one another daily; diligently availing ourselves of the public assembly, and so much the more, as we see the day approaching.

May the Holy Spirit engrave upon the heart of both writer and reader these most precious exhortations so thoroughly characteristic of our glorious Christianity—"*Let us draw near*"—"*Let us hold fast*"—"*Let us consider one another!*"

CHRISTIAN PERFECTION WHAT IS IT?

THERE ARE FEW THOUGHTFUL students of the New Testament who have not, at some time or another, felt a little perplexed as to the real force and application of the word "perfect," which is of frequent occurrence. This word is used in such a variety of connections that it is deeply important we should be clear as to what the Holy Ghost means by it in each particular case. We believe the context will, generally speaking, guide as to a right understanding of the just sense and application of the word in any given passage.

We are aware that the subject of "Christian perfection" has given rise to much theological strife and controversy; but we must at the outset assure our readers that it is not by any means our intention to take up the question in a controversial way; we shall merely seek to bring under their notice the various passages in the New Testament in which the word "perfect" occurs, or at least some of the leading instances of its use, trusting the Lord to use what He may give us to write, for the glory of His name and the profit of those precious souls for whom we ever desire to write. We shall not trace the word in the order in which it occurs, but rather in that order which the real need of the soul would naturally suggest. In this way we shall find that the first great aspect of Christian perfection is presented to us in the ninth verse of the ninth chapter of Hebrews, and may be denominated *perfection as to the state of the conscience.*

"Which was a figure for the time then

present, in which were offered both gifts and sacrifices, that could not make him that did the service *perfect* [$\tau\epsilon\lambda\epsilon\iota\tilde{\omega}\sigma\alpha\iota$] as pertaining to the conscience." The apostle, in this passage, is drawing a contrast between the sacrifices under the Mosaic economy, and the sacrifice of Christ. The former could never give a perfect conscience, simply because they were imperfect in themselves. It was impossible that the blood of a bullock or of a goat could ever give a perfect conscience. Hence, therefore, the conscience of a Jewish worshiper was never perfect. He had not, if we may use the expression, reached his moral end as to the condition of his conscience. He could never say that his conscience was perfectly purged, because he had not yet reached a perfect sacrifice.

With the Christian worshiper, however, it is different. He has, blessed be God, reached his moral end. He has arrived at a point, so far as the state of his conscience is concerned, beyond which it is utterly impossible for him to go. He cannot get beyond the blood of Jesus Christ. He is perfect as to his conscience. As is the sacrifice, so is the conscience that rests thereon. If the sacrifice is imperfect, so is the conscience. They stand or fall together. Nothing can be simpler, nothing more solid, nothing more consolatory, for any awakened conscience. It is not at all a question of what I am; *that* has been fully and forever settled. I have been found out, judged, and condemned in myself. "In me, that is in my flesh, dwelleth no good." I have got to the end of myself, and there I have reached the blood of Christ. I want no more. What could be added to that most precious blood? Nothing. I am perfect, as to the state of my conscience. I do not want an ordinance, a sacrament, or a ceremony, to perfect the condition of my conscience. To say so, to think so, would be to cast dishonor upon the sacrifice of the Son of God.

The reader will do well to get a clear and firm hold of this foundation-point. If there be any darkness or uncertainty as to this, he will be wholly unable to understand or appreciate the various aspects of "Christian perfection" which are yet to pass in review before us. It is quite possible that many pious people fail

to enjoy the unspeakable blessing of a perfect conscience by reason of self-occupation. They look in at self, and not finding aught there to rest upon—who ever did?—they deem it presumption to think of being perfect in any respect whatever. This is a mistake. It may be a pious mistake, but it is a mistake. Were we to speak of perfection in the flesh (what many, alas, are vainly aiming at), then, verily, true piety might recoil with just horror from the presumptuous and silly chimera.

But, thank God, our theme is not perfection in the flesh, through any process of improvement, moral, social, or religious. This would be poor, dreary, depressing work indeed. It would be setting us to look for perfection in the old creation, where sin and death reign. To look for perfection amid the dust of the old creation were a hopeless task. And yet how many are thus engaged! They are seeking to *improve man and mend the world;* and yet, with all this, they have never reached, never understood—yea, they actually deny—the very first and simplest aspect of Christian perfection, namely, perfection as to the state of the conscience in the presence of God.

This latter is our thesis, and we want the anxious reader to understand it in its simplicity, in order that he may see the solid foundation of his peace laid down by the very hand of God Himself. We want him, ere he lays aside this paper, to enter into the joyful sense of sins perfectly forgiven, and his conscience perfectly purged by the blood of Jesus. The entire matter hinges upon the question of the sacrifice. What has God found in that sacrifice? Perfection. Well, then, that perfection is for you, anxious one, and you should at once and forever enjoy it.

Remember, it is not a question as to what you are, nor yet as to what you think about the blood of Christ. No, the question is, What does God think about the blood of His own Son? This makes all so clear. Say, is it clear to you? Can you now rest in it? Is your conscience set free by being brought in contact with a perfect sacrifice? Oh that it may be so! May God's Spirit now show you the fulness and perfectness of Christ's atoning work with such clearness, vividness and power that your whole being may be emancipated, and your heart filled with praise and thanksgiving!

It makes the heart bleed to think of the thousands of precious souls kept in darkness and bondage when they ought to be walking in the light and liberty which flow from a perfectly purged conscience. So many things are mixed up with the simple testimony of the Word and Spirit of God as to the value of Christ's work that it is wholly impossible for the heart to get liberated. You will get a little bit of Christ, and a little bit of self; a little bit of grace, and a little bit of law; a little bit of faith, and a little bit of works. Thus the soul is kept hovering between confidence and doubt, hope and fear, just as one or other of the ingredients predominates in the mixture, or happens to be tasted at the moment. How rare is the gem of full, free, present, and eternal salvation! We would fain cause that gem to sparkle in all its divine and heavenly lustre under the gaze of the reader at this moment. Then shall the chains of his spiritual bondage drop off. If the Son shall make him free he shall be free indeed, and thus be able to rise in the power of this freedom and trample the legal system beneath his feet.

The more we ponder the question now before us—and we have pondered it a good deal—the more we are convinced that the true secret of all the error, confusion and perplexity in which so many are involved in reference to it will be found in the fact that they do not clearly understand death and resurrection—the new birth—the new creation. Were this grand truth only laid hold of in power it would make all clear as to the state of the conscience. So long as I am seeking to tranquilize my conscience by efforts after self-improvement, so long I must be either miserable or self-deceived. It does not matter in the least what means I adopt in carrying on the process; the issue must be one and the same. If I attempt to take up the profession of Christianity for the purpose of bettering *self*—improving nature or mending my condition in the old creation—I must be a total stranger to the bliss of a perfect conscience. "All flesh is as grass." The old creation lies under the withering infuences of sin and its curse. A risen Christ is the Head of the new creation—"the beginning of the creation of God"—"the first-begotten from among the dead" (ἐκ τῶν νεκρῶν).

Here in very deed is perfection for the conscience. What more do I want? I see the One who hung upon the cross, charged with the full weight of all my sins, now crowned with glory and honor at the right hand of God, amid the full blaze of Heaven's majesty. What can be added to this? Do I want ordinances, rites, ceremonies, or sacraments? Surely not. I dare not add aught to the death and resurrection of the eternal Son of God. The ordinances of baptism and the Lord's Supper symbolize and celebrate that grand reality; and, so far, they are precious to the Christian—most precious. But when, instead of being used to symbolize and celebrate death and resurrection, they are used to displace it—used as patches upon the old creation, as crutches for the old man—they must be regarded as a snare, a curse, from which may the Lord deliver the souls of His people!

We would fain dwell upon this our first point because of its immense importance in this day of ordinances, traditionary religion, and self-improvement. We should like to ponder it—to elaborate, illustrate, and enforce it—in order that the reader may get a clear, full, bold grasp of it. But we look to God the Holy Ghost to do His own work in this matter; and if He will graciously bring the heart under the power of the truth which has been so feebly unfolded, then indeed will there be both ability and leisure to look at the second great aspect of Christian perfection, namely, *perfection as to the object of the heart.*

Here, again, we are ushered into the new creation. Christ died to give me a perfect conscience. He lives to give me a perfect object. But it is very clear that until I have tasted the deep blessedness of the former, I can never be properly occupied with the latter. I must have a perfect conscience ere my heart can be at leisure to go out after the Person of Christ. How few of us really taste the sweetness of communion with a risen Christ! How little do any of us know of that fixedness of heart upon Him as our one paramount, engrossing, undivided object! We are occupied with our own things. The world creeps in, in one way or another; we live in the region of nature; we breathe the atmosphere—the dark, heavy, murky atmosphere—of the old creation; self is indulged; and thus our spiritual vision becomes dimmed, we lose our sense of peace, the soul becomes disturbed, the heart unhinged, the Holy Ghost grieved, the conscience exercised. Then the eye is turned in upon self and back upon its actings. The time that else might be spent in holy and happy occupation with our Object is, and must be, devoted to the business of self-judgment—heavy, but needed work!—in order to get back into the enjoyment of what we should never have lost, even a perfect conscience.

Now, the moment the eye is turned off from Christ darkness must set in—ofttimes darkness that may be felt. It is only as the eye is single that the body is full of light. And what is a single eye but having Christ for our one object? It is thus that light divine pours in upon us, until every chamber of our moral being becomes lighted up, and we become lights for others, "as when the bright shining of a candle doth give thee light." In this way the soul is kept happily free from obscurity, perplexity, and anxiety. It finds all its springs in Christ. It is independent of the world, and can move on, singing—

> Salvation in that name is found,
>   Cure for my grief and care;
> A healing balm for every wound:
>   All, all I want is there.

It is impossible for words to convey the power and blessedness of having Jesus ever before the heart as an object. It is perfection, as we have it in Philippians 3:15, where the apostle says, "Let us therefore, as many as be *perfect* (τέλειοι), be thus minded: and if in anything ye be differently minded (ἑτέρως), God shall reveal even this unto you." When Christ stands before the heart as our absorbing and satisfying object, we have reached our moral end so far as an object is concerned; for how can we ever get beyond the Person of Christ, in whom dwelleth all the fulness of the Godhead bodily, and in whom are hid all the treasures of wisdom and knowledge? Impossible. We cannot get beyond the blood of Christ, for the conscience; neither can we get beyond the Person of Christ, for the heart; we have therefore reached our moral end in both; we have perfection as to the state of the conscience, and as to the object of the heart.

Here, then, we have both peace and power—peace for the conscience, and power over the affections. It is when the conscience finds sweet repose in the blood that the emancipated affections can go forth and find their full play around the Person of Jesus. And oh, what tongue can tell, what pen unfold, the mighty moral results of gazing upon Christ? "But we all, with open face, beholding as in a glass the glory of the Lord, are changed into the same image, from glory to glory, even as by the Spirit of the Lord" (2 Cor. 3:18). Observe, "*Beholding . . . are changed.*" There is no legal bondage—no restless effort—no anxious toiling. We gaze, and gaze, and—what then? Continue to gaze, and as we gaze we become morally assimilated to the blessed Object, through the transforming power of the Holy Ghost. The image of Christ is engraved upon the heart, and reflected back in ten thousand ways in our practical career, from day to day.

Remember, this is the only true idea of Christianity. It is one thing to be a religious man, it is quite another to be a Christian. Paul was a religious man before his conversion; but he was a Christian afterwards. It is well to see this. There is plenty of religion in the world, but, alas, how little Christianity! And why? Simply because Christ is not known, not loved, not cared for, not sought after. And even where His work is looked to for salvation—where His blood is trusted for pardon and peace—how little is known or thought of Himself! We are ready enough to take salvation through the death of Jesus, but oh, how far off do we keep from His blessed Person! How little does He get His true place in our hearts! This is a serious loss. Indeed, we cannot but believe that the pale, flickering light of modern profession is the fruit of habitual distance from Christ, the central sun of Christianity.

How can there possibly be light, heat, or fruitfulness, if we wander amid the gloomy vaults and dark tunnels of this world's pleasures, its politics, or its religion? It is vain to expect it. And even where we make salvation our object—when we are occupied with our spiritual condition, feeding upon our experiences and looking after our frames and feelings—we must become weak and low, inasmuch as these things are certainly not Christ.

There are many who, as we say, have retired from the world, have given up its balls, its parties, its theatres, its exhibitions, its concerts, its flower shows, its numberless and nameless vanities, who, nevertheless, have not found their object in a risen and glorified Christ. They have retired from the world, but have gone in upon themselves. They are seeking an object *in their religion;* they are engrossed with forms of pietism; they are feeding upon the workings of a morbid conscience or a superstitious mind; or they are trafficking in the experience of yesterday. Now, these persons are just as far from happiness—as far from the true idea of Christianity, as the poor pleasure-hunters of this world. It is quite possible to give up pleasure-hunting and become a religious mope—a morbid, melancholy mystic—a spiritual hypochondriac. What do I gain by the change? Nothing; unless, indeed, it be a vast amount of self-deception. I have retired from the world around, to find an object in the world within—a poor exchange!

How different is this from the true Christian! There he stands, with a tranquilized conscience and an emancipated heart, gazing upon an Object that absorbs his whole soul. He wants no more. Talk to him about this world's pleasure? Ask him, has he been to this or that exhibition? What is his calm and dignified reply? Will he merely tell you of the sin, the harm, of such things? Nay; what then? "I have found my *all* in Christ. I have reached my moral end. I want no more." This is the Christian's reply. It is a poor affair when we come to talk of the harm of this or that. It often happens that persons who speak thus are occupied, not with Christ, but with their own reputation, their character, their consistency with themselves. Of what use is all this? Is it not self-occupation, after all? What we want is to keep the eye fixed on Christ; then the heart will follow the eye, and the feet will follow the heart. In this way our path will be as the shining light, shining more and more until it becomes lost in the blaze of the perfect and everlasting day of glory.

May God, in His infinite mercy, grant to the writer and reader of these pages to know more of what it is to have reached our moral end, both as to the state of the conscience and as to the object of the heart!

In considering the subject of Christian perfection, it might seem sufficient to say that the believer is perfect in a risen Christ: "Complete in Him which is the head of all principality and power." This, surely, comprehends everything. Nothing can be added to the completeness which we have in Christ. All this is blessedly true; but does it not still hold good that the inspired writers use the word "perfect" in various ways? And is it not important that we should understand the sense in which the word is used? This, we presume, will hardly be questioned. We cannot suppose for a moment that any thoughtful reader of Scripture would be satisfied to dismiss the matter without prayerfully seeking to understand the exact force and just application of the word in each particular passage in which it occurs. It is plain that the word "perfect" in Heb. 9:9 is not applied in the same way as it is in Phil. 3:15. And is it not right—is it not profitable—is it not due to our own souls and to the sacred volume—to seek, through grace, to understand the difference? For our part, we cannot question it; and in this confidence we can happily pursue our examination of the subject of Christian perfection by calling the reader's attention, in the third place, to *perfection in the principle of our walk.*

This is unfolded to us in Matt. 5:48: "Be ye therefore perfect ($\tau\acute{\epsilon}\lambda\epsilon\iota o\iota$), even as your Father which is in heaven is perfect." "How," it may be asked, "can we be perfect as our

Father which is in Heaven? How can we reach to such an elevated point as this? How can we attain to so lofty a standard? We can understand our being perfect as to the conscience, inasmuch as this perfection is based upon what Christ has done for us. And we can also understand our being perfect as to the object of the heart, inasmuch as this perfection is based upon what Christ is to us. But to be perfect as our Father in Heaven seems entirely beyond us."

To all this it may be said that our blessed Lord does not ask us to do impossibilities. He never issues a command without furnishing the needed grace to carry it out. Hence, therefore, when He calls upon us to be perfect as our Father, it is plain that He confers upon us a holy privilege, that He invests us with a high dignity, and it is our place to seek to understand and appropriate both the one and the other.

What, then, is meant by our being perfect as our Father in Heaven? The context of Matt. 5:48 furnishes the answer: "But I say unto you, Love your enemies, bless them that curse you, do good to them that hate you, and pray for them which despitefully use you and persecute you; that ($\delta\pi\omega\varsigma$) ye may be the sons ($\upsilon\iota o\iota$) of your Father which is in heaven; for He maketh His sun to rise on the evil and on the good, and sendeth rain on the just and on the unjust. . . . Be ye therefore perfect, even as your Father which is in heaven is perfect."

Here we have a lovely phase of Christian perfection, namely, perfection in the principle of our walk. We are called to walk in grace toward all, and in so doing to be imitators of God as dear children. Our Father sends His sunshine and His showers even upon His enemies. He deals in grace with all. This is our model. Are we formed upon it?

Search and see. Are you perfect in the principle of your walk? Are you dealing in grace with your enemies and those who are in your debt? Are you demanding your rights? Are you, in principle, taking your fellow by the throat, and saying, "Pay me that thou owest?" If so, you are not "perfect as your Father." He is dealing in grace, and you are dealing in righteousness. Were He to act as

you are acting, the day of grace would close, and the day of vengeance open. Had He dealt with you as you are now dealing with others, you should long since have been in that place where hope is unknown.

Let us ponder this. Let us see to it that we are not misrepresenting our heavenly Father. Let us aim at perfection in the principle of our daily walk. It will cost us something. It may empty the purse, but it will fill the heart; it may contract our pecuniary resources, but it will enlarge our spiritual circle. It will bring us into closer contact and deeper fellowship with our heavenly Father. Is not this worth something? Truly it is. Would that we felt its worth more deeply! Would that we felt more of the dignity conferred upon us in our being called to represent, in this evil, selfish, dark world, our heavenly Father, who pours in rich profusion His blessings upon the unthankful and the unholy. There is no use in preaching grace if we do not act it. It is of little avail to speak of God's dealing in long-suffering mercy if we are dealing in high-handed justice.

But, it may be said by some, "How ever could we carry out such a principle? We should be robbed and ruined. How could business be carried on if we are not to enforce our rights? We should be imposed upon and plundered by the unprincipled and the designing." This is not the mode in which to arrive at a just conclusion on our point. An obedient disciple never says, "How?" The question is, "Does the Lord Jesus call upon me to be perfect as my Father in heaven is perfect?" Assuredly. Well, then, am I aiming at this when I summon my fellow-creature to a bar of justice? Is this like my Father? Is this what He is doing? No; blessed be His name! He is on a throne of grace. He is reconciling the world. He is not imputing trespasses. This is plain enough. It only needs full subjection of heart. Let us bow our souls beneath the weight of this most glorious truth. May we gaze upon this most lovely aspect of Christian perfection, and seek to aim at the attainment of it.

If we pause to reason about results, we shall never reach the truth. What we want is, that moral condition of soul that fully owns the power and authority of the Word. Then, though there may be failure in detail, we have always a touchstone by which to test our ways, and a standard to which to recall the heart and conscience. But if we reason and argue—if we deny that it is our privilege to be perfect in the sense of Matt. 5:48—if we justify our going to *law* when our Father is not going to law, but acting in the most unqualified *grace*, we deprive ourselves of that perfect model on which our character and ways should ever be formed.

May God the Holy Spirit enable us to understand, to submit to, and carry out in practical life, this perfect principle! It is most lamentable to see the children of God adopting in daily life a course of acting the direct opposite of that adopted by their heavenly Father. We ought to remember that we are called to be His moral representatives. We are His children by spiritual regeneration, but we are called to be His sons in moral assimilation to His character and practical conformity to His ways. "Do good to them that hate you . . . *that ye may be* the sons of your Father which is in heaven." Striking words! In order to our being morally and characteristically the sons of God, we are called to do good to our enemies. This is what He does, and we are called to be like Him. Alas, how little we enter into this! How unlike we are! Oh for a more faithful representation!

Time and space would fail us to dwell, as we should like to do, upon this deeply practical part of our subject; we must therefore pass on, in the fourth place, to the consideration of *perfection in the character of our service.*

"I have not found thy works perfect (πεπληρωμένα) before God" (Rev. 3:2). The English reader should be informed that the word here rendered "perfect" is not the same as that used in the three passages already referred to. It is usually translated "fulfilled"—"finished"—"accomplished." Its use in reference to the works of the church of Sardis teaches us a deeply solemn and heart-searching lesson. There was a name to live; but the works were not fulfilled under the immediate eye of God. There is nothing more dangerous to a Christian than to have "*a name.*" It is a positive snare of the devil.

Many a professor has fallen by means of being occupied with a name. Many a useful servant has been destroyed by the effort to keep up a name. If I have gotten a reputation in any department of service—as an active evangelist—a gifted teacher—a clear and attractive writer—a man of prayer—a man of faith—a person of remarkable sanctity, or great personal devotedness—a benevolent person—a name for anything, in short—I am in imminent danger of making shipwreck. The enemy will lead me to make my reputation my object instead of Christ. I shall be working to keep up a name instead of the glory of Christ. I shall be occupied with the thoughts of men instead of doing all my work under the immediate eye of God.

All this demands intense watchfulness and rigid censorship over myself. I may be doing the most excellent works, but if they are not fulfilled in the presence of God they will prove a positive snare of the devil. I may preach the gospel—visit the sick—help the poor—go through the entire range of religious activity—and never be in the presence of God at all. I may do it for a name—do it because others do it, or expect me to do it. This is very serious. It demands real prayer—self-emptiness—nearness to and dependence upon God—singleness of eye—holy consecration to Christ. Self continually intrudes upon us. Oh this self, self, self, even in the very holiest things; and all the while we may appear to be very active and very devoted. Miserable delusion! We know of nothing more terrible than to have a religious name without spiritual life, without Christ, without a sense of God's presence possessing the soul.

Let us look closely into this. Let us see that we begin, continue, and end our work under the Master's eye. This will impart a purity and a moral elevation to our service beyond all price. It will not cripple our energy, but it will tend to raise and intensify our action. It will not clip our wings, but it will guide our movements. It will render us independent of the thoughts of men, and fully deliver us from the slavery of seeking to maintain a name, or keep up a reputation—miserable, degrading bondage! May the good Lord grant us full deliverance from it! May He give us grace to fulfil our works, whatever they may be, few or many, small or great, in His own blessed presence!

Having said thus much in reference to the *character* of our service, we shall close with a few lines on *perfection in our equipment for service.*

"All Scripture is given by inspiration of God, and is profitable for doctrine, for reproof, for correction, for instruction in righteousness: that the man of God may be *perfect* (ἄρτιος) throughly furnished unto all good works" (2 Tim. 3:16-17). Here, again, we have a different word, and one which only occurs in this one place in the entire New Testament. It is most expressive. It signifies *present readiness* for any exigence. The man who is acquainted with, and subject to the Word of God, is ready for every emergency.

He has no need to go and cram for an occasion—to consult his authorities—to make himself up on a point. He is *ready now.* If an anxious inquirer comes, he is ready; if a curious inquirer comes, he is ready; if a skeptic comes, he is ready; if an infidel comes, he is ready. In a word, he is always ready. He is perfectly equipped for every occasion.

The Lord be praised for all these aspects of Christian perfection! What more do we want? Perfection as to the conscience; perfection in object; perfection in walk; perfection in the character of service; perfection in our equipment. What remains? What wait we for? Just this—perfection in glory—perfect conformity in spirit, and soul, and body, to the image of our glorified Head in Heaven!

May the Lord so work on our hearts by His Spirit, producing that which is well-pleasing in His sight, that we may stand "perfect and complete in all the will of God!"

THE MINISTRY OF RECONCILIATION

"AND ALL THINGS ARE OF GOD, who hath reconciled us to Himself by Jesus Christ, and hath given to us the ministry of reconciliation; to wit, that God was in Christ, reconciling the world unto Himself, not imputing their trespasses unto them; and hath committed unto us the word of reconciliation. Now then we are ambassadors for Christ, as though God did beseech you by us: we pray you in Christ's stead, be ye reconciled to God. For He hath made Him to be sin for us, who knew no sin; that we might be made the righteousness of God in Him" (2 Cor. 5:18-21).

The fifth chapter of Second Corinthians is a most weighty section of inspiration. Its closing lines contain the special thesis of the following pages; but ere we proceed with it, we must call the reader's attention to some most interesting and important points presented in the course of the chapter.

And, first of all, let us dwell for a moment on the opening sentence, "*We know.*" In it we

have the language of Christian certainty. It does not say, "We *hope.*" Still less does it say, "We *fear,*" or "We *doubt.*" No; such language would not express that unclouded certainty and calm assurance which it is the privilege of the very feeblest child of God to possess. And yet, alas, how few, even of the children of God, enjoy this blessed certainty—this calm assurance! Many there are who look upon it as the height of presumption to say, "We know." They seem to think that doubts and fears argue a proper condition of soul—that it is impossible for anyone to be sure—that the most we can expect is to cherish a vague hope of reaching Heaven when we die.

Now, it must be admitted that if we ourselves had aught to do with the ground of certainty or assurance, then it would indeed be the very height of folly to think of being sure; then assuredly our hope would be a very vague one. But, thanks be to God, it is not so. We having nothing whatever to do with the ground of our certainty, it lies entirely outside of ourselves, and it must be sought only and altogether in the eternal Word of God. This renders it blessedly simple. it makes the whole question hinge upon the truth of God's Word. Why am I sure? Because God's Word is true. A shadow of uncertainty or misgiving on my part would argue a want of authority or security in the Word of God. It really comes to this: Christian certainty rests on the faithfulness of God. Before you can shake the former, you must shake the latter.

We can understand this simple principle by our dealings with one another. If my fellow man makes a statement to me, and I express the smallest doubt or misgiving, or if I feel it without even expressing it, I am calling in question his truthfulness, or credibility. If he is a faithful, competent authority, I have no business to entertain a single doubt. My certainty is linked with his credibility. If he is a competent authority, I may enjoy perfect repose as to the matter concerning which he has spoken. Now, we all know what it is to receive in the most unqualified way the testimony of man, and to repose with calmness therein. It is not a question of feeling, but of receiving without a single question a plain statement, and resting on the authority of a competent witness. Well, then, as we have it in the First Epistle of John, "If we receive the testimony of man, the testimony of God is greater." So, also, our Lord said to the men of His time, "If I say the truth, why do ye not believe Me?" (John 8) He appeals to the truth of what He says as the reason why, or the ground on which, He expected to be believed.

This is a very weighty principle, and one which demands special attention on the part of all anxious inquirers, as also on the part of all who undertake to deal with such. There is a strong and constant tendency to look *within* for the ground of assurance—to build upon certain feelings, experiences, and exercises, either past or present—to look back at some special process through which we have passed, or to look in at certain impressions or convictions of our own minds, and to find in these the ground of our confidence, the warrant for our faith. This

will never do. It is impossible to find settled peace or calm repose in this way.

Feelings, however true and real, change and pass away. Experiences, however genuine, may prove defective. Impressions and convictions may prove utterly false. None of these things, therefore, can form a solid ground of Christian certainty. This latter must be sought and found in God's Word alone. It is not in feelings, not in experiences, not in impressions or convictions, not in reasonings, not in human traditions or doctrines, but simply in the unchangeable, eternal Word of the living God. That Word which is settled forever in Heaven, and which God has magnified according to all the stability of His name, can alone impart peace to the mind and stability to the soul.

True, it is only by the gracious ministry of the Holy Ghost that we can properly grasp and ever hold fast to the Word of God; but still it is His Word, and that Word *alone*, that forms the ground of Christian certainty and the true basis and authority for the Christian in the entire range of practical life and action. We cannot be too simple as to this. We can only adopt the opening sentence of our chapter, and say, "We know," when we take God's Word as the all-sufficient ground of our personal confidence. It will not do to be in any wise propped up by human authority. Thousands of the people of God have been made to taste the bitterness of leaning upon the commandments and doctrines of men. It is sure to end in disappointment and confusion, sooner or later.

The edifice which is built upon the sand of human authority must fall at some time or other; whereas that which is founded on the rock of God's eternal truth shall stand forever. God's Word imparts its own stability to the soul that leans upon it. "Therefore thus saith the Lord God, Behold, I lay in Zion for a foundation a stone, a sure foundation; he that believeth shall not make haste" (Isa. 28:16).

As is the foundation, so is the faith that builds thereon. Hence the solemn importance of seeking to lead souls to build *only* upon God's precious Word. Look at the anxiety of the apostle Paul in reference to this matter. Hear what he says to the Corinthians who were in such danger of being led away by human leadership and human authority. "And I, brethren, when I came to you, came not with excellency of speech or of wisdom, declaring unto you *the testimony of God*. For I determined not to know anything among you, save Jesus Christ and Him crucified. And I was with you in weakness, and in fear, and in much trembling. And my speech and my preaching was not with enticing words of man's wisdom, but in demonstration of the Spirit and of power. That your faith should not stand in the wisdom of men, but in the power of God" (1 Cor. 2:1-5).

Here is a grand model for all preachers and teachers. Paul declared the "testimony of God," nothing more, nothing less, nothing different. And not only so, but he delivered that testimony in such a way as to connect the souls of his hearers immediately with the living God. Paul did not want the Corinthians to lean upon him; nay, he "trembled" lest they should be tempted to do so. He would have done them a grievous wrong had he in anywise come in between their souls and the true source of all authority—the true foundation of confidence and peace. Had he led them to build upon himself, he would have robbed them of God, and this would have been a wrong indeed.

No marvel, therefore, that he was among them "in fear and in much trembling." They were evidently very much prone to set up and follow after human leaders, and thus miss the solid reality of personal communion with and dependence upon the living God. Hence the jealous care of the apostle in confining himself to the testimony of God; in delivering to them *only* that which he had received of the Lord (see 1 Cor. 11:23; 15:3), lest the pure water should suffer in its passage from its source in God to the souls of the Corinthians—lest he should in the smallest degree impart the color of his own thoughts to the precious truth of God.

We see the same thing in the First Epistle to the Thessalonians. "For this cause also," says the faithful servant of Christ, "thank we God without ceasing, because, when ye received the word of God which ye heard of us, ye received it *not as the word of men*, but,

as it is in truth, the word of God, which effectually worketh also in you that believe" (chap. 2:13). Had he been seeking his own things, he would have been glad to obtain influence over the Thessalonians by linking them on to himself and leading them to lean upon him. But no; he rejoices in seeing them in living connection, in direct and realized association with God Himself.

This is always the effect of true ministry, as it is ever the object of the true minister. Unless the soul be livingly linked with God, there is really nothing done. If it be merely following men—receiving what they say because they say it—an attachment to certain preachers or teachers because of something in their style and manner, or because they seem to be very holy, very separated, or very devoted—all this will come to naught. Those human links will soon be snapped asunder. The faith that stands in any measure in the wisdom of men will prove hollow and worthless. Nothing will prove permanent, nothing will endure, but that faith which rests on the testimony and in the power of the only true God.

We earnestly invite your attention to this point. We do indeed feel its importance at the present moment. The enemy is seeking diligently to lead souls away from God, away from Christ, away from the holy Scriptures. He is seeking to get them to build on something short of *the truth*. He does not care what it is, provided it is not Christ. It may be reason, tradition, religiousness, human priesthood, fleshy pietism, holiness in the flesh, sectarianism, morality, good works, service (so called), human influence, patronage, philanthropy, anything short of Christ, short of God's Word, short of a lively, personal, direct faith in the living God Himself.

Now it is the sense of this pressing home upon the heart that leads us to urge with earnestness upon the reader the necessity of being thoroughly clear as to the ground on which he is at this moment standing. We want him to be able to say in the face of all around him, "*I know*." Nothing less than this will stand. It will not do to say, "*I hope*." No; there must be certainty. There must be the ability to say, "We know that if our earthly house of this tabernacle were dissolved, *we have* a building of God, an house not made with hands, eternal in the heavens." This is the language of faith, the language of a Christian. All is calm, clear, and sure, because all is of God.

There may be an "if" with regard to "the earthly house." It may be dissolved, it may crumble into dust. All that belongs to this scene may bear the stamp of death; it may change and pass away, but the Word of the Lord endureth forever, and the faith that grasps and rests upon that Word partakes of its eternal stability. It enables one to say, "*I know* that *I have*." Naught but faith can say this. Reason can only say, "I doubt"; superstition, "I fear"; only faith can say, "I know and am sure."

An infidel teacher once said to a dying woman whom he had indoctrinated with his infidel notions, "Hold fast, Mary." What was her reply? "I can't hold fast, for you have never given me anything to hold by." Cutting rebuke! He had taught the poor woman to doubt, but he had given her nothing to believe; and then, when flesh and heart were failing, when earthly scenes were passing away and the dread realities of eternity were crowding in upon her soul's vision, infidelity altogether failed her; its wretched cobwebs could afford no refuge, no covering, in view of death and judgment.

How different the condition of the believer —of the one who, in all simplicity of heart and humility of mind, takes his stand on the solid rock of Holy Scripture! Such an one can calmly say, "*I am now ready* to be offered, and the time of my departure is at hand. I have fought a good fight, I have finished my course, I have kept the faith; henceforth there is laid up for me a crown of righteousness, which the Lord, the righteous judge, shall give me at that day: and not to me only, but to all them, also, that love His appearing" (2 Tim. 4: 6-8).

It is more than probable that some may find it difficult to reconcile the calm certainty expressed in the first verse of our chapter with the groan of verse 2. But the difficulty will vanish the moment we are enabled to see the true reason of the groan. "For in this we groan, earnestly desiring to be clothed upon with our house which is from heaven, if so be that, being clothed, we shall not be found naked. For we that are in this tabernacle do groan, being burdened; not for that we would be unclothed, but clothed upon, that mortality might be swallowed up of life."

Here we see that the very certainty of having "a building of God, an house not made with hands, eternal in the heavens," makes us groan to possess it. The apostle did not groan in doubt or uncertainty. He did not groan under the weight of guilt or fear. Still less did he groan because he could not satisfy the desires of the flesh or of the mind, or because he could not surround himself with this world's perishable possessions. No; he longed for the heavenly building—the divine, the real, the eternal. He felt the heavy burden of the poor, crumbling tabernacle; it was a grievous hindrance to him. It was the only link with the scene around, and as such it was a heavy clog of which he longed to be rid.

But, most clearly, he would not, and could not, have groaned for the heavenly house if he had a single question on his mind with respect to it. Men are never anxious to get rid of the body unless they are sure of possessing something better; nay, they grasp this present life with intense eagerness, and tremble at the thought of the future, which is all darkness and uncertainty to them. They groan at the thought of quitting the body; the apostle groaned because he was in it.

This makes all the difference. Scripture never contemplates such a thing as a Christian groaning under sin, guilt, doubt, or fear; or sighing after the riches, honors or pleasures of this vain, sin-stricken world. Alas, alas, they do thus groan through ignorance of their true position in a risen Christ and their proper portion in the heavens! But such is not the ground or character of the groan in the Scripture now before us; Paul saw with distinctness his house in the heavens; and, on the other hand, he felt the heavy burden of the tabernacle of clay; and he ardently longed to lay aside the latter and be clothed with the former.

Hence, then, there is the fullest harmony between "*we know*" and "*we groan*." If we did not know for a certainty that we have a building of God, we should like to hold our earthly house as long as possible. We see this constantly. Men cling to life. They leave nothing untried to keep body and soul together. They have no certainty as to Heaven. They cannot say, "*we know*" that "*we have*" anything there. On the other hand, they have a terrible dread of the future, which to their vision is wrapped up in clouds and thick darkness. They have never committed themselves in calm confidence to God and His Word; they have never felt the tranquilizing power of His love. They have viewed Him as an angry Judge instead of seeing Him as the sinner's Friend—a just God and a Saviour—the righteous Justifier. No marvel, therefore, if they shrink with terror from the thought of meeting Him.

But it is a totally different thing with a man who knows God as his Father—his Saviour—his best Friend; who knows that Jesus died to save him from his sins, and from all the consequences thereof. Such an one can say:

I have a home above,
  From sin and sorrow free;
A mansion which eternal Love
  Designed and formed for me.

The Father's gracious hand
  Has built this blest abode;
From everlasting it was planned,
  The dwelling-place of God.

The Saviour's precious blood
  Has made my title sure;
He passed through death's dark, raging flood,
  To make my rest secure.

These are the breathings of simple faith, and they perfectly harmonize with the groans of a spirit "that looks beyond its cage and longs to flee away." The believer finds his body of sin and death a heavy burden, and longs to be free from the encumbrance, and to be clothed upon with a body suited to his new and eternal state—a new creation body—a body perfectly free from every trace of mortality. This cannot be until the morning of resurrection, that glorious moment, long looked for, when the dead in Christ shall rise and the living saints be changed, in a moment; when death shall be swallowed up in victory, and mortality shall be swallowed up of life.

It is for this we groan, not that we would be unclothed, but clothed upon. The unclothed state is not *the* object, though we know that to be absent from the body is to be present with the Lord; and to depart and be with Christ is far better. The Lord Jesus is waiting that glorious consummation, and we wait in sympathy with Him. Meanwhile, "the whole creation groaneth and travaileth in pain together until now. And not only so, but ourselves also, which have the firstfruits of the Spirit, even we ourselves groan within ourselves, waiting for the adoption, to wit, the redemption of our body. For we are saved in hope: but hope that is seen is not hope: for what a man seeth, why doth he yet hope for? But if we hope for that we see not, then do we with patience wait for it" (Rom. 8:22-25).

Thus, then, we have before us a very distinct answer to the question, "Why does the believer groan?" He groans, being burdened. He groans in sympathy with a groaning creation, with which he is linked by means of a body of sin and death—a body of humiliation. He sees around him, day by day, the sad fruits of sin. He cannot pass along the streets of our cities and towns without having before his eyes a thousand proofs of man's sad state. He hears on one side the wail of sorrow; on another, the cry of distress. He sees oppression, violence, corruption, strife, heartless villany and its victims. He sees the thorn, and the briar. He notes the various disturbing forces which are abroad in the physical, the moral, and the political world. He marks the varied forms of disease and misery around him.

The cry of the poor and the needy, the widow and the orphan, falls sadly upon his ear and upon his heart; and what can he do but send up from the deepest depths of his spiritual nature a sympathetic groan, and long for the blissful moment when "the creation itself shall be delivered from the bondage of corruption into the liberty of the glory of the sons of God"? It is impossible for a true Christian to pass through a world like this without groaning. Look at the blessed Master Himself; did not He groan? Yes, verily. Mark Him as He approached the grave of Lazarus, in company with the two weeping sisters. "When Jesus therefore saw her weeping, and the Jews also weeping which came with her, he groaned in the spirit, and was troubled, and said, Where have ye laid him? They said unto him, Lord, come and see. Jesus wept" (John 11:33-35).

Whence came those tears and groans? Was He not approaching the grave of His friend as the Prince of Life—the Quickener of the dead—the Conqueror of death—the Spoiler of the grave? Why, then, did He groan? He groaned in sympathy with the objects of His love, and with the whole scene around Him. His tears and groans emanated from the profound depths of a perfect human heart which felt, according to God, the true condition of the human family and of Israel in particular. He beheld around Him the varied fruits of sin. He felt for man, He felt for Israel. "In all their afflictions He was afflicted." He was a Man of sorrows and acquainted with grief. He never even cured a person without bearing upon His spirit the reality of that with which He was dealing. He did not, He would not, lightly bid away death, disease, and sorrow.

No: He entered into it all, as man; and that, too, according to the infinite perfections of His divine nature. He bore it all upon His spirit, in the reality of it, before God. Though perfectly free from it all, and above it all, yet did He in grace voluntarily enter into it most thoroughly, so as to taste, and prove, and know it all, as none else could know it.

All this is fully expressed in Matt. 8, where we read the following words: "When the even was come, they brought unto Him many that were possessed with devils; and He cast out the spirits with His word, and healed all that were sick; that it might be fulfilled which was spoken by Esaias the prophet, saying, *Himself took our infirmities, and bare our sicknesses*" (ver. 16-17).

We have very little idea of what the heart of Jesus felt as He passed through this sorrowful, because sinful, world; and we are far too apt to miss the reality of His sufferings by confining them merely to what He endured on the cross, and also by supposing that because He was God over all, blessed for ever, He did not feel all that a human heart is capable of feeling. This is a sad loss. Indeed we may say it is an incalculable loss. The Lord Jesus, as the Captain of our salvation, was made perfect through sufferings. See Heb. 2, where the inspired writer distinguishes carefully between "the suffering of death," and the "suffering" of the Captain of our salvation.

In order to save sinners from *wrath*, "He tasted death for every man," and having done so, we see Him "crowned with glory and honor." But in order to "*bring many sons to glory*," He had to be "perfected through sufferings." And now all true believers have the unspeakable privilege of knowing that there is One at the right hand of the Majesty in the heavens who, when in this world of sin and woe, tasted every form of suffering and every cup of sorrow which it was possible for any human heart to know. He could say, "Reproach hath broken My heart, and I am full of heaviness: and I looked for some to take pity, but there was none, and for comforters, but I found none" (Ps. 69:20).

How deeply affecting is all this! But we cannot pursue this subject here. We have merely touched upon it in connection with the question, "Why does the believer groan?" We trust that the reader will see clearly the true answer to this inquiry; and that it will be most evident to his mind that the groans of a Christian proceed from the divine nature which he actually possesses, and cannot therefore, by any possibility, be occasioned by doubts or fears, on the one hand, nor yet by selfish desires or the insatiable cravings of nature, on the other. But that, on the contrary, the very fact of his possessing everlasting life, through faith in Christ, and the blessed assurance of having a house not made with hands, eternal in the heavens, causes him to long for that blessed, indestructible building, and to groan because of his connection with a groaning creation, as well as in sympathy therewith.

If any further proof were needed, on this

deeply interesting question, we have it in verses 5 and 6 of our chapter (2 Cor. 5), where the apostle goes on to say, "Now He that hath wrought us for the selfsame thing is God, who also hath given unto us the earnest of the Spirit. Therefore we are *always confident* (not doubting or fearing), knowing that whilst we are at home in the body we are absent from the Lord (for we walk by faith, not by sight), we are confident, I say, and willing rather to be absent from the body, and to be present with the Lord" (ver. 5-8).

Here we have two grand cardinal truths laid down, namely, first, The believer is God's workmanship; and secondly, God has given him the earnest of the Spirit. Most marvelous —most glorious facts! Facts which demand the attention of the reader. Everyone who simply and heartily believes on the Lord Jesus Christ is God's workmanship. God has created him anew in Christ Jesus.

Clearly, therefore, there can be no possible ground for questioning his acceptance with God, inasmuch as God can never call in question His own work. He will, assuredly, no more do this in His new creation, than He did in the old. When God looked upon His work, in the opening of the book of Genesis, it was not to judge it or call it in question, but to announce it very good, and express His complacency in it. So now, when God looks upon the very feeblest believer, He sees in him His own workmanship, and most assuredly, He is not going, either here or hereafter, to call in question His own work. God is a rock, His work is perfect, and the believer is God's work; and because he is His work He has sealed him with the Holy Ghost.

The same truth is stated in Ephesians 2, where we read, "For we are God's workmanship, created in Christ Jesus unto good works, which God hath before ordained that we should walk in them." This, we may truly say, is a point of the weightiest moment. It claims the grave attention of the reader who desires to be thoroughly established in the truth of God as to what a Christian—what Christianity really is. It is not a ruined, lost, guilty sinner seeking to work himself up into something or other fit for God. It is the very reverse.

It is God, in the riches of His grace, on the ground of the atoning death of Christ, taking up a poor, dead, worthless, condemned thing—a guilty, hell-deserving sinner, and creating him anew in Christ Jesus. It is, as it were, God beginning *de novo*—on the new, as we may say—to form man in Christ, to place him on a new footing altogether, not now as an innocent being on a creation basis, but as a justified one, in a risen Christ. It is not man's old condition improved by human effort of any sort or description; but it is God's new workmanship in a risen, ascended, and glorified Christ.

It is not man's own garment pieced or patched by human device in any shape or form whatever; but it is God's new garment introduced in the Person of Christ, who having, in infinite grace, gone down into the dust of death, and endured, on man's behalf, the judgment of sin, the righteous wrath of a sin-hating God, was raised from the dead by the glory of the Father, and is become the Head of the new creation—"The beginning of the creation of God" (Rev. 3:14).

Now, it must be perfectly clear that if our Lord Jesus Christ be, in very deed "the *beginning*" of God's creation, then we must begin at the beginning, else we have done absolutely nothing at all. We may labor and toil—we may do our very utmost, and be perfectly sincere in our doing—we may vow and resolve—we may seek to improve our state, to alter our course, to mend our ways, to live in a different way—but all the while we are in the old creation, which has been completely set aside, and is under the judgment of God; we have not begun at "the beginning" of God's new creation, and, as a necessary consequence, we have gained nothing at all. We have been spending our strength for nought and in vain. We have been putting forth efforts to improve a thing which God has condemned and set aside altogether. We are, to use a very feeble figure indeed, like a man who is spending his time, his pains, and his money in painting and papering a house that has been condemned by the government surveyor, on account of the rottenness of the foundation, and which must be taken down at once.

What should we say to such a man? Should we not deem him very foolish? Doubtless. But if it be folly to paint and paper a condemned house, what shall we say to those who are seeking to improve a condemned nature—a condemned world? We must say this, at least, they are pursuing a course which must, sooner or later, end in disappointment and confusion.

Oh that this were understood and entered into! Would to God that Christians more fully entered into it! Would to God that all Christian writers, preachers, and teachers entered into it, and set it forth distinctly with pen and voice! At the least, we earnestly desire that the reader should thoroughly grasp it. We are most fully persuaded that it is pre-eminently "truth for the times." It is truth to meet the need of thousands of souls—to remove their burdens, relieve their hearts and consciences—solve their difficulties—chase away their clouds.

There are, at this moment, throughout the length and breadth of Christendom, countless multitudes engaged in the fruitless work of painting and papering a condemned house—a house on which God has pronounced judgment, because of the hopelessly ruined condition of its foundations. They are seeking to do little jobs of repairs here and there throughout the house, forgetting, or perhaps not knowing, that the whole building is very shortly to be demolished by order of the divine government. Some are doing this with the utmost sincerity, amid much sore exercise of soul, and many tears, because they cannot succeed in satisfying their own hearts even, much less the claims of God.

For God demands a perfect thing, not a patched-up ruin. There is no use in seeking to cover with paper and paint old walls tottering on a rotten foundation. God cannot be deceived by surface work, by shallow outside appearances. The foundations are bad, the whole thing must come down, and we must put our whole trust in Him who is "the beginning of the creation of God."

Pause here for a moment's calm and serious reflection. Ask yourself the question, "Am I seeking to patch up a ruin? Am I seeking to improve the old nature? Or have I really found my place in God's new creation, of which a risen Christ is the Head and Beginning?" Remember, we beseech you, that you cannot possibly engage in more fruitless toil than seeking to make yourself better. Your efforts may be sincere, but they must, in the long run, prove worthless. Your paper and paint may be all good and genuine enough, but you are putting them on a condemned ruin.

You cannot say of your unrenewed nature that it is "God's workmanship"; and, most assuredly, *your* doings, *your* good works, *your* religious exercises, *your* efforts to keep the ten commandments—nothing, in short, that *you* can do, could possibly be called "God's workmanship." It is yours, and not God's. He cannot acknowledge it. He cannot seal it with His Spirit. It is all false and good for nothing. If you cannot say, "He that hath wrought us for the selfsame thing is God," you have really nothing. You are yet in your sins. You have not begun at God's beginning. You are yet "in the flesh": and the voice of Holy Scripture declares that "they that are in the flesh *cannot* please God" (Rom. 8).

This is a solemn and sweeping sentence. A man out of Christ is "in the flesh"; and such a man cannot please God. He may be most religious, most moral, most amiable, most benevolent, a most excellent master, a generous friend, a liberal giver, a genial companion, a patron of the poor, upright and honorable in all his dealings, he may be an eloquent preacher and a popular writer, and all the while not be "*in Christ*," but "in the flesh," and therefore he "cannot please God."

Can aught be more solemn than this? Only to think of how far a person may go in all that is deemed excellent among men, and yet not be in Christ, but in his sins—in the flesh—in the old creation—in the condemned house. And be it noted that it is not a question of gross sins, of scandalous living, in all its varied, hideous shapes of immorality, in its deeper and dark shades; no, the declaration of Holy Scripture is, that "they that are in the flesh cannot please God." This, truly, is most soul-subduing, and calls for deep and solemn reflection on the part of every thoughtful and earnest soul.

But it may be that, to the reader's view, difficulties and stumbling blocks still surround this most weighty subject. He may still be utterly at a loss to know what is meant by the expression, "In the flesh." If so it will, we fondly hope, help him not a little to remember that Scripture speaks of *two men*—"the first man" and "the Second Man." These two men are presented as the heads of two distinct races. Adam *fallen* is the head of one race; Christ *risen* is the Head of the other race.

Now, the very fact of there being "a Second Man" proves that the first man had been set aside: for if the first man had proved faultless, then should no place have been sought for the second. This is clear and unquestionable. The first man is a total wreck—an irreparable ruin. The foundations of the old edifice have given way; and albeit, in man's view, the building seems to stand, and to be capable of being repaired, yet, in God's view it is completely set aside, and a Second Man—a new edifice—set up, on the solid and imperishable ground of redemption.

Hence, we read, in Gen. 3 that God "*drove out the man;* and He placed at the east of the garden of Eden cherubims, and a flaming sword which turned *every way*, to keep the way of the tree of life." In other words, the first man was driven out, and every possible way of return was closed against him, as *such*. He could only get back by "a new and living way," namely, through the rent veil of the Saviour's flesh. The flaming sword "turned every way," so that there was positively no way by which the first man could ever get back to his former state.

The only hope, now, was through "the seed of the woman"—"the Second Man." The flaming sword declared, in symbolic yet impressive language, the truth, which comes out in the New Testament divested of all symbol and shadow, namely, that "they that are in the flesh *cannot* please God"—"Ye must be born again." Every unconverted man, woman, and child is part and parcel of the first man, fallen, ruined, set aside, and driven out. He is a member of the first Adam—the old race—a stone in the old condemned building.

Thus it stands, if we are to be guided by Scripture. The head and his race go together. As is the one, so is the other; what is true of the one is true of the other. They are, in God's view, absolutely identical. Was the first Adam fallen when he became the head of a race? Was he driven out? Was he completely set aside? Yes, verily, if we are to believe Scripture; then the unconverted, the unregenerated reader of these lines is fallen, driven out, and set aside. As is the head, so is the member—each member in particular—all the members together. They are inseparable, if we are to be taught by divine revelation.

But, further, was every possible way of return finally closed against the fallen head? yes, Scripture declares that the flaming sword turned "*every way*, to keep the way of the tree of life." Then it is utterly impossible that the unconverted—the unregenerate can improve himself or make himself fit for God. If the fallen head could not get back to the tree of life, neither can the fallen member. "They that are in the flesh cannot please God." That is, they that are on the old footing, in the old creation, members of the first Adam, part and parcel of the old edifice, cannot please God. "Ye must be born again." Man must be renewed in the very deepest springs and sources of his being. He must be "God's workmanship, created in Christ Jesus unto good works, which God hath before prepared that we should walk in them." He must be able to say, in the language of our text, "He that has wrought us for the selfsame thing is God."

But this leads us to another point. How is anyone to get into this marvelous position? How can any soul take up such language? How can anyone whose eyes have been opened to see his utter and hopeless ruin, as connected with the first man, as standing in the old creation, as a stone in the old edifice—how can such an one ever reach a position in which he can please God? The Lord be praised, Scripture gives an answer, full, clear, and distinct, to this serious question.

A Second Man has appeared upon the scene—the Seed of the woman, and, at the same time, God over all, blessed for ever. In

Him all begins afresh. He came into this world born of a woman, made under the law, pure and spotless, free from every taint of sin, personally apart from every claim of sin and death, standing in the midst of a ruined world, a guilty race, Himself that pure, untainted grain of wheat. We see Him lying as a babe in the manger. We see Him growing up as a youth beneath the parental roof. We see Him as a man working in a carpenter's shop at Nazareth. We see Him baptized in Jordan, where all the people were baptized confessing their sins—Himself sinless, but fulfilling all righteousness, and, in pefect grace, identifying Himself with the repentant portion of the nation of Israel.

We see Him anointed with the Holy Ghost for the work that lay before Him. We see Him in the wilderness faint and hungry, unlike the first man who was placed in the midst of a paradise of creature delights. We see Him tempted of Satan and coming off victorious. We trace Him along the pathway of public ministry—and such a ministry! What incessant toil! What weariness and watching! What hunger and thirst! What sorrow and travail! Worse off than the fowls and the foxes, the Son of man had not where to lay His head. The contradiction of sinners by day, the mountain-top by night.

Such was the marvelous life of this blessed One. But this was not all. He died! Yes, He died under the weight of the first man's guilt, He died to take away the sin of the world, and alter completely the ground of God's relationship with the world, so that God might deal with man and with the world on the new ground of redemption, instead of the old ground of sin. He died for the nation of Israel. He tasted death for every man. He died the just for the unjust. He suffered for sins. He died and was buried, according to the Scriptures. He went through all—met all—paid all—finished all. He went down into the dust of death, and lay in the dark and silent tomb. He descended into the lower parts of the earth. He went down to the very bottom of everything. He endured the sentence passed on man.

He paid the penalty, bore the judgment, drained the cup of wrath, went through every form of human suffering and trial, was tempted in all points, sin excepted. He made an end of everything that stood in the way, and, having *finished all,* He gave up His spirit into the hand of His Father, and His precious body was laid in a tomb on which the smell of death had never passed.

Nor was this all. He rose! Yes, He rose triumphant over all. He rose as the Head of the new creation—"The beginning of the creation of God"—"The first-begotten from among the dead"—"The first-born among many brethren." And now the Second Man is before God, crowned with glory and honor, not in an earthly paradise, but at the right hand of the Majesty in the heavens.

This Second Man is the last Adam, because there is none to come after Him, we cannot get beyond the last. There is only one Man before God now. The first is set aside. The last is set up. And as the first was the fallen head of a fallen race, so the last is the risen Head of a saved, justified, and accepted race. The Head and His members are inseparably identified—all the members together, and each member in particular. We are accepted in Him.

"As He is, so are we in this world" (1 John 4:17). There is nothing before God but Christ. The Head and the body, the Head and each individual member are indissolubly joined together—inseparably and eternally one. God thinks of the members as He thinks of the Head—loves them as He loves Him. Those members are God's workmanship, incorporated by His Spirit into the body of Christ, and in God's presence, having no other footing, no other rank, position, or station whatsoever but "in Christ." They are no longer "in the flesh, but in the Spirit." They can please God, because they possess His nature, and are sealed by His Spirit, and guided by His Word. *"He that hath wrought them is God,"* and God must ever delight in His own workmanship. He will never find fault with or condemn the work of His own hand. "God is a rock, His work is perfect," and hence the believer, as God's workmanship, must be perfect. He is *"in Christ"* and that is enough—enough for God—enough for faith—enough for ever.

And, now, if it be asked, "How is all this to be attained?" Scripture replies, "*by faith.*" "Verily, verily, I say unto you, He that heareth My word, and believeth on Him that sent Me, *hath* everlasting life, and shall not come into judgment; but is passed from death unto life" (John 5:24).

The reader who has traveled intelligently with us through the opening lines of our chapter will be in a position to understand something of the solemn and momentous subject to which we now approach, namely, the judgment-seat of Christ. If indeed it be true that the believer is God's workmanship —if he is actually a member of Christ—associated with the second Adam—bound up in the bundle of life with the risen and glorified Lord, if all this be true—and God's Word declares it is—then it must be perfectly evident that the judgment-seat of Christ cannot, by any possibility, touch the Christian's position, or prove, in any wise, unfriendly to him.

No doubt it is a most solemn and serious matter, involving the most weighty consequences to every servant of Christ, and designed to exert a most salutary influence upon the heart and conscience of every man. But it will do all this just in proportion as it is viewed from the true standpoint, and no further. It is not to be supposed that anyone can reap the divinely appointed blessing from meditating on the judgment-seat, if he is looking forward to it as the place where the grand question of his eternal salvation is to be settled. And yet how many are thus regarding it! How many of God's true people are there, who, from not seeing the simple truth involved in these words, "He that hath wrought us for the selfsame thing is God," are anticipating the judgment-seat of Christ as something that may, after all, condemn them.

This is greatly to be deplored, both because it dishonors the Lord, and completely destroys the soul's peace and liberty. For how, let us ask, is it possible for anyone to enjoy peace so long as there is a single question about salvation to be settled? We conceive it is wholly impossible. The peace of the true believer rests on the fact that every

possible question has been divinely and eternally settled; and as a consequence, no question can ever arise, either before the judgment-seat of Christ, or at any other time. Hear what our Lord Jesus Christ saith in reference to this great question: "Verily, verily, I say unto you, He that heareth My word, and believeth on Him that sent Me, *hath* everlasting life, and shall not come into condemnation [or judgment]; but is passed from death unto life" (John 5:24).

It is important to understand that the word used by our Lord in the above passage is not "condemnation" but "judgment." He assures the believer that he shall never come into judgment; and this, too, be it observed, in immediate connection with the statement that "the Father judgeth no man, but hath committed all judgment unto the Son" (ver. 22). And, again, "For as the Father hath life in Himself, so hath He given to the Son to have life in Himself; and hath given Him authority to execute judgment also, because He is the Son of man" (ver. 26-27).

Thus, then, the One to whom all judgment is committed—who alone has authority to execute judgment, by the Father's just decree—this blessed One assures us that if we harken to His Word, and believe on Him that sent Him, we shall never come into judgment at all.

This is clear and conclusive. It must tranquilize the heart completely. It must roll away every cloud and mist, and conduct the soul into a region where no question can ever arise to disturb its deep and eternal repose. If the One who has all judgment in His hand, and all authority to execute it—if *He* assures me that I shall never come into judgment, I am perfectly satisfied. I believe His Word, and rest in the happy assurance that whatever the judgment-seat of Christ may prove to others, it cannot prove unfriendly to me. I know that the Word of the Lord endureth for ever, and that the Word tells me I shall never come into judgment.

But it may be that the reader finds it difficult, if not impossible, to reconcile this entire exemption from judgment with the solemn fact stated by our Lord, that "for every idle word that men shall speak, they shall give account thereof in the day of judgment." But there is really no difficulty in the matter. If a man has to meet judgment at all, he must give account for every idle word. How awfully solemn the thought! There is no escaping it. Were it possible for a single idle word to be let pass, it would be a dishonor to the judgment-seat. It would be a sign of weakness and incompetency which is utterly impossible. It were blasphemy against the Son of God to suppose that a single stain could escape His scrutinizing gaze. If the reader comes into judgment, that judgment must be perfect, and, hence, his comdemnation must be inevitable.

We would press this serious matter upon the attention of the unconverted reader. It imperatively demands his immediate and earnest consideration. There is a day rapidly approaching when every idle word, and every foolish thought, and every sinful act, will be brought to light, and he will have to answer for it. Christ, as a Judge, has eyes like unto a flame of fire, and feet like unto fine brass—eyes to detect, and feet to crush the evil. There will be no escape. There will be no mercy then: all will be stern and unmitigated judgment.

"I saw a great white throne, and Him that sat on it, from whose face the earth and the heaven fled away; and there was found no place for them. And I saw the dead, small and great, stand before God: and the *books* were opened; and another *book* was opened, which is the book of life; and the dead were judged out of those things which were written in the *books*, according to their *works*. And the sea gave up the dead which were in it, and death and the grave gave up the dead which were in them; and they were judged *every man according to their works*. And death and the grave were cast into the lake of fire. This is the second death. And whosoever was not found written in the book of life was cast into the lake of fire" (Rev. 20:11-15).

Mark here the difference between "the books" and "the book of life." The entire scene sets forth the judgment of the wicked dead—of those who have died in their sins, from first to last. "The book of life" is opened;

but there is no judgment for those whose names are written therein by the hand of electing and redeeming love. "The books" are opened—those awful records written in characters deep, broad, and black—those terrible catalogues of the sins of every man, woman, and child, from the beginning to the end of time. There will be no escaping in the crowd. Each one will stand in his own most intense individuality in that appalling moment. The eye of each will be turned in upon himself, and back upon his past history. All will be seen in the light of the great white throne, from which there is no escape.

The skeptic may reason against all this. He may say, "*How* can these things be? *How* could all the dead stand before God? *How* could the countless millions, who have passed away since the foundation of the world find sufficient space before the judgment-seat?" The answer is very simple to the true believer, whatever it may be to the skeptic; God who made them, will make a place for them to stand for judgment, and a place to lie in everlasting torment. Tremendous thought? "God hath appointed a day in the which He will judge the world in righteousness, by that Man whom He hath ordained; whereof He hath given assurance unto all men, in that He hath raised Him from the dead" (Acts. 17:31).

And be it remembered that "*every man* will be judged according to *his* works." The solemn session of the judgment referred to in Revelation 20 will not be an indiscriminate act. Let none suppose this. There are "*books*" —rolls—records. "*Every man*" will be judged. How? "According to *his* works. Nothing can be more precise and specific. Each one has committed his own sins, and for them he will be judged and punished everlastingly. We are aware that many cherish the notion that people will only be judged for rejecting the gospel. It is a fatal mistake. Scripture teaches the direct contrary. It declares that people will be judged according to their works.

What are we to learn from the "many stripes" and the "few stripes" of Luke 12? What is the force of the words "more tolerable" in Matthew 11? Are we not plainly taught by these words that there will be a difference in the degrees of judgment and punishment? And does not the apostle most distinctly teach us in Ephesians 4 and Colossians 3 that the wrath of God cometh upon the children of disobedience (or unbelief) "because of" certain sins against which he solemnly warns the saints?

No doubt the rejection of the gospel leaves people on the ground of judgment, just as the true belief of the gospel takes people off that ground. But the judgment will be, in every case, according to a man's works. Are we to suppose that the poor ignorant savage, who has lived and died amid the gloomy shades of heathen darkness, will be found in the same "book," or punished with the same severity as a man who has lived and died in the total rejection of the full blaze of gospel light and privilege? Not for a moment, so long as the words "more tolerable" stand on the page of inspiration. The savage will be judged according to his works, and the baptized sinner will be judged according to his works, but assuredly it will be more tolerable for the former than the latter. God knows how to deal with people. He can discriminate, and He declares that He will give to each according to his works.

Think of this, we beseech you. Think deeply, think seriously. If thou art unconverted, think of it for thyself, for, assuredly, it concerns thee. And if thou art converted, think of it for others, as the apostle says, "Knowing the terror of the Lord, we persuade men." It is impossible for anyone to reflect upon the great and awful fact of judgment to come, and not be stirred up to warn his fellows. We believe it is of the very last possible importance that the consciences of men should be acted upon by the solemn truth of the judgment-seat of Christ—that they should be made to feel the seriousness of having to do with God as a Judge.

Should the reader, whoever he be, have been led to feel this—if he has been roused by this weighty matter—if he is, even now, asking the question, "What must I do?" the answer is blessedly simple. The gospel declares that the One who will, ere long, act as a Judge, is now revealed as a Justifier—even a Justifier of the ungodly sinner that believeth in Jesus. This changes the aspect of things entirely. It is not that the thought of the judgment-seat loses a single jot or tittle of its gravity and solemnity. Quite the contrary. It stands in all its weight and magnitude.

But the believer looks at it from a totally different point of view. In place of looking at the judgment-seat of Christ as a guilty member of the first Adam, he looks at it as a justified and accepted member of the Second. In place of looking forward to it as the place where the question of his eternal salvation or perdition is to be decided, he looks to it as one who knows that he is God's workmanship, and that he can never come into judgment, inasmuch as he has been taken clean off the ground of guilt, death, and judgment, and placed, through the death and resurrection of Christ, on a new ground altogether, even the ground of life, righteousness, and cloudless favor.

It is most needful to be clear as to this grand fundamental truth. Very many even of the people of God are clouded in reference to it, and hence it is that they are afraid when they think of the judgment-seat. They do not know God as a Justifier. Their faith has not grasped Him as the One who raised up Jesus our Lord from the dead. They are looking to Christ to keep God out as a Judge, very much in the same way as the Israelites looked to the blood to keep out the destroyer. See Exod. 12. It is true and real enough, so far as it goes; but it falls very far short of the truth revealed in the New Testament. There is a vast difference between keeping God out as a Destroyer and a Judge, and bringing Him in as a Saviour and a Justifier. An Israelite would have dreaded, above all things, God's coming in to him. Why? Because God was passing through the land as a Destroyer. The Christian, on the contrary, delights to be in the presence of God. Why? Because He has revealed Himself as a Justifer. How? By raising up Jesus our Lord from the dead.

There are three forms of expression used by the inspired apostle in Rom. 3 and 4 which should be carefully pondered. In chap. 3:26, he speaks of "believing in Jesus." In chap. 4:5, he speaks of "believing in Him that justifieth the ungodly." And, ver. 24, he speaks of "believing in Him that raised up Jesus our Lord from the dead."

Now, there is no distinction in Scripture without a difference; and when we see a distinction it is our business to inquire as to the difference. What then, is the difference between believing in Jesus, and believing in Him that raised up Jesus? We believe it to be this. We may often find souls who are really looking to Jesus and believing in Him, and yet they have, deep down in their hearts a sort of dread of meeting God. It is not that they doubt their savlation, or that they are not really saved. By no means. They are saved, inasmuch as they are looking to Christ, by faith, and all who so look are saved in Him with an everlasting salvation. All this is most blessedly true: but still there is this latent fear or dread of God, and shrinking from death. They know that Jesus is friendly to them, inasmuch as He died for them; but they do not see so clearly the friendship of God.

Hence it is that we find so many of God's people in uncertainty and spiritual distress. Their faith has not yet laid hold of God as the One who raised up Jesus our Lord from the dead. They are not quite sure of how it may go with them. At times they are happy, because by virtue of the new nature, of which they are assuredly the partakers, they get occupied with Christ: but at times they are miserable, because they begin to look at themselves, and they do not see God as their Justifier, and as the One who has condemned sin in the flesh. They are thinking of God as a Judge with whom some question still remains to be settled. They feel as if God's eye were resting on their indwelling sin, and as if they had, in some way or other, to dispose of that question with God.

Thus it is, we feel persuaded, with hundreds of the true saints of God. They do not see God as the Condemner of sin in Christ on the cross, and the Justifier of the believing sinner in Christ rising from the dead. They are looking to Christ on the cross to screen them from God as a Judge, instead of looking to God as a Justifier, in raising up Christ from the dead. Jesus was delivered for our offences, and raised again for our justification. Our sins are forgiven; our indwelling sin, or evil nature, is condemned and set aside. It has no existence *before God*. It is in us, but He sees us only in a risen Christ; and we are called to *reckon* ourselves dead, and by the power of God's Spirit, to mortify our members, to deny and subdue the evil nature which still dwells in us, and will dwell until we are passed out of our present condition, and find our place forever with the Lord.

This makes all so blessedly clear. We have already dwelt upon the fact, that "they that are in the flesh cannot please God;" but the believer is not in the flesh, though the flesh be in him. He is in the *body*, and on the *earth*, as to the fact of his existence; but he is neither in the *flesh*, nor of the *world*, as to the ground or principle of his standing. "Ye," says the Holy Ghost, "are not in the flesh, but in the Spirit" (Rom. 8). "They," says our blessed Lord, "are not of the world, even as I am not of the world" (John 17).

What a sweet relief to a heart bowed down under a sense of indwelling sin, and not knowing what to do with it! What solid peace and comfort flow into the soul when I see God condemning my sin in the cross, and justifying me in a risen Christ! Where are my *sins?* Blotted out. Where is my *sin?* Condemned and set aside. Where am I? Justified and accepted in a risen Christ. I am brought to God without a single cloud or misgiving. I am not afraid of my Justifier. I confide in Him, love Him, and adore Him. I joy in God, and rejoice in hope of His glory.

Thus, then, we have, in some measure, cleared the way for the believer to approach the subject of the judgment-seat of Christ, as set forth in ver. 10 of our chapter, which we shall here quote at length, in order that the reader may have the subject fully before him in the veritable language of inspiration. "For we must all appear [or rather, be manifested] before the judgment-seat of Christ; that every one may receive the things done in his body, according to that he hath done, whether it be good or bad."

Now there is, in reality, no difficulty or ground of perplexity here. All we need is to look at the matter from a divine standpoint, and with a simple mind, in order to see it clearly. This is true in reference to every subject treated of in the Word of God, and specially so as to the point now before us. We have no doubt whatever that the real secret of the difficulty felt by so many in respect to the question of the judgment-seat of Christ is self-occupation. Hence it is we so often hear such questions as the following, "Can it be possible that all our sins, all our failures, all our infirmities, all our naughty and foolish ways, shall be published, in the presence of assembled myriads, before the judgment-seat of Christ?"

Well, then, in the first place, we have to remark that Scripture says nothing of the kind. The passage before us, which contains the great, broad statement of the truth on this weighty subject, simply declares that "we must all be manifested before the judgment-seat of Christ." But how shall we be manifested? Assuredly, *as we are*. But how is that? As God's workmanship—as perfectly righteous, and perfectly holy, and perfectly accepted in the Person of that very One who shall sit on the judgment-seat, and who Himself bore in His own body on the tree all the judgment due to us, and made a full end of the entire system in which we stood.

All that which, as sinners, we had to meet, Christ met in our stead. Our *sins* He bore; our *sin* He was condemned for. He stood in our stead and answered all responsibilities which rested upon us as men alive in the flesh, as members of the first man, as standing on the old creation-ground. The Judge Himself is our righteousness. We are in Him. All that we are and all that we have, we owe it to Him and to His perfect work. If we, as sinners, had to meet Christ as a Judge, escape were utterly impossible; but, inasmuch as He is our righteousness, condemnation is utterly impossible. In short, the matter is reversed. The atoning death and triumphant resurrection of our Divine Substitute have completely changed everything, so that the effect of the judgment-seat of Christ will be to make manifest that there is not, and cannot be, a single stain or spot on that workmanship of God which the saint is declared to be.

But whence this dread of having all our naughtiness exposed at the judgment-seat of Christ? Does not He know all about us? Are we more afraid of being manifested to the gaze of men and angels than to the gaze of our blessed and adorable Lord? If we are manifested to Him, what matters it to whom beside we are known? How far are Peter and David and many others affected by the fact that untold millions have read the record of their sins, and that the record thereof has been stereotyped on the page of inspiration? Will it prevent their sweeping the strings of the golden harp, or casting their crowns before the feet of Him whose precious blood has obliterated for ever all their sins, and brought them, without spot, into the full blaze of the throne of God? Assuredly not.

Why then need any be troubled by the thought of their being thoroughly manifested before the judgment-seat of Christ? Will not the Judge of all the earth do right? May we not safely leave all in the hands of Him who has loved us and washed us in His own blood? Cannot we trust ourselves implicitly to the One who loved us with such a love? Will He expose us? Will He—can He, do aught inconsistent with the love that led Him to give His precious life for us? Will the Head expose the body, or any member thereof? Will the Bridegroom expose the bride? Yes, He will, in one sense. But how? He will publicly set forth, in view of all created intelligences, that there is not a speck or a flaw, a spot or wrinkle, or any such thing, to be seen upon that Church which He loved with a love that many waters could not quench.

Ah! Christian reader, dost thou not see how that nearness to the heart of Christ, as well as the knowledge of His perfect work, would completely roll away the mists which enwrap the subject of the judgment-seat? If thou art washed from thy sins in the blood of Jesus, and loved by God as Jesus is loved, what reason hast thou to fear that judgment-seat, or to shrink from the thought of being manifested before it? None whatever. Nothing can possibly come up there to alter thy standing, to touch thy relationship, to blot thy title, or cloud thy prospect. Indeed we are fully persuaded that the light of *the judgment-seat* will chase away many of the clouds that have obscured *the mercy-seat*.

Many, when they come to stand before that judgment-seat, will wonder why they ever feared it for themselves. They will see their mistake and adore the grace that has been so much better than all their legal fears. Many who have hardly ever been able to read their title here, will read it there, and rejoice and wonder—they will love and worship. They will then see, in broad daylight, what poor, feeble, shallow, unworthy thoughts they had once entertained of the love of Christ, and of the true character of His work. They will perceive how sadly prone they ever were to measure Him by themselves, and to think and feel as if His thoughts and ways were like their own. All this will be seen in the light of that day, and then the burst of praise—the rapturous hallelujah—will come forth from many a heart that, when down here, had been robbed of its peace and joy by legal and unworthy thoughts of God and His Christ.

But, while it is divinely true that nothing can come out before the judgment-seat of Christ to disturb, in any way, the standing or relationship of the very feeblest member of the body of Christ, or of any member of the family of God, yet is the thought of that judgment most solemn and weighty. Yes, truly, and none will more feel its weight and solemnity than those who can look forward to it with perfect calmness. And be it well remembered, that there are two things indispensably needful in order to enjoy this calmness of spirit. First, we must have a title without a blot; and, secondly, our moral and practical state must be sound. No amount of mere evangelical clearness as to our title will avail unless we are walking in moral integrity before God.

It will not do for a man to *say* that he is not afraid of the judgment-seat of Christ because Christ died for him, while, at the same time, he is walking in a loose, careless, self-indulgent way. This is a most dreadful delusion. It is alarming in the extreme to find persons drawing a plea from evangelical clearness to shrink from the holy responsibility resting upon them as the servants of Christ. Are we to speak idle words because we know we shall never come into judgment? The bare thought is horrible; and yet we may shrink from such a thing when clothed in plain language before us, while, at the same time, we allow ourselves to be drawn, through a false application of the doctrines of grace, into most culpable laxity and carelessness as to the claims of holiness.

All this must be sedulously avoided. The grace that has delivered us from judgment should exert a more powerful influence upon our ways than the fear of that judgment. And not only so, but we must remember that while we, *as sinners*, are delivered from judgment and wrath, yet, *as servants*, we must give account of ourselves and our ways. It is not a question of our being exposed here or there to men, angels, or devils. No; "we must give account to God" (Rom. 14:11-12). This is far more serious, far more weighty, far more influential, than our being exposed in the view of any creature. "Whatsoever ye do, do it heartily, as *to the Lord*, and not unto men; knowing that of *the Lord* ye shall receive the reward of the inheritance; for ye serve *the Lord* Christ. But he that doeth wrong shall receive for the wrong which he hath done: and there is no respect of persons" (Col. 3:23-25).

This is most serious and salutary. It may be asked, "When shall we have to give account to God? When shall we receive for the wrong?" We are not told, because that is not the question. The grand object of the Holy Ghost in the passages just quoted is to lead the conscience into holy exercise in the presence of God and of the Lord Christ. This is good and most needful in a day of easy profession, like the present, when there is much said about grace, free salvation, justification without works, our standing in Christ. Is it that we want to weaken the sense of these things? Far be the thought. Yea, we would, in every possible way, seek to lead souls into the divine knowledge and enjoyment of those most precious privileges. But then we must remember the adjusting power of *truth*.

There are always two sides to a question, and we find in the pages of the New

Testament the clearest and fullest statements of grace, lying side by side with the most solemn and searching statements as to our responsibility. Do the latter obscure the former? Assuredly not. Neither should the former weaken the latter. Both should have their due place, and be allowed to exert their moulding infuence upon our character and ways.

Some professors seem to have a great dislike to the words "duty" and "responsibility"; but we invariably find that those who have the deepest sense of grace have also, and as a necessary consequence, the truest sense of duty and responsibility. We know of no exception. A heart that is duly influenced by divine grace is sure to welcome every reference to the claims of holiness. It is only empty talkers about grace and standing that raise an outcry about duty and responsibility. God deals in moral realities. He is real with us, and He wants us to be real with Him. He is real in His love, and real in His faithfulness; and He would have us real in our dealings with Him, and in our response to His holy claims. It is of little use to say "Lord, Lord" if we live in the neglect of His commandments. It is the merest sham to say "I go sir" if we do not go. God looks for obedience in His children. "He is a rewarder of them that *diligently* seek Him."

May we bear these things in mind, and remember that all must come out before the judgment-seat of Christ. "We must all be manifested" there. This is unmingled joy to a really upright mind. If we do not unfeignedly rejoice at the thought of the judgment-seat of Christ, there must be something wrong somewhere. Either we are not established in grace, or we are walking in some false way. If we know that we are justified and accepted before God in Christ, and if we are walking in moral integrity, as in His presence, the thought of the judgment-seat of Christ will not disturb our hearts.

The apostle could say, "We are made manifest to God; and I trust also are made manifest in your consciences." Was Paul afraid of the judgment-seat? Not he. But why? Because he knew that he was accepted, as to his person, in a risen Christ; and, *as to*

his ways, he "labored that whether present or absent he might be acceptable to Him." Thus it was with this holy man of God and devoted servant of Christ. "And herein do I exercise myself, to have always a conscience void of offence toward God and toward men" (Acts 24:16). Paul knew that he was accepted *in* Christ, and therefore he labored to be acceptable to Him in all his ways.

These two things should never be separated, and they never will be in any divinely taught mind or divinely regulated conscience. They will be perfectly joined together, and, in holy harmony, exert their formative power over the soul. It should be our aim to walk, even now, in the light of the judgment-seat. This would prove a wholesome regulator in many ways. It will not, in any wise, lead to legality of spirit. Impossible. Shall we have any legality when we stand before the judgment-seat of Christ? Assuredly not. Well, then, why should the thought of that judgment-seat exert a legal influence now?

In point of fact, we feel assured there is, and can be, no greater joy to an honest heart than to know that everything shall come clearly and fully out, in the perfect light of that solemn day that is approaching. We shall see all then as Christ sees it—judge of it as He judges. We shall look back from amid the blaze of divine light shining from the judgment-seat, and see our whole course in this world. We shall see what blunders we have made—how badly we did this, that, and the other work—mixed motives here—an under current there—a false object in something else. All will be seen then in divine truth and light.

Is it a question of our being exposed to the whole universe? By no means. Should we be concerned, whether or no? Certainly not. Will it, can it, touch our acceptance? Nay, we shall shine there in all the perfectness of our risen and glorified Head. The Judge Himself is our righteousness. We stand in Him. He is our all. What can touch us? We shall appear there as the fruit of His perfect work. We shall even be associated with Him in the judgment which He executes over the world.

Is not this enough to settle every question? No doubt. But still we have to think of our individual walk and service. We have to look to it that we bring no wood, hay, and stubble into the light of the coming day, for as surely as we do we shall suffer loss, though we ourselves shall be saved through the fire. We should seek to carry ourselves now as those who are already in the light, and whose one desire is to do what is well pleasing to our adorable Lord, not because of the fear of judgment, but under "the vast constraining influence" of His love.

"The love of Christ constraineth us, because we thus judge, that if one died for all, then were all dead: and that He died for all, that they which live should not henceforth live unto themselves, but unto Him who died for them and rose again." This is the true motivespring in all Christian service. It is not the fear of judgment impelling, but the love of Christ constraining us; and we may say, with fullest assurance, that never shall we have so deep a sense of that love as when we stand before the judgment-seat of Christ.

> When this passing world is done,
> When has sunk yon radiant sun,
> When I stand with Christ on high,
> Looking o'er life's history,
> Then, Lord, shall I fully know,
> Not till then, how much I owe.

There are many other points of interest and value in this marvelous chapter; but we feel we must bring our paper to a conclusion; and, most assuredly, we could not do this more suitably than by unfolding, as God's Spirit may enable us, that theme which has been before us all along, "The Ministry of Reconciliation," to which we shall now direct the reader's attention as briefly as we can.

We may view it under three distinct heads; namely, first, the *foundation* on which this ministry rests; secondly, the *objects* toward whom it is exercised; thirdly, the *features* by which it is characterized.

And first, then, as to the foundation on which the ministry of reconciliation rests. This is set before us, in the closing verse of our chapter.

"For He [God] hath made Him [Christ] to be sin for us, who knew no sin; that we might be made the righteousness of God in Him."

We have here three parties, namely, God, Christ, and sin. This latter is simply the expression of what we are by nature. There is in *"us"* naught but *"sin,"* from the crown of the head to the sole of the foot, the whole man is sin. The principle of sin pervades the entire system of fallen humanity. The root, trunk, branches, leaves, blossom, fruit—all is sin. It is not only that we have committed sins; we are actually *born* in sin. True, we have, all of us, our characteristic sins. We have not only, all of us, "gone astray," but "we have turned every one to his own way." Each has pursued his own specific path of evil and folly; and all this is the fruit of that thing called "sin." The outward life of each is but a stream from the fountain—a branch from the stem; that fountain is sin.

And what, let us ask, is sin? It is the acting of the will in opposition to God. It is doing our own pleasure—doing what we like ourselves. This is the root—this the source of sin. Let it take what shape, or clothe itself in what forms it may; be it gross or be it most refined in its actings, the great root-principle, the parent stem, is self-will, and this is sin. There is no necessity for entering into any detail; all we desire is that the reader should have a clear and thorough sense of what sin is, and not only so, but that he, by nature, is sinful. Where this great and solemn fact takes full possession of the soul, by the power of the Holy Ghost, there can be no settled rest until the soul is brought to lay hold on the truth set forth in 2 Corinthians 5:21.

The question of sin had to be disposed of ere there could be so much as a single thought of reconciliation. God could never be reconciled to sin. But fallen man was a sinner by practice and sinful in nature. The very sources of his being were corrupt and defiled, and God was holy, just, and true. He is of purer eyes than to behold evil, and cannot look upon iniquity. Hence, then, between God and sinful humanity there could be no such thing as reconciliation. True it is—most blessedly true—that God is good, and merciful, and gracious. But He is also holy; and holiness and sin could never coalesce.

What was to be done? Hear the answer: "God hath made Christ to be sin." But where?

Look well at this. Where was Christ made sin? Was it in His birth? or in Jordan's flood? or in the garden of Gethsemane? Nay; though, most assuredly, in that garden the shadows were lengthening, the darkness was thickening, the gloom was deepening. But where and when was the holy, spotless, precious Lamb of God made sin? *On the cross, and only there!* This is a grand cardinal truth—a truth of vital importance—a truth which the enemy of God and His Word is seeking to darken and set aside in every possible way. The devil is seeking, in the most specious manner, to displace the cross. He cares not how he compasses this end. He will make use of anything and everything in order to detract from the glory of the Cross, that great central truth of Christianity round which every other truth circulates, and on which the whole fabric of divine revelation rests as upon an eternal foundation.

"He hath made Him to be sin." Here lies the root of the whole matter. Christ, on the cross, was made sin for us. He died, and was buried. Sin was condemned. It met the just judgment of a holy God who could not pass over a single jot or tittle of sin; nay, He poured out His unmingled wrath upon it in the Person of His Son, when that Son was "made sin."

It is a serious error to believe that Christ was bearing the judgment of God during His lifetime, or that aught save the death of Christ could meet the question of sin. He might have become incarnate—He might have lived and labored on this earth—He might have wrought His countless miracles— He might have healed, and cleansed, and quickened—He might have prayed, and wept, and groaned; but not any of these things, nor yet all of them put together, could blot out a single stain of that dreadful thing *"sin."* God the Holy Ghost declares that "without shedding of blood there is no remission" (Heb. 9:22).

Now, then, if the holy life and labors of the Son of God—if His prayers, tears, and groans could not put away sin; how do you think that your life and labors, your prayers, tears, and groans, your good works, rites, ordinances, and ceremonies could ever put away sin? The fact is, that the life of our blessed Lord only proved man more and more guilty. It laid the topstone upon the superstructure of his guilt, and therefore left the question of sin wholly unsettled.

Nor was this all. Our blessed Lord Himself declares, over and over again, the absolute and indispensable necessity of His death. "Except a corn of wheat fall into the ground and *die*, it abideth *alone*; but if it *die*, it bringeth forth much fruit" (John 12). "Thus it is written, and thus *it behoved* [or was necessary for] Christ to suffer" (Luke 24:46). "How then shall the Scriptures be fulfilled that thus it *must* be" (Matt. 26)?

In a word, death was the only pathway of life, the only basis of union, the only ground of reconciliation. All who speak of incarnation as being the basis of our union with Christ deny, in the plainest way, the whole range of truth connected with a dead and risen Christ. Many may not see this; but Satan sees it, and he sees too how it will work. He knows what he is about, and surely the servants of Christ ought to know what is involved in the error against which we are warning our readers.

The fact is, the enemy does not want souls to see that, in the death of Christ, sentence was passed on fallen human nature and upon the whole world. This was not the case in incarnation at all. An incarnate Christ put man to the test—a dead Christ put man to death—a risen Christ takes the believer into union with Himself. When Christ came in the flesh, fallen man was still under probation. When Christ died on the cross, fallen man was wholly condemned.

When Christ rose from the dead, He became the head of a new race, each member of which, being quickened by the Holy Ghost, is viewed by God as united to Christ, in life, righteousness, and favor—he is viewed as having been dead, as having passed through judgment, and as being now as free from all condemnation as Christ Himself. "He hath made Him to be sin for us, [He] who knew no sin, that we might be made the righteousness of God in Him."

Now, it must be plain to the reader who bows to Scripture, that incarnation did not, and could not accomplish all this. Incarnation did not put away sin. Need we stop here to dwell upon the glories of the mystery of incarnation? Will anyone imagine that we take away from the value, or mar the integrity of that priceless fundamental truth, because we deny that it puts away sin, or forms the basis of our union with Christ? We trust not. That incarnation was essentially necessary for the accomplishment of redemption is plain to all. Christ had to become a man in order to die. "Without shedding of blood is no remission." He had to give His flesh for the life of the world.

But this only goes to prove the absolute necessity of death. It was the *giving* of His flesh, not the *taking* of it, that laid the foundation of the whole fabric—life, pardon, peace, righteousness, union, glory, all. Apart from death, there is, and could be, absolutely nothing. Through death we have all.

But we cannot pursue this profound subject any further now. Enough has been said to set forth its connection with our special thesis—the ministry of reconciliation. When we read that "God hath made Christ to be sin for us," we must see that this involved nothing less than the death of the cross. "*Thou*," says that blessed One, "hast brought *Me* into the dust of death" (Ps. 22). What an utterance! Who can fathom the mighty depths of those words—"Thou"—"Me"—and "death"? Who can enter into the question, "My God, My God, why hast *Thou* forsaken *Me?*" Why did a holy, righteous God forsake His only begotten, well-beloved, eternal Son? The answer contains the solid basis of that marvelous ministry whereof we speak. Christ was made sin. He not only bore our *sins* in His own body on the tree; but He was made sin. He stood charged with the entire question of sin. He was "the Lamb of God bearing away the sin of the world."

As such He gloriously vindicated God, in the very scene where He had been dishonored. He glorified Him in respect to that very thing by which His majesty had been insulted. He took upon Himself the whole matter—placed Himself beneath the weight of the whole burden, and completely cleared the ground on which God could lay the foundations of the new creation. He opened those eternal flood-gates which sin had closed, so that the full tide of divine love might roll down along that channel which His atoning death alone could furnish; so long as sin was *in* question, reconciliation must be *out* of the question. But Christ, being made sin, died and put it away forever, and thus changed entirely the ground and character of God's dealing with man and with the world.

The death of Christ, then, as we have seen, is the alone basis of reconciliation. That divine work has opened the way for placing men and things in their right relationship to God, and on their proper footing before Him. And this, be it remembered, is the true sense and meaning of reconciliation. Sin had alienated "men" from God, and set "*things*" entirely astray, and hence both men and things needed to be reconciled, or set straight; and the death of Christ has cleared the way for this.

It is well to see clearly the distinction between "atonement" and "reconciliation." They are often confounded, through inattention to Scripture; and the honored translators of our excellent Authorized Version have not, with sufficient accuracy, marked this distinction. For example, in Rom. 5:11, they have the word "atonement" where it ought to be rendered "reconciliation" and in Heb. 2:17, we have the word "reconciliation" where it ought to be "atonement."

Nor is the distinction by any menas unimportant. The word "atonement," or "propitiation," occurs, in some one or other of its forms, six times in the Greek New Testament. (See carefully Luke 18:13; Rom. 3:25; Heb. 2:17; 9:5; 1 John 2:2; 4:10.) The word "reconciliation" occurs, in one or other of its forms, thirteen times in the New Testament. (See Rom 5:10-11; 11:15; 1 Cor. 7:11; 2 Cor. 5:18-20; Eph. 2:16; Col. 1:20-21.)

If the reader will take the trouble of examining and comparing these passages, he will see that atonement and reconciliation are not the same thing, but that the former is the foundation of the latter. Sin had made man an enemy and thrown things into confusion; and in Col. 1:20-21, we read, "And, having made peace through the blood of His cross [here is the foundation], by Him to reconcile all *things* unto Himself; by Him, I say, whether they be things in earth, or things in heaven. And *you*, that were sometime alienated, and enemies in your mind by wicked works, yet now *hath He reconciled*, in the body of His flesh, *through death*, to present you holy, and unblamable, and unreprovable in His sight." Here we have the death of Christ set forth as the ground of the reconciliation of both men and things.*

Now this leads to another point of immense importance. We often hear it said that "the death of Christ was necessary in order *to reconcile God to man*." This is a pious mistake, arising from inattention to the language of the Holy Ghost, and indeed to the plain meaning of the word "reconcile." God never changed—never stepped out of His normal and true position. He abideth faithful. There was, and could be, no derangement, no confusion, no alienation, so far as He was concerned; and hence there could be no need of reconciling Him to us. In fact, it was exactly the contrary. Man had gone astray; he was the enemy, and needed to be reconciled. But this was wholly impossible if *sin* were not righteously disposed of; and sin could only be disposed of by *death*—even the death of One, who, as being a man, could die, and being God, could impart all the dignity, value, and glory of His divine Person to the atoning sacrifice which He offered.

Wherefore, then, as might be expected, Scripture never speaks of reconciling God to man. There is no such expression to be found within the covers of the New Testament. "God was in Christ reconciling the world [in its broad aspect—men and things] unto Himself, not imputing their trespasses unto them." And again, "All things are of God, who hath reconciled *us* to Himself by Jesus Christ." In a word, it is God, in His infinite mercy and grace, through the atoning death of Christ, bringing us back to Himself, and placing us not merely in the original place, or on the original footing, or in the original

relationship; but, as was due to the work of Christ, giving us back far more than we had lost, and introducing us into the marvelous relationship of sons, and setting us in His presence, in divine and eternal righteousness, and in the infinite favor and acceptableness of His own Son Jesus Christ our Lord.

Amazing grace! Stupendous and glorious plan! What a ministry! And yet need we wonder when we think of the death of Christ as the foundation of it all? When we remember that "Christ was made sin for us," it seems but the necessary counterpart that "we should be made the righteousness of God in Him." It would have been no adequate result of such a work as Christ accomplished, to have brought men and things back to the Adamic or old creation ground. This would never have satisfied the heart of God in any way, whether as respects Christ's glory or our blessing. It would not have furnished an answer to that omnipotent appeal of John 17: "I have glorified Thee on the earth: I have finished the work which Thou gavest Me to do. And *now*, O Father, glorify Thou Me, with Thine own self, with the glory which I had with Thee before the world was" (ver. 4-5). Who can gauge the depth and power of those accents as they fell upon the ear of the God and Father of our Lord Jesus Christ?

But we must not enlarge, much as we should like to do so. Little remains to be said as to the *objects* of the ministry of reconciliation, inasmuch as we have, in a measure, anticipated them by speaking of "men and things," for these are, in very deed, the objects, and they are included in that comprehensive word "world." "God was in Christ, reconciling the world unto Himself." We would merely add here, that it is utterly impossible for any creature under heaven to exclude himself from the range of this most precious ministry. Before the reader can shut himself out from the application of all this grace to himself, he must prove that he does not belong to the world. This he cannot do, and hence he must see that God is beseeching him to be reconciled.

---

* If the reader will turn, for a moment, to 1 Cor. 7: 11, he will see the use of the word reconciliation. "But and if she depart, let her remain unmarried, or be *reconciled* to her husband." In classical Greek the word is applied to the *changing* money: the *exchanging* one thing for another; *exchanging* prisoners; the changing a person from *enmity to friendship*. In short, everywhere the distinction is maintained between "atonement," or "propitiation" and "reconciliation." The former is ἱλασμος , the latter, καταλλαγη .

But this leads us to look, for a moment, at the *features* which characterize this glorious ministry.

First, let us mark God's attitude. He is beseeching sinners. What a thought! It seems too much for the heart to conceive. Only think, reader, of the Most High and Mighty God, the Creator of the ends of the earth—the One who has power to destroy both soul and body in hell—think of Him as beseeching and praying you to be friends with Him! It is not a question of your praying to Him and His hearing you. No: but the very reverse—He is praying you. And for what does He ask you? Is it to do anything or to give anything? Nay; He simply asks you to be friends with Him because He has befriended you at the cost of His own Son. Think of this. He spared not His only begotten and well-beloved Son, but bruised Him in your stead. He made Him to be sin for you. He judged your sin in the person of His Son, on the cross, in order that He might be able to reconcile you. And now He stretches forth His arms and opens His heart to you, and prays you to be reconciled—to be friends with Him. Surpassing grace! It really seems to us as though human language can only tend to weaken and impoverish this grand reality.

We would only further suggest that the force of ver. 20 is greatly weakened by the word "you," which, as the reader will observe, ought not to be inserted. It makes it appear as though the apostle were beseeching the Corinthian saints to be reconciled, whereas he is only setting forth the terms and the style adopted by all "ambassadors" for Christ wherever they went through the wide world—the language in which they were to address "every creature" under heaven. It is not, "Do this or that"—"Give this or that." It was not command or prohibition; but simply, "Be reconciled."

Then, what encouragement to the poor trembling heart that feels the burden of sin and guilt to be assured that God will not impute, will not reckon, one of his sins! This is another precious feature of the ministry of reconciliation. *"Not* imputing their trespasses unto them." This must set the heart at rest. If God tells me that He will not count one of my trespasses to me, because He has already counted them to Jesus on the cross, this may well tranquilize my spirit and emancipate my heart. If I believe that God means what He says, perfect peace must be my portion. True, it is only by the Holy Ghost that I can enter into the power of this glorious truth; but what the Holy Ghost leads me to believe and rest in is, that God does not, and will not, blessed be His name, impute a single sin to me, because He has already imputed *all* to Christ.

But this leads us to the third feature of the ministry of reconciliation.

If God will not impute my trespasses to me then what will He impute? Righteousness—even the righteousness of God. We cannot attempt to unfold the nature and character of this righteousness. We may do so on another occasion, if the Lord permit; but here we confine ourselves to the statement contained in the passage before us, which declares that God hath made Christ, who knew no sin, to be sin for us who were all sin, that we might become the righteousness of God *in Him*. Most glorious truth! Sin is made an end of, as regards the believer. Christ lives as our subsisting righteousness, before God, and we live in Him. There is not so much as one single entry to our debit in the book of divine justice; but there is a risen and glorified Christ to our credit. Nor is this all. Not only are our sins gone, our guilt cancelled—our old self completely ignored—not only are we made the righteousness of God in Jesus; but we are loved by God as Jesus is loved—accepted in Him—one with Him in all that He is and has, as a risen, victorious, ascended, and glorified Man at God's right hand. Higher than this it is impossible to go.

And now we must close, and we do it reluctantly. We do it with a certain painful consciousness of the feebleness and poverty of our handling of this lofty and comprehensive theme. But all this we must leave in the Master's hand. He knows all about the subject and the treatment thereof—all about the reader and the writer of these lines. To Him we commit all, while we make one solemn, closing appeal to the unconverted, unawakened reader.

Let us remind you that this glorious ministry will very soon close. The acceptable year, the day of salvation, shall ere long come to an end. The ambassadors shall soon be all called home and their embassy be closed forever. The door shall soon be shut, and the day of vengeance set in in terror and wrath upon a Christ-rejecting world. Let us entreat of you to flee from the wrath to come. Remember that the One who is now praying and beseeching you to be reconciled, has uttered the following awful words, "Because I have called, and ye refused; I have stretched out My hand, and no man regarded. But ye have set at nought all My counsel, and would none of My reproof; I also will laugh at your calamity; I will mock when your fear cometh" (Prov. 1:24-26). May the reader escape the unutterable horrors of the day of wrath and judgment!

The Church—
The Body of Christ

EVANGELIZATION

A WORD TO THE EVANGELIST

WE TRUST it may not be deemed out of place if we venture to offer a word of counsel and encouragement to all who have been and are engaged in the blessed work of preaching *the gospel of the grace of God*. We are, in some measure, aware of the difficulties and discouragements which attend upon the path of every evangelist, whatever may be his sphere of labor or measure of gift; and it is our heart's desire to hold up the hands and cheer the hearts of all who may be in danger of falling under the depressing power of these things. We increasingly feel the immense importance of an earnest, fervent gospel testimony everywhere; and we dread exceedingly any falling off therein. We are imperatively called to "do the work of an evangelist," and not be moved from that work by any arguments or considerations whatsoever.

Let none imagine that, in writing thus, we mean to detract, in the smallest degree, from the value of teaching, lecturing, or exhortation. Nothing is further from our thoughts. "These things ought ye to have done, and not to leave the other undone." We mean not to compare the work of the evangelist with that of the teacher, or to exalt the former at the expense of the latter. Each has its own proper place, its own distinctive interest and importance.

But is there not a danger, on the other hand, of the evangelist abandoning his own precious work in order to give himself to the work of teaching and lecturing? Is there not a danger of the evangelist becoming merged in the teacher? We fear there is; and it is under the influence of this very fear that we pen these few lines. We observe, with deep concern, some who were once known amongst us as earnest and eminently successful evangelists, now almost wholly abandoning their work and becoming teachers and lecturers.

This is most deplorable. *We really want evangelists.* A true evangelist is almost as great a rarity as a true pastor. Alas! how rare are both! The two are closely connected. The evangelist gathers the sheep; the pastor feeds and cares for them. The work of each lies very near the heart of Christ—the Divine Evangelist and Pastor; but it is with the former we have now more immediately to do—to encourage him in his work, and to warn him against the temptation to turn aside from it. We cannot afford to lose a single ambassador just now, or to have a single preacher silent.

We are perfectly aware of the fact that there is in some quarters a strong tendency to throw cold water upon the work of evangelization. There is a sad lack of sympathy with the preacher of the gospel; and, as a necessary consequence, of active co-operation with him in his work. Further, there is a mode of speaking of gospel preaching which argues but little sympathy with the heart of Him who wept over impenitent sinners, and who could say, at the very opening of His blessed ministry, "The Spirit of the Lord is upon Me, because He hath anointed Me *to preach the gospel to the poor*" (Isa. 61; Luke 4). And again, "Let us go into the next towns, that I may preach there also: for therefore came I forth" (Mark 1: 38).

Our blessed Lord was an indefatigable preacher of the gospel, and all who are filled with His mind and spirit will take a lively interest in the work of all those who are seeking in their feeble measure to do the same. This interest will be evinced, not only by earnest prayer for the divine blessing upon the work, but also by diligent and persevering efforts to get immortal souls under the sound of the gospel.

This is the way to help the evangelist, and this way lies open to every member of the Church of God—man, woman, or child. All can thus help forward the glorious work of evangelization. If each member of the assembly were to work diligently and prayerfully in this way, how different would it be with the Lord's dear servants who are seeking to make known the unsearchable riches of Christ.

But, alas! how often is it otherwise. How often do we hear even those who are of some repute for intelligence and spirituality, when referring to meetings for gospel testimony, say, "Oh, I am not going there; it is *only* the gospel." Think of that! "*Only the gospel.*" If they would put the idea into other words, they might say, "It is *only* the heart of God—*only* the precious blood of Christ—*only* the glorious record of the Holy Ghost."

This would be putting the thing plainly. Nothing is more sad than to hear professing Christians speak in this way. It proves too clearly that their souls are very far away from the heart of Jesus. We have invariably found that those who think and speak slightingly of the work of the evangelist are persons of very little spirituality; and on the other hand, the most devoted, the most true hearted, the best taught saints of God, are always sure to take a profound interest in that work. How could it be otherwise? Does not the voice of Holy Scripture bear the clearest testimony to the fact of the interest of the Trinity in the work of the gospel? Most assuredly it does.

Who first preached the gospel? Who was the first herald of salvation? Who first announced the good news of the bruised Seed of the woman? The Lord God Himself, in the garden of Eden. This is a telling fact in connection with our theme. And further, let us ask, who was the most earnest, laborious, and faithful preacher that ever trod this earth? The Son of God. And who has been preaching the gospel for the last eighteen centuries? The Holy Ghost sent down from Heaven.

Thus then we have the Father, the Son, and the Holy Ghost all actually engaged in the work of evangelization; and if this be so,

who are we to dare to speak slightingly of such a work? Nay, rather may our whole moral being be stirred by the power of the Spirit of God so that we may be able to add our fervent and deep Amen to those precious words of inspiration, "How beautiful are the feet of them that preach the gospel of peace, and bring glad tidings of good things!" (Isa. 52:7; Rom. 10:15)

But it may be that these lines shall be scanned by some one who has been engaged in the work of preaching the gospel, and is beginning to feel rather discouraged. It may be that he has been called to preach in the same place for years, and he feels burdened by the thought of having to address the same audience, on the same subject, week after week, month after month, year after year. He may feel at a loss for something new, something fresh, some variety. He may sigh for some new sphere, where the subjects which are familiar to him will be new to the people. Or, if this cannot be, he may feel led to substitute lectures and expositions for the fervid, pointed, earnest preaching of the gospel.

If we have in any measure set forth the reader's feelings on this subject, we think it will greatly help him in his work to bear in mind that the one grand theme of the true evangelist is Christ. The power to handle that theme is the Holy Ghost. The one to whom that theme is to be unfolded is the poor lost sinner. Now, Christ is ever new; the power of the Holy Ghost is ever fresh; the soul's condition and destiny ever intensely interesting.

Furthermore, it is well for the evangelist to bear in mind, on every fresh occasion of rising to preach, that his unconverted hearers are totally ingnorant of the gospel, and hence he should preach as though it were the first time they had ever heard the message, and the first time he had ever delivered it. For, be it remembered, the preaching of the gospel, in the divine acceptation of the phrase, is not a mere barren statement of evangelical doctrine—a certain form of words enunciated over and over again in wearisome routine. Far, very far from it. The gospel is really the large loving heart of God welling up and flowing forth toward the poor lost sinner in streams of life and salvation. It is the presentation of the atoning death and glorious resurrection of the Son of God; and all this in the present energy, glow, and freshness of the Holy Ghost, from the exhaustless mine of Holy Scripture.

Moreover, *the* one absorbing object of the preacher is to win souls for Christ, to the glory of God. For this he labors and pleads; for this he prays, weeps, and agonizes; for this he thunders, appeals, and grapples with the heart and conscience of his hearer. His object is not to teach doctrines, though doctrines may be taught; his object is not to expound Scripture, though Scripture may be expounded. These things lie within the range of the teacher or lecturer; but let it never be forgotten, the preacher's object is to bring the Saviour and the sinner together—to win souls to Christ. May God by His Spirit keep these things ever before our hearts, so that we may have a deeper interest in the glorious work of evangelization!

We would, in conclusion, merely add a word of exhortation in reference to the Lord's Day evening. We would, in all affection, say to our beloved and honored fellow-laborers, Seek to give that one hour to the great business of the soul's salvation. There are 168 hours in the week, and, surely, it is the least we may devote *one* of these to this momentous work. It so happens that during that interesting hour we can get the ear of our fellow-sinner. Oh, let us use it to pour in the sweet story of God's free love and of Christ's full salvation.

THE WORK OF AN EVANGELIST

Acts 16:8-31

We ventured to offer a word to the evangelist, which we now follow up with a paper on the evangelist's work; and we cannot do better than select, as the basis of our remarks, a page from the missionary record of one of the greatest evangelists that ever lived. The passage of Scripture that stands at the head of this article furnishes specimens of three distinct classes of hearers, and also the method in which they were met by the great apostle of the Gentiles, guided, most surely, by the Holy Ghost.

We have, first, *the earnest seeker*; secondly, *the false professor*; and thirdly, *the hardened sinner*. These three classes are to be met everywhere, and at all times, by the Lord's workman; and hence we may be thankful for an inspired account of the right mode of dealing with such. It is most desirable that those who go forth with the gospel should have skill in dealing with the various conditions of soul that come before them, from day to day; and there can be no more effectual way of attaining this skill than the careful study of the models given us by God the Holy Ghost.

Let us then, in the first place, look at the narrative of *the earnest seeker*.

The laborious apostle, in the course of his missionary journeyings, came to Troas, and there a vision appeared to him in the night, "There stood a man of Macedonia, and prayed him, saying, Come over into Macedonia and help us. And after he had seen the vision, immediately we endeavored to go into Macedonia, assuredly gathering that the Lord had called us for to preach the gospel unto them. Therefore loosing from Troas, we came with a straight course to Samothracia, and the next day to Neapolis; and from thence to Philippi, which is the chief city of that part of Macedonia, and a colony: and we were in that city abiding certain days.

"And on the Sabbath we went out of the city by a river side, where prayer was wont to be made; and we sat down, and spake unto the women which resorted thither. And a certain woman named Lydia, a seller of purple, of the city of Thyatira, which worshiped God, heard us; whose heart the Lord opened, that she attended unto the things that were spoken of Paul. And when she was baptized, and her household, she besought us, saying, If ye have judged me to be faithful to the Lord, come into my house and abide there. And she constrained us" (Acts 16: 8-15).

Here, then, we have a touching picture—something well worth gazing at and pondering. It is a picture of one who, having through grace gotten a measure of light, was living up to it, and was earnestly seeking for more. Lydia, the seller of purple, belonged to the same interesting generation as the eunuch of Ethiopia, and the centurion of Caesarea. All three appear on the page of inspiration as quickened souls not emancipated—not at rest—not satisfied. The eunuch had gone from Ethiopia to Jerusalem in search of something on which to rest his anxious soul. He had left that city still unsatisfied, and was devoutly and earnestly hanging over the precious page of inspiration. The eye of God was upon him, and He sent His servant Philip with the very message that was needed to solve his difficulties, answer his questions, and set his soul at rest.

God knows how to bring the Philips and the eunuchs together. He knows how to prepare the heart for the message and the message for the heart. The eunuch was a worshiper of God; but Philip is sent to teach him how to see God in the face of Jesus Christ. This was precisely what he wanted. It was a flood of fresh light breaking in upon his earnest spirit, setting his heart and conscience at rest, and sending him on his way rejoicing. He had honestly followed the light as it broke in upon his soul, and God sent him more.

Thus it is ever. "To him that hath shall more be given." There never was a soul who sincerely acted up to his light that did not get more light. This is most consolatory and encouraging to all anxious inquirers. If the reader belongs to this class, let him take courage. If he is one of those with whom God has begun to work, then let him rest assured of this, that He who hath begun a good work will perform the same until the day of Jesus Christ. He will, most surely, perfect that which concerneth His people.

But let no one fold his arms, settle upon his oars, and coolly say, "I must wait God's time for more light. I can do nothing—my efforts are useless. When God's time comes I shall be

all right; till then, I must remain as I am." These were not the thoughts or feelings of the Ethiopian eunuch. He was one of the earnest seekers; and all earnest seekers are sure to be happy finders. It must be so, for "God is a rewarder of them that diligently seek Him" (Heb. 11:6).

So also with the centurion of Caesarea. He was a man of the same stamp. He lived up to his light. He fasted, he prayed, and gave alms. We are not told whether he had read the sermon on the mount: but it is remarkable that he exercised himself in the three grand branches of practical righteousness set forth by our Lord in the sixth chapter of Matthew.* He was molding his conduct and shaping his way according to the standard which God had set before him. His righteousness exceeded the righteousness of the scribes and Pharisees, and therefore he entered the kingdom. He was, through grace, a real man, earnestly following the light as it streamed in upon his soul, and he was led into the full blaze of the gospel of the grace of God. God sent a Peter to Cornelius, as he had sent a Philip to the eunuch. The prayers and alms had gone up as a memorial before God, and Peter was sent with a message of full salvation through a crucified and risen Saviour.

Now it is quite possible that there are persons who, having been rocked in the cradle of easy-going evangelical profession, and trained up in the flippant formalism of a self-indulgent, heaven-made-easy religion, are ready to condemn the pious conduct of Cornelius, and pronounce it the fruit of ignorance and legality. Such persons have never known what it was to deny themselves a single meal, or to spend an hour in real, earnest prayer, or to open their hand, in true benevolence, to meet the wants of the poor. They have heard and learnt, perchance, that salvation is not to be gained by such means—that we are justified by faith without works—that it is to him that worketh not, but believeth on Him that justifieth the ungodly.

All this is most true; but what right have

* The reader will notice that in Matthew 6:1, the marginal reading is the correct one: "Take heed that ye do not your *righteousness* before men, to be seen of them." Then we have the three departments of this righteousness, namely, alms-giving (ver. 2); prayer (ver. 3); fasting (ver. 16). These were the very things Cornelius was doing. In short, he feared God, and was working righteousness, according to his measure of light.

we to imagine that Cornelius was praying, fasting, and giving alms in order to earn salvation? None whatever—at least if we are to be governed by the inspired narrative, and we have no other means of knowing aught about this truly excellent and interesting character. He was informed by the angel that his prayers and his alms had gone up as a memorial before God. Is not this a clear proof that these prayers and alms were not the trappings of self-righteousness, but the fruits of a righteousness based on the knowledge which he had of God? Surely the fruits of self-righteousness and legality could never have ascended as a memorial to the throne of God; nor could Peter ever have said concerning a mere legalist that he was one who feared God and worked righteousness.

Ah, no; Cornelius was a man thoroughly in earnest. He lived up to what he knew, and he would have been quite wrong to go further. To him the salvation of his immortal soul, the service of God, and eternity, were grand and all-absorbing realities. He was none of your easy-going professors, full of flippant, vapid, worthless talk, but *doing* nothing. He belonged to another generation altogether. He belonged to the *working*, not the *talking* class. He was one on whom the eye of God rested with complacency, and in whom the mind of heaven was profoundly interested.

So was our friend of Thyatira, Lydia, the seller of purple. She belonged to the same school—she occupied the same platform as the centurion and the eunuch. It is truly delightful to contemplate these three precious souls—to think of one in Ethiopia; another at Caesarea; and a third at Thyatira or Philippi. It is particularly refreshing to contrast such downright thorough-going, earnest souls, with many in this our day of boasted light and knowledge, who have got the plan of salvation, as it is termed, in their heads, the doctrines of grace on the tongue, but the world in the heart; whose absorbing object is self, self, self—miserable object!

We shall have occasion to refer more fully to these latter under our second head; but, for the present, we shall think of the earnest Lydia; and we must confess it is a far more grateful exercise. It is very plain that Lydia,

like Cornelius and the eunuch, was a quickened soul; she was a worshiper of God; she was one who was right glad to lay aside her purple-selling, and betake herself to a prayer-meeting, or to any such like place where spiritual profit was to be had, and where there were good things going. "Birds of a feather flock together," and so Lydia soon found out where a few pious souls, a few kindred spirits, were in the habit of meeting to wait on God in prayer.

All this is lovely. It does the heart good to be brought in contact with this deep-toned earnestness. Surely the Holy Ghost has penned this narrative, like all Holy Scripture, for our learning. It is a specimen case, and we do well to ponder it. Lydia was found diligently availing herself of any and every opportunity; indeed she exhibited the real fruits of divine life, the genuine instincts of the new nature. She found out where saints met for prayer, and took her place among them. She did not fold her arms and settle down on her lees, to wait, in antinomian indolence and culpable idleness, for some extraordinary undefinable thing to come upon her, or some mysterious change to come over her. No; she went to a prayer-meeting— the place of expressed need—the place of expected blessing: and there God met her, as He is sure to meet all who frequent such scenes in Lydia's spirit.

God never fails an expectant heart. He has said, "They shall not be ashamed that wait for Me"; and, like a bright and blessed sunbeam on the page of inspiration, shines that pregnant, weighty, soul-stirring sentence, "God is a rewarder of them that *diligently* seek Him." He sent a Philip to the eunuch in the desert of Gaza. He sent a Peter to the centurion, in the town of Caesarea. He sent a Paul to a seller of purple, in the suburbs of Philippi; and He will send a message to the reader of these lines, if he be a really earnest seeker after God's salvation.

It is ever a moment of deepest interest when a prepared soul is brought in contact with the full gospel of the grace of God. It may be that that soul has been under deep and painful exercise for many a long day, seeking rest but finding none. The Lord has been working by His Spirit, and preparing the ground for the good seed. He has been making deep the furrows so that the precious seed of His Word may take permanent root, and bring forth fruit to His praise. The Holy Ghost is never in haste. His work is deep, sure and solid. His plants are not like Jonah's gourd, springing up in a night and perishing in a night. All that He does will stand, blessed be His name. "I know that whatsoever God doeth, it shall be forever." When He convicts, converts, and liberates a soul, the stamp of His own eternal hand is upon the work, in all its stages.

Now, it must have been a moment of intense interest when one in Lydia's state of soul was brought in contact with that most glorious gospel which Paul carried (Acts 16: 14). She was thoroughly prepared for his message; and surely his message was thoroughly prepared for her. He carried with him truth which she had never heard and never thought of. As we have already remarked, she had been living up to her light; she was a worshiper of God; but we are bold to assert that she had no idea of the glorious truth which was lodged in the heart of that stranger who sat beside her at the prayer-meeting. She had come thither—devout and earnest woman that she was—to pray and to worship, to get some little refreshment for her spirit, after the toils of the week. How little did she imagine that at the meeting she should hear the greatest preacher that ever lived, save One, and that she should hear the very highest order of truth that had ever fallen upon mortal ears.

Yet thus it was. And, oh, how important it was for Lydia to have been at that memorable prayer meeting! How well it was she had not acted as so many, nowadays, act, who after a week of toil in the shop, the warehouse, the factory, or the field, take the opportunity of lying in bed on Sunday! How many there are whom you will see at their post from Monday morning till Saturday night, working away with all diligence at their calling, but for whom you will look in vain at the meeting on the Lord's day. How is this? They will tell you, perhaps, that they are so worn out on Saturday night that they

have no energy to rise on Sunday, and therefore they spend this day in sloth, lounging, and self-indulgence. They have no care for their souls, no care for eternity, no care for Christ. They care for themselves, for their families, for the world, for money-making; and hence you will find them up with the dawn of Monday and off to their work.

Lydia did not belong to this class at all. No doubt she attended to her business, as every rightminded person will. We dare say—indeed, we are sure—she kept very excellent purple, and was a fair, honest trader, in every sense of the word. But she did not spend her Sabbath in bed, or lounging about her house, or nursing herself up, and making a great fuss about all she had to do during the week. Neither do we believe that Lydia was one of those self-occupied folk whom a shower of rain is sufficient to keep away from a meeting. No; Lydia was of a different stamp altogether. She was an earnest woman, who felt she had a soul to save, and an eternity before her, and a living God to serve and worship.

Would to God we had more Lydias in this our day! It would give a charm, and an interest, and a freshness to the work of an evangelist, for which many of the Lord's workmen have to sigh in vain. We seem to live in a day of terrible unreality as to divine and eternal things. Men, women, and children are real enough at their money-making, their pursuits, and their pleasures; but oh, when the things of God, the things of the soul, the things of eternity, are in question, the aspect of people is that of a yawning indifference. But the moment is rapidly approaching—every beat of the pulse, every tick of the watch, brings us nearer to it—when the yawning indifference shall be exchanged for "weeping, wailing, and gnashing of teeth." If this were more deeply felt, we should have many more Lydias, prepared to lend an attentive ear to Paul's gospel.

What force and beauty in those words, "Whose heart the Lord opened, that *she attended* unto the things that were spoken of Paul." Lydia was not one of those who go to meetings to think of anything and everything but the things that are spoken by the Lord's messengers. She was not thinking of her purple, or of the prices, or the probable gains or losses. How many of those who fill our preaching rooms and lecture halls follow the example of Lydia? Alas! we fear but very few indeed. The business, the state of the markets, the state of the funds, money, pleasure, dress, folly—a thousand and one things are thought of, and dwelt upon, and attended to, so that the poor vagrant, volatile heart is at the ends of the earth instead of *"attending"* to the things that are spoken.

All this is very solemn, and very awful. It really ought to be looked into and thought of. People seem to forget the responsibility involved in hearing the gospel preached. They do not seem to be in the smallest degree impressed with the weighty fact that the gospel never leaves any unconverted person where it finds him. He is either saved by receiving, or rendered more guilty by rejecting it. Hence it becomes a serious matter to hear the gospel. People may attend gospel meetings as a matter of custom, as a religious service, or because they have nothing else to do, and the time would hang heavy upon their hands; or they may go because they think that the mere act of going has a sort of merit attached to it. Thus thousands attend preachings at which Christ's servants, though not Pauls in gift, power, or intelligence, unfold the precious grace of God in sending His only begotten Son into the world to save us from everlasting torment and misery. The virtue and efficacy of the atoning death of the divine Saviour—the Lamb of God—the dread realities of eternity —the awful horrors of hell, and the unspeakable joys of Heaven—all these weighty matters are handled, according to the measure of grace bestowed upon the Lord's messengers, and yet how little impression is produced! They "reason of righteousness, temperance, and judgment to come," and yet how few are made even to "tremble!"

And why? Will anyone presume to excuse himself for rejecting the gospel message on the ground of his inability to believe it? Will he appeal to the very case before us, and say, "The Lord opened her heart; and if He would only do the same for me, I, too, should attend; but until He does, I can do nothing"? We reply, and with deep seriousness, Such an argument will not avail thee in the day of judgment. Indeed we are most thoroughly convinced that thou wilt not dare to use it then. Thou art making a false use of Lydia's charming history. True it is, blessedly true, the Lord opened her heart; and He is ready to open thine also, if there were in thee but the hundredth part of Lydia's earnestness.

There are two sides to this great question, as there are to every question. It is all very well, and sounds very forcible, for thee to say, "I can do nothing." But who told thee this? Where hast thou learnt it? We solemnly challenge thee, in the presence of God, Canst thou look up to Him and say, "I can do nothing— I am not responsible"? Say, is the salvation of thy never-dying soul just *the* one thing in which thou canst do nothing? Thou canst do a lot of things in the service of the world, of self, and of Satan; but when it becomes a question of God, the soul, and eternity, you coolly say, "I can do nothing—I am not responsible."

Ah! it will never do. All this style of argument is the fruit of a one-sided theology. It is the result of the most pernicious reasoning of the human mind upon certain truths in Scripture which are turned the wrong way and sadly misapplied. But it will not stand. This is what we urge upon the reader. It is of no possible use arguing in this way. The sinner is responsible; and all the theology, and all the reasoning, and all the fallacious though plausible objections that can be scraped together, can never do away with this weighty and most serious fact.

Hence, therefore, we call upon the reader to be, like Lydia, in earnest about his soul's salvation—to let every other question, every other point, every other subject, sink into utter insignificance in comparison with this one momentous question—the salvation of his precious soul. Then, he may depend upon it, the One who sent Philip to the eunuch, and sent Peter to the centurion, and sent Paul to Lydia, will send some messenger and some message to him, and will also open his heart to attend. Of this there cannot possibly be a doubt, inasmuch as Scripture declares that

"God is not willing that any should perish, but that all should come to repentance." All who perish, after having heard the message of salvation—the sweet story of God's free love, of a Saviour's death and resurrection—shall perish without a shadow of an excuse, shall descend into hell with their blood upon their guilty heads. Their eyes shall then be open to see through all the flimsy arguments by which they have sought to prop themselves up in a false position, and lull themselves to sleep in sin and worldliness.

But let us dwell for a moment on "the things that were spoken of Paul." The Spirit of God hath not thought proper to give us even a brief outline of Paul's address at the prayer-meeting. We are therefore left to other passages of Holy Scripture to form an idea of what Lydia heard from his lips on that interesting occasion. Let us take, for example, that famous passage in which he reminds the Corinthians of the gospel which he had preached to them. "Moreover, brethren, I declare unto you the gospel which I preached unto you, which also ye have received, and wherein ye stand; by which also *ye are saved*, if ye keep in memory what I preached unto you, unless ye have believed in vain. For I delivered unto you first of all that which I also received, how that Christ died for our sins according to the Scriptures; and that He was buried, and that He rose again the third day according to the Scriptures" (1 Cor. 15:1-4).

Now we may safely conclude that the foregoing passage of Scripture contains a compendium of the things that were spoken of Paul at the prayer-meeting at Philippi. The grand theme of Paul's preaching was Christ—Christ for the sinner—Christ for the saint—Christ for the conscience—Christ for the heart. He never allowed himself to wander from this great centre, but made all his preachings and all his teachings circulate round it with admirable consistency. If he called on men, both Jews and Gentiles, to repent, the lever with which he worked was Christ. If he urged them to believe, the object which he held up for faith was Christ, on the authority of Holy Scripture. If he reasoned of righteousness, temperance, and judgment to come, the One that gave cogency and moral power to his reasoning was Christ. In short, Christ was the very gist and marrow, the sum and substance, the foundation and top stone of Paul's preaching and teaching.

But, for our present purpose, there are three grand subjects, found in Paul's preaching, to which we desire to call the reader's attention. These are, first, the grace of God; secondly, the Person and work of Christ; and thirdly, the testimony of the Holy Ghost as given in the Holy Scriptures.

We do not attempt to go into these vast subjects here; we merely name them, and entreat the reader to ponder them, to muse over them, and seek to make them his own.

1. The grace of God—His free, sovereign favor—is the source from whence salvation flows—salvation in all the length, breadth, height, and depth of that most precious word—salvation which stretches, like a golden chain, from the bosom of God, down to the very deepest depths of the sinner's guilty and ruined condition, and back again to the throne of God—meets all the sinner's necessities, overlaps the whole of the saint's history, and glorifies God in the highest possible manner.

2. Then, in the second place, the Person of Christ and His finished work are the *only* channel through which salvation can possibly flow to the lost and guilty sinner. It is not the Church and her sacraments, religion and its rites and ceremonies—man or his doings in any shape or form. It is the death and resurrection of Christ. "He died for our sins, was buried, and rose again the third day." This was the gospel which Paul preached, by which the Corinthians were saved, and the apostle declares, with solemn emphasis, "If any man preach any other gospel, let him be accursed." Tremendous words for our day!

3. But, thirdly, the authority on which we receive the salvation is the testimony of the Holy Ghost in Scripture. It is "according to the Scriptures." This is a most solid and comforting truth. It is not a question of feelings, or experiences, or evidences; it is a simply question of faith in God's Word wrought in the heart by God's Spirit.

It is a serious reflection for the evangelist, that wherever God's Spirit is at work, there Satan is sure to be busy. We must remember and ever be prepared for this. The enemy of Christ and the enemy of souls is always on the watch, always hovering about to see what he can do, either to hinder or corrupt the work of the gospel. This need not terrify or even discourage the workman; but it is well to bear it in mind and be watchful. Satan will leave no stone unturned to mar or hinder the blessed work of God's Spirit. He has proved himself the ceaseless, vigilant enemy of that work, from the days of Eden down to the present moment.

Now, in tracing the history of Satan, we find him acting in two characters, namely, as a serpent, or as a lion—using craft or violence. He will try to deceive; and, if he cannot succeed, then he will use violence. Thus it is in this sixteenth chapter of the Acts. The apostle's heart had been cheered and refreshed by what we moderns should pronounce, "a beautiful case of conversion." Lydia's was a very real and decided case, in every respect. It was direct, positive, and unmistakable. She received Christ into her heart, and forthwith took Christian ground by submitting to the deeply significant ordinance of baptism. Nor was this all. She immediately opened her house to the Lord's messengers. Hers was no mere lip profession. It was not merely *saying* she believed. She proved her faith in Christ, not only by going down under the water of baptism, but also by identifying herself and her household with the name and cause of that blessed One whom she had received into her heart by faith.

All this was clear and satisfactory. But we must now look at something quite different. The serpent appears upon the scene in the person of *the deceiver*.

"It came to pass, as we went to prayer, a certain damsel possessed with a spirit of divination met us, which brought her masters much gain by soothsaying. The same

followed Paul and us, and cried, saying, These men are the servants of the most high God, which show unto us the way of salvation. And this did she many days. But Paul, being grieved, turned and said to the spirit, I command thee in the name of Jesus Christ to come out of her. And he came out the same hour" (vers. 16-18).

Here, then, was a case eminently calculated to test the spirituality and integrity of the evangelist. Most men would have hailed such words from the lips of this damsel as an encouraging testimony to the work. Why then was Paul grieved? Why did he not allow her to continue to bear witness to the object of his mission? Was she not saying the truth? Were they not the servants of the most high God? And were they not showing the way of salvation? Why be grieved with—why silence such a witness? Because it was of Satan; and, most assuredly, the apostle was not going to receive testimony from him. He could not allow Satan to help him in his work. True, he might have walked about the streets of Philippi owned and honored as a servant of God, if only he had consented to let the devil have a hand in the work. But Paul could never consent to this. He could never suffer the enemy to mix himself up with the work of the Lord. Had he done so, it would have given the deathblow to the testimony at Philippi. To have permitted Satan to put his hand to the work, would have involved the total shipwreck of the mission to Macedonia.

It is deeply important for the Lord's workman to weigh this matter. We may rest assured that this narrative of the damsel has been written for our instruction. It is not only a statement of what has occurred, but a sample of what may and indeed what does occur every day.*

Besides, christendom is full of false profession. There are multitudes of false professors at this moment, throughout the wide domain of Christian profession. It is sad to have to say it, but so it is, and we must press the fact upon the attention of the

---

* An evangelist will not travel far in our day to find persons who will take him warmly by the hand, and profess lively interest in his work. A moment's intercourse with them, however, will disclose them to be agents of "Christian Science," of "Millennial Dawn," of "Seventh Day Adventism," or of some one or other of like systems—messengers of Satan, all professing Christianity, though in reality destroyers of it; pluming themselves with its name, only to get inside and work destruction the more easily. [ED.]

reader. We are surrounded, on all sides, by those who give a merely nominal assent to the truths of the Christian religion. They go on, from week to week, and from year to year, professing to believe certain things which they do not in reality believe at all. There are thousands who, every Lord's Day, profess to believe in the forgiveness of sins, and yet, were such persons to be examined, it would be found that they either do not think about the matter at all, or, if they do think, they deem it the very height of presumption for any one to be sure that his sins are forgiven.

This is very serious. Only think of a person standing up in the presence of God and saying, "I believe in the forgiveness of sins," and all the while he does not believe any such thing! Can anything be more hardening to the heart, or more deadening to the conscience than this? It is our firm persuasion that the forms and the formularies of professing Christianity are doing more to ruin precious souls than all the forms of moral pravity put together. It is perfectly appalling to contemplate the countless multitudes that are at this moment rushing along the well-trodden highway of religious profession, down to the eternal flames of hell. We feel bound to raise a warning note. We want the reader most solemnly to take heed as to this matter.

We have only instanced one special formulary, because it refers to a subject of very general interest and importance. How few, comparatively, are clear and settled as to the question of forgiveness of sins! How few are able, calmly, decidedly, and intelligently, to say, "*I know* that my sins are forgiven!" How few are in the real enjoyment of full forgiveness of sins, through faith in that precious blood that cleanseth from all sins! How solemn, therefore, to hear people giving utterance to such words as these, "I believe in the forgiveness of sins," while, in fact, they do not believe their own very utterance!

Is the reader in the habit of using such a form of words? Does he believe it? Say, are *thy* sins forgiven? Art thou washed in the precious atoning blood of Christ? If not, why not? The way is open. There is no hindrance.

Thou art perfectly welcome, this moment, to the free benefits of the atoning work of Christ. Though thy sins be as scarlet; though they be black as midnight, black as hell; though they rise like a dreadful mountain before the vision of thy troubled soul, and threaten to sink thee into eternal perdition; yet do these words shine with divine and heavenly lustre on the page of inspiration, "*The blood of Jesus Christ, God's Son, cleanseth us from all sin*" (1 John 1:7).

But mark, friend, do not go on, week after week, mocking God, hardening thine own heart, and carrying out the schemes of the great enemy of Christ, by a false profession. This marks the damsel possessed by a spirit of divination, and here her history links itself with the present awful condition of christendom. What was the burden of her song, during those "many days" in the which the apostle narrowly considered her case? "These men are the servants of the most high God, which *show unto us* the way of salvation." But she was not saved—she was not delivered—she was, all the while, under Satan's power herself.

Thus it is with christendom—thus it is with each false professor throughout the length and breadth of the professing Church. We know of nothing, even in the deepest depths of moral evil, or in the darkest shades of heathenism, more truly awful than the state of careless, hardened, self-satisfied, fallow-ground professors, who on each successive Lord's Day give utterance, either in their prayers or their singing, to words which, so far as they are concerned, are wholly false.

The thought of this is, at times, almost overwhelming. We cannot dwell upon it. It is really too sorrowful. We shall therefore pass on, having once more solemnly warned the reader against every shade and degree of false profession. Let him not say or sing aught that he does not heartily believe. The devil is at the bottom of all false profession, and by means thereof he seeks to bring discredit on the work of the Lord.

But how truly refreshing to contemplate the actings of the faithful apostle in the case of the damsel. Had he been seeking his own ends, or had he been merely a minister of religion, he might have welcomed her words as a tributary stream to swell the tide of his popularity, or promote the interest of his cause. But Paul was not a mere minister of religion; he was a minister of Christ—a totally different thing. And we may notice that the damsel does not say a word about Christ. She breathes not the precious, peerless name of Jesus. There is total silence as to Him. This stamps the whole thing as of Satan. "No man can call Jesus Lord but by the Holy Ghost." People may speak of God, and of religion; but Christ has no place in their hearts. The Pharisees, in the ninth of John, could say to the poor man, "Give God the praise"; but in speaking of Jesus, they could say, "This man is a sinner."

Thus it is ever in the case of corrupt religion, or false profession. Thus it was with the damsel in Acts 16. There was not a syllable about Christ. There was no truth, no life, no reality. It was hollow and false. It was of Satan; and hence Paul would not and could not own it; he was grieved with it and utterly rejected it.

Would that all were like him! Would that there were the singleness of eye to detect, and the integrity of heart to reject the work of Satan in much that is going on around us! Such an eye Paul, through grace, possessed. He was not to be deceived. He saw that the whole affair was an effort of Satan to mix himself up with the work, that thus he might spoil it altogether. "But Paul, being grieved, turned and said to the spirit, I command thee, in the name of Jesus Christ, to come out of her. And he came out the same hour."

This was true spiritual action. Paul was not in any haste to come into collision with the evil one, or even to pronounce upon the case at all; he waited many days; but the very moment that the enemy was detected he is resisted and repulsed with uncompromising decision. A less spiritual workman might have allowed the thing to pass, under the idea that it might turn to account and help forward the work. Paul thought differently; and he was right. He would take no help from Satan. He was not going to work by such an agency; and hence, in the name of Jesus

Christ—that name which the enemy so sedulously excluded—he puts Satan to flight.

But no sooner was Satan repulsed as the serpent, than he assumed the character of a lion. Craft having failed, he tried violence. "And when her masters saw that the hope of their gains was gone, they caught Paul and Silas and drew them into the market-place unto the rulers, and brought them to the magistrates, saying, These men, being Jews, do exceedingly trouble our city, and teach customs which are not lawful for us to receive, neither to observe, being Romans. And the multitude rose up together against them; and the magistrates rent off their clothes, and commanded to beat them. And when they had laid many stripes upon them, they cast them into prison, charging the jailor to keep them safely" (Acts 16:19-23).

Thus the enemy seemed to triumph; but be it remembered that Christ's warriors gain their most splendid victories by apparent defeat. The devil made a great mistake when he cast the apostle into prison. Indeed it is consolatory to reflect that he has never done anything else but make mistakes, from the moment that he left his first estate down to the present moment. His entire history, from beginning to end, is one tissue of errors.

And thus, as has been already remarked, the devil made a great mistake when he cast Paul into prison at Philippi. To nature's view it might have seemed otherwise; but in the judgment of faith, the servant of Christ was much more in his right place in prison for the truth's sake, than outside at his Master's expense. True, Paul might have saved himself. He might have been an honored man, owned and acknowledged as "a servant of the most high God," if he had only accepted the damsel's testimony, and suffered the devil to help him in his work. But he could not do this, and hence he had to suffer. "And the multitude [ever fickle and easily swayed] rose up together against them: and the magistrates rent off their clothes, and commanded to beat them. And when they had laid many stripes upon them, they cast them into prison, charging the jailor to keep them safely. Who, having received such a charge, *thrust* them into the inner prison, and made their feet fast in the stocks" (ver. 22-24).

Here, then, some might have said, was an end to the work of the evangelist in the city of Philippi. Here was an effectual stop to the preaching. Not so; the prison was the very place, at the moment, for the evangelist. His work was there. He was to find a congregation within the prison walls which he could not have found outside. But this leads us, in the third and last place, to the case of *the hardened sinner.*

It was very unlikely that the jailor would ever have found his way to the prayer-meeting at the river side. He had little care for such things. He was neither an earnest seeker, nor a deceiver. He was a hardened sinner, pursuing a very hardening occupation. Jailors, from the occupation of their office, are, generally speaking, hard and stern men. No doubt there are exceptions. There are some tender-hearted men to be found in such situations; but, as a rule, jailors are not tender. It would hardly suit them to be so. They have to do with the very worst class of society. Much of the crime of the whole country comes under their notice; and many of the criminals come under their charge. Accustomed to the rough and the course, they are apt to become rough and coarse themselves.

Now, judging from the inspired narrative before us, we may well question if the Philippian jailor was an exception to the general rule with respect to men of his class. Certainly he does not seem to have shown much tenderness to Paul and Silas. "He *thrust* them into the *inner* prison, and made their feet *fast* in the stocks." He seems to have gone to the utmost extreme in making them uncomfortable.

But God had rich mercy in store for that poor, hardened, cruel jailor; and, as it was not at all likely that he would go to hear the gospel, the Lord sent the gospel to him; and, moreover, He made the devil the instrument of sending it. Little did the jailor know whom he was thrusting into the inner prison—little did he anticipate what was to happen ere another sun should rise. And we may add, little did the devil think of what he was doing

when he sent the preachers of the gospel into jail, there to be the means of the jailor's conversion. But the Lord Jesus Christ knew what He was about to do, in the case of a poor hardened sinner. He can make the wrath of man to praise Him and restrain the remainder.

> He everywhere hath sway,
> And all things serve His might,
> His ev'ry act pure blessing is,
> His path unsullied light.
>
> When He makes bare His arm,
> Who shall His work withstand?
> When He His people's cause defends,
> Who then shall stay His hand?

It was His purpose to save the jailor; and so far from Satan's being able to frustrate that purpose, he was actually made the instrument of accomplishing it. "God's purpose shall stand; and He will do all His pleasure." And where He sets His love upon a poor, wretched, guilty sinner, He will have him in Heaven, spite of all the malice and rage of hell.

As to Paul and Silas, it is very evident that they were in their right place in the prison. They were there *for the truth's sake*, and therefore *the Lord was with them.* Hence they were perfectly happy. What, though they were confined within the gloomy walls of the prison, with their feet made fast in the stocks, prison walls could not confine their spirits. Nothing can hinder the joy of one who has the Lord with him. Shadrach, Meshach, and Abednego, were happy in the fiery furnace. Daniel was happy in the lions' den; and Paul and Silas were happy in the dungeon of Philippi: "And at midnight Paul and Silas prayed, and sang praises to God: and the prisoners heard them."

What sounds to issue from the inner prison! We may safely say that no such sounds had ever issued thence before. Curses and execrations and blasphemous words might have been heard; sighs, cries, and groans come forth from those walls. But to hear the accents of prayer and praise, ascending at the midnight hour, must have seemed strange indeed. Faith can sing as sweetly in a dungeon as at a prayer-meeting.

It matters not where we are, provided always that we have God with us. His presence lights up the darkest cell, and turns a dungeon into the very gate of Heaven. He can make His servants happy anywhere, and give them victory over the most adverse circumstances, and cause them to shout for joy in scenes where nature would be overwhelmed with sorrow.

But the Lord had His eye upon the jailor. He had written his name in the Lamb's book of life before the foundation of the world, and He was now about to lead him into the full joy of His salvation. "And suddenly there was a great earthquake, so that the foundations of the prison were shaken: and immediately all the doors were opened, and every one's bands were loosed" (ver. 26).

Now if Paul had not been in full communion with the mind and heart of Christ, he would assuredly have turned to Silas and said, "Now is the moment for us to make our escape. God has most manifestly appeared for us, and set before us an open door. If ever there was an opening of divine Providence surely this is one." But no; Paul knew better. He was in the full current of His blessed Master's thoughts, and in full sympathy with his Master's heart. Hence he made no attempt to escape. The claims of *truth* had brought him into prison; the activities of *grace* kept him there. Providence opened the door; but faith refused to walk out. People talk of being guided by Providence; but if Paul had been so guided, the jailor would never have been a jewel in his crown.

"And the keeper of the prison awaking out of his sleep and seeing the prison doors open, he drew out his sword, and would have killed himself, supposing that the prisoners had been fled" (ver. 27). This proves, very plainly, that the earthquake, with all its attendant circumstances, had not touched the heart of the jailor. He naturally supposed, when he saw the doors open, that the prisoners were all gone. He could not imagine a number of prisoners sitting quietly in jail when the doors lay open and their chains were loosed. And then what was to become of him if the prisoners were gone? How could he face the authorities? Impossible. Anything

but that. Death, even by his own hand, was preferable to that.

Thus the devil had conducted this hardened sinner to the very brink of the precipice, and he was about to give him the final and fatal push over the edge, and down to the eternal flames of hell; when lo, a voice of love sounded in his ear. It was the voice of Jesus through the lips of His servant—a voice of tender and deep compassion—"*Do thyself no harm.*"

This was irresistible. A hardened sinner could meet an earthquake; he could meet death itself; but he could not withstand the mighty melting power of love. The hardest heart must yield to the moral influence of love. "Then he called for a light, and sprang in, and came *trembling*, and fell down before Paul and Silas, and brought them out, and said, Sirs, what must I do to be saved?" Love can break the hardest heart. And surely there was love in those words, "Do thyself no harm," coming from the lips of one to whom he had done so much harm a few hours before.

Be it noted, there was not a single syllable of reproach, or even of reflection, uttered by Paul to the jailor. This was Christ-like. It was the way of divine grace. If we look through the Gospels, we never find the Lord casting reproach upon the sinner. He has tears of sorrow; He has touching words of grace and tenderness; but no reproaches—no reflections—no reproach to the poor distressed sinner. We cannot attempt to furnish the many illustrations and proofs of this assertion; but the reader has only to turn to the gospel story to see its truth. Look at the prodigal; look at the thief. Not one reproving word to either.

Thus it is in every case; and thus it was with God's Spirit in Paul. Not a word about the harsh treatment—the thrusting into the inner prison—not a word about the stocks. "Do thyself no harm." And then, "Believe on the Lord Jesus Christ, and thou shalt be saved, and thy house."

Such is the rich and precious grace of God. It shines, in this scene, with uncommon lustre. It delights in taking up hardened sinners, melting and subduing their hard hearts, and leading them into the sunlight of a full salvation; and all this in a style peculiar to itself. Yes, God has His style of doing things, blessed be His name; and when He saves a wretched sinner, He does it after such a fashion as fully proves that His whole heart is in the work. It is His joy to save a sinner—even the very chief—and He does it in a way worthy of Himself.

Let us look at the fruit of all this. The jailor's conversion was most unmistakable. Saved from the very brink of hell, he was brought into the very atmosphere of heaven. Preserved from self-destruction, he was brought into the circle of God's salvation; and the evidences of this were as clear as could be desired. "And they spake unto him the Word of the Lord, and to all that were in his house. And he took them the same hour of the night, and washed their stripes; and was baptized, he and all his straightway. And when he had brought them into his house, he set meat before them, and rejoiced, *believing in God, with all his house.*"

What a marvelous change! The ruthless jailor has become the generous host! "If any man be in Christ, he is a new creature; old things are passed away: behold, all things are become new." How clearly we can now see that Paul was right in not being guided by *providences!* How much better and higher to be led by the "eye" of God! What an eternal loss it would have proved to him had he walked out at the open door! How much better to be conducted out by the very hand that had thrust him in—a hand once the instrument of cruelty and sin, now the instrument of righteousness and love! What a magnificent triumph! What a scene, altogether!

How little had the devil anticipated such a result from the imprisonment of the Lord's servants! He was thoroughly outwitted. The tables were completely turned upon him. He thought to hinder the gospel, and, behold! he was made to help it on. He had hoped to get rid of two of Christ's servants, and, lo! he lost one of his own. Christ is stronger than Satan; and all who put their trust in Him and move in the current of His thoughts shall most assuredly share in the triumphs of His grace now, and shine in the brightness of His glory forever.

Thus much, then, as to "the work of an evangelist." Such are the scenes through which he may have to pass—such the cases with which he may have to come in contact. We have seen the earnest seeker satisfied; the deceiver silenced; the hardened sinner saved. May all who go forth with the gospel of the grace of God know how to deal with the various types of character that may cross their path! May many be raised up to do the work of an evangelist!

LETTERS TO AN EVANGELIST

Letter 1

I HAVE BEEN MUCH INTERESTED, and I trust profited, of late, by tracing, through the Gospels and the Acts, the various notices of the work of evangelization; and it has occurred to me that it may not be amiss to present to you, as one much occupied in the blessed work, a few of the thoughts that have suggested themselves to my mind. I shall feel myself much more free in this way, than if I were writing a formal treatise.

First of all, I have been greatly struck with the simplicity with which the work of evangelizing was carried on in primitive times; so very unlike a great deal of what obtains among us. It seems to me that we moderns are quite too much hampered by conventional rules—too much fettered by the habits of christendom. We are sadly deficient in what I may call spiritual elasticity. We are apt to think that in order to evangelize there must be a special gift; and even where there is this special gift, there must be a great deal of machinery and human arrangement. When we speak of doing the work of an evangelist, we, for the most part, have before our minds great public halls, and crowded audiences, for which there is a demand for considerable gift and power for speaking.

Now you and I thoroughly believe, that in order to preach the gospel publicly, there must be a special gift from the Head of the Church; and, moreover, we believe according to Eph. 4:11, that Christ has given, and does still give, "evangelists." This is clear, if we are to be guided by Scripture. But I find in the Gospels, and in the Acts of the Apostles, that a quantity of most blessed evangelistic work was done by persons who were not specially gifted at all, but who had an earnest love for souls, and a deep sense of the preciousness of Christ and His salvation. And, what is more, I find in those who were specially gifted, called, and appointed by Christ to preach the gospel, a simplicity, freedom, and naturalness in their mode of working, which I greatly covet for myself and for all my brethren.

Let us look a little into Scripture. Take that lovely scene in John 1:36-45. John pours out his heart in testimony to Jesus: "Behold the Lamb of God!" His soul was absorbed with the glorious Object. What was the result? "Two disciples heard him speak, and they followed Jesus." What then? "One of the two which heard John speak, and followed Him, was Andrew, Simon Peter's brother." And what does he do? "*He first findeth his own brother* Simon, and saith unto him, We have found the Messias, which is, being interpreted, the Christ. And he brought him to Jesus." Again, "The day following, Jesus would go forth into Galilee, and findeth Philip, and saith unto him, Follow Me . . . *Philip findeth Nathanael,* and saith unto him, We have found Him, of whom Moses in the law, and the prophets, did write, Jesus of Nazareth, the son of Joseph . . .*Come and see.*"

Here then, is the style of thing for which I earnestly long: this individual work, this laying hold of the first man that comes in our way, this finding one's own brother, and bringing him to Jesus. I do feel we are deficient in this. It is all right enough to gather congregations, and address them, as God gives ability and opportunity. I would not pen a single word to detract from the value of such a line of work. By all means hire rooms, halls, and theatres; put out bills inviting people to come; leave no lawful means untried to spread the gospel. Seek to get at souls as best you can. Far be it from me to cast a damp upon any who are seeking to carry on the work in this public way.

But does it not strike you that we want more of the individual work? more of the private, earnest, personal dealing with souls? Do you not think that if we had more "Philips" we should have more "Nathanaels"? If we had more "Andrews," we should have more "Simons"? I cannot but believe it. There is amazing power in an earnest personal appeal. Do you not often find that it is after the more formal public preaching is finished, and the close personal work begins, that souls are reached? How is it then that there is so little of this latter? Does it not often happen at our public preachings, that when the formal address is delivered, a hymn sung, and a word of prayer offered, all disperse without any attempt at individual work?

I speak not now, mark you, of the preacher—who cannot possibly reach every case, but of the scores of Christians who have been listening to him. They have seen strangers enter the room, they have sat beside them; they have, it may be, noticed their interest, seen the tear stealing down the cheek; and yet they have let them pass away without a single loving effort to reach them, or to follow up the good work.

No doubt it may be said, "It is much better to allow the Spirit of God to follow up His own Work. We may do more harm than good. And besides, people do not like to be spoken to: they will look upon it as an impertinent intrusion, and they will be driven away from the place altogether." There is considerable weight in all this. I fully appreciate it; and I am sure you do likewise. I fear great blunders are committed by injudicious persons intruding upon the sacred privacy of the soul's deep and holy exercises. It needs tact and judgment; in short, it needs direct spiritual guidance to be able to deal with souls; to know whom to speak to, and what to say.

But allowing all this, as we do in the fullest possible manner, there is, as a rule, something lacking in connection with our public preachings. Is there not a want of that deep, personal, loving interest in souls which will express itself in a thousand ways that act powerfully on the heart? I confess that I have often been pained by what has come under my own notice in our preaching-rooms. Strangers come in and are left to find a seat wherever they can. No one seems to think of them. Christians are there, and they will hardly move to make room for them. No one offers them a Bible or hymn-book. And when the preaching is over, they are allowed to go as they came; not a loving word of inquiry as to whether they enjoyed the truth preached; not even a kindly look which might win confidence and invite conversation. On the contrary, there is a chilling reserve, amounting almost to repulsiveness.

All this is very sorrowful; and perhaps you will tell me that I am drawing too highly colored a picture. Alas! the picture is only too true. And what makes it all the more deplorable is, that one knows as a fact that many persons frequent our preaching-rooms and lecture-halls in the deepest exercise, and they are only longing to open their hearts to some one who could offer them a little spiritual counsel; but through timidity, reserve, or nervousness, they shrink from making any advance, and have but to retire to their homes and to their bedchambers, lonely and sad, there to weep in solitude because no man cares for their precious souls. Now I feel persuaded that much of this might be remedied if those Christians who attend the gospel preachings were more *on the look out* for souls: if they would attend, not so much for their own profit, as in order to be co-workers with God, in seeking to bring souls to Jesus.

No doubt it is very refreshing to Christians to hear the gospel fully and faithfully preached. But it would not be the less refreshing because they were intensely interested in the conversion of souls, and in earnest prayer to God in the matter. Besides, it could in no wise interfere with their personal enjoyment and profit to cultivate and manifest a lively and loving interest in those who surround them, and to seek at the close of the meeting to help any who may need and desire to be helped. It has a surprising effect upon the preacher, upon the preaching, upon the whole meeting, when the Christians who attend are really entering into, and discharging, their high and holy responsibilities to Christ and to souls. It imparts a certain tone and creates a certain atmosphere which must be felt in order to be understood; but when once felt it cannot easily be dispensed with.

But, alas, how often is it otherwise! How cold, how dull, how dispiriting is it at times to see the whole congregation clear out the moment the preaching is over! No loving, lingering groups gathering round young converts or anxious inquirers. Old experienced Christians have been present; but, instead of pausing with the fond hope that God would graciously use them to speak a word in season to him that is weary, they hasten away as though it were a matter of life and death that they should be home at a certain hour.

Do not suppose that I wish to lay down rules for my brethren. Far be the thought. I am merely, in the freest possible manner, pouring out the thoughts of my heart to one with whom I have been linked in the work of the gospel for many years. I feel convinced there is a something lacking. It is my firm persuasion that no Christian is in a right condition, if he is not seeking in some way to bring souls to Christ. And, on the same principle, no assembly of Christians is in a right condition if it be not a thoroughly evangelistic assembly. We should all be on the lookout for souls; and then we may rest assured we should see soul-stirring results. But if we are satisfied to go on from week to week, month to month, and year to year, without a single leaf stirring, without a single conversion, our state must be truly lamentable.

But I think I hear you saying, "Where is all the Scripture we were to have had? where the many quotations from the Gospels and the Acts?" Well, I have gone on jotting down the thoughts which have for some considerable time occupied my mind. But if you so desire, I shall write you a second letter on the subject. Meanwhile, may the Lord, by His Spirit, make us more earnest in seeking the salvation of immortal souls, by every legitimate agency. May our hearts be filled with genuine love for precious souls, and then we shall be sure to find ways and means of getting at them!

Letter 2

There is one point in connection with our subject which has much occupied my mind; and that is, the immense importance of cultivating an earnest faith in the presence and action of the Holy Ghost. We want to remember, at all times, that we can do nothing, and that God the Holy Ghost can do all. It holds good in the great work of evangelization, as in all beside, that it is "not by might, nor by power, but by My Spirit, saith the Lord of hosts." The abiding sense of this would keep us humble, and yet full of joyful confidence. Humble, because we can do nothing; full of joyful confidence, because God can do all. Moreover, it would have the effect of keeping us very sober and quiet in our work—not cold and indifferent, but calm and serious, which is a great matter just now. I was much struck with a remark lately made by an aged workman, in a letter to one who had just entered the field. "Excitement," says this writer, "is not power, but weakness. Earnestness and energy are of God."

This is most true and most valuable. But I like the two sentences taken together. If we were to take either apart, I think you and I would prefer the latter; and for this reason: there are many, I fear, who would regard as "excitement" what you and I might really consider to be "earnestness and energy." Now I do confess, I love a deep-toned earnestness in the work. I do not see how a man can be otherwise than deeply and thoroughly in earnest, who realizes in any measure the awfulness of eternity, and the state of all those who die in their sins. How is it possible for any one to think of an immortal soul standing on the very brink of hell, and in danger at any moment of being dashed over, and not be serious and earnest?

But this is not excitement. What I understand by excitement is the working up of mere nature, and the putting forth of such efforts of nature as are designed to work on the natural feelings—all high pressure—all that is merely sensational. This is all worthless. It is evanescent. And not only so, but it superinduces weakness. We never find aught of this in the ministry of our blessed Lord or His apostles: and yet what earnestness! what untiring energy! what tenderness! We see an earnestness which wore the appearance of being beside oneself; an energy which hardly afforded a moment for rest or refreshment; and a tenderness which could weep over impenitent sinners. All this we see; but no excitement. In a word, all was the fruit of the Eternal Spirit; and all was to the glory of God. Moreover, there was ever that calmness and solemnity which becomes the presence of God, and yet that deep earnestness which proves that man's serious condition was fully realized.

Now, dear brother, this is precisely what we want, and what we ought diligently to cultivate. It is a signal mercy to be kept from all merely natural excitement; and, at the same time, to be duly impressed with the magnitude and solemnity of the work. Thus the mind will be kept properly balanced, and we shall be preserved from the tendency to be occupied with *our* work merely because it is ours. We shall rejoice that Christ is magnified, and souls are saved, whoever be the instrument used.

I have been thinking a good deal lately of that memorable time, now exactly ten years ago, when the Spirit of God wrought so marvelously in the province of Ulster. I think I gathered up some valuable instruction from what then came under my notice. That was a time never to be forgotten by those who were privileged to be eyewitnesses of the magnificent wave of blessing which rolled over the land. But I now refer to it in connection with the subject of the Spirit's action. I have no doubt whatever that the Holy Ghost was grieved and hindered in the year 1859, by man's interference.

You remember how that work began. you remember the little school-house by the road side, where two or three men met, week after week, to pour out their hearts in prayer to God, that He would be pleased to break in upon the death and darkness which reigned around: and that He revive His work, and send out His light and His truth in converting power. You know how these prayers were heard and answered. You and I were privileged to move through these soul-stirring scenes in the province of Ulster; and I doubt not the memory of them is fresh with you, as it is with me, this day.

Well, what was the special character of that work in its earlier stages? Was it not most manifestly a work of God's Spirit? Did not He take up and use instruments the most unfit and unfurnished, according to human thinking, for the accomplishment of His gracious purpose? Do we not remember the style and character of the agents who were chiefly used in the conversion of souls? Were they not for the most part "unlearned and ignorant men?"

Further, can we not distinctly recall the fact that there was a most decided setting aside of all human arrangement and official routine? Working men came from the field, the factory, and the workshop, to address crowded audiences; and we have seen hundreds hanging in breathless interest upon the lips of men who could not speak five words of good grammar. In short, the mighty tide of spiritual life and power rolled in upon us, and swept away for the time being a quantity of human machinery, and ignored all question of man's authority in the things of God and the service of Christ.

Now we can well remember, that just in so far as the Holy Ghost was owned and honored, did the glorious work progress; and, on the other hand, in proportion as man intruded himself, in bustling self-importance, upon the domain of the Eternal Spirit, was the work hindered and quashed. I saw the truth of this illustrated in numberless cases. There was a vigorous effort made to cause the living water to flow in official and denominational channels, and this the Holy Ghost would not sanction. Moreover, there was a strong desire manifested, in many quarters, to make sectarian capital out of the

blessed movement; and this the Holy Ghost resented.

Nor was this all. The work and the workman were *lionized* in all directions. Cases of conversion which were judged to be "striking" were blazed abroad and paraded in the public prints. Travelers and tourists from all parts visited these persons, took notes of their words and ways, and wafted the report of them to the ends of the earth. Many poor creatures, who had up to that time lived in obscurity, unknown and unnoticed, found themselves, all of a sudden, objects of interest to the wealthy, the noble, and the public at large. The pulpit and the press proclaimed their sayings and doings; and, as might be expected, they completely lost their balance. Knaves and hypocrites abounded on all hands.

It became a grand point to have some strange and extravagant experience to tell; some remarkable dream or vision to relate. And even where this ill-advised line of action did not issue in producing knavery and hypocrisy, the young converts became heady and high-minded, and looked with a measure of contempt upon old established Christians, or those who did not happen to be converted after their peculiar fashion—"stricken," as it was termed.

In addition to this, some very remarkable characters—men of desperate notoriety, who seemed to be converted, were conveyed from place to place and placarded about the various streets, and crowds gathered to see them and hear them recount their history; which history was very frequently a disgusting detail of immoralities and excesses which ought never to have been named. Several of these remarkable men afterwards broke down, and returned with increased ardor to their former practices.

These things I witnessed in various places. I believe the Holy Ghost was grieved and hindered, and the work marred thereby. I am thoroughly convinced of this: and hence it is that I think we should earnestly seek to honor the blessed Spirit; to lean upon Him in all our work; to follow where He leads, not run before Him. His work will stand: "Whatsoever God doeth it shall be forever." "The works that are done upon the earth, He is the doer of them." The remembrance of this will ever keep the mind well balanced. There is great danger of young workmen getting so excited about *their* work, *their* preaching, *their* gifts, as to lose sight of the blessed Master Himself. Moreover, they are apt to make preaching the *end* instead of the *means*. This works badly in every way. It injures themselves, and it mars their work.

The moment I make preaching my end, I am out of the current of the mind of God, whose end is to glorify Christ; and I am out of the current of the heart of Christ, whose end is the salvation of souls, and the full blessing of His Church. But where the Holy Ghost gets His proper place, where He is duly owned and trusted, there all will be right. There will be no exaltation of man; no bustling self-importance; no parading of the fruits of our work; no excitement. All will be calm, quiet, real, and unpretending. There will be the simple, earnest, believing, patient waiting upon God. Self will be in the shade; Christ will be exalted.

I often recall a sentence of yours. I remember your once saying to me, "Heaven will be the best and safest place to hear the results of our work." This is a wholesome word for all workmen. I shudder when I see the names of Christ's servants paraded in the public journals, with flattering allusion to their work and its fruits. Surely those who pen such articles ought to reflect upon what they are doing: they should consider that they may be ministering to the very thing which they ought to desire to see mortified and subdued. I am most fully persuaded that the quiet, shady, retired path is the best and safest for the Christian workman. It will not make him less earnest but the contrary. It will not cramp his energy, but increase and intensify it.

God forbid that you or I should pen a line or utter a sentence which might in the most remote way tend to discourage or hinder a single worker in all the vineyard of Christ. No, this is not the moment for aught of this kind. We want to see the Lord's laborers thoroughly in earnest; but we believe, most assuredly, that true earnestness will ever result from the most absolute dependence upon God the Holy Ghost.

But only see how I have run on! And yet I have not referred to those passages of Scriptures of which I spoke in my last. Well, dearly beloved in the Lord , I am addressing one who is happily familiar with the Gospels and Acts, and who therefore knows that the great Workman Himself, and all those who sought to tread in His blessed footsteps, owned and honored the Eternal Spirit as the One by whom all their works were to be wrought.

I must now close for the present, my much loved brother and fellow-laborer; and I do so with a full heart, commending you, in spirit and soul and body, to Him who has loved us, and washed us from our sins in His own blood, and called us to the honored post of workers, in His gospel field. May He bless you and yours, most abundantly, and increase your usefulness a thousandfold!

Letter 3

There is another point which stands intimately connected with the subject of my last letter, and that is, the place the Word of God occupies in the work of evangelization. In my last letter, as you will remember, I referred to the work of the Holy Ghost, and the immense importance of giving Him His proper place. How clearly the precious Word of God is connected with the action of the Holy Spirit, I need not say. Both are inseparably linked in those memorable words of our Lord to Nicodemus—words so little understood—so sadly misapplied: "Except a man be born of water and of the Spirit, he cannot enter into the kingdom of God" (John 3).

Now, you and I, fully believe that in the above passage the Word is presented under the figure of "water." Thank God, we are not disposed to give any credit to the ritualistic absurdity of baptismal regeneration. We are, I believe, most thoroughly convinced that no one ever did, ever will, or ever could, get life by water baptism. That all who believe in Christ ought to be baptized we fully admit; but this is a totally different thing from the fatal error that substitutes an ordinance for the atoning death of Christ, the regenerating power of the Holy Ghost, and the life-giving virtues of the Word of God. I shall not waste your time or my own in combating this error, but at once assume that you agree with me in thinking that when our Lord speaks of being "born of water and of the Spirit," He refers to the Word and the Holy Ghost.

Thus, then, the Word is the grand instrument to be used in the work of evangelization. Many passages of holy Scripture establish this point with such clearness and decision as to leave no room whatever for dispute. In the first chapter of James, ver. 18, we read, "Of His own will begat He us *with the word of truth.*" Again, in 1 Pet. 1:23, we read, "Being born again, not of corruptible seed, but of incorruptible, *by the word of God,* which liveth and abideth forever." I must quote the whole passage because of its immense importance in connection with our subject: "For all flesh is as grass, and all the glory of man as the flower of grass. The grass withereth, and the flower thereof falleth away; but the word of the Lord endureth forever. *And this is the word which by the gospel is preached unto you.*"

This last clause is of unspeakable value to the evangelist. It binds him, in the most distinct manner, to the Word of God as the instrument—the only instrument—the all-sufficient instrument, to be used in his glorious work. He is to give the Word to the people; and the more simply he gives it the better. The pure water should be allowed to flow from the heart of God to the heart of the sinner, without receiving a tinge from the channel through which it flows. The evangelist is to preach the Word; and he is to preach it in simple dependence upon the power of the Holy Ghost. This is the true secret of success in preaching.

But while I urge this great cardinal point in the work of preaching—and I believe it cannot be too strongly urged—I am very far indeed from thinking that the evangelist should give his hearers a quantity of truth. So far from this, I consider it a very great mistake. He ought to leave this to the teacher, lecturer, or pastor. I often fear that

very much of our preaching shoots over the heads of the people, owing to the fact of our seeking rather to unfold truth than to reach souls. We rest satisfied, it may be, with having delivered a very clear forcible lecture, a very interesting and instructive exposition of Scripture, something very valuable for the people of God; but the unconverted hearer has sat unmoved, unreached, unimpressed. There has been nothing for him. The lecturer has been more occupied with his lecture than with the sinner—more taken up with his subject than with the soul.

Now I am thoroughly convinced that this is a serious mistake, and one to which we all—at least I am—very apt to fall. I deplore it deeply and I earnestly desire to correct it. I question if this very mistake may not be viewed as the true secret of our lack of success. But I should not perhaps say "*our* lack" but *my* lack. I do not think—so far as I know aught of your ministry—that you are exactly chargeable with the defect to which I am now just referring. Of this, however, you will be the best judge yourself; but of one thing I am certain, namely, that the most successful evangelist is the one who keeps his eye fixed on the sinner, who has his heart bent on the salvation of souls, yea, the one with whom the love for precious souls amounts almost to a passion. It is not the man who unfolds the most truth, but the man who longs most after souls, that will have the most seals to his ministry.

I assert all this, mark you, in the full and clear recognition of the fact with which I commenced this letter, namely, that the Word is the grand instrument in the work of conversion. This fact must never be lost sight of, never weakened. It matters not what agency may be used to make the furrow, or in what form the Word may clothe itself, or by what vehicle it may be conveyed; it is only by "the Word of truth" that souls are begotten.

All this is divinely true, and we would ever bear it in mind. But do we not often find that persons who undertake to preach the gospel (particularly if they continue long in one place) are very apt to leave the domain of the evangelist—most blessed domain!—and travel into that of the teacher and lecturer? This is what I deprecate and deeply deplore. I know I have erred in this way myself, and I mourn over the error. I write in all loving freedom to you—the Lord has of late deepened immensely in my soul the sense of the vast importance of earnest gospel preaching. I do not—God forbid that I should—think the less of the work of a teacher or pastor. I believe that wherever there is a heart that loves Christ, it will delight to feed and tend the precious lambs and sheep of the flock of Christ, that flock which He purchased with His own blood.

But the sheep must be gathered before they can be fed; and how are they to be gathered but by the earnest preaching of the gospel? It is the grand business of the evangelist to go forth upon the dark mountains of sin and error, to sound the gospel trumpet and gather the sheep; and I feel convinced that he will best accomplish this work, not by elaborate exposition of truth; not by lectures however clear, valuable, and instructive; not by lovely unfoldings of prophetic, dispensational, or doctrinal truth—most precious and important in the right place—but by fervid, pointed, earnest dealing with immortal souls; the warning voice, the solemn appeal, the faithful reasoning of righteousness, temperance, and judgment to come—the awakening presentation of death and judgment, the dread realities of eternity, the lake of fire and the worm that never dies.

In short, it strikes me we want awakening preachers. I fully admit that there is such a thing as *teaching* the gospel, as well as *preaching* it. For example, I find Paul teaching the gospel in Rom. 1—8, just as I find him preaching the gospel in Acts 13 or 17. This is of the very last importance at all times, inasmuch as there are almost sure to be a number of what we call "exercised souls" at our public preachings, and these need an emancipating gospel—the full, clear, elevated, resurrection gospel.

But admitting all this, I still believe that what is needed for successful evangelization is not so much a great quantity of truth as an intense love for souls. Look at that eminent evangelist George Whitefield. What think

you was the secret of his success? No doubt you have looked into his printed sermons. Have you found any great breadth of truth in them? I question it. Indeed I must say I have been struck with the contrary. But oh! there was that in Whitefield which you and I may well covet and long to cultivate. There was a burning love for souls—a thirst for their salvation—a mighty grappling with the conscience—a bold, earnest, face-to-face dealing with men about their past ways, their present state, their future destiny.

There were the things that God owned and blessed; and He will own and bless them still. I am persuaded—I write as under the very eye of God—that if our hearts are bent upon the salvation of souls, God will use us in that divine and glorious work. But on the other hand, if we abandon ourselves to the withering influences of a cold, heartless, godless fatalism; if we content ourselves with a formal and official statement of the gospel—a very cheerless sort of thing; if, to use a vulgar phrase, our preaching is on the principle of "take it or leave it," need we wonder if we do not see conversions? The wonder would be if there were any to see.

No; I believe we want to look seriously into this great practical subject. It demands the solemn and dispassionate consideration of all who are engaged in the work. There are dangers on all sides. There are conflicting opinions on all sides. But I cannot conceive how any Christian man can be satisfied to shirk the responsibility of looking after souls. A man may say, "I am not an evangelist; that is not my line; I am more of a teacher, or a pastor." Well, I understand this; but will any one tell me that a teacher or pastor may not go forth in earnest longing after souls? I cannot admit it for a moment.

Nay more; it does not matter in the least what a man's gift is, or even though he should not possess any prominent gift at all, he can and ought, nevertheless, to cultivate a longing desire for the salvation of souls. Would it be right to pass a house on fire, without giving warning, even though one were not a member of the fire brigade? Should we not seek to save a drowning man, even though we could not command the use of a patent life-boat? Who in his senses would maintain aught so monstrous? So, in reference to souls, it is not so much a gift or knowledge of truth that is needed, as a deep and earnest longing for souls—a keen sense of their danger, and a desire for their rescue.

Letter 4

When I took up my pen to address you in my first letter, I had no idea that I should have occasion to extend the series to a fourth. However, the subject is one of intense interest to me; and there are just two or three points further on which I desire very briefly to touch.

In the first place I deeply feel our lack of a prayerful spirit in carrying on the work of evangelization. I have referred to the subject of the Spirit's work; and also to the place which God's Word ought ever to get; but it strikes me we are very deficient in reference to the matter of earnest, persevering, believing prayer. This is the true secret of power. "We," say the apostles, "will give ourselves continually to prayer and to the ministry of the Word."

Here is the order: "Prayer, and the ministry of the Word." Prayer brings in the power of God; and this is what we want. It is not the power of eloquence, but the power of God; and this can only be had by waiting upon Him. "He giveth power to the faint; and to them that have no might He increaseth strength. Even the youths shall faint and be weary, and the young men shall utterly fall: but they that wait upon the Lord shall renew their strength; they shall mount up with wings as eagles; they shall run, and not be weary; and they shall walk, and not faint" (Isa. 40:29-31).

It seems to me that we are far too mechanical, if I may so express myself, in the work. There is too much of what I may call going through a service. I greatly fear that some of us are more on our legs than on our knees; more in the railway carriage than in the closet; more on the road than in the sanctuary; more before men than before God. This will never do. It is impossible that our preaching can be marked by power and

crowned with results, if we fail in waiting upon God. Look at the blessed Master Himself—that great Workman. See how often He was found in prayer. At His baptism; at His tranfiguration; previous to the appointment and mission of the twelve. In short, again and again we find that blessed One in the attitude of prayer. At one time He rises up a great while before day, in order to give Himself to prayer. At another time He spends the whole night in prayer, because the day was given up to work.

What an example for us! May we follow it! May we know a little better what it is to agonize in prayer. How little we know of this!—I speak for myself. It sometimes appears to me as if we were so much taken up with preaching engagements that we have no time for prayer—no time for closet work—no time to be alone with God. We get into a sort of whirl of public work; we rush from place to place, from meeting to meeting, in a prayerless, barren condition of soul. Need we wonder at the little result? How could it be otherwise when we so fail in waiting upon God? *We* cannot convert souls—God alone can do this; and if we go on without waiting on Him, if we allow public preaching to displace private prayer, we may rest assured our preaching will prove barren and worthless. We really must "give ourselves to prayer" if we would succeed in the "ministry of the Word."

Nor is this all. It is not merely that we are lacking in the holy and blessed practice of private prayer. This is, alas! too true, as I have said. But there is more than this. We fail in our public meetings for prayer. The great work of evangelization is not sufficiently remembered in our prayer-meetings. It is not definitely, earnestly, and constantly kept before God in our public reunions. It may occasionally be introduced in a cursory, formal manner, and then dismissed. Indeed, I feel there is a great lack of earnestness and perseverance in our prayer-meetings generally, not merely as to the work of the gospel, but as to other things as well. There is frequently great formality and feebleness. We do not seem like men in earnest. We lack the spirit of the widow in Luke 18, who overcame the unjust judge by the bare force of her importunity. We seem to forget that God will be inquired of; and that He is a rewarder of them that diligently seek Him.

It is of no use for any one to say, "God can work without our earnest pleading; He will accomplish His purposes; He will gather out His own." We know all this; but we know also that He who has appointed the end has appointed the means; and if we fail in waiting on Him, He will get others to do His work. The work will be done, no doubt, but we shall lose the dignity, the privilege, and the reward of working. Is this nothing? Is it nothing to be deprived of the sweet privilege of being co-workers with God, of having fellowship with Him in the blessed work which He is carrying on? Alas! that we prize it so little. Still we do prize it; and perhaps there are few things in which we can more fully taste this privilege than in united earnest prayer. Here every saint can join. Here all can add their cordial Amen. All may not be preachers; but all can pray—all join in prayer; all can have fellowship.

And do you not find that there is always a stream of deep and real blessing where *the assembly* is drawn out in earnest prayer for the gospel, and for the salvation of souls? I have invariably seen it, and hence it is always a source of unspeakable comfort, joy, and encouragement to my heart when I see the assembly stirred up to pray, for then I am sure God is going to give copious showers of blessing.

Moreover, when this is the case, when this most excellent spirit pervades the whole assembly, you may be sure there will be no trouble as to what is called "the responsibility of the preaching." It will be all the same who does the work, provided it is done as well as it can be. If the assembly is waiting upon God, in earnest intercession for the progress of the work, it will not be a question as to the one who is to take the preaching, provided Christ is preached and souls are blessed.

Then there is another thing which has of late occupied my mind a good deal; and that is our method of dealing with young converts. Most surely there is immense need of care

and caution, lest we be found accrediting what is not the genuine work of God's Spirit at all. There is very great danger here. The enemy is ever seeking to introduce spurious materials into the assembly, in order that he may mar the testimony and bring discredit upon the truth of God.

All this is most true, and demands our serious consideration. But does it not seem to you that we often err on the other side? Do we not often, by a stiff and peculiar style, cast a chill upon young converts? Is there not frequently something repulsive in our spirit and deportment? We expect young Christians to come up to a standard of intelligence which has taken us years to attain. Nor this only. We sometimes put them through a process of examination which only tends to harass and perplex.

Now assuredly this is not right. The Spirit of God would never puzzle, perplex, or repulse a dear anxious inquirer—never, no never. It could never be according to the mind or heart of Christ to chill the spirit of the very feeblest lamb in all His blood-bought flock. He would have us seeking to lead them on gently and tenderly—to soothe, nourish, and cherish them, according to all the deep love of His heart. It is a great thing to lay ourselves out, and hold ourselves open to discern and appreciate the work of God in souls, and not to mar it by placing our own miserable crotchets as stumbling-blocks in their pathway.

We need divine guidance and help in this as much as in any other department of our work. But, blessed be God, He is sufficient for this as for all beside. Let us only wait on Him: let us cling to Him, and draw upon His exhaustless treasury for each case as it arises, for exigence of every hour. He will never fail a trusting, expectant, dependent heart.

I must now close this series of letters. I think I have touched most, if not all, of the points which I had in my mind. You will, I trust, bear in mind that I have, in all these letters, simply jotted down my thoughts in the utmost possible freedom, and in all the intimacy of true brotherly friendship. I have not been writing a formal treatise, but pouring out my heart to a beloved friend and yoke-fellow. This must be borne in mind by all who may read these letters.

May God bless and keep you. May He crown your labors with His richest and best blessing! May He keep you from every evil work, and preserve you unto His own everlasting kingdom!

Letter 5

It seems as though I must once more take up my pen to address you on certain matters connected with the work of evangelization, which have forced themselves upon my attention for some time past. There are three distinct branches of the work which I long to see occupying a far more definite and prominent place among us; and these are, the tract depot, the gospel preaching, and the Sunday-school.

It strikes me that the Lord is awakening attention to the importance of the tract depot as a valuable agency in the work of evangelization; but I question if we, on this side of the Atlantic, are thoroughly in earnest on the subject. How is this? Have books and tracts lost their interest and value in our eyes? Or does the fault lie in the mode of conducting our tract depots? To my mind there seems to be something lacking in reference to this matter.

I would fain see a well-conducted depot in every important town; by "well-conducted" I mean one taken up and carried on as a direct service to the Lord, in true love for souls, deep interest in the spread of the truth, and at the same time in a sound business way. I have known several depots fall to the ground through lack of business habits on the part of the conductors. They seemed very earnest, sincere persons, but quite unfit to conduct a business. In short, they were persons in whose hands any business would have fallen through. Then in many places there is the most deplorable failure as to the valuable and interesting work of conducting a depot.

How can we best reach the people for whom the tracts and books are prepared? I believe by having the books and tracts exposed for sale in a shop window, where

that is possible, so that people may see them as they pass, and step in and purchase what they want. Many a soul has been laid hold of in this way. Many, I doubt not, have been saved and blessed by means of tracts, seen for the first time in a shop window or arranged on a counter. But where there is no such opportunity, the assembly's meeting-room is the tract depot's natural home.

There is, manifestly, a real want of a tract depot in every large town, conducted by some one of intelligence and sound business habits, who would be able to speak to persons about the tracts, and to recommend such as might prove helpful to anxious inquirers after truth. In this way, I feel persuaded, much good might be done. The Christians in the town would know where to go for tracts, not only for their own personal reading, but also for general distribution. Surely if a thing is worth doing at all, it is worth doing well; and if the tract depot be not worth attending to, we know not what is.

The tract depot must be taken up in direct service to Christ. I feel assured that where it is so taken up and so carried on, in energy, zeal, and integrity, the Lord will own it and He will make it a blessing. Is there no one who will take up this valuable work for Christ's sake and not for the sake of remuneration? Is there no one who will enter upon it in simple faith, looking to the living God?

Here lies the root of the matter. For this branch of the work, as for every other branch, we need those who trust God and deny themselves. It seems to me that a grand point would be gained if the tract depot were placed on its proper footing, and viewed as an integral part of the evangelistic work, to be taken up in responsibility to the Lord and carried on in the energy of faith in the living God. Every branch of gospel work—the depot, the preaching, the Sunday-school— must be carried on in this way. It is all well and most valuable to have fellowship—full cordial fellowship, in all our service; but if we wait for fellowship and co-operation in the starting of work which comes within the range of personal, as well as collective, responsiblity, we shall find ourselves very much behind—or the work may not be done at all.

I shall have occasion to refer more particularly to this point, when I come to treat of the preaching and the Sunday-school. All I want now, is to establish the fact that the tract depot is a branch, and a most important and efficient branch, of evangelistic work. If this be thoroughly grasped by our friends, a great point is gained. I must confess to you that my moral sense has often been grievously offended by the cold, commercial style in which the publishing and sale of books and tracts are spoken of—a style befitting perhaps a mere commercial business, but most offensive when adopted in reference to the precious work of God.

I admit in the fullest way—nay, I actually contend for it—that the proper management of the depot demands good sound business habits, and upright business principles. But at the same time I am persuaded that the tract depot will never occupy its true ground—never realize the true idea, never reach the desired end—until it is firmly fixed on its holy basis, and viewed as an integral part of that most glorious work to which we are called—even the work of active, earnest, persevering evangelization.

And this work must be taken up in the sense of responsibility to Christ, and in the energy of faith in the living God. It will not do for an assembly of Christians, or some wealthy individual, to take up an inefficient protégé, and commit to such an one the management of the affair in order to afford a means of living. It is most blessed for all to have fellowship in the work; but I am thoroughly convinced that the work must be taken up in direct service to Christ, to be carried on in love for souls, and real interest in the spread of the truth.

Letter 6

I have, in some of the earlier letters of this series, dwelt upon the unspeakable importance of keeping up with zeal and constancy, a faithful preaching of the gospel—a distinct work of evangelization, carried on in the energy of love to precious souls, and with direct reference to the glory of Christ—a work bearing entirely upon the unconverted, and therefore quite distinct from the work of teaching, lecturing, or exhorting, in the bosom of the assembly; which latter is, I need not say, of equal importance in the mind of our Lord Christ.

My object in referring again to this subject is to call your attention to a point in connection with it, respecting which, it seems to me, there is a great want of clearness amongst some of our friends. I question if we are, as a rule, thoroughly clear as to the question of individual responsibility in the work of the gospel. I admit, of course, that the teacher or lecturer is called to exercise his gift, to a very great extent, on the same principle as the evangelist; that is, on his own personal responsibility to Christ; and that the assembly is not responsible for his individual services; unless indeed he teach unsound doctrine, in which case the assembly is bound to take it up.

But my business is with the work of the evangelist; and he is to carry on his work outside of the assembly. His sphere of action is the wide, wide world. "Go ye into all the world, and preach the gospel to every creature." Here is the sphere and here the object of the evangelist—"*All* the world"—"*Every* creature."

He may go forth from the bosom of the assembly, and return thither again laden with his golden sheaves; nevertheless he goes forth in the energy of personal faith in the living God, and on the ground of personal responsibility to Christ; nor is the assembly responsible for the peculiar *mode* in which he may carry on his work.

No doubt the assembly is called into action when the evangelist introduces the *fruit* of his work in the shape of souls professing to be converted, and desiring to be received into fellowship at the Lord's table. But this is another thing altogether, and must be kept distinct.

The evangelist must be left free: this is what I contend for. He must not be tied down to certain rules or regulations, nor cramped by special conventionalities. There are many things which a large-hearted evangelist will feel perfectly free to do which might not commend themselves to the spiritual judgment and feelings of some in the assembly; but, provided he does not traverse any vital or fundamental principle, such persons have no right to interfere with him.

When I use the expression, "spiritual judgment and feelings," I am taking the very highest possible view of the case, and treating the objector with the highest respect. I feel this is but right and proper. Every true man has a right to have his feelings and judgment—not to speak of conscience—treated with all due respect. There are, alas! everywhere, men of narrow mind, who object to everything that does not square with their own notions—men who would fain tie the evangelist down to the exact line of things and mode of acting which according to their thinking would suit the assembly of God's people when gathered for worship at the table of the Lord.

All this is a thorough mistake. The evangelist should pursue the even tenor of his way, regardless of all such narrowness and meddling. Take, for example, the matter of singing hymns. The evangelist may feel perfectly free to use a class of hymns or gospel songs which would be wholly unsuitable for the assembly. The fact is, he *sings* the gospel for the same object that he *preaches* it, namely, to reach the sinner's heart. He is just as ready to sing "Come" as to preach it.

Such is the judgment which I have had on this subject for many years, though I am not quite sure if it will fully commend itself to your spiritual mind. It strikes me we are in danger of slipping into christendom's false notion of "establishing a cause," and "organizing a body." Hence it is that the four walls in which the assembly meets are regarded by many as a "chapel," and the evangelist who happens to preach there is looked upon as "the minister of the chapel."

All this has to be carefully guarded against: but my object in referring to it now is to clear up the point with respect to the gospel preaching. The true evangelist is not the minister of any chapel; or the organ of any congregation; or the representative of a body; or the paid agent of any society. No; he is the ambassador of Christ—the messenger of a God of love—the herald of glad tidings. His heart is filled with love to souls; his lips anointed by the Holy Ghost; his words clothed with heavenly power. Let him alone! Fetter him not by your rules and regulations! Leave him to his work and to his Master!

And further, bear in mind that the Church of God can afford a platform broad enough for all sorts of workmen and every possible style of work, *provided only* that foundation truth be not disturbed. It is a fatal mistake to seek to reduce every one and every thing to a dead level. Christianity is a living, a divine reality. Christ's servants are sent by Him, and to Him they are responsible. "Who art thou that judgest another man's servant? To his own master he standeth or falleth" (Rom. 14).

We may depend upon it these things demand our serious consideration, if we do not want to have the blessed work of evangelization marred in our hands.

I have just one other point that I would refer to before closing my letter, as it has been rather a vexed question in certain places—I allude to what has been termed "the responsibility of the preaching." How many of our friends have been and are harassed about this question! And why? I am persuaded that it is from not understanding the true nature, character, and sphere of the work of evangelization. Hence we have had some persons contending for it that the Sunday evening preaching should be left open. "Open to what?" That is the question. In too many cases it has proved to be "open" to a character of speaking altogether unsuited to many who had come there, or who had been brought by friends, expecting to hear a full, clear, earnest gospel. On such occasions our friends have been disappointed, and the unconverted perfectly unable to understand the meaning of the service. Surely such things ought not to be; nor would they be if men would only discern the simplest thing possible, namely, the distinction between all meetings in which Christ's servants exercise their ministry on their own personal responsibility, and all meetings which are purely reunions of the assembly, whether for the Lord's Supper, for prayer, or for any other purpose whatsoever.

Letter 7

Through want of space I was obliged to close my last letter without even touching upon the subject of the Sunday-school: I must, however, devote a page or two to a branch of work which has occupied a very large place in my heart for thirty years. I should deem my series incomplete were this subject left untouched.

Some may question how far the Sunday-school can be viewed as an integral part of the work of evangelization. I can only say it is mainly in this light I regard it. I look upon it as one great and most interesting branch of gospel work. The superintendent of the Sunday-school and the teacher of the Sunday-school class are workers in the wide gospel field, just as distinctly as the evangelist or preacher of the gospel.

I am fully aware that a Sunday-school differs materially from an ordinary gospel preaching. It is not convened in the same way, or conducted in the same manner. There is, if I may so express myself, a union of the parent, the teacher, and the evangelist, in the person of the Sunday-school worker. For the time being he takes the place of the parent: he seeks to do the duty of a teacher; but he aims at the object of the evangelist—that priceless object, the salvation of the souls of the precious little ones committed to his charge. As to the mode in which he gains his end—as to the details of his work—as to the varied agencies which he may bring to bear, he alone is responsible.

I am aware that exception is taken to the Sunday-school on the ground that its tendency is to interfere with parental or domestic training. Now I must confess that I cannot see any force whatever in this objection. The true object of the Sunday-school is not to supersede parental training, but to help it where it exists, or to supply its lack where it does not exist. There are, as you and I well know, hundreds of thousands of dear children who have no parental training at all. Thousands have no parents, and thousands

more have parents who are far worse than none. Look at the multitudes that throng the lanes, alleys, and courtyards of our large cities and towns, who seem hardly a degree above mere animal existence—yea, many of them like little incarnate demons.

Who can think upon all these precious souls without wishing a hearty God-speed to all *true* Sunday-school workers, and earnestly longing for more thorough earnestness and energy in that most blessed work?

I say *"true"* Sunday-school workers, because I fear that many engage in the work who are not true, not real, not fit. Many, I fear, take it up as a little bit of fashionable religious work, suited to the younger members of the religious communities. Many, too, view it as a kind of set-off to a week of self-indulgence, folly, and worldliness. All such persons are an actual hindrance rather than a help to this sacred service.

Then again, there are many who sincerely love Christ, and long to serve Him in the Sunday-school, but who are not really fitted for the work. They are deficient in tact, energy, order, and rule. They lack that power to adapt themselves to the children, and to engage their young hearts, which is so essential to the Sunday-school worker.

It is a great mistake to suppose that every one who stands idle in the market-place is fit to turn into this particular branch of Christian labor. On the contrary, it needs a person thoroughly fitted of God for it; and if it be asked, "How are we ever to be supplied with suited agents for this branch of evangelistic service?" I reply, Just in the same way as you are to be supplied in any other department—by earnest, persevering, believing prayer.

I am most thoroughly persuaded that if Christians were more stirred up by God's Spirit to feel the importance of the Sunday-school—if they could only seize the idea that it is, like the tract depot and the preaching, part and parcel of that most glorious work to which we are called in these closing days of christendom's history—if they were more permeated by the idea of the evangelistic nature and object of Sunday-school work, they would be more instant and earnest in prayer, both in the closet and in the public assembly, that the Lord would raise up in our midst a band of earnest, devoted, whole-hearted Sunday-school workers.

This is the lack; and may God, in His abounding mercy, supply it! He is able, and surely He is willing. But then He will be waited on and inquired of; and "He is the rewarder of them that *diligently* seek Him." I think we have much cause for thankfulness and praise for what has been done in the way of Sunday-schools during the last few years. I well remember the time when many of our friends seemed to overlook this branch of work altogether. Even now many treat it with indifference, thus weakening the hand and discouraging the hearts of those engaged in it.

But I shall not dwell upon this, inasmuch as my theme is the Sunday-school, and not those who neglect or oppose it. I bless God for what I see in the way of encouragement. I have often been exceedingly refreshed and delighted by seeing some of our very oldest friends rising from the table of their Lord, and proceeding to arrange the benches on which the dear little ones were soon to be ranged to hear the sweet story of a Saviour's love. And what could be more lovely, more touching, or more morally suited, than for those who had just been remembering the Saviour's dying love to seek, even by the arrangement of the benches, to carry out His living words, "Suffer the little children to come unto Me"?

There is very much I should like to add as to the mode of working the Sunday-school; but perhaps it is just as well that each worker should be wholly cast upon the living God for counsel and help as to details. We must ever remember that the Sunday-school, like the tract depot and the preaching, is entirely a work of individual responsibility. This is a grand point; and where it is fully understood, and where there is real earnestness of heart and singleness of eye, I believe there will be no great difficulty as to the particular mode of working. A large heart, and a fixed purpose to carry on the great work and fulfil the glorious mission committed to us, will effectually deliver us from the withering influence of crotchets and prejudices—those miserable obstructions to all that is lovely and of good report.

May God pour out His blessing on all Sunday-schools, upon the pupils, the teachers, and the superintendents! May He also bless all who are engaged, in any way, in the instruction of the young! May He cheer and refresh their spirits by giving them to reap many golden sheaves in their special corner of the one great and glorious gospel field!

"PUBLICLY AND FROM HOUSE TO HOUSE"

THE SENTENCE which we have just penned is taken from Paul's farewell address to the elders of Ephesus, as recorded in Acts 20. It is a very suggestive sentence, and sets forth in a most forcible manner the intimate connection between the work of the teacher and that of the pastor. "I kept back nothing that was profitable unto you," says the blessed apostle, "but have showed you and have taught you publicly, and from house to house."

Paul was not only an apostle, he combined, in a striking way, the evangelist, the pastor and the teacher. The two last named are closely connected, as we see from Eph. 4:11. It is important that this connection be understood and maintained. The teacher unfolds truth; the pastor applies it. The teacher enlightens the understanding; the pastor looks to the state of the heart. The teacher supplies the spiritual nutriment; the pastor sees to the use that is made of it. The teacher occupies himself more with the Word; the pastor looks after the soul. The teacher's work is for the most part public; the pastor's work, chiefly in private. When combined in one person, the teaching faculty imparts immense moral power to the pastor, and the pastoral element imparts affectionate tenderness to the teacher.

The reader must not confound a pastor with an elder or bishop. The two are quite distinct. Elder and bishop are frequently interchangeable, but pastor is never confounded with either. Elder is a local charge; pastor is a gift. We have nothing about elders or bishops in 1 Corinthians 12 and 14, or Ephesians 4, though in these Scriptures we have the fullest unfolding of the subject of gifts. We must carefully distinguish between gift and local charge. Elders or bishops are for rule and oversight. Teachers and pastors are to feed and edify. An elder may be a teacher or pastor, but he must keep the two things distinct. They rest upon a different footing altogether, and are never to be confounded.

However, our object in this brief article is not to write a treatise on ministry, or to dwell elaborately upon the difference between spiritual gift and local charge, but simply to offer to our readers a few words on the immense importance of the pastoral gift in the Church of God, in order that they may be stirred up to earnest prayer to the great Head of the Church, that He may graciously be pleased to shed forth this precious gift more abundantly in our midst. We are not straitened in Him. The treasury of spiritual life is not exhausted; and our Lord Christ loves His Church, and delights to nourish and cherish His body, and to supply its every need out of His own infinite fulness.

That there is urgent need of pastoral care throughout the Church of God, few can deny who know what pastorship is, and who are at all acquainted with the true condition of the Church. How rare is the true spiritual pastor! It is easy to take the name, and assume the office; but, in point of fact, pastorship is neither a name nor an office, but a living reality—a divinely-imparted gift—something communicated by the Head of the Church for the growth and blessing of His members. A true pastor is a man who is not only possessed of a real spiritual gift, but also animated by the very affections of the heart of Christ toward every lamb and sheep of His blood-bought flock.

Yes, we repeat it, "*every* lamb and sheep." A true pastor is a pastor all over the world. He is one who has a heart, a message, a ministry, for every member of the body of Christ. Not so the elder or bishop. His is a local charge, confined to the locality in which such charge is entrusted. But the pastor's range is the whole Church of God, as the evangelist's range is the wide, wide world. In New York, in London, in Paris, or Canton, a pastor is a pastor, and he has his blessed work everywhere. To imagine a pastor, confined to a certain congregation to which he is expected to discharge the functions of evangelist, teacher, elder, or bishop, is something altogether foreign to the teaching of the New Testament.

But how few real pastors are to be found in our midst! How rare is the pastor's gift, the pastor's heart! Where shall we find those who duly combine the two grand and important elements contained in the heading of this paper—"Publicly and from house to house"? A man may, perhaps, give us a brief address on the Lord's day, or a lecture on some week-day; but where is the "house to house" side of the question? Where is the close, earnest, diligent looking after individual souls day by day? Very often it happens that the public teaching shoots completely over the head; it is the house to house teaching that is sure to come home to the heart. How frequently it happens that something uttered in public is entirely misunderstood and misapplied, until the loving pastoral visit during the week supplies the true meaning and just application.

Nor is this all. How much there is in a pastor's range that the public teacher never can compass! No doubt public teaching is most important; would that we had many times more of it than we have. The teacher's work is invaluable, and when mellowed by the deep and tender affection of a pastor's heart, can go a great way indeed in meeting the soul's manifold necessities. But the loving pastor who earnestly, prayerfully, and faithfully goes from house to house, can get at the deep exercises of the soul, the sorrows of the heart, the puzzling questions of the mind, the grave difficulties of the conscience. He can enter, in the profound sympathy of an affectionate heart, into the thousand little circumstances and sorrows of the path. He can kneel down with the tried, the tempted, the crushed, and the sorrowing one before the mercy-seat, and they can pour out their hearts together, and draw down sweet consolation from the God of all grace and the Father of mercies.

The public teacher cannot do this. No doubt, if, as we have said, he has something of the pastoral element in him, he can anticipate in his public address a great deal of the soul's private exercises, sorrows, and difficulties. But he cannot fully meet the soul's individual need. This is the pastor's holy work. It seems to us that a pastor is to the soul what a doctor is to the body. He must understand disease and medicine. He must be able to tell what is the matter. He must be able to discern the spiritual condition to apply the true remedy. Ah, how few are these pastors! It is one thing to take the title, and another thing to do the work.

Christian reader, we earnestly entreat you to join us in fervent believing prayer to God to raise up true pastors amongst us. We are in sad need of them. The sheep of Christ are not fed and cared for. We are occupied so much with our own affairs, that we have not time to look after the beloved flock of Christ.

And even on these occasions, when the Lord's people assemble in public, how little there is for their precious souls! What long barren pauses and silence of poverty! What aimless hymns and prayers we hear! How little leading of the flock through the green pastures of Holy Scripture, and by the still waters of divine love! And then, all through the week, few loving pastoral calls, few tender solicitous inquiries after soul or body. There seems to be no time. Every moment is swallowed up in the business of providing for ourselves and our families. It is, alas! the old sad story; "All seek their own, not the things that are Jesus Christ's."

How different it was with the blessed apostle. He found time to make tents, and also to "teach publicly and from house to house." He was not only the earnest evangelist, ranging over continents and planting churches, but he was also the loving pastor, the tender nurse, the skilful spiritual physician. He had a heart for Christ and for His body, the Church, and for every member of that body. Here lies the real secret of the matter. It is wonderful what a loving heart can accomplish. If I really love the Church, I shall desire its blessing and progress, and seek to promote these according to my ability.

May the Lord raise up in the midst of His people pastors and teachers after His own heart—men filled with His Spirit, and animated by a genuine love for His Church—men competent and ready to teach—"*publicly and from house to house.*"

"THE REGIONS BEYOND"

2 Corinthians 10:16

"*TO PREACH THE GOSPEL in the regions beyond you.*"

These words, while they set forth the largeheartedness of the self-denying and devoted apostle, do also furnish a fine model for the evangelist, in every age. The gospel is a traveler; and the preacher of the gospel must be a traveler likewise. The divinely-

qualified and divinely-sent evangelist will fix his eye upon "*the world.*" He will embrace, in his benevolent design, the human family. From house to house; from street to street; from city to city; from province to province; from kingdom to kingdom; from continent to continent; from pole to pole. Such is the range of "the good news," and the publisher thereof. "The regions beyond" must ever be the grand gospel motto. No sooner has the gospel lamp cast its cheering beams over a district, than the bearer of that map must think of the regions beyond. Thus the work goes on. Thus the mighty tide of grace rolls, in enlightening and saving power, over a dark world which lies in "the region of the shadow of death."

> Waft, waft, ye winds, the story,
> And you, ye waters roll,
> Till, like a sea of glory,
> It spreads from pole to pole.

Christian reader, are you thinking of "the regions beyond you"? This expression may, in your case, mean the next house, the next street, the next village, the next city, the next kingdom, or the next continent. The application is for your own heart to ponder; but say, are you thinking of "the regions beyond you"? I do not want you to abandon your present post, at all; or, at least, not until you are fully persuaded that your work, at that post, is done. But, remember, the gospel plough should never stand still. *"Onward"* is the motto of every true evangelist. Let the shepherds abide by the flocks; but let the evangelists betake themselves hither and thither, to gather the sheep. Let them sound the gospel trump, far and wide, over the dark mountains of this world, to gather together the elect of God. This is the design of the gospel. This should be the object of the evangelist, as he sighs after "the regions beyond."*

When Caesar beheld, from the coast of Gaul, the white cliffs of Britain, he earnestly longed to carry his arms thither. The evangelist, on the other hand, whose heart beats in unison with the heart of Jesus, as he casts his eye over the map of the world, longs to carry the gospel of peace into regions which have heretofore been wrapped in midnight gloom, covered with the dark mantle of superstition, or blasted beneath the withering influences of "a form of godliness without the power."

It would, I believe, be a profitable question for many of us to put to ourselves, how far we are discharging our holy responsibilities to "the regions beyond." I believe the Christian who is not cultivating and manifesting an evangelistic spirit, is in a deplorable condition. I believe, too, that the assembly which is not cultivating and manifesting an evangelistic spirit is in a dead state. One of the truest marks of spiritual growth and prosperity, whether in an individual, or in an assembly, is earnest anxiety after the conversion of souls. This anxiety will swell the bosom with most generous emotions; yea, it will break forth, in copious streams of benevolent exertion, ever flowing toward "the regions beyond." It is hard to believe that "the Word of Christ" is "dwelling richly" in any one who is not making some effort to impart that Word to his fellow sinners. It matters not what may be the amount of the effort; it may be to drop a few words in the ear of a friend, to give a tract, to pen a note, to breathe a prayer. But one thing is certain, namely, that a healthy vigorous Christian will be an evangelistic Christian—a teller of good news—one whose sympathies, desires, and energies, are ever going forth toward "the regions beyond." "I must preach the gospel to other cities also, therefore am I sent." Such was the language of the divine Evangelist.

It is very doubtful whether many of the servants of Christ have not erred in allowing themselves, through one influence or another, to become too much localized—too much tied to one place. They have dropped into routine work—into a round of stated preaching, in the same place, and, in many cases, have paralyzed themselves and paralyzed their hearers also. I speak not, now, of the labors of the pastor, the elder, or the teacher, which must, of course, be carried on in the midst of those who are the proper subjects of such labors. I refer more particularly to the evangelist. Such an one should never suffer himself to become localized. The world is his sphere—"the regions beyond," his motto—to gather out God's elect, his object—the current of the Spirit, his line of direction. If the reader

---

* The conversion of the world is not the object of the divinely instructed evangelist, but the gathering out of a people to the Lord's name—a people for the heavens—the body of Christ—the Church of God (Acts 15:14).

should be one whom God has called and fitted to be an evangelist, let him remember these four things, the sphere, the motto, the object, and the line of direction which all must adopt, if they would prove fruitful laborers in the gospel field.

Finally, whether the reader be an evangelist or not, I would earnestly entreat him to examine how far he is seeking to further the gospel of Christ. We really must not stand idle. Time is short! Eternity is rapidly posting on! The Master is most worthy! Souls are most precious! The season for work will soon close! Let us, then, in the name of the Lord, be up and doing. And when we have done what we can, in the regions around, let us carry the precious gospel into "*the regions beyond.*"

Go, labor on, while it is day,
The world's dark night is hastening on;
Speed, speed thy work, cast sloth away;
It is not thus that souls are won.

Men die in darkness at thy side,
Without a hope to cheer the tomb;
Take up the torch and wave it wide,
The torch that lights time's thickest gloom.

Go on, faint not, keep watch, and pray;
Be wise the erring soul to win;
Go forth into the world's highway,
Compel the wanderer to come in.

"LET US GO AGAIN"

Acts 15:36

"LET US GO AGAIN and visit our brethren in every city where we have preached the word of the Lord, and see how they do." In the preceding paper we presented to the notice of our readers, a motto for the evangelist, in the expression, "To preach the gospel in the regions beyond." This is the grand object of the evangelist, let his gift or sphere of action be what it may.

But, the pastor has his work as well as the evangelist; and we are desirous to furnish a motto for him likewise. Such a motto we have in the words, "*Let us go again.*" We are not merely to regard this expression as the narrative of what was done, but a model of what ought to be done. If the evangelist is responsible to preach the gospel in the regions beyond, so long as there are regions to be evangelized, the pastor is responsible to "go again and visit his brethren," so long as there are brethren to be visited. The evangelist forms the interesting connection; the pastor maintains and strengthens that connection. The one is the instrument of creating that beautiful link, the other of perpetuating it. It is quite possible that the two gifts may exist in the same person, as in Paul's case; but whether this be so or not,

each gift has its own specific sphere and object. The business of the evangelist is to call out the brethren; the business of the pastor is to look after them. The evangelist goes, *first*, and preaches the Word of the Lord; the pastor goes *again* and visits those upon whom that Word has taken effect. The former calls out the sheep, the latter feeds and takes care of them.

The order of these things is divinely beautiful. The Lord would not gather out His sheep and leave them to wander uncared for and unfed. This would be wholly unlike His gracious, tender, thoughtful way. Hence, He not only imparts the gift whereby His sheep are to be called into existence, but also that whereby they are to be fed and maintained. He has His own interest in them, and in every stage of their history. He watches over them, with intense solicitude, from the moment in which they hear the first quickening accents, until they are safely folded in the mansions above. His desire to gather the sheep tells itself forth in the large-heartedness of the expression, "the regions beyond"; and His desire for their well-being breathes in the words, "let us go again." The two things are intimately connected. Wherever the Word of the Lord has been preached and received, there you have the formation of mysterious, but real and most precious links between Heaven and earth. The eye of faith can discern the most beauteous link of divine sympathy between the heart of Christ in Heaven, and "every city" where "the Word of the Lord" has been preached and received. This is as true now, as it was eighteen hundred years ago. There may be many things to hinder our spiritual perception of this link; but it is there for all that. God sees it, and faith sees it likewise. Christ has His eye—an eye beaming with intense interest, and radiant with tender love—upon every city, every town, every village, every street, every house in which His Word has been received.

The assurance of this is most comforting to every one who feels that he has, in very deed, received the Word of the Lord. Were we called upon to prove from Scripture, the truth of our assertion, we should do so by the following quotation: "And there was a certain disciple at Damascus, named Ananias; and to him said the Lord in a vision, Ananias. And he said, Behold, I am here, Lord. And the Lord said unto him, Arise and go into *the street* which is called Straight, and inquire in *the house* of Judas for one called Saul, of Tarsus: for behold *he prayeth*" (Acts 9: 10-11. Can aught be more touching than to hear the Lord of glory giving, with such minuteness, the address of His newly-found sheep? He gives the street, the number, so to speak, and the very occupation at the moment. His gracious eye takes in everything connected with each one of those for whom He gave His precious life. There is not a circumstance, however trivial, in the path of the very feeblest of His members, in which the blessed Lord Jesus is not interested. His name be praised for such a comforting assurance. May we be enabled to enter, more fully, into the reality and power of such a truth!

Now, our gracious Shepherd would fill the heart of each one acting under Him with His own tender care for the sheep; and He it was who animated the heart of Paul to express and carry out the design embodied in the words, "let us go again." It was the grace of Christ flowing down into the heart of Paul, and giving character and direction to the zealous service of that most devoted and laborious apostle. "I have taught you publicly and *from house to house*" (Acts 20: 20). What an example! Think of the apostle, with all his gigantic labors, finding time to visit from house to house; and that for three years in one town!

And observe the force of the words "*go again*." It does not matter how often you have been there before. It may be once, twice, or thrice. This is not the question. "Let us go again," is the motto for the pastoral heart, for there is always a demand for the pastoral gift. Matters are ever and anon springing up, in the various places in which "the Word of the Lord" has been preached and received, demanding the labors of the divinely-qualified pastor. No human language could adequately set forth the value and importance of real pastoral work. Would there were more of it amongst us! It often nips in the bud evils which might grow to terrible proportions. This is, in an especial manner, true, in this day of spiritual poverty. There is immense demand—a demand on the evangelist, to think of "the regions beyond"—a demand on the pastor to "go *again* and visit his brethren, in every city" where "the Word of the Lord" has been preached, "and see how they do."

Reader, do you possess aught of pastoral gift? If so, think, I pray you, of those comprehensive words, "let us go again." Have you been acting on them? Have you been thinking of your "brethren"—of those "who have obtained like precious faith"—those who, by receiving "the Word of the Lord," have become spiritual brethren? Are your interests and sympathies engaged on behalf of "every city" in which a spiritual link has been formed with the Head above? Oh, how the heart longs for a greater exhibition of holy zeal and energy, of individual and independent devotedness—independent, I mean, not of the sacred fellowship of the truly spiritual, but of every influence which would tend to clog and hinder that elevated service to which each one is distinctly called, in responsibility to the Master *alone*. Let us beware of the trammels of cumbrous machinery, of religious routine, of false order. Let us beware, too, of indolence, of love of personal ease, of a false economy, which would lead us to attach an undue importance to the matter of expense. The silver and the gold are the Lord's, and His sheep are far more precious to Him than silver and gold. His words are, "Lovest thou Me? feed My sheep." And if only there is the *heart* to do this, the *means* will never be wanting. How often may we detect ourselves spending sums of money, *unnecessarily*, on the table, the wardrobe, and the library, which would be amply sufficient to carry us to "the regions beyond," to preach the gospel, or to "every city," in order to "visit our brethren"!

May the Lord grant unto us an earnest self-denying spirit, a devoted heart to Him and to His most holy service, a true desire for the spread of His gospel, and the prosperity of His people. May the time passed of our lives suffice us to have lived and labored for self and its interests, and may the time to come be given to Christ and His interests. Let us not allow our treacherous hearts to deceive us by plausible reasonings about domestic, commercial, or other claims. All such should be strictly attended to, no doubt. A well-regulated mind will never offer to God a sacrifice arising out of the neglect of any just claim. If I am at the head of a family, the claims of that family must be duly responded to. If I am at the head of a business, the claims of that business must be duly met. If I am a hired servant, I must attend to my work. To fail in any of these, would be to dishonor the Lord, instead of serving Him.

But, allowing the widest possible margin for all righteous claims, let us ask, are we doing all we can for "the regions beyond," and for "our brethren, in every city where we have preached the Word of the Lord"? Has there not been a culpable abandonment both of evangelistic and pastoral work? Have we not allowed domestic and commercial ties to act unduly upon us? And what has been the result? What have we gained? Have our children turned out well, and our commercial interests prospered? Has it not often happened that, where the Lord's work has been neglected, the children have grown up in carelessness and worldliness? And as to business, have we not often toiled all the night, and gazed on an empty net in the morning? On the other hand, where the family and the circumstances have been left, with artless confidence, in the hand of Jehovah-jireh, have they not been far better cared for? Let these things be deeply pondered, with an honest heart and a single eye, and we shall be sure to arrive at just conclusions.

I cannot lay down the pen without calling the reader's attention to the fulness of the expression, "see how they do." How very much is involved in these words! "How they do," publicly, socially, privately. "How they do," in doctrine, in association, in walk. "How they do," spiritually, morally, relatively. In a word, "how they do," in every way. And, be it well remembered, that this seeing how our brethren do must never resolve itself into a curious, prying, gossiping, busybody spirit— a spirit that wounds and heals not, that meddles and mends not. To all who would visit us in such a spirit as this, we should, assuredly, say, "be far from hence." But, to all who would carry out Acts 15:36, we desire to say "our hands, our hearts, our houses, are wide open; come in, ye blessed of the Lord. 'If ye have judged me to be faithful to the Lord, come into my house and abide.'"

O Lord, be pleased to raise up evangelists to visit "the regions beyond," and pastors to visit, again and again, "the brethren in every city."

"Lovest thou Me? . . . Feed My lambs. . . . Lovest thou Me? . . . Shepherd My sheep" (John 21: 15-16).

"And when the chief Shepherd shall appear, ye shall receive a crown of glory that fadeth not away" (1 Peter 5: 4).

ISRAEL AND THE NATIONS

Psalm 67

IT WOULD GREATLY TEND to give clearness and definiteness to missionary effort to keep fully before our minds God's original purpose in sending the gospel to the Gentiles, or nations. This we have stated in the most distinct manner in Acts 15. "Simeon hath declared," says James, "how God at the first did visit the Gentiles, *to take out of them* a people for His name."

It gives no warrant for the idea, so persistently held by the professing Church, that the whole world is to be converted by the preaching of the gospel. To convert the world is one thing; to take out of the nations a people is quite another.

The latter, and not the former, is God's present work. It is what He has been doing since the day that Simon Peter opened the kingdom of heaven to the Gentile in Acts 10; and it is what He will continue to do until the moment so rapidly approaching, in which the last elect one is gathered out, and our Lord shall come to receive His people unto Himself.

Let all missionaries remember this. They may rest assured it will not clip their wings, or cripple their energies; it will only guide their movements, by giving them a divine aim and object. Of what possible use can it be for a man to propose as the end of his labors something wholly different from that which is before the mind of God? Ought not a servant to seek to do his master's will? Can he expect to please his master by pursuing other than his clearly expressed object?

It is blessedly true, that all the earth shall yet be filled with the knowledge of the Lord as the waters cover the sea. There is no question as to this. All Scripture bears witness to it. To quote the passages would literally fill a volume. All Christians are agreed on this point, and hence there is no need to adduce evidence.

But the question is, how is this grand and glorious result to be brought about? Is it the purpose of God to use the professing Church as His agent, or a preached gospel as His instrument, in the conversion of the world? Scripture says No; with a clearness which ought to sweep away every doubt.

Here let it be distinctly understood that we delight in all true missionary effort. We heartily wish God's speed to every true missionary—to every one who has left home, and kindred, and friends, and all the comforts and privileges of civilized life, in order to carry the glad tidings of salvation into the dark places of the earth. We desire to render hearty thanks to God for all that has been accomplished in the fields of foreign missions; though we cannot approve some modes by which the work is carried on. We consider there is a lack of simple faith in God, and of subjection to the authority of Christ, and the guidance of the Holy Ghost. There is too much of human machinery, and looking to the world for aid.

But all this is not our present object. The point with which we are occupied in this brief paper is this—*will* God make use of the professing Church to convert the nations? We ask not, *has* He done so? for, were we to put the question thus, we could only receive an unqualified negative; for the professing Church has been at work for eighteen long centuries; and what is the result?

Let the reader take a glance at a missionary map, and he will see in a moment. Look at those large patches of black, designed to set forth the dismal regions over which heathenism bears sway. Look at the red, the green, the yellow, setting forth popery, the Greek church, and Mohammedanism. And where is—we say not true Christianity, but even nominal Protestantism? That is indicated by those spots of blue which, if all put together, make but a small fraction indeed. As to what even this Protestantism is we need not now stop to inquire.

What, then, say the Scriptures on the great question of the conversion of the nations? Take, for example, the lovely psalm that stands at the head of this paper. It is but one proof among a thousand, but, we need hardly say, perfectly harmonizes with the testimony of all Scripture. We give it in full.

"God be merciful unto us, and bless us; and cause His face to shine upon us; that Thy way may be known upon earth, Thy saving health among all nations. Let the people praise Thee, O God; let all the people praise Thee. O let the nations be glad, and sing for joy: for Thou shalt judge the people righteously, and govern the nations upon earth. Let the people praise Thee, O God, let all the people praise Thee. Then shall the earth yield her increase; and God, even our own God, shall bless us. *God shall bless us;* and all the ends of the earth shall fear Him."

Here, then, the simple truth shines before us. It is when God shall have mercy upon Israel—when He shall cause His light to shine upon Zion—then will His way be known upon earth, His saving health among all nations. It is through *Israel*, not through the professing Church, that God will yet bless the nations.

That the "us" of the foregoing psalm refers to Israel, no intelligent reader of Scripture needs to be told. Indeed, as we all know, the great burden of the Psalms, the Prophets, and the entire Old Testament, is Israel. There is not a syllable about the Church in the Old Testament. Types and shadows there are in which—now that we have the light of the New Testament—we can see the truth of the Church prefigured. But without that light no one could, by any possibility, find the truth of the Church in Old Testament Scripture. That great mystery was, as the inspired apostle tells us, *"hid"*—not in the Scriptures (for whatever is contained in the Scriptures is no longer hid, but revealed) but it was "hid in God;" and was not, and could not, be revealed until Christ, being rejected by Israel, was crucified and raised from the dead.

So long as the testimony to Israel was

pending, the doctrine of the Church could not be unfolded. Hence, although at the day of Pentecost we have the *beginning of the Church*, yet it was not until Israel had rejected the testimony of the Holy Ghost in Stephen that a special witness was called out in the person of Paul, to whom *the doctrine of the Church* was committed. We must distinguish between the fact and the doctrine; indeed it is not until we reach the last chapter of the Acts that the curtain finally drops upon Israel; and Paul, the prisoner at Rome, fully unfolds the grand mystery of the Church which from ages and generations had been hid in God, but was now made manifest. Let the reader ponder Romans 16:25-26; Ephesians 3:1-11; Colossians 1:24-27.

We cannot attempt to go fully into this glorious subject here; indeed, to refer to it at all is a digression from our present line. But we deem it needful just to say thus much, in order that the reader may fully see that Psalm 67 refers to Israel; and, seeing this, the whole truth will flow into his soul, that the conversion of the nations stands connected with Israel, and not with the Church. It is through Israel, and not through the Church, that God will yet bless the nations. It is His eternal purpose that the seed of Abraham, His friend, shall yet be pre-eminent in the earth, and that all nations shall be blessed in and through them. "Thus saith the Lord of Hosts, In those days it shall come to pass, that ten men shall take hold, *out of all languages of the nations*, even shall take hold of *the skirt of him that is a Jew*, saying, *We will go with you;* for we have heard that God is with you" (Zech. 8:23).

It would be an easy and a delightful task to prove from the New Testament, that, previous to the restoration and blessing of Israel, and therefore previous to the conversion of the nations, the true Church of God, the body of Christ, shall have been taken up to be for ever with the Lord, in the full and ineffable communion of the Father's house; so that the Church will not be God's agency in the conversion of the Jews as a nation, any more than in that of the Gentiles. But we do not desire at this time to do more than establish the two points above stated.

THE REMNANT

PAST AND PRESENT

IT IS AT ONCE INTERESTING, instructive, and encouraging to trace through Scripture the history of what is called "The Remnant." We may remark at the outset that the fact of there being a remnant proves the failure of the ostensible witness or professing body, whether Jewish or Christian. If all were faithful there would, of course, be no moral ground for a remnant, nothing to distinguish a few from the general body of professors. The remnant, at any time, will be found to consist of those who feel and own the common failure and ruin, and count on God, and cleave to His Word. These are the great characteristic marks of the remnant in every age. We have failed, but God is faithful, and His mercy is from everlasting to everlasting.

Now in tracing the history of the remnant in Old Testament times we find that the lower down we go in the nation's history, the richer the display of divine grace; and, further, the deeper the moral gloom, the brighter the flashes of individual faith. This is fraught with the most blessed encouragement for every true-hearted child of God and servant of Christ who feels and owns the ruin of the whole professing Church. It is cheering beyond expression for every faithful soul to be assured that, however the Church has failed, it is the privilege of the individual believer to enjoy as full and precious fellowship with God, and pursue as true a path of discipleship as ever was known in the brightest days of the Church's history. Let us turn to Scripture for illustration.

In 2 Chronicles 30 we have a refreshing and encouraging record of a passover kept in the reign of Hezekiah, when the visible unity of the nation was broken up; and failure and ruin had come in. We do not attempt to quote the whole passage, much as we should like to do so, for it is most precious and soul-stirring.

We merely give the closing lines as bearing upon our thesis.

"So there was great joy in Jerusalem: *for since the time of Solomon the son of David king of Israel there was not the like in Jerusalem.*" Here then we have a lovely illustration of the grace of God meeting those of His people who owned their failure and sin and took their true place in His presence. Hezekiah and those with him were fully convinced of their low condition, and hence they did not presume to keep the passover in the first month. They availed themselves of the provision of grace, as recorded in Numbers 9, and kept the feast in the second month. "For a multitude of the people . . . had not cleansed themselves, yet did they eat the passover otherwise than it was written. But Hezekiah prayed for them, saying, The good Lord pardon *every one that prepareth his heart to seek God*, the Lord God of his fathers, though . . . not according to the purification of the sanctuary. And the Lord harkened to Hezekiah, and healed the people" (chap. 30: 18-20).

Here we see divine grace meeting, as it ever does, those who truly confess their failure and weakness. There was no assumption or pretension, no hardness or indifference, no attempt to hide their true condition, no setting up to be all right; no, they took their true place, and cast themselves on that exhaustless grace which never fails to meet a contrite heart.

What was the result? "The children of Israel that were present at Jerusalem kept the feast of unleavened bread seven days *with great gladness:* and the Levites and the priests praised the Lord day by day, singing with loud instruments unto the Lord. And Hezekiah spake comfortably [to the heart] unto all the Levites that taught the good knowledge of the Lord: and they did eat throughout the feast seven days, offering peace offerings, and making confession to the Lord God of their fathers. And the whole assembly took counsel to keep other seven days: and they kept other seven days with gladness" (chap. 30:21-23).

Now we may rest assured that all this was most grateful to the heart of Jehovah, God of Israel. True there was weakness, failure, short-coming. Things were not externally what they were in Solomon's day. Doubtless many may have looked upon Hezekiah's acting as presumptuous in convening such an assembly under the circumstances. Indeed, we are told that his touching and beautiful invitation was mocked and laughed to scorn throughout Ephraim, Manasseh, and Zebulun.

Thus it is, alas! too often. The actings of faith are not understood, because the precious grace of God is not understood. But "divers of Asher and Manasseh and Zebulun *humbled themselves*, and came to Jerusalem," and they were richly rewarded by coming in for a feast of fat things such as had not been celebrated since the days of Solomon. There is no limit to the blessing which grace has in store for the broken and contrite heart. If all Israel had responded to Hezekiah's touching appeal, they would have shared in the blessing; but they were *unbroken*, and therefore *unblessed!* Let us all remember this; we may rest assured it has a voice and a needed lesson for us. May we hear and learn!

We shall now pass on to the reign of the pious and devoted king Josiah, when the nation was on the very eve of dissolution. Here we have a very striking and beautiful illustration of our thesis. We do not attempt to go into details, having done so elsewhere.*

We shall merely quote the few closing lines. "And the children of Israel that were present kept the passover at that time, and the feast of unleavened bread seven days. *And there was no passover like to that kept in Israel from the days of Samuel the prophet; neither did all the kings of Israel* keep such a passover as Josiah kept, and the priests, and the Levites, and all Judah and Israel that were present, and the inhabitants of Jerusalem. In the eighteenth year of the reign of Josiah was this passover kept" (2 Chron. 35:17-19).

What a very remarkable testimony! In Hezekiah's passover we are carried back to the brilliant reign of Solomon; but here we have something brighter still. And if it be asked what it was that threw such a halo of glory around Josiah's passover, we believe it was the fact of its being the fruit of holy and reverent obedience to the Word of God in the midst of abounding ruin and corruption, error and confusion. The activities of faith in an obedient and devoted heart were thrown into relief by the dark background of the nation's condition.

All this is full of encouragement and comfort for every true lover of Christ. Many might have thought it very presumptuous of Josiah to pursue such a course at such a moment and under such circumstances; but it was the very reverse of presumption, as we may gather from the blessed message sent to him from the Lord by the mouth of Huldah, the prophetess; "Thus saith the Lord God of Israel concerning the words which thou hast heard; *Because thy heart was tender, and thou didst humble thyself before God*, when thou heardest His words against this place, and against the inhabitants thereof, and humbledst thyself before Me, and didst rend thy clothes, and weep before Me; I have even heard thee also, saith the Lord" (chap. 34: 26-27).

Here we have the moral basis of Josiah's remarkable career; and most assuredly there was nothing savoring of presumption therein. A contrite heart, weeping eyes, and rent garments are not the accompaniments of presumption or self-confidence. No; they are the precious results of the Word of God acting on the heart and conscience and leading to a course of deep-toned personal devotedness, most cheering and edifying to contemplate. Oh, that there were more of it amongst us! Truly the heart longs for it. May the Word of

---

* See "The Life and Times of Josiah," in this volume.

God so tell upon our whole moral being that instead of yielding to the condition of things around us we may live above it and pass through it as witnesses to the eternal reality of the truth of God and the imperishable virtues of the name of Jesus.

But we must pass on from the interesting history of Josiah, and present some further illustrations of our theme. Hardly had that beloved servant of God passed off the scene when every trace of his blessed work was swept away, and the heavy tide of judgment, long held back in the long-suffering mercy of God, rolled over the land. Jerusalem was laid in ruins, its temple burnt to the ground, and all the people who escaped were carried captive to Babylon, there to hang their harps on the willows and weep over the faded light of other days.

But, blessed forever be the God of all grace, He never leaves Himself without a witness; and hence, during the long and dreary period of Babylonish captivity, we find some most striking and beautiful proofs of the statement that the greater the ruin the richer the grace, and the deeper the gloom the brighter the flashes of individual faith. There was then, as there ever is, "a remnant according to the election of grace"—a little band of devoted men who loved the Lord and were true to His Word amid the pollutions and abominations of Babylon, and who were prepared to face the fiery furnace and the lions' den for the truth of God.

The opening chapters of the book of Daniel furnish some magnificent results of individual faith and devotedness. Look, for example, at chap. 2:46. Where in the history of the nation of Israel have we aught more striking than what is here recorded? Earth's greatest monarch humbled before a captive exile and giving forth this wonderful testimony: "The king answered unto Daniel, and said, Of a truth it is, that your God is a God of gods, and a Lord of kings, and a revealer of secrets, seeing thou couldest reveal this secret."

But where did Daniel get the power to reveal the king's secret? Verses 17 and 18 supply the lovely answer: "Then Daniel went to his house, and made the thing known to Hananiah, Mishael, and Azariah, his companions: that they would desire mercies of the God of heaven concerning this secret." Here we have a prayer-meeting in Babylon. These dear men were of one heart and one mind. They were one in their purpose to refuse the king's meat and wine. They were resolved, by the grace of God, to tread the holy path of separation, though captive exiles in Babylon; and they got together for prayer, and received an abundant answer.

Can aught be finer than this? What an encouragement to the Lord's beloved people in darkest days to hold fast Christ's Word, and not deny His precious name! Is it not most refreshing and edifying to find amid the dark days of Babylonish captivity a few true-hearted men treading in holy fellowship the path of separation and dependence? They stood for God in the king's palace, and God was with them in the furnace and in the lions' den, and conferred upon them the high privilege of standing before the world as the servants of the Most High God. They refused the king's meat; they would not worship the king's image; they kept God's Word and confessed His name utterly regardless of consequences.

They did not say, "We must go with the times; we must do as others do; there is no need to make ourselves singular; we must outwardly conform to the public worship, the religion of the state, and hold our own private opinions all the same; we are not called to withstand the faith of the nation; being in Babylon, we must conform to Babylon's religion."

Thank God, Daniel and his beloved companions did not adopt this contemptible, time-serving policy. No! and what is more, they did not draw a plea, from the complete wreck of Israel's national polity, for lowering the standard of individual faithfulness. They felt—could not but feel, the ruin. They confessed their sin, and the sin of the nation; they felt that, so far as they were concerned, sackcloth and ashes became them; they would bow down their whole moral being beneath that solemn word, "O Israel, thou hast destroyed thyself." All this was, alas, too true; but that was no reason why they should defile themselves with the king's meat, worship the king's image, or give up the worship of the one true and living God. Ah, *God* was before their eyes, and Him they served and obeyed.

All this is full of the most precious teaching for all the Lord's people at the present moment. There are two special evils which we have to guard against. We must beware of ecclesiastical pretension or boasting in mere church position, without an exercised conscience and the holy fear of God. This is a terrible evil, against which every beloved child of God should most sedulously watch. We must never forget that the professing Church is a hopeless wreck, and that any human effort to restore it is a delusion. We are not called, and hence not qualified, to restore it. The Holy Ghost is nevertheless forming the body of Christ, and hastening its completion for the Lord's return.

But, on the other hand, we are not to draw a plea from the ruin of the church for laxity as to truth, or sluggishness in our personal walk. We are in great danger of this. There is no reason whatever why any child of God, or servant of Christ, should do or sanction what is wrong, or continue for an hour in association with aught that has not for its authority, "Thus saith the Lord." "Let *every one* that nameth the name of the Lord *depart* from iniquity." And what then? Stand alone? Do nothing? Not so, thanks and praise to our ever-gracious God! But "follow righteousness, faith, love, peace, *with them* that call on the Lord out of a pure heart"—a heart true to Christ and His interests.

But we must pursue our subject, and ask the reader to turn to Neh. 8. We have been looking at the remnant before the captivity and during the captivity; and now we are called to look at them after the captivity; brought back, by the rich mercy of God, into their own beloved land. We shall not attempt to go into details, but just take one weighty fact in illustration of our special thesis—a fact of immense importance for the whole Church of God at the present moment.

We shall quote a few verses of this lovely Scripture: "So they read in *the book* in *the law of God distinctly, and gave the sense, and*

caused them to understand the reading. . . . And on the second day were gathered together the chief of the fathers of all the people, the priests, and the Levites, unto Ezra the scribe, even *to understand the words of the law*. And they found written in the law which the Lord had commanded by Moses, that the children of Israel should dwell in booths in the feast of the seventh month. . . . And all the congregation of them that were come again out of the captivity made booths, and sat under the booths: for *since the days of Joshua the son of Nun* unto that day had not the children of Israel done so. And there was very great gladness. Also day by day, from the first day unto the last day, he read in the book of the law of God. And they kept the feast seven days; and on the eighth day was a solemn assembly, according unto the manner."

This is very striking. Here we find a feeble remnant gathered round the Word of God, holding a reading-meeting, and getting to understand the truth and feel its power on the heart and conscience. And what was the result? Nothing less than the celebration of the feast of tabernacles, which had never been kept since the days of Joshua the son of Nun. Throughout the days of the judges, the days of Samuel the prophet, the days of the kings—even the brilliant days of David and Solomon—the feast of tabernacles had never been celebrated. It was reserved for a feeble company of returned exiles to keep, amid the ruins of Jerusalem, this precious and beautiful festival—the type of Israel's glorious future.

Was this presumption? Nay, it was simple obedience to the Word of God. It was written in the Book—written for them; they acted upon it. "And there was very great gladness." There was no pretension, no setting up to be anything, no boasting, no attempt to hide their true condition; they were a poor, feeble, despised remnant, taking their true place, broken and contrite, confessing their failure, deeply conscious that it was not with them as it was in the days of Solomon, David, and Joshua. But they heard the Word of God—heard and understood—bowed to its holy authority—

kept the feast. "And there was very great gladness." This surely is another striking and beautiful illustration of our theme, that the greater the ruin, the richer the grace; and the deeper the gloom, the brighter the flashes of individual faith. At all times, and in all places, the contrite and confiding heart is met by unqualified, unbounded grace.

We shall now turn, for a moment, to the last page of Old Testament Scripture—the prophecy of Malachi. Many years have rolled by since the bright days of Ezra and Nehemiah, and we have here a most sorrowful picture of Israel's condition. Alas, alas! "the down grade" has been rapidly trodden. It is the same sad story—"O Israel, thou hast destroyed thyself!" Let us quote a few sentences:

"Ye offer polluted bread upon Mine altar; and ye say, Wherein have we polluted Thee? In that ye say the table of the Lord is contemptible. . . . Who is there even among you that would shut the doors for naught? neither do ye kindle fire on Mine altar for naught. I have no pleasure in you, saith the Lord of hosts, neither will I accept an offering at your hand. . . . Ye say, The table of the Lord is polluted; and the fruit thereof, even His meat, is contemptible. Ye said also, Behold, what a weariness is it! and ye have snuffed at it, saith the Lord of hosts; and ye brought that which was torn, and the lame, and the sick; thus ye brought an offering: should I accept this of your hand? saith the Lord" (chap. 1:7,10,12-13; see also chap. 3: 5-9).

What a deplorable condition of things! It is simply heart-breaking to contemplate. The public worship of God brought into utter contempt; the ministers of religion working only for hire; venality and corruption in connection with the holy service of God; every form of moral pravity practiced amongst the people. In short, it was a scene of deep moral gloom, depressing beyond expression to all who cared for the Lord's interests.

Yet, even in the midst of this terrible scene, we have a most touching and exquisite illustration of our thesis. As ever, there is a remnant—a beloved company who honored and loved the Lord, and found in Him their centre, their object, their delight. "Then they that feared the Lord spake often one to another; and the Lord harkened, and heard, and a book of remembrance was written before Him for them that feared the Lord, and that thought upon His name. And they shall be Mine, saith the Lord of hosts, in that day when I make up My jewels [My special treasure]; and I will spare them, as a man spareth his own son that serveth him."

How lovely is all this! What a contrast to the general condition of things! We may range through the entire history of the nation, and find nothing like this. Where do we read of "a book of remembrance written before the Lord"? Nowhere; not even amidst the brilliant victories of Joshua and David, or the splendors of Solomon. It may be said there was no need. That is not the point. What we have to ponder is the striking fact that the words and ways of this feeble remnant, in the very midst of abounding wickedness, were so refreshing to the heart of God that He had a book of remembrance written about them. We may safely assert that the communings of these beloved ones were more grateful to the heart of God than the singers and trumpeters in Solomon's day. "They spake often one to another." "They feared the Lord, and thought upon His name." There was individual devotedness, personal attachment; they loved the Lord; and this drew them together.

Nothing can be more lovely. Would there were more of it in our midst! Those dear people were not doing anything very great or showy in man's view; but ah, they loved the Lord, they thought of Him, and their common attachment to Him drew them together to speak of Him; and this gave a charm to their reunions which gratified and refreshed the heart of God! It stood out in bright and beauteous relief from the dark background of hirelingism and heartless routine with which they were surrounded. They were not bound together by certain views or opinions which they held in common, though doubtless they had their views and opinions; neither were they held together by ritualistic services or ceremonial

observances; no, they had something far
better and higher than any of these things;
they were drawn and knit together by
deep-toned personal devotedness to the
Lord, and this was agreeable to His heart. He
was weary with the whole system of
ritualism, but refreshed by the genuine
devotedness of a few precious souls who got
together as often as they could to speak one
to another, and to encourage one another in
the Lord.

Would that there were more of this
amongst us! We long for it, and our one
earnest desire in writing this paper is to
promote it. We greatly dread the withering,
paralyzing influence of mere formalism or
religious routine—getting into a groove, and
going on day after day, week after week,
year after year, in a poor, cold, formal
manner, most offensive to the loving heart of
our adorable Lord and Saviour, who desires
to be surrounded by a company of whole-
hearted, devoted followers, true to His
name, true to His Word, true to one another
for His sake, seeking to serve Him in every
right way, while ardently looking out for His
blessed appearing. May the Spirit of God
work mightily in the hearts of all His people,
healing, restoring, reviving, and maintaining
a faithful company to welcome the heavenly
Bridegroom! Let us cry to our gracious God
day and night for this.

I am anxious to present two or three
illustrations drawn from the precious pages
of the New Testament. In the opening of
Luke's Gospel we have a lovely picture of a
remnant in the midst of a hollow, heartless
profession. We listen to the spiritual heart-
utterances of Mary, Elizabeth, Zacharias,
and Simeon. We read of Anna the prophetess, who spoke of Jesus to all who looked for
redemption in Jerusalem. I remember hearing my beloved and revered old friend J.N.D.
[Darby] say in reference to Anna, "I am sure I
do not know how she managed to get at them
at all, but she did." Yes, she did, because she
loved the Lord and loved His dear people,
and delighted to find them out and speak of
Him. It is just our beloved remnant in
Malachi over again. Nothing can be more
lovely or refreshing. It was the exquisite and

fragrant fruit of deep-toned love to the Lord
in contrast with the wearisome forms of dead
religiousness.

We shall now pass on to the Epistle of
Jude. Here we find apostate christendom in
all its appalling forms of wickedness, just as
in Malachi we had apostate Judaism. But our
object just now is not apostate christendom,
but the Christian remnant. Thanks and praise
to our gracious God, there is always a
remnant marked off from the mass of corrupt
profession, and characterized by genuine
attachment to Christ, to His interests, and to
every member of His beloved body.

It is to this remnant that the inspired
apostle addresses his solemn and weighty
Epistle. It is not to any special assembly, but
"To them that are *sanctified* by God the
Father, and *preserved* in Jesus Christ,
called: mercy unto you, and *peace*, and *love*,
be multiplied."

Blessed position! Precious portion! "Separated," "preserved," "called"—this is the position. "Mercy," "peace," "love"—this is the
portion. And all this made sure to every true-
hearted child of God on the face of the earth
ere a single word is written about the
overwhelming tide of apostasy which was so
soon to roll over the whole professing Church.

We repeat, and would emphasize the
expression, "to every true-hearted child of
God." As in Israel of old, so in the professing
Church, the remnant will be found to consist
of those who are true to Christ, hold fast His
Word in the face of everything, are devoted
to His precious interests, and who love His
appearing. In a word, it must be a living
reality, and not mere church-membership or
nominal fellowship here or there, with this or
that. Moreover it is not assuming to be, but
really being, of the remnant—not the name,
but the spiritual power; so the apostle says, "I
will know, not the speech . . . but the power."
A weighty word for us all.

And now let us turn for a few moments to
the precious words of exhortation addressed
to the Christian remnant. May the Spirit
clothe them with power to our souls!

"But, beloved, remember ye the words
which were spoken before of the apostles of
our Lord Jesus Christ." They are directed to

the Holy Scriptures, and to these alone. It is not to human tradition of any kind; not to the Fathers; not to the decrees of general councils; not to the commandments and doctrines of men; not to any of these, or all put together, which can only bewilder, perplex, and mislead; but to the pure and precious Word of God, that perfect revelation which in His infinite goodness He has put into our hands, and which can make a little child "wise unto salvation" and make a man "*perfect*, thoroughly furnished unto *all good works*" (2 Tim. 3).

The Lord be praised for this unspeakable favor! No human language can set forth the importance of having a divinely settled authority for our path. All we want is to be absolutely and completely governed by it, to have it hidden in our hearts, acting on our consciences, forming our character, governing our conduct *in everything*. To give the Word of God this place is one of the marked characteristics of the Christian remnant. It is not the worthless, baseless formulary, "The Bible, and the Bible only, is the religion of Protestants." Protestantism is not the Church of God, it is not the Christian remnant.

The Reformation was the result of a blessed work of the Spirit of God; but Protestantism, in all its denominational branches, is what man has made of it. In it human organization has displaced the living work of the Spirit, and the form of godliness has displaced the power of individual faith. No mere *ism*, call it what you please, can ever be regarded as the Church of God or the Christian remnant. It is of the very utmost moral importance to see this. The professing Church has utterly failed, its corporate unity is hopelessly gone, just as we see in the history of Israel. But the Christian remnant is made up of all those who truly feel and own the ruin, who are governed by the Word and led by the Spirit, in separation from what is contrary to that Word, to wait for their Lord.

Let us see how all this comes out in Jude's address to the remnant. "But ye, beloved, building up yourselves on your most holy faith, praying in the Holy Ghost, keep yourselves in the love of God, looking for the mercy of our Lord Jesus Christ unto eternal life."

Here then we have a lovely view of the true Christian remnant and their occupation among themselves. Nothing can be more beautiful. We may be asked, to whom does this charming passage apply? We answer, to those—whoever and wherever they are—addressed in the first verse of the Epistle: "To them that are sanctified by God the Father, and preserved in Jesus Christ, and called." Nothing can be more simple or more blessed. It is perfectly obvious that these words do not and cannot apply to mere professors; neither can they apply to any ecclesiastical body under the sun. In a word, they apply to the living members of the body of Christ. All such should be found together building up themselves on their most holy faith, praying in the Holy Ghost, keeping themselves in the love of God, and looking out for their Lord.

This is the Christian remnant, just as in Malachi 3 we have the Jewish remnant. Nothing can be more lovely. It is the position in which all true Christians should be found. There is no pretension to setting themselves up to be anything, no attempt to ignore the sad and solemn fact of the utter ruin of the professing Church. It is a Christian remnant in the midst of christendom's ruins, true to the Person of Christ, true to His Word; knit together in true Christian love—not the love of sect, party, clique, or coterie, but love in the Spirit, love to all who love our Lord Jesus Christ in sincerity; love expressing itself in true devotedness to Christ and His precious interests; and loving ministry to all who belong to Him and seek to reflect Him in all their ways. It is not resting in mere position, regardless of condition—a terrible snare of the devil—but a healthy union of the two in a life characterized by sound principle and gracious practice; the kingdom of God established in the heart and developing itself in the whole practical career.

Such then is the position, the condition, the practice of the true Christian remnant; and we may rest assured that, where these things are realized and carried out, there will be as rich enjoyment of Christ, as full communion with God, and as bright a testimony to the glorious truth of New

Testament Christianity as ever was known in the brightest days of the Church's history. In a word, there will be that which will glorify the name of God, gratify the heart of Christ, and tell with living power on the hearts and consciences of men. May God, in His infinite goodness, give us to see these bright realities in this dark and evil day—a fresh illustration of the soul-stirring fact that the greater the ruin, the richer the grace; the deeper the gloom, the brighter the flashes of individual faith.

Look for a moment at the address to the fourth of the seven churches, as given in the second chapter of Revelation. The church of Thyatira gives us the history of the Church during those long, dreary centuries of the Middle Ages, when gross darkness covered the earth, when poverty—that darkest moral blot—prevailed in the well-known character of Jezebel.

In the address to this assembly we find a marked change, indicated by three plain facts—namely: first, a remnant is for the first time addressed: secondly, the Lord's coming is for the first time introduced; and, thirdly, the hearing ear is no longer looked for in the assembly at large, but in the *overcomer*. Now these facts prove beyond all question that in Thyatira all hope of corporate restoration is abandoned. "I gave her space to repent . . . and she repented not." The case is hopeless as regards the professing body. But here the remnant is singled out and cheered—not with the hope of a converted world or a restored church, but with the bright and blessed hope of the Lord's coming as the bright and morning star. "But unto you I say, the remnant* in Thyatira, as many as have not this doctrine [διδαχήν, the same root as διδάσκειν, what Jezebel was doing], and which have not known the depths of Satan, as they speak; I will put upon you none other burden. But that which ye have hold fast *till I come*."

Here then we have a deeply interesting view of the Christian remnant. It is not the church restored, but a distinct company clear of Jezebel's teaching and Satan's depths, and

going on to the end. It is of the utmost importance that the reader should be clear in reference to the fact that the last four churches run on synchronously to the end. It simplifies the whole subject immensely, and gives us a very definite, practical view of the Christian remnant. There is no mention of a remnant until we get to Thyatira. Then all hope of corporate restoration is given up. This simple fact overturns the church of Rome from its very foundations. It is presented to us as an apostate and idolatrous system, threatened with the judgment of God: and a remnant are addressed who have nothing to do with her. So much for the boasted, universal, infallible church of Rome.

But what of Sardis? Is this the church restored? Nothing of the kind. "Thou hast *a name* that thou livest, and *art dead*." This is not a restored or reformed church, but *threatened* with Christ's coming *as a thief*, instead of being cheered with "the bright and morning star." In a word, it is Protestantism with "a name," but the works "not perfect before God." And what then? The Christian remnant. "*A few names* even in Sardis which have not defiled their garments; and *they* [He does not say *thou*] shall walk with Me in white: for they are worthy." We have here a vivid and most striking contrast between dead, cold, nominal profession and a few true-hearted, earnest lovers of Christ—between form and power, death and life.

In the last two assemblies we have the contrast continued, enlarged, and enforced. Philadelphia gives us a most precious picture of a company of true Christians, humble, lowly, feeble, but true to Christ; holding fast His Word, and not denying His name—Christ and His Word treasured in the heart and confessed in the life—a living reality, not a lifeless form. The moral beauty of this is excellent. The very contemplation of it is refreshing and edifying indeed. In short, it is Christ reproduced by the Holy Ghost in a beloved remnant. There is no pretension to be anything, no assumption of great things. Christ is all: His Word, His name, how precious! We seem to have gathered up and

---

* The word rendered "remnant" in the above passage is λυιπoῖς, and is from the same root as the word "remnant" in Romans 11: 5, which is λίμμα. Both are from λείπω, to leave.

concentrated here the lovely moral traits of the various remnants that have come under our notice, brought out in full blow and yielding a fragrant perfume.

Now all this is most grateful to the heart of Christ. It is not a question of great service rendered, mighty works performed, anything striking or splendid in the eyes of men. No; it is something far more precious to the Lord, namely, the deep, calm, thorough appreciation of Himself and His precious Word. This is far more to Him than the most showy services and costly sacrifices. What He looks for is a place in the heart. Without this all is worthless. But the very feeblest breathing of the heart's affections after Himself is most precious.

Let us harken to our adorable Lord as He pours out His loving heart to this dear Philadelphian company—this true Christian remnant. "These things saith He that is holy, He that is true, He that hath the key of David, He that openeth, and no man shutteth; and shutteth, and no man openeth; I know thy works: behold, I have set before thee an open door, and no man can shut it: for thou hast a little strength, and hast kept *My word*, and hast not denied *My name*. Behold, I will make them of the synagogue of Satan"—those who take their stand on the boasted ground of traditionary religion— "which *say* they are Jews, and are not, but do lie; behold, I will make them to come and worship before thy feet, and to know that *I have loved thee*"—precious, blessed fact, the basis and guarantee of all, for time and eternity!—"Because thou hast kept the word of My *patience* [not My *power*], I will also keep thee from the hour of temptation, which shall come upon all the world, to try them that dwell upon the earth" ($\tau o \dot{\upsilon} \varsigma \varkappa \alpha \tau o \iota \varkappa o \tilde{\upsilon} \nu$-$\tau \alpha \varsigma$, those finding their home on the earth, in contrast to those whose citizenship is in Heaven).

The Lord Christ most graciously pledges Himself to keep His beloved assembly from the terrible hour of trial that is coming upon this whole scene. He will have His heavenly people with Himself in their heavenly home ere a single seal is opened, a trumpet sounded, or a vial poured out. All praise to His name for this bright, blessed, tranquilizing, joyful hope! May we live in the power of it while we wait for the full fruition!

But we must quote the remainder of this most exquisite address, so full of comfort and consolation. "Behold, I come quickly: hold that fast which thou hast, that no man take thy crown. Him that overcometh will I make a pillar in the temple of *My God*, and he shall go no more out: and I will write upon him the name of *My God*, and the name of the city of *My God*, new Jerusalem, which cometh down out of heaven from *My God*: and *My new name*."

Nothing can exceed the grace that shines in all this. Jehovah spoke gracious words to His beloved remnant in the days of Malachi. "*They shall be Mine* . . . in that day when I make up *My jewels*; and I will spare them, as a man spareth his own son that serveth him. Then shall ye return, and discern between the righteous and the wicked, between him that serveth God and him that serveth Him not. For, behold, the day cometh that shall burn as an oven; and all *the proud*, yea, and all that *do wickedly*, shall be stubble: and the day that cometh shall burn them up, saith the Lord of hosts, that it shall leave them neither root nor branch. But unto you that"—what? That have done great things, made great sacrifices, made a great profession, had a great name? No; but—"*fear My name* shall the Sun of righteousness arise with healing in His wings; and ye shall go forth, and grow up as calves of the stall. And ye shall tread down the wicked; for they shall be ashes under the soles of your feet in the day that I shall do this, saith the Lord of hosts" (Mal. 3:17—4:3).

There are points of similarity and points of contrast in the Jewish and Christian remnants which we cannot go into just now, inasmuch as our object in referring to both is to illustrate our special theme, namely, that in darkest days we find a devoted remnant dear to the heart of God, the heart of Christ, and who are addressed in the most tender and endearing terms, comforted by the most precious assurances, and cheered by the brightest hopes. This we believe to be the special subject laid upon the heart to present to the whole Church of God, for the purpose of encouraging every member of the beloved body of Christ on the face of the earth to stand apart from all that is contrary to His mind as revealed in His Word, and to be found in the position, attitude and spirit of the true Christian remnant, waiting for the coming of our beloved Lord.

One point marks the distinction between the two remnants in the clearest way. It is this: the Jewish remnant is cheered by the hope of the Sun of righteousness; whereas to the Christian remnant is granted the far higher, brighter and sweeter privilege of looking out for the bright and morning Star. A little child can understand the difference between these two things. The morning star appears in the heavens long before the sun rises; and in like manner the Church will meet her Lord as "the bright and morning Star" before the beams of the Sun of righteousness fall in healing power on the God-fearing remnant of Israel.

And now a word, in conclusion, as to Laodicea. Nothing can be more vivid or striking than the contrast between it and Philadelphia in every respect. We have here the last phase of the professing Chrisitan body. It is just about to be spewed out as something insufferably nauseous to Christ. It is not a question of gross immorality. It may to man's eye present a very respectable appearance; but to the heart of Christ its condition is most repulsive. It is characterized by lukewarmness and indifference. "I know thy works, that thou art neither cold nor hot: I would thou wert cold or hot. So then because thou art lukewarm, and neither cold nor hot, I will spew thee out of My mouth."

How awfully solemn to find the professing Church in such a condition! And to think how soon we pass from the attractions of Philadelphia—so grateful to the heart of Christ, so refreshing to His spirit—to the withering atmosphere of Laodicea, where there is not a single redeeming feature! We have heartless indifference as to Christ and His interests, combined with the most

deplorable self-gratulation. "Thou sayest, I am rich, and increased with goods, and *have need of nothing;* and knowest not that thou art wretched, and miserable, and poor, and blind, and naked: I counsel thee to buy of Me gold tried in the fire, that thou mayest be rich; and white raiment, that thou mayest be clothed, and that the shame of thy nakedness do not appear; and anoint thine eyes with eyesalve, that thou mayest see."

How solemn is all this! People boasting of their riches, and of their having need of nothing, and Christ outside. They have lost the sense of divine righteousness, symbolized by "gold," and practical human righteousness, as symbolized by "white raiment," and yet full of themselves and their doings—the very reverse of the dear Philadelphian company. There, He reproves nothing; here, He commends nothing. There, Christ is all; here, He is actually outside, and the Church is all. In a word, it is perfectly appalling to contemplate. We are just at the close. We have got to the last solemn phase of the Church as God's witness on the earth.

Yet even here, in the face of this most deplorable condition of things, the infinite grace and changeless love of the heart of Christ shine out in all their undimmed lustre. He is outside; this tells what the Church is. But He is knocking, calling, waiting: this tells what He is, eternal and universal homage to His name! "As many as I love, I rebuke and chasten: be zealous therefore, and repent." The gold, the white raiment and the eyesalve are offered. Love has various offices to discharge, various characters in which to clothe itself; but it is the same love still—"the same yesterday, and to-day, and forever," even though it has to "rebuke and chasten." Here His attitude and His action speak volumes, both as to the Church and as to Himself. "Behold, I stand at the door, and knock: *if any man* hear My voice, and open the door, I will come in to *him,* and will sup with him, and *he with Me.*"*

In the church of Sardis the remnant is spoken of as "a few names"; in Laodicea there

---

* Here it is not to the outside sinner, but to the professing Church the Lord makes this most solemn and weighty appeal. It is not Christ knocking at the door of the sinner's heart (true as that is also), but at the door of those in the professing Church. How telling! how suggestive! Oh, may professing Christians ponder it!

is an "if" as to one; but even if there be a single hearing ear, if there be one to open the door, that one is assured of the high privilege, the immense favor, of supping with Christ—of having that precious one as Guest and Host. "I with him, and he with Me." When the corporate witness has reached the very lowest point, individual faithfulness is rewarded with intimate fellowship with the heart of Christ. Such is the infinite and everlasting love of our beloved Saviour and Lord. Oh, who would not trust Him and praise Him and love Him and serve Him?

And now, beloved Christian reader, I would earnestly and affectionately entreat you to join in petition to our ever-gracious God to stir up the hearts of His beloved people all over the world to seek a more pronounced, whole-hearted, devoted discipleship; to turn away from everything contrary to His Word; to be true to His Word and to His name in this dark and evil day; and thus realize the truth, which has passed before us in this paper, that *the greater the ruin, the richer the grace; the deeper the gloom, the brighter the outshining of individual faith.*

P.S.—I feel I must not let this paper go forth without adding a word on the immense importance of keeping up a full, clear, earnest gospel testimony. "Do the work of an evangelist" is a charge given by the beloved apostle from his prison at Rome to his dear son Timothy, in view of the total ruin of the professing Church; and truly the circumstances under which these words were penned impart a touching interest to them. Come what may, Timothy was to continue to announce the glad tidings of God's salvation. He might be tempted to give up in despair, and say, "All is going to pieces, people will not listen to the gospel"—"will not endure sound doctrine."

Faith says, "No; we must never give up. God's gospel must be preached to every creature under heaven. And even though men reject it, God is glorified and His heart is refreshed by the precious message of His love being told out in the ears of perishing sinners." We would encourage the heart of every beloved evangelist on the face of the earth by reminding him that however the Church has failed as God's witness to the world, yet the precious gospel tells out what He is to every poor, broken-hearted, bankrupt sinner who will only trust Him. The thought of this has cheered us during forty-eight years of evangelistic work, when the condition of the Church was heartbreaking to contemplate.

In speaking of the work of an evangelist, we must not confine it to public halls and rooms, which, of course, demand a distinct gift from the Head of the Church. We believe it is the sweet privilege of every child of God to be in a condition of soul to tell the glad tidings to individual souls in private life; and we must confess we long to see more of this. It matters not what our position in life or sphere of action may be, we should earnestly and prayerfully seek the salvation of those with whom we come in contact. If we fail in this, we are not in communion with the heart of God and the mind of Christ. In the Gospels and Acts we see a great deal of this lovely individual work. "Philip findeth Nathanael." "Andrew first findeth his own brother Simon."

We want more of this earnest, beautiful, personal work in private. It is refreshing to the heart of God. We are apt to get into a groove and rest satisfied with asking people to come to public halls and rooms—all right and good in its place, and most important. We would not pen a line to detract from the value of this service; but at the same time we cannot help feeling our sad deficiency in loving, personal dealing with souls. But this requires nearness to God in our inward life; which may well cause serious searching of our hearts before God, for it is the root of our deficiency.

May the gracious Lord stir up the hearts of all His beloved people to a more lively interest in the blessed work of evangelization, at home and abroad, in public and in private!

THE GREAT COMMISSION

Part 1

"AND HE SAID UNTO THEM, These are the words which I spake unto you while I was yet with you, that all things must be fulfilled which were written in the law of Moses, and in the Prophets, and in the Psalms, concerning Me. Then opened He their understanding, that they might understand the Scriptures, and said unto them, *Thus it is written*, and thus it behoved Christ to suffer, and to rise from the dead on the third day; and that repentance and remission of sins should be preached in His name among all nations, beginning at Jerusalem. And ye are witnesses of these things. And behold, I send the promise of My Father unto you: but tarry ye in the city of Jerusalem, until ye be endued with power from on high" (Luke 24:44-49).

This splendid passage of Holy Scripture sets before us the great commission which the risen Lord entrusted to His apostles just as He was about to ascend into the heavens, having gloriously accomplished all His blessed work upon earth. It is truly a most wonderful commission, and opens up a very wide field of truth, through which we may range with much spiritual delight and profit. Whether we ponder *the commission itself*, its *basis*, its *authority*, its *power*, or its *sphere*, we shall find it all full of most precious instruction. May the blessed Spirit guide our thoughts, while we meditate, first of all, upon *the commission itself*.

The apostles of our Lord and Saviour Jesus Christ were specially charged to preach "repentence and remission of sins." Let us all remember this. We are prone to forget it, to the serious damaging of our preaching, and of the souls of our hearers. Some of us are apt to overlook the first part of the commission, in our eagerness, it may be, to get to the second. This is a most serious mistake. We may rest assured that it is our truest wisdom to keep close to the veritable terms in which our blessed Lord delivered His charge to His earliest heralds. We cannot omit a single point, not to say a leading branch of the commission, without serious loss in every way. Our Lord is infinitely wiser and more gracious than we are, and we need not fear to preach with all possible plainness what He told His apostles to preach, namely, "repentance and remission of sins."

Now the question is, are we all careful to maintain this very important connection? Do we give sufficient prominence to the first part of the great commission? Do we preach "repentance?"

We are not now inquiring what repentance is; that we shall do, if God permit. But, whatever it is, do we preach it? That our Lord commanded His apostles to preach it is plain; and not only so, but He preached it Himself, as we read it in Mark 1:14-15: "Now after that John was put in prison, Jesus came into Galilee, preaching the gospel of the kingdom of God, and saying, The time is fulfilled, and the kingdom of God is at hand; repent ye and believe the gospel."

Let us carefully note this record. Let all preachers note it. Our divine Master called upon sinners to repent and believe the gospel. Some would have us to believe that it is a mistake to call upon persons dead in trespasses and sins to do anything. "How," it is argued, "can those who are dead repent? They are incapable of any spiritual movement. They must first get the power ere they can either repent or believe."

What is our reply to all this? A very simple one indeed—Our Lord knows better than all the theologians in the world what ought to be preached. He knows all about man's condition —his guilt, his misery, his spiritual death, his utter helplessness, his total inability to think a single right thought, to utter a single right word, to do a single right act; and yet He called upon men to repent. This is quite enough for us. It is no part of our business to seek to reconcile seeming differences. It may seem to us difficult to reconcile man's utter powerlessness with his responsibility; but "God is His own interpreter, and He will make it plain." It is our happy privilege, and our bounden duty, to believe what He says, and do what He tells us. This is true wisdom, and it yields solid peace.

Our Lord preached repentance, and He commanded His apostles to preach it; and they did so constantly. Harken to Peter on the day of Pentecost. "Then Peter said unto them, Repent, and be baptized, every one of you, in the name of Jesus Christ, for the remission of sins, and ye shall receive the gift of the Holy Ghost." And again, "Repent ye, therefore, and be converted, that your sins may be blotted out when the times of refreshing shall come from the presence of the Lord." Harken to Paul also, as he stood on Mars' Hill, at Athens: "But now *God commandeth all men everywhere* to repent; because He hath appointed a day in which He will judge the world in righteousness, by that Man whom He hath ordained; whereof He hath given assurance unto all men, in that He hath raised Him from the dead."

So also, in his touching address to the elders of Ephesus, he says, "I kept back nothing that was profitable [blessed servant!] but have showed you, and have taught you publicly, and from house to house, testifying both to the Jews, and also the Greeks, *repentance toward God*, and faith toward our Lord Jesus Christ." And again, in his address to king Agrippa, he says, "Whereupon, O king Agrippa, I was not disobedient unto the heavenly vision, but showed first unto them of Damascus, and at Jerusalem, and throughout all the coasts of Judea, and then to the Gentiles, that *they should repent*, and turn to God, and *do works meet for repentance*."

Now, in the face of this body of evidence—with the example of our Lord and His apostles so fully and clearly before us—may we not very lawfully inquire whether there is not a serious defect in much of our modern preaching? Do we preach repentance as we

ought? Do we assign to it the place which it gets in the preaching of our Lord, and of His early heralds? It is vanity and folly, or worse, to talk about its being legal to preach repentance, to say that it tarnishes the lustre of the gospel of the grace of God to call upon men dead in trespasses and sins to repent, and do works meet for repentance. Was Paul legal in his preaching? Did he not preach a clear, full, rich, and divine gospel? Have we got in advance of Paul? Do we preach a clearer gospel than he? How utterly preposterous the notion! Well, but he preached repentance. He told his hearers that "God now commandeth all men everywhere to repent." Does this mar the gospel of the grace of God? Does it detract from its heavenly fulness and freeness? As well might you tell a farmer that it lowered the quality of his grain to plough the fallow ground before sowing.

No doubt it is of the very last possible importance to preach the gospel of the grace of God, or, if you please, the gospel of the glory, in all its fulness, clearness, and power. We are to preach the unsearchable riches of Christ—to declare the whole counsel of God, to present the righteousness of God and His salvation, without limit, condition, or hindrance of any kind—to publish the good news to every creature under heaven.

We should, in the very strongest possible manner, insist upon this. But at the same time we must jealously keep to the terms of "the great commission." We cannot depart the breadth of a hair from these without serious damage to our testimony, and to the souls of our hearers. If we fail to preach repentance, we are "keeping back" something "profitable." What should we say to a husbandman, if we saw him scattering his precious grain along the beaten highway? We should justly pronounce him out of his mind. The ploughshare must do its work. The fallow ground must be broken up ere the seed is sown; and we may rest assured that, as in the kingdom of nature, so in the kingdom of grace, the ploughing must precede the sowing. The ground must be duly prepared for the seed, else the operation will prove altogether defective. Let the gospel be preached as God has given it to us in His Word. Let it not be shorn of one of its moral glories; let it flow forth as it comes from the deep fountain of the heart of God, through the channel of Christ's finished work, on the authority of the Holy Ghost.

All this is not only most fully admitted but peremptorily insisted upon; but at the same time we must never forget that our Lord and Master called upon men to "repent and believe the gospel"; that He strictly enjoined it upon His holy apostles to preach repentance; and that the blessed apostle Paul, the chief of apostles, the profoundest teacher the Church has ever known, did preach repentance, calling upon men everywhere to repent and do works meet for repentance.

And here it may be well for us to inquire what this repentance is which occupies such a prominent place in "the great commission," and in the preaching of our Lord and of His apostles. If it be—as it most surely is—an abiding and universal necessity for man—if God commands all men everywhere to repent—if repentance is inseparably linked with remission of sins—how needful it is that we should seek to understand its true nature!

What, then, is repentance? May the Spirit Himself instruct us by the Word of God! He alone can. We are all liable to err—some of us have erred—in our thoughts on this most weighty subject. We are in danger, while seeking to avoid error on one side, of falling into error on the other. We are poor, feeble, ignorant, erring creatures, whose only security is in our being kept continually at the feet of our blessed Lord Jesus Christ. He alone can teach us what repentance is, as well as what it is not. We feel most fully assured that the enemy of souls and of the truth has succeeded in giving repentance a false place in the creeds, and confessions, and public teachings of christendom; and the conviction of this makes it all the more needful for us to keep close to the living teachings of Holy Scripture.

We are not aware of any formal definition of the subject furnished by the Holy Ghost. He does not tell us in so many words what repentance is; but the more we study the Word in reference to the great question, the more deeply we feel convinced that true repentance involves the solemn judgment of ourselves, our condition, and our ways, in the presence of God; and, further, that this judgment is not a transient feeling, but an abiding condition—not a certain exercise to be gone through as a sort of title to the remission of sins, but the deep and settled habit of the soul, giving seriousness, gravity, tenderness, brokenness, and profound humility, which shall overlap, underlie, and characterize our entire course.

We seriously question if this aspect of the subject is sufficiently understood. Let not the reader mistake us. We do not mean for a moment to teach that the soul should be always bowed down under the sense of unforgiven sin. Far be the thought! But we greatly fear that some of us, in running away from *legality* on the question of repentance, have fallen into *levity*. This is a serious error. We may depend upon it that levity is no remedy for legality: were it proposed as such, we should have no hesitation in pronouncing the remedy much worse than the disease. Thank God we have His own sovereign remedy for levity, on the one hand, and legality on the other. *"Truth"*—insisting upon "repentance," is the remedy for the former. *"Grace"*—publishing "remission of sins," is the remedy for the latter. And we cannot but believe that the more profound our repentance, the fuller will be our enjoyment of remission.

We are inclined to judge that there is a sad lack of depth and seriousness in much of our modern preaching. In our anxiety to make the gospel simple, and salvation easy, we fail to press on the consciences of our hearers the holy claims of truth. If a preacher now-a-days were to call upon his hearers to "repent and turn to God, and to do works meet for repentance," he would, in certain circles, be pronounced legal, ignorant, below the mark, and such like. And yet this was precisely what the blessed apostle Paul did, as he himself tells us. Will any of our modern evangelists have the temerity to say that Paul was a legal or an ignorant preacher? We trust not. Paul carried with him the full, clear, precious gospel of God—the gospel of the grace, and the gospel of the glory. He preached the kingdom of God—He unfolded the glorious mystery of the Church—yea, that mystery was specially committed to him.

But let all preachers remember that Paul preached repentance. He called upon sinners to judge themselves—to repent in dust and ashes, as was meet and right they should. He himself had learnt the true meaning of repentance. He had not only judged himself once in a way, but he *lived* in the spirit of self-judgment. It was the habit of his soul, the attitude of his heart, and it gave a depth, solidity, seriousness and solemnity to his preaching of which we modern preachers know but little. We do not believe that Paul's repentance ended with the three days and three nights of blindness after his conversion. He was a self-judged man all his life long. Did this hinder his enjoyment of the grace of God or of the preciousness of Christ? Nay, it gave depth and intensity to his enjoyment.

All this, we feel persuaded, demands our most serious consideration. We greatly dread the light, airy, superficial style of much of our modern preaching. It sometimes seems to us as if the gospel were brought into utter contempt and the sinner led to suppose that he is really conferring a very great favor upon God in accepting salvation at His hands. Now we most solemnly protest against this. It is dishonoring to God, and lowering His gospel; and, as might be expected, its moral effect on those who profess to be converted is most deplorable. It superinduces levity, self-indulgence, worldliness, vanity, and folly. Sin is not felt to be the dreadful thing it is in the sight of God. Self is not judged. The world is not given up. The gospel that is preached is what may be called "salvation made easy" to the flesh—the most terrible thing we can possibly conceive—terrible in its effect upon the soul—terrible in its results in the life. God's sentence upon the flesh and the world gets no place in the preaching to which we refer. People are offered a salvation which leaves self and the world practically unjudged, and the consequence is, those who profess to be converted by this gospel exhibit a lightness

and unsubduedness perfectly shocking to people of serious piety.

Man must take his true place before God, and that is the place of self-judgment, contrition of heart, real sorrow for sin, and true confession. It is here the gospel meets him. The fulness of God ever waits on an empty vessel, and a truly repentant soul is the empty vessel into which all the fulness and grace of God can flow in saving power. The Holy Ghost will make the sinner *feel* and *own* his real condition. It is He alone who can do so: but He uses preaching to this end. He brings the Word of God to bear on man's conscience. The Word is His hammer, wherewith He breaks the rock in pieces—His plowshare, wherewith He breaks up the fallow ground. He makes the furrow, and then casts in the incorruptible seed, to germinate and fructify to the glory of God. True, the furrow, how deep soever it may be, can produce no fruit. It is the seed, and not the furrow; but there must be the furrow for all that.

It is not, need we say, that there is anything meritorious in the sinner's repentance. To say so could only be regarded as audacious falsehood. Repentance is not a good work whereby the sinner merits the favor of God. All this view of the subject is utterly and fatally false. True repentance is the discovery and hearty confession of our utter ruin and guilt. It is the finding out that my whole life has been a lie, and that I myself am a liar. This is serious work. There is no flippancy or levity when a soul is brought to this. A penitent soul in the presence of God is a solemn reality; and we cannot but feel that were we more governed by the terms of "the great commission," we should more solemnly, earnestly and constantly call upon men "to repent and turn to God and do works meet for repentance"—we should preach "repentance" as well as "remission of sins."

Part 2

Since writing our last paper, we have been much interested in the way in which repentance is presented in those inimitable parables in Luke 15. There we learn, in a manner the most touching and convincing, not only the abiding and universal necessity —the moral fitness in every case of true repentance—but also that it is grateful to the heart of God. Our Lord, in His marvelous reply to the scribes and Pharisees, declares that "there is joy in heaven over one sinner that repenteth." And again, "Likewise, I say unto you, there is joy in the presence of the angels of God over one sinner that repenteth."

Now this gives us a very elevated view of the subject. It is one thing to see that repentance is binding upon man, and another and very much higher thing to see that it is grateful to God. "Thus saith the high and lofty One that inhabiteth eternity, whose name is Holy: I dwell in the high and holy place, with him also that is of a contrite and humble spirit, to revive the spirit of the humble, and to revive the heart of the contrite ones." A broken heart, a contrite spirit, a repentant mind, gives joy to God.

Let us ponder this fact. The scribes and Pharisees murmured because Jesus received sinners. How little they understood Him! How little they knew of the object that brought Him down into this dark and sinful world! How little they knew of themselves! It was the "lost" that Jesus came to seek. But scribes and Pharisees did not think themselves lost. They thought they were all right. They did not want a Saviour. They were thoroughly unbroken, unrepentant, self-confident: and hence they had never afforded one atom of joy in Heaven. All the learning of the scribes, and all the righteousness of the Pharisees, could not waken up a single note of joy in the presence of the angels of God. They were like the elder son in the parable who said, "Lo, these many years do I serve thee, neither transgressed I at any time thy commandment; and yet thou never gavest me a kid, that I might make merry with my friends."

Here we have a true specimen of an unbroken heart and an unrepentant spirit—a man thoroughly satisfied with himself. Miserable object! He had never touched a chord in the Father's heart—never drawn out the Father's love—never felt the Father's embrace—never received the Father's welcome. How could he? He had never felt himself lost. He was full of himself, and therefore had no room for the Father's love. He did not feel that he owed anything, and hence he had nothing to be forgiven. It rather seemed to him that his father was his debtor. "Lo, these many years do I serve thee; and yet thou never gavest me a kid." He had not received his wages.

What egregious folly! And yet it is just the same with every unrepentant soul—every one who is building upon his own righteousness. He really makes God his debtor. "I have served Thee; but I have never gotten what I earned." Miserable notion! The man who talks of his duties, his doings, his sayings, his givings, is really insulting God. But on the other hand, the man who comes with a broken heart, a contrite spirit, repentant, self-judged—that is the man who gives joy to the heart of God.

And why? Simply because such a one feels his need of God. Here lies the grand moral secret of the whole matter. To apprehend this is to grasp the full truth on the great question of repentance. A God of love desires to make His way to the sinner's heart, but there is no room for Him so long as that heart is hard and impenitent. But when the sinner is brought to the end of himself, when he sees himself a helpless, hopeless wreck, when he sees the utter emptiness, hollowness and vanity of all earthly things; when like the prodigal he comes to himself and feels the depth and reality of his need, then there is room in his heart for God, and—marvelous truth!—God delights to come and fill it. "To this man will I look." To whom? To the man who does his duty, keeps the law, does his best, lives up to his light? Nay; but "to him who is of a contrite spirit."

It will perhaps be said that the words just quoted apply to Israel. Primarily, they do; but morally they apply to every contrite heart on the face of the earth. And, further, it cannot be said that Luke 15 applies specially to Israel. It applies to all. "There is joy in the presence of the angels of God over one sinner that"—What? Does his duty? Nay, it does not even say, "that believeth." No doubt believing is essential in every case; but the interesting point here is that a truly repentant sinner causes joy in Heaven. A person may say, "I fear I do not believe." Well, but do you repent? Have your eyes been opened to see your true condition before God? Have you taken your true place before God as utterly lost? If so, you are one of those over whom there is joy in Heaven.

What gave joy to the shepherd's heart? Was it the ninety and nine sheep that went not astray? Nay, it was finding the lost sheep.* What gave joy to the woman's heart? Was it the nine pieces in her possession? Nay, it was finding the one lost piece. What gave joy to the father's heart? Was it the service and the obedience of the elder son? Nay, it was getting back his lost son. A repentant, broken-hearted, returning sinner wakens up Heaven's joy. "Let *us* eat and be merry." Why? Because the elder son has been working in the fields and doing his duty? No; but "This my son was *dead*, and is alive again; he was *lost*, and is found."

All this is perfectly wonderful. Indeed, it is so wonderful that if we had it not from the lips of Him who is the Truth, and on the eternal page of divine inspiration, we could not believe it. But, blessed be God, there it stands, and none can gainsay it. There shines the glorious truth that a poor, self-convicted, broken-hearted, penitent, though hell-deserving sinner, gives joy to the heart of God. Let people talk as they will about keeping the law and doing their duty: it may go for what it is worth; but be it remembered there is no such clause within the covers of the volume of God—no such sentence ever dropped from the lips of our Lord Jesus Christ as "There is joy in heaven over one sinner that does his duty."

A *sinner's duty!* What is it? "God commandeth *all* men *everywhere* to repent." What is it that can really define our duty? Surely the divine command. Well, here it is, and there is no getting over it. God's command to all men, in every place, is to repent. His commandment binds them to do it; His goodness leads them to it; His judgment warns them to it; and, above all, and most marvelous of all, He assures us that our repentance gives joy to His heart. A penitent heart is an object of profoundest interest to the mind of God, because that heart is morally prepared to receive what God delights to bestow, namely, "remission of sins"—yea, all the fulness of divine love. A man might spend millions in the cause of religion and philanthropy, and not afford one atom of joy in Heaven. What are millions of money to God? A single penitential tear is more precious to Him than all the wealth of the universe. All the offerings of an unbroken heart are a positive insult to God; but a single sigh from the depths of a contrite spirit goes up as a fragrant incense to His throne and to His heart.

No man can meet God on the ground of duty; but God can meet any man—the very chief of sinners—on the ground of repentance, for that is man's true place; and we may say with all possible confidence that when the sinner, as he is, meets God as He is, the whole question is settled once and forever. "I said, *I will confess* my transgressions unto the Lord, and *Thou forgavest* the iniquity of my sin." The moment man takes his true place—the place of repentance—God meets him with a full forgiveness, a divine and everlasting righteousness. It is His joy to do so. It gratifies His heart and it glorifies His name to pardon, justify and accept a penitent soul that simply believes in Jesus. The very moment the prophet cried, "Woe is me; for I am undone"—"Then *flew* one of the seraphims with a live coal from off the altar" to touch his lips, and to purge his sins (Isa. 6:5-7).

Thus it is always. The fulness of God ever waits on an empty vessel. If I am full of myself, full of my own fancied goodness, my own morality, my own righteousness, I have no room for God, no room for Christ. "He filleth the *hungry* with good things; but the

---

* Let the reader note that the "ninety and nine just persons that need no repentance" and the elder son that "never transgressed his father's commandment" is the expression of their own thoughts as to themselves. When *God's* judgment of man is expressed, the Scriptures declare, "There is none righteous, no, not one. . . . They are all gone out of the way . . . there is none that doeth good, no, not one" (Rom. 3: 10, 12). [Ed.]

rich He hath sent *empty* away." A self-emptied soul can be filled with the fulness of God; but if God sends a man empty away, whither can he go to be filled? All Scripture, from Genesis to Revelation, goes to prove the deep blessedness as well as the moral necessity of repentance. It is the grand turning-point in the soul's history—a great moral epoch which sheds its influence over the whole of one's after life. It is not, we repeat, a transient exercise, but an abiding moral condition. We are not now speaking of how repentance is produced; we are speaking of what it is according to Scripture, and of the absolute need of it for every creature under Heaven. It is the sinner's true place; and when through grace he takes it, he is met by the fulness of God's salvation.

Here we see the lovely connection between the first and second clauses of "the great commission," namely, "repentance and remission of sins." They are inseparably linked together. It is not that the most profound and genuine repentance forms the meritorious ground of remission of sins. To say or to think so would be to set aside the atonement of our Lord Jesus Christ, for in that, and *in that alone*, have we the divine ground on which God can righteously forgive us our sins. This we shall see more fully when we come to consider the "*basis*" of "the great commission."

We are now occupied with the commission itself; and in it we see those two divinely settled facts, repentance and remission of sins. The holy apostles of our Lord and Saviour were charged to preach among all nations—to declare in the ears of every creature under heaven "repentance and remission of sins." Every man, be he Jew or Gentile, is absolutely commanded by God to repent; and every repentant soul is privileged to receive, on the spot, the full and everlasting remission of sins. And we may add, the deeper and more abiding the work of repentance, the deeper and more abiding will be the enjoyment of remission of sins. The contrite soul lives in the very atmosphere of divine forgiveness; and as it inhales that atmosphere, it shrinks with ever-increasing horror from sin in every shape and form.

Let us turn for a moment to the Acts of the Apostles, and see how Christ's ambassadors carried out the second part of His blessed commission. Hear the apostle of the circumcision addressing the Jews on the day of Pentecost. We cannot attempt to quote the whole of his address; we merely give the few words of application at the close. "Therefore let all the house of Israel know assuredly that God hath made that same Jesus whom ye have crucified both Lord and Christ."

Here the preacher bears down upon the consciences of his hearers with the solemn fact that they had proved themselves to be at issue with God Himself about His Christ. What a tremendous fact! It was not merely that they had broken the law, rejected the prophets, refused the testimony of John the Baptist; but they had actually crucified the Lord of glory, the eternal Son of God. "Now when they heard this, they were pricked in their heart, and said unto Peter and to the rest of the apostles, Men, brethren, what shall we do? Then Peter said unto them, *Repent*, and be baptized every one of you in the name of Jesus Christ, for *the remission of sins*, and ye shall receive the gift of the Holy Ghost" (Acts 2:36-38).

Here are the two parts of the great commission brought out in all their distinctness and power. The people are charged with the most awful sin that could be committed, namely, the murder of the Son of God; they are called upon to repent, and assured of full remission of sins and the gift of the Holy Ghost. What wondrous grace shines forth in all this! The very people that had mocked and insulted the Son of God, and crucified Him, even these, if truly repentant, were assured of the complete pardon of all their sins, and of this crowning sin amongst the rest. Such is the wondrous grace of God—such the mighty efficacy of the blood of Christ—such the clear and authoritative testimony of the Holy Ghost—such the glorious terms of "the great commission."

But let us turn for a moment to Acts 3. Here the preacher, after charging his hearers with this awful act of wickedness against God, even the rejection and murder of His Son, adds these remarkable words: "And now, brethren, I wot that through ignorance ye did it, as did also your rulers. But those things, which God before had showed by the mouth of all His prophets, that Christ should suffer, *He hath so fulfilled. Repent* ye therefore, and be converted, that *your sins may be blotted out.*"

It is not possible to conceive anything higher or fuller than the grace that shines out here. It is a part of the divine response to the prayer of Christ on the cross, "Father, forgive them, for they know not what they do." This surely is royal grace. It is victorious grace—grace reigning through righteousness. It was impossible that such a prayer should fall to the ground. It was answered in part on the day of Pentecost. It will be answered in full at a future day, for "All Israel shall be saved; as it is written, There shall come out of Zion the Deliverer, and shall turn away ungodliness from Jacob."

Mark particularly the words "Those things which God before had shewed . . . He hath so fulfilled." Here the preacher brings in God's side of the matter: and this is salvation. To see only man's part in the cross would be eternal judgment. To see God's part, and to rest in it is eternal life, full remission of sins, divine righteousness, everlasting glory.

The reader will doubtless be reminded here of the touching scene between Joseph and his brethren. There is a striking analogy between Acts 3 and Genesis 14. "Now therefore," says Joseph, "be not grieved, nor angry with yourselves, that ye sold me hither; for God did send me before you to preserve life. . . . And God sent me before you to preserve you a posterity in the earth, and to save your lives by a great deliverance. *So now it was not you that sent me hither, but God.*"

But when were these words uttered? Not until the guilty brethren had felt and owned their guilt. Repentance preceded the remission. "They said one to another, We are verily guilty concerning our brother, in that we saw the anguish of his soul, when he besought us, and we would not hear; therefore is this distress come upon us." Joseph "spake roughly" to his brethren at the first. He brought them through deep waters,

and made them feel and confess their guilt. But the very moment they took the ground of repentance, he took the ground of forgiveness. The penitent brethren were met by a pardoning Joseph, and the whole house of Pharaoh was made to ring with the joy which filled the heart of Joseph on getting back to his bosom the very men that had flung him into the pit.

What an illustration of "repentance and remission of sins!" It is ever thus. It is the joy of the heart of God to forgive us our sins. He delights in causing the full tide of His pardoning love to flow into the broken and contrite heart.

Yes, if you have been brought to feel the burden of your guilt, then be assured it is your privilege this very moment to receive a divine and everlasting remission of all your sins. The blood of Jesus Christ has perfectly settled the question of your guilt, and you are now invited to rejoice in the God of your salvation.

Part 3

We shall now turn for a few moments to the ministry of the apostle of the Gentiles, and see how he fulfilled the great commission. We have already heard him on the subject of "repentance." Let us hear him also on the great question of "remission of sins."

Paul was not of the twelve. He did not receive his commission from Christ on earth, but, as he himself distinctly and repeatedly tells us, from Christ in heavenly glory. Some have spent not a little time and pains in laboring to prove that he was of the twelve, and that the election of Matthias in Acts 1 was a mistake. But it is labor sadly wasted, and only proves an entire misunderstanding of Paul's position and ministry. He was raised up for a special object, and made the depositary of a special truth which had never been made known to any one before, namely, the truth of the Church—the one body composed of Jew and Gentile, incorporated by the Holy Ghost, and linked, by His personal indwelling, to the risen and glorified Head in Heaven.

Paul received his own special commission,

of which he gives a very beautiful statement in his address to Agrippa, in Acts 26, "Whereupon, as I went to Damascus, with authority and commission from the chief priests"—what a different "commission" he received ere he entered Damacus!—"at midday, O king, I saw in the way a light from heaven, above the brightness of the sun, shining round about me and them which journeyed with me. And when we were all fallen to the earth, I heard a voice speaking unto me, and saying in the Hebrew tongue, Saul, Saul, why persecutest thou Me? it is hard for thee to kick against the pricks. And I said, Who art thou, Lord? And He said, I am Jesus, whom thou persecutest." Here the glorious truth of the intimate union of believers with the glorified Man in Heaven, though not stated, is beautifully and forcibly implied.

"But rise, and stand upon thy feet, for I have appeared unto thee for this pupose, to make thee a minister and a witness both of these things which thou hast seen, and of those things in the which I will appear unto thee; delivering thee from the people and the Gentiles, unto whom now I send thee, to open their eyes, and to turn them from darkness to light, and from the power of Satan unto God, that they may receive remission of sins" (the same word as in the commission to the twelve in Luke 24) "and inheritance among them which are sanctified, by faith that is in Me."*

What depth and fulness in these words! What a comprehensive statement of man's condition! What a blessed presentation of the resources of divine grace! There is a very remarkable harmony between this commission to Paul and that to the twelve in Luke 24. It will perhaps be said there is nothing about repentance. True, the word does not occur; but we have the moral reality, and that with singular force and fulness. What mean the words, *"To open their eyes"*? Do they not most certainly involve the discovery of our condition? Assuredly. A man who has his eyes opened is brought to the knowledge of himself, the knowledge of his condition, the knowledge of his ways; and this is true

repentance. It is a wonderful moment in a man's history when his eyes are opened. It is the grand crisis, the momentous epoch, the one turning-point. Till then he is blind—morally and spiritually blind. He cannot see a single divine object. He has no perception of anything pertaining to God, to Christ, to Heaven.

This is truly humbling to proud human nature. Think of a clear-headed, highly educated, deeply learned, intellectual man, a profound thinker, a powerful reasoner, a thorough philosopher, who has won the honors, the medals, the degrees, that this world's universities can bestow; and yet he is blind to everything spiritual, heavenly, divine. He gropes in moral darkness. He thinks he sees, assumes the right to judge and pronounce upon things, even upon Scripture and upon God Himself. He undertakes to decide what is fitting for God to say and to do. He sets up his own mind as the measure in the things of God. He reasons upon immortality, upon eternal life, and eternal punishment. He deems himself perfectly competent to give judgment in reference to all these solemn and weighty matters; and all the while his eyes have never been opened. How much is his judgment worth? Nothing! Who would take the opinion of a man who, if his eyes were only opened, would reverse that opinion in reference to everything heavenly and divine? Who would think for a moment of being guided by a blind man?

But how do we know that every man in his natural, unconverted state is blind? Because, according to Paul's commission, the very first thing which the gospel is to do for him is "to open his eyes." This proves, beyond all question, that he must be blind. Paul was sent to the people and to the Gentiles—that is, to the whole human family—to open their eyes. This proves, to a divine demonstration, that all are by nature blind.

But there is more than this. Man is not only blind, but he is in "darkness." Supposing for a moment that a person has his eyesight, of what use is it to him if he is in the dark? It is the double statement as to man's state and

---

* "By faith" is connected with remission of sins and inheritance among the sanctified.

position. As to his state, he is blind. As to his position, he is in darkness; and when his eyes are opened, and divine light streams in upon his soul, he then judges himself and his ways according to God. He sees his folly, his guilt, his rebellion, his wild, infidel reasonings, his foolish notions, the vanity of his mind, his pride and ambition, his selfishness and worldliness—all these things are judged and abhorred. He repents, and turns right round to the One who has opened his eyes and poured in a flood of living light upon his heart and conscience.

Further, not only is man—every man—Jew and Gentile, blind and in darkness, but, as if to give the climax of all, he is under the power of Satan. This gives a terrible idea of man's condition. He is the slave of the devil. He does not believe this. He imagines himself free—thinks he is his own master—fancies he can go where he pleases, do what he likes, think for himself, speak and act as an independent being. But he is the bondslave of another, he is sold under sin, Satan is his lord and master. Thus Scripture speaks, and it cannot be broken. Man may refuse to believe, but that cannot in the least change the fact. A condemned criminal at the bar may refuse to believe the testimony from the witness table, the verdict from the jury-box, the sentence from the bench; but that in nowise alters his terrible condition. He is a condemned criminal all the same.

So with man as a sinner; he may refuse the plain testimony of Scripture, but that testimony remains notwithstanding. Even if the thousand millions that people this globe were to deny the truth of God's Word, that Word would still stand unmoved. Scripture does not depend for its truth upon man's belief. It is true whether he believes it or not. Blessed forever is the man who believes; doomed forever is the man who refuses to believe; but the Word of God is settled forever in Heaven, and it is to be received on its own authority, apart from all human thoughts for or against it.

This is a grand fact, and one demanding the profound attention of every soul. Everything depends upon it. The Word of God claims our belief because it is His Word. If we want any

authority to confirm the truth of God's Word, we are in reality rejecting God's Word altogether, and resting on man's word. A man may say, "How do I know that the Bible is the Word of God?" We reply, It carries its own divine credentials with it; and if these credentials do not convince, all the human authority under the sun is perfectly worthless. If the whole population of the earth were to stand before me, and assure me of the truth of God's Word, and that I were to believe on their authority, it would not be saving faith at all. It would be faith in men, and not faith in God; but the faith that saves is the faith that believes what God says because God says it.

It is not that we undervalue human testimony, or reject what are called the external evidences of the truth of the Holy Scripture. All these things must go for what they are worth; they are by no means essential in laying the foundation of saving faith. We are perfectly sure that all genuine history, all true science, all sound human evidence, must go to establish the divine authenticity of the Bible; but we do not rest our faith upon them, but upon the Scriptures to which they bear witness; for if all human evidence, all science, and every page of history, were to speak against Scripture, we should utterly and absolutely reject them; reverently and implicitly believe it. Is this narrow? Be it so. It is the blessed narrowness in which we gladly find our peace and our portion forever. It is the narrowness that refuses to admit the weight of a feather as an addition to the Word of God. If this be narrowness—we repeat it with emphasis, and from the very centre of our ransomed being—let it be ours forever.

If to be broad we must look to man to confirm the truth of God's Word, then away with such broadness; it is the broad way that leadeth straight down to hell. No, your life, your salvation, your everlasting peace, blessedness and glory, depend upon your taking God at His Word, and believing what He says because He says it. This is faith—living, saving, precious faith. May you possess it!

God's Word, then, most distinctly declares

that man in his natural, unrenewed, unconverted state is Satan's bondslave. It speaks of Satan as "the god of this world," as "the prince of the power of the air, the spirit that now worketh in the children of disobedience." It speaks of man as "led captive by the devil at his will." Hence, in Paul's commission, the third thing which the gospel is to do is to turn man from "the power of Satan to God." Thus his eyes are opened; divine light comes streaming in; the power of Satan is broken, and the delivered one finds himself, peacefully and happily, in the presence of God. Like the demoniac in Mark 5, he is delivered from his ruthless tyrant, his cruel master; his chains are broken and gone; he is clothed and in his right mind, and sitting at the feet of Jesus.

What a glorious deliverance! It is worthy of God in every aspect of it, and in all its results. The poor blind slave, led captive by the devil, is set free; and not only so, but he is brought to God, pardoned, accepted, and endowed with an eternal inheritance among the sanctified. And all this is by faith, through grace. It is proclaimed in the gospel of God to every creature under heaven—not one is excluded. The great commission, whether we read it in Luke 24 or in Acts 26, assures us that this most precious, most glorious salvation is unto all.

Let us listen for a moment to our apostle as he discharges his blessed commission in the synagogue at Antioch of Pisidia. Most gladly would we transcribe the whole of his precious discourse, but our limited space compels us to confine ourselves to the powerful appeal at the end. "Be it known unto you therefore, men and brethren, that through *this Man*" (Jesus Christ, crucified, risen, and glorified) "is preached"—not promised in the future, but preached *now*, announced as a present reality—is preached "*unto you* the remission of sins. And by Him all who believe *are* justified from *all things*, from which ye could not be justified by the law of Moses."

From these words we learn, in the clearest possible manner, that every soul in that synagogue was called upon, there and then, to receive into his heart the blessed message which fell from the preacher's lips. Not one was excluded. "*Unto you* is the word of this salvation sent." If any one had asked the apostle if the message was intended for him, what would have been the reply? "Unto *you* is the word of this salvation sent." Was there no preliminary question to be settled? Not one. All the preliminaries had been settled at the cross. Was there no question as to election or predestination? Not a syllable about either in the whole range of this magnificent and comprehensive discourse.

Is there no such question? Not in that "great commission" whereof we speak. No doubt the grand truth of election shines in its proper place on the page of inspiration. But what is its proper and divinely appointed place? Most assuredly not in the preaching of the evangelist, but in the ministry of the teacher or pastor. When the apostle sits down to instruct believers, we hear such words as these: "Whom He did foreknow, He also did *predestinate*." And again: "Knowing, brethren beloved, your *election* of God."

Let it never be lost sight of, when he stands up as an ambassador of Christ, the herald of salvation, he proclaims in the most absolute and unqualified manner a present, a personal, a perfect salvation to every creature under heaven; and every one who heard him was responsible there and then to believe. And every one who reads him now is equally so. If any one had presumed to tell the preacher that his hearers were not responsible, that they were powerless, and could not believe—that it was only deceiving them to call upon them to believe—what would have been his reply? We think we are warranted in saying that a full and overwhelming reply to this, and every such preposterous objection, is wrapped up in the solemn appeal with which the apostle closes his address, "*Beware*, therefore, lest that come upon you which is spoken of in the prophets: Behold, ye despisers, and wonder, and perish; for I work a work in your days, a work which ye shall in no wise believe, though a man declare it unto you."

Part 4

Having in the former papers dwelt a little upon the *terms* of "the great commission," we shall now, in dependence upon divine teaching, seek to unfold the truth as to the *basis*. It is of the greatest importance to have a clear understanding of the solid ground on which "repentance and remission of sins" are announced to every creature under heaven. This we have distinctly laid down in our Lord's own words, "*It behooved Christ to suffer, and to rise from the dead the third day.*"

Here lies, in its impregnable strength, the foundation of the glorious commission whereof we speak. God—blessed forever be His holy name—has been pleased to set before us with all possible clearness the moral ground on which He commands all men everywhere to repent, and the righteous ground on which He can proclaim to every repentant soul the perfect remission of sins.

We have already had occasion to guard the reader against the false notion that any amount of repentance on the part of the sinner could possibly form the meritorious ground of forgiveness. But inasmuch as we write for those who may be ignorant of the foundations of the gospel, we feel bound to put things in the very simplest possible form, so that all may understand. We know how prone the human heart is to build upon something of our own—if not upon good works, at least upon our penitential exercises. Hence, it becomes our bounden duty to set forth the precious truth of the atoning work of our Lord Jesus Christ as the only righteous ground of the forgiveness of sins.

True, all men are commanded to repent. It is meet and right that they should. How could it be otherwise? How can we look at that accursed tree on which the Son of God bore the judgment of sin and not see the absolute necessity of repentance? How can we harken to that solemn cry breaking forth from amid the shadows of Calvary, "My God, My God, why hast Thou forsaken Me?" and not own, from the deepest depths of our moral being, the moral fitness of repentance?

If indeed sin is so terrible, so absolutely hateful to God, so perfectly intolerable to His holy nature, that He had to bruise His well beloved and only begotten Son on the cross in order to put it away, does it not well become the sinner to judge himself, and repent in dust and ashes? Had the blessed Lord to endure the hiding of God's countenance because of our sins, and we not be broken, self-judged and subdued on account of these sins? Shall we with impenitent heart hear the glad tidings of full and free forgiveness of sins—a forgiveness which cost nothing less than the unutterable horrors and agonies of the cross? Shall we, with flippant tongue, profess to have peace—a peace purchased by the ineffable sufferings of the Son of God? If it was absolutely necessary that Christ should suffer for our sins, is it not morally fitting that we should repent of them?

Nor is this all. It is not merely that it becomes us, once in a way, to repent. There is far more than this. The spirit of self-judgment, genuine contrition and true humility must characterize every one who enters at all into the profound mystery of the sufferings of Christ. Indeed, it is only as we contemplate and deeply ponder those sufferings that we can form anything approaching to a just estimate of the hatefulness of sin on the one hand, and the divine fulness and perfectness of remission on the other. Such was the hatefulness of sin, that it was absolutely necessary that Christ should suffer; but—all praise to redeeming love!— such were the sufferings of Christ, that God can forgive us our sins according to the infinite value which He attaches to those sufferings. Both go together; and both, we may add, exert a formative influence, under the powerful ministry of the Holy Ghost, on the Christian character from first to last. Our sins are all forgiven; but "it behooved Christ to suffer"; and hence, while our peace flows like a river, we must never forget the soul-subduing fact that the basis of our peace was laid in the ineffable sufferings of the Son of God.

This is most needful, owing to the excessive levity of our hearts. We are ready enough to receive the truth of the remission of sins, and then go on in an easy, self-indulgent, world-loving spirit, thus proving how feebly we enter into the sufferings of our blessed Lord, or into the real nature of sin. All this is truly deplorable, and calls for the deepest exercise of soul.

There is a sad lack amongst us of that real brokenness of spirit which ought to characterize those who owe their present peace and everlasting felicity and glory to the sufferings of Christ. We are light, frivolous, and self-willed. We avail ourselves of the death of Christ to save us from the consequences of our sins, but our ways do not exhibit the practical effect of that death in its application to ourselves. We do not walk as those who are dead with Christ—who have crucified the flesh with its affections and lusts—who are delivered from this present evil world. In a word, our Christianity is sadly deficient in depth of tone; it is shallow, feeble, and stunted. We profess to know a great deal of truth; but it is to be feared it is too much in theory—therefore not turned to practical account as it should be.

It may, perhaps, be asked, What has all this to do with "the great commission"? It has to do with it in a very intimate way. We are deeply impressed with a sense of the superficial way in which the work of evangelization is carried on at the present day. Not only are the *terms* of the great commission overlooked, but the *basis* seems to be little understood. The sufferings of Christ are not duly dwelt upon and unfolded. The atoning work of Christ is presented in its sufficiency for the sinner's need—and no doubt this is a signal mercy. We have to be profoundly thankful when preachers and writers hold up the precious blood of Christ as the sinner's only plea, instead of preaching up rites, ceremonies, sacraments, good works (falsely so-called), creeds, churches, religious ordinances, and such-like delusions.

All this is most fully admitted. But at the same time we must give expression to our deep and solemn conviction that much of our modern evangelical preaching is extremely shallow and bald; and the result of that preaching is seen in the light, airy, flippant style of many of our so-called converts. Some of us seem so intensely anxious to make everything so easy and simple for the sinner that the preaching becomes extremely one-sided.

Thanks be to God, He has indeed made all easy and simple for the needy, broken-hearted, penitent sinner. He has left him nothing to do, nothing to give. It is "to him that worketh not, but believeth on Him that justifieth the ungodly." It is not possible for any evangelist to go too far in stating this side of the question. No one can go beyond Rom. 4:5 in setting forth salvation by free grace, through faith, without works of any sort or description.

But then, we must remember that the blessed apostle Paul—the greatest evangelist that ever lived, except his divine Master—did not confine himself to this one side; and neither should we. He pressed the claims of divine holiness. He called upon sinners to judge themselves, and he called upon believers to subdue and deny themselves. He did not preach a gospel that left people at ease in the world, satisfied with themselves, and occupied with earthly things. He did not tell people that they were saved from the flames of hell and were therefore free to enjoy the follies of earth.

This was not Paul's gospel. He preached a gospel which, while it fully met the sinner's deepest need, did also most fully maintain God's glory—a gospel which, while it came down to the very lowest point of the sinner's condition, did not leave him there. Paul's gospel not only set forth a full, clear, unqualified, unconditional, present *forgiveness of sins*, but also, just as fully and clearly, the *condemnation of sin*, and the believer's entire deliverance from this present evil world. The death of Christ, in Paul's gospel, not only assured the soul of complete deliverance from the just consequences of sins, as seen in the judgment of God in the lake of fire, but it also set forth, with magnificent fulness and clearness, the complete snapping of every link with the world, and entire deliverance from the present power and rule of sin.

Now, here is precisely where the lamentable deficiency and culpable one-sidedness of our modern preaching are so painfully manifest. The gospel which one often hears nowadays is, if we may be allowed to use of such a term, a carnal, earthly, worldly gospel. It offers a kind of ease, but it is fleshly, worldly ease. It gives confidence, but it is rather a carnal confidence than the confidence of faith. It is not a delivering gospel. It leaves people in the world, instead of bringing them to God.

What must be the result of all this? We can hardly bear to contemplate it. We greatly fear that, should our Lord tarry, the fruit of much of what is going on around us will be a terrible combination of the very highest profession with the very lowest practice. It cannot be otherwise. High truth taken up in a light, carnal spirit tends to lull the conscience and quash all godly exercise of soul as to our habits and ways in daily life. In this way people escape from legality only to plunge into levity, and truly the last state is worse than the first.

We earnestly hope that the Christian reader may not feel unduly depressed by the perusal of these lines. God knows we would not pen a line to discourage the feeblest lamb in all the precious flock of Christ. We desire to write in the divine presence. We have entreated the Lord that every line of this paper, and of all our papers, should come directly from Himself to the reader.

Hence, therefore, we must ask the reader—and we do so most faithfully and affectionately—to ponder what is here put before him. We cannot hide from him the fact that we are most seriously impressed with the condition of things around us. We feel that the tone and aspect of much of the so-called Christianity of this our day are such as to awaken the gravest apprehension in the mind of every thoughtful observer. We perceive a terribly rapid development of the features of the last days, as detailed by the pen ·of inspiration. "This know also that, in the last days, perilous times shall come. For men shall be *lovers of their own selves*, covetous, boasters, proud, blasphemers, *disobedient to parents*, unthankful, unholy, without natural affection, truce-breakers, false accusers, incontinent, fierce, *despisers of those that are good*, traitors, *heady, high-minded, lovers of pleasure rather than lovers of God, having a form of godliness, but denying the power thereof:* from such turn away" (2 Tim. 3: 1-5).

What an appalling picture! How solemn to find the same evils that characterize the heathen, as recorded in Rom. 1, reproduced in connection with the profession of Christianity! Should not the thought of this awaken the most serious apprehensions in the mind of every Christian? Should it not lead all who are engaged in the holy service of preaching and teaching amongst us to examine themselves closely as to the tone and character of their ministry, and as to their own private walk and ways? We want a more searching style of ministry on the part of evangelists and teachers. There is a lack of hortatory and prophetic ministry. By prophetic ministry we mean that which brings the conscience into the immediate presence of God. (See 1 Cor. 14: 1-3, 23-26.)

In this we are lamentably deficient. There is a vast amount of objective truth in circulation amongst us—more, perhaps, than ever since the days of the apostles. Books and periodicals by hundreds and thousands, tracts by thousands and millions, are sent forth annually.

Do we object to this? Nay; we bless God for it. But we cannot shut our eyes to the fact that by far the largest proportion of this vast mass of literature is addressed to the intelligence, and not enough to the heart and conscience. Now, while it is quite right to enlighten the understanding, it is quite wrong to neglect the heart and conscience. We feel it to be a most serious thing to allow the intelligence to outstrip the conscience— to have more truth in the head than in the heart—to profess principles which do not govern the practice. Nothing can be more dangerous. It tends to place us directly in the hands of Satan. If the conscience be not kept tender, if the heart be not governed by the fear of God, if a broken and contrite spirit be not cultivated, there is no telling what depths we may plunge into. When the conscience is kept in a sound condition, and the heart is humble and true, then every fresh ray of light that shines in upon the understanding ministers strength to the soul and tends to elevate and sanctify our whole moral being.

This is what every earnest spirit must crave. All true-hearted Christians must long for increased personal holiness, more likeness to Christ, more genuine devotedness of heart, a deepening, strengthening and expanding of the kingdom of God in the soul—that kingdom which is righteousness, and peace, and joy in the Holy Ghost.

May we all have grace to seek after these divine realities! May we diligently cultivate them in our own private life, and seek in every possible way to promote them in all those with whom we come in contact! Thus shall we in some measure stem the tide of hollow profession around us, and be a living testimony against the powerless *form* of godliness so sadly dominant in this our day.

Christian reader! art thou one with us in this current of thought and feeling? If so, then let us most earnestly entreat thee to join us in earnest prayer to God that He will graciously raise our spiritual tone by drawing us closer to Himself, and filling our hearts with love to Him and earnest desire for the promotion of His glory, the progress of His cause, and the prosperity of His people.

Part 5

In pursuing our subject, we have yet to consider the *authority* and the *sphere* of "the great commission;" but ere proceeding to treat of these we must dwell a little longer on the *basis*. The commission is truly a great one, and would need a solid foundation on which to rest it; and such it has, blessed be God, in the atoning death of His Son. Nothing less than this could sustain such a magnificent fabric; but the grace that planned the commission has also laid the foundation; so that a full remission of sins can be preached among all nations, inasmuch as God has been glorified, in the death of Christ, as to the entire question of sin.

This is a grand point for the reader to seize. It lies at the very foundation of the Christian system. It is the keystone of the arch of divine revelation. God has been glorified as to sin. His judgment has been executed upon it. The claims of His throne have been vindicated as to it. The insult offered to His divine majesty has been flung back in the enemy's face. If the sweet story of remission of sins had never fallen upon a human ear or entered a human heart, the divine glory would none the less have been most perfectly maintained.

The Lord Jesus Christ did, by His most precious death, wipe off the stain which the enemy sought to cast upon the eternal glory of God. A testimony has been given in the cross, to all created intelligence, as to God's thoughts about sin. It can there be seen, with all possible clearness, that a single trace of sin can never enter the precincts of the divine presence. God is of purer eyes than to behold evil, and cannot look on iniquity. Sin, wherever found, must be met by divine judgment.

Where does all this come most fully and forcibly out? Assuredly in the cross. Harken to that solemn and most mysterious cry, "My God, My God, why hast Thou forsaken Me?" What means this wondrous inquiry? Who is the speaker? Is he one of Adam's fallen posterity? Is he a sinner? Surely not; for were he such, there would be no moral force whatever in the question. There never was a sinner on the face of this earth who, so far as he was personally concerned, did not richly deserve to be forsaken of a holy, sin-hating God. This must never be forgotten. Some people entertain most foolish notions as to this point. They have, in their own vain imagination, invented a god to suit themselves—one who will not punish sin—one who is so tender, so kind, so benevolent, that he will connive at evil and pass it over as though it were nothing.

Now, nothing is more certain than that this god of the human imagination is a false one, just as false as any of the idols of the heathen. The God of the Bible, the God of Christianity, the God whom we see at the cross, is not like this. Men may reason as they will; but sin must be condemned—it must be met by the just and inflexible judgment of a sin-hating God.

We repeat the question, Who uttered those words at the opening of Ps. 22? If He was not a sinner, who was he? Wonderful to declare, He was the only spotless, perfectly holy, pure and sinless Man that ever trod this earth. He was more. He was the eternal Son of the Father, the object of God's ineffable delight, who had dwelt in His bosom from all eternity, "the brightness of His glory and the exact expression of His substance."

Yet He was forsaken of God! yes, that holy and perfect One, who knew no sin, whose human nature was absolutely free from every taint, who never had a single thought, never uttered a single word, never did a single act that was not in the most perfect harmony with the mind of God; whose whole life, from Bethlehem to Calvary, was a perfect sacrifice of sweetest odor presented to the heart of God. Again and again we see Heaven opening upon Him, and the voice of the Father is heard giving expression to His infinite complacency in the Son of His bosom. And yet, He it is whose voice is heard in that bitter cry, "My God, My God, why hast Thou forsaken Me?"

Marvelous question! It stands alone in the annals of eternity. No such question had ever been asked before; no such question has ever been asked since; and no such question can ever be asked again. Whether we consider the One who asked the question, or the One of whom it was asked, or the answer, we must admit that it is perfectly unique. That God should forsake such an One is the most profound and marvelous mystery that could possibly engage the attention of men or angels. Human reason cannot fathom its depths. No created intelligence can comprehend its mighty compass.

Yet there it stands, a stupendous fact before the eye of faith. Our blessed Lord Himself assures us that it was absolutely necessary. "Thus it is written, and thus it *behooved* Christ to suffer." But why was it necessary? Why should the only perfect, sinless, spotless Man have to suffer? Why should He be forsaken of God? The glory of God, the eternal counsels of redeeming love, man's guilty, ruined, helpless condition—all these things rendered it indispensable that Christ should suffer. There was no other way in which the divine glory could be maintained; no other way in which the claims of the throne of God could be answered; no other way in which Heaven's majesty could be vindicated; no other way in which the eternal purposes of love could be made good; no

other way in which sin could be fully atoned for, and finally taken away out of God's creation; no other way in which sins could be forgiven; no other way in which Satan and all the powers of darkness could be thoroughly vanquished; no other way in which God could be just, and yet the Justifier of any poor ungodly sinner; no other way in which death could be deprived of its sting, or the grave of its victory; no other way in which any or all of these grand results could be reached save by the sufferings and death of our adorable Saviour, our Lord Jesus Christ.

But, blessed forever be His holy name, He went through it all. He went down under the heavy billows and waves of God's righteous wrath against sin. He took the sinner's place, stood in his stead, sustained the judgment, paid the penalty, died the death, answered every question, met every demand, vanquished every foe; and having done all, He ascended into the heavens and took His seat on the throne of God, where He is now crowned with glory and honor as the divine and all-glorious Accomplisher of the entire work of man's redemption.

Such, then, is the *basis* of "the great commission" whereof we speak. Need we wonder at the *terms*, when we contemplate the basis? Can there be anything too good, anything too great, anything too glorious, for the God of all grace to bestow upon us poor sinners of the Gentiles, seeing He has been so fully glorified in the death of Christ? That most precious death furnishes a divinely righteous ground on which our God can indulge the deep and everlasting love of His heart in the perfect remission of our sins. It has removed out of the way every barrier to the full flood-tide of redeeming love which can now flow through a perfectly righteous channel, to the very vilest sinner that repents and believes in Jesus.

A Saviour-God can now publish a full and immediate remission of sins to every creature under heaven. There is positively no hindrance. God has been glorified as to the question of sin; and the time is coming when every trace of sin shall be forever obliterated from His fair creation, and those words of John the Baptist shall have their full accomplishment, "Behold the Lamb of God that taketh away the sin of the world." Meanwhile, the heralds of salvation are commanded to go forth to the ends of the earth and publish, without let or limitation, perfect remission of sins to every soul that believes. It is the joy of God's heart to pardon sins; and it is due to the One who bore the judgment of sin on the cross that in His name forgiveness of sins should be thus freely published, fully received, and abidingly enjoyed.

But what of those who reject this glorious message—who shut their ears against it and turn away their hearts from it? This is the solemn question. Who can answer it? Who can attempt to set forth the eternal destiny of those who die in their sins, as all must who refuse God's only basis of remission? Men may reason and argue as they will; but all the reasoning and argument in the world cannot set aside the Word of God, which assures us in manifold places, and in terms so plain as to leave no possible ground for questioning, that all who die in their sins—all who die out of Christ—must inevitably perish eternally, must bear the consequences of their sins, in the lake that burneth with fire and brimstone.

To quote the passages in proof of the solemn truth of eternal punishment would require a small volume. We cannot attempt it here; nor is it necessary, inasmuch as we have gone into the subject again and again in other places.

We would here put a question which arises naturally out of our present thesis. It is this: Was Christ judged, bruised, and forsaken on the cross—did God visit His only begotten and well beloved Son with the full weight of His righteous wrath against sin—and shall impenitent sinners escape? We solemnly press this question on all whom it may concern. Men talk of its being inconsistent with the idea of divine goodness, tenderness and compassion that God should send any of His creatures to hell. We reply, Who is to be the judge? Is man competent to decide as to what is morally fitting for God to do? And further, we ask, What is to be the standard of judgment? Anything that human reason can grasp? Assuredly not. What then? *The cross*

on which the Son of God died, the Just for the unjust—this, and this only, is the great standard by which to judge the question as to sin's desert.

Who can harken to that bitter cry emanating from the broken heart of the Son of God, "My God, My God, why hast Thou forsaken Me?" and question the eternal punishment of all who die in their sins? Talk of tenderness, goodness, and compassion! Where do these shine out most brightly and blessedly? Surely in "the great commission" which publishes full and free forgiveness of sins to every creature under heaven. But would it be just, or good, or compassionate, to suffer the rejecter of Christ to escape? If we would see the goodness, kindness, mercy and deep compassion of God, we must look at the cross. "He spared not His own Son, but delivered Him up for us all." "It pleased Jehovah to bruise Him. He hath put Him to grief." "He hath made Him who knew no sin to be sin for us, that we might become the righteousness of God in Him."

If men reject all this, and go on in their sins, in their rebellion, in their infidel reasonings and impious speculations—what then? If men maintain that suffering for sin is not necessary, and that there is another and a better way of disposing of the matter—what then? Our Lord declared in the ears of His apostles that "it was necessary that Christ should suffer"—that there was no other way possible by which the great question could be settled. Whom are we to believe? Was the death of Christ gratuitous? Was His heart broken for nothing? Was the cross a work of supererogation? Did Jehovah bruise His Son and put Him to grief for an end which might be gained some other way?

How monstrous are the reasonings, or rather the ravings, of infidelity! Infidel doctors begin by throwing overboard the Word of God—that peerless and perfect revelation; and then, when they have deprived us of our divine guide, with singular audacity, they present themselves before us, and undertake to point out for us a more excellent way; and when we inquire what that way is, we are met by a thousand and one fine-spun theories, no two of which agree in anything save in shutting out God and His Word.

True, they talk plausibly about a God; but it is a God of their own imagination—one who will connive at sin—who will allow them to indulge in their lusts, and passions, and pleasures, and then take them to a heaven of which they really know nothing. They talk of mercy, and kindness, and goodness; but they reject the only channel through which these can flow, namely, the cross of our Lord Jesus Christ. They speak not of righteousness, holiness, truth, and judgment to come. They would fain have us to believe that God put Himself to needless cost in delivering up His Son. They would ignore that marvelous transaction which stands alone in the entire history of the ways of God—the atoning death of His Son. In one word, the grand object of the devil, in all the skeptical, rationalistic and infidel theories that have ever been propounded in this world, is to shut out completely the Word of God, the Christ of God, and God Himself.

We solemnly call upon all our readers, specially our young friends, to ponder this. It is our deep and thorough conviction that the harboring of a single infidel suggestion is the first step on that inclined plane which leads straight down to the dark and terrible abyss of atheism—down to the blackness of darkness forever.

We shall have occasion to recur to the foregoing line of thought when we come to consider the *authority* on which "the great commission" comes to us. We have been drawn into it by the sad fact that in every direction, and on every subject, we are assailed by the contemptible reasonings of infidelity; and we feel imperatively called upon to warn all with whom we come in contact against infidel books, infidel lectures, infidel theories in every shape and form. *May the inspired Word of God be more and more precious to our hearts! May we walk in its light, feel its sacred power, bow to its divine authority, hide it in our hearts, feed upon its treasures, own its absolute supremacy, confess its all-sufficiency, and utterly reject all teaching which dares to touch the integrity of the Holy Scriptures.*

Part 6

We have seen that the *basis* of "the great commission" is the death and resurrection of our Lord and Saviour Jesus Christ. This must never be lost sight of. "It behooved Christ to suffer, and to rise from the dead the third day." It is a risen Christ that sends forth His heralds to preach "repentance and remission of sins." The incarnation and the crucifixion are great cardinal truths of Christianity; but it is only in resurrection they are made available for us in any way. Incarnation—precious and priceless mystery though it be—could not form the groundwork of remission of sins, for "without shedding of blood is no remission" (Heb. 9:22). We are justified by the *blood*, and reconciled by the *death* of Christ.

But it is in resurrection that all this is made good unto us. Christ was delivered for our offenses, and raised again for our justification (Rom. 4:25; 5:9-10). "For I delivered unto you first of all that which I also received, how that Christ died for our sins according to the Scriptures; and that He was buried, and that He rose again the third day according to the Scriptures" (1 Cor. 15: 3-4).

Hence, therefore, it is of the very last possible importance, for all who would carry out our Lord's commission, to know in their own souls, and to set forth in their preaching, the grand truth of resurrection. The most cursory glance at the preaching of the earliest heralds of the gospel will suffice to show the prominent place which they gave to this glorious fact.

Harken to Peter on the day of Pentecost, or rather to the Holy Ghost, just come down from the risen, ascended and glorified Saviour. "Ye men of Israel, hear these words: Jesus of Nazareth, a man approved of God among you by miracles, and wonders, and signs, which God did by Him in the midst of you, as ye yourselves also know: Him being delivered by the determinate counsel and foreknowledge of God, ye have taken, and by wicked hands have crucified and slain: *whom God hath raised up,* having loosed the pains of death: because it was not possible that He should be holden of it. . . . *This Jesus* hath God raised up, whereof we all are witnesses. Therefore being by the right hand of God exalted, and having received of the Father the promise of the Holy Ghost, He hath shed forth this which ye now see and hear" (Acts 2).

So also in chapter 3: "The God of Abraham, and of Isaac, and of Jacob, the God of our fathers, hath glorified His Son Jesus; whom ye delivered up, and denied Him in the presence of Pilate, when he was determined to let Him go. But ye denied the Holy One and the Just, and desired a murderer to be granted unto you; and killed the Prince of life, *whom God hath raised from the dead;* whereof we are witnesses. . . . Unto you first *God, having raised up His Son Jesus*, sent Him to bless you, in turning away every one of you from his iniquities. . . . And as they spake unto the people, the priests, and the captain of the temple, and the Sadducees, came upon them, being grieved that they taught the people, and *preached through Jesus the resurrection from the dead.*"

Their preaching was characterized by the prominent place which it assigned to the glorious, powerful and telling fact of resurrection. True, there was the full and clear statement of incarnation and crucifixion, with the great moral bearings of these facts. How could it be otherwise? The Son of God had to become a man to die, in order that by death He might glorify God as to the entire question of sin; destroy the power of Satan; rob death of its sting, and the grave of its victory; put away forever the sins of His people, and associate them with Himself in the power of eternal life in the new creation, where all things are of God, and where a single trace of sin or sorrow can never enter. Eternal and universal homage and adoration to His peerless name!

Let all preachers remember the place which resurrection holds in apostolic preaching and teaching. "With great power gave the apostles witness." Of what? Incarnation or crucifixion merely? Nay; but "of the resurrection of the Lord Jesus." This was the stupendous fact that glorified God and His Son Jesus Christ. It was this that attested, in the view of all created intelligences, the

divine complacency in the work of redemption. It was this that demonstrated, in the most marvelous way, the complete and eternal overthrow of the kingdom of Satan and all the powers of darkness. It was this that declared the full and everlasting deliverance of all who believe in Jesus—their deliverance, not only from all the consequences of their sins, but from this present evil world, and from every link that bound them to that old creation which lies under the power of evil.

No marvel, therefore, if the apostles, filled as they were with the Holy Ghost, persistently and powerfully presented the magnificent truth of resurrection. Hear them again before the council—a council composed of the great religious leaders and guides of the people. "The God of our fathers raised up Jesus, whom ye slew, and hanged on a tree." They were at issue with God on the all-important question as to His Son. They had slain Him, but God raised Him from the dead. "Him hath God exalted with His right hand, a Prince and a Saviour, for to give repentance to Israel, and remission of sins."

So also in Peter's address to the Gentiles, in the house of Cornelius, speaking of Jesus of Nazareth, he says, "whom they slew, and hanged on a tree, *Him God raised up the third day, and showed Him openly:* not to all the people, but unto witnesses chosen before of God, to us who did eat and drink with Him after He rose from the dead."

The Holy Ghost is careful to set forth the weighty and, to us, profoundly interesting fact that "God raised up His Son Jesus." This fact has a double bearing. It proves that God is at issue with the world, seeing He has raised, exalted and glorified the very One whom they slew and hanged on a tree. But, blessed throughout all ages be His holy name, it proves that He has found eternal rest and satisfaction as to us, and all that was or could be against us, seeing He has raised up the very One who took our place and stood charged with all our sin and guilt.

But all this will come more fully out as we proceed with our proofs.

Let us now listen for a moment to Paul's address in the synagogue at Antioch. "Men, brethren, children of the stock of Abraham, and whosoever among you feareth God, to you is the word of this salvation sent. For they that dwell at Jerusalem, and their rulers, because they knew Him not, nor yet the voices of the prophets which are read every Sabbath day, they have fulfilled them in condemning Him. And though they found no cause of death in Him, yet desired they Pilate that He should be slain. And when they had fulfilled all that was written of Him, they took Him down from the tree, and laid Him in a sepulchre.

"But God raised Him from the dead. And He was seen many days of them which came up with Him from Galilee to Jerusalem, who are His witnesses unto the people. And we declare unto you glad tidings, how that the promise which was made unto the fathers, God hath fulfilled the same unto us their children, in that He hath raised up Jesus; as it is also written in the second psalm, Thou art My Son, this day have I begotten Thee. And as concerning that *He raised Him up from the dead*, no more to return to corruption, He said on this wise, I will give you the sure mercies of David. Wherefore He saith also in another psalm, Thou shalt not suffer Thy Holy One to see corruption. For David, after he had served his own generation by the will of God, fell on sleep, and was laid unto his fathers, and saw corruption: but *He whom God raised again* saw no corruption."

Then follows the powerful appeal which, though not bearing upon our present line of argument, we cannot omit in this place. "Be it known unto you therefore, men and brethren, that through this Man is preached unto you the forgiveness of sins: and *by Him* all that believe *are justified from all things*, from which ye could not be justified by the law of Moses. *Beware* therefore, lest that come upon you which is spoken of in the prophets: Behold, ye despisers, and wonder, and perish; for I work a work in your days, a work which ye shall in no wise believe, though a man declare it unto you" (Acts 13: 26-41).

We shall close our series of proofs from the Acts of the Apostles by a brief quotation from Paul's address at Athens. "Forasmuch then as we are the offspring of God, we ought not to think that the Godhead is like unto gold, or silver, or stone, graven by art and man's device. And the times of this ignorance God overlooked; but now commandeth all men everywhere to repent; because He hath appointed a day in the which He will judge the world in righteousness by that Man whom He hath ordained; whereof He hath given assurance unto all, *in that He hath raised Him from the dead*" (Acts 17).

This is a very remarkable and deeply solemn passage. The proof that God is going to judge the world in righteousness—a proof offered to all—is that He has raised His ordained Man from the dead. He does not here name the Man; but at verse 18 we are told that some of the Athenians deemed the apostle a setter forth of strange gods, "because he preached unto them *Jesus and the resurrection.*"

From all this it is perfectly plain that the blessed Apostle Paul gave a most prominent place in all his preachings to the glorious truth of resurrection. Whether he addresses a congregation of Jews in the synagogue at Antioch, or an assembly of Gentiles on Mars Hill at Athens, he presents a risen Christ. In a word, he was characterized by the fact that he preached not merely the incarnation and the crucifixion, but the resurrection; and this, too, in all its mighty moral bearings—its bearing upon man in his individual state and destiny; its bearing upon the world as a whole, in its history in the past, its moral condition in the present, and its certain doom in the future; in its bearing upon the believer, proving his absolute, complete and eternal justification before God, and his thorough deliverance from this present evil world.

We have to bear in mind that in apostolic preaching the resurrection was not presented as a mere doctrine, but as a living, telling, mighty moral fact—a fact, the magnitude of which is beyond all power of human utterance or thought. The apostles, in carrying out "the great commission" of their Lord, pressed the stupendous fact that God had raised Jesus from the dead—had raised the Man who was nailed to the cross and buried in the grave. In short, they preached a resurrection gospel. Their preaching was governed by these words, "It was necessary that Christ should suffer, and rise from the dead the third day."

We shall now turn for a moment to the Epistles, and see the wondrous way in which the Holy Ghost unfolds and applies the fact of resurrection. But ere doing so we would call the reader's attention to a passage which is sadly misunderstood and misapplied. The apostle, in writing to the Corinthians, says, "We preach Christ crucified." These words are continually quoted for the purpose of casting a damper on those who earnestly desire to advance in the knowledge of divine things. But a moment's serious attention to the context would be sufficient to show the true meaning of the apostle. Did he confine himself to the fact of the crucifixion? The bare idea, in the face of the body of Scripture which we have quoted, is simply absurd. The fact is, the glorious truth of resurrection shines out in all his discourses.

What, then, does the apostle mean when he declares, "We preach Christ crucified"? Simply this, that the Christ whom he preached was the One whom the world crucified. He was a rejected, outcast Christ—one assigned by the world to a malefactor's gibbet. What a fact for the poor Corinthians, so full of vanity and love for this world's wisdom! A crucified Christ was the one whom Paul preached, "to the Jews a stumblingblock, and unto the Greeks foolishness; but to those that are called, both Jews and Greeks, Christ the power of God, and the wisdom of God. Because the foolishness of God is wiser than men, and the weakness of God is stronger than men."

Remarkable words! words divinely suited to people prone to boast themselves in the so-called wisdom and greatness of this world—the vain reasonings and imaginations of the poor human mind, which all perish in a moment. All the wisdom of God, all His power, all His greatness, all His glory, all that He is, in short, comes out in a crucified Christ. The cross confounds the world, vanquishes Satan and all the powers of darkness, saves all who believe, and forms the solid foundation of the everlasting and universal glory of God.

We shall now turn for a moment to a very beautiful passage in Rom. 4, in which the inspired writer sets forth the subject of resurrection in a most edifying way for us. Speaking of Abraham, he says, "Who against hope believed in hope, that he might become the father of many nations, according to that which was spoken, So shall thy seed be. And being not weak in faith, he considered not his own body now dead, when he was about a hundred years old, neither yet the deadness of Sarah's womb; *he staggered not* at the promise of God through unbelief,"—which is always sure to stagger,—"but was *strong in faith, giving glory to God*"—as faith always does; "and being *fully persuaded* that what He had promised He was able also to perform. And therefore it was imputed to him for righteousness."

And then, lest any should say that all this applied only to Abraham, who was such a devoted, holy, remarkable man, the inspiring Spirit adds, with singular grace and sweetness, "Now it was not written for his sake alone, that it was imputed to him, but for us also, to whom it shall be imputed, if we believe on Him that"—what? Gave His Son? Bruised His Son on the cross? Not merely this, but "*that raised up Jesus our Lord from the dead*."

Here lies the grand point of the apostle's blessed and powerful argument. We must, if we would have settled peace, believe in God as the One who raised up Jesus from the dead, and who in so doing proved Himself friendly to us, and proved too His infinite satisfaction in the work of the cross. Jesus, having been "delivered for our offenses," could not be where He now is if a single one of these offenses remained unatoned for. But, blessed forever be the God of all grace, He raised from among the dead the One who had been delivered for our offenses; and to all who believe in Him righteousness shall be reckoned. "It behooved Christ to suffer, and to rise from the dead the third day." See how this glorious theme, the *basis* of the great commission, expands under our gaze as we pursue our study of it!

One more brief quotation shall close this paper. In Heb. 13 we read, "*Now the God of peace, that brought again from the dead* our Lord Jesus, that great Shepherd of the sheep, through the blood of the everlasting covenant.*"

This is uncommonly fine. The God of judgment met the Sin-bearer at the cross, and there, with Him, entered thoroughly into and definitively settled the question of sin. Then, in glorious proof that all was done—sin atoned for—guilt put away—Satan silenced —God glorified—all divinely accomplished— "the God of peace" entered the scene, and raised from the dead our Lord Jesus, that "great Shepherd of the sheep."

How glorious is all this! How enfranchising to all who simply believe! Jesus is risen. His sufferings are over forever. God has exalted Him. Eternal Justice has wreathed His blessed brow with a diadem of glory; and, wondrous fact, that very diadem is the eternal demonstration that all who believe are justified from all things, and accepted in a risen and glorified Christ. Eternal and universal hallelujahs to the Father, and to the Son, and to the Holy Ghost!

Part 7

We are now called to consider the deeply important subject of the *authority* on which the great commission proceeds. This we have presented to us in that one commanding and most comprehensive sentence, *"It is written"* —a sentence which ought to be engraved in characters deep and broad on the tablet of every Christian's heart.

Nothing can possibly be more interesting or edifying than to note the way in which our blessed Lord on all occasions and under all circumstances exalts the Holy Scriptures. He, though God over all, blessed forever, and as such the Author of all Scripture, yet, having taken His place as man on the earth, He plainly sets forth what is the bounden duty of every man, and that is to be absolutely, completely and abidingly governed by the authority of Scripture. See Him in conflict with Satan! How does He meet him? Simply as each one of us should meet

him—by the written Word. It could be no example to us had our Lord vanquished him by the putting forth of divine power. Of course He could, there and then, have consigned him to the bottomless pit or the lake of fire, but that would have been no example for us, inasmuch as we could not so overcome.

But on the other hand, when we find the blessed One referring to Holy Scripture, when we find Him appealing again and again to that divine authority, when we find Him putting the adversary to flight simply by the written Word, we learn in the most impressive manner the place, the value and the authority of the Holy Scriptures.

Is it not of the very last possible importance to have this great lesson impressed upon us at the present moment? Unquestionably it is. If ever there was a moment in the history of the Church of God when it behooved Christians to bow down their whole moral being to this very lesson, it is the moment through which we are just now passing. On all hands the divine authority, integrity, plenary inspiration and all-sufficiency of Holy Scripture are called in question. The Word of God is openly insulted and flung aside. Its integrity is called in question, and that too in quarters where we should least expect it. At our colleges and universities our young men are continually assailed by infidel attacks upon the blessed Word of God.

Men who are in total spiritual blindness, and who therefore cannot possibly know anything whatever about divine things, and are utterly incompetent to give an opinion on the subject of Holy Scripture, have the cool audacity to insult the sacred volume, to pronounce the five books of Moses an imposture, to assert that Moses never wrote them at all!

What is the opinion of such men worth? Not worth the weight of a feather. Who would think of going to a man who was born in a coal mine, and had never see the sun, to get his judgment as to the properties of light, or the effect of the sun's beams upon the human constitution? Who would think of going to one who was born blind to get his opinion upon colors, or the effect of light and shade? Surely no one in his senses. Well, then, with how much more moral force, may we not ask, who would think of going to an unconverted man—a man dead in trespasses and sins—a man spiritually blind, wholly ignorant of things divine, spiritual, and heavenly—who would think for a moment of going to such a one for a judgment on the weighty question of Holy Scripture? And if such a one were audacious enough, in ignorant self-confidence, to offer an opinion on such a subject, what man in his sober senses would think of giving the slightest heed?

It will perhaps be said, "The illustration does not apply." Why not? We admit it fails in force, but most certainly not in its moral application. Is it not a commonly received axiom amongst us that no man has any right to give an opinion on a subject of which he is totally ignorant? No doubt. Well, what does the blessed apostle say as to the unconverted man? We quote the whole context for the reader. It is morally grand, and its interest and value just now are unspeakable.

"And I, brethren, when I came to you, came not with excellency of speech or of wisdom, declaring unto you the testimony of God. For I determined not to know anything among you save Jesus Christ, and Him crucified. And I was with you in weakness, and in fear, and in much trembling. And my speech and my preaching were not with enticing words of man's wisdom, but in demonstration of the Spirit and of power: *that your faith"*—mark these words,— *"should not stand in the wisdom of men, but in the power of God."* Howbeit we speak wisdom among them that are perfect; yet not the wisdom of this world, nor of the princes of this world, that come to naught.

"But we speak the wisdom of God in a mystery, even the hidden wisdom which God ordained before the world unto our glory: which none of the princes of this world knew; for had they known it, they would not have crucified the Lord of glory. But, as it is written, Eye hath not seen, nor ear heard, neither have entered into the heart of man, the things which God hath prepared for them that love Him. *But God hath revealed them*

to us by His Spirit";—otherwise they could not possibly be known—"for the Spirit searcheth all things, yea, the deep things of God. For what man knoweth the things of a man, save the spirit of man which is in him? Even so *the things of God knoweth no man*, but the Spirit of God. Now we"—all true believers, all God's children—"have received, not the spirit of the world, but the Spirit which is of God; that we might know the things that are freely given to us of God.

"Which things also we speak, not in the words which man's wisdom teacheth, but which the Holy Ghost teacheth; comparing spiritual things with spiritual"—or, communicating spiritual things through a spiritual medium. "But the natural man receiveth not the things of the Spirit of God; neither can he know them"—be he ever so wise and learned—"because they are spiritually discerned. But he that is spiritual judgeth all things, yet he himself is judged of no man. For who hath known the mind of the Lord, that he may instruct Him? But we have the mind of Christ" (1 Cor. 2: 1-16).

We dare not offer an apology for giving so lengthened an extract from the Word of God. We deem it invaluable, not only because it proves that it is only by divine teaching that divine things can be understood, but also because it completely withers up all man's pretensions to give judgment as to Scripture. If the natural man cannot know the things of the Spirit of God, then it is perfectly plain that all infidel attacks upon the Word of God are absolutely unworthy of the very smallest attention.

In fact, all infidel writers, be they ever so clever, ever so wise, ever so learned, are put out of court; they are not to be listened to for a moment. The judgment of an unconverted man in reference to the Holy Scriptures is more worthless than the judgment of an uneducated plowman as to the use of the differential calculus, or the truth of the Copernican system. As to each, we have only to say, he knows nothing whatever about the matter. His thoughts are absolutely good for nothing.

But how truly delightful and refreshing to turn from man's worthless notions, and see the way in which our blessed Lord Jesus Christ prized and used the Holy Scriptures! In His conflict with Satan, He appeals three times over to the book of Deuteronomy. "*It is written*" is His one simple and unanswerable reply to the suggestions of the enemy. He does not reason. He does not argue or explain. He does not refer to His own personal feelings, evidences, or experiences. He does not argue from the great facts of the opened heavens, the descending Spirit, the voice of the Father—precious and real as all these things were. He simply takes His stand upon the divine and eternal authority of the Holy Scriptures, and of that portion of the Scriptures in particular which modern infidels have audaciously attacked. He uses as His authority that which they are not afraid to pronounce an imposture! How dreadful for them! What will be their end, unless they repent?

Not only did the Son of God—Himself, as God, the Author of every line of Holy Scripture—use the Word of God as His only weapon against the enemy, but He made it also the basis and the material of His public ministry. When His conflict in the wilderness was over, "He returned in the power of the Spirit into Galilee: and there went out a fame of Him through all the region round about. And He taught in their synagogues, being glorified of all. And He came to Nazareth, where He had been brought up; and, *as His custom was*, He went into the synagogue on the Sabbath day, and *stood up for to read*"—*His custom was to read the Scriptures publicly.*

"And there was delivered unto Him the book of the prophet Esaias." Here He puts His seal upon the prophet Isaiah, as before upon the law of Moses. "And when He had opened the book, He found the place where it was written, The Spirit of the Lord is upon Me, because He hath anointed Me to preach the gospel to the poor; He hath sent Me to heal the broken-hearted, to preach deliverance to the captives, and recovering of sight to the blind, to set at liberty them that are bruised, to preach the acceptable year of the Lord" (Luke 4).

Let us turn now to that most solemn parable of the rich man and Lazarus, at the close of Luke 16, in which we have a solemn testimony from the Master's own lips to the integrity, value and surpassing importance of "Moses and the Prophets"—the very portions of the divine Word which infidels impiously assail. The rich man in torment— alas, no longer rich, but miserably and eternally poor!—entreats Abraham to send Lazarus to warn his five brethren, lest they also should come into that place of torment. Mark the reply! Mark it, all ye infidels, rationalists, and skeptics! Mark it, all ye who are in danger of being deluded and turned aside by the impudent and blasphemous suggestions of infidelity!

"Abraham saith unto him, They have Moses and the Prophets; *let them hear them.*" Yes; "hear them"—hear those very writings which infidels tell us are not divinely inspired at all, but documents palmed upon us by impostors pretending to inspiration. Assuredly the rich man knew better; indeed, the devil himself knows better. There is no thought of calling in question the genuineness of "Moses and the Prophets;" but perhaps "if one went unto them from the dead, they will repent." Hear the weighty rejoinder! "And he said unto him, If they hear not Moses and the Prophets, neither will they be persuaded though one rose from the dead."

Now we must confess we rejoice exceedingly in the grandeur of this testimony. Nothing can be clearer, nothing higher, nothing more thoroughly confirmatory as to the supreme authority and divine integrity of "Moses and the Prophets." We have the blessed Lord Himself setting His seal to the two grand divisions of Old Testament Scripture; and hence we may with all possible confidence commit our souls to the authority of these holy writings; and not only to Moses and the Prophets, but to the whole canon of inspiration, inasmuch as Moses and the Prophets are so largely and so constantly quoted everywhere, are so intimately, yea, indissolubly, bound up with every part of the New Testament, that all must stand or fall together.

We must pass on, and turn for a moment to

the last chapter of Luke—that precious section which contains "the great commission" whereof we speak. We might refer with profit and blessing to those occasions in which our blessed Lord, in His interviews with Pharisees, Sadducees, and lawyers, ever and only appeals to the Holy Scriptures. In short, whether in conflict with men or devils, whether speaking in private or in public, whether for His public ministry or for His private walk, we find the perfect Man, the Lord from Heaven, always putting the very highest honor upon the writings of Moses and the Prophets, thus commending them to us in all their divine integrity, and giving us the very fullest and most blessed encouragement to commit our souls, for time and eternity, with absolute confidence, to those peerless writings.

We turn to Luke 24, and listen to the glowing words uttered in the ears of the two bewildered travelers to Emmaus—words which are the sure and blessed remedy for all bewilderment—the perfect solution of every honest difficulty—the divine and all-satisfying answer to every upright inquiry. We do not quote the words of the perplexed disciples; but here is the Master's reply. "Then said He unto them, O fools and slow of heart to believe *all that the prophets have spoken!*"

Alas! nowadays a man is counted a fool if he does believe all that the prophets have spoken. In many learned circles, yea, and in not a few religious circles likewise, the man who avows—as every true man ought—his hearty belief in every line of Holy Scripture, is almost sure to be met with a sneer of contempt. It is deemed clever to doubt the genuineness of Scripture—fatal, detestable cleverness, from which may the good Lord deliver us!—cleverness which is sure to lead the soul that is ensnared by it down into the dark and dreary abyss of atheism, and the darker and more dreary abyss of hell. From all such cleverness, we again say, from the profoundest depths of our moral being, may God, in His mercy, deliver us and all our young people!

Have we not much cause to bless the Lord for these words of His addressed to His poor perplexed ones on their way to Emmaus? They may seem severe; but it is the necessary severity of a pure, a perfect, and a divinely wise love. "O fools, and slow of heart to believe all that the prophets have spoken! Ought not Christ to have suffered these things, and to enter into His glory? And"—mark these words!—"beginning at *Moses and all the Prophets*, He expounded unto them *in all the Scriptures* the things concerning Himself." He Himself—all homage to His glorious Person!—is the divine centre of all the things contained in the Scriptures from cover to cover. He is the golden chain that binds into one marvelous and magnificent whole every part of the inspired volume, from Genesis to Revelation.

Hence the man that touches a single section of the sacred canon is guilty of the heinous sin of seeking to overthrow the Word of God; and of such a man even charity itself must say he knows neither the Christ of God nor God Himself. The man who dares to tamper in any way with the Word of God has taken the first step on that inclined plane that leads inevitably down to eternal perdition. Let men beware, then, how they speak against the Scriptures; and if some *will* speak, let others beware how they listen.

If there were no infidel listeners, there would be few infidel lecturers. How awful to think that there should be either the one or the other in this our highly favored land! May God have mercy upon them, and open their eyes ere it be too late! Five minutes in hell will quash forever all the infidel theories that ever were propounded in this world. Oh, the egregious folly of infidelity!

We return to our chapter, which furnishes one more proof of the place assigned by our risen Lord to the Holy Scriptures. After having manifested Himself in infinite grace and tranquilizing power to His troubled disciples, having shown them His hands and His feet, and assured them of His personal identity by eating in their presence, "He said unto them, These are the words which I spake unto you while I was yet with you, that *all things must be fulfilled which were written in the law of Moses, and in the Prophets, and in the Psalms*, concerning Me.

Then opened He their understanding, that they might understand the Scriptures, and said unto them, Thus *it is written*."

Here again we have the divine seal put upon all the grand divisions of the Old Testament. This is most comforting and strengthening for all pious lovers of Scripture. To find our Lord Himself on all occasions, and under all circumstances, referring to Scripture, using it at all times and for all purposes, feeding upon it Himself and commending it to others, wielding it as the sword of the Spirit, bowing to its holy authority in all things, appealing to it as the only perfect standard, test and touchstone, the only infallible guide for man in this world, the only unfailing light amid all the surrounding moral gloom—all this is comforting and encouraging in the very highest degree, and it fills our hearts with deepest praise to the Father of mercies who has so provided for us in all our weakness and need.

Here we might close this branch of our subject, but we feel bound to furnish our readers with two more uncommonly fine illustrations of our thesis; one from the Acts, and one from the Epistles. In Acts 24 the apostle Paul, in his address to Felix, thus expresses himself as to the ground of his faith: "But this I confess unto thee, that after the way which they call heresy, so worship I the God of my fathers, *believing all things which are written in the Law and in the Prophets*." So, then, he reverently believed in Moses and the Prophets. He fully accepted the Old Testament Scriptures as the solid foundation of his faith, and as the divine authority for his entire course. Now how did Paul know that the Scriptures were given of God? He knew it in the only way in which any one can know it, namely, by divine teaching.

God alone can give the knowledge that the Holy Scriptures are His own very revelation to man. If He does not give it, no one can; if He does, no one need. If I want human evidence to accredit the Word of God, it is not the Word of God to me. The authority on which I receive it is higher than the Word itself. Supposing I could by reason or human learning work my way to the rational conclusion that the Bible is the Word of God, then my faith would merely stand in the wisdom of man, and not in the power of God. Such a faith is worthless; it does not link me with God, and therefore leaves me unsaved, unblessed, uncertain. It leaves me without God, without Christ, without hope. Saving faith is believing what God says because *He* says it, and this faith is wrought in the soul by the Holy Spirit. Intellectual faith is a cold, lifeless, worthless faith, which only deceives and puffs up; it never can save, sanctify, or satisfy.

We turn now to 2 Tim. 3: 14-17. The aged apostle, at the close of his marvelous career, from his prison at Rome, looking back at the whole of his ministry, looking around at the failure and ruin so sadly apparent on every side, looking forward to the terrible consummation of the "last days," and looking beyond all to "the crown of righteousness which the Lord, the righteous Judge, shall give *in that day*," thus addresses his beloved son: "But *continue thou* in the things which thou hast learned and *hast been assured of*, knowing of whom thou hast learned; and that *from a child thou hast known the Holy Scriptures, which are able to make thee wise unto salvation* through faith which is in Christ Jesus. *All Scripture is given by inspiration of God*, and is profitable for doctrine, for reproof, for correction, for instruction in righteousness; that *the man of God may be perfect* [complete], *thoroughly furnished unto all good works*."

All this is unspeakably precious to every true lover of the Word of God. The place here assigned, and the virtues here attributed, to the Holy Scriptures are beyond all price. In short, it is utterly impossible to overstate the value and importance of the foregoing quotation. It is deeply touching to find the revered and beloved old veteran, in the full power of the Holy Ghost, recalling Timothy to the days of his childhood, when, at the knees of his pious mother, he drank at the pure fountain of inspiration. How did the dear child know that these holy writings were the Word of God? He knew it just in the same way that the blessed apostle himself knew it, by their divine power and effect upon his heart and conscience through the Holy Ghost.

Did the Holy Scriptures need man's credentials? What an insult to the dignity of Scripture to imagine that any human seal or guarantee is necessary to accredit it to the soul! Do we want the authority of the Church, the judgment of the Fathers, the decrees of councils, the consent of the doctors, the decision of the universities, to accredit the Word of God? Far away be the thought! Who would think of bringing out a rushlight at noon to prove that the sun shines, or to bring home its beams in their genial virtue to the human frame? What son would think of taking his father's letter to an ignorant crossing-sweeper to have it accredited and interpreted to his heart?

These figures are feebleness itself when used to illustrate the egregious folly of submitting the Holy Scriptures to the judgment of any human mind. No, the Word of God speaks for itself. It carries its own powerful credentials with it. Its own internal evidences are amply sufficient for every pious, right-minded, humble child of God. It needs no letter of commendation from men. No doubt external evidences have their value and their interest. Human testimony must go for what it is worth. We may rest assured that the more thoroughly all human evidence is sifted, and the nearer all human testimony approaches to the truth, the more fully and distinctly will all concur in demonstrating the genuineness and integrity of our precious Bible.

Further, we must declare our deep and settled conviction that no infidel theory can hold water for a moment; no infidel argument can pass muster with an honest mind. We invariably find that all infidel assaults upon the Bible recoil upon the heads of those who make them. Infidel writers make fools of themselves, and leave the divine volume just where it always was, and where it always will be, like an impregnable rock, against which the waves of infidel thought dash themselves in contemptible impotency.

There stands the Word of God in its divine majesty, in its heavenly power, in its beautiful simplicity, in its matchless glory, in its unfathomed because unfathomable depths, in its never-failing freshness and power of adaptation, in its marvelous comprehensiveness, in its vastness of scope, its perfect unity, its thorough uniqueness. The Bible stands alone. There is nothing like it in the wide world of literature; and if anything further were needed to prove that that book which we call "The Bible" is in very deed the living and eternal Word of God, it may be found in the ceaseless efforts of the devil to prove that it is not.

"*Forever,* O Lord, Thy word is *settled in heaven.*" What remains, beloved reader, for thee? Just this: "Thy word have I *hid in my heart,* that I might not sin against Thee." Thus it stands, blessed be His holy name; and when we have His Word hid in the depths of our hearts, the theories and the arguments, the reasonings or the ravings, the questionings and the conclusions of skeptics, rationalists, and infidels, will be to us of less moment than the pattering of rain upon the window.

Thus much as to the weighty question of the "*authority*" upon which the great commission proceeds. The immense importance of the subject, and the special character of the moment through which we are passing, must account for the unusual length of this article. We feel profoundly thankful for an opportunity of bearing our feeble testimony to the power, authority, all-sufficiency, and divine glory of "the Holy Scriptures." "Thanks be to God for His unspeakable gift!"

Part 8

In full keeping with all that has passed in review before us is the *sphere* of "the great commission," as set forth in that comprehensive clause, "*Among all nations.*" Such was to be the wide range of those heralds whom the risen Lord was sending forth to preach "repentance and remission of sins." Theirs was emphatically a world-wide mission. In Matt. 10 we find something quite different. There the Lord, in sending forth the twelve apostles, "commanded them, saying, Go not into the way of the Gentiles, and into any city of the Samaritans enter ye not."

This was to be a mission exclusively to the house of Israel. There was no message for the Gentiles, no word for the poor Samaritans. If these messengers approached a city of the uncircumcised, they were on no account to enter it. The ways of God—His dispensational dealings—demanded a circumscribed sphere for the twelve apostles sent forth by the Messiah in the days of His flesh. "The lost sheep of the house of Israel" were to be the special objects of their ministry.

But in Luke 24 all is changed. The dispensational barriers are no longer to interfere with the messengers of grace. Israel is not to be forgotten, but the Gentiles are to hear the glad tidings. The sun of God's salvation must now pour its living beams over the whole world. Not a soul is to be excluded from the blessed light. Every city, every town, every village, every hamlet, every street, lane and alley, hedge and highway, must be diligently and lovingly searched out and visited, so that "every creature under heaven" might hear the good news of a full and free salvation.

How like our God is all this! How worthy of His large, loving heart! He would have the tide of His salvation flowing from pole to pole, and from the river to the ends of the earth. His righteousness is unto all, and the sweet tale of His pardoning love must be wafted far and wide over a lost and guilty world. Such is His most gracious purpose, however tardy His servants may be in carrying it out.

It is of the greatest importance to have a clear view as to this branch of our subject. It brings out the character of God in a very magnificent light, and it leaves man wholly without excuse. Salvation is sent to the Gentiles. There is absolutely no limit, and no obstacle. Like the sun in the heavens, it shines on all. If a man will persist in hiding himself in a mine or in a tunnel, so that he cannot see the sun, he has none but himself to blame. It is no defect in the sun if all do not enjoy his beams. He shines for all. And in like manner, "the grace of God that bringeth salvation unto all men hath appeared." No one need perish because he is a poor lost sinner, for "God will have all to be saved, and to come to the knowledge of the truth." "He willeth not that any should perish, but that all should come to repentance."

And then, that not a single feature might be lacking to set forth with all possible force and fulness the royal grace which breathes in "the great commission," our blessed Lord does not fail to point out to His servants the remarkable spot which was to be the centre of their *sphere*. He tells them to "begin at Jerusalem." Yes, Jerusalem, where our Lord was crucified; where every indignity that human enmity could invent was heaped upon His divine Person; where a murderer and a robber was preferred to "God manifest in the flesh"; where human iniquity had reached its culminating point in nailing the Son of God to a malefactor's cross—there the messengers were to begin their blessed work; that was to be the centre of the sphere of their gracious operations; and from thence they were to travel to the utmost bounds of the habitable globe. They were to begin with "Jerusalem sinners"—with the very murderers of the Son of God, and then go forth to publish everywhere the glorious tidings, so that all might know that precious grace of God which was sufficient to meet the crimson guilt of Jerusalem itself.

How glorious is all this! The guilty murderers of the Son of God were the very first to hear the sweet tale of pardoning love, so that all men might see in them a pattern of what the grace of God and the blood of Christ can do. Truly the grace that could pardon Jerusalem sinners can pardon any one; the blood that could cleanse the betrayers and murderers of the Christ of God can cleanse any sinner outside the precincts of hell. These heralds of salvation, as they made their way from nation to nation, could tell their hearers where they had come from; they could tell of that superabounding grace of God which had commenced its operations in the guiltiest spot on the face of the earth, and which was amply sufficient to meet the very vilest of the sons of Adam.

Sovereign grace o'er sin abounding:
   Ransomed souls the tidings swell;
'Tis a deep that knows no sounding;
   Who its length or breadth can tell?

Precious grace of God! May it be published with increased energy and clearness throughout the divinely appointed sphere. Alas, that those who know it should be so slow to make it known to others! That slowness is, most surely, not of God. He absolutely delights in the publication of His saving, pardoning grace. He tells us that the feet of the evangelist are beautiful upon the mountains. He assures us that the preaching of the cross is a sweet savor to His heart. Ought not all this to quicken our energies in the blessed work? Ought we not in every possible way to seek to carry out the gracious desire of the heart of God? Why are we so slow? Why so cold and indolent? Why so easily discouraged and repulsed? Why so ready to make excuses for not speaking to people about their souls?

There stands the great commission shining on the eternal page of inspiration in all its moral grandeur—its *terms*, its *basis*, its *authority*, its *sphere!* The work is not yet done. Nearly nineteen hundred years have rolled past since the risen Saviour sent forth His messengers; and still He waits, in sweet, long-suffering mercy, not willing that any should perish. Why are we not more willing-hearted in carrying out the gracious desire of His heart? It is not by any means necessary that we should be great preachers, or powerful public speakers, in order to carry on the precious work of evangelization. What we want is a heart in communion with the heart of God, the heart of Christ, and that will surely be a heart for souls. We do not, and cannot, believe that one who is not led out in loving desire after the salvation of souls can really be in communion with the mind of Christ. We cannot be in His presence and not think of the souls of those around us. For whoever cared for souls as He did? Mark His marvelous path!—His ceaseless toil as a teacher and preacher!—His thirst for the salvation and blessing of souls!

And has He not left us an example that we should follow His steps? Are we doing so in this one matter of making known the blessed gospel? Are we seeking to imitate Him in His earnest diligence in seeking the lost? See Him at the well of Sychar! Mark His whole deportment! Listen to His earnest, loving words! Note the joy and refreshment of His spirit as He sees one poor sinner receiving His message! "I have meat to eat that ye know not of;" "Lift up your eyes, and look on the fields; for they are white already to harvest. And he that reapeth receiveth wages, and gathereth fruit unto life eternal; that both he that soweth and he that reapeth may rejoice together."

We would earnestly entreat the Christian reader to consider this great subject in the divine presence. We deeply feel its importance. We cannot but judge that, amid all the writing and reading, all the speaking and hearing, all the coming and going, there is a sad lack of deep-toned, earnest, solemn dealing with individual souls. How often do we rest satisfied with inviting people to come to the preaching, instead of seeking to bring them directly to Christ? How often do we rest content with the periodical preaching, instead of earnestly seeking, all the week through, to persuade souls to flee from the wrath to come? No doubt it is good to preach, and good to invite people to the preaching; but we may rest assured there is something more than all this to be done, and that something must be sought in deeper communion with the heart and mind of Christ.

Some there are who speak disparagingly of the blessed and holy work of evangelization. We tremble for them. We feel persuaded they are not in the current of the Master's mind, and hence we utterly reject their thoughts. It is to be feared that their hearts are cold in reference to an object that engages the heart of God. If so, they would need to humble themselves in His presence, and seek to get their souls restored to a true sense of the magnitude, importance and interest of the grand question before us. At least let them beware of how they seek to discourage and hinder others whose hearts the Lord has moved to care for precious, immortal souls.

The present is most assuredly not the time for raising difficulties, and starting questions which can only prove stumbling-blocks in the pathway of earnest workers. It becomes us to seek in every right way to strengthen the hands of all who are endeavoring, according to their measure, to publish the glad tidings, and make known the unsearchable riches of Christ. Let us see that we do so, so far as in us lies; and above all things, let us never utter a sentence calculated to hinder any one in the blessed work of winning souls to Christ.

There is one more point in our subject which we feel must not be omitted, and that is the *power* by which "the great commission" was to be carried out. To leave this out would be a great defect, a serious blank indeed; and we are the more anxious to notice it, inasmuch as the special form in which the power was communicated links itself, in a very remarkable way, with that which has been before us. If the *sphere* was to be "all nations," the *power* must be adapted thereto; and, blessed be God, so it was.

Our blessed Lord, in closing His commission to His disciples, said, "And ye are witnesses of these things. And behold, I send the promise of My Father upon you; but tarry ye in the city of Jerusalem, until ye be endued with power from on high." This promise was fulfilled, this power was communicated on the day of Pentecost. The Holy Ghost came down from the ascended and glorified Man, to qualify His servants for the glorious work for which He had called them. They had to "tarry" until they got the power. How could they go without it? Who but the Holy Ghost could speak adequately of the love of God, of the person, work and glory of Christ? Who but He could enable any one to preach repentance and remission of sins? Who but He could properly handle all the weighty subjects comprehended in "the great commission?" In a word, the power of the Holy Ghost is absolutely essential in every branch of Christian service, and all who go to work without it will find it to be barrenness, misery, and desolation.

We must call the reader's special attention to the form in which the Holy Ghost came down on the day of Pentecost. It is full of deepest interest, and lets us into the precious secret of the heart of God in a most touching manner.

Let us turn to chapter 2 of the Acts of the Apostles.

"And when the day of Pentecost was fully come, they were *all with one accord in one place*"—instructive and suggestive fact!—"And suddenly there came a sound from heaven as of a rushing mighty wind, and it filled all the house where they were sitting. And there appeared unto them *cloven tongues*, like as of fire, and it sat upon each of them. And they were all filled with the Holy Ghost"—He had full possession of their hearts and minds, full sway over their whole moral being—blessed condition!—"And they began to speak with *other tongues*" (not in the absurd and unintelligible jargon of cunning impostors or deluded fanatics, but) "as the Spirit gave them utterance. And there were dwelling at Jerusalem Jews, devout men, *out of every nation under heaven*." Note this fact.

"Now when this was noised abroad, the multitude came together, and were confounded, because that *every man heard them speak in his own language*."—How real—how telling!—"And they were all amazed, and marveled, saying one to another, Behold, are not all these which speak Galileans? And how *hear we every man in our own tongue wherein we were born?*"—not merely wherein we were educated—"Parthians, and Medes, and Elamites, and the dwellers in Mesopotamia, and in Judea, and Cappadocia, in Pontus and Asia, Phrygia and Pamphylia, in Egypt, and in the parts of Libya about Cyrene, and strangers of Rome, Jews and proselytes, Cretes and Arabians, *we do hear them speak in our tongues* the wonderful works of God."

What a marvelous occurrence! How marked the coincidence! God so ordered it, in His infinite wisdom and perfect grace, that there should be assembled in the city of Jerusalem, at the exact moment, people from every nation on the face of the whole earth, in order that—even should the twelve apostles fail to carry out their commission—all might hear, in the very dialect in which their mothers first whispered into their infant ears the accents of a mother's love, the precious tidings of God's salvation.

Can anything exceed this in interest? Who can fail to see in the fact here recorded that it was the loving desire of the heart of God to reach every creature under Heaven with the sweet story of His grace? The world had rejected the Son of God, had crucified and slain Him; but no sooner had He taken His seat at the right hand of God than down came the august Witness, God the Spirit, to speak to man—to every man—to speak to him, not in accents of withering denunciation, not in the thundering anathemas of judgment, but in accents of deep and tender love, to tell him of full remission of sins through the blood of the cross.

True, He called on man to judge himself, to repent, to take his only true and proper place. Why not? How could it be otherwise? Repentance is—as we have already fully shown and earnestly insisted upon in these papers—a universal and abiding necessity for man. But the Spirit of God came down to speak face to face with man, to tell him in his own mother tongue of the wonderful works of God. He did not speak to a Hebrew in Latin, or a Roman in Greek; but He spoke to each in the very dialect in which he was born, thus proving to a demonstration—proving in the most affecting manner possible—that it was God's gracious desire to make His way to man's heart in deepest, richest, fullest grace. All homage to His name!

How different it was when the law was to be published from mount Sinai! If all the nations of the earth had been assembled round that fiery mount, they could not have understood one word—unless, indeed, any one happened to know the Hebrew tongue. The law was addressed to one people, it was wrapped up in one language, it was enclosed in the ark. God took no pains to publish the record of man's duty in every language under Heaven. But when grace was to be published, when the glad tidings of salvation were to be sounded abroad, when testimony was to be borne to a crucified, risen, ascended and coming Saviour and Lord, then, verily, God the Holy Ghost came down, for the purpose of fitting His messengers to speak to every man in a tongue which he could understand.

Facts are powerful arguments, and assuredly the above two facts, in reference to the law and the gospel, must speak to every heart, in a manner the most convincing, of the matchless grace of God. God did not send forth heralds to publish the law to "all nations." No—this was reserved for "the great commission" on which we have been dwelling, and which we now earnestly commend, with all its great subjects, to the serious attention of every reader.

DAVID'S COMPANIONS AND PAUL'S FRIENDS

2 Samuel 23 and Romans 16

HOW PRECIOUS are those specific links which are formed by the hand of God! There is the great *general* link which connects us with all the children of God—all the members of the body of Christ; but there are *specific* links which we should ever recognize and seek to strengthen and perpetuate, in every right way.

We were lately looking, with much interest and profit, at David's mighty men in 2 Samuel 23, and Paul's friends at Rome in

Romans 16. Out of the many thousands of Israel—circumcised members of the congregation, children of Abraham—there were comparatively few who distinguished themselves by personal devotedness and whole-hearted consecration. Even among those few there were marked differences. There were "the thirty," "the three," and "the first three." Each gets his own specific place on the page of the book of responsible, practical life, according to what he was or what he had done. Moreover, we are told particularly what each one did and how he did it. Nothing is forgotten, but all is faithfully recorded; and no one can ever get another's place. Each does his own work, fills his own niche, and gets his own reward.*

So also in Romans 16. Nothing can be more marked or striking than the beautiful discrimination which characterizes this exquisite Scripture. First of all, mark the way in which Phebe is commended to the assembly at Rome. "I commend unto you Phebe our sister." On what ground? Is it that she is "breaking bread" or "in fellowship" at Cenchrea? No; but "she is *a servant of the assembly*"; and "she has been a *succourer of many, and of myself also.*"

He presents, in touching and forcible language, the moral basis of her claim upon the hospitality and succour of the assembly. To say that a person is "breaking bread" is, alas! no guarantee of personal devotedness. It ought to be; but it is not. And hence, to expect the sympathy, succour, and confidence of the Lord's people on that ground is unwarrantable. Even the blessed apostle himself, when he asks for the prayers of the brethren, presents the moral basis of his claim. "Brethren, pray for us." On what ground? Is it because we are "breaking bread" or "in fellowship"? Nothing of the kind; but because "we trust we have a good conscience, in all things willing to live honestly."

Then mark the notice of Priscilla and Aquila. What had they done? They had been the apostle's helpers. They had laid down their own necks for his life. And he adds: "Unto whom not only I give thanks, but also all the assemblies of the Gentiles." This is uncommonly fine. They had purchased to themselves a good degree. They had worked their way into the confidence and esteem of the apostle and of all the assemblies. Thus it must be. We cannot jump, all in a moment, into people's confidence and affection. We must commend ourselves by a life of practical righteousness and personal devotedness. "Commending ourselves to *every man's conscience*, in the sight of God" (2 Cor. 4: 2).

Again, look at the exquisite touch in verse 12: "Salute Tryphena and Tryphosa, who *labour* in the Lord. Salute the beloved Persis, which *laboured much* in the Lord." See what lovely discrimination is here! Why does he not class all three together? The reason is plain: because two had only labored, while the third had labored *much*. Each one gets his and her place, according to what they were, and according to what they had done.

Nor would Tryphena and Tryphosa have had any cause of envy and jealousy against Persis, because she was characterized as "beloved" while they were not; or because the word "much" was added to her labor and withheld from theirs. Ah! no; envy and jealousy are the pernicious fruit of a miserable self-occupation; they can find no place in a heart wholly devoted to Christ and His precious interests.

Now, I look upon 2 Samuel 23 and Romans 16 as specimen pages of the book of responsible, practical life, in which each one is written down according to what he is and according to what he has done. It is, of course, all by grace. Each one will delight to say that "by the grace of God I am what I am." Moreover, all the children of God and members of Christ, are equally "*accepted* in the beloved," all stand in one common relationship. The very feeblest member of the body of Christ is loved by God as Christ is loved. The Head and the members cannot be separated. As He is so are they. The feeblest child in the family has his own place in the Father's heart, with which no one can ever interfere (Eph. 1:6; John 17:26; 1 John 4:17).

All this is blessedly true, and nothing can ever touch it. But when we turn to the grand question of practical life and personal devotedness, what endless variety! We see "the three," "the first three," and "the thirty." It is one thing to be "*accepted,*" and another thing to be "*acceptable*" or agree-

---

* We may observe the same thing in the case of the twelve apostles. We read much more about "Peter, James, and John" than about the other nine. And not only so, but even in the case of those three, we mark a difference, for one is specially named as "the disciple whom Jesus loved," and who leaned on His breast at supper.

Thus it is all through the Word. Look at Abraham and Lot; Elijah and Obadiah; the Shunammite and the Sareptan.

Christian reader, let us earnestly seek a closer walk with God—deeper intimacy with the mind of Christ.

able. It is one thing to be a beloved child and another thing to be a devoted servant. There is the love of relationship and the love of complacency.

These things must not be confounded. And, most assuredly, it should be the earnest desire of every "accepted" child of God to be an "acceptable" servant of Christ. Oh! may it be so more and more in this day of cold indifference and self-seeking, in which so many seem to rest satisfied with the mere fact of being in fellowship, as it is called—the form of breaking bread; and so few, comparatively, are pressing after that high standard of personal devotedness which, we may rest assured, is "agreeable" to the heart of Christ.

Let us not be misunderstood. True fellowship in the Spirit—the communion of saints—is precious beyond all expression;

and the breaking of bread, in truth and sincerity, in remembrance of our adorable Lord and Saviour Jesus Christ, who loved us and gave Himself for us, is one of the very highest and richest privileges for those whose hearts are true to Him. All this is clearly understood and fully admitted.

But, on the other hand, we must never forget the strong tendency of our poor hearts to rest in mere forms and formularies when the power is gone. It is one thing to be in nominal fellowship and go through the outward form of breaking bread, and another thing altogether to be an earnest, devoted, pronounced disciple of Christ. This latter is what we should all ardently long for; but to rest in the former is a miserable delusion, deadening the conscience, hardening the heart, and deceiving the soul.

"THE DEW OF HERMON"

Psalm 133

THE EXPRESSION "the dew of Hermon" has, it seems, long proved "a geographical puzzle" to some. But to one who has the mind of Christ it is no puzzle, but a most striking and beautiful figure. Hermon is the very loftiest peak in all the land of Palestine, and from its snowy cap, when all the surrounding country is parched, the refreshing dew descends upon the mountains of Zion; and this is one of the figures used by the Holy Ghost to illustrate the beauty and pleasantness of brethren dwelling together in unity.

Let us quote the entire psalm.

"Behold how good and how pleasant it is for brethren to dwell together in unity! It is like the precious ointment upon the head, that ran down upon the beard, even Aaron's beard, that went down to the skirts of his garments. As the dew of Hermon that descended upon the mountains of Zion;* for

there the Lord commanded the blessing, even life for evermore."

Here we have two lovely illustrations of unity among brethren. It is like ointment descending from the head of the high priest to the skirts of his garment; and it is like the dew descending, in refreshing power, from Hermon's snowy top.

How truly delightful! And yet they are but figures used to set forth the divine idea of unity among brethren. But how is the unity to be promoted? By living sufficiently near to our great priestly Head to catch the fragrant ointment as it descends from Him—to be living so near the Man in the glory as that the refreshing dew of His grace may drop upon our souls, thus rendering us fragrant and fruitful to His praise.

This is the way to *dwell* in unity with our brethren. It is one thing to talk about unity,

---

* The interpolated words, "and as the dew," spoil the beauty of the figure.

and another thing altogether to dwell in it. We may profess to hold "the unity of the body," and "the unity of the Spirit"—most precious and glorious truths surely—and all the while be really full of selfish strife, party spirit, and sectarian feeling, all of which are entirely destructive of practical unity. If brethren are to dwell together in unity, they must be receiving the ointment from the Head, the refreshing showers from the true Hermon. They must live in the very presence of Christ, so that all their points and angles may be moulded off, all their selfishness judged and subdued, all their own peculiar notions set aside, all their *cues* and crotchets flung to the winds. Thus there will be large-ness of heart, breadth of mind, and depth of sympathy. Thus we shall learn to bear and forbear. It will not then be loving those who think with us and feel with us as to some pet theory or other. It will be loving and embracing "all who love our Lord Jesus Christ in sincerity."

The blessed Head loves all His members, and if we are drinking into His spirit, if we are learning of Him, we shall love all likewise. No doubt, those who keep His commandments enjoy His special love—the love of com-placency; and so we cannot but specially love those in whom we trace most of His blessed Spirit. But this is a totally different thing from loving people because they adopt *our* line of truth, or *our* peculiar views. It is Christ, and not self; and this is what we want, if we are to "*dwell together in unity.*"

Look at that charming picture presented in Philippians 2. There truly we see, first of all, the divine Head Himself, and from Him the ointment descending to the skirts of His garments. Where did Paul get the grace to enable him to be ready to be poured out as a drink-offering upon the sacrifice of his brethren? What was it that made Timothy care for other people? What led Epaphro-ditus to put his life in his hand to supply his

brethren's lack? What is the one grand answer to all these questions? Simply this: these beloved servants of Christ lived so in their Master's presence, and drank so deeply into His Spirit, they dwelt so near the Man in the glory, that the fragrant ointment, and the refreshing dew, fell upon their souls abun-dantly, and made them channels of blessing to others.

This, be assured of it, is the grand secret of getting on together. If brethren are to dwell together in unity, they must have the "ointment" and the "dew" dropping contin-ually upon them. They must live close to Christ, and be occupied with Him, so that they may shew forth His virtues, and reflect His blessed image.

Then, what joy to be enabled, in any little measure, to refresh the heart of God! He delights to see His children walking in love. It is He who says, "Behold, how good and how pleasant it is for brethren to dwell together in unity!" Surely this ought to stir our hearts to seek in every possible way to promote this lovely unity. It should lead us to sink self and all its belongings, to surrender everything that might tend in any measure to alienate our hearts from Christ, or from one another. The Holy Ghost exhorts us to "*endeavour*" to keep the unity of the Spirit in the bond of peace." Let us remember this. It is the unity of the Spirit, not the unity of the body, we are to keep in the uniting bond of peace. This will cost us something. The word "endeavouring" shews that it cannot be done without sacrifice. But the One who so graciously exhorts us to the service will ever supply the needed grace. The ointment and the dew will flow down from Him in refreshing power, knitting our hearts together in holy love, and enabling us to deny ourselves, and surrender everything which might tend to hinder that true unity which we are imperatively called upon to maintain.

DIVERSITY AND UNITY

IT IS AT ONCE INTERESTING and instructive to mark the varied lines of truth presented in the New Testament, all finding their common centre in that blessed One who is the truth. We see this, both in the Gospels and in the Epistles. Each of the four Evangelists, under the direct guidance and power of the Holy Ghost, gives us a distinct view of Christ. Matthew presents Him in His Jewish relations—as the Messiah, the Son of David, Son of Abraham—heir of the promises made to the fathers. Mark presents Him as the earnest workman, the diligent servant, the laborious minister, the incessant preacher and teacher. Luke gives us "The Man Christ Jesus," in His human relations, Son of man, Son of Adam. John is occupied with the Son of God, Son of the Father, the heavenly Man, in His heavenly relationships.

Thus each one has his own specific line. No two are alike, but all agree. There is lovely variety, but the most perfect harmony; there is diversity and unity. Matthew does not interfere with Mark; nor Mark with Luke; nor Luke with John. There is no collision, because each moves in his own proper orbit, and all revolve round the one grand centre.

Nor could we do without any one of the four. There would be a serious blank if one were missing; and it is the Holy Spirit's purpose and joy to set forth every ray of the moral glory of the Son of God. Each Gospel fulfils his own service, under the guiding hand of the Holy Ghost.

So also is it in the Epistles. Paul's line of things is as distinct from Peter's, as Peter's is from John's, or John's from James'. No two are alike, but all agree. There is no collision, because, like the four Evangelists, each moves in his own appointed orbit, and all revolve round the one common centre. The orbit is distinct, but the centre is one. Paul gives us the great truth of man's relation with God, on the ground of accomplished redemption, together with the counsels of God as to Israel and the Church. Peter gives us the Christian pilgrimage and God's government of the world. James insists upon practical righteousness. John opens up the grand theme of eternal life; first with the Father, then manifested in the Son, communicated unto us, and finally displayed in the glorious future.

Now, it would be the very height of folly on our part to institute any invidious comparison between those varied lines of truth, or the beloved and honored instruments by whom those lines are presented to us. How silly it would be to set up Matthew against Mark, Mark against Luke, Luke against John, or John against all the rest! How puerile it would be for any one to say, "I go in for Paul's line of things, only. James seems below the mark. Peter and John I do not appreciate. Paul is the man for me. His ministry suits me."

All this we should, at once, denounce as sinful folly, not to be tolerated for a moment. The varied lines of truth all converge upon one glorious and blessed centre. The varied instruments are all employed by one and the self-same inspiring Spirit, for the one grand object of presenting the varied moral glories of Christ. We want them all. We could no more afford to do without Matthew or Mark than we could do without Luke or John; and it is no part of our business to undervalue Peter or James, because they do not give such a lofty or comprehensive range of truth as Paul or John. Each is needful in his place. Each has his work to do, his appointed line of things to attend to, and we should be doing serious damage to our own souls, as well as marring the integrity of divine revelation, if we were to confine ourselves to any one particular line of truth, or attach ourselves exclusively to any one particular instrument or vessel.

The early Corinthians fell into this grave error, and thus called forth a sharp rebuke from the blessed Apostle Paul. Some were of Paul; some of Apollos, some of Cephas; some of Christ. All were wrong; and those who said they were of Christ were quite as wrong as any of the others. They were carnal, and walked as men. It was a grievous folly to be puffed up for one against another, inasmuch as they were all Christ's servants, and all belonged to the whole Church.

Nor is it otherwise now in the Church of God. There are varied kinds of workmen, and varied lines of truth; and it is our happy privilege, not to say our holy duty, to recognize and rejoice in them all. To be puffed up for one against another, is to be "carnal and walk as men." To depreciate any of Christ's servants is to depreciate the truth which he carries, and to forsake our own mercies. "All things are yours; whether Paul, or Apollos, or Cephas, or the world, or life, or death, or things present, or things to come; all are yours; and ye are Christ's; and Christ is God's."

This is the true and the divine way to look at the matter; and this, too, is the way to avoid sects, parties, cliques and coteries in the Church of God. There is one body, one Head, one Spirit, one divine and perfect revelation—the Holy Scriptures. There are many members, many gifts, many lines of truth, many distinct characters of ministry. We need them all, and therefore God has given them all.

But, most surely, God has not given the various gifts and ministries for us to set one against another, but that we may humbly and thankfully avail ourselves of all, and profit by them according to His gracious purpose in giving them. If all were Pauls, where were the Peters? If all were Peters, where were the Johns?

Nor this only; but what must be the effect of going in for any one particular line of truth, or character of ministry? What but to produce an imperfect Christian character? We are all sadly prone to one-sidedness, and nothing more ministers to this evil than an inordinate attachment to some one particular branch of truth, to the exclusion of other branches equally important. It is by "*the truth*" we are sanctified—by all, not by *some* truth.

We should delight in every department of truth, and give a cordial welcome to each vessel or instrument which our God may be pleased to use in ministering His truth to our souls. To be puffed up for one against another is to be more occupied with the vessel than with the truth which the vessel contains, more occupied with man than with God—a grievous mistake! "Who then is Paul, or who is Apollos, but ministers by whom ye believed, even as *the Lord gave to every man.*"

Here lies the grand principle. God has various instruments for His work, and we should value them all as *His* instruments, and nothing more. It has ever been Satan's object to lead the Lord's people to set up heads of schools, leaders of parties, centres of cliques, thus splitting up the Church of God into sects, and destroying its visible unity. Let us not be ignorant of his devices; but in every possible way "*endeavour* to keep the unity of the Spirit in the uniting bond of peace."

How is this great object to be attained? By keeping near the Centre—by abiding in Christ—by habitual occupation with Himself —by drinking deeply into His spirit, and walking in His footsteps—by lying at His feet, in true brokenness of spirit and humility of mind—by thorough consecration to His service, the furtherance of His cause, the promotion of His glory, the prosperity and blessing of every beloved member of His body.

Thus shall we be delivered from strife and contention, from the discussion of profitless questions and baseless theories, from partiality, prejudice, and predilection. We shall be able to see and appreciate all the varied lines of truth converging upon the one divine Centre, the varied rays of light emanating from the one eternal Source. We shall rejoice in the great fact that, in all the ways and works of God, in every department of nature and grace, in things on earth and things in Heaven, in time and eternity, it is not a dull uniformity but a delightful variety. In a word, God's universal and eternal principle is "*diversity and unity.*"

"THERE IS ONE BODY"

Psalm 93; 1 Corinthians 3:16, and 6:19

THESE SCRIPTURES set forth a truth which I believe to be of cardinal importance to every one of us, individually as well as corporately: the Church as a whole is the temple of God; and every believer is made such as really, as literally, as absolutely as the temple of old in which God dwelt, only, of course, in a different way. He dwells in each individual believer. Mark that fact; ponder it. It is not a question of opinion; it is God's truth. If people do not bow to Scripture, it is of no use to argue with them.

The truth presented here is not one about which you may think this or that. *God has a house here on the earth.* Take in that fact; ponder it. Do not say it is what we *ought* to be, but what we *are;* and then see the conduct that flows from it; see what becomes God's house: "Holiness becometh Thy house, O Lord, for ever."

This is the basis of the truth which underlies all discipline from the time that God had a house on earth. We never hear a word about God dwelling with man until redemption is accomplished. But the moment that Israel is out of Egypt, on the shore of the Red Sea, the first note that falls on our ear from the lips of a redeemed people is: "I will prepare Him a habitation." And the moment the last pin is put into the earthly tabernacle, the glory of God comes down to take up His abode in the midst of His people.

But His presence demands and secures holiness. Read Joshua 6—7, and see how we get there two grand consequences of the self-same presence: Jericho in ruins, and the heap of stones in the valley of Achor. One man dared to defile the assembly of God! How solemn it is! It was a fine thing to see those bulwarks crumbling to dust beneath the feet of God's people. But mark: the same

presence that laid Jericho in ruins could not allow that one man's sin to escape notice. The Holy Ghost has penned these records for us, and it is our bounden duty to hang over them; and to seek to drink into our souls the instruction in them.

The very instincts of faith ought to have taught Joshua that there was some hindrance. God's people were His habitation. That fact gave them a characteristic which marked them off from every other nation upon earth. No other nation knew aught of that great privilege but Israel. But God is God; He will be true to Himself; He will take care of His great name. Joshua thought the glory of that great name was involved: but there are more ways than one to maintain that glory.

If Jehovah is present to give victory over His enemies, He is also present to discipline His people. "Israel hath sinned!" God does not say, One man has sinned—find him out. No; it is the six hundred thousand of Israel, because Israel is one nation; one Divine Presence in their midst stamped and marked and formed their unity. Do not try to reason about it, brethren, but bow down your whole moral being to that truth. Do not judge it, but let it judge you. "Israel hath sinned;" that is the reason why they could not get the victory. And Israel must come up man by man, so that he who has transgressed the covenant of Jehovah may be taken. God cannot go on with unjudged evil. Weakness is no hindrance, wickedness is. Can God lend the sanction of His presence to evil? Never! If we are God's dwelling-place, we *must* be holy. This is one of those eternal principles which can never be given up.

But the question is raised: How could it be said that Israel had sinned? Six hundred thousand innocent people! The answer is, *the nation is one*, and that unity has to be maintained and confessed.

In Leviticus 24 we read, that twelve loaves were placed on the golden table before the Lord continually, with the seven lamps of the golden candlestick to throw their light upon them. The end of the same chapter shows us a man brought outside the camp, where all Israel is to stone him with stones. Why this grouping of passages? It is full of meaning. The grouping of Scripture is among some of its brightest glories; the very way in which the Holy Ghost groups His materials commands our attention. Every fact, every circumstance tends to illustrate its infinite depths and its moral glories.

Why, then, do we find this connection in Leviticus? For the simple purpose of illustrating this great principle: faith's power to grasp the eternal truth of Israel's unity, and to confess it in the face of everything—a magnificent, practical truth. There is first the divine side: what Israel was in God's mind; and then, what Israel might become under God's discipline. And it ever behoves the faithful company to confess and maintain the original truth of God, even in the midst of the ruin around. I earnestly, urgently press the necessity as from God to-day, to maintain the great truth of the unity of the body of Christ as that which we have to hold, maintain, and confess in the face of everything.

Elijah on mount Carmel, when the kingdom was divided, called for twelve stones with which to build the altar. But Israel is no longer twelve tribes, it might be said; Israel's unity is broken and gone. No; it is an indissoluble unity, a unity which is never to be surrendered. Israel is twelve while God's eye rests on the twelve loaves on the golden table, on the twelve stones in Aaron's breastplate. Faith holds fast that truth, and Elijah builds his altar of twelve stones. The unity is never to be given up, though it may be like a chain flung across a river, with the tide flowing over it, so that you cannot see it. The Church was one on the day of Pentecost; it will be one in the glory; and it is as true to-day that there is one body and one Spirit, as it was when the Holy Ghost penned the fourth of Ephesians. How is this unity formed? By the Holy Ghost; it is union with the Man at the right hand of God.

Thus I get three substantial reasons for a life of holiness: I am not to dishonor Him to whom I am united; I am not to grieve the Spirit by whom I am united; and I am not to grieve the members to whom I am united.

I feel responsibility to urge this truth upon you. Let not the devil cheat you of the blessing of walking in it. See that you realize its formative, influential power. Think how your state and walk at this moment are affecting the saints elsewhere. "If one member suffer, all the members suffer with it." All Israel was affected by Achan's sin. He thought nobody saw, nobody knew, and quietly hid the forbidden thing in his tent. If this is your state, there is a complete stoppage at once: there is no more power put forth on your behalf by God; there is power truly, but power not to act for you in *victory*, but to act towards you in *discipline;* power to smash you to pieces.

Let us not measure the Word of God by our consciences, or by our sensibilities, but in simplicity believe what it says. We read that there is one Spirit uniting every member to the Head in glory, and uniting every single member on the earth to every other. In this body a saint out of communion is like a waster in a candle; he affects his fellow-saints. Confess this great truth, own it simply, whatever the condition. Never deny it, never give it up.

You say, Brethren are smashed up! I answer, I am not to be occupied with brethren, but with the truth of God. Take your eyes off brethren, and fix them on the truth of God. Are you conscientiously gathered on the ground of the one body? I speak freely and pointedly to you, because I believe this truth is assailed. "He that is joined to the Lord is one spirit," and is joined to all who belong to Him. There is no such thing as independence in the Word of God. The assembly in one place is the corporate local expression of the Church of God, as we saw of the twelve tribes of Israel in the Old Testament.

Why did Daniel pray towards Jerusalem?

The house of God was not there to the eye of man; but it was there to faith. Faith still recognizing it prays towards it, though the lions' den be its reward.

Again, when Paul was before Agrippa, the nation scattered among all peoples from one end of the earth to the other, but Paul will speak of "the promise unto which our twelve tribes hope to come:" and the noun is in the singular (*dodecaphulon*). Could Paul have *shown* them?

Nor can you talk "joining" this body. If you are converted to Christ, all the "joining" is done! you are "added to the Lord;" you are part of that which man cannot touch for a moment; no one can cut off one single member of the body of Christ, which, according to the eternal purpose of God, and according to the operation of the Holy Ghost, is united to Him.

There is no need to organize this body. No, thank God, it is not man's work at all. The Holy Ghost came down at Pentecost to form it, and here it is still. And when our Lord Jesus comes to take it to the glory, it will be "the *holy* city, the new Jerusalem, prepared as a bride adorned for her husband," in which He will show forth "the exceeding riches of His grace, in His kindness toward us through Christ Jesus."

THE CHRISTIAN PRIESTHOOD

WE WANT THE READER to open His Bible and read 1 Pet. 2:1-9. In this lovely Scripture he will find three words on which we will ask him to dwell with us for a little. They are words of weight and power—words which indicate three great branches of practical Christian truth—words conveying to our hearts a fact which we cannot too deeply ponder, namely, that Christianity is a living and divine reality. It is not a set of doctrines, however true; a system of ordinances, however imposing; a number of rules and regulations, however important.

Christianity is far more than any or all of these things. It is a living, breathing, speaking, active, powerful reality—something to be seen in the every day life—something to be felt in the scenes of personal, domestic history, from hour to hour—something formative and influential—a divine and heavenly power introduced into the scenes and circumstances through which we have to move, as men, women, and children, from Sunday morning to Saturday night. It does not consist in holding certain views, opinions, and principles, or in going to this place of worship or that.

Christianity is the life of Christ communicated to the believer—dwelling *in* him—and flowing out *from* him, in the ten thousand little details which go to make up our daily practical life. It has nothing ascetic, or sanctimonious about it. It is genial, pure, elevated, holy, divine. Such is Christianity. It is Christ dwelling in the believer, and reproduced, by the power of the Holy Ghost, in the believer's daily practical career.

But let us turn to our three words; and may the Eternal Spirit expound their deep and holy meaning to our souls!

First, then, we have the word "living." "To whom coming, as unto a living Stone, disallowed indeed of men, but chosen of God, and precious, ye also, as living stones, are built up."

Here we have what we may call the foundation of Christian priesthood. There is evidently an allusion here to that profoundly interesting scene in Matt. 16 to which we must ask the reader to turn for a moment.

"When Jesus was come into the coasts of Caesarea Philippi, He asked His disciples, saying, Whom do men say that I, the Son of Man, am?* And they said, Some say Thou art

---

* Let the reader note this title "*Son of Man.*" It is infinitely precious. It is a title indicating our Lord's rejection as the Messiah, and leading out into that wide, that universal sphere over which He is destined, in the counsels of God, to rule. It is far wider than Son of David, or Son of Abraham, and has peculiar charms for us, inasmuch as it places Him before our hearts as the lonely, out-

John the Baptist; some, Elias; and others, Jeremias, or one of the prophets."

There was endless speculation, simply because there was no real heart-work respecting the blessed One. Some said this, some said that; and, in result, no one cared who or what He was; and hence He turns away from all this heartless speculation, and puts the pointed question to His own, "But whom say ye that I am?" He desired to know what they thought about Him—what estimate their hearts had formed of Him. "And Simon Peter answered and said, Thou art the Christ, the Son of the *living* God."

Here we have the true confession. Here lies the solid foundation of the whole edifice of the Church of God and all true practical Christianity—"Christ the Son of the *living* God." No more dim shadows—no more powerless forms—no more lifeless ordinances —all must be permeated by this new, this divine, this heavenly life which has come into this world, and is communicated to all who believe in the name of the Son of God.

"And Jesus answered and said unto him, Blessed art thou, Simon Bar-jona; for flesh and blood hath not revealed it unto thee, but My Father which is in heaven. And I say also unto thee, That thou art Peter; and upon this rock I *will build* My Church; and the gates of hell shall not prevail against it."

Now, it is evidently to this magnificent passage that the apostle Peter refers in the second chapter of his first Epistle, when he says, "To whom coming, as unto a *living* stone, disallowed indeed of men, but chosen of God, and precious, ye also, as *living* stones [the same words], are built up," etc. All who believe in Jesus are partakers of His risen, victorious, *rock* life. The life of Christ, the Son of the living God, flows through all His members, and through each in particular. Thus we have the *living* God, the *living* Stone, the *living* stones. It is all life together—life flowing down from a living source, through a living channel, and imparting itself to all believers, thus making them living stones.

Now, this life having been tried and tested, in every possible way, and having come forth victorious, can never again be called to pass through any process of trial, testing, or judgment whatsoever. It has passed through death and judgment. It has gone down under all the waves and billows of divine wrath, and come forth at the other side in resurrection, in divine glory and power—a life victorious, heavenly, and divine, beyond the reach of all the powers of darkness. There is no power of earth or hell, men or devils, that can possibly touch the life which is possessed by the very smallest and most insignificant stone in Christ's assembly.

All believers are built upon the living Stone, Christ; and are thus constituted living stones. He makes them like Himself in every respect, save of course, in His incommunicable deity, Is He a living Stone? They are living stones. Is He a precious Stone? They are precious stones. Is He a rejected Stone? They are rejected stones—rejected, disallowed of men. They are, in every respect, identified with Him. Ineffable privilege!

Here, then, we repeat, is the solid foundation of the Christian priesthood—the priesthood of all believers. Before any one can offer up a spiritual sacrifice, he must come to Christ, in simple faith, and be built on Him as the foundation of the whole spiritual building. "Wherefore also it is contained in the Scripture [Isa. 28:16], Behold, I lay in Sion a chief corner-stone, elect, precious; and he that believeth in Him shall not be confounded."

How precious are these words! God Himself has laid the foundation, and that foundation is Christ; and all who simply believe in Christ—all who give Him the confidence of their hearts—all who rest satisfied with Him, are made partakers of His resurrection-life, and thus made living stones.

How blessedly simple is this! We are not asked to assist in laying the foundation. We are not called upon to add the weight of a feather to it. God has laid the foundation, and all we have to do is to believe and rest

cast Stranger, and yet as the One who links Himself in perfect grace with us in all our need—One whose footprints we can trace all across this dreary desert. "The Son of Man hath not where to lay His head." And yet it is as Son of Man that He shall, by-and-by, exercise that universal dominion reserved for Him according to the eternal counsels of God. See Daniel 7.

thereon; and He pledges His faithful word that we shall never be confounded. The very feeblest believer in Jesus has God's own gracious assurance that he shall never be confounded—never be ashamed—never come into judgment. He is as free from all charge of guilt and every breath of condemnation as that living Rock on whom he is built.

Are you on this foundation? Are you built on Christ? Have you come to Him as God's living Stone, and given Him the full confidence of your heart? Are you thoroughly satisfied with God's foundation? or are you seeking to add something of your own—your own works, your prayers, your ordinances, your vows and resolutions, your religious duties? If so, if you are seeking to add the smallest jot to God's foundation, you may rest assured, you will be confounded. God will not suffer such dishonor to be offered to His tried, elect, precious, chief corner Stone. Think you that He could allow aught, no matter what, to be placed beside His beloved Son, in order to form, with Him, the foundation of His spiritual edifice? The bare thought were an impious blasphemy. No; it must be Christ alone. He is enough for God, and He may well be enough for us; and nothing is more certain than that all who reject, or neglect, turn away from, or add to, God's foundation, shall be covered with everlasting confusion.

Having glanced at the foundation, let us look at the superstructure. This will lead us to the second of our three weighty words. "To whom coming as unto a *living* Stone . . . ye also, as living stones, are built up a spiritual house, a *holy* priesthood, to offer up spiritual sacrifices, acceptable to God by Jesus Christ."

All true believers are holy priests. They are made this by spiritual birth, just as Aaron's sons were priests in virtue of their natural birth. The apostle does not say, Ye *ought to be* living stones, and, Ye ought to be holy priests. He says ye *are* such. No doubt, being such, we are called upon to act accordingly; but we must be in a position before we can discharge the duties belonging to it. We must be in a relationship before we can know the affections which flow out of it.

We do not become priests by offering priestly sacrifices. But being, through grace, made priests, we are called upon to present the sacrifice.

If we were to live a thousand years twice told, and spend all that time working, we could not work ourselves into the position of holy priests; but the moment we believe in Jesus—the moment we come to Him in simple faith—the moment we give Him the full confidence of our hearts, we are born anew into the position of holy priests, and are then privileged to draw nigh and offer the priestly sacrifice. How could any one, of old, have constituted himself a son of Aaron? Impossible. But being born of Aaron, he was thereby made a member of the priestly house. We speak not now of capacity, but simply of the position. This latter was reached not by effort, but by birth.

Now let us inquire as to the nature of the sacrifice which, as holy priests, we are privileged to offer. We are "to offer up spiritual sacrifices, acceptable to God by Jesus Christ." So also in Heb. 13:15, we read, "By Him therefore let us offer the sacrifice of praise to God continually, that is, the fruit of our lips giving thanks to His name."

Here, then, we have the true nature and character of that sacrifice which, as holy priests, we are to offer. It is praise—"praise to God continually." Blessed occupation! Hallowed exercise! Heavenly employment! This is not to be an occasional thing. It is not merely at some peculiarly favored moment, when all looks bright and smiling around us. It is not to be merely amid the glow and fervor of some specially powerful public meeting, when the current of worship flows deep, wide, and rapid. No; the word is, "praise *continually*." There is no room, no time for complaining or murmuring, fretfulness and discontent, impatience and irritability, lamenting about our surroundings, whatever these may be, complaining about the weather, finding fault with those who are associated with us, whether in public or in private, whether in the congregation, in the business, or in the family circle.

Holy priests should have no time for any of these things. They are brought nigh to God, in holy liberty, peace, and blessing. They breathe the atmosphere and walk in the sunlight of the divine presence, in the new creation, where there are no materials for a sour and discontented mind to feed upon. We may set it down as a fixed principle—an axiom—that whenever we hear anyone pouring out a string of complaints about circumstances, his neighbors, etc., such an one is not realizing the place of holy priesthood, and, as a consequence, not exhibiting its practical fruits. A holy priest should "rejoice in the Lord always"—ever ready to praise God. True, he may be tried in a thousand ways; but he brings his trials to God in communion, not to his fellow-man in complaining. "Hallelujah" is the proper utterance of the very feeblest member of the Christian priesthood.

Now look, for a moment, at the third and last branch of our present theme. This is presented in that highly expressive word "royal." The apostle goes on to say, "But ye are a chosen generation, a *royal* priesthood. . . that ye should show forth the virtues of Him who hath called you out of darkness into His marvelous light."

This completes the lovely picture of the Christian priesthood.* As *holy* priests, we draw nigh to God, and present the sacrifice of praise. As *royal* priests we go forth among our fellow-men, in all the details of practical daily life, to show forth the virtues—the graces—the lovely moral features of Christ. Every movement of a royal priest should emit the fragrance of the grace of Christ.

Mark again, the apostle does not say, *Ye ought to be* royal priests. He says ye *are*; and as such we are to show forth the virtues of Christ. Nothing else becomes a member of the royal priesthood. To be occupied with myself, to be taking counsel for my own ease, my own interest, my own enjoyment, to be seeking my own ends, and caring about my own things, is not the act of a royal priest at all. Christ never did so; and I am told to show forth His virtues. He, blessed be His name,

grants to His people, in this the time of His absence, to anticipate the day when He shall come forth as a Royal Priest, and sit upon His throne, and send forth the benign influence of His dominion to the ends of the earth. We are called to be the present expression of the kingdom of Christ—the expression of Himself.

Let none suppose that the actings of a royal priest are to be confined to the matter of *giving*. This would be a grave mistake. No doubt, a royal priest will give, and give liberally if he has it; but to limit him to the mere matter of communicating would be to rob him of some of the most precious functions of his position. The very man who penned the words on which we are dwelling said on one occasion—and said it without shame, "Silver and gold have I none"; and yet at that very moment, he was acting as a royal priest, by bringing the precious virtue of the name of Jesus to bear on the impotent man (Acts 3). The blessed Master Himself, we know, possessed no money; but He went about doing good; and so should we: nor do we need money to do it. Indeed it very often happens that we do mischief instead of good with our silver and gold. We may take people off the ground on which God has placed them, namely, the ground of honest industry, and make them dependent upon human alms. Moreover, we may often make hypocrites and sycophants of people by our injudicious use of money.

Hence, therefore, let no one imagine that he cannot act as a royal priest without earthly riches. What riches are required to speak a kindly word—to drop the tear of sympathy—to give the soothing, genial look? None whatever save the riches of God's grace—the unsearchable riches of Christ, all of which are laid open to the most obscure member of the Christian priesthood. I may be poorly clad, without a penny in the world, and yet carry myself truly as a royal priest, by diffusing around me the fragrance of the grace of Christ.

---

* The intelligent reader does not need to be told that all believers are priests; and, further, that there is no such thing as a priest upon earth, save in the sense in which all true Christians are priests. The idea of a certain set of men, calling themselves priests in contrast with the people—a certain *caste* distinguished by title and dress from the body of Christians, is not Christianity at all, but Judaism or intelligently worse. All who read the Bible and bow to its authority will be perfectly clear as to these things.

Perhaps we cannot more suitably close these few remarks on the Christian priesthood, than by giving a very vivid illustration drawn from the inspired page—the narrative of two beloved servants of Christ who were enabled, under the most distressing circumstances, to acquit themselves as holy and royal priests.

Turn to Acts 16:19-34. Here we have Paul and Silas thrust into the innermost part of the prison at Philippi, their backs covered with stripes, and their feet fast in the stocks, in the darkness of the midnight hour. What were they doing? murmuring and complaining? Ah, no! They had something better and brighter to do. Here were two really "living stones," and nothing that earth or hell could do could hinder the life that was in them expressing itself in its proper accents.

But what, we repeat, were these living stones doing? these partakers of the rock-life —the victorious, resurrection-life of Christ— how did they employ themselves? Well, then, in the first place, as *holy* priests they offered the sacrifice of praise to God. Yes, "at midnight, Paul and Silas prayed and sang praises to God." How precious is this! How morally glorious! How truly refreshing! What are stripes, or stocks, or prison walls, or gloomy nights, to living stones and holy priests? Nothing more than a dark background to throw out into bright and beauteous relief the living grace that is in them. Talk of circumstances! Ah, it is little any of us know of trying circumstances. Poor things that we are, the petty annoyances of daily life are often more than enough to cause us to lose our mental balance. Paul and Silas were really in trying circumstances; but they were there as living stones and holy priests.

Yes, and they were there as royal priests, likewise. How does this appear? Certainly not by scattering silver and gold. It is not likely the dear men had much of these to scatter. But oh, they had what was better, even "the virtues of Him who had called them out of darkness into His marvelous light." And where do these virtues shine out? In those touching words addressed to the jailer, "*Do thyself no harm*." These were the accents of a *royal* priest, just as the song of praise was the voice of a *holy* priest. Thank God for both! The voices of the holy priests went directly up to the throne of God and did their work there; and the words of the royal priests went directly to the jailer's hard heart and did their work there. God was glorified and the jailer saved by two men rightly discharging the functions of "*the Christian priesthood*."

EACH MEMBER—A HELP OR A HINDRANCE: WHICH?

A QUESTION FOR ALL IN THE ASSEMBLY

OF THE MANY FAVORS conferred upon us by our ever-gracious Lord, one of the very highest is the privilege of being present in the assembly of His beloved people, where He has recorded His name. We may assert with all possible confidence that every true lover of Christ will delight to be found where He has promised to be. Whatever may be the special character of the meeting; whether it be round the Lord's table, to show forth His death; or round the Word, to learn His mind; or round the mercy-seat, to tell Him our need, and draw from His exhaustless treasury, every devoted heart will long to be there: and we may rest assured that any one who wilfully neglects the assembly is in a cold, dead, dangerous state of soul. To neglect the assembling of ourselves is to take the first step on the inclined plane that leads down to the total abandonment of Christ and His precious interests. See Heb. 10:25-27.

And here, at the very outset, we would remind the reader that the object of this brief paper is not to discuss the oft-raised question, "How are we to know what meeting to go to?" This is, assuredly, a question of cardinal importance, which every Christian— man, woman, and child—is bound and privileged to have divinely settled ere he takes his place in an assembly. To go to a meeting without knowing the ground on which such meeting is gathered, is to act in ignorance or indifference wholly incompatible with the fear of the Lord and the love of His Word.

But we repeat, this question is not now before us. We are not occupied with the ground of the meeting, but with *our state and conduct on the ground*—a question, surely, of vast moral importance to every soul professing to be gathered in or to the name of Him who is holy and true. In a word, our thesis is distinctly stated at the head of this article. We assume that the reader is clear as to the ground of the assembly, and hence our immediate business with him just now is to raise the solemn question in his heart and conscience, "Am I a help, or a hindrance, to the assembly?" That each individual member is either the one or the other is as clear as it is weighty and practical.

If the reader will just open his Bible, and read, thoughtfully and prayerfully, 1 Cor. 12, he will find most clearly established the great practical truth that each member of the body exerts an influence on all the rest; just as, in the human body, if there be anything wrong with the very feeblest and most obscure member, all the members feel it, through the head. If there be a broken nail, or broken tooth, a foot out of joint; any limb, muscle or nerve out of order, it is a hindrance to the whole body. Thus it is in the Church of God, the body of Christ: "If one member suffer, all the members suffer with it; or if one member be honored, all the members rejoice with it." The state of each member affects the whole body. Hence it follows that each member is either a help or a hindrance to all. What a

profound truth! Yes, and it is as practical as it is profound.

Be it remembered that the apostle is not speaking of any mere local assembly, but of the whole body, of which, no doubt, each particular assembly ought to be the local expression. Thus he says, in addressing the assembly at Corinth, "Now *ye are the body of Christ*, and members in particular." True, there were other assemblies; and had the apostle been addressing any of them on the same subject, he would have used the same language; for what was true of each was true of all; and what was true of the whole was true of each local expression. Nothing can be clearer, nothing simpler, nothing more deeply practical. The whole subject furnishes three most precious and powerful motives for a holy, earnest, devoted life—namely, first, that we may not dishonor the Head to whom we are united; secondly, that we may not grieve the Holy Spirit by whom we are united; and, thirdly, that we may not injure the members with whom we are united.

Can anything exceed the moral power of such motives as these? Oh that they were more fully realized among God's beloved people! It is one thing to hold and teach the doctrine of the unity of the body, and quite another thing to enter into and exhibit its holy formative power. Alas, the poor human intellect may discuss and traffic in the highest truths, while the heart, the conscience and the life have never felt their holy influence! This is a most solemn consideration for every one. May we ponder it in our hearts, and may it tell upon our whole life and character. May the truth of the "one body" be a grand moral reality to every member of that body on the face of the earth.

Here we might close, feeling, as we do, that if the glorious truth on which we have been dwelling were held in the living power of faith by all the Lord's beloved people, then, assuredly, *all* the precious practical results would follow. But in sitting down to write, there was one special branch of the subject prominently before the mind; and that is, the way in which the various meetings are affected by the condition of soul, the attitude of heart, and the state of mind, of all who attend. We repeat, and with emphasis, all who attend—not merely all who audibly take part, but all who form the meeting.

No doubt a special and very weighty responsibility rests on those who take any part in the ministry, whether it be in giving out a hymn, engaging in prayer or thanksgiving, reading the Word, teaching, or exhortation. All who do so should be very sure that they are simply the instruments in the hands of the Lord for whatever they undertake to do. Otherwise they may do serious damage to the meeting. They may quench the Spirit, hinder the worship, interrupt the communion, mar the integrity of the occasion.

All this is most serious, and calls for holy watchfulness on the part of all who engage in any branch of ministry in the assembly. Even a hymn may prove a hindrance; it may interrupt the current of the Spirit in the assembly. Yea, the precious Word of God may be read out of place. In short, whatever is not the direct fruit of the Spirit can only hinder the edification and blessing of the assembly. All who take part in the ministry should have the distinct sense that they are led by the Spirit in what they do. They should be governed by the one commanding, absorbing object—the glory of Christ in the assembly, and the blessing of the assembly in Him. "Let all things be done unto edifying" (1 Cor. 14:26). If it be not thus, they had better be quiet, and wait on the Lord. They will render more glory to Christ and more blessing to the assembly by quiet waiting than by restless action and unprofitable talking.

But while feeling and owning the gravity of all that has to be said in reference to the holy responsibility of all who minister in the assembly, we are thoroughly persuaded that the tone, character, and general effect of public meetings are very intimately connected with *the moral and spiritual condition of all*. It is this, we confess, that weighs upon the heart, and leads us to pen this brief address to every assembly under the sun. Every soul in the meeting is either a help or a hindrance, a contributor or a waster. All who attend in a devout, earnest, loving spirit; who come

simply to meet the Lord Himself; who flock to the assembly as the place where His precious name is recorded; who delight to be there because He is there—all such are a real help and blessing to a meeting. May God increase their number. If all assemblies were made up of such blessed elements, what a different tale would have to be told!

And why not? It is not a question of gift or knowledge, but of grace and godliness, true piety and prayerfulness. In a word, it is simply a question of that condition of soul in which every child of God and every servant of Christ ought to be, and without which the most shining gifts and the most extensive knowledge are a hindrance and a snare. Mere gift and intelligence, without an exercised conscience and the fear of God, may be, and have been, used of the enemy for the moral ruin of souls. But where there is true humility, and that seriousness and reality which the sense of the presence of God ever produces, there you have what will most surely, gift or no gift, impart depth of tone, freshness, and a spirit of worship, to an assembly.

There is a vast difference between an assembly of people gathered round some gifted man, and one gathered simply to the Lord Himself, on the ground of the one body. It is one thing to be gathered *by* ministry, and quite another to be gathered *to* it. If people are merely gathered to ministry, when the ministry goes they are apt to go too. But when earnest, true-hearted, devoted souls are gathered simply to the Lord Himself, then, while they are most thankful for true ministry when they can get it, they are not dependent upon it. They do not value gift less, but they value the Giver more. They are thankful for the streams, but they depend *only* upon the Fountain.

It will invariably be found that those who can do best without ministry, value it most when they get it. In a word, they give it its true place. But those who attach undue importance to gift, who are always complaining of the lack of it, and cannot enjoy a meeting without it, are a hindrance and a source of weakness to the assembly.

Alas, there are other hindrances and

sources of weakness which demand the serious consideration of all. We should, each one of us, as we take our places in the assembly, honestly put the question to our hearts, "Am I a help, or a hindrance—a contributor, or a waster?" If we come in a cold, hard, careless state of soul—come in a merely formal manner, unjudged, unexercised, unbroken; in a fault-finding, murmuring, complaining spirit, judging everything and everybody except ourselves—then, most assuredly, we are a serious hindrance to the blessing, the profit and the happiness of the meeting. We are the broken nail, the broken tooth, or the foot out of joint. How sorrowful, how humiliating, how terrible is all this! May we watch against it, pray against it, firmly disallow it.

But, on the other hand, those who present themselves in the assembly in a loving, gracious, Christlike spirit; who delight to meet their brethren, whether round the table, round the fountain of Holy Scripture, or round the mercy-seat for prayer; who, in their hearts' deep and tender affections, embrace all the members of the beloved body of Christ; whose eyes are not dimmed, nor their affections chilled by dark suspicions, evil surmisings, or unkindly feelings toward any around them; who have been taught of God to love their brethren, to look at them "from the top of the rocks," and see them "in the vision of the Almighty"; who are ready to profit by whatever the gracious Lord sends them, even though it may not come through some brilliant gift or favorite teacher—all such are a divinely sent blessing to the assembly, wherever they are. Again we say, with a full heart, may God add to their number. If all assemblies were composed of such, it would be the very atmosphere of Heaven itself; the name of Jesus would be as ointment poured forth; every eye would be fixed on Him, every heart absorbed with Him, and there would be a more powerful testimony to His name and presence in our midst than could be rendered by the most brilliant gift.

May the gracious Lord pour out His blessing upon all His assemblies throughout the whole earth. May He deliver them from every hindrance, every weight, every stumbling-block, every root of bitterness. May the hearts of all be knit together in sweet confidence and true brotherly love. May He crown with His richest blessing the labors of all His beloved servants at home and abroad, cheering their hearts and strengthening their hands, giving them to be stedfast and unmovable, always abounding in His precious work, in the assurance that their labor is not in vain.

THE LORD'S SUPPER

Preface

THE INSTITUTION OF THE LORD'S SUPPER must be regarded, by every spiritual mind, as a peculiarly touching proof of the Lord's gracious care and considerate love for His Church. From the time of its appointment until the present hour, it has been a steady, though silent, witness to a truth which the enemy, by every means in his power, has sought to corrupt and set aside, namely, that redemption is an accomplished fact to be enjoyed by the weakest believer in Jesus. Eighteen centuries have rolled away since the Lord Jesus appointed "the bread and the cup" in the eucharist as the significant symbols of His broken body and His blood shed for us; and notwithstanding all the heresy, all the schism, all the controversy and strife, the war of principles and prejudices which the blotted page of ecclesiastical history records, this most expressive institution has been observed by the saints of God in every age.

True, the enemy has succeeded, throughout a vast section of the professing Church, in wrapping it up in a shroud of dark superstition: in presenting it in such a way as actually to hide from the view of the communicant the grand and eternal reality of which it is the memorial; in displacing Christ and His accomplished sacrifice by a powerless ordinance—an ordinance, moreover, which by the very mode of its administration proves its utter worthlessness and opposition to the truth. (See note to page 806.) Yet, notwithstanding Rome's deadly error in reference to the ordinance of the Lord's Supper, it still speaks to every circumcised ear and every spiritual mind the same deep and precious truth—it "shows the Lord's death till He come." The body has been broken, the blood has been shed *once* no more to be repeated; and the breaking of bread is but the memorial of this emancipating truth.

With what profound interest and thankfulness, therefore, should the believer contemplate "the bread and the cup"! Without a word spoken, there is the setting forth of truths at once the most precious and glorious: grace reigning—redemption finished—sin put away—everlasting righteousness brought in—the sting of death gone—eternal glory secured—"grace and glory" revealed as the free gift of God and the Lamb—the unity of the "one body," as baptized by "one Spirit." What a feast! It carries the soul back, in the twinkling of an eye, over a lapse of eighteen hundred years, and shows us the Master Himself, "in the same night in which He was betrayed," sitting at the supper table, and there instituting a feast which, from that solemn moment, that memorable night, until the dawn of the morning, should lead every believing heart at once backward to the cross and forward to the glory.

This feast has ever since, by the very simplicity of its character, and yet the deep significance of its elements, rebuked the superstition that would deify and worship it, the profanity that would desecrate it, and the infidelity that would set it aside altogether: and furthermore, while it has rebuked all these, it has strengthened, comforted, and refreshed the hearts of millions of God's beloved saints. It is sweet to think of this—sweet to bear in mind, as we assemble on the first day of the week round the supper of the Lord, that apostles, martyrs, and saints have gathered round that feast, and found therein, according to their measure, refreshment and blessing.

Schools of theology have arisen, flourished, and disappeared; doctors and fathers have accumulated ponderous tomes of divinity; deadly heresies have darkened the atmosphere, and rent the professing church from one end to the other; susperstition and fanaticism have put forth their baseless theories and extravagant notions; professing Christians have split into sects innumerable —all these things have taken place; but the Lord's Supper has continued, amid the darkness and confusion, to tell out its simple yet comprehensive tale. "As oft as ye eat this bread, and drink this cup, ye do show* the Lord's death till He come" (1 Cor. 11:26).

Precious feast! Thank God for the great privilege of celebrating it! And yet is it but a sign, the elements of which must, in nature's view, be mean and contemptible. Bread broken, wine poured out—how simple! Faith alone can read, in the sign, the thing signified; and therefore it needs not the adventitious circumstances which false religion has introduced in order to add dignity, solemnity, and awe to that which derives all its value, its power, and its impressiveness from its being a memorial of an eternal fact which false religion denies.

May you and I enter with more freshness and intelligence into the meaning of the Lord's Supper, and with deeper experience into the blessedness of breaking that bread which is "the communion of the body of Christ," and drinking of that cup which is "the communion of the blood of Christ."

THE LORD'S SUPPER

"For I have received of the Lord that which also I delivered unto you, That the Lord

---

* The Greek word translated "show" is more exactly rendered "announce" or "proclaim"—same word as in 1 Cor. 9:14. [ED.]

Jesus, the same night in which He was betrayed, took bread: and when He had given thanks, He brake it, and said, Take, eat; this is My body, which is broken for you: this do in remembrance of Me. After the same manner also He took the cup, when He had supped, saying, This cup is the new testament in My blood: this do ye, as oft as ye drink it, in remembrance of Me. For as often as ye eat this bread, and drink this cup, ye do show the Lord's death till He come" (1 Cor. 11:23-26).

I desire to offer a few brief remarks on the subject of the Lord's Supper, for the purpose of stirring up the minds of all who love the name and institutions of Christ to a more fervent and affectionate interest in this most important and refreshing ordinance.

We should bless the Lord for His gracious consideration of our need in having established such a memorial of His dying love, and also in having spread a table at which *all* His members might present themselves without any other condition than the indispensable one of personal connection with and obedience to Him. The blessed Master knew well the tendency of our hearts to slip away from Him, and from each other, and to meet this tendency was *one*, at least, of His objects in the institution of the Supper. He would gather His people around His own blessed Person; He would spread a table for them where, in view of His broken body and shed blood, they might remember Him, and the intensity of His love for them, and from whence, also, they might look forward into the future, and contemplate the glory of which the cross is the everlasting foundation. There, if anywhere, they would learn to forget their differences, and to love one another; there they might see around them those whom *the love of God* had invited to the feast, and whom *the blood of Christ* had made fit to be there.

However, in order that I may the more easily and briefly convey to the mind of my reader what I have to say on this subject, I shall confine myself to the four following points, viz.:

1. The nature of the ordinance of the Lord's Supper.

2. The circumstances under which it was instituted.

3. The persons for whom it was designed.

4. The time and manner of its observance.

Part 1

First, as to the nature of the ordinance of the Lord's Supper. This is a cardinal point. If we understand not the nature of the ordinance, we shall be astray in all our thoughts about it. The Supper, then, is purely and distinctly a feast of thanksgiving —thanksgiving for grace already received. The Lord Himself, at the institution of it, marks its character by giving thanks. "He took bread . . . when He had given thanks," etc. Praise, and not prayer, is the suited utterance of those who sit at the table of the Lord.

True, we have much to pray for, much to confess, much to mourn over; but the table is not the place for mourners: its language is, "Give strong drink unto him that is ready to perish, and wine unto those that be of heavy hearts. Let him drink and forget his poverty, and remember his misery no more." Ours is "a cup of blessing," a cup of thanksgiving, the divinely appointed symbol of that precious blood which has procured our ransom. "The bread which we break, is it not the communion of the body of Christ?" How, then, could we break it with sad hearts or sorrowful countenances?

Could a family circle, after the toils of the day, sit down to supper with sighs and gloomy looks? Surely not. The supper was the great family meal, the only one that was sure to bring *all the family together*. Faces that might not have been seen during the day were sure to be seen at the supper table, and no doubt they would be happy there. Just so it should be at the Lord's Supper: the family should assemble there; and when assembled, they should be happy, unfeignedly happy, in the love that brings them together. True, each heart may have its own peculiar history—its secret sorrows, trials, failures, and temptations, unknown to all around; but these are not the objects to be contemplated at the supper: to bring them into view is to dishonor the Lord of the feast, and make the cup of blessing a cup of sorrow.

The Lord has invited us to the feast, and commanded us, notwithstanding all our shortcomings, to place the fulness of His love and the cleansing efficacy of His blood between our souls and everything; and when the eye of faith is filled with Christ, there is no room for aught beside. If my sin be the object which fills my eye and engages my thoughts, of course I must be miserable, because I am looking right away from what God commands me to contemplate; I am remembering my misery and poverty, the very things which God commands me to forget. Hence the true character of the ordinance is lost, and, instead of being a feast of joy and gladness, it becomes a season of gloom and spiritual depression; and the preparation for it, and the thoughts which are entertained about it are more what might be expected in reference to mount Sinai than to a happy family feast.

If ever a feeling of sadness could have prevailed at the celebration of this ordinance, surely it would have been on the occasion of its first institution, when, as we shall see when we come to consider the second point in our subject, there was everything that could possibly produce deep sadness and desolation of spirit; yet the Lord Jesus could "give thanks"; the tide of joy that flowed through His soul was far too deep to be ruffled by surrounding circumstances. He had a joy even in the breaking and bruising of His body and in the pouring forth of His blood which lay far beyond the reach of human thought and feeling. And if He could rejoice in spirit, and give thanks in breaking that bread which was to be to all future generations of the faithful the memorial of His broken body, should not we rejoice therein, we who stand in the blessed results of all His toil and passion? Yes; it becomes us to rejoice.

It may be asked, Is there no preparation necessary? Are we to sit down at the table of the Lord with as much indifference as if we were sitting down to any ordinary supper table? Surely not—we need to be right in our souls, and the first step toward this is peace with God—that sweet assurance of our eternal salvation which most certainly is not the result of human sighs or penitential tears, but the simple result of the finished work of the Lamb of God, attested by the Spirit of God. Apprehending this by faith, we apprehend that which makes us perfectly fit for God. Many imagine that they are putting honor upon the Lord's table when they approach it with their souls bowed down into the very dust, under a sense of the intolerable burden of their sins. This thought can only flow from the legalism of the human heart, that ever-fruitful source of thoughts at once dishonoring to God, dishonoring to the cross of Christ, grievous to the Holy Ghost, and completely subversive of our own peace. We may feel quite satisfied that the honor and purity of the Lord's table are more fully maintained when *the blood of Christ* is made the *only* title than if human sorrow and human penitence were superadded.*

---

* It is needful to bear in mind that, while the blood of Christ is that alone which introduces the believer, in holy boldness, into the presence of God, yet it is nowhere set forth as our centre, or bond of union. Truly precious is it for every blood-washed soul to remember, in the secret of the divine presence, that the atoning blood of Jesus has rolled away for ever his heavy burden of sin. Yet the Holy Ghost can only gather us to the person of a risen and glorified Christ, who, having shed the blood of the everlasting covenant, is gone up into Heaven in the power of an endless life, to which divine righteousness inseparably attaches. A living Christ, therefore, is our centre and bond of union. The blood having answered for us to God, we gather round our risen and exalted Head in the heavens. "I, if I be lifted up from the earth, will draw all men unto *Me*." We behold in the cup in the Lord's Supper the symbol of shed blood; but we are neither gathered round the cup nor the blood, but round Him who shed it. The blood of the Lamb has put away every obstacle to our fellowship with God; and in proof of this the Holy Ghost has come down to baptize believers into one body, and gather them round the risen and glorified Head. The wine is *the memorial* of a life shed out for sin: the bread is *the memorial* of a body broken for sin: but we are not gathered round a life poured out, nor round a body broken, but round a living Christ, who dieth no more, who cannot have His body broken any more, or His blood shed any more. This makes a serious difference; and when looked at in connection with the discipline of the house of God, the difference is immensely important.

Very many are apt to imagine that when any one is put away from or refused communion, the question is raised as to their being a link between his soul and Christ. A moment's consideration of this point in the light of Scripture will be sufficient to prove that no such question is raised. If we look at the case of the "wicked person" in 1 Cor. 5, we see one put away from the communion of the Church on earth who was nevertheless a Christian, as people say. He was not, therefore, put away because he was not a Christian: such a question was never raised; nor should it be in any case. How can we tell whether a man is eternally linked with Christ or not? Have we the custody of the Lamb's book of life? Is the discipline of the Church of God founded upon what we *can* know, or upon what we *cannot?* Was the man in 1 Cor. 5 linked eternally with Christ, or not? Was the Church told to inquire? Even suppose

However, the question of preparedness will come more fully before us as we proceed with our subject; I shall therefore state another principle connected with the nature of the Lord's Supper, viz., that there is involved in it an intelligent recognition of the oneness of the body of the Christ. "The bread which we break, is it not the communion of the body of Christ? For we, being many, are one bread, and one body; for we are all partakers of that one bread." Now there was sad failure and sad confusion in reference to this point at Corinth: indeed, the great principle of the Church's oneness would seem to have been totally lost sight of there. Hence the apostle observes that "when ye come together into one place, this is not to eat the Lord's Supper, for every one taketh before other *his own* supper" (1 Cor. 11:20-21). Here, it was isolation, and not unity; an individual, and not a corporate question: "*his own supper*" is strikingly contrasted with "*the Lord's Supper.*"

The *Lord's* Supper demands that the body be fully recognized: if the one body be not recognized, it is but sectarianism: the Lord Himself has lost His place. If the table be spread upon any narrower principle than that which would embrace the whole body of Christ, it is become a sectarian table, and has lost its claim upon the hearts of the faithful. On the contrary, where a table is spread upon this divine principle, which embraces *all* the members of the body *simply as such*, every one who refuses to present himself at it is chargeable with schism, and that, too, upon the plain principles of 1 Cor. 11. "There must," says the apostle, "be heresies among

you, that they which are approved may be made manifest among you."

When the great Church principle is lost sight of by any portion of the body, there must be heresies, in order that the approved ones may be made manifest! and under such circumstances it becomes the business of each one to approve himself, and so to eat. The "approved" ones stand in contrast with the heretics, or those who were doing their own will.*

But do not the numerous denominations at present existing in the professing Church altogether preclude the idea of ever being able to gather the whole body together? and, under such circumstances, is it not better for each denomination to have their own table? If there be any force in this question, it merely goes to prove that the people of God are no longer able to act upon God's principles, but that they are left to the miserable alternative of acting on human expediency. Thank God, such is not the case. The truth of the Lord endureth forever, and what the Holy Ghost teaches in 1 Cor. 11 is binding upon every member of the Church of God.

There were divisions, and heresies, and unholiness, existing in the assembly at Corinth, just as there are divisions, and heresies, and unholiness, existing in the professing Church now; but the apostle did not tell them to set up separate tables on the one hand, nor yet to cease from breaking bread on the other. No; he presses upon them the principles and the holiness connected with "the Church of God," and tells those who could approve themselves accordingly to eat. The expression is, "*So let him eat.*" We are to

---

we could see a man's name written in the book of life, that would not be the ground of receiving him into the assembly on earth, or retaining him there. That which the Church is held responsible for, is to keep herself pure in doctrine, pure in practice, and pure in association, and all this on the ground of being God's house. "Thy testimonies are very sure; holiness becometh Thy house, O Lord, for ever." When any one was separated, or "cut off," from the congregation of Israel, was it because of not being an Israelite? By no means; but because of some moral or ceremonial defilement which could not be tolerated in God's Assembly. In Achan's case (Josh. 7), although there were six hundred thousand souls ignorant of his sin, yet God says, "*Israel hath sinned.*" Why? Because they were looked at as God's Assembly, and there was defilement there which if not judged, all would have been broken up.

---

* Those who are competent to do so can look at the original of this important chapter, where they will see that the word translated "approved" (ver. 19) comes from the same root as that translated "examine himself" (vers. 28). Thus we see that the man who approves himself takes his place amongst the approved, and is the very opposite of those who were amongst the heretics. Now the meaning of a heretic is not merely one who holds false doctrine, though one may be a heretic in so doing, but one who persists in the exercise of *his own will*. The apostle knew that there must be heresies at Corinth, seeing that there were sects: those who were doing their own will were acting in opposition to God's will, and thus producing division; for God's will had reference to the whole body. Those who were acting heretically were despising the Church of God.

eat, therefore: our care must be to eat "*so*," as the Holy Ghost teaches us; and that is in the true recognition of the holiness and oneness of the Church of God.*

When the Church is despised, the Spirit must be grieved and dishonored, and the certain end will be spiritual barrenness and freezing formalism: and although men may substitute intellectual for spiritual power, and human talents and attainments for the gifts of the Holy Ghost, yet will the end be "like the heath in the desert." The true way to make progress in the divine life is to live for the Church, and not for ourselves. The man who lives for the Church is in full harmony with the mind of the Spirit, and must necessarily grow.

On the contrary, the man who is living for himself, having his thoughts revolving round, and his energies concentrated upon, himself, must soon become cramped and formal, and, in all probability, openly worldly. Yes; he will become worldly, in some sense of that extensive term; for the world and the Church stand in direct opposition, the one to the other; nor is there any aspect of the world in which this opposition is more fully seen than in its religious aspect. What is commonly called the *religious world* will be found, when examined in the light of the presence of God, to be more thoroughly hostile to the true interests of the Church of God than almost anything.

But I must hasten on to other branches of our subject, only stating another simple principle connected with the Lord's Supper,

to which I desire to call the special attention of the Christian reader; it is this: the celebration of the ordinance of the Lord's Supper should be the distinct expression of the unity of *all* believers, and not merely of the unity of a certain number gathered on certain principles, which distinguish them from others. If there be any term of communion proposed, save the all-important one of faith in the atonement of Christ, and a walk consistent with that faith, the table becomes the table of a sect, and possesses no claims upon the hearts of the faithful.

Futhermore, if by sitting at the table I must identify myself with any one thing, whether it be principle or practice, not enjoined in Scripture, as a term of communion, there also the table becomes the table of a sect. It is not a question of whether there may be Christians there or not; it would be hard indeed to find a table amongst the reformed communities of which some Christians are not partakers. The apostle did not say, "there must be heresies among you, that they which are *Christians* may be made manifest among you." No; but "that they which are *approved.*" Nor did he say, "Let a man prove himself a Christian, and so let him eat." No; but "let a man approve himself," i.e., let him shew himself to be one of those who are not only upright in their consciences as to their individual act in the matter, but who are also confessing the oneness of the body of Christ. When men set up terms of communion of their own, there you find the principle of heresy; there, too, there must be schism.

---

* It may be well to add a word here for the guidance of any simple-hearted Christian who may find himself placed in circumstances in which he called upon to decide between the claims of different tables which might seem to be spread upon the same principle. To confirm and encourage such an one in a truthful course of action, I should regard as a most valuable service.

Suppose, then, I find myself in a place where two or more tables have been spread; what am I to do? I believe I am to inquire into the *origin* of these various tables, to see how it became needful to have more than one table. If, for example, a number of Christians meeting together have admitted and retained amongst them any unsound principles, affecting the person of the Son of God, or subversive of the unity of the Church of God on earth; if, I say, such principles be admitted and retained in the assembly, or if persons who hold and teach them be received and acknowledged by the assembly; under such painful and humiliating circumstances the faithful can no longer be there. Why? Because I cannot take my place at it without identifying myself with manifestly unchristian principles. The same remark, of course, applies if the case be that of corrupt conduct unjudged by the assembly.

Now, if a number of Christians should find themselves placed in the circumstances above described, they would be called upon to maintain the purity of the truth of God while acknowledging as ever the oneness of the body. We have not only to maintain the *grace* of the Lord's table, but the *holiness* of it also. Truth is not to be sacrificed in order to maintain unity, nor will *true* unity ever be interfered with by the strict maintenance of truth.

It is not to be imagined that the unity of the body of Christ is interfered with when a community based upon unsound principles, or countenancing unsound doctrine or practice, is separated from. The Church of Rome charged the Reformers with schism because they separated from her; but we know that the Church of Rome lay, and still lies, under the charge of schism because she imposes false doctrine upon her members. Let it only be ascertained that the truth of God is called in question by any community, and that, to be a member of that community, I must identify myself with unsound doctrine or corrupt practice, and then it cannot be schism to separate from such a community; nay, I am bound to separate.

On the contrary, where a table is spread in such a manner and upon such principles as that a Christian, subject to God, can take his place at it, then it becomes schism not to be there; for, by being there, and by walking consistently with our position and profession there, we, so far as in us lies, confess the oneness of the Church of God—that grand object for which the Holy Ghost was sent from Heaven to earth.

The Lord Jesus, having been raised from the dead, and having taken His seat at the right hand of God, sent down the Holy Ghost to earth for the purpose of forming one body. Mark, to form *one body*—not many bodies. He has no sympathy with the many bodies, as such; though He has blessed sympathy with many members in those bodies, because they, though being members of sects or schisms, are nevertheless, members of the one body; but He does not form the many bodies, but the one body, for "by one Spirit are we all baptized into one body, whether we be Jews or Gentiles, whether we be bond or free; and have all been made to drink into one Spirit" (1 Cor. 12:13).

I desire that there may be no misunderstanding on this point. I say the Holy Ghost cannot approve the schisms in the professing Church, for He Himself has said of such, "I praise you not." He is grieved by them—He would counteract them; He baptizes all believers into the unity of the one body, so that it cannot be thought, by any intelligent mind, that the Holy Ghost could sustain schisms, which are a grief and a dishonor to Him.

We must however, distinguish between the Spirit's dwelling in the Church, and His dwelling in individuals. He dwells in the body of Christ, which is the Church (see 1 Cor. 3:17; Eph. 2:22); He dwells also in the body of the believer, as we read, "your body is the temple of the Holy Ghost, which is in you, which ye have of God" (1 Cor. 6:19). The only body or community, therefore, in which the Spirit can dwell, is *the whole Church of God;* and the only person in which He can dwell is the believer. But, as has already been observed, the table of the Lord, in any given locality, should be the exhibition of the unity of the whole Church. This leads us to another principle connected with the nature of the Lord's Supper.

It is an act whereby we not only shew the death of the Lord until He come, but whereby we also give expression to a fundamental truth, which cannot be too strongly or too frequently pressed upon the minds of Christians, at the present day, viz., that *all believers are "one loaf—one body."* It is a very common error to view this ordinance merely as a channel through which grace flows to the soul of the individual, and not as an act bearing upon the whole body, and bearing also upon the glory of the Head of the Church.

That it is a channel through which grace flows to the soul of the individual communicant there can be no doubt, for there is blessing in every act of obedience. But that individual blessing is but a very small part of it, can be seen by the attentive reader of 1 Cor. 11. It is the Lord's death and the Lord's coming, that are brought prominently before our souls in the Lord's Supper; and where any one of these elements is excluded there must be something wrong. If there be anything to hinder the complete showing forth of the Lord's death, or the exhibition of the unity of the body, or the clear perception of the Lord's coming, then there must be something radically wrong in the principle on which the table is spread, and we only need a single eye, and a mind entirely subject to the Word and Spirit of Christ, in order to detect the wrong.

Let the Christian reader, now, prayerfully examine the table at which he periodically takes his place and see if it will bear the threefold test of 1 Cor. 11, and if not, let him, in the name of the Lord, and for the sake of the Church, abandon it. There are heresies, and schisms flowing from heresies, in the professing Church, but "let a man approve himself, and so let him eat" the Lord's Supper; and if, once for all, it be asked, What means the term "approved"? it may be answered, It is in the first place, to be personally true to the Lord in the act of breaking bread; and in the next place, to shake off all schism, and take our stand, firmly and decidedly, upon the broad principle which will embrace all the members of the flock of Christ.

We are not only to be careful that we ourselves are walking in purity of heart and life before the Lord; but also, that the table of which we partake has nothing connected with it that could at all act as a barrier to the unity of the Church. It is not merely a personal question. Nothing more fully proves the low ebb of Christianity at the present day, or the fearful extent to which the Holy Ghost is grieved, than the miserable selfishness which tinges, yea, pollutes, the thoughts of professing Christians.

Everything is made to hinge upon the mere question of self. It is *my* forgiveness—*my* safety—*my* peace—*my* happy frames and feelings, and not the glory of Christ, or the welfare of His beloved Church.

Well, therefore, may the words of the prophet be applied to us, "Thus saith the Lord, Consider your ways. Go up to the mountain and bring wood, and *build the house;* and I will take pleasure in *it* and *I will be glorified.* Ye looked for much, and lo, it came to little; and when ye brought it home, I did blow upon it. Why? saith the Lord of hosts. Because of *My house* that is waste, and ye run every man to *his own* house" (Hag. 1:7-9).

Here is the root of the matter. Self stands in contrast with the house of God; and, if self be made the object, no marvel that there should be a sad lack of spiritual joy, energy, and power. To have these, we must be in fellowship with the Spirit's thoughts. He thinks of the body of Christ; and, if we are thinking of self, we must be at issue with Him; and the consequences are but too apparent.

Part 2

Having now treated of what I conceive to be by far the most important point in our subject, I shall proceed to consider, in the second place, the circumstances under which the Lord's Supper was instituted. These were particularly solemn and touching. The Lord was about to enter into dreadful conflict with all the powers of darkness—to meet all the deadly enmity of man; and to drain to the dregs the cup of Jehovah's righteous wrath against sin. He had a terrible morrow before Him—the most terrible that had ever been encountered by man or angel; yet, notwithstanding all this, we read that "on *the same night* in which He was betrayed, He took bread."

What unselfish love is here! "The same night"—the night of profound sorrow—the night of His agony and bloody sweat—the night of His betrayal by one, and His denial by another, and His desertion by all of His disciples—on that very night, the loving heart of Jesus was full of thoughts about His Church—on that very night He instituted the ordinance of the Lord's Supper. He appointed the bread to be the emblem of His body broken, and the wine to be the emblem of His blood shed; and such they are to us now, as often as we partake of them, for the Word assures us that "as often as ye eat *this bread* and drink *this cup,* ye do show *the Lord's death,* till He come."

Now, all this, we may say, attaches peculiar importance and sacred solemnity to the Supper of the Lord; and, moreover, gives us some idea of the consequences of eating and drinking unworthily.*

The voice which the ordinance utters in the circumcised ear is ever the same. The bread

---

* It is usual to apply the term "unworthily," in this passage, to *persons* doing the act, whereas it really refers to the *manner* of doing it. The apostle never thought of calling in question the Christianity of the Corinthians; nay, in the opening address of his Epistle, he looks at them as "the Church of God which is at Corinth, sanctified in Christ Jesus, called saints" (or saints by calling). How could he use this language in the first chapter, and in the eleventh call in question the worthiness of these saints to take their seat at the Lord's Supper? Impossible. He looked upon them as saints, and as such he exhorted them to celebrate the Lord's Supper in a worthy manner. The question of any but true Christians being there, is never raised; so that it is utterly impossible that the word "unworthily" could apply to *persons.* Its application is entirely to the *manner.* The persons were worthy, but their manner was not; and they were called, as saints, to judge themselves as to their *ways,* else the Lord might judge them in their *persons* as was already the case. In a word, it was as true Christians they were called to judge themselves. If they were in doubt as to that, they were utterly unable to judge anything. I never think of setting my child to judge as to whether he is my child or not; but I expect him to judge himself as to his habits, else, if he do not, I may have to do, by chastening, what he ought to do by self-judgment. It is because I look upon him as my child, that I will not allow him to sit at my table with soiled garments and disorderly manners.

and the wine are deeply significant symbols; the bruised corn and the pressed grape being both combined to minister strength and gladness to the heart: and not only are they significant in themselves, but they are also to be used in the Lord's Supper, as being the very emblems which the blessed Master Himself ordained on the night previous to His crucifixion; so that faith can behold the Lord Jesus presiding at *His own table*—can see Him take the bread and the wine, and hear Him say, "Take, eat; this is My body"; and again, of the cup, "Drink ye *all* of it. For this is My blood of the New Testament which is shed for many for the remission of sins."

In a word, the ordinance leads the soul back to the eventful night already referred to—brings before us all the reality of the cross and passion of the Lamb of God, in which our whole souls can rest and rejoice; it reminds us, in the most impressive manner, of the unselfish love and pure devotedness of Him, who, when Calvary was casting its dark shadow across His path, and the cup of Jehovah's righteous wrath against sin, of which He was about to be the bearer, was being filled for Him, could, nevertheless, busy Himself about us, and institute a feast which was to be both the expression of our connection with Him, and with all the members of His body.

May we not infer, that the Holy Ghost made use of the expression "*the same night*," for the purpose of remedying the disorders that had arisen in the church at Corinth? Was there not a severe rebuke administered to the selfishness of those who were taking "*their own supper*," in the Spirit's reference to the same night in which the Lord of the feast was betrayed? Doubtless there was. Can selfishness live in the view of the cross? Can thoughts about our own interests, or our own gratification, be indulged in the presence of Him who sacrificed Himself for us? Surely not. Could we heartlessly and wilfully despise the Church of God—could we offend or exclude beloved members of the flock of Christ, while gazing on that cross on which

the Shepherd of the flock, and the Head of the body, was crucified?* Ah, no; let believers only keep near the cross—let them remember "the same night"—let them keep in mind the broken body and shed blood of the Lord Jesus Christ, and there will soon be an end to heresy, schism, and selfishness.

If we could only bear in mind that the Lord Himself presides at the table, to dispense the bread and wine; if we could hear Him say, "Take this, and divide it among yourselves," we should be better able to meet *all* our brethren on the *only* Christian ground of fellowship which God can own. In a word, the Person of Christ is God's centre of union. "I," said Christ, "if I be lifted up from the earth, will draw all men unto *Me*." Each believer can hear his blessed Master speaking from the cross, and saying of his fellow believers, "*Behold thy brethren;*" and, truly, if we could distinctly hear this, we should act, in a measure, as the beloved disciple acted towards the mother of Jesus; our hearts and our homes would be open to all who have been thus commended to our care. The word is, "*Receive ye one another, as Christ also received us to the glory of God.*"

There is another point worthy of notice, in connection with the circumstances under which the Lord's Supper was instituted, namely, its connection with the Jewish Passover. "Then came the day of unleavened bread, when the Passover must be killed. And He sent Peter and John, saying, Go and prepare us the Passover, that we may eat. . . . And *when the hour was come*, He sat down, and the twelve apostles with Him. And He said unto them, With desire I have desired to eat this Passover with you before I suffer; for I say unto you, I will not any more eat thereof, until it be fulfilled in the kingdom of God. And He took the cup [i.e., the cup of the Passover], and gave thanks, and said, Take this and divide it among yourselves; for I say unto you, I will not drink of the fruit of the vine until the kingdom of God shall come" (Luke 22:7-18).

---

* The reader will bear in mind that the test does not touch the question of scriptural discipline. There may be many members of the flock of Christ who could not be received into the Assembly on earth, inasmuch as they may possibly be leavened by false doctrine, or wrong practice. But, though we might not be able to receive them, we do not, by any means, raise the question as to their being in the Lamb's book of life. This is not the province nor the prerogative of the Church of God. "*The Lord* knoweth them that are His; and let every one that nameth the name of Christ depart from iniquity" (2 Tim. 2:19).

The Passover was, as we know, the great feast of Israel, first observed on the memorable night of their happy deliverance from the thraldom of Egypt. As to its connection with the Lord's Supper, it consists in its being the marked *type* of that of which the Supper is the *memorial.* The Passover pointed *forward* to the cross; the Supper points *back* to it. But Israel was no longer in a fit moral condition to keep the Passover, according to the divine thoughts about it; and the Lord Jesus on the occasion above referred to, was leading His apostles away altogether from the Jewish element to a new order of things. It was no longer to be a lamb sacrificed, but bread broken and wine drunk in commenoration of a sacrifice *once* offered, the efficacy of which was to be eternal. Those whose minds are bowed down to Jewish ordinances, may still look, in some way or another, for the periodical repetition, either of a sacrifice, or of something which is to bring them into a place of greater nearness to God.*

Some there are who think that in the Lord's Supper the soul makes, or renews, a covenant with God, not knowing that if we were to enter into covenant with God, we should inevitably be ruined; as the only possible issue of a covenant between God and man is the failure of one of the parties (i.e., man), and consequent judgment. Thank God, there is no such thing as a covenant with us. The bread and wine, in the Supper, speak a deep and wondrous truth; they tell of the broken body and shed blood of the Lamb of God—the Lamb of God's own providing. Here the soul can rest with perfect complacency; it is *the New Testament in the blood of Christ,* and not a covenant between God and man. Man's covenant had signally failed, and the Lord Jesus had to allow the cup of the fruit of the vine (the emblem of joy in the earth) to pass Him by. Earth had no joy for Him—Israel had become "the degenerate plant of a strange vine;" wherefore, He had only to say, "I will not drink of the fruit of the vine, until the Kingdom of God shall come." A long and dreary season was to pass over Israel, ere her King could take any joy in her moral condition: but, during the time, "the Church of God" was to "keep the feast" of unleavened bread, in all its moral power and significance, by putting away the "old leaven of malice and wickedness," as the fruit of fellowship with Him whose blood cleanseth from all sin.

However, the fact of the Lord's Supper having been instituted immediately after the Passover, teaches us a very valuable principle of truth, viz., this: the destinies of the Church and of Israel are inseparably linked with the cross of the Lord Jesus Christ. True, the Church has a higher place, even identification with her risen and glorified Head; yet all rests upon the cross. Yes; it was on the cross that the pure sheaf of corn was bruised and the juices of the living vine pressed forth

* The church of Rome has so entirely departed from the truth set forth in the Lord's Supper, that she professes to offer, in the mass, "an unbloody sacrifice for the sins of the living and the dead." Now, we are taught, in Heb. 9:22, that "without shedding of blood is no remission"; consequently, the church of Rome has no remission of sins for her members. She robs them of this precious reality, and instead thereof, gives them an anomalous and utterly unscriptural thing, called "an unbloody sacrifice, or mass." This, which according to her own practice and the testimony of Heb. 9:22, can never take away sin, she offers day by day, week by week and year by year. A sacrifice without blood must, if Scripture be true, be a sacrifice without remission. Hence, therefore, the sacrifice of the mass is a positive blind raised by the devil, through the agency of Rome, to hide from the sinner's view the glorious sacrifice of Christ, "once offered," and never to be repeated. "Christ, being raised from the dead, dieth no more; death hath no more dominion over Him" (Rom. 6:9). Every fresh sacrifice of the mass only declares the inefficiency of all the previous sacrifices, so that Rome is only mocking the sinner with an empty shadow. But she is consistent in her wickedness, for she withholds the cup from the laity, and teaches her members that they have body and blood and all in the wafer. But, if the blood be still in the body, it is manifestly not shed, and then we get back to the same gloomy point, namely, "no remission." "Without shedding of blood is no remission."

How totally different is the precious and most refreshing institution of the Lord's Supper, as set before us in the New Testament. There we find the bread broken, and the wine poured out—the significant symbols of a body broken, and of blood shed. The wine is not in the bread, because the blood is not in the body, for, if it were, there would be "no remission." In a word, the Lord's Supper is the distinct memorial of an eternally accomplished sacrifice; and none can communicate thereat, with intelligence or blessing, save those who know the full remission of sins. It is not that we would, by any means, make knowledge a term of communion, for very many of the children of God, through bad teaching, and various other causes, do not know the perfect remission of sins, and were they to be excluded on that ground, it would be making *knowledge* a term of communion, instead of *life* and *obedience.* Still, if I do not know, experimentally, that redemption is an accomplished fact, I shall see but little meaning in the symbols of bread and wine; and, moreover, I shall be in great danger of attaching a species of efficacy to the memorials, which belongs only to the great reality to which they point.

by the hand of Jehovah Himself, to yield strength and gladness to the hearts of His heavenly and earthly people forever. The Prince of Life took from Jehovah's righteous hand the cup of wrath, the cup of trembling, and drained it to the dregs in order that He might put into the hands of His people the cup of salvation, the cup of God's ineffable love, that they might drink and forget their poverty, and remember their misery no more. The Lord's Supper expresses all this. There the Lord presides; there the redeemed should meet in holy fellowship and brotherly love, to eat and drink before the Lord; and while they do so, they can look back at their Master's *night* of deep sorrow, and forward to His day of glory—that "morning without clouds," when "He shall come to be glorified in His saints, and to be admired in all them that believe."

Part 3

We shall now consider, in the third place, the persons for whom, and for whom *alone*, the Lord's Supper was instituted.

The Lord's Supper, then, was instituted for the Church of God—the family of the redeemed. All the members of that family should be there; for none can be absent without incurring the guilt of disobedience to the plain command of Christ and His inspired apostle; and the consequence of this disobedience will be positive spiritual decline and a complete failure in testimony for Christ. Such consequences, however, are the result only of wilful absence from the Lord's table. There are circumstances which, in certain cases, may present an insurmountable barrier, though there might be the most earnest desire to be present at the celebration of the ordinance, as there ever will be where the mind is spiritual; but we may lay it down as a fixed principle of truth that no one can make progress in the divine life who wilfully absents himself from the Lord's table. "*All* the congregation of Israel" were commanded to keep the passover (Exod. 12). No member of the congregation could with impunity be absent. "The man that is clean, and is not in a journey, and forbeareth to

keep the passover, even the same soul shall be cut off from among his people: because he brought not the offering of the Lord in his appointed season, that man shall bear his sin" (Num. 9:13).

I feel that it would be rendering really valuable service to the cause of truth, and a furtherance of the interests of the Church of God, if an interest could be awakened on this important subject. There is too much lightness and indifference in the minds of Christians as to the matter of their attendance at the table of the Lord; and where there is not this indifference, there is an unwillingness arising from imperfect views of justification. Now both these hindrances, though so different in their character, spring from one and the same source, viz., selfishness.

He who is indifferent about the matter will selfishly allow trifling circumstances to interfere with his attendance: he will be hindered by family arrangements, love of personal ease, unfavorable weather, trifling or, as it frequently happens, imaginary bodily ailments—things which are lost sight of or counted as nothing when some worldly object is to be gained. How often does it happen that men who have not spiritual energy to leave their houses on the Lord's day have abundant natural energy to carry them some miles to gain some worldly object on Monday. Alas that it should be so! How sad to think that worldly gain could exert a more powerful influence on the heart of the Christian than the glory of Christ and the furtherance of the Church's benefit! for this is the way in which we must view the question of the Lord's Supper. What would be our feelings, amid the glory of the coming kingdom, if we could remember that, while on earth, a fair or a market, or some such worldly object, had commanded our time and energies, while the assembly of the Lord's people around His table was neglected?

Beloved Christian reader, if you are in the habit of absenting yourself from the assembly of Christians, I pray you to ponder the matter before the Lord ere you absent yourself again. Reflect upon the pernicious effect of your absence in every way. You are failing in your testimony for Christ; you are injuring the souls of your brethren, and you are hindering the progress of your own soul in grace and knowledge. Do not suppose that your actings are without their influence on the whole Church of God: you are at this moment either helping or hindering every member of that body on earth. "If *one* member suffer, all the members suffer with it." This principle has not ceased to be true, though professing Christians have split into so many different divisions. Nay, it is so divinely true, that there is not a single believer on earth who is not acting either as a helper to, or a drain upon, the whole body of Christ.

If there be any truth in the principle already laid down (viz., that the assembly of Christians and the breaking of bread in any given locality is, or ought to be, the expression of the unity of the whole body), you cannot fail to see that if you absent yourself from that assembly, or refuse to join in giving expression to that unity, you are doing serious damage to all your brethren as well as to your own soul. I would lay these considerations on your heart and conscience, in the name of the Lord, looking to Him to make them influential.*

But not only does this culpable and pernicious indifference of spirit act as a hindrance to many, in presenting themselves at the Lord's table; imperfect views of justification produce the same unhappy result. If the conscience be not perfectly purged, if there be not perfect rest in God's testimony about the finished work of Christ, there will either be a shrinking from the Supper of the Lord, or an unintelligent celebration of it. Those only can show the Lord's death who know, through the teaching of the Holy Spirit, the value of the Lord's death. If I regard the ordinance as a means whereby I am to be brought into a place of greater nearness to God, or whereby I am to

obtain a clearer sense of my acceptance, it is impossible that I can rightly observe it. I must believe, as the gospel commands me to believe, that *all* my sins are *forever* put away ere I can take my place with any measure of spiritual intelligence at the Lord's table. If the matter be not viewed in this light, the Lord's Supper can only be regarded as a kind of step to the altar of God, and we are told in the law that we are not to go up by steps to God's altar, lest our nakedness be discovered (Exod. 20:26). The meaning of which is, that all human efforts to approach God must issue in the discovery of human nakedness.

Thus we see that if it be indifference that prevents the Christian from being at the breaking of bread, it is most culpable in the sight of God, and most injurious to his brethren and himself; and if it be an imperfect sense of justification that prevents, it is not only unwarrantable, but most dishonoring to the love of the Father, the work of the Son, and the clear and unequivocal testimony of the Holy Ghost.

But it is not unfrequently said, and that, too, by those who profess spirituality and intelligence, "I derive no spiritual benefit by going to the assembly: I am as happy in my own room, reading my Bible." I would affectionately ask such, Are we to have no higher object before us in our actings than our own happiness? Is not obedience to the command of our blessed Master—a command delivered on "the same night in which He was betrayed"—a far higher and nobler object to set before us than anything connected with self? If He desires that His people should assemble in His name, for the express object of showing forth His death till He come, shall we refuse because we feel happier in our own rooms? He tells us to be there: we reply "We feel happier at home." Our happiness, therefore, must be based on disobedience; and, as such, it is an unholy happiness. It is much better, if it should be so, to be unhappy

* I can only feel myself responsible to present myself in the assembly when it is gathered on proper Church ground, i. e., the ground laid down in the New Testament. People may assemble, and call themselves the Church of God, in any given locality, but if they do not exhibit the characteristic features and principles of the Church of God as set forth in Holy Scripture, I cannot own them. If they refuse, or lack spiritual power, to judge worldliness, carnality, or false doctrine, they are evidently not on proper Church ground: they are merely a religious fraternity, which, in its collective character, I am in no wise responsible before God to own. Hence the child of God needs much spiritual power, and subjection to the Word, to be able to carry himself through all the windings of the professing Church in this peculiarly evil and difficult day.

in the path of obedience than happy in the path of disobedience. But I verily believe, the thought of being happier at home is a mere delusion, and the end of those deluded by it will prove it such.

Thomas might have deemed it indifferent whether he was present with the other disciples, but he had to do without the Lord's presence, and to wait for eight days, until the disciples came together on the first day of the week; for there and then the Lord was pleased to reveal Himself to his soul. And just so will it be with those who say, "We feel happier at home than in the assembly of believers." They will surely be behindhand in knowledge and experience; yea, it will be well if they come not under the terrible woe denounced by the prophet: "Woe to the idol shepherd that *leaveth the flock!* the sword shall be upon his arm, and upon his right eye; his arm shall be clean dried up, and his right eye shall be utterly darkened" (Zech. 11:17). And again, "Not forsaking the assembling of ourselves together, *as the manner of some is;* but exhorting one another, and so much the more as ye see the day approaching. For if we sin wilfully, after that we have received the knowledge of the truth, there remaineth no more sacrifice for sins, but a certain fearful looking for of judgment and fiery indignation, which shall devour the adversaries" (Heb. 10:25-27).

As to the objection upon the grounds of the barrenness and unprofitableness of Christian assemblies, it will generally be remarked that the greatest spiritual barrenness will always be found in connection with a captious and complaining spirit; and I doubt not that if those who complain of the unprofitableness of meetings, and draw from thence an argument in favor of their remaining at home, were to spend more time in secret waiting on the Lord for His blessing on the meetings, they would have a very different experience.

Now, having shown from Scripture who ought to be at the breaking of bread, we shall proceed to consider who ought *not.* On this point Scripture is equally explicit: in a word, then, none should be there who are not members of the true Church of God. The

same law which commanded *all* the congregation of Israel to eat the passover, commanded all uncircumcised strangers *not* to eat; and now that Christ our Passover has been sacrificed for us, none can keep the feast (which is to extend throughout this entire dispensation), nor break the bread nor drink the wine in true remembrance of Him, save those who know the cleansing and healing virtues of His precious blood. To eat and drink without this knowledge, is to eat and drink unworthily—to eat and drink judgment; like the woman in Num. 5 who drank the water of jealousy, to make the condemnation more manifest and awfully solemn.

Now it is in this that christendom's guilt is specially manifest. In taking the Lord's Supper, the professing church has, like Judas, put her hand on the table with Christ and betrayed Him; she has eaten with Him, and at the same time lifted up her heel against Him. What will be her end? Just like the end of Judas. "He, then, having received the sop, *went immediately out:* and"—the Holy Ghost adds, in awful solemnity—"*it was night.*" Terrible night! The strongest expression of divine love only elicited the strongest expression of human hatred.

So will it be with the false professing Church collectively, and each false professor individually; and all those who, though baptized in the name of Christ, and sitting down at the table of Christ, have nevertheless been His betrayers, will find themselves at last thrust out into outer darkness—involved in a night which shall never see the beams of the morning—plunged in a gulf of endless and ineffable woe. And though they may be able to say to the Lord, "We have eaten and drunk in Thy presence, and Thou hast taught in our streets," yet His solemn, heartrending reply will be, while He shuts the door against them, "Depart from Me! I never knew you." O reader, think of this, I pray you; and if you be yet in your sins, defile not the Lord's table by your presence; but instead of going thither as a hypocrite, repair to Calvary as a poor ruined and guilty sinner, and there receive pardon and cleansing from Him who died to save just such as you are.

Part 4

Having now considered, through the Lord's mercy, the nature of the Lord's Supper; the circumstances under which it was instituted; and the persons for whom it was designed; I would only add a word as to what Scripture teaches us about the time and manner of its celebration.

Although the Lord's Supper was not *first* instituted on the first day of the week, yet the twenty-fourth of Luke and the twentieth of Acts are quite sufficient to prove, to a mind subject to the Word, that that is the day on which the ordinance should specially be observed. The Lord broke bread with His disciples on "the first day of the week" (Luke 24:30); and "on the first day of the week the disciples came together to break bread" (Acts 20:7). These Scriptures are quite sufficient to prove that it is not once a month, nor once in three months, nor once in six months, that disciples should come together to break bread, but once a week at least, and that upon the first day of the week.

Nor can we have any difficulty in seeing that there is a moral fitness in the first day of the week for the celebration of the Lord's Supper: it is the resurrection day—the Church's day, in contrast with the seventh, which was Israel's day; and as, in the institution of the ordinance, the Lord led His disciples away from Jewish things altogether (by refusing to drink of the fruit of the vine—the passover cup—and then instituting another ordinance), so, in the day on which that ordinance was to be celebrated, we observe the same contrast between heavenly and earthly things. It is in the power of resurrection that we can rightly show the Lord's death.

When the conflict was over, Melchizedek brought forth bread and wine, and blessed Abram, in the name of the Lord. Thus, too, our Melchizedek, when all the conflict was over and the victory gained, came forth in resurrection with bread and wine, to strengthen and cheer the hearts of His people, and to breathe upon them that peace which He had so dearly purchased.

If, then, the first day of the week be the day on which Scripture teaches the disciples to break bread, it is clear that man has no authority to alter the period to once a month, or once in six months. And I doubt not, when the affections are lively and fervent toward the Person of the Lord Himself, the Christian will desire to show the Lord's death as frequently as possible: indeed, it would seem, from the opening of Acts, that the disciples broke bread daily. This we may infer from the expression "breaking bread from house to house" (or "at home"). However, we are not left to depend upon mere inference as to the question of the first day of the week being the day on which the disciples came together to break bread: we are distinctly taught this, and we see its moral fitness and beauty.

Thus much as to the *time*. And now one word about the *manner*. It should be the special aim of Christians to show that the breaking of bread is their grand and primary object in coming together on the first day of the week. They should show that it is not for preaching or teaching that they assemble, though teaching may be a happy adjunct, but that the breaking of bread is the leading object before their minds. It is the work of Christ which we show forth in the Supper, wherefore it should have the first place; and when it has been duly set forth, there should be a full and unqualified opening left for the work of the Holy Ghost in ministry. The office of the Spirit is to set forth and exalt the name, the Person, and the work of Christ; and if He be allowed to order and govern the assembly of Christians, as He undoubtedly should, He will ever give the work of Christ the primary place.

I cannot close this paper without expressing my deep sense of the feebleness and shallowness of all that I have advanced, on a subject of really commanding interest. I do feel before the Lord, in whose presence I desire to write and speak, that I have so failed to bring out the full truth about this matter, that I almost shrink from letting these pages see the light. It is not that I have a shadow of doubt as to the truth of what I have endeavored to state; no: but I feel that, in writing upon such a subject as the breaking of bread, at the time when there is such sad confusion among professing Christians, there is a demand for pointed, clear, and lucid statements, to which I am little able to respond.

We have but little conception of how entirely the question of the breaking of bread is connected with the Church's position and testimony on earth; and we have as little conception of how thoroughly the question has been misunderstood by the professing Church. The breaking of bread ought to be the distinct enunciation of the fact that all believers are *one body;* but the professing Church, by splitting into sects, and by setting up a table for each sect, has practically denied that fact.

In truth, the breaking of bread has been cast into the back-ground. The table, at which the Lord should preside, is almost lost sight of, by being placed in the shade of the pulpit, in which man presides: the pulpit, which, alas! is too often the instrument of creating and perpetuating disunion, is, to many minds, the commanding object; while the table, which if properly understood would perpetuate love and unity, is made quite a secondary thing. And even in the most laudable effort to recover from such a lamentable condition of things, what complete failure have we seen.

What has the evangelical alliance effected? It has effected this, at least, it has developed a need existing among professing Christians, which they are confessedly unable to meet. They want union, and are unable to attain it. Why? Because they will not give up everything which has been *added* to the truth to meet together according to the truth, to break bread as disciples. I say, *as disciples*, and not as churchmen, Independents, Baptists, etc. It is not that all such may have much valuable truth, I mean those of them who love our Lord Jesus Christ: they certainly may; but they have no *truth* that should prevent them from meeting *together* to break bread.

How could truth ever hinder Christians from giving expression to the unity of the Church? Impossible! A sectarian spirit in those who hold truth may do this, but truth never can. But how is it now in the professing Church? Christians, of various communities, can meet for the purpose of reading, praying, and singing together during the week, but when the first day of the week arrives, they have not the least idea of giving the only real and effectual expression of their unity, which the Holy Ghost can recognize, which is the breaking of bread. "We being many are one bread and one body; for we are *all* partakers of that *one* bread."

The sin at Corinth was their not tarrying one for another. This appears from the exhortation with which the apostle sums up the whole question (1 Cor. 11), "Wherefore, my brethren, when ye come together to eat, tarry one for another." Why were they to tarry one for another? Surely, in order that they might the more clearly express their unity. But what would the apostle have said, if, instead of coming together, into one place, they had gone to different places, according to their different views of truth? He might then say with, if possible, greater force, "Ye cannot eat the Lord's Supper."

It may, however, be asked, "How could all the believers in London meet in one place?" I reply, if they could not meet in one place, they could, at least, meet on one principle. But how did the believers at Jerusalem meet together? The answer is, they were *"of one accord."* This being so, they had little difficulty about the question of a meeting-room. "Solomon's porch," or anywhere else, would suit their purpose. They gave expression to their unity, and that, too, in a way not to be mistaken. Neither various localities, nor various measures of knowledge and attainment, could, in the least, interfere with their unity. There was "one body and one Spirit."

Finally, I would say, the Lord will assuredly honor those who have faith to believe and confess the unity of the Church on earth; and the greater the difficulty in the way of doing so, the greater will be the honor. The Lord grant to all His people a single eye, and a humble and honest spirit.

Thy broken body, gracious Lord,
　Is shadowed by this broken bread;
The wine which in this cup is poured
　Points to the blood which Thou hast shed.

And while we meet together thus,
  We show that we are one in Thee;
Thy precious blood was shed for us—
  Thy death, O Lord, has set us free.

Brethren in Thee, in union sweet—
  Forever be Thy grace adored—

'Tis in Thy name, that now we meet,
  And know Thou'rt with us, gracious Lord.

We have one hope—that Thou wilt come:
  Thee in the air we wait to see,
When Thou wilt take Thy people home,
  And we shall ever reign with Thee.

THE ASSEMBLY OF GOD

THE ALL-SUFFICIENCY OF THE
NAME OF JESUS

IN A DAY LIKE THE PRESENT, when almost every new idea becomes the centre or gathering-point of some new association, we cannot but feel the value of having divinely formed convictions as to what the assembly of God really is. We live in a time of unusual mental activity, and hence there is the more urgent need of calm and prayerful study of the Word of God. That Word, blessed be its Author, is like a rock amid the ocean of human thought. There it stands unmoved, notwithstanding the raging of the storm and the ceaseless lashing of the waves. And not only does it thus stand unmoved itself, but it imparts its own stability to all who simply take their stand upon it. What a mercy to make one's escape from the heavings and tossings of the stormy ocean, and find a calm resting place on that everlasting Rock.

This, truly, is a mercy. Were it not that we have "the law and the testimony," where should we be? Whither should we go? What should we do? What darkness! What confusion! What perplexity! A thousand jarring voices fall, at times, upon the ear, and each voice seems to speak with such authority, that if one is not well taught and grounded in the Word, there is a great danger of being drawn away, or, at least, sadly unhinged. One man will tell you that *this* is right; another will tell you *that* is right; a third will tell you that *everything* is right; and a fourth will tell you that *nothing* is right. With reference to the question of church position, some go *here*; some go *there;* some go *everywhere;* and some go *nowhere.*

Now, under such circumstances, what is one to do? All cannot possibly be right. And yet, surely, there is something right. It cannot be that we are *compelled* to live in error, in darkness, or uncertainty. "*There is a path*," blessed be God, though "no fowl knoweth it, and the vulture's eye hath not seen it. The lion's whelps have not trodden it, nor the fierce lion passed by it." Where is this safe and blessed path? Hear the divine reply: "Behold *the fear of the Lord*, that is wisdom: and *to depart from evil* is understanding" (Job 28).

Let us, therefore, in the fear of the Lord, in the light of His infallible truth, and in humble dependence upon the teaching of the Holy Spirit, proceed to the examination of the subject which stands at the head of this paper; and may we have grace to abandon all confidence in our own thoughts, and the thoughts of others, so that we may heartily and honestly yield ourselves up to be taught only of God.

Now, in order to get fairly into the grand and all-important subject of the assembly of God, we have first to state *a fact;* and, secondly, to ask *a question.* The fact is this, *There is an assembly of God on the earth.* The question is, *What is that assembly?*

Part 1

First then, as to our *fact.* There is such a thing as the assembly of God on the earth.

This is a most important fact, surely. God has an assembly on the earth. I do not refer to any merely human organization, such as the Greek Church; the Church of Rome; the Church of England; the Church of Scotland; or to any of the various systems which have sprung from these, framed and fashioned by man's hand, and carried on by man's resources. I refer simply to that assembly which is gathered by God the Holy Ghost, round the Person of God the Son, to worship and hold fellowship with God the Father.

If we set forth upon our search for the assembly of God, or for any expression thereof, with our minds full of prejudice, preconceived thoughts, and personal predilections; or if, in our searchings, we seek the aid of the flickering light of the dogmas, opinions, and traditions of men, nothing is more certain than that we shall fail to reach the truth. To recognize God's assembly, we must be exclusively taught by God's Word, and led by God's Spirit; for, of God's assembly, as well as of the sons of God, it may be said, "the world knoweth it not."

Hence, then, if we are, in any wise, governed by the spirit of the world; if we desire to exalt man; if we seek to commend ourselves to the thoughts of men; if our object be to gain the attractive ends of a plausible and soul-ensnaring expediency, we may as well, forthwith, abandon our search for any true expression of the assembly of God, and take refuge in that form of human organization which most fully commends itself to our thinkings or our conscientious convictions.

Further, if our object be to find a religious community in which the Word of God is read, or in which the people of God are found, we may speedily satisfy ourselves, for it would be hard indeed to find a section of the professing Christian body in which one or both of these objects might not be realized.

Finally, if we merely aim at doing all the good we can, without any question as to how we do it; if *Per fas aut nefas*, "right or wrong," be our motto in whatever we undertake; if we are prepared to reverse those weighty words of Samuel, and say that, "To sacrifice is better than to obey, and the fat of rams better than to harken," then is it worse than vain for us to pursue our search for the assembly of God, inasmuch as that assembly can only be discovered and approved by one who has been taught to flee from the thousand flowery pathways of human expediency, and to submit his conscience, his heart, his understanding, his whole moral being to the supreme authority of "Thus saith the Lord."

In one word, then, the obedient disciple knows that there is such a thing as God's assembly: and he it is, too, that will be enabled, through grace, to understand what is a true expression of it. The sincere student of Scripture knows, full well, the difference between that which is founded, formed, and governed by the wisdom and the will of man, and that which is gathered round, and governed by Christ the Lord. How vast is the difference! It is just the difference between God and man.

But we may here be asked for the Scripture proofs of our fact that there is such a thing on the earth as *the* assembly of God, and we shall, at once, proceed to furnish these; for we may be permitted to say that, without the authority of the Word, all statements are utterly valueless. What, therefore, saith the Scripture?

Our first proof shall be that famous passage, in Matthew 16, "When Jesus came into the coast of Caesarea Philippi, He asked His disciples, saying, Whom do men say that I, the Son of man, am? And they said, Some say that Thou art John the Baptist; some, Elias; and others, Jeremias, or one of the prophets. He saith unto them, But whom say ye that I am? And Simon Peter answered and said, Thou art the Christ, the Son of the living God. And Jesus answered and said unto him, Blessed art thou, Simon Bar-jona: for flesh and blood hath not revealed it unto thee, but My Father which is in heaven. And I say also unto thee, that thou art Peter; and upon this rock I will build My assembly* (ἐκκλησίαν); and the gates of hell shall not prevail against it" (vers. 13-18).

---

* The same Greek word, *ecclesia*, has been rendered both "church" and "assembly" in our English translation—"assembly" gives the true meaning.

Here our blessed Lord intimates His purpose to build an assembly, and sets forth the true foundation of that assembly, namely, "Christ, the Son of the living God." This is an all-important point in our subject. The building is founded on the Rock, and that Rock is not the poor failing, stumbling, erring Peter, but *Christ*, the eternal Son of the living God; and every stone in that building partakes of the Rock-life which, as being victorious over all the power of the enemy, is indestructible.*

Again, passing over a section of Matthew's Gospel, we come to an equally familiar passage: "Moreover, if thy brother shall trespass against thee, go and tell him his fault between thee and him alone: if he shall hear thee, thou hast gained thy brother. But if he will not hear thee, then take with thee one or two more, that in the mouth of two or three witnesses every word may be established. And if he shall neglect to hear them, tell it unto the assembly, but if he neglect to hear the assembly, let him be unto thee as a heathen man and a publican. Verily I say unto you, Whatsoever ye shall bind on earth shall be bound in heaven; and whatsoever ye shall loose on earth, shall be loosed in heaven. Again, I say unto you, that if two of you shall agree on earth as touching anything that they shall ask, it shall be done for them of My Father which is in heaven. For where two or three are *gathered* together *in My name*, there am I in the midst of them" (chap. 18:15-20).

We shall have occasion to refer to this passage again, under the second division of our subject. It is here introduced merely as a link in the chain of Scripture evidence of the fact that there is such a thing as the assembly of God on the earth. This assembly is not a name, a form, a pretence, an assumption. It is a divine reality—an institution of God, possessing His seal and sanction. It is a something to be appealed to in all cases of personal trespass and dispute which cannot be settled by the parties involved. This assembly may consist of only "two or three"

in any particular place—the smallest plurality, if you please; but there it is, owned of God, and its decisions ratified in Heaven.

Now, we are not to be scared away from the truth on this subject, by the fact that the church of Rome has attempted to base her monstrous pretensions on the two passages which we have just quoted. That church is not God's assembly, built on the Rock Christ, and gathered in the name of Jesus; but a human apostasy, founded on a failing mortal, and governed by the traditions and doctrines of men. We must not, therefore, suffer ourselves to be deprived of God's reality by reason of Satan's counterfeit. God has His assembly on the earth, and we are responsible to confess the truth of it, and to be a practical expression of it. This may be difficult, in a day of confusion like the present. It will demand a single eye—a subject will—a mortified mind. But let the reader be assured of this, that it is his privilege to possess as divine certainty as to what is a true expression of the assembly of God, as surely as the truth concerning his own salvation through the blood of the Lamb; nor should he be satisfied without this.

I should not be content to go on for an hour without the assurance that I am, in spirit and principle, associated with those whose ground of gathering is purely their common membership in the assembly of God—that assembly which includes all saints. I say, in spirit and principle, because I may happen to be in a place where there is no such local expression of the assembly; in which case I must be satisfied to hold fellowship, in spirit, with all those who are thus gathered.

This simplifies the matter amazingly. If I cannot have a true expression of God's assembly, I shall have nothing. It will not do to point me to a religious community, with some Christians therein, the gospel preached, and the ordinances administered. I must be convinced that in very truth, they are gathered on that ground which, in my heart and conscience, frees them from the charge of sectarianism. I can own the children of God

---

* It is of the utmost importance to distinguish between what Christ builds, and what man builds. "The gates of hell" shall assuredly prevail against all that is merely of man; and hence it would be a fatal mistake to apply to man's building words which only apply to Christ's. Man may build with "wood, hay, stubble," alas! he does; but all that our Lord Christ builds shall stand forever. The stamp of eternity is upon every work of His hand. All praise to His glorious name!

individually anywhere; but sectarianism I cannot own or sanction.

No doubt this will give offence. It will be called bigotry, narrow-mindedness, intolerance, and the like. But this need not discourage us. All we have to do is to ascertain the truth as to God's assembly, and cleave to it, heartily and energetically, at all cost. If God has an assembly—and Scripture says He has—then let me be with those who maintain its principles, and nowhere else. It must be in this as in all other matters, truth or nothing. If there be a local expression of that assembly, well; be there in person. If not, be content to hold spiritual communion with all who humbly and faithfully own and occupy that holy ground.

It may sound and seem like liberality to be ready to sanction and go with everything and everybody. It may appear very easy and very pleasant to be in a place "where everybody's will is indulged, and nobody's conscience is exercised"—where we may hold what we like, and say what we like, and do what we like, and go where we like. All this may seem very delightful—very plausible—very popular—very attractive; but oh! it will be barrenness and bitterness in the end; and, in the day of the Lord, it will assuredly be burnt up as so much wood, hay, and stubble, that cannot stand the action of His judgment.

But let us proceed with our Scripture proofs. In the Acts of the Apostles, or rather, the Acts of the Holy Ghost, we find the assembly formally set up. A passage or two will suffice: "And they, continuing daily with one accord in the temple, and breaking bread from house to house, did eat their meat with gladness and singleness of heart, praising God, and having favor with all the people. And the Lord added to the assembly, daily, such as should be saved" (Acts 2:46-47). Such was the original, simple apostolic order. When a person was converted, he thereby belonged to the assembly and took his place in it: there was no difficulty in the matter, there were no sects or parties, each claiming to be considered *a* church, a cause, or an interest. There was just the one thing, and that was the assembly of God, where He dwelt, acted, and ruled. It was not a system formed according to the will, the judgment, or even the conscience of man. Man had not, as yet, entered upon the business of church-making. This was God's work. It was just as exclusively God's province and prerogative to baptize the saved into one body by one Spirit, as to save the scattered.*

Why, we may justly inquire, should it be different now? Why should the regenerated seek to belong to something else than that to which they already belong—the assembly of God? Is not that sufficient? Assuredly. Should they seek aught else? Assuredly not. We repeat, with emphasis, *"Either that or nothing."*

True it is, alas! that failure, and ruin, and apostasy have come in. Man's wisdom, and his will; or, if you please, his reason, his judgment, and his misguided conscience have wrought, in matters ecclesiastical, and the result appears before us in the almost numberless and nameless sects and parties of the present moment. Still, we are bold to say, that the ground of assembling as at the beginning, simply as being members of the assembly of God, remains the same, spite of all the failure, the error, and the confusion, which have come in. The difficulty in reaching it practically may be great, but its reality, when reached, is unaltered, and unalterable.

In apostolic times the assembly stood out, in bold relief, from the dark background of

---

* There is no such thing in Scripture as being a member of *a* church. Every true believer is a member of *the* Church of God—the body of Christ, and can therefore no more be, properly, a member of anything else, than my arm can be a member of any other body.

The only true ground on which believers can gather is set forth in that grand statement, "There is one body, and one Spirit." And again, "We being many are one loaf, and one body" (Eph. 4:4; 1 Cor. 10:17). If God declares that there is but "one body," it must be contrary to His mind to own more than that one.

Now, while it is quite true that no given number of believers in any given place can be called "the body of Christ," or "the assembly of God"; yet they should be gathered on the ground of that body and that assembly, and on no other ground. We call the reader's special attention to this principle. It holds good at all times, in all places, and under all circumstances. The fact of the ruin of the professing Church does not touch it. It has been true since the day of Pentecost; is true at this moment; and shall be true until the Church is taken to meet her Head and Lord in the clouds, that *"there is one body."* All believers belong to that body; and they should meet on that ground, and on no other.

Judaism on the one hand, and Paganism on the other. It was impossible to mistake it; there it stood, a grand reality! a company of living men, gathered, indwelt, ruled and regulated by God the Holy Ghost, so that the unlearned or unbelieving coming in, were convinced of all, and constrained to acknowledge that God was there. (See carefully, 1 Cor. 12, 14 throughout.)

Thus, in this Gospel of Matthew, our blessed Lord intimates His purpose of building an assembly. This assembly is historically presented to us in the Acts of the Apostles. Then, when we turn to the Epistles of Paul, we find him addressing the assembly in seven distinct places, namely, Rome, Corinth, Galatia, Ephesus, Philippi, Colosse, and Thessalonica; and finally, in the opening of the book of Revelation, we have addresses to seven distinct assemblies. Now, in all these places, the assembly of God was a plain, palpable, real thing, established and maintained by God Himself. It was not a human organization, but a divine institution—a testimony—a light bearer for God, in each place.

Thus much as to our Scripture proofs of the fact that God has an assembly on the earth, gathered, indwelt, and governed by the Holy Ghost who is the true and only Vicar of Christ upon earth. The Gospel prophetically intimates the assembly; the Acts historically presents the assembly; and the Epistles formally address the assembly. All this is plain. And if it be broken into fragments now, it is for us to be gathered on the ground of the *one* assembly of God, and to be a true expression of it.

And let it be carefully noted that we will listen to nothing on this subject but the voice of Holy Scripture. Let not reason speak, for we own it not. Let not tradition lift her voice, for we wholly disregard her. Let not expediency thrust itself upon us, for we shall give it no place whatever. We believe in the all-sufficiency of Holy Scripture—that it is sufficient to furnish the man of God thoroughly—to equip him perfectly for all good works (2 Tim. 3:16-17). The Word of God is either sufficient or it is not. We believe it to be amply sufficient for every exigency of God's assembly. It could not be otherwise if God be its author. We must either deny the divinity or admit the sufficiency of the Bible. There is not a single hair's breadth of middle ground. It is impossible that God could have written an imperfect, an insufficient book.

This is a very grave principle in connection with our subject. Many of our protestant writers have, in assailing popery, maintained the sufficiency and authority of the Bible; but it does seem very plain to us that they are always at fault when their opponents turn sharp round upon them and demand proof from Scripture for many things sanctioned and adopted by protestant communities.

There are many things adopted and practised in the national establishment and other protestant communities, which have no sanction in the Word; and when the shrewd and intelligent defenders of popery have called attention to these things, and demanded authority for them, the weakness of mere protestantism has been strikingly apparent.

If we admit, for a moment, that, in some things, we must have recourse to tradition and expediency, then who will undertake to fix the boundary line? If it be allowable to depart from Scripture at all, how far are we to go? If the authority of tradition be admitted at all, who is to fix its domain? If we leave the narrow and well-defined pathway of divine revelation, and enter upon the wide and bewildering field of human tradition, has not one man as much right as another to make a choice?

The gates of hell shall assuredly prevail against every human system—against all those corporations and associations which men have set on foot. And in no case has that triumph been, even already, made more awfully manifest than in that of the church of Rome itself, although it has arrogantly laid claim to this very declaration of our Lord as the bulwark of its strength. Nothing can withstand the power of the gates of hell but the assembly of the living God, for that is built upon "the living Stone." Now the local expression of that assembly may be but "two or three gathered in the name of Jesus," a poor, feeble, despised handful.

It is well to be clear and decided as to this.

Christ's promise can never fail. He has, blessed be His name, come down to the lowest possible point by which the assembly can be represented, even "*two.*" How gracious! How tender! How considerate! How like Himself! He attaches all the dignity—all the value—all the efficacy of His own divine and deathless name to an obscure handful gathered round Himself.

It must be very evident to the spiritual mind that the Lord Jesus, in speaking of the "two or three" thought not of those vast systems which have sprung up in ancient, mediaeval, and modern times, throughout the eastern and western world, numbering their adherents and votaries, not by "twos or threes," but by kingdoms, provinces, and, parishes. It is very plain that a baptized kingdom, and "two or three" living souls gathered in the name of Jesus, do not and cannot mean the same thing. Baptized christendom is one thing, and the assembly of God is another. What this latter is, we have yet to unfold; we are here asserting that they are not, and cannot be, the same thing. They are constantly confounded, though no two things can be more distinct.*

If we would know under what figure Christ presents the baptized world, we have only to look at the "leaven" and the "mustard tree" of Matt. 13. The former gives us the internal, and the latter the external character of "the kingdom of heaven"—of that which was originally set up in truth and simplicity—a real thing, though small, but which, through Satan's crafty working, has become inwardly a corrupt mass, though outwardly a far-spreading, showy, popular thing in the earth, gathering all sorts beneath the shadow of its patronage. Such is the lesson—the simple but deeply solemn lesson to be learnt by the spiritual mind from the "leaven" and the "mustard-tree" of Matt. 13. And we may add, one result of learning this lesson would be an ability to distinguish between "the kingdom of heaven" and "the assembly of God."

The former may be compared to a wide morass, the latter to a running stream passing through it, and in constant danger of losing its distinctive character, as well as its proper direction, by intermingling with the surrounding waters. To confound the two things is to deal a deathblow to all godly discipline and consequent purity in the assembly of God.

If the kingdom and the assembly mean one and the same thing, then how should we act in the case of "that wicked person" in 1 Cor. 5? The apostle tells us "to put him away." Where are we to put him? Our Lord Himself tells us distinctly that "the field is *the world*"; and again, in John 17, He says that His people are not of the world. This makes all plain enough.

But men tell us, in the very face of our Lord's statement, that the field is the assembly, and the tares and wheat, ungodly and godly, are to grow together, that they are on no account to be separated. Thus the plain and positive teaching of the Holy Ghost in 1 Cor. 5 is set in open opposition to the equally plain and positive teaching of our Lord in Matt. 13; and all this flows from the effort to confound two distinct things, namely, "the kingdom of heaven" and "the assembly of God."

It would not by any means comport with the object of this paper to enter further upon the interesting subject of "the kingdom." Enough has been said, if the reader has thereby been convinced of the immense importance of duly distinguishing that kingdom from the assembly. What this latter is we shall now proceed to inquire; and may God the Holy Ghost be our teacher!

Part 2

In handling our question as to the assembly of God, it will give clearness and precision to our thoughts to consider the four following points, namely:

First, what is the *material* of which the assembly is composed?

Secondly, what is the *centre* round which the assembly is gathered?

---

* The reader will need to ponder the distinction between the Church viewed as "the body of Christ," and as "the house of God." He may study Eph. 1:22; 1 Cor. 12 for the former. Eph. 2:21; 1 Cor. 3; 1 Tim. 3 for the latter. The distinction is as interesting as it is important.

Thirdly, what is the *power* by which the assembly is gathered?

Fourthly, what is the *authority* on which the assembly is gathered?

1. And, first, then, as to the material of which God's assembly is composed; it is, in one word, those possessing salvation, or eternal life. We do not enter the assembly in order to be saved, but as those who are saved. The word is, *"On* this rock I will build My Church." He does not say, "On My Church I will build the salvation of souls." One of Rome's boasted dogmas is this— "There is no salvation out of the true Church." Yes, but we can go deeper still, and say, "Off the true Rock there is no church." Take away the Rock, and you have nothing but a baseless fabric of error and corruption. What a miserable delusion, to think of being saved by that!

Thank God, it is not so. We do not get to Christ through the Church, but to the Church through Christ. To reverse this order is to displace Christ altogether, and thus have neither Rock, nor Church, nor salvation. We meet Christ as a life-giving Saviour, before we have anything to say to the assembly at all; and hence we could possess eternal life, and enjoy full salvation, though there were no such thing as the assembly of God on the earth.*

We cannot be too simple in grasping this truth, at a time like the present, when ecclesiastical pretention is rising to such a height. The church, falsely so called, is opening her bosom with delusive tenderness, and inviting poor sin-burdened, world-sick, and heavy-laden souls to take refuge therein. She, with crafty liberality, throws open her treasury door, and places her resources at the disposal of needy, craving, yearning souls. And truly those resources have

powerful attractions for those who are not on "the Rock." There is an ordained priesthood, professing to stand in an unbroken line with the apostles. Alas! how different the two ends of the line! There is a continual sacrifice. Alas! a bloodless one, and therefore a worthless one (Heb. 9:22). There is a splendid ritual. Alas! it seeks its origin amid the shadows of a by-gone age—shadows which have been for ever displaced by the Person, the work, and the offices of the eternal Son of God. For ever be His peerless name adored!

The believer has a very conclusive answer to all the pretensions and promises of the Romish system. He can say he has found his *all* in a crucified and risen Saviour. What does he want with the sacrifice of the mass? He is washed in the blood of Christ. What does he want with a poor, sinful, dying priest, who cannot save himself? He has the Son of God as his priest. What does he want with a pompous ritual, with all its imposing adjuncts? He worships in spirit and in truth, within the holiest of all, whither he enters with boldness, through the blood of Jesus.

Nor is it merely with Roman Catholicism we have to do in the establishment of our first point. We fear there are thousands besides Roman Catholics who, in heart, look to the church, if not for salvation, at least to be a stepping-stone thereto. Hence the importance of seeing clearly that the materials of which God's assembly is composed are those possessing salvation, in whom is eternal life; so that whatever be the object of that assembly it most certainly is not to provide salvation for its members, seeing that all its members are saved ere they enter it at all.

God's assembly is a houseful of saved ones from one end to the other. Blessed fact! It is not an institution set on foot for the purpose of providing salvation for sinners, nor yet

---

* The reader will do well to note the fact that, in Matt. 16, we have the very earliest allusion to the Church, and there our Lord speaks of it as a future thing. He says, "On this rock I *will* build My Church." He does not say, "I *have* been, or I *am* building." In short the Church had no existence until our Lord Christ was raised from the dead and glorified at the right hand of God. Then, but not until then, the Holy Ghost was sent down to baptize believers, whether Jews or Gentiles, into one body, and unite them to the risen and glorified Head in Heaven. This body has been on the earth since the descent of the Holy Ghost; is here still, and shall be until Christ comes to fetch it to Himself. It is a perfectly unique thing. It is not to be found in Old Testament Scripture. Paul expressly tells us it was not revealed in other ages; it was hid in God, and never made known until it was committed to him. (See carefully, Rom. 16:25-26; Eph. 3:3-11; Col. 1:24-27.) True it is—most blessedly true—that God had a people in Old Testament times. Not merely the nation of Israel, but a quickened, saved, spiritual people, who lived by faith, went to Heaven and are there "the spirits of just men made perfect." But the Church is never spoken of until Matt. 16, and there only as a future thing. As to the expression used by Stephen, "The church in the wilderness" (Acts 7:38), it is pretty generally known that it simply refers to the congregation of Israel. The *termini* of the Church's earthly history are Pentecost (Acts 2), and the rapture (1 Thess. 4:16-17).

for providing for their religious wants. It is a saved, living body, formed and gathered by the Holy Ghost, to make known to "Principalities and powers in the heavenlies, the manifold wisdom of God," and to declare to the whole universe the all-sufficiency of the name of Jesus.

Now, the great enemy of Christ and the Church is well aware of what a powerful testimony the assembly of God is called and designed to yield on the earth; and therefore he has put forth all his hellish energy to quash that testimony in every possible way. He hates the name of Jesus, and everything tending to glorify that name. Hence his intense opposition to the assembly as a whole, and to each local expression thereof, wherever it may happen to exist. He has no objection to a mere religious establishment set on foot for the purpose of providing for man's religious wants, whether maintained by government or by voluntary effort. You may set up what you please. You may join what you please. You may be what you please; anything and everything for Satan but the assembly of God, and the practical expression of it in any given place. That he hates most cordially, and will seek to blacken and blast by every means in his power. But those consolatory accents of the Lord Christ fall with divine power on the ear of faith: "On this rock I will build My assembly, and the gates of hell shall not prevail against it."

2. This conducts us naturally to our second point, namely, What is the centre round which God's assembly is gathered? The centre is Christ—the living Stone, as we read in the Epistle of Peter, "To whom coming as unto a living stone, disallowed indeed of men, but chosen of God, and precious, ye also, as living stones, are built up a spiritual house, a holy priesthood, to offer up spiritual sacrifices, acceptable to God by Jesus Christ" (chap. 2:4-5).

It is around the Person of a living Christ, then, that God's assembly is gathered. It is not round a doctrine, however true; nor round an ordinance, however important; but round a living, divine Person. This is a great cardinal and vital point which must be distinctly seized, tenaciously held, and faithfully and constantly avowed and carried out. "To whom coming." It is not said "To *which* coming." We do not come to a thing, but to a Person. "Let us go forth therefore unto *Him*" (Heb. 13). The Holy Ghost leads us *only* to Jesus. Nothing short of this will avail.

We may speak of joining *a* church, becoming a member of a congregation, attaching ourselves to a party, a cause, or an interest. All these expressions tend to darken and confuse the mind, and hide from our view the divine idea of the assembly of God. It is not our business to join anything. When God converted us, He joined us by His Spirit to Christ and to all the members of Christ, and that should be enough for us. Christ is the only centre of God's assembly.

And, we may ask, is not He sufficient? Is it not quite enough for us to be "joined to the Lord"? Why add aught thereto? "Where two or three are gathered together *in My name*, there am I in the midst of them" (Matt. 18:20). What more can we need? If Jesus is in our midst, why should we think of setting up a human president? Why not unanimously and heartily allow Him to take the president's seat, and bow to Him in all things? Why set up human authority, in any shape or form, in the house of God?

But this is done, and it is well to speak plainly about it. Man is set up in that which professes to be an assembly of God. We see human authority exercised in that sphere in which divine authority alone should be acknowledged. It matters not, so far as the foundation principle is concerned, whether it be pope, parson, priest, or president. It is man set up in Christ's place. It may be the pope appointing a cardinal, a legate, or a bishop to his sphere of work; or it may be a president appointing a man to exhort or to pray for ten minutes. The principle is one and the same. It is human authority acting in that sphere where only God's authority should be owned. If Christ be in our midst, we can count on Him for everything.

Now, in saying this, we anticipate a very probable objection. It may be said by the advocates of human authority, "How could an assembly ever get on without some human presidency? Would it not lead to all sorts of confusion? Would it not open the door for everyone to intrude himself upon the assembly, quite irrespective of gift or qualification?

Our answer is a very simple one. Jesus is all-sufficient. We can trust Him to keep order in His house. We feel ourselves far safer in His gracious and powerful hand than in the hands of the most attractive human president. We have all spiritual gifts treasured up in Jesus. He is the fountain-head of all ministerial authority. "He hath the seven stars." Let us only confide in Him, and the order of our assembly will be as perfectly provided for as the salvation of our souls. This is just the reason of our connecting, in the title of this pamphlet, "The all-sufficiency of the name of Jesus" with the "Assembly of God." We believe that the name of Jesus is, in very truth, all-sufficient, not only for personal salvation, but for all the exigencies of the assembly—for worship, communion, ministry, discipline, government, everything. Having Him, we have all and abound.

This is the real marrow and substance of our subject. Our one aim and object is to exalt the name of Jesus; and we believe He has been dishonored in that which calls itself His house. He has been dethroned, and man's authority has been set up. In vain does He bestow a ministerial gift; the possessor of that gift is not free to exercise it without the seal, the sanction, and the authority of man. And not only is this so, but if man thinks proper to give his seal, his sanction and authority, to one possessing not a particle of spiritual gift—yea, it may be, not a particle of spiritual life—he is nevertheless a recognized minister. In short, man's authority without Christ's gift makes a man a minister; whereas Christ's gift without man's authority does not. If this be not a dishonor done to the Lord Christ, what is?

Christian reader, pause here, and deeply ponder this principle of human authority. We confess we are anxious you should get to the root of it, and judge it thoroughly, in the light of Holy Scripture, and the presence of God. It is, be assured of it, the grand point of distinction between the principles of the assembly of God and every human system of

religion under the sun. If you look at all those systems, from Romanism down to the most refined form of religious association, you will find man's authority recognized and demanded. With that you may minister; without it you must not. On the contrary, in the assembly of God, Christ's gift *alone* makes man a minister, apart from all human authority. "Not of men, neither by man, but by Jesus Christ, and God the Father, who raised Him from the dead" (Gal. 1:1). This is the grand principle of ministry in the assembly of God.

Now, in classing Romanism with all the other religious systems of the day, let it, once for all, be distinctly understood that it is *only* in reference to the principle of ministerial authority. God forbid that we should think of comparing a system which shuts out the Word of God, and teaches idolatry, the worship of saints and angels, and a whole mass of gross, abominable error and superstition, with those systems where the Word of God is held up, and more or less of scriptural truth promulgated. Nothing can be further from our thoughts. We believe popery to be Satan's master-piece, in the way of a religious system, although many of the people of God have been, and may yet be, involved therein.

Further, let us at this stage plainly aver that we believe the saints of God are to be found in every Protestant community, both as ministers and members; and that the Lord uses them in many ways—blesses their work, service, and personal testimony.

And, finally, we feel it right to declare that we would not move a finger to touch any one of those systems. It is not with the systems we have to do; the Lord will deal with them. Our business is with the saints in those systems, to seek by every spiritual and scriptural agency to get them to own and act upon the divine principles of the assembly of God.

Having said thus much, in order to prevent misunderstanding, we return with increased power to our point, namely, that the thread of human authority runs through every religious system in christendom, and that, in good truth, there is not a hair's breadth of consistent standing ground between the church of Rome and a true expression of the assembly of God. We believe that an honest seeker after truth, setting out from amid the dark shadows of popery, cannot possibly halt until he finds himself in the clear and blessed light of that which is a true expression of God's assembly. He may take years to travel over the intervening space. His steps may be slow and measured; but if only he follows the light, in simplicity and godly sincerity, he will find no rest between those two extremes. The ground of the assembly of God is the true position for all the children of God. Alas! they are not all there; but this is only their loss and their Lord's dishonor. They should be there because not only is God there, but He is allowed to act and *rule* there.

This latter is of all-importance, inasmuch as it may be truly said, Is not God everywhere? And does He not act in various places? True, He is everywhere, and He works in the midst of palpable error and evil. But He is not allowed to *rule* in the systems of men, seeing that man's authority is really supreme, as we have already shown. And in addition to this, if the fact of God's converting and blessing souls in a system be a reason why we should be there, then we ought to be in the church of Rome, for how many have been converted and blessed in that awful system? Even in the recent revival we have heard of persons being stricken in Roman Catholic chapels. What proves too much proves nothing at all, and hence no argument can be based on the fact of God's working in a place. He is sovereign, and may work where He pleases. We are to be subject to His authority, and work where we are commanded. My Master may go where He pleases, but I must go where I am told.

But some may ask, "Is there no danger of incompetent men intruding their ministry upon an assembly of God? And in the event of this, where is the difference between that assembly and the systems of men?" We reply, assuredly there is very great danger. But then such a thing would be *despite*, not in virtue of, the principle. This makes all the difference. Yes, indeed, we have seen mistakes and failures which are most humiliating.

Let no one imagine that, while we contend for the truth concerning the assembly of God, we are at all ignorant or forgetful of the dangers and trials to which any carrying out its principles are exposed. Far from it. No one could be for twenty-eight years on that ground without being painfully conscious of the difficulty of maintaining it. But then the very trials, dangers, and difficulties only prove to be so many proofs—painful if you please, but proofs of the truth of the position; and were there no remedy but an appeal to human authority—a setting up of man in Christ's place—to return to worldly systems, we should without hesitation pronounce the remedy to be far worse than the disease. For were we to adopt the remedy, we should have the very worst symptoms of the disease, not to be mourned over as disease, but gloried in as the fruits of so-called order.

But blessed be God, there is a remedy. What is it? "*There am I* in the midst." This is enough. It is not, "There is a pope, a priest, a parson, or a president in their midst, at their head, in the chair, or in the pulpit." No thought of such a thing, from cover to cover of the New Testament. Even in the assembly of God at Corinth, where there was most grievous confusion and disorder, the inspired apostle never hints at such a thing as a human president, under any name whatsoever. "*God is the author* of peace in all the assemblies of the saints" (1 Cor. 14:33). God was there to keep order. They were to look to Him, not to a man, under any name. To set up man to keep order in God's assembly is sheer unbelief, and an open insult to the Divine Presence.

Now, we have been often asked to adduce Scripture in proof of the idea of the divine presidency in an assembly. We at once reply, "There am I"; and "God is the Author." On these two pillars, even had we no more, we can triumphantly build the glorious truth of divine presidency—a truth which *must* deliver all, who receive and hold it from God, from every system of man, call it by what name you please. It is, in our judgment, impossible to recognize Christ as the centre and sovereign ruler in the assembly, and continue to sanction the setting up of man.

When once we have tasted the sweetness of being under Christ, we can never again submit to the servile bondage of being under man. This is not insubordination or impatience of control. It is only the utter refusal to bow to a false authority—to sanction a sinful usurpation. The moment we see man usurping authority in that which calls itself the church, we simply ask, "Who are you?" and retire to a sphere where God alone is acknowledged.

"But then, there are errors, evils, and abuses even in this very sphere." Doubtless; but if there are, we have the Word of God to correct them. And hence, if an assembly should be troubled by the intrusion of ignorant and foolish men—men who have never yet measured themselves in the presence of God—men who boldly overleap the wide domain over which common sense, good taste, and moral propriety preside, and then vainly talk of being led by the Holy Spirit—restless men, who *will* be at something, and who keep the assembly in a continual state of nervous apprehension, not knowing what is to come next—should any assembly be thus grievously afflicted, what should they do? Abandon the ground in impatience, chagrin, and disappointment? give all up as a myth, a fable, an idle chimera? go back to that from which they once came out? Alas! this is what some have done, thus proving that they never understood what they had been doing; or if they had understood it, that they had not faith to pursue it. May the Lord have mercy upon such, and open their eyes that they may see from whence they have fallen, and get a true view of the assembly of God, in contrast with the most attractive of the systems of men.

But what is an assembly to do when abuses creep in? Correct them by the Word of God. This is God's authoritative voice.

We are fully aware of the difficulties and trials connected with any expression of the assembly of God. We believe its difficulties and trials are perfectly characteristic. There is nothing under the canopy of Heaven that the devil hates as he hates that. He will leave no stone unturned to oppose it. We have seen this exemplified again and again. An evan-

gelist may go to a place and preach the all-sufficiency of the name of Jesus for the salvation of the soul, and he will have thousands hanging on his lips. Let the same man return, and, while he preaches the same gospel, take another step and proclaim the all-sufficiency of that same Jesus for all the exigencies of an assembly of believers, and he will find himself opposed on all hands. Why is this? Because the devil hates the very feeblest expression of the assembly of God.

You may see a town left for ages and generations to its dark and dull routine of religious formalism—a dead people gathering once a week to hear a dead man go through a dead service, and all the rest of the week living in sin and folly. There is not a breath of life, not a leaf stirring. The devil likes it well. But let some one come and unfurl the standard of the name of Jesus—Jesus for the soul and Jesus for the assembly—and you will soon see a mighty change. The rage of hell is excited, and the dark and dreadful tide of opposition rises.

This, we most fully believe, is the true secret of many of the bitter attacks that have been recently made on those who maintain the principles of the assembly of God. No doubt we have to mourn over many mistakes, errors, and failures. We have given much occasion to the adversary in various ways. We have been a poor blotted epistle, a faint and feeble witness, a flickering light. For all this we have to be deeply humbled before our God. Nothing could be more unbecoming in us than pretention or assumption, or the putting forth of high-sounding ecclesiastical claims. The dust is our place. Yes, beloved brethren, the place of confession and self-judgment becomes us, in the presence of our God.

Still, we are not to let slip the glorious principles of the assembly of God because we have so shamefully failed in carrying them out: we are not to judge the truth by our exhibition of it, but to judge our exhibition by the truth. It is one thing to occupy divine ground, and another thing to carry ourselves properly thereon; and while it is perfectly right to judge our practice by our principles, yet truth is truth for all that, and we may rest assured that the devil hates the truth which characterizes the assembly. A mere handful of poor people, gathered in the name of Jesus, as members of His body, to break bread in remembrance of Him, is a thorn in the side of the devil. True it is that such an assembly evokes the wrath of men, inasmuch as it throws their office and authority overboard, and they cannot bear that. Yet we believe the root of the whole matter will be found in Satan's hatred of the special testimony which such an assembly bears to the all-sufficiency of the name of Jesus for every possible need of the saints of God.

This is a truly noble testimony, and we earnestly long to see it more faithfully carried out. We may fully count upon intense opposition. It will be with us as it was with the returned captives in the days of Ezra and Nehemiah. We may expect to encounter many a Rehum and many a Sanballat. Nehemiah might have gone and built any other wall in the whole world but the wall of Jerusalem, and Sanballat would never have molested him. But to build the wall of Jerusalem was an unpardonable offence. And why? Just because Jerusalem was God's earthly centre, round which He will yet gather the restored tribes of Israel. This was the secret of the enemy's opposition. And mark the affected contempt. "If a fox go up, he shall even break down their stone wall." And yet Sanballat and his allies were not able to break it down. They might cause it to cease because of the Jews' lack of faith and energy; but they could not break it down when God would have it up.

How like is this to the present moment! Surely there is nothing new under the sun. There is affected contempt, but real alarm. And, oh! if those who are gathered in the name of Jesus were only more true in heart to their blessed Centre, what testimony there would be! What power! What victory! How it would tell on all around. "Where two or three are gathered together in My name, there am I." There is nothing like this under the sun, be it ever so feeble and contemptible. The Lord be praised for raising up such a witness for Himself in these last days. May He greatly increase its effectiveness, by the power of the Holy Ghost!

Part 3

We must now very briefly glance at our third point, namely, what is the power by which the assembly is gathered. Here again man and his doings are set aside. It is not man's will choosing, nor man's reason discovering; nor man's judgment dictating; nor man's conscience demanding; it is the Holy Ghost gathering souls to Jesus. As Jesus is the only centre, so the Holy Ghost is the only gathering power. The one is as independent of man as the other. It is "where two or three are *gathered*." It does not say "where two or three are *met*." Persons may meet together round any centre, on any ground, by any influence, and merely form a society, an association, a community. But the Holy Ghost gathers saved souls only to Christ.

An assembly may not embrace all the saints of God in a locality. In such a case they cannot be called the assembly of God in that place. But if they are assembled as members of the body of Christ, they occupy the ground of the assembly of God.

This is a very simple truth. A soul led by the Holy Ghost will gather only to the name of the Lord; and if we gather to aught else, be it a point of truth, or some ordinance or another, we are not in that matter led by the Holy Ghost. It is not a question of life or salvation. Thousands are saved by Christ that do not own Him as their centre. They are gathered to some form of church government, some favorite doctrine, some special ordinance, some gifted man. The Holy Ghost will never gather to any one of these. He gathers only to a risen Christ. This is true of the whole Church of God upon earth; and each local assembly, wherever convened, is the expression of the whole.

Now, the *power* in an assembly will very much depend upon the measure in which each member thereof is gathered in integrity of heart to the name of Jesus. If I am gathered to a party holding peculiar opinions—if I am attracted by the people, or by the teaching—if, in a word, it be not the power of the Holy Ghost, leading me to the true Centre of God's assembly, I shall only prove a hindrance, a weight, a cause of weakness. I shall be to an assembly what a waster is to a candle; and instead of adding to the general light and usefulness, I shall do the very reverse.

All this is deeply practical. It should lead to much exercise of heart and self-judgment as to what has drawn me to an assembly, and as to my ways therein. We are fully persuaded that the tone and testimony of an assembly have been greatly weakened by the presence of persons not understanding their position. Some present themselves there because they get teaching and blessing there which they cannot get anywhere else. Some come because they like the simplicity of the worship. Others come looking for love. None of these things are up to the mark. We should be in an assembly simply because the name of Jesus is the only standard set up there, and the Holy Spirit has "gathered" us thereto.

No doubt ministry is most precious, and we shall have it, in more or less power, where all is ordered aright. So also as to simplicity of worship: we are sure to be simple, and real, and true, when the Divine Presence is realized, and the sovereignty of the Holy Ghost fully owned and submitted to. And as to love, if we go *looking for it* we shall surely be thoroughly disappointed: but if we are enabled to *cultivate* and *manifest it*, we shall be sure to get a great deal more than we expect or deserve.

it will generally be found that those persons who are perpetually complaining of want of love in others are utterly failing in love themselves; and, on the other hand, those who are really walking in love will tell you that they receive a thousand times more than they deserve. Let us remember that the best way to get water out of a dry pump is to pour a little water in. You may work at the handle until you are tired, and then go away in fretfulness and impatience, complaining of that horrible pump; whereas, if you would just pour in a little water, you would get in return a gushing stream to satisfy your utmost desire.

We have but little conception of what an assembly would be were each one distinctly led by the Holy Ghost, and gathered *only* to Jesus. We should not then have to complain of dull, heavy, unprofitable, trying meetings.

We should have no fear of an unhallowed intrusion of mere nature and its restless doings—no *making* of prayer—no talking for talking's sake—no hymn-book seized to a fill a gap. Each one would know his place in the Lord's immediate presence—each gifted vessel would be filled, fitted, and used by the Master's hand—each eye would be directed to Jesus—each heart occupied with Him. If a chapter were read, it would be the very voice of God. If a word were spoken, it would tell with power upon the heart. If prayer were offered, it would lead the soul into the very presence of God. If a hymn were sung, it would lift the spirit up to God, and be like sweeping the strings of the heavenly harp. We should have no ready-made sermons—no teaching or preaching prayers, as though we would explain doctrines to God, or tell Him a whole host of things about ourselves—no praying *at* our neighbors, or asking for all manner of graces for them, in which we ourselves are lamentably deficient—no singing for music's sake, or being disturbed if harmony be interfered with. All these evils should be avoided. We should feel ourselves in the very sanctuary of God, and enjoy a foretaste of that time when we shall worship in the courts above, and go no more out.

We may be asked, "Where will you find all this down here?" Ah! this is the question. It is one thing to present a *beau ideal* on paper, and another thing to realize it in the midst of error, failure, and infirmity. Through mercy, some of us have tasted, at times, a little of this blessedness. We have occasionally enjoyed moments of Heaven upon earth. Oh, for more of it! May the Lord, in His great mercy, raise the tone of the assemblies everywhere! May He greatly enlarge our capacity for more profound communion and spiritual worship! May He enable us so to walk, in private life, from day to day so as to judge ourselves and our ways in His holy presence, that at least we may not prove a lump of lead or a waster to any of God's assemblies.

Then, even though we may not be able to reach in experience the true expression of the assembly, yet let us never be satisfied with anything less. Let us honestly aim at the loftiest standard, and earnestly pray to be lifted up thereto. As to the *ground* of God's assembly, we should hold it with jealous tenacity, and never consent for an hour to occupy any other.

As to the tone and character of an assembly, they may and will vary immensely, and will depend upon the faith and spirituality of those gathered. Where the tone of things is felt to be low—when meetings are felt to be unprofitable—where things are said and done repeatedly which are felt by the spiritual to be wholly out of place, let all who feel it wait on God—wait continually—wait believingly—and He will assuredly hear and answer. In this way the very trials and exercises which are peculiar to an assembly will have the happy effect of casting us more immediately upon Him, and thus the eater will yield meat, and the strong sweetness.

We must count upon trials and difficulties in any expression of the assembly, just because it is *the* right and divine way for God's people on earth. The devil will put forth every effort to drive us from that true and holy ground. He will try the patience, try the temper, hurt the feelings, cause offence in nameless and numberless ways—anything and everything to make us forsake the true ground of the assembly.

It is well to remember this. We can only hold the divine ground by faith. This marks the assembly of God, and distinguishes it from every human system. You cannot get on there save by faith. And, further, if you want to be somebody, if you are seeking a place, if you want to exalt *self*, you need not think of any true expression of the assembly. You will soon find your level there, if it be in any measure what it should be. Fleshly or worldly greatness, in any shape, will be of no account in such an assembly. The Divine Presence withers up everything of that kind, and levels all human pretension.

Finally, you cannot get on in the assembly if you are living in secret sin. The Divine Presence will not suit you. Have we not often experienced in the assembly a feeling of uneasiness, caused by the recollection of many things which had escaped our notice during the week? Wrong thoughts—foolish words—unspiritual ways—all these things crowd in upon the mind, and exercise the conscience, in the assembly! How is this? Because the atmosphere of the assembly is more searching than that which we have been breathing during the week. We have not been in the presence of God in our private walk. We have not been judging ourselves: and hence, when we take our place in a spiritual assembly, our hearts are detected—our ways are exposed in the light; and that exercise which ought to have gone on in private—even the needed exercise of self-judgment, must go on at the table of the Lord. This is poor, miserable work for us, but it proves the power of the presence of God in the assembly.

Things must be in a miserably low state in any assembly when hearts are not thus detected and exposed. It is a fine evidence of the power of the Holy Spirit in an assembly when careless, carnal, worldly, self-exalting, money-loving, unprincipled persons are compelled to judge themselves in God's presence, or, failing this, are driven away by the spirituality of the atmosphere. Such an assembly is no place for these. They can breathe more freely outside.

Now, we cannot but judge that numbers that have departed from the ground of the assembly have done so because their practical ways did not comport with the purity of the place. No doubt it is easy, in all such cases, to find an excuse in the conduct of those who are left behind. But if the *roots* of things were in every case laid bare, we should find that many leave an assembly because of inability or reluctance to bear its searching light. "Thy testimonies are very sure; holiness becometh Thy house, O Lord, forever." Evil *must* be judged, for God cannot sanction it. If an assembly does not, it is not practically God's assembly at all, though composed of Christians, as we say. To pretend to be an assembly of God, and not judge false doctrine and evil ways, would involve the blasphemy of saying that God and wickedness can dwell together.

The assembly of God must keep itself pure, because it is His dwelling-place. Men may sanction evil, and call it liberality and large-heartedness so to do; but the house of

God must keep itself pure. Let this great practical truth sink down into our hearts, and produce its sanctifying influence upon our course and character.

Part 4

A very few words will suffice to set forth, in the last place, "the *authority*" on which the assembly is gathered. It is the Word of God alone. The charter of the assembly is the eternal Word of the living and true God. It is not the traditions, the doctrines, nor the commandments of men. A passage of Scripture, to which we have more than once referred in the progress of this paper, contains at once the standard round which the assembly is gathered, the power by which it is gathered, and the authority by which it is gathered—"the name of Jesus"—"the Holy Ghost"—"the Word of God."

Now these are the same all over the world. Whether I go to New Zealand, to Australia, to Canada, to London, to Paris, to Edinburgh, or Dublin, the Centre, the gathering Power, and the authority are one and the same. We can own no other centre but Christ; no gathering energy but the Holy Ghost: no authority but the Word of God; no characteristic but holiness of life and soundness in doctrine.

Such is a true expression of the assembly of God, and we cannot acknowledge aught else. Saints of God we can acknowledge, love, and honor as such, wherever we find them; but human systems we look upon as dishonoring to Christ, and hostile to the true interest of the saints of God. We long to see all Christians on the true ground of the assembly. We believe it to be the place of real blessing and effective testimony. We believe there is a character of testimony yielded by carrying out the principles of the assembly which cannot be yielded otherwise, even were each member a Whitefield in evangelistic power.

We say this not to lower evangelistic work. God forbid. We would that all were Whitefields. But then we cannot shut our eyes to the fact that many affect to despise the assembly, under the plea of going out as evangelists; and when we trace their path, and examine the results of their work, we find that they have no provision for the souls that have been converted by their means. They seem not to know what to do with them. They quarry the stones, but do not build them together. The consequence is that souls are scattered hither and thither, some pursuing a desultory course, others living in isolation, all at fault as to true Church ground.

Now, we believe that all these should be gathered on the ground of the assembly of God, to have "fellowship in the breaking of bread and in prayer." They should "come together on the first day of the week, to break bread," looking to the Lord Christ to edify them by the mouth of whom He will. This is the simple path—the normal, the divine idea, needing, it may be, more faith to realize it, because of the clashing and conflicting elements of the present day, but none the less simple and true on that account.

We are aware, of course, that all this will be pronounced proselytizing, and party spirit, by those who seem to regard it as the very *beau ideal* of Christian liberality and large-heartedness to be able to say, "I belong to nothing." Strange, anomalous position! It just resolves itself in this: it is *somebody* professing *nothingism* in order to get rid of all responsibility, and go with all and everything. This is a very easy path for nature, and amiable nature, but we shall see what will come of it in the day of the Lord. Even now we regard it as positive unfaithfulness to Christ, from which may the good Lord deliver His people.

But let none imagine that we want to place the evangelist and the assembly in opposition. Nothing is further from our thoughts. The evangelist should go forth from the bosom of the assembly, in full fellowship therewith; he should work not only to gather souls to Christ, but also bring them to an assembly, where divinely-gifted pastors might watch over them, and divinely-gifted teachers instruct them. We do not want to clip the evangelist's wings, but only to guide his movements. We are unwilling to see real spiritual energy expended in desultory service.

No doubt it is a grand result to bring souls to Christ. Every soul linked to Jesus is a work done forever. But ought not the lambs and sheep to be gathered and cared for? Would any one be satisfied to purchase sheep, and then leave them to wander whithersoever they list? Surely not. But whither should Christ's sheep be gathered? Is it into the folds of man's erection, or into an assembly gathered on divine ground? Into the latter unquestionably; for that, we may rest assured, however feeble, however despised, however blackened and maligned, is the place for all the lambs and sheep of the flock of Christ.

Here, however, there will be responsibility, care, anxiety, labor, a constant demand for watchfulness and prayer; all of which flesh and blood would like to avoid, if possible. There is much that is agreeable and attractive in the idea of going through the world as an evangelist, having thousands hanging on one's lips, and hundreds of souls as the seals of one's ministry: but what is to be done with these souls? by all means show them their true place with those gathered on the ground of the assembly of God, where, notwithstanding the ruin and apostasy of the professing body, they can enjoy spiritual communion, worship, and ministry.

This will involve much trial and painful exercise. It was so in apostolic times. Those who really cared for the flock of Christ had to shed many a tear, send up many an agonizing prayer, spend many a sleepless night. But, then, in all these things, they tasted the sweetness of fellowship with the chief Shepherd; and when He appears, their tears, their prayers, their sleepless nights will be remembered and rewarded; while those who are building up human systems will find them all come to an end, to be heard of no more forever; and the false shepherds, who ruthlessly seize the pastoral staff only to use it as an instrument of filthy gain to themselves, shall have their faces covered with everlasting confusion.

But, we may be asked, "Is it not worse than useless to seek to carry out the principles of the assembly of God, seeing that the professing Church is in such complete ruin?"

We reply by asking, "Are we to be disobedient because the church is in ruin? Are we to continue in error because the dispensation has failed?" Surely not. We own the ruin, mourn over it, confess it, take our share in it, and in its sad consequences, seek to walk softly and humbly in the midst of it, confessing ourselves to be most unfaithful and unworthy.

But though we have failed, Christ has not failed. He abideth faithful; He cannot deny Himself. He has promised to be with His people to the end of the age. Matt. 18:20 holds as good to-day as it did 1800 years ago. "Let God be true and every man a liar."

We utterly repudiate the idea of men setting about church-making, or pretending to ordain ministers. We look upon it as a pure assumption, without a single shadow of Scripture authority. It is God's work to gather His Church and raise up ministers. We have no business to form ourselves into a church, or to ordain office-bearers. No doubt the Lord is very gracious, tender, and pitiful. He bears with our weakness, and overrules our mistakes, and where the heart is true to Him, even though in ignorance, He will assuredly lead on into higher light.

But we must not use God's grace as a plea for unscriptural acting, any more than we should use the church's ruin as a plea for sanctioning error. We have to confess the ruin, count on the grace, and act in simple obedience to the Word of the Lord. Such is the path of blessing at all times. The remnant, in the days of Ezra, did not pretend to the power and splendor of Solomon's days, but they obeyed the Word of Solomon's Lord, and they were abundantly blessed in their deed. They did not say, "Things are in ruin, and therefore we had better remain in Babylon, and do nothing." No; they simply confessed their own and their people's sin, and counted on God. This is precisely what we are to do. We are to own the ruin, and count on God.

Finally, if we be asked, "Where is the true expression of this assembly of God now?" We reply, "Where Christ is truly the Centre of gathering; the one body the ground; the Holy Spirit the Leader; the Holy Scriptures the sole authority; and holiness the practice."

Are you assembled on this divine ground? If so, cling to it with your whole soul. Are you in this path? If so, press on with all the energies of your moral being. Never be content with anything short of His dwelling in you, and your conscious nearness to Him. Let not Satan rob you of your proper portion by leading you to rest in a mere name. Let him not tempt you to mistake your ostensible *position* for your real *condition*. Cultivate secret communion—secret prayer—constant self-judgment. Be especially on your guard against every form of spiritual pride. Cultivate lowliness, meekness, and brokenness of spirit, tenderness of conscience, in your own private walk. Seek to combine the sweetest grace towards others with the boldness of a lion where truth is concerned. Then will you be a blessing in the assembly of God, and an effective witness of the all-sufficiency of the name of Jesus.

JERICHO and ACHOR

PRIVILEGE AND RESPONSIBILITY

Joshua 6—7

Part 1

THE CHRISTIAN READER will do well to turn, first of all, to the two chapters named above, and give them a careful reading. They furnish a very striking and impressive record of the double effect of God's presence with His people. In chapter 6 we are taught that the Divine Presence insured victory over the power of the enemy. In chapter 7 we learn that the Divine Presence demanded judgment upon evil in the bosom of the congregation. The ruins of Jericho demonstrate the one; the great heap of stones in the valley of Achor attests the other.

Now, these two things must never be separated. We see them vividly illustrated in every page of the history of God's people, both in the Old and in the New Testament. The self-same Presence that secures victory demands holiness. Let us never forget this. Yea, let us keep it ever in the remembrance of our hearts. It has an individual as well as a collective application. If we are to walk with God, or, rather, if He is to walk with us, we must judge and put away everything inconsistent with His holy presence. He cannot sanction unjudged evil in His people. He can pardon, heal, restore, and bless; but He is intolerant of evil. *"Our God* is a consuming fire." "The time is come that judgment must *begin* at the house of God."

Should the thought of this discourage or depress any true-hearted child of God, or servant of Christ? Certainly not. It should neither discourage nor depress, but it should make us very watchful over our hearts, very careful as to our ways, our habits of thought and conversation. We have nothing to fear while God is with us, but He cannot possibly sanction evil in His people; and every true lover of holiness will heartily bless Him for this. Could we possibly desire it to be otherwise? Would we wish the standard of holiness to be lowered at all? God forbid.

All those who love His name can give thanks at the remembrance of His holiness, and rejoice in the truth that holiness becometh His house forever? "Be ye holy, for I am holy." It is not by any means on the pharisaic principle, wrapped up in the words, "Stand by thyself; I am holier than thou." Thank God, it is not this. It is not a question of what *we* are, but of what *He* is. Our character and conduct are to be formed by the truth of what God is. Marvelous grace! Precious privilege!

God must have His people like Himself. If they forget this, He will surely remind them of it. If He, in infinite grace, links His name and His glory with us, it behooves us to look well to our habits and ways, lest we bring any reproach on that name. Is this legal bondage? Nay, it is the holiest liberty. We may rest perfectly assured of this, that we are never further removed from legality than when treading that path of true holiness which becomes all those who bear the name of Christ. "Having therefore these promises, dearly beloved, let us cleanse ourselves from all filthiness of the flesh and spirit, perfecting holiness in the fear of God."

This great truth holds good at all times. We see it in the ruins of Jericho. We read it in the valley of Achor. What was it that caused the frowning walls and towering bulwarks of Jericho to fall down at the sound of rams' horns and the shout of the people? The presence of Jehovah. And it mattered not if it was but the city of Jericho or the whole land of Canaan, before that invincible Presence.

But what means the humiliating defeat before the insignificant city of Ai? How comes it to pass that the hosts of Israel, so recently triumphant at Jericho, have to flee ignominiously before a mere handful of men at Ai? Ah, the answer tells a sorrowful tale! Here it is; let us harken to it, and ponder it in the deepest depths of our heart. Let us seek to profit by it. Let us be solemnly warned by it. It has been written for our admonition. The Holy Ghost has taken the pains to record it for our learning. Woe be to the one who turns a deaf ear to the warning voice!

"But the children of Israel committed a trespass in the accursed thing: for Achan, the son of Carmi, the son of Zabdi, the son of Zerah, of the tribe of Judah, took of the accursed thing: and the anger of the Lord was kindled against"—whom? Achan merely? or his household, or his family, or his tribe? Nay, but "against the children of Israel"! The whole assembly was involved in the evil. How was this? The Divine Presence imparted a unity to the whole assembly; it bound them all together in such a manner as to involve all in the sin of the one.

It was one assembly, and hence it was impossible for any one to take independent ground. The sin of each was the sin of all, because God was in their midst, and He could not countenance unjudged evil. The whole congregation was involved, and had to clear

itself of the evil ere Jehovah could lead it on to victory. Had He allowed them to triumph at Ai, it would have argued that He was indifferent to the sin of His people, and that He could give the sanction of His presence to "an accursed thing," which were simply blasphemy against His holy name.

"And Joshua sent men from Jericho to Ai, which is beside Beth-aven, on the east side of Bethel, and spake unto them, saying, Go up and view the country. And the men went up and viewed Ai. And they returned to Joshua, and said unto him, Let not all the people go up; but let about two or three thousand men go up and smite Ai"—more easily said than done—"and make not all the people to labor thither; for they are but few"—yet quite too many for Israel with an Achan in the camp. "So there went up thither of the people about three thousand men; and they fled before the men of Ai. And the men of Ai smote of them about thirty and six men: for they chased them from before the gate even unto Shebarim, and smote them in the going down: wherefore the hearts of the people melted, and became as water.

"And Joshua rent his clothes, and fell to the earth upon his face before the ark of the Lord until the eventide, he and the elders of Israel, and put dust upon their heads."

Here was a strange and unlooked-for experience. "And Joshua said, Alas, O Lord God, wherefore hast Thou at all brought this people over Jordan, to deliver us into the hand of the Amorites, to destroy us? would to God we had been content, and dwelt on the other side Jordan! O Lord, what shall I say, when Israel turneth their backs before their enemies? For the Canaanites and all the inhabitants of the land shall hear of it, and shall environ us round, and cut off our name from the earth: and what wilt Thou do unto Thy great name?"

Joshua, that beloved and honored servant of God, did not see, did not understand, that it was the very glory of that "great name" which necessitated the defeat at Ai, just as it had achieved the victory at Jericho. But there were other elements in that glory besides power. There was holiness, and that holiness rendered it impossible for Him to lend the sanction of His presence where there was unjudged evil. Joshua should have concluded that there was something wrong in the condition of the people. He ought to have known that the hindrance was with Israel, and not with Jehovah. The same grace that had given them victory at Jericho would have given it at Ai, if things were right.

But, alas, they were not right; and hence defeat, and not victory, was the order of the day. How could there be victory with an accursed thing in the camp? Impossible! Israel must judge the evil, or Jehovah must judge Israel. To have given them a victory at Ai would have been a reproach and a dishonor to the One whose name was called upon them. The Divine Presence absolutely demanded judgment upon the evil; and until that was executed, further progress in the conquest of Canaan was out of the question. "Be ye clean that bear the vessels of the Lord." "Holiness becometh Thy house, O Lord, for ever."

"And the Lord said unto Joshua, Get thee up; wherefore liest thou thus upon thy face? *Israel hath sinned*"—not merely Achan—"and they have also transgressed My covenant which I commanded them: for they have even taken of the accursed thing, and have also stolen, and dissembled also, and they have put it even among their own stuff. *Therefore the children of Israel could not stand before their enemies*, but turned their backs before their enemies, because they were accursed: neither will I be with you any more, except ye destroy the accursed from among you."

This is peculiarly solemn. The whole congregation is held responsible for the evil. "A little leaven leaveneth the whole lump." Unbelief may inquire how all are involved in the sin of one; but the Word of God definitely settles the question—"*Israel* hath sinned"— "*they* have taken"—"*they* have stolen"— "*they* have dissembled." The assembly was one; one in privilege, one in responsibility. As such, the sin of one was the sin of all, and all were called upon to clear themselves thoroughly by putting away the accursed thing from among them. There was not a single member of the large congregation who was not affected by Achan's sin.

This may seem strange to mere nature, but such is the solemn and weighty truth of God. It was true in the assembly of Israel of old, and assuredly it is not less true in the Church of God now. No one could take independent ground in the assembly of Israel; how much less can he take it in the Church of God? There were over six hundred thousand people who, to speak after the manner of men, were wholly ignorant of what Achan had done; and yet God's word to Joshua was, "Israel hath sinned." All were involved; all were affected; and all had to clear themselves ere Jehovah could again lead them on to victory.

The presence of God in the midst of the assembly formed the unity of all; and the presence of the Holy Ghost in the Church of God, the body of Christ now on the earth, binds all up in one divine, indissoluble unity. Hence, to talk of independency is to deny the very foundation-truth of the Church of God, and to prove beyond all question that we understand neither its nature nor its unity as set forth on the page of inspiration.

And if evil creeps into an assembly, how is it to be met? Here it is: "Up, sanctify the people, and say, Sanctify yourselves against to-morrow: for thus saith the Lord God of Israel, There is an accursed thing in the midst of thee, O Israel: thou canst not stand before thine enemies, until ye take away the accursed thing from among you." Were they one in privilege? Were they one in the enjoyment of the glory and strength which the Divine Presence secured? Were they one in the splendid triumph at Jericho? Who would deny all this? Who would wish to deny it? Why, then, seek to question their oneness in responsibility—their oneness in respect to the evil in their midst, and all its humbling consequences?

Surely, if there was unity in anything, there was unity in everything. If Jehovah was the God of Israel, He was the God of all, the God of each; and this grand and glorious fact was the solid basis both of their high privileges and their holy responsibilities. How could evil exist in such an assembly, and a single member be unaffected by it? How could there be an accursed thing in their very midst, and a single member not be defiled? Impossible. We may reason and argue about it until the tongue cleaves to the roof of the mouth, but all the reasoning and argument in the world cannot touch the truth of God, and that truth declares that "a little leaven leaveneth the whole lump."

But how is the evil to be discovered? The presence of God reveals it. The self-same power that had leveled the walls of Jericho, detected, revealed, and judged the sin of Achan. It was the double effect of the same blessed Presence, and Israel was called to share in the one as well as in the other. To attempt to separate the two is folly, ignorance, or wickedness. It cannot be done, and ought not to be attempted.

Part 2

We must ever remember, that, in the history of God's ways with His people, privilege and responsibility are intimately bound up together. To talk of privilege, or think of enjoying it, while neglecting the responsibility, is a gross delusion. No true lover of holiness could think for a moment of separating them; nay, he must ever delight in strengthening and perpetuating the precious link.

Thus, for example, in Israel's case, who could estimate aright the high privilege of having Jehovah dwelling in their midst? By day and by night, there He was, to guide and guard, shield and shelter them; to meet their every need, to give them bread from heaven, and bring them forth water out of the rock. His presence was a safeguard against every foe; no weapon formed against them could prosper; not a dog might move his tongue against them; they were at once invulnerable and invincible; with God in their midst they had nothing whatever to fear. He charged Himself with all their wants, whether great or small. He looked after their garments, that they might not wax old; He looked after their feet, that they might not swell; He covered them with the shield of His favor, so that no arrow might touch them; He stood between them and every foe, and flung back in the enemy's face every accusation.

Thus much as to the high privilege. But mark the corresponding and connected responsibility. See how both are indissolubly bound up together in the following weighty words: "For the Lord thy God walketh in the midst of thy camp, to deliver thee, and to give up thine enemies before thee: *therefore shall thy camp be holy; that He see no unclean thing in thee, and turn away from thee.*"

Precious privilege! Solemn responsibility! Who would dare to dissolve the hallowed connection? Had Jehovah deigned to come down into their midst, and walk with them, and tabernacle among them? Had He, in infinite grace, condescended to be their traveling companion? Was He there for the exigence of every hour? Yes, blessed be His name. If so, then what did His presence demand? We have seen something of what His presence *secured;* but what did it *demand?* Holiness!

Israel's whole conduct was to be regulated by the great fact of the Divine Presence in their midst. Not only their great public national institutions, but their most private habits, were to be brought under the controlling influence of Jehovah's presence with them. He regulated what they were to eat, what they were to wear, how they were to carry themselves in all the scenes, circumstances and relationships of daily life. By night and by day, sleeping and waking, sitting in the house or walking by the way, alone or in company, He looked after them. Nothing was to be allowed in any wise inconsistent with the holiness and purity which became the presence of the Holy One of Israel.

Was all this irksome? Were the privileges irksome? Was it irksome to be fed, clothed, guided, guarded, and cared for in every possible way? Was it irksome to repose beneath the overshadowing wings of the God of Israel? Surely not. Why, then, should it be irksome to keep their persons, their habits, and their dwellings clean? Must not every true heart, every upright mind, every tender conscience, accept as thoroughly the responsibility which the Divine Presence necessarily involves as the privileges which it infallibly secures? Yea, rather must we not rank the very responsibility itself among our richest and rarest privileges? Unquestionably. Every true lover of holiness will esteem it a signal mercy—a very high order of blessing—to walk in company with One whose presence detects and condemns every form of evil. "Thy testimonies are very sure; holiness becometh Thy house, O Lord, for ever."

The foregoing train of thought will enable us in some measure to understand the history of Achan, in Josh. 7—a history solemn and impressive in the highest degree—a history which utters in our hearing, with deepest emphasis, words which our careless hearts are only too ready to forget, "God is greatly to be feared in the assembly of His saints, and to be had in reverence of all them that are about Him." Had Achan remembered this, it would have taught him the holy necessity of nipping in the very bud the covetousness of his heart, and thus have spared the whole assembly the humiliating defeat at Ai, and all the consequent sorrow and discipline. How terrible to think of one man, for the sake of a little personal gain, which at best could last but for a moment, plunging a whole congregation into the deepest trouble! and, what was worse than all, dishonoring and grieving that blessed One who had deigned, in His infinite goodness, to take up His abode in their midst!

How well it would be if each one of us, when tempted to commit any secret sin, would just pause and ask himself the question, "How can I do this thing, and grieve the Holy Spirit of God who dwells in me, and bring leaven into the assembly of God's people?" We ought to remember that our private walk has a direct bearing upon all the members of the body. We are either helping or hindering the blessing of all. We are none of us independent atoms; we are members of a body incorporated by the presence of the Holy Ghost; and if we are walking in a loose, carnal, worldly, self-indulgent spirit, we are grieving the Spirit, and injuring all the members.

"But God hath tempered the body together . . . that there should be no schism in the body; but that the members should have the same care one for another. And whether one member suffer, all the members suffer with it; or one member be honored, all the members rejoice with it" (1 Cor. 12:24-26).

It may seem hard, to some, to grasp this great practical truth—hard to see how our private condition and conduct can affect our fellow-members; but the simple and obvious fact is, we must either admit this, or maintain the unscriptural and foolish notion that each Christian is an independent person, having no connection with the whole body of believers. If he be a member of a body, all the members of which are bound together, and linked with the Head by the personal indwelling of the Holy Ghost, then, verily, it follows that his walk and ways affect all his fellow-members just as really as, if any member of the human body suffers, all the other members feel it. If there is anything wrong with the hand, the foot feels it. How is this? Because the head feels it. The communication, in every instance, is with the head first, and from the head to the members.

Now, though Achan was not a member of a body, but merely of a congregation, yet we see how his private conduct affected the whole assembly. This is all the more striking, inasmuch as the great truth of the one body was not unfolded, and could not be until—redemption being a grand, accomplished fact—the Head took His seat on the throne of God, and sent down the Holy Ghost to form the body, and link it, by His personal presence and indwelling, to the Head in Heaven. If the secret sin of Achan affected every member of the congregation of Israel, how much more (may we not say?) doth the secret sin of any member of the body of Christ affect all the members thereof!

Let us never forget this weighty truth. May we keep it ever in the remembrance of our hearts, that so we may see the urgent need of a careful, tender, holy walk; that we may not dishonor our glorious Head, grieve the blessed indwelling Spirit, or injure the feeblest member of that body of which, by the sovereign grace of God and the precious blood of Christ, we form a part.

But we must call special attention to the way in which the sin of Achan was traced home to him. It is all most solemn. He had little idea whose eye was resting upon him when he was carrying on his secret wickedness. He would, no doubt, think himself all right, and very successful, when he had the money and the garment safely hidden in his tent. Fatal, guilty, wretched treasure! Unhappy man! How dreadful is the love of money! How terrible is the blinding power of sin! It hardens the heart, deadens the conscience, darkens the understanding, ruins the soul, and in the case before us brought defeat and disaster upon the whole people of which he formed a part.

"And the Lord said unto Joshua, Get thee up; wherefore liest thou thus upon thy face?" There is a time for lying on the face, and there is a time for standing on our feet; a time for devout prostration, and a time for decided action. The instructed soul will know the time for each.

"Israel hath sinned, and they have also transgressed My covenant which I commanded them; for they have even taken of the accursed thing, and have also stolen, and dissembled also, and they have put it even among their own stuff. Therefore the children of Israel could not stand before their enemies, but turned their backs before their enemies, because they were accursed: neither will I be with you any more, except ye destroy the accursed from among you. Up, sanctify the people, and say, Sanctify yourselves against to-morrow: for thus saith the Lord God of Israel, There is an accursed thing in the midst of thee, O Israel: *thou canst not stand before thine enemies*, until ye take away the accursed thing from among you."

How peculiarly solemn is all this! how very arresting! how soul-subduing! God's people—those who bear His name, and profess to hold His truth, who stand identified with Him in this world—must be holy. He cannot lend the sanction of His presence to that which is unholy or impure. Those who enjoy the high privilege of being associated with God are solemnly responsible to keep themselves unspotted from the world, else He must take down the rod of discipline and do His strange work in their midst. "Be ye clean that bear the vessels of the Lord."

"Thou canst not stand before thine enemies, until ye take away the accursed thing from among you. In the morning therefore ye shall be brought according to your tribes: and it shall be, that the tribe which the Lord taketh shall come according to the families thereof; and the family which the Lord shall take shall come by households; and the household which the Lord shall take shall come man by man."

Ah, this was coming to close quarters! The sinner might seek to persuade himself that discovery was impossible; he might cherish the fond hope of escaping amid the many thousands of Israel. Miserable delusion! He might be sure his sin would find him out. The self-same Presence that secured individual blessing, secured with equal fidelity the detection of the most secret individual sin. Escape was impossible. If Jehovah was in the midst of His people to lay Jericho in ruins at their feet, He was there also to lay bare, in its deepest roots, the sin of the congregation, and to bring forth the sinner from his hiding-place to bear the penalty of his wickedness.

How searching are God's ways! First, the twelve tribes are summoned, that the transgressor might be manifested. Then, one tribe is fixed upon. Nearer still! the family is fixed upon! and yet nearer! the very household is actually singled out; and, last of all, *"man by man"!* Thus, out of six hundred thousand people, the all-searching eye of Jehovah reads the sinner through and through, and marks him off before the assembled thousands of Israel.

"And it shall be that he that is taken with the accursed thing shall be burnt with fire, he and all that he hath: because he hath transgressed the covenant of the Lord, and because he hath wrought folly in Israel.

"So Joshua rose up early in the morning, and brought Israel by their tribes; and the tribe of Judah was taken: and he brought the family of Judah; and he took the family of the Zarhites: and he brought the family of the Zarhites man by man; and Zabdi was taken: and he brought his household man by man; and Achan, the son of Carmi, the son of Zabdi, the son of Zerah, of the tribe of Judah, was taken."

"Our God is a consuming fire." He cannot tolerate evil in the ways of His people. This accounts for the solemn scene before us. The natural mind may reason about all this—it may marvel why the taking of a little money and a garment from amid the spoils of a doomed city should involve such awful consequences and entail such a severe punishment. But the natural mind is incapable of understanding the ways of God.

And may we not ask the objector, How could God sanction evil in His people? How could He go on with it? What was to be done with it? If He was about to execute judgment upon the seven nations of Canaan, could He possibly be indifferent to sin in His people? Most assuredly not. His word is, "You only have I known of all the families of the earth; therefore will I punish you for your iniquities." The very fact of His taking them into relationship with Himself was the ground of His dealing with them in holy discipline.

It is the height of folly for man to reason about the severity of divine judgment, or the apparent lack of proportion between the sin and the punishment. All such reasoning is false and impious. What was it that brought in all the misery, the sorrow, the desolation, the sickness, pain, and death—all the untold horrors of the last six thousand years? What was the source of it all? Just the one little act—as man would call it—of eating a bit of fruit? But this little act was that terrible thing called sin—yea, rebellion—against God!

And what was needed to atone for this? How was it to be met? What stands over against it as the only adequate expression of the judgment of a holy God?—What? The burning in the valley of Achor? Nay. The everlasting burnings of hell? Nay; something far deeper and more solemn still. What? The cross of the Son of God! The awful mystery of the death of Christ!—that terrible cry, "My God, My God, why hast Thou forsaken Me?" Let men remember this, and cease to reason.

Part 3

It is always well for the Christian to be able to give a calm and decided answer to the objection which infidelity is sure to offer to the actings of divine government. The answer is this: "Shall not the Judge of all the earth do right?" If the creature is to be allowed to judge the Creator, there is an end of all government in the vast universe of God. Hence, when we hear men daring to pronounce judgment upon the ways of God, and undertaking to decide what is or what is not fit for God to do, this grand preliminary question invariably suggests itself, "Who is to be judge?" Is man to judge God? or is God to judge man? If the former, there is no God at all; and if the latter, then man has to bow his head in reverent silence, and own his utter ignorance and folly.

The fact is, if man could fathom the government of God, he would no longer be man, but God. What contemptible folly, therefore, for a poor, shallow, ignorant, short-sighted mortal to attempt to pronounce an opinion upon the profound mysteries of divine government! His opinion is not only utterly worthless, but, in the judgment of every truly pious mind, positively impious and blasphemous—a daring insult offered to the throne, to the nature and to the character of God, for which he will, most assuredly, have to answer before the judgment-seat of Christ, unless he repent and find pardon through the blood of the cross.

The foregoing line of thought has suggested itself in connection with the solemn scene in the valley of Achor. The unbelieving mind may be disposed to start an objection on the ground of the apparent severity of the judgment; to institute a comparison between the offence and the punishment; to call in question the equity of Achan's children being involved in their father's sin.

To all this we simply reply, "Are we competent to judge?" If any one thinks he is, it is tantamount to saying that God is not fit to govern the world, but should give place to man. This is the real root of the whole matter. Infidelity wants to get rid of God altogether, and set up man in His place. If God is to be God, then, most certainly, His ways, the actings of His government, the mysteries of His providence, His purposes, His counsels and His judgments must lie far beyond the range of the greatest human or angelic mind.

Neither angel, man nor devil can comprehend Deity. Let men own this, and hush into eternal silence their puny, ignorant, and contemptible reasonings. Let them take up the language of Job when his eyes were opened: "Then Job answered the Lord, and said, I know that Thou canst do everything, and that no thought can be withholden from Thee. Who is he that hideth counsel without knowledge? therefore have I uttered that I understood not; things too wonderful for me, which I knew not. Hear, I beseech Thee, and I will speak: I will demand of Thee, and declare Thou unto Me. I have heard of Thee by the hearing of the ear; but now mine eye seeth Thee: wherefore I abhor myself, and repent in dust and ashes." When the soul gets into this attitude, there is an end of all infidel questions. Till then there is little use in discussion.

Let us now turn for a few moments to contemplate the solemn scene in the valley of Achor; and let us remember that "whatsoever things were written aforetime, were written for our learning." May we learn to watch with holy jealousy the incipient workings of evil in our hearts. It is on these men ought to sit in judgment, and not on the pure and perfect actings of divine government.

Joshua's address to Achan is solemn, weighty, and powerful: "My son, give, I pray thee, glory to the Lord God of Israel, and make confession unto Him; and tell me now what thou hast done; hide it not from me."

Here is the all-important matter. "Give glory to Jehovah, God of Israel." All hinges upon this. The Lord's glory is the one perfect standard by which all is to be judged—the perfect gauge by which everything is to be measured—the perfect touchstone by which all is to be tried. The one great question for the people of God in all ages and in all dispensations is this: *What is suited to the glory of God?* In comparison with this, all other questions are less than secondary.

It is not a question of what is suitable to us, or what we can tolerate or agree with. This is a very minor consideration indeed. What we have ever to look to, and think of, and provide for, is the glory of God. We have to ask ourselves the question, in reference to everything that comes before us, "Will this comport with the glory of God?" If not, let us, by His grace, fling it aside.

Well would it have been for Achan had he thought of this when his eye rested on the cursed treasure! What misery it would have saved him! What sorrow and trouble it would have saved his brethren! But, alas, people forget all this when lust dims the eye and vanity and folly possess the heart! and onward they go until the heavy judgment of a holy, sin-hating God overtakes them. And then, forsooth, men presume to comment upon such judgment as unworthy of a gracious and beneficent Being. Ignorant presumption! They would fain have a god of their own imagination, one like themselves, who can make light of sin and tolerate all sorts of evil. The God of the Bible, the God of Christianity, the God of the Cross, the God and Father of our Lord Jesus Christ, does not suit such infidel reasoners. Their deep heart-utterance to Him is, "Depart from us, for we desire not the knowledge of Thy ways."

"And Achan said, Indeed I have sinned against the Lord God of Israel, and thus and thus have I done: when I saw among the spoils a goodly Babylonish garment, and two hundred shekels of silver, and a wedge of gold of fifty shekels weight, then I coveted them, and took them; and, behold, they are hid in the earth in the midst of my tent, and the silver under it."

Here the dark, defiling stream is traced up to its source in the heart of this unhappy man. Oh, how little did he think whose eye was resting on him during the entire progress of this melancholy and disastrous affair! He thought of but one thing, namely, the gratification of his covetousness. He *saw*, he *coveted*, he *took*, he *hid;* and there, no doubt, he thought the matter would end. He would have his treasure, and no one would be the wiser.

But, ah, the eye of Jehovah, the God of Israel, was upon him—that holy eye, from which no secret thing is hidden, which penetrates the depths of the human heart, and takes in at a glance all the hidden springs of human action. Yes, God saw it all, and He would make Israel see it, and Achan also. Hence the lamentable defeat at Ai, and all that followed.

How perfectly solemn!—the whole assembly involved in shameful defeat and disaster—Joshua and the elders of Israel, with rent garments and dust upon their heads, prostrate on their faces from morning till evening! And then, the divine challenge and rebuke! the solemn muster of the hosts of Israel, tribe by tribe, family by family, household by household, man by man!

And why all this? Just to trace the evil to its source, bring it out, and have it judged in the sight of every creature. All created intelligence must be made to see and confess that the throne of God can have no fellowship with evil. The same power that had leveled the walls of Jericho, and executed judgment upon its guilty inhabitants, was to be manifested in detecting Achan's sin, and in evoking from the very depths of his convicted heart the confession of his terrible guilt. He, in common with all his brethren, had heard Jehovah's solemn charge, "And ye, in any wise keep yourselves from the accursed thing, lest ye make yourselves accursed, when ye take of the accursed thing, and make"—not merely any one individual's tent, but—"*the camp of Israel* a curse, and trouble it. But all the silver, and gold, and vessels of brass and iron, are consecrated unto the Lord: they shall come into the treasury of the Lord."

All this was plain enough. No one could mistake it. It only needed an attentive ear and an obedient heart. It was as plain as the commandment delivered to Adam and Eve amid the bowers of Eden. But Achan, like Adam, transgressed the plain and positive command. Instead of hiding it in his heart, that he might not sin against God, he trampled it under his feet, that he might gratify his sinful desire. He fixed his covetous gaze upon the accursed thing, in itself nothing but a wretched pile of dust, but, through Satan's power and Achan's erring heart, turned into an occasion of sin, shame, and sorrow.

O how sad, how sorrowful, how terrible a thing it is to allow the poor heart to go after the wretched things of this world! What are they all worth? If we could have all the garments that were ever made in Babylon; all the gold and silver that ever issued from the mines of Peru, California, and Australia; all the pearls and diamonds that ever glittered on the kings, princes and nobles of this world—could they give us one hour's true happiness? Could they send a single ray of heavenly light into the soul? Could they impart to us one moment's pure, spiritual enjoyment? Not they. In themselves they are but perishable dust, and when used of Satan a positive curse, misery, and degradation.

Not all the riches and material comforts which this world could offer are worth one hour's holy communion with our heavenly Father and our precious Saviour. Why should we covet this world's wretched wealth? Our God will supply all our need according to His riches in glory by Christ Jesus. Is not this enough? Why should we put ourselves within the range of Satan's power by setting our hearts upon the riches, honors, or pleasures, of a world which is ruled by the arch-enemy of God and of our souls? How well it would have been for Achan had he rested content with what the God of Israel had given him! How happy he might have been had he been satisfied with the furniture of his tent, the smile of Jehovah, and the answer of a good conscience!

But he was not; and hence the appalling scene in the valley of Achor, the record of which is enough to strike terror into the stoutest heart. "So Joshua sent messengers, and they ran unto the tent; and, behold, it was hid in his tent, and the silver under it. And they took them out of the midst of the tent, and brought them unto Joshua, and unto all the children of Israel, and laid them out before the Lord. And Joshua, and *all Israel* with him, took Achan the son of Zerah, and the silver, and the garment, and the wedge of gold, and his sons, and his daughters, and his oxen, and his asses, and his sheep, and his tent, and all that he had: and they brought them unto the valley of Achor. And Joshua said, Why hast thou troubled us? the Lord shall trouble thee this day. And *all Israel* stoned him with stones, and burned them with fire, after they had stoned them with stones. And they raised over him a great heap of stones unto this day. So the Lord turned from the fierceness of His anger. Wherefore the name of that place was called, The valley of Achor (that is, trouble), unto this day" (Josh. 7:19-26).

How deeply solemn is all this! What a warning note it sounds in our ears! Let us not attempt, under the false influence of one-sided notions of grace, to turn aside the holy edge of such a passage of Scripture. Let us read with earnest attention the inscription on that awful monument in the valley of Achor. What is it? "God is greatly to be feared in the assembly of His saints, and to be had in reverence of all them that are about Him." And again, "If any man defile the temple of God, him will God destroy." And further, "Our God is a consuming fire."

Weighty, solemn, searching words these!—much needed, surely, in these days of flippant, easy-going profession, when the doctrines of grace are so much on our lips, but the fruits of righteousness so little seen in our lives. May we learn from them the urgent need of watchfulness over our hearts, and over our private life, that evil may be judged and nipped in the bud, so that it may not bring forth its sad, shameful and sorrowful fruit in our practical career, to the gross dishonor of the Lord and the grievous sorrow of those with whom we are linked in the bonds of fellowship.

Part 4

There is a very interesting allusion to "the valley of Achor" in Hos. 2 at which we may just glance in passing, though it does not connect itself with the special line of truth which we have had before us in this series of papers.

Jehovah, in speaking of Israel, by His prophet says: "Therefore, behold, I will allure her, and bring her into the wilderness, and speak comfortably unto her. And I will give her her vineyards from thence, and *the valley of Achor for a door of hope; and she shall sing there*, as in the days of her youth, and as in the day when she came up out of the land of Egypt" (ver. 14-15).

What touching grace shines in these words! "The valley of Achor"—the place of "trouble"—the place of deep sorrow and shame—the place of humiliation and judgment—the place where the fire of Jehovah's righteous wrath consumed the sin of His people—*there* shall be "a door of hope" for Israel by and by; there, too, she shall sing as in the days of her youth. How wonderful to hear of songs of praise in the valley of Achor! What glorious triumphs of grace! What a bright and blessed future for Israel!

"It shall be at *that day*, saith the Lord, that thou shalt call me Ishi [my husband], and shalt call me no more Baali [my lord]. For I will take away the names of Baalim out of her mouth, and they shall no more be remembered by their name . . . . *And I will betroth thee unto Me for ever;* yea, I will betroth thee unto Me in righteousness, and in judgment, and in loving-kindness, and in mercies: I will even betroth thee unto Me in faithfulness: and thou shalt know the Lord."

From this digression to "the valley of Achor" in the future, we now return to our special theme; and in so doing we shall ask the reader to turn with us, for a few moments, to the opening chapters of the Acts. Here we find the same grand results of the presence of God in the midst of His people as we have seen in the opening of the book of Joshua; only in a much more glorious manner, as we might expect.

On the day of Pentecost, God the Holy Ghost came down to form the assembly, and take up His abode therein. This great and glorious fact was grounded on the accomplishment of the work of atonement, as attested by the resurrection of our Lord Jesus Christ, and His glorification at the right hand of God.

We cannot attempt to unfold this truth in all its bearings in this brief article; we merely call the reader's attention to the two practical points which have been before us—namely, the privilege and responsibility connected with the Lord's presence in the midst of His people. If He was there to *bless*—as He most surely was—He was also, and quite as surely, there to *judge*. The two things go together, and we must not attempt to separate them.

And first, then, we see the effect and blessings of the Divine Presence in the assembly: "And all that believed were together, and had all things common; and sold their possessions and goods, and parted them to all, as every man had need." The blessed effect of the realized presence of the Holy Ghost was to bind their hearts together in a holy and loving fellowship; to cause them to let go earthly things, and to lead them to merge their personal interests in the common good.

Precious fruits! Would that we saw more of them! No doubt times are changed; but God is not changed, and the effect of His realized presence is not changed. True, we are not in Acts 2. Pentecostal times are passed away; christendom has lapsed in complete failure; the professing Church has hopelessly fallen. All this is sadly true; but Christ our Head abides in all His living power and unchangeable grace.

"The foundation of God standeth sure"—as sure, as safe and as solid to-day as it was on the day of Pentecost. No change here, blessed be God; hence we may say, with all possible confidence, that where His presence is realized, even though it be only by "two or three" gathered to the name of Jesus, there the same lovely fruits will be found. Hearts will be knit together; earthly things will be surrendered; personal interests will be merged. It is not a question of throwing our goods into a common heap, but of the grace which once took that special form, and which at all times would lead us, not merely to surrender our possessions, but ourselves, for the good of others.

It is a very grave mistake indeed for any one to say, or to think, that because we are not in Pentecostal times we cannot count on the presence of God with us in the path of holy obedience to His will. Such a thought should be judged as sheer unbelief. We are certainly shorn of many of the Pentecostal gifts, but we are not bereft of the Giver. The blessed Comforter abides with us; and it is our happy privilege to be in a position in which we can enjoy His presence and ministry.

The thing is *to be* in that position; not merely to *say* we are in it, to boast of being in it, but *really* to be in it. We may well apply here the pointed question of the blessed apostle, "What doth it profit, my brethren, though a man *say*" he is on divine ground, if he be not really there? Assuredly it profits nothing.

But let us not forget that although we are not in Acts 2, but in the Second Epistle to Timothy; although we are not in the refreshing scenes of Pentecost, but in the "perilous times" of "the last days," yet the Lord is with those "who call on Him out of a pure heart," and His presence is all we want. Let us only trust Him, use Him, lean upon Him. Let us see to it that we are in a position in which we can count on His presence—a position of entire separation from all that He judges to be "iniquity"—from the "dishonorable vessels" in "the great house," and from all those who, having a form of godliness, deny the power thereof.

These, we may rest assured, are the absolutely essential conditions on which the Divine Presence can be realized by any company of Christians. We may come together, and form ourselves into an assembly; we may profess to be on divine ground; we may call ourselves the assembly of God; we may appropriate to ourselves all those passages of Scripture which only apply to those who are really gathered by the Holy Ghost in the name of Jesus; but if the essential conditions are not there; if we are not "calling on the Lord out of a pure heart"; if we are mixed up with "iniquity"; if we are associated with "dishonorable vessels"; if we are walking hand in hand with lifeless professors who deny in practice the power of godliness—what then? Can we expect to realize the Lord's presence? As well might Israel have expected it with Achan in the camp. It cannot be. In order to reach divine results, there must be divine conditions. To look for the former without the latter is vanity, folly, and wicked presumption.

We are not now treating, or even touching, the great question of the soul's salvation.

This, precious and important as it is to all whom it may concern, is not at all our subject in this series of papers on "Jericho and Achor." We are dealing with the solemn and weighty question of the privilege and responsibility of those who profess to be the Lord's people, gathered to His name; and we are specially anxious to impress upon the mind of the reader that, notwithstanding the hopeless ruin of the professing Church, its utter failure in its responsibility to Christ as His witness and light-bearer in the world, yet it is the happy privilege of "two or three" to be gathered in His name, apart from all the evil and error around, owning our common sin and failure, feeling our weakness, and looking to Him to be with us and bless us according to the unchangeable love of His heart.

Now, to those thus gathered, there is no limit whatever to the measure of blessing which our ever gracious and faithful Lord can bestow. "He has the seven spirits of God, and the seven stars"—the fulness of spiritual power, ministerial gift and authority for His Church. Such is His style and title in addressing the church at Sardis, which, we believe, prophetically sets before us the history of Protestanism.

It is not said, as in the address to Ephesus, that He "holds the seven stars in His right hand." There is a grave difference as to this; and it is our bounden duty to recognize both the difference and the cause. When the Church began, on the day of Pentecost, and during the days of the apostles, Christ, the Head, not only *possessed* all spiritual gift, power and authority for His Church, but was owned as *the actual administrator* thereof. He held the stars in His right hand. There was no such thing known or thought of as human authority in the assembly of God. Christ was owned as Head and Lord. He had received the gifts, and He dispensed them according to His sovereign will.

Thus it should ever be. But, alas, man has intruded upon the hallowed sphere of Christ's authority. He presumes to meddle in the appointment of ministry in the Church of God. Without so much as a single atom of divine authority, without any ability whatso-

ever to impart the necessary gift for ministry, he nevertheless takes upon himself the solemn responsibility of calling, appointing, or ordaining to the ministry in the Church of God. As well might the writer of these lines undertake to appoint a man as an admiral in Her Majesty's fleet, or a general in her army, as for any man, or body of men, to appoint a man to minister in the Church of God. It is a daring usurpation of divine authority. None can impart ministerial gift, and none can appoint to any branch of the ministry but Christ, the Church's Head and Lord; and all who undertake to do so will have to account to Him for so doing.

It may be that many who thus act, and many more who sanction or are identified with such acting, are not aware of what they are doing; and our God is gracious and merciful in bearing with our feebleness and ignorance. All this is blessedly true; but as to the principle of human authority in the Church of God, it is utterly false, and should be rejected with holy decision by every one who loves, reverences and adores the great Head of the Church and Lord of the assembly, who, blessed be His name, still *has* the seven Spirits of God and the seven stars. He has them now just as positively as in apostolic times; and all who take their true place, the place of self-judgment and humiliation; all who are truly own our common sin and failure, our departure from first love, first principles; all who really, in true humility of mind, look to Christ alone for all they want; all who, in real earnestness of heart and godly sincerity, bow to His Word and confess His name—all such will assuredly prove the reality of His presence; they will find Him amply sufficient for all their need. They can count on Him for the supply of all ministerial gift, and for the maintenance of all godly order in their public reunions.

True, they will feel—must feel—that they are not in the days of Acts 2, but in the days of 2 Timothy. Yet Christ is sufficient for these, as He was for those. The difficulties are great, but His resources are infinite. It were folly to deny that there are difficulties; but it is sinful unbelief to question the all-sufficiency of our ever-gracious and faithful Lord. He has promised to be with His people right on to the end. But He cannot sanction hollow pretension, or proud assumption. He looks for reality, for truth in the inward parts. He will have us in our right place, owning our true condition. There He can meet us according to His infinite fulness, and according to the eternal stability of that grace which reigns through righteousness unto eternal life.

But oh, let us never forget that our God delights in uprightness of heart and integrity of purpose. He will never fail a trusting heart; but He must be trusted really. It will not do to speak of trusting Him while in reality we are leaning on our own appliances and arrangements. Here is precisely where we so sadly fail. We do not leave room for Him to act in our midst. We do not leave the platform clear for Him. Thus we are robbed, and that to an extent of which we have little idea, of the blessed manifestation of His presence and grace in our assemblies. His Spirit is quenched and hindered, and we are left to feel our barrenness and poverty, when we might be rejoicing in the fulness of His love and in the power of His ministry. It is utterly impossible that He can ever fail those who, owning the truth of the condition, earnestly look to Him. He cannot deny Himself; and He can never say to His people that they have reckoned too largely on Him.

It is not that we are to look for any special display of power in our midst, anything that might attract public attention, or make a noise in the world. There are no tongues, no gifts of healing, no miracles, no extraordinary manifestations of angelic action on our behalf. Neither are we to look for anything similar to the case of Ananias and Sapphira—the sudden and awful execution of divine judgment, striking terror into the hearts of all, both inside and outside the assembly.

Such things are not to be looked for now. They would not comport with the present condition of things in the Church of God. No doubt our Lord Christ has all power in Heaven and on earth, and He could display that power now just as He did in Pentecostal times, if it so pleased Him. But He does not so

act, and we can readily understand the reason. It is our place to walk softly, humbly, tenderly. We have sinned, and failed, and departed from the holy authority of the Word of God. We must ever bear this in mind, and be content with a very low and retired place. It would ill become us to seek a name or a position in the earth. We cannot possibly be too little in our own eyes.

But at the same time we can, if in our right place, and in a right spirit, fully count on the presence of Jesus with us; and we may rest assured that where He is—where His most gracious presence is felt—there we may look for the most precious results, both in the way of binding our hearts together in true brotherly love, in causing us to sit loose to all earthly possessions and earthly ties, in leading us forth in grace and kindness toward all men, and also in putting away from among us all who would defile the assembly by unsound doctrine or unholy morals.

P.S.—It is of the utmost importance for the Christian reader to bear in mind that, whatever be the condition of the professing Church, it is his privilege to enjoy as high communion and to tread as high a path of individual devotedness as ever was known in the very brightest days of the Church's history. We must never draw a plea from the condition of things around us for lowering the standard of individual holiness and devotedness. *There is no excuse for continuing a single hour in connection with anything that will not stand the test of Holy Scripture.*

True, we feel the condition of things—cannot but feel it: would we felt it more! But it is one thing to feel it, and go through it with Christ, and another thing to sink under it and go on with the evil, and give up in despair.

May the Lord, in His infinite grace, produce in the hearts of all His people a more profound and influential sense of their privileges and responsibilities, both individually and collectively, that thus there may be a truer and brighter testimony for His name, and a devoted band of worshipers, workers and witnesses, gathered out to wait for His coming!

THE DISCIPLINE OF THE ASSEMBLY

ITS GROUND, NATURE, AND OBJECT

"THY TESTIMONIES are very sure: holiness becometh Thy House, O Lord, for ever" (Ps. 93: 5).

Here we have, plainly set before us, the real ground of discipline in the assembly. The place of God's presence must be holy: "Be ye holy, for I am holy." It is not upon the miserable principle of "stand by thyself, I am holier than thou." No, thank God, it is not this. It is not upon the ground of what we are, but what God is, that discipline is exercised. To allow unjudged evil, either in doctrine or practice, in the assembly, is tantamount to saying that God and evil can go on together—which is simply wickedness.

But some persons maintain that we are not to judge, and Matthew 7: 1 is quoted in proof. We reply that the passage has nothing to say to the assembly: it simply teaches us, as individuals, not to judge motives. Further on in the chapter, we are told to beware of false prophets. How can we beware, if we are not to judge? "By their fruits ye shall know them." So that, even as individuals, we are to judge conduct. We are not to judge *motives* but *fruits*. In 1 Corinthians 5, the assembly is peremptorily called to judge and put away an evil doer.

"In the name of our Lord Jesus Christ, when ye are gathered together, and my spirit, with the power of our Lord Jesus Christ, to deliver such an one unto Satan for the destruction of the flesh, that the spirit may be saved in the day of the Lord Jesus." And then, at the end of the chapter, we read: "Do not ye judge them that are within? But them that are without God judgeth. Therefore put away from among yourselves that wicked person."

This is clear and conclusive. The assembly is solemnly bound to exercise discipline—bound to judge and put away evil-doers. To refuse to do so is to become a leavened lump; and, most assuredly, God and unjudged leaven cannot go on together.

Mark, we speak of *unjudged* leaven. We know, alas, that there is evil in every member of the assembly; but if it is judged and refused, it does not defile the assembly, or hinder the enjoyment of the Divine Presence. It was not the evil in the man's nature that caused him to be put away, but the evil in his life. If he had judged and refused the sin in his nature, the assembly would not have been called to judge and refuse him. All this is as simple as it is solemn. An assembly that refuses to judge evil, in doctrine or morals, is not an assembly of God. There may be children of God in it, but they are in a false and dangerous position; and if the assembly persists in refusing to judge the evil, they should, with firm decision, turn away from it. They are solemnly called upon to do so: "Let every one that nameth the name of the Lord depart from iniquity."

But there are many who do not understand the truth as to the assembly, or its discipline, and they bring forward Matthew 13:30 as a proof that evil-doers are not to be put away from the assembly, or the Lord's table. The tares and the wheat are to grow together until the harvest, they say. Yes; but where? In the assembly? Nay; but in the field, and "the field is the *world*"—not the Church. To argue that, because the tares and wheat are to grow together in the world, therefore evil-doers are to be knowingly allowed in the assembly, is to place the teaching of our Lord

Jesus Christ, in Matthew 13, in direct opposition to the teaching of the Holy Spirit in 1 Corinthians 5. Hence, this argument cannot stand for a moment, but must be flung to the winds. To confound the kingdom of Heaven, in the Gospel of Matthew, with the Church of God, in the Epistles of Paul, is to mar the integrity of the truth of God, and plunge the Lord's people into utter confusion. Indeed, no human language could adequately set forth the deplorable consequences of such a system of teaching. But this is a digression from our subject, to which we must return.

Having proved from the plainest statements of Holy Scripture that the assembly is solemnly bound to judge those that are within, and put away evil-doers, we shall now proceed to consider the nature, character, and spirit of the discipline which the assembly is called to exercise. Nothing can be more solemn or more affecting than the act of putting away a person from the Lord's table. It is the last sad and unavoidable act of the whole assembly, and it should be performed with broken hearts and weeping eyes. Alas, how often it is otherwise! How often does this most solemn and holy duty take the form of a mere official announcement that such a person is out of fellowship. Need we wonder that discipline, so carried out, fails to tell with power upon the erring one, or upon the assembly?

How then should the discipline be carried out? Just as 1 Corinthians 5 directs. When the case is so patent, so clear, that all discussion and deliberation is at an end, the whole assembly should be solemnly convened for the special purpose—for, most assuredly, it is of sufficient gravity and importance to command a special meeting. All should, if possible, attend, and seek grace to make the sin their own, to go down before God in true self-judgment, and eat the sin offering. The assembly is not called to deliberate or discuss. If there is any demand for discussion, the assembly is not called to act. The case should be thoroughly investigated, and all the facts collected by those who care for the interests of Christ and His Church; and when it is thoroughly settled, and the evidence perfectly conclusive, then the whole

assembly is called to perform, in deep sorrow and humiliation, the sad act of putting away from among themselves the evil-doer. It is an act of holy obedience to the Lord's command.

We cannot but feel that, were the assembly's discipline carried out in this spirit, we should see very different results. How different is this from the formal reading out of a notice in the course, or at the close, of an ordinary meeting—a notice often unheard by many. It is an entirely different thing, and it would be attended with very different results, both as to the assembly and the person put away. There would be a much more profound sense, on all hands, of the gravity and solemnity of the assembly's discipline. And oh, what urgent need there is of this in all our assemblies! We are sadly prone to be light and trifling.

We would repeat, and emphasize the statement, that the putting away of a person from the Lord's table, as well as the reception, must be the act of the whole assembly. No one has any right to tell another to remain away from the table. If I know of any brother who is living in sin, I should seek to exercise his conscience in a pastoral way. I should warn him, and seek to lead him to self-judgment. If he persists, I should bring his case before those who really care for the honor of Christ and the purity of His assembly. Then, if there be no hope, and no possible ground for demur, the assembly should be called together to act, and the occasion might be used for setting before the consciences of all the solemnity of the ground occupied by the assembly, and the holiness that becometh the house of the Lord forever.

We cannot too strongly protest against the idea of the whole assembly being called to discuss cases of discipline. We may well say, "Doth not even nature itself teach" the unseemliness of bringing the details of a case of immorality, for example, before a promiscuous assembly? It is contrary to God, and contrary to nature.

In conclusion, one word as to the object of the assembly's discipline. The inspired apostle tells us, in 1 Cor. 5, that it is salvation —"that the spirit may be saved in the day of the Lord Jesus." This is very precious. It is worthy of the God of all grace. The man is delivered to Satan for the destruction of that odious thing which has caused his humiliating fall, *that his spirit may be saved in the day of the Lord Jesus.*

Let us never forget this. We should ever be on the lookout for this precious result when any one has to be put away. We should wait much on the Lord to own the action of the assembly in this way. We should not put away evil-doers in order to get rid of a disgrace or a trouble to us, but to maintain the holiness of the Lord's house, and for the ultimate salvation of those put away.

And here we may remark that the discipline of the assembly can never interfere with the unity of the body. Some persons speak of cutting off the members of the body of Christ, when any are refused or put away by the assembly. This is a grave mistake. The man in 1 Cor. 5 was a member of the body, and nothing could touch that blessed membership. He was put away, not because he was unconverted, but because he defiled the assembly. But the discipline was used for the ultimate blessing of a member of the body. No member of the body can ever be cut off. All are indissolubly joined to the Head in Heaven, and to the members on earth, by the Holy Ghost. "By one Spirit we are all baptized into one body."

This is divinely simple and clear, and moreover it is a conclusive answer to the statement so constantly made, namely, that, provided a person is a Christian, he ought not to be put away or refused by the assembly. No such question is ever raised. To put away a person for not being a Christian is opposed to the spirit and teaching of the Word of God. Even under the Old Testament economy people were not put outside the camp for not being the seed of Abraham, or circumcised members of the congregation, but because they were ceremonially defiled. See Num. 5.

P.S.—There is a character of discipline presented in 2 Thess. 3 which demands our serious attention: "Now we command you, brethren, in the name of our Lord Jesus Christ, that ye *withdraw yourselves* from every brother that walketh disorderly, and not after the tradition which he received of us. . . . If any man obey not our word by this epistle, note that man, and have no company with him, that he may be ashamed. Yet count him not as an enemy, but admonish him as a brother."

This is what we may call personal discipline in private life—a very important thing, much needed, alas, but not generally understood. It is not a case calling for the action of the assembly, but for faithful personal dealing. The disorderly walking referred to is a brother not working, but going about as an idle busybody. Such a one was to be admonished, and avoided. Now we cannot help thinking that this form of discipline is much called for. There are many whose ways, though not of such a character as to call for excommunication, do, nevertheless, demand faithful dealing: for example, persons going in debt, living beyond their means, dressing in a vain, fashionable style, unbecoming a Christian; and many other things inconsistent with the holiness, purity and solemnity of the Lord's table and the assembly. If all such cases were dealt with according to the apostolic command in 2 Thess. 3, we believe it would prove a real blessing to many.

We need hardly add that it needs much grace, much spiritual wisdom, much of the mind of Christ, much nearness to God, to carry out this sort of discipline; but we are persuaded it demands the prayerful attention of Christians; and we may confidently count on the grace of God to enable us to act for Him in this matter.

"HOLY BRETHREN"

"WHEREFORE, holy brethren, partakers of the heavenly calling, *consider* the Apostle and High Priest of our confession, Jesus" (Heb. 3:1).

"And let us *consider* one another, to provoke unto love and good works" (Heb. 10:24).

The two passages we have just penned, are very intimately connected. Indeed, they are bound together by the simple fact, that the inspired writer makes use of the same word in each; and, further, that this word occurs only in these two places throughout the whole of this marvelous treatise.*

We are to consider Jesus; and we are to consider all those who belong to Him, wherever they are. These are the two grand departments of our work. We are to apply our minds diligently to Him and to His interests on the earth, and thus be blessedly delivered from the miserable business of thinking about ourselves or our own interests: a morally glorious deliverance, most surely, for which we may well praise our glorious Deliverer.

However, before proceeding to the great subjects which we are called to consider, we must dwell, for a little, on the wonderful title bestowed by the Holy Spirit upon all believers—all true Christians. He calls them, "holy brethren." This, truly, is a title of great moral dignity. He does not say, we *ought to be* holy. No; he says we *are*. It is a question of the title or standing of every child of God on the face of the earth. No doubt, having through sovereign grace this holy standing, we ought to be holy in our walk; our moral condition ought ever to answer to our title. We should never allow a thought, word, or act, in the smallest degree inconsistent with our high position as "holy brethren." Holy thoughts, holy words, holy actings are alone suited to those upon whom infinite grace has bestowed the title of "holy brethren."

Let us never forget this. Let us never say, never think, that we cannot maintain such a dignity, or live up to such a standard. The very same grace which has bestowed upon us the dignity, will ever enable us to support it; and we shall see, in the progress of this paper, how this grace acts—the mighty moral means used to produce a practical walk in accordance with our holy calling.

But let us inquire on what does the apostle ground the title of "holy brethren"? It is of all possible importance to be clear as to this. If we do not see that it is wholly independent of our state, our walk, or our attainments, we can neither understand the position nor its practical results. We may assert with all confidence, that the very holiest walk that ever was exhibited in this world, the highest spiritual state that ever was attained, could never form the basis of such a position as is set forth in the title of which we speak. Nay, more; we are bold to affirm that not even the work of the Spirit in us, blessedly essential as it is in every stage of the divine life, could entitle us to enter upon such a dignity. Nothing in us, nothing of us, nothing about us, could ever form the foundation of such a standing as is set forth in the title "holy brethren."

* The English word, "consider," occurs four times throughout the Epistle to the Hebrews; but it represents three different Greek words. In chapter 7:4, "Consider how great this man was." Here the word is $\theta \epsilon \omega \rho \epsilon \tilde{\iota} \tau \epsilon$, which occurs, in its various inflections, about fifty-six times in the Greek Testament, but only in this one instance is it rendered by the word "consider." Its simple and general meaning is to "see" or "perceive."

Again, in Hebrews 12:3, we have, "Consider Him who endured such contradiction," etc. Here the word is $\dot{\alpha} \nu \alpha \lambda o \gamma \acute{\iota} \sigma \alpha \sigma \theta \epsilon$, which occurs only in this place throughout the entire New Testament, and expresses the idea of comparison or analogy.

But in the two verses which stand at the head of this paper, the word is $\kappa \alpha \tau \alpha \nu o \acute{\epsilon} \omega$, which has an intensive force, and signifies an earnest application of the mind.

On what then is it grounded? Hebrews 2:11 furnishes the reply. "For both He that sanctifieth and they who are sanctified are *all of one: for which cause He is not ashamed* to call them brethren." Here we have one of the most profound and comprehensive statements of truth contained within the covers of the divine volume. Here we see how we become "holy brethren"; even by association with that blessed One who went down into death for us, and who, in resurrection, has become the foundation of that new order of things in which we have our place; the Head of that new creation to which we belong; the Firstborn among the many brethren of whom He is not ashamed, inasmuch as He has placed them on the same platform with Himself, and brought them to God not only in the perfect efficacy of His work, but in all His own perfect acceptability and infinite preciousness. "The Sanctifier and the sanctified are all of one."*

Wonderful words! let the reader ponder them. Let him specially note the vast, yea, the immeasurable difference between these two words "Sanctifier and sanctified." Such was our blessed Lord, personally, intrinsically, in His humanity, that He was capable of being the Sanctifier. Such were we personally, in our moral condition, in our nature, that we needed to be sanctified. But—eternal and universal homage to His name!—such is the perfection of His work, such the "riches" and the "glory of His grace" that it can be said, "As He is so are we in this world"—"the Sanctifier and the sanctified are all of one"— all on one common ground, and that for ever.

Nothing can exceed this as to title and standing. We stand in all the glorious results of His accomplished work, and in all the acceptance of His Person. He has linked us with Himself, in resurrection-life, and made us sharers of all He has and all He is as man—His deity, of course is incommunicable.

But let us note very particularly all that is involved in the fact that we *needed* to be "sanctified." It sets forth in the clearest and most forcible manner the total, hopeless, absolute ruin of every one of us. It matters not, so far as this aspect of the truth is concerned, who we were or what we were in our personal history or our practical life. We may have been refined, cultivated, amiable, moral, and, after a human fashion, religious; or we may have been degraded, demoralized, depraved, the very scum of society. In a word, we may have been morally and socially as far apart as the poles; but inasmuch as all needed to be sanctified, the highest as well as the lowest, ere we could be addressed as "holy brethren," there is evidently "no difference." The very worst needed nothing more, and the very best could do with nothing less. Each and all were involved in one common ruin, and needed to be sanctified, or set apart, ere we could take our place amongst the "holy brethren."

And now, being set apart, we are all on one common ground; so that the very feeblest child of God on the face of the earth belongs as really and truly to the "holy brethren" as the blessed apostle Paul himself. It is not a question of progress or attainment, precious and important as it most surely is to make progress, but simply of our common standing before God, of which the "First-born" is the blessed and eternal definition.

But we must here remind the reader of the vast importance of being clear and well-grounded as to the relationship of the "First-born" with the "many brethren." This is a grand foundation-truth, as to which there must be no vagueness or indecision. Scripture and is clear and emphatic on this great cardinal point. But there are many who will not listen to Scripture. They are so full of their own thoughts that they will not take the trouble to search and see what Scripture says on the subject. Hence you find many maintaining the fatal error that incarnation is

---

* It is a fact of deepest interest, that, to "Mary Magdalene, out of whom went seven devils," was granted the privilege of announcing to the disciples the glad tidings of the new and wondrous relationship into which they were introduced. "Go to *My brethren,*" said the risen Saviour, "and say unto them, I ascend unto *My* Father and *your* Father; and to *My* God and *your* God." It is John who, by the Holy Ghost, records this profoundly interesting fact.

Never before had such an announcement been made. But now the great work was done, the battle over, the victory gained, the foundation of the new edifice laid; and Mary Magdalene was made the herald of the most glorious tidings that ever fell on mortal ears.

the ground of our relationship with the First-born. They look upon the Incarnate One as our "Elder Brother," who, in taking human nature upon Him, took us into union with Himself, or linked Himself on to us.

Now such an error involves most frightful consequences. In the first place, it involves a positive blasphemy against the Person of the Son of God—a denial of His absolutely spotless, sinless, perfect manhood. He, blessed be His name, was such in His humanity that the angel could say to the virgin of Him, "That holy thing which shall be born of thee shall be called the Son of God." His human nature was absolutely holy. As a man He knew no sin. He was the only man that ever lived of whom this could be said. He was unique. He stood absolutely alone. There was, there could be, no union with Him in incarnation. How could the Holy and the un-holy, the Pure and the impure, the Spotless and the spotted ever be united? Utterly impossible! Those who think or say they could, do greatly err, not knowing the Scriptures or the Son of God.

Further: those who speak of union in incarnation are most manifestly the enemies of the cross of Christ; for what need was there of the cross, the death or the blood of Christ, if sinners could be united to Him in incarnation? Surely none whatever. There was no need of atonement, no need of propitiation, no need of the substitutionary sufferings and death of Christ, if sinners could be united to Him without them.

Hence we see how entirely this system of doctrine is of Satan. It dishonors the Person of Christ, and sets aside His precious atonement. And in addition to all this, it overthrows the teaching of the entire Bible on the subject of man's guilt and ruin. In short, it completely sweeps away the great foundation-truths of our glorious Christian-ity, and gives us instead a Christless, infidel system. This is what the devil has ever been aiming at; it is what he is aiming at still; and thousands of so-called Christian teachers are acting as his agents in the terrible business of seeking to abolish Christianity. Tremendous fact for all whom it may concern!

Let us reverently harken to the teaching of Holy Scripture on this great subject. What mean those words which fell from the lips of our Lord Jesus Christ, and are repeated for us by God the Holy Ghost, "Except a corn of wheat fall into the ground and *die*, it abideth alone"? Who was this corn of wheat? Himself, blessed be His holy name. He had to die in order to "bring forth much fruit." If He was to surround Himself with His "many breth-ren," He had to go down into death in order to take out of the way every hindrance to their eternal association on the new ground of resurrection. He, the true David, had to go forth single-handed to meet the terrible foe, in order that He might have the deep joy of sharing with His brethren the spoils of His glorious victory. Eternal halleluiahs to His peerless name!

There is a very beautiful passage bearing upon our subject in Mark 8. We shall quote it for the reader: "And He began to teach them, that the Son of man *must suffer* many things, and be rejected of the elders, and of the chief priests, and scribes, and be killed, and after three days rise again. And He spake that saying openly. And Peter took Him, and began to rebuke Him." In another Gospel we are told what Peter said: "Pity Thyself, Lord: this shall not be unto Thee." Mark the Lord's reply; mark His attitude: "But when He had turned about and *looked on His disciples*, He rebuked Peter, saying, Get thee behind Me, Satan, for thou savorest not the things that be of God, but the things that be of men."

This is perfectly beautiful. It not only presents a truth to the understanding, but lets in upon the heart a bright ray of the moral glory of our adorable Lord and Saviour Jesus Christ, eminently calculated to bow the soul in worship before Him. "He turned and looked upon His disciples." It is as though He would say to His erring servant, "If I adopt your suggestion, if I pity myself, what will become of these?" Blessed Saviour! He did not think of Himself.

"He stedfastly set His face to go to Jerusalem," well knowing what awaited Him there. He went to the cross, and there endured the wrath of God, the judgment of sin, all the terrible consequences of our condition, in order to glorify God with respect to our sins, and that He might have the ineffable and eternal joy of surrounding Himself with the "many brethren" to whom He could, on resurrection ground, declare the Father's name. "*I will* declare Thy name unto *My brethren.*" He looked forward to this from amid the awful shadows of Calvary, where He was enduring for us what no created intelligence can ever fathom. If ever He was to call us "brethren," He must *all alone* meet death and judgment on our behalf.

Now why all this if incarnation was the basis of our union or association?* Is it not perfectly plain that there could be no link between Christ and us save on the ground of accomplished atonement? How could there be a link with sin unatoned for, guilt uncanceled, the claims of God unanswered? Utterly impossible. To maintain such a thought is to fly in the face of divine revelation and sweep away the very foundations of Christianity; and this, as we very well know, is precisely what the devil is ever aiming at.

However, we shall not pursue the subject further here. It may be that the great majority of our readers are thoroughly clear and settled on the point, and that they hold it as a great cardinal and essential truth. Still, we feel it of importance just now to bear a very distinct testimony to the whole Church of God on this most blessed subject. We feel persuaded that the error which we have been combating—the notion of union with Christ in incarnation—forms an integral part of a vast infidel and antichristian system which holds sway over thousands of professing Christians, and is making fearful progress throughout the length and breadth of christendom. It is the deep and solemn conviction of this that leads us to call the attention of the beloved flock of Christ to one of the most precious and glorious subjects that could possibly occupy their hearts, namely, their title to be called "holy brethren."

We shall now turn for a few moments to the exhortation addressed to the "holy brethren, partakers of the heavenly calling." As we have already observed, we are not exhorted *to be* holy brethren: we are *made* such. The place and the portion are ours through infinite grace, and it is on this blessed fact that the inspired apostle grounds his exhortation, "Wherefore, holy brethren, partakers of the heavenly calling, consider the Apostle and High Priest of our profession, Jesus."

The titles bestowed on our blessed Lord in this passage present Him to our hearts in a very wonderful manner. They take in the wide range of His history from the bosom of the Father down to the dust of death; and from the dust of death back to the throne of God. As the Apostle, He came from God to us; and as the High Priest, He has gone back to God for us. He came from Heaven to reveal God to us, to unfold to us the very heart of God, to make us know the precious secrets of His bosom.

"God, who at sundry times and in divers manners spake in times past unto the fathers by the prophets, hath in these last days spoken unto us by His Son, whom He hath appointed heir of all things, by whom also He made the worlds; who being the brightness of His glory, and the express image of His person, and upholding all things by the word of His power, when He had by Himself purged our sins, sat down on the right hand of the Majesty on high."

What a marvelous privilege to have God revealed to us in the Person of Christ! God has spoken to us in the Son. Our blessed Apostle has given us the full and perfect revelation of God. "No man hath seen God at any time; the only begotten Son, which is in the bosom of the Father, He hath declared Him." "God, who commanded the light to shine out of darkness, hath shined in our hearts, to give the light of the knowledge of the glory of God in the face of Jesus Christ" (John 1; 2 Cor. 4).

All this is unspeakably precious. Jesus has revealed God to our souls. We could know

---

* We do not mean that union with Christ as Head of the body is taught in Heb. 2:11. For the unfolding of that glorious truth we must look elsewhere. It comes not within the range of the Epistle to the Hebrews. See Eph. 1:22-23; 5:30. But whether we view Him as Head of the body, or as the First-born among many brethren, Scripture most distinctly and emphatically teaches us that His death on the cross was absolutely essential to our union, or association, with Christ. *No death, no union.* The corn of wheat had to fall into the ground and die, in order to bring forth much fruit.

absolutely nothing of God if the Son had not come and spoken to us. But—thanks and praise to our God!—we can say with all possible certainty, "*We know* that the Son of God is come, and hath given us an understanding, that we may know Him that is true: and we are in Him that is true, even in His Son Jesus Christ. This is the true God, and eternal life."

We can now turn to the four Gospels; and as we gaze upon that blessed One who is there presented to us by the Holy Ghost, in all that lovely grace which shone out in all His words, and works, and ways, we can say, That is God. We see Him going about doing good, and healing all that were oppressed of the devil; we see Him healing the sick, cleansing the leper, opening the eyes of the blind, unstopping the ears of the deaf, feeding the hungry, drying the widow's tears, weeping at the tomb of Lazarus, and say, That is God. Every ray of moral glory that shone in the life and ministry of the Apostle of our confession was the expression of God. He was the brightness of the divine glory, and the exact impression of the divine essence.

> Thou art the everlasting Word,
>   The Father's only Son;
> God manifest, God seen and heard,
>   The Heavens' beloved One.
>
> In Thee most perfectly expressed,
>   The Father's self doth shine;
> Fulness of Godhead too; the Blest—
>   Eternally Divine.

How precious is all this to our souls! To have God revealed in the Person of Christ, so that we can know Him, delight in Him, find all our springs in Him, call Him Abba Father, walk in the light of His blessed countenance, have fellowship with Him and with His Son Jesus Christ, know the love of His heart, the very love wherewith He loves the Son—what deep blessedness! what fulness of joy! How can we ever sufficiently praise the God and Father of our Lord Jesus Christ for His marvelous grace in having introduced us into

such a sphere of blessing and privilege, and set us in such a wondrous relationship with Himself in the Son of His love! Oh, may our *hearts* praise Him! May our *lives* praise Him! May it be the one grand aim and object of our whole moral being to magnify His name!

We must now turn for a little to another great branch of our subject. We have to "consider the High Priest of our confession." This, too, is fraught with richest blessing for every one of the "holy brethren." The same blessed One who, as the Apostle, came to make Him known to our souls, has gone back to God for us. He came to speak to us about God; and He is gone to speak to God about us. He appears in the presence of God for us; He bears us up on His heart continually; He represents us before God to maintain us in the integrity of the position into which His precious atoning work has introduced us. His blessed priesthood is the divine provision for our wilderness path. Were it merely a question of our standing or title, there would be no need of priesthood; but inasmuch as it is a question of our actual state and practical walk, we could not get on for one moment if we had not our great High Priest ever living for us in the presence of God.

Now there are three most precious departments of our Lord's priestly service presented in the Epistle to the Hebrews. In the first place we read, in chap. 4, "Seeing then that we have a great high priest, that is passed through the heavens, Jesus the Son of God, let us hold fast our confession. For we have not a high priest which cannot be touched with the feeling of our infirmities; but was in all points tempted like as we are, except sin."*

Only think of the deep blessedness of having One at the right hand of the Majesty in the heavens who is *touched* with the feeling of your infirmities, who enters into all your sorrows, who feels for you and with you in all your exercises, trials, and difficulties! Think of having a Man on the throne of God— a perfect human heart, One on whom you can count in all your weakness, heaviness, and

---

* "Yet without sin," as given in the Authorized Version, does not convey the correct thought of the original, which is, "tempted in all things in like manner [to us], sin apart," or "sin excepted." [Ed.]

conflict; in everything, in short, except sin! With this, blessed be His name, He can have no sympathy.

But oh, what pen, what human tongue, can adequately set forth the deep, deep blessedness of having a Man in the glory whose heart is with us in all the trials and sorrows of our wilderness path! What a precious provision! What a divine reality! The One who has all power in Heaven and on earth now lives for us in Heaven. We can count on Him at all times. He enters into all our feelings in a way that no earthly friend could possibly do. We can go to Him and tell him things which we could not name to our dearest friend on earth, inasmuch as none but He can fully understand us.

Our great High Priest understands all about us. He has passed through every trial and sorrow that a perfect human heart could know. Hence He can perfectly sympathize with us, and He delights to minister to us in all our seasons of sorrow and affliction, when the heart is crushed and bowed beneath a weight of anguish which only He can fully enter into. Precious Saviour! Most merciful High Priest! May our hearts delight in Thee! May we draw more largely upon the exhaustless springs of comfort and consolation that are found in Thy large and loving heart for all Thy tried, tempted, sorrowing, suffering brethren here below!

In Hebrews 7:25 we have another very precious branch of our Lord's priestly work, and that is His intercession—His active intervention on our behalf, in the presence of God. "Wherefore He is able to save them to the uttermost that come unto God by Him, seeing He ever liveth to make intercession for them."

What comfort is here for all the "holy brethren"! What strong consolation! What blessed assurance! Our great High Priest bears us upon His heart continually before the throne. All our affairs are in His blessed hands, and can never fall through. He lives for us, and we live in Him. He will carry us right through to the end. Men speak about "the final perseverance of the saints." Scripture speaks of the final perseverance of our divine and adorable High Priest. Here we

rest. He says to us, "Because I live, ye shall live also."

"If, when we were enemies, we were reconciled to God by *the death of His Son*," (the only possible way in which we could be reconciled) "much more, being reconciled, we shall be saved by His life"—that is, His life up in Heaven. He has made Himself responsible for every one of the "holy brethren," to bring them through all the difficulties, trials, snares, and temptations of the wilderness, right home to glory. Universal and everlasting homage to His blessed name!

We cannot, of course, attempt to go elaborately into the great subject of priesthood in a paper like this; we can do little more than touch upon the three salient points indicated above, and quote for the reader the passages of Scripture in which those points are presented.

In Hebrews 13:15 we have the third branch of our Lord's service for us in the heavenly sanctuary. "*By Him*, therefore, let us offer the sacrifice of praise to God continually, that is, the fruit of our lips, giving thanks to His name."

What a comfort to know that we have One in the presence of God to present our sacrifices of praise and thanksgiving! How sweetly it encourages us to bring such sacrifices at all times! True, they may seem very poor, very meagre, very imperfect; but our great High Priest knows how to separate the precious from the vile; He takes our sacrifices, and presents them to God in all the perfect fragrance of His own Person and ministry. Every little breathing of the heart, every utterance, every little act of service, goes up to God, not only divested of all our infirmity and imperfection, but adorned with all the excellency of the One who ever liveth in the presence of God, not only to sympathize and intercede, but also to present our sacrifices of thanksgiving and praise.

All this is full of comfort and encouragement. How often have we to mourn over our coldness, barrenness, and deadness, both in private and in public! We seem unable to do more than utter a groan or a sigh. Well, Jesus—it is the fruit of His grace—takes that groan or that sigh, and presents it to God in all His own preciousness. This is part of His present ministry for us in the presence of our God, a ministry which He delights to discharge—blessed be His name! It is His joy to bear us upon His heart before the Throne. He thinks of each one in particular, as if He had but that one to think of.

It is wonderful; but so it is. He enters into all our little trials and sorrows, conflicts and exercises, as though He had nothing else to think of. Each one has the undivided attention and sympathy of that large, loving heart, in all that may rise in our passage through this scene of trial and sorrow. He has gone through it all. He knows, as we say, every step of the road. We can discern His blessed footprints all across the desert; and look up through the opened heavens and see Him on the throne, a glorified Man, but the same Jesus who was down here upon earth—His circumstances changed, but not His tender, loving, sympathizing heart: "The same yesterday, to-day, and for ever."

Such then, is the great High Priest, whom we are exhorted to "consider." Truly we have all we want in Him. His sympathy, perfect; His intercession, all-prevailing; His presentation of our sacrifices, ever acceptable. Well may we say, "We have all, and abound."

In conclusion, let us glance for a moment at the precious exhortation in Hebrews 10:24: "Let us *consider* one another, to provoke unto love and good works."

How morally lovely is the connection! The more attentively we consider Him, the more we shall be fitted and disposed to consider all who belong to Him, whoever and wherever they may be. Shew us a man full of Christ, and we will shew you a man full of love, and care, and interest for every member of the body of Christ. It must be so. It is simply impossible to be near Christ, and not have

the heart filled with the sweetest affections for all that belong to Him. We cannot consider Him without being reminded of them, and led out in service, prayer, and sympathy, according to our little measure.

If you hear a person talking loudly of his love for Christ, his attachment to Him and delight in Him, and, all the while, having no love for His people—no readiness to spend and be spent for them, no self-sacrifice on their behalf—you may be sure it is all hollow, worthless profession. "Hereby perceive we the love, because He laid down His life for us; and we ought to lay down our lives for the brethren. But whoso hath this world's good, and seeth his brother have need, and shutteth up his bowels from him, how dwelleth the love of God in him? My little children, let us not love in word, neither in tongue, but in deed, and in truth." And again, "This commandment have we from Him, that he who loveth God, love his brother also" (1 John 3:16-18; 4:21).

These are wholesome words for all of us. May we apply our hearts most diligently to them! May we, by the powerful ministry of the Holy Ghost, be enabled to respond with all our hearts, to these two weighty and needed exhortations, to "Consider the Apostle and High Priest of our confession," and to "Consider one another!" And let us bear in mind, that the proper consideration of one another will never take the form of prying curiosity, or unwarrantable *espionage*—things which can only be regarded as the curse and bane of all Christian society. No; it is the very reverse of all this. It is a loving, tender care, expressing itself in every form of refined, delicate, and seasonable service—the lovely fruit of true communion with the heart of Christ.

The Lord's Coming

"READY"

WE WANT THE READER to dwell for a few moments on the little word "ready." If we mistake not, he will find it to be a word of immense depth and suggestive power, as used by the Holy Ghost in Scripture. We shall just now refer to four passages in which our word occurs; and may the One who penned these passages be pleased to open and apply them in divine power and freshness to the heart of both writer and reader.

1. And first we shall turn to 1 Peter 1: 5, where it is used in connection with the word *"salvation."* Believers are said to be "kept by the power of God through faith unto salvation, *ready* to be revealed in the last time."

Here, then, we are taught that salvation is ready to be revealed at this moment; for we are, as John tells us, in "the last times." And be it noted that salvation as here used is not to be confined to the mere matter of the *soul's* deliverance from hell and perdition: it refers, rather, to the deliverance of the *body* of the believer from the power of death and corruption. In short, it takes in all that stands in anywise connected with the glorious appearing of our Lord and Saviour Jesus Christ. We already possess the salvation of our souls, as we are told in the very context from which our text is taken. "Receiving the end of your faith, even the salvation of your souls. . . . Wherefore gird up the loins of your mind, be sober, and hope to the end for the grace that is to be brought unto you *at the revelation of Jesus Christ.*"

Thus we learn in the clearest way that the "salvation ready to be revealed" is linked on to "the revelation of Jesus Christ." This is confirmed, were confirmation needful, by Hebrews 9:28, where we read, "So Christ was once offered to bear the sins of many; and unto them that look for Him shall He appear the second time, apart from sin, unto *salvation.*"

From all this we learn that the salvation which is *ready* to be revealed is at the second coming of our Lord Jesus Christ. For this we are taught, as Christians, to look at any moment. There is literally nothing so far as God is concerned, nothing so far as the work of Christ is concerned, nothing so far as the testimony of the Holy Ghost is concerned, to hinder our hearing "the shout of the archangel and the trump of God" this very night, this very hour. All is done that needed to be done. Atonement is made, redemption is accomplished, God has been glorified by the work of Christ, as is proved by the fact of Christ's present place on the throne of the Majesty in the heavens. From the moment that our Lord Christ took His seat upon that throne, it could always be said that "salvation is *ready* to be revealed."

But it could not have been said before. Salvation could not be said to be ready until the divine groundwork thereof was laid in the death and resurrection of the Saviour. But when once that most glorious work of all works was accomplished, it could at any moment be said that "salvation is ready to be revealed." "The Lord said unto my Lord, Sit Thou at My right hand, until I make Thine enemies Thy footstool" (Ps. 110: 1).

2. The apostle Peter gives us another instance and application of our word in chap. 4: 5, where he refers to some "who shall give account to Him that is *ready to judge* the quick and the dead."

Here the word stands before us in a form of awful solemnity. If on the one hand it be true that *salvation* is ready to be revealed for the everlasting joy of God's redeemed, it is equally true on the other hand that *judgment* is ready to take its course, for the everlasting misery of those who neglect God's proffered salvation.* The one is as true, and as pointed, and as forcible, as the other. There is nothing to wait for in respect to the judgment, any more than there is in respect to the salvation. The one is as *"ready"* as the other.

God has gone to the utmost in demonstrating His grace; and man has gone to the utmost in demonstrating his guilt. Both have reached their climax in the death of Christ; and when we see Him crowned with glory and seated on the throne, we have the most powerful evidence that could possibly be afforded that nothing remains but for salvation to be revealed on the one hand, and for judgment to take its course on the other.

Hence it follows that man is no longer under probation. It is a grand mistake for any one to think so. It falsifies man's entire position and state. If I am under probation; if God is still testing me; if He is even now occupied in testing whether I am good for aught; if I am capable of producing any fruit for Him—if this be indeed the case, then it is not and cannot be true that "He is *ready* to judge." Nature is not ripe for judgment so long as a probationary process is pending, if there is yet something to wait for ere judgment can take its course.

But no; we feel bound to press upon you the fact that the period of your probation is over forever, and the period of God's long-suffering is nearly run out. It is of the utmost importance to seize this truth. It lies at the very foundation of the sinner's position. Judgment is actually impending. It is "ready" at this moment to fall upon the head of the unrepentant—the reader of these lines, should he be one of them. The entire history of human nature—of man, of the world—has been wound up and closed forever. The cross of Christ has made perfectly manifest the guilt and ruin of the human race. It has put an end to man's probationary season; and from that solemn hour until now the true position of the world as a whole, and of each individual sinner—man, woman, and child—has been that of a culprit tried, found guilty, and condemned,

but the sentence not executed. This is the present awful position of the unconverted, unbelieving reader.

Wilt thou not think of this? Fellow immortal soul, wilt thou not, even this very moment, bend the undivided attention of thy soul to this eternal question? We must speak plainly and pointedly. We feel in some small degree the awfulness of the sinner's state and prospect, in view of these weighty words, *"ready to judge."* We are convinced that the present is a moment which calls for serious and faithful dealing with the souls of our readers. We do not, as God is our witness, want to write essays or sermons; we want to reach souls. We want the reader to be assured of this; that he is not now reading an article on a religious subject prepared for some literary purpose, but a solemn appeal made to his heart and conscience in the immediate presence of "Him who is ready to judge the quick and the dead."

3. But this leads us to the third passage of Holy Scripture in which our weighty motto occurs. The reader will find it in Luke 12: 40: "Be ye therefore *ready* also; for the Son of man cometh at an hour when ye think not."

If salvation is "ready" to be revealed, and if judgment is "ready" to be executed, what becomes us but to be "ready" also?

And in what does this readiness consist? How are we to be ready? It strikes us that there are two things included in the answer.

First, we must be "ready" in *title*; and, secondly, we must be "ready" in our moral *state*—ready in conscience, and ready in heart. The one is founded upon the work of Christ *for* us; the other is connected with the work of the Spirit *in* us. If we are simply resting by faith on the finished work of Christ, if we are leaning exclusively on what He has done and what He is, then are we in very truth ready in title, and we may rest assured of being with Him when He comes.

But, on the other hand, if we are leaning upon our fancied goodness, upon any righteousness which we think we possess, upon not having done any harm to any one, upon

---

* As regards the solemn subject of eternal punishment, we shall just refer the reader to three passages of Scripture which establish the truth of it beyond all question: Mark 9:43-48, the fire is *unquenchable*, and the worm *never dies;* Luke 16:26, the great gulf is *fixed;* John 3:36, the wrath of God *abideth.*

our not being worse than some of our neighbors, upon our church-membership, upon our attention to the ordinances of religion; if we are leaning upon any or all of these things, or if we are adding these things to Christ, then we may be assured we are not ready in title, not ready in conscience. God can accept nothing, absolutely nothing, as a title, but Christ. To bring aught else is to declare that Christ is not needful: to bring aught besides is to affirm that He is not enough. But God has borne ten thousand testimonies to the fact that we can do with nothing less, and that we want nothing more, than Christ. Hence, therefore, Christ is our all-essential and all-sufficient title.

But, then, there is such a thing as professing to be ready in title while at the same time we are not ready in our moral condition or practical state. This demands our gravest attention. There is a vast amount of easy-going evangelical profession abroad at the present moment. The atmosphere is permeated by the rays of gospel light. The darkness of the Middle Ages has been chased away by the brightness of a free gospel and an open Bible.

We are thankful for a free gospel and an open Bible. But we cannot shut our eyes to the fact that there is a fearful amount of laxity, unsubduedness, and self-indulgence going hand in hand with the evangelical profession of the day. We notice with the deepest anxiety many young professors who have, or seem to have, a very clear insight, so far as the intellect goes, into the truth of the sinner's title, who, if we are to judge from their style, deportment, and habits, are not "ready" in their moral condition—in the real state of their hearts. We are at times, we must confess, sadly cast down when we see our young friends decking their persons in the vain fashions of a vain and sinful world; feeding upon the vile literature that issues in such frightful profusion from the press; and actually singing vain songs and engaging in light and frivolous conversation. It is impossible to reconcile such with "Be ye also ready."

We may perhaps be told that these things are externals, and that the grand point is to be occupied with Christ. It may be said—it has been said—"Provided we have Christ in our hearts, it does not matter what we have on our heads or in our hands." We reply, "If we really have Christ in our hearts, it will regulate what we put on our heads and take into our hands; yea, it will exert a *manifest* influence upon our whole deportment and character."

We should like to ask some of our young friends this question: "Would you like the Lord Christ to come and find you reading a love-story, or singing a song?" We feel assured you would not. Well, then, let us, in the name of the Lord, see to it that we do not engage in anything which does not comport with our being "*ready.*"

We specially urge this upon the young Christian reader. Let this question be ever before us, "Am I ready?—ready in title, ready in state, ready in conscience, ready in heart?" The times are really very solemn, and it behooves us to think seriously of our true state. We feel persuaded that there is a lack of real, godly heart-exercise amongst us. There are, we fear, many—God only knows how many—who are not ready; many who would be taken aback and terribly surprised by death or the coming of the Lord. There are things said and done by those who occupy the very highest platform of profession which we dare not indulge in if we are really *looking* for the Lord.

God grant that the reader may know what it is to be ready in title and ready in state; that he may have a purged conscience and a truly exercised heart. Then he will be able to enter into the meaning of the fourth and last passage, to which we call his attention. It occurs in Matt. 25:10.

4. "And while they [the foolish virgins] went to buy, the bridegroom came; and they that were *ready* went in with him to the marriage; and the door was shut."

How solemn! How awfully solemn! Those who were *ready* went in, and those who were not ready were shut out. Those who have life in Christ, who are indwelt by the Holy Ghost, will be ready. But the mere professor—the one who has truth in the head and on the lip, but not in the heart; who has the lamp of profession, but not the Spirit of life in Christ—will be shut out into outer darkness —in the everlasting misery and gloom of hell.

Let us, as we take a solemn leave of you, put this question home to your very inmost soul, "*Art thou ready?*"

OUR STANDARD AND OUR HOPE

THERE ARE TWO VERY IMPORTANT principles presented in Revelation 3:3, 11, which are profoundly interesting, but clear, simple, easily grasped, and full of power, when understood—two distinct things which characterize the overcomer. The first is the truth that has been communicated; and the second, the hope that is set before us.

We find these two things illustrated in Israel's history, and in the history of the Church of God—what He has given us, and what is held out before us. These two things are to form your character and mine. We are not to be influenced by the character of things around, or the present condition of the people of God; but we are to be influenced by what God *has* given, and what He *will* give. We are apt to be discouraged and disheartened by the state of things around, and to surrender everything because of the ruin, and thus get paralyzed; but if you get hold of these two things, or rather if they get hold of you, they will enable you to stem the tide, and to be an overcomer. You are to remember what you have received and heard, and cherish the hope of glory.

We have Protestantism before us in Sardis. You must always distinguish between a work of the Spirit of God and the state of things resulting from it through man's interference, human management, earthly machinery, stereotyping the form when the power was gone. The Reformation was a distinct work of the Spirit of God, a wave of spiritual power. Protestantism is the powerless form which, through human weakness and Satan's craft, has followed that glorious season of divine visitation.

Fifty years ago there was a very distinct movement of the Spirit of God, which drew many out of the enclosures of christendom. But what use has been made of it? When the energy, freshness, and bloom of the Spirit had departed, what followed, in many cases? Why, people slipped into what may be called dead brethrenism, and there is nothing worse than that, because the corruption of the best thing is the worst corruption. What is our moral safeguard? Simply to hold fast what we have received, and to live in the blessed hope of Christ's coming, to realize in our own souls the power of what God has given and what He will give.

We find illustrations of this in Old Testament times. All the great reformatory movements in Israel were characterized by this very thing. It was so in Jehoshaphat's time, and in Hezekiah's time. The Lord calls back His people to the original standard, to what they had received at the first. Hezekiah goes back to Moses, as his authority to maintain the divine standard in the celebration of the passover. Many might have said, Oh, it is all hopeless; your national unity is gone. Even Solomon had left abominations behind him. The devil suggests to lower the standard because of the ruin; but Hezekiah did not listen to that. He was an overcomer. A tide of blessing rolled in, such as had not been known since the days of Solomon (2 Chron. 30).

So, again, in the days of Josiah: a child was on the throne; a woman filling the prophetic office; Nebuchadnezzar almost at the gates. What did Josiah do? The book of the law was read. Instead of lowering the standard on account of the state of things, he acted on the

Word of God; that was his standard of action, and he kept the passover in the first month. The result was, there had not been such a passover since the days of Samuel.

Thus was it with Hezekiah and Josiah; and we have a still more beautiful example of it in Ezra and Nehemiah. In those days a feast was kept which had not been observed since the days of Joshua the son of Nun. It was reserved for that poor, little remnant to keep that feast. They were overcomers; they went back to God, and to what He had given at the beginning.

Again, Daniel, Shadrach, Meshach, and Abednego gained a magnificent victory when they refused to eat the king's meat. They would not yield one hair's breadth. Were not they overcomers? They might have said, God in His governmental dealings has sent us into captivity; why should we refuse to eat the king's meat? But no! they were enabled to hold up the standard of God in the midst of the ruin around.

It was the same with Daniel. He stood in unshaken faithfulness, and gained a splendid victory. It was not to make a show that he opened his windows, and prayed towards Jerusalem, but to maintain the truth of God; he prayed towards God's centre, and he was called the servant of the living God. If these had surrendered, they would have lost their victories, and God would have been dishonored.

All this bears upon us in a very distinct way, in the midst of Protestantism. It makes the Word of God of unspeakable value to us. It is not a question of setting up our own opinion or authority, but we are called on to maintain the truth of God, and nothing else; and if you do not get hold of that, you do not know where you are. It might have been said to Josiah, when he broke down the high places built by Solomon (2 Kings 23: 13), Who are you, to set yourself up against Solomon, and the institutions set up by a great man like him? But it was not a question of Josiah *versus* Solomon, but of God *versus* error.

And now, as to our second great principle, namely, that our character is also to be formed by what is before us—the coming of the Lord. But mark here, the church of Sardis, instead of being cheered by the Church's proper hope, the bright and Morning Star, is warned, "If, therefore, thou shalt not watch, I will come on thee as a thief, and thou shalt not know what hour I will come upon thee." This is how He will come upon the world —as a thief. We belong to the region of light; our proper hope is the Morning Star, which is only seen by those who are watching during the night. The reason why Sardis is warned, instead of cheered by the hope of His coming, is, that it has sunk down to the world's level: low, lifeless, sapless Christianity; and it will overtake them as a thief.

This is what Protestantism is threatened with, and what you are threatened with, if you let yourself go down with the stream, like a dead fish. The Lord is awakening the hearts of His people to a deeper sense of this. He is giving them to see that nothing will do, save downright reality. If we have not this, we have nothing. It is one thing to have doctrines in the mind, and another thing altogether to have Christ in the heart and Christ in the life.

He is coming for *me*, and I have to watch for the bright and Morning Star. Now let my heart rise up, and overcome the condition of things around. If I find saints in that condition, I seek to rouse them out of it. If you want to instruct saints, you must bring them back to the truth you have received, what God gave at the beginning. Build on what God has given you, and on the hope that is set before you. I find it a great thing to say to any one, Are you prepared to abandon everything that will not bear the test of the Word of God—to take your stand on that?

Hold fast the standard of the truth of God, and do not accept anything less; even though you may be alone. If a regiment were cut to pieces, and only one man left, if he hold the colors, the dignity of the regiment is maintained. It is not a question of results, but of being true to Christ, to be really alive in a scene which is characterized by having "a name to live, while dead." We want something more than mere profession. Even the breaking of bread may become an empty formality. We want more power and freshness, more living devotedness to the Person of Christ. We are called to overcome. The hearing ear is found only with the overcomer.

May our hearts be stirred up to desire it increasingly.

PRE-MILLENNIAL DOCTRINE OR WAITING FOR THE SON?

Revelation 1:5-7

IN A DAY LIKE THE PRESENT, when knowledge on every question is so widely diffused, it is most needful to press upon the conscience of the Christian reader the vast distinction between merely holding the *doctrine* of the Lord's second coming and actually waiting for His appearing (1 Thess. 1:10). Many, alas! hold and, it may be, eloquently preach, the doctrine of a second advent who really do not know *the Person* whose advent they profess to believe and preach. This evil must be faithfully pointed out and dealt with. The present is an age of knowledge—of religious knowledge; but oh! knowledge is not life, knowledge is not power—knowledge will not deliver from sin, or Satan, from the world, from death, from hell. Knowledge, I mean, short of the knowledge of God in Christ. One may know a great deal of Scripture, a great deal of prophecy, a great deal of doctrine, and, all the while, be dead in trespasses and sins.

There is, however, one kind of knowledge which necessarily involves eternal life, and that is the knowledge of God, as He is revealed in the face of Jesus Christ. "This is life eternal, to know Thee the only true God, and Jesus Christ whom Thou hast sent" (John 17: 3). Now, it is impossible to be living in the daily and hourly expectation of "the coming of the Son of Man," if the Son of Man be not experimentally known. I may take up the prophetic record, and by mere study, and the exercise of my intellectual faculties, discover the doctrine of the Lord's second coming, and yet be totally ignorant of Christ, and living a life of entire alienation of heart from Him.

How often has this been the case! How many have astonished us with their vast fund of prophetic knowledge—a fund acquired, it may be, by years of laborious research, and yet, in the end, proved themselves to have been displaying unhallowed light—light not acquired by prayerful waiting upon God! Surely the thought of this should deeply affect our hearts and solemnize our minds, and lead us to inquire whether or not *we* know the blessed Person who, again and again, announces Himself as about to "come quickly"; else, if we know Him not, we may find ourselves of the number of those addressed by the prophet in the following startling words: "Woe unto you that desire the day of the Lord! to what end is it for you? The day of the Lord is darkness, and not light. As if a man did flee from a lion, and a bear met him; or went into the house, and leaned his hand on the wall and a serpent bit him. Shall not the day of the Lord be darkness and not light? even very dark and no brightness in it?" (Amos 5: 18-20)

The second chapter of Matthew furnishes us with a very striking illustration of the difference between mere prophetic knowledge of Christ—between the exercise of the intellect on the letter of Scripture, and the drawings of the Father to the Person of Christ. The wise men, manifestly led by the finger of God, were in true and earnest search of Christ, and they found Him. As to scriptural knowledge, they could not, for a moment have competed with the chief priests and scribes; yet what did the scriptural knowledge of the latter do for them? Why, it rendered them efficient instruments for Herod, who called them together for the purpose of making use of their Biblical knowledge in his deadly opposition to God's Anointed. They were able to give him chapter and verse, as we say. But, while they were assisting Herod by their knowledge, the wise men were, by the drawings of the Father, making their way to Jesus. Blessed contrast! How much happier to be a worshipper at the feet of Jesus, though with slender knowledge, than to be a learned scribe, and a heart cold, dead, and distant from that blessed One! How much better to have the heart full of lively affection for Christ than to have the intellect stored with the most accurate knowledge of the letter of Scripture!

What is the melancholy characteristic of the present time? A wide diffusion of scriptural knowledge with little love for Christ, and little devotedness to His work; abundant readiness to quote Scripture, like the scribes and chief priests, but little purpose of heart, like the wise men, to open the treasures and present to Christ the willing offerings of a heart filled by the sense of what He is. What we want is personal devotedness, and not the mere empty display of knowledge. It is not that we would undervalue scriptural knowledge; God forbid, if that knowledge be found in connection with genuine discipleship. But if it be not, I ask, of what value is it? None whatever. The most extensive range of knowledge, if Christ be not its centre, will avail just nothing; yea, it will, in all probability, render us more efficient instruments in Satan's hand for the furthering of his purposes of hostility to Christ. An ignorant man can do but little mischief; but a learned man, without Christ, can do a great deal.

The verses which stand at the head of this paper present to us the divine basis on which to found all scriptural knowledge, more especially prophetic knowledge. Before any one can utter his hearty amen to the announcement, "Behold He cometh with clouds," he must, without any question, be able to join in the blessed burst of praise, "To Him that loved us, and washed us from our sins in His own blood." The believer knows the One who is coming, because He has loved him, and washed him from his sins. The believer expects the everlasting Lover of his soul. The meek and lowly One who served, suffered, and was emptied down here, will speedily come in the clouds of Heaven, with power and great glory, and *all* who know Him will welcome Him with glad hosannahs—they will be able to say, "This is the Lord, *we have waited for* Him, we will rejoice and be glad in His salvation." But, alas! there are, it is to be feared, very many who hold and argue about the Lord's coming who are not waiting for Him at all, who are living for themselves in the world, and "mind earthly things." How terrible to be found talking about the Lord's coming, and yet, when He does come, *to be left behind*! Oh! think of this; and if you are really conscious that you know not the Lord, then let me entreat of you to behold Him shedding His precious blood to wash you from your sins, and learn to confide in Him, to lean upon Him, to rejoice in Him and *in Him alone*.

But if you can look up to Heaven, and say, "Thank God, I do know Him, and I am waiting for Him," then let me remind you of what the Apostle John says, as to the practical result of this blessed hope. "Every man that hath this hope *in him*, purifieth himself, even as *He* is pure." Yes, this must ever be the result of waiting for the Son from Heaven; but not at all so of the mere prophetic doctrine. Many of the most impure, profane and ungodly characters, that have made their appearance in the world, have held, in theory, the second advent of Christ; but they were not *waiting for the Son*, and therefore they did not, and could not purify themselves. It is impossible that any one can be waiting for Christ's appearing, and not make efforts after increased holiness, separation, and devotedness of heart: "Behold, I come quickly; blessed is he that watcheth." Those who know the Lord Jesus Christ, and love His appearing, will daily seek to shake off everything contrary to their Master's mind; they will seek to become more and more conformed to Him in all things. Men may hold the doctrine of the Lord's coming, and yet grasp the world and the things thereof with great eagerness; but the true hearted servant will ever keep his eye steadily fixed on his Master's return, remembering His blessed words, "I will come again and receive you unto Myself, that where I am, there ye may be also" (John 14:3).

What a day will that be when the Saviour appears!
How welcome to those who have shared in His cross!
A crown incorruptible then will be theirs—
A rich compensation for suffering and loss.

THE LORD'S COMING

INTRODUCTION

THE ATTENTIVE READER of the New Testament will find in its pages three solemn and weighty facts presented to his view; namely, first, that the Son of God has come into this world and gone away; secondly, that the Holy Ghost has come down to this earth, and is here still; and, thirdly, that the Lord Jesus is coming again.

These are the three great subjects unfolded in the New Testament Scriptures; and we shall find that each of them has a double bearing: it has a bearing upon the world and a bearing upon the Church; upon the world, as a whole, and upon each unconverted man, woman, and child in particular; upon the Church, as a whole, and upon each individual member thereof, in particular. It is impossible for any one to avoid the bearing of these three grand facts upon his own personal condition and future destiny.

Be it noted, we are not speaking of doctrines—though, no doubt, there are doctrines—but of facts—facts presented in the simplest possible manner by the various inspired writers employed to set them forth. There is no attempt at garnishing or setting off. The facts speak for themselves; they are recorded and left to produce their own powerful effect upon the soul.

1. And, first of all, let us look at the fact that the Son of God, has been in this world of ours. "God so loved the world that He gave His only begotten Son." "The Son of God has come." He came in perfect love, as the very expression of the heart and mind, the nature and character of God. He was the brightness of God's glory, and the express image of His Person, and yet a lowly, humble, gracious, social man; one who was to be seen, from day to day, about the streets; going from house to house; kind and affable to all; easily approached by the very poorest; taking up little children in His arms, in the most tender, gentle, winning way; drying the widow's tears; soothing the stricken and sorrowing heart; feeding the hungry, healing the sick; cleansing the poor leper; meeting every form of human need and misery; at the bidding of all who stood in need of succor and sympathy. "He went about doing good." He was the unwearied servant of man's necessities. He never thought of Himself, or sought His own interest in any one thing. He lived for others. It was His meat and His drink to do the will of God, and gladden the sad and weary hearts of the sons and daughters of men. His loving heart was ever flowing out in streams of blessing to all who felt the pressure of this sin-stricken, sorrowful world.

Here, then, we have a marvelous fact before our eyes. This world has been visited—this world has been trodden by that blessed One of whom we have spoken—the Son of God—the Creator and Sustainer of the universe—the lowly, self-emptied and loving, gracious Son of Man—Jesus of Nazareth— God over all blessed for ever, and yet a spotless, holy, absolutely perfect man. He came in love to men—came into this world as the expression of perfect love to those who had sinned against God, and deserved nothing but eternal perdition because of their sins. He came not to crush, but to heal—not to judge, but to save and to bless.

What has become of this blessed One? How has the world treated Him? It has cast Him out! It would not have Him! It preferred a robber and a murderer to this holy, gracious, perfect Man. The world got its choice. Jesus and a robber were placed before the world, and the question was put, "Which will you have?" What was the answer? "Not this man, but Barabbas." "The chief priests and elders persuaded the multitude that they should ask Barabbas and destroy Jesus. The governor answered and said unto them. Whether of the twain will ye that I release unto you? They said, Barabbas" (Matt. 27:20-21). The religious leaders and guides of the people—the men who ought to have led them in the right way—persuaded the poor ignorant multitude to reject the Son of God, and accept a robber and a murderer instead!

Remember, you are in a world that has been guilty of this terrible act. And not only so, but unless you have truly repented and believed on the Lord Jesus Christ, you are part and parcel of that world, and you lie under the full guilt of that act. This is most solemn. The whole world stands charged with the deliberate rejection and murder of the Son of God. We have the testimony of no less than four inspired witnesses to this fact. Matthew, Mark, Luke, and John all bear record that the whole world—the Jew and the Gentile—kings and governors, priests, and people—all classes, sects, and parties, agreed to crucify the Son of God—all agreed to murder the only perfect man that ever appeared on this earth—the perfect expression of God—God over all blessed for ever. We must either pronounce the four evangelists to be false witnesses, or admit that the world as a whole, and each constituent part thereof, is stained with the awful crime of crucifying the Lord of glory.

This is the true standard by which to measure the world, and by which to measure the condition of every unconverted man, woman, and child in the world. If I want to know what the world is I have only to reflect that the world is that which stands charged before God with the deliberate murder of His Son. Tremendous fact! A fact which stamps the world, in the most solemn manner, and

places it before us in characters of appalling blackness. God has a controversy with this world. He has a question to settle with it—an awful question—the mere mention of which should make men's ears to tingle and their hearts to quake. A righteous God has to avenge the death of His Son. It is not merely that the world accepted a vile robber and murdered an innocent man; this, in itself, would have been a dreadful act. But no; that innocent man was none other than the Son of God, the beloved of the Father's heart.

What a thought! The world will have to account to God for the death of His Son—for having nailed Him to a cross between two thieves! What a reckoning it will be! How red will be the day of vengeance! How awfully crushing the moment in the which God will draw the sword of judgment to avenge the death of His Son! How utterly vain the notion that the world is improving! Improving!—though stained with the blood of Jesus. Improving!—though under the judgment of God for that act. Improving!—though having to account to a righteous God for its treatment of the beloved of His soul, sent in love to bless and save. What blind fatuity! What wild folly! Ah, no! improvement there can be none till the besom of destruction and the sword of judgment have done their terrible work in avenging the murder—the deliberately planned and determinedly executed murder of the blessed Son of God. We cannot conceive any delusion more fatally false than to imagine that the world can ever be improved while it lies beneath the awful curse of the death of Jesus. That world which preferred Barabbas to Christ can know no improvement. There is naught before it save the overwhelming judgment of God.

Thus much as to the weighty fact of the absence of Jesus, in its bearing upon the present condition and future destiny of the world. But this fact has another bearing. It bears upon the Church of God as a whole, and upon the individual believer. If the world has cast Christ out, the heavens have received Him. If man has rejected Him, God has exalted Him. If man has crucified Him, God has crowned Him. We must carefully distinguish these two things. The death of

Christ, viewed as the act of the world—the act of man—involves naught but unmitigated wrath and judgment. On the other hand, the death of Christ, viewed as the act of God, involves naught but full and everlasting blessedness to all who repent and believe. A passage or two from the divine Word will prove this.

Let us turn for a moment to Psalm 69, which so vividly presents our blessed and adorable Lord suffering from the hand of man, and appealing to God for vengeance. "Hear Me, O Lord; for Thy loving kindness is good: turn unto Me according to the multitude of Thy tender mercies. And hide not Thy face from Thy servant; for I am in trouble: hear Me speedily: draw nigh unto My soul, and redeem it: deliver Me, because of Mine enemies. Thou hast known My reproach, and My shame, and My dishonor: *Mine adversaries are all before Thee.* Reproach hath broken My heart, and I am full of heaviness: and I looked for some to take pity, but there was none; and for comforters, but I found none. They gave Me also gall for My meat, and in My thirst they gave Me vinegar to drink. Let their table become a snare before them: and that which should have been for their welfare, let it become a trap. Let their eyes be darkened, that they see not; and make their loins continually to shake. Pour out Thine indignation upon them, and let Thy wrathful anger take hold of them" (verses 16-28).

All this is deeply and impressively solemn. Every word of this appeal will have its answer. Not a syllable of it shall fall to the ground. God will assuredly avenge the death of His Son. He will reckon with the world—with men for the treatment which His only begotten Son has received at their hands. We deem it right to press this home upon the heart and conscience of the reader. How awful the thought of Christ making intercession *against* people! How appalling to hear Him calling upon God for vengeance upon His enemies! How terrible will be the divine response to the cry of the injured Son!

But let us look at the other side of the picture. Turn to Psalm 22, which presents the blessed One suffering under the hand of God.

Here the result is wholly different. Instead of judgment and vengeance, it is universal and everlasting blessedness and glory. "I will declare Thy name unto My brethren; in the midst of the congregation will I praise Thee. Ye that fear the Lord, praise Him; all ye the seed of Jacob, glorify Him; and fear Him, all ye the seed of Israel. . . . My praise shall be of Thee in the great congregation; I will pay My vows before them that fear Him. The meek shall eat and be satisfied; they shall praise the Lord that seek Him; your heart shall live for ever. All the ends of the world shall remember and turn unto the Lord; and all the kindreds of the nations shall worship before Thee. For the kingdom is the Lord's; and He is the governor among the nations. . . . A seed shall serve Him; it shall be accounted to the Lord for a generation. They shall come, and shall declare His righteousness unto a people that shall be born, that He hath done this" (verses 22-31).

These two quotations present, with great distinctness, the two aspects of the death of Christ. He died, as a martyr, for righteousness, under the hand of man. For this, man will have to account to God. But He died, as a victim, for sin, under the hand of God. This is the foundation of all blessing to those that believe in His name. His martyr-sufferings bring down wrath and judgment upon a godless world: His atoning sufferings open up the everlasting well-springs of life and salvation to the Church, to Israel, and to the whole creation. The death of Jesus consummates the world's guilt; but secures the Church's acceptance. The world is *stained*, and the Church *purged*, by the blood of the cross.

Such is the double bearing of the first of our three great New Testament facts. Jesus has come and gone—come, because God loved the world—gone, because the world hated God. If God were to ask the question—and He will ask it—"What have you done with My Son?" What is the answer? "We hated Him, cast Him out, and crucified Him. We preferred a robber to Him."

But the Christian, the true believer, can look up to Heaven and say, "My absent Lord is there, and there for me. He is gone from this wretched world, and His absence makes the entire scene around me a moral wilderness—a desolate waste."

He is not here. This stamps the world with a character unmistakable in the judgment of every loyal heart. The world would not have Jesus. This is enough. We need not marvel at any tale of horror now. Police reports, grand jury calendars, the statistics of our cities and towns need not surprise us. The world that could reject the divine personification of all human goodness, and accept a robber and a murderer instead, has proved its moral turpitude to a degree not to be exceeded. Do we wonder when we discover the hollowness and heartlessness of the world? Are we surprised when we find out that it is not to be trusted? If so, it is plain we have not interpreted aright the absence of our beloved Lord.

What does the cross of Christ prove? That God is love? No doubt. That Christ gave His precious life to save us from the flames of an everlasting hell? Blessedly true, all praise to His peerless name! But what does the cross prove as regards the world? That its guilt is consummated, and its judgment sealed. The world, in nailing to the cross the One who was perfectly good, proved, in the most unanswerable manner, that it was perfectly bad. "If I had not come and spoken unto them, they had not had sin: but now they have no cloak for their sin. He that hateth Me hateth My Father also. If I had not done among them the works which none other man did, they had not had sin; but now have they both seen and hated both Me and My Father. But this cometh to pass, that the word might be fulfilled that is written in their law, They hated Me without a cause" (John 15:22-26).

2. We must now glance for a moment at our second weighty fact. God the Holy Ghost has come down to this earth. It is now over eighteen long centuries since the blessed Spirit descended from Heaven; and He has been here ever since. This is a stupendous fact. There is a divine Person on this earth; and His presence—like the absence of Jesus—has a double bearing: it has a bearing upon the world, and a bearing upon the Church—upon the world as a whole, and upon every man, woman and child therein; upon the Church as a whole, and upon every individual member thereof in particular. As regards the world, this august witness descended from Heaven to convict it of the terrible crime of rejecting and crucifying the Son of God. As regards the Church, He came as the blessed Comforter, to take the place of the absent Jesus, and comfort by His presence and ministry the hearts of His people. Thus, to the world, the Holy Ghost is a powerful *Convicter;* to the Church He is a precious *Comforter.*

A passage or two of holy Scripture will establish these points in the heart and mind of the pious reader who bows in lowly reverence to the authority of the divine Word. Let us turn to chapter 16 of John's Gospel. "But now I go My way to Him that sent Me; and none of you asketh Me, Whither goest Thou? But because I have said these things unto you, sorrow hath filled your heart. Nevertheless I tell you the truth; it is expedient for you that I go away: for if I go not away, the Comforter will not come unto you; but if I depart, I will send Him unto you. And when He is come, He will *convict* [ἐλέγξει] the world of sin, and of righteousness, and of judgment. Of sin, because they believe not on Me; of righteousness, because I go to My Father, and ye see Me no more; of judgment, because the prince of this world is judged" (verses 5-11).

Again in John 14 we read, "If ye love Me, keep My commandments. And I will pray the Father, and He shall give you another Comforter, that He may abide with you for ever; even the Spirit of truth; whom the world cannot receive because it seeth Him not, neither knoweth Him: but ye know Him for He dwelleth with you, and shall be in you" (verses 15-19).

These quotations prove the double bearing of the presence of the Holy Ghost. We cannot attempt to dwell upon this subject in this brief introduction; but we trust the reader may be led to study if for himself, in the light of holy Scripture; and we are persuaded that the more he thus studies it, the more deeply he will feel its interest and immense practical importance. Alas! that it should be so little understood; that Christians should so little see what is involved in the personal presence of the eternal Spirit, God the Holy Ghost, on this earth—its solemn consequences as regards the world, and its precious results as regards the assembly as a whole, and each individual member in particular.

Oh! that God's people everywhere may be led into a deeper understanding of these things; that they may consider what is due to that divine Person who dwells in them and with them; that they may have a jealous care not to "grieve" Him in their private walk, or "quench" Him in their public assemblies!

THE FACT ITSELF

In approaching this most glorious subject, we feel that we cannot do better than to lay before the reader the distinct testimony of holy Scripture to the broad fact itself, that our Lord Jesus Christ will come again—that He will leave the place which He now occupies on His Father's throne, and come in the clouds of heaven, to receive His people to Himself; to execute judgment upon the wicked; and set up His own everlasting and universal kingdom.

This fact is as clearly and fully set forth in the New Testament as either of the other two facts to which we have already referred. It is as true that the Son of God is coming from Heaven, as that He is gone to Heaven, or that the Holy Ghost is still on this earth. If we admit one fact, we must admit all: and if we deny one, we must deny all; inasmuch as all rest upon precisely the same authority. They stand or fall together. Is it true that the Son of God was refused, cast out, crucified? Is it true that He has gone away into Heaven? Is it true that He is now seated at the right hand of God, crowned with glory and honor? Is it true that God the Holy Ghost came down to this earth, fifty days after the resurrection of our Lord; and that He is still here?

Are these things true? As true as Scripture can make them. Then just as true is it that our blessed Lord will come again, and set up His kingdom upon this earth—that He will literally, and actually, and personally come from Heaven, take to Himself His great

power and reign from pole to pole, and from the river to the ends of the earth.

It may perhaps seem strange to some of our readers that we should deem it needful to undertake the proof of such a plain truth as this; but be it remembered that we are writing on this subject as though it were perfectly new to the reader; as if he had never heard of such a thing as the Lord's second coming; or as if, having heard of it, he still calls it in question. This must be our apology for handling this precious theme in so elementary a manner.

Now for our proofs.

When our adorable Lord was about to take leave of His disciples, He sought, in His infinite grace, to comfort their sorrowing hearts by words of sweetest tenderness. "Let not your heart be troubled; ye believe in God, believe also in Me. In My Father's house are many mansions; if it were not so I would have told you. I go to prepare a place for you. And if I go and prepare a place for you, *I will come again*, and receive you unto Myself; that where I am, there ye may be also" (John 14: 1-3).

Here we may have something most definite. Indeed it is as definite as it is cheering and consolatory. "I will come again." He does not say, I will send for you. Still less does He say, "You will come to me when you die." He says nothing of the kind. To send an angel, or a legion of angels, would not be the same thing as coming Himself. No doubt it would be very gracious of Him, and very glorious for us, if a multitude of the heavenly host were sent, with horses of fire and chariots of fire, to convey us triumphantly to Heaven. But it would not be the fulfilment of His own sweet promise. And most surely He will do what He promised to do. He will not say one thing and do another. He cannot lie or alter His Word. And not only this, but it would not satisfy the love of His heart to send an angel or a host of angels to fetch us. He will come Himself.

What touching grace shines in all this! If I am expecting a very dear and valued friend by train, I shall not be satisfied with sending a servant or an empty cab to meet him; I shall go myself. This is precisely what our loving

Lord means to do. He is gone to Heaven; and His entrance there prepares and defines His people's place. Amid the many mansions of the Father's house, there would be no place for us if our Jesus had not gone before; and then, lest there should be in the heart any feeling of strangeness at the thought of our entrance into that place, He says, with such sweetness, "I will come again, and receive you unto Myself, that where I am there ye may be also." Nothing short of this can fulfil the gracious promise of our Lord, or satisfy the love of His heart.

Be it carefully noted that this promise has no reference whatever to the death of the individual believer. Who can imagine that, when our Lord said, "I will come again," He really meant that we should go to Him through death? How can we presume to take such liberties with the plain and precious words of our Lord? Surely if He meant to speak of our going to Him, through death, He could and would have said so. But He has not said so, because He did not mean so; nor is it possible that He could say one thing and mean another. His coming for us, and our going to Him, are totally different things; and being different ideas, they would have been clothed in different language.

Thus, for example, in the case of the penitent thief on the cross, our Lord does not speak of coming to fetch him; but He says, "To-day shalt thou be with Me in paradise." We really must remember that Scripture is as divinely definite as it is divinely inspired, and hence it never could and it never does confound two things so totally different as the Lord's coming and the Christian's falling asleep.

It may be well, at this point, to remark that there are but four passages in the entire New Testament in which allusion is made to the subject of the Christian passing through the article of death. The first is that passage in Luke 23 already referred to: "To-day shalt thou be with Me in paradise." The second occurs in Acts 7, "Lord Jesus, receive my spirit." The third is that most familiar and lovely utterance in 2 Corinthians 5, "Absent from the body, present with the Lord." The fourth occurs in that charming first of

Philippians, "Having a desire to depart, and to be with Christ; which is far better."

These most precious passages make up the sum of Scripture testimony on the interesting question of the disembodied state. There is a passage in Revelation 14 often misapplied to this subject: "Blessed are the dead which die in the Lord *from henceforth:* Yea, saith the Spirit, that they may rest from their labors; and their works do follow them." But this has no application to Christians now, though no doubt all such who die in the Lord are blessed, and their works do follow them. The reference, however, is to a time yet future, when the Church shall have left this scene altogether, and other witnesses make their appearance. In a word, Revelation 14:13 bears upon apocalyptic times, and must be so viewed if we would avoid confusion.

We must now resume our subject, and proceed with our proofs, and in so doing we shall ask the reader to turn to the first chapter of the Acts of the Apostles. The blessed Lord had just gone up from this earth, in the presence of His holy apostles. "And while they looked steadfastly toward heaven as He went up, behold, two men stood by Him in white apparel; which also said, Ye men of Galilee, why stand ye gazing up into heaven? This same Jesus, which is taken up from you into heaven, shall so come in like manner as ye have seen Him go into heaven" (verses 10-11).

This is intensely interesting, and furnishes a most striking proof of our present thesis. Indeed it is impossible to avoid its force. Alas! that any should seek or desire to avoid it! From the manner in which the angelic witnesses speak to the men of Galilee it would seem like tautology; but, as we well know, there is—there can be—no such thing in the volume of God. It is, therefore, lovely fulness, divine completeness, that we see in this testimony. From it we learn that the self-same Jesus who left this earth, and ascended into Heaven, in the presence of a number of witnesses, shall *so come in like manner as* they had seen Him go into Heaven. How did He go? He went up personally, literally, actually, the very same person who had just been conversing familiarly with them—whom they had seen with their eyes, heard with their ears, handled with their hands—who had eaten in their presence, and "showed Himself alive after His passion by many infallible proofs." Well then, "He shall so come in like manner."

> He who with hands uplifted,
>   Went from this earth below,
> Shall come again all gifted,
>   His blessing to bestow.

Here we may ask—though it be rather anticipating what may come before us in a future paper—Who saw the blessed Lord as He went up? Did the world? Nay; not one unconverted, unbelieving person ever laid his eyes upon our precious Lord from the moment that He was laid in the tomb. The last sight the world got of Jesus was as He hung on the cross, a spectacle to angels, men, and devils. The next sight they will get of Him will be when, like the lightning flash, He shall come forth to execute judgment, and tread, in terrible vengeance, the winepress of the wrath of Almighty God. Tremendous thought!

None, therefore, but His own saw the ascending Saviour, as none but they had seen Him from the moment of His resurrection. He showed Himself, blessed be His holy name! to those who were dear to His heart. He assured and comforted, strengthened and encouraged their souls by these "many infallible proofs" of which the inspired narrator speaks to us. He led them to the very confines of the unseen world, just so far as men could go while still in the body; and there He allowed them to see Him ascending into Heaven; and while they gazed upon this glorious sight He sent the precious testimony home to their very hearts. "This same Jesus"—no other, no stranger, but the same loving, sympathizing, gracious, unchanging friend—"whom ye have seen go into heaven, shall so come in like manner as ye have seen Him go into heaven."

Is it possible for testimony to be more distinct or satisfactory? Could proof be more clear or conclusive? How can any counter argument stand for a moment, or any objection be raised? Either those two men in white apparel were false witnesses, or our

Jesus shall come again in the exact manner in which He went away. There is no middle ground between those two conclusions. We read in Scripture that, "in the mouth of two or three witnesses shall every word be established;" and therefore in the mouth of two heavenly messengers—two heralds from the region of light and truth, we have the word established that our Lord Jesus Christ shall come again in actual bodily form, to be seen by His own first of all, apart from all others, in the holy intimacy and profound retirement which characterized His departure from this world. All this, blessed be God, is wrapped up in the two little words, "*as*" and "*so*."

We cannot attempt, in a brief paper like the present, to adduce all the proofs which are to be found in the pages of the New Testament. We have given one from the Gospels and one from the Acts, and we shall now ask the reader to turn with us to the Epistles. Let us take, for example, the First Epistle to the Thessalonians. We select this Epistle because it is acknowledged to have been the earliest of Paul's writings; and further, because it was written to a company of very young converts. This latter point is valuable, inasmuch as we sometimes hear it stated that the truth of the Lord's coming is not suitable to bring before the minds of young believers. That the Apostle Paul did not think it unsuitable is evident from the fact that of all the Epistles which he wrote not one contains so much about the Lord's coming as that which he penned for the newly converted Thessalonians. The fact is, when a soul is converted and brought into the full light and liberty of the gospel of Christ, it becomes divinely natural for such a one to look for the Lord's coming. That most precious truth is an integral part of the gospel. The first coming and the second coming are most blessedly bound up together by the divine link of the personal presence of the Holy Ghost in the Church.

On the other hand, where the soul is not established in grace; where peace and liberty are not enjoyed; where a defective gospel has been received, there it will be found that the hope of the Lord's coming will not be cherished, for the simple reason that the soul is, of necessity, occupied with the question of its own state and prospects. If I am not certain of my salvation—if I do not know that I have eternal life—that I am a child of God—I cannot be looking out for the Lord's return. It is only when we know what Jesus has done for us at His first coming that we can with bright and holy intelligence look out for His second coming.

But let us turn to our Epistle. Take the following sentences from the first chapter: "For our gospel came not unto you in word only, but also in power, and in the Holy Ghost, and in much assurance. . . . So that ye were ensamples to all that believe in Macedonia and Achaia. For from you sounded out the word of the Lord, not only in Macedonia and Achaia, but also in every place your faith to God-ward is spread abroad; so that we need not to speak anything. For they themselves show of us what manner of entering in we had unto you, and how ye turned to God from idols to serve the living and true God; and *to wait for His Son from Heaven*, whom He raised from the dead, even Jesus, which delivered us from the wrath to come" (1 Thess. 1: 5-10).

Here we have a fine illustration of the effect of a full clear gospel, received in simple earnest faith. They turned from idols, to serve the living and true God, and to wait for His Son. They were actually converted to the blessed hope of the Lord's coming. It was an integral part of the gospel which Paul preached; and an integral part of their faith. Was it a reality to turn from idols? Doubtless. Was it a reality to serve the living God? Unquestionably. Well then it was just as real, just as positive, just as simple, their waiting for God's Son from Heaven. If we question the reality of one, we must question the reality of all, inasmuch as all are bound up together and form a beauteous cluster of practical Christian truth.

If you had asked a Thessalonian Christian what he was waiting for, what would have been his reply? Would he have said, "I am waiting for the world to improve by means of the gospel which I myself have received? or, I am waiting for the moment of my death when I shall go to be with Jesus?" No. His reply would have been simply this, "I am waiting for the Son of God from heaven." This, and nothing else, is the proper hope of the Christian, the proper hope of the Church. To wait for the improvement of the world is not Christian hope at all. You might as well wait for the improvement of the flesh, for there is just as much hope of the one as the other.

As to the article of death—though no doubt it may intervene—it is never once presented as the true and proper hope of the Christian. It may, with the fullest confidence, be asserted that there is not so much as a single passage in the entire New Testament in which death is spoken of as the hope of the believer; whereas, on the other hand, the hope of the Lord's coming is bound up, in the most intimate manner, with all the concerns and associations and relationships of life, as we may see in the Epistle before us. Thus, if the apostle would refer to the interesting question of his own personal connection with the beloved saints at Thessalonica, he says, "For what is our hope, or joy, or crown of rejoicing? Are not even ye in the presence of our Lord Jesus Christ at His coming? For ye are our glory and joy."

Again, if he thinks of their progress in holiness and love, he adds, "And the Lord make you to increase and abound in love one toward another, and toward all men, even as we do toward you; to the end He may stablish your hearts unblamable in holiness before God, even our Father, *at the coming of our Lord Jesus Christ* with all His saints" (1 Thess. 3:12-13).

Finally, if the apostle would seek to comfort the hearts of his brethren in reference to those who had fallen asleep, how does he do it? Does he tell them that they should soon follow them? Nay; this would have been in full keeping with Old Testament times, as David says of his departed child, "I shall go to him, but he shall not return to me" (2 Sam. 12:23). But it is not thus that the Holy Ghost instructs us in 1 Thessalonians— quite the reverse. "I would not," he says, "have you to be ignorant, brethren, concerning them which are asleep, that ye sorrow not, even as others which have no hope. For if we believe that Jesus died and rose again, even so them also which sleep in Jesus will God bring with Him. For this we say unto you by the word of the Lord, that [not they which shall be, but] *we* which *are* alive and remain unto the coming of the Lord shall not prevent [come before or take precedence of] them which are asleep. For the Lord Himself shall descend from heaven with a shout, with the voice of the archangel, and with the trump of God: and the dead in Christ shall rise first. Then *we* which are alive and remain shall be caught up together with them in clouds, to meet the Lord in the air; and so shall we ever be with the Lord. Wherefore comfort one another with these words" (1 Thess. 4:13-18).

It is impossible for any proof to be more simple, direct, and conclusive than this. The Thessalonian Christians, as we have already remarked, were converted to the hope of the Lord's return. They were taught to look out for it daily. It was as much a part of their Christianity to believe that He *would* come, as to believe that He *had* come and gone. Hence it came to pass that when some of their number were called to pass through death, they were taken aback; they had not anticipated this; and they feared lest the departed should miss the joy of that blissful and longed-for moment of the Lord's return. The apostle therefore writes to correct their mistake; and, in so doing, he pours a fresh flood of light upon the whole subject, and assures them that the dead in Christ—which includes all who had or shall have fallen asleep; in short, those of Old Testament times as well as those of the New—should rise first, that is, before the living are changed, and all shall ascend together to meet their descending Lord.

We shall have occasion to refer to this remarkable passage again, when handling other branches of this glorious subject. We merely quote it here as one of the almost innumerable proofs of the fact that our Lord will come again, personally, really, and actually; and that His personal coming is the true and proper hope of the Church of God collectively, and of the believer individually.

We shall close this paper by reminding the Christian reader that he can never sit down to the table of his Lord without being reminded of this glorious hope, so long as those words shine on the page of inspiration, "For as often as ye eat this bread, and drink this cup, ye do show the Lord's death till"—when? Till ye die? Nay; but—*'till He come"* (1 Cor. 11:26). How precious is this! The table of the Lord stands between those two marvelous epochs, the cross and the advent—the death and the glory. The believer can look up from the table and see the beams of the glory gilding the horizon. It is our privilege, as we gather, on each Lord's day, round the Lord's table, to show forth the Lord's death, to be able to say, "This may be the last occasion of celebrating this precious feast; ere another Lord's day dawn upon us, He Himself may come." Again we say, How precious is this!

THE DOUBLE BEARING OF THE FACT

Having, as we trust, fully established the fact of the Lord's coming, we have now to place before the reader the double bearing of that fact—its bearing upon the Lord's people, and its bearing upon the world. The former is presented, in the New Testament, as the coming of Christ to receive His people to Himself; the latter is spoken of as "the day of the Lord"—a term of frequent use also in Old Testament Scriptures.

These things are never confounded in Scripture, as we shall see when we come to look at the various passages. Christians do confound them, and hence it is that we often find "that blessed hope" overcast with heavy clouds, and associated in the mind with circumstances of terror, wrath, and judgment, which have nothing whatever to do with the *coming* of Christ for His people, but are intimately bound up with "the *day* of the Lord."

Let the Christian reader, then, have it settled in his heart, on the clear authority of holy Scripture, that the grand and specific hope for him ever to cherish is the coming of Christ for His people. This hope may be realized this very night. There is nothing whatever to wait for—no events to transpire amongst the nations—nothing to occur in the history of Israel—nothing in God's government of the world—nothing, in short, in any shape or form whatsoever, to intervene between the heart of the true believer and his heavenly hope. Christ may come for His people to-night. There is actually nothing to hinder. No one can tell when He *will* come; but we can joyfully say that, at any moment, He *may* come. And, blessed be His name, when He does come for us, it will not be with the accompanying circumstances of terror, wrath, and judgment. It will not be with blackness and darkness and tempest. These things will accompany "the day of the Lord," as the Apostle Peter plainly tells the Jews in his first great sermon, on the day of Pentecost, in which he quotes the following words from the solemn prophecy of Joel, "And I will show wonders in heaven above, and signs in the earth beneath: blood and fire and vapor of smoke: the sun shall be turned into darkness, and the moon into blood, before"—what? the coming of the Lord for His people? Nay; but before *"that great and notable day of the Lord* come."

When our Lord shall come to receive His people to Himself no eye shall see Him, no ear shall hear His voice, save His own redeemed and beloved people. Let us remember the words of the angelic witnesses in the first of Acts. Who saw the blessed One ascending into the heavens? None but His own. Well, "He shall so come in like manner as ye have seen Him go into heaven." *As* was the going, *so* shall be the coming, if we are to bow to Scripture. To confound the day of the Lord with His coming for His Church is to overlook the plainest teachings of Scripture, and to rob the believer of his own true and proper hope.

Here perhaps we cannot do better than to call attention to a very important and interesting passage in the Second Epistle of Peter: "For we have not followed cunningly devised fables when we made known unto you the power and coming of our Lord Jesus Christ, but were eye-witnesses of His majesty. For He received from God the Father honor and glory, when there came such a voice to Him from the excellent glory, This is My beloved Son, in whom I am well pleased. And this voice which came from heaven we heard when we were with Him in the holy mount. We have also the word of prophecy more sure [or confirmed], whereunto ye do well that ye take heed, as unto a light that shineth in a dark place, until the day dawn, and the day-star arise in your hearts" (chap. 1:16-19).

This passage demands the reader's most attentive consideration. It sets forth, in the clearest possible manner, the distinction between "the word of prophecy" and the proper hope of the Christian, namely, "the morning star." We must remember that the great subject of prophecy is God's government of the world in connection with the seed of Abraham. "When the Most High divided to the nations their inheritance, when He separated the sons of Adam, He set the bounds of the people according to the number of children of Israel. For the Lord's portion is His people; Jacob is the lot of His inheritance" (Deut. 32:8-9).

Here then is the scope and theme of prophecy—Israel and the nations. A child can understand this. If we range through the prophets, from the opening of Isaiah to the close of Malachi, we shall not find so much as a single line about the Church of God—its position, its portion, or its prospects. No doubt the word of prophecy is deeply interesting, and most profitable for the Christian to study; but it will be all this just in proportion as he understands its proper scope and object, and sees how it stands in contrast with his own special hope. We may fearlessly assert that it is as utterly impossible for any one to study the Old Testament prophecies aright who does not clearly see the true place of the Church.

We cannot attempt to enter upon the subject of the Church in this brief paper. It has been repeatedly referred to and unfolded elsewhere, and we can now merely ask the reader to weigh and examine the statement which we here deliberately make, namely, that there is not so much as a single syllable about the Church of God, the body of Christ, from cover to cover of the Old Testament. Types, shadows, illustrations, there are, which, now that we have the full-orbed light of the New Testament, we can see, understand, and appreciate. But it was not possible for any Old Testament believer to see the great mystery of Christ and the Church, inasmuch as it was not revealed. The inspired apostle expressly tells us that it was "*hid*," not in the Old Testament Scriptures, but "in God," as we read in Ephesians 3, "And to make all men see what is the fellowship [or rather the administration] of the mystery, which from the beginning of the world hath been *hid in God*, who created all things by Jesus Christ" (verse 9). So also in Colossians we read, "Even the mystery which *hath been hid* from ages and from generations, but now is made manifest to His saints" (chap. 1:26).

These two passages establish the truth of our statement beyond all question, for those who are willing to be governed absolutely by the authority of holy Scripture; they teach us that the great mystery—Christ and the Church—is not to be found in the Old Testament. Where have we in the Old Testament a word about Jews and Gentiles forming one body, and being united by the Holy Ghost to a living Head in Heaven? How could such a thing possibly be, so long as "the middle wall of partition" stood as an insuperable barrier between the circumcised and the uncircumcised? If one were asked to name a special feature of the old economy he would at once reply, "The rigid separation of Jew and Gentile." On the other hand, if he were asked to name a special feature of the Church, or Christianity, he would as readily reply, "The intimate union of Jew and Gentile in one body." In short, the two conditions stand in vivid contrast, and it was wholly impossible that both could hold good at the same time. So long as the middle wall of partition stood, the truth of the Church could not be revealed; but the death of Christ having thrown down that wall, the Holy Ghost descended from Heaven to form the one body, and link it, by His presence and indwelling, to the risen and glorified Head in

the heavens. Such is the great mystery of Christ and the Church, for which there could be no less a basis than accomplished redemption.

Now we entreat the reader to examine this matter for himself. Let him search the Scriptures to see if these things be indeed true. This is the only way to get at the truth. We must lay aside all our own thoughts and reasonings, our prejudices and predilections, and come like a little child, to the holy Scriptures. In this way we shall learn the mind of God on this most precious and interesting subject. We shall find that the Church of God, the body of Christ, did not exist, as a fact, until after the resurrection and ascension of Christ, and the consequent descent of the Holy Ghost on the day of Pentecost. And further, we shall find that the full and glorious doctrine of the Church was not brought out until the days of the apostle Paul (compare Rom. 16:25-26; Eph. 1—3; Col. 1:25-29). Finally, we shall see that the actual and unmistakable boundary lines of the Church's earthly history are Pentecost (Acts 2) and the rapture or taking up of the saints (1 Thess. 4:13-17).

Thus we reach a position from which we can get a view of the Church's proper hope; and that hope is, most assuredly, "the bright and morning star." Of this hope the Old Testament prophets utter not a syllable. They speak largely and clearly of "the day of the Lord"—a day of judgment upon the world and its ways (see Isaiah 2:12-22 and parallel Scriptures). But "the day of the Lord," with all its attendant circumstances of wrath, judgment, and terror, must never be confounded with His coming for His people. When our blessed Lord comes *for* His people there will be nothing to terrify. He will come in all the sweetness and tenderness of His love to receive His loved and redeemed people to Himself. He will come to finish up the precious story of His grace. "To them that look for Him shall He appear [ὀφθήσεται] the second time, without [that is, apart from all question of] sin, unto salvation" (Heb. 9).* He will come as a bridegroom to receive the

---

* The clause, "them that look for Him," refers to all believers. It does not mean, as some suppose, those only who hold the truth of the Lord's second coming. This would make our place with Christ at His coming dependent upon knowledge, instead of upon our union with Him by the presence and power of the Holy Ghost. The Spirit of God, in the above passage, most graciously takes for

bride; and when He thus comes none but His own shall hear His voice or see His face. If He were to come this very night for His people—and He may, for aught we know—if the voice of the archangel and the trump of God were to be heard to-night, then all the dead in Christ—all who have been laid to sleep by Jesus—all the saints of God, both those of Old Testament and New Testament times, who lie sleeping in our cemeteries and graveyards, or in the ocean's depths—all these would rise from their temporary sleep. All the living saints would be changed in a moment, and all would be caught up to meet their descending Lord, and return with Him to the Father's house (John 14:3; 1 Thess. 4:16-17; 1 Cor. 15:51-52).

This is what is meant by the rapture or catching up of the saints, and has nothing to do directly with Israel or the nations. It is the distinct and only proper hope of the Church; and there is not so much as a single hint of it in the entire Old Testament. If any one asserts that there is, let him produce it. If there be such a thing, nothing is easier than to furnish it. We solemnly and deliberately declare there is no such thing. For all that respects the Church—its standing, its calling, its portion, its prospects—we must turn to the pages of the New Testament, and, of those pages, mainly the Epistles of Paul. To confound "the word of prophecy" with the hope of the Church is to damage the truth of God, and mislead the souls of His people. That the enemy has succeeded in doing all this, throughout the length and breadth of the professing Church is, alas! too true. And hence it is that so very few Christians have really Scriptural thoughts about the coming of their Lord. They are looking into prophecy for the Church's hope—they confound "the Sun of righteousness" with "the morning star"—they mix up the coming of Christ *for* His people, and His coming *with* them—they make His "coming" or "state of presence" to be identical with His "appearing" or "manifestation."

All this is a most serious mistake, against which we desire to warn our readers. When Christ comes with His people, "every eye shall see Him." When He is manifested, His people will be manifested also. "When Christ our life shall appear [or be manifested], then shall ye also appear with Him in glory" (Col. 3:4). When Christ comes to execute judgment, His saints come with Him. "Behold, the Lord cometh *with* ten thousand of His saints, to execute judgment upon all" (Jude 14-15). So also in Revelation 19, the rider on the white horse is followed by the armies in Heaven upon white horses, clothed in fine linen, white and clean. These armies are not angels, but saints; for we do not read of angels being clothed in white linen, which is expressly declared, in this very chapter, to be "the righteousness of saints" (verse 8).

Now, it is most evident that, if the saints accompany their Lord when He comes in judgment, they must be with Him previously. The fact of their going to Him is not presented in the book of Revelation, unless it be involved—as we doubt not it is—in the catching up of the man child, in chapter 12. The man child is, most surely, Christ; and inasmuch as Christ and His people are indissolubly joined in one, they are most completely identified with Him, blessed for ever be His holy and precious name!

But, clearly, it does not at all lie within the scope of the book of Revelation to give us the coming of Christ *for* His people, or their being caught up to meet Him in the air, or their return to the Father's house. For these blessed events or facts, we must look elsewhere, as, for example, in John 14:3; 1 Corinthians 15:23, 51-52; 1 Thessalonians 4:14-17. Let the reader ponder these three passages. Let him drink into his very soul their clear and precious teaching. There is nothing difficult about them, no obscurity, no mist or vagueness whatever. A babe in Christ can understand them. They set forth in the clearest and simplest possible manner, the true Christian hope, which—we repeat it emphatically, and urge it upon the reader as the direct and positive teaching of holy

granted that all God's people are looking, in some way or another, for the precious Saviour; and verily so they are. They may not see eye to eye as to all the details. They may not all enjoy equal clearness of view or depth and fulness of apprehension; but, most surely, they would all be glad at any moment to see the One who loved them and gave Himself for them.

Scripture—is the coming of Christ to receive His people, all His people, to Himself, to take them back with Him to His Father's house, there to remain with Him, while God deals governmentally with Israel and the nations, and prepares the way, by His judicial actings, for bringing in the First-begotten into the world.

Now, if it be asked, "Why have we not the coming of Christ for His people in the book of Revelation?" Because that book is pre-eminently a book of judgment—a governmental, judicial book, at least chapter 1 to 20. Hence even the Church is presented as under judgment. We do not see the Church in chapters 2 and 3 as the body or the bride of Christ; but as a responsible witness on the earth, whose condition is being carefully examined and rigidly judged by Him who walks amongst the candlesticks.

It would not, therefore, comport with the character or object of this book to introduce, directly, the rapture of the saints. It shows us the Church on the earth, in the place of responsibility. This it gives us, in chapters 2 and 3, under the head of "the things that are." But from that to chapter 19, there is not a single syllable about the Church on earth. The plain fact is, the Church will not be on earth during that solemn period. She will be with her Head and Lord, in the divine retirement of the Father's house. The redeemed are seen in Heaven, under the title of the twenty-four crowned elders, in chapters 4—5. There, blessed be God, they will be, while the seals are being opened, the trumpets sounded, and the vials poured out. To think of the Church as being on the earth, from Revelation 6 to 18—to place her amid the apocalyptic judgments—to pass her through "the great tribulation"—to subject her to "the hour of temptation which shall come upon all the world, to try them that dwell upon the earth"—would be to falsify her position, to rob her of her chartered privileges, and to contradict the clear and positive promise of her Lord."*

No, beloved Christian reader; let no man deceive you, by any means. The Church is seen on earth in Revelation 2—3. She is seen in Heaven, together with the Old Testament saints, in chapters 4—5. We are not told, in the Revelation, how she gets there; but we see her there, in high communion and holy worship; and then, in chapter 19, the rider on the white horse comes forth, *with* His saints, to execute judgment upon the beast and the false prophet—to put down every enemy and every evil, and to reign over the whole earth for the blissful period of a thousand years.

Such is the plain teaching of the New Testament, to which we earnestly invite the attention of our readers. And let no one suppose that our object is to find an easy path for Christians in thus teaching, as we do most emphatically, that the Church will not be in "the great tribulation"—will not come into "the hour of temptation." Nothing of the kind. The fact is, the true and normal condition of the Church, and therefore of the individual Christian, in this world, is tribulation. So says our Lord: "In the world ye shall have tribulation." And again, "We glory in tribulation."

It cannot, therefore, be a question of avoiding that which is our appointed portion in this world, if only we are true to Christ. But the fact is, that the entire truth of the Church's position and prospect is involved in this question, and this is our reason for urging it so upon the prayerful attention of our readers.

The great object of the enemy is to drag down the Church of God to an earthly level—to set Christians entirely astray as to their divinely appointed hope—to lead them to confound things which God has made to differ, to occupy them with earthly things—to cause them to so mix up the *coming* of Christ for His people with His *appearing* in judgment upon the world, that they may not be able to cultivate those bridal affections and heavenly aspirations which become them as members of the body of Christ. He would fain have them looking out for various earthly events to come between them and their own proper hope, in order that they may not be—as God would have them—ever

---

* We shall have occasion, in a future paper, to show that, after the Church has been removed to Heaven, the Spirit of God will act both among the Jews, and also among the Gentiles. See Revelation 7.

on the very tip-toe of expectation, looking out, with ardent desire, for the appearing of "the bright and morning Star."

Well doth the enemy know what he is about; and surely we ought not to be ignorant of his devices, but rather give ourselves to the study of the Word of God, and thus learn, as we most surely shall, "the double bearing" of the glorious fact of the Lord's coming.

"THE COMING" AND "THE DAY"

We must now ask the reader to turn with us for a little to the two Epistles to the Thessalonians. As we have already remarked, these Christians were converted to the blessed hope of the Lord's return. They were taught to look for Him day by day. It was not merely the doctrine of the advent received and held in the mind, but a divine Person constantly expected by hearts that had learnt to love Him and long for His coming.

But, as we can easily imagine, the Thessalonian Christians were ignorant of many things connected with this blessed hope. The apostle had been "*taken* from them for a short time, in presence, not in heart." He had not been allowed to remain long enough amongst them to instruct them in the details of the subject of their hope. They knew that Jesus was to return—that self-same blessed One who had graciously delivered them from the wrath to come. But as to any distinction between His coming *for* His people and coming *with* them—between His "state of presence" and His "appearing" —His "coming" and His "day," they were, at first, wholly ignorant.

Hence, as might be expected, they fell into various errors and mistakes. It is wonderful how speedily the human mind wanders away into the wildest and grossest confusion and error. We need to be guarded on all sides by the pure, solid, all-adjusting truth of God. We must have our souls evenly balanced by divine revelation, else we are sure to plunge into all manner of false and foolish notions. Thus some of the Thessalonians conceived the idea of giving up their honest callings. They ceased to labor with their hands, and went about idle.

This was a great mistake. Even though we were perfectly certain that our Lord would come this very night, it would be no reason why we should not, most diligently and faithfully, attend to our daily round of duty, and do all that devolved upon us in that particular sphere in which His good hand has placed us. So far from this, the very fact of expecting the blessed Master would strengthen our desire to have everything done as it ought to be up to the very moment of His return, so that not so much as a single righteous claim should be left neglected. In point of fact, the hope of the Lord's speedy return, when held in power in the soul, is most sanctifying, purifying, and adjusting in its influence upon Christian life, conduct, and character. We know, alas! that even this most glorious truth may be held in the region of the understanding, and flippantly professed with the lips, while the heart and the life, the course, conduct, and character, remain wholly unaffected by it. But we are expressly taught by the inspired Apostle John, that "every man that hath this hope in him purifieth himself, even as He is pure" (1 John 3:3). And, most surely, this "purifying" embraces all that which goes to make up our whole practical life, from day to day.

But there was another grave mistake into which those dear Thessalonians fell, and out of which the blessed apostle, like a true and faithful pastor, sought to recover them. They imagined that their departed Christian friends would not have part in the joy of the Lord's return. They feared that they would fail to participate in that blissful and longed-for moment.

Now while it is quite true that this very mistake proves how vividly these Christians realized their blessed hope, still it was a mistake, and needed to be corrected. But let us carefully note the correction: "I would not have you to be ignorant, brethren, concerning them which are asleep, that ye sorrow not, even as others which have no hope. For if we believe that Jesus died and rose again, even so them also which sleep in Jesus [or are laid to sleep by Jesus] will God bring with Him."

Mark this. He does not seek to comfort

these sorrowing friends by the assurance that they should, ere long, follow the departed. Quite the reverse. He assures them that Jesus would bring the departed back with Him. This is plain and distinct, and founded upon the great fact that "Jesus died for us and rose again."

But the apostle does not stop here, but goes on to pour a flood of fresh light upon the understanding of His dear children in the faith. "For this we say unto you by the word of the Lord, that we which are alive and remain unto the coming of the Lord, shall not prevent [or precede] them which are asleep. For the Lord Himself shall descend from heaven with a shout, with the voice of the archangel, and with the trump of God: and the dead in Christ shall rise first [that is, before the living are changed]. Then we which are alive and remain shall be caught up together with them in [the] clouds, to meet the Lord in the air: and so shall we ever be with the Lord. Wherefore comfort one another with these words."

Here, then, we have presented to us what is commonly spoken of amongst us as the rapture of the saints—a most glorious, soul-stirring, and enrapturing theme surely —the brightest hope of the Church of God, and of the individual believer. The Lord *Himself* shall descend from Heaven with a summons designed only for the ears and the hearts of His own. Not one uncircumcised ear shall hear—not one unrenewed heart be moved by, that heavenly voice, that divine trumpet call. The dead in Christ, including, as we believe, the Old Testament saints, as well as those of the New, who shall have departed in the faith of Christ—all those shall hear the blessed sound, and come forth from their sleeping places. All the living saints shall hear it, and be changed in a moment. And oh! what a change! The poor crumbling tabernacle of clay exchanged for a glorified body, like unto the body of Jesus.

Look at yonder bent and withered frame— that body racked with pain, and worn out with years of acute suffering. It is the body of a saint. How humiliating to see it like that! Yes; but wait a little. Let but the trumpet sound, and in one moment that poor crushed and withered frame shall be changed, and make like to the glorified body of the descending Lord.

And there, in yonder lunatic asylum, is a poor lunatic. He has been there for years. He is a saint of God. How mysterious! True; we cannot fathom the mystery; it lies beyond our present narrow range. But so it is; that poor lunatic is a saint of God, an heir of glory. He too shall hear the voice of the archangel and the trump of God, and leave his lunacy behind him for ever, while he mounts into the heavens, in his glorified body, to meet his descending Lord.

Oh! what a brilliant moment! How many sick chambers and beds of languishing shall be vacant then! What marvelous changes shall then take place! How the heart bounds at the thought, and longs to sing, in full chorus, that lovely hymn,

Christ, the Lord, will come again,
None shall wait for Him in vain:
I shall then His glory see;
Christ will come and call for me.

Then, when the archangel's voice
Calls the sleeping saints to rise,
Rising millions shall proclaim
Blessings on the Saviour's name.

This is our redeeming God!
Ransomed hosts will shout aloud:
Praise, eternal praise, be given
To the Lord of earth and Heaven!

Amen and amen!

How glorious the thought of those "rising millions"! How truly delightful to be amongst them! How precious the hope of seeing that blessed One who loveth us and who gave Himself for us! Such is the hope of the Christian, a hope concerning which there is not a single line from cover to cover of the Old Testament. "The word of prophecy" is of all importance. We do well to take heed to it. It is an unspeakable mercy for those who find themselves in a dark place to have a bright lamp to cast its light athwart the gloom. But let the Christian bear in mind that what he wants is to have "the day star arising in his heart"; in other words, to have his whole heart governed by the hope of seeing Jesus as the bright and morning Star. When the heart is thus filled and ruled by the proper Christian hope, then the eye can intelligently scan the prophetic chart: it can take in the whole field of prophecy as our God has graciously opened it before us, and find interest and profit in every page and in every line. But, on the other hand, we may rest assured that the man who looks into prophecy in order to find the Church or its hope there has his face turned the wrong way. He will find "the Jew" there, and "Gentile" there, but not "the church of God." We earnestly trust that not one of our readers will fail to lay hold of this fact—a fact, we may safely say, of the very deepest moment.

But it will perhaps be asked, "Of what use, then, is prophecy? If indeed it be true that we cannot find aught about the Church on the prophetic page, of what possible use can it be to Christians? Why should we be told to take heed to it if it does not immediately concern us?" We reply, Is nothing of any value to us save what immediately concerns ourselves? Shall we take no interest in anything unless we ourselves form the immediate subject thereof? Is it nothing to us to have the counsels and purposes and plans of God laid open before us? Do we lightly esteem the high favor of having the thoughts of God communicated to us in His holy Word of prophecy? Surely it was not thus that Abraham treated the divine communications made to him in Genesis 18: "Shall I hide from Abraham that thing which I do?" And what was that thing? Did it immediately concern Abraham? Not at all. It concerned Sodom and the neighboring cities, and Abraham had no stake in them. But did that prevent his interest in the divine communication? Did it hinder his appreciation of the mark of special favor in his being made the honored and trusted depository of the thoughts of God? Surely not. We may safely assert that the faithful patriarch highly esteemed the privilege conferred upon him.

And so should we. We should study prophecy with all the interest arising from the fact that therein we have unfolded to us, with divine precision, what God is about to do on this earth with Israel and with the nations. Prophecy is God's history of the future; and just in proportion as we love Him shall we delight to study His history; not indeed, as some have said, that we may know its truth by its fulfilment, but that we may possess all that absolute, that divine certainty as to the future which God's Word is capable of imparting. Nothing can be more absurd, in the judgment of faith, than to suppose that we must wait until the accomplishment of a prophecy to know that it is true. What an insult offered—unwittingly, no doubt—to the peerless revelation of our God.

But we must now turn, for a moment, to the solemn subject of "the day of the Lord." This is a term of frequent occurrence in Old Testament Scriptures. We cannot attempt to quote all the passages; but we shall refer to one or two, and then the reader can follow up the subject for himself.

In Isaiah 2 we read, "For the day of the Lord of hosts shall be upon every one that is proud and lofty, and upon every one that is lifted up, and he shall be brought low. . . . And the loftiness of man shall be bowed down, and the haughtiness of men shall be made low: and the Lord alone shall be exalted *in that day*. And the idols he shall utterly abolish. And they shall go into the holes of the rocks, and into the caves of the earth, for fear of the Lord, and for the glory of His majesty, when He ariseth to shake terribly the earth."

So also in Joel 2. "Blow ye the trumpet in Zion, and sound an alarm in My holy mountain: let all the inhabitants of the land tremble; for the day of the Lord cometh, for it is nigh at hand. A day of darkness and of gloominess, a day of clouds and of thick darkness, as the morning spread upon the mountains; a great people and a strong; there has not been ever the like, neither shall be any more after it, even to the years of many generations . . . the earth shall quake before them; the heavens shall tremble; the sun and the moon shall be dark, and the stars shall withdraw their shining . . . for the day of the Lord is great and very terrible; and who can abide it?"

From these and similar passages, we learn

that "the day of the Lord" stands associated with the deeply solemn thought of judgment upon the world—upon apostate Israel—upon man and his ways—upon all that which the human heart prizes and longs after. In short, the day of the Lord stands in striking contrast with man's day. Man has the upper hand now, the Lord will have the upper hand then.

Now, while it is perfectly true that all the Lord's people can rejoice in the prospect of that day, which, though it will open in judgment upon the world, shall, nevertheless, be marked by the universal reign of righteousness; yet we must remember that the peculiar hope of the Christian is not the day with its awful accompaniments of judgment, wrath, and terror; but the coming or presence of Jesus, with its precious accompaniments of peace and joy, love and glory. The Church shall have met her Lord, and returned with Him to the Father's house, before that terrible day bursts upon the world. It will be her blissful portion to taste the ineffable communion of that heavenly home, for an indefinite period previous to the opening of the day of the Lord. Her eyes shall be gladdened by the sight of "the bright and morning Star," long before even "the Sun of righteousness" shall arise, in healing virtue, upon the pious portion of the nation of Israel—the God-fearing remnant of the seed of Abraham.

We are intensely anxious that the Christain reader should thoroughly enter into this grand and important distinction. We feel persuaded that it will have an immense effect upon all his thoughts and views and hopes of the future. It will enable him to see, without a single intervening cloud, his true prospect as a Christian. It will deliver him from all mist, vagueness, and confusion; and further, it will divest his mind of all that feeling of dread with which so many even of the Lord's dear people contemplate the future. It will teach him to look for the Saviour—the blessed Bridegroom—the everlasting Lover of his soul, and not for judgments and terror, eclipses and earthquakes, convulsions and revolutions, it will keep his spirit tranquil and happy, in the sure and certain hope of

being with Jesus, ere that great and terrible day of the Lord come.

See how the faithful apostle labored to lead his dear Thessalonian converts into the clear understanding of the difference of "the coming" and "the day."

"But of the times and seasons, brethren, ye have no need that I write unto you. For yourselves know perfectly that the day of the Lord so cometh as a thief in the night. For when *they* [not ye] shall say, Peace and safety; then sudden destruction cometh upon them, as travail upon a woman with child; and they shall not escape. But ye, brethren, are not in darkness, that that day should overtake you as a thief. Ye are all the children of light, and the children of the day; we are not of the night, nor of darkness"— The Lord be praised!—"Therefore let us not sleep, as do others; but let us watch and be sober. For they that sleep, sleep in the night; and they that are drunken, are drunken in the night. But let us, who are of the day, be sober, putting on the breastplate of faith and love, and for an helmet, the hope of salvation. For God hath not appointed us to wrath, but to obtain salvation by our Lord Jesus Christ, who died for us, that, whether we wake or sleep [that is, are dead or alive] we should live together with Him. Wherefore comfort yourselves together and edify one another, even as also ye do" (1 Thessalonians 5:1-11).

Here we have the distinction set forth with unmistakable clearness. The Lord Himself shall come for us as the Bridegroom. The day of the Lord shall come upon the world as a thief. Is it possible for contrast to be more striking? How can any one confound these two things? They are as distinct as any two things can be. A bridegroom and a thief are surely two different things; and just as different are the coming of the Lord for His waiting people and the coming of His day upon a slumbering or intoxicated world.

Some perhaps may find a difficulty in the fact that the church in Sardis is addressed in such solemn words as these, "If therefore thou shalt not watch, I will come on thee as a thief, and thou shalt not know what hour I will come upon thee" (Rev. 3:3). The difficulty will vanish when we reflect that, in the case of Sardis, the professing body is looked upon as having a mere name to live while dead. It has sunk to the level of the world, and can only see things from the world's standpoint. The church has failed utterly; it has fallen from its high and holy position; it is under judgment; it cannot therefore be cheered by the Church's proper hope; but is threatened by the world's terrible doom. We do not see the church here as the body or bride of Christ, but as the responsible witness for God on the earth— the golden candlestick which ought to have held forth the divine light of testimony in this dark world, in the absence of her Lord. But alas! the professing Church has sunk lower and become darker than even the world itself. Hence the solemn threatening. The exception confirms the rule.

We shall proceed with this subject as presented in 2 Thessalonians.

It is a fact full of the richest comfort and consolation to the heart of a true believer, that our God, in His marvelous grace, ever makes the eater to yield meat, and the strong, sweetness. He brings light out of darkness, life out of death, and causes the bright beams of His glory to shine amid the most disastrous ruin caused by the enemy's hand. The truth of this is illustrated on every page of the inspired volume, and it should fill our hearts with peace and our mouths with praise.

Hence it is that the varied doctrinal errors and practical evils, into which the early Christians were permitted to fall, have been overruled of God, and used for the instruction, guidance, and solid profit of the Church to the close of her earthly history.

Thus, for example, the error of the Thessalonian Christians in reference to their departed brethren was made the occasion of pouring such a flood of divine light upon the Lord's coming, and upon the rapture of the saints, that it is impossible for any simple mind that bows to Scripture ever to fall into a similar mistake. They looked for the Lord to come, and in that they were right. They expected Him to set up His kingdom on the earth, and in that they were right, as to the broad fact.

But they made a great mistake in leaving out the heavenly side of this glorious hope. Their intelligence was defective—their faith lacking. They did not see the two parts—the double bearing of the advent of Christ—His descent into the air to receive His people to Himself, and His appearing in glory to set up His kingdom in manifested power. Hence they feared that their departed brethren would necessarily be absent from the sphere of blessing—the circle of glory. This mistake is divinely corrected, as we have seen, in the First Epistle, chapter 4. The heavenly side of the hope—the Christian's proper portion—is placed before the heart as the true corrective for the error in reference to the sleeping saints. Christ will gather all (and not merely part of) His people to Himself; and if there is to be any advantage—a shade of difference in the matter—it will be on the side of those very people about whom they were mourning. "The dead in Christ shall rise first."

But from the Second Epistle to the Thessalonians we learn that those dear young converts had been led into another grave error—an error, not as to the dead, but as to the living—a mistake, not respecting "the coming," but respecting "the day of the Lord." In the one case they feared that the dead would not participate in the blissful triumph of "the coming"; and in the other case they feared that the living were actually, at the very moment, involved in the terrors of the day.

Such is the mistake with which the inspired apostle deals in his second letter to the Thessalonian believers; and nothing can exceed the tenderness and delicacy, and yet withal the wisdom and faithfulness of his dealing.

The Christians at Thessalonica were passing through intense persecution and tribulation; and it is very evident that the enemy, by means of false teachers, sought to upset their minds, by leading them to think that "the great and terrible day of the Lord" had actually arrived, and that the troubles through which they were passing were the accompaniments of that day. If this were so the entire teaching of the apostle was proved false; for if there was one truth that shone forth more brightly and prominently in his teaching than another, it was the association and identification of believers with Christ— an association so intimate, an identification so close, that it was impossible for Christ to appear in glory without His people. "When Christ, who is our life, shall appear, then shall ye also appear with Him in glory." But He must appear in order to introduce "the day."

Furthermore, when the day of the Lord does actually arrive it will not be to trouble His people, but, on the contrary, to trouble their persecutors. Of this the apostle reminds them, in the most simple, forcible manner, in his very opening lines: "We are bound to thank God always for you, brethren, as it is meet, because that your faith groweth exceedingly, and the charity of every one of you all toward each other aboundeth, so that we ourselves glory in you in the churches of God for your patience and faith in all your persecutions and tribulations that ye endure; which is a manifest token of the righteous judgment of God, that ye may be counted worthy of the kingdom of God, for which ye also suffer: seeing *it is a righteous thing with God to recompense tribulation to them that trouble you; and to you who are troubled rest with us,* when the Lord Jesus shall be revealed from heaven and with His mighty angels, in flaming fire, taking vengeance on them that know not God [Gentiles], and that obey not the gospel of our Lord Jesus Christ [Jews]" (chapter 1:3-8).

Thus, not only was the Christian position involved in this matter, but the very glory of God—His actual righteousness. If, indeed, the day of the Lord brought tribulation to Christians, then was there no truth in the doctrine—the grand prominent doctrine of Paul's teaching—that Christ and His people are one; and moreover it would impugn the righteousness of God. In short, then, if Christians were in tribulation, it was morally impossible that the day of the Lord could have set in, for when that day comes, it will be rest for believers, as their public recompense, in the kingdom—not merely in the Father's house; which is not the point here. The tables will be completely turned. The Church will be in rest, the Church's troublers in tribulation. During man's day, the Church is called to tribulation; but in the day of the Lord all will be reversed.

Note this carefully. It is not the question of Christians suffering tribulation. They are actually called to it in this world, so long as wickedness has the upper hand. Christ suffered, and so must they. But the point we want to fasten upon the mind and heart of the Christian is, that when Christ comes to set up His kingdom, it is utterly impossible that His people can be in trouble. Thus the entire teaching of the enemy, by which he sought to upset the Thessalonian believers, was proved to be utterly fallacious. The apostle sweeps away the very foundation of the whole fabric by the simple statement of the precious truth of God. This is the divine way of delivering people from false notions and vain fears. Give them the truth, and error must flee before it. Let in the sunshine of God's eternal Word, and all the mists and clouds of false doctrine must be rolled away.

Let us, for a moment, examine the further teaching of our apostle, in this remarkable writing. In so doing, we shall see how thoroughly he establishes the distinction between "the coming" and "the day"—a distinction which the reader will do well to ponder.

"Now we beseech you, brethren, by [or on the ground of] the coming of our Lord Jesus Christ, and our gathering together unto Him, that ye be not soon shaken in mind, or be troubled, neither by spirit, nor by word, nor by letter, as from us, as that the day of the Lord is present."*

Apart altogether from the question of various readings, a moment's reflection will suffice to show the simple minded Christian that the apostle could not possibly mean to

---

* We have no pretensions whatever to scholarship; we are merely gleaners in the deeply interesting field of criticism in which others have reaped a golden harvest. We do not mean to occupy our readers with arguments in defence of readings given in the text; but we feel that there is no use in giving them what we consider to be erroneous. We believe there is no doubt whatever that the true reading of 2 Thessalonians 2, is as we have given it above, "as that the day of the Lord is present," the word ἐνέστηκεν can only be thus rendered. It occurs in Romans 3:38, where it is translated "things *present.*" So also in 1 Corinthians 3:22, "things *present*"; chapter 7:25, "*present* distress"; Galatians 3:4, "*present* evil world"; Hebrews 9:9, "time then *present.*"

teach the Thessalonians that the day of the Lord was not, even then, at hand. Scripture can never contradict itself. No one sentence of divine revelation can possibly collide with another. But if the reading given in our excellent Authorized Version were correct, it would stand in direct opposition to Romans 13:12, where we are plainly and expressly told that "the day is at hand." What "day"? The day of the Lord, most surely, which is always the term used in connection with our individual responsibility in walk and service.

This is a point of much interest and practical value. If the reader will take the trouble to examine the various passages in which "the day" is spoken of, he will find that they have reference, more or less, to the question of work, service or responsibility. For instance, "That ye may be blameless [not at the *coming*, but] in the *day* of our Lord Jesus Christ" (1 Cor. 1:8). Again, "Every man's work shall be made manifest, for the *day* shall declare it" (1 Cor. 3:13). "Without offence till the day of Christ" (Phil. 1:10). "Henceforth there is laid up for me a crown of righteousness, which the Lord, the righteous judge, shall give me at *that day*" (2 Timothy 4:8).

From all these passages, and many more which might be adduced, we learn that "the day of the Lord" will be the grand time for reckoning with the workers; for the divine appraisal of service; for the setting of all questions of personal responsibility; for the distribution of rewards—the "ten cities" and the "five cities."

Thus, wherever we turn, in whatever way we look at the subject, we are more and more confirmed in the truth of the clear distinction between our Lord's "coming," or "state of presence," and His "appearing," or "day." The former is ever held up before the heart as the bright and blessed hope of the believer, which may be realized at any moment. The latter is pressed rather upon the conscience, in deep solemnity, as bearing upon the entire practical career of those who are set in this world to work and witness for an absent Lord. Scripture never confounds these things, however much we may do it; nor is there a single sentence from cover to

cover of the holy volume which teaches that believers are not always to be looking out for the coming of the Lord, and eager to bear in mind that "the day is at hand." It is only "that evil servant"—referred to in our Lord's discourse in Matthew 24—that "says in his heart, My Lord delayeth His coming"; and there we see the terrible results which must ever flow from the harboring of such a thought in the heart.

We shall now return for a moment to 2 Thessalonians 2—a passage of Scripture which has given rise to much discussion amongst prophetic expositors, and presented considerable difficulty to the students of prophecy.

It is very evident that the false teachers had been seeking to disturb the minds of the Thessalonians by leading them to think that they were, even then, surrounded by the terrors of the day of the Lord. Not so, says the apostle; that cannot be. Before ever that day opens we must all be gathered to meet the Lord in the air. He beseeches them, on the ground ($\dot{v}\pi\dot{\varepsilon}\rho$) of the Lord's coming and our gathering together unto Him, not to be troubled about the day. He had already opened to them the heavenly side of the Lord's coming. He had taught them that they, as Christians, belonged to the day; that their home and their portion and their hope were all in that very region from which the day was to shine out. It was wholly impossible, therefore, that the day of the Lord could involve any terror or trouble to those who were actually, through grace, the sons of the day.

Further, even in looking at the subject from the earthly side of it, the false teachers were all wrong. "Let no man deceive you by any means: for [that day shall not come] except there come a falling away first, and that man of sin be revealed, the son of perdition; who opposeth and exalteth himself above all that is called God, or that is worshipped; so that he, as God, sitteth in the temple of God, showing himself that he is God. Remember ye not that when I was with you I told you these things. And now ye know what withholdeth that he might be revealed in his time. For the mystery of iniquity doth already work: only he who now letteth will let, until he be taken out of the way. And then shall that wicked be revealed, whom the Lord shall consume with the spirit of His mouth, and shall destroy with the brightness of His coming [for the appearing of His presence]. Even him whose coming is after the working of Satan, with all power and signs and lying wonders, and with all deceivableness of unrighteousness in them that perish; because they received not the love of the truth, that they might be saved" (verses 3-10).

Here, then, we are taught that ere the day of the Lord arrives, the lawless one, the man of sin, the son of perdition, must be revealed. The mystery of iniquity must rise to a head. Man shall set himself up in open opposition to God, nay, shall even assume to himself the name and the worship of God. All this has to be developed on the earth before that great and terrible day of the Lord shall burst in judgment upon the scene. For the present there is a barrier, a hindrance to the manifestation of this awful personage. We are not told here what this barrier or hindrance is. God may vary it at different times.* But we learn, most distinctly, from the book of Revelation that ere the mystery of iniquity culminates in the person of the man of sin, the Church shall have been removed from this scene altogether. It is impossible to read, with an enlightened eye, Revelation 4—5 and not see that the Church shall be in the very innermost circle of heavenly glory ere a single seal is opened, a single trumpet sounded, a single vial poured out. We do not believe that any one can understand the book of the Apocalypse who does not see this.

We may have occasion to go more freely into this profoundly interesting point by-and-by. We can only now entreat the reader to study the subject for himself. Let him ponder Revelation 4—5, and ask God to interpret their precious contents to his soul. In this way we feel persuaded that he will learn that the twenty-four crowned elders set forth the heavenly saints, who shall be gathered round the Lamb, in glory, before a single line of the prophetic portion of the book is fulfilled.

We should like to put a very plain question to the reader—a question which can only be answered rightly in the immediate presence of God. It is this, What is it thou art looking for? What is thy hope? Art thou looking forward to certain events which are to transpire on this earth, such as the revival of the Roman Empire, the development of the ten kingdoms; the gathering back of the Jews to their own land of Palestine; the rebuilding of Jerusalem; the appearance of Antichrist; the great tribulation; and finally, the appalling judgments which shall, most surely, usher in the day of the Lord?

Are these the things which fill the vision of thy soul? Is it for these thou art looking and waiting? If so, be assured of it thou art not governed by the Church's proper hope. It is quite true that all these things which we have named shall come to pass in their appointed time; but not one of them should be allowed to come between thee and thy proper hope. They all stand on the prophetic page: they are all recorded in God's history of the future; but they were never intended to cast a shadow athwart the Christian's bright and blessed hope. That hope stands forth in glorious relief from the background of prophecy. What is it? Yes, we again say, what is it? It is the appearing of the bright and morning Star—the coming of the Lord Jesus, the blessed Bridegroom of the Church.

This, and naught else, is the true and proper hope of the Church of God. "I will give him the morning star" (Rev. 2:23). "Behold the bridegroom cometh" (Matt. 25). When, we may ask, does the morning star appear in the natural world? Just before the dawning of the day. Who sees it? The one who has been watching during the dark and dreary hours of the night. How plain, how practical, how telling the application. The Church is supposed to be watching—to be lovingly wakeful—to be looking out—to be

---

* Some have considered that the hinderer or hindrance was the Roman Empire; others that it is the Holy Ghost in the Church. To this latter we have inclined for many years, though it may be there is a measure of truth in the former. This, at least, we know from other parts of Scripture, that ere the lawless one appears on the scene, the Church will have been safely and blessedly housed in her own eternal home above—her prepared place. How precious the thought of this!

putting forth that inquiry of the intensely longing heart, "Why tarry the wheels of his chariot?" Alas! the Church has failed in this. But that is no reason why the individual believer should not be in the full present power of the blessed hope. "Let *him* that heareth say, Come." This is deeply personal. Oh! that the writer and the reader of these lines may realize habitually the purifying, sanctifying, elevating power of this heavenly hope! May we understand and exhibit the practical power of those words of the Apostle John, "Every man that hath this hope in him purifieth himself, even as He is pure."

THE TWO RESURRECTIONS

It may be that some of our readers will feel startled by the title of this paper. Accustomed, from their earliest days, to look at this great question through the medium of christendom's standards of doctrine and confessions of faith, the idea of two resurrections have never once entered their minds. Nevertheless Scripture does speak, in the most distinct and unequivocal terms, of a "resurrection of life," and a "resurrection of judgment"—two resurrections, distinct in character, and distinct in time.

There will be at least a thousand years between the two. If men teach otherwise—if they build up systems of divinity, and set forth creeds and confessions of faith contrary to the direct and positive teaching of holy Scripture, they must settle that with their Lord, as must all who commit themselves to their guidance. But remember, reader, it is your bounden duty and ours to harken only to the authority of the Word of God, and to bow down, in unqualified submission, to its holy teaching. Let us, then, reverently inquire, what saith the Scripture on the subject indicated at the head of this article? May God the Spirit guide and instruct!

We shall first quote that remarkable passage in chapter 5 of John's Gospel: "Verily, verily, I say unto you, he that heareth My word and believeth on Him that sent Me, hath everlasting life, and shall not come into judgment; but is passed from death unto life. Verily, verily, I say unto you, the hour is coming, and now is, when the dead shall hear the voice of the Son of God; and they that hear shall live. For as the Father hath life in Himself; so hath He given to the Son to have life in Himself; and hath given Him authority to execute judgment also, because He is the Son of man. Marvel not at this; for the hour is coming, in the which all that are in the graves shall hear His voice, and shall come forth, they that have done good, unto the resurrection of life; and they that have done evil, unto the resurrection of judgment."*

Here, then, we have, indicated in the most unmistakable terms, the two resurrections. True, they are not distinguished as to time, in this passage; but they are as to character. We have a *life* resurrection; and a *judgment* resurrection, and nothing can be more distinct than these. There is no possible ground here on which to build the theory of a promiscuous resurrection. The resurrection of believers will be eclectic; it will be on the same principle, and partake of the same character as the resurrection of our blessed and adorable Lord; it will be a resurrection from among the dead. It will be an act of divine power, founded upon accomplished redemption, whereby God will interpose on behalf of His sleeping saints, and rise them up from among the dead, leaving the rest of the dead in their graves for a thousand years (Revelation 20:5).

There is an interesting passage in Mark 9 which throws great light on this subject. The opening verses contain the record of the transfiguration; and then we read, "As they came down from the mountain, He charged

---

* The English reader should be informed that, in the entire passage, John 5:22-26, the words "judgment," "condemnation," "damnation," are all expressed by the same word in the original, and that word is simply "judgment," κρίσις, the process, not the result. It is much to be deplored that our Authorized Version should not have so rendered the word throughout. It would have made the teaching of the passage so very much clearer. It is with extreme reluctance that we ever venture to touch our unrivalled English Bible, but it is, at times, absolutely necessary for the truth's sake, and for the sake of our readers. As to the rendering of verse 24, it really comes to the same thing whether we say "condemnation" or "judgment," inasmuch as if there be judgment at all, its issue must be condemnation. But why not be accurate?

them that they should tell no man what things they had seen, till the Son of man were risen from the dead. And they kept that saying with themselves, questioning one with another what the rising from [ἐκ, from among] the dead should mean."

The disciples felt that there was something special, something entirely beyond the ordinary orthodox idea of the resurrection of the dead, and verily so there was, though they understood it not then. It lay beyond their range of vision at that moment.

Let us turn to Philippians 3, and harken to the breathings of one who thoroughly entered into and appreciated this grand Christian doctrine, and fondly cherished this glorious and heavenly hope. "That I may know Him, and the power of His resurrection, and the fellowship of His sufferings, being made conformable unto His death: if by any means I might attain unto the resurrection from among the dead" [ἐξανάστασιν] (verses 10-11).

A moment's just reflection will suffice to convince the reader that the apostle is not speaking here of the great broad truth of "the resurrection of the dead," inasmuch as every one must rise again. But there was something specific before the heart of this dear servant of Christ, namely, "a resurrection from among the dead"—an eclectic resurrection— a resurrection formed on the model of Christ's resurrection. It was for this he longed continually. This was the bright and blessed hope that shone upon his soul and cheered him amid the sorrows and trials, the toils and the difficulties, the buffetings and the conflicts of his extraordinary career.

It may be asked, "Does the apostle always use this distinguishing little word (ἐκ) when speaking of resurrection?" Not always. Turn, for example, to Acts 24:15: "And have hope toward God, which they themselves also allow, that there shall be a resurrection of the dead, both of the just and unjust." Here, there is no word to indicate the Christian or heavenly side of the subject, for the simplest possible reason that the apostle was speaking to those who were utterly incapable of entering into the Christian's proper hope— far more incapable than even the disciples in

Mark 9. How could he possibly unbosom himself in the presence of such men as Tertullus, Ananias, and Felix? How could he speak to them of his own specific and fondly cherished hope? No; he could only take his stand on the great broad truth of resurrection, common to all orthodox Jews. Had he spoken of a "resurrection from among the dead," he could not have added the words, "which they themselves also allow," for they did not "allow" anything of the kind.

What a contrast between this precious servant of Christ, defending himself from his accusers, in Acts 24, and unbosoming himself to his beloved brethren, in Philippians 3! To the latter he can speak of the true Christian hope in the full-orbed light which the glory of Christ pours upon it. He can give utterance to the inmost thoughts, feelings, and aspirations of the great, large, loving heart, with its earnest throbbings after the life-resurrection in the which he shall be satisfied as he wakes up in the likeness of his blessed Lord.

But we must return, for a moment, to our first quotation, from John 5. It may perhaps present a difficulty to some of our readers in laying hold of the truth of the Christian's hope of resurrection, that our Lord makes use of the word "hour" in speaking of the two classes. "How," it is argued, "can there be a thousand years between the two resurrections, when our Lord expressly tells us that all shall occur within the limits of an hour?"

To this question we have a double reply. In the first place, we find our Lord making use of the self-same word, "hour," at verse 25, where He is speaking of the great and glorious work of quickening dead souls. "Verily, verily, I say unto you, The hour is coming, and now is, when the dead shall hear the voice of the Son of God; and they that hear shall live."

Now, here we have a work which has been going on for nearly nineteen long centuries. During all that time, here spoken of as an "hour," the voice of Jesus, the Son of God, has been heard calling precious souls from death to life. If, therefore, in the very same discourse, our Lord used the word "hour" when speaking of a period which has already extended to well-nigh two thousand years, what difficulty can there be in applying the word to a period of one thousand years?

Surely, none whatever, as we judge. But even if any little difficulty yet remained it must be thoroughly met by the direct testimony of the Holy Ghost in Revelation 20, where we read, "But the rest of the dead lived not again till the thousand years were finished. *This is the first resurrection.* Blessed and holy is he that hath part in the first resurrection: on such the second death hath no power, but they shall be priests of God, and of Christ, and shall reign with him a thousand years" (verses 5-6).

This settles the question absolutely and forever, for all those who are willing to be taught exclusively by holy Scripture, as every true Christian ought to be. There will be two resurrections, the first and the second: and there will be a thousand years between the two. To the former belong all the Old Testament saints—referred to in Hebrews 12 under the title of the spirits of just men made perfect—then the Church of the firstborn ones—and finally all those who shall be put to death during "the great tribulation," and throughout the entire period between the rapture of the saints and the appearing of Christ in judgment upon the beast and his armies, in Revelation 19.

To the latter, on the other hand, belong all those who shall have died in their sins, from the days of Cain, in Genesis 4, down to the last apostate from millennial glory, in Revelation 20.

How solemn is all this! How real! How soul-subduing! If our Lord were to come to-night what a scene would be enacted in all our cemeteries and graveyards! What tongue, what pen can portray—what heart can conceive—the grand realities of such a moment? There are thousands of tombs in which lie mingled the ashes of the dead *in* Christ and the ashes of the dead *out* of Christ. In many a family vault may be found the ashes of both. Well, then, when the voice of the archangel is heard all the sleeping saints shall rise from their graves, leaving behind them those who have died in their sins, to remain in the darkness and silence of the tomb for a thousand years.

Yes, such is the direct and simple testimony of the Word of God. True, it does not enter into any curious details. It does not furnish any food for a morbid imagination or idle curiosity. But it sets forth the solemn and weighty fact of a first and second resurrection—a resurrection of life and everlasting glory, and a resurrection of judgment and everlasting misery. There is, positively, no such thing in Scripture as a promiscuous resurrection—a common rising of all at the same time. We must abandon this idea altogether, like many others which we have received to hold, in which we have been trained from our earliest days, which have grown with our growth and strengthened with our strength, until they have become actually ingrained as a part of our very mental, moral, and religious constitution, so that to part with them is like the sundering of limb from limb, or rending the flesh from our bones.

Nevertheless it must be done if we really desire to grow in the knowledge of divine revelation. There is no greater hindrance to our getting into the thoughts of God than having our minds filled with our own thoughts, or the thoughts of men. Thus, for example, in reference to the subject of this paper, almost all of us have, at one time, held the opinion that all will rise together, both believers and unbelievers, and all stand together to be judged. Whereas, when we come to Scripture, like a little child, nothing can be simpler, nothing clearer, nothing more explicit than its teaching as to this question. Revelation 20:5 teaches us that there will be an interval of a thousand years between the resurrection of the saints and the resurrection of the wicked.

It is of no use to speak of a resurrection of spirits. Indeed it is a manifest piece of absurdity; for inasmuch as spirits cannot die they cannot be raised from the dead. Equally absurd is it to speak of a resurrection of principles. There is no such thing in Scripture. The language is as plain as plainness itself. "The rest of the dead lived not again until the thousand years were finished. This is the first resurrection." Why should any one seek to set aside the plain force of such a passage? Why not bow to it? Why not get rid, at once, of all our old and fondly cherished notions, and receive with meekness the engrafted Word?

Does it not seem plain that if Scripture speaks of a *first* resurrection, then it must follow that all will not rise together? Why should it be said, "Blessed and holy is he that hath part in the first resurrection," if all are to rise at the same time?

In fact it seems to us impossible for any unprejudiced mind to study the New Testament and yet hold to the theory of a promiscuous resurrection. It is due to the glory of Christ, the Head, that His members should have a specific resurrection—a resurrection like His own—a resurrection from among the dead. And verily, so they shall. "Behold I show you a mystery: we shall not all sleep, but we shall all be changed, in a moment, in the twinkling of an eye, at the last trump: for the trumpet shall sound, and the dead shall be raised incorruptible, and we shall be changed. For this corruptible must put on incorruption, and this mortal must put on immortality. So when this corruptible shall have put on immortality, then shall be brought to pass the saying that is written, Death is swallowed up in victory. O, death, where is thy sting? O, grave, where is thy victory? The sting of death is sin; and the strength of sin is the law. But thanks be to God which giveth us the victory through our Lord Jesus Christ. Therefore, my beloved brethren, be ye steadfast, unmovable, always abounding in the work of the Lord, forasmuch as ye know that your labor is not in vain in the Lord" (1 Corinthians 15).

THE JUDGMENT

There is something peculiarly painful in the thought of having so frequently to come in collision with the generally received opinions of the professing Church. It looks presumptuous to contradict, on so many subjects, all the great standards and creeds of christendom. But what is one to do? Were it indeed a mere question of human opinion it might seem a piece of bold and unwarrant-

able temerity for any one individual to set himself in direct opposition to the established faith of the whole professing Church—a faith which has held sway for centuries over the minds of millions.

It is not at all a question of human opinion or of a difference of judgment amongst even the very best of men. It is entirely a question as to the teaching and authority of holy Scripture. There have been, and there are, and there will be, schools of doctrine, varieties of opinion, and shades of thought; but it is the obvious duty of every child of God and every servant of Christ to bow down, in holy reverence, and harken to the voice of God in Scripture. If it be merely a matter of human authority, it must simply go for what it is worth; but, on the other hand, if it be a matter of divine authority, then all discussion is closed, and our place—the place of all—is to bow and believe.

Thus, in our last paper we were led to see that there is no such thing in Scripture as a general resurrection—a common rising of all at the same time. We trust our readers have, like the Bereans of old, searched the Scriptures as to this, and that they are now prepared to accompany us in our examination of the Word of God as to the subject of the judgment.

The great question at the outset is this, Does Scripture teach the doctrine of a general judgment? Christendom holds it; but does Scripture teach it? Let us see.

In the first place, as to the Christian individually, and the Church of God, collectively, the New Testament sets forth the precious truth that there is no judgment at all. So far as the believer is concerned judgment is past and gone. The heavy cloud of judgment has burst upon the head of our divine Sin-bearer. He has exhausted, on our behalf, the cup of wrath and judgment, and planted us on the new ground of resurrection, to which judgment can never, by any possibility, apply. It is just as impossible that a member of the body of Christ can come into judgment as that the divine Head Himself can do so. This seems a very strong statement to make; but is it true? If so, its strength is part of its moral value and glory.

For what, let us ask, was Jesus judged on the cross? For His people. He was made sin for us. He represented us there. He stood in our stead. He bore all that was due to us. Our entire condition, with all its belongings, was dealt with in the death of Christ; and so dealt with that it is utterly impossible that any question can ever be raised. Has God any question to settle with Christ, the Head? Clearly not. Well, then, neither has He any question to settle with the members. Every question is divinely and definitively settled, and, in proof of the settlement, the Head is crowned with glory and honor, and seated at the right hand of the Majesty in the heavens.

Hence, to suppose that Christians are to come to judgment, at any time, or on any ground, for any object whatsoever, is to deny the very foundation truth of Christianity, and to contradict the plain words of our Lord Jesus Christ, who has expressly declared, in reference to all who believe in Him, that they "shall not come into judgment" (John 5:24).

In point of fact, the idea of Christians being arraigned at the bar of judgment to try the question of their title and fitness for Heaven is as absurd as it is unscriptural. For example, how can we think of Paul or the penitent thief standing to be judged as to their title to Heaven—after having been there already for nearly two thousand years? But thus it must be if there be any truth in the theory of a general judgment. If the great question of our title to Heaven has to be settled at the day of judgment, then clearly it was not settled on the cross; and if it was not settled on the cross, then most surely we shall be damned; for if we are to be judged at all it must be according to our works, and the only possible issue of such a judgment is the lake of fire.

If, however, it be maintained that Christians shall only stand in the judgment in order to make it manifest that they are clear through the dead of Christ, then would the day of judgment be turned into a mere formality, the bare thought of which is most revolting to every pious and well regulated mind.

But, in truth, there is no need of reasoning on the point. One sentence of holy Scripture is better far than ten thousand of man's most cogent arguments. Our Lord Christ hath declared, in the clearest and most emphatic terms, that believers "shall not come into judgment." This is enough. The believer was judged over eighteen hundred years ago in the Person of his Head; and to bring him into judgment again would be to ignore completely the cross of Christ in its atoning efficacy; and most assuredly God will not, cannot allow this. The very feeblest believer may say, in thankfulness and triumph, "So far as I am concerned, all that had to be judged is judged already. Every question that had to be settled is settled. Judgment is past and gone forever. I know my work must be tried, my service appraised; but as to myself, my person, my standing, my title, all is divinely settled. The Man who answered for me on the tree is now crowned on the throne; and the crown which He wears is the proof that there remains no judgment for me. I am waiting for a life resurrection."

This, and nothing short of this, is the proper language of the Christian. It is simply due to the work of the cross that the believer should thus feel and thus express himself. For such a one to be looking forward to the day of judgment for a settlement of the question of his eternal destiny is to dishonor his Lord and deny the efficacy of His atoning sacrifice. It may sound like humility and savor of piety to hover in doubt. But we may rest assured that all who harbor doubts, all who live in a state of uncertainty, all who are looking forward to the day of judgment for a final settlement of their affairs, all such are more occupied with themselves than with Christ. They have not yet understood the application of the cross to their sins and to their nature. They are doubting the Word of God and the work of Christ, and this is not Christianity. There is—there can be—no judgment for those who, sheltered by the cross, have planted a firm foot on the new and everlasting ground of resurrection. For such all judgment is over forever, and nothing remains but a prospect of cloudless glory and everlasting blessedness in the presence of God and of the Lamb.

However, it is not at all improbable that all

this while the mind of the reader has been recurring to Matthew 25:31-46 as a Scripture which directly establishes the theory of a general judgment; and we feel it to be our sacred duty to turn with him for a moment to that very solemn and important passage; at the same time reminding him of the fact that no one Scripture can possibly clash with another, and hence if we read, in John 5:24, that believers shall not come into judgment, we cannot read in Matthew 25 that they shall. This is a fixed and invulnerable principle—a general rule to which there is, and can be, no exception. Nevertheless, let us turn to Matthew 25.

"When the Son of man shall come in His glory, and all the holy angels with Him, then shall He sit upon the throne of His glory. And before Him shall be gathered all nations; and He shall separate them one from another, as a shepherd divideth his sheep from the goats."

Now, it is most necessary to pay strict attention to the precise terms made use of in this Scripture. We must avoid all looseness of thought, all that haste, carelessness, and inaccuracy which have caused such serious damage to the teaching of this weighty Scripture, and thrown so many of the Lord's people into the utmost confusion respecting it.

First of all, let us see who are the parties arraigned. "Before Him shall be gathered *all nations*." This is very definite. It is the living nations. It is not a question of individuals, but of nations—all the Gentiles. Israel is not here, for we read in Numbers 23:9, that "the people shall dwell alone, and shall not be reckoned among the nations." If Israel were to be included in this scene of judgment, then would Matthew 25 stand in palpable contradiction to Numbers 23, which is wholly out of the question. Israel is never reckoned amongst the Gentiles, on any ground or for any object whatever. Looked at from a divine point of view, Israel stands alone. They may, because of their sins, and under the governmental dealings of God, be scattered among the nations; but God's Word declares that they shall not be reckoned among them; and this should suffice for us.

If then it be true that Israel is not included

in the judgment of Matthew 25 then, without proceeding one step further, the idea of its being a general judgment must be abandoned. It cannot be general, if all are not included; but Israel is never included under the term "Gentiles." Scripture speaks of three distinct classes, namely, "The Jew, and the Gentile, and the church of God," and these three are never confounded. But, further, we have to remark that the Church of God is not included in the judgment of Matthew 25. Nor is this statement based merely upon the fact which has been already gone into of the Church's necessary exemption from judgment; but also upon the grand truth that the Church is taken from among the nations, as Peter declared in the council at Jerusalem. "God did visit the Gentiles to *take out of them* a people for His name." If then the Church be taken out of the nations, it cannot be reckoned among them; and thus we have additional evidence against the theory of a general judgment in Matthew 25. The Jew is not there; the Church is not there; and therefore the idea of a general judgment must be abandoned as something wholly untenable.

Who then are included in this judgment? The passage itself supplies the answer to any simple mind. It says, "Before Him shall be gathered all *nations*." This is distinct and definite. It is not a judgment of individuals, but of nations, as such. And further, we may add that not one of those here indicated shall have passed through the article of death. In this it stands in vivid contrast with the scene in Revelation 20:11-15, in the which there will not be one who has not died. In short, in Matthew 25, we have the judgment of "the quick"; and in Revelation 20 the judgment of "the dead." Both these are referred to in 2 Timothy 4, "I charge thee before God, and the Lord Jesus Christ, who shall judge the quick and the dead at His appearing and His kingdom." Our Lord Christ shall judge the living nations at His appearing; and He shall "judge the dead, small and great," at the close of His millennial reign.

Let us glance, for a moment, at the mode in which the parties are arranged in the judgment, in Matthew 25: "He shall set the sheep on His right hand, but the goats on the left." Now, the almost universal belief of the professing Church is that "the sheep" represent all the people of God, from the beginning to the end of time; and that "the goats," on the other hand, set forth all the wicked, from first to last. But, if this be so, what are we to make of the third party referred to here, under the title of "these My brethren"? The King addresses both the sheep and the goats in respect to this third class. Indeed the very ground of judgment is the treatment of the King's brethren. It would involve a manifest absurdity to say that the sheep were themselves the parties referred to. If that were so the language would be wholly different, and in place of saying, "Inasmuch as ye have done it unto one of the least of these My brethren" we should hear the King saying, "Inasmuch as ye have done it to one another," or "amongst yourselves."

We consider that were there no other argument and no other Scripture on the subject, this one point would prove fatal to the theory of a general judgment. It is impossible not to see three parties in the scene, namely, "the sheep," and "the goats," and "these My brethren"; and if there are three parties it cannot possibly be a general judgment, inasmuch as "these My brethren" are not included either in the sheep or the goats.

No, it is not a general judgment at all, but a very partial and specific one. It is a judgment of living nations, previous to the opening of the millennial kingdom. Scripture teaches us that after the Church has left the earth a testimony will go forth to the nations; the gospel of the kingdom shall be borne, by Jewish messengers, far and wide, over the earth, into those regions which are wrapped in heathen darkness. These nations which shall receive the messengers and treat them kindly will be found on the King's right hand. Those, on the contrary, who shall reject them and treat them unkindly will be found on His left. "These My brethren" are Jews—the brethren of the Messiah.

The treatment of the Jews is the ground on which the nations will be judged by-and-by;

and this is another argument against a general judgment. We know full well that all those who have lived and died in the rejection of the gospel of Christ will have something more to answer for than unkindness to the King's brethren. And, on the other hand, those who shall surround the Lamb in heavenly glory will do so on a very different title from aught that their works can furnish.

In short, there is not a single feature in the scene, not a single fact in the history, not a single point in the narrative which does not make against the notion of a general judgment. And not only so, but the more we study Scripture, the more we know of the ways of God; the more we know of His nature, His character, His purposes, His counsels, His thoughts; the more we know of Christ, His Person, His work, His glory; the more we know of the Church, its standing before God in Christ, its completeness, its perfect acceptance in Christ; the more closely we study Scripture; the more profoundly we meditate therein—the more thoroughly convinced we must be that there can be no such thing as a general judgment.

Who that knows aught of God could suppose that He would justify His people to-day and arraign them in judgment to-morrow—that He would blot out their transgressions to-day and judge them according to their works to-morrow? Who that knows aught of our adorable Lord and Saviour Jesus Christ could suppose that He would ever arraign His Church, His body, His bride, before the judgment seat in company with all those who have died in their sins? Could it be possible that He would enter into judgment with His people for sins and iniquities of which He has said, "I will remember no more"!

But enough, We fondly trust that the reader is now most fully persuaded in his own mind that there is, and can be, no such thing as a promiscuous resurrection—no such thing as a general judgment.

We cannot now enter upon the judgment in Rev. 20:11-15 further than to say that it is a post-millennial scene, and that it includes all the wicked dead, from the days of Cain down to the last apostate from millennial glory.

There will not be one there who has not passed through the article of death—not one there whose name has been set down in life's fair book—not one there who shall not be judged according to his own very deeds—not one there who shall not pass from the dread realities of the great white throne into the everlasting horrors and ineffable torments of the lake that burneth with fire and brimstone. How awful! How terrible! How perfectly dreadful!

What sayest thou to these things? Art thou a true believer in Jesus? Art thou washed in His precious blood? Art thou sheltered in Him from coming judgment? If not, let me entreat thee now, with all tenderness and earnestness, to flee, this very hour, from the wrath to come! Flee to Jesus, who now waits to receive thee to His loving bosom, and to present you to God in the full value of His atoning work, and in the full credit of His peerless name.

THE JEWISH REMNANT

Matt. 24:1-44 forms a part of one of the most profound and comprehensive discourses that ever fell on human ears—a discourse which takes in, in its marvelous sweep, the destiny of the Jewish remnant; the history of christendom; and the judgment of the nations. At the last-named subject we have already glanced. It remains for us now to consider the subject of the remnant of Israel, and the history of professing Christianity, whether genuine or spurious.

First, let us look at the Jewish remnant.

In order to understand Matt. 24:1-44, it will be needful for us to place ourselves at the standpoint of those whom our Lord was addressing at the moment. If we attempt to import into this discourse the light which shines in the Epistle to the Ephesians, we shall only involve our minds in confusion, and miss the solemn teaching of the passage which now lies open before us. We shall find nothing about the Church of God, the body of Christ, here. The teaching of our Lord is divinely perfect, and hence we cannot, for a moment, imagine anything premature therein. But it would be premature to have

introduced a subject which, as yet, was hid in God. The great truth of the Church could not be unfolded until Christ, being cut off as the Messiah, had taken His place at the right hand of God, and sent down the Holy Ghost, to form by His presence the one body, composed of Jew and Gentile.

Of this we hear nothing in Matt. 24. We are entirely on Jewish ground, surrounded by Jewish circumstances and influences. The scenery and the allusions are all purely Jewish. To attempt to apply the passage to the Church would be to miss completely our Lord's object, and to falsify the real position of the Church of God. The more closely we examine the Scripture, the more clearly we shall see that the persons addressed occupy a Jewish standpoint, and are on Jewish ground, whether we think of those very persons whom our Lord was then addressing, or those who shall occupy the self-same ground at the close, when the Church shall have left the scene altogether.

At the close of Matt. 23, our Lord sums up His appeal to the leaders of the Jewish nation with the following words of awful solemnity: "Fill ye up then the measure of your fathers. Ye serpents, ye generation of vipers! how can ye escape the damnation of hell? Wherefore, behold, I send unto you prophets, and wise men, and scribes: and some of them ye shall kill and crucify; and some of them shall ye scourge in your synagogues, and persecute them from city to city. That upon you may come all the righteous blood shed upon the earth, from the blood of righteous Abel unto the blood of Zecharias, son of Barachias, whom ye slew between the temple and the altar. Verily I say unto you, All these things shall come *upon this generation*. O Jerusalem, Jerusalem, thou that killest the prophets, and stonest them which are sent unto thee, how often would I have gathered thy children together, even as a hen gathereth her chickens under her wings, and ye would not! Behold, your house is left unto you desolate. For I say unto you, Ye shall not see Me henceforth till ye shall say, Blessed is He that cometh in the name of the Lord" (verses 32-39).

Thus closes Messiah's testimony to the

apostate nation of Israel. Every effort that love, even divine love, could put forth had been tried, and tried in vain. Prophets had been sent, and stoned; messenger after messenger had gone and pleaded, and reasoned, and warned, and entreated; but to no purpose. Their mighty words had fallen upon deaf ears and hardened hearts. The only return made to all these messengers was shameful handling, stoning, and death.

At length, the Son Himself was sent, and sent with this touching utterance: "It may be they will reverence My Son, when they see Him." Did they? Alas! no. When they saw Him, there was no beauty that they should desire Him. The daughter of Zion had no heart for her King. The vineyard was under the control of wicked husbandmen. "The husbandmen said among themselves, This is the heir, come, let us kill Him, that the inheritance may be ours."

Thus much as to the moral condition of Israel, in view of which our Lord spoke those unusually awful words quoted above; and, then, "He went out and departed from the temple." How reluctant He was to do this we know; for, blessed be His name, whenever He leaves a place of mercy, or enters a place of judgment, He moves with a slow and measured pace. Witness the departure of the glory, in the opening chapters of Ezekiel. "Then the glory of the Lord departed from off the threshold of the house, and stood over the cherubims. And the cherubims lifted up their wings, and mounted up from the earth in my sight; when they went out, the wheels also were beside them, and every one stood at the door of the east gate of the Lord's house; and the glory of the God of Israel was over them above" (chap. 10:18-19). "Then did the cherubims lift up their wings, and the wheels beside them; and the glory of the God of Israel was over them above. And the glory of the Lord went up from the midst of the city, and stood upon the mountain which is on the east side of the city" (chap. 11:22-23).

Thus, with slow and measured pace, did the glory of the God of Israel take its departure from the house at Jerusalem. Jehovah lingered near the spot, reluctant to depart.* He had come, with loving alacrity, with His whole heart and with His whole soul, to dwell in the midst of His people, to find a home in the very bosom of His assembly; but He was *forced* away by their sins and iniquities. He would fain have remained; but it was impossible; and yet He proved, by the very mode of His departure, how unwilling He was to go.

Nor was it otherwise with Jehovah Messiah, in Matt. 23. Witness His touching words, "How often would I have gathered thy children together, even as a hen gathereth her chickens under her wings, and ye would not!" Here lay the deep secret *"I would."* This was the heart of God. *"Ye would not."* This was the heart of Israel. He, too, like the glory in the days of Ezekiel, was forced away; but not, blessed be His name, without dropping a word which forms the precious basis of hope as to the brighter days to come, when the glory shall return, and the daughter of Zion shall welcome her King with joyful accents. "Blessed is He that cometh in the name of Jehovah."

But, until that bright day dawn, darkness, desolation, and ruin, make up the sum of Israel's history. The very thing which the leaders sought, by the rejection of Christ, to avert, came upon them, in stern and awful reality. "The Romans shall come, and take away both our place and nation." How literally, how solemnly this was fulfilled! Alas! their place and their nation were gone already, and the significant movement of Jesus, in Matt. 24:1, was but the passing sentence, and writing desolation upon the whole Jewish system. "Jesus went out and departed from the temple." The case was hopeless. All must be given up. A long period of darkness and dreariness must pass over the infatuated nation—a period which shall culminate in that "great tribulation" which must precede the hour of final deliverance.

---

* Contrast with this reluctant departure His ready entrance into the tabernacle in Exodus 20; and into the temple, 2 Chron. 7:1. No sooner was the habitation ready for Him, than down He came to occupy it, and fill it with His glory. He was as quick to enter as He was slow to depart. And not only so, but ere the book of Ezekiel closes, we see the glory coming back again; and "Jehovah Shammah" stands engraved in everlasting characters upon the gates of the beloved city. Nothing changeth God's affection. Whom He loves, and as He loves, He loves to the end. "The same yesterday, to-day, and forever."

But, as in the days of Ezekiel, there were those who sighed and cried over the sins and sorrows of the nation, so in the days of Matt. 24, there was a remnant of godly souls who attached themselves to the rejected Messiah, and who cherished the fond hope of redemption and restoration for Israel. Very dim indeed were their perceptions, and their thoughts full of confusion. Nevertheless their hearts, as touched by divine grace, beat true to the Messiah, and they were full of hope as to Israel's future.

Now, it is of the utmost importance that the reader should recognize and understand the position of this remnant, and that it is with it our Lord is occupied in His marvelous discourse on the mount of Olives. To suppose for a moment that the persons here addressed were on Christian ground would involve the abandonment of all true thoughts of what Christianity is, and the ignoring of a company whose existence is recognized throughout the Psalms, the Prophets, and various parts of the New Testament. There was, and there always is, "a remnant according to the election of grace." To quote the passages which present the history, the sorrows, the experiences, and the exercises of that remnant would demand a volume, and hence we shall not attempt it; but we are extremely desirous that the reader should seize the thought that this godly remnant is represented by the handful of disciples which gathered round our Lord on the mount of Olives. We feel persuaded that if this be not seen, the true scope, bearing, and application of this remarkable discourse must be lost.

"And Jesus went out and departed from the temple; and His disciples came to Him for to show Him the buildings of the temple. And Jesus said unto them, See ye not all these things? Verily I say unto you there shall not be left one stone upon another that shall not be thrown down. And as He sat upon the mount of Olives the disciples came unto Him privately, saying, Tell us, when shall these things be? and what shall be the sign of Thy coming, and of the end of the world [or age, αἰῶνος]?

The disciples were, naturally, occupied with earthly and Jewish objects and expec-

tations—the temple and its surroundings. This must be borne in mind if we would understand their question and our Lord's reply. As yet they had no thought beyond the earthly side of things. They looked for the setting up of the kingdom, the glory of the Messiah, the accomplishment of the promises made to the fathers. They had not yet fully taken in the solemn and momentous fact that the Messiah was to be "cut off and have nothing" (Dan. 9:26). True, the blessed Master had, from time to time, sought to prepare their minds for the solemn event. He had faithfully warned them in reference to the dark shadows that were to gather round His path. He had told them that the Son of Man should be delivered to the Gentiles to be mocked and scourged and crucified.

But they understood Him not. Such sayings seemed dark, hard, and incomprehensible; and their hearts still fondly clung to the hope of national restoration and blessing. They longed to see the star of Jacob in the ascendant. Their minds were full of expectancy as to the restoration of the kingdom to Israel. As yet they knew nothing—how could they?—of that which was to spring out of the rejection and death of the Messiah. The Lord had no doubt spoken of building an assembly; but as to the position and privileges of that assembly, its calling, its standing, its hopes, they knew absolutely nothing. The thought of a body composed of Jew and Gentile, united by the Holy Ghost to a living and glorified Head in the heavens, had never entered—how could it have entered?—their minds. The middle wall of partition was still standing; and one of their number—the very foremost amongst them—had, long after, to be taught, with much difficulty, to take in the idea of even admitting the Gentiles into the kingdom.

All this, we repeat, must be taken into account if we would read aright our Lord's reply to the inquiry as to His coming and the end of the age. There is not a single syllable about the Church, as such, from beginning to end of that reply. Up to verse 14, He passes on to the end, giving a rapid survey of the events which should transpire amongst the nations. "Take heed," He says, "that no man deceive you. For many shall come in My name saying, I am Christ; and shall deceive many. And ye shall hear of wars, and rumors of wars: see that ye be not troubled: for all these things must come to pass, but the end is not yet. For nation shall rise against nation, and kingdom against kingdom; and there shall be famines, and pestilences, and earthquakes, in divers places. All these are the beginning of sorrows. Then shall they deliver you up to be afflicted, and shall kill you: and ye shall be hated of all nations for My name's sake. And then shall many be offended, and shall betray one another, and shall hate one another. And many false prophets shall rise and shall deceive many. And because iniquity shall abound, the love of many shall wax cold. But he that shall endure to the end, the same shall be saved. And this gospel of the kingdom shall be preached in all the world for a witness unto all nations: and then shall the end come."

Here then we have a most comprehensive sketch of the entire period from the moment in which our Lord was speaking, down to the time of the end. But the reader will need to bear in mind that there is an unnoticed interval—a parenthesis, a break—in this period, during which the great mystery of the Church is unfolded.

This interval or break is entirely passed over in this discourse, inasmuch as the time had not arrived for its development. It was as yet "hid in God," and could not be unfolded until the Messiah was finally rejected and cut off from the earth and received up into glory. The entire of this discourse would have its full and perfect accomplishment, although such a thing as the Church had never been heard of. For, let it never be forgotten, the Church forms no part of the ways of God with Israel and the earth. And as to the allusion, in verse 14, to the preaching of the gospel, we are not to suppose that it is at all the same thing as "The glorious gospel of the grace of God," as preached by Paul. It is styled, "This gospel of the kingdom"; and, moreover, it is to be preached, not for the purpose of gathering the Church, but "as a witness to all nations." We must not confound things which God, in His infinite wisdom, has made to differ. The Church must not be confounded

with the kingdom; nor yet the gospel of the grace of God with the gospel of the kingdom. The two things are perfectly distinct; and, if we confound them, we shall understand neither the one nor the other. And, further, we would desire to press upon the reader the absolute necessity of seeing the break, parenthesis, or unnoticed interval in which the great mystery of the Church is inserted. If this be not clearly seen, Matt. 24 cannot be understood.

At verse 15, He seems to call His hearers back a little, as it were, to something very specific—something with which a Jewish believer would be familiar from the fact of Daniel's allusion to it. "When ye, therefore, shall see the abomination of desolation, spoken of by Daniel the prophet, stand in the holy place (whoso readeth let him understand): then let them which be in Judea flee into the mountains. Let him which is on the housetop not come down to take anything out of his house: neither let him which is in the field return back to take his clothes. . . . But pray ye that your flight be not in the winter, neither on the Sabbath day. For then shall be great tribulation, such as was not since the beginning of the world to this time, no, nor ever shall be."

All this is most definite. The quotation from Daniel 12 fixes the application beyond all question. It proves that the reference is not to the siege of Jerusalem, under Titus; for we read in Daniel 12 that, "At that time thy people shall be delivered"; and, most clearly, they were not delivered in the days of Titus. No; the reference is to the time of the end. The scene is laid at Jerusalem. The persons addressed and contemplated are Jewish believers—the pious remnant of Israel, in the great tribulation, after the Church has left the scene. How can any imagine that the persons here instructed are viewed as on church ground? What force would there be to such in the allusion to the winter or the Sabbath day?

Then, again, "If any man shall say unto you, Lo, here is Christ, or there, believe it not . . . . If they shall say unto you, Behold He is in the desert, go not forth: Behold He is in the secret chambers, believe it not." What possible application could such words have to persons who are instructed to wait for God's Son from Heaven, and who know that ere He returns to this earth they shall have met Him in the clouds and returned with Him to the Father's house? Could any Christian, instructed in his proper hope, be deceived by persons saying that Christ is here or there, in the desert or in the secret chambers? Impossible. Such a one is looking out for the Bridegroom to come from Heaven; and he knows that it is wholly out of the question that Christ can appear on this earth without bringing all His people with Him.

Thus, the simple truth settles everything; and all we want is to be simple in taking it in. The simplest Christian knows full well that his Lord will not appear to him like a flash of lightning, but as the bright and morning Star, and hence he understands that Matt. 24 cannot apply to the Church, though most surely the Church can study it with interest and profit, as it can all the other prophetic Scriptures; and, we may add, the interest will be all the more intense, and the profit all the deeper, in proportion as we see the true application of such Scriptures.

Limited space forbids our entering as fully as we could wish into the remaining portion of this marvelous discourse; but the more closely each sentence is examined, the more fully each circumstance is weighed, the more clearly we must see that the persons addressed are not on proper Christian ground. The entire scene is earthly and Jewish, not heavenly and Christian. There is ample instruction supplied for those who shall find themselves, by-and-by, in the position here contemplated; and nothing can be clearer than that the entire paragraph, from verse 15-42, refers to the period which shall elapse between the rapture of the saints and the appearing of the Son of Man.

Some may perhaps feel a difficulty in understanding verse 34: "This generation shall not pass till all these things be fulfilled." But we must remember that the word "generation" is constantly used in Scripture in a moral sense. It is not to be confined to a certain number of persons actually living at the time, but takes in the *race*. In the passage

before us it simply applies to the Jewish race; but the wording is such as to leave the question of time entirely open, so that the heart might ever be kept in readiness for the Lord's coming. There is nothing in Scripture to interfere with the constant expectation of that grand event. On the contrary, every parable, every figure, every allusion is so worded as to warrant each one to look for the Lord' return in his own lifetime, and yet to leave margin for the elongation of the time according to the long-suffering grace of a Saviour God.

CHRISTENDOM

What varied thoughts and feelings are awakened in the soul by the very sound of the word "christendom"! It is a terrible word. It brings before us, at once, that vast mass of baptized profession which calls itself the church of God, but is not; which calls itself Christianity, but is not. Christendom is dark and a dreadful anomaly. It is neither one thing nor the other. It is not "the Jew or the Gentile, or the church of God." It is a corrupt mysterious mixture, a spiritual malformation, the masterpiece of Satan, the corrupter of the truth of God, and the destroyer of the souls of men, a trap, a snare, a stumblingblock, the darkest moral blot in the universe of God. It is the corruption of the very best thing, and therefore the very worst of corruptions. It is that thing which Satan has made of professing Christianity. It is worse, by far, than Judaism; worse by far than all the darkest forms of paganism, because it has higher light and richer privileges, makes the very highest profession, and occupies the very loftiest platform. Finally, it is that awful apostasy for which is reserved the very heaviest judgments of God—the most bitter dregs in the cup of His righteous wrath.

True it is, blessed be God, there are a few names even in christendom who, through grace, have not defiled their garments. There are some brilliant embers amid the smouldering ashes—precious stones amid the terrible *debris*. But as to the mass of Christian profession to which the term christendom applies, nothing can be more appalling, whether we think of its present condition or its future destiny. We doubt if Christians generally have anything like an adequate sense of the true character and inevitable doom of that which surrounds them. If they had it would solemnize their minds, and cause them to feel the urgent need of standing apart, in holy separation, from christendom's ways, and distinct testimony against its spirit and principles.

But let us turn again to our Lord's profound discourse on the mount of Olives, in which, as we have already observed, He deals with the subject of the Christian profession. This He does in three distinct parables, namely, the household servant; the ten virgins; and the talents. In each and all we have the two things noticed above, the genuine and the spurious; the true and the false; the bright and the dark; that which is of Christ, and that which is of Satan; that which belongs to Heaven, and that which emanates from hell.

We shall glance at the three parables which embody, in their brief compass, a vast mine of most solemn and practical instruction.

Turn to Matt. 24:45-47. "Who, then, is a faithful and wise servant, whom his lord hath made ruler over his household, to give them meat in due season? Blessed is that servant, whom his lord, when he cometh shall find so doing. Verily I say unto you that he shall make him ruler over all his goods."

Here, then, we have at once the source and object of all ministry in the house of God. "Whom *his lord* hath made ruler." This is the source. "To give them meat in due season." This is the object.

These things are of the very highest possible moment, and they are worthy of the reader's most profound thought. All ministry in the house of God, whether in Old or New Testament times, is of divine appointment. There is no such thing recognized in Scripture as human authority in appointing to the ministry. Neither is there such a thing as a self-constituted ministry. None but God can make or appoint a minister of any sort or description. Thus, in Old Testament times,

Jehovah appointed Aaron and his sons to the priesthood; and if a stranger presumed to meddle with the functions of the holy office, he was to be put to death. Even the king himself dared not touch the priestly censer, for we are told of Uzziah, king of Judah, that, "When he was strong, his heart was lifted up to his destruction; for he transgressed against the Lord his God, and went into the temple of the Lord to burn incense upon the altar of incense. And Azariah the priest went in after him, and with him fourscore priests of the Lord, that were valiant men. And they withstood Uzziah the king, and said unto him, It appertaineth not unto thee, Uzziah, to burn incense unto the Lord, but to the priests the sons of Aaron, that are consecrated to burn incense; go out of the sanctuary: for thou hast trespassed: neither shall it be for thine honor from the Lord God. . . . *And Uzziah the king was a leper unto the day of his death*" (2 Chron. 26).

Such was the solemn result—the awful consequence of man's daring intrusion upon that which was wholly of divine appointment. Has this no voice for christendom? Assuredly it has. It sounds a warning note in our ears. It tells the professing Church, in accents not to be mistaken, to beware of human intrusion upon a domain which belongs only to God. "Every high priest taken from among men is ordained *for* [not *by*] men in things pertaining to God, that he may offer both gifts and sacrifices for sins. . . . *And no man taketh this honor unto himself*, but he that is called [not of men but] of God, as was Aaron."

Nor was this principle of divine appointment confined to the high and holy office of the tabernacle. No man dare put his hand to the most insignificant part of that sacred structure unless by Jehovah's direct authority. "The Lord spake unto Moses, saying, See *I have called* by name Bezaleel the son of Uri, the son of Hur, of the trible of Judah." Nor could Bezaleel choose his companions in labor, or appoint whom he would to the work, any more than he could choose or appoint himself. No; this, too, was divine. "And I," says Jehovah, "Behold *I have given* with him Aholiab." Thus Aholiab, as well as Bezaleel, held his commission immediately from Jehovah Himself, the only true source of all ministerial authority.

Nor was it otherwise in the case of the prophetic office and ministry. God alone could make, and fit, and send a prophet. Alas! there were those of whom Jehovah had to say, "I have not sent them, yet they ran." They were unhallowed intruders upon the domain of prophecy, just as there were upon the office of the priesthood; but all such brought down upon themselves the judgment of God.

Is this great principle changed? Has ministry been shifted from its ancient base? Has the living stream been diverted from its divine source? Is it true that this more precious and glorious institution has been shorn of its lofty dignities? Can it be possible that, under the times of the New Testament, ministry has been cast down from its divine excellency? Has it become a mere human appointment? Can man appoint his fellow, or appoint himself to any one branch of ministry in the house of God?

What answer is to be returned to these questions? No doubtful one, thank God; but a distinct and emphatic *No!* Ministry was, is, and ever shall be, divine; divine in its source; divine in its nature; divine in its every feature and principle. "There are diversities of gifts, but the same Spirit. And there are differences of administration, but the same Lord. And there are diversities of operations, but it is the same God which worketh all in all" (1 Cor. 12:4-6). "But now hath *God* set the members every one of them in the body *as it hath pleased Him.*" "And *God* hath set some in the church; first, apostles; secondarily prophets; thirdly, teachers; after that, miracles; then gifts of healing, helps, governments, diversities of tongues" (verses 18, 28). "But unto every one of us is given grace according to the measure of the gift of Christ. Wherefore He saith, when He ascended up on high, He led captivity captive, and gave gifts unto men. . . . And He gave some, apostles; and some, prophets; and some, evangelists; and some, pastors and teachers; for the perfecting of the saints, for the work of the ministry, for the edifying of the body of Christ; till we all come in the unity of the faith, and of the knowledge of the Son of God, unto a perfect man, unto the measure of the stature of the fulness of Christ" (Eph. 4:7-13).

Here lies the grand source of all ministry in the Church of God, from first to last—from the foundation laid in grace, to the topstone, in glory. It is divine and heavenly, not human or earthly. It is not of man or by man, but of Jesus Christ, and God the Father who raised Him from the dead, and in the power of the Holy Ghost (see Gal. 1). There is no such thing recognized in Scripture as human authority in any one branch of ministry in the Church. If it be a question of gift, it is emphatically stated to be "the gift of Christ." If it be a question of assigned position, we are, with equal clearness and emphasis, told that "God hath set the members." If it be a question of local charge, whether elder or deacon, it was entirely of divine appointment, by apostolic hands or apostolic delegates.

All this is so clear, so distinct, so palpable, on the very surface of Scripture, that it is only necessary to say, "How readest thou?" And the more we penetrate beneath the surface—the more we are conducted by the Eternal Spirit into the profound and precious depths of inspiration—the more thoroughly convinced we shall be that ministry, in its every department and every branch, is divine in its source, nature, and principles. The truth of this shines out in full-orbed brightness, in the Epistles; but we have the germ of it in the words of our Lord in Matt 25:45, "Whom his lord hath made ruler over his household." The household belongs to the Lord, and He alone can appoint the servants, and this He does according to His own sovereign will.

Equally plain is the object of ministry, as stated in this parable, and elaborated in the Epistles. "To give them meat in due season." "For the edifying of the body of Christ"— "that the church may receive edifying." It is this that lies near the loving heart of Jesus. He would have His household perfected—His Church edified—His body nourished and cherished. For this end, He bestows gifts, and maintains them in the Church, and will maintain them until they shall be no longer needed.

But alas! there is a dark side of the picture. For this we must be prepared since we have the picture of christendom before us. If there is a "faithful wise, and blessed servant," there is also "an evil servant" who "says in his heart, My lord delayeth his coming." Mark this. It is in *the heart* of the wicked servant that the thought originates as to the delay of the coming.

And what is the result? "He shall begin to smite his fellows servants, and to eat and drink with the drunken." How awfully this has been exemplified in the history of christendom, we need not say. Instead of true ministry flowing from the risen and glorified Head in the heavens, and promoting the edification of the body, the blessing of souls, and the prosperity of the household, we have a false clerical authority, arbitrary rule, a lording it over God's heritage, a grasping after this world's wealth and power, fleshly ease, self-indulgence, and personal aggrandizement, priestly domination in its nameless and numberless forms and practical consequences.

The reader will do well to apply his heart to the understanding of these things. He will need to seize, with clearness and power, the distinction between clericalism and ministry. The one is a thoroughly human assumption; the other, a purely divine institution. The former has its source in man's evil heart; the latter has its source in a risen and exalted Saviour, who, being raised from the dead, received gifts for men, and sheds them forth upon His Church, according to His own will. That is a positive scourge and curse; this, a divine blessing to men. In fine, this in its root-principle flows from Heaven and leads back thither; that in its root-principle flows from hell and leads thither again.

All this is most solemn, and it should exert a mighty influence upon our souls. There is a day coming when the Lord Christ will deal, in summary justice, with that which man has dared to set up in His house. We speak not of individuals—though surely it is a most serious and terrible thing for any one to put his hand unto, or have aught to do with, that on which such awful judgment is about to be executed—but we speak of a positive system—a great principle which runs, in a deep and dark current, through the length and breadth of the professing Church—we speak of clericalism and priestcraft, in all its forms and in all its ramifications.

Against this dreadful thing we solemnly warn our readers. No human language can possibly depict the evil of it, nor can human language adequately set forth the deep blessedness of all true ministry in the Church of God. The Lord Jesus not only bestows ministerial gifts, but, in His marvelous grace, He will abundantly reward the faithful and diligent exercise of those gifts. But as to that which man has set up, we read its destiny in those burning words, "The lord of that servant shall come in a day when he looketh not for him, and in an hour that he is not aware of, and shall cut him asunder, and appoint him his portion with the hypocrites; there shall be weeping and gnashing of teeth."

May the gracious Lord deliver His servants and His people from all participation in this great wickedness which is perpetrated in the very bosom of that which calls itself the church of God. And, on the other hand, may He lead them to understand, to appreciate, and to exercise that true, that precious, that divine ministry which emanates from Himself, and is designed, in His infinite love, for the true blessing and growth of that Church which is so dear to His heart. We are in danger, very great danger, while seeking (as we most surely should) to keep clear of the evil of clericalism—of rushing into the opposite extreme of despising ministry.

This must be carefully guarded against. We have ever to bear in mind that ministry in the Church is of God. Its source is divine. Its nature is heavenly and spiritual. Its object is the calling out, the building up of the Church of God. Our Lord Christ imparts the varied gifts, evangelists, pastors, and teachers. He holds the great reservoir of spiritual gifts. He has never given it up, and He never will. Spite of all that Satan has wrought in the professing Church; spite of all the actings of "that evil servant"; spite of all man's daring assumption of authority which in no wise belongs to him; spite of all these things, our risen and glorified Lord "hath the seven stars." He possesses all ministerial gifts, power, and authority. It is He alone who can make any one a minister. Unless He impart a gift there can be no true ministry. There may be hollow assumption—guilty usurpation—empty affectation—worthless talking; but not one atom of true, loving, divine ministry can there be unless where our sovereign Lord is pleased to bestow the gift. And even where He does bestow the gift that gift must be "stirred up," and diligently cultivated, else "the profiting" will not "appear unto all." The gift must be exercised in the power of the Holy Ghost, else it will not promote the divinely appointed end.

But we are rather anticipating what is yet to come before us in the parable of the talents, so we shall close here by simply reminding the reader that the weighty subject on which we have been dwelling has direct reference to the coming of our Lord, inasmuch as all true ministry is carried on in view of that great and glorious event. And not only so, but the counterfeit, the corrupt, the evil thing will be judicially dealt with when the Lord Christ shall appear in His glory.

THE TEN VIRGINS

We now approach that solemn section of our Lord's discourse in which He presents the kingdom of Heaven under the similitude of "ten virgins." The instruction contained in this most weighty and interesting parable is of wider application than that of the servant to which we have already referred, inasmuch as it takes in the whole range of Christian profession, and is not confined to ministry either within the house or outside. It bears directly and pointedly upon Christian profession, whether true or false.

"Then shall the kingdom of heaven be likened unto ten virgins, which took their lamps, and went forth to meet the bridegroom." Some have considered that this parable refers to the Jewish remnant; but it does not seem that this idea is borne out, either by the context in which this parable

occurs or by the terms in which it is couched.

As to the entire context, the more closely we examine it the more clearly we shall see that the Jewish portion of the discourse ends with chapter 24: 44. This is so distinct as not to admit of a question. Equally distinct is the Christian portion, extending, as we have seen, from chapter 24: 45 to chapter 25: 30; while from 25: 31 to the end, we have the Gentiles. Thus the order and fulness of this marvelous discourse must strike any thoughtful reader. It presents the Jew, the Christian, and the Gentile, each on his own distinct ground, and according to his own distinctive principles. There is no merging of one thing in another, no confounding of things that differ. In a word, the order, the fulness, and the comprehensiveness of this profound discourse are divine, and fill the soul "with wonder, love, and praise." We rise from the study of it, as a whole, with those words of the apostle upon our lips, "O, the depth of the riches both of the wisdom and knowledge of God! how unsearchable are His judgments, and His ways past finding out."

And then, when we examine the precise terms made use of by our Lord in the parable of the ten virgins we must see that it applies not to Jews but to Christian professors—it applies to us—it utters a voice, and teaches a solemn lesson to the writer and the reader of these lines.

Let us apply our hearts thereto.

"Then shall the kingdom of heaven be likened unto ten virgins, which took their lamps, and went forth to meet the bridegroom."

Primitive Christianity was especially characterized by the fact here indicated, namely, a going forth to meet a returning and an expected bridegroom. The early Christians were led to detach themselves from present things, and go forth, in the spirit of their minds, and in the affections of their hearts, to meet the Saviour whom they loved, and for whom they waited. It was not, of course, a question of going forth from one place to another; it was not local, but moral, and spiritual. It was the outgoing of the heart after a beloved Saviour whose return was eagerly looked for day by day.

It is impossible to read the Epistles to the various churches and not see that the hope of the Lord's sure and speedy return governed the hearts of the Lord's dear people in early days. "They waited for the Son from heaven." They knew He was to come and take them away, to be with Himself forever; and the knowledge and power of this hope had the effect of detaching their hearts from present things. Their bright, heavenly hope caused them to sit loose to the things of earth. They looked for the Saviour." They believed that He might come at any moment, and hence the concerns of this life were just to be taken up and attended to for the moment—properly, thoroughly attended to, no doubt—but only, as it were, on the very tip-toe of expectation.

All this is conveyed to our hearts, briefly but clearly, by the expression, "They went forth to meet the bridegroom." This could not be intelligently applied to the Jewish remnant, inasmuch as they will not go forth to meet their Messiah, but, on the contrary, they will remain in their position and amid their circumstances until He come and plant His foot on the mount of Olives. They will not look for the Lord to come and take them away from this earth to be with Him in Heaven; but He will come to bring deliverance to them in their own land, and make them happy there under His own peaceful and blessed reign during the millennial age.

But the call to Christians was to "go forth." They are supposed to be always on the move; not settling down on the earth, but going out in earnest and holy aspirations after that heavenly glory to which they are called, and after the heavenly Bridegroom to whom they are espoused, and for whose speedy advent they are taught to wait.

Such is the true, the divine, the normal idea of the Christian's attitude and state. And this lovely idea was marvelously realized and practically carried out by the primitive Christians. But alas! we are reminded of the fact that we have to do with the spurious as well as the true in christendom. There are "tares" as well as "wheat" in the kingdom of Heaven; and thus we read of these ten virgins, that "five of them were wise, and five were foolish." There are the true and the false, the genuine and the counterfeit, the real and the hollow, in professing Christianity.

Yes, and this is to continue unto the time of the end, until the Bridegroom come. The tares are not converted into wheat, nor are the foolish virgins converted into wise ones. No, never. The tares will be burnt and the foolish virgins shut out. So far from a gradual improvement by the means now in operation —the preaching of the gospel and the various beneficent agencies which are brought to bear upon the world—we find, from all the parables, and from the teaching of the entire New Testament, that the kingdom of Heaven presents a most deplorable admixture of evil; a corrupting process; a grievous tampering with the work of God, on the part of the enemy; a positive progress of evil in principle, in profession, and in practice.

And all this goes on to the end. There are foolish virgins found when the Bridegroom appears. Whence come they if all are to converted before the Lord comes? If all are to be brought to the knowledge of the Lord by the means now in operation, then how comes it to pass that when the Bridegroom comes, there are quite as many foolish as wise?

But it will perhaps be said that this is but a parable, a figure. Granted; but a figure of what? Not surely of a whole world converted. To assert this would be to offer a grievous insult to the holy volume, and to treat our Lord's solemn teaching in a manner in which we would not dare to treat the teaching of a fellow mortal.

No, the parable of the ten virgins teaches, beyond all question, that when the Bridegroom comes, there will be foolish virgins on the scene, and clearly, if there are foolish virgins, all cannot have been previously converted. A child can understand this. We cannot see how it is possible, in the face of even this one parable, to maintain the theory of a world converted before the coming of the Bridegroom.

But let us look a little closely at these foolish virgins. Their history is full of admonition for all Christian professors. It is very brief, but awfully comprehensive.

"They that were foolish took their lamps, and took no oil with them." There is the outward profession, but no inward reality—no spiritual life—no unction—no vital link with the source of eternal life—no union with Christ. There is nothing but the lamp of profession, and the dry wick of a nominal, notional, head belief.

This is peculiarly solemn. It bears down with tremendous weight upon that vast mass of baptized profession which surrounds us, at the present moment, in which there is so much of outward semblance, but so little of inward reality. All profess to be Christians. The lamp of profession may be seen in every hand; but ah! how few have the oil in their vessels, the spirit of life in Christ Jesus, the Holy Ghost dwelling in their hearts. Without this, all is utterly worthless and vain. There may be the very highest profession; there may be a most orthodox creed; one may be baptized; he may receive the Lord's supper; be a regularly enrolled and duly recognized member of a Christian community; be a Sunday-school teacher; an ordained minister of religion; one may be all this, and not have one spark of divine life, not one ray of heavenly light, not one link with the Christ of God.

Now there is something peculiarly awful in the thought of having just enough religion to deceive the heart, deaden the conscience, and ruin the soul—just enough religion to give a name to live while dead—enough to leave one without Christ, without God, and without hope in the world—enough to prop the soul up with a false confidence, and fill it with a false peace, until the Bridegroom come, and then the eyes are opened when it is too late.

Thus it is with the foolish virgins. They seem to be very like the wise ones. An ordinary observer might not be able to see any difference, for the time being. They all set out together. All have lamps. And, moreover, all turn aside to slumber and sleep, the wise as well as the foolish. All rouse up at the midnight cry, and trim their lamps. Thus far there is no apparent difference. The foolish virgins light their lamps—the lamp of profession lighted up with the dry wick of a

lifeless, notional, nominal faith; alas! a worthless—worse than worthless—thing, a fatal soul-destroying delusion.

Here the grand distinction—the broad line of demarcation—comes out with awful, yea, with appalling clearness. "The foolish said unto the wise, Give us of your oil; for our lamps *are going out*" (see margin). This proves that their lamps had been lighted; for had they not been lighted, they could not go out. But it was only a false, flickering, transient light. It was not fed from a divine source. It was the light of mere lip profession, fed by a head belief, lasting just long enough to deceive themselves and others, and going out at the very moment when they most needed it, leaving them in the dreadful darkness of eternal night.

"Our lamps are going out." Terrible discovery! "The Bridegroom is at hand, and our lamps are going out. Our hollow profession is being made manifest by the light of His coming. We thought we were all right. We professed the same faith, had the same shaped lamp, the same kind of wick; but alas! we now find to our unspeakable horror, that we have been deceiving ourselves, that we lack the one thing needful, the spirit of life in Christ, the unction from the Holy One, the living link with the Bridegroom. Whatever shall we do? O ye wise virgins, take pity upon us, and share with us your oil. Do, do, for mercy's sake, give us a little, even one drop of that all-essential thing, that we may not perish forever."

It is all utterly vain. No one can give of his oil to another. Each has just enough for himself. Moreover, it can only be had from God Himself. A man can give *light*, but he cannot give *oil.* This latter is the gift of God alone. "The wise answered, saying, Not so; lest there be not enough for us and you: but go ye rather to them that sell and buy for yourselves. And while they went to buy, the Bridegroom came; and they that were ready went in with him to the marriage; *and the door was shut.*" It is of no use looking to Christian friends to help us or prop us up. No use in flying hither and thither for some one to lean upon—some holy man, or some eminent teacher—no use building upon our church, or our creed, or our sacraments. *We want oil.* We cannot do without it. Where are we to get it? Not from man, not from the church, not from the saints, not from the fathers. We must get it from God; and He, blessed be His name, gives freely. "The gift of God is eternal life, through Jesus Christ our Lord."

But, mark, it is an individual thing. Each must have it for himself. No man can believe, or get life for another. Each must have to do with God for himself. The link which connects the soul with Christ is intensely individual. There is no such thing as second-hand faith. A man may teach us religion, or theology, or the letter of Scripture; but he cannot give us oil; he cannot give us faith; he cannot give us life. "It is the *gift* of God." Precious little word, "gift." It is like God. It is free as God's air; free as His sunlight; free as His refreshing dew-drops. But, we repeat, and with solemn emphasis, each one must get it for himself, and have it in himself. "None can by any means redeem his brother, nor give to God a ransom for him: that he should still live forever and not see corruption. For the redemption of their soul is precious, and it ceaseth forever" (Psalm 49: 7-9).

What sayest thou to these solemn realities? Art thou a wise or a foolish virgin? Hast thou gotten life in a risen and glorified Saviour? Art thou a mere professor of religion, content with the mere ordinary dead routine of church-going, having just sufficient religion to make thee respectable on earth, but not enough to link thee with Heaven?

We earnestly beseech thee to think seriously of these things. Think of them now. Think how unspeakably dreadful it will be to find thy lamp of profession going out and leaving thee in obscure darkness—darkness that may be felt—the outer darkness of an everlasting night. How terrible to find the door shut behind that brilliant train which shall go in to the marriage; but shut in thy face! How agonizing the cry, "Lord, Lord, open unto us!" How withering, how crushing the response, "I know you not."

O, do give these weighty matters a place in thy heart now, while yet the door is open, and while yet the day of grace is lengthened out in God's marvelous long suffering. The moment is rapidly approaching in the which the door of mercy shall be closed against thee forever, when all hope shall be gone, and thy precious soul be plunged in black and eternal despair. May God's spirit rouse thee from thy fatal slumber, and give thee no rest until thou findest it in the finished work of the Lord Jesus Christ, and at His blessed feet in adoration and worship.

We shall just for a moment glance at the wise virgins. The great distinguishing feature which, according to the teaching of this parable, marks them off from the foolish virgins is that when starting at the first they "took oil in their vessels with their lamps." In other words, what distinguishes true believers from mere professors is that the former have in their hearts the grace of God's Holy Spirit; they have gotten the spirit of life in Christ Jesus; and the Holy Ghost dwelling in them as the seal, the earnest, the unction, and the witness. This grand and glorious fact characterizes now all true believers in the Lord Jesus Christ—a stupendous, wondrous fact, most surely—an immense and ineffable privilege, which should ever bow our souls in holy adoration before our God and our Lord Jesus Christ, whose accomplished redemption has procured for us this great blessing.

How sad to think that, notwithstanding this high and holy privilege, we should have to read, as in the words of our parable, "They all slumbered and slept!" All alike, wise as well as foolish, fell asleep. The Bridegroom tarried, and all, without exception, lost the freshness, fervor, and power of the hope of His coming, and fell fast asleep.

Such is the statement of our parable, and such is the solemn fact of the history. The whole professing body fell asleep. "That blessed hope" which shone so brightly on the horizon of the early Christians, very speedily waned and faded away; and as we scan the page of church history for eighteen centuries, from the Apostolic Fathers to the opening of the current century, we look in vain for any intelligent reference to the Church's specific hope—the personal return of the blessed

Bridegroom. In fact, that hope was virtually lost to the Church; nay, more, it became almost heresy to teach it. And even now, in these last days, there are hundreds of thousands of professed ministers of Christ who dare not preach or teach the coming of the Lord as it is taught in Scripture.

True it is, blessed be God, we notice a mighty change within the last half century. There has been a great awakening. God is, by His Holy Spirit, recalling His people to long-forgotten truths, and amongst the rest, to the glorious truth of the coming of the Bridegroom. Many are now seeing that the reason why the Bridegroom tarried was simply because God was long-suffering to usward, not willing that any should perish, but that all should come to repentance. Precious reason!

But they are also seeing that, spite of this long-suffering, our Lord is at hand. Christ is coming. The midnight cry has gone forth, "Behold, the Bridegroom cometh; go ye out to meet Him." May millions of voices re-echo the soul-stirring cry until it passes in its mighty moral power, from pole to pole, and from the river to the ends of the earth, rousing the whole Church to wait, as one man, for the glorious appearing of the blessed Bridegroom of our hearts.

Brethren beloved in the Lord, awake! Let every soul be roused. Let us shake off the sloth and the slumber of worldly ease and self-indulgence—let us rise above the withering influence of religious formality and dull routine—let us fling aside the dogmas of false theology, and go forth, in the spirit of our minds and in the affections of our hearts, to meet our returning Bridegroom. May His own solemn words come with fresh power to our souls, "Watch therefore, for ye know neither the day nor the hour." May the language of our hearts and our lives be, "Even so, come, Lord Jesus."

The dark stream of evil is flowing apace;
Awake, and be doing, ye children of grace,
Let's seek with compassion the souls that are
    lost,
Well knowing the price their redemption
    has cost.
While singing with rapture the Saviour's great
    love,

And waiting for Him to translate us above—
"It may be to-morrow, or even to-night"—
Let our loins be well girded, and lamps
burning bright.

THE TALENTS

It only remains for us now to consider that portion of our Lord's discourse in which He again takes up the deeply solemn subject of ministerial responsibility during the time of His absence. That this stands closely connected with the hope of His coming is evident from the fact that having summed up the parable of the ten virgins with these most weighty words, "Watch therefore, for ye know neither the day nor the hour," He goes on to say, "For as a man travelling into a far country, who called his servants, and delivered unto them his goods."

There is a material difference between the parable of the talents and that of the servant in chapter 24:45-51. In the latter, we have ministry inside the house. In the former, on the other hand, we have ministry abroad in the world. But in each we find the grand foundation of all ministry, namely, the gift and authority of Christ. "He called *His own* servants, and delivered unto them *His* goods." The servants are His, and the goods are His. No one but the Lord Christ can put a man into the ministry, as none but He can impart spiritual gift. It is utterly impossible for any one to be a minister of Christ unless He calls him and fits him for the work. This is so plain as not to admit of a single question. A man may be a minister of religion; he may preach the doctrines of the gospel, and teach theology; but a minister of Christ he cannot possibly be unless Christ calls him to, and gifts him for, the work. If it be a question of ministry inside the house, it is "whom his lord hath made ruler over his house." And if it be a question of ministry abroad in the world, we are told that "He called his own servants and delivered unto them his goods."

This great root-principle of ministry is powerfully embodied in these words of one of the greatest ministers that ever lived, when he says, "I thank Christ Jesus our Lord, *who hath enabled me*, for that He counted me faithful, *putting me into the ministry*" (1 Tim. 1:12).

Thus it must be in every case, whatever be the measure, the character, or the sphere of ministry. The Lord Christ alone can put any one into the ministry, and enable him to fulfil it. If it be not this, it will be either a man putting himself into the ministry, or his fellow man doing it, both of which are alike opposed to the mind of God, and to all the principles of the true ministry as taught in the Word. If we are to be guided by Scripture, we must see that all ministry in or out of the house must be by divine appointment and divine ability. If it be not thus, it is worse than worthless. A man may set himself up as a minister, or he may be set up by his fellows; but it is all utterly vain. It is not from Heaven—it is not of God—it is not by Jesus Christ; and, in the sequel, it will be made manifest and judged as a most horrible and daring usurpation.

It is of the very last importance that the Christian reader should thoroughly seize this grand principle of ministry. It is as simple as it is solemn. And, moreover, that it rests on a basis truly divine cannot be questioned by any one who bows down—as every Christian ought— with unqualified and absolute submission, to the authority of the divine Word. Let the reader take his Bible, and read carefully every line therein which bears upon the subject of ministry. If he turns to the parable of the house-steward, he will read, "Whom *his lord* hath made ruler." He does not make himself ruler; neither is he appointed by his fellows. The appointment is divine.

So, also, in the parable of the talents, the master calls his own servants, and delivers unto them his goods. The call and the equipment are divine.

We have another aspect of the same truth in Luke 19. "A certain nobleman went into a far country, to receive for himself a kingdom, *and to return*. And he called his ten servants, and delivered them ten pounds, and said unto them, Occupy *till I come*." The difference between Luke and Matthew appears to be this: in the former, human responsibility; in the latter, divine sovereignty is prominent.

But in both the great root-principle is distinctly maintained and unanswerably established, namely, that all ministry is by divine appointment.

The same truth meets us in the Acts of the Apostles. When one was to be appointed to fill the place of Judas, the appeal is made to Jehovah, "Thou, Lord, which knowest the hearts of all, show whether of these two *Thou hast chosen*; that he may take part of this ministry and apostleship."

Even where it is a question of local charge, as of deacons, in chapter 6, or of elders, in chapter 14, it is by direct apostolic appointment. In other words, it is divine. A man could not even appoint himself to a deaconship, much less to an eldership. In the case of the former, inasmuch as the deacons were to take charge of the people's property, these latter were, in the grace and lovely moral order of the Spirit, permitted to select men in whom they could confide; but the appointment was divine, whether of deacons or elders. Thus, whether it be a question of gift or of local charge, all rests on a purely divine basis. This is *the* all-important point.

Again, if we turn to the Epistles, the same great truth shines in full and undimmed lustre before us. Thus, at the opening of Romans 12, we read, "For I say, through the grace given unto me, to every man that is among you, not to think of himself more highly than he ought to think; but to think soberly, according as *God hath dealt to every man the measure of faith*. For as we have many members in one body, and all members have not the same office; so we being many, are one body in Christ, and every one members one of another. Having then *gifts differing according to the grace that is given us*," etc. In 1 Cor. 12 we read, "*But now hath God set the members every one of them in the body* as it hath pleased Him" (verse 18). And again, "*God hath set some in the church, first, apostles*," etc. (verse 28). So also in Ephesians 4, "But unto every one of us is given grace according to the measure of *the gift of Christ*."

All these Scriptures, and many more that might be quoted, go to establish the truth which we are intensely anxious to impress upon our readers, namely, that ministry in all its departments, is divine—is of God—is from Heaven—is by Jesus Christ. There is positively no such thing in the New Testament as human authority to minister in the Church of God. Turn where we may, throughout its sacred pages, and we find only the same blessed doctrine as is contained in that one brief sentence in our parable, "He called his own servants, and delivered unto them his goods." The whole New Testament doctrine of ministry is embodied here; and we earnestly entreat the Christian reader to let this doctrine take full possession of his soul, and exert its full sway over his conduct, course and character.*

It may perhaps be asked, "Is there no adaptation of the vessel to the ministerial gift deposited therein?" Unquestionably there is; and this very adaptation is distinctly presented in the words of our parable, "Unto one he gave five talents, to another two, and to another one; to every man *according to his several ability*."

This is a point of deepest interest, and it must never be lost sight of. The Lord knows what use He means to make of a man. He knows the character of gift which He purposes to deposit in the vessel, and He shapes the vessel and moulds the man accordingly. We cannot doubt that Paul was a vessel specially formed of God for the place he was afterwards to fill, and the work he had to do. And so in every case. If God designs a man to be a public speaker, He gives him lungs, He gives him a voice, He gives him a physical constitution adapted to the work which He designs him to do. The gift is from God; but there is always the most distinct reference to the ability of the man.

If this be lost sight of, our apprehension of the true character of ministry will be very defective indeed. We must never forget the two things, namely, the divine gift, and the human vessel in which the gift is deposited. There is the sovereignty of God, and the responsibility of man. How perfect and how beautiful are all the ways of God! But alas! man mars everything, and the touch of the human finger only dims the lustre of divine workmanship. Still, let us never forget that ministry is divine in its source, its nature, its power, and its object. If the reader rises from this paper convinced in heart and soul of this grand truth, we have so far gained our object in penning it.

"What has all this subject of ministry to do with the Lord's coming?" Much every way. Does not our blessed Lord introduce the subject again and again, in His discourse on the mount of Olives? And is not this entire discourse a reply to the question of the disciples, "What shall be the sign of Thy coming and the end of the age?" Is not His coming the great prominent point of the discourse as a whole, and of each section of it in particular? Unquestionably.

And what is the next prominent theme? Is it not ministry? Look at the parable of the servant made ruler over the household. How is he to serve? In view of his Lord's return. The ministry links itself on, as it were, to the departing and the return of the Master. It stands between, and is to be characterized by, these two grand events. And what is it that leads to failure in the ministry? Losing sight of the Lord's return. The evil servant says in his heart, "My Lord delayeth His coming," and, as a consequence, "he begins to smite his fellow servants, and to eat and drink with the drunken."

So also in the parable of the talents. The solemn and soul-stirring word is "Occupy till I come." In short, we learn that ministry, whether in the house of God or abroad in the world, is to be carried on in full view of the Lord's return. "After a long time the lord of those servants cometh and reckoneth with them." All the servants are to keep continually before their minds the solemn fact that there is a reckoning time coming. This will regulate their thoughts and feelings in reference to every branch of their ministry. Harken to the following weighty words in which one servant seeks to animate another, "I charge thee therefore before God, and the Lord Jesus Christ, who shall judge the quick and the dead at His appearing and

---

* We do not, by any means, restrict the application of the "talents" to direct, specific, spiritual gifts. We believe the parable takes in the wide range of Christian *service:* just as the parable of the ten virgins takes in the wide range of Christian *profession*.

His kingdom: preach the word; be instant in season, out of season; reprove, rebuke, exhort, with all long-suffering and doctrine. For the time will come when they will not endure sound doctrine; but after their own lusts shall they heap to themselves teachers, having itching ears. And they shall turn away their ears from the truth, and shall be turned unto fables. But watch thou in all things, endure afflictions, do the work of an evangelist, make full proof of thy ministry. For I am now ready to be offered, and the time of my departure is at hand. I have fought a good fight. I have finished my course, I have kept the faith. Henceforth there is laid up for me a crown of righteousness, which the Lord, the righteous judge, shall give me *at that day*; and not to me only, *but unto all them also that love His appearing*" (2 Tim. 4: 1-8).

Does not this touching and weighty passage show how intimately the subject of ministry stands connected with the Lord's coming? The blessed apostle—the most devoted, gifted, and effective workman that ever wrought in the vineyard of Christ—the most skillful steward that ever handled the mysteries of God—the wise master builder— the great minister of the Church and preacher of the gospel—the incomparable servant—this rare and precious vessel carried on his work, fulfilled his ministry, and discharged his holy responsibilities in full view of *"that day."* He looked forward, and is still looking, to that solemn and glorious occasion when the Righteous Judge shall place on his brow "the crown of righteousness." And he adds, with such affecting sweetness, "not to me only, but unto all them also that love His appearing."

This is peculiarly touching. There will be a crown of righteousness in "that day," not merely for the gifted, laborious, and devoted Paul, but for every one that loves the appearing of our Lord and Saviour Jesus Christ. No doubt Paul shall have gems in his crown of peculiar lustre; but, lest any one should think that the crown of righteousness was only for Paul, he adds these lovely words, "unto all them also that love His appearing." The Lord be praised for such

words! May they have the effect of stirring up our hearts, not only to love the appearing of our Lord, but also to serve with more intense and whole-hearted devotedness in view of that glorious day! That the two things are very closely connected we may see in the sequel of the parable of the talents. We can do little more than quote the words of our Lord.

When the servants had received the talents, we read, "Then he that had received the five talents went and traded with the same, and made them other five talents. And likewise he that had received two, he also gained other two. But he that had received one went and digged in the earth and hid his lord's money. After a long time the lord of those servants cometh, and reckoneth with them. And so he that had received five talents came and brought other five talents, saying, Lord, thou deliveredst unto me five talents; behold I have gained besides them five talents more. His lord said unto him, Well done, good and faithful servant: thou hast been faithful over a few things, I will make thee ruler over many things: enter thou into the joy of thy lord. He also that had received two talents came and said, Lord, thou deliveredst unto me two talents; behold, I have gained two other talents beside them. His lord said unto him, Well done, good and faithful servant: thou hast been faithful over a few things; I will make thee ruler over many things: enter thou into the joy of thy lord."

It is interesting and instructive to note the difference between the parable of the talents as given in Matthew, and the parable of the ten servants, in Luke 19. In the former, it is a question of divine sovereignty; in the latter, of human responsibility. In that, each receives a like sum; in this, one receives five, another two, according to the master's will. Then, when the day of reckoning comes, we find in Luke a definite reward according to the work; whereas, in Matthew, the word is, "I will make thee ruler over many things; enter thou into the joy of thy lord." They are not told what they are to have, or how many things they are to rule over. The master is sovereign both in His gifts and rewards; and the crowning point of all is, "Enter thou into the joy of thy lord."

This, to a heart that loves the Lord, is beyond everything. True, there will be the ten cities and the five cities. There will be ample, distinct, and definite reward for responsibility discharged, service rendered, and work done. All will be rewarded. But above and beyond all, shines this precious word, "Enter thou into the joy of thy lord." No reward can possibly come up to this. The sense of the love that breathes in these words will lead each one to cast his "crown of righteousness" at the feet of his Lord. The very crown which the righteous Judge shall give, we shall willingly cast at the feet of a loving Saviour and Lord. One smile from Him will touch the heart far more deeply and powerfully than the brightest crown that could be placed on the brow.

Who would not work? Who hid his lord's money? Who proved to be "a wicked and slothful servant?" The man who did not know his master's heart—his master's character—his master's love. "Then he which had received the one talent, came and said, Lord, I know thee, [?] that thou art an hard man, reaping where thou hast not sown, and gathering where thou hast not strewed; and I was afraid, and went and hid thy talent in the earth: lo, there thou hast that is thine. His Lord answered and said unto him, Thou wicked and slothful servant, thou knewest that I reap where I sowed not, and gather where I have not strewed. Thou oughtest therefore to have put my money to the exchangers, and then at my coming, I should have received mine own with usury. Take therefore the talent from him, and give it unto him which hath ten talents. For unto every one that hath shall be given, and he shall have abundance; but from him that hath not shall be taken away even that which he hath. And cast ye the unprofitable servant into outer darkness: there shall be weeping and gnashing of teeth."

How awfully solemn! How striking the contrast between the two servants! One knows, and loves, and trusts, and serves his Lord.* The other belies, fears, distrusts, and does nothing. The one enters into the joy of his lord, the other is cast out into outer darkness, into the place of weeping and wailing and gnashing of teeth. How solemn! How soul-subduing is all this! And when does it all come out? When the Master returns!

CONCLUSION

The theme is intensely interesting, deeply practical, and abundantly fruitful. Moreover, it is very suggestive, and opens up an extensive field of vision for the spiritual mind to range through with an interest that never flags, because the subject is inexhaustible.

However, we must close our meditations on this most marvelous line of truth; but ere doing so, we are anxious to call the reader's attention, as briefly as possible, to one or two things which have been barely hinted at in the progress of these papers. We deem them not only interesting, but of real practical value in helping to a clearer understanding of many branches of the great subject which has been engaging our attention.

The reader who has traveled in company with us through the various branches of our subject will remember a cursory reference to what we ventured to call "an unnoticed interval—break—or parenthesis" in the dealings of God with Israel and with the earth. This is a point of the deepest interest; and we hope to be able to show the reader that it is not some curious question, a dark mysterious subject, or a favorite notion of some special school of prophetic interpretation. Quite the contrary. We consider it to be a point which throws a flood of light on very many branches of our general subject. Such we have found it for ourselves, and as such we desire to present it to our readers. Indeed we strongly question if any one can rightly understand prophecy or his own true position and bearings, who does not see the unnoticed

---

* We may add, in connection with the foregoing remarks, on ministry, that every Christian has his and her own specific place and work to do. All are solemnly responsible to the Lord to know their place and fill it, to know their work and do it. This is a plain practical truth, and most fully confirmed by the principle upon which we have been insisting, namely, that all ministry and all work must be received from the Master's hand, carried on under His eye, and in full view of His coming. These things must never be forgotten.

interval or break above referred to.

But let us turn directly to the Word, and open at chapter 9 of the book of Daniel.

The opening verses of this remarkable section show us the beloved servant of God in profound exercise of soul in reference to the sad condition of his much loved people Israel—a condition into which, through the Spirit of Christ, he most thoroughly enters. Though not having himself personally participated in these actings which had brought ruin upon the nation, yet he identifies himself, most completely, with the people, and makes their sins his own in confession and self-judgment before his God.

We cannot attempt to quote from Daniel's remarkable prayer and confession on this occasion; but the subject which immediately concerns us now is introduced in verse 20.

"And while I was speaking, and praying, and confessing my sin and the sin of my people Israel, and presenting my supplication before the Lord my God for the holy mountain of my God; yea, while I was speaking in prayer, even the man Gabriel, whom I had seen in the vision at the beginning, being caused to fly swiftly, touched me about the time of the evening oblation. And he informed me and talked with me, and said, O Daniel, I am now come forth to give thee skill and understanding. At the beginning of thy supplications the commandment came forth, and I am come to show thee; for thou art greatly beloved: therefore understand the matter, and consider the vision. Seventy weeks are determined [or portioned out] upon thy people, and upon thy holy city, to finish the transgression, and to make an end of sins, and to make reconciliation for iniquity, and to bring in everlasting righteousness, and to seal up the vision and prophecy, and to anoint the Most Holy."

Now we cannot, in our limited space, enter upon any elaborate argument to prove that the "seventy weeks," in the above quotation, mean really four hundred and ninety years. We assume this to be the fact. We believe that Gabriel was commissioned to instruct the beloved prophet, and to inform him of the fact that, from the going forth of the decree to rebuild Jerusalem, a period of four hundred and ninety years was to elapse, and that then Israel would be brought into blessing.

This is as simple and definite as anything can be. We may assert, with all possible confidence, that it is not so certain that the sun shall rise, at the appointed moment, tomorrow morning, as that at the close of the period above named by the angelic messenger, Daniel's people shall be brought into blessing. It is as sure as the throne of God. Nothing can hinder. Not all the powers of earth and hell combined shall be allowed to stand in the way of the full and perfect accomplishment of the Word of God by the mouth of Gabriel. When the last sand of the four hundred and ninetieth year shall have run out of the glass, Israel shall enter upon the possession of all their destined pre-eminence and glory. It is impossible to read Daniel 9:24, and not see this.

But, it may be, the reader feels disposed to ask—and ask, too, with astonishment, "Have not the four hundred and ninety years expired long ago?" We reply, Certainly not. Had they done so, Israel would be now in their own land, under the blessed reign of their own loved Messiah. Scripture cannot be broken; nor can we play fast and loose with its statements, as though they might mean anything or everything, or nothing at all. The word is precise. "Seventy weeks are portioned out upon thy people." Neither more nor less than seventy weeks. If this be taken to mean literal weeks, the passage has no sense or meaning whatever. It would be an insult to our readers to occupy time in combating such an absurdity as this.

But if, as we are most thoroughly persuaded, Gabriel meant seventy weeks of years, then have we a period most distinct and definite before us—a period extending from the moment in which Cyrus issued his decree to restore Jerusalem, to the moment of Israel's restoration.

Still, however, the reader may feel led to ask, "How can these things be? It is very much more than four hundred and ninety years, four times told, since the king of Persia issued his decree, and yet there is no sign of Israel's restoration. There must surely be some other mode of interpreting the seventy weeks."

We can only repeat our statement, that the four hundred and ninety years are not out yet. There has been a break—a parenthesis —a long unnoticed interval. Let the reader look closely at Daniel 9:25-26: "Know therefore and understand, that from the going forth of the commandment to restore and to build Jerusalem, unto the Messiah the Prince, shall be seven weeks [49 years] and threescore and two weeks [434 years]; the street shall be built again, and the wall, even in troublous times;" or, as the margin reads it, "in strait of times," that is, the street and the wall of Jerusalem were built in the shorter of the two periods named, or in forty-nine years. "And after threescore and two weeks [434 years from the rebuilding of Jerusalem], shall Messiah be cut off, and have nothing" (see margin).

Here then we reach the marked, memorable, and solemn epoch. The Messiah, instead of being received, is cut off. In place of ascending the throne of David, He goes to the cross. Instead of entering upon the possession of all the promises, He has nothing. His only portion—so far as Israel and the earth were concerned—was the cross, the vinegar, the spear, the borrowed grave.

Messiah was rejected, cut off, and had nothing. What then? God signified His sense of this act, by suspending for a time His dispensational dealings with Israel. The course of time is interrupted. There is a great gap. Four hundred and eighty-three years are fulfilled; seven yet remain—a cancelled week, and all the time since the death of the Messiah has been an unnoticed interval—a break or parenthesis, during which Christ has been hidden in the heavens, and the Holy Ghost has been working on earth in forming the body of Christ, the Church, the heavenly bride. When the last member shall have been incorporated into this body, the Lord Himself shall come and receive His people to Himself, to conduct them back to the Father's house, there to be with Him in the ineffable communion of that blessed home, while God will, by His governmental dealings, prepare

Israel and the earth for the introduction of the First-begotten into the world.

Now as to this interval and all that was to occur therein, Gabriel maintains a profound reserve. Whether he understood aught of it is not the question. It is clear he was not commissioned to speak of it, inasmuch as the time was not come for so doing. He passes, with marvelous and mysterious abruptness, over ages and generations—steps from headland to headland of the prophetic chart, and dismisses in a short sentence or two, a lengthened period of nearly two thousand years. The siege of Jerusalem by the Romans is thus briefly noticed, "The people of the prince that shall come shall destroy the city and the sanctuary." Then, a period which has already lasted for eighteen centuries is thus disposed of, "And the end thereof shall be with a flood, and unto the end of the war desolations are determined."

Then, with intense rapidity, we are conducted on to the time of the end, when the last of the seventy weeks, the last seven of the four hundred and ninety years, shall be accomplished. "And he [the Prince] shall confirm the covenant with many [of the Jews] *for one week* [seven years]; and in the midst of the week he shall cause the sacrifice and the oblation to cease, and for the over-spreading of abominations he shall make it desolate, even until the consummation, and that determined shall be poured upon the desolator" (margin).

Here then we reach the end of the four hundred and ninety years which were determined or portioned out upon Daniel's people. To attempt to interpret this period without seeing the break and the long unnoticed interval, must of necessity plunge the mind in utter confusion. It cannot possibly be done. Numberless theories have been started; endless calculations and speculations have been attempted; but in vain. The four hundred and ninety years are not accomplished yet; nor will they have their accomplishment until the Church has left this scene altogether, and gone to be with her Lord in her bright heavenly home. Revelation 4—5 show us the place which the heavenly saints shall occupy during the last of

Daniel's seventy weeks; while from chapters 6—18 we have the various actings of God in government, preparing Israel and the earth for the bringing in of the first-begotten in the world.*

We are very anxious to make these matters clear to the reader. It has greatly helped us in the understanding of prophecy, and cleared away many difficulties. We feel thoroughly persuaded that no one can understand the book of Daniel, or indeed the general scope of prophecy, who does not see that the last of the seventy weeks remains to be fulfilled. Not one jot or tittle of God's Word can ever pass away, and seeing He has declared that "seventy weeks were portioned out upon Daniel's people," and that at the close of that period they should be brought into blessing, it is plain that this period is not yet expired. But unless we see the break, and the dropping of time, consequent upon the rejection of the Messiah, we cannot possibly make out the fulfilment of Daniel's seventy weeks, or four hundred and ninety years.

Another important fact for the reader to seize is this, the Church forms no part of the ways of God with Israel and the earth. The Church does not belong to time, but to eternity. She is not earthly, but heavenly. She is called into existence during an unnoticed interval—a break or parenthesis consequent upon the cutting off of the Messiah. To speak after the manner of men, if Israel had received the Messiah, then the seventy weeks or four hundred and ninety years would have been fulfilled; but Israel rejected her King, and God has retired to His place until they acknowledge their iniquity. He has suspended His public dealings with Israel and the earth, though most surely controlling all things by His providence, and keeping His eye upon the seed of Abraham, ever beloved for the father's sake.

Meanwhile He is calling out from Jews and Gentiles that body called the Church, to be the companion of His Son in heavenly glory—to be thoroughly identified with Him in His present rejection from this earth, and to wait in holy patience for His glorious advent.

All this marks off the Christian's position in the most definite manner possible. His portion and his prospects, too, are thus defined with equal clearness. It is vain to look into the prophetic page in order to find the Church's position, her calling, or her hope. They are not there. It is entirely out of place for the Christian to be occupied with dates and historic events, as though he were in anywise involved therein. No doubt, all these things have their proper place and their value, and their interest, as connected with God's dealings with Israel and with the earth. But the Christian must never lose sight of the fact that he belongs to Heaven, that he is inseparably linked with an earth-rejected, Heaven-accepted Christ—that his life is hid with Christ in God—that it is his holy privilege to be looking out, daily and hourly, for the coming of his Lord. There is nothing to hinder the realization of that blissful hope at any moment. There is but one thing that causes the delay, and that is, "the long-suffering of our Lord, not willing that any should perish, but that all should come to repentance"—precious words these for a lost and guilty world! The salvation is *ready* to be revealed; and God is *ready* to judge. There is nothing now to wait for but the gathering in of the last elect one, and then—oh! most blessed thought—our own dear and loving Saviour will come and receive us to Himself to be with Him where He is, and to go no more out forever.

Then when the Church has gone to be with her Lord in the heavenly home, God will resume His public actings with Israel. They will be brought into great tribulation, during the week already referred to. But at the close of that period of unexampled pressure and trial, their long-rejected Messiah will appear for their relief and deliverance. He will come forth as the rider on the white horse,

---

* It is, we are aware, a question among the expositors, whether the events detailed in Revelation 6—18 will occupy a whole week or only a half. We do not here attempt to offer an opinion. Some consider that the public ministry of John the Baptist and that of our Lord occupied a week, or seven years, and that in consequence of Israel's rejection of both, the week is cancelled, and remains yet to be fulfilled. It is an interesting question; but it in no wise affects the great principles which have been before us, or the interpretation of the book of Revelation. We may add that the expressions "forty and two months"—"twelve hundred and sixty days" "time, times, and the dividing of time," indicate the period of half a week, or three years and a half.

accompanied by the heavenly saints. He will execute summary judgment upon His enemies, and take to Himself His great power and reign. The kingdoms of this world shall become the kingdoms of our Lord and of His Christ. Satan shall be bound for a thousand years; and the whole universe shall repose beneath the blissful and benignant rule of the Prince of peace.

Finally, at the close of the thousand years, Satan shall be loosed, and permitted to make one more desperate effort—an effort issuing in his eternal defeat and consignment to the lake of fire, there to be tormented with the beast and the false prophet throughout the everlasting ages.

Then follows the resurrection and judgment of the wicked dead, and their consignment to the lake that burneth with fire and brimstone—tremendous and appalling thought! No heart can conceive—no tongue can tell—the horrors of that lake of fire.

But hardly is there a moment to dwell upon the dark and awful picture, ere the unutterable glories of the new heavens and the new earth burst upon the vision of the soul; the holy city is seen descending from Heaven, and these seraphic sounds fall upon the ear, "Behold, the tabernacle of God is with men, and He will dwell with them, and they shall be His people, and God Himself shall be with

them, and be their God. And God shall wipe away all tears from their eyes; and there shall be no more death, neither sorrow, nor crying, neither shall there be any more pain; for the former things are passed away. And He that sat upon the throne, said, Behold I make all things new."

O beloved Christian reader, what scenes are before us! What grand realities! What brilliant moral glories! May we live in the light and power of these things! May we cherish that blessed hope of seeing the One who loved us and gave Himself for us—who would not enjoy His glory alone, but endured the wrath of God in order that He might link us with Himself, and share with us all His love and glory for ever. Oh! to live for Christ and wait for His appearing!

High in the Father's house above
  My mansion is prepared;
There is the home, the rest I love,
  And there my bright reward.

With Him I love, in spotless white,
  In glory I shall shine;
His blissful presence my delight,
  His love and glory mine.

All taint of sin shall be removed,
  All evil done away;
And I shall dwell with God's Beloved,
  Through God's eternal day.

TITLE INDEX

The number in parentheses indicates the volume
in which the article appeared in the six-volume set.